The Republic for Which It Stands

The Oxford History of the United States

David M. Kennedy, *General Editor*

ROBERT MIDDLEKAUFF
THE GLORIOUS CAUSE
The American Revolution, 1763–1789

GORDON S. WOOD
EMPIRE OF LIBERTY
A History of the Early Republic, 1789–1815

DANIEL WALKER HOWE
WHAT HATH GOD WROUGHT
The Transformation of America, 1815–1848

JAMES M. MCPHERSON
BATTLE CRY OF FREEDOM
The Civil War Era

RICHARD WHITE
THE REPUBLIC FOR WHICH IT STANDS
The United States during Reconstruction and the Gilded Age, 1865–1896

DAVID M. KENNEDY
FREEDOM FROM FEAR
The American People in Depression and War, 1929–1945

JAMES T. PATTERSON
GRAND EXPECTATIONS
The United States, 1945–1974

JAMES T. PATTERSON
RESTLESS GIANT
The United States from Watergate to Bush v. Gore

GEORGE C. HERRING
FROM COLONY TO SUPERPOWER
U.S. Foreign Relations since 1776

THE REPUBLIC FOR WHICH IT STANDS

The United States during Reconstruction and the Gilded Age, 1865–1896

RICHARD WHITE

OXFORD
UNIVERSITY PRESS

OXFORD
UNIVERSITY PRESS

Oxford University Press is a department of the University of Oxford.
It furthers the University's objective of excellence in research, scholarship,
and education by publishing worldwide. Oxford is a registered trade mark of
Oxford University Press in the UK and certain other countries.

Published in the United States of America by Oxford University Press
198 Madison Avenue, New York, NY 10016, United States of America.

Library of Congress Cataloging-in-Publication Data
Names: White, Richard, 1947– author.
Title: The republic for which it stands : the United States during
Reconstruction and the Gilded Age, 1865–1896 / Richard White.
Other titles: United States during Reconstruction and the
Gilded Age, 1865–1896
Description: New York City : Oxford University Press, [2017] |
Series: The Oxford history of the United States |
Includes bibliographical references and index.
Identifiers: LCCN 2017002719 (print) | LCCN 2017016846 (ebook) |
ISBN 9780190619060 (Updf) | ISBN 9780190619077 (Epub) |
ISBN 9780199735815 (hardcover : alk. paper)
Subjects: LCSH: Reconstruction (U.S. history, 1865–1877) |
United States—History—1865–1921. | United States—Politics
and government—1865–1933.
Classification: LCC E668 (ebook) | LCC E668 .W58 2017 (print) |
DDC 973.8—dc23
LC record available at https://lccn.loc.gov/2017002719

1 2 3 4 5 6 7 8 9
Printed by Edwards Brothers Malloy, United States of America

To my family

I pledge allegiance to my Flag and the Republic for which it stands, one Nation, indivisible, with liberty and justice for all.

—Original pledge by Francis Bellamy, *Youth's Companion*, 1892

Acknowledgments

I have written a book about a time of rapid and disorienting change and failed politics, and now I finish it in a parallel universe. Fittingly, I decided to write this book about the Gilded Age, in part for the money, but the era came to fascinate me. I lost myself in it.

I needed money because my mother had dementia. She died more than a year before this book was finished. I would lie if I said I didn't at times find my retreat into the late nineteenth century, with all of its turmoil, pain, and suffering, a relief. The past is the secret refuge of historians. It was a retreat my wife, stuck in the present and sharing the care for my mother over nearly ten years, did not have. This only increases my love for her and my gratitude to her.

The Gilded Age delivered me up to the doorstep of my own family history in the United States. One of my grandparents was the child of Jewish immigrants from Poland who arrived during the Gilded Age. My Jewish grandfather came from Belarus around the turn of the century. My maternal grandmother came from Ireland about the same time. My Irish grandfather, following his relatives, came later. One grandfather was an illegal immigrant; the other was nearly deported back to Russia. They stepped into the world whose origins I describe here. They did not have easy lives. Both of my Irish grandparents returned to where they came, but not at the same time. They lived apart in different countries for years. They left children here.

My family now, as my brothers and sister, children, and nephews have married, contains Catholics, Protestants, Jews, agnostics, and atheists. Some come from Mexico; part of my nephew's wife's family comes from India. Some have roots stretching back deep into America for generations.

Their connections, including mine, still include people from the places where they or their parents originated.

My mother and father and my grandparents, though dead; my wife, and children and grandchildren; my siblings, cousins, nieces, and nephews; and my in-laws are inseparable from the writing of this book. I was simply going to dedicate this book to my own messy, contentious, diverse, and irreplaceable family, but it is necessary to say something more because I realized that I had somehow arrived at a time when my country, which I love in my own perverse way, is making devotion to family antithetical to devotion to country, in a way that ironically echoes the Gilded Age. I find this easier to describe and analyze as an historian than indulge or endure as a citizen.

I have had much help in writing this book. Friends and colleagues have saved me from mistakes, but I am sure they have not saved me from all of them. Elliott West, Daniel Czitrom, Jon Levy, Daniel Carpenter, Willie Forbath, Jen Seltz, Matthew Klingle, Gavin Jones, Gavin Wright, Rachel St. John, and Destin Jenkins all read parts of this manuscript. David Blight and Michael Kazin read most of it. I owe them a debt of gratitude.

David Blight, Beth Lew-Williams, and Louis Warren allowed me to see manuscripts of their forthcoming books, which aided me immensely.

Jennifer Peterson was up to any task I asked of her. She caught mistakes in the text, did research, and helped gather photographs. Branden Adams and Gabriel Lee gave aid at a critical time.

David Kennedy, the editor for *The Oxford History of the United States* series and my colleague at Stanford, is as skilled a writer as he is an historian. He and Susan Ferber, my editor at Oxford, read several drafts of this book, so many that it eventually must have seemed like a bad penny that would never go away. Every reading they gave it made it better. Whatever the book's shortcomings, they are not responsible, but they deserve credit for its merits. The final product is much better for both their editorial interventions, which I deeply appreciate.

Geoff McGhee did extraordinary work on the charts and maps. They were, as usual, far more difficult to compile and design than I imagined they would be.

Joellyn Ausanka was the editor who oversaw this book's final copyediting and production. She saved the volume from what seemed impending disaster. My software failed, but luckily she did not. I owe her a debt of gratitude beyond my thanks for the obvious skill her work displays.

Thomas Finnegan, the copy editor, has tightened the prose, helped eliminate lingering infelicities, and forced me to clarify arguments.

I also am grateful to the Stanford Humanities Center. I began working on this book during my fellowship year there.

High school teachers who took Gilder Lehrman seminars over several years have allowed me to test and polish the ideas and themes of this book. The seminars with the teachers are one of the highlights of my summers. Their questions, comments, and queries shaped the book in ways they may or may not recognize. The Gilder Lehrman Institute is a national treasure.

I owe an immense debt to the generations of scholars, many though hardly all of whom are cited in the bibliographic essay. I have used their work in creating this volume. Knowing how difficult it is to recreate and understand the past, I can only be impressed by those who did it so well.

My agent, Georges Borchardt, appears when necessary and takes care of business. If only everything worked so well. I deeply appreciate him.

And, of course, and always, there is Beverly.

Contents

Part III: The Crisis Arrives

Maps

Editor's Introduction

Before the Civil War, Americans commonly said that "the United States *are.*" After the war, despite grousing from fussy pedants, it gradually became standard usage to say that "the United States *is.*"

That grammatically anomalous and long-contested transition in popular speech to conceiving the nation in the singular rather than the plural serves as an apt metaphor for the compelling story that Richard White tells in *The Republic for Which It Stands*. To be sure, the Civil War brought formal constitutional resolution to the questions of slavery and secession. It also conferred unprecedented power on the federal government that now reigned over the restored Union. But in the remaining decades of the nineteenth century, Americans strenuously and sometimes violently struggled to define the character and purpose of the "one nation" that had emerged from the war—even as many of them continued to battle against federal authority.

This volume in *The Oxford History of the United States* richly chronicles those contests. Few of them were fully settled then or even later. Many yielded bitterly ironic consequences. Americans in the post–Civil War years may have inhabited a unified nation, but they were far from a unified people.

A renowned historian of the American West, White reminds readers of the continuing centrality of the West to the nation's history across the long arc of the nineteenth century. Conflict over the status of slavery in the far western territories torn by musket and sword from Mexico in 1848 had been the proximate cause of the Civil War. ("Mexico will poison us," Ralph Waldo Emerson had tellingly predicted.) What White calls the "Greater Reconstruction" of the postwar years focused not only on rehabilitating the defeated South, but also, no less importantly, on the application of newly invigorated federal power—conspicuously including military power—to subdue the native peoples of the West and to build the infrastructure that would facilitate the western region's settlement and its incorporation into America's headlong industrial revolution. From this perspective, Abraham Lincoln figures not simply as the Great Emancipator, but also as the faithful legatee of his great political hero, Whig statesman Henry Clay, whose prewar advocacy for the "American System" of federally sponsored internal improvements, federally catalyzed economic development, and continentally scaled national institutions provided the template for Republican policies both during and long after the Civil War. As White convincingly argues, the tortured and ultimately failed effort to reconstruct the conquered Confederacy was but part of a much larger story of ambitiously conceived, though often ill-starred, nation-building efforts in late nineteenth-century America.

Underlying and informing those efforts was a vision of an ideal America that White movingly evokes in his opening pages describing the solemn procession of Abraham Lincoln's funeral train to his hometown and burial place in Springfield, Illinois, "the figurative Nazareth of the nation." In that imaginatively idealized setting of a Midwestern small town, mostly white Protestant Americans would live productive, orderly, self-reliant lives. They would dwell in tidy homes in tranquil communities that knew neither grinding poverty nor ostentatious wealth. Wage-labor would be but a way station on the path to self-reliance and security.

The longing for a nation composed of such citizens, living and working in such places, White argues, was the deepest impulse that had animated the prewar abolitionist movement. It also drove the political imperative to give to future generations, as Lincoln put it, a West that would be "a clean bed, with no snakes in it," a place uncorrupted by "forced rivalry with negro slaves." That yearning endured and deepened through the years of Civil War. It shaped the aspirations of countless Americans as the postwar period began to unfold.

But by century's end that vision had died an inglorious death. In the states of the former Confederacy, emancipated freedmen and freedwomen found themselves rigidly segregated and all but re-enslaved in an iron cage of law and custom known as Jim Crow. The West became not Lincoln's peaceable kingdom but a new war zone, where settlers and soldiers alike ruthlessly reduced the native peoples to immiserated isolation on ever-shrinking reservations. The greatest nation-building enterprise of them all, the transcontinental railroad completed in 1869, proved a feeble engine of economic development but a fecund breeder of financial and political corruption. In the rapidly industrializing and urbanizing North, the growth of behemoth corporations swamped the hope of Americans both native-born and newly arrived that they would lead lives of economic autonomy and personal freedom. State and federal troops closed the fist of federal power over hapless "wage-slaves" in bloody clashes at places like Homestead, Pennsylvania, and Pullman, Illinois. By century's end, a new class of hyper-wealthy industrial potentates cast their shadows across the land, wielding power unimaginable to previous generations. The Republican Party, once the vehicle of emancipation, free soil, and free labor, had become their obedient servant. By then, little was left of those once-cherished illusions about racial equality and self-determination for common people.

Witnessing this spectacle of disappointment prompted Mark Twain and his co-author, Charles Dudley Warner, to write a satirical novel in 1873 that gave a name to the era: *The Gilded Age*. That legendary moniker has stubbornly persisted, right down to the subtitle of this volume. But as White impressively demonstrates, the post–Civil War decades deserve to be remembered and understood for far more than their endemic venality, vulgarity, moral turpitude, and smothered hopes. Those same years can also instruct us about the kinds of issues that have afflicted subsequent generations down to our own—including the stresses of disruptive technological innovation, uncontrollable cycles of economic boom and bust, widening disparities in wealth and income, unprecedented immigrant inflows, political polarization and legislative deadlock, the obsolescence of legacy institutions when faced with baffling changes in an ever more kinetic marketplace, as well as the timeless human predicament of scaling even the most honorable hopes to the unforgiving metrics of recalcitrant reality.

All these themes Richard White develops with the skill of a seasoned historical analyst, even while he writes with the panache and sensitivity of an accomplished novelist. Irony is the dominant tone of his account, though it is sounded with empathy and respect for those whose lives he recounts. He peoples his pages with a parade of personalities both famous and infamous, familiar and obscure—from the triumphant general turned inept president, Ulysses Grant, to the principled lawyer, Albion Tourgée, who argued and lost the notorious 1896 segregation case of *Plessy v. Ferguson*; from the august Brahmin historian Henry Adams to the freed slave of the same name who fought against anti-black terrorism in postwar Louisiana; from the railroad magnates Leland Stanford, Collis P. Huntington, and Henry Villard to the relentless temperance advocate Frances Willard and antilynching crusader Ida B. Wells; from the vainglorious General George Armstrong Custer to the cunning Lakota strategist, Red Cloud; and from the legendary to the real-life steel-drivin' man, John Henry.

All the volumes in *The Oxford History of the United States* strive to bring the most comprehensive and current historical scholarship to experts as well as to general readers. *The Republic for Which It Stands* admirably meets—indeed exceeds—that standard. Richard White has succeeded in doing what many historians have attempted but few have achieved. He has deeply reconceptualized a complex, consequential moment in the history of the Republic, one whose challenges and dilemmas echo robustly in our own time.

David M. Kennedy

The Republic for Which It Stands

Introduction

> Wandering between two worlds, one dead,
> The other powerless to be born...

Matthew Arnold's famous lines from "Stanzas from the Grand Chartreuse" have long served as an epigram for nineteenth-century Europeans whose past seemed far more certain than their future. Arnold, the English poet adored by American liberals, looking out from a French monastery in 1850, evoked the tensions and confusion of emerging industrial modernity. What he said of Europe applied to the post–Civil War United States as well, if only as a borrowed garment.

In 1865 an older American nation had died, a casualty of the Civil War. Abraham Lincoln's lesson taken from the Gospel of Mark, that "a house divided against itself cannot stand," had been rewritten in blood. The old Union had perished in a fratricidal war, but Northerners did not doubt that, again in Lincoln's words, "this nation, under God, shall have a new birth of freedom." They would resurrect the best of the old society with the cancer of slavery cut out.

Americans did give birth to a new nation, but it was not the one they imagined. How the United States at the end of the nineteenth century turned out to be so different from the country that Lincoln conjured and Republicans confidently set out to create is the subject of this book.

Arnold's metaphor of gestation and birth imagined two discrete worlds, one quickening as the other died, but Americans had, unknowingly, conceived twins in 1865. The first twin embodied the world they anticipated emerging from the Civil War, and it died before ever being born. The second, unexpected, twin lived, forever haunted by its sibling.

Americans have been of two minds of that surviving twin ever since. They have recognized that it carried some of the noblest instincts and ambitions of the triumphant republic even if these were more fully embodied in its vanished sibling: a world of equal opportunity, a uniform set of rights, and a homogeneous citizenship guaranteed by the federal government. This was the world Radical Republicans like Thaddeus Stevens imagined in a Greater Reconstruction that would remake the country—West as well as South—in the mold of the Free Labor North. Ideally, every community in the United States would become a replica of Springfield, Illinois, Abraham Lincoln's hometown and the figurative Nazareth of the nation. The country would be Protestant and roughly egalitarian without either of the "dangerous classes": the very rich or the very poor. Independent production would be the norm and wage labor but a stage in life. Historians often write of Reconstruction and the Gilded Age as if they were separate and consecutive eras, but the two gestated together.

Actual Reconstruction considerably scaled back the vaunting ambitions of the most radical of the Republicans. It denied rights and protections to other men and all women even as it guaranteed them to white and black men, but still the audacity of the Thirteenth, Fourteenth, and Fifteenth Amendments of the Constitution that ended slavery, granted citizenship, and gave the vote to ex-slaves remains inspiring. Rarely have Americans moved so boldly or so quickly.

Greater Reconstruction presented only one aspect of the Gilded Age. When Mark Twain and Charles Dudley Warner wrote *The Gilded Age: A Tale of Today* in 1873, they gave a forgettable novel a memorable title that has come to stand for the entire late nineteenth century. The pithy title covered a convoluted plot whose moral was the danger of privileging speculation over honest labor. The "Gilded Age" exposed the rot beneath the gilded surface. Historians once embraced corruption as diagnostic of the age, but for the past half century they have downplayed its importance. They have been wrong to do so. The Gilded Age was corrupt, and corruption in government and business mattered. Corruption suffused government and the economy. "Friendship" defined the relation between public officials and businessmen, and officials from postmasters to deputy sheriffs and judges received fees for services. Lavish subsidies went to private corporations such as the transcontinental railroads, and the government subcontracted public responsibilities from prisons, Indian reservations, moral regulation, and more to churches, corporations, and other private organizations.[1]

In this volume of *The Oxford History of the United States*, the Gilded Age begins in 1865 with Reconstruction and ends with the election of William McKinley. This period for a long time devolved into historical flyover country. Writers and scholars departed the Civil War, taxied through Reconstruction, and embarked on a flight to the twentieth

---

1. Mark Twain and Charles Dudley Warner, *The Gilded Age: A Tale of to-Day*, 2 vols. (New York: Harper & Brothers, 1915, orig. ed. 1873).

century and the Progressives, while only rarely touching down in between. Such neglect has changed with recent scholarship that has revealed a country transformed by immigration, urbanization, environmental crisis, political stalemate, new technologies, the creation of powerful corporations, income inequality, failures of governance, mounting class conflict, and increasing social, cultural, and religious diversity.

Failed presidencies proliferated across the Gilded Age. Critical periods in American history tend to be epitomized by a dominant political figure: Jefferson, Jackson, Lincoln, Wilson, the two Roosevelts, Reagan. But the Gilded Age does not induce hagiography. Its presidents come from the Golden Age of Facial Hair, none of them seemingly worth remembering for any substantial achievement. There was no Age of Harrison.

Political parties mattered far more than presidents, but these parties were not particularly ideological. They tapped deeper loyalties that arose out of the Civil War and religious, ethnic, and sectional identities. People became Republicans and Democrats because of who they were more than because of the principles they espoused. Both parties contained members across an ideological spectrum.

The Republican Party dominated American politics at the end of the Civil War, but it changed after the war. The split between radical, moderate, and conservative that defined the wartime party's divisions yielded to a split between those Republicans whose beliefs mirrored those of the old Whig Party, and liberals. Whiggish Republicans believed in a strong and interventionist government, and during the Civil War they put those beliefs into practice, passing the Homestead Act; the Morrill Tariff; the Morrill Act, funding state land grant universities; and subsidizing transcontinental and other railroads. After the war, they possessed no more patience with laissez-faire than they had before or during it. Gilded Age liberals sprang from a noble European and American lineage whose opposition to hierarchies and privileges made them enemies of the Catholic Church, monarchy, aristocracy, and human slavery. Nineteenth-century liberals stressed individual freedom, private property, economic competition, and small government. These ideological distinctions do not map easily onto the political beliefs of the late twentieth and early twenty-first century. Liberals, in particular, produced a varied progeny now scattered across the modern political spectrum. Modern liberals have inherited their namesakes' concern with individual rights, but they do not tie those rights as closely to property as nineteenth-century liberals, and they have abandoned their distrust of government intervention in the economy. In this respect, they are more like Whigs. Nineteenth-century liberals, with their devotion to laissez faire and property rights and their faith in competition, were closer to twentieth and twenty-first century conservatives and closer still to libertarians. During the Civil War, Gilded Age liberals had temporarily accepted the need for a powerful central government—the so-called Yankee Leviathan—in the war against slavery, but they feared such centralized power after the war, which put them in opposition to Regular Republicans.

Politics changed over the period, but politics and politicians did not change nearly so rapidly as ordinary life and ordinary Americans. During the Gilded Age, the actions of millions mattered more than the actions of a few. The cumulative efforts of tens of thousands of tinkerers transformed technology. People moved from the countryside into cities and, in much smaller numbers, from the east to the west. Mass immigration made the United States, in today's parlance, diverse and multicultural even as the country tried, and failed, to bridge the racial chasm that slavery had created. Then, as now, large numbers of native-born Americans did not regard diversity as a good thing, and the arrival of Catholic and Jewish immigrants spawned a nativist reaction. One of the ironies of the Gilded Age was that during this period the United States both completed the

"Home Sweet Home," the title of this Currier and Ives print, was the refrain of a popular song in a now-forgotten English opera. It became a favorite of both Union and Confederate soldiers and captures the sentimentalized home that loomed so large in Victorian culture. Library of Congress, LC-USZC2-2590.

four-centuries-long conquest of Indian peoples by Europeans and their descendants and then treated Indians like immigrant Europeans: a people to be acculturated and assimilated.

Americans assessed these changes in terms of the home, a symbol so ubiquitous and seemingly so bland that it can vanish while in plain sight. The home became the beating heart of an expansive political program that would create black homes, impose "proper" homes on Indian peoples, exclude Chinese (deemed both a threat to American homes and incapable of creating their own), and expand the white home into the West. Home embodied all the gendered and racialized assumptions of American republicanism and the American economy. It contained manly men and womanly women united in monogamous marriage to reproduce families. It originally provided a site of production as well as reproduction. The threat to the home—from industrialization, great wealth, and urbanization—became a threat to the entire society. Farmers and workers mobilized the home in defense of their interests. Those who failed to secure proper homes were cast as a danger to the white home—as happened to Chinese, blacks, Indians, and to a lesser degree some European immigrants. They became the targets of horrendous violence and repression, which the perpetrators always cast as self-defense. The struggle over Reconstruction, as well as the class struggle that emerged in the 1870s, ended up as a struggle over the home.

Invoking the gendered home involved seizing a weapon of considerable power. Frances Willard, of the Woman's Christian Temperance Union, realized this. Her broad campaign of home protection made her into one of the most formidable and powerful political figures of the century. She was hardly alone. Buffalo Bill Cody placed it at the center of popular culture, and President Rutherford B. Hayes deployed it to buttress Republican programs and the creation of a nascent social welfare system.

Willard was both a feminist and an evangelical Christian, and the United States remained a profoundly evangelical Protestant culture whose reforming zeal had hardly been exhausted by the success of abolition. Evangelical Protestantism had been the great wellspring of American reform since the 1830s, and its current had widened to take in not only an expanding country but also the world. Temperance reform became its great cause, but this was one among many. Americans exported missionaries and reformers in an attempt to create what historian Ian Tyrrell has called "America's moral empire."

American engagement with the world managed to be both expansive and defensive. The United States defined itself against Europe, and Americans regarded most of the rest of the world as barbarous. Americans exported missionaries and reformers as well as wheat and cotton, while trying to shut themselves off from those European manufacturers that threatened American industry. At the same time, immigrants made the United States a polyglot nation, filled with people from Europe, Canada, Asia, and Mexico. Nor were ideas easily banished. American students, intellectuals, and officials traveled to Europe and brought back European notions and philosophies.

Yet to simply track the United States as another swimmer in a vast transnational current misses all the complexities of the Gilded Age. Most of the changes examined in this volume took place on national and regional scales, not the transnational. Transnational developments mattered, but during the Gilded Age the nation took shape in response to these larger changes rather than as a simple reflection of them. The existence of a larger global economy, for example, led to an American nationalist reaction—the tariff—that profoundly shaped the American economy and American politics.

Abraham Lincoln, the politician whose memory and legacy dominated the Gilded Age, died as this book begins, but he never really vanished. The novelist and critic William Dean Howells captured part of the reason when he reviewed John Hay's and John Nicolay's monumental biography of the president in 1890. Howells wrote that "if America means anything at all, it means the sufficiency of the common, the insufficiency of the uncommon." Lincoln had come to be both the personification of the American common people and the nation's greatest—and most uncommon—president. Howells thought it was the nation's common people and common traits that most mattered.[2]

Howells, famous then and largely forgotten since, knew most everyone, but he always remained detached. He watched, and he wrote. His interventions in politics remained minor. Howells was a Midwesterner, and this was the great age of the Midwest. Originally a committed liberal, he came to acknowledge liberalism's failures and insufficiencies, and then struggled to imagine alternatives. He did so as a writer, and he and his fellow Realists created invaluable portraits of the age. In his confusion, his intelligence, and his honesty, he reminds us that for those living through the Gilded Age it was an astonishing and frightening period, full of great hopes as well as deep fears. When Howells cryptically embraces the common, it is worth listening to him. Understanding his judgment of the "sufficiency of the common, the insufficiency of the uncommon" provides a lens for assessing the Gilded Age.

2. "Editor's Study," February 1891, William Dean Howells, *Editor's Study*, ed. James W. Simpson (Troy, NY: Whitston, 1983), 298.

The Gilded Age produced uncommon men and women. They abound in this volume, but in Howells's lifetime, and during the twentieth century, businessmen who amassed wealth on a scale never seen before in American history became the face of the period. Contemporary caricaturists and later historians named them the Robber Barons, but this, as well as their later incarnation as farsighted entrepreneurs, gave them too much credit. They never really mastered the age. When Howells wrote of "the insufficiency of the uncommon," he probably had them in mind, seeing them as insufficient to the demands of the period for the same reasons as Charles Francis Adams, who had aspired to be one of them and then dismissed them his *Autobiography*.

> I have known tolerably well, a good many "successful" men—"big" financially—men famous during the last half-century, and a less interesting crowd I do not care to encounter. Not one that I have ever known would I care to meet again, either in this world or the next; nor is one of them associated in my mind with the idea of humor, thought or refinement. A set of mere money-getters and traders, they were essentially unattractive and uninteresting.[3]

In a period that began with such exalted hopes and among a people so willing to proclaim their virtue as were Americans, sufficient seems condemning with faint praise, but a sobered Howells writing in the midst of what seemed a prolonged economic, political, and social crisis expressed a restrained optimism. Howells did not romanticize the "common people." The failure of Reconstruction in the South was, in part, their failure. They often at least consented to the corruption of democratic governance. And for most of the Gilded Age the "common people" questioned whether they really had much in common as race, religion, ethnicity, class, and gender divided the nation. Yet their actions transformed the country, even if they undertook perhaps the most consequential of these actions—the movement into wage labor—unwillingly and under duress.

In judging them sufficient, Howells settled down in between the dystopian and utopian fantasies that marked the age. Millions of ordinary Americans had remade the country with their work, their movements, their agitation, their tinkering, their broad and vernacular intellectualism that neither aspired to nor created a high culture, and even with their amusements. They had not succumbed to the long economic and social

---

3. Charles Francis Adams, *An Autobiography, 1835–1915, with a Memorial Address Delivered November 17, 1915, by Henry Cabot Lodge* (Boston: Houghton Mifflin 1916), 190.

crisis that threatened to overwhelm the country. What they accomplished was sufficient. It was a foundation on which to build.

Howells and his contemporaries never escaped the great gravitational pull of the Civil War. The era began with the universal conviction that the Civil War was the watershed in the nation's history and ended with the proposition that the white settlement of the West defined the national character. Changing the national story from the Civil War to the West amounted to an effort to escape the shadow of the Gilded Age's vanished twin and evade the failure of Reconstruction. Rewriting the Civil War as a mere interruption of the national narrative of western expansion minimized the traumas and vestiges of the Civil War and downplayed the significance of the transformation of Gilded Age economy and society. But too much had changed, and too much blood had been spilled in the War, for such a simple story of continuity to be fully persuasive. The twin, never born, shadowed the Gilded Age. A vision of a country unachieved lingered, and quarrels over what should come next remained unresolved.

Howells settled for the sufficient. It was not a judgment he came to easily; nor is it the kind of judgment we expect from Americans. How he made it, and why he judged the common life of his country sufficient, involves a long story, a history of the Gilded Age.

Part I

Reconstructing the Nation

Prologue
Mourning Lincoln

On Good Friday, April 14, 1865, John Wilkes Booth shot Abraham Lincoln in Ford's Theatre in Washington, D.C. Lincoln died the next day. For a country inclined to see the war as God's judgment on the national sin of slavery, the shooting on the day the Christian savior died was deeply symbolic. William Dean Howells was then a young journalist and aspiring novelist. He had written a campaign biography of Lincoln and been rewarded with the post of consul in Venice. Lincoln's death, he thought, fell "upon every American like a personal calamity." It blackened the national future, "but thank God they cannot assassinate a whole Republic: the People is immortal."[1]

The People might be immortal, but who counted as "the People" was open to question. Not everyone mourned. Many Southerners, at least privately, rejoiced, and so did some Northern Copperheads, though public celebration was dangerous. That there would be vengeance was certain, but whether it would extend beyond the assassins was unclear. Calls for the extermination of the traitors were common, and most Southerners fell within the net of treason. Gen. Carl Schurz thought the Confederates should be grateful that most of their troops had already surrendered because if the Union army were still on the march the slaughter would have

---

1. The basic account is drawn from Dorothy Kunhardt, *Twenty Days: A Narrative in Text and Pictures of the Assassination of Abraham Lincoln and the Twenty Days and Nights That Followed—the Nation in Mourning, the Long Trip Home to Springfield*, ed. Philip B. Kunhardt (New York: Harper & Row, 1965); Victor Searcher, *The Farewell to Lincoln* (New York: Abingdon Press, 1965); Merrill D. Peterson, *Lincoln in American Memory* (New York: Oxford University Press, 1994), 14–24; Martha Hodes, *Mourning Lincoln* (New Haven, CT: Yale University Press, 2015), 46–91; Richard Wightman Fox, *Lincoln's Body: A Cultural History* (New York: Norton, 2015), 3–123; W. D. Howells to W. C. Howells, Apr. 28, 1865, William Dean Howells, *Selected Letters*, ed. George Warren Arms (Boston: Twayne, 1979), 1: 215; "A Nation in Tears," *Chicago Tribune*, Apr. 17, 1865 (Chicago: ProQuest Historical Newspapers), 2; "American Self-Control," *Chicago Tribune*, Apr. 19, 1865; "News by Telegraph," *Chicago Tribune*, Apr. 20, 1865, 1.

rivaled that of Attila the Hun. Mary Butler in Pennsylvania called for "death to all traitors," and she included among them her cousin and suitor Frank. But calls for vengeance quickly narrowed first to the Southern leadership and then to the assassins themselves.

With rage focused on Booth and his fellow conspirators, real and imagined, the nation gave way to grief. "A Nation in Tears" read the *Chicago Tribune's* headline on April 17. The trial and execution of Booth's accused co-conspirators would be far less than fair, but despite the nation's fury, there was little violence against Confederate sympathizers.[2]

Lincoln had been shot in a theater, but it was unthinkable that he should die there. For many American Protestants theaters were profane, and the president's presence there on Good Friday was disturbing. Doctors had quickly moved his body to William Petersen's boarding house across the street, where Lincoln had died without speaking or recovering consciousness. The price of black crepe soared as the work of interpretation began. The first draft belonged to the Radical Republicans. At a ceremony in New York the day Lincoln died, Rep. James Garfield of Ohio—known as "the praying Colonel" during the Civil War—had explained why God had allowed the assassination of "the kindest, gentlest...friend" that the people of the South could expect. It was because Lincoln was too good and too kind. God had made Lincoln his instrument to save the Union, and he had become Christ-like and a martyr, but God would use sterner men to reconstruct the South. Across the North hundreds of Protestant ministers echoed this theme.[3]

Lincoln's wake and extended funeral began on Tuesday, April 18, when the East Room of the White House opened for the first of many public viewings of his body. Benjamin French, then the commissioner of public buildings and a past Grand Master of the Freemasons of the District of Columbia, designed a catafalque —the raised structure on which the body was exhibited—modeled after the Lodge of Sorrows featured in Masonic funerals. From 9:30 that morning until 5:30 that evening mourners, six or seven abreast, filed through the White House, draped, inside and out, in black. It was a mark of the age that of the six hundred people invited to the East Room ceremony only seven were women. Six of the women were the wives and daughters of the invited eminent men; the other was the nurse who had cared for Willie Lincoln before his death in 1862.

2. Hodes, 46–91, 117–38, particularly 21, 23; William Alan Blair, *With Malice toward Some: Treason and Loyalty in the Civil War Era* (Chapel Hill: University of North Carolina Press, 2014), 234–35; "A Nation in Tears"; "American Self-Control."

3. Fox, 34–36, 51–52, 56–58, 66–68; Hodes, 4–5.

That following day a solemn procession carried the body of the slain president down Pennsylvania Avenue to the Capitol, where Lincoln would lay in state. This was a northern ceremony because the North *was*, for the moment, the nation. Its sectional values of free labor were the values Lincoln both proclaimed and embodied, and they had become by virtual default the national values. The South lay in defeat and ruins. But ironically Lincoln's victory tolled the knell for the world that produced him. The Civil War that seemed to ensure the triumph of a free labor society—of small individual producers bound together by contract freedom—was really a rather large step in the demise of that society. The Union was already changed and on the verge of far greater changes than the mourners could anticipate. Defeat certainly doomed the South. Victory had just as certainly doomed the North. Americans surely knew that the nation was changing, but Northerners thought that it was the South that would embody the changes, morphing into a sunny version of the North. Unionists regarded the war as a surgery necessary to excise the cancer of slavery and thought the bloody operation had restored the health of the republic.[4]

The war begun to save the union had become, as Maine's Sen. Lot Morrill would say in 1866, a second American revolution. Slavery and the extremes of states' rights—the hallmarks of the South—were dead. Without slavery, there would have been no war. The South fought in defense of slavery; it had said so, vociferously and repeatedly, and the South had lost. The federal government was more powerful than ever. These things were settled. The revolution confirmed the Northern order even as it overthrew the Southern. The revolution intended to make the South a reflection of the North.[5]

The changes that the North celebrated were on display in Washington in 1865. Black mourners—men, women, and children—crowded the streets in front of the White House as the pallbearers started the body on its long journey. A *Chicago Tribune* reporter wrote, "The sight was novel. Four years since a procession of this description could no more have passed unmolested through the streets of the National Capital than it

4. Hodes, 145–56. Drew Gilpin Faust gives a superb analysis of the funeral and the nation's grief. Faust, *This Republic of Suffering: Death and the American Civil War* (New York: Knopf, 2008), 156–61.
5. Eric Foner, *Reconstruction: America's Unfinished Revolution, 1863–1877* (New York: Harper & Row, 1988), 245; James Oliver Horton, "Confronting Slavery and Revealing the Lost Cause," *Cultural Resource Management* 24, no. 4 (1998): 1–6; Chandra Manning, *What This Cruel War Was Over: Soldiers, Slavery, and the Civil War* (New York: Knopf, 2007), 1–18, passim.

could have passed over Long Bridge from Virginia into the District of Columbia without passes from their slave driving masters."[6]

More astonishing still would be the Twenty-second U.S. Colored Troops, marching with trailed arms, who preceded Lincoln's coffin along Pennsylvania Avenue when it left the White House. No one had intended that black soldiers lead the otherwise carefully orchestrated parade. The regiment had swung into line off a side street and found itself at the head of the procession. But then to many, black people were an unending source of surprise. Few in 1861 could have imagined regiments of black men armed to fight white men, and few whites in 1865 imagined black people at the forefront of the struggle over Reconstruction in the South.[7]

The capital exhibited the triumph of not just the nation but also the state. The ceremony became the domain of the federal government rather than the family. Three men central to the immediate future of that government sat in the East Room when the funeral began on Wednesday, April 19. Each was already wary of the others. Gen. Ulysses S. Grant, who had declined an invitation to accompany the Lincolns to Ford's Theatre the night of the assassination, sat near the body, as did the new president, Andrew Johnson, and Edwin Stanton, the secretary of war. From the immediate family, only Lincoln's son Robert was present. Mary Todd Lincoln remained confined to bed, and her younger son Tad, too, stayed in the family quarters. Sitting with Robert Lincoln were Abraham Lincoln's brothers-in-law and two of Mary Lincoln's first cousins, as well as Lincoln's two secretaries, John Nicolay and John Hay, men who were considered part of his official household.

Four ministers—a Baptist, a Presbyterian, an Episcopalian, and a Methodist—conducted the White House funeral service. The United States in 1865 was an overwhelmingly Protestant country with a feared Catholic minority, and Protestant ecumenism was ecumenism enough. Many Christians had distrusted Lincoln early in his career. His religious beliefs were not orthodox, but Lincoln had always understood the political importance of Protestantism in the United States, and he had cultivated northern evangelicals without sharing their postmillennialism or their fixation on a personal savior.[8]

In the East Room the public officials and ministers participated in the transformation of Abraham Lincoln into a symbol of a chosen Protestant

6. Hodes, 146; "News by Telegram," 1.
7. Hodes, 146.
8. Searcher, 72–78. Richard J. Carwardine, "Lincoln, Evangelical Religion, and American Political Culture in the Era of the Civil War," *Journal of the Abraham Lincoln Association* 18, no. 1 (1997): 27–55.

nation, but the procession marked him as the fallen leader of a powerful modern state—the Yankee Leviathan—that had crushed the South in the biggest war ever fought in North America. The voice of the state sounded in the minute guns that boomed throughout the march and in the muffled drums of the thirty military bands. It could be seen in the columns of soldiers.

The funeral train carrying the dead president finally left Washington on Friday, April 21, traveling back to Springfield, Illinois, Lincoln's hometown, by roughly the same seventeen-hundred-mile route that had brought the president to Washington in 1861. Some of those who had escorted him in death had earlier escorted him in life. In a reminder that Lincoln was a father touched by personal as well as national tragedy, the train also carried the remains of his young son Willie, who had died during Lincoln's presidency. The train proceeded among a somber and adoring people, many of whom had not thought nearly so highly of Lincoln during his lifetime. Henry Ward Beecher—abolitionist minister, brother of novelist Harriet Beecher Stowe, and the leading figure of American evangelicalism—spoke for the nation. The martyr moved

> in triumphal march, mightier than when alive. The nation rises up at every stage of his coming. Cities and states are his pall-bearers and the cannon speaks the hours with solemn progression....Wail and weep here; God makes it echo joy and triumph there. Pass on! Four years ago, Oh Illinois, we took from thy midst an untried man, and from among the people; we return him to you a mighty conqueror. Not thine any more, but the nation's; not ours, but the world's.[9]

The procession down Pennsylvania Avenue had displayed military organization and the technology of war, but the journey home to Springfield displayed equally formidable American organizations and a technology of peace. The telegraph already knit the country together, coordinating sermons and ceremonies that took place simultaneously across the North. Largely a tool of newspapers and financiers, the telegraph carried the schedule of funeral arrangements and told those in one place what had happened in another. Some in the North waited for the funeral procession to come to them; others flocked to the cities where the great ceremonies took place. If any distance was involved, they came by rail, for, in the North at least, the age of steam, iron, and coal had arrived.[10]

The bodies of the father and the beloved son would travel to Baltimore, Harrisburg, Philadelphia, New York, Albany, Buffalo, Cleveland, Columbus,

9. Hodes, 144–56; Faust, 156–61; Fox, 110–21; *Chicago Tribune*, Apr. 28, 1865.
10. Richard R. John, *Network Nation: Inventing American Telecommunications* (Cambridge, MA: Belknap Press of Harvard University Press, 2010), 52–53, 78–80, 145–47.

Indianapolis, and Chicago, before arriving in Springfield. The train was to run at a maximum speed of twenty miles an hour, with a preferred speed of only five miles per hour.[11]

In the cities vast throngs watched and marched in processions that stretched for miles past buildings draped in black; sometimes, as in Philadelphia, there was disorder and tumult. In New York space at windows with prime views of the procession supposedly rented for $25. Mostly there was an orderly grief, a surprising patience in lines to view the body, which by New York was already beginning to darken visibly. Perhaps more impressive than the great ceremonies were the receptions at towns and villages where the train stopped briefly or not at all. The crowds stood silent, men's, and sometimes women's, heads uncovered, people softly weeping. Farmers, their wives, and children gathered along the tracks. Bonfires silhouetted them against the night. At many places a tableaux of thirty-six young women dressed in white with black sashes carrying flags representing the thirty-six states stood in silent witness.[12]

The journey started in the East but the train's destination was the Midwest, the region that Americans then usually called the West. The rest of the century would in many ways belong to the Midwest. By 1870 its population exceeded that of the New England and the Middle Atlantic States combined. Outside of their great cities, these Midwesterners were a largely white, Protestant, and rural people. Like other Americans, their letters and diaries noted Lincoln's passing and recorded their grief. They thought "time stood still," but they also noted the ongoing daily tasks of a still largely preindustrial nation. Midwestern farms produced most of the country's food, and its shops—there were relatively few large factories—made the region the country's fastest growing manufacturing section, doubling its share of manufacturing jobs during the 1860s. By 1900 it would surpass New England's manufacturing output and was rivaling the Middle Atlantic States.[13]

Men and women born in the Midwest, if not always living there, would soon dominate American culture and politics. William Dean Howells, the editor and novelist who became one of the most influential of them, would describe "the best sort of American" as a "Westerner... with Eastern

11. "News by Telegraph," *Chicago Tribune*, Apr. 22, 1865; Robert Reed, *Lincoln's Funeral Train: The Epic Journey from Washington to Springfield* (Atglen, PA: Schiffer, 2014), 20; Fox, 110.
12. Hodes, 152; *Chicago Tribune*, Apr. 27, 1865, 1; Kunhardt.
13. Hodes, 170; David R. Meyer, "Midwestern Industrialization and the American Manufacturing Belt in the Nineteenth Century," *Journal of Economic History* 49, no. 4 (1989): 921–26.

finish." The national and financial capitals would remain in the East, primarily in New York, and the myth of the nation would eventually move still further westward into the Great Plains and Rocky Mountains and beyond, but those who wielded power in Congress and the White House were largely Midwesterners. The presidency would be the special province of Midwesterners. Andrew Johnson was from Tennessee; all but two other presidents for the remainder of the century would be born in Ohio. Howells and Missouri's Mark Twain were Midwestern writers who claimed national audiences. Dwight Moody, who would succeed Beecher as the era's most prominent evangelist, was born in New England but made his mark in Chicago. Robert Ingersoll, the country's leading orator and religious skeptic, had also been born in the East but moved to Illinois. Prominent Midwestern reformers, women such Frances Willard, who would eventually head the Woman's Christian Temperance Union, and Jane Addams of Chicago's Hull House were more likely to remain in the Midwest, but their influence, too, went far beyond their own region. In bringing Lincoln home, Mary Lincoln, who did not accompany the train, reinforced an idea firmly in place by the end of the century that the Midwest, in a vast and varied country, was the heartland, the supposedly quintessential American place.[14]

If the Midwest was the heartland, then Chicago, despite being in many ways the most atypical place in it, was the heartland's capital. It was the funeral train's last stop before Springfield, and measured by rapid growth and diversity Chicago was perhaps the most vibrant, if raucous, city in the country. It had sprung from a near swamp, doubled in population during the 1860s, and by 1870 would number about 350,000 people. It was, as historian William Cronon has put it, "Nature's Metropolis," drawing in the productions of northern forests and western prairies and the energy of the vast interior. Lincoln's funeral train arrived on May 1 and pulled out on a trestle that stretched into Lake Michigan. It had rained for a week before the train's arrival, and the funeral procession proceeded through dirt streets with the mud swept into giant embankments along their edges. Lincoln lay in state at the Cook County Court House, where a reported 40,000 people viewed the body on the first day alone.[15]

Americans mourned individually, but they also mourned collectively, and when they did it was not as a homogeneous national mass but rather as a collection of groups. Americans, particularly American men, were joiners. That the Masons had commandeered the symbolism of the state

14. Quote, W. D. Howells to Whitelaw Reid, Oct. 22, 1880, Howells, 2: 269.
15. William Cronon, *Nature's Metropolis: Chicago and the Great West* (New York: Norton, 1991), 299–300; "The City," *Chicago Tribune*, May 2, 1865.

funeral was no accident; they were the most powerful of numerous voluntary organizations. The grouping of mourners at Chicago conveyed much
about the North. They marched in five divisions, each with its clubs,
orders, and sodalities, some ethnic, some religious, some by craft, and
none open to all: the Knights Templar, the Lodges of the Ancient Order
of Free and Accepted Masons, the Independent Order of Odd Fellows,
the Fenian Brotherhood, the Young Men's Association, the Holland and
Belgian Society, the St. Joseph's Society, French Mutual Aid Society,
German Roman Catholic Benevolent Society, Society Svea, Order of
Hamgair, Society Nova, German Workingman's Association, Old Free
Order of Chaidaer (Cholduer), Turnverein, Sons of Hermann, Ancient
United Order of Druids, North Chicago Workingmen's Relief Society,
Social Arbeiter Verein, Germania Bruderbund, Hebrew Benevolent Asso-
ciation, Chicago Bildungs Verein, German Stone Cutters' Association,
German Masons and Bricklayers' Society, Cabinet Makers' Society,
Butchers' Association, and on and on with United Sons of Erin, the
Colored Citizens of Chicago, and the Chicago Fire Department bringing
up the rear. Not all these groups were equal. Most were segregated by race
as well as gender, and, in a foretaste of the way freedom would be seasoned with inequality, black people marched near the very end of the
parade in Washington and Chicago; in New York the city council had
tried to prevent them from marching at all.[16]

The solemnity of the dead president's progress was mixed with anxiety.
There was, for example, a nearly obsessive concern with the condition of
the president's body. It was "blackening," and there were debates over
whether the coffin should continue to be opened for viewing. Undertakers
at every stop rouged and powdered the face. Lincoln was, after all, now
just a corpse, but the *Chicago Tribune* took pains to dispute any decay.
The *Tribune* acknowledged some darkening but also reported Lincoln's
lifelike appearance—"as if calmly slumbering." The embalmer, Dr.
Charles Brown, who kept his method secret, had promised that the body
would "never know decay."

It was hard to preserve the body, and it proved equally hard to preserve
the intricate paraphernalia of the funeral. In Washington and nearly every
city thereafter memento seekers took tiny pieces from the catafalques.
Thousands of visitors to Lincoln's old home in Springfield nearly stripped
it of living vegetation, chipped off paint, and carried away bricks.[17]

16. "Funeral of the President," *Chicago Tribune*, May 1, 1865, 3–4. Proquest Digital
    Microfilm.
17. "From Springfield," May 4, 1865; Hodes, 144; Peterson, 26–35; Fox, 65; "The City,"
    Chicago Tribune, May 2, 1865.

Interment in Springfield took place on May 4. Mary Lincoln was still distraught and conspicuously absent. She bore no affection for the town nor for most of its residents, but she had decided Oak Ridge Cemetery in Springfield was where Lincoln would have wanted to be buried. It was early May and the lilacs were in bloom when the funeral train arrived. In the memories of those who came that day—and in the millions who would later read Walt Whitman's elegiac poem, "When Lilacs Last in the Dooryard Bloom'd"—the dead Lincoln and fragrance of lilacs would always be connected. The town buried him in a simple tomb in an isolated cemetery. Eventually, Springfield would build the grander structure town leaders desired.

Old resentments and tensions did not change the fact that this was Lincoln's home.

The town had grown quickly, but it had only ninety-four hundred people—roughly one-third of them born abroad—when the war began. The town could seem unprepossessing, but at the outbreak of the war it had bustled with activity. It was the state capital. It had a woolen mill, a broom factory, and a planing mill as well as car factories and repair shops for its railroads. In its industry, ambition, and zeal for improvement, Springfield emblematized Lincoln, his life, and the America that was disappearing far better than the grand monuments to him that the nation would eventually build. Methodist Bishop Matthew Simpson, who preached the funeral service, put the president to rest figuratively as well as physically in the Midwestern prairie for "his home was in the growing West, the heart of the Republic...." Lincoln came home, Simpson declared, not just to the prairie but also to the people, who would not "be subject to tyrants or autocrats, or to class rule of any kind."[18]

The iconography of home was everywhere in Gilded Age America, but perhaps no region featured it as prominently as the Midwest. The mythic stories of American republicanism all paired individualism and the home. The story of Lincoln was of the type: a story of both triumphant individualism—a man whose fate was in his own hands—and the home. Born poor, Lincoln rose to the presidency. His story began with his birth in a

18. "The Obsequies at Springfield," *New York Tribune*, May 5, 1865; Bonnie E. Paul and Richard E. Hart, *Lincoln's Springfield Neighborhood* (Charleston, SC: History Press, 2015), 76–77; "The Obsequies at Springfield," *Daily National Republican*, May 5, 1865; Paul M. Angle, *Here I Have Lived: A History of Lincoln's Springfield, 1821–1865* (Springfield, IL: Abraham Lincoln Association, 1935), 165–66, 184, 187; Matthew Simpson, "Funeral Address Delivered at the Burial of President Lincoln, Rev. Matthew Simpson, May 4, 1865, Methodist Episcopal Church, Springfield, Illinois," in *The Martyred President: Sermons Given on the Occasion of the Assassination of Abraham Lincoln* (Atlanta: Pitts Theology Library, Emory University).

Kentucky log cabin—the American manger—and culminated in his rise to the White House. His life's trajectory traced the course between two homes: one the humblest imaginable, little better than slave cabins, and the other the residence of the nation's first family. The creation and growth of the home became the great trope of Lincoln's Midwest.

But this focus on the beginning and end of Lincoln's journey omitted the critical center of his life: Springfield, which he always considered home. Lincoln's friend James Matheny had written in the Springfield City Directory of 1858, "Every man in our midst who has evidenced a reasonable industry, coupled with care and prudence, has a home of his own, humble though it be, yet nevertheless, it is a 'home'—and what costly palace is more than that." Springfield, its surrounding farms, and innumerable places like it were the culmination of the ambitions of the men and women of Lincoln's and his children's generations. As the residents aged, publishing houses in the Midwest sent out agents to sell subscriptions to county histories. Their main feature was biographical sketches written from material provided by the subscribers. The purchasers, in effect, commemorated their own lives in illustrated volumes colloquially known as mug books because they contained portraits of the subscribers. They also contained illustrations of their homes that reveal how they understood their lives. In the picture of the finished prosperous farm with its large house is an inset of a cabin, often labeled "Our first home in the woods." The paired pictures captured the arc of these Americans' lives and the achievement of their ambitions: the creation of a prosperous home.[19]

Perhaps the most revealing memorial to Lincoln was not a memorial at all. It was the census of 1860, the most common of American state documents. There he was on line 16, page 140 of Schedule 1 for Springfield: Abraham Lincoln, fifty-one years old, lawyer, owner of home worth $5,000, $12,000 in personal property, born in Kentucky. Wife, thirty-six-year-old Mary, no property listed, born also in Kentucky. They had three sons, Robert sixteen, Willie nine, Thomas seven. Living with him were two servants, M. Johnson, eighteen, female, and Philip Dinkell, fourteen, male.

Before arriving at Lincoln's house, the census taker had just visited three other families. Lotus Niles, a forty-year-old "secretary"—equivalent to a manager today—headed one of them. He was born in New York and

---

19. Quoted in Paul and Hart, 72–74; Richard White, "Frederick Jackson Turner and Buffalo Bill," in James Grossman, ed., *The Frontier in American Culture: An Exhibition at the Newberry Library, August 26, 1994–January 7, 1995* (Chicago: The Library, 1994), 19–26.

This picture of Ira A. and Susan J. Warren of Calhoun County, Michigan,
comes from one of the "Mugbooks," or subscription county histories popular
after the Civil War. It captured the presumed trajectory of American lives:
humble beginnings symbolized by the cabin in the woods, a life of hard work,
and the reward of a prosperous farm and home. From *History of Calhoun
County, Michigan* by H. B. Peirce (Philadelphia: L. H. Everts & Co., 1877).

had accumulated $7,000 in real estate and $2,500 in personal property.
Next was Edward Brigg, a forty-eight-year-old teamster (or wagon driver)
from England, with $4,000 in real estate and $300 in personal property.
Then came fifty-year-old Henry Corrigan, born in Ireland. He had the
highest net worth in the neighborhood, with $30,000 in real estate but
only $300 in personal property. His son ran the livery stable Corrigan
owned. These were all prosperous men, but the next family the census
taker visited was that of D. J. Snow, his wife, Margaret, and two sons, four
and two. Snow listed no occupation and had a net worth of $350. Just
beyond him on the list was a bricklayer, Richard Ives, with $4,000 in real
estate and $4,500 in personal property. Lawyer, secretary, livery stable
owner, man with no profession and no wealth, and bricklayer all presumably lived adjacent to each other in the same neighborhood. There was
considerable inequality in the United States, with the top 1 percent controlling 37 percent of the nation's wealth, but that top 1 percent hardly
controlled unimaginable wealth. This was a town and a country where

not much property separated bricklayers, lawyers, stable owners, and managers. Lincoln was one of the richer men in Springfield, but neither he nor his neighbors were very wealthy.[20]

The message of the sermons, the speeches, and the journey itself was that the martyred president had left the Union secure, its values affirmed, and liberty triumphant. A new magazine, *The Nation*, which would become the voice of liberal — in the nineteenth-century sense of the word — opinion for the rest of the century, published its first issue on July 5, 1865. Its editors saw themselves as standing at a turning point not just in American but also in world history.

> It is not simply the triumph of American democracy that we rejoice over, but the triumph of democratic principles everywhere, for this is involved in the successful issue of our struggle with the rebellion.... We utter no idle boast, when we say that if the conflict of the ages, the great strife between the few and the many, between privilege and equality, between law and power, between opinion and the sword, was not closed on the day on which Lee threw down his arms, the issue was placed beyond doubt.[21]

Lincoln proved more malleable in death than in life. The assassination, the end of slavery, and the religious imagery and sermons surrounding his funeral speeded Lincoln's transformation into "Father Abraham." A man who in life could never shed his sense of tragedy and suffering, whose celebration of the possibilities of the republic never blinded him to its faults, would in death become, as historian Robert Carwardine has put it, a "prophet and agent of American mission."[22]

20. Carole Shammas, "A New Look at Long-Term Trends in Wealth Inequality in the United States," *American Historical Review* 98, no. 2 (1993): 424; U.S. Bureau of the Census; U.S. National Archives and Records Service, "Population schedules of the eighth census of the United States, 1860, Illinois [microform], reel 226, Sangamon County, Schedule 1, Springfield, Illinois," 140.

21. Nancy Cohen, *The Reconstruction of American Liberalism, 1865–1914* (Chapel Hill: University of North Carolina Press, 2002), 25.

22. Searcher, 70; Carwardine, 55.

1

In the Wake of War

In April 1865 the United States was divided into three parts. The North dominated the nation. The South lay broken and battered, although the most defiant Southerners still regarded it as rightfully a separate country. Beyond the Missouri River lay the West, claimed but hardly controlled by the American Union. There dwelled independent peoples who called themselves Dine, Lakotas, and dozens of other names, but whom Americans collectively called Indians. For four years the three sections had known little but war, and the inhabitants of each, like the inhabitants of Caesar's Gaul, had reason to account themselves brave. Yet all were about to feel the power and policies of an enlarged federal government, a victorious Union army, and an expansive capitalism.

The triumphant North demanded three things of the defeated South: acknowledgment of the emancipation of its slaves; contract freedom for all citizens, black and white; and national reunification. Emancipation, freedom, and reunification were still just words. Their meanings remained unfixed. The image of the new country would emerge only as the lines connecting these ideological dots were drawn. As former North Carolina governor David L. Swain recognized, "With reference to emancipation, we are at the beginning of the War." This struggle over the results and meaning of the Civil War—and the meaning of black freedom—would be fought throughout the rest of the century in all sections of the country, but it began in 1865 in the South with Reconstruction.[1]

The foundations of black freedom had been laid in the contraband camps and the Union Army during the Civil War. Initially, the former slaves were stateless: no longer slaves but not yet citizens. They were

1. Steven Hahn, *A Nation under Our Feet: Black Political Struggles in the Rural South, from Slavery to the Great Migration* (Cambridge, MA: Belknap Press of Harvard University Press, 2003), 130; Eric Foner, *Reconstruction: America's Unfinished Revolution, 1863–1877* (New York: Harper & Row, 1988), 129; David W. Blight, *Race and Reunion: The Civil War in American Memory* (Cambridge, MA: Belknap Press of Harvard University Press, 2001), 31.

dependent on federal aid, but they made themselves useful both as soldiers and laborers. Through their labor and service the freedpeople, in the language of the period, entered into contracts with the federal government, creating social relationships of mutual and reciprocal obligations that marked their independent status. In the contraband camps and army the freedpeople had exchanged useful service for rights and protection and by doing so breached what had once seemed an impenetrable barrier between black people and the possibility of citizenship.[2]

I

The task after the war was to regularize and clarify the status of freedpeople and force the Southern states to accept that new status. The Republicans took up this task after Gen. Robert E. Lee's surrender. In 1865 the Republican Party controlled both houses of Congress. Salmon Chase of Ohio, a former secretary of the treasury in Lincoln's cabinet, was chief justice of the U.S. Supreme Court. The Republicans were the party of nationalism, economic improvement, personal independence, and, more tentatively, universal rights. In the immediate aftermath of the war it was easy to cast the rival Democrats as the party of treason, backwardness, hierarchy, and slavery.[3]

Washington, D.C., the nation's still vaguely Southern capital, acted as the hub connecting the three sections. Washington was a bedraggled city of frame houses, muddy streets, open spaces, and about seventy-five thousand people, roughly a third of whom were black. The city was the emerging and still incongruous North American Rome, both republican and imperial, both grand and shoddy. Rising among dirt and squalor were the great granite, sandstone, and marble hulks of official buildings. The Capitol dome had finally been completed, but the canal running along the edge of the Mall was an open sewer, which reeked, as John Hay said, of "the ghosts of 20,000 drowned cats." From the White House the bucolic countryside of Mt. Vernon and Alexandria was visible across the Potomac, but at the end of the war the middle ground of such a view was a stockyard full of cattle to feed Union troops. Near it was the embarrassing stub—153 feet of the projected 600 feet—of the Washington

---

2. I take this formulation from Chandra Manning, *Troubled Refuge: Struggling for Freedom in the Civil War* (New York: Knopf, 2016), 218.

3. William Alan Blair, *With Malice toward Some: Treason and Loyalty in the Civil War Era* (Chapel Hill: University of North Carolina Press, 2014), 271–86.

Monument, begun seventeen years earlier, but left only partially built after funds had run out.[4]

Many of the capital's public buildings and monuments—including the toga-clad statue of George Washington exiled from the Capitol rotunda to the park outside—were classical in inspiration. There were victorious generals in abundance, but no Caesar.[5]

The authority and power of the federal government, so visible in Washington, were less visible elsewhere. The South in the spring of 1865 was conquered, but only thinly occupied by federal forces. Neither Northerners nor Southerners knew what the peace that followed the war and its carnage would look like, what form Northern occupation would take, or how Southerners, black and white, would react. Indians, not white settlers, were still a majority in most places west of the 100th meridian. The shape U.S. policy would take there remained unclear.

Carl Schurz captured the venom that suffused American social relations in the conquered South in an incident that took place in a Savannah hotel. Schurz was a German émigré and refugee from the failed European revolutions of 1848. He had settled in Missouri and become a general in the Union army. He knew what it meant to lose a revolution, and he knew that defeat did not necessarily change minds. He was in 1865 a Radical, sent to the South by the president to report on conditions there. He did not worry much about young Southern men "of the educated or semi-educated" class. They swaggered in courthouse squares, and Schurz overheard their talk in hotels and on the streets. They were of a type and potentially dangerous, but they did not immediately concern Schurz.

What troubled him were the sentiments of Southern women, for whom Schurz had greater respect than he did for Southern men. At a hotel's common table, he sat opposite "a lady in black, probably mourning. She was middle-aged, but still handsome." Schurz was sitting next to a young Union lieutenant, in uniform, and the lady seemed agitated. During the meal, the woman reached for a dish of pickles. The lieutenant with a polite bow offered it to her. "She withdrew her hand as if it had touched

4. Kate Masur, *An Example for All the Land: Emancipation and the Struggle over Equality in Washington, D.C.* (Chapel Hill: University of North Carolina Press, 2010), 146; Dorothy Kunhardt, *Twenty Days: A Narrative in Text and Pictures of the Assassination of Abraham Lincoln and the Twenty Days and Nights That Followed—the Nation in Mourning, the Long Trip Home to Springfield*, ed. Philip B. Kunhardt (New York: Harper & Row, 1965), 111–17.

5. For classicism, see: Caroline Winterer, *The Culture of Classicism: Ancient Greece and Rome in American Intellectual Life, 1780–1910* (Baltimore, MD: Johns Hopkins University Press, 2002); Garry Wills, *Cincinnatus: George Washington and the Enlightenment* (Garden City: Doubleday & Company, 1984), 55, 67–74.

something loathsome, her eyes flashed fire and with a tone of wrathful scorn and indignation she said: 'So you think a Southern woman will take a dish of pickles from a hand that is dripping with the blood of her countrymen?'" The incongruity of the pickles and the passion amused Schurz, but the scene also struck him as "gravely pathetic." It augured "ill for the speedy revival of a common national spirit" because women composed a "hostile moral force of incalculable potency."[6]

A comparable loathing seethed in the North. Harriet Beecher Stowe was as hostile to the South at the end of the war as she had been toward slavery in the 1850s. In her fiction, Southern whites were not like Northern whites. Stowe had popularized the term "white trash" to Northern audiences in her *A Key to Uncle Tom's Cabin*, which she had published to demonstrate the factual basis of her best-selling novel. Slavery, Stowe had written, had produced "a poor white population as degraded and brutal as ever existed in the most crowded districts of Europe." Even when these whites had gained enough wealth to own slaves, the slaves were "in every respect, superior to their owners."[7]

When Sidney Andrews, a correspondent for the antislavery papers the *Chicago Tribune* and the *Boston Advertiser*, went south in 1865, he might well have been traveling through the landscape of Stowe's novel. In describing the "common inhabitant" of white rural North Carolina, Andrews found "insipidity in his face, indecision in his step, and inefficiency in his whole bearing." His day was "devoid of dignity and mental or moral compensation." He was all talk and little work, fond of his apple-jack and fonder still of his tobacco. To Andrews, the "whole economy of life seems radically wrong, and there is no inherent energy which promises reformation." How armies whose backbone was men like this had managed to hold off the North for four years Andrews did not explain. He didn't have too; his prejudices were those of his readers.[8]

6. Schurz was more dismissive of Southern women in his original letter of July 31, 1865. Joseph H. Mahaffey, "Carl Schurz's Letters from the South," *Georgia Historical Quarterly* 35, no. 3 (1951): 246; Carl Schurz, *The Reminiscences of Carl Schurz*, ed. Frederic Bancroft and William Archibald Dunning (New York: McClure, 1907), 3: 178–81.

7. Edward J. Blum, *Reforging the White Republic: Race, Religion, and American Nationalism, 1865–1898* (Baton Rouge: Louisiana State University Press, 2005), 98–99; Nancy Isenberg, *White Trash: The 400-Year Untold History of Class in America* (New York: Viking, 2016), 135–36; Harriet Beecher Stowe, *A Key to Uncle Tom's Cabin; Presenting the Original Facts and Documents Upon Which the Story Is Founded. Together with Corroborative Statements Verifying the Truth of the Work* (Boston: J. P. Jewett & Co., 1853), 184–85.

8. Isenberg, 178–80; selection from Sidney Andrews, *The South Since the War* (Boston: Ticknor and Fields, 1866); Harvey Wish, *Reconstruction in the South, 1865–1877:*

Familiarity, however, did not necessarily change Northern opinions. Despite some outrages by Union soldiers toward the freedpeople, many of them came to despise the ex-Confederates for their continued resistance, the violence they directed at freedpeople, and their attacks on individual soldiers, agents of the Freedmen's Bureau, and northern teachers. Lt. Col. Nelson Shaurman, after service in Georgia, thought Georgians the "most ignorant, degraded white people I have ever seen…were it not for the military power—of which they have a wholesome fear—there would be scenes of cruelty enacted that would disgrace savages." The soldiers sought to cow, not convert, the ex-Confederates, and military posts succeeded in doing so.[9]

In the wake of the war journalists, travelers, and soldiers conducted what amounted to a political reconnaissance of the South. John Townsend Trowbridge, a popular author touring the southern battlefields, sat in the Atlanta rail yards on a foggy, rainy morning and described the shattered remnant of what had once been the city looming in the mist. Squat wooden buildings thrown up as temporary replacements were scattered among the ruins. General William Tecumseh Sherman's men—"the inevitable Yankee" as the great Southern diarist, Mary Chesnut, had called them—had left "windrows of bent railroad iron by the track." There were "piles of brick; a small mountain of old bones from the battle-fields, foul and wet with the drizzle…with mud and litter all around."[10]

In the spring of 1865 southwestern Georgia was one of the Southern places that seemed to northern travelers untouched by the war. The land lay green and bounteous. Black people plowed the earth, planted cotton, and, until the arrival of Union troops who came only after Appomattox, suffered under the lash as if slavery still lived and the old South was merely dozing and not dead. Clara Barton, who had done much to alleviate the suffering of Northern soldiers during the war and who would later found the Red Cross, saw the region differently. She thought it "not the gate of hell, but hell itself." Roughly thirteen thousand Union soldiers lay buried there in mass graves at the Confederate prison camp at Andersonville.[11]

First-Hand Accounts of the American Southland after the Civil War (New York: Farrar, Straus and Giroux, 1965), 20–21.

9. Gregory P. Downs, After Appomattox: Military Occupation and the Ends of War (Cambridge, MA: Harvard University Press, 2015), 54–56.

10. J. T. Trowbridge, The South: A Tour of Its Battlefields and Ruined Cities, a Journey through the Desolated States, and Talks with the People (Hartford, CT: L. Stebbins, 1866), 460; Mary Boykin Miller Chesnut, Mary Chesnut's Civil War, ed. C. Vann Woodward (New Haven, CT: Yale University Press, 1981), 780, Apr. 5, 1865.

11. Stephen B. Oates, A Woman of Valor: Clara Barton and the Civil War (New York: Free Press, 1994), 309–36, 368; Susan E. O'Donovan, Becoming Free in the Cotton

Union soldiers had come to southwest Georgia during the war, but they had come as prisoners. Most had died there, and their bones were what brought Clara Barton. For many American families the war had not been fully resolved at Appomattox because their fathers, sons, and husbands had simply vanished. The dead at Andersonville were among the half of the Union dead who had been buried unidentified or left unburied on the battlefields, rendering the South "one vast charnel house."[12]

By recent estimates, somewhere between 650,000 and 850,000 men died in the Civil War, with a reasonable figure being about 752,000. Roughly 13 percent of men of military age in the slave states died during the war, twice the figure (6.1 percent) of men born in the free states or territories. More were incapacitated. In Mississippi 20 percent of the state's revenues in 1866 went to artificial limbs for veterans.[13]

The Union Army had burial records for about one-third of its estimated fatalities. The vast effort of both victors and vanquished to identify and inter their dead reflected the deep divisions left by the war and how difficult the creation of a common citizenry would be. The dead provoked the living to keep the old animosities alive. White Southerners often refused to say what they knew of the location of Union dead, and Union reburial parties often refused to bury the remains of Confederates. Barton would help locate more than twenty thousand of the Union's dead and spark a systematic effort to reinter them in national cemeteries. A suggestion that the national cemetery in Marietta, Georgia, include the Confederate dead, however, horrified local women who protested any "promiscuous mingling" of the remains of the Confederates with "the remains of their enemies." The South launched its own private efforts to reinter its abundant dead.[14]

Freedpeople proved the most helpful in finding the graves of Union soldiers. In Charleston, South Carolina, they had cared for the graves of two hundred Union prisoners who had died there. On May 1, 1865, under the protection of a brigade of Union soldiers, they honored the dead in what was probably the country's first Decoration Day. The Union and

South (Cambridge, MA: Harvard University Press, 2007), 111–15; Lee W. Formwalt, "The Origins of African-American Politics in Southwest Georgia: A Case Study of Black Political Organization During Presidential Reconstruction, 1865–1867," *Journal of Negro History* 77, no. 4 (1992).

12. Drew Gilpin Faust, *This Republic of Suffering: Death and the American Civil War* (New York: Knopf, 2008), 211–49, 267; Oates, 309–36, 368.

13. J. David Hacker, "A Census-Based Count of the Civil War Dead," *Civil War History* 57, no. 4 (2011): 312, 338, 342, 348; Eugene R. Dattel, *Cotton and Race in the Making of America: The Human Costs of Economic Power* (Chicago: Ivan R. Dee, 2009), 225.

14. Oates, 309–36, 368; Faust, 225.

Confederate dead—grotesquely anonymous in the piles of bones, bitterly yet tenderly remembered by the living—still bred hatreds and resentments that were not going to melt quickly away with peace.[15]

Congress was in recess in the spring of 1865 when the Confederacy collapsed following Lee's surrender, Lincoln's assassination, the gradual surrender of the other Southern armies, and the capture on May 10 of Jefferson Davis. It was left to a new president—and his cabinet, the army, and Southerners, both black and white—to determine the fate of the South.

Congress had passed the Thirteenth Amendment abolishing slavery before adjourning, but it took until December for enough states to ratify it, and only then was slavery legally extinguished in the loyal border states of Kentucky and Delaware. Emancipation remained a work in progress. The Emancipation Proclamation, the flight of the slaves, and the advance of Union armies during the war had brought freedom, of a sort, but it had also brought hunger, suffering, and death to many of those who seized that freedom. The federal government had enlisted able-bodied black men as laborers and soldiers, but often consigned their families to contraband camps or neglected them entirely. They died by the tens of thousands. Freedom that amounted to no more than the ability to sell one's labor at what a buyer was willing to pay was a more constrained freedom than slaves had imagined.[16]

In the spring and summer of 1865 many Southerners were unwilling to grant even that limited freedom. In large swaths of the interior South only the arrival of soldiers actually ended slavery. Returning rebels, in violation of the law, moved to evict the wives and families of black soldiers from their homes.[17]

Even with the arrival of troops, Carl Schurz wrote that Southerners still thought that the freedmen would not work without coercion and that "the blacks at large belong to the whites at large." As long as these beliefs persisted, emancipation would yield "systems intermediate between slavery as it formerly existed in the south, and free labor as it exists in the north, but more nearly related to the former than to the latter." The North had achieved only the "negative part" of emancipation, ending the system of

15. Faust, 211–49.
16. Jim Downs, *Sick from Freedom: African-American Illness and Suffering During the Civil War and Reconstruction* (New York: Oxford University Press, 2012), 18–64.
17. Downs, *After Appomattox*, 39–44; Manning, 243; Alie Thomas to Brother, July 30, 1865, Emily Waters to Husband, July 16, 1865, in Ira Berlin, ed., *Families and Freedom: A Documentary History of African-American Kinship in the Civil War Era* (New York: New Press, 1997), 131–32.

chattel slavery; the hard part, instituting a system of free labor, remained to be done.[18]

During spring and summer of 1865, Mary Chesnut chronicled the descent of South Carolina, the heartland of the Confederacy, into a snarling mix of rumor, resentment, self-recrimination, blame, rage, and self-pity. The elite of the Old South proved as recalcitrant in defeat as they had been in the glory days of their rebellion. They had gambled virtually everything on the attempt to create a slave state, "dedicated," as historian Stephanie McCurry has put it, "to the proposition that all men were not created equal," and they had lost the gamble. Sherman's army had looted and burned and driven home the enormity of the catastrophe they had engendered. Their slaves had deserted them and welcomed the Yankees. In the face of all this, Chesnut's friends saw the Yankees as barbarians and their own slaves as pitiful and deluded. The old Southern elite thought of themselves as victims.[19]

That the victimization they most feared did not come to pass did nothing to diminish their sense of persecution. Above all, whites dreaded vengeance from their own ex-slaves. White Southerners had always wavered between contentions that their slaves were treated with kindness and considered part of the slaveholder's family and a fear of seething collective black anger and individual grievances that had to be restrained by force lest they erupt in vengeance and retaliation. With emancipation, all their latent fears of retaliatory violence against a system sustained by the lash and gun haunted them. Southerners proclaimed that emancipation would result in "all the horrors of St. Domingo" and the Haitian Revolution. But as Schurz reported in 1865, and the slaveholders themselves admitted, "the transition of the southern negro from slavery to freedom was untarnished by any deeds of blood, and the apprehension [of African American violence]...proved utterly groundless." There was violence in the South, but it was usually at the hands of white outlaws, bushwhackers, and unreconciled Confederates. Black people were victims, not perpetrators. Their collective restraint was remarkable. Chesnut heard the fears of Santo Domingo, but in the daily interactions she witnessed "both parties, white and black, talked beautifully." Characteristically, she discerned something more beneath the beautiful talk: when the ex-slaves "see an opening to better themselves they will move on."[20]

18. Carl Schurz, *Report on the Condition of the South*, 39th Congress, Senate Ex. Doc. 1st Session, No. 2, Project Gutenberg (1865).
19. Chesnut, 792ff.; Stephanie McCurry, *Confederate Reckoning: Power and Politics in the Civil War South* (Cambridge, MA: Harvard University Press, 2010), 1.
20. Schurz, *Report*; Chesnut, May 21, 1865, 821, and July 4, 1865, 834.

As the spring of 1865 wore on, the clash of armies ceased, and both the North and South waited to see what President Johnson would do. "We sit and wait until the drunken tailor who rules the U.S.A. issues a proclamation and defines our anomalous position," Chesnut wrote in her diary. Frederick Douglass sensed danger. An escaped slave, he had become a leading abolitionist and the most famous black man in America. He warned that Southern hostility toward blacks had, if anything, increased because African American soldiers had helped defeat the rebellion. He cautioned the North not to trust the South, but to wait and see "in what new skin this old snake will come forth next."[21]

Theoretically the victorious Union Army held control, but that control depended on two things. The first was the physical occupation of the South. The second was the legal right of the army to govern the South under war powers, which, in turn, depended on deciding whether war continued after the defeat of the Southern armies.[22]

When Lee surrendered, the South was barely occupied by the army and slavery only partially uprooted. Nearly 75 percent of the enslaved remained in slavery. Force had begun the abolition of slavery, and only force could fully end it. In April the Union Army held some eighty towns and cities, but elsewhere the armies had either passed through leaving devastation in their wake or never appeared. Occupying the South meant controlling an area the size of Western Europe, roughly eight hundred counties, spread over 750,000 square miles, and containing nine million people. By September the army had some 324 garrisons and at least 630 outposts of one sort or another, but the actual number could have been much higher since reporting was spotty and unsystematic. But neither the high command nor the officers and men had much of a stomach for a long occupation of the South. With the war won, the soldiers in the volunteer units—the vast bulk of the army—were ready to muster out, and most officers wanted no part of occupation.[23]

Even as the army expanded across the South, its numbers diminished. Both the North and South had used the rhetoric of home—perhaps the central symbol of the age—to justify the Civil War, and with the fighting done, Union soldiers clamored to go home. Even more significantly, the country could not afford to maintain a million-man army. A brief financial panic in March 1865 forced the government to intervene secretly to

21. Chesnut, 814, May 16, 1865, "In What New Skin Will the Old Snake Come Forth," May 10, 1865, in Frederick Douglass, *The Frederick Douglass Papers: Series One, Speeches, Debates, and Interviews* (New Haven, CT: Yale University Press, 1979), 4: 80–85.
22. Downs, *After Appomattox*, 1–25.
23. Ibid., 14, 23–25, 41–42, 47–48, 89–97; James E. Sefton, *The United States Army and Reconstruction, 1865–1877* (Baton Rouge: Louisiana State University Press, 1967), 7–8.

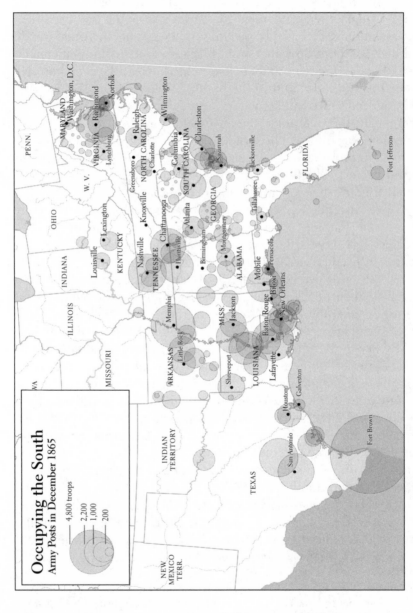

Map adapted by Geoff McGhee from Gregory P. Downs, *After Appomattox*; Basemaps: Minnesota Population Center; National Historical Information System; Natural Earth Data.

buy its own bonds to maintain prices. The problem was paradoxical. With Union victory certain, the price of gold dropped, and since the government depended on the sale of bonds whose interest was paid in gold, the yield of bonds dropped and the market for them fell. It appeared the government might not be able to meet its obligations. The crisis convinced officials that they must quickly cut expenses and pay down the debt. The North demobilized just as army officers realized the demands occupation of the South would place on the army.[24]

The curtain call of the Union army that won the Civil War was the Grand Review on May 23 and May 24 in Washington, where for two days Gen. George Meade's and Gen. Sherman's armies paraded through the city. Grant, who as general-in-chief commanded both of them, doubted that "an equal body of men of any nation, take them man for man, officer for officer, was ever gotten together...." It was a celebration of a democracy in arms. As the *Philadelphia North American* put it, only a democracy could trust such a mass of armed men in the capital. "Is it not as great a tribute to free government as was ever paid?" And it was a sign of the limits of that democracy; the black regiments that had fought so long and so well were excluded.[25]

As the regiments disbanded with the longest-serving dismissed first, Grant put fifty thousand of those soldiers that remained under Philip Sheridan and shifted them to the Mexican border, which like all American borders remained porous, with Indians and *tejanos, nuevo mexicanos,* Sonorans, and *californios* moving in both directions. Sheridan had begun the Civil War as a lieutenant and become one of Grant's most trusted generals. Lincoln described the five-foot, five-inch Sheridan as "a brown, chunky little chap, with a long body, short legs, not enough neck to hang him and such long arms that if his ankles itch he can scratch them without stooping." Sending Sheridan signaled the seriousness of American concerns about the border.[26]

24. Downs, *After Appomattox*, 92–93, 97–99.
25. Ulysses S. Grant, *Personal Memoirs of U.S. Grant* (New York: C. L. Webster & Co., 1886; Dover reprint, 1995), 454. Stuart McConnell, *Glorious Contentment: The Grand Army of the Republic, 1865–1900* (Chapel Hill: University of North Carolina Press, 1992), 4, 8.
26. For the western part of the U.S.-Mexican border, Rachel St. John, *Line in the Sand: A History of the Western U.S.–Mexico Border* (Princeton, NJ: Princeton University Press, 2011), 1–89; Andrew R. Graybill, *The Red and the White: A Family Saga of the American West* (New York: Norton, 2013), 113. For a lucid overview of borders and boundary making, Tamar Herzog, *Defining Nations: Immigrants and Citizens in Early Modern Spain and Spanish America* (New Haven, CT: Yale University Press, 2003), 1–23.

Grant, and many Republicans, saw the Mexican Liberals under Benito Juarez as the Mexican equivalent of Republicans and anticipated intervening on the side of Juarez's revolutionaries against the Emperor Maximilian, installed by the French in 1864 and supported by the Confederacy. The planned intervention would disproportionately involve black troops because black regiments having been formed later would be discharged later. The shift of so many soldiers to Texas led to complaints in the fall about insufficient troops in the rest of the old Confederacy. The number of Union soldiers in the Confederacy fell from roughly 1 million in April to 125,000 by November and 90,000 by the end of January 1866. Those who remained were often on foot, for the army began selling horses, reducing the cavalry in Mississippi to fewer than 100 men by October. Away from the railroads, infantry could not chase down mounted nightriders who terrorized freedpeople.[27]

Hamlin Garland later captured both the joy and the melancholy of the Union soldiers' return home in his *Son of the Middle Border*. He wrote of "a soldier with a musket on his back, wearily plodding his way up the low hill just north of the gate." It was his father, Dick Garland, home from campaigning with Grant and Sherman. But it was his "empty cottage" that was at the center of the scene. The Garland family happened to be at a neighbor's house. They saw him approaching and rushed to overtake him, only to find him "sadly contemplating his silent home." His wife, approaching him, found her husband "so thin, so hollow-eyed, so changed" that she had to ask to make sure that the man in front of her was indeed Richard Garland. His daughter knew him. His small sons did not. Decades later Hamlin Garland remembered the "sad reproach in his voice. 'Won't you come and see your poor old father when he comes from the war?'" The war left a restlessness in Dick Garland. He never explained his sadness on seeing his home, but no current home would ever be enough again. The Garlands' lives thereafter would be a continuous whirl west.[28]

Such restlessness was part of the war's legacy. The veterans had been "touched by fire," as Oliver Wendell Holmes would famously put it twenty years later. The ordeal had changed them. But while the Civil War

27. Downs, *After Appomattox*, 27–28, 89–90, 96; Hahn, 133; Sefton, 11–24; Gregory P. Downs, "The Mexicanization of American Politics: The United States' Transnational Path from Civil War to Stabilization," *American Historical Review* 117 (2012): 393–95; William A. Dobak and Thomas D. Phillips, *The Black Regulars, 1866–1898* (Norman: University of Oklahoma Press, 2001), 4–5; Paul Andrew Hutton, *Phil Sheridan and His Army* (Lincoln: University of Nebraska Press, 1985), 20–21.
28. Hamlin Garland, *A Son of the Middle Border* (New York: Grosset & Dunlap, 1928), 1–3.

abundantly bestowed death with one hand, it had, with the other, offered young men opportunities. Men in their twenties and early thirties rose quickly to positions of authority within the military and in the government. The postwar world relieved most of them from danger, but it also constrained their possibilities. The army shrank and soldiers flooded back into a quieter life, but one without the promise of early advance and authority. Henry Adams, great-grandson and grandson to presidents and secretary to his father, the wartime ambassador to Great Britain, felt this acutely, and he captured the sense of displacement in his famous *Education*. "All his American friends and contemporaries who were still alive," he recalled, "looked singularly commonplace without uniforms, and hastened to get married and retire into back streets and suburbs until they could find employment." John Hay, a Midwesterner and Lincoln's secretary, would "bury himself in second-rate legations for years." Charles Francis Adams, Jr., Henry's brother, "wandered about, with brevet brigadier rank, trying to find employment."[29]

In the spring following the war the confusion and disorientation of the young men who fought the war and held office mirrored that of the government itself. President Andrew Johnson was the great anomaly of the postwar United States. Born in Tennessee and a Jacksonian Democrat for most of his career, he was not only one of the few Southerners in power, but also the single most powerful man in the country. Lincoln had named him vice president on his 1864 Union ticket. Johnson was born poor and as a young man worked as a tailor, but he had prospered and owned slaves before the war. He never forgot his own beginnings, and despite his political success, he could never conceive of himself as anything but an outsider. He was often his own worst enemy. He had done himself no favors at Lincoln's second inaugural. Already sick, he had spent the preceding night drinking with John Forney, an editor, secretary of the Senate, and one of the more corrupt political fixers of a corrupt age. He had resumed drinking in the morning, and illness and alcohol produced a rambling, insulting inaugural speech that was rescued only by being largely inaudible to much of the audience. He never lived it down. In Chesnut's slur, he was the drunken tailor.[30]

Still, following Lincoln's assassination, he drew on the public sympathy that flowed to him and for a brief season had a relatively free hand. Rhetorically, Johnson initially breathed fire. "Treason," he declared, "must be made odious, and traitors must be punished and impoverished.

29. Henry Adams, *The Education of Henry Adams: An Autobiography* (New York: Heritage Press, 1942, orig. ed. 1918), 195–96.
30. Hans L. Trefousse, *Andrew Johnson: A Biography* (New York: Norton, 1989), 188–91.

Their great plantations must be seized and divided into small farms...."
The new president was impatient with the astonishing assumption by
Confederate governors and legislatures that their authority had not evaporated with defeat and that they would continue in office. Despite his actions later, he largely supported military occupation in 1865 and defended
the extension of war powers. The war was not over until Southern
resistance ceased, peace reigned, and the old Confederate states were readmitted into Congress.[31]

Johnson, however, soon softened. Politically, he grew close to Secretary
of State William Seward. Seward, wounded at home by another assassin
on the night that Booth murdered Lincoln, had become the leading
Republican advocate of leniency toward the South. He worried about the
growth of a powerful central state. When the Comte de Gasparin, a
French author and reformer, criticized the government for not immediately providing for black suffrage, Seward responded by emphasizing
curbs on federal power. He argued that, beyond denying amnesty to the
leaders and upholders of the rebellion and maintaining "military control
until the civil power is reorganized," the federal government could do
nothing. To resort to coercion would be a "policy of centralization, consolidation and imperialism...repugnant to the spirit of individual liberty"
and something "unknown to the habits of the American people." It was an
extraordinary statement in a country that had just resorted to four years of
coercion to restore the Union, centralized and consolidated federal power,
ended slavery and thus deprived Southerners of property, and enacted a
western policy—including Seward's future purchase of Alaska—that was
avowedly imperial. Seward's position became one that many Southerners,
particularly those who had initially opposed secession, embraced.[32]

While Congress was in recess, Secretary of War Edwin Stanton formed,
at first tentatively, a counterpoint to Johnson and Seward. Radical
Republicans, who advocated a thorough remaking of the South, initially
thought they could work with Johnson and tried to influence him by
channeling their suggestions through Stanton. Before becoming Lincoln's
secretary of war, Stanton was a successful Ohio lawyer and James
Buchanan's attorney general in the lame duck days of that disastrous

31. Michael Perman, *Reunion without Compromise: The South and Reconstruction: 1865–*
    1868 (Cambridge: Cambridge University Press, 1973), 43–44, 57–59; Brooks D.
    Simpson, *The Reconstruction Presidents* (Lawrence: University Press of Kansas, 1998),
    68; Downs, *After Appomattox*, 64–65; Foner, 177.
32. Perman, 4, 30–31; Michael Les Benedict, *The Fruits of Victory: Alternatives in Restoring*
    the Union, 1865–1877 (Philadelphia: Lippincott, 1975), 10; Brooks D. Simpson, *Let Us*
    Have Peace: Ulysses S. Grant and the Politics of War and Reconstruction, 1861–1868
    (Chapel Hill: University of North Carolina Press, 1991), 110–11.

administration. Stanton was a mean-spirited and dour man. He had been born sickly and asthmatic, but it was not poor health that soured him. The death of his first wife and his daughter and the suicide of his brother had left him first grief-stricken and then hardened. Irritated during a trial by the clever opening statement of an opposing attorney, Stanton had begun his remarks by saying, sarcastically, "Now that this extraordinary flow of wit has ceased, I will begin." The other lawyer could not resist the opening. "Wit always ceases when you begin," he said. The courtroom erupted in laughter (but Stanton won the case).[33]

Where most biographers incline to hagiography, Stanton's biographers sometimes strain for tolerance. Autocratic, duplicitous, and humorless, Stanton had initially scorned Abraham Lincoln, the funniest—at least intentionally—president the United States ever had, as a man of little consequence and less ability, and he always remained surer of himself than he was of Lincoln. Ulysses Grant, who disliked Stanton, "acknowledged his great ability" and also his "natural disposition to assume all power and control in all matters that he had anything whatever to do with." Stanton seemed to take pleasure in disappointing people and denying their requests, even as he constantly overreached his authority.[34]

Stanton and Johnson had much in common. Both were outsiders: isolated and unpleasant, rigid and self-righteous. Neither had been Republicans at the outbreak of the Civil War. Both owed their places to Lincoln, and both were magnets for trouble. In terms of personality they occupied the same pole; like magnets, they repelled.

The cabinet's task in May 1865 was to construct a plan for reconstituting the Southern governments. At Lincoln's death there were a hodgepodge of approaches to governing the conquered states. Stanton presented the option of black suffrage to accompany black freedom, but he did not insist on it.[35]

On May 29, 1865, President Johnson issued his first two Reconstruction proclamations. They created the road map—vague as it was in its particulars—for Reconstruction and the return of civil government in the South. The first proclamation, issued under the constitutional power of the president to grant pardons, gave amnesty to most ex-Confederates on their taking an oath of loyalty to the United States and accepting the end of slavery. He imagined ordinary Southern whites taking power, displacing

33. Foner, 181; Benjamin Platt Thomas, *Stanton: The Life and Times of Lincoln's Secretary of War*, ed. Harold Melvin Hyman (New York: Knopf, 1962), 1–92, quote 57.
34. William Marvel is not the first Stanton biography to take a jaundiced view of his subject. William Marvel, *Lincoln's Autocrat: The Life of Edwin Stanton* (Cambridge, MA: Harvard, 2015); Grant, 2: 105, 536–37.
35. Downs, *After Appomattox*, 65–66; Foner, 181–82; Benedict, 12.

the old elite. Blacks would remain on the bottom with certain civil rights but no right to political participation. The second, issued under his war-time powers as commander-in-chief, created the provisional government for North Carolina and provided a template that the other Southern governments were supposed to follow. In North Carolina all of those able to vote before the Civil War and who fell within the scope of Johnson's pardons could vote. This formulation denied freedmen the franchise while granting it to men who had rebelled against the United States. By leaving suffrage qualifications up to the new legislatures, it ensured that blacks would not vote in the South. Johnson appointed William W. Holden, a secessionist who had become a peace candidate in 1864, as governor. Holden would supervise the election of a convention that would amend the state's constitution to create "a republican form of government."[36]

The proclamations embodied both recognition of the necessary political realities in a nation perched between war and peace and some of the most spectacular misjudgments in the history of American politics. Even as Johnson maintained war powers to govern the South, he alienated the Radical Republicans, who read conditions in the South more accurately than Johnson. The proclamations also badly underestimated the freed-people. They would not be passive. Finally, the proclamations, insofar as they partially restored civil law, undercut the only effective agents of federal power—the army and the Freedmen's Bureau—in the South. To Johnson's dismay, Southern sheriffs and posses would try to arrest and imprison Northern soldiers.[37]

The proclamations revealed how poorly Johnson fitted the historical moment. He had a weakness for principles, which, combined with his stubbornness, meant that once he had reasoned himself into a position, that position, intended to be an intellectual fortress, often became a prison. Since the Constitution did not give the Confederate states any right to leave the Union, he concluded that they had never been out of the Union at all. And if they had never been out of the Union, then they retained all their rights under the Constitution. And if they retained their rights, then they could determine who could vote and hold office. He as president could not demand that they implement universal male suffrage for citizens or grant black suffrage. The South might have rebelled, and that rebellion might have been crushed, but the president and Congress, by Johnson's logic, had no more authority over the South when the war ended than when it had begun. Lincoln had dismissed this question of the

36. Isenberg, 177–78; Foner, 182–83; Eric L. McKitrick, *Andrew Johnson and Reconstruction* (Chicago: University of Chicago Press, 1960), 7.
37. Downs, *After Appomattox*, 65–68; Foner, 221.

status of the states as a "pernicious abstraction" and the Radicals thought the question was "profitless." Johnson pursued it, and his logic had constructed his prison. Leland Stanford, a wartime governor of California, was among those who saw the problems with such a stance. A man had no right to commit murder, Stanford said, but that did not mean that men did not commit murders that and they should not be punished.[38]

Johnson's answer to such objections was that he was making a distinction between individual treason and collective treason. He had no intention, at least initially, of letting individual traitors escape unscathed. He wanted to protect Southern states, not Confederate leaders. But no matter how logically plausible Johnson's argument might seem, even he had to make exceptions to it. He, after all, was appointing provisional governors, ordering new state constitutional conventions, and demanding certain terms for reunion: agreement to the abolition of slavery, renunciation of secession, and, later, repudiation of the Confederate debt. None of this, as Schurz pointed out, was part of contemporary constitutional theory. If he could do these things, Radicals asked, why could he not demand the vote for the black male population?[39]

In practice, Johnson was willing to stretch his authority when it served his desire for rapid reintegration and amnesty. Legally, few or none of the new Southern governors he appointed were eligible for office. Congress had in 1862 demanded that all federal officials swear to the so-called ironclad oath, that they were now and had always been loyal to the United States. Versions of this oath were required for congressmen and embedded in the new constitutions of Tennessee, Missouri, and Maryland. Amnesty did not do away with the requirement, but Johnson chose to ignore the law. When it became apparent that qualified appointees for the U.S. revenue offices being reopened in the South could not be found if the ironclad oath was required, Johnson substituted an oath specifying only future loyalty to the United States.[40]

Although he ignored the ironclad oath, Johnson still targeted the leading rebels. He had exempted fourteen separate classes of rebels from amnesty; the most significant were high-ranking Confederate officials and those holding taxable property valued at more than $20,000. These high officials and the rich would have to apply individually for pardons. Without a pardon, they were barred from participating in public affairs and their property was liable to confiscation. Despite the general amnesty

38. Downs, *After Appomattox*, 66–67; Foner, 178–79.
39. Downs, *After Appomattox*, 71; Foner, 179; Simpson, *The Reconstruction Presidents*, 80.
40. For oaths, Joseph A. Ranney, *In the Wake of Slavery: Civil War, Civil Rights, and the Reconstruction of Southern Law* (Westport, CT: Praeger, 2006), 36–37; Thomas, 447.

and his appointments in the South, Johnson seemed serious about punishing the men who had led the South into rebellion, but by the end of the summer he would be pardoning hundreds of people a day and restoring their property to them.[41]

In appointing the remainder of the provisional governors for the former Confederate states during May, June, and July 1865, Johnson again ignored the oath requirements; but he did pick men who had either opposed secession or not taken a leading role in precipitating it, even if they later served the Confederacy. He sought to strengthen Unionists in the South where he could find them and find collaborators among the more moderate Confederates, usually old Whigs, where he could not. His policy was to make leniency "the spring of loyal conduct and proper legislation rather than to impose upon them laws and conditions by external force." Outside of abolishing slavery and renouncing secession, he did not demand a commitment to transforming the South.[42]

II

Johnson's proclamations marked the beginning of Presidential Reconstruction, and they complicated a muddled political situation. It often seemed that the defining quality of Presidential Reconstruction was the president's sporadic absence from it. The president's authority came from his war powers. When disorder and violence continued after the surrender of Confederate armies, war powers and martial law remained in force. Neither Johnson nor the Republican Congress considered the mere defeat of Confederate armies to constitute peace. Wartime and war powers continued until civil government was fully restored. Johnson could, and did, intervene to curtail the reach of martial law, but his interventions were often piecemeal and sporadic.

Officers on the ground had great leeway. As during the war, the provost marshals assigned to most Northern armies determined Southerners' freedom to travel, controlled their access to supplies, and governed the towns and cities. Under the Confiscation Act of 1862, they could seize the property of disloyal citizens in the South, and they often undertook the organization and supervision of labor by freedmen.[43]

41. Perman, 122; Downs, *After Appomattox*, 79; Foner, 183.
42. Perman, 60–68, 70–74; Foner, 187–88.
43. Perman, 59; Downs, *After Appomattox*, 2–3, 14–17; Harold M. Hyman, "Stanton, and Grant: A Reconsideration of the Army's Role in the Events Leading to Impeachment," *American Historical Review* 66, no. 1 (1960): 85–87; P. Moore Wilton, "Union Army Provost Marshals in the Eastern Theater," *Military Affairs* 26, no. 3 (1962): 120–26.

With the collapse of the Confederacy, the army ruled the South as a conquered territory under martial law, and military responsibilities kept increasing. The army acted as a relief agency, a police force, a court, a public works bureau, and a school system. Although Johnson's proclamations restored limited civil government in the South, they did not end martial law, which persisted for all of 1865 and much of 1866. Dual authority ensured endless jurisdictional clashes between military courts run by the provost marshals, courts run by the Freedmen's Bureau, and civil courts.[44]

Johnson was actively hostile to the Freedmen's Bureau. Congress had established the Bureau of Refugees, Freedmen and Abandoned Lands on March 3, 1865, before Lincoln's assassination. In creating the bureau, Congress gave new power to the federal government, which it would do repeatedly. More unusually, it created and staffed an agency designed to execute that power. It was, to be sure, a temporary agency, expiring a year after the Confederacy expired, but until then the Freedmen's Bureau had the authority to govern "all subjects relating to refugees and freedmen from the rebel states." In large swaths of the South the bureau's authority over refugees allowed it to give from two to four times as much aid to whites as blacks. Its real power depended on the military. It never had more than nine hundred agents in the field at any one time.[45]

The Freedmen's Bureau fell under the jurisdiction of Edwin Stanton and the War Department. At its head was Maj. Gen. Oliver Otis Howard, the "Christian General." Howard had lost his arm in the war, but not his belief in the millennial mission of the United States. The feelings of Howard and the superintendents he appointed toward the freedpeople arose from Northern evangelical faith in uplift and personal and national salvation. All of Howard's original assistant commissioners were Protestant. Most were college-educated at a time when few attended college, and virtually all were from the Northeast and Midwest. Most had served in the military, but few were career soldiers. Like Howard, they did not think black people were their equals, but they shared his immediate goal of bringing them opportunity and justice, by which they meant "protection, land, and schools." Unlike the Radical Republicans in

44. Perman, 132–33; Downs, *After Appomattox*, 74–78; Sefton, 5–11.
45. Paul A. Cimbala, *Under the Guardianship of the Nation: The Freedmen's Bureau and the Reconstruction of Georgia, 1865–1870* (Athens: University of Georgia Press, 1997), 1, 22–29; Mark Wahlgren Summers, *The Ordeal of the Reunion* (Chapel Hill: University of North Carolina Press, 2014), 57; Paul A. Cimbala, *The Freedmen's Bureau: Reconstructing the American South after the Civil War* (Malabar, FL: Krieger, 2005), ix, 8; 23–24; Isenberg, 178; Downs, *After Appomattox*, 46–47.

Congress, Howard did not stress the vote. His goal was not immediate black political influence.[46]

Abolitionist women, working inside and outside the bureau, were among the most forceful advocates of aid to freedpeople. They connected the Freedmen's Bureau with larger ambitions to use government to push reform, and saw the employment of women by the bureau and elsewhere in the government as a step toward equal rights and suffrage for women. Josephine Griffing's vehement advocacy of freedpeople and women's rights within the bureau led to her dismissal.[47]

Only a slim majority in Congress recognized that the freedpeople needed substantial assistance and were willing to grant it under the general welfare clause of the Constitution. The bureau had four divisions: Land, Educational, Legal, and Medical. The ex-slaves were sick and needed care; they were largely illiterate and needed education. Health and literacy seemed obvious requirements for contract freedom that would involve negotiating the sale of bodily labor. The Legal Division would supervise the contracts the freedpeople negotiated with their ex-owners.[48]

Land became the most contentious issue. The Land Division was the bureau's feeblest branch but one that reflected both the freedmen's deepest hopes and the grudging congressional recognition that contract freedom alone might be too weak a reed to support the hopes of emancipation. The ex-slaves wanted land, particularly the abandoned and confiscated land held by the federal government. A Virginia freedman, Bayley Wyatt, made the case for the ex-slaves' right to land powerfully and simply: "we has a right to [that] land.... [D]idn't we clear the land and raise de crops.... And didn't dem large cities in the North grow up on de cotton and de sugars and de rice dat we made?" Rufus Saxton of the Freedmen's Bureau echoed this. The land would be payment for "two hundred years of unrequited toil." Many of the four million freedpeople believed the land would be given them at Christmas of 1865 or in 1866.[49]

46. Cimbala, Under the Guardianship of the Nation, 1, 22–29; Cimbala, The Freedmen's Bureau, ix, 8, 11, 13–14, 28; William S. McFeely, Yankee Stepfather: General O. O. Howard and the Freedmen (New Haven, CT: Yale University Press, 1968), 11–12, 17–19, 62–64, 69–81, 88–89.
47. Carol Faulkner, Women's Radical Reconstruction: The Freedmen's Aid Movement (Philadelphia: University of Pennsylvania Press, 2006), 90–95.
48. Downs, Sick from Freedom, 61–64.
49. Hahn, 9, 127–52; Leon F. Litwack, Been in the Storm So Long: The Aftermath of Slavery, (New York: Knopf, dist. Random House, 1979), 363; Foner, 105; Cimbala, The Freedmen's Bureau, 52–53.

Although Congress had passed wartime measures to distribute confiscated land among "loyal refugees and freedmen," the federal government controlled only 900,000 acres taken during the war. The law creating the Freedmen's Bureau authorized that agency to set aside individual allotments of no more than 40 acres each from confiscated and abandoned lands for loyal refugees and freedmen. They were to rent it for up to three years with the prospect of eventual purchase.[50]

For some freedmen, the policy had already borne enough fruit that the issue was not receiving lands, but keeping them. Much of the land seized by Northern armies had benefited whites rather than blacks. Freed slaves had cultivated lands in the Sea Islands, lower Louisiana, and the Mississippi Valley, but not always in ways of their own choosing. Many had worked for wages, growing cotton for loyal planters, Northern carpet-baggers, and speculators who leased the land from the federal government. But as the war drew to a close, Gen. Sherman's Special Field Order No. 15, issued on Jan. 15, 1865, established what amounted to a black reservation on the Sea Islands off the South Carolina and Georgia coasts and along coastal rivers as far south as the St. John's River in Florida. Here forty thousand freedpeople obtained plots of land covering 400,000 acres.[51]

During the war General Sherman had made Rufus Saxton "the inspector of settlements and plantations" for this reservation. By the time O. O. Howard made him an assistant commissioner of the Freedmen's Bureau for the state of Georgia, he had become a champion of freedmen and a believer in the necessity of land redistribution. In August 1865 Saxton wrote that when the ex-slave "is made a landholder, he becomes practically an independent citizen, and a great step towards his future elevation had been made."[52]

Like Saxton, Howard initially relied on land acquisition as the engine that would turn freedpeople from slaves to citizens. Given the eventual decline of so many Southern white small landholders into tenancy and poverty, in hindsight landholding hardly seems a panacea. In 1865, though, redistribution of land abandoned by fleeing planters or seized by Union armies still looked like a motor for change. It would weaken the hold of the old planter elite on Southern society. It would create a landowning class among the freedmen that would ensure their devotion to the Republican Party. And it would undercut the system of subordinated labor on which plantation agriculture depended. If black people owned land, they would have an

---

50. Hahn, 129; Cimbala, *The Freedmen's Bureau*, 8.
51. Foner, 50–61; Cimbala, *The Freedmen's Bureau*, 4–5.
52. Cimbala, *Under the Guardianship of the Nation*, 2–5.

alternative to the gang labor that Southerners believed cotton demanded. By Howard's own estimation, however, the government had confiscated 0.002 percent of land in the South, and so only a fraction of freedpeople could have obtained farms without much greater confiscation.[53]

Thaddeus Stevens, the Radical Republican leader in the House, was ready to confiscate more land, but land confiscation and redistribution touched deep ideological nerves in the United States. In one sense, massive land redistribution was the basis of the American republic. The U.S. government took Indian lands, peaceably through treaties if it could and forcibly or through fraud and war when it thought necessary. The government then redistributed these ceded or conquered lands to white citizens. Southern redistribution, in essence, was about whether Southern whites could be treated as Indians and Southern blacks could be treated like white men. Furthermore, the wide distribution of land had deep roots in republican theory from Jefferson onward. Americans regarded land as the key source of personal independence and an independent citizenry as the cornerstone of the republic. As the *New Orleans Tribune*—the voice of Louisiana Radicalism and black rights—wrote, "There is...no true republican government, unless the land and wealth in general, are distributed among the great mass of the inhabitants...no more room in our society for an oligarchy of slaveholders or property holders." This belief in the broad distribution of property as the core of a republican society and the dangers the concentration of wealth presented had numerous variants that could be found in Jefferson, Jackson, and Lincoln.[54]

The redistribution of land to freedmen, however, prompted opposition, practical and principled, that extended well beyond those whose lands were at risk. Some objected that the legislative confiscation of the estates of traitors without individual trials violated the Constitution's prohibition on bills of attainder. This objection seemed to carry more weight when the land would go to black men than just to white men. Johnson had argued for the redistribution of plantations to whites. The forty acres and a mule that freedmen hoped for meant that independent black farmers would compete with small white farmers. Ordinary Southern whites saw their status threatened. It was hard for them to see white independence as not depending on black subordination. They denounced it as agrarianism, a word associated with policies that redistributed property downward.[55]

53. Downs, *After Appomattox*, 79; Cimbala, *The Freedmen's Bureau*, 54–55.
54. Foner, 63; Hahn, 142.
55. Simpson, *The Reconstruction Presidents*, 77; Daniel W. Hamilton, *The Limits of Sovereignty: Property Confiscation in the Union and the Confederacy During the Civil*

Saxton and other assistant commissioners who sought to distribute land found themselves stymied. In Georgia, the bureau controlled no land outside the coastal reservation. In Mississippi, Assistant Commissioner Samuel Thomas considered a policy of leasing land to freedmen but abandoned it because it would "require a hero to execute it, and military force to protect the Freedmen during the term of the lease." He warned that without adequate protection, the Emancipation Proclamation itself would be a dead letter in Mississippi. To leave the freedmen to the care of the state of Mississippi "with all their prejudices and independent of national control" would be to relegate the freedpeople to virtual slavery.[56]

On July 28, 1865, Howard issued Circular 13, ordering the assistant commissioners to divide the confiscated and abandoned lands under federal control into forty-acre plots for lease to freedmen, who were to have three years to purchase the land at its 1860 value. Future pardons by the president would not affect the status of abandoned or confiscated property. The circular attracted opposition beyond the South, and the key opponent was Johnson.[57]

Within a month, Johnson overturned the order. He stripped the bureau of the right to allocate lands, a right embodied in its congressional charter, and ordered the army to stop distributions. It would take until the next year for the freedmen's hopes for redistribution to die. Howard floated a much smaller plan that Johnson also rejected. Some assistant commissioners hedged and delayed on the restoration of lands that had been redistributed through 1866. Thaddeus Stevens would attempt to resurrect the issue by advocating the confiscation of the lands of all Confederates worth $10,000 or more for redistribution. This would provide enough land for the freedmen but leave the lands of 90 percent of the residents of the South untouched. But in renewing the bureau in July 16, 1866, Congress validated the restoration of lands to white Southerners in the Sherman Reservation, the belt of abandoned plantations in the Georgia Sea Islands and coast that Gen. Sherman had turned over to freedmen.[58]

War (Chicago: University of Chicago Press, 2007), 26; Ranney, 44–45; Sven Beckert, *The Monied Metropolis: New York City and the Consolidation of the American Bourgeoisie, 1850–1896* (Cambridge: Cambridge University Press, 2001), 161–62; Foner, 235–37.

56. Cimbala, *The Freedmen's Bureau*, 16; Cimbala, *Under the Guardianship of the Nation*, 3.

57. McFeely, 91–106; Cimbala, *The Freedmen's Bureau*, 52–53.

58. Cimbala, *The Freedmen's Bureau*, 56–57; Hahn, 146; Palmer Beverly Wilson and Holly Byers Ochoa, "Reconstruction, September 6, 1865," *Pennsylvania History* 60, no. 2 (1993): 203; Downs, *After Appomattox*, 78–79; McFeely, 107–29.

With Johnson having blocked the redistribution of land, the Freedmen's Bureau put enormous pressure on the freedmen to enter into contracts. Agents regarded labor as the quickest way to wean the freedmen from dependence on the government, to resurrect the Southern economy, and to teach the freedmen the lessons of free labor. Contracts, as Howard put it, were not only a mark of freedom but a form of discipline: "If they can be induced to enter into contracts, they are taught that there are duties as well as privileges of freedom." By signing contracts black people would prove that they "deserved" freedom.[59]

Such language was revealing. Howard imagined the Freedmen's Bureau as part of a larger effort to regenerate the nation. Like many Protestants of the period, he had partially secularized the old Protestant notion of rebirth. Ideas of rebirth and regeneration virtually always required suffering, and this was the prescription for freedmen. Eliphalet Whittlesey, the assistant commissioner for North Carolina, saw blacks as entering a hard apprenticeship. Only suffering, he believed, could make them "the equal of the Anglo-Saxon." Slavery, apparently, had not been hardship enough.[60]

Republicans embraced contract freedom like a secular gospel. The Freedmen's Bureau promoted contract freedom, articulated its meaning, and praised its virtues. The agents of the bureau presented freedom as a series of contracts, particularly labor contracts and marriage contracts. Some ex-slaves and many blacks who had been free before the war embraced it. In November 1865 delegates to a freedmen's convention in South Carolina extolled the right to sell their labor, the right to be paid for their work, the right to move from job to job, and the guarantee of the "sanctity of our family" as markers of freedom.[61]

Actual labor contracts, however, varied widely and were often hard to mistake for freedom. There were standard bureau contracts, but there were also contracts written by the employers. And there were oral contracts. In some places, such as the sugar fields of Louisiana, slaves would use contracts to their own benefit. The bureau hoped to supervise all contracts, but white Southerners often had the contracts executed before a local magistrate. Given the discrepancy in the power and status of

59. Amy Dru Stanley, *From Bondage to Contract: Wage Labor, Marriage, and the Market in the Age of Slave Emancipation* (Cambridge: Cambridge University Press, 1998), 36–37.

60. McFeely, *Yankee Stepfather*, 17–19, 71–83, 89–90; T. J. Jackson Lears, *Rebirth of a Nation: The Making of Modern America, 1877–1920* (New York: Harper, 2009), 18–19, 31, 56–57; Cimbala, *The Freedmen's Bureau*, 15, 17–18, 62, 64–76; Edwards, 67–68.

61. Stanley, 38–40; Laura F. Edwards, *Gendered Strife & Confusion: The Political Culture of Reconstruction* (Urbana: University of Illinois Press, 1997), 47.

those making the contracts, the illiteracy of many ex-slaves, and white Southerners' resort to violence and coercion, the possibilities of abuse were manifold.[62]

The first labor contracts negotiated by the Freedmen's Bureau certainly seemed evidence that the new order differed only in the details from the old. In South Carolina, Charles C. Soule, a white officer in the black Fifty-fifth Massachusetts Infantry, described how he talked to thousands of whites and blacks, explaining to the whites "the necessity of making equitable contracts with their workmen, of discontinuing corporal punishment and of referring all cases of disorder and idleness to the military authorities." In this, he seemed messenger of a new order. But to freedpeople he also said, "Every man must work under orders... and on a plantation the head man who gives all the orders is the owner of the place. Whatever he tells you to do you must do at once, and cheerfully. Remember that all your working time belongs to the man who hires you." Soule told the freedpeople "you will have to work hard, and get very little to eat, and very few clothes to wear," and husbands and wives on separate plantations would not live together. The new freedom might seem reminiscent of the old slavery. But, "remember even if you are badly off, no one can buy or sell you." Soule thought, "only actual suffering, starvation, and punishment will drive many of them to work." It was no wonder that many ex-slaves initially regarded men like Soule as "rebels in disguise."[63]

Contracts could produce exactly the kind of subordinated labor force ex-slave owners desired. The bureau's fear of black dependency often *created* black dependency by driving freedpeople into contracts that impoverished them and made them reliant on their old masters. Bureau agents were right in thinking that the mere fact of a contract forced the white employer to recognize the black employee as his legal equal, but this triumph was purely nominal and yielded only marginal benefits to black laborers. At their extreme, contracts were little more than slavery under another name. In South Carolina in the immediate aftermath of the war, William Tunro in South Carolina asked his former slaves to sign a contract for life. Refusal led first to the expulsion of Robert Perry, his wife, and two others from the plantation, and then to their pursuit and murder by Tunro's neighbors.[64]

62. Cimbala, *The Freedmen's Bureau*, 64–76; Edwards, 67–68.
63. Julie Saville, *The Work of Reconstruction: From Slave to Wage Laborer in South Carolina, 1860–1870* (Cambridge: Cambridge University Press, 1994), 28–29; Carole Emberton, *Beyond Redemption: Race, Violence, and the American South after the Civil War* (Chicago: University of Chicago Press, 2013), 56–57.
64. Hahn, 153–56; Saville, 23.

Contracts could replicate conditions that the freedmen thought emancipation had ended forever. In many areas of the South contracts ran for a year. The freedmen agreed to labor "for their rations and clothing in the usual way," which is to say the same way as they labored under slavery. Many often received very little beyond this. *The New Orleans Tribune*, the most consistent advocate for the rights of the freedmen, attacked the idea that an annual contract was compatible with free labor. Why, it asked, was it necessary for freedmen to have to sign yearlong contracts when northern workers could quit their jobs and take another at any time? Answering its own question, it said the aim of the contracts was to replicate the old system and tie the laborers to the plantation.[65]

Freedmen rebelled against such contracts, but as bad as the contracts were, the bureau at least tried to ensure that white employers upheld their terms. The very fact that a black person had any recourse against abuse by a white person outraged many Southerners. John F. Couts of Tennessee found the mere presence of the bureau was humiliating.

> The Agent of the Bureau...requires citizens (former owners) to make and enter into *written contracts* for hire of their *own* negroes....When a negro is not *properly* paid or fairly dealt with and *reports* the facts, then a squad of Negro soldiers is sent after the *offender*, who is *escorted* to town to be dealt with as per the negro testimony. In the name of God how long is such things to last.[66]

Just as American Indian peoples would later complain of the fraud and injustice of the Bureau of Indian Affairs while nonetheless seeing it as a necessary line of defense against even more rapacious whites, so most freedmen, with all their justified criticisms of the Freedmen's Bureau, saw it as necessary protection against white Southerners.[67]

Johnson saw the bureau differently. His revocation of Howard's Circular 13 formed part of his wider war against the bureau. He systematically drove from office those agents denounced by white Southerners as too sympathetic to the freedmen. Howard, still a good soldier, neither publicly objected nor prevented the purge. Many of the men who replaced Howard's agents were Southern men with Southern attitudes. They often abused the freedmen and actively sought to subvert the bureau and use it as a shield against the army. The army, however, also maintained a presence within the bureau since freedmen's agents were often recruited from the Veteran Reserve Corps. These military men, many of them amputees,

65. O'Donovan, 126–32; Downs, *After Appomattox*, 110–11; McFeely, 150; Foner, 166–70; Cimbala, *The Freedmen's Bureau*, 66–67.
66. Foner, 168.
67. Ibid., 167–69; O'Donovan, 132–38.

proved harder to purge. They were sometimes prompted by sympathy for the ex-slaves, but as often from a desire to make sure that the sacrifices of the war—and their own quite visible sacrifices—would not be in vain. They were tough men, hard to coerce, which meant in some cases they were murdered.[68]

Such murders spotlighted the deep hatred of white Southerners for the Freedmen's Bureau. In Mississippi, Assistant Commissioner Thomas recognized by the end of 1865 that the "simple truth is that the Bureau is antagonistic to what white people believe to be in their interest." They were "determined to get rid of it, and are not particular as to the means adopted to gain their end."[69]

Politically, Johnson used the presence of the army and the Freedmen's Bureau as both a carrot and a stick. Both he and Southerners recognized that without the army and the bureau the federal government lacked the capacity to enforce the laws Congress passed. If Southerners failed to accept his minimal conditions for readmission, then war powers, martial law, the army, and the Freedmen's Bureau would remain. If the ex-Confederates cooperated with him, the army and the Freedmen's Bureau would vanish from the South and the future political status of the freedmen would be left to the states.

What white Southerners would do to the freedmen if left unrestrained became clear as Presidential Reconstruction proceeded in the summer and fall of 1865 and Johnson's hope that the "plain people" of the South would reject the old planter elite were dashed. Ironically, Johnson himself now became an agent of the elite's return. Largely following the recommendations of his governors, he had pardoned those who had supported the Confederacy on the condition that they take an oath of loyalty to the United States and accept the end of slavery. He also agreed to pardon anyone elected to office, eliminating the advantage those loyal to the Union would have held. Schurz reported that some Southerners found the loyalty oath repugnant and humiliating and refused to take it, but for others it was merely instrumental. It gave them back their votes and potentially their power. They treated it with scorn and ridicule, but they took it. Johnson initially denied pardons to the highest-ranking Confederates; they had to apply for personal pardons. Petitioning for pardons became women's work, and it was both personal and tawdry. Lobbyists provided access to Johnson for a fee; the wives and daughters of Confederate leaders appeared, petitioned, and if necessary, begged and wept. The president issued seven thousand pardons by 1866. Southerners saw in amnesty,

68. Cimbala, *The Freedmen's Bureau*, 27–31; O'Donovan, 221–23.
69. Cimbala, *The Freedmen's Bureau*, 35.

the pardons, and the denial of votes to blacks Johnson's intention to pro-mote "a white man's government," with control over suffrage vested in the states.[70]

Johnson seems to have thought that pardoning leading Confederates would make them both grateful to him and dependent on him, but he soon learned that the opposite was true. He found *his* policies interpreted in the light of *their* actions, and men he had opposed, and whom Union armies had defeated, were now riding him. Even as border states disen-franchised ex-Confederates in the years immediately following the war, his provisional governors in the old Confederacy made appointments and adopted policies that saddled him with men the Republican Congress would never accept. South Carolina Gov. Benjamin Perry had "put upon their legs a set of men who...like the Bourbons have learned nothing and forgotten nothing." The Southern Bourbons, as they were known, were the most reactionary elements of the old plantation elite. Creating a Bourbon South was not Johnson's intent, but he did not encourage the alternatives. Those Southerners who urged even limited black suffrage, like ex-Confederate postmaster general John H. Reagan, became, at least for the moment, pariahs. To the old Southern elite, such as the ex-vice president of the Confederacy Alexander Stephens, the South depended on "the subordination of the African race." Or, as a white Mississippian put it, "Our negroes have...a tall fall ahead of them. They will learn that freedom and independence are different things."[71]

III

Johnson was aware of events in the South. He had dispatched emissaries to inquire "into the existing condition of things" and to suggest appropri-ate measures. Not all of these emissaries shared his convictions or his policies. Certainly, Carl Schurz did not. Johnson promised him that his accommodation with the older Southern leadership was tentative and contingent on their cooperation. He would withdraw the extended hand if there were not reciprocity and true reconciliation. But when Schurz reported to Johnson on his return, he thought the president "wished to suppress my testimony as to the condition of things in the South."[72]

70. Perman, 70–81, 123–31; Foner, 184–85, 188–201; Summers, 67.
71. Foner, 192–93; Perman, 102–3, 153; Schurz, *Reminiscenses*, 178–80; Hahn, 152; David Montgomery, "Strikes in Nineteenth-Century America," *Social Science History* 4, no. 1 (1980): 94; Blair, 271–73.
72. Perman, 41; Schurz, *Reminiscences*, 3: 202.

Schurz's letters and the report he eventually submitted could not have been clearer: accommodation was not working. "Treason," he wrote, "does, under existing circumstances, not appear odious in the south." Southerners were "loyal" only insofar as "the irresistible pressure of force" had forced them to renounce independence, and loyalty was little more than "the non-commission of acts of rebellion." He warned Johnson not to have any illusions about the governments taking form under his proclamations. Southerners met even Johnson's minimal requirements only in order to rid themselves of federal troops. They complained bitterly of receiving no compensation for their slaves and had not given up hope of eventually being paid. Many wanted the debts owed by the Confederate states assumed by the newly reorganized states, and they promised resistance to any federal excise taxes that would go to pay the Union war debt. But Southern recalcitrance was greatest in regard to the freedmen. Southerners continued to believe black people unfit for freedom, offering evidence not particularly persuasive to Northerners. "I heard," Schurz reported, "a Georgia planter argue most seriously that one of his negroes had shown himself certainly unfit for freedom because he impudently refused to submit to a whipping."[73]

Outside of the protection of federal troops, freedmen who showed signs of independence and resistance risked their lives. The provost marshal at Selma, Alabama, Maj. J. P. Houston, reported "twelve cases, in which I am morally certain the trials have not been had yet, that negroes were killed by whites. In a majority of cases the provocation consisted in the negroes' trying to come to town or to return to the plantation after having been sent away. The cases above enumerated, I am convinced, are but a small part of those that have actually been perpetrated."[74]

The violence went beyond that. Once freedpeople ceased to have value as property, Schurz wrote,

> the maiming and killing of colored men seems to be looked upon by many as one of those venial offences which must be forgiven to the outraged feelings of a wronged and robbed people. Besides, the services rendered by the negro to the national cause during the war, which make him an object of special interest to the loyal people, make him an object of particular vindictiveness to those whose hearts were set upon the success of the rebellion." Southerners seemed irrevocably committed to the idea that "the elevation of the blacks will be the degradation of the whites.[75]

73. Schurz, *Report*, 17.
74. Ibid., 18.
75. Ibid., 20.

Murders, whipping, and physical compulsion would, Schurz asserted, "continue to be so until the southern people will have learned, so as never to forget it, that a black man has rights which a white man is bound to respect," but when that moment was to arrive was anything but clear. For Schurz, the South in the summer of 1865 foreshadowed the future.[76]

Henry Adams—a black man born into slavery in Georgia—came to Shreveport in Caddo Parish, Louisiana, in the latter part of 1865. He had been, as he put it, "at hard work my whole life." He was a faith doctor, a railsplitter, and a striving man, and he lived what Schurz described. In December 1865 he had a little wagon and was transporting produce to Shreveport when "a crowd of white men" waylaid him. They robbed him, took everything he had, and tried to kill him. Adams was not a man easily discouraged. The next year he traveled to De Soto Parish. He passed through a grim landscape. Six miles south of Shreveport, he saw the body of "a colored man" hanging from the limb of an oak tree. Six miles north of Keachi whites had burned the wagon "belonging to a colored man…with all his things: even his mules were burned." Near Sunny Grove he saw "the head of a colored man lying on the side of the road." He was again waylaid, this time by five men who demanded to know to whom he belonged. He replied he did "belong to God, but not to any man." "Well, by God," they said, "negroes can travel through here that don't belong to somebody, and we will fix you up right here." He was on "a pretty good horse," and that pretty good horse and the whites' bad marksmanship saved his life. White violence prompted Adams' enlistment in the army. He rose to quartermaster sergeant, learned to read and write, and was discharged in 1869.[77]

The sullen resentment of the South, hardly surprising in the face of defeat and suffering, was as much in evidence at the Southern conventions ordered by Johnson as on the roads traveled by Adams. Some states refused to nullify secession, but simply repealed it with the implication that they could pass it again if they wished. Others would not abolish slavery but instead simply acknowledged that it had ceased to exist from force of arms. Mississippi petulantly refused to ratify the Thirteenth Amendment, outlawing slavery. It did so only in 1995, 130 years after enough states had ratified it for it to take effect. Johnson had added to his

---

76. Schurz, 20.
77. U.S. Congress. Senate Select Committee to Investigate the Causes of the Removal of the Negroes from the Southern States to the Northern States. *Report and Testimony of the Select Committee of the United States Senate to Investigate the Causes of the Removal of the Negroes from the Southern States to the Northern States: In Three Parts* (U.S. GPO, 1880), 2: 101, 123, 128–29, 137–39, 154.

requirements that the states repudiate their Confederate war debts, yet both Mississippi and South Carolina refused to do so.[78]

Johnson did not condone most of these outrages, and through much of the summer he supported the actions of the military in the South, but he lost his ability to control events. He made things worse with his overruling the policy of land distribution and removing key officials, thus crippling the Freedmen's Bureau. August and September saw him increasingly siding with the provisional governments in conflicts with the military. In August Gov. William Sharkey of Mississippi created a state militia, certain to be dominated by ex-Confederates. The Union commander, Maj. Gen. Henry W. Slocum, had ordered the plan dropped, and Johnson initially backed him, but then reversed himself. "The people must be trusted," he said. It went without saying that the people to be trusted were white, not black, people. That same month Johnson announced that black regiments would be removed from the South because whites found their presence humiliating and they were a danger to plantation discipline. Generals retained black soldiers in the South, but they tended to withdraw them to garrison duty along the coast. White veterans mustered out of the Union army were allowed to purchase their weapons. When black veterans in Louisiana were mustered out, they had to turn in their guns.[79]

With Johnson increasingly undermining the army and the Freedmen's Bureau, the new Southern legislatures acted as if they had a free hand to impose their own racial order. Black people would have a choice: work for white people or starve. The only question, hardly a trivial one, was how they would work.[80]

Mississippi enacted the first Black Code in the fall of 1865, and other states followed. U.S. Supreme Court Justice Samuel Miller asserted that the codes did "but change the form of slavery," but they were not a return to slavery. African Americans had civil rights—including contract rights—they did not possess under slavery: to marry, hold property, sue, and be sued. Yet the codes reminded both Northerners and freedpeople of a return to slavery because the most egregious of them—those in South Carolina, Mississippi, and Texas—defined black people as agricultural and domestic workers and their white employers as "masters." The laws were as close to apartheid as the United States ever came. They gave

---

78. McKitrick, 9–10.
79. Downs, *After Appomattox*, 80, 108–9, 111; Foner, 190; Hahn, 155; Perman, 43, 99–100, 135–36; Richard M. Valelly, *The Two Reconstructions: The Struggle for Black Enfranchisement* (Chicago: University of Chicago Press, 2004), 26–27.
80. Litwack, 365; Ranney, 45–46.

employers near absolute control of their laborers during the hours of labor (which South Carolina defined as from sunrise to sunset) and when they were not working. Employers retained the right of physically punishing their workers and docking their pay. In Florida black workers could be whipped for "impudence and disrespect."[81]

Southern legislatures recognized in Northern vagrancy laws a particularly useful means of subordinating black labor while contending that they, like the North, accepted freedom of contract. They exploited what seemed on the surface a glaring contradiction in the triumph of free labor: that men and women who asked for alms could be compelled to labor against their wishes in a jail or workhouse. Defenders of contract freedom, however, asserted that vagrancy laws actually validated contract freedom. Beggars had violated the rules of contract. They had asked for goods for which they gave nothing in exchange. They had left the world of the market and sought refuge in charity, dependence, and paternalism. Southern lawmakers contended that in passing vagrancy laws they did nothing that the North had not already done, and that in aiming them at the freedmen they only compelled them to work as the Freedmen's Bureau itself did. If the North could compel white paupers to work, why couldn't the South compel black paupers to work? If vagrants could be compelled to work, then the next step was to make virtually all black people vagrants and paupers under the law. In the North the new industrial economy would generate vagrants and paupers, but Southern legislatures in 1865 sought to manufacture them by legislation.[82]

The general impoverishment of the ex-slaves made them particularly vulnerable to vagrancy laws. Although in certain sections of the South both custom and informal economies had allowed some slaves to accumulate property and many soldiers had saved their wages, most freedmen had no easy access to cash. The black codes were designed to make sure that lack of cash became a legally punishable offense, and they ensured that agricultural labor and domestic service were the only ways for African Americans to get cash. Mississippi defined "vagrant" so broadly that those who neglected their calling, did not support themselves or their families, or failed to pay annual poll taxes were all vagrants. In Alabama "any runaway, stubborn servant or child," any worker "who loiters away his time," or failed to comply with a labor contract was deemed a vagrant. The laws themselves thus produced vagrants, who could be punished by being forced to labor. Mississippi demanded special labor certificates for black

81. Downs, *After Appomattox*, 84–87; Ranney, 45–46.
82. Noralee Frankel, *Freedom's Women: Black Women and Families in Civil War Era Mississippi* (Bloomington: Indiana University Press, 1999), 56–58; Stanley, 98–100.

workers, and failure to possess them as well as failure to pay fines for labor violations or petty criminal infractions could all result in forced labor. Any black workers who quit their jobs without what their employers regarded as a good reason were subject to arrest, and arrest, of course, could result in hiring out for forced labor.[83]

What vagrancy laws did to adults, apprenticeship laws did to children. Except for a few "industrious" and "honest" freedpeople, the black codes declared black parents incapable of raising children. Southern courts sundered black families as effectively as the slave trade by assigning black children, without their or their parents' consent, to white employers. Sometimes, as in North Carolina, Mississippi, and Kentucky, the courts sent children back to their old masters. The South created two distinct sets of laws, one pertaining to whites and the other to blacks.[84]

Southern whites grew quite proficient at using the contracts as tools for the subordination of black labor. Southern whites could escape the Freedmen's Bureau's supervision of contracts by turning to Southern courts to enforce their own contracts with black workers. They also made agreements among themselves not to compete for laborers and not to rent or sell lands to black people. If all else failed, there was always violence. A barrage of beatings, whippings, mutilations, rapes, and murders of freedpeople by whites accompanied the black codes.[85]

Johnson may have sympathized with the racism that inspired the black codes, but he did not endorse the codes. He did, however, accept the new government's legitimacy without granting them full authority. The military remained in place and martial law remained in force. These were the ambiguities of Presidential Reconstruction in practice.[86]

IV

Until Congress was called to session in December 1865, the Republicans could do little about Johnson's policies, and they were hardly united about what they should do when they returned. They had achieved much during the Civil War. With Southerners gone and the remaining Democrats in a minority, Republicans had passed an ambitious program

---

83. Dylan C. Penningroth, *The Claims of Kinfolk: African American Property and Community in the Nineteenth-Century South* (Chapel Hill: University of North Carolina Press, 2003), 45–78; Ranney, 46–47; Litwack, 366–71; Hahn, 141–42.
84. Edwards, 39; Frankel, 136–45; Ranney, 47–48.
85. Hahn, 155, 157; Cimbala, *The Freedmen's Bureau*, 70, 75; Frankel, 69; Litwack, 278–80.
86. Downs, *After Appomattox*, 84–87.

of national improvements to create small farms, build a modern railroad infrastructure, and fund universities. To finance the Civil War, they had borrowed and printed money backed only by the credit of the government. They remade the financial and banking systems to allow them to increase the national debt, which provided the funds to pay and supply armies. The national debt grew from about $65 million to $2.7 billion, about 30 percent of the Union's gross national product in 1865. To generate revenue, Congress had created an income tax and raised the tariff. The higher tariff reduced imports and thus did not yield a great deal more in taxes than a lower one, but it achieved another Republican purpose: shielding American industry from foreign competition. Republicans had forged as vigorous a political program for nation building as the United States would see until the New Deal of the 1930s.[87]

This powerful federal government—the Yankee Leviathan—made Reconstruction not only a practical matter, but also an issue with ideological implications that divided Republicans. Some Radicals accepted the increase in federal power as permanent and beneficial. Other Radicals reverted to their antebellum liberalism. They countenanced the growth of federal power as a necessary war measure but, like other Republicans wary of too radical a Reconstruction of the South, were unwilling to accept it as the new status quo. These divisions, in part, reflected Republican origins. The party had arisen from an amalgamation of Whigs, who embraced government interventions in the economy, and orthodox liberals—many of them antislavery Democrats—to whom both government intervention in the economy and slavery were anathema.

Although the Republicans remained a sectional party rooted in the North, Radical Republicans were nationalists committed to a homogeneous citizenry of rights-bearing individuals, all identical in the eyes of a newly powerful federal government. The Civil War had undercut antebellum arguments for states' rights, which had become tainted, a code not for restraint and limited government but for slavery and oppression. Homogeneous citizenship formed the foundation of the Radical vision of Reconstruction. In practice it came to mean full civil, political, and social equality for freedpeople and confiscation and redistribution of land in the South. The core support of the Radicals lay in New England and areas settled by New Englanders, although other areas could also produce Radicals. Opponents, such as Democrat James Brooks of New York, denounced a homogeneous citizenship as undesirable and impossible.[88]

87. Richard Franklin Bensel, *Yankee Leviathan: The Origins of Central State Authority in America, 1859–1877* (Cambridge: Cambridge University Press, 1990), 162–73, 243–51.
88. Foner, 228–35, 237; Downs, 46.

Intellectually and ideologically, those committed to the full Radical program never constituted a majority of the party's representatives, but the Radicals formed the most influential wing of the Republican Party. The party's most powerful figures—Charles Sumner in the Senate and Thaddeus Stevens in the House—were Radicals who looked beyond the restoration of the old Union and sought to create a new nation from the ruins of the old.[89]

As long as the Radicals emphasized the larger Republican goals of nationalism, free labor, and contract freedom, they could exert tremendous influence. The Republicans' political bet was that military victory and the success of their policies would remake the South and West in the image of the North, create a new national identity under a dominant federal government, and achieve benefits for their party. Freedmen in the South and Indians in the West were to be "raised up." Republican programs for the South and West were of a piece, and they were a variant of a larger pattern of state building in Italy, Germany, Mexico, Argentina, Japan, and elsewhere.[90]

But broad common goals did not resolve underlying tensions between liberals and other Radicals. Liberalism, held strongly by some Republicans and weakly or hardly at all by others, was less a glue holding the party together than a solvent that, once the war was over, threatened to dissolve its unity. Liberalism had arisen in opposition to European aristocracy, monarchy, and established churches, particularly the Catholic Church. Liberals easily accepted the idea of a homogeneous citizenry since they conceived of society as a collection of autonomous rights-bearing individuals rather than an assemblage of classes, ethnic groups, or other collectivities. They made the contract between buyer and seller the template for all social relations. The endless web of individual contracts was how society constituted itself.[91]

Orthodox liberals embraced a laissez-faire economy, something other Radicals either paid lip service to or ignored, and a minimal government that was incompatible with Radical ambitions. Although liberals in Europe and the United States acknowledged the need for state intervention at numerous levels, they thought that economic well-being should be

89. Michael Les Benedict, *A Compromise of Principle: Congressional Republicans and Reconstruction, 1863–1869* (New York: Norton, 1974), 26–33, 34–35, 37–38.

90. Thomas Bender, *A Nation among Nations: America's Place in World History* (New York: Hill and Wang, 2006), 172–81.

91. Daniel T. Rodgers, *Atlantic Crossings: Social Politics in a Progressive Age* (Cambridge, MA: Belknap Press of Harvard University Press, 1998), 78–79; Michael Les Benedict, "Laissez-Faire and Liberty: A Re-Evaluation of the Meaning and Origins of Laissez-Faire Constitutionalism," *Law and History Review* 3, no. 2 (1985), 293–331; Stanley, 1–24.

left largely to markets, which they equated with freedom and regarded as natural. Drawing on a deep Protestant heritage, liberals believed free choice as essential to morality and freedom and made the economy into a moral realm that depended on the free choice of its actors. Yet paradoxically for a group that arose in reaction to an established and entrenched European order, liberals were also fearful of a freedom that manifested itself in the popular movements, popular religion, and popular culture that flourished in the wake of war. Liberals tended to be ensconced in the elite institutions of American society.[92]

Earlier in American history both Jeffersonians and Jacksonians paired democracy and laissez-faire. And some liberals with Jacksonian roots preserved that earlier orientation. Isaac Sherman, a New York businessman and financier and a reliable bankroller of liberal causes and publications, testified before the New York Assembly in 1875 that his goal was "to limit the sphere of Government and the number and sphere of officials" in order to give more room to "individual judgment and individual enterprise and competition, the great motor force in all free government." Because markets seemed to epitomize individual judgment, enterprise, and competition, liberals like Sherman held fast to a belief in the autonomy and moral authority of markets. As the Reverend Lyman Atwater proclaimed, "economics and ethics largely interlock." The market was the metaphor and model for all social order.

A rising generation of younger liberals held more complicated views. Rhetorically, E. L. Godkin of the *Nation* conflated all freedom with free markets: "the liberty to buy and sell, and mend and make, where, when, and how we please." Godkin, however, also acknowledged the limitations of markets in practice. He, at least in his early years, did not regard permanent wage labor as contract freedom. He and other younger liberals also differed from Sherman in their distrust of democracy. Godkin was eager to curtail political freedoms that he thought produced corruption and threatened anarchy. He recognized that the United States had become a multicultural nation deeply divided by class, and, since he thought democracy could work only in small homogeneous communities, American democracy had become dangerous.[93]

Liberalism and Radical Republicanism were ideologies—simplified and idealized versions of how society should operate—and not descriptions of the far more complicated ways the North did operate. Northerners,

92. Rodgers, 77–79.
93. Joyce Appleby, "Republicanism and Ideology," *American Quarterly* 37, no. 4 (1985): 470; Nancy Cohen, *The Reconstruction of American Liberalism, 1865–1914* (Chapel Hill: University of North Carolina Press, 2002), 56.

in general, were both decidedly less liberal than doctrinaire liberals desired and less Radical than ardent Radicals wished. They were quite ready to regulate the economy and social life, if not always at the federal level, and they did not wholeheartedly endorse ideas of homogeneous citizenship. There were two intertwined threads of American thinking about freedom, rights, and equality. The brightly colored thread naturalized rights and made them universal: "all men are created equal." The second, more inconspicuous but also arguably more powerful, thread localized rights. This thread represented how Americans thought and acted in their specific and bounded communities. They understood each other less as discrete individuals than as members of groups defined by sex, race, wealth, kinship, religion, and persistence in the community. These groups were unequal, and their inequality was marked by differences in status and privilege. Local governance consisted of a collective order of duties and privileges rather than universal rights. As long as citizenship remained local, as it always had been in the United States, citizens were manifestly unequal.[94]

Americans endowed their local governments with remarkable powers. Such governments in the United States had long regulated "public safety, public economy, public mobility, public morality, and public health." They controlled whom people could marry, what they could print, and what they could send through the mail. They regulated how citizens conducted their businesses, how they built their houses, what they could do in them, and how they managed their livestock. They determined where, and if, people could carry firearms and where and with whom their children went to school. Local governments intervened constantly in daily life. It never occurred to the vast majority of Americans that property was beyond public regulation or control or that its use should be left solely to private arrangements. But neither were Northerners necessarily ready to put this regulatory authority in the hands of the *federal* government.[95]

As long as the Civil War raged, military necessity had suppressed the ideological contradictions between laissez-faire liberalism and the neo-Whig policies of other Radicals. Liberals could regard the Yankee Leviathan as an aberration, if a necessary one, produced by the requirements of war. Once the government ended slavery, free labor and contract freedom would flourish and the state would shrink and recede.

The ratification of the Thirteenth Amendment threatened to dissolve the Republican consensus. With slavery abolished, the most ardent liberals

94. Masur, 4–5.
95. William J. Novak, *The People's Welfare: Law and Regulation in Nineteenth-Century America* (Chapel Hill: University of North Carolina Press, 1996), 51 and passim.

among the Radicals thought their work largely done. By distilling the essence of freedom into the right of self-ownership and the ability to dispose of one's labor by mutually agreed contracts, Republicans had forged a weapon that cut through defenses of slavery. Slaves did not own their own bodies, let alone their labor; they worked under compulsion. At the moment when the fetters were removed and the kneeling slaves stood as free men and women, the most ardent liberals thought victory achieved. William Lloyd Garrison, the nation's leading abolitionist, proclaimed the new age: "Where are the slave auction-blocks...the slave-yokes and fetters....They are all gone! From chattels to human beings...Freedmen at work as independent laborers by voluntary contract."[96]

The slaves had supposedly entered a world of individualism, where their fate was in their own hands. As Clinton Fisk, assistant commissioner of the Freedmen's Bureau for Kentucky and Tennessee, told the ex-slaves quite sincerely, "Every man is, under God, just what he makes of himself." William Dean Howells, who was in 1865 writing for the *Nation*, exuded liberal orthodoxy when he endorsed Herbert Spencer's contention, already old in 1865, that all the state owed a man was a fair start in life.[97]

Other Radicals, like white Southerners, were less blind to the realities of the freedpeople's condition. Contract freedom had, after all, triumphed over slavery only through the armed power of the federal government. Stevens and Sumner recognized that people experienced freedom only under the protection of the government's police power.[98]

Despite the exhaustion following four years of brutal war, these Radicals did not think that the Thirteenth Amendment was the end of the struggle. Instead 1865 seemed to them a "golden moment" that needed to be seized. This idea animated a "Greater Reconstruction," covering the West as well as the South.[99]

The Radicals' struggles to use the power of the federal government to attain this dream predictably created a contest between the Republicans on the one hand and Johnson and the Democrats and conservative Republicans who supported him on the other, but it also exacerbated tensions within the Republican Party. Alarmed by the desire of some Radicals for land redistribution and their far-reaching claims for equality, Republican conservatives pulled back. They would end slavery and

96. Benedict, *A Compromise of Principle*, 36–37; Stanley, 4.
97. Cimbala, *The Freedmen's Bureau*, 63; Kenneth Schuyler Lynn, *William Dean Howells: An American Life* (New York: Harcourt Brace Jovanovich, 1971), 131.
98. Downs, *After Appomattox*, 46, 134.
99. Elliott West, *The Last Indian War: The Nez Perce Story* (New York: Oxford University Press, 2009), xx–xxi; Cohen, 28–29.

guarantee freedpeople some basic civil rights, but they would proceed cautiously from there. They did not share the Radicals' desire to remake the South "root and branch." They still hoped for an accommodation with President Johnson. In between the Radicals and the Conservatives, and holding the balance of power were the moderate Republicans. For them restoring the Union often took priority over securing the rights of the freedpeople. The Moderates determined the shifting balance between the Radicals and conservative Republicans, which would be critical to Reconstruction politics.[100]

Liberal Republicans were the wild card. With the ratification of the Thirteenth Amendment, some liberals shed their Radicalism as easily as soldiers removed their uniform, but thanks to Andrew Johnson and the Southerners who eventually supported him, many liberals did not desert Radicalism easily or quickly. The Black Codes did not look like either free labor or contract freedom. By the end of 1865, as Congress prepared to return to Washington, it seemed that Johnson's policies were squandering the fruits of victory and rewarding the actions of traitors.

Racism further complicated the nation's politics. Racism, like other beliefs, came in degrees. Many Radicals and most Republicans were racist; it would have been astonishing had they not been. Most Northerners in 1865 initially proved unwilling to move beyond granting civil liberties to black people. They balked at granting them political freedom—suffrage and the right to hold office—let alone social equality. Johnson was also a racist, but his racism was extreme. Johnson had what his private secretary described as "a morbid distress and feeling against the negroes." In this he reflected his Tennessee Unionist supporters. "It is hard to tell," William Brownlow, an old Tennessee Whig, declared of East Tennessee's Unionists, "which they hate most, the Rebels, or the negroes." In a discourse of white victimization common in the late nineteenth century, Johnson thought poor whites rather than blacks the real victims of slavery. Slaves had joined with their masters to keep the poor white man "in slavery by depriving him of a fair participation in the labor and productions of the rich land of the country."[101]

With the war over, Johnson feared the situation would worsen if the mass of freedmen obtained the vote. They would always be pliable tools of their masters on whom they would remain dependent. Giving African

100. Summers, 83–86; Benedict, *A Compromise of Principle*, 26–33, 42–56, 142–43; Moderate, Radical, and Conservative were porous categories, and politicians moved between them; Foner, 236–38; McKitrick, *Andrew Johnson and Reconstruction*, 53-55, 77–84.
101. Thomas, 440; Eric McKitrick, "Andrew Johnson, Outsider," in McKitrick, *Andrew Johnson: A Profile*, 68–77; Foner, 181; Simpson, *The Reconstruction Presidents*, 76.

Americans the franchise thus seemed to him antithetical to his ambition of ensuring that the Southern "plain folks"—the whites with whom Johnson sympathized most deeply—dominated the postbellum South. Privately, he supposedly declared that "this is a country for white men, and, by God, as long as I am President, it shall be a government for white men."[102]

So long as Reconstruction seemed to be about the transfer of power from the old Southern elite to the plain people of the South, Johnson was enthusiastically for it. When Radicals, however, pressed for equal rights, citizenship, and even suffrage for the freedmen, then Johnson's devotion to a white republic surged to the fore. He thought that in this he had the sympathy of the Northern electorate, which thought of suffrage as a privilege rather than a right. In the fall of 1865 proposals to extend the vote to black men went down to defeat in Connecticut, Wisconsin, and Minnesota.[103]

The status quo, however, was rapidly changing, and the man pushing the change most aggressively and rapidly was Thaddeus Stevens of Pennsylvania. Stevens came to consider Andrew Johnson "at heart a damn scoundrel," and when Congress came into session in December 1865, Stevens's opinions mattered. Stevens vociferously attacked the idea that the United States was a "white man's country" and that its government was a "white man's government." In this, he diverged not only from President Johnson but also from most Republicans. Stevens could not eliminate American racism, but that was not his aim. He wanted to topple as many of its supports as he could and link it to a failed past. The doctrine of a "white man's government" was a sibling of deceased Chief Justice Roger Taney's ruling in the *Dred Scott* decision that black men were "beings of an inferior order, and altogether unfit to associate with the white race, either in social or political relations, and so far inferior that they had no rights which the white man was bound to respect." That "infamous sentiment," Stevens said with characteristic bluntness, had "damned the late Chief Justice to ever lasting fame; and, I fear, to everlasting fire." The upholders of white men's government risked the same fate.[104]

102. Foner, 183–84, 186–87.
103. Ibid., 218–19, 222–24; Heather Cox Richardson, *The Death of Reconstruction: Race, Labor, and Politics in the Post–Civil War North, 1865–1901* (Cambridge, MA: Harvard University Press, 2001), 12–15; Simpson, *The Reconstruction Presidents*, 85–86.
104. Thaddeus Stevens, Speech on Reconstruction, Dec. 18, 1865, Furman University: Thaddeus Stevens Papers On-line, http://history.furman.edu/benson/hst41/blue/stevens1.htm; Wish, 96–97; Annette Gordon-Reed, *Andrew Johnson* (New York: Times Books/Henry Holt, 2011), 100.

Stevens wanted the franchise extended to black men, and he wanted to grant them a share of the Southern property that their labor had created. His egalitarianism went only so far. Women would remain outside the electoral process. The fixation of some Republican reforms on racial injustice could blind them to a staggering array of other problems emerging in an American society that denied women many of the rights Stevens wanted for black men. Those reformers who saw the inequities of gender and class most clearly, however, were, in turn, often aggressively racist in anchoring reform in the defense of white manhood and the white home. There was also an undeniable smugness in the Radicals' assumption that blacks, Southern whites, Indians, and poor Northerners all needed to turn themselves into replicas of successful and independent Northern white men. Still, Stevens's position was a brave and remarkable one in 1865.[105]

The touchstone for American politics of Reconstruction at the end of 1865 was a question: What would Lincoln have done? Lincoln's ideal of a "government of the people, by the people, for the people" animated Reconstruction, but the phrase retained both its power and its ambiguity. Who were the people? The inhabitants of the United States often hated each other, and yet they could not avoid each other. Most Americans appealed to ideals of freedom, family, and home, but they often regarded other Americans as a threat to those ideals. Race, religion, ethnicity, and language divided Americans, but hate extended well beyond these bright markers. To say that Lincoln's policy probably would have fallen somewhere between the most punitive treatment of the South and the virtual abandonment of the ex-slaves that Johnson and his most ardent supporters advocated does not say much at all. It was in this expansive territory that Republican policies took root. Policy, in any case, was never going to be the product of a single individual, and the implementation of any policy would prove far more difficult than its formulation. The Civil War produced great structural change in the United States, and the forces set in motion were beyond the capacity of any individual to control, as Lincoln himself admitted.[106]

When Congress reconvened, the government was forced to confront those changes, not only in the South, which dominated national attention, but also in the North and West. Reconstruction involved the West as well as the South, and although the North might consider itself the template for the new society destined to emerge from the war, that template had begun to show its own cracks and fissures.

105. Foner, 231–33.
106. Eric Foner, *The Fiery Trial: Abraham Lincoln and American Slavery* (New York: Norton, 2010), 331–36.

2

Radical Reconstruction

Killing Presidential Reconstruction could be done with congressional votes, but creating a substitute was akin to building a house during a hurricane, or rather two houses, since Republicans were also trying to create replicas of Lincoln's Springfield in the West. On the one hand, there were clear structural necessities: how to readmit the Southern states, how to pacify and occupy the West, how to define the new powers of the federal government, and how to turn former slaves into citizens. On the other hand there were questions of design: How full would be the equality offered freedpeople? What would be the relationship with Indian peoples once fighting stopped? And then there was the political weather, the buffeting onrush of events, many of them destructive and violent. That the builders in the 1860s were on the ground in the South and West and the architects' offices were, in effect, in Washington D.C. only compounded the problem. Congress could neither remake the South nor create a free labor West by proclamation. This would have to be done in hundreds of Southern towns and counties and across a vast expanse of the West. To one degree or another, it would depend on force and whether Congress or the president controlled the force embodied in war powers.

In December 1865, Congress faced the immediate practical question of whether to seat the newly elected Southern representatives arriving in Washington. If Congress seated the Southern delegations, the war power would come to an end once civil government was restored in all states. Southern Democrats, their representation increased by the abolition of slavery and with it the end of the three-fifths clause, would, in combination with Democrats from the North, threaten Republican dominance. As an Illinois Republican put it, "the reward of treason would be increased representation in the House" and an increase in the Southern electoral vote. Thaddeus Stevens foresaw a Democratic Party dominated by the South in possession of Congress and the White House: "I need not depict the ruin that would follow." To avert ruin, he suggested a Joint Committee on Reconstruction to decide the issue, and it became the focal point for investigations of conditions in the South. In testimony behind closed doors, soldiers, Freedmen's Bureau agents, and Southern Unionists recited a litany of ongoing Southern violence, crime, and injustice against freedpeople and Radicals.[1]

Moderate Republicans did not wish to break with Johnson, but they, as fully as Radicals, were determined to suppress the atrocities committed by ex-Confederates. Should accommodation with Johnson fail, the Radicals prepared the ground for unilateral action by Congress. They had three powerful constitutional weapons. The first was familiar: the right of Congress to determine its own membership, that is the power to reject members even if they had won election in their states. The second, untested, weapon was the constitutional clause guaranteeing every state a republican form of government. This was, in Senator Charles Sumner's words, a "sleeping giant." Nothing else in the Constitution gave "Congress such supreme power over the states." The third were the war powers that allowed the continuing occupation of the South.[2]

The power of the constitutional clause hinged on the definition of republican government, and Sumner, with his usual erudition, seized the ground for the Radicals. His speech stretched over two days in February 1866 and demanded forty-one columns of small print in the *Congressional Globe*. Sumner asserted that without equality of citizens before the law and full consent of the governed, a government could not be considered republican. It defined a standard that the North no more met than the South.[3]

In January 1866 Republicans offered the president two bills that they regarded as a workable compromise between the Radicals' desire to remake the South and Johnson's desire to readmit the South as it was to the Union. One bill expanded the duties of the Freedmen's Bureau and extended its life; the second guaranteed freedpeople basic civil rights. The proposed legislation gave the Freedmen's Bureau jurisdiction in cases involving black people in the South and assigned the agency direct

---

1. Richard M. Valelly, *The Two Reconstructions: The Struggle for Black Enfranchisement* (Chicago: University of Chicago Press, 2004), 28–29; Gregory P. Downs, *After Appomattox: Military Occupation and the Ends of War* (Cambridge, MA: Harvard University Press, 2015), 113–19; " 'Reconstruction,' December 18, 1865 in Congress," in Beverly Wilson Palmer and Holly Byers Ochoa, eds., *The Selected Papers of Thaddeus Stevens* (Pittsburgh: University of Pittsburgh Press, 1998), Volume 2: April 1865–August 1868, 51.

2. Eric Foner, *Reconstruction: America's Unfinished Revolution, 1863–1877* (New York: Harper & Row, 1988), 228–47; Michael Les Benedict, *A Compromise of Principle: Congressional Republicans and Reconstruction, 1863–1869* (New York: Norton, 1974), 142–43; Eric L. McKitrick, *Andrew Johnson and Reconstruction* (Chicago: University of Chicago Press, 1960), 274–76.

3. Downs, 118–29; Foner, 232–33.

responsibility for protecting their rights. To do so, it could call on the military. Bureau agents could intervene against state officials denying blacks "civil rights belonging to a white person" and arraign those officials in federal court. This was Congress's response to Southern outrages and the Black Codes, but the bills did not give freedmen the vote, and they did not redistribute land. The Radicals supported them because the bills were all they initially could get and because they hoped that more ambitious measures would follow.[4]

The second proposal was the Civil Rights Bill of 1866, which passed the Senate in early February. It gave teeth to the Thirteenth Amendment and represented a breathtaking extension of federal power. In the words of Sen. Lyman Trumbull of Illinois, it guaranteed to all citizens the "fundamental rights belonging to every man as a free man": the right to make contracts, to sue in court, and have the state protect their property and person. Federal marshals, attorneys, and bureau agents could bring suit in federal court against any state officials or state laws that violated these protections. Maine Senator Lot Morrill proclaimed, "This species of legislation is absolutely revolutionary. But are we not in the midst of a revolution?"[5]

The revolution extended a homogeneous national citizenship with a specific set of rights over the entire country, but it had clear limits. The Civil Rights Act secured only *civil* equality, giving the freedpeople access to the legal system and protection from some kinds of discriminatory laws. It did not give them *political* equality: the right to vote and hold office. Nor did it give them *social* equality: free and equal access to public venues, from streetcars and railroad cars to theaters and schools. Primary jurisdiction for enforcing civil rights still remained in the state courts. Once state laws were stripped of overt discrimination, de facto discrimination by sheriffs, judges, or ordinary citizens would be hard to prevent under the act.[6]

In February Johnson vetoed the Freedmen's Bureau bill. He denounced it as unconstitutional and expensive and as encouraging black "indolence." Congress sustained, if barely, this veto, but Johnson remained the kind of man who was angry even in victory. As was the custom, on Washington's Birthday a crowd gathered before the White House to serenade the president, and Johnson gave an impromptu speech that provided more evidence that he should never give impromptu speeches. He

4. Foner, 239–51.
5. Downs, 121–23; Foner, 243–45.
6. Kate Masur, *An Example for All the Land: Emancipation and the Struggle over Equality in Washington, D.C.* (Chapel Hill: University of North Carolina Press, 2010), 117–18; Foner, 243–45.

equated Stevens, Sumner, and the abolitionist Wendell Phillips with the Confederate leadership. They were, he said, as bad as traitors since they too aimed to undermine the Constitution. The president referred to himself 210 times in a speech of little more than an hour, or three times every minute.[7]

As indiscreet as Johnson was in public, he was worse in private. A former slave owner, he rebuffed and insulted a black delegation headed by Frederick Douglass. Johnson told the delegation that it was poor whites, not blacks, who were the real victims of slavery in the South. After the delegates left, he told his private secretary: "Those damned sons of bitches thought they had me in a trap. I know that damned Douglass; he's just like any nigger, & he would sooner cut a white man's throat than not."[8]

There was method in Johnson's madness. His goal was a coalition of conservatives who would cross party and sectional boundaries to maintain a white man's republic. On March 27, Johnson vetoed the Civil Rights Bill as an attack on the rights of white people and as a move to centralize all power in the federal government. He began his veto message with the denunciation of a country that would protect "the Chinese of the Pacific States, Indians subject to taxation, the people called Gipsies, as well as the entire race designated as blacks, people of color, negroes, mulattoes and persons of African blood." This was the "mongrel republic" of Democratic nightmares.[9]

He also indicated that only he could speak for the nation; Congress spoke for parochial interests. This was a "modest" assertion, one of his enemies pointed out, for a man who became president only because of an assassin's bullet. Johnson's political calculation was that by framing the issue as a dual contest between the rights of whites and the rights of blacks, and between the expansion of the federal government and the preservation of local governments, he could not lose.[10]

Indiana Republican Oliver P. Morton, however, went straight to the weakness of Johnson's strategy. The battle remained what it had been all along: a choice between loyalty and treason, between North and South. Morton hoisted what became known as the bloody shirt: the call to remember northern sacrifices and the Democrats' taint of treason. "Every unregenerate rebel lately in arms against his government," Morton said,

7. McKitrick, 293–95; Foner, 247–49.
8. Hans L. Trefousse, *Andrew Johnson: A Biography* (New York: Norton, 1989), 241–42.
9. McKitrick, 314–19; Nancy Isenberg, *White Trash: The 400-Year Untold History of Class in America* (New York: Viking, 2016), 182–83; Michael Perman, *Reunion without Compromise: The South and Reconstruction: 1865–1868* (Cambridge: Cambridge University Press, 1973), 190–93; Foner, 250–51.
10. Foner, 249–51; McKitrick, 314–19.

"calls himself a Democrat." So did every bounty jumper, deserter, every man who "murdered Union prisoners by cruelty and starvation," every man who "shoots down negroes in the streets, burns up negro school-houses and meeting houses, and murders women and children by the light of their own flaming dwellings." The list went on as Morton mounted to his climax, aligning the president with the Democrats:

> And this party . . . proclaims to an astonished world that the only effect of vanquishing armed rebels in the field is to return them to seats in Congress, and to restore them to political power. Having failed to destroy the constitution by force, they seek to do it by construction, with . . . the remarkable discovery that the rebels who fought to destroy the constitution were its true friends, and that the men who shed their blood and gave their substance to preserve it were its only enemies.

Morton was not a Radical; he was a leader of Indiana's conservative Republicans.[11]

On April 6, 1866, Congress overrode Johnson's veto of the Civil Rights Bill. It was the first time in American history that Congress had overridden a presidential veto of a major piece of legislation. The Senate, however, obtained its necessary two-thirds majority only by expelling a New Jersey Democrat. In July the second attempt to extend the life of the Freedmen's Bureau succeeded. In passing a new bill over Johnson's veto, Congress gave the bureau power to enforce the Civil Rights Act and reinstated bureau courts.[12]

The passage of the Civil Rights Act signaled a permanent break between Johnson and Congress, but Johnson in his fury also alienated the army and deepened his estrangement from the secretary of war. Both Stanton and Union army officers felt increasingly threatened by civil suits for actions taken during the war and its aftermath. Grant, who had initially pushed demobilization, had changed his mind. He issued General Orders No. 3 in January 1866 to protect soldiers in the South from lawsuits, and had then allowed his commanders to use its rather vague and general provisions to protect freedpeople from the Black Codes. In an attempt to stop Congress from using war powers, on April 2 Johnson proclaimed the end of the rebellion everywhere but in Texas, though in practice the proclamation did not end martial law because the power to declare war, and restore peace, belonged to Congress and Southern representatives had not yet been restored to Congress. And even Johnson sought to limit rather than eliminate army authority. Officers were not

11. McKitrick, 318–19.
12. Ibid., 317–23; Foner, 250–51; William S. McFeely, *Yankee Stepfather: General O. O. Howard and the Freedmen* (New Haven, CT: Yale University Press, 1968), 246, 268, 271.

supposed to use military tribunals "where justice can be attained through the medium of civil authority," but they could use them when civil courts abused freedmen or Unionists and when state laws conflicted with federal laws. Still, the army remained nervous as Southern officials tried to arrest and sue U.S. soldiers. Far from defending the army and its officers, Johnson welcomed the Supreme Court's *ex parte Milligan* and *Garland* decisions in 1866, which indicated limits, as yet unclear, on the reach of martial law, and the *Cummings* decision in 1867, which ruled the iron-clad oath unconstitutional.[13]

The threatened army was also a weakened and overextended army. As the terms of volunteer enlistments expired, it continued to dwindle. By July 1866 there were only twenty-eight thousand soldiers in the entire South, and eighty-seven hundred of them were in Texas. Grant came to oppose further reductions of the military, but he, as well as Johnson, had initially sanctioned them despite warnings from officers on the ground. As the number of soldiers diminished, rural outposts were abandoned. By January 1866 the number of posts had already been reduced to 207; by September there were only 101. Without cavalry the troops could not patrol outside of towns and along rail lines. A Freedmen's commissioner in Texas expressed the basic spatial logic of Reconstruction: "The wrongs increase just in proportion to their distance from the United States authorities." As an army commander complained, it was impossible to stop Southern stragglers and marauders by telegraph. He needed cavalry. The change was particularly stark in the Deep South. There were only five posts in Mississippi by September 1866, five in Georgia, seven in Alabama, and fourteen in South Carolina.[14]

These troops were enough to give hope to freedpeople and Unionists but outside of the towns not enough to provide protection. Congress, concerned about both the cost of the military and the longstanding American fear of a standing army, debated the size of a new permanent force. The compromise army bill that resulted did not produce sufficient soldiers to provide garrisons everywhere needed in the South and the West, and for coastal forts. There would be ten cavalry regiments, two of which would be segregated black units, and forty-five infantry—four of which would be black and stationed largely in the West. On paper it would be fifty-four thousand men, about three times the size of the army in 1860 and smaller

13. Benjamin Platt Thomas, *Stanton: The Life and Times of Lincoln's Secretary of War,* ed. Harold Melvin Hyman (New York: Knopf, 1962), 473–88, 516–17; Downs, 105–6, 126, 146–48, 156–57; Harold M. Hyman, "Stanton, and Grant: A Reconsideration of the Army's Role in the Events Leading to Impeachment," *American Historical Review* 66, no. 1 (1960): 85–93; Thomas, 473–88, 516–17.
14. Downs, *After Appomattox,* 89–91, 103–8, 142, 152, 257–63.

than the number of troops stationed in the South outside of Texas at the beginning of 1866.[15]

I

The demobilization of the army gave unreconciled Confederates freedom and confidence. With one hand, the government had passed new laws and assumed new powers; with the other, it had eliminated much of its ability to enforce them. Efforts to create black independence faltered not only because of the conviction of some bureau agents that black people were by nature dependent but also because those who sought to protect black rights often lacked the means to do so outside of the cities and towns. There were too few agents, and there were far too few soldiers to call on to suppress violence and provide necessary aid.[16]

The bureau was typical of the federal government's administrative apparatus in the wake of the Civil War. On paper, it was powerful, with a sweeping mandate and the legal means to enforce it. On the ground, it was understaffed, underfinanced, and incapable of achieving its goals. Hugo Hillebrandt, a Freedmen's Bureau agent in North Carolina, lacked neither courage nor conviction. Born in Hungary, he had fought with Lajos Kossuth in the Hungarian Revolution, joined Garibaldi's Italian Revolution, and enlisted in the Union Army. Wounded at Gettysburg, he joined the Freedmen's Bureau in 1866. He found himself largely powerless as whites stole horses and mules from freedmen. Hillebrandt commanded four soldiers with no horses. When in May 1866 a freedwoman traveled to his office in Kinston to report the murder of a Union soldier nineteen miles away, Hillebrandt, who had been warned not to proceed without adequate force, could do nothing except let the body rot in the road.[17]

Without troops to overawe them, guerrillas and outlaws became more aggressive. In rural areas across the Deep South the withdrawal of troops was the prelude to violence and chaos. Southerners burned churches, shot isolated soldiers, and killed hundreds of freedpeople. In response

15. Downs, *After Appomattox*, 132–33, 141–45, 152–53.
16. Foner, 190; Steven Hahn, *A Nation under Our Feet: Black Political Struggles in the Rural South, from Slavery to the Great Migration* (Cambridge, MA: Belknap Press of Harvard University Press, 2003), 155; Downs, 145; Perman, 43, 99–100, 135–36.
17. Gregory P. Downs, *Declarations of Dependence: The Long Reconstruction of Popular Politics in the South, 1861–1908* (Chapel Hill: University of North Carolina Press, 2011), 90–98.

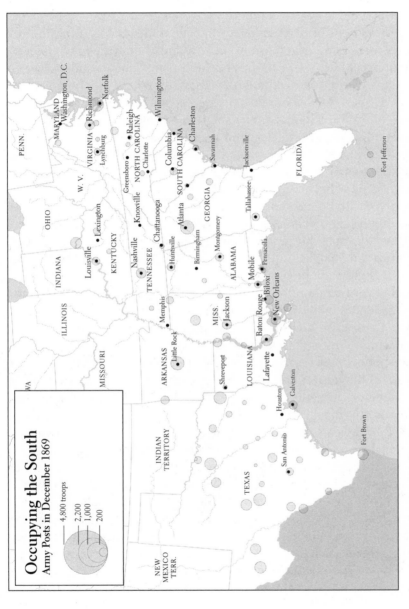

Map adapted by Geoff McGhee from Gregory P. Downs, *After Appomattox*; Basemaps: Minnesota Population Center; National Historical Information System; Natural Earth Data.

black refugees fled to garrisoned cities and towns while other freedmen, particularly in places with Union veterans, organized for self-defense. Black dockworkers in St. Augustine, Florida, armed and created what whites called a secret military organization. Elsewhere, in Jackson County, freedmen armed to protect a school.[18]

The movement of black refugees into the cities both during the war and after increased racial tensions and produced new waves of violence. In Memphis clashes between mustered-out black soldiers and the largely Irish police led to a confrontation on May 1, 1866, in which two policeman were shot. The police, supplemented by largely Irish mobs, descended on South Memphis, first singling out black men in uniform—current or discharged soldiers—and then killing blacks indiscriminately. In ensuing days the rioting spread back into Memphis proper. Gen. George Stoneman, in charge of the Union garrison, refused to intervene, although some of his subordinates did, largely ineffectually. For three days white mobs, with police and firemen as their core, attacked blacks, torching freedmen's schools and churches, killing, and raping. They invaded a shantytown housing the families of black soldiers. Forty-eight people died. All but two were blacks, and a large swath of black Memphis lay in ruins. No one was indicted; no one was punished.[19]

A little over two months later, violence ripped through New Orleans. Ex-Confederates had won the 1866 local elections in which blacks could not vote. Louisiana Radicals called a convention in New Orleans with the goal of enfranchising blacks and disenfranchising "rebels." The New Orleans police force, consisting largely of Confederate veterans, plotted to break up the convention. On July 30 the police and a white mob attacked a march of twenty-five convention delegates and two hundred supporters, mostly black veterans. The police and white mob were well armed; the Radicals were not. When the mob invaded the convention hall, they denounced the American flag as "a dirty rag" and ignored the white handkerchiefs the white Unionists waved as a sign of surrender. They beat to death or shot any black man they could seize. A carpetbagger described how, as a wagon carried away corpses one of the black men thought dead raised himself up, only to be shot through the head by a policeman. General Phil Sheridan, in charge of the occupation of Louisiana as well as Texas, called it an "absolute massacre by the police...perpetrated without the shadow of necessity." By the time federal troops drove off the police, thirty-seven people, all Radicals and thirty-four of them

18. Downs, *After Appomattox*, 145–46.
19. Stephen V. Ash, *A Massacre in Memphis* (New York: Hill & Wang, 2013): for tensions, 42–54, 62–86; for outbreak, 93–99; for riot, 100–58; for toll, 180–82.

black, were dead. Johnson would defend the New Orleans authorities and blame the riot on the Radicals.[20]

The slaughters in Memphis and New Orleans shocked the North both because of the carnage and because of their snarling challenge to federal authority. These were not attacks by nightriders; police led the crowds. Southern governments created under Presidential Reconstruction seemed little more than progeny of the Confederacy and children even more brutal than their parent. The Radicals used the violence to persuade the Northern electorate of the need for occupation of the South and the necessity for the Fourteenth Amendment, guaranteeing black civil rights.[21]

The Republicans had proposed the Fourteenth Amendment to the Constitution to enshrine the Civil Rights Bill of 1866 in the Constitution itself. They wanted to protect it from the Supreme Court and future congresses, a particular danger since the end of slavery meant the demise of the three-fifths clause, which would add a million and a half people and twenty congressional seats to the South's total. Unless black people could vote, those seats would probably be overwhelmingly Democratic. Politically, the Republicans also needed to provide a route to eventual peace as an alternative to Johnson's April announcement that organized resistance had ceased everywhere but in Texas. Johnson had not rescinded martial law or restored habeas corpus. His proclamation was purely for political and rhetorical effect.[22]

The struggle to ratify the Fourteenth Amendment would continue into July 1868, but its critical framing came in the spring of 1866. The Republicans were divided. Stevens wanted the amendment to enfranchise blacks and strip leading rebels of political rights, but Republicans had not forged a consensus on either. They were also divided over whether suffrage should be extended to women, as a petition presented by Susan B. Anthony and Elizabeth Cady Stanton demanded. As finally approved by Congress, the amendment did not include black suffrage, but it sought to exact a price for treason. All those Confederates who had served in federal or state governments or in the military before the war and had taken an oath to uphold the Constitution were made ineligible for political

---

20. Foner, 261–64; George C. Rable, *But There Was No Peace: The Role of Violence in the Politics of Reconstruction* (Athens: University of Georgia Press, 1984), 51–56; Paul Andrew Hutton, *Phil Sheridan and His Army* (Lincoln: University of Nebraska Press, 1985), 22–23.

21. In the case of Louisiana, the government had been created under Lincoln's wartime Reconstruction. Foner, 264; Perman, 209–28; Carole Emberton, *Beyond Redemption: Race, Violence, and the American South after the Civil War* (Chicago: University of Chicago Press, 2013), 50–51; Downs, *After Appomattox*, 149.

22. Foner, 253–61; Downs, *After Appomattox*, 127–28.

office without a two-thirds vote of Congress. The proposed amendment also torpedoed Southern plans to have the United States assume the Confederate debt and pay pensions to Confederate soldiers. Both would now be unconstitutional. At the same time, it ensured the payment of the Union war debt. Stevens guaranteed that ratifying the amendment would be a necessary but not sufficient requirement for the readmission of the Confederate states into the Union. If any state attempted to abridge the suffrage of male voters, except for crimes or participation in the rebellion, then it would lose a proportional amount of its representation in Congress.[23]

The broad principles of the Fourteenth Amendment were clear. The Republicans sought to abrogate judicial interpretations of the Constitution that, in the name of federalism, had limited the extension of a uniform set of rights applicable to all citizens everywhere in the Union. Congress intended the new amendment to extend the guarantees of the Bill of Rights so that they protected citizens against actions by the states as well as by the federal government. The equal protection clause was supposed to ensure that no state discriminated among its own citizens or against the citizens of another state. The amendment would protect both new black citizens and white Unionists in the South. The Republicans desired a national citizenship with uniform rights. Ultimately the amendment was Lincolnian: it sought, as had Lincoln, to make the sentiments of the Declaration of Independence the guiding light of the republic. It enshrined in the Constitution broad principles of equality, the rights of citizens, and principles of natural rights prominent in the Declaration of Independence and in Republican ideals of free labor and contract freedom.[24]

Still, Stevens was disappointed. He thought it patched "up the worst portions of the ancient edifice" rather than freeing all American institutions "from every vestige of human oppression." He regarded the amendment as an imperfect proposition, but he accepted it "because I live among men and not among angels." He believed that events were moving in his direction and more would be possible later. War powers remained

23. Michael Kent Curtis, No State Shall Abridge: The 14th Amendment and the Bill of Rights (Durham, NC: Duke University Press, 1986), 83–91; Perman, 209–28; William E. Nelson, The Fourteenth Amendment: From Political Principle to Judicial Doctrine (Cambridge, MA: Harvard University Press, 1988), 45–46, 57–58; Foner, 253–63.
24. Amy Dru Stanley, From Bondage to Contract: Wage Labor, Marriage, and the Market in the Age of Slave Emancipation (Cambridge: Cambridge University Press, 1998), 55; Pauline Maier, American Scripture: Making the Declaration of Independence (New York: Random House, 1998); Curtis, 70–77, 80–81, 86–89; Nelson, 64–90, 110–11.

in force, Southern delegates had not been seated, and the next Congress might go further.[25]

The Southern violence that helped Republicans sell the Fourteenth Amendment undercut Johnson's attempts to legitimize the new Southern governments and to form a coalition to counter the Radical and moderate Republicans. The National Union Convention that gathered in Philadelphia in mid-August in the wake of the riots represented Johnson's attempt to join Southern conservatives with northern Democrats and conservative Republicans to form the basis for a new political party. But the convention only clarified the disunity among conservatives. There would be no new party, instead just a pledge from those in attendance to offer support for candidates in either party who would support Johnson. Despite the failure of the convention, Johnson decided to stake his political future on the congressional elections of 1866. He would campaign against the Radicals.[26]

At the heart of Johnson's fall campaign was his bitter opposition to the Fourteenth Amendment. He pushed hard to restore power to the South before it could be ratified and take effect. In October the governor of Virginia requested surplus federal arms to equip his reactivated militia composed largely of Confederate veterans. Johnson acquiesced over Grant's objections, further alienating Grant and the army. In order to gain greater control over the army, Johnson schemed to send Grant off as ambassador to Mexico and to remove Secretary of War Stanton from office. Grant, Stanton, and Johnson became afraid to turn their backs on each other. Grant refused to go to Mexico and was far too popular for Johnson simply to dismiss. Stanton mistakenly feared Grant was double-crossing him and would betray him and side with Johnson. Stanton grew increasingly sympathetic to the Radicals and backed the Fourteenth Amendment that Johnson opposed.[27]

II

When whites in 1865 warned the freedpeople that there was a big difference between freedom and independence, they highlighted a fundamental struggle that raged from the first days that the ex-slaves seized their freedom. It was a struggle of small daily battles that can be lost sight of amidst the larger political battles of Reconstruction. The contracts that

25. Downs, *After Appomattox*, 130; Foner, 253–55.
26. Foner, 264–68; Perman, 209–28; Downs, *After Appomattox*, 130–31.
27. Hyman, 93–95; Trefousse, 257; Thomas, 499–507.

the Freedmen's Bureau offered were a step up from slavery, but they were not independence from the dictates of white people, which freedpeople craved. Contracts still consigned black people to gang labor in fields even if, unlike the Black Codes, they seemed to make that labor consensual. The ex-slaves did not get the land they expected at Christmas of 1865 or in 1866, and those who had gained land lost it, but this did not change their determination to avoid the coerced field labor that had defined slavery for most of them.

White Southerners fixated on forcing black people into field labor because the cotton economy seemed to depend on it, but also because they considered such labor suitable to the nature of black people. In the immediate wake of the war, black people starved, sickened, and suffered horrific violence—and tens of thousands died. Southern whites and many Northerners did not consider this primarily a result of Southern persecution or failures of Northern policy. It was a result of the nature of black people, who were not capable of taking care of themselves once free.[28]

The definition of the nature of black people was critical to their treatment and the resources allocated to them; those who claimed to be able to identify the supposedly innate qualities of black people would in large measure get to determine their fate. Southern whites had long considered black people not only theirs to own but also theirs to define. This did not change with emancipation. A Virginian who told a northern reporter, "No nigger, free or slave, in these Southern States, nor in any part of the known world, ever would work or ever will work unless he's made to" voiced the consensus of the South. The white South remained determined to have blacks continue to be dependent on whites, even as they asserted that the end of slavery erased their old paternalist obligations to slaves.[29]

The South regarded the lash—the great symbol of coerced labor—and even more extreme violence as the necessary tools of order and prosperity. Without coercion, there would be only poverty and chaos. Radical Republicans, in turn, seized on the whip as the symbol of continued Southern barbarism and defiance.[30]

---

28. Jim Downs, *Sick from Freedom: African-American Illness and Suffering During the Civil War and Reconstruction* (New York: Oxford University Press, 2012), 6–8, 14–17.

29. Heather Cox Richardson, *The Death of Reconstruction: Race, Labor, and Politics in the Post-Civil War North, 1865–1901* (Cambridge, MA: Harvard University Press, 2001), 11; Leon F. Litwack, *Been in the Storm So Long: The Aftermath of Slavery* (New York: Knopf, dist. Random House, 1979), 363; Laura F. Edwards, *Gendered Strife & Confusion: The Political Culture of Reconstruction* (Urbana: University of Illinois Press, 1997), 33.

30. Emberton, 40–45.

Radical Republicans—black and white—presumed that black men and white men shared a common nature, and that centuries of slavery, the disruption and havoc of a long war, and the misery of hungry, sick, and desperate people would all burn off like a morning fog if black men could be men. Being male was mere biology; being a man meant protecting and supporting a wife, family, and home. A Thomas Nast drawing turned into a lithograph by the print shop of King and Baird in Philadelphia in 1865 captured the iconography of black freedom, black manhood, the home, and the actual desires of freedpeople. Nast contrasted scenes from slavery and freedom that he alternated around the lithograph's borders, but the centerpiece, overlapping with a smaller portrait of Lincoln, was a family at home that was indistinguishable except for the color of its occupants from portrayals of white families. A black father sat surrounded by his wife, children, and mother. He was presumably the same father portrayed as soldier and wage earner on the picture's borders.

The Nast lithograph, seemingly so clichéd and sentimental, actually undercuts a set of easy assumptions about Gilded Age Americans, black and white. To a greater degree than later Americans appreciate, they thought in terms of collectivities rather than individuals. They imagined their society as consisting of families, congregations, the wide

In *Emancipation* Thomas Nast positions the home as the goal and reward of ex-slaves following the Civil War. The drawings on the margins trace the history of black slavery and freedom; the centerpiece is the reward, the black home. Library of Congress, LC-DIG-pga-03898.

array of voluntary organizations who had massed for Lincoln's funeral processions. They gauged the success of an economy, and a life, more by its ability to produce homes than its ability to produce wealth. Americans gendered the home as a female space, but they also defined manhood around a very simple test: the ability to maintain and protect a family home.

The question—contested by Southern whites, freedpeople, and Northern whites alike—was whether a portrayal such as Nast's was a foolish fiction or the emerging reality. Were the freedmen, in fact, men? Freedmen asserted their manhood, but George Fitzhugh, a leading Southern intellectual speaking for the South, denied it. Fitzhugh had been one of the most extreme, effective, and clever defenders of slavery before the war, and he skillfully attacked the freedmen by attacking the Freedmen's Bureau, which he described as a "Negro Nursery." He claimed that the Republicans were acknowledging what the slaveholders had long known: "we told them the darkeys were but grown-up children that needed guardians, like all children." In compelling the freedmen to work and in taking care of their needs, the agents of the bureau had merely replaced the old masters. To be citizens, he argued, the freedmen "must first be made men, and the Bureau is a practical admission and assertion that they are not men."[31]

Fitzhugh's attack played on the fears of both Northerners, who suspected that the freedpeople were naturally dependent, and those of freedpeople, who suspected that the bureau's agents were at the time acting as if they had replaced the old masters in enforcing black dependency. The bureau often did internalize the slurs of white Southerners. Compelling black people to do field labor became a primary task of bureau officials, who worried about black reliance on federal aid. Real emancipation involved a freedom from idleness and vagrancy, which only work could secure.[32]

Dependence was real. The suffering of freedpeople in the wake of the war had made many of them reliant on federal aid, but in this they were no different from white refugees. Still, this was charity, and to many bureau officials a reliance on charity was a form of slavery because it rendered its recipients dependent. Even though in some places, such as Alabama in 1865 and 1866, far more whites drew rations from the bureau than blacks, and even though over the life of the agency roughly a third of

31. Emberton, 65; Downs, *Sick from Freedom*, 72–74, Downs, *Declarations of Dependence*, 1–14.
32. Paul A. Cimbala, *The Freedmen's Bureau: Reconstructing the American South after the Civil War* (Malabar, FL: Krieger, 2005), 40–44, 64; Edwards, 25, 45–54, 66–67.

all rations went to Southern whites, the bureau's agents were fixated on black dependency.[33]

The worst bureau contracts did deny independence and represented an implicit denial of black manhood, but such contracts did even more harm to women, particularly single women with children. One of the agonizing tragedies of slavery was the separation of families through the sale of parents or children; freedom promised to end this, but instead the sundering of mothers and children took new forms. During slavery, masters had welcomed black children in the same way they had welcomed colts and calves, as signs of future wealth. But in the postbellum era, unless they could obtain indentures on them through the Black Codes, employers regarded the children who came with their house servants as nuisances. They either refused to take them in at all or pressured their mothers to send them off to relatives.[34]

Black women, married or unmarried, most acutely recognized that the new order was not a clear choice between independence and dependence. Freedmen asserted their manhood in the same manner as white men: the ownership of their wives and their labor. They challenged the racial order of the South while accepting and reinforcing its gendered power structure. Freedmen had grasped the essence of the marriage contract and pithily restated it. "I consider her my property," said one North Carolina freedman of his wife. And a Tennessee freedman declared of his wife, "I married her to wait on me." The Freedmen's Bureau usually allowed a married freedman to make labor contracts covering his wife and children since married freedwomen could not make contracts. Freedwomen, understandably, often did not see this as freedom. An antislavery feminist, Frances Gage, reported that freedwomen told her, "You give us a nominal freedom, but you leave us under the heel of our husbands."[35]

Black women often got to choose only between competing patriarchs, but in the Reconstruction South acknowledging black male privilege offered them and their children some protection. Black men began to negotiate contracts with plantation owners for a squad or company, usually made up of relatives. Planters had to make concessions that they did not have to make to individuals. The squads might include women, but

33. Downs, *Declarations of Dependence*, 75–100; Cimbala, 42–43; Noralee Frankel, *Freedom's Women: Black Women and Families in Civil War Era Mississippi* (Bloomington: Indiana University Press, 1999), 153–54; Michael W. Fitzgerald, *The Union League Movement in the Deep South: Politics and Agricultural Change During Reconstruction* (Baton Rouge: Louisiana State University Press, 1989), 18–19.

34. Frankel, 153–54; Downs, *Sick from Freedom*, 132.

35. Stanley, 48–50.

married women tried to withdraw from full-time field labor. They sought to devote most of their work to creating their own homes and raising their children. When black women delegated the negotiation of their labor contracts to black men to escape the conditions imposed by white men, they still often recognized the dangers of such dependence.[36]

These negotiations to resist the restoration of forced labor were part of the larger political and social effort of black people to reconstitute in freedom a set of kinship connections, political practices, and voluntary organizations whose roots lay in slave times. Black heads of households sought to command the labor of their wives and children to work on their own crops and maintain their own households. Their resistance to gang labor prevented plantation owners from reassembling their labor forces, but most of the old elite held onto their land. A new system of tenancy and sharecropping emerged. Sharecroppers—who got a quarter to a third of the crop that they produced—and renters, who paid a fixed rent for the land, did the actual farming. Such arrangements represented a compromise between the planters' desire to bind labor to the land and the freedpeople's desire for their own land and autonomy.[37]

Black sharecroppers and tenants shed the old vestiges of slavery, but they did not escape exploitation. Richard Crump, an ex-slave, recounted the experience of many: "We made crops on shares for three years after freedom, and then we commenced to rent. They didn't pay everything they promised. They taken a lot of it away from us. They said figures didn't lie. You know how that was. You dassent [sic] dispute a man's word then." Planters had been labor lords defined by their slave holdings; after the war they had become landlords defined by their land holdings.[38]

Because independence proved elusive, freedpeople did cultivate ties of dependence, although not in the way Fitzhugh had imagined. That

---

36. Julie Saville, *The Work of Reconstruction: From Slave to Wage Laborer in South Carolina, 1860–1870* (Cambridge: Cambridge University Press, 1994), 103–10; Hahn, 66–73, 83; Thavolia Glymph, *Out of the House of Bondage: The Transformation of the Plantation Household* (Cambridge: Cambridge University Press, 2008), 168–71, 179; Susan E. O'Donovan, *Becoming Free in the Cotton South* (Cambridge, MA: Harvard University Press, 2007), 162–207; Edwards, 24–65, 145–83; for a full discussion of black families, sexual relations, and gender relations, see Frankel, 79–118, 146–54.

37. Stanley Engerman, "Slavery and Its Consequences for the South in the Nineteenth Century," in *The Cambridge Economic History of the United States*, ed. Stanley L. Engerman and Robert E. Gallman (Cambridge: Cambridge University Press, 1996), 357. The continuities between black struggles for freedom and autonomy in slave and postslavery times are the theme of Hahn, *Nation Under Our Feet*; Gavin Wright, *Old South, New South: Revolutions in the Southern Economy since the Civil War* (New York: Basic Books, 1986), 84–89, 93–94; Frankel, 64–65, 71–78.

38. Wright, 17–50; Litwack, 448.

the bureau and the army were in retreat in late 1865 and 1866 did not mean they were everywhere without power to which freedpeople could appeal for physical protection and for enforcement of contracts and tenancy agreements. The result was a relationship of dependence at odds with ideals of free labor, manhood, and independence, but very much of a kind with the patronage that defined so much of the era. In action bureau agents often functioned like other Gilded Age politicians. They aided those who could make compelling appeals or could claim obligations.[39]

It is hard to think of sharecropping and tenancy as a triumph, but in the first years of Reconstruction, as planters first refused to acknowledge the end of slavery and then resorted to violence to coerce freedpeople back into gang labor, they were victories of a sort. These were not the black homes Nast imagined; instead they were part of a more complicated reality in which black families were poised between independence and dependence both on landlords they feared and resented and on federal authorities whose assistance they needed. Freedpeople and white Southerners recognized that this world of tangled and desperate struggles allowed no easy division to be made between dependence and independence. These were distinctions not readily apparent in the tumult of Southern life.

What was developing in the South was a coercive labor system, which although not slavery, was not free labor either. It depended on extralegal violence, coercive laws, burdensome debt relations, and the use of convict labor to limit alternatives. The South was demonstrating that there were routes to capitalist development—both agricultural and industrial—that did not rely on free labor. The beneficiaries of this system—both those denounced as Bourbons and those praised as harbingers of a New South—were not opposed to economic progress. They embraced it; they just realized that they could achieve it without free labor.

III

As the presence of federal troops dwindled in late 1865 and early 1866, the battle between Congress and the president over the next form Reconstruction would take paralleled simultaneous political conflicts within the South. There political organization and organization for self-defense merged. The two were always connected.

39. Downs, *Declarations of Dependence*, 2–13, 76–77, 85–86.

The congressional campaign of 1866 featured a Unionist president who headed a Republican administration campaigning against the majority of the Republican Party. To defeat the Radicals and ensure the rejection of the Fourteenth Amendment, Johnson made a "swing around the circle," traveling from the East through the Midwest. He ended up delighting his enemies and appalling many of his supporters. With each stop, the crowds became more hostile, and Johnson grew angrier. He argued with hecklers, compared himself to the crucified Christ, and found himself abused in the press. To buttress his appeal, he brought along Grant, but this only led to his own speeches being drowned out by calls for the general. To Union veterans like Hamlin Garland's father, "Grant, Lincoln, Sherman, and Sheridan were among the noblest men of the world, and he [Dick Garland] would not tolerate any criticism of them." Grant's presence only made Johnson seem a smaller man.[40]

In the 1860s there was no single election day, and by September when the Republicans carried Maine, the signs of a sweeping Republican victory were apparent. The Republicans carried the country north of the Mason Dixon line, increasing both their majority in Congress and the number of Radicals in their ranks. They rightly considered themselves "masters of the situation." If they stuck together, they could override the president on any legislation that he vetoed.[41]

The election of 1866 dashed the hopes of ex-Confederates for easy readmission and also for the rise of a new conservative party, while it raised the hopes of Southern Unionists and freedmen for new state governments under their control. Congress had already turned Washington, D.C., and the territories into laboratories for their policies and had pushed for political equality. Congress had enfranchised blacks in D.C. and made universal manhood suffrage a condition for the organization of new Western territories. The Republicans required Southern ratification of the Fourteenth Amendment if Confederate states were to be considered for readmission to the Union. Only Tennessee accepted these terms and reentered the Union in 1866. In the remaining ten states of the Confederacy a grand total of thirty-three legislators—or about three per state—voted in favor of the amendment. Southern conservatives, for lack of alternatives, embraced "masterly inactivity." They refused all compromise and waited for the Republicans to collapse. Congressional Democrats from the North sought to expedite that collapse by exacerbating

40. Trefousse, 264–65; Downs, 164–66; Hamlin Garland, *A Son of the Middle Border* (New York: Grosset & Dunlap, 1928), 8.
41. Trefousse, 267, 271; Foner, 265–72; Perman, 248–49.

Republican divisions. They sometimes sided with the Radicals to pass measures that they thought would prove disastrous and hasten the end of Republican rule.[42]

The Republicans of the new Fortieth Congress responded by retreating to their caucus to work out their divisions before a bill came to the floor. When they succeeded, their two-thirds majority allowed them to reduce the president of the United States to little more than a legislative nuisance. But governing involved more than legislating. Johnson still retained his power as commander-in-chief, and the army was critical to the plans Congress contemplated for reconstructing the South. Johnson also had power over the Freedmen's Bureau, a department he loathed, which was housed in the War Department. Bitter and angry, Johnson moved increasingly closer to the old Southern leadership that he had spent his career opposing. He continued to replace Freedmen's Bureau officials who had Radical sympathies with conservative Southerners.[43]

To deal with the South, the Republicans in February passed the Reconstruction Act of 1867. Along with the supplementary acts that followed, it became the centerpiece of what was variously called Congressional, Radical, or Military Reconstruction. Like so much of the legislation of the period, it was poorly written and unwieldy but also powerful and consequential. It divided the Confederate South, except Tennessee, into five military districts. The army was to protect freedpeople and Unionists from attacks on their lives and property and to supervise the calling of the state constitutional conventions. Congress required that blacks be able to vote for the delegates to the new constitutional conventions, while the Reconstruction Act denied the right to vote to those who had lost the right to hold office because of rebellion against the United States. Southern Unionists in particular insisted on these provisions to ensure the end of rebel rule. In terms of republican theory, however, they created an uncomfortable exception to the principle of government resting on the consent of the governed. The governments formed under the new constitutions could ratify the Fourteenth Amendment and apply to reenter the Union. Until these new governments were formed, the state governments created under Presidential Reconstruction remained in place, although the military could remove officials for violation of the Reconstruction Act.[44]

42. Foner, 271–72; Trefousse, 264–65; Perman, 229–65; Masur, 272–76.
43. Benedict, 26; McFeely, 291–302; Downs, 146–55; Foner, 271–76.
44. Foner, 276–77; Perman, 269–72.

In some ways, the original Reconstruction Act was the high-water mark of Republican Radicalism and demonstrated the limits of power based on legislation alone. At least on paper, Congress had dramatically enlarged federal power and black rights. In December 1866 only about 0.5 percent of black adult males could vote. In December 1867 the figure rose to 80.5 percent, with the entire increase coming in the old Confederacy. This was sufficient for a group of Republicans, some of them Radicals, who were willing to move toward peace and the readmission of the Confederate states. The fate of Reconstruction in the still-defiant South would turn on access to the ballot and the strength of the new governments that voters would create. Other Radicals, however, led by Sumner and Stevens, did not believe the vote would be sufficient. They worked to maintain war powers, believing only force could protect black voters and civil rights, and they continued to push for confiscation and redistribution as well as integrated school systems. These bills failed. So, too, did their attempt to block an Occupation Bill that set the terms of peace. Peace Republicans set the terms: the Confederate states would have to pass new constitutions with biracial suffrage. There was a caveat. Until they did, war powers remained in force, and Congress had largely, but not completely, wrested control of those powers from the president.[45]

Freedmen began to organize politically well before the Reconstruction Act guaranteed they could vote for delegates to the new constitutional conventions. They had no real alternative to the Republicans. As Douglass put it, "The Republican Party is the ship and all else is the sea." The Union League or Loyal League brought the freedmen on board. In Philadelphia, New York, and Boston Union Leagues were patriotic and patrician men's clubs, but in the South they became secret political clubs affiliated with the Republican Party. In upland Alabama and North Carolina some black men actively participated in Union Leagues organized by white men. But in many of these cases, white acknowledgment of black rights was contingent and partial. White Unionists needed allies against ex-Confederates, but they did not see blacks as their political equals and were not committed to black rights beyond the present emergency. In most of the South, therefore, blacks organized independent Union Leagues.[46]

45. Richardson, 41–52; Foner, 275–80, 307–9; Valelly, 3; Downs, *After Appomattox*, 162–65, 168–74, 178.
46. Downs, *After Appomattox*, 193, 195; Trefousse, 264–65; Hahn, 177–89; Michael Kazin, *American Dreamers: How the Left Changed a Nation* (New York: Knopf, 2011), 66; Fitzgerald, 22–23, 10–16, 47–53.

Black people were new citizens, but they were also longtime Americans with typical American habits. Before the Civil War free blacks had begun to organize into voluntary societies, which ranged from churches to fraternal organizations with the usual accouterments of secret signs and rituals. The enthusiasm of antebellum Northern blacks for fraternal organizations had alarmed Douglass, who had denounced them as distractions from the fight against slavery. After the war, however, voluntary associations provided a foundation for political organization. A parade of freedpeople in Mobile on July 4, 1865, featured not only two regiments of black troops, but the Mechanics and Draymen's Association, the Steamboatmen's Association, the firemen's Association, the Benevolent Society, the Daughters of Zion, the Sons of Zion, the Missionary Society, the Young Men's Association, and more.[47]

Fertilized by the Reconstruction Act of 1867, the league grew at different rates in different places. The ability of freedmen to organize often depended on the ability and willingness of northern military officers and agents of the Freedmen's Bureau to aid and protect them. In Alabama, where the Union Republican Congressional Executive Committee, the Freedmen's Bureau, the African Methodist Episcopal (AME) Church, and the occupying army nurtured it, the league blossomed. In neighboring Mississippi, where protection was often lacking, the league withered. Since as the number of soldiers fell army protection was most dependable in cities and towns, league chapters often first took root there and spread into the countryside.[48]

How the Union Leagues operated in different areas of the South depended on demography. In 1870 in South Carolina, Mississippi, and Louisiana black people formed a majority of the population, and in Virginia, Georgia, Florida, and Alabama they formed a large minority ranging from 42 percent in Virginia to 49 percent in Florida. But in all of these states overwhelmingly black counties existed alongside counties with very few black people. The black belt counties of Alabama and Mississippi were originally named for their soil, formed in the shallows of an ancient sea, not their people, but cotton and slavery had concentrated black people there. In areas where blacks formed fewer than 20 percent of the population, Union Leagues were not a threat to white dominance of local politics. Where the population was overwhelmingly

47. Litwack, 465–68, 471; Fitzgerald, 31–33; Hahn, 232–33; Valelly, 36–37; Stephen Kantrowitz, "'Intended for the Better Government of Man': The Political History of African American Freemasonry in the Era of Emancipation," *Journal of American History* 96, no. 4 (2010): 1001.
48. Hahn, 177–89; Fitzgerald, 22–23, 110–16, 147–53; Downs, *After Appomattox*, 193, 195.

black, there was initially little whites could do but complain. But where blacks numbered from one-third to two-thirds of the total population, whites were openly antagonistic, and the Union League was often forced to operate in secret.[49]

Despite white alarm at the growth of the Union Leagues and the resistance of black workers to gang labor, it seemed for a moment in the spring and summer of 1867 that Southern conservatives had learned from the Civil War and would pull back from the violence washing over the South. Men who had rushed into a disastrous conflict now paused on the brink of a second struggle. Some of them urged that the South accept defeat and collaborate with moderate Republicans in seeking an accommodation. The alternatives, they thought, would be far worse. Accommodationists feared that resistance would make Reconstruction so protracted that the cost to whites would exceed the benefits of any eventual success. No matter whether moderates like former governor Joseph E. Brown of Georgia considered policy, expediency, or self-interest, they all counseled accommodation. Wealthy Southerners still feared Radical plans for confiscation of property would be resurrected unless the South cooperated.[50]

The accommodationists, however, had illusions of their own. Convinced of black dependency, they believed that Southern whites knew the ex-slaves, had cared for them, and would look out for them, while Northerners would merely exploit them. But the masters found that their own houses and fields swarmed with Republicans unimpressed with their paternalism. As the Mississippi planter, former Whig, and future moderate Republican governor James Lusk Alcorn observed, "All which our people claim for the influence of the 'old master' on the freedmen is neither more or less than nonsense." With blacks resistant to the appeals of their former masters and most white Southerners dubious about any compromise with Republicans, the movement for accommodation proved stillborn.[51]

The political lines in the South hardened. The freedmen, except for those who depended on white patronage or were coerced by whites, were Republicans. The majority of Southern whites were Democrats, but a substantial number of whites in the South attached themselves to the Republican Party. They were willing, at least initially, to defend black

49. Foner, 283–85; Hahn, 180–88.
50. Mark Wahlgren Summers, *The Ordeal of the Reunion* (Chapel Hill: University of North Carolina Press, 2014), 118; Perman, 272–74, 282–84.
51. Perman, 272–74, 282–303; Hahn, 163–64, 198–200, 204; Foner, 291–94.

suffrage, and in alliance with blacks they gave the Republicans a majority of eligible voters in most Southern states, but it was a tenuous and fragile alliance.[52]

There were two major groups of white Republicans in the South. The first were the so-called scalawags. Most had opposed secession, even if they later fought for the Confederacy. Others had remained Unionists during the Civil War. They had been thickest in the hill and mountain counties of the Appalachians, particularly in Alabama, Tennessee, and West Virginia, which had seceded from Virginia and become a new state. The Alabama hill country, like the border states, had seen a civil war within the Civil War as Unionists and Confederates fought and killed one other. A mutual campaign of murder and terror had continued during Presidential Reconstruction. This bitter legacy had led many Alabama Unionists to make common cause with freedmen. The Alabama Grand Council of the Union League argued that "in the nature of things the black man is your friend.... Shall we have him for our ally, or the rebel for our master?" Like the freedmen, they sought a political life denied them before the war.[53]

The second group of whites who welcomed the black vote was the carpetbaggers (a term that seems not to have gained currency until 1868): Northerners who had moved to the South either as soldiers or seekers of opportunity in the wake of the war. Mostly male, young, and ambitious, carpetbaggers identified their own future with a progressive Republican South. To them, progress meant "free institutions, free schools, and the system of free labor." The search for opportunity led them into politics. They saw their politics as benefiting the freedmen and the freedmen's votes as benefiting them.[54]

Freedmen, scalawags, and carpetbaggers depended on each other. "We must keep together, scalawags, carpetbaggers and niggers," a white Republican in North Carolina said, but the very need to say it meant that the task was challenging. These Southern Republicans had fundamental interests in common, particularly their fear of the old Southern elite, but they did not have all concerns in common.[55]

52. Kazin, 66; Downs, *Declarations of Dependence*, 91; Foner, 283–85; Perman, 269–72.
53. Hahn, 198–200, 204, 208–9; Fitzgerald, 1–28, 42–43; Foner, 298–303; Kantrowitz, 1001; Summers, 286–303.
54. Thomas C. Holt, *Black over White: Negro Political Leadership in South Carolina During Reconstruction* (Urbana: University of Illinois Press, 1977), 3–4, 131, 153; Foner, 295–97, 302, 317–33; Hahn, 205–15.
55. Hahn, 208–9, 251–53; Foner, 348.

Most critically, their economic interests differed considerably. The scalawags wanted debt relief and low taxes. The usual form of debt relief—homestead protection and stay laws—prevented the seizure of land by creditors or tax collectors for debts incurred before 1865. Debt relief, however, would also aid the scalawags' enemies, the rich and heavily indebted planters, while hurting the black rural poor. With the defeat of redistribution, freedmen regarded tax sales and forced sales to pay debts as bringing cheap land onto the market and providing one of the few ways that they could obtain farms. Those black people who had gained freedom before the war, however, often had both some property and white patrons. They did not necessarily share the freedpeople's desire to redistribute the property of their patrons.[56]

Carpetbaggers and scalawags also often opposed each other. Carpetbaggers objected to debt relief because they feared that it would scare off the capital on which development depended. They also wanted state subsidies for infrastructure, particularly railroads. Scalawags, in turn, were skeptical of plans for railroad subsidies because they would raise taxes.[57]

The spread of the Union League provided a first step in a larger Republican effort to control the state constitutional conventions mandated by the Reconstruction Act. Registration of new voters involved political education, and political education produced not just black voters, but black registrars and eventually black delegates. A new political class was emerging. A wealthy Alabamian punned, "The political horizon is darkening."[58]

The state constitutional conventions followed one after another in a narrow period between Alabama's, which met on November 5, 1867, and Florida's convention on January 20, 1868. Only Texas, whose convention did not meet until June 1, 1868, and which did not produce a constitution until the following February, fell outside this window. A second election followed in each state to ratify the constitutions and select officials in the new governments.[59]

56. Holt, 58–61, 69, 128–31; Richardson, 53–57; Summers, 131–32; Michael Perman, *The Road to Redemption: Southern Politics, 1869–1879* (Chapel Hill: University of North Carolina Press, 1984), 31–32.
57. Holt, 3–4, 131, 153; Summers, 126, 131–32; Foner, 295–97, 302, 317–33.
58. Hahn, 191–98, quote, 198.
59. Ibid., 202–15; Peter Kolchin, *First Freedom: The Responses of Alabama's Blacks to Emancipation and Reconstruction* (Westport, CT: Greenwood Press, 1972), 163; Martin E. Mantell, *Johnson, Grant, and the Politics of Reconstruction* (New York: Columbia University Press, 1973), 72–73; "Constitutional Convention of 1869," in

The conventions reflected Republican divisions. The largely white areas of the South elected Southern white men—the scalawags. More heavily black areas elected carpetbaggers and black representatives. The black representatives from urban areas tended to be men freed before the war, many of them of mixed race. In every state but South Carolina, Louisiana, and Florida, white delegates outnumbered black delegates, often heavily. In most states, white Southern Unionists dominated the delegations. Carpetbaggers formed about one-sixth of the total number of delegates.[60]

For all their divisions, scalawags, carpetbaggers, and freedmen usually held to core democratic principles. They mandated universal manhood suffrage, making exceptions only in the case of traitors by denying the vote to leading Confederates. "Manhood and not property or color," as one Virginia delegate put it, was to be the basis of suffrage. The conventions abolished property qualifications and reduced residency qualifications. Principles were clear, but practices tended to be more ambiguous. In Florida and Georgia moderate Republicans, not Radicals, controlled the conventions and passed rules that would confine and limit the influence of black voters. Overall, the constitutions were surprisingly conservative documents.[61]

The Republican Party had achieved quick and remarkable success in 1867. It had swept the South and written the new constitutions. But the most astute Republicans recognized that this was but the beginning of the struggle. As Governor William Brownlow of Tennessee observed, "Never was such a conflict witnessed as we are to have."[62]

The signs of the coming struggle were already apparent. Southern conservatives had never had any real chance to dominate the conventions. Their boycotts of the elections that selected delegates made little difference, but in some states they did have a real chance to reject the new constitutions. Congress had so sloppily drafted the Reconstruction Acts that they required a majority of registered voters, not just a majority of those who actually voted, to approve the constitutions. Abstaining was thus as good as voting no, and suppressing the vote by intimidating black voters promised to pay real dividends. Since the existing governments established during Presidential Reconstruction were to remain in power

---

A *Handbook of Texas Online* (Austin: Texas State Historical Association). https://tshaonline.org/handbook/online/articles/mhco6.

60. Foner, 316–30; Summers, 130–33; Holt, 37–38, 43.
61. Hahn, 212–15; Saville, 156–57; Summers, 133; Foner, 327–33.
62. Foner, 307.

until there was a new constitution, rejecting the constitutions would preserve the status quo with Democrats in control. Even with continuing military occupation, conservatives thought this preferable to being ruled by Republicans.[63]

The call of Southern conservatives for principled and practical resistance to the new constitutions became inseparable from calls for white solidarity. Calls for white solidarity, in turn, quickly shaded into intimidation of blacks. And when economic intimidation by white employers proved insufficient, they turned to terror.

Many organizations arose to terrorize the South, but the Ku Klux Klan became the most notorious. Founded in Tennessee in 1866, the Klan emerged as the armed wing of the Democratic Party. It struck hard in Alabama and harder still in Mississippi. Klan night riding arose easily out of the antebellum slave patrols. Recruits were easy to find in a countryside full of bitter ex-soldiers inured to violence and unreconciled to defeat, but the Klan seems to have recruited largely from the sons of well-to-do slaveholding families who had lost wealth and standing following the war.[64]

Terror quickly jumped from white attempts to suppress black economic independence to efforts to thwart black suffrage and destroy the Union Leagues. White terrorists assassinated Republican leaders in broad daylight. During October 1866 estimates put the number of black people murdered in Caddo Parish, Louisiana, at forty-two. In Bossier Parish a Negro hunt resulted in the murder of at least 162 freedpeople. Ironically, the success of freedpeople in escaping gang labor made them more vulnerable to the Klan. Scattered tenants and sharecroppers were easier targets than families gathered in what had been old slave quarters. In Mississippi intimidation and terror succeeded in defeating the constitution. In Alabama terror was but an element in a more complicated mix that derailed the constitution.[65]

Terror created a political dilemma for the Republicans. Violence often accompanied American elections. Private militia companies paraded to the polls and partisans brawled. Parties hired thugs to intimidate

63. Foner, 332–33; Holt, 3–4, 35, 73; Perman, *Reunion without Compromise*, 304–12, 328–36.
64. Summers, 147–50; Perman, *Reunion without Compromise*, 340; Michael W. Fitzgerald, "Ex-Slaveholders and the Ku Klux Klan: Exploring the Motivations of Terrorist Violence," in Bruce E. Baker, Brian Kelly, and Eric Foner, eds., *New Perspectives on the History of the South: After Slavery: Race, Labor, and Citizenship in the Reconstruction South* (University Press of Florida, 2013), 143–156; Foner, 329–33; Fitzgerald, *Union League Movement*, 55, 56.
65. Foner, 425–26; Fitzgerald, *Union League Movement*, 55, 56; Summers, 147–50; Perman, *Reunion without Compromise*, 340.

the opposition. But until Reconstruction, violence did not lead to soldiers intervening in elections. Americans elected men with military reputations to office, but the army itself was supposed to remain outside of politics. Terror in the South made the army critical to politics. In the absence of effective state militias, only the army could protect voters and candidates.[66]

Mississippi, Alabama, Texas, and also Virginia failed to reenter the Union in time for the 1868 elections. In the remaining Southern states the Republicans won electoral victories, but these did not always yield the results Radicals and freedmen expected. In Georgia, with the cooperation of Republican moderates, Democrats expelled all the black members from the legislature. They argued, accurately enough, that the law guaranteed blacks the right to vote, but it did not guarantee them the right to hold office.[67]

IV

Johnson's struggle against the Radicals precipitated serious Republican attempts to remove the president from office. The drive for impeachment sprang from Johnson's contest with Edwin Stanton, but it was hard to separate the accusations against Johnson, which were important, from the larger political context. Impeaching Johnson would install a new president and would influence the upcoming 1868 election. Because the country lacked a vice president following the assassination of Lincoln, the 1792 law governing presidential succession would make Sen. Benjamin Wade, as president pro tempore of the U.S. Senate, president of the United States if Johnson were impeached and convicted. Wade was a Radical and already a candidate for the Republican nomination for president. William Dean Howells, who had briefly read law in Wade's Ohio law office, thought him a man not only of "great native power, but of wider cultivation" than most recognized. He had made his reputation by standing up "against the fierce proslavery leaders in Congress with an intrepidity even with their own." Making enemies did not scare him. Many moderates, who hated Wade, feared Johnson's impeachment would give Wade both the presidency and the Republican nomination in 1868. Chief Justice Salmon Chase, who would

66. Thomas, 531; Emberton, 136–62; Downs, *After Appomattox*, 118; Fitzgerald, 51–57, 79–90.
67. Foner, 453–54.

preside over the trial in the Senate, was also from Ohio, and he too wanted to be president. He, too, hated Wade. Wade, for his part, rightly saw Grant as his rival for the Republican nomination, and knew that unless something dramatic happened—such as Johnson's removal from office and Wade's ascension to the presidency—Grant was almost certainly going to be the nominee. Virtually every major politician involved in the trial thus had issues other than Andrew Johnson's innocence or guilt on his mind.[68]

When Congress reconvened after Johnson's interim removal of Stanton, it refused to approve the secretary's dismissal. In January 1868 Stanton reclaimed his office, and when Grant supported him, Johnson felt betrayed. With both Stanton and Grant potential rivals in the presidential election that coming fall, his political future and his desire to end Reconstruction in the South seemed to depend on removing Stanton.[69]

Stanton had originally intended to resign his office once Congress vindicated and reinstated him, but the Republicans urged him to stay. Without military protection, Reconstruction would fail, and Stanton was critical in blocking Johnson's subversion of the Reconstruction Act. Radicals promised to breathe life into the impeachment proceedings should Johnson take any further action against the secretary of war.[70]

Johnson, nonetheless, once more dismissed Stanton and appointed Gen. Lorenzo Thomas—old, garrulous, and ineffectual—as interim secretary of war. When Johnson sent Thomas to inform Stanton of his dismissal, Stanton refused to yield the office. Instead, he went to court. The next Saturday morning Thomas, hung over and hungry, was arrested for violating the Tenure of Office Act, which Republicans had passed to prevent the removal of officials appointed with the Senate's consent until the Senate had approved their successor. Undeterred, Thomas made bail and returned to Stanton's office on Monday. Stanton put his arm around Thomas's shoulder, tousled his hair, and sent for a bottle. They had a few amiable drinks. "The next time you have me arrested, please do not do it before I get something to eat," Thomas told Stanton. He left again. Congress was not so amiable. News of Thomas's appointment created an uproar, and on a snowy February 4, 1868, the House, voting along party lines, impeached Johnson for violating the Tenure of Office Act.[71]

68. Hans L. Trefousse, *Impeachment of a President: Andrew Johnson, the Blacks, and Reconstruction* (New York: Fordham University Press, 1999), 156–57; Foner, 333–36; Summers, 136–40; for Howells on Wade, William Dean Howells, *Years of My Youth, and Three Essays* (Bloomington: Indiana University Press, 1975), 93–94.
69. William S. McFeely, *Grant: A Biography* (New York: Norton, 1981), 262–71.
70. Thomas, 583–91.
71. Ibid., 583–91; Foner, 333–34; William Marvel, *Lincoln's Autocrat: The Life of Edwin Stanton* (Cambridge, MA: Harvard University Press, 2015); 439–41.

Much was at stake: the fate of four million freedpeople, the question of who would govern the South, and the constitutional relationship between the branches of government. What should have been high political drama began as comic opera.

Stanton barricaded himself in his office. His furious wife, tiring of the turmoil, urged him to resign and refused to send him the linens and food he requested. He put the building under heavy guard. His partisans saw him as heroic, but his enemies, and some of his friends, regarded him as ridiculous. William Tecumseh Sherman joked that he had less protection when traveling through Indian country than Stanton had in the heavily garrisoned War Department. Others laughed at the guards, telling Stanton no one would dare steal the building now.[72]

Impeachment went forward because Republican moderates were convinced that a defiant Johnson was illegally subverting the will of Congress and attempting to block the Reconstruction of the South. Southern Unionists, whose political, and sometimes actual, lives rested on the outcome, hated Johnson. Republican anger and frustration initially overcame Republican differences.[73]

Johnson, as usual, counted on popular support and was, as usual, deluded; his lawyers, most of whom were Republicans and all of whom were very good political tacticians, counted on time and delay. The longer the process took, the more emotions faded, as divisions reemerged and festered. Political rivalries could then shape the outcome. Even when they had passed the Tenure of Office Act, some senators had doubted whether it applied to Stanton since Lincoln had appointed him. While few saw Johnson as anything but impolitic and racist, these were not grounds for removal.[74]

Johnson's lawyers got Johnson to do what he should have done long before: shut his mouth. They banned interviews, speeches, and told him not to testify. As the trial stretched into May, the defense became more confident. Johnson opened behind-the-scenes negotiations with some Republican moderates.[75]

The Senate eventually acquitted Johnson, falling one vote short of the two-thirds needed to convict. Seven Republicans voted for acquittal. They did not put principle over politics; nor did they suffer political martyrdom as a consequence. Most remained prominent Republican politicians.

72. Thomas, 581–94; Trefousse, *Impeachment of a President*, 133–36.
73. Trefousse, *Impeachment of a President*, 131–45.
74. Annette Gordon-Reed, *Andrew Johnson* (New York: Times Books/Henry Holt, 2011), 135–38.
75. Trefousse, *Impeachment of a President*, 146–64; Foner, 335–37; Trefousse, *Andrew Johnson: A Biography*, 317–19.

Andrew Johnson rewarded the most celebrated of them, Edmund Ross of Kansas, with presidential patronage within weeks. Thaddeus Stevens deplored the outcome, but the "Old Commoner" was so sick that his black servants had to carry him around the Capitol.[76]

With Johnson acquitted, the Republican convention nominated Ulysses Grant for president, while the Republicans in Congress moved to buttress their position in the next election by readmitting those Southern states with approved and ratified constitutions. Since ratification of the Fourteenth Amendment was a condition of readmission, that amendment had won the approval of enough states in early July 1868 to become part of the Constitution. But because the Radicals still did not trust the South, Congress drafted the Fifteenth Amendment, which would prohibit states from ever restricting suffrage on the grounds of "race, color or previous condition of servitude." Ratifying it would become a requirement for readmission for those Southern states still under military rule.[77]

With the exception of California, every free state had ratified it. Californians, citing the state's diversity as a danger, objected to any movement beyond white male suffrage. Future Democratic senator John S. Hager described a California population that included "not only…the negro, but the Digger Indian, the Kanaka, the New Zealander, the Lascar, and the Chinese." Ratification did not end the struggle over the amendment and its meaning. Its final version emerged through important compromises, and its text underwent a descent from clarity to ambiguity in order to secure passage. Its ultimate language seems designed to mask disagreements about particulars while preserving agreement on general principles.[78]

In the long run, the critical ambiguity of the amendment was its distinction between citizens and "persons." The framers of the amendment may have meant only to protect the rights of aliens, who were persons but not citizens. This they succeeded in doing, creating a set of constitutional rights for immigrants into the United States even when they were not citizens. But the courts also eventually expanded the definition of person by defining corporations as persons. What this meant and how much of the amendment's guarantee of equal protection under the law

76. Trefousse, *Impeachment of a President*, 165–79; *Andrew Johnson*, 323–27.

77. Foner, 338.

78. Downs, *After Appomattox*, 127–30, 202–3; Joshua Paddison, *American Heathens: Religion, Race, and Reconstruction in California* (Berkeley: published for the Huntington-USC Institute on California and the West by University of California Press; 2012), 11, 17–18; Foner, 253–55.

rights of due process was owed corporations has evolved, and been disputed, ever since.[79]

Impeachment had failed to remove Johnson, but the amendment he so hated had become law. Impeachment had proved in a different way to become a defining political moment. Of the principals, only Grant would emerge more powerful than before. Thaddeus Stevens died in August 1868. His funeral drew crowds second only to Lincoln's. Following his wishes, he was buried in an integrated cemetery in Pennsylvania. Grant refused to choose Wade as his vice president, and Wade lost his bid for reelection to the Senate in 1868. Grant largely ignored Stanton for months, but then nominated him to fill a vacancy on the Supreme Court. Before the Senate could confirm him, the ravages of Stanton's asthma killed him on Christmas Eve 1869. Chase, who had moved from Radicalism into the Democratic Party in a vain quest for the presidency, did not get the nomination. He died in 1873. Andrew Johnson's political career was over. By his death in 1875 his ironic achievement was secure. He had weakened the Southern Unionists from whom he had sprung and strengthened their conservative ex-Confederate enemies.[80]

After twenty-one ballots, the Democrats in 1868 nominated the wartime governor of New York, Horatio Seymour. They were pushed by New York bankers and financiers frightened that the Democrats would nominate George Pendleton of Ohio. Pendleton was a soft-money man who wished to keep greenbacks in circulation. A return to the gold standard was coming to be a defining issue, splitting both parties along regional lines. Midwestern Democrats distrusted Seymour and his hard-money stance. Their party's choice for vice president was worse. Francis Blair, Jr., came from a corrupt and reactionary Missouri political dynasty tied to Andrew Johnson. Blair shared with Johnson a pathological fear of racial mixing that he thought would produce a "mongrel nation, a nation of bastards." He mistook the opinions of the Blair family for the opinions of the nation and made the Republicans, whom Democrats had been denouncing as revolutionary, seem the party of moderation and stability. Grant ran on the slogan, "Let us have peace," while Blair promised to use the army to restore "white people" to power in the South and disperse the new governments controlled by "a semi-barbarous race of blacks" whose goal was to "subject the white women to their unbridled lust." Even Democrats

79. Curtis, 78–80, 117–32; Stanley, 57–58; William J. Novak, *The People's Welfare: Law and Regulation in Nineteenth-Century America* (Chapel Hill: University of North Carolina Press, 1996), 9; Nelson, 49–59, 110–11, 116–17; Ruth Bloch and Naomi R. Lamoreaux, "Corporations and the Fourteenth Amendment," working paper, in possession of author.

80. Trefousse, *Impeachment of a President*, 180–90; Thomas, 627–39; Foner, 344.

denounced his "stupid and indefensible" actions. The Republicans declared that Seymour "was opposed to the late war, and Blair was in favor of the next one."[81]

The campaigns to defeat Radical constitutions in the Deep South proved a dress rehearsal for the 1868 election. The Fourteenth Amendment disenfranchised only the Southern elite who had violated oaths of office. Many of the new Southern constitutions granted suffrage to all eligible ex-Confederates. Georgia, North Carolina, and Florida had no clauses disenfranchising ex-Confederates in their constitutions, and Louisiana had only a nominal one. The vast majority of ex-Confederates could vote. Democratic victories seemed likely if the Democrats could suppress the black vote. White employers redeployed their economic arsenal. The secret ballot was decades away, and employers threatened to dismiss workers who voted Republican. They seized the crops of tenants who attended league rallies. Merchants denied credit to freedmen who voted Republican. To coercion they added terror.[82]

The election of 1868 in the South was one of the most violent in American history. When white terrorists expanded their attacks from recalcitrant black laborers to black voters, the increase in black self-defense organizations spawned rumors among whites of black aggression. Many white Southerners justified their own violence as preemptive and defensive.[83]

How this reign of terror developed is apparent in the journals of an extraordinary Southern woman, Ella Gertrude Clanton Thomas. Ella Thomas was from Georgia, and she had been an antebellum Southern belle: rich, beautiful, and well educated. She was so used to depending on the labor of black women that she recalled she had wiped dishes dry only twice in her life before the end of the Civil War. She was thirty-four years old in 1868. Although her husband had bought a substitute to serve in the Confederate Army, he became one of those angry, and often increasingly pathetic, Southern men, who never could cope with the changes and economic losses of the war. Bitter, depressed, and a hypochondriac, he was also incompetent. A business failure in 1868 accelerated his downward slide. His wife was made of sterner stuff. Although embarrassed by financial failures, she accepted emancipation and the outcome of the war. "It is humiliating," she wrote, "very indeed to be a conquered people,

81. Summers, 142–44; Nicolas Barreyre, "Les échelles de la monnaie: Souveraineté monétaire et spatialisation de la politique américaine après la guerre de sécession," *Annales, Sciences Sociales* 69, no. 2 (2014): 454–55; Isenberg, 182; Foner, 338–41.
82. Perman, *The Road to Redemption*, 7–15; for Alabama, Kolchin, 174–75; Foner, 342–43; Fitzgerald, 209–10; Mantell, 132–34.
83. Saville, 222–31; Foner, 337–45; O'Donovan, 342–43; Rable, 68–70; Emberton, 155.

but the sky is so bright, the air so pure, the aspect of nature so lovely that I can but be encouraged and hope for something which will benefit us." Slavery had caused the war, and slavery was wrong. Like the more famous Southern diarist Mary Chesnut, she understood much that escaped her husband.[84]

In the days preceding the election of 1868, rumors spread among the whites around Augusta that armed blacks were coming to burn them out. Such rumors were common across the South. Talk of this and the election dominated Ella's conversations, and she conversed with both whites and blacks. Ella Thomas and the black women who worked as her servants had no official place in politics, but they were immersed in politics. That the freedpeople were overwhelmingly Republican was clear to her. Her young servant Ned told her that "uncle Mac said if he had a son who was willing to be a Democrat he would cut his throat." The freedmen knew the whites were afraid of them; they were equally afraid of white violence. They planned to march to the polls as a company to protect themselves.[85]

In Thomas's diary these days unfolded like scenes in a melodrama, with the action confined to the kitchen, the parlor, and the crawl space beneath the house. In one scene, her husband burst in, his coat covered in cobwebs, and sent Ned off so he wouldn't be overheard. He had been under the house, crawling about trying to hear their black servants' conversations. Alarmed and confused himself, he alarmed and confused the servants by telling them that "they" were coming to burn the house down that night. Ella Thomas didn't eavesdrop on servants. She walked into the kitchen and talked with them. She told them the white people did not want trouble, but would fight. Patsey, one of her servants, replied that she would stand with her husband, Bob, a Radical. Black women like Patsey became domestic enforcers for the Republicans across the South. They steeled men, shaming those who caved to white pressure and abandoning husbands and lovers who voted Democratic. Ella Thomas secretly admired this. She told her black employees that she was glad they were free.

84. Martha Hodes, *Mourning Lincoln* (New Haven, CT: Yale University Press, 2015), 166; *The Secret Eye: The Journal of Ella Gertrude Clanton Thomas, 1848–1889*, ed. Virginia Ingraham Burr (Chapel Hill: University of North Carolina Press, 1990), 1–16; Glymph, 143–45, 179–82.

85. For similar fears, Lou Falkner Williams, *The Great South Carolina Ku Klux Klan Trials, 1871–1872* (Athens: University of Georgia Press, 1996), 19–27; *The Secret Eye*, 293–96; Jonathan M. Bryant, "'Surrounded on All Sides by an Armed and Brutal Mob': Newspapers, Politics, and Law in the Ogeechee Insurrection, 1868–1869," in Baker, Kelly, and Foner, *New Perspectives on the History of the South*, 58–61.

Mr. Thomas overheard this conversation when he was again lurking beneath the floorboards.[86]

Ella Thomas wrote in the privacy of her diary "that I do not in my heart wonder that the Negroes vote the Radical ticket, and to have persuaded them otherwise would be against my own conscience." The right to vote was within their grasp, and who "can guarantee that they will ever have it extended to them again? If the women of the North once secured to me the right to vote whilst it might be 'an honour thrust upon me,' I think I should think twice before I voted to have it taken from me." These were sentiments she dared not utter outside her own household.[87]

On Election Day angry crowds of black men and white men clashed in Augusta. Federal troops appeared, and the police arrested a few black men. This seemed to restore quiet, but then a shot from the crowd killed Albert Ruffin, a deputy sheriff and white Radical.[88]

This violence was mild compared with what occurred elsewhere. In September in Albany in southwest Georgia, the Young Men's Democratic Club had ordered and received five cases of repeating rifles. When 150 freedmen and a few women arrived in Camilla in Mitchell County for a Republican rally, they came en masse for protection with an array of old shotguns, sticks, and pistols for which they lacked ammunition. About half were unarmed. The sheriff ordered them not to enter town with their arms. They refused. The whites who awaited them were deputized and had repeating rifles. They fired at nearly point blank range into the rally on the town square. They hunted the fleeing survivors down with dogs. Shootings and whippings continued for days. At least ten and as many as fifty freedpeople died in the attack and in the days that followed. Black Republicans had a choice: flee, be killed, or vote Democrat. Seymour carried Georgia.[89]

Terrorism also helped carry Louisiana for the Democrats. Armed whites in St. Landry Parish killed as many as 200 blacks in the course of the campaign. The army general in charge refused to intervene, instead warning blacks to stay away from the polls. He rejoiced that the "ascendance of the negro in this state is approaching its end." A congressional investigation put the state's election toll at 1,081 dead. To counter the violence, General Meade and General Thomas, despite the end of martial law, deployed troops to protect polling places. The troops accomplished enough that

86. Hahn, 227–28; entry Nov. 1, 1868, in *The Secret Eye*, 293–96; Glymph, 152–54, 221, 225; Fitzgerald, 212; Saville, 169–70.
87. Entry, Nov. 2, 1868, in *The Secret Eye*, 296–98.
88. Ibid., Nov. 3, 1868, 298–300.
89. O'Donovan, 260–62; Hahn, 289–91.

terror achieved its goal only in Louisiana and Georgia; elsewhere Grant carried the election. Republican dominance in the North remained largely intact. Grant got a safe 53 percent of the national vote and won the Electoral College vote 214–80.[90]

With the inauguration of Grant, most of the South was back in the Union. Only Virginia, Texas, and Mississippi had not been readmitted. Georgia's readmission would be rescinded when it purged black representatives from the legislature. Reconstruction was hardly over, but it would proceed with reconstructed Republican governments in place across much of the South.

In the wake of the election, Congress in 1869 sent the Fifteenth Amendment to the states for ratification. It ended limitations on the right to vote by "race, color or previous condition of servitude." The requisite number of states ratified it in 1870. Douglass heralded it as the completion of a "grand revolution." It was, however, not the universal suffrage amendment that Ella Thomas privately, and many northern women in the antislavery movement publicly, desired. The presence or absence of single words had immense significance. The word "citizens" excluded Chinese since they were ineligible for citizenship. And the absence of the word "sex" from allowable exclusions meant states could deny women the vote, as all but the territories of Utah and Wyoming did. In 1870 in response to the Fifteenth Amendment, the citizens of Michigan made a simple but far-reaching alteration to their 1850 constitution. They struck out the word "white."[91]

In seeking to deracialize citizenship, Reconstruction emphasized its gendering. There was not a single set of rights. There was one set of rights for men and another, lesser, set for women. Nothing made this clearer than the ubiquitous marriage contract, which sutured together male authority and female subordination. Legally, women agreed to obey and serve their husbands in exchange for protection. The marriage contract was, however, a unique contract. Under the legal doctrine of coverture the identities of married women were subsumed into those of their husbands. His decisions were her decisions; her property was his property. He was the public face of the family and legally responsible for her and their children. Manhood, legally as well as culturally, meant protecting and supporting; womanhood meant serving and obeying. Because the wife's

90. Mantell, 143–47; Allen W. Trelease, *White Terror: The Ku Klux Klan Conspiracy and Southern Reconstruction* (New York: Harper & Row, 1971), 129, 135; Downs, *After Appomattox*, 206–9; Foner, 342–43.

91. *The History of Michigan Law*, ed. Paul Finkelman, Martin J. Hershock, and Clifford W. Taylor (Athens: Ohio University Press, 2006), 197–98, 444–49; Richardson, 80.

identity, property, and autonomy vanished into that of her husband she could make no further contracts. The marriage contract thus was a contract that took away a wife's right to make future contracts. Although legislatures had softened coverture somewhat in the years before the Civil War and allowed an easier escape through divorce, only an unmarried adult woman had legal standing and full control over her property.[92]

To the minority of white women who were both liberals and active in the fight for women's rights, this gendering of liberalism was nonsensical, and to women who had long been active in the movement for the abolition, failure to enact universal suffrage seemed a betrayal. White women suffragists had formed the American Equal Rights Association in 1866, but the Fifteenth Amendment divided them. Lucy Stone became a leader of the American Woman Suffrage Association, which supported the extension of the suffrage to black men. Elizabeth Cady Stanton and Susan B. Anthony, who had fought to keep black rights and women's rights linked, opposed the Fifteenth Amendment until women received the vote. They felt betrayed by Wendell Phillips, whose conviction that this was the black man's hour and that women's suffrage was impossible in the present generation, denied them access to funds to campaign for universal suffrage. They thought women's suffrage a real possibility. The debate turned ugly. Stanton contrasted the freedmen's "incoming pauperism, ignorance, and degradation, with the wealth, education, and refinement of the women of the republic." She followed with attacks on immigrants and the working class and argued that it was better "to be the slave of an educated white man, than of a degraded, ignorant black one." Stanton and Anthony formed the National Woman Suffrage Association. Stanton allied herself with George Francis Train, the flamboyant and corrupt promoter of the Union Pacific Railway, who joined racism and women's suffrage even more blatantly than Stanton, and then in 1868 endorsed the Democrats and Frank Blair, agreeing with Blair that suffrage for black men ensured the rape and abuse of white women.[93]

92. Nancy F. Cott, *Public Vows: A History of Marriage and the Nation* (Cambridge, MA: Harvard University Press, 2000), 28, 52–55; Stanley, 10–11.
93. Ellen Carol DuBois, *Feminism and Suffrage: The Emergence of an Independent Women's Movement in America, 1848–1869* (Ithaca, NY: Cornell University Press, 1978), 58–104; Faye E. Dudden, *Fighting Chance: The Struggle over Woman Suffrage and Black Suffrage in Reconstruction America* (New York: Oxford University Press, 2011), 10–11, 153–60; Lori D. Ginzberg, *Elizabeth Cady Stanton: An American Life* (New York: Hill and Wang, 2009), 121–23; Louise Michele Newman, *White Women's Rights: The Racial Origins of Feminism in the United States* (New York: Oxford University Press, 1999), 56–63.

Douglass was pained by Stanton's stance. He advocated a Sixteenth Amendment to give women the vote and praised Stanton personally. But he also argued that the case for black suffrage was more urgent than women's suffrage. "When women, because they are women, are hunted down through the cities of New York and New Orleans; when they are dragged from their houses and hung upon lamp-posts; when their children are torn from their arms, and their brains dashed out upon the pavement; when they are objects of insult and outrage at every turn...then they will have an urgency to obtain the ballot equal to our own." Many other advocates of women's suffrage, male and female, took a similar position.[94]

The Radicals were fissuring. As in so many other things, Henry Ward Beecher, the country's leading liberal Protestant, was a flag in the wind. Beecher had a foot—and usually a sister—in both suffrage camps. Before the Civil War, he agreed with his sister Catharine that women were "to act as the conservators of the domestic state." He did not oppose women's suffrage but thought it premature and politically impossible. During and immediately after the war he became an advocate of universal suffrage. He retreated to neutrality when the women's rights movement erupted into its own civil war. His half-sister Isabella Beecher Hooker, who was an uneasy ally of Stanton, seemed to draw him to that side, but Lucy Stone persuaded him to become president of the American Woman Suffrage Association. Briefly there was a hope of reconciliation between the rival associations, but the animosities were personal as well as ideological. Henry's wife, Eunice, disliked Stanton and her ally and Beecher's old associate, Theodore Tilton. She refused to let them in her house. Catharine Beecher publicly opposed Henry's advocacy of immediate women's suffrage and Harriet Beecher Stowe joined her sister in opposition. She wrote her brother, "The man is and ought to be the head of the woman...." Voting would undermine women's place in the home. Caught between his sisters, rival organizations, and the deeper ideological crosscurrents they represented, Beecher retreated to his old belief that, whatever its merits, women's suffrage was premature and politically impossible. It became the conventional liberal stance.[95]

It was not just Stanton and Anthony who pulled back from black rights. The Republicans were determined to make Washington, D.C., "an example for all the land." Congress had decreed the vote for freedmen, but as freedmen gained suffrage they demanded full equality. They desired not only civil and political equality, but also social equality: an end to

94. Dudden, 61–87; Ginzberg, 124–25.
95. Clifford Edward Clark, *Henry Ward Beecher: Spokesman for a Middle-Class America* (Urbana: University of Illinois Press, 1978), 197–207.

racial discrimination in schools; on public transport; in theaters, restaurants, and hotels; and in hiring. The resistance they ran into included many white Republicans. They did gain access to Washington's new streetcars and a share of city and federal government jobs, but they were far less successful in integrating schools and in attempts to gain social equality.[96]

The reaction against attempts by black people to gain full equality merged with the reaction against increased taxes and corruption that sprang from the improvements funded by the Republican government of D.C. It was not Democrats but Republicans in Congress who began to restrict black suffrage rights. In 1871 Congress stripped Washington of its right to self-government, making it a federal territory with the chief officials appointed by Congress. Henry Cooke, Jay Cooke's brother, became governor and began a period of elite rule and limits on democratic governance in the name of economic progress. City funds found their way into Jay Cooke's bank. In 1874 the still-Republican Congress went further. It stripped D.C. of even territorial government status. The city would be run by a commission appointed by Congress; its citizens, black and white, lost the vote, while racial discrimination against blacks continued in schools, on jobs, and in housing. The limits of "equality" even among Republicans were becoming apparent.[97]

When he was inaugurated, Ulysses S. Grant became the first American president who had actually resided in the trans-Missouri West. He had been an army officer in California and the Washington Territory before the Civil War. The West had been for him a place of some hope, much greater failure, and ultimately loneliness and depression, which drove him out of the army. When Grant in 1868 embraced the larger goals of Reconstruction—homogeneous citizenship, contract freedom, and a free labor economy—he would apply them to a South that he had helped conquer and to a West that in some ways had conquered him. In his inaugural, he endorsed the Fifteenth Amendment, which granted universal male suffrage for all citizens, as a necessary step toward homogeneous citizenship. Then, to the surprise of many, he turned to Indian policy, writing that "the proper treatment of the original occupants of this land—the Indians—is one deserving of careful study. I will favor any course toward them which tends to their civilization and ultimate citizenship." This was a logical extension of Reconstruction. Whether this was good or bad news for Indians remained to be seen.[98]

96. Masur, 122–72.
97. Ibid., 207–27, 246–55.
98. McFeely, *Grant: A Biography*, 46–48, 289.

3

The Greater Reconstruction

On November 29, 1864, at Sand Creek in the Territory of Colorado, Col. John Chivington, a former Methodist minister, attacked a camp of Cheyennes who thought themselves under military protection. With Cheyenne men absent hunting, Chivington's command slaughtered roughly two hundred Indians, mostly women and children, in a bloody dawn assault that typified American tactics against Great Plains tribes. The Sand Creek massacre ignited war across the central Great Plains, which would continue even as the Civil War came to an end.[1]

A mix of antislavery and racism had driven western Republicans to arms during the Civil War, but troops raised to counter the Confederate threat often fought Indians. Chivington had fought Confederates in New Mexico before Colorado Republican Gov. John Evans appointed him to command Colorado's Third Regiment of Volunteer Cavalry, raised in 1864 to counter a perceived Indian threat. In California, Republicans had not originated genocidal wars aimed at the "extermination" of Indians who resisted white occupation, but under Gov. Leland Stanford they had continued them, as well as policies that provided for indenture and forced labor of Indian children. Forced labor officially ended with the Emancipation Proclamation, but unfree labor in California continued longer in practice.[2]

An attack by American troops on Indian women and children was not how the mythic version of American settlement was supposed to proceed. Troops were not supposed to be involved at all; the Indians, like the bison, were supposed to fade quietly away. John Gast's famous 1872 lithograph "American Progress" portrayed the ideal course of events, drawing on traditional views of expansion. Indians and bison retreated—virtually vanishing

1. Elliott West, *The Contested Plains: Indians, Goldseekers, & the Rush to Colorado* (Lawrence: University Press of Kansas, 1998), 299–307.
2. Stacey L. Smith, *Freedom's Frontier: California and the Struggle over Unfree Labor, Emancipation, and Reconstruction* (Chapel Hill: University of North Carolina Press, 2014), 189–92; Benjamin Madley, *An American Genocide: The United States and the California Indian Catastrophe* (New Haven, CT: Yale University Press, 2016), 299–335.

John Gast's "American Progress" (1872) is one of the most famous, and misinterpreted, lithographs in American history. More suited to antebellum ideas about Manifest Destiny than government- and corporate-sponsored expansion after the war, it is notable for what it leaves out. There is no army fighting Indians; the railroad follows, rather than leads. There is no government surveying and giving away land. The towns and cities are in the East rather than springing up quickly in the West. Library of Congress, LC-USZC4-668.

off the print's edge—while white Americans advanced. The American vanguard advanced on horseback and in covered wagons. In the middle ground, farmers plowed the earth, and behind them came railroad trains, and the telegraph. Floating above them all was a female figure draped in a white, diaphanous gown with the star of empire on her brow, a telegraph wire in one hand and a schoolbook, emblem of the public common schools, in the other. The lithograph pictured expansion as a providential folk movement that involved neither armies nor the state. It contradicted the realities of expansion during and after the Civil War.

Congress couldn't wait on Providence. The old expansion was too slow, too limited, and insufficient to save the country in the midst of a crisis. Congress had dispatched troops to conquer Indians and funded state efforts to slaughter them. They overcame the reasonable reluctance of American railroad men to build railroads in advance of actual settlement, and the unwillingness of most American farmers to establish farms in areas that lacked ready access to markets, by offering subsidies to both. Congress reversed the order of march depicted in Gast's "American Progress." Endowed with federal subsidies, railroads would build in advance of actual settlement. Soldiers, who appeared nowhere on Gast's canvas, would protect them, and the railroads, along with the federal government, would induce settlers to follow.

The violence unleashed by the Civil War in the West, like the violence in the South, needed to be mitigated and suppressed. In early March 1865, a little more than a month before Lee surrendered at Appomattox, Congress had responded to chaos and fighting in the West by creating a Joint Special Committee "to investigate into the present condition of the Indian tribes, and especially into the manner in which they are treated by the civil and military authorities of the United States." Committee chair Sen. James R. Doolittle of Wisconsin was a devout Baptist whose beliefs paralleled those of evangelicals drawn to the Freedmen's Bureau. He regarded the Declaration of Independence as the "new gospel of man's redemption," which made the Fourth of July "the birthday of God's Republic." His committee toured the West in three groups; it was the Western equivalent of Northern travelers reporting back from the South.[3]

The desire for peace and the persistence of war fed both the Western and Southern variants of the Greater Reconstruction, and in both sections Congress sought a blueprint for a new nation. In the West, too, Congress promoted free labor, contract freedom, and economic development that would yield even more American homes. Both Indians and ex-Confederates distrusted and resisted the coming of this new order, but they had little else in common. Confederates had aspired to independence, but they had failed to create a nation. The Indians remained semisovereign nations in treaty relation with the United States. The American struggle with them was imperial rather than an internecine conflict between citizens of the United States.

Northerners blamed the South for the Civil War, but in the fall of 1865 American negotiators at the Treaty of the Little Arkansas—in actuality a set of treaties—admitted that Americans had proved the war through "gross and wanton outrages" that had taken place at Sand Creek. They apologized and sought peace, but they also required access for the railroad and stagecoach lines projected across the southern and central Great Plains. For the next decade, Indian wars and railroads would remain linked. The treaties at the Little Arkansas created immense reservations

3. Francis Paul Prucha, *The Great Father: The United States Government and the American Indians* (Lincoln: University of Nebraska Press, 1984), 1: 485–86; West, 299–307.

Indian Lands in January 1864

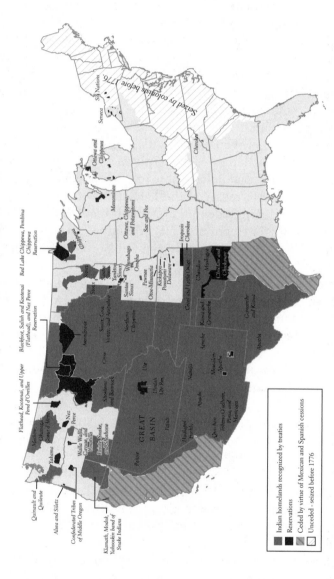

Quinault and
Quileute

Alsea and Siletz

Confederated Tribes
of Middle Oregon

Klamath, Modoc,
Yahooskin band of
Snake Indians

Makah
Clallam
Coeur d'Alene

Walla Walla,
Cayuse, and
Umatilla

Pathas Snake,
and Shoshone

Nez
Perce

Yakama

Flathead, Kootenai, and Upper
Pend d'Oreilles

Blackfoot, Salish and Kootenai
(Flathead), and Nez Perce
Reservation

Red Lake Chippewa, Pembina
Chippewa
Reservation

Chippewa

Sioux

Menominee

Ottawa and
Chippewa

Seneca

Sénit Nation

Chemehuevi

Ottawa, Chippewa,
and Potawatomi

Sac and Fox

Yankton
Sioux

Winnebago

Santee
Sioux

Omaha

Pawnee
Otoe-Missouria

Kickapoo
Powdatomi
Delaware

Osage and Little Osage

Iroquois
Cherokee

Cherokee

Wyandot

Choctaw and
Chickasaw

Assiniboine

Crow

Northern
Cheyenne

Shoshone
and Bannock

Ute

Uintah
Ute-Hoc

Great
Basin

Paiute

Hualapai
Pueblo

Que-chan
Tohono-O'odham,
Pima, and
Maricopa

Navaho

Apache

Mexican
Pueblo

Austin

Comanche and
Kiowa

Comanche

Kansai and
Comanche

Apache

Cahuancho and
Kiowa

Seized by colonists before 1776

	Indian homelands recognized by treaties
	Reservations
	Ceded by virtue of Mexican and Spanish cessions
	Unceded - seized before 1776

Sources: Based on data from Claudio Saunt, Sergio Bernardes, David Holcomb, and Daniel Reeves, University of Georgia, "The Invasion of America: How the United States Took Over an Eighth of the World," http://invasionofamerica.ehistory.org/; Minnesota Population Center. National Historical Geographic Information System: Version 11.0 [Database]. Minneapolis: University of Minnesota, 2016 (state boundaries).

carved out of Texas, Kansas, and the Indian Territory (modern Oklahoma), but after Kansas and Texas objected to reservations within their borders, the government excluded that land from the reservations.[4]

During the rest of the 1860s American soldiers, treaty commissioners, and Congressional investigators crisscrossed the Central and Southern Plains, often at cross-purposes with each other. They talked to Indians, fought Indians, chased Indians, and investigated the treatment of Indians. They provoked war as often as they made peace.

War erupted because Americans threatened resources critical to the survival of Plains tribes. As the army reorganized and withdrew from the South, it deployed into the West, creating new posts, most of them small, isolated, and designed to protect the very travelers and railroad construction crews who precipitated conflict. The initial deployments were disasters. Companies sent west in 1865 refused direct orders to fight Indians. They wanted to go home. Three hundred men deserted three Illinois regiments.

The new forts demonstrated how undermanned and overextended the army was. Fort Phil Kearny in 1866 was one of three new posts to protect travelers on the Bozeman Trail, which followed the eastern front of the Rockies from the Oregon Trail to the gold fields of Montana. The travelers threatened some of the last prime bison grounds on the northern plains. The fort, about 150 miles north of Fort Laramie on the Oregon Trail, came under siege from Lakotas under a prominent *Ogle Tanka Un* or war leader, Red Cloud. The Indians cut the soldiers' animals off from the surrounding grasslands and soldiers from the scattered timber they needed for fuel. When Capt. William J. Fetterman marched out of Fort Phil Kearny to rescue a wood cutting party on December 21, 1866, most of his men were on foot because the fort's horse herd was so weakened and depleted. Fetterman had supposedly boasted that with eighty men he could ride through the entire Sioux nation, but his death alongside all eighty of his entire command did not result from his arrogance. It came instead from the deficiencies of a fort without easy access to either wood or grass, and his following the orders he received to cut off the Lakota attackers. Instead, they ambushed him. It was a costly and embarrassing defeat that became grist for rivalries within the army when Fetterman's commander sought to place the blame for the disaster on him. The truth of the fight disappeared beneath a mountain of recriminations, cover-ups, myth making, and self-serving accounts.[5]

4. West, 308–9; Francis Paul Prucha, *American Indian Policy in Crisis: Christian Reformers and the Indian, 1865–1900* (Norman: University of Oklahoma Press 1976), 13–14.

5. For desertions and refusal to fight, see Gregory Downs, *After Appomattox: Military Occupation and the Ends of War* (Cambridge, MA: Harvard University Press, 2015), 102; Calitri Shannon Smith, "'Give Me Eighty Men': Shattering the Myth of the Fetterman Massacre," *Montana: The Magazine of Western History* 54, no. 3 (2004): 44–59.

Fort Wallace on the Smoky Hill River in Kansas provoked a similar conflict that also revolved around travelers, grass, horses, and wood. In creating the fort, the soldiers destroyed a large grove of cottonwoods that gave the river its Cheyenne name, Bunch of Timber. A mountain man, Uncle Dick Wootton, recalled later that the Arapahos and Cheyennes threatened to kill a white man for every tree the whites had cut down at Bunch of Timber. And, he added, "I reckon they did it."[6]

In January 1867 the Doolittle Committee finally issued its report; it was scathing, blaming the fighting on "the aggression of lawless whites." Gen. Winfield Scott Hancock, however, apparently did not read the report. Operating on faulty intelligence of impending Indian attacks, he launched a grandiosely titled Expedition for the Plains that spring. It consisted of eighteen companies of soldiers, including eight companies of the newly formed Seventh Cavalry under Lt. Col. George Armstrong Custer, and an artillery battery. Hancock marched prepared for "peace or war." His intent was to remove Indians "infesting the country traveled by our over-land routes." But the Cheyennes, Arapahos, and Kiowas that he was looking for were in their own country. It was the whites who were invaders.[7]

Hancock found members of the most militant of the Cheyenne warrior societies, the Dog Soldiers, and their Lakota and Arapaho allies on the Pawnee Fork of the Arkansas River. The Cheyennes, with the memory of Sand Creek still fresh, fled. Hancock burned their village. Custer, as flamboyant an officer as any in the army, pursued the fleeing Indians, who left a trail of burned ranches, stagecoach stations, and dead whites along the Smoky Hill River. Tired of fruitlessly chasing Indians, Custer force-marched his men, who did not love him, back to Fort Harker so he could visit his wife, who did. He was court-martialed for being absent without leave, for "conduct to the prejudice of good order and discipline," specifically for taking horses and a large escort so he could conduct private business and for ordering deserters killed on sight without trial, which resulted in the death of at least one soldier. Finally, he was charged with abandoning soldiers attacked by Indians. He was found guilty of all charges, but the sentence proved mild. He was suspended from the army without pay for a year. Grant, as the commander of the army, decided not to refer the murder to a civil court for trial.[8]

6. West, 275–76, 308–10; William R. Petrowski, "The Kansas Pacific Railroad in the Southwest," *Arizona and the West* 11, no. 2 (1969): 129–46.

7. Prucha, *The Great Father*, 485–92; Paul Andrew Hutton, *Phil Sheridan and His Army* (Lincoln: University of Nebraska Press, 1985), 30–33; William Y. Chalfant, *Hancock's War: Conflict on the Southern Plains* (Norman, OK: Arthur H. Clark, 2010), 157ff.

8. T. J. Stiles, *Custer's Trials: A Life on the Frontier of a New America* (New York: Knopf, 2015), 255–57, 273–76, 293–98; Chalfant, 157ff.; Hutton, 30–33.

Congress again tried to put an end to the fighting by establishing the Indian Peace Commission in June 1867. This time the army suspended offensive operations and operated in tandem with the reformers. The government intended the commission to be an exercise in coercive benevolence. The commissioners, some of whom were reformers and some soldiers, were to deal with Indians as members of semisovereign tribes.[9]

The question for the commissioners was not whether the United States would expand into Indian country, but rather how. Their goal was to overcome Indians without the necessity of expensive wars and embarrassing atrocities such as Sand Creek. The immediate requirement was to open up a corridor across the Central Plains that would allow transcontinental railroads already building west—particularly the Union Pacific and Kansas Pacific—to proceed. As the commissioners stated in their final report, "Civilization must not be arrested in its progress by a handful of savages." The West was to be the home of "an industrious, thrifty, and enlightened civilization." The question was one of means and not ends.[10]

The Indian Peace Commission was a major step in the Greater Reconstruction of the West, a project that involved a vast spatial rearrangement of a kind that later generations would call nation building and still later generations would call ethnic cleansing. Existing populations would be concentrated and moved; new peoples would migrate into the region. Both involved demarcating a new Western space in a region where jurisdictional, sovereign, and property lines had never been firm. The railroad land grants, the surveying of the public domain, the Homestead Act, and an Indian policy that marked specific tribal territories and then created reservations were all aspects of the new spatial arrangement. The new lines would be drawn in blood. Preparing the way for and building railroads often provoked the Indian wars they were supposed to prevent.[11]

Advocates of the Peace Commission could appear as "friends of the Indian," because the alternative was on such vivid display. Wars of extermination—genocide—would decline in California following the Civil War, but they continued in the Southwest, particularly in Arizona. Americans, sometimes with the collaboration of the army and sometimes on their own, waged an avowed war of "extermination against the Apaches," a group the *Weekly Arizonian* described in 1873 as "the most

9. Prucha, *The Great Father*, 488–92.
10. Prucha, *American Indian Policy in Crisis*, 20–21.
11. The idea of parallel Southern and Western Reconstructions is one that I have borrowed from Elliott West, particularly in his superb book *The Last Indian War: The Nez Perce Story* (New York: Oxford University Press, 2009); Brian Balogh, *A Government out of Sight: The Mystery of National Authority in Nineteenth-Century America* (Cambridge: Cambridge University Press, 2009), 292.

treacherous, blood-thirsty, implacable fiends that roam anywhere on the face of the earth." The government disavowed extermination. Yet in practice the Peace Commission and the peace policy that followed sought the same ends as army officers who urged violent solutions: the cession of Indian lands, the confinement of Indian peoples to reservations, and their transformation into monogamous Christians who would live like surrounding whites. Outside of California, parts of Oregon, Nevada, and Arizona, this was a program of coerced assimilation rather than extermination.[12]

In October 1867 the commissioners met the Comanches and other southern plains tribes at Medicine Lodge Creek in what is now Kiowa County, Kansas, to negotiate a treaty to replace the failed Little Arkansas treaties. Initially, the large majority of Cheyennes were not present; they were fifty miles away conducting the Massaum ceremony, the most sacred in their ceremonial cycle. The Cheyennes cleansed the Sacred Arrows, among the holiest objects they possessed, and in doing so renewed the world. At Medicine Lodge the commissioners negotiating with the Comanches, Kiowas, Arapahos, and Plains Apaches were outlining a new world of agriculture and reservations. The Indians made clear they wanted no part of it. When it became apparent from the speeches in council that the Indians would not agree to the treaty as presented, the commissioners obfuscated. Given the lack of interpreters and long chains of interpretation through several languages, confusion was inevitable. The government later claimed, and the Indians later denied, that the Medicine Lodge Treaty abrogated the commitments made at the Little Arkansas to compensate the Cheyennes and Arapahos for Sand Creek. When points were in dispute, the commissioners sometimes prevaricated. The Indians living south of the Arkansas River believed they had retained their country and the right to hunt buffalo wherever they found them. They would take the Americans' advice on farming within reservations should the buffalo disappear. These were not, however, the terms of the treaty, and the commissioners did not alter the treaty to reflect the Indians' understanding. The Senate made things worse. Distracted by their battles with President Johnson, senators would not consider the treaty for a year and so the promised annuities were delayed.[13]

When the Cheyennes arrived, the council with them proceeded in much the same way as those with the other tribes, although many of the

12. Madley, 317–59; Karl Jacoby, *Shadows at Dawn: A Borderlands Massacre and the Violence of History* (New York: Penguin Press, 2008), 112–29.

13. Chalfant, 465–90; Hutton, 33–35; West, *The Contested Plains*, 310–11; Prucha, *American Indian Policy in Crisis*, 20, 117.

leading chiefs remained too suspicious of Americans to sign anything. The Cheyennes thought they had agreed only to allow travelers to pass through their territory on overland trails and permitted whites to build the railroads. In return they received annuities and retained the country between the Arkansas and the Platte rivers. The treaty actually deprived them of that country. Capt. Albert Barnitz, who was at the treaty negotiations, had no illusions about the results. The Cheyennes, he wrote, "have no idea that they are giving up, or have ever given up … the country north of the Arkansas. The treaty amounts to nothing, and we will certainly have another war, sooner or later, with the Cheyennes."[14]

In a sense, the war with the Comanches never ceased, although the Comanches did not regard themselves as at war with the United States. They took the American promise in the Medicine Lodge Treaty of 1867 of the right to hunt below the Arkansas River as an acknowledgment of their ownership of the land and their right to keep Texans out of Comancheria. Comanches appeared at their Indian Territory agency to collect annuities under the treaty and then returned to Texas to raid there and into New Mexico and Mexico. They viewed their relations with the United States as different from their relations with the Texans, Mexicans, and other Indian nations. In 1868 the tacit truce between the army and the Comanches badly frayed, and a Comanche band skirmished with Sheridan's troops.[15]

Like the Comanches, Gen. Phil Sheridan in 1867 did not regard Texas as being at peace with the United States; nor was he particularly sympathetic to those Texans who had settled in Comancheria and faced attack from the people they had dispossessed. Sheridan's opinion mattered because he commanded the Fifth Military District, which included Texas and Louisiana. He also had the support of Ulysses S. Grant. As one of Grant's aides put it, the two generals had "the friendship of chieftains." As the government sought peace on the Great Plains in the summer of 1867, simmering controversy between Texas Gov. James W. Throckmorton and Sheridan had come to a head. Their confrontation fed the crisis in Washington, D.C., that would lead to President Johnson's impeachment and helped fuel Grant's election, but just as significantly, it radiated west, illustrating how events in the South and West linked into a Greater Reconstruction.[16]

14. Chalfant, 493–501; Hutton, 33–35.
15. Pekka Hämäläinen, *The Comanche Empire* (New Haven, CT: Yale University Press, 2008), 324–25.
16. "James W. Throckmorton," in *Handbook of Texas Online*, https://tshaonline.org/handbook/online/articles/fth36; Gregory P. Downs, *After Appomattox: Military Occupation and the Ends of War* (Cambridge, MA: Harvard University Press, 2015), 182.

Texas and Sheridan embodied the southern and western variants of Reconstruction. Sheridan disliked both Texas and Texans. He appropriated a joke applied to many places in the United States after the Civil War. Asked how he liked Texas, he replied, "If I owned hell and Texas, I would rent out Texas and live in hell."[17]

Freedpeople in Texas could be excused for thinking that Texas was, in fact, hell. According to a Freedmen's Bureau official, they were "frequently beaten unmercifully, and shot down like wild beasts, without any provocation." Ex-Confederates insisted they were provoked, and they listed the provocations: "putting on airs," "sassiness," "impudence," "insolence," and "disrespect."[18]

The relentless violence against freedpeople outraged Sheridan, who was a dangerous man to antagonize. Throckmorton opposed the pending Fourteenth Amendment and thought the Texas legislature should have the opportunity to reject the Thirteenth, which was the product of "a parcel of experimenting, humbugging, rascally, fanatical hounds of hell who have served the devil all their lives." He predictably refused to protect Unionists and freedpeople. This was not a promising route for reentering the Union, and Throckmorton became Sheridan's enemy. In his short, brave, and often thoroughly unpleasant person, Phil Sheridan personified the latent power of the federal government, and if any man deserved Phil Sheridan, it was Throckmorton.[19]

The violence against freedpeople occurred in many places across the South, but the confrontation between Throckmorton and Sheridan in Texas also involved the deaths of white settlers at the hands of Indians. The Comanches had used the Civil War to reemerge as a formidable enemy of Texas and reclaim parts of their homeland. They raided to rebuild their horse and cattle herds, which compensated for the reduced numbers of bison. As they had for a century, the Comanches took captives in Texas, Mexico, and New Mexico to replenish their own diminished

17. Hutton, 22–25; William L. Richter, "'It Is Best to Go in Strong-Handed': Army Occupation of Texas, 1865–1866," *Arizona and the West* 27, no. 2 (1985), 113–42.

18. Hutton, 20, 25; Leon F. Litwack, *Been in the Storm So Long: The Aftermath of Slavery* (New York: Knopf, distributed by Random House, 1979), 278–80; "James W. Throckmorton"; Mark W. Summers, *The Ordeal of the Reunion: A New History of Reconstruction* (Chapel Hill: University of North Carolina Press, 2014), 100–101; Eric Foner, *Reconstruction: America's Unfinished Revolution, 1863–1877* (New York: Harper & Row, 1988), 119, 307.

19. The best account of Sheridan is Hutton, *Phil Sheridan and His Army*, 20–25; Edward M. Coffman, *The Old Army: A Portrait of the American Army in Peacetime, 1784–1898* (New York: Oxford University Press, 1986), 238–39; Summers, 99–100; "James W. Throckmorton."

numbers. Throckmorton demanded that the military cease interfering with civil officials in Texas and that Sheridan deploy his troops to protect border settlements.[20]

Although the Union Army stationed more troops in Texas than in any other Confederate state, they were insufficient to cover all needs. Sheridan had to choose between applying force to protect citizens—freedpeople and Southern Unionists—or to conquer Indians who were resisting invasion from ex-Confederates. He preferred to protect freedpeople and white Unionists. He stated the issue in Texas succinctly: "If a white man is killed by the Indians on an extensive frontier, the greatest excitement will take place, but over the killing of many freedmen in the settlements, nothing is done." Throckmorton appealed to President Johnson, who overruled Sheridan, leading Sheridan, with the implicit support of Grant, to defy Johnson. Using his authority under the Reconstruction Act, Sheridan removed Throckmorton from office in late July 1867. Johnson, in retaliation, removed the "tyrant" Sheridan the next day.[21]

Johnson transferred Sheridan to the West, having him exchange places with General Hancock, who was sympathetic to the president. Hancock had proved better at precipitating Indian wars than winning them, and he was happy enough to leave the Great Plains behind. Sheridan moved to the District of Missouri, part of the larger Department of the Missouri under the command of William Tecumseh Sherman. There, he would shed his reticence about attacking Indians and become the mailed fist of the Greater Reconstruction.[22]

Reconstruction in the West involved the same paradox as in the South: the expansion of individualism and contract freedom—hallmarks of a liberalism ideologically opposed to strong governments—under the sponsorship of a newly powerful state. As in the South, the federal government assumed new powers and demanded rapid and transformative change. The federal task was easier in the West. The transformation at the heart of the Greater Reconstruction had begun earlier there, and the U.S. territorial system (which some Radicals had wished to use as a model to reconstruct the South), allowed the president to appoint the governors and Congress to veto acts of territorial legislatures. The territories west of the Missouri River took much longer to transition to statehood than had been the case farther east. This was partially because Protestants feared a Catholic state (New Mexico) and a Mormon state (Utah), and partially

20. Hämäläinen, 312–17.
21. "James W. Throckmorton"; Downs, 142–44, 182–83; Foner, 119, 307; Hutton, 20, 24–25; Richter, "'It Is Best to Go in Strong-Handed'," 133–34.
22. Coffman, 239; Hutton, 24–27.

because of political rivalries revolving around control of the Senate, but it was largely the result of the slow pace of settlement in the arid and semi-arid West. Congress created thirteen Western territories between 1861 and 1888, but during those years only four—Kansas (1861), Nevada (1864), Nebraska (1867), and Colorado (1876)—joined California and Oregon as Western states.[23]

In the West the federal government boldly undertook policies considered too radical for the old Confederacy. Acting as an imperial state against semisovereign tribes, it forced the cession of Indian lands and redistributed them to both individuals and corporations, in effect instituting the land redistribution that was rejected in the South. Congress voted direct federal subsidies to corporations, something they largely refused to do in the South. The army attacked and disciplined noncitizen Indians in ways the government never attempted with citizen Southerners after the Civil War.[24]

In 1867 American achievements in the West still consisted largely of bold talk. The United States claimed rather than controlled most of the land west of the Missouri River. Most of the Great Plains, the Great Basin, and the Rockies remained Indian Territory, a legal classification for unceded land. Yet conquest had begun. In the Far West only the Modocs, Nez Perce, and Bannocks would mount violent resistance to the Americans in the 1870s. In the Great Plains, Rockies, and the Southwest there was much wider opposition, including the Apaches, Comanches, Utes, Lakotas, Cheyennes, and Arapahos, none of whom had as yet been decisively defeated. American citizens had penetrated the interior West, but their settlements remained ruptures in the much larger expanse of Indian country. By and large only precious metals and wheat, which went by ocean from California, could be profitably shipped to the East and Europe. Indians and non-Indians west of the Missouri lived in a world that, although deeply affected by an emerging industrial order, still relied on human and animal muscles as well as wood for the energy that sustained life. In such things the West resembled northern Mexico, which it blended into, creating a common borderland that neither the United States nor Mexico could fully control, and western Canada, whose borders also existed largely on paper. The West was far more like the *pampas* of Argentina and southern Chile

23. Elliott West has suggested that the Greater Reconstruction began earlier in the West than in the South. Elliott West, "Reconstructing Race," *Western Historical Quarterly* 34, no. 1 (2003): 6–26; Richard White, *"It's Your Misfortune and None of My Own": A History of the American West* (Norman: University of Oklahoma Press, 1991), 171–77.
24. Prucha, *The Great Father*, 491–92.

than the eastern United States. All would undergo similar transformations during the late nineteenth century.[25]

Reconstructing this vast territory into a replica of the Northeast and Midwest was made even more daunting by the same limited administrative capacity that hindered the government in the South. The army, as blunt a tool as it was, remained the most effective instrument for achieving the government's ends. In the West as in the South, the presence of the army was the best indicator of Greater Reconstruction's chances of success, and neither region had sufficient soldiers to control events.[26]

The Civil War Army had been the iron fist of an armed democracy, but the postwar regular army of thirty thousand men managed to be both the American democracy's least democratic place outside of a prison and a reflection of the nation's hardening class divisions and growing inequality. African Americans, immigrants—mostly Germans and Irish—and the poor supplied most of the army's manpower, and they had virtually no chance of advancing into the officer corps. A person did not have to be desperate to enlist in the regular army, but it helped. Men enlisted, as General Sherman observed, during "winters and hard times" and deserted in the spring or while on campaign. Enlisted men's pay might be a refuge in times of depression, but it fell well below civilian wages in good times. Between 1867 and 1891 the annual desertion rate was about 15 percent, with a peak of 33 percent in 1871 and 1872. Courts-martial did not stem the tide. With good reason, ordinary soldiers regarded military justice as an oxymoron. Yet the army paradoxically became a tool of last resort to secure a democracy in the South and extend by force democratic governance at the expense of Indian peoples across the West.[27]

Except for the ex-slaves, the army was a Northern and immigrant institution, in part because northern cities were where the army opened its recruiting offices. The recruitment of black units proved slow. A few black

25. Benjamin Madley, "California's Yuki Indians: Defining Genocide in Native American History," *Western Historical Quarterly* 39, no. 3 (2008): 303–32; for the Comanches, Hämäläinen, 321–41. Rachel St. John, *Line in the Sand: A History of the Western U.S.-Mexico Border* (Princeton, NJ: Princeton University Press, 2011), 50–79; for the fighting following the Civil War, Hutton; for a survey of Western Indian wars, Robert M. Utley, *The Indian Frontier of the American West, 1846–1890* (Albuquerque: University of New Mexico Press, 1984); Benjamin Hoy, *A Wall of Many Heights: The Uneven Enforcement of the Canadian–United States Border* (Stanford, CA: Stanford University Press, 2015), 203–95.

26. Elliott West, whose term the Greater Reconstruction I borrow, has dated the beginning of this larger Reconstruction well before the Civil War. West, "Reconstructing Race," 6–36.

27. Coffman, 218, 220, 224–25, 346–49, 371–81; Kevin Adams, *Class and Race in the Frontier Army: Military Life in the West, 1870–1890* (Norman: University of Oklahoma Press, 2009), 20–24, 156–58.

veterans immediately reenlisted; others returned to the army as they rec-ognized the limited opportunities for black men in the Reconstruction South. After 1869, black soldiers, serving under white officers, made up about 10 percent of the regular army, and black cavalry about 20 percent of its mounted force.[28]

A rigid caste line separated officers and men. Soldiers were poor when they entered and poor when they left, which was why so many deserters stole and then sold their equipment. Officers were quite liter-ally officers and gentlemen, and the government paid them and granted them privileges that allowed them to live as gentlemen. Promotions arrived with glacial slowness, but deflation increased the real value of officers' wages so even a second lieutenant received a salary that put him in the top 10 percent of Americans in income. Officers read widely, and they wrote: ethnology, natural history, geology, poetry, and fiction. Officers' wives lived at the posts and the officer corps entertained lav-ishly. Servants, often soldiers, prepared the meals. As Elizabeth Custer, George Armstrong Custer's wife, remembered, "Nothing seemed to annoy my husband more than to find me in the kitchen." Champagne, oysters, ice cream, and fresh vegetables graced officers' tables. Hardtack, beans, and often rancid bacon were the regular fare of enlisted men, who if they did not buttress their rations with their own purchases faced the danger of scurvy. Soldiers received little military training and were notoriously bad shots. They were laborers in uniform—building forts, improving roads, and repairing buildings. Their own barracks were vile, and if they had families, the living quarters around the posts as late as the 1890s were described by the surgeon general as "wretched" and "a disgrace."[29]

Yet for all its failings, the army was comparatively honest and efficient. It was an armed bureaucracy, which is why the government employed it or delegated its officers at various times to administer Indian reservations, staff the Freedmen's Bureau, police new national parks, conduct geologi-cal surveys, and enforce land laws. At the end of the Civil War the govern-ment lacked alternative reliable bureaucratic institutions.

28. Coffman, 328–33; Adams, 25–28, 64–72; William A. Dobak and Thomas D. Phillips, *The Black Regulars, 1866–1898* (Norman: University of Oklahoma Press, 2001), 3–24.

29. Coffman, 215–34, 265, 278–79, 305–9, 336–37, 340–46, 350–57; Sherry L. Smith, *Sagebrush Soldier: Private William Earl Smith's View of the Sioux War of 1876*, ed. William Earl Smith (Norman: University of Oklahoma Press, 1989), 7–8, 22–23, 78–86, 106–18; Don Rickey, *Forty Miles a Day on Beans and Hay: The Enlisted Soldier Fighting the Indian Wars* (Norman: University of Oklahoma Press, 1963), 17–32; Adams, 18–20, 38–46, 48–64, 156–57.

I

The weakness of existing federal institutions in the West, the inordinate dependence on the army for basic tasks of governance, and eruption of violence on the Great Plains would have mattered less if Congress had not so greatly expanded the government's ambitions in the West by passing some of the most consequential legislation in American history. In the space of a few years during the Civil War, Congress restructured both the methods and the pace of American expansion. The Pacific Railway Acts (1862, 1864) and other land grant legislation that followed, the Morrill Act (1862), and the Homestead Act (1862), respectively sought to create basic infrastructure over roughly two-thirds of the nation's territory, establish a public university system, and provide free farms for anyone—man or woman, citizen or immigrant eligible for citizenship—who was willing to work the land for five years to gain title. Although most of the elements in these acts had been proposed before, their combination and successful passage was revolutionary. The government abandoned the lingering constraints on American expansion and subsidized the rapid occupation of the remainder of the continent by American farmers, miners, and businesspeople.

Railroad land grants were central to this new dispensation. Deeply in debt and fearing the loss of California and other Western territories to the Confederacy, Congress sought to use land to secure capital to build railroads they thought necessary to hold the West for the Union. It was an audacious gamble, an attempt to use largely unceded Indian lands to subsidize the railroads that would expedite the conquest of Indians while simultaneously spurring the development of Indian homelands by Americans. It spawned Indian treaties and conflicts with the Indians that otherwise could have been postponed.

Congress resorted to taxless finance because it had few other choices if it wanted to build transcontinental railroads in the 1860s. Private capital was unwilling to build them because for those seeking a profit from selling transportation the scheme was mad. So how else could a country that was burdened with war debt and so near insolvency that it was precipitously dismantling its army and endangering Reconstruction in the South embark on a project that demanded large federal subsidies to succeed? By using land grants and federal credit, the promoters of the railroad could secure the necessary capital at no ultimate cost to the taxpayer or the government beyond the price of acquiring the land from the Indians. Taxless finance was the equivalent of the free lunch that nineteenth-century saloons served to attract customers; what the government gave with one hand, it intended to recoup with the other. Just as the price of the lunch was folded into the cost of the drinks that customers bought, so too the cost of the gift to the railroads would be folded into the ultimate cost of the remaining land.

To understand how taxless finance was supposed to work, imagine a railroad line as the crease in a black-and-red checkerboard. Each of the black squares in the checkerboard corresponded to a section of public land a mile square. The government gave these sections to the railroad company, while each of the red squares remained part of the public domain and available to settlers. For the original Pacific Railway, as the combination of the Union Pacific from Omaha to Sacramento was called, this checkerboard extended ten miles on each side of the tracks. Land grants to other roads stretched even further out from the tracks. The government, however, doubled the price of the red squares from $1.25 – the base rate – to $2.50 per acre. On paper, the government had lost nothing through subsidies to the railroad; the country had gained railroads, and the railroads, by quickly selling off the checkerboard's black squares, as required in the acts, would promote settlement and raise money to pay back the loans necessary to build the road. Even as formidable a critic as Henry George, eventually the most famous reformer in the nation, initially regarded the logic behind the land grants as "plausible and ably urged."[30]

Congress was taken with this system, and railroad promoters seeking subsidies lobbied avidly for it. To get aid, railroads gave in return; the promoters were free with stocks and bonds in Washington. Congressmen proved much more likely to see the value of those railroads they had a stake in. Oakes Ames, both a congressman from Massachusetts and a director of the Union Pacific, brushed aside the qualms of colleagues as he proffered shares in the Crédit Mobilier, the construction and finance company of the Union Pacific, which was certain to make money no matter what happened to the railroad. "There is no law nor reason," he declared, "legal or moral why a member of Congress should not own stock in a road any more than why he should not own a sheep when the price of wool is to be affected by tariff." Ames's choice of investments was better than his choice of analogies. Just as there were rather transparent reasons a member of Congress should not accept an offer to buy a flock of sheep at a discount and then vote to impose a tariff on wool, there were reasons congressmen

30. For survey, Hildegard Binder Johnson, *Order Upon the Land: The U.S. Rectangular Land Survey and the Upper Mississippi Country* (New York: Oxford University Press, 1976); Henry George, *Our Land and Land Policy*, Complete Works of Henry George (New York: Doubleday, Page and Company, 1904, orig. ed. 1871), 8: 24.

should not accept an offer to acquire stock in a corporation whose profit-ability depended on the legislation that came before them.[31]

Between 1862 and 1872 Congress gave individual railroads gifts the size of small and medium states. The federal grant to the Union Pacific roughly equaled the acreage of New Hampshire and New Jersey combined. The main line of the Central Pacific got slightly more land than there was in Maryland. The Kansas Pacific, one of the branches connecting with the Union Pacific trunk, had to settle for the equivalent of Vermont and Rhode Island. The Northern Pacific received the equivalent of New England. In all, the land grant railroads east and west of the Mississippi received 131,230,358 acres from the United States. If all these federal land grants had been concentrated into a single state, think of it as "Railroadiana," it would have ranked third, behind Alaska and Texas, in size. The railroads also received state land grants totaling 44,224,175 acres, or an area roughly the size of Missouri, with 33 million acres alone coming from Texas, whose lands were not part of the federal public domain. Finally, cities and towns gave the railroads valuable lands for depots and yards as well as other subsidies.[32]

The strongest indication that the logic of taxless finance might be flawed was the refusal of experienced railroad men, who looked to make a profit on the sale of transportation, to undertake the transcontinentals even with the subsidies. They left the Pacific Railway to storekeepers, such as the Big Four who undertook the Central Pacific, and speculators. The owners of the Union Pacific, Central Pacific, and Kansas Pacific hoped to make a killing not by running railroads but by gathering subsidies, insider construction contracts, and financial manipulation.[33]

Serious building began only at the end the war. Of the numerous transcontinentals subsidized by Congress, only the Pacific Railway actually extended its lines to the Pacific Coast in the 1860s and 1870s. That it succeeded where other transcontinentals failed had less to do with the skill of its managers than with a second subsidy that only a few railroads received. The government loaned the Pacific Railway U.S. bonds, whose interest the government would pay until the bonds came due and whose principal the government guaranteed. By selling these bonds, rather than their own far riskier bonds, to start construction, these roads operated on state credit.

31. Richard White, *Railroaded: The Transcontinentals and the Making of Modern America* (New York: Norton, 2011), 62–66.

32. I have borrowed this from White, *Railroaded*, 24–25; "Public Aids to Transportation: Volume II: Aids to Railroads and Related Subjects" (Washington, DC: U.S. GPO, 1938), table 13, 29, 111; "Report of the Auditor of Railroad Accounts, House Ex. Doc. 1, 46th Congress, 2nd Session" (1911); ibid., table 13, 113–15.

33. White, *Railroaded*, 1–38.

The grant inadvertently provided a bonus. The legislation was so badly written that the railroads had to pay only simple rather than compound interest, and they did not have pay back either interest or principal for thirty years. To sweeten the deal further, the government took merely a second mortgage, which gave private investors who bought the first issue of the railroads' own bonds priority in collecting the money owed them.[34]

Railroad land grants and loans of federal credit were simply the first layer in a cake of subsidies to induce Western settlement. The 1862 Homestead Act provided the opportunity for farmers to claim 160 acres of land on the public domain. If a settler worked the claim for five years, he or she would pay only a small fee to gain title. As one congressional advocate put it, the act was suitable reward for "the soldiers of peace—that grand army of the sons of toil, whose lives from the cradle to the grave are at constant warfare with the elements, with the unrelenting obstacles of nature and the merciless barbarities of savage life."[35]

Giving land to both corporations and settlers might seem to make an oddly layered cake since land given to corporations could not go directly to homesteaders. Congress, however, reasoned that Western lands had little value without the access to markets provided by railroads. And Congress believed that there would be plenty of land left for homesteading outside the railroad checkerboard. In 1867 the public domain contained 1.145 billion acres. Subtracting the railroad land grants (125 million acres), the lands granted or eventually granted to states (140 million acres), and eventual Indian reservations (175 million acres) still left 705 million acres of land for homesteaders.[36]

Land seemed so abundant because Congress ignored both a popular early nineteenth-century myth about the West that was already in decline— the Great American Desert—and the environmental reality that had helped prop up the myth: aridity. Over much of the West there was not enough dependable rainfall to sustain agriculture without irrigation. The 100th meridian forms an invisible north-south line that roughly divides the lands to the east, on which crops can usually be grown without irrigation, from

34. White, *Railroaded*, 22–23.
35. Benjamin Horace Hibbard, *A History of the Public Land Policies* (Madison: University of Wisconsin Press, 1965), 327–33, 383–85; "The Homestead Act, Free Land Policy in Operaton, 1862–1935," in Paul W. Gates, *The Jeffersonian Dream: Studies in the History of American Land Policy and Development*, ed. Allan G. Bogue and Margaret Beattie Bogue (Albuquerque: University of New Mexico Press, 1996), 40–43.
36. Paul Wallace Gates, "The Homestead Law in an Incongruous Land System," *American Historical Review* 41, no. 4 (1936); Paul W. Gates, *History of Public Land Law Development* (Washington, DC: [for sale by the Superintendent of Documents, U.S. GPO], 1968), 395–99.

those on the west, which require irrigation. The line is only a rough one because the climate on the Great Plains is cyclical; periods of drought and years of adequate rainfall alternate unpredictably. Staying east of the 100th meridian did not entirely eliminate danger. Between the 98th and 100th meridians, agriculture was risky but usually successful.

Congress acted as if fertile prairies, arid plains, and scorching deserts were all the same. The same land laws, the same survey grid, and the same set of subsidies extended across the public domain from the Mississippi to the Pacific, no matter the value of the land. In imposing a homogeneous grid on a varied landscape, Congress created a set of fundamentally spatial problems that would come back to haunt the country.

Congress did eventually adjust, but in a way that made things worse. The Homestead Act proved relatively useless in the semi-arid region beyond the 100th meridian, but lawmakers passed additional legislation— the Timber Culture Act (1873) and the Desert Land Act (1877)—to supplement it. Both embodied dreams of environmental transformation, and both enabled considerable fraud. The Timber Culture Act imagined turning patches of the Great Plains into forest and promised 160 acres to anyone planting and maintaining 40 acres of trees in the "western prairies." An 1878 amendment reduced the acres to be planted to 10. The act might better have been called the Fictitious Forest Act. Most of those who planted trees saw them die, and speculators did not bother to plant at all. They claimed to have planted trees in order to hold the land until they could force an actual settler to purchase a relinquishment. Dead trees and trees never planted amounted to the same thing in the end. The General Land Office (GLO) reported large areas with many Timber Culture claims and no trees. The government granted two million acres under the act in Kansas, Nebraska, and South Dakota.[37]

The land system proved dysfunctional and often corrupt. It granted land to those who did not need it and did not develop it, while denying it to many of those who did need it, but that was not the intent. In the late 1860s the various pieces of legislation seemed to fit together like parts of a jigsaw puzzle. Each would complement others and create a harmonious whole. The key pieces depended on the railroads building quickly, expeditiously disposing of their land grants at low cost, and having the General Land Office efficiently administer the resulting flood of transactions.

37. Donald Worster, A River Running West: The Life of John Wesley Powell (New York: Oxford University Press, 2001), 339; Hibbard, 414–20.

II

No pieces in the Western puzzle were more important than the railroads, but the railroads faced conditions that varied widely across the West. The Middle Border, the arid interior, and the Pacific Coast differed in physical conditions and in Indian resistance, and the railroads in each served different functions. The so-called transcontinentals (which were not true transcontinentals since their termini were usually on the Missouri River) had tracks in all three regions, but in many respects they functioned as separate though connected railroads rather than a single line. The St. Louis and Chicago roads of the Middle Border, which linked those cities to the lands east of the 100th meridian, formed the first and most powerful system. The roads along the Pacific Coast constituted a second system. The trunk line of the Pacific Railway that ran between California and the 100th meridian was the third system, which later transcontinentals paralleled and amplified. This third system created the weak link.

In the Middle Border whites already heavily outnumbered Indians. Both settlers and railroads desired Indian lands, and the battle between them created bitter political conflicts to which the Indians became mere bystanders. The corruption of the Lincoln, Johnson, and Grant administrations put the tribes in an impossible position. During the Civil War, Sen. Samuel Pomeroy of Kansas, who provided the inspiration for Senator Dilworthy, "the golden tongued statesman," of Mark Twain's co-authored novel *The Gilded Age*, perfected the device of using Indian treaties to give Indian lands directly to railroads at bargain prices. The epitome of the technique came when James Joy, who acquired the Leavenworth, Lawrence, and Galveston Railroad in 1869, tried to push through Congress an 1868 treaty with the Osage in Kansas that granted the railroad eight million acres of Osage land for twenty cents an acre, nothing down. This treaty came before Congress amidst huge public uproar in 1871.[38]

White settlers were outraged; they had squatted on the Osage Reservation in the expectation the Indians would be evicted and the land would be theirs. They were right about the eviction. What the squatters did not expect was to have to pay Joy for the land they had seized from the Indians. Among the squatters was the Ingalls family, whose residence in Kansas from 1869 to 1871 inspired Laura Ingalls Wilder's *Little House on the*

---

38. H. Craig Miner and William E. Unrau, *The End of Indian Kansas: A Study of Cultural Revolution, 1854–1871* (Lawrence: Regents Press of Kansas, 1978), 47–48, 116–19, 121–32; Paul W. Gates, *Fifty Million Acres: Conflicts over Kansas Land Policy, 1854–1890* (New York: Atherton Press, 1966), 137–39, 153–93; Mark Twain and Charles Dudley Warner, *The Gilded Age: A Tale of to-Day*, 2 vols. (New York: Harper & Brothers, 1915, orig. ed. 1873), 1: 198.

Prairie. That the Ingalls family was squatting, illegally taking Indian land, was not featured in the *Little House* books.[39]

Barring overbuilding, railroads east of the 100th meridian would not lack for traffic. The settlement of the Middle Border formed one of the clearest American successes of the 1860s and 1870s, and the railroads were central to it. In 1873 the directors of the Burlington and Missouri claimed that without the B&M the land along its route would have "remained almost an entirely unoccupied territory." This seemed railroad hyperbole, but it was largely true. Railroads were necessary to the settlement of the region; except for lands along the Mississippi and Missouri Rivers, there was no other way to get crops to market.[40]

Most of the railroads, both the transcontinentals and those lines running into Chicago and St. Louis, that actually completed their lines—a major caveat—disposed of their land east of the 100th meridian as the act required. Not only did the law require that they do so, but the railroads needed revenue from land sales and traffic to pay interest on their bonds. Rapid settlement was in the railroads' best interest since all the western railroads were freight roads hauling bulk commodities: wheat, lumber, coal, corn, and livestock. The settlers would produce the grain and livestock and consume the coal and lumber as well as manufactured goods that the railroads carried west. The so-called Chicago Roads—the Burlington system, the Rock Island, the Chicago and Northwestern, and others—became the most powerful in the West. They connected in Chicago with the great eastern trunk lines, the New York Central, the Pennsylvania Railroad, and the Baltimore and Ohio.[41]

To ensure settlement, the Burlington, the Kansas Pacific, and others running through Iowa, Kansas, and Nebraska quickly created publicity bureaus to attract settlers. They subsidized newspapermen to write stories boosting the areas through which they ran. They advertised in Europe as

39. Frances W. Kaye, "Little Squatter on the Osage Diminished Reserve: Reading Laura Ingalls Wilder's Kansas Indians," *Great Plains Quarterly* 23, no. 2 (Spring 2000), 123–40; Penny T. Linsenmayer, "A Study of Laura Ingalls Wilder's *Little House on the Prairie*," *Kansas History* 24 (Autumn 2001), 169–85.

40. David M. Emmons, *Garden in the Grasslands: Boomer Literature of the Central Great Plains* (Lincoln: University of Nebraska Press, 1971), 25–46; James B. Hedges, "The Colonization Work of the Northern Pacific Railroad," *Mississippi Valley Historical Review* 13, no. 3 (1926), 311–42; Richard C. Overton, *Burlington West: A Colonization History of the Burlington Railroad* (Cambridge, MA: Harvard University Press, 1941), 388, 455; Gilbert Courtland Fite, *The Farmers' Frontier, 1865–1900* (New York: Holt, Rinehart and Winston, 1966), 28–33.

41. William Cronon, *Nature's Metropolis: Chicago and the Great West* (New York: Norton, 1991), 83–93; White, *Railroaded*, 158–59; Scott Nelson, *A Nation of Deadbeats: An Uncommon History of America's Financial Disasters* (New York: Knopf, 2012), 157.

well as the United States. The Kansas Pacific printed circulars and book-lets in Swedish, German, Danish, Welsh, Italian, and other languages. The efforts of these roads complemented those of land bureaus estab-lished by the states. The railroads charged more for their land than did the government, but the railroads, unlike the government, allowed settlers to buy on credit and provided excursion tours so they could view their poten-tial new homes.[42]

Following the channels created by the railroads, migrants moved west, hewing roughly to the line of latitude on which they began their journey. In the 1860s, northern New England, New York, Pennsylvania, and Ohio all had more emigration than immigration, with Ohio and New York being the biggest net losers. For the rest of the century every state east of the Mississippi had more emigration than immigration, as did Utah, Nevada, Louisiana, Missouri, and Iowa. Kansas, Iowa, and Missouri received the most immigrants. Iowa, the most dynamic state, held the anomalous position of having slightly more emigrants than im-migrants while still ranking third among the states with the most people moving in.[43]

The problem with the government's subsidies to railroads in the Middle Border was that they were unnecessary. Experienced railroad men saw that freight railroads could yield a profit with or without subsi-dies; subsidies were a windfall to induce them to build railroads that they would have built anyway. To get the land, they built more quickly. The best evidence for this is South Dakota, which, by historical accident, was the only state in the Middle Border not to get substantial land grant rail-roads. Nevertheless by the 1880s it had a railroad network as dense as and more efficient than those of neighboring states. There was no need to subsidize railroads that would have been built, albeit more slowly, with-out subsidies.[44]

If the land grants were not necessary to secure railroads in the Middle Border, then their main effect was to lessen the amount of land available for homesteading. Taxless finance forced farmers to pay for land they would have otherwise gotten for free. Those who did homestead had to take less desirable land further away from the railroad lines or take 80

42. Emmons, 27–30, 104–24; Allan G. Bogue, "An Agricultural Empire," in *The Oxford History of the American West*, ed. Clyde A. Milner, Carol A. O'Connor, and Martha A. Sandweiss (New York: Oxford University Press, 1994), 285–87; Walter T. K. Nugent, *Into the West: The Story of Its People* (New York: Knopf, 1999), 69.

43. Fred A. Shannon, *The Farmer's Last Frontier: Agriculture, 1860–1897* (New York: Harper and Row, 1968, orig. ed. 1945), 38–39.

44. John Hudson, "Two Dakota Homestead Frontiers," *Annals of the Association of American Geographers* 63, no. 4 (1973): 448; White, *Railroaded*, 485–90.

rather than 160 acres in the government land available in the checkerboard. There were other consequences; the rapid settlement stimulated by railroads led to immense amounts of grain and livestock that glutted markets and drove down prices, leading to an agricultural crisis that sporadically plagued farmers for most of the rest of the century. Finally, the withdrawal of land until railroads determined their final route frustrated settlers seeking title, and the rush of settlers into the West overwhelmed the easily overwhelmed General Land Office.

The situation along the Pacific Coast was both similar, in that railroads served a metropolitan center, in this case San Francisco, and different, in that they largely served as feeders for ocean commerce. The Central Pacific and, later the Southern Pacific, were profitable railroads so long as they ferried traffic in and out of San Francisco and other ports on San Francisco Bay. Like the roads on the Middle Border, they certainly profited by the subsidies, but their monopoly over traffic in California until the 1880s made the West Coast lines of the Big Four (who preferred to call themselves "the Associates") lucrative as long as they remained within California. There was no reason for the federal government to subsidize a system that became a hated monopoly and, because of their land grants, controlled land as well as traffic.[45]

The third part of the railroad system was the long stretch between the 100th meridian and the Pacific Coast. This stretch of railroad was instrumental in repositioning the army to the West, in creating the Peace Commission, and in other expansions of federal activity. It deeply influenced events, but it had lost its original rationale before it was ever built. With the Confederacy defeated, there was no longer any danger of California leaving the Union. Nor with the Suez Canal, under construction half a world away, was there any hope of capturing the China trade. Building railroads through remote mountains, immense deserts, and arid plains where there was precious little traffic demanded new justifications.

Indians provided part of the new rationale. In 1867 General Sherman proclaimed the Pacific Railway "the solution of the Indian question." Railroad officials formed a hallelujah chorus. As Grenville Dodge of the Union Pacific later wrote, "Experience proves the Railroad line through Indian Territory a Fortress as well as a highway." That there might be no need to fight the Indians if railroads were not being built into their country went unremarked. The wars railroads helped provoke became justification for their construction.[46]

45. White, *Railroaded*, 162–69.
46. Hutton, 41; White, *Railroaded*, xxiii.

Developing the interior of the continent, always a component of the plan, now took pride of place as an economic rationale for the transcontinentals. The question was, What would railroads carry in the vast expanse between the 100th meridian and the Pacific Coast?

Clarence King recognized an opportunity this question presented. Only twenty-five years old in 1867, but possessed of "supreme audacity," he lobbied for, and obtained, the command of a federal survey to explore the 40th Parallel between the Rockies and the Sierras and catalog the mineral resources along the route of the Pacific Railway. Knowledge became a federal production, and the point of knowledge was development. King might have been the most complicated man in America. Secretive, and eventually leading a double life, he was also paradoxically a genius at self-promotion. While working on the California Geological Survey, he had written sketches of life in the Sierras that he sent to William Dean Howells's *Atlantic Monthly*; they were published as *Mountaineering in California* in 1872. The book remains a classic of scientific adventure.[47]

King's civilian survey formed a small step in the development of the Western bureaucracies that made the West the kindergarten of the American state. It gave the government an administrative capacity that extended beyond the army. The Army Corps of Topographical Engineers had been critical to both the American exploration of the West and the creation of an initial infrastructure of crude roads. Lt. George Wheeler tried to recapture the army's antebellum domination of exploration, but King and other civilian surveys proved formidable competitors. The West proved not to be big enough for both the civilian surveys and the army. In the summer of 1873 surveyors from Wheeler's command and Ferdinand Hayden's Geological Survey met on remote mountain peaks around the headwaters of the Arkansas, duplicating each other's work.[48]

King, Hayden, and John Wesley Powell hitched their careers to the rise of federal power. Along with Powell, King became, as oxymoronic as it may sound, the era's first charismatic bureaucrat. Working first with the California Geological Survey, he climbed mountains and exposed diamond hoaxes. Powell, the reserved scientific amateur in contrast to King's flamboyant man of science, more than matched him in adventure and

47. Martha A. Sandweiss, *Passing Strange: A Gilded Age Tale of Love and Deception across the Color Line* (New York: Penguin Press, 2009), 47–70; William H. Goetzmann, *Exploration and Empire: The Explorer and the Scientist in the Winning of the American West* (New York: Knopf, 1966), 358–89, 435–66; Clarence King, *Mountaineering in the Sierra Nevada* (New York: Scribner's, 1911); Patricia O'Toole, *The Five of Hearts: An Intimate Portrait of Henry Adams and His Friends, 1880–1918* (New York: C. N. Potter, 1990), 33.

48. White, *"It's Your Misfortune and None of My Own,"* 130–35; Goetzmann, 467, 477–88.

attracting the attention of the press. And he outlasted him. The one-armed Union veteran successfully ran the Colorado River through the Grand Canyon in 1869. Ultimately, he would become the most influential federal bureaucrat in the West.[49]

The geological surveys were both a way to justify the railroads and a gift to private development; Congress gave a second gift to miners that was nearly as valuable as the land it gave to railroads. The Land Ordinance of 1785 had reserved "one third part of all gold, silver, lead and copper mines" for the public, and later legislation reserved coal lands and waterpower sites. For all practical purposes, however, the government had abandoned its original claims before the Civil War. During the California Gold Rush miners created an extralegal code, which became law in the Mining Act of 1872. It granted open access for exploration on public lands and the exclusive right to mine a discovery. The law was democratic in that claims were cheap—$2.50 to $5.00 an acre—and limited in size, and claimants could retain their claims only as long as they worked them. Controversies over competing claims, however, made them expensive and kept lawyers busy for the rest of the century and beyond. Mining companies could and would extract hundreds of millions of dollars of minerals with enormous environmental consequences and no compensation to the public, which was left bearing the cost when things went badly.[50]

In California hydraulic mining, which washed away the sides of mountains to get at the underlying gold, sluiced so much debris into the rivers that it raised the riverbeds above adjoining farmlands. In floods the debris settled on fields and orchards, creating the rock piles that scar the Sacramento Valley to this day. Without expensive dredging, the rivers became unnavigable. The debris eventually made its way into San Francisco Bay, smothering oyster beds and harming fisheries. Not until 1884 did the courts ban the dumping of hydraulic mining wastes in the rivers.[51]

49. Worster, 201–96; Goetzmann, 358–89.
50. Carl J. Mayer, "The 1872 Mining Law: Historical Origins of the Discovery Rule," *University of Chicago Law Review* 53, no. 2 (1986): 624–28; Rodman W. Paul, *Mining Frontiers of the Far West, 1848–1880* (New York: Holt, Rinehart and Winston, 1963), 172–75.
51. Paul A. David and Gavin Wright, "Increasing Returns and the Genesis of American Resource Abundance," *Industrial and Corporate Change* 6, no. 2 (1997): 217–20; Robert Lloyd Kelley, *Gold Vs. Grain, the Hydraulic Mining Controversy in California's Sacramento Valley: A Chapter in the Decline of the Concept of Laissez Faire* (Glendale, CA: A. H. Clark, 1959); Andrew C. Isenberg, *Mining California: An Ecological History* (New York: Hill and Wang, 2005), 17–53.

In the arid interior Indians resisted expansion of the railroads. The federal government judged the Pacific Railway to be critical for American policy, but other roads and trails could be sacrificed. Peace commissioners met the northern plains tribes at Fort Laramie in the spring of 1868, although the Lakotas fighting under Red Cloud to close the Bozeman Trail did not come to the council. Those Lakotas present agreed to withdraw from the area south of the Platte River and to cease attacks on the railroads and their construction crews. In return, they were to receive annuities and services, including education. The Americans, for their part, agreed to abandon the Bozeman Trail and the forts that guarded it. The sacrifice was a small one. The new transcontinental railroad would allow the United States to construct a new trail to the Montana gold fields along the west side of the Big Horn Mountains. Red Cloud signed only after the army burned its forts north of Fort Fetterman in the summer of 1868.[52]

The treaty also represented a compromise between the intentions of the reformers to educate, acculturate, confine, and pacify the Lakotas, and the Lakotas' desire to preserve their northern buffalo grounds from penetration by the Americans. In addition to paying the Indians annuities and granting them services, the commissioners recognized the country north of the Platte and east of the Big Horn Mountains as unceded Indian country. The United States prohibited any white person from settling, occupying, or even passing through the region without the consent of the Indians. At the same time, however, the treaty provided for the eventual subdivision of the reserved land into individual holdings and the transformation of the Lakotas into Christian farmers, something most of them had no intention of becoming. American violations of the treaty would eventually yield more war and, still later, spawn litigation that continues into the twenty-first century.[53]

The Americans secured treaties, but they did not secure peace. They simply changed the location of the fighting. Warfare became most intense between the Platte River and the Arkansas River, which the commissioners regarded as an American corridor through which the railroads could build and migrants could move. Fighting also continued in Texas. The Comanches interpreted the Medicine Lodge Treaty as a validation of their claims in exchange for rights of passage granted to Americans but

---

52. Prucha, *The Great Father*, l: 493–94.
53. Ibid., 493–95; Charles J. Kappler, compiler and ed., "Treaty with the Sioux, Brule, Oglala, Miniconjou, Yanktonai, Hunkpapa, Blackfeet, Cuthead, Sans Acrs, and Santee—and Arapaho, 1868, Apr. 29, 1868. | 15 Stats., 635. | Ratified, Feb. 16, 1869. | Proclaimed, Feb. 24, 1869, in Indian Affairs: Laws and Treaties, Vol. II, Treaties" (Washington, DC: U.S. GPO, 1904), 998–1007.

not Texans. The Comanche attacks that prompted Governor Throckmorton's rage were not checked by the treaty.[54]

How little the treaties had done to curb the violence became apparent in August 1868 when a Cheyenne, Arapaho, and Lakota war party riding against the Pawnees turned instead against American settlers on the Saline and Solomon rivers in Kansas. They killed fifteen men and raped five women. Sheridan, now in command on the southern Great Plains, acted predictably. His troops' goal, in the words of his commander, General Sherman, was to ensure that "these Indians, the enemies of our race and our civilization, shall not be able to begin and carry out their barbarous warfare." In the flash of an eye, with the Peace Commission barely departed, the policy of peace gave way to racial war.[55]

Military officers could sound bloodthirsty, but it is a mistake to equate them with the Indian haters who certainly did exist in the West. Sherman was no friend of the Indians despite being named after Tecumseh, the great Shawnee leader. He became a member of the Peace Commission, but he never believed that the treaties would yield peace; yet even he protested American policy. "The poor Indians are starving," he said. "We kill them if they attempt to hunt and if they keep within the Reservation, they starve." Other generals would be even more sympathetic to the Indians they fought, and many high-ranking regular army officers were at best ambivalent about their role in smashing Indian resistance. Gen. George Crook regarded the Indians as a wronged people, blaming "greed and avarice on the part of the whites," for the Indian wars, and in this he echoed Gen. John M. Schofield's denunciation of government Indian policy as "greed and cruelty." Even Sheridan thought that "we took away their country and their means of support, broke up their mode of living, their habits of life, introduced disease and decay among them, and it was for this and against this they made war. Could any one expect less?"[56]

In the summer of 1868, the army once more proved no match for mobile Plains warriors, who inflicted significant damage on American settlers, killing 110 people. When the army managed to confront and fight them, the army usually lost. Maj. Frank North's Pawnee Scouts—Pawnees who fought as a separate army unit—proved more effective.[57]

54. Hämäläinen, 322–24.
55. West, *The Contested Plains*, 311; Hutton, 38.
56. Adams, 16–17; Prucha, *The Great Father*, 489–90; Hutton, 33–35, 180–82; David Haward Bain, *Empire Express: Building the First Transcontinental Railroad* (New York: Viking, 1999), 349–52; Coffman, 255–56; Richard N. Ellis, "The Humanitarian Generals," *Western Historical Quarterly* 3, no. 2 (April 1972): 169–78.
57. West, *The Contested Plains*, 310–12; Hutton, 35–51; Mark Van de Logt, *War Party in Blue: Pawnee Scouts in the U.S. Army* (Norman: University of Oklahoma Press, 2010), 80–109.

What the army could not accomplish on the open plains in the summer, it could achieve in the winter when the Indians were confined to the river valleys for shelter and to feed their horse herds. Sheridan deployed the Seventh Cavalry under the command of Custer, who had been reinstated. Custer's destination was the Washita River in Indian Territory. The Cheyenne peace chiefs Big Mouth and Black Kettle, whose band had been the victims at Sand Creek, asked for peace, but they were told that only Sheridan could grant it. Warriors from their bands had been raiding, and Sheridan was no longer interested in negotiating. His instructions to Custer were to find the Cheyennes and their allies along the Washita River, "to destroy their villages and ponies; to kill or hang all warriors, and bring back all women and children." Sheridan was not particular about which Cheyennes Custer attacked.[58]

Custer followed the trail of a Cheyenne raiding party to the Washita. There were certainly raiders in Black Kettle's camp, but Black Kettle had long been the leading advocate of peace among the Cheyennes. The Seventh Cavalry attacked at dawn on November 27, 1868. Most of the village was sleeping. One of Black Kettle's last acts was to fire his rifle into the air to wake his people. He then caught one of his horses, mounted it with his wife, and tried to escape the onrushing soldiers. The troopers shot him and his wife down in the middle of the river, where they died.

The soldiers killed about a dozen warriors along with twenty or more women and children at the Washita. Many more were wounded. Custer lost twenty men, including an entire detachment that was cut off as Kiowas, Arapahos, and Cheyenne warriors swarmed in from villages down river—villages a more adroit or cautious commander would have known were there. Custer, never one to downplay his success, exaggerated the number of warriors who died and reduced the number of women and children. He destroyed the lodges and supplies that the Cheyennes would need for the winter. He methodically shot the village horse herd. He took captive more than fifty women and children. When he rejoined Sheridan, Custer and other army officers arranged to have the youngest and prettiest captive women brought to their tents at night.[59]

Custer was already famous for his exploits during the Civil War, but his attack at the Washita made his reputation as an Indian fighter. An attack on a sleeping village, the killing of twenty women and children and a handful of warriors would seem a pretty slim basis on which to build a

58. Hutton, 56–63.
59. Jerome A. Greene, *Washita: The U.S. Army and the Southern Cheyennes, 1867–1869* (Norman: University of Oklahoma Press, 2004), 116–38; Chalfant, 513–14; Stiles defends Custer's actions and tactics during the fight, 316–27; Hutton, 60–76.

western military reputation, but reputation in the wake of the Civil War was more about self-promotion than soldiering. Custer was a master of self-promotion. He already had a clear path to follow. Sam Patch, Davy Crockett, and P. T. Barnum had pioneered American celebrity. Custer followed them. He recounted his exploits in the *Galaxy Magazine* between 1872 and 1874, and serialized articles became a book, *My Life on the Plains*.[60]

The dead Cheyennes enhanced Custer's fame, but they also earned him enemies. By targeting Black Kettle and the most peaceful of the Cheyennes, Custer brought back all the memories of Sand Creek and loosed a wave of objections from reformers and Indian Department personnel. Custer's numerous enemies, within and outside the army, attacked him. Sheridan defended him. For such a hard man, Sheridan was remarkably thin-skinned. He bridled at criticism and justified the dead Cheyenne women and children by building on the actual Smoky Hill river raids to conjure up graphic, detailed, and apparently largely invented depictions of innumerable white women repeatedly raped and then murdered. He portrayed Custer as their savior.[61]

The real loss for the Indians at Washita was measured not in the warriors killed, but in the recognition by other bands that they, too, were vulnerable in their winter camps. Continued campaigning by Sheridan's troops did not lead to a climactic battle; it did not have to. No longer safe, the Indians were hungry and cold and had weakened horses. All but a few Kiowas refused to join the Cheyennes and Arapahos in renewed war, and more and more of the southern Plains Indians agreed to move onto the reservations where both rations and troops awaited them.[62]

By summer only the Dog Soldiers under Tall Bull seemed bent on war. They headed north hoping for Lakota and Arapaho allies along the Platte and found a few. Sheridan sent the Fifth Cavalry to pursue them. Their chief scout was William F. Cody, a man who lusted for celebrity as much as George Armstrong Custer and was far smarter. But Pawnee Scouts, not Cody, tracked down the Dog Soldiers and their Lakota allies. The Americans attacked Tall Bull's camp at Summit Springs in northeastern Colorado on July 8, 1869. The Dog Soldiers fought bitterly, bravely, and ultimately hopelessly. They shot the two white women they held captive even as the attacking Americans and Pawnees shot down Cheyenne women and children. Tall Bull died fighting while covering the retreat of

60. Greene, 193; George A. Custer, *My Life on the Plains* (Chicago: Lakeside Press, 1952); Paul E. Johnson, *Sam Patch, the Famous Jumper* (New York: Hill and Wang, 2003), 161–84.
61. Greene, 192–93; Hutton, 95–100.
62. Hutton, 77–114.

his family, after killing his horse and using its body as a shelter. Wolf with Plenty of Hair looped his dog rope around his body, drove in the red stake to which the rope was tied, and prepared to die in place. He fell, his body riddled with bullets, the stake still in the ground. The battle at Summit Springs ended the Dog Soldiers as an effective military force. It also secured the American corridor across the Great Plains. The railroads could proceed with little risk.[63]

The Union Pacific building westward and the Central Pacific eastward joined their tracks at Promontory Summit, Utah, on May 10, 1869. Those completing the railroad self-consciously dramatized the moment. There was first of all the golden spike. Prepared beforehand and unfortunately inscribed with the wrong date, it was ceremonially tapped and then removed. Two engines, one from each railroad, stood nose to nose surrounded by the dignitaries brought to the site for the speeches and celebration. When Leland Stanford, the president of the Central Pacific and ex-governor of California, tapped the final spike, which was wired to the telegraph paralleling the track, it sent a signal east as far as New York and west to Sacramento and San Francisco that triggered celebrations thousands of miles away. As badly built as the road was over large stretches, it was a great technological achievement. Technology had apparently subdued nature, and development could now proceed.[64]

Economically, the completion of the Pacific Railway turned out to be anticlimactic. Completing a railroad was not equivalent to running trains on it, at least successfully, and nature was not so easily subdued. The winters of 1869–70 and 1871–72 shut down large portions of the Central Pacific and Union Pacific for weeks at a time, stranding passengers and goods. The problems on the Central Pacific only encouraged other railroads — the Atlantic and Pacific, the Texas and Pacific, the Northern Pacific — to plunge ahead, confident they had better routes and that lines on a map would translate into parallel lines of iron. They would not arrive for years, if ever; meanwhile, the Pacific Railway hardly proved a boon to the West Coast.

In the late 1860s business interests on the West Coast radiated optimism about the railroads, but Henry George, a printer and radical journalist, had a sense of foreboding. In 1867 J. W. Forney, the well-connected newspaperman who drank with Andrew Johnson the night before he gave his ill-fated inauguration speech in 1864, visited San Francisco. For the most part, he stressed the familiar and recited the pieties of progress. San

---

63. West, *The Contested Plains*, 308–16; Hutton, 110–11; Louis S. Warren, *Buffalo Bill's America: William Cody and the Wild West Show* (New York: Knopf, 2005), 111–13.
64. White, *Railroaded*, 37–38.

Francisco was a progressive American place—a prosperous and substantial city of nearly two hundred thousand, with impressive buildings, good hotels, churches and synagogues, banks, steamship companies, and railroads—that faced out over the Pacific and connected with Asia and Latin America.

At the city's edges, the substantial and the American, however, seemed to melt into the exotic. There was, Forney wrote, "a Chinese city" within San Francisco, which had itself not lost its "pervading Spanish tone." The climate was Mediterranean and "grapes, oranges, figs, and pomegranates of the tropics" grew alongside the more familiar fruits and grains of the North. The city, which would be dominated by Irish and German immigrants for much of the century, had nearly as many students in Catholic schools as public schools, and it had a substantial Jewish population. The ride from the city to the Cliff House, then six miles outside San Francisco on the Pacific, was, Forney wrote, like "a ride into the suburbs of Cairo or Alexandria, in Egypt. All was Oriental—the low houses, the Eastern sand and verdure, the veiled hills in the distance gave the scene a strange glamour hard to define." But when he looked at the four-in-hand driven by William Ralston, the president of the Bank of California and then the richest man in the city, "the delusion was exchanged for the fact that I had an American host, who, like our chief, Colonel Scott," combined "brain-labor" with conviviality and balanced his moneymaking with "works of charity and benevolence." California had the "flowers and the fruits of the tropics" but men like Ralston were "the sturdy growth of the North, who do not lose their vigor by transplantation." J. W. Forney and William Ralston expected that California would only grow more Northern and prosperous with the arrival of the transcontinental railroad in 1869.[65]

Henry George was one of the few skeptics. George loved California. Although a venomous racist where Chinese and African Americans were concerned, he praised the city and state's "cosmopolitanism, a certain freedom and breadth of common thought and feeling, natural to a community made up from so many difference sources, to which every man and woman had been transplanted—all travelers to some extent, and with native angularities of prejudice and habit more or less worn off." The result had been "a feeling of personal independence and equality, a general hopefulness and self-reliance and a certain large-heartedness and open-handedness which were born of the comparative evenness with which property was distributed, the high standard of wages and comfort, and the latent feeling of every one that he might 'make a strike,' and certainly could not be kept down long." Instead of connecting California's

65. "'San Francisco through Eastern Eyes'," *San Francisco Evening Bulletin*, Sep. 19, 1872.

diversity and difference with the exotic, George used them to configure a community whose core values were much like Lincoln's Springfield. The railroad, he feared, would destroy his California.[66]

In 1868 George had published "What the Railroad Will Bring Us" in the *Overland Monthly*. Like Forney, he praised San Francisco's growth and California's possibilities, but overestimated the immediate impact of the transcontinentals. Unlike Ralston, Forney, and other boosters, however, he warned that the benefits of the railroad would be more than offset by the losses Californians would incur. Men like Ralston, who were speculators and "captains of industry," employed men in "gangs" undercutting the "personal independence—the basis of all virtues" that had characterized the state and its people. George feared that the benefits of the railroads would flow to the Ralstons of the world; the losses would be borne by working people. The spawn of California's millionaires would be its numerous and desperate poor.[67]

Neither George's fears nor Ralston's hopes ever fully came to fruition. California and San Francisco grew far more slowly after the arrival of the Pacific Railway than they had before it. The explosive growth California expected the railroad to carry did not arrive on schedule. In 1860 California, with 379,994 people, dwarfed the newer states of the Middle Border in population, although not in the number of farms. It had more than twice the population of Minnesota and three times the population of Kansas. It soon lost that lead. California certainly grew, reaching 1,208,130 people by 1890, but its growth rate and population fell behind its rivals. Kansas was bigger than California by 1880 and had 1,427, 096 people by 1890, when Minnesota, with 1,301,826 people, was also more populous. Minnesota also had more than twice as many farms as California in 1890, while Kansas had three times as many. California at least compared favorably with Nevada, which lost population after the arrival of the railroad. In comparison with the Middle Border, California's economy stagnated.

Shipping goods from the West Coast to Gulf and Eastern ports by steamship and then by railroad across Panama remained far cheaper and often nearly as fast as shipping them by rail. In 1873 Jay Gould of the Union Pacific complained of competition from steamships, saying that it was "outrageous that we have to carry our California business at so low rates." First the Union Pacific and Central Pacific, and later other transcontinentals, paid the Pacific Mail Steamship Company to raise its rates and shrink its fleet in order to maintain traffic on the transcontinental. A government

66. Henry George, "'What the Railroad Will Bring Us'," *Overland Monthly and Out West Magazine* 1, no. 4 (October 1868): 297–306.
67. Ibid.

subsidy for railroads, and another for the Pacific Mail, thus ended with an arrangement to raise the cost of commerce.[68]

The irony of public subsidies to the railroads was that subsidized railroads were most successful where they least needed subsidizing: within the Middle Border and along the Pacific Coast. Chicago and St. Louis anchored the railroads of the Middle Border and received the wheat, corn, and cattle they funneled out of the fat lands of America. San Francisco anchored the Central Pacific and later the Southern Pacific, railroads that poured the wheat of the Central Valley into the ports of San Francisco Bay. These systems were the bookends of the transcontinentals, but commercially neither system really needed to be linked to the other. Little traffic flowed between them, and the traffic from the Mississippi Valley and the East could go more cheaply by water.

The railroad land grants acted as a kind of black hole, drawing in settlers and distorting the rest of the land system. Lands near the railroads were preferable to those farther away and settlers were willing to pay for railroad lands rather than take up free land on the public domain. But this was not their only effect. As the West beyond the 100th meridian failed to develop as rapidly as predicted, the railroad lands there threatened to become a burden to the railroads. They were reluctant to survey the land or take title to it since this would open the land to taxation. About 90 percent of the Central Pacific's land in Nevada and Utah was patented only in the 1890s. By law the subsidized railroads had to sell their land within a few years of completion. East of the 100th meridian this was not a problem, but west of it the railroads would be saved from forfeiting their land grants only by the courts. In *Platt v. Union Pacific Railroad*, the Supreme Court accepted the argument that the railroads mortgaging their lands had disposed of them under the terms of the law.[69]

In 1869 Americans remained hopeful about the West's place in the Greater Reconstruction. Despite all the blunders and misjudgments, the creation of a free labor society in the Middle Border was under way. Elsewhere in the West the process already seemed more dubious, but the larger ideals of free labor and contract freedom and their ultimate result— the republican home—still seemed within the grasp of those who strived.

68. Maury Klein, *Union Pacific* (Garden City, NY: Doubleday, 1987), 314; White, *Railroaded*, 47–48, 165–67.
69. David Maldwyn Ellis, "The Forfeiture of Railroad Land Grants, 1867–1894," *Mississippi Valley Historical Review* 33, no. 1 (1946): 27–60; Leslie E. Decker, *Railroads, Lands, and Politics: The Taxation of the Railroad Land Grants, 1864–1897* (Providence, RI: Brown University Press, 1964), 52–55, 60, 70–116; *Platt v. Union Pacific R. Co.*, 99 US 48, 25 L. Ed. 424 (1879); White, *Railroaded*, 130.

4

Home

In its simplest form the Greater Reconstruction boiled down to Springfield, Illinois. This was as close as any actual place could be to the template that the North planned to use in recasting the South, as well as the West. Springfield and its surrounding farms were the world of Lincoln. Ideologically, this was the North of free labor and contract freedom, with few rich and few poor. Although saturated with immigrants, culturally, it was Protestant, particularly evangelical Protestant. Wage labor was a possible, even likely, stage of life, but it was expected to be a stop on the road to independence and not a permanent condition. Most of all it was the world of homes, with all that the word implied in late nineteenth-century America.

Home was a concept so pervasive that it is easy to dismiss it as a cliché and to miss its particular resonance in this historical moment. In *Uncle Tom's Cabin* Harriet Beecher Stowe conflated home, religion, morality, safety, and freedom. When George escapes slavery and reunites with his wife and child in an abolitionist Quaker home, Stowe wrote:

> This, indeed, was a home—*home*—a word that George had never yet known a meaning for; and a belief in God, and trust in his providence, began to encircle his heart, as, with a golden cloud of protection and confidence, dark, misanthropic, pining; atheistic doubts, and fierce despair melted away before the light of living gospel breathed in living faces, preached by a thousand unconscious acts of love and good will....[1]

Home, in the fullest meaning, links to other concepts—manhood and womanhood—which took shape around it, and to another concept that was disappearing from common use by the end of the century: a competency or competence. Home with these satellite notions provided the frame in which ordinary nineteenth-century Americans understood their

1. Harriet Beecher Stowe, *Uncle Tom's Cabin* (London: John Cassell, Ludgate Hill, 1852), 120.

own lives, the economy, and the national goals of Reconstruction in the South and West.

Home and competence linked to manhood and womanhood because a man had to achieve a competence to support and protect a wife and mother who would reproduce and nurture future citizens. The "wifely wife" and the "motherly mother," in the words of the escaped slave, reformer, and schoolteacher Harriet Jacobs, were as much the mark of the home as the man whose labor sustained it.[2]

The production of homes was the ultimate rationale for the economy, for the nation itself, and for the public policies and the activist government embraced by Republicans. Ultimately the Republic rested on homes; the creation of homes blurred the lines between public and private, and production and reproduction, so that they bled into each other. The Homestead Act underlined the connections between creating homes and economic development, but then so too did the tariff, which Republicans promoted as ensuring high wages, which allowed workingmen to establish and maintain homes. Americans thought it impossible to have too many homes.

In the social conflicts that pitted ex-Confederates against freedmen, workers against employers, whites against Indians, immigrants against the native-born, and sometimes women against men, Americans appealed to home. Home became the most prized ideological ground. Those who seized it held a cultural fortress.

The idea of the home both stimulated and limited individual striving. A successful economy would yield independent men who would protect the homes and families that would reproduce republican citizens. But too much striving became restlessness or greed, which threatened not only a family's home but also other families' homes and associated cultural values of manhood, independence, and citizenship. Wealth needed to be distributed to ensure the maximum number of homes.

In this American world, the rich and the very poor were the dangerous classes because both poverty and excessive wealth threatened homes. What would later be called the American dream was in the years following the Civil War less a desire for riches than for a sum that guaranteed security and the moderate level of prosperity necessary to maintain a home. A prosperous farm represented a competence. For workingmen a wage that could support a family with a reserve to sustain it through hard times constituted that competence. When a person through hard work or good fortune exceeded a competency and possessed enough to support

2. Amy Dru Stanley, *From Bondage to Contract: Wage Labor, Marriage, and the Market in the Age of Slave Emancipation* (Cambridge: Cambridge University Press, 1998), 139.

himself and his family for his lifetime, he very often retired. In 1863 at age twenty-nine Charles Schofield, a successful textile manufacturer in Philadelphia, sold his interest in his firm for $40,000 and "retired with a competency." Schofield considered himself "sufficiently opulent."[3]

Abraham Lincoln had both embraced and symbolized the opportunity, achievement, and progress that a competence represented. In 1860 he had told an audience in New Haven, Connecticut, "I am not ashamed to confess that twenty-five years ago I was a hired laborer, mauling rails, at work on a flat-boat—just what might happen to any poor man's son." But in the free states a man knew that "he can better his condition...there is no such thing as a freeman being fatally fixed for life, in the condition of a hired laborer....The man who labored for another last year, this year labors for himself, and next year he will hire others to labor for him." If a man "continues through life in the condition of the hired laborer, it is not the fault of the system, but because of either a dependent nature which prefers it, or improvidence, folly, or singular misfortune." The "free labor system opens the way for all—gives hope to all, and energy, and progress, and improvement of condition to all." After his death, Lincoln's personal trajectory from log cabin to White House served as the apotheosis of free labor. Anything was possible for those who strived.[4]

Republicans imagined their future constituency in the South and West as strivers in the mold of Lincoln and Schofield. The task, the *Nation* declared after Appomattox, was to transform the South in the image of the North, "to renew [its] soil, to raise unheard of crops, to clear the forest and drain the swamp, to impress the water-power into service, to set up the cotton-mill alongside of the corn-field, to build highways, to explore mines, and in short to turn the slothful, shiftless Southern world upside down."[5]

In the Midwest the "mug books," commemorative county histories that showed the results of a lifetime of labor in the progress of individual farms from cabins in clearings to whitewashed farmhouses and outbuildings, captured not just the making of farms but also the creation of homes. When P. B. S. Pinchback, once, so it was rumored, a riverboat gambler and very briefly a black governor of Louisiana, and an elected, but never seated, senator and representative, said that all black men required was "a white man's chance," he used a gambler's phrase to express a desire for an

3. Philip Scranton, *Proprietary Capitalism: The Textile Manufacture at Philadelphia, 1800–1885* (Cambridge: Cambridge University Press, 1983), 68–69.
4. James M. McPherson, *Battle Cry of Freedom: The Civil War Era* (New York: Oxford University Press, 1988), 28.
5. Daniel T. Rodgers, *The Work Ethic in Industrial America: 1850–1920*, 2nd ed. (Chicago: University of Chicago Press, 2014), 32.

extension of such American possibilities across the color line. Indians posed more of a challenge, but even though they still held their land communally, Choctaws, Creeks, and Cherokees all contained a striving class whose economic ambitions seemed to mirror those of whites. These commercial farmers and ranchers could seem the incarnation of an assimilated American Indian, at least economically. A reconstructed United States would be a progressive nation of small producers. There would be no hereditary elite and few rich or poor. Competition, in theory, would eliminate both.[6]

Lincoln spoke in a familiar idiom of progress and self-reliance, and the home was both the product and the site for the reproduction of these values. Unless the work of American males produced homes, they were not men. Unless women helped create and control a domestic space, they could not be true women. Without the home, the country could not reproduce republican citizens. Homes sheltered and largely confined girls, who were not encouraged to explore a larger world, and prepared boys for a life of independence that would allow them to support homes of their own. Separated from this larger cultural universe, disputes over politics and the economy made little sense.[7]

The home ordered society, but it also produced a set of American paradoxes. On the one hand, the home redeemed male individualism and independence from selfishness while creating an arena for female independence. Manliness demanded independence because, as the *New York Times* put it in 1879, it prohibited men "under any circumstances from depending on anybody but themselves for the maintenance of their family." This would seem to leave women without responsibility for maintaining home and family; yet when the Civil War had provided the great test of American manhood, men had abandoned the home and left it to their wives to sustain. John Logan, a leading figure in the Grand Army of the Republic, in celebrating Union volunteers who had rushed to the front to protect the nation had stated the paradox: they had left their wives to maintain "that place of Heaven called home." The Civil War showed that women, albeit at considerable cost, could maintain a home without

6. The best collection of Midwestern mug books is at the Newberry Library in Chicago: Peggy Tuck Sinko, "'Mug Books' at the Newberry Library," *Origins* 8, no. 1 (1992): 3–5; "'Senator P. B. S. Pinchback, His Frank Criticism Upon a Late Personal Attack,' February 12, 1876," in *P.B.S. Pinchback Papers, P.S. Clippings* (Washington, DC: Moorland Spingam Research Center, Howard University); Alexandra Harmon, *Rich Indians: Native People and the Problem of Wealth in American History* (Chapel Hill: University of North Carolina Press, 2010), 133–70.

7. Steven Mintz, *Huck's Raft: A History of American Childhood* (Cambridge, MA: Belknap Press of Harvard University Press, 2004), 134–35.

men. After the war women did not *cede* responsibility for the domestic space; they *enlarged* it. The farther women could push the boundaries of the domestic sphere into public life after the war, the greater their own influence.[8]

To protect the home, some women stepped outside the home. By the 1880s women, particularly among the new urban middling classes, expanded the reform and benevolent associations of the antebellum era such as the Young Women's Christian Association and Protestant foreign and home missionary societies and then created a growing number of secular reform organizations. Virtually all of these associations, in the words of historian Anne Firor Scott, clung to the idea of a "woman as a moral being whose special responsibility was to bring the principles of a well-run Christian home into community life." The title of the home mission magazine was revealingly *Our Homes*, and Frances Willard made "home protection" the great goal of the Woman's Christian Temperance Union. Such high-minded concern with home had definite class accents that in middle-class women's clubs could descend into laments over the "servant problem," yet even these centered on the home.[9]

The majority of women embraced the home and saw it as a source of advantage, but a minority regarded it—insofar as it was based on the marriage contract—as a source of fundamental inequality. The great symbol of such inequality was the legal doctrine of coverture, under which the wife lost her legal identity with marriage. In a society supposedly devoted to free labor, coverture merged the labor of the wife with the person of her husband and deprived her of the ability to make any contract after agreeing to the marriage contract. Elizabeth Cady Stanton posed the challenge directly in 1868: "If the contract be equal, whence come the terms 'marital power,' 'marital rights,' obedience and restraint,' dominion and control'? According to man's idea, as set forth in his creeds and codes, marriage is a condition of slavery." Stanton went to the heart of the paradox of the republican home. The home—the cultural, social, and economic basis of American freedom and democracy—was, she said, based on slavery and the abrogation of contract freedom. The home depended on marriage, and marriage demanded the legal subordination of women. But any attack on the subordination of women in the marriage contract was, by the same logic, an assault on the home, and to escape or at least reduce the paradox,

8. Stuart McConnell, *Glorious Contentment: The Grand Army of the Republic, 1865–1900* (Chapel Hill: University of North Carolina Press, 1992), 136, 220.
9. Anne Firor Scott, *Natural Allies: Women's Associations in American History* (Urbana: University of Illinois Press, 1991), 80–81, 85, 88–90, 111, 114, 121.

mid- and late-nineteenth-century married women's property acts gradually modified and restrained coverture.[10]

I

The expansion of the nation involved the expansion of homes. And since in the decades following the Civil War, the United States remained a predominantly rural nation, the ideal home continued to be the farm home, which combined ideas of a competency, independence, family, and free labor. The Republicans had placed all of this into a single powerful political package with the Homestead Act.

The Homestead Act had its greatest success in the Middle Border. That success, and the social and economic promise of the free labor home, can be summed up in the experience of Henry Ise. Ise was a German immigrant who had enlisted in the Union Army under his given name, Eisenmanger. His captain, who couldn't be bothered to pronounce or spell Eisenmanger, changed it to Ise. After the war, Henry returned to Illinois riding atop a freight car and then moved to Iowa. He worked for four years as a prairie breaker in Iowa, part of the itinerant crews armed with heavy cast iron plows, pulled by at least eight oxen, that cut through and turned the matted grassland. He illustrated how the older patterns of farming and farm making that relied on kin were changing as tenancy and farm labor rose. For Ise, as for Lincoln, this was just a stage in life. He saved enough to buy a farm, but then he lost the wallet containing his savings.[11]

He began again, and in 1871 he decided to homestead in Kansas on the north fork of the Solomon River between the 98th and 99th meridians in country where farming was arduous but possible. In 1872 he returned to eastern Kansas to work for wages and earn the money needed for farm implements and cattle. He also came for a wife. He married Rosa Haag for love, but her labor was as necessary for the success of the farm as his. Together they returned to his homestead in the summer of 1873. Nothing in this combination of homesteading, work, and marriage was unusual. Its end result was a home of the kind memorialized in mug books.[12]

10. Stanley, 3, 176.
11. John Mack Faragher, *Sugar Creek: Life on the Illinois Prairie* (New Haven, CT: Yale University Press, 1986), 96–101; John Ise, with additional material by Von Rothenberger, *Sod and Stubble* (Lawrence: University Press of Kansas, 1996), 8–16.
12. Ise, 8–16.

Republicans had designed the Homestead Act to invite both men and women — except Confederates who had taken up arms against the government — to invest five years of their labor in improving a tract of land, up to 160 acres. The unstated assumption, usually correct, was that the successful development of this tract demanded the labor of both men and women and thus the creation of a home and family. At the end of five years, labor on the land would have created a home, family, a competence, and independence. The Homestead Act created the template that had yielded the Ises their farm.

The resourcefulness, self-reliance, and determination of settler families as celebrated in mug books or in the later Little House books are how Americans have remembered and portrayed western expansion following the Civil War. Taken family by family, the story becomes one of self-reliance, the predicted results of the triumph of contract freedom.

The story was never so simple. The Ises' success was the exception rather than the rule. Hundreds of thousands of families acquired free land through the Homestead Act, but over the course of the act, for every four families that succeeded, six, to one degree or another, failed or bailed, abandoning the land, selling their right to others, or choosing to purchase the claim rather than waiting five years for title.[13]

The success varied over time and space, with success most likely in the lands east of the 100th meridian in the years immediately following the Civil War. In Minnesota, roughly two-thirds of the homestead claims entered in the state between 1863 and 1875 proved successful — a much larger success rate than what homesteaders achieved overall. Kansas was closer to the national average. There 40 percent of the claims filed between 1863 and 1890 on nearly thirty million acres of land under the Homestead Act and the associated Timber Culture Act eventually yielded a free patent. Some of the remaining 60 percent gained farms by using commutation, a legal device that allowed purchase before the five years were up, to gain title to another three million acres. And an unknown, but probably significant, number of farmers realized some gain by selling the rights to their claims and improvements to others before they had "proved up," that is submitted proof of fulfilling the conditions necessary to get title. Homesteaders in Kansas successfully established 94,448 farms, roughly half of the state's farms (but not the farm acreage) by 1890.[14]

13. Todd Arrington, "Final Patents by Decade," National Park Service, "Homesteading by the Numbers: Homestead National Monument," National Park Service. https://www .nps.gov/home/learn/historyculture/bynumbers.htm.
14. Paul W. Gates, *History of Public Land Law Development* (Washington, DC: for sale by the Superintendent of Documents, U.S. GPO, 1968), 402, 410–11, 416–17; Gates, *Fifty*

Homestead Final Entries, 1868–1900

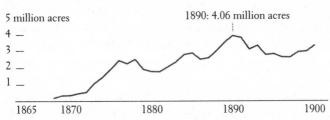

Source: U.S. Department of the Interior, Annual Report of the Commissioner of the General Land Office, 1946.

Final patents are one measure of the success of the Homestead Act; others are the amount of land claimed under, and the percentage of farms established through, it. In the 1860s and 1870s, the years when settlers covered the Middle Border and the lands east of the 98th meridian in farms, most did not acquire their land through the Homestead Act. They bought it from the government, the railroads, or speculators.

In the 1860s Americans created 615,908 new farms, a 23 percent increase. Homesteaders, however, filed only 142,410 applications between 1863, when the government began accepting claims, and 1870. Even if every application proved successful—and only a minority in fact succeeded—the act accounted for fewer than 25 percent of the new farms created. Except for Wisconsin and Michigan, little land remained for homesteading in the Midwest east of the Mississippi River. Illinois, for example, created 59,463 new farms in the 1860s, but only 7 were entered under the Homestead Act.[15]

The 1870s brought little change. Settlers created 1,348,985 new farms, but filed 318,572 homestead entries. Even in Minnesota more settlers established farms through preemptions and land purchases than homesteading. Only in the 1880s did homestead claims (477,052) make up a large portion of new farms (555,734), but this would not prove a particularly good thing. Many of these claims came west of the 100th meridian, and many farmers would eventually fail.[16]

The Homestead Act succeeded best in places like South Dakota, where homesteaders encountered little railroad land and few large-scale speculators. Settlement proceeded more quickly and more densely

Million Acres: Conflicts over Kansas Land Policy, 1854–1890 (New York: Atherton Press, 1966), 238–40.

15. Gates, History of Public Land Law Development, 401–2, 411–12; Fred A. Shannon, The Farmer's Last Frontier: Agriculture, 1860–1897 (New York: Harper and Row, 1968, orig. ed. 1945), 38–39.

16. Gates, History of Public Land Law Development, 402, 410–11, 416–17.

in South Dakota, where railroads by and large did not get land grants and followed or barely preceded settlement, than in North Dakota with its large land grants. In Nebraska, which was checkered with railroad grants, far more acres (9,435,796) went to the railroads between 1863 and 1872 or were purchased than were homesteaded or preempted (1,471,761).[17]

The lands granted to railroads or sold to large speculators, particularly under the Swamp Land Act of 1850, which conveyed large acreages into the hands of purchasers for a pittance, proved a great limiting factor on the success of the Homestead Act and its companions, but there were others. In California, Spanish and Mexican land grants created a barrier to homesteading. Large tracts were granted to states through the Morrill Act and other measures. Indians retained other land for reservations.[18]

Bringing this hodgepodge of laws and methods of distribution together would have been difficult for an efficient bureaucracy, but there was no efficient bureaucracy; there was only the General Land Office. Creaky and corrupt, the GLO modernized only gradually. It was described as a "den of thieves and robbers" as early as the Jackson Administration, and, if anything, it grew worse following the Civil War. In charge of administering an unwieldy land system, its officials were often in league with local landholders and speculators. Depending on private contractors, it was incapable of surveying what amounted to two-thirds of a continent with the rapidity and accuracy the legislation passed during the Civil War demanded. The GLO lacked the staff to process the paperwork and issue the patents—land titles—that rapid settlement required. There were eighty-two registers and eighty-two receivers at local land offices scattered across the United States. Their fees—for this was still very much a fee-based system—and the opportunities for fraud made them potentially lucrative appointments. In addition there were surveyors general (fifteen by 1889), deputy surveyors, and clerks in Washington, D.C., to keep a central record and issue patents. The GLO ran a race with the settlers, speculators, and railroads in which it was so perennially behind that it sometimes seemed to be going backwards. Dealing with the Land Office frustrated

17. Richard White, *Railroaded: The Transcontinentals and the Making of Modern America* (New York: Norton, 2011), 484–86; Gates, *History of Public Land Law Development*, 401–2, 409–11; "The Homestead Act, Free Land Policy in Operation, 1862–1935," in *The Jeffersonian Dream: Studies in the History of American Land Policy and Development*, ed. Allan G. Bogue and Margaret Beattie Bogue (Albuquerque: University of New Mexico Press, 1996), 48.

18. Gates, *History of Public Land Law Development*, 323–33, 379, 394–97, 715.

generations of honest land seekers, but its slow and grinding ways became a comfort to timber thieves, squatters, and other illegal claimants.[19]

Even after proving up a claim or purchasing land, it often took settlers years to get a patent, and incompetence—and fraud—meant that there could be more than one claimant to a tract of land. This resulted in long, expensive legal battles between rival claimants and opportunities for land office officials. Morgan Bates became the Republican lieutenant governor of Michigan in the late 1860s, but that office was no more important to him than his appointment as register of the land office at Grand Traverse, Michigan, under the Lincoln and Grant administrations. Along with Reuben Goodrich, who was the receiver at the same land office, the two well-connected Republican politicians used their appointments to plunder Odawa and Chippewa Indians through illegal claims on their reservations, to embezzle funds, and to collect fees far beyond their modest salaries. Bates was said to have gotten $50,000 out of the land office during his first term as register, of which only $2,000 was honestly earned. In 1880 the per capita income in Michigan was only $183, and it was falling. "You have no idea," G. P. Griswold wrote Austin Blair, a Michigan congressman, "how quick a register or receiver can make a fortune out of the people where as much land is sold as at this office." Field officers made excessive charges against applicants, who often willingly paid them in order to avoid the strict enforcement of the law.[20]

When the government failed to monitor the veracity of claims and instead relied on citizens to challenge illicit claims, it created a system that pitted settlers against each other. A successful farm might represent only the triumph of one farmer over another; the creation of one home negated another. The delay in obtaining patents could also, however, benefit farmers, since, until patented, the lands could not be taxed. Freedom from taxes came at a price, hurting schools and community development, while the lack of clear title prevented farmers from using their land as collateral for loans. By the 1870s Congress recognized that the lack of administrative capacity in the General Land Office had created a backlog in surveying and patenting land that was thwarting the promise of the Homestead Act. Large acreages awaited adjudication to determine

19. Daniel P. Carpenter, *The Forging of Bureaucratic Autonomy: Reputations, Networks, and Policy Innovation in Executive Agencies, 1862–1928* (Princeton, NJ: Princeton University Press, 2001), 56–57; Gates, *History of Public Land Law Development*, 127–28, 421.

20. G. P. Griswold to Austin Blair, Feb. 8, 1869, in *Blair, Austin, Papers, 1838–1921, Correspondence* (Burton Historical Library, Detroit Public Library). Nicholas R. Parrillo, *Against the Profit Motive: The Salary Revolution in American Government, 1780–1940* (New Haven, CT: Yale University Press, 2013), 119–20.

ownership. Demands for reform of both the land system and the GLO gained momentum.[21]

Compared with the South, however, homesteading in the Middle Border was a rousing success. There was a separate Southern Homestead Act passed in 1866, in part to compensate the freedmen for the failure to redistribute Southern lands. Until January 1, 1867, forty-six million acres of public land in Alabama, Arkansas, Florida, Louisiana, and Mississippi were open only to loyal refugees and freedpeople; after that, the public lands in the South were open to general entry. The act required five years' residence and fees to gain title to a maximum claim of eighty acres. Only about 41 percent of the claimants, black or white, ever made good. Just some seven thousand black families gained land before the law was repealed in 1876.[22]

Men like Henry Ise were common, but they were not typical, and even their success did not necessarily represent a triumph of individualism. Homesteads, after all, were gifts of the state, which had acquired the lands that went into them from Indians by treaty, conquest, or fraud. In every case, there lurked at least the threat of military force. Homesteaders often found the land they desired contested by railroads, which also often benefited from the largesse of the state that subsidized them. Without railroads, however, farmers had no access to markets.

Hamlin Garland, who grew from a boy to a promising writer over the course of American settlement of the Middle Border and West, was less concerned with the structural problems of American land policy than what he thought were personal and social failings that could kill the home even as they allowed farmers to live. Garland did not shy away from the costs that the restlessness and ambition of his father, Dick Garland, and men like him imposed on home and family. They established homes, but their actions often simultaneously threatened and undermined them. This became a consistent trope of Hamlin Garland's writing about the Middle Border.

Americans regarded the farm as both home and business, and this combination prevented it from ever being fully the haven from a heartless world that Victorians idealized. Back from the Civil War, Dick Garland

21. Roy M. Robbins, *Our Landed Heritage: The Public Domain, 1776–1970*, 2nd, rev. ed. (Lincoln: University of Nebraska Press, 1976), 218–19; Gates, *History of Public Land Law Development*, 399–401, 421, 425–27, 454–61.

22. Paul A. Cimbala, *The Freedmen's Bureau: Reconstructing the American South after the Civil War* (Malabar, FL: Krieger, 2005), 57–61; Gates, *History of Public Land Law*, 335, 443-47; Steven Hahn, *A Nation under Our Feet: Black Political Struggles in the Rural South, from Slavery to the Great Migration* (Cambridge, MA: Belknap Press of Harvard University Press, 2003), 141–42.

quickly grew discontented with his Wisconsin farm with "its up-tilted, horse-killing fields," and its stumps and ravines. It was a home, surrounded by relatives and family, but not as productive a farm as he desired. He sold it to settle in Minnesota on a farm with "not a hill on it big enough for a boy to coast on." It was "right on the edge of Looking Glass Prairie" with "a pure spring of water, and a fine grove of trees just where," as he said, "I want them, not where they have to be grubbed out." The new farm's lure overwhelmed the ties of his old home place, where he had been married, where his children were born, and around which his parents and relatives lived. He presumed his relatives would follow. Only a year later an even better farm beckoned. The Garlands again sold and acquired a new farm in Iowa amidst a "russet ocean" of grass on an unbroken prairie. "A mighty spreading and shifting was going on all over the West," and the Garlands were a quite typical part of it. This would not be their last move.[23]

The prairie's "russet ocean" would gradually disappear as settlers hired "prairie breakers." "Breaking" the land connotes a conquest and domination of nature, but the phrase was in many ways misleading. When Hamlin Garland later wrote his best-known book, *Main-Travelled Roads*, he had a character riding his sulky-plow, talking to his horses, and "finishing a land." The plowings and harrowings necessary to have the wild grasses yield to cultivated grains constituted what many American farmers, in an old Jeffersonian sense, thought of as finishing. Human labor was the necessary, and quite natural, last step necessary to bring a landscape into its intended final form.[24]

As he grew older, Hamlin Garland was increasingly appalled by the burden his father's ambitions placed on his mother. A later book, *A Daughter of the Middle Border*, which was really a continuation of Garland's own memoir, began with his mother in "failing health" in the 1890s. The "work of a farm household had become an intolerable burden." Hamlin Garland crafted Dick Garland into a literary character, who embodied the ambiguities of western settlement. Dick Garland created homes and then sacrificed them for business, selling them to start grander ventures further west. Hamlin's father's success as a farmer and his failure as a father and husband were intertwined. It was the willingness of men

23. Hamlin Garland, *A Son of the Middle Border* (New York: Grosset & Dunlap, 1928), 42, 61, 80; *Historical Statistics of the United States, Earliest Times to the Present: Millennial Edition*, ed. Scott Sigmund Gartner, Susan B. Carter, Michael R. Haines, Alan L. Olmstead, Richard Sutch, and Gavin Wright (New York: Cambridge University Press, 2006), fig. Da-G, Acreage of major crops: 1866–1999.

24. For settlement of prairies, Gilbert Courtland Fite, *The Farmers' Frontier, 1865–1900* (New York: Holt, Rinehart and Winston, 1966), 43–44, 48–50; Hamlin Garland, *Main-Travelled Roads* (New York: Signet, New American Library, 1962), 141–42.

like Garland to exploit the labor of their wives and children, to divert income to modernizing and improving the farm, and, if necessary, to relocate that allowed household production in wheat to outcompete larger farms that relied largely on wage labor. Dick Garland embodied the democratic manhood and economic striving that Radical Republicans wanted to transplant in the West. His son made him into something more.[25]

Hamlin Garland's stories of his father added up the domestic cost of commercial success. Striving created the homes that were the central cultural symbol of the age, but unrestrained striving could destroy them. Garland's best literary work amounts to a wrenching account of rural life in the nineteenth century and especially of the price paid by women who tried to keep homes alive on family farms in an industrializing society. "Why," he asked as his father uprooted them again to move from Iowa to the Dakotas, "should this suffering be? Why should mother be wrenched from all her dearest friends and forced to move away to a strange land?" This was not just a literary conceit. Americans sentimentalized the home and particularly the farm home, but they also regarded that home as property and thus collateral for other ventures. A land system open to both those seeking profit from speculative sales and those seeking to establish permanent homes was bound to have conflicts, but when it was put together with as much haste and inattention to detail as the American system, the results could lead to endless litigation and controversy.[26]

If the goal of the system the Republicans designed during the Civil War and deployed during the first years of the Greater Reconstruction was rapid settlement and development, then it was a tremendous success in the Middle Border. But if the goal was stable, independent farms and homes, then the results were much more mixed. The Middle Border would become the center of antimonopoly agitation in the years to come, and much of that agitation revolved around the defense of homes already sabotaged from within.

II

One aim of Reconstruction was to induce blacks in the South or to coerce Indians in the West into adopting free labor and replicating the Protestant

25. Hamlin Garland, *A Daughter of the Middle Border* (New York: Macmillan, 1921), xxii; Harriet Friedmann, "World Market, State, and Family Farm: Social Bases of Household Production in the Era of Wage Labor," *Comparative Studies in History and Society* 20 (October 1978).

26. Garland, *A Son of the Middle Border*, 238; for litigation and controversy, Gates, *History of Public Land Law*, 205, 324, 355, 421, 426, 603, 666.

home. In the South the Republicans imagined black strivers in the mold of Henry Ise and Dick Garland and black homes like those in mug books, but the Radicals' attempt to redistribute the lands of traitors to freedmen and poor Southern Unionists as they redistributed Indian land to western settlers had failed, and the Southern Homestead Act had produced few farms. Black homes would have to be supported by men who were not fully independent, but instead depended on sharecropping, renting, and wage labor. At stake in the efforts of freedmen was Reconstruction itself. Republicans thought this was the chance for freedmen to prove themselves men. For the Klan and similar organizations, it was a chance to prove that black men could never be men because they could not support and protect homes. They could, like Indians in the West, only be a threat to white homes.

In a trope that would last well beyond Reconstruction, white Southerners contended black men threatened white homes and white women, but in practice it was white men who relentlessly and quite purposefully targeted black homes. Slavery was dead, but white Southerners had no intention of abandoning racial hierarchy and the dependence that tied black people to the households of white people. In theory free black citizens could challenge the conditions and terms of their work, they could move when and where they desired, they could establish their own households and marry whom they wished, they enjoyed the same political and civil rights as any other citizen. White men who thought they should rightfully control them and their labor would have no say. This was what the political scientist Marek Steedman has called "the nightmare scenario" of those who still "aspired to the status of masters." When the Klan and other white regulators intervened to enforce the old order, the results were shocking and bloody.[27]

Eliza Pinkston was a freedwoman, born a slave in Alabama, who tried to negotiate the tricky terrain between being an appendage of a white household and living in an independent black home. White planters and employers presumed they still controlled black lives and politics, and the majority of the white community thought themselves entitled to enforce such control. Eliza found herself trapped between the struggles of men, black and white, and the ambitions of a black community for a new racial and economic order and the fears of a white community over the loss of an old one.[28]

27. Marek D. Steedman, *Jim Crow Citizenship: Liberalism and the Southern Defense of Racial Hierarchy* (New York: Routledge, 2012), 101.
28. Ibid., 61–77.

Charles Tidwell was a white man, a tenant farmer who had never owned slaves, but it never occurred to him that he could not command black people or that he could not have ready sexual access to black women. He had a daughter by a black woman, and his white son—David, who was called Sonny—assumed he had the same sexual privileges as his father. In the late 1860s and early 1870s Eliza had apparently worked for the Tidwells both in Alabama and Louisiana, and part of the work was sex. As Eliza put it, "I never was sot up as a mistress, I worked; but when night-time came I done duty too." She had given birth to twins, who had died. She understood that this was neither marriage, nor an approximation of it. "I could not be called 'Mrs. Tidwell' it was always 'Eliza Finch.'" She paid a price among both blacks and whites: "People looked on me with such scorn, no matter if I was well dressed. Wherever I would go they would say, 'That's David Tidwell's piece." Her "color," she said, "didn't look on me with honor."[29]

Leaving David Tidwell and marrying Henry Pinkston—whom she said she loved "with all my heart"—brought her "honor"; it freed her from a relationship that freedpeople regarded as a replication of slave times in which sex was part of a larger relationship of dependence. Sonny Tidwell tried unsuccessfully to prevent the marriage, but his threats forced the Pinkstons to move to a neighboring parish. The Pinkstons were not free of the Tidwells, who in the early 1870s tried to force Henry, and Eliza, to attend Democratic meetings—or speakings as they were called—and avoid Republican meetings. Henry refused to be intimidated, and he demanded Eliza follow his lead, even though Eliza regarded his course as reckless: "it seems like you don't care no more for your life than you do for a rabbit's life." For Henry, it was about manhood: "I is not a man having a thing in him without speaking it out. I will go yonder if I get killed." Eliza was not convinced. She never accepted the elections of the mid-1870s on Republican terms—as a choice between freedom and a return to slavery— but she recognized that whites could and would unleash horrific violence against the Republicans.[30]

When Eliza saw a white man writing down Henry's name at the meeting, she turned to the Tidwells to prevent what she saw coming. They did nothing. The white man doing the writing was one of a group of regulators, young men moving "in the best circles of society" who acted as enforcers for the Democrats. The regulators, who brought along two "colored" men, were careful to attack the Pinkstons at home. The whole idea of a black home was as much their target as the Pinkstons. They castrated

29. Steedman, 60–67.
30. Ibid., 67–69.

Henry and broke his ribs. They raped Eliza, broke her skull, slashed her, and cut her Achilles tendon. They killed the Pinkstons' baby, and they killed Henry. The message could not have been clearer. Freedpeople could not have independent homes, black men could not protect them, black women could not live within them, and black parents could not reproduce the children that would sustain them. Submission—social, political, economic, and sexual—was to be the only protection from such attacks.[31]

Eliza Pinkston was a tragic character in a larger story of attempts by whites to prevent the creation of independent black homes. The Klan's attacks were inseparable from issues of home and manhood because Southern whites by and large could not separate racial relations from relations of dependence organized around households. Southern white men portrayed black men and white Radicals as threats to the white home and family. They proclaimed that a black man could not create or protect his home and family, while a black woman was too lascivious to maintain it. To protect the old order, they struck at black homes and at black families. The testimonies given in court and before federal investigators are a heartbreaking repetition of rape, beatings, mutilation, and murder.[32]

In the West the campaign for Indian homes also failed. Of all the challenges to homemaking, none seemed more daunting than that posed by Western Indians, whom Americans regarded as having homelands but no proper homes. Indians created an obstacle to American homemaking. Americans had long regarded Indians as a collection of deficiencies. Their religions were deficient, their economies were deficient, their cultures were deficient, and their families were deficient. American efforts to "civilize" Indians focused on correcting these deficiencies: making them Protestant, organizing them into patrilineal nuclear families, and giving them homes. Treaties from the 1850s onward had provisions to divide Indian lands in severalty—that is, made into private property—and use them as the basis for Indian homes with monogamous nuclear families whose gender roles mimicked those of white Protestants.[33]

The *Annual Report of the Commissioner of Indian Affairs* for 1868 included the report of the Peace Commissioners sent to negotiate the treaties intended to end warfare on the Great Plains. The commissioners laid out what needed to be done. Indians were to be confined to particular

31. Ibid., 68–71.
32. Hannah Rosen, *Terror in the Heart of Freedom: Citizenship, Sexual Violence, and the Meaning of Race in the Postemancipation South* (Chapel Hill: University of North Carolina Press, 2009), 185–221.
33. Francis Paul Prucha, *American Indian Policy in Crisis: Christian Reformers and the Indian, 1865–1900* (Norman: University of Oklahoma Press, 1976), 105–6.

districts, where agriculture and manufactures would be introduced among them and their children forced to attend schools. "Their barbarous dialects should be blotted out and the English language substituted," the commissioners wrote; this would help break down tribal barriers and "fuse them into one homogeneous mass." But the ultimate goal was to place them on a "homestead" that they would improve. Women would "be taught to weave, sew and to knit." Polygamy would be punished, and they would be encouraged to build houses with "the gathering there of those comforts which endear the home." With the establishment of Christian homes, their civilization would be complete.[34]

This is the program Grant had in mind when in his inaugural address in 1869 he announced that the goal for Indians was "their civilization and ultimate citizenship." Like freedpeople, they were to melt into the homogeneous citizenship that was the Republican ideal. But where freedpeople faced extralegal coercion and violence to prevent their establishing homes, Indians would face legal coercion and, if necessary, violence to force them to establish proper homes. To advance his policy, Grant organized the Board of Indian Commissioners, composed of Protestant philanthropists, and gave them joint control with the secretary of interior over the money Congress appropriated for Indian Affairs. The commissioners recommended that the treaty system itself be abandoned. Existing treaties would be enforced, although they should be abrogated with Indian consent when possible. The Indians were to move to reservations, which were to be divided in severalty. Indians should learn English and become Christian since the "religion of our blessed Saviour is believed to be the most effective agent for the civilization of any people." Until they became Christian, self-supporting, American citizens, Indians would remain wards of the government.[35]

In formulating his Indian policy, Grant sought a precarious balance between the Christian reformers, whose support he sought, and the army officers, whom he thought best able to administer Indian reservations. Grant made his old aide-de-camp Ely Parker, a Seneca Indian, the commissioner of Indian affairs. Parker ultimately was a military man. Only soldiers, he thought, "when they make a promise will keep it and when they make a threat will execute it." He believed that Indians did not

34. U.S. Department of the Interior, "Annual Report of the Commissioner of Indian Affairs, 1868" (Washington, DC: U.S. GPO, 1868), 504.
35. Francis Paul Prucha, *The Great Father: The United States Government and the American Indians* (Lincoln: University of Nebraska Press, 1984), 1: 501–11.

respect the civilian Indian agents because "they neither kept their promises nor executed their threats."[36]

Parker, with his military preferences, would have to work with a new Board of Indian Commissioners who distrusted the military. What Christian reformers and the army agreed on was, in the words of the *Army and Navy Journal*, the Indian Office's "unbroken record of slaughter and swindle," but they took opposite positions on reform. Military officers thought of themselves as the natural guardians of the Indians and as possessing an administrative capacity and ability to coerce that were absent elsewhere in the government. General Sherman argued that only the transfer of responsibility for the Indians to the War Department rather than Interior would solve the "Indian problem." Sherman thought, "To labor with their own hands, or even to remain in one place, militates with all the hereditary pride of the Indian, and *force* must be used to accomplish the result." Proper homes could only be established by compulsion. The dispute over transfer to the War Department would last through the 1870s.[37]

The army itself sabotaged the ultimate goal of having the Office of Indian Affairs placed within the War Department and military officers delegated from the army to staff Indian reservations. On January 23, 1870, an army detachment led by Col. Eugene M. Baker killed 173 members of Heavy Runner's band of Piegan Indians—largely women, old men, and children—who were camped on the Marias River in Montana. Baker was looking for Piegan raiders, but he found the wrong band: a village full of people sick and dying of smallpox. Although warned this was the wrong band, he attacked anyway, unleashing what reformers condemned as a "sickening slaughter." Sheridan made things worse. He defended Baker by conjuring up visions of universal murder and rape—in effect, marking Indians as bloody savages who threatened the white home and white womanhood. No one presented any evidence that any member of Heavy Runner's band had murdered or raped anyone.[38]

While committing some atrocities, the army also failed to prevent others. Whites and *vecinos* (as Spanish speakers referred to their community members) accused Western Apaches of being savage enemies of their homes, but in 1871 the Apaches had believed army promises that they

36. Edward M. Coffman, *The Old Army: A Portrait of the American Army in Peacetime, 1784–1898* (New York: Oxford University Press, 1986), 255; Prucha, *American Indian Policy in Crisis*, 75–77.

37. Prucha, *American Indian Policy in Crisis*, 72–82, quote, 75; Coffman, 255.

38. Andrew R. Graybill, *The Red and the White: A Family Saga of the American West* (New York: Norton, 2013), 105–41; Paul Andrew Hutton, *Phil Sheridan and His Army* (Lincoln: University of Nebraska Press, 1985), 113–17, 186–200.

would be safe if they came in and settled at Aravaipa Canyon near Tucson. The promises were sincere, but they bound the army and not American settlers in Tucson, or the *vecinos* — Mexican inhabitants absorbed into the United States as citizens with the Gadsden Purchase — or the Tohono O'odham, the desert farmers of Sonora and Arizona. In April 1871 members of all three groups attacked the Western Apaches camped in the canyon. The slaughter was brutal and methodical. Roughly 150 people, overwhelmingly women and children, died, either shot or with their skulls crushed by war clubs. The twenty-nine children who were captured were doomed to servitude or slavery unless they escaped. The army's promise ultimately meant nothing, although the Camp Grant Massacre so outraged both the military and reformers that there was a trial of the perpetrators. No one was convicted. The army, having failed to protect Apaches, proceeded to wage war against them. In 1873 General Crook forced the Apaches into reservations where, despite sporadic outbreaks, most would remain.[39]

Baker's attack and Sheridan's defense of it vitiated Grant's message of peace. Such assaults, justified in the name of protecting white women and white homes, did nothing to create Indian homes and instead slaughtered Indian women and children. Grant, who was always too loyal to his old friends, supported Sheridan, promoting him to command the entire Division of the Missouri, the second-highest rank in the army behind Sherman. Rep. Daniel Voorhees of Indiana pointed out the "curious spectacle" of Grant welcoming both Quakers — "missionaries of a gospel of peace" whom he appointed as agents on some reservations — and "General Sheridan, stained with the blood of innocent women and children." Congress forbade army officers from taking civil appointments. Congressional motives were, as usual, mixed. Those shocked by the slaughter, and fearful of the transfer of the Indian Office to the War Department, joined the congressmen who did not want to lose valuable patronage appointments.[40]

The drive to institute monogamy and establish nuclear families on individual allotments, with male breadwinners providing for a wife who governed a clearly demarcated domestic space, remained a central aspect of American Indian policy for the remainder of the century. In popular culture it yielded to a far more prominent image: the Indian as a threat to the white family. This theme was an old one, but it took on new prominence

39. Karl Jacoby, *Shadows at Dawn: A Borderlands Massacre and the Violence of History* (New York: Penguin Press, 2008), 1–2, 183–88.
40. Prucha, *The Great Father*, 1: 512–15.

with the rise of the penny press, dime novels, and by the 1880s, the Wild West Show.

Few monitored the pulse of popular culture better than William Cody, better known as Buffalo Bill, and by the end of the nineteenth century the "Attack on the Settler's Cabin" had emerged as perhaps the central element of his Wild West. It displayed Cody's genius in reducing the complicated story of American expansion down to the extension of the home into a wild interior. The Wild West was always about race violence, manhood, and the home. Its intended audience was the respectable middle classes. They thrilled to watching white men ward off "savage" dangers to the home in order to advance civilization.[41]

Beneath the surface, the Wild West was a complicated performance. The trope of the savage threat to white homes proved quite adaptable in the Gilded Age; not only Indians but also radical workers and immigrants could be cast in the role. In the United States, however, the audience for

This poster for Buffalo Bill's Wild West and Congress of Rough Riders of the World from the late 1890s shows American Indians attacking pioneers in covered wagons. In the common reversal of the actual history, it makes Indians defending their lands into savages who threaten the white family and home. Library of Congress, LC-DIG-ppmsca-13514.

41. Louis S. Warren, *Buffalo Bill's America: William Cody and the Wild West Show* (New York: Knopf, 2005), 39, 238.

the Wild West shows also contained immigrants, who in the 1880s and 1890s applauded the defense of the white home even as they were denounced in the popular press as dangerous savages whose own whiteness was in question. Nativists made immigrants a threat to the American home, but workingmen and antimonopolists, many of them immigrants themselves, turned the white home into a lethal weapon against Chinese immigrants.

When Sinophobes accused the Chinese of being unassimilable and a threat to a free labor society, the evidence they mustered revolved around the home. "Home life as we understand and honor it," they said of the Chinese, "is unknown to them." White Californians believed that virtually all of the Chinese women in America were prostitutes, "held in slavery by their own people for the basest purposes." And many of them were, in fact, coerced into prostitution. Far more important than the supposed deficiencies of Chinese families, however, was their threat to white families: "They crowd our men of families out of employment, and leave them

A PICTURE FOR EMPLOYERS

One frame of this cartoon, entitled "A Picture for Employers," bears the caption, "Why *They* can live on 40 cents a day, and *they* can't" shows Chinese in a crowded opium den, eating rats. The other frame portrays an American workingman arriving home to his wife and children. The moral was clear: the Chinese, who lacked homes, threatened white homes. From *Puck*, Aug. 21, 1878. Library of Congress, LC-USZC2-1242.

to want and destitution. They make hoodlums and criminals of our boys, and drive our girls to worse than death by working for wages which to them means starvation."[42]

Protestant women established rescue homes for Chinese prostitutes in San Francisco, but they faced intense opposition from those who wanted all Chinese, men and women, banished rather than rescued. Terence Powderly, the head of the Knights of Labor, in an accusation that says much about the sexual activities of adolescent boys, claimed Chinese prostitutes had infected "thousands of boys" from eight to fifteen with venereal disease. These boys would, doctors asserted, then later infect their wives and through them their children.[43]

III

White attitudes about the dangers blacks, Indians, and Chinese posed to the white Protestant home bubbled up out of longstanding racial attitudes, but they also reflected a real and deep anxiety about the home. In the late nineteenth century the home was equated with the nuclear family, and if the prevalence of nuclear families and their existence in identifiable households were the measure of the health of the home, then the home was ubiquitous and thriving. Roughly 90 percent of American families had two parents present in the late nineteenth century.[44]

Yet the anxiety over the home remained palpable; it arose from three very different sources. One was the racial threat to the white home by outsiders. This could, and did, slide over into threats posed by Mormons and Catholics. The second was concern over children growing up with only one parent—particularly a female parent—or none. The final, and most complicated, source was male discontent over female domination of the domestic space that defined the Victorian home, and the partial

---

42. White, *Railroaded*, 300–301.

43. Ibid.; Joshua Paddison, *American Heathens: Religion, Race, and Reconstruction in California* (Berkeley: published for the Huntington-USC Institute on California and the West by University of California Press, 2012), 50–53; Peggy Pascoe, *Relations of Rescue: The Search for Female Moral Authority in the American West, 1874–1939* (New York: Oxford University Press, 1990), 13–17, 94–97.

44. Herbert S. Klein, *A Population History of the United States* (Cambridge: Cambridge University Press, 2004), 141; Stephen Ruggles, "Family and Household Composition," in *Historical Statistics of the United States, Earliest Times to the Present: Millennial Edition*, fig. Ae-C. Marital status of mothers with children younger than age 18: 1880–1990.

withdrawal of men from that space into male havens ranging from the saloon to fraternal orders such as the Masons and Odd Fellows.

Even with the vast majority of children in homes with two parents present, that still left 13 percent of white children and 30 percent of black children in homes with only a single parent. Single parent homes were three to four times more likely to have female than male heads as the century progressed. In addition there were orphans, either institutionalized or left to life on the streets. Such children loomed much larger in Victorian fiction than Victorian society: Tom Sawyer, Huckleberry Finn, and the numerous dime novel heroes of Horatio Alger were among the most famous. But in a society where as late as 1900 20–30 percent of all children lost a parent before the age of fifteen, being orphaned remained a lively possibility. Divorce was a minor cause of the absence of parents, ranking far behind death and desertion.[45]

Homeless children—the street urchins, newspaper boys, and shoeshine boys—numbered in the thousands in New York by the 1870s, and in both his fiction and his life Horatio Alger was obsessed with them. Before and during the Civil War, he aspired to being a serious novelist and a poet. He never earned enough to support himself, and so he turned first to teaching and then to the ministry to supplement his income. When drafted, he was turned down for his myopia and his height: 5 feet 2 inches. In 1864 his life changed. He was appointed minister at the First Unitarian Church in Brewster, Massachusetts, and he decided to devote himself to juvenile fiction. As he put it later, "I leased my pen to the boys, and the world has been spared much poor poetry and ambitious prose." It also "would pay me better."[46]

The writing succeeded better than the ministry. Modern definitions of sexuality are no more appropriate to the late nineteenth century than modern definitions of race; they were both being invented as time went on. Horatio Alger was sexually attracted to men, but sexual contact between men did not in the nineteenth century mark men as homosexual. Sexual contact between men might be a sin—like masturbation—but it did not yet signify that men who indulged in it occupied a distinct sexual category. Alger was, however, particularly sexually attracted to boys, and this crossed a quite clear moral boundary. Rumors circulated during his

45. Klein, 141; Alexander B. Callow, *The Tweed Ring* (New York: Oxford University Press, 1969), 54–55; Ruggles, fig. Ae-C. Marital status of mothers with children younger than age eighteen: 1880–1990; Mintz, 157; Table Ae38–78: Related and unrelated subfamilies, by race and sex of reference person and subfamily type: 1850–1990, in *Historical Statistics of the United States, Earliest Times to the Present: Millennial Edition.*

46. Callow, *The Tweed Ring,* 54–55; Gary Scharnhorst and Jack Bales, *The Lost Life of Horatio Alger, Jr.* (Bloomington: Indiana University Press, 1985), 58–62.

ministry. The church investigated and reported he had committed "a crime of no less magnitude than the abominable and revolting crime of unnatural familiarity with boys. . . ." Alger resigned his ministry and left for New York City.[47]

In New York he set to work writing juvenile fiction in religious publications and those aimed at schoolchildren. He became fascinated by the so-called street Arabs of New York, the city's thousands of homeless children. He befriended them, aided them, and opened his rooms to them, which, given his activities in Brewster, would seem to be the moth returning to the flame. Perhaps it was. He would never marry and never have a conventional Victorian home, but a series of boys came to live or vacation with him. There was no further mention of scandal. He seemed to think of his work with them as a kind of penance.[48]

They were also a source of profit; the street Arabs inspired *Ragged Dick*, his first and most successful book, published serially in 1867. The book eschewed the violence and sex of the streets of New York. It was didactic moral fiction with simple characters, but it was also full of local color. *Ragged Dick* created the template for virtually all of Alger's subsequent juvenile writing. Although he gave his heroes differing names, situations, and adventures, the hero was always the same, and he was usually a homeless boy. The moral of the stories never changed. They were stories of overcoming adversity, of learning proper values, and of rising in the world.[49]

Ragged Dick was an honest street urchin in living in a box in an alley in New York City. A bootblack, he smoked, went to theaters, and spent all the money that came his way; his problem was bad values, not a bad heart. The book was a *Bildungsroman*, the story of an education.[50]

The lessons begin when Dick meets a middle-class boy, Frank, and his uncle. The adult sponsor was Alger's great innovation in the genre. The uncle tells Dick, "Remember that your future position depends mainly on yourself, and that it will be high or low as you choose to make it." In Alger's version of America, a homeless, illiterate child, living in a box in an alley, needs only good advice if he is made of the right stuff. To indicate that not all poor children are made of the right stuff, Alger

47. Ibid., 66–67; Estelle Freedman and John D'Emilio, *Intimate Matters: A History of Sexuality in America*, ed. Estelle B. Freedman (New York: Harper & Row, 1988), 121–24; George Chauncey, *Gay New York: Gender, Urban Culture, and the Making of the Gay Male World, 1890–1940* (New York: Basic Books, 1994), 13, 21–27.
48. Scharnhorst and Bales, 70–79.
49. Ibid., 80–83.
50. Horatio Alger, *Ragged Dick: Or Street Life in New York with the Boot-Blacks* (New York: John C. Winston, 1910; 1st ed. 1868), 9–13.

introduces an Irish villain—Mickey Maguire—whose name conveys his shortcomings.

What follows is a course in self-improvement and progress. Dick starts saving money, stops drinking and hanging out with the guys, and learns to read and write. He learns the "satisfaction of self-denial" and the pleasures of property. These are juvenile novels, of course, and there is only so much lecturing on thrift and sobriety that a dime novel audience can sustain. Dick's gradual rise in society is speeded by his diving off a ferry to save a young girl, who turns out to be rich. The novel is unclear on the utility of saving poor girls.[51]

"Ragged Dick is Ragged Dick no longer; he is now Richard Hunter, Esq.: He has taken a step upward and is determined to mount still higher." *Ragged Dick* taught hard work, ambition, and self-discipline. These were values Lincoln would have espoused, and Alger presents them as not only sufficient for Lincoln's world, but also for the industrializing and urban world of the 1880s. A man's fate was still in his hands.[52]

But the United States was never so simple in either ideology or fact, and it was growing more complicated in ways that overwhelmed Alger. His rags-to-riches stories, later remembered as the definitive literature of the age, were in trouble by the early 1880s. They raised the ire of moral reformers, particularly female reformers, because they neglected women and the home.

Alger wrote pulp fiction: mass-produced, commercial literature. The predictability of the stories was part of their appeal, but readers increasingly demanded exotic settings, adventure, and novel incidents. Alger's urban settings were growing stale, and during the 1870s the dime novel had moved to the West and a world of Indian fighting, armed robbery, and violence. In his Pacific Series, Alger too had gone West. Reformers objected to the violence and crime of dime novels, but their objections went deeper than that. They thought Alger's stories were only a step above the *Police Gazette*, with its sensational accounts of crime, criminals, and the demimonde. Critics claimed such literature did more than exploit and sensationalize crime and delinquency; they thought such writing caused them. What surprised Alger was that critics of the dime novel would lump him with the likes of Ned Buntline, a newspaperman and nativist associated with New York's Protestant gangs, as well as a dime novelist who helped make Wild Bill Hickok and Buffalo Bill famous. Alger proclaimed his responsibility to "exert a wholesome influence on his young readers," instilling "honesty, industry, frugality, and a worthy ambition." A novelist,

51. Alger, quotes, 114, 209, Mickey McGuire, 129ff.; Scharnhorst and Bales, 83.
52. Alger, 262.

he thought, could teach through the medium of a story much more effectively than by lecturing or preaching.[53]

Women social reformers objected, however, that Alger's heroes did not
live in families and did not have homes. They lacked maternal influence.
Although his plots were unrealistic, his social milieus were too realistic.
The novels thus supposedly created dangerous and unrealizable ambitions among immigrants and working-class boys who should be content
with their lot, while their graphic social settings prompted dangerous
emotions among middle-class boys attracted to the independence, freedom from adult supervision, and exotic lives of Alger's heroes.[54]

Evangelical women were not alone in seeing popular literature and
children free from parental control as dangers to the home and nation.
Anthony Comstock was a devout evangelical Protestant and the head of
the New York Society for the Suppression of Vice, which spun off from
the Young Men's Christian Association in 1873. He opposed contracep-
tion, abortion, pornography, and obscenity as threats to the family. His
leading funders and supporters came disproportionately from the Social
Register and included prominent businessmen. He waged a war on lust in
general, but above all Comstock made Americans quail when faced with
the specter of the masturbating boy.[55]

Comstock was obsessed with obscenity because he felt it threatened
what he and supporters regarded as normal sexuality necessary for the reproduction of families and the home. "Lust," he proclaimed, "defiles the
body, debauches the imagination, corrupts the mind, deadens the will,
destroys the memory, sears the conscience, hardens the heart, and damns
the soul," but most of all it threatened the family. By weakening the family,
lust threatened the entire social order.[56]

Adultery, or the lesser alienation of affections, also threatened the home
because one man in penetrating another man's wife alienated her affections, violated his domestic space, took his property, and attacked his
home. Sexual liaisons that threatened the home became the issue at the

53. Alison M. Parker, *Purifying America: Women, Cultural Reform, and Pro-Censorship
   Activism, 1873–1933* (Urbana: University of Illinois Press, 1997), 198–202; Gary
   Scharnhorst, *Horatio Alger, Jr.* (Boston: Twayne, 1980), 66–67; Scharnhorst and Bales,
   The Lost Life of Horatio Alger, Jr., 118–23.
54. Parker, 198–202; Scharnhorst, *Horatio Alger, Jr*, 66–67; Scharnhorst and Bales, *The
   Lost Life of Horatio Alger, Jr.*, 118–23.
55. Nicola Kay Beisel, *Imperiled Innocents: Anthony Comstock and Family Reproduction
   in Victorian America* (Princeton, NJ: Princeton University Press, 1997), 3–7, 53–57.
56. Gaines M. Foster, *Moral Reconstruction: Christian Lobbyists and the Federal
   Legislation of Morality, 1865–1920* (Chapel Hill: University of North Carolina Press,
   2002), 47.

root of the Beecher-Tilton trial, the great private scandal of the 1870s, in which Theodore Tilton sued Henry Ward Beecher for the alienation of his wife's affections. The *New York Herald* declared that no event since the assassination of Lincoln had stirred such interest.[57]

Except for Ulysses S. Grant, Henry Ward Beecher may have been the most famous man in the United States in the 1870s. The *Andover Review* called him "the foremost private citizen of the Republic," and he displayed the contradictions of the liberal republic. Beecher was rational and practical, but he was also effusive and emotional, an overflowing vessel of Romantic feeling.[58]

These were the traits of liberal evangelical Protestantism, and Beecher—handsome, eloquent, and well-connected—was the leading figure of liberal Protestantism, which was above all the religion of the home. To have him be accused of the seduction of the wife of one of his close associates and tried for adultery could only be a sensation. It was hardly a private matter; he was accused of home wrecking, striking at the root of Protestant America. The courts assumed that women were sexual victims and men predators. If adultery took place, it was the man's fault. To conservatives, Beecher's religion of love and feeling rather than duty and restraint had nurtured the scandal that overwhelmed him. The charges, the countercharges, the defenses, and the testimony were wildly contradictory, but what they bared at the very least was a home that was the seat if not of adultery then of deep unhappiness and men engaged, as Tilton put it, in a mutual attack on "home and hearth."[59]

Beecher officiated at Horace Greeley's funeral in 1872, and it was fitting that another presidential candidate in 1872, the beautiful, flamboyant, articulate Victoria Woodhull, would make public the charges of adultery that until then had circulated privately. Woodhull was an advocate of free love, which simply meant the freedom of men and women to follow their hearts, making and dissolving relationships as their affections changed. She and her sister, Tennessee Claflin, became the most notorious radicals of the 1860s and 1870s by combining scandalous personal lives with outspoken opinions, but all they really demanded was full contract freedom for women. "There is," Woodhull wrote, "neither right nor duty beyond the uniting—the contracting—individuals." All free love asserted was contract freedom. Marriage was a contract, and it consisted of whatever

57. Laura Hanft Korobkin, *Criminal Conversations: Sentimentality and Nineteenth-Century Legal Stories of Adultery*, Casebook ed. (New York: Columbia University Press, 1998), 20–26, 57; Richard Wightman Fox, *Trials of Intimacy: Love and Loss in the Beecher-Tilton Scandal* (Chicago: University of Chicago Press, 1999), 106–7, 381 n. 22.
58. Fox, 21, 22–23.
59. Korobkin, 160–66; Fox, 1–32, 54–55, 66, 68, 75.

the parties involved agreed to do. Like any contract, it could be dissolved by mutual consent. Women were supposed to be, by nature, domestic creatures, nurturing and unsuited for public life beyond what affected the home. Woodhull and Claflin became public figures, publishing their own newspaper; they were neither domestic nor private. Their opponents regarded them as unnatural and monsters, but they just wanted to turn the marriage contract into a contract like any other.[60]

Free love proved so shocking to Victorians not because of its embrace of sexuality but because it put personal satisfaction and emotional connections above the home, whose stability society needed and demanded. Beecher had denounced Woodhull for her views, and she regarded him as a hypocrite. She accused him of adultery with Elizabeth Tilton, the wife of his former close associate Theodore Tilton. When she had heard rumors of the affair from Elizabeth Cady Stanton, with whom, as one memoirist put it, "a secret was not safe for an hour," she published them. Stanton had heard the story from Elizabeth Tilton herself; Tilton, both before and after the story broke, would repeat it and recant it several times. The scandal led to a famous trial in 1875.[61]

Beecher embodied Christian manhood. He preached that in "the actual conflicts of life men find more that follows manhood in its essential elements, in its trustworthiness, in its fidelity, in its enterprise, its largeness of spirit, than can be found under any dome or any temple, or before any altar." In daily life "God fashions character, and makes manhood noble." Theodore Tilton accused Beecher of having failed the test. He was not a man.[62]

Beecher's effusive and emotional side had led him into a complicated nineteenth-century intimacy with Theodore and Elizabeth Tilton. They all did, in some real but uncertain way, love each other. This led to Theodore's suit for alienation of affection and to Beecher's trial for adultery; it involved a public battle between Beecher and Theodore Tilton and an equally public and scandalous battle between Elizabeth and Theodore Tilton. As E. L. Godkin summarized the legal battle, in the name of "protect[ing] domestic happiness and purity" the Tiltons had invited "the whole world to see the Furies tearing a Household to pieces." The trial ended in a hung jury. The nation ultimately did not—could not—accept the thought that Beecher could have betrayed his home and

60. Freedman and D'Emilio, 161–65; Stanley, 3, 176, 261–62.
61. Lori D. Ginzberg, *Elizabeth Cady Stanton: An American Life* (New York: Hill and Wang, 2009), 145.
62. "Religion in Daily Life," in Henry Ward Beecher, *Sermons in Plymouth Church, Brooklyn...September 1873–March 1874* (New York: Fords, Howard, & Hulburt, 1882), 10–11, 18–19.

family and that of the Tiltons. As an article in *Harper's Weekly* put it, "The case is one of conspiracy against a good and great, though careless man." His "pure life and noble character" withstood the shock. The Church Council of Plymouth Church exonerated him, excommunicated those parishioners who thought him guilty, and voted him $100,000 for the expenses of the trial. Popular sentiment supported him.[63]

IV

By accusing Henry Ward Beecher of subverting home and marriage, Elizabeth Tilton had forced him onto the most fraught and dangerous ground in American society. Women had seized "that place of Heaven called home," and they could use it as a base to attack men who threatened it through drink, domestic violence, and desertion. They simultaneously pushed the boundaries of the home far beyond the walls of any dwelling.

In joining the temperance movement, women did not so much challenge existing gender roles as they sought to protect the home. The social consequences of drunkenness and alcoholism bore heavily on women, even though relatively few of them drank. Drunken husbands did beat their wives, abuse their children, and neglect their homes. They not only spent their wages on drink, but they could spend those of their wives, since under law a wife had no claim on her husband's earnings while he controlled hers. Even at the end of the century, wives in thirty-seven states had no rights to their children if they left their husbands. The drunken husband bared the inequities of the social order, the burdens placed on women, and women's lack of recourse. The Woman's Christian Temperance Union drew women into political activities, and once in, women expanded the concerns of the WCTU beyond drink.[64]

Frances Willard had not originally been active in the temperance movement. She had spent the 1860s and early 1870s somewhat adrift. She made and broke marital engagements. She wondered if she really wanted a career in education. She developed intense female friendships and took

63. Far and away the most nuanced account of the Tilden-Beecher relationship is in Fox, *Trials of Intimacy*, 225–27, quote p. 255; for a biography of Beecher, Clifford Edward Clark, *Henry Ward Beecher: Spokesman for a Middle-Class America* (Urbana: University of Illinois Press, 1978).

64. Ian R. Tyrrell, *Reforming the World: The Creation of America's Moral Empire* (Princeton, NJ: Princeton University Press, 2010), 13–15, 20–27; Ruth Birgitta Anderson Bordin, *Woman and Temperance: The Quest for Power and Liberty, 1873–1900* (Philadelphia: Temple University Press, 1981), 7–9, 12–14.

a Grand Tour of Europe and the Near East. She learned languages and studied art and antiquities. When she returned home, she became president of the Evanston Ladies College, affiliated with Northwestern University, and then dean of women at Northwestern. She resigned in a battle over her authority. The Reverend Charles Fowler, to whom she had once been engaged and who had become president of Northwestern, forced her out. He had the will of Napoleon, she explained, while she had the will of Queen Elizabeth.[65]

Under Willard the WCTU sought, in her words "to make the whole world HOMELIKE," but by then her own struggles had brought considerable nuance to her own attitudes toward the home. In the 1860s Willard was still young and unknown and struggling with her conflicting desires for independence and a home of her own. Her father was dying of consumption, as tuberculosis—the great killer of the nineteenth century—was known. She took her turns sitting with him, and he conveyed his last wishes. He wanted her to have a home. He wanted Frances to "be married to a strong, healthy, kind man who can take good care of you & make you happy." He "rejoiced" when she told him that she had broken off with the man she thought she loved because he was sickly.

She did not rejoice. She had conflicts of her own between her deep and ardent friendships with women and her more ambivalent relationships with men. But she recognized how the demands of manhood limited her own choices. Her dying father talked disconnectedly and often incoherently, but his incapacity did not sap his authority. She grew depressed, conscious of how "far from my choice are my present surroundings—circumstances—occupations." Employing an economic metaphor for the emotional price manhood exacted from women, she reached for the first time the "sober judgment" that "life did not pay." Her whole career would revolve around making the world more "homelike," but she would never live in a home headed by a man again. She would combine the threat to the home and a critique of women's subordination within it into a powerful weapon for a variety of social reforms.[66]

Home and marriage were hard to master. Frances Willard would never marry, but Abigail Scott Duniway did, and it was her very desire to maintain her home that drove her into the public sphere. Abigail Scott was born in a log cabin, took the overland trail west to Oregon as a child, and

65. Ruth Birgitta Anderson Bordin, *Frances Willard: A Biography* (Chapel Hill: University of North Carolina Press, 1986), 34–53, 56–64, 87–88.
66. Entries for Dec. 18, 1867, Nov. 27, 1867, Nov. 31, 1867, Jan. 8, 1868, Jan. 9, 1868, Jan. 24, 1868, Frances E. Willard, *Writing out My Heart: Selections from the Journal of Frances E. Willard, 1855*, ed. Carolyn De Swarte Gifford (Urbana: University of Illinois, 1995), 257–58, 259, 260–62; Bordin, *Frances Willard*, 34–37, 44–48.

married Benjamin Duniway, a rancher and prospector. He was kind, but he proved far better at producing children than supporting them. He accrued debts. The sheriff served the summons to pay the debts on Abigail Duniway since her husband was in Idaho prospecting, hoping to raise money to save his farm. As Duniway noted, "When that obligation was made, I was my husband's silent partner—a legal nonentity—with no voice or power for self-protection under the sun; but, when penalty accrued, I was his legal representative." Duniway, already teaching school to help support the family, moved the children to Portland. In the winter of late 1870 and early 1871 she weaned her sixth and last child and started a newspaper, the *New Northwest,* devoted to women's rights and suffrage. Her husband had failed to provide the competency that would sustain a home, leaving it to his wife to do so.[67]

Instead of appealing to white manhood as the key protection for the home, the WCTU implicitly sought protection for "defenseless" women and children against drunken men. A skilled and popular orator, Willard in 1876 had changed the title of her standard temperance lecture to "Home Protection." She phrased her early demands for women's suffrage as a home protection ballot. This had little to do with individualism or individual moral reform. Women needed the ballot because the WCTU needed government—local, state, and federal—to pass moral legislation necessary to protect the home.[68]

The political power of women was not immediately visible. Women could not form an important voting bloc when the vast majority could not vote. And even though women participated in many reform movements, they usually did not lead them. The acceptance by the majority of women of the idea of separate spheres and distinct male and female natures seemed a guarantee of public subordination. Men would dominate the public sphere, while ceding the private sphere to women. But the injection of home and family into the most basic political conflicts of the republic created the opportunity that Willard seized. She was expert at taking the common belief in separate spheres for men and women and turning it into an argument for equality. Responsible for home, family, the education and health of children, and morality, women could not help but expand their activities into the public sphere. She and other women reformers created an imperial home whose boundaries constantly expanded. Anything that affected the home and family became the political concern of women and a rationale for extending suffrage to them. Attacks

67. Moynihan, 1, 26–42, 53, 73–75, 82–90.
68. Foster, 36; Bordin, *Frances Willard,* 100, 110–11; Parker, 4–7, 126–27; Bordin, *Woman and Temperance,* 58–61.

on drink were part of efforts to enlarge the sphere of what historian Peggy Pascoe has called female moral authority.[69]

V

The success of reformers, particularly female reformers, of making home protection the rationale for political action against Indians, Mormons, pornographers, saloonkeepers, and others, spoke to the political power of the home, but the greater danger remained subversion from within. This betrayal of the home did not come from spectacular infidelities, as was the subject of the Beecher-Tilton trial, but instead from subtler developments. As part of the long struggle of women to take control of their own bodies and childbearing, female fertility steadily declined, leading to charges by the end of the century that Protestant white women were failing in their duty to the home by restricting the number of children they bore. These charges usually came from middle- and upper-class men. But men from these same classes were simultaneously engaged in a quiet withdrawal from the home. This was not the withdrawal of workingmen seeking camaraderie and relief in a saloon, but instead the retreat into fraternal lodges, as devoted to temperance as the WCTU, that became a defining feature of the period.

In 1800 the United States had a birth rate higher than any ever recorded for a European country, but it fell steeply and consistently throughout the century. The total fertility rate, which is the average number of children borne by a woman before she reaches menopause, had fallen 50 percent by 1900. An average woman bore 7.04 children in 1800 but only 3.56 in 1900. By later standards the rate was high, roughly equaling the mid-twentieth-century baby boom, but it brought the United States into line with other nineteenth-century nations. Its birth rate by the end of the century equaled Great Britain's and only slightly exceeded Sweden's. These trends were most apparent among native-born middle-class women, far less apparent among immigrant and Catholic women, but strong among the daughters of immigrants. For a decline to be this steep, it had to stretch across the society in both urban and rural areas.[70]

69. Pascoe, xvi–xx.
70. Miriam King and Steven Ruggles, "American Immigration, Fertility, and Race Suicide at the Turn of the Century," *Journal of Interdisciplinary History* 20, no. 3 (1990): 348, 352–53, 360–61; Klein, 124–25; Carl N. Degler, *At Odds: Women and the Family in America from the Revolution to the Present* (New York: Oxford University Press, 1980), 180–82.

The reasons for the decline are broadly clear but somewhat puzzling in their timing. Over the century as a whole, the decline corresponded to a movement into the cities where children were expensive to raise and where their labor, at least among the middle and upper classes, was unnecessary. But the decline began in rural areas long before urban areas began to grow. There it seemed more closely tied to parents' inability to provide their children with land. In urban areas in the late nineteenth century, lower fertility correlated with declining labor participation and increasing education of children. Among workers, smaller families correlated with higher standards of living. The decline was, however, not clearly related to infant and childhood mortality, which dropped after, not before, the fertility rate declined. Women reduced the fertility rate by marrying later and spacing children farther apart as families grew. The spacing may have been through *coitus interruptus*, the so-called rhythm method, or continence, particularly after the first years of marriage, but by the 1870s there were widespread advertisements for and use of condoms, diaphragms, douches, and folk remedies. If birth control failed, there was abortion—either self-induced or surgical. The numbers are unclear, but contemporaries estimated abortions at one to every five or six live births in the 1850s. A Michigan Board of Health estimate in the 1880s claimed that one-third of all pregnancies ended in an abortion. For all the uncertainties, the signs point to women voluntarily controlling their fertility.[71]

Birth control and smaller families brought increasing tension between evangelical reformers (women as well as men), the rising medical profession, and the practices of American women. The alliance between Comstock and female reformers had never been close. They proceeded along parallel tracks rather than boarding the same train. The WCTU had by 1883 established a Department for the Suppression of Impure Literature, but it and other women's groups eventually grew critical of Comstock and his methods. Friction increased as Comstock waged war on birth control and abortion as well as what he regarded as obscene literature. Many doctors who were alarmed by the declining birth rate joined the attack on abortion. They broadened the definition of abortion by attacking the belief in quickening, which did not mark a woman as truly carrying a child until the point when she felt the

71. Daniel Scott Smith, "Differential Mortality in the United States before 1900," *Journal of Interdisciplinary History* 13, no. 4 (1983): 735–36; Freedman and D'Emilio, *Intimate Matters*, 58–66; Michael R Haines and Barbara Anderson, "New Demographic History of the Late 19th-Century United States," *Explorations in Economic History* 25 (1988): 345–46, 348, 353–54; Degler, 124–25, 182–83; John F. McClymer, "Late Nineteenth-Century American Working-Class Living Standards," *Journal of Interdisciplinary History* 17, no. 2 (1986): 392–95; Klein, 107–9, 111–12, 118–26.

fetus move in her womb, usually at about three months. A woman seeking a miscarriage before then did not abort because she wasn't yet considered to be carrying a child. Between 1860 and 1890, forty states and territories outlawed abortion, with most rejecting the quickening doctrine.[72]

The clashes between women and an increasingly influential male medical profession over reproduction and abortion were signs that the division of the home, with the man as protector and provider and the woman as the master of the expanding domestic space, was growing unstable. A gendered guerrilla war had erupted along domestic boundaries. Male fraternal organizations resisted enlarged claims to female moral authority.

By 1896 roughly 5.5 million of the country's 19 million adult men belonged to one or more fraternal lodges. The largest, the Odd Fellows, had 810,000 members, and the most influential, the Freemasons, had 750,000. Fraternal organizations did not embrace fraternité; most were racially segregated, and the various lodges reflected clear class distinctions. Masons, who established the standard of respectability and had the highest fees, had the greatest percentage of businessmen, merchants, professionals, and better-paid clerks. The Odd Fellows were in the middle, and below them were the largely working-class Knights of Pythias. At the bottom were the immigrant and black fraternities and mutual benefit societies.[73]

Fraternalism, like the home, captured the large swath of the Gilded Age that went beyond individualism and self-interest. It did not so much disavow striving as channel it into a set of male rituals and ranks that emphasized brotherhood and concern for others. If manhood involved the refusal "under any circumstances from depending on anybody but themselves for the maintenance of their family," then fraternal orders softened the demands of manhood and acknowledged the impossibility of such extreme independence. When through injury (either in war or work), sickness, or bad luck men could not support their families, they sometimes needed help from their brothers. Men did not beg, but obligations between "brothers" voluntarily agreed to and acknowledged could provide aid. The Odd Fellows demanded "Friendship, Faith, and Charity" from their membership.[74]

72. Freedman and D'Emilio, *Intimate Matters*, 146–47, 159–60 ; Parker, 24, 36, 39–40, 129.
73. Martha Hodes, *Mourning Lincoln* (New Haven, CT: Yale University Press, 2015), 162–63; Anthony D. Fels, "The Square and Compass: San Francisco's Freemasons and American Religion, 1870–1900" (Ph.D. diss., Stanford University, 1987), 67–70; David G. Hackett, *That Religion in Which All Men Agree: Freemasonry in American Culture* (Berkeley: University of California Press, 2014), 127, 129, 130, 271.
74. McConnell, 88.

The fraternal lodges set themselves apart from the sunny middle-class Christianity of liberal evangelicals. They acknowledged human weakness and mortality, and celebrated restraint. Although they sprang from similar social roots as their evangelical neighbors, judging by statistics from San Francisco, most were not affiliated with any church even though they required belief in God. Masons who did have a religious affiliation were most likely to be Episcopalians or of other liturgical denominations that interposed ritual between Christians and their God. The fraternal orders proclaimed that true knowledge did not come from an immediate personal relationship with God, but originated in study, symbolism, and rituals, many derived from the Bible. They claimed an affinity with Christianity, but excised references to Christ, and replaced Christian rituals with those, which for all their biblical references, were of their own making. They, in effect, secularized religious ritual and maintained that morality and redemption could be attained through human reason.[75]

The rituals of the lodges echoed an earlier Calvinism. Becoming a lodge brother, in the words of historian Mark Carnes, involved being "blindfolded, bound, and brought before the emblem of mortality." Evangelical reform, and the strong anti-Masonic movement before the Civil War, influenced the postwar lodges. They abandoned their earlier devotion to mere fellowship and bonhomie, banned liquor, and embraced temperance. At the same time they insisted on their masculine exclusiveness as a necessary wall between them and a feminized evangelical Christianity and a feminized home. All of this had a great appeal. Their membership soared.[76]

Men forged all kinds of useful connections within their lodges and provided assistance, charity, and insurance to members, but there was no need for the elaborate rituals, ranks, and costumes that made up the quotidian activities of a lodge if this was all the lodges sought to achieve. There was no need to play-act roles—masons, Indians, foresters, priests, or knights—supposedly derived from older, simpler, more communal societies in order to get burial insurance. Members of the Grand Army of the Republic had been soldiers, but their organization grew only when it dropped its military hierarchy and assumed the form of a fraternal order.[77]

No one who did not want to be pushed to the fringes of American society could disavow the home, and the fraternal lodges certainly did not do so. Instead they provided a counterpoint to the gendered evangelical

75. Fels, 254–56, 315, 439; Mark C. Carnes, *Secret Ritual and Manhood in Victorian America* (New Haven, CT: Yale University Press, 1989), 46.
76. Carnes, 26–28, 54–61, 76–79.
77. McConnell, 31, 38, 45.

home, mimicking it while purging it of women, and proclaiming their respect for and support of it. Lodge members claimed to, and did, aid the widows and orphans of members, but they did so from within the lodge. Several nights a week the lodges drew men away from "that place of Heaven called home" into a homosocial world full of invented rituals that emphasized the relations between fictional fathers and sons rather than husbands and wives, or for that matter, actual fathers and sons. The fraternal orders appropriated family relations: father, son, and brother to have surrogate fathers and sons reborn into families of fraternal patriarchs. By banning women, they struck back at women's increasing power in the home, churches, and society.[78]

Having done all this, lodge members claimed that their goal was only to produce better fathers, sons, and husbands. The rituals of the final and highest degrees of Masonry sought to produce men purified of masculine passion and aggression who were capable of nurturing and paternal emotions. They would not be men whose intemperance or ambition or passions threatened the home. They would be the emblems of the perfected home.[79]

All the major developments of the Gilded Age had to pass, one way or another, through the doors of the home, which sat at the juncture of politics, public policy, gender relations, racial relations, social reform, the economy, and childrearing. The conflicts of the 1860s and 1870s continued for the rest of the century, and Americans framed the new conflicts that arose as conflicts over the home. They sentimentalized the home, but they were also coldly realistic about its power. It was the political and social ground that could not be ceded.

78. Carnes, 105, 120, 122, 126–27.
79. Ibid., 140, 149.

5

Gilded Liberals

The Republican Party originated as an awkward coalition of ex-Whigs, who advocated federal policies to aid and subsidize development, and laissez-faire liberals, who distrusted both a strong federal government and those who benefited from its intervention. Opposition to slavery and the desire to develop the West free from slavery had held the party together, but with the defeat of the Confederacy, the fissures dividing the party's factions gaped ever wider.

"Liberal" in the nineteenth-century United States and Europe designated people who in many, but not all, respects would be called conservatives in the twenty-first century. They embraced minimal government, a free market economy, individualism, and property rights; they attacked slavery, aristocracy, monarchy, standing armies, the Catholic Church, and hereditary authority.

In the years following the Civil War, the fragmentation of that liberal consensus had just begun. The bulk of liberals remained individualists and republicans, but they were less reliably democrats. An expanded democracy with immigrant and black voters frightened them.

Given liberals' suspicion of established institutions, it might seem odd that during the Gilded Age, they had ensconced themselves in American universities, the elite press, and Protestant churches, but they did. Liberal ideas dominated the Northern commercial and professional middle class, and this allowed even young liberals such as Henry James, Henry and Charles Francis Adams, Clarence King, and William Dean Howells to speak with precocious authority, even as they and other liberal writers often demeaned many of their readers. When Northern congregants went to their Congregational, Presbyterian, Unitarian, and Universalist churches, their preachers were liberals. When their children who attended universities took classes, their professors were liberals. And when Americans read the *Nation*, *Atlantic Monthly*, and *North American Review*, they read the words of liberals. Liberal sometimes seemed all that was respected, learned, and conventional.[1]

1. Sidney Fine, *Laissez Faire and the General-Welfare State: A Study of Conflict in American Thought, 1865–1901* (Ann Arbor: University of Michigan Press, 1956), 47–56;

Howells, a young writer from Ohio with impeccable Republican connections, knew that the respectable literary career he desired depended
on liberal credentials. He had been an employee of Henry Cooke, the
brother of Jay Cooke. Howells had written a Lincoln campaign biography. These Republican credentials had earned him an appointment as
consul in Venice. His writings on Italy had launched his literary career.
But when he returned from Italy in 1865 and entered into the intellectual
circles of New York and Boston, his liberalism began to distance him from
his former Republican sponsors.

Howells found work writing for E. L. Godkin's the *Nation*. Godkin was
an Irish Protestant immigrant, but the magazine's founders were New
Englanders, Boston Brahmins who located the offices in New York.
Howells received $40 a week and the freedom to write for other outlets.
Godkin introduced him to Charles Eliot Norton, one of the *Nation's*
founders, who was a Harvard faculty member and co-editor of the *North
American Review*. He was the country's leading liberal intellectual, whom
Howells would later praise for his "civic righteousness" and "esthetic con-
science." Howells wrote for both journals, sharing their liberal politics
and cultural views.[2]

The forte of liberal intellectuals was criticism (though not necessarily
self-criticism). There was a disjuncture, largely unexamined, between the
liberal belief that freedom of contract—the negotiation of individual
choices in a free market—would inevitably ensure progress, and their increasing dismay at what free political choice and people's taste in culture
yielded. When in 1866 Howells left New York for Boston to become assistant editor of the *Atlantic Monthly*, he joined Norton's intellectual circle.
Norton thought that there were "few greater sins than the dissemination
of second-rate literature." He recoiled from a society that was, in the words
of one of his 1865 essays, "The Paradise of Mediocrities," consumed with
the tawdry, the cheap, and the fake. "Of all civilized nations," Norton
thought the United States "the most deficient in the higher culture of the
mind, and not in the culture only but also in the conditions on which this
culture mainly depends."[3]

Nancy Cohen, *The Reconstruction of American Liberalism, 1865–1914* (Chapel Hill:
University of North Carolina Press, 2002), 11–13. For hard money, a bedrock of liberal-
ism, Irwin Unger, *The Greenback Era: A Social and Political History of American
Finance, 1865–1879* (Princeton, NJ: Princeton University Press, 1964), 120–44.

2. Kenneth Schuyler Lynn, *William Dean Howells: An American Life* (New York:
Harcourt Brace Jovanovich, 1971), 130–31; W. D. Howells to Elinor Howells, Nov. 17,
1865, Dec. 22, 1865, in William Dean Howells, *Selected Letters*, ed. George Warren
Arms (Boston: Twayne, 1979), 1: 237–38.

3. "Charles Eliot Norton: A Reminiscence," *North American Review* 198, no. 697 (1913):
837; Leslie Butler, *Critical Americans: Victorian Intellectuals and Transatlantic Liberal
Reform* (Chapel Hill: University of North Carolina Press, 2007), 42–43, 97, 121, 135–36,

Liberals believed that culturally and politically the people needed the guidance and uplift that only they could provide. They joined the British writer Matthew Arnold in seeking to spread the "sweetness and light" of high culture among the masses. Arnold wished "numbers" to follow "brains." American liberals wanted to equip the "numbers" with brains, but both sacralized a high culture that consisted of "the best that has been thought or said in the world." They disparaged popular tastes and the "Philistinism" of both the middling classes and the nouveau riche of the republic.[4]

Liberals adopted a trickle-down theory of culture. Norton imagined "superior institutions of learning" such as Harvard as "head-waters of the stream of education by which the general intellectual and moral life of the community is supplied and sustained." Liberal ministers assigned a similar role to religion. Liberal theology emphasized salvation and uplift rather than sin and suffering, and it had great appeal among the middling classes of the cities. Henry Ward Beecher appeared every Sunday on a platform at his Plymouth Church in Brooklyn around which were seats arranged in a semicircle for three thousand congregants. His collections of sermons became a staple of popular literature.[5]

The liberal defense of culture often involved attacks on women writers and lecturers whom they feared were dangerously feminizing society. In 1868 when Henry James reviewed Anna Dickinson's novel *What Answer?* in the *Nation*, he was an aspiring novelist. Dickinson was twenty-six, a year older than James, and she was far more famous than he. She had gained notoriety as a flamboyant and popular public speaker on the lyceum circuit. She had addressed Congress and spoken widely on black civil rights, women's rights, and temperance. In *What Answer?* she defended interracial marriage. James attacked Dickinson, but his target was not interracial marriage; he instead denied the capacity of Anna Dickinson—and women writers and reformers in general—to have anything worthwhile to say about racial relations or any other serious public subject. He lumped the books of most American women writers into one "earnest," "sentimental," and "didactic" heap. These women used good causes as an excuse to produce bad art. James would eventually put Dickinson to the service of great

143, 163–65; Charles Eliot Norton, "The Paradise of Mediocrities," *The Nation* 1, no. 2 (1865): 43–44; Lawrence W. Levine, *Highbrow/Lowbrow: The Emergence of Cultural Hierarchy in America* (Cambridge, MA: Harvard University Press, 1988), 214–15.

4. Butler, 120–23, 131–35, 163–65; Levine, 214–15.

5. Butler, 167–69; Clifford Edward Clark, *Henry Ward Beecher: Spokesman for a Middle-Class America* (Urbana: University of Illinois Press, 1978), 88–89; *Louis C. Tiffany and the Art of Devotion*, ed. Patricia Pongracz (New York: Museum of Biblical Art, 2012); Lynn, 89–91, 134, 143–44.

art, as she became his inspiration for Verena Tarrant, the young, beautiful, and charismatic speaker for women's rights in his novel *The Bostonians*. Susan B. Anthony, who took on Dickinson as a protégée following the Civil War, became the model for Olive Chancellor. In James's novel, Verena ultimately deserted reform and Olive Chancellor for the reactionary Southerner Basil Ransom.[6]

Women writers, James argued, did more than produce bad art; they threatened to produce bad and weak men unable to support homes. James declared women to be prisoners of sentiment, making them incapable of serious thought or work outside the domestic sphere. Women writers deformed fictional men and threatened to deform actual men. James denounced the title character in the Rebecca Harding Davis novel *Dallas Galbraith*, for example, as a "hysterical schoolgirl," and "like nothing in trousers." Davis exalted self-sacrifice and altruism over individualism and competition. Dallas Galbraith had accepted a partner's guilt as his own and served five years in prison.[7]

Henry Adams, too, disparaged female attempts at self-improvement. Young women were "unconscious of the pathetic impossibility of improving those poor little hard, thin, wiry, one-stringed instruments which they call their minds, and which haven't range enough to master one big emotion much less to express it in words or figures." To be fair, Adams did not think the intellectual achievements of American men much better. His comments were twins to those of his friend, Clarence King: "The New York girl is certainly a phenomenon. What she would doubtless call her mind is a mere crazy quilt of bright odds and ends. Bits of second-hand opinion cut bias, snips of polite error patched in with remnants of truth which don't show the whole pattern, little rags of scandal &c &c all deftly sewn together in a pretty chromatic chaos."[8]

6. "'Injurious Works and Injurious Criticism'," *The Nation* 7, no. 174 (Oct. 19, 1868); J. Matthew Gallman, *America's Joan of Arc: The Life of Anna Elizabeth Dickinson* (New York: Oxford University Press, 2006), 66–94, 103; Joan D. Hedrick, *Harriet Beecher Stowe: A Life* (New York: Oxford University Press, 1994), 350–53. James himself read Stowe's novel and found it "under the circumstances... a work of singular & delicious perfection," Henry James to Alice James, Aug. 31, 1869, in Henry James, *The Complete Letters of Henry James, 1855–1872*, ed. Pierre A. Walker and Greg W. Zacharias (Lincoln: University of Nebraska Press, 2006), 2:84; Henry James, *The Bostonians*, ed. A. S. Byatt (New York: Random House, 2003), 437.

7. Hedrick, 350–51.

8. Adams to Robert Cunliffe, Aug. 31, 1875, in *Henry Adams, Selected Letters*, ed. Ernest Samuels (Cambridge, MA: Belknap Press of Harvard University Press, 1992), 2: 138 Patricia O'Toole, *The Five of Hearts: An Intimate Portrait of Henry Adams and His Friends, 1880–1918* (New York: C. N. Potter, 1990), 184.

In their disparagement of women writers and their dismissal of the idea of female intellectuals, these liberal men could appear simple misogynists, but they nevertheless sustained complicated relationships with women. Adams maintained a deep intellectual partnership with his wife, Marian Hooper Adams, known as Clover, and King eventually settled into a double life and secret marriage. Adams spent the 1870s as a Harvard history professor, and he and King became close friends. Together with Clover, John Hay, and his wife, Clara Stone, they formed the self-designated and close knit "Five of Hearts."[9]

Liberal intellectual ambitions extended beyond high culture. Liberals were paradoxical ideologues who, although convinced they already knew the answer to all the big questions, were devoted to the pragmatic investigation of society. The American Social Science Association (ASSA) was perhaps the most important liberal institution of the Gilded Age. Intellectuals, professionals, journalists, businessmen, and politicians founded the ASSA in Boston in 1865, modeling it after the British National Association for the Promotion of Social Science. They intended it to collect the facts and apply the principles that would reveal "the general laws that govern social relations." Ostensibly a national group, the association drew heavily from New England, New York, and Pennsylvania. In 1868 Henry Villard took the salaried position of secretary and for all practical purposes ran the association for the next several years. Villard, a German immigrant and journalist, had established his own liberal connections by marrying Fanny Garrison, the daughter of the famous abolitionist William Lloyd Garrison. He was particularly interested in the methods of financing the new railroad corporations, and he would eventually control the Northern Pacific Railroad.[10]

The ASSA's mandate was not just to study society but also to reform it. The association advocated removing essential government functions from elected officials and placing them in the hands of independent commissions staffed by experts and professionals, like the men, and a few women, who belonged to the association. They would study the problems and

9. Martha A. Sandweiss, *Passing Strange: A Gilded Age Tale of Love and Deception across the Color Line* (New York: Penguin Press, 2009), passim.

10. Henry Villard, "Historical Sketch of Social Science," *Journal of Social Science* 1 (June 1869): 1; Thomas L. Haskell, *The Emergence of Professional Social Science: The American Social Science Association and the Nineteenth Century Crisis of Authority* (Urbana: University of Illinois Press, 1977), 91–118, 132; Villard, "Introductory Note," *Journal of Social Science*, no. 1 (June 1869); Dietrich G. Buss, *Henry Villard: A Study of Transatlantic Investments and Interests, 1870–1895* (New York: Arno Press, 1978), 15–26; Villard, *Memoirs of Henry Villard: Journalist and Financier, 1835–1900* (Westminster: Archibald Constable, 1904), 2: 270.

discover the facts; then, the solutions, or so they assumed, would be relatively obvious. The association's officers and the speakers were a Who's Who of Gilded Age liberalism. The articles in their *Journal of Social Science* composed a catalog of liberal issues: immigration, opposition to the income tax, administration of charities, suffrage, elections, crime and punishment, education, trade, currency reform, and health. Under Villard the association became an organization devoted to civil service reform, and it retained this focus through the 1870s.[11]

The liberal intellectuals and reformers of the ASSA recognized that industrial society presented them with a new order of things. They retained their belief in individual autonomy, but also they recognized a social interdependence that demanded cooperation and mutuality. Reconciling their belief in an autonomous individual with recognition of a social order over which the individual had decreasing control seemed a surmountable challenge. They attempted to overcome it by invoking and modifying Auguste Comte, the French philosopher and positivist. They imagined a natural harmony of classes, races, and sexes, but cooperation across these social boundaries demanded the supervision of educated elites such as, for example, members of the American Social Science Association.[12]

The natural laws that mandated harmony also provided the ways to ensure it. Liberals appealed to statistics to smooth over the contradictions between their search for universal laws that determined the structure of human society and their continued belief that society revolved around the choices made in a free market by autonomous individuals whose fate was supposedly in their own hands. "Statistics," the *Journal* proclaimed, "lie at the basis of all sound legislation and of social science in all its departments." Through statistics discrete individual choices and actions could be aggregated and quantified, and their larger patterns discerned.[13]

The census and the insurance industry became mother lodes of a new statistical knowledge and the means to reconcile individualism and deterministic laws. Life insurance, seemingly the most mundane of endeavors, encapsulated the switch from the older providential thinking that placed a person's fate in God's hands. Where once Americans had embraced

11. See volumes 1–5 [1869–1873], *Journal of Social Science Containing the Transactions of the American Association* (New York: Leypoldt & Holdt, 1869–1873); Haskell, 91–121; Ari Arthur Hoogenboom, *Outlawing the Spoils: A History of the Civil Service Reform Movement, 1865–1883* (Urbana: University of Illinois Press, 1961), 55–58, 62, 64–65.

12. Jeffrey P. Sklansky, *The Soul's Economy: Market Society and Selfhood in American Thought, 1820–1920* (Chapel Hill: University of North Carolina Press, 2002), 109–12.

13. "The International Statistical Congress," *Journal of Social Science* 5 (1873): 136; Haskell, 98; Theodore M. Porter, *The Rise of Statistical Thinking, 1820–1900* (Princeton, NJ: Princeton University Press, 1986), 62–63.

providence, they now hedged it. Life had become property, and it belonged in an insurance company's hands rather than God's. Rev. Beecher, paid by New York's Equitable Life Assurance Society, argued that men had an obligation to do all they could, and nobody had a "right to trust in providence." He told the devout that a man had a duty "to do all he knows how to do," and that providence "did not pay a premium on indolence." The industry began in England but blossomed in the United States, selling policies among urban middle-class men, who, unlike farmers who bequeathed land, would have their livelihoods buried with them.[14]

American life insurance companies combined careful demographic statistics, large numbers, and the laws of probability to discern social regularities that were reconcilable with individual choice and responsibility. Applying "mathematical principles to the laws of nature" did not negate the importance of individual choice but rather highlighted the obligation of free men to assume responsibility for the risk that came with self-ownership. Insurance proclaimed the compatibility of individualism and predictable laws of nature.[15]

Such arguments sought to salvage an individualism increasingly out of step with industrial society. The core ideas of individualism—that a person's fate should be in his (or her) own hands and that freedom gave citizens the opportunity and the responsibility to make of themselves what they could—seemed almost quaint in the new, urban, and industrial United States. When industrial work crippled and epidemic diseases killed, and where chance—freaks of fortune—produced what John Maynard Keynes, the economist, would later call "the radical uncertainties of capitalism," luck as much as effort seemed to dictate outcomes. But the law of large numbers could fold the radical uncertainty of any individual life into the serene laws of probability. When any individual was going to die was unknown, but the number of a large population who would die in an average year was predictable. Collectivizing risk and considering the community as a whole rather than the individual was a form of "communism," but the practice paradoxically allowed people to maintain their belief in individualism. Probability could compensate for the limits of human knowledge.[16]

14. Sheppard Homans, "Life Insurance," *Journal of Social Science* 2 (1870): 159–60; Jonathan Levy, *Freaks of Fortune: The Emerging World of Capitalism and Risk in America* (Cambridge, MA: Harvard University Press, 2012), 61, 70–82, 86–87, Beecher quote 76.
15. Homans, 159–60; Levy, 5, 61, 70–82, 84, 86–87.
16. Louis Menand, *The Metaphysical Club: A Story of Ideas in America* (New York: Farrar, Straus and Giroux, 2001), 370–72, 407–11; Levy, 14, 80–84, 86.

The beauty of insurance was that the market freedom that liberals embraced, or so they argued, mitigated the very hazards that capitalism and economic growth created. By insuring the future productive capacity of a worker, the market could offload risk onto life insurance companies. The companies, in turn, by investing the money they amassed from premiums, could create new capital necessary for the economic growth that provided individual opportunities—and new risks. Much of this capital went into western farm mortgages, which, along with government subsidies, fueled the tremendous expansion of both agriculture and farm indebtedness. The 43 life insurance companies in the United States in 1860 grew to 163 by 1870.[17]

Liberal enthusiasm for actuarial tables paled before their enthusiasm for the census. James Garfield, then an Ohio congressman, told the association in 1870 that statistics had "developed the truth that society is an organism whose elements and forces conform to laws as constant and pervasive as those which govern the material universe; and that the study of these laws will enable man to ameliorate his condition, to emancipate himself from countless evils which were once thought beyond his control; and will make him the master, rather than the slave of nature."[18]

Bewitched by how aggregated individual choice yielded collective regularities, and statistics yielded probabilities, liberals had found what they regarded as a scientific solution to the problem of reconciling free choice and contract freedom and social stability. They concluded that all regularities were necessities. Social science would identify the range of human behavior and mark the boundaries beyond which it was useless and dangerous for governments to go. Liberals fervently believed in progress: things not only changed, but they changed for the better. But such progress was slow and followed natural laws; it was not the progress of evangelical reformers who imagined a world changed by individual moral efforts, or of labor radicals who thought of a world reorganized to dismantle existing class privilege. If immutable laws determined progress, then the safest route to change involved an understanding of those laws and a repression of all attempts to violate them. Governance was a matter of creating expert administrators, who would act as a kind of police, blocking those who would violate the natural laws and noting legitimate exceptions to those laws. Seeking to reconcile individualism and natural laws, liberals made the market an expression of both. They regarded the market as natural because, as writer Louis Menand has put it, "they had already decided that nature operated like the market."[19]

17. Levy, 17, 60–64, 156–64.
18. James A. Garfield, "American Census," *Journal of Social Science* 2, no. 1 (1870): 31–32.
19. Menand, 195.

Francis Amasa Walker epitomized the expert in government, reconciling the supposedly natural laws of the market with administrative governance. Taken in isolation, his statements made him seem the most doctrinaire of liberals, a man who defined as socialistic "all efforts, under popular impulse, to enlarge the functions of government, to the diminution of individual initiative and enterprise, for a supposed public good." Taken literally, such an expansive definition of socialism meant that virtually every positive action taken by governments, from delivering the mail or cleaning the streets to providing for schools, amounted to the kind of socialism that Walker opposed. Although insisting that "it is eminently desirable to reduce the action of the organized public force to the minimum," Walker argued that, although contrary to laissez-faire, it was the duty of the state to educate its population, provide "a strict system of sanitary administration," and secure "by special precautions the integrity of banks of savings...."[20]

Walker's career created a paradigm for the liberal expert in government. He followed up his service as superintendent of the 1870 census by becoming the commissioner of Indian affairs and then supervising the Tenth Census of 1880. The First U.S. Census had asked each household only four questions. Walker's Tenth Census gathered information on people, businesses, farms, hospitals, churches, and more. The census takers posed 13,010 questions. The questions created categories, which were ways of "making up people" in that the classifications themselves became a reality that defined the people contained within them. Eventually, he would serve as president of the Massachusetts Institute of Technology and of both the American Statistical Association and the American Economic Association.[21]

Like other liberals devoted to laissez-faire and supposedly universal economic laws, Walker inserted exceptions to them as a kind of asterisk, but far from embarrassing the liberals, such exceptions were marks of their certitude. Unlike the uneducated electorate, they had studied and discerned social laws and were capable of understanding their limits. Walker did not distrust government so much as democratic governance, which he and other liberals linked to inefficiency and corruption. Their solution was to

---

20. Michael Les Benedict, "Laissez-Faire and Liberty: A Re-Evaluation of the Meaning and Origins of Laissez-Faire Constitutionalism," *Law and History Review* 3, no. 2 (1985): 306; R. Daniel Wadhwani, "Protecting Small Savers: The Political Economy of Economic Security," in Richard R. John, ed., *Ruling Passions: Political Economy in Nineteenth-Century America*, (College Station: Pennsylvania State University Press, 2006), 126.

21. Porter, 154–57; Margo J. Anderson, *The American Census: A Social History* (New Haven, CT: Yale University Press, 1988), 84, 98–104; Ian Hacking, *The Taming of Chance* (Cambridge: Cambridge University Press, 1990), 2–3, 6.

turn to rule by expert commissioners insulated from popular politics. These would, like the courts, prove a check on democracy.

I

To turn their cultural dominance and their principles into politics, Liberal Republicans originally invested great hope in Ulysses S. Grant, regarded by many at the end of the Civil War as the "great man of the day, perhaps the age." He was the country's most famous citizen. He wanted the presidency not because of a desire for power or to forward an agenda but because he deeply needed public approval. Liberals anticipated that after extending universal male suffrage to the South, Grant would break the back of the old Southern "aristocracy," end Reconstruction, curb government power, uproot the spoils system and corruption, end protection and subsidies, and institute the gold standard. Partially liberals misjudged Grant; but mostly they overestimated their own influence within the Republican Party and the nation. The liberals' hopes for Grant turned to dust between 1868 and 1872. His financial and economic policies, the spoils system with its associated corruption, and his foreign policy—particularly his desire to annex Santo Domingo—all contributed to a rich stew of disappointment and alienation.[22]

Liberals worshipped the gold standard, which they regarded as the solution to the problems of the financial system created by the Civil War. The economic cost of Union victory had been high: inflation, debt, a diversion of millions of men from production to destruction, and the loss or crippling of hundreds of thousands of workers. But to liberals these problems paled before a financial system based on a fiat currency. During the war the government had issued greenbacks, a paper currency, in order to pay soldiers and buy supplies. Essentially federal IOUs backed by the credit of the government, greenbacks were unredeemable in either gold or silver. By war's end there were nearly half a billion dollars' worth of them in circulation. Their value fluctuated against American gold coins and against the British pound, but gold and gold-backed currency always had the greater value.[23]

22. William S. McFeely, *Grant: A Biography* (New York: Norton, 1981), 169–70, 232–35, 278–84; Andrew L. Slap, *The Doom of Reconstruction: The Liberal Republicans in the Civil War Era* (New York: Fordham University Press, 2006), 98–111.

23. Richard Franklin Bensel, *Yankee Leviathan: The Origins of Central State Authority in America, 1859–1877* (Cambridge: Cambridge University Press, 1990), 152, 254–58; Unger, 13–16; Matthias Morys, "The Emergence of the Classical Gold Standard," *Centre for*

Greenbacks, along with national bank notes and specie, constituted the three forms of money in circulation. The origins of national bank notes, also not redeemable for gold or silver, were complicated. During the Civil War Republicans had turned national debt into a tool for creating money by constructing a national banking system that simultaneously funded the debt and created the nation's first standard currency. The government required national banks to hold a certain percentage of their capital reserves in federal bonds. In return, the banks could (up to a certain limit) issue standardized national bank notes that circulated as money in proportion to the federal bonds they held. To make this a deal that the banks could not refuse, the government levied a prohibitive tax on banknotes issued by state-chartered banks, driving them from circulation. The arrangement proved lucrative for national banks. They bought bonds with greenbacks, collected interest paid in gold on the bonds, and then used those bonds to issue bank notes, which they loaned to collect additional interest. In 1875, U.S. bond issues formed 63 percent of the investments of New York City national banks.[24]

There was also a nominal currency of gold and silver coins (specie); it was nominal because dollar denomination coins were so scarce as to be invisible in ordinary transactions. The value of the gold in the coins was higher than their face value and so, except in California, they disappeared from everyday circulation. Gold, however, remained essential for financing international trade and to paying interest on government bonds.[25]

Liberals considered only currency redeemable in gold as real money—so-called hard money. Making all money—greenbacks and banknotes—redeemable in gold became for them the only sure cure for inflation. They wanted the United States to follow Great Britain onto the gold standard.[26]

The gold standard divided both parties along practical, ideological, and moral lines. The practical consequences revolved around the deflationary consequences of a gold standard. Theoretically, under the gold standard the government could issue no more greenbacks than it could redeem in gold, and the nation's money supply would thus contract. Congress, however, had already had an unpleasant experience with contraction. In 1866 it had authorized President Johnson's secretary of treasury,

Historical Economics and Related Research at York: Cherry Discussion Papers Series, Cherry DP 12/01 (2012): 14–47.

24. Bensel, 258, 260–62, 263; Gretchen Ritter, *Goldbugs and Greenbacks: The Antimonopoly Tradition and the Politics of Finance in America* (Cambridge: Cambridge University Press, 1997), 66–71.
25. Ritter, 73–78.
26. Claudia D. Goldin and Frank D. Lewis, "The Economic Cost of the American Civil War: Estimates and Implications," *Journal of Economic History* 35, no. 2 (1975), 299–326.

Hugh McCulloch, to reduce the number of greenbacks, and the currency deflated at the rate of 8 percent a year. This proved particularly hard on the South and West, which had far less money circulating per capita than the East. When, as the opponents of retraction had predicted, a recession struck in 1866, Congress slowed retraction. And when the recession continued into 1868, Congress suspended McCulloch's authority to retire greenbacks.[27]

The financial maneuvers of Isaac Sherman, a leading liberal advocate of the gold standard, illustrated how debtors gained from inflation and lost with deflation, and why creditors favored a gold standard. During the Civil War Sherman was a rich man, an ardent free-soil Republican, an abolitionist, and a creditor. He recognized that greenbacks would bring inflation, which would hurt him. He lamented that his existing loans would be worth only "60 cents on a dollar" and thus it was "my ox that is to be gored." As greenbacks sank in value requiring $289 in greenbacks to buy $100 worth of gold in 1864, Sherman recognized an opportunity. Government policy allowed bonds to be purchased with cheap greenbacks while interest would be paid in expensive gold. If he bought $1,000 worth of bonds for greenbacks with greenbacks selling for one-third the price of gold, the result would be interest rates nearly triple the nominal rate of 6 percent. He did well, and if the government paid back the principal on the bonds in more valuable gold equivalent dollars, he would do even better.[28]

Sherman and other advocates of the gold standard regarded their stance as more than self-interest. They made it a moral choice, and opponents of the gold standard responded in kind, making the debate over monetary policy often seem more theological than political. Liberals often framed the decision between gold and greenbacks as a choice between sin and salvation. Carl Schurz consistently described the redemption of U.S. bonds with greenbacks—even though they had been bought with greenbacks—as immoral. The liberal publicist Edward Atkinson, funded by Isaac Sherman, equated the adoption of greenbacks with theft. He declared circulation of greenbacks a crime, and he demanded that crimes be

27. Unger, 41–42; Richard Eugene Sylla, *The American Capital Market, 1846–1914: A Study of the Effects of Public Policy on Economic Development* (New York: Arno Press, 1975), 52–54; Walter T. K. Nugent, *Money and American Society, 1865–1880* (New York: Free Press, 1968), 45, 92–94.; Richard H. Timberlake, Jr., "Ideological Factors in Specie Resumption and Treasury Policy," *Journal of Economic History* 24, no. 1 (1964): 32; Richard H. Timberlake, *The Origins of Central Banking in the United States* (Cambridge, MA: Harvard University Press, 1978), 94–97.

28. James A. Henretta, "Isaac Sherman and the Trials of Gilded Age Liberalism," *American Nineteenth Century History* 4, no. 1 (2003): 80–83.

suppressed no matter what the cost. Nature demanded gold; it, along with silver, had intrinsic value.[29]

Atkinson admitted deflation, unemployment, and bankruptcies would follow an immediate return to the gold standard: "Much real hardship will ensue; because, if we have broken a great economic law in declaring that to be real money which is not money, the innocent must suffer with the guilty, precisely as in the case of the infraction of a great moral law, the criminal causes misery and suffering to others than himself."[30]

The more wealth became a matter of paper—stocks, bonds, and bank checks—the more liberals fetishized gold. Gold was ancient and natural and not modern and manufactured. It was rare, could not be reproduced, and held its value. Paper, on the other hand, could, like Confederate currency or the stocks and bonds of failed companies, seem a fortune one day and end up as the lining of trunks the next. Paper threatened to render the world flimsy, ephemeral, and open to constant negotiation, which made it all the more necessary that order be restored and all value be reducible to gold. Liberals regarded gold as wealth you could touch—it was real—while greenbacks were fictional, a mere representation of wealth.[31]

In reality, the gold standard was neither ancient nor natural. Both the international gold standard and American dependence on a fiat currency were new and revolutionary. The British, who formally adopted the gold standard in 1819, were virtually alone until the 1860s when others followed. Like the United States, most nations had previously relied on various forms of bimetallism or silver-backed currencies. The unprecedented increase in gold supplies that began with the discoveries in California and Australia had driven silver out of circulation in Europe and made a gold standard practicable. Necessity had forced the United States to print greenbacks during the Civil War to pay for goods and services.[32]

The difference in value between greenbacks and gold certainly did create real problems, which a gold standard would remove. With the gold

29. Carl Schurz, *The Reminiscences of Carl Schurz*, ed. Frederic Bancroft and William Archibald Dunning (New York: McClure, 1907), 3: 286–91; Kathryn Taylor Morse, *The Nature of Gold: An Environmental History of the Klondike Gold Rush* (Seattle: University of Washington Press, 2003), 22–23.

30. Edward Atkinson, *On the Collection of Revenue*, rev. ed. (New York: American Free Trade League, 1869), 20; Sven Beckert, *The Monied Metropolis: New York City and the Consolidation of the American Bourgeoisie, 1850–1896* (Cambridge: Cambridge University Press, 2001), 163–64; Ritter, 141–42.

31. Morse, 16–39; Beckert, 226.

32. Bensel, 152, 254–58, 294, n. 114; Unger, 13–16; Morys, 14–47. Milton Friedman and Anna Jacobson Schwartz, *A Monetary History of the United States* (Princeton, NJ: Princeton University Press, 1963), 51–52.

standard, merchants engaged in international trade would not incur the transaction costs of resorting to the Gold Room, the New York exchange devoted to buying gold with currency. It would also eliminate the higher interest rates that American borrowers and bond sellers had to pay for foreign capital. By increasing the confidence of foreign investors in American securities, the gold standard would lower interest rates on American bonds. It would also create a boon for bankers, since if the United States went on the gold standard, bank notes would become redeemable in gold, substantially increasing their value. Such advantages inclined many bankers to become hard-money men. But as critics of the gold standard pointed out, and as retraction in the 1860s had demonstrated, facilitating foreign trade and stabilizing the currency would come at a high price, and the ultimate economic result might not be stability at all.[33]

The halt in the policy of contraction of the greenbacks worried liberals in large part because it delayed transition to the gold standard, but initially they were reassured because Grant took what they regarded as a sound position on both the debt and currency questions. The government had not specified how the wartime bonds' principal would be repaid. Since at the height of inflation in 1864 a greenback dollar had been worth only 34 percent of a gold dollar, redeeming the bond in gold represented as much as a tripling of the original investment in addition to the interest already paid. Bondholders would reap a wonderful windfall if the government paid in gold. Taxpayers would assume an additional burden. If, however, the government redeemed its bonds with greenbacks, there would be no windfall.[34]

Initially, a large majority of the Republicans in Congress agreed with Sen. John Sherman, the brother of Gen. William Tecumseh Sherman (but no relation to Isaac Sherman), who held that redemption in greenbacks would amount to an unconscionable "repudiation" of the debt. They argued for repayment in gold. But a coalition of Midwestern Democrats and Republicans emerged to challenge this policy, as well as any policy to reduce the number of greenbacks in circulation.[35]

Following Grant's inauguration in March 1869, Congress passed the Public Credit Act, promising to redeem the war bonds in gold. The next year Congress authorized the refunding of the national debt. Investors could exchange existing bonds for new bonds running for another ten to

33. Alan M. Taylor and Maurice Obstfeld, "Sovereign Risk, Credibility and the Gold Standard: 1870–1913 Versus 1925–31," *National Bureau of Economic Research Working Paper Series*, no. Working Paper 9435 (2002): 1–6, 15–24; Morys, 34–48.
34. Unger, 15–16, 22–23, 132; Nugent, 126–27; Bensel, 318–19.
35. Unger, 73–74; Nugent, 109–10, 121–33, 139, 185–86.

fifteen years at lower interest rates. All would be redeemable in gold coin, and all were tax-exempt. Congress bolstered the public credit with repayment spread out over a much longer period.[36]

A victory on the debt still left the currency question unresolved, and liberals pushed for a resumption of the policy of reducing the number of greenbacks in circulation to ease transition to the gold standard. Grant, who had failed at business, seems to have had few deep-seated economic convictions. He had come into office favoring contraction, but his actual program when George Boutwell was his secretary of treasury was far more pragmatic. Boutwell accomplished a task of considerable intricacy in keeping a balance between the gold needed for foreign trade, the national bank notes issued by the federal banks, and greenbacks. The moving parts had to be kept well greased or the financial machinery was likely to seize up, as it regularly threatened to do. Boutwell's efforts to defuse financial crises were often hair-raising, but they succeeded. Liberals believed such intervention would be unnecessary on the gold standard. Eastern bankers and financiers wanted predictability and stability that they did not think the Treasury could continue to achieve. They pressured for a gold standard that they thought would ensure the predictability they desired, while cementing in place the advantages the new banking system had already given them.[37]

Neither Grant nor Boutwell, whom Henry Adams scorned as a "lugubrious joke," showed any enthusiasm for bankrupting constituents in order to uphold liberal principles and please bankers. Boutwell adopted a policy of letting the economy "grow up to the Civil War money stock." With settlers starting farms in the West, the South rebuilding, and northern industry expanding, the economy would soon need all the available money supply. The value of greenbacks would rise with the expansion of the economy rather than through the reduction of the money supply, and at some future date the resumption of specie—that is gold—payments could proceed with less pain. This was, in essence, how resumption did eventually take place on January 2, 1879, but it happened far more slowly than liberals wished.[38]

With the Grant administration unwilling to abandon the greenbacks, the liberals took to the courts. In 1870, the liberals won a partial victory when the Supreme Court decided *Hepburn v. Griswold*. The Court

36. Eric Foner, *Reconstruction: America's Unfinished Revolution, 1863–1877* (New York: Harper & Row, 1988), 344; Nugent, 126, 128; Bensel, 317–19.
37. Bensel, 254–55, 277; Unger, 165–72.
38. Bensel, 291–92; Nicolas Barreyre, "Sectionalisme et politique aux États-Unis: Le midwest et la reconstruction, 1865–1877" (Ph.D., École des Hautes Études en Sciences Sociales, 2008), 319–20; Henry Adams, *The Education of Henry Adams: An Autobiography* (New York: Heritage Press, 1942; orig. ed. 1918), 263–67.

undermined the legitimacy of fiat currency by ruling that creditors could demand specie to repay any obligations made before the law authorized the issuance of greenbacks. This was an astonishing verdict and it threatened to wreak havoc, so Grant immediately appointed two new justices to the court. They were both railroad attorneys, and they both knew that *Griswold* meant railroads would have to pay interest on antebellum bonds in gold, thus significantly raising their costs. In 1871, to the anger of liberals, the court reversed itself in *Knox v. Lee* and *Parker v. Davis*. As the gold standard seemed to be pushed further into the future, it pulled liberal hopes for laissez-faire increasingly beyond reach.[39]

These setbacks depleted liberal confidence in both Grant and the U.S. Treasury Department and made them even more enamored of the gold standard. Already Anglophiles, they tended to trust the Bank of England more than the secretary of the treasury. With the gold standard, the United States would, in effect, cede control of its interest rates and money supply to Great Britain, the world's largest creditor nation. The gold standard depended on a country having access to enough gold to redeem its currency on demand. When London controlled a large proportion of that gold, Great Britain and the Bank of England acquired inordinate influence over the fiscal and economic policies of other governments. The gold standard created what economists have called a "golden straitjacket." Debtor nations would exchange control over their monetary policy for capital mobility and stable exchange rates. Although the cost of borrowing abroad would fall, the United States would lose the ability to drive domestic interest rates below international interest rates. Gold dollars would flee abroad if interest rates elsewhere were higher.[40]

Free trade was as sacred as the gold standard to orthodox liberals, and the tariff joined fiat currency as a bête noire. The tariff, however, provided more than half of federal revenue between 1865 and 1871, including the gold necessary to pay interest on bonds. No government could eliminate it, but Congress could reform and simplify it since relatively few goods — such as sugar and coffee — provided the bulk of the revenue. Even a liberal ideologue like E. L. Godkin was flummoxed by the tariff. He was a free trader, but he hesitated to publish articles by the ardent free trader Edward Atkinson because it would alienate other investors in the *Nation*. The tariff drew a sharp line between liberals and Republican Party

39. Bensel, 292–93; "Hepburn V. Griswold—75 U.S. 603 (1869)," (1869); McFeely, 387; Timberlake, *The Origins of Central Banking in the United States*, 100–101.

40. Bensel, 293–97; Jay C. Shambaugh, Maurice Obstfeld, and Alan M. Taylor, "The Trilemma in History: Tradeoffs among Exchange Rates, Monetary Policies, and Capital Mobility," *Review of Economics and Statistics* 87, no. 3 (2005): 423.

regulars who put protection of American industries at the heart of their economic policy.[41]

II

Economic policy was only one element that alienated liberals from Republican regulars. Reconstruction increasingly disturbed liberals as it became apparent that black suffrage alone would not eliminate the necessity for continued federal intervention. In the 1870 elections, white terrorists brazenly attacked Republicans, resulting in losses in Alabama, Tennessee, Texas, North Carolina, and Georgia, which sent the state's grand titan of the Ku Klux Klan to Congress. But the response more than the attacks alarmed liberals.[42]

Liberals would have preferred not to have to make a choice between men like Wyatt Outlaw and the Klan, but they effectively did. Wyatt Outlaw, the son of a slave mother and a white father, was a carpenter in Alamance County, North Carolina. He also operated a store and bar that catered to railroad workers, black and white. He helped found the local African Methodist Church and was a prominent leader of the Loyal Republican League, many of whose members were black railroad workers pledged not to "countenance any social or political aristocracy." He was, by the standards of the time, a man.[43]

The Alamance Klan was also about manhood, but in this case white manhood rather than black manhood. Their initiations, even by nineteenth-century standards, were oddly homoerotic. The new member would have a noose placed around his neck and be partially strangled while regular members with great horns on their head barked and growled as they rubbed their horns on his body. The Klan preferred to whip its victims in their own front yards in front of their families to demonstrate their impotence and inability to protect home and family; sometimes they sexually mutilated them.[44]

41. Bensel, 299; E. L. Godkin to Edward Atkinson, July 17, 1865, and "To the Nation Stockholders," Aug. 23, 1865, in The Gilded Age Letters of E. L. Godkin, ed. William Martin Armstrong (Albany: State University of New York Press, 1974), 39–40, 53; Richard Franklin Bensel, The Political Economy of American Industrialization, 1877–1900 (Cambridge: Cambridge University Press, 2000), 10.

42. Gregory P. Downs, After Appomattox: Military Occupation and the Ends of War (Cambridge, MA: Harvard University Press, 2015), 213–17, 220–21, 229–30, 233–34.

43. Scott Reynolds Nelson, Iron Confederacies: Southern Railways, Klan Violence, and Reconstruction (Chapel Hill: University of North Carolina Press, 1999), 98–110.

44. Ibid., 110–12.

The Republicans carried Alamance County in the election of 1868, and the Klan and the White Brotherhood were determined to take it back. When they menaced Outlaw and his followers, Outlaw turned to local authorities rather than the Loyal League. This was a mistake, but also a sign of his trust that governments supported by black men could protect black homes. But local officials could not protect Outlaw from the one hundred or more white men who in February 1870 dragged him from his bed before his children and mother and hanged him in front of the county courthouse. They mutilated his body, and then, in case that was not warning enough, they attached a sign: "Beware you guilty black and white."[45]

Outlaw's lynching formed part of a string of outrages. In nearby Caswell County, Robin Jacobs, a freedman, was murdered. The next day another freedman was tied to a tree while fifteen Klansmen raped his wife in succession. Another band of white men raped another freedwoman and "afterwards stuck their knives in various parts of her body." To climax the violence, white conservatives murdered a Republican state senator and former Freedmen's Bureau agent, John W. Stephens. Grant's sensitivity to accusations that he was a military despot left him reticent to challenge even these crimes. He hoped the new Reconstruction governments could restore order. North Carolina tried.[46]

North Carolina Gov. William W. Holden reacted forcefully to the murder of Wyatt Outlaw and the atrocities that followed. In part he duplicated actions in Arkansas where in 1868 the governor had mobilized the militia, including black soldiers, to smash the Klan, but Holden would neither rely on a predominantly black militia to protect black people nor trust white juries in the affected areas. Holden declared martial law, mobilized largely white Unionists of western North Carolina, and suppressed the Klan in nine counties. He attempted to try his prisoners before a military commission, but the prisoners appealed for due process under the same Fourteenth Amendment that they had bitterly opposed. They were remanded to local courts, which were unlikely to convict white men for crimes against black people.[47]

45. Steven Hahn, A Nation under Our Feet: Black Political Struggles in the Rural South, from Slavery to the Great Migration (Cambridge, MA: Belknap Press of Harvard University Press, 2003), 274–75; Nelson, 100–114.
46. Gregory P. Downs, Declarations of Dependence: The Long Reconstruction of Popular Politics in the South, 1861–1908 (Chapel Hill: University of North Carolina Press, 2011), 123–24; Allen W. Trelease, White Terror: The Ku Klux Klan Conspiracy and Southern Reconstruction (New York: Harper & Row, 1971), 208–23.
47. Trelease, 208–25; Downs, After Appomattox, 216–17, 231–32; Hahn, 283–86; Foner, 439–41; Downs, Declarations of Dependence, 125.

Holden defeated the Klan, but the Democrats portrayed themselves as the real victims of violence, painting the Republicans as politically repressive tools of the railroads. They succeeded in impeaching Holden and driving him from office. An aggressive and powerful federal government and accusations of intervention on behalf of the railroads rang liberal alarm bells, for liberals feared both. Southern Democrats did not invent the railroads' role in attempts to suppress the Klan. As the violence spread and intensified in South Carolina, many of the attacks took place around the railroad lines being built there. Secretary of the Interior Columbus Delano wanted to protect the railroads controlled by Tom Scott, a central figure in both the Pennsylvania Railroad and in the new Southern systems.[48]

Prior to the congressional elections of 1870, Congress had passed the Enforcement Act, which made it a federal crime for two or more persons to act together or go in disguise to deprive any person of a right or privilege of citizenship or to punish them for exercising it. The president could use the armed forces of the United States to enforce the law. Except in Kentucky, however, Grant did not employ the Enforcement Act.[49]

For reasons that went well beyond the railroads, the Klan appalled Attorney General Amos T. Akerman, a northerner who had moved to Georgia before the Civil War and stayed. He urged Grant to intervene. A Senate investigation of Southern violence in 1871 produced a second Enforcement Act, and a special congressional session that spring yielded the Ku Klux Klan Act, which gave the president the power to suspend the right of habeas corpus and use federal troops to suppress attempts to deprive citizens of their civil rights. Still Grant hesitated.[50]

In October 1871 Grant finally acted. The Klan had virtually taken over York and surrounding South Carolina counties. Three troops of the Seventh Cavalry, the same regiment employed by Sheridan in Texas and by Hancock against Cheyennes on the Great Plains, were already present. They aided the U.S. marshal in making arrests. The Klan ripped up the railroad to hinder the federal forces. Hundreds fled; hundreds more — so-called pukers — confessed. They provided evidence against almost two hundred Klan leaders and the most violent members.[51]

The trials became a contest between present and former U.S. attorneys general. Reverdy Johnson, who as James Buchanan's attorney general had argued against Dred Scott in the Supreme Court, was the lead defense

48. Nelson, 112–14, 136–37; Slap, 113–14.
49. Foner, 454–56; Downs, *After Appomattox*, 223–28; Trelease, 385–87.
50. Trelease, 385–98; Foner, 457–58.
51. Lou Falkner Williams, *The Great South Carolina Ku Klux Klan Trials, 1871–1872* (Athens: University of Georgia Press, 1996), 40–59; Nelson, 136–37; Trelease, 362–80.

attorney. Henry Stanbery, who had been Andrew Johnson's attorney general, assisted him. Attorney General Akerman, determined to break the Klan, guided the prosecution from afar. He thought the elimination of the Klan both right and necessary for preserving the Republican Party in the South.[52]

The guilt of the defendants on the conspiracy charges was hardly in doubt, but larger constitutional issues concerned the meaning of the Fourteenth Amendment. Did it extend only to acts of the federal government or also to acts by the states, individuals, and associations? And in the prosecution of a federal crime, could a federal court try common law crimes, such as murder, traditionally reserved to state courts? These questions went to the heart of the Republicans' expansion of federal power and the goal of a national citizenship. The issues were posed, but for the moment the courts did not rule on them. When the first suspects were convicted, usually by majority black juries, the remaining suspects confessed to charges of conspiracy. The punishments were as mild as the crimes behind the conspiracy charges—murder, rape, torture, and mutilation—were gruesome. The longest prison term was five years. The government broke the Klan in South Carolina, but many of the Klan's leaders had fled and escaped punishment.[53]

Attorney General Akerman had demonstrated the potency of the combination of even small numbers of cavalry and prosecution under the Enforcement Acts, but though he won the battle in South Carolina, he lost the internecine battles within Grant's cabinet. Secretary of State Hamilton Fish advocated leniency toward the Klan and the South. Akerman had refused to approve contested western land grants to companies controlled by Jay Gould and by Collis P. Huntington, one of the Associates of the Central Pacific and Southern Pacific. They wanted Akerman removed. Secretary of Interior Delano changed his position. What Gould and Huntington wanted, Delano wanted. He joined Fish in pressuring Grant to dismiss his attorney general. Grant complied and then, under pressure from the liberal Republicans, undertook a policy of pardon and clemency for Klansmen. Akerman returned to Georgia.[54]

The federal attack on the Klan proved the final straw for liberals worried about the expanding powers of the federal government, and liberal Republicans joined Democrats in opposing federal action. Sen. Lyman Trumbull, who originally supported Reconstruction, became alarmed at growing federal power and passed over into opposition, as did Carl Schurz.

52. McFeely, 370–74; Williams, 54–55.
53. Trelease, 399–408; Williams, 19, 46–61, 81, 100, 107–12; Foner, 454–56.
54. Williams, 125–27; McFeely, 368–73.

The same Congress that passed the Ku Klux Klan Act passed a bill for amnesty for most Southerners disqualified for office under the Fourteenth Amendment. It would become law the following year.[55]

Neither Schurz nor other Liberal Republicans repudiated the constitutional achievements of Reconstruction; they would keep the Thirteenth, Fourteenth, and Fifteenth Amendments, but otherwise they would leave the South to local governments, which, they hoped, would become the domain of men of "property and enterprise." Schurz, Trumbull, and Godkin thought that the fate of the freedmen was now in their own hands. "The removal of white prejudice against the negro," the *Nation* had editorialized as early as 1867, "depends almost entirely on the negro himself." Schurz, representing a border state, had politically expedient reasons to move away from the Radicals. He split from the Missouri Radicals by endorsing the re-enfranchisement of Confederates in Missouri, and he also voted against the Ku Klux Klan Act, which he regarded as "insane." He thought the crimes of the Klan exaggerated and the result of Northern interference. He seriously thought that black rights would be more secure under conservative Southerners than Republican governments. Time would soon give the lie to that belief.[56]

Other liberals drew parallels between black voters in the South and immigrant voters in the North. *New York Tribune* correspondent James Pike united liberal perceptions of a corrupt New York City with the corruption of the Reconstruction South. Pike had been an ardent abolitionist and Lincoln's minister to the Netherlands. When he came home following the war, he wrote a widely cited article on South Carolina, "A State in Ruins." Its villains were carpetbaggers and freedpeople, who had deserved the violence brought down on them. "The men who lead and manage . . . the State Government are thieves and miscreants, ignorant and corrupt." They had impoverished the state and driven out capital. A democracy that placed black over white could not endure.[57]

Pike was right about two things, and wrong about most everything else. First, reflecting the population of the state, more than half the men elected to state and public office in South Carolina between 1867 and 1876 were black, although being black made various shades of skin color a disguise for a quite diverse and factionalized group of people. Second, the government was corrupt, but it was not particularly corrupt when

55. Slap, 112–14; Mark W. Summers, *The Ordeal of the Reunion: A New History of Reconstruction* (Chapel Hill: University of North Carolina Press, 2014), 270–71, 309.
56. Foner, 456, 498, 500; Hoogenboom, 83; McFeely, 380–81.
57. Adam-Max Tuchinsky, *Horace Greeley's New-York Tribune: Civil War-Era Socialism and the Crisis of Free Labor* (Ithaca, NY: Cornell University Press, 2009), 225–26.

measured against other governments of the era. He was wrong in seeing black politicians as the pliant tools of whites, wrong in failing to recognize the considerable democratic accomplishments of the South Carolina legislature, and wrong about the source of violence in the state. As historian Thomas Holt has argued, it sprang from "an almost religious crusade to restore white supremacy."[58]

Pike wrote the article, which would become a staple of reactionary folklore, without actually visiting the state. His source was Sen. William Sprague of Rhode Island, who had invested heavily in the South and lost. Attacks on reconstruction and corruption became two of the legs on the liberal stool, and Pike also illuminated the third one: immigrants and the urban political machines they supported. New York repelled Pike. He disliked its "stink," and he disliked its people: "those who are not German are Irish, those who are not Irish are Chinese, & those who are not Chinese are nigger."[59]

Pike's article was part of a larger liberal brief for rule by the "better classes." Corrupt Southern governments and urban immigrant machines demonstrated the dangers of an expanded male suffrage. In the North and the South, the "better classes" had to resume their appropriate role. This could only happen in the South if the heavy hand of federal Reconstruction were lifted. It could happen in the North only if the better classes crushed the immigrant machines, which was what the liberals saw happening in New York in the early 1870s.

III

Against the better classes, liberals counterpoised the dangerous classes. The very rich were part of the dangerous classes, but the more urgent threats came from immigrants and black people, and although not all immigrants were regarded as dangerous, many were. The dangerous classes made the "savage" threat to the home as real in Northern cities as on the Great Plains. Liberals regarded the dangerous classes as the source of crime and vagrancy. Immigrants and the poor supported the urban political machines that liberals thought the great font of corruption, inefficiency, and waste. When liberals soured on democracy, they had the immigrant poor—particularly the Irish—in mind.

58. Thomas C. Holt, *Black over White: Negro Political Leadership in South Carolina During Reconstruction* (Urbana: University of Illinois Press, 1977), 1–5, and passim.
59. Tuchinsky, 225–26.

The Irish came to the United States poor and desperate, victims of the Great Famine, which they blamed on British policies. They thought of themselves as exiles and refugees. Bishop John Hughes called them "The scattered debris of the Irish Nation." The United States contained Irish before there was an Ireland, just as Germans came to the United States before there was a Germany. The project of becoming American and becoming Irish or German were all the result of diasporas. The Irish in America, many of them ex-Union soldiers and predominantly working-class, had formed the Fenians, which, along with the Irish Republican Brotherhood in Ireland, worked to establish a democratic Irish republic. By 1867 the Fenians were a revolutionary organization, factionalized and riven with British spies, that already had struck at Canada.[60]

The Fenians created conflicts with Great Britain, but the gangs of New York epitomized the dangerous classes: the Gophers, Dead Rabbits, Gorillas, East Side Dramatic and Pleasure Club, the Limburger Roarers, and the Battle Row Ladies Social and Athletic Club, led by Battle Annie Walsh, the "Sweetheart of Hell's Kitchen." They concentrated in lower Manhattan, not just Chelsea and the Bowery, but a set of neighborhoods whose names told their story: Hell's Kitchen, Satan's Circus, Rag Pickers' Row, Cat Alley, Rotten Row, The Great Eastern, Sebastopol, Bummers' Retreat, Mulligan Alley, Cockroach Row, and the Five Points. These streets, rutted and garbage-strewn, teemed with vehicles, animals, and people. They contained perhaps fifteen thousand beggars and thousands of homeless children. The tenement population numbered half a million. Nearly twenty thousand people lived in dank, dark, miserable basements. The antithesis of the home, tenements were already familiar in the 1860s and would grow more familiar thereafter. Charles Dickens had denounced them in his visit to New York before the war. They became a staple of the popular press in the 1870s and into the 1880s and beyond.[61]

As novelists and reformers would detail for the rest of the century, immigrants and workers lived in a city at once grand and horrible. It was a place, as nineteenth-century writers put it, of palaces and hovels. Immediately after the Civil War, New York numbered nearly one million people; it was the nation's financial capital, the leading port, and one of the major manufacturing centers. Across the East River, Brooklyn, then a separate city,

60. David Thomas Brundage, *Irish Nationalists in America: The Politics of Exile, 1798–1998* (New York: Oxford University Press, 2016), 87–90.
61. Alexander B. Callow, *The Tweed Ring* (New York: Oxford University Press, 1969), 54–55, 59; Bonnie Yochelson and Daniel J. Czitrom, *Rediscovering Jacob Riis: Exposure Journalism and Photography in Turn-of-the-Century New York* (New York: New Press, 2007), 32–77; "Tenement Life in New York," *Harper's Weekly*, Mar. 22, 1879, 226–27.

had an additional four hundred thousand people. Together, New York City and Brooklyn possessed the nation's greatest concentration of immigrants. In a nation that in 1870 remained overwhelmingly Protestant and 86 percent native-born, New York City by contrast was about 50 percent Catholic and 44 percent immigrant. The Irish-born made up 21 percent of the city and German-born 16 percent.[62]

Approximately one-half of New York's population lived within a tight belt that stretched a mile and a half between Canal and Fourteenth streets. They dwelled in a fetid sink of misery. The infant death rate in the tenements was twice that in private homes, and in the 1860s New York had a higher death rate (40 per 1,000) than any city in the western world. The city passed a law to regulate tenements in 1867, but enforcement was another matter. Tammany Hall, the Democratic organization that usually controlled the party and the city, did virtually nothing to alleviate the high rents for filthy tenements extorted by grasping landlords, the dirty streets, overflowing sewers, the crime, and the abysmal sanitation that were the curses of New York's poor.[63]

New York was also the center of American's consolidating bourgeoisie in the European sense of the word: a self-conscious upper class that coalesced after the defeat of the South partially in reaction to the proletarianization of the city. In New York the antebellum merchant elite with their ties to the South, cotton, and the Democratic Party yielded to a new class whose wealth came from industry and finance. Some of the industrialists and railroad men, Cornelius Vanderbilt for one, had made their money in New York. Others like Huntington moved to New York to be closer to investment banks and to Washington, D.C. A second tier of wealth—lawyers and high executives—surrounded them, and leading families intermarried. The bourgeoisie in the 1860s and 1870s considered themselves the epitome of the better classes.[64]

Everything that happened in New York was magnified. The city contained the country's leading newspapers as well as the Associated Press,

62. *Historical Statistics of the United States, Earliest Times to the Present: Millennial Edition,* ed. Scott Sigmund Gartner, Susan B. Carter, Michael R. Haines, Alan L. Olmstead, Richard Sutch, and Gavin Wright (New York: Cambridge University Press, 2006), table Aa 22–35, Selected Population Characteristics; *Ninth Census of the United States. Statistics of Population: Tables I to VIII Inclusive* (Washington, DC: U.S. GPO, 1872), 212, table 3; Seymour J. Mandelbaum, *Boss Tweed's New York* (New York: Wiley, 1965), 8–9; Jay P. Dolan, *The Immigrant Church: New York's Irish and German Catholics, 1815–1865* (Baltimore: Johns Hopkins University Press, 1975), 15.

63. Mandelbaum, 8, 12–14, 66; Edwin G. Burrows and Mike Wallace, *Gotham: A History of New York City to 1898* (New York: Oxford University Press, 1999), 919–22.

64. Beckert, 3, 5–8, 131–32, 170–72, 178–80, 191.

which in aggregating the news increasingly determined the information that would reach the American people as a whole. News from New York, advertisements from New York, and stories about New York became ubiquitous in other urban and small town newspapers.[65]

Just as New York towered over other American cities so William Marcy Tweed—Boss Tweed—and Tammany Hall loomed over New York, particularly in the cartoons of another liberal, Thomas Nast. Nast portrayed Tweed as corpulent and imperious but also as seedy and devious. Always, he was greedy and a thief. The Tammany Tiger, in one of Nast's most famous cartoons, feasted on the Republic while Tweed, as Roman emperor, looked on.

Nast turned Tweed into a caricature—a wonderfully effective caricature—that greased his downfall, but only once Tweed began to slip. Until then Nast was but a nuisance. Tweed was a more complicated man than

One of Thomas Nast's powerful anti-Tammany cartoons, it plays off Boss Tweed's supposed response to accusations of fraud. The caption reads: "The Tammany Tiger Loose—'What are you going to do about it?'" In a play on wild animals devouring Christians in the Roman Coliseum, Tweed as an emperor watches the Tammany Tiger, which, having dispatched Justice and Liberty, is about to devour the Republic. *Harper's Weekly*, Nov. 11, 1871. From the Collection of Macculloch Hall Historical Museum, Morristown, NJ.

65. Cameron Blevins, "Space, Nation, and the Triumph of Region: A View of the World from Houston," *Journal of American History* 100, no. 1 (2014): 122–47.

Nast made him. In his corruption, greed, and ability to knit together government and private capital, he was not that different from Huntington or Jay Gould. Indeed, Gould could not have created the ring that looted the Erie railroad or escaped from the repercussions of his gold corner without the help of judges controlled by Tammany.

Tweed was the first modern boss of an urban political machine. He would have many imitators. Tweed stood a little under six feet, but he packed onto that frame 300 pounds, and sported a diamond "that glittered like a planet on his shirt front." He contained a whole bundle of contradictions. A Scots-Irish Presbyterian, he headed a predominantly Irish Catholic organization. He could dominate a room, but not a public platform. As a speaker, he was often incoherent. He could be crude and vulgar, but he neither smoked nor drank. He was a family man who doted on his wife and children and gave lavishly to charity. In the bitter winter of 1870, he personally donated $50,000 to buy food for the poor. His enemies denounced it as conscience money, saying he stole more than that in a day. Tweed's personal contributions were a trickle in a stream of money, much of it public, that the Tweed Ring funneled to private charities and schools, largely but not exclusively Catholic.[66]

Like most successful bosses, Tweed was a broker, not a dictator. He brought together the state capital at Albany, usually dominated by upstate Republicans, and New York City, the fiefdom of Democrats. Before Tweed's arrival and after his departure, the state of New York did everything it could to weaken New York City. The state legislature sapped the city government's power by controlling its charter and loading it with independent commissions. This was not unique; city governments lost power throughout much of the Gilded Age. To truly govern New York City required controlling the city's hopelessly unwieldy government and the state legislature. Tweed did both. He dominated Tammany Hall through a network of Democratic clubs in every ward and assembly district. Tammany, in turn, controlled New York City. Tweed held no city office himself, but he was a state senator and chair of the senate's State Finance Committee. The governor felt Tammany's influence. Employing the so-called Black Horse Cavalry—a group of Republican and Democratic legislators for sale to the highest bidder—Tweed managed the legislature. In 1870 Tweed used his power to deliver the "Tweed Charter," which bestowed much more authority on New York City's government.[67]

66. Callow, 10–12, 152–58; James J. Connolly, *An Elusive Unity: Urban Democracy and Machine Politics in Industrializing America* (Ithaca, NY: Cornell University Press, 2010), 30, 37; Mandelbaum, 66–75.
67. Edward T. O'Donnell, *Henry George and the Crisis of Inequality: Progress and Poverty in the Gilded Age* (New York: Columbia University Press, 2015), 100–102; Jon

Tweed recognized that the Republican ideal of a homogeneous citizenry was an illusion, and in this he mirrored the convictions of his immigrant constituency. As Patrick Ford, an Irish American radical who had worked on William Lloyd Garrison's *Liberator* and emerged from the abolitionist movement to become the editor of the *Irish World*, wrote: "This people are not one. In blood, in religion, in traditions, in social and domestic habits, they are many." Tweed governed a city riven by class, ethnicity, and religion. It could be governed by coalitions but not by appealing to a civic republicanism or common values. In New York City, Tweed joined together businessmen and the swarming immigrant poor. Domination of the city's government gave the Tweed Ring an estimated twelve thousand jobs, which it distributed largely through the Democratic clubs. Jobs went to the politically ambitious and the working poor. Charters and contracts for public works rewarded his allies among businessmen and bankers regardless of whether they were Republican or Democrat. All was financed through the sale of city bonds, negotiated by the city's bankers. The city was a vast corrupt bargain that, until the early 1870s, brought profits and low taxes to business, and plunder to Tammany Hall, which ensured its power by distributing some of the take to its members through contracts, jobs, and charity.[68]

The new County Courthouse became the great symbol of Tammany rule. Budgeted at $250,000, the carpets alone eventually cost $350,000. The total cost had reached $13 million by 1871, and the building still was not finished. The courthouse had become a siphon to pour public money into the pockets of the Tweed Ring, which received 65 percent of every padded bill. The remaining 35 percent went to the contractor. Similar waste, extravagance, and corruption affected everything from street projects to the building of the Brooklyn Bridge. Despite spiraling public debt, New York's most influential businessmen protected Tweed. In 1870 they dominated an investigating committee, chaired by John Jacob Astor, that whitewashed the ring's manipulation of New York's finances. Why shouldn't they? Tweed channeled far more wealth upward than downward, while conciliating an immigrant working class they feared.[69]

Initially, liberal opposition to Tweed was as futile as it was furious. Thomas Nast and *Harper's Weekly* waged their war of outrage and ridicule against Tammany. The *New York Times* frothed and protested. It attacked Tweed

---

C. Teaford, *The Unheralded Triumph, City Government in America, 1870–1900* (Baltimore: Johns Hopkins University Press, 1984), 19–20, 18–82.

68. Connolly, 29, 42–47; Burrows and Wallace, 932–33, 1004.

69. Callow, 199–202.

and his henchmen in classic republican terms: they were a corrupt faction, a small number of men who formed a "ring," to use the terminology of the period, that betrayed an honest citizenry. The antidemocratic language that would come to characterize liberal reform in New York was present, but not yet dominant.[70]

Two events—a bloody sectarian riot and a sleighing accident—brought Tweed down. The events were unconnected, but they could be combined into a story of social breakdown, the growth of dangerous classes, and political corruption. The riot created a cultural panic, but it was not the work of urban savages; it sprang from hostilities between immigrant Catholics and native Protestants. These were the tensions Tweed had promised to contain. The riot signaled his failure. The sleighing accident was a contingent event. A man had made some money and spent it, as many of the wealthy did, on expensive trotting horses, and his death created a window on how extensive fraud had become.

In July 1871 New York City exploded. To celebrate the anniversary of the 1690 Battle of the Boyne, which had secured British rule in Ireland, the Protestant Loyal Order of Orange requested police permission to march through New York. Violence had erupted along the route of this annual march a year earlier, and the Irish American press protested that the march was a provocation, part of a larger nativist project to make American mean Protestant and "Saxon." The police, backed by Tweed's Tammany Hall, refused to permit the march.

Protestant New Yorkers exploded in anger at what they regarded as discrimination against the native-born and Protestant. They pointed to the city's endorsement of the annual St. Patrick's Day parade, and its aid to Catholic charities and schools, which in the 1860s instructed about twenty thousand students. They pointed to the Fenians' botched invasion of Canada in 1866, the first of several attempts. Horace Greeley's *Tribune* asserted that the Irish "under the leadership of Mr. William M. Tweed, had taken possession of the City and State."[71]

Tweed backed down, and on July 12, 1871, the Orangemen marched. Five thousand Protestant militia accompanied the marchers, many of whom were armed; most Catholic militia remained confined to their armories. The soldiers supplemented fifteen hundred police. Both the Catholic Church and the Fenian leadership urged Irish Catholics to show restraint, but some lodges of the Ancient Orders of Hibernians advocated resistance.

---

70. Beckert, 174–75; the ring probably stole between $60 million and $200 million, depending on how the thefts are calculated. Mandelbaum, 77–79; Connolly, 28–46; Callow, 78–86, 102–3, 164–65, 168, 240–43, 279, 299.
71. Burrows and Wallace, 1002–5; Mandelbaum, 34.

Irish quarrymen, railroad workers, longshoremen, and more gathered along parts of the parade route.[72]

When crowds blocked Eighth Avenue and stones rained down on the parade, scattered shots rang out. The police charged and the troops without orders began to fire point blank into the largely Irish masses that poured in from Twenty-fourth Street. The violence continued until Fifth Avenue, where the parade entered a bubble of supportive Protestant bystanders. At Fourteenth Street, New York was again a world of angry Catholics.[73]

The parade left in its wake along Eighth Avenue the bloodied, the dying, and the dead. A reporter for the *New York Herald* reported basement steps "smeared and slippery with human blood and brains while the land beneath was covered two inches deep with clotted gore, pieces of brain, and the half digested contents of a human stomach and intestines." The mud on the streets was stained red. Sixty civilians died, most of them Irish. Three guardsmen perished. The Orangemen suffered comparatively little; one was wounded. The *Irish World* denounced the "Slaughter on Eighth Avenue." Twenty thousand Irish converged on the morgue the next day. The police commissioner, Protestant banker Henry Smith, said his only regret was that there was not a larger number killed. For Smith the "dangerous classes" understood only force.[74]

By the time the riot erupted, the sleighing accident had already occurred, but its consequences were not yet apparent. In January 1871 James Watson, the county auditor who managed the finances of the ring, died while exercising his trotting horses. Watson, thinking there was "too rough a crowd" on the road, was returning home when another sleigh driver, believed to be intoxicated, lost control of his horse, which collided with Watson's sleigh. A hoof struck Watson in the head. He left a widow and two children, who were "believed to be amply provided for." It seemed at the time simply a personal tragedy.[75]

Divisions within Tammany, however, produced a new auditor, who was bitter over money he thought the ring owed him. He eventually released inside information to the *New York Times*. The backlash over the Orange riots in July 1871 coincided with the *Times'* publication of the leaked information under the blaring headline "Gigantic Frauds of the Ring Exposed." The evidence alarmed European bankers, who ceased underwriting city bonds. With the city facing bankruptcy, Tammany's constituency fractured. German immigrants in particular deserted the machine,

72. Burrows and Wallace, 1005–6.
73. Ibid., 1006–7.
74. Ibid., 1005–8.
75. "Death of County Auditor Watson," *New York Times*, Jan. 31, 1871.

but it was the New York financial and business community, which had profited from the marketing of the city's debt and feared going down with Tweed, that led the attack. They organized a tax strike and obtained an injunction prohibiting the city from borrowing or selling bonds. Tweed was arrested in late October. He retained his state Senate seat in the election of 1871, but most of his allies fell. Indicted in December, he would, after an unsuccessful attempt to flee the country, spend the rest of his life on trial or in prison.[76]

The Committee of Seventy that organized the opposition to Tweed was a diverse group, but liberal reformers were among them, and it was the liberals who first injected a critical antidemocratic element into the attack on the Tweed Ring. They gradually altered the committee's republican language into a rhetoric of class conflict. The committee had initially portrayed the conflict as being between virtuous citizens from all walks of life and Tweed and his plundering gang. Godkin and other liberals, ironically much like Tweed, challenged the very possibility of a united and homogeneous citizenry. As early as 1866, the *Nation* had denounced the "swarm of foreigners...ignorant, credulous, newly emancipated, brutalized by oppression, and bred in the habit of regarding the law as their enemy." The people were not only diverse, as *Irish World* editor Patrick Ford had contended, but that very diversity made them dangerous. They represented a threat to property and order, and their votes could be purchased. Godkin did not denounce immigrants per se; like Nast, he was an immigrant. His target was the poor of the tenements, whose lives seemed to embody the disintegration of the American home.[77]

The *Nation* urged on an antidemocratic reaction. The magazine called for the formation of a vigilance committee since "the revolution of force must sooner or later follow." It demanded the disenfranchisement of the poor and regarded municipal democracy as a "ridiculous anachronism." Liberals abandoned the old Jacksonian/Lincolnian embrace of equality and the dream of a homogeneous citizenry that sprang from it. They promoted the writing of social and political inequality into law. The reformers wanted the city run as a corporation, with the property-owning taxpayers as shareholders. Allowing all male citizens to vote in a municipal election was like allowing the employees of a railroad corporation to vote along with stockholders. Workers should not be able to say how a corporation

76. Beckert, 183–95; Mandelbaum, 79–80; Burrows and Wallace, 1009–11.
77. The older standard account of the liberals is John G. Sproat, *The Best Men: Liberal Reformers in the Gilded Age* (New York: Oxford University Press, 1968); for an account of the emergence of the liberal Republicans on the national level, Slap, xi–xiii; Connolly, 45–51.

should be run, and citizens should not be able to say how a city was to be run. This was a predictable analogy from people who thought the market was the model for society. Workers, however, no more accepted the premise that they should have no say in how a corporation was run than they accepted the conclusion that they should not take part in municipal governance.[78]

The array of metaphors and policies that sprang from the riot and the fall of Tweed indicated threats to Republican ideas of homogeneous citizens, the home, and manhood in northern cities. Savagery was a versatile metaphor, identifying those who were not and apparently could not be men. Like other savages, the dangerous classes could not maintain homes; they could only threaten them.

Liberal Republicans had set off down the path that would reconcile them with old enemies in the South. They turned denunciations of corruption into denunciations of democracy, whose particular targets were the newly enfranchised. The denunciations of Tammany and immigrant voters echoed in the South with denunciations of carpetbaggers and black voters, which led liberals to have a new sympathy with Southern elites. The "best men," North and South, believed that expanding the franchise was a mistake. It inevitably yielded corruption. Here were the additions to the core liberal ideology that could spark political revolt against the regular Republicans.

IV

The attack on Tammany consolidated the liberal attack on the local political status quo, but the liberals were also organizing on the federal level against President Grant. Sen. Carl Schurz of Missouri became a particular bane of Grant because Schurz spearheaded virtually every liberal issue in Congress. An ardent free trader and a leading opponent of Reconstruction, he also led the attack on Grant's policy on Santo Domingo and on the spoils system. What Schurz was *not* was anti-immigrant. When he had won election to the U.S. Senate in 1868, it marked more than a personal triumph. It was a sign of the growing importance, particularly in the Midwest, of German Americans, who were the largest single group of immigrants to the United States in the nineteenth century. Chicago, St. Louis, and Milwaukee had a strong German American flavor, and rural areas and small towns from Minnesota to Missouri, and down into the Texas

78. Connolly, 50–51; Beckert, 189, 190–92.

hill country, were often predominantly German-speaking, with German newspapers and schools. They were largely Republican in Missouri, although in neighboring Illinois many Catholic Germans were Democrats, but everywhere they were uneasy with those Republicans who came from evangelical roots, favored prohibition, and clung to antebellum nativism. In Missouri, the sitting Republican Senator, Charles Drake, had opposed Schurz. He delivered a nativist rant against German Americans as "an ignorant crowd, who did not understand English, read only their German newspapers, and were led by corrupt and designing rings." The backlash against Drake secured Schurz's nomination, which, given the Republican control of the legislature, was as good as election.[79]

By 1871 Schurz had broken with Grant, desiring "the questions connected with the Civil War to be disposed of forever, to make room as soon as possible for the new problems of the present and future." Like E. L. Godkin of the *Nation* and Lyman Trumbull, the Illinois senator who had helped author the Thirteenth Amendment, he thought the political pendulum had swung too far toward federal power and was ready to push it back. They had principled reasons to oppose Grant's policies, but many liberals were also losers within factional struggles in their state Republican parties and were eager to regain lost advantages. Grant punished Schurz by awarding patronage to his enemies in Missouri.[80]

Grant's attempt to annex Santo Domingo—the modern-day Dominican Republic—fed the liberal fears of executive power, corruption, and the growing presence of "inferior" peoples in the American republic; but even without racial and ideological issues, the activities of Grant's private secretary, Orville Babcock, would have raised eyebrows. Babcock had been a trusted member of Grant's staff, and he became Grant's friend. He owned land in Santo Domingo, and he rather remarkably negotiated a treaty of annexation with a corrupt and endangered Dominican regime without the prior knowledge of Grant's secretary of state, Hamilton Fish.

During the Civil War Santo Domingo had been reannexed by Spain, part of a resurgent Spain's effort to strengthen its American presence and part of the larger European intervention into the Americas whose central

79. For these Midwestern communities and their maintennce of German culture, see Kathleen Conzen, "Making Their Own America: Assimilation Theory and the German Peasant Pioneer," in *German Historical Institute Annual Lecture Series* (New York: BERG, 1990), 17; Hans L. Trefousse, *Carl Schurz, a Biography* (Knoxville: University of Tennessee Press, 1982), 172–74; Schurz, 3: 298; Kathleen Neils Conzen, *Germans in Minnesota* (St. Paul: Minnesota Historical Society Press, 2003).

80. Frederic Bancroft and William A. Dunning, "A Sketch of Carl Schurz's Political Career, 1869–1906," in Schurz, *Reminiscences*, 3: 332; Slap, 122; Foner, 500–501.

piece was the invasion of Mexico and the French establishment of Maximilian I as Emperor. As in Mexico, occupation led to a revolt, which began in 1863. Spanish racism and fear of the return of slavery fed it. American sympathizers had sent arms. In 1865 the Spanish withdrew.[81]

Despite the popularity of the restoration of Santo Domingo's independence, the new president, Buenaventura Báez, began secret negotiations with Babcock in 1869. The regime conducted a dubious plebiscite to approve the treaty, which Grant submitted to Senate in 1870. Babcock secured the support of other Americans who had invested in Dominican land and the U.S. Navy, which desired a Caribbean base. The treaty seemed an odd new form of antebellum filibustering. Where the original filibusterers had tried to extend Southern slavery, the backers of the annexation of Santo Domingo were Northerners, including Frederick Douglass, and black Southerners. They justified the annexation as a way to provide land for freedpeople. The ex-slaves would supposedly become American colonists and carriers of American institutions, thus weakening slavery in Cuba and Puerto Rico.[82]

Opposition created an unlikely coalition. Grant's liberal opponents regarded the Santo Domingo treaty as a sign of the administration's reckless willingness to continue to add black peoples to the republic and of the corruption of the political process. Schurz, convinced that Anglo-Saxons could not thrive in a tropical country and that the result would be the ruin of the republic, led the opposition in the Senate. He denounced Grant's use of force by dispatching a naval vessel to protect the sitting government of the country without congressional authorization. Charles Sumner, chairman of the powerful Senate Foreign Relations Committee and hardly a liberal, also opposed the treaty. He thought it endangered the independence of neighboring Haiti, the hemisphere's only black republic. The vote in the Senate tied at 28–28, nowhere near the necessary two-thirds majority. Grant would try again and fail again.[83]

Grant was a soldier, inclined to see opposition as insubordination and disloyalty. He had taken the unprecedented step of visiting Sumner at his home and asking for his support. He thought he had it, and his reaction to what he regarded as a betrayal had lasting repercussions. Sumner had honed his own sharp tongue on Southern slaveholders, and he turned it on Grant. He equated Grant with Presidents Pierce, Buchanan, and

81. Anne Eller, "Dominican Civil War, Slavery, and Spanish Annexation, 1844–1865," in *American Civil Wars: The United States, Latin America, Europe, and the Crisis of the 1860s*, ed. Don H. Doyle (Chapel Hill: University of North Carolina Press, 2017), 8, 14–15, 17–21.
82. Summers, 220–26; McFeely, 338–41; Eller, 21–22; Foner, 494–95.
83. Slap, 117–19; Foner, 496.

Johnson, a trio that amounted to a rogue's gallery for most Republicans. Grant persuaded the Republicans to strip Sumner of his chairmanship and funneled party patronage to his friends the so-called Stalwarts: Senators Conkling of New York and Morton of Indiana, and Rep. Benjamin Butler of Massachusetts. They used patronage to build powerful state machines. The emerging Liberal Republicans reviled them all.[84]

South Carolina, the Tweed Ring, the New York City riots, and Santo Domingo fanned the fire of liberal rebellion; the only source of liberal outrage not yet prominent in the newspapers was the ubiquitous corruption of the Grant administration itself, which was as yet largely known only to insiders. A government that just a few years before had imagined remaking the republic had begun to sink beneath the weight of a thousand peculations. In 1871 Whitelaw Reid, another ex-abolitionist disillusioned with Reconstruction and democracy, was Horace Greeley's managing editor at the *New York Tribune*. He wrote privately, "All Administrations, I suppose, are more or less corrupt; certainly the depth of corruption this one has reached is scarcely suspected as yet, even by its enemies."[85]

How much Reid knew is unclear, but as it turned out there was a lot to know. The most famous of the scandals, the Whiskey Ring, was up and running by 1870 when Gen. John A. McDonald, the supervisor of internal revenue at St. Louis, organized the previously random corruption of internal revenue agents into a centralized operation stretching out to New Orleans, Chicago, Peoria, Milwaukee, and Indianapolis. The Whiskey Ring flourished by not collecting the tax on every gallon of distilled spirits; instead it issued revenue stamps in exchange for bribes. When whiskey was supposed to be taxed at $2 a gallon and sold for $1.25 a gallon, it did not take advanced math to guess something was amiss. The agents didn't keep all of the money; they kicked back 40 percent of the profits to higher government officials, including Babcock. Other proceeds went to finance the Republican Party. The ring stole millions from the Treasury and would not be finally suppressed until Benjamin Bristow became secretary of the treasury in 1874 and launched a campaign against it that would last into 1876.[86]

Not all the scandals were so lucrative, but the ability of the tawdry and petty to reach into high places was perhaps even more revealing and disturbing. In the War Department, the wife of the new secretary, William

---

84. McFeely, 340–46, 351–52; Summers, 225–27; Foner, 496.
85. David M. Jordan, *Roscoe Conkling of New York: Voice in the Senate* (Ithaca, NY: Cornell University Press, 1971), 221.
86. Mark W. Summers, *The Era of Good Stealings* (New York: Oxford University Press, 1993), 91–98, 103–4, 184–91, 267–69; Jordan, 221–23.

Belknap, arranged with her husband's knowledge for Caleb Marsh to receive the appointment as Indian trader at Fort Sill in Indian Territory in exchange for half the profits being returned to her. The existing trader then agreed to pay Marsh $12,000 a year to leave the post to him, and Marsh, being a man of his word, paid half to Belknap's wife. When she died, Belknap married her sister. Marsh continued to pay Belknap, who passed the old kickback on to his new wife. The arrangement continued for years. Only when the House started impeachment provisions did Belknap resign.[87]

Grant stubbornly defended the flagrantly guilty, but the problems went beyond Grant. Hitching the profit motive to public service in an expanding and industrializing country inevitably dragged the country into a swamp of corruption, and under Grant it wallowed there.

Liberals lacked knowledge of the details, but they were already convinced of the rottenness of the spoils system. In 1869 at the advent of the first Grant administration Henry Adams had published an article in the *North American Review* denouncing the "hungry army of political adventurers" who descended on Washington for the roughly fifty-three thousand federal jobs, most of which changed hands with every new administration. The Post Office Department accounted for nearly half of these jobs, with the Treasury Department coming in second. For Adams and other liberals, the spoils system made a mockery of good governance and the Constitution. The office seekers absorbed the attention of elected officials, received jobs for which they were unqualified, and fed corruption as they sought to profit from their offices. Congress, by arrogating the power to appoint office holders serving under the executive branch, a right to which it had no constitutional authority, violated the constitutional separation of powers.[88]

Schurz became the principal liberal Republican voice for civil service reform, although he had not originally embraced the issue. His brother had secured the lucrative appointment of collector of revenue for the port of Chicago, and Schurz sought other appointments for his constituents. When he failed to get his expected share of patronage, he wearied of the endless lines of office seekers who sucked up his time. He found the whole process unseemly. Thomas Allen Jenckes, a Republican of Rhode Island, had launched the crusade for civil service reform in 1864, but Schurz made it his issue.[89]

---

87. Jordan, 222–23; Summers, *Era of Good Stealings*, 133–34, 261–63.
88. Henry Brooks Adams, "Civil-Service Reform," *North American Review* 109, no. 225 (1869): 445; Hoogenboom, 1–2.
89. Adams, "Civil-Service Reform," 445; Hoogenboom, 1–69.

Civil service reform involved far more than honest government. It was part of the liberals' larger antidemocratic initiative, which envisioned restrictions on suffrage and the reining in of the powers of elected officials. Liberal reformers believed in limited government, but they also sought to make that government more disciplined, more effective, more centralized, and less democratic. They attacked local democracy and the political patronage associated with it, as well as the delegation of powers to corporations and other private entities.

Grant had to pay at least lip service to civil service reform, and in 1871 he accepted the recommendation of the Civil Service Commission for competitive examinations. The results were minimal because particular rules and exams for each department had to be drawn up, because there was resistance in some departments, and because opponents of civil service reform in Congress cut or blocked appropriations for the commission. To liberals, civil service reform became another example of how Grant gave only token support to reform. Eventually in March 1875 the competitive examinations would be abandoned entirely.[90]

By 1872 liberals who had once had hopes for the Grant administration scorned the president. Half a century later, their disappointment still rankled. Henry Adams wrote that the "progress of evolution from President Washington to President Grant, was alone evidence enough to upset Darwin." Adams had been rather less ironic and distanced in 1871, writing Schurz that "between the Force Bill, the Legal Tender case, San Domingo and Tammany, I see no constitutional government any longer possible." Adams later claimed that the Grant administration "was not even sensibly American" and lacked American ideas. The great ironist quite unironically boiled "American" down to liberal and reduced the Republicans to a lazy betrayal and a policy of drift that allowed too many of the policies put in place during the war to endure and the problems that arose in the wake of war to fester.[91]

Liberal Republicans spun their own peculiar cocoon of hope and fear to shelter the chrysalis of a new party. Among their threads of hope were the overthrow of Tweed and the coalition that had achieved it, the first successes of civil service reform, the defeat of Grant's attempts to annex Santo Domingo, and the seeming dominance of liberalism among educated and genteel Northerners. But it was the threads of fear that predominated.

Benjamin Butler gave them a sharp lesson in the difficulties of turning their principles into electoral politics. Convinced of the threat the

90. Ibid., 85–134.
91. Slap, 125; Adams, *The Education of Henry Adams*, quote, 247, 262–63, 266–67.

"dangerous" classes posed to property, order, and rule by the "better classes," liberals were appalled by the willingness of Stalwart Republican politicians to cater to voters. In 1871 French workers seized power, formed the Paris Commune, and ruled Paris in the wake of the Franco-Prussian War. They terrified liberals, creating a revolutionary symbol that would not be displaced until the Bolshevik Revolution. Butler praised the commune. In Massachusetts everything wrong with the Republican Party seemed distilled in Butler, who looked like a pudgy, disheveled pirate and was a master of machine politics. He adroitly used patronage appointments to the Massachusetts Naval Shipyards, customs offices, and post offices to build a potent political organization. A not particularly successful but nonetheless famous general, he acted as a champion for veterans in Congress. Recognizing the increasing importance of the Irish Catholic vote, he championed their causes and supported the Fenians. Although wealthy himself, he allied with workingmen and unions. He thought women should vote. The more a cause outraged respectable liberal opinion, the more likely Butler was to embrace it.[92]

Worse, Butler humiliated the Brahmin liberals who challenged him. Richard Henry Dana, Jr., the author of *Two Years Before the Mast*, a prominent Massachusetts lawyer and a member of one of Boston's leading families, ran against him for Congress in 1868 because of Butler's advocacy of redemption of war bonds with greenbacks. Butler responded with an attack that made class and democracy key issues. As Charles Francis Adams put it in the biography he later wrote of Dana, Butler attacked "his opponent's personal habits and peculiarities, his ancestry and his supposed aristocratic tendencies, his equipage, his gloves and his apparel...." The attacks, Adams admitted, were telling. In a three-way election, Dana got only eighteen hundred votes out of more than twenty thousand cast. Butler won in a landslide.[93]

V

Liberals in 1872 had confidence that they knew what needed to be done to reform American governance. The defeat of Tammany encouraged them to believe that their political moment had arrived. Since other liberals wrote virtually everything liberals read, they lived in a kind of echo chamber

92. Foner, 491; William D. Mallam, "Butlerism in Massachusetts," *New England Quarterly* 33, no. 2 (1960): 186–203.
93. Charles Francis Adams, *Richard Henry Dana: A Biography*, rev. 3rd ed. (Boston: Houghton Mifflin, 1891), 2: 347–48.

in which they mistook their own voices for the sound of America. In 1872 William Dean Howells announced in the *Atlantic Monthly* the rise of "a movement—it is yet too early to call it a party." In explaining this movement's rise, Howells pointedly referenced both scandals in municipal government and the failings of the Grant administration.[94]

The era's problem, as Howells saw it, was adjusting the ideal of liberty to the necessity of order. The movement's solution was to sever "administration" from democracy in order "to effect reforms in the machinery of politics and in administration" and "to evolve order out of chaos, government out of anarchy." Howells's account of the necessary reforms amounted to a manifesto for Gilded Age liberalism: abolition of the tariff, civil service reform, return to the gold standard, curbing of democracy through limitations on suffrage, replacement of elected officials with appointed officials, and prevention of any extension of suffrage to women.[95]

Many liberals had become convinced that the Republican Party was beyond hope. Their dislike of Grant's and the Stalwarts' positions on free trade and the gold standard caused them to lose faith in the efficacy of the Republican Party as a vehicle for laissez-faire. They were correct. The bulk of the party lacked any devotion to laissez-faire. Although not opposed to regulation by experts, liberals regarded regulation by democratic legislatures as worse than no regulation at all. They denounced the Grant administration's corruption and its patronage ties to the powerful Republican state organizations. Unable to defeat Grant within the Republican Party, these liberals resolved in the spring of 1872 to nominate their own candidate.[96]

A cadre of liberals, largely Northeastern intellectuals and journalists leavened with dissident Republican politicians, had set their hopes on the nomination of Charles Francis Adams, Sr. Only genealogically was he was an ideal candidate. He was the son and grandson of presidents, with impeccable antislavery credentials. The Free Soil Party had nominated him for vice president in 1848, and he had been elected as a Republican congressman from Massachusetts. He had been Lincoln's minister to England and served as a special envoy and negotiator under Grant. His sons, particularly Henry and Charles Francis, Jr., were leading liberals. He responded to interest in making him the Liberal Republican nominee with a letter that could be generously described as confused, and less

94. W. D. Howells, "Politics," *Atlantic Monthly*, January 1872, 124–28; Cohen, 110–12.
95. Ibid.
96. Brian Balogh, *A Government out of Sight: The Mystery of National Authority in Nineteenth-Century America* (Cambridge: Cambridge University Press, 2009), 314; Hoogenboom, 84–87; Foner, 488, 499–500.

generously as contradictory, arrogant, and daft. He was a terrible candidate whose supporters mismanaged their attempt to nominate him, but the Liberal Republicans managed to find a worse one.[97]

The convention in Cincinnati in May 1872 nominated Horace Greeley, the antebellum champion of free labor and an assortment of other reform causes. He was a man Godkin considered "a conceited, ignorant, half cracked, obstinate old creature." Nominating him was "a most serious and dangerous thing." A party of liberals had nominated a candidate who opposed the key liberal tenet of free trade. But this was a problem with the new party as a whole. Every specific liberal policy position acted like a magnet, pulling in adherents who did not necessarily embrace other policy positions. Only liberal ideologues embraced all the positions.[98]

Greeley was a man formed by antebellum America, and he longed for a world of self-reliance and cooperation, of social mobility grounded in the independence of small property holding. He refused to accept the emerging new conditions that these old ideals faced. He recoiled from accepting a permanent, wage-earning working class.[99] Unwilling to accept the idea of a class struggle, he was nonetheless aware of the deteriorating condition of labor, and so he embraced a protective tariff, anathema to the liberals, as a way to protect wages. Paradoxically, it was his aversion to social conflict that allowed many of his positions to overlap with those of liberals. He also opposed strikes, refused to embrace legislation for the eight-hour day, urged reconciliation between ex-Confederates and Unionists, and repudiated Reconstruction. Along with his support of the gold standard, this made him liberal enough to win the nomination.[100]

To many of Greeley's old allies in the struggle against slavery, he seemed a vacillating old man at sea in a new and confusing world. Frederick Douglass denounced Greeley's abandonment of the black struggle for freedom and economic independence and his desire for reconciliation with the white South. Greeley was "an uncertain man; an inconsistent man; one whom you do not know today and can give no guess what he will do to-morrow, what he will say to-morrow, what principles he will

97. Slap, 132–63; Edward Chalfant, *Better in Darkness: A Biography of Henry Adams: His Second Life, 1862–1891* (Hamden, CT: Archon Books, 1994), 262–65.

98. Godkin to Carl Schurz, May 19, 1872, in Godkin, *The Gilded Age Letters of E. L. Godkin*, 186–87; Hoogenboom, 84, 112–16; Michael E. McGerr, *The Decline of Popular Politics: The American North, 1865–1928* (New York: Oxford University Press, 1986), 60.

99. Tuchinsky, 178–79.

100. Slap, 141–56; Tuchinsky, 184–86, 210, 228–35.

advocate, what measures he will propose." The arch-Radical Charles Sumner first refused to join the liberals since he hated Charles Francis Adams, but he eventually backed Greeley because he hated Grant even more.[101]

Sumner deserted the Republicans as many liberals were returning to the Republican fold. Godkin refused to support Greeley. Howells, who remained Republican, thought the Greeley party essentially the old Democrats. Greeley was offering the South states' rights and the acknowledgment of white supremacy in the guise of amnesty and reconciliation. The South would not get everything the conservative Bourbons wanted, but it would get quite a bit. The very threat of Greeley's candidacy led Republicans to lower the tariff by 10 percent and approve the Amnesty Act, which for all practical purposes ended the restrictions on ex-Confederates imposed by the Fourteenth Amendment. The Democrats also nominated Greeley. In practice many Democrats in the South could not vote for a man who was the South's "unrepentant life-long enemy" despite the advantages he offered them.[102]

The contradictions of the Liberal-Republican, Democratic alliance, the continuing personal popularity of Grant, and the persisting sectional loyalties of the Civil War proved too much for Greeley. The vote in the South for Democratic candidates fell in 1872 from 1868 in what was the least violent election in the South during Reconstruction. The Republicans actually won back some of the Southern states that the Democrats had redeemed. In the North, the Regular Republicans vigorously waved the bloody shirt to rally their voters. Suffrage restriction, prohibition, and attacks on the Irish were not policies that appealed to the North's Democratic base, which was as unenthusiastic about Greeley as Southern Democrats. Turnout fell dramatically. The Republicans regained two-thirds majorities in both Houses of Congress. Greeley did not carry a single electoral vote north of the Mason-Dixon line. Grant captured 55 percent of the popular vote. No presidential candidate would get a higher percentage for the rest of the century. "I was the worst beaten man that ever ran for that high office," Greeley wrote. "And I have been assailed so bitterly that I hardly know whether I was running for President or the penitentiary." A month later Greeley was dead.

101. "Vote The Regular Republican Ticket," *New York Times*, July 25, 1872, in Frederick Douglass, *The Frederick Douglass Papers: Series One, Speeches, Debates, and Interviews* (New Haven, CT: Yale University Press, 1979), 4: 321; Slap, 134; Summers, 307–8.

102. Slap, 183, 190–97; Foner, 502–3, 506; W. D. Howells to Franklin Sanborn, Aug. 25, 1872, Howells, *Selected Letters*, 1: 399–400.

Liberal New York mourned; for the moment old divisions were forgotten. Henry Ward Beecher gave his eulogy, and Isabella Beecher, Henry's sister, sat alongside Elizabeth Tilton in the church. The liberals would never again attempt to form a separate party, though they were not going away.[103]

103. Michael F. Holt, *By One Vote: The Disputed Presidential Election of 1876* (Lawrence: University Press of Kansas, 2008), 1–9; Summers, 309–21; Foner, 509–10; Debby Applegate, *The Most Famous Man in America: The Biography of Henry Ward Beecher* (New York: Doubleday, 2006), 424–25.

6

Triumph of Wage Labor

The Stalwart Republicans who backed Grant made prosperity—not great wealth but a competence—a showpiece of free labor. Outside of the sharp recession following the war that accompanied contraction of the currency, the late 1860s and early 1870s were prosperous years.[1]

Prosperity formed part of free labor's promise but not its goal. "My dream," a Radical congressman said in 1866, "is of a model republic, extending equal protection and rights to all men....The wilderness shall vanish, the church and school-house will appear;...the whole land will revive under the magic touch of free labor." The "revived land," "the vanishing wilderness," "the magic touch of free labor" were what Republicans meant by progress, which, spreading over the West and South, included, but was greater than, economic prosperity. But in the early 1870s some began to worry that prosperity had commandeered free labor, subordinating its other ambitions.[2]

When, six years into Reconstruction, Attorney General Amos T. Akerman voiced such concerns, he worried that material progress was all that remained of the larger progress Republicans had sought. He had been philosophical in December 1871 when Ulysses S. Grant asked for his resignation and effectively aborted his successful war against the South Carolina Klan. Akerman thought that "such atrocities as Ku-Kluxery" could not hold northern "attention...the Northern mind being active and full of what is called progress runs away from the past." In having the North's lust for progress cause it to forget rather than uproot the legacy of slavery, Akerman separated what the Radicals had sought to join.[3]

1. Robert J. Gordon, *The Rise and Fall of American Growth: The U.S. Standard of Living since the Civil War* (Princeton, NJ: Princeton University Press, 2016), 28–30. Paul W. Rhode, "Gallman's Annual Output Series for the United States, 1834–1909," *National Bureau of Economic Research Working Papers Series* Working Paper 8860, April 2002: 28. The caution here is that annual figures are not fully reliable but the broader trends are.
2. Eric Foner, *Reconstruction: America's Unfinished Revolution, 1863–1877* (New York: Harper & Row, 1988), 235.
3. Lou Falkner Williams, *The Great South Carolina Ku Klux Klan Trials, 1871–1872* (Athens: University of Georgia Press, 1996), 125–27; William S. McFeely, *Grant: A Biography* (New York: Norton, 1981), 368–73.

Akerman's analysis, though understandable, was too neat. Neither the Radicals in Congress nor the carpetbaggers and freedmen in Southern state governments imagined that they had to choose between Reconstruction and economic progress. They continued to think that prosperity would ensure the success of the Greater Reconstruction. Northern Radicals and Southern carpetbaggers wagered that Southern whites would embrace prosperity, even at the price of supporting Reconstruction policies that extended economic opportunities to black men. They counted on prosperity as a balm of Gilead that would, as the American spiritual had it, "make the wounded whole."[4]

Despite corruption and their own racism, most Republicans sincerely embraced free labor and continued to believe in its transformative capacity and its egalitarian assumptions. In the South, Reconstruction governments established public school systems, hospitals, and asylums. They sought ways to clear the course for black self-making; they desired black independence.[5]

One of the most popular campaign posters in the 1872 presidential election, "The Workingman's Banner" pictured the Republican candidates as workingmen. Ulysses S. Grant was "The Galena Tanner," and his vice president, Henry Wilson, was the "The Natick Shoemaker." Grant had been a tanner, or rather, when he could not avoid it, he worked for his father, who had a tannery; Wilson had been a shoemaker, although he more accurately was the owner of a shoe factory. But these were white lies, since the line between skilled workmen and the owners of shops and small factories was still quite permeable. The Republicans aimed at symbolic rather than literal truth. They proclaimed themselves the party of free labor and independence.[6]

Prosperity was supposed to glue shut the cracks in a free labor ideology that embraced individualism, the production of homes, and a republican economy. The idea of self-making, embodied in the first generation of clerks flocking to business in the larger cities, supported some of these ideals better than others. In his visit to the United States in 1867–68, Charles Dickens memorably captured the paradoxical uniformity of self-made young men: "300 boarding houses in West 14th Street, exactly alike, with 300 young men, exactly alike, sleeping in 300 hall bedrooms, exactly alike, with 300 dress suits, exactly alike, lying on so many chairs, exactly

4. Mark W. Summers, *Railroads, Reconstruction, and the Gospel of Prosperity: Aid under the Republicans, 1865–1877* (Princeton, NJ: Princeton University Press, 1984), 85–97.

5. Foner, 364–72.

6. McFeely, 56, 66, 381–82.

This Currier and Ives lithograph (ca. 1872) portrays Grant and his vice president as working men. Grant did work for a while in his father's tanning shop; he hated it and was a terrible workman and businessman. Wilson did train as a shoemaker, but he ended up as a shoe manufacturer. Library of Congress, LC-DIG-ds-00680.

alike, beside the bed." These young men fitted uneasily within the republican home.[7]

In the years immediately after the war the glue weakened. Workers, employers, and liberal ideologues began to split up the free labor platform and choose the parts they needed. Workers emphasized the goals of free labor: independent producers, a general equality, and the production of republican citizens. By and large, liberals chose the means by which antebellum free labor had sought to gain these ends: contract freedom and laissez-faire. Employers mixed and matched; they wanted to have their cake and eat it too. They had no objection to city, state, or federal interventions in the economy in order to redistribute income, so long as it was redistributed upward. In Chicago the railroads that fought against the eight-hour day happily accepted the legislature's donation of Chicago's immensely valuable lakefront. They stressed contract freedom and laissez-faire only when it suited their interests.

Yet in 1872 the apparent successes of free labor indicated that it could still sustain the differences among its advocates and outrun its tensions and troubles. During the first Grant administration that success appeared brightest in the Midwest and Middle Border. It seemed to validate both free labor and Republican neo-Whig economic policies since the Civil War.

I

The American economy during the first Grant administration did two things extremely well. American farmers flooded Europe with wheat and eventually cotton while producing large amounts of corn, pork, and beef for domestic consumers. This productivity depended on a second success. Americans invested heavily in farms, infrastructure, and capital goods. They built the railroads required to haul crops, and they produced the iron, timber, and machinery required for the railroads and farms. This represented a political and spatial achievement as well as economic. Unlike Europe, the United States erased internal boundaries that impeded the passage of resources and commodities even as it erected external boundaries to protect American production.[8]

7. Michael Zakim, "Producing Capitalism: The Clerk at Work," in Michael Zakim and Gary J. Kornblith, eds., *Capitalism Takes Command: The Social Transformation of Nineteenth-Century America* (Chicago: University of Chicago Press, 2012), 223–48; Edwin G. Burrows and Mike Wallace, *Gotham: A History of New York City to 1898* (New York: Oxford University Press, 1999), 970.

8. Robert J. Gordon, "Two Centuries of Economic Growth: Europe Chasing the American Frontier," *National Bureau of Economic Research Working Paper Series* (2004), http://www.nber.org/papers/w10662.

The investment in capital goods and infrastructure during the first Grant administration proved unprecedented. From 1869 through 1873, investment in new capital goods was 20.5–23.5 percent of the gross national product. In the five years between 1855 and 1859 it had ranged from 12.5 percent to 15.7 percent. The new railroads, farms, steam engines, factories, and growing cities formed the fruits of that investment.[9]

The entire republic was mad for railroads. The United States added 29,589 miles of track between 1868 and 1873. The vast majority of it, 19,380 miles, was in the Midwest, Middle Border, and South. Every year from 1869 to 1872 set a new record for track laid in the United States, peaking in 1872 with 7,439 miles. Railroads spidered across the American landscape, creating a dense web of iron tracks that gave the United States more miles per capita than any nation in the world. Government—local, state, and federal—subsidized these railroads, and railroads, in turn, demanded iron, steel, timber, locomotives, and freight cars. The American tariff ensured that they bought the bulk of what they required from American manufacturers.[10]

For all the astonishing expansion of the railroads and the growth in manufacturing, the most important sector of the American economy remained agriculture. Only in 1880 did commerce's 29 percent share of the economy edge out agriculture's 28 percent share. It took until 1890, when agriculture's portion had fallen to 19 percent, for manufacturing and mining at 30 percent each to exceed it. This decline paradoxically emphasized agriculture's larger success. Manufacturing, mining, and commerce could grow only because farmers steadily shed workers no longer needed to feed the country. The absolute number of workers in agriculture continued to rise until the twentieth century, but agriculture's share of the national workforce fell. By 1900 it had declined to 40 percent, from a majority in 1860. Those workers, however, still produced more than the country could consume.[11]

9. Paul W. Rhode, "Gallman's Annual Output Series for the United States, 1834–1909," *National Bureau of Economic Research Working Papers Series* Working Paper no. 8860, April 2002: 28.

10. *Historical Statistics of the United States, Earliest Times to the Present: Millennial Edition*, ed. Scott Sigmund Gartner, Susan B. Carter, Michael R. Haines, Alan L. Olmstead, Richard Sutch, and Gavin Wright (New York: Cambridge University Press, 2006), table Df882–885—Railroad mileage built: 1830–1925; Richard White, *Railroaded: The Transcontinentals and the Making of Modern America* (New York: Norton, 2011), 50; Scott Reynolds Nelson, *Iron Confederacies: Southern Railways, Klan Violence, and Reconstruction* (Chapel Hill: University of North Carolina Press, 1999), 120.

11. Robert E. Gallman, "Economic Growth and Structural Change in the Long Nineteenth Century," in *The Cambridge Economic History of the United States*, ed. Stanley L. Engerman and Robert E. Gallman (Cambridge: Cambridge University Press, 1996), 2: 50; *Historical Statistics of the United States, Earliest Times to the*

The new western farms provided a multiplier effect. Farmers needed machinery, lumber, livestock, and a house. Without prairie farms, Cyrus McCormick's reapers would have lacked a market, and most of the white pines of Wisconsin and Michigan would have remained standing. Since the most common way to acquire a new farm was to sell an existing one, farmers took capital from older sections of the country or Europe and invested it in a new region. For varying periods, most also became wage laborers, using their wages to sustain their families until the farm became productive. Cabins, dugouts, sod houses, and tarpaper shacks that cost little beside the labor to construct them provided initial shelter, but no one wanted to endure a "soddy," with its snakes, insects, dust, dirt, and drips, any longer than necessary. In the best of circumstances, with good weather, good prices for crops, and settlement during early spring, which allowed the quick planting of a crop, a farmer had only to wait months rather than years before his farm yielded crops to support his family. Then the sod house gave way to a frame house.[12]

Enough Americans and European immigrants could afford to pay this toll in the 1860s and 1870s to make the Midwest and Middle Border into a cornucopia. The antebellum center of corn production, the Corn Belt, had included parts of the upper South, but by 1880 Illinois, Iowa, and Missouri and parts of Kansas, Nebraska, and Wisconsin formed its heart. Expansion drove innovation, the biological modification of corn, and the animals that ate it. Farmers bred new varieties of Dent corn — the type of corn then most commonly raised as animal feed — and bred hogs and cattle into four-footed factories that turned the corn into more-valuable meat.[13]

When measured by production per acre, American farmers were not efficient, but they were remarkably efficient when measured by production per worker. In the Midwest, West, and Middle Border, machines

Present: Millennial Edition, table Ee569–589 — Exports of selected commodities: 1790–1989; John C. Hudson, Making the Corn Belt: A Geographical History of Middle-Western Agriculture (Bloomington: Indiana University Press, 1994), 147–49; James Livingston, "The Social Analysis of Economic History and Theory: Conjectures on Late Nineteenth-Century American Development," American Historical Review 92, no. 1 (1987): 72–73; Richard Schneirov, "Thoughts on Periodizing the Gilded Age: Capital Accumulation, Society, and Politics, 1873–1898," Journal of the Gilded Age and Progressive Era 5, no. 3 (2006): 203–4; Jeffrey G. Williamson, "Watersheds and Turning Points: Conjectures on the Long-Term Impact of Civil War Financing," Journal of Economic History 34, no. 3 (1974): 637–38.

12. Gilbert Courtland Fite, The Farmers' Frontier, 1865–1900 (New York: Holt, Rinehart and Winston, 1966), 39–48.

13. Hudson, 130–41.

relentlessly replaced human labor. Between 1840 and 1880 technology reduced the number of hours humans had to work to produce 100 bushels of wheat from 233 to 152; for corn the equivalent figures fell from 276 to 180. During the wheat harvest of 1874 Dick Garland used "a new model of the McCormick self-rake." The machine demanded four horses. One son rode the lead horse; Dick drove the reaper; and another son, Hamlin, and four hired men took "'stations' behind the reaper" to bind the cut grain. They worked from dawn to sunset, fueled by massive meals cooked by Garland's mother. The harvest was semimechanized, but at the end of the day Garland still ached. Even with the machines, the reaping took four weeks: first barley, then wheat, and then oats. Then came stacking and storing, which was still handwork in the 1870s.[14]

Farmers engineered a massive ecological transformation, turning native grasslands in the Middle Border and California into a sea of domesticated grains. "We were all worshippers of wheat," Hamlin Garland wrote of the 1870s, a decade when the value of U.S. wheat and flour exports ballooned from $68 million in 1870 to $226 million in 1880. The wheat fed new mills with new technologies, some the products of American invention, others gained from industrial espionage in Europe. Charles Pillsbury's flour and Cadwallader Washburn's Gold Medal flour became national brands. They made Minneapolis the miller to the world. Between 1868 and 1872 domestic wheat prices fell by half. Bleached, white, superfine flour became a national staple. In Southern households white flour biscuits increasingly replaced cornbread.[15]

Cotton and wheat drove the American export economy. In 1872 cotton and the combination of wheat and flour dwarfed everything else, with tobacco coming in a distant third. Only wood manufactures at $15 million formed a significant manufactured export, and they amounted to just 8 percent of the export value of cotton. At the end of the nineteenth century exports accounted for 20 percent to 25 percent of farm income. Corn remained the country's leading crop in terms of output, but it left the

14. Ibid., 147–49; Hamlin Garland, *Main-Travelled Roads* (New York: Signet, New American Library, 1962), 141–42; Garland, *A Son of the Middle Border* (New York: Grosset & Dunlap, 1928), 148–54; *Historical Statistics of the United States, Earliest Times to the Present: Millennial Edition*, table Ee569–589 — Exports of selected commodities: 1790–1989; "Labor Hours per Unit of Production," table Da 1142–71.

15. Jeremy Atack, Fred Bateman, and William Parker, "The Farm, the Farmer, and the Market," in *Cambridge Economic History of the United States*, 2: 258–64; Garland, *A Son of the Middle Border*, 148–54; Nelson, 120; W. Bernard Carlson, "Technology and America as a Consumer Society, 1870–1900," in *The Gilded Age: Perspectives on the Origins of Modern America*, ed. Charles W. Calhoun, 2nd ed. (Lanham, MD: Rowman & Littlefield, 2007), 33–35.

country largely in the form of animal flesh after having fattened cattle and hogs. American exports reduced the cost of food in Europe faster than at any time since the Neolithic era. European peasants could not compete with cheap American grain and meat. Forced off the land, many of them immigrated to the United States. Some became American farmers; more became American workers.[16]

The construction of railroads, the expansion of agriculture, and the explosion of small shops and factories in key Midwestern cities yielded a booming economy of "More" that fulfilled the ambitions of Midwestern strivers. An economy of "More" did not denote an economy of greed. "More" involved collective expansion rather than individual accumulation. Although Americans put considerable weight on the numerical signs of material progress—numbers of farms, bushels of wheat, tons of ore, miles of railroad tracks—these numbers were also surrogates for things that were harder to calculate. They marked the increase in homes and families, and the maintenance of the values that supported them. For most Americans the economy made sense as a set of material arrangements whose purpose was the creation of homes, with their gendered division of labor and reproduction of republican citizens. In the Midwest and the Middle Border, free labor seemed to be working as intended, producing widespread prosperity and republican homes. This was Whiggish free labor dependent on government subsidies, tariffs, and other interventions; it was far from liberal laissez-faire. It created a society that Southern Radical governments sought to emulate, but they lacked the resources and advantages that the federal government bestowed outside the South.

The Civil War's legacy dogged Southerners. Slavery had been the basis of the Southern economy, and the South, particularly when it turned first to black codes and later to prison and convict labor, never fully gave up attempts to create new systems of coerced labor. Slavery had turned human beings into capital. In the antebellum South, slaves had been collateral, and mortgaging them had been the most common way to raise money. The Thirteenth Amendment ended that practice at the same time other forms of Southern capital either vanished or went into sharp decline. Southern investors had bought war bonds to support the Confederacy, but with defeat those bonds were worthless and the capital

16. Table Ee569–589—Exports of selected commodities: 1790–1989, in *Historical Statistics of the United States, Earliest Times to the Present: Millennial Edition*; Robert E. Lipsey, "U.S. Trade and the Balance of Payments, 1800–1913," in *Cambridge Economic History of the United States*, 2: 704–5; Scott Nelson, *A Nation of Deadbeats: An Uncommon History of America's Financial Disasters* (New York: Knopf, 2012), 158, 161; Harold G. Vatter, *The Drive to Industrial Maturity: The U.S. Economy, 1860–1914* (Westport, CT: Greenwood Press, 1975), 63.

they represented lost. The Fourteenth Amendment ended any chance of their redemption. Land and other resources remained, but land prices, without an enslaved labor supply, were plummeting. States that had once taxed slaves for revenue depended on taxing the land instead.[17]

The new national banking system provided the South with few new sources of capital. Because the South had left the Union when the North created the system, there were few national banks there, and those few were prohibited from taking land as collateral. Many banks chartered by the states did not do sufficient business to afford the capital reserve requirements necessary to get a national charter, and without the charter they could not issue bank notes. Large numbers of state banks shut their doors.[18]

The South, like the Midwest, found itself starved not only of gold but also of national bank notes, whose possession in 1866 ranged between $2.50 and $8.00 per inhabitant. In the Northeast there was $77 in circulation per inhabitant. As late as 1880, the South had a quarter of the country's population but only 10 percent of its currency. Those state banks that survived in the North and South found a niche by financing local merchants and making loans on farms and other real estate. To draw interest, they invested their reserves in the national banks, which clustered in the Northeast, the Mid-Atlantic, and the larger cities of the Midwest. Until 1874 the National Banking Act of 1864 concentrated money in New York City by requiring national banks to maintain a 25 percent reserve against their deposits and notes in the large New York City national banks. By 1870 the city's banks contained nearly a quarter of all American banking resources, and the national banks controlled 87 percent of these assets. This spatial distribution of banks, in turn, influenced manufacturing since manufacturers borrowed from the national banks to finance their operations. The easier the access businesses had to a national bank, the easier their access to credit and cash.[19]

17. Gavin Wright, *Old South, New South: Revolutions in the Southern Economy since the Civil War* (New York: Basic Books, 1986), 87–89.
18. Richard H. Timberlake, *The Origins of Central Banking in the United States* (Cambridge, MA: Harvard University Press, 1978), 87–88; Sven Beckert, *The Monied Metropolis: New York City and the Consolidation of the American Bourgeoisie, 1850–1896* (Cambridge: Cambridge University Press, 2001), 149; Richard Franklin Bensel, *Yankee Leviathan: The Origins of Central State Authority in America, 1859–1877* (Cambridge: Cambridge University Press, 1990), 268–72.
19. Nicolas Barreyre, "Les échelles de la monnaie: Souveraineté monétaire et spatialisation de la politique américaine après la guerre de sécession," *Annales, Sciences Sociales* 69, no. 2 (2014): 450; Beckert, 149; Timberlake, 87–88; Gretchen Ritter, *Goldbugs and Greenbacks: The Antimonopoly Tradition and the Politics of Finance in America* (Cambridge: Cambridge University Press, 1997), 68–69, 70–73.

The Republicans counted on prosperity to win over Southerners even as their economic policies punished the South. Given the cost of the bloody war and the rise of Southern terrorism during Reconstruction, economic retribution was both self-defeating and understandable. Congressional Radicals never calibrated their economic policies to exact punishment from ex-Confederates while sparing Unionists. The Radicals continued a wartime excise tax on cotton, which made American cotton less competitive on world markets and hindered Southern attempts to regain their old share of European cotton markets. Congress eliminated the tax in 1868 just before cotton boomed.[20]

Congress also refused to give the South subsidies proportional to those that went to the West and Northeast. The tariff paid down the Union war debt while funding the federal government and protecting key industries, but, except for sugar, it sheltered little that the South produced while driving up the costs of much of what it consumed. Between 30 and 40 percent of the tariff burden fell on exporters of agricultural products. They sold on unprotected competitive markets while buying goods in a protected market that produced higher prices. Because cotton remained the country's leading export, the South shouldered a disproportionate burden. Federal subsidies created the Western railroad system and improved river navigation and harbors in the Northeast and Pacific Coast, but they did little for the South except improve navigation at the mouth of the Mississippi. Southern rivers, ports, and harbors received a fraction of the funds devoted to the Eastern and Pacific states, and even the critical levees along the Mississippi River languished. For the rest of the century Southerners contended that the banking system, the tariff, and federal subsidies for internal improvements discriminated against the South, and they clearly did.[21]

The only man capable of gaining subsidies for the South seemed to be Tom Scott, who rose to prominence as an executive of the Pennsylvania Railroad. Like Collis P. Huntington, he loomed large in both the West and South. In 1870 the House of Representatives passed the Holman Resolution, promising no further railroad land grants. In 1871 the House ignored its own resolution and passed a last huge land grant to Scott's

20. Summers, 8; Sven Beckert, *Empire of Cotton: A Global History* (New York: Knopf, 2014), 274–94; Bensel, 331–32, 343–45.
21. Douglas A. Irwin, "Tariff Incidence in America's Gilded Age," *Journal of Economic History* 67, no. 3 (September 2007): 584, 596; Christopher Morris, *The Big Muddy: An Environmental History of the Mississippi and Its Peoples from Hernando De Soto to Hurricane Katrina* (New York: Oxford University Press, 2012), 151–64; Bensel, 331–32, 343–45.

Texas Pacific Railroad (which became the Texas and Pacific Railway) to link the South and West.[22]

Southern governments, both Democratic and Republican, were thrown back on the South's own meager resources to create prosperity. Even under siege, the Radical governments did the South considerable good in improving public institutions. To fund these reforms, the Radicals put their hopes in railroads and cotton. They felt they had to prime the pump, and so they lavished state subsidies on railroad corporations and raised taxes to pay for the subsidies. They thought they had little choice.[23]

At the end of the Civil War, the South had a considerable railroad system, much of it fully or partially controlled by the states. These railroads became the bait to lure Northern capital to the South. Southern governments sold the lines to private corporations for a pittance in exchange for promises of new investment to rebuild and extend them. They also allowed railroad corporations to use state bonds to raise funds, bestowed land grants on the railroads, granted them tax exemptions, and gave them special privileges to cut timber and take stone from state lands. States provided additional public capital by purchasing railroad stocks and bonds. What the railroads could not get from the states, they sought from counties and towns. As in the West, public resources were turned into private capital. It would have been a miracle if such policies went forward without corruption. There was no miracle.[24]

Like the Western land grants, the policies of Republican state governments in the South were, on paper at least, plausible. In their existing condition many of the railroads were nearly worthless; Southern Republicans wagered that giving away worn, wrecked, or incomplete railroads to gain functioning railroads was worth the cost. To pay for the subsidies to railroad corporations, they raised taxes on land.

The Republican willingness to redistribute resources to corporations was not matched by a redistribution of resources to small farmers. Only in South Carolina did the government intervene to help poor men secure

22. Paul W. Gates, *History of Public Land Law Development* (Washington, DC: [for sale by the Superintendent of Documents, U.S. GPO], 1968), 380–81; Leslie E. Decker, *Railroads, Lands, and Politics: The Taxation of the Railroad Land Grants, 1864–1897* (Providence: Brown University Press, 1964), passim, particularly 243–50; White, 123.

23. Foner, 379–89; Nelson, 4–6, Summers, 9–10, 24–25.

24. Summers details the aid and subsidies, 9–10, 24–25, 29–30, 36, 39–46, 65–84, 87–90, 100–12, 123–36, 168–73, 182–83, 214–17, 236, 243–44; for Southern rail system, see William G. Thomas, *The Iron Way: Railroads, the Civil War, and the Making of Modern America* (New Haven, CT: Yale University Press, 2011); Roger Ransom and Richard Sutch, "Capitalists without Capital: The Burden of Slavery and the Impact of Emancipation," *Agricultural History* 62, no. 3 (1988): 138–39.

depreciated lands or lands forfeited for taxes. Elsewhere, with land dropping in value and taxes on it increasing, Radicals hoped redistribution would require no government intervention beyond tax policy. They intended such a backdoor reallocation of land to replace the direct redistribution they could not obtain from Congress. It did not materialize. Overall the plantation elite did not sell their land at fire sale prices or lose it to the tax collector. When South Carolina granted debt relief to the benefit of large planters, plans for redistribution faltered in the state where they had the greatest chance of success.[25]

Southern legislatures did change the law to provide credit for the farmers seeking to grow cotton. Legislators passed bills permitting liens on unplanted cotton, which allowed crops that did not yet exist to become collateral to secure credit in the Southern economy. With the best of intentions, they saddled the South with a crop lien system that would burden the region for generations.[26]

II

Many of those who fattened on federal subsidies in the West were first to the trough in the South. Isaac Sherman, who argued for laissez-faire as vehemently as anyone in the country, did not allow his economic principles to stop his investments in Southern railroads, which fed off state aid. Huntington and Scott had no scruples over subsidies, and they came running wherever they caught a whiff of them in either the South or the West. The two men remained connected, usually as enemies and rivals, throughout the late 1860s and 1870s. Scott was ebullient and charming; Huntington was publicly dour; privately, his wit usually drew blood. Only

25. Nelson, *Iron Confederacies*, 116, 121; Foner, 328–29, 382–83; Robin L. Einhorn, *American Taxation, American Slavery* (Chicago: University of Chicago Press, 2006), 107–8, 203–4, 209, 231–35; Wright, 17–50; Summers, 36–46; Thomas C. Holt first made the important argument about debt relief in the 1970s, in *Black over White: Negro Political Leadership in South Carolina During Reconstruction* (Urbana: University of Illinois Press, 1977), 129–30.

26. Edward L. Ayers, *The Promise of the New South: Life after Reconstruction* (New York: Oxford University Press, 1992), 13–15; Steven Hahn, *The Roots of Southern Populism: Yeomen Farmers and the Transformation of the Georgia Upcountry, 1850–1890* (New York: Oxford University Press, 1983), 170–203; Wright, 110.

in their backgrounds, their financial ability, their daring, and their corruption were they similar.[27]

Huntington was born in the Litchfield Hills of Connecticut above the appropriately named Poverty Hollow. The town overseers had taken him away from his family as an adolescent and bound him out to work for local farmers. He eventually went west to California, became a Sacramento merchant, and took up the Central Pacific when knowledgeable railroad men would not touch it.[28]

Tom Scott, as everyone called Thomas A. Scott, knew a great deal about railroads, but his background was as impoverished and his honesty as suspect as Huntington's. Passed from his mother to his older siblings after the death of his father, he became a clerk and eventually moved up through the ranks of the Pennsylvania Railroad. By the Civil War he was the Pennsylvania's vice president and later became president. In what was probably the work of John W. Forney, the *Philadelphia Sunday Morning News* described him with as much admiration as exaggeration as

> a one man power, who sets up and pulls down, and rules with omnipotent sway. Able, unscrupulous, shrewd, knowing how to make the interests of thousands of imitators of a smaller pattern run in the same groove with his own, he has probably done more to corrupt legislation, debauch politics, make bribery a science, elevate it to the rank of profession and enshrine it among the fine arts, than any man in this country.[29]

The two men collided in Virginia. Huntington took control of the struggling Chesapeake and Ohio, whose first terminus on the Ohio River would become the eponymous Huntington, West Virginia. Scott moved to create a north-south system to rival the east-west ambitions of the transcontinentals. He combined pieces of a reconstructed and extended antebellum railroad system into a corridor running from Richmond, Virginia, to Atlanta, Georgia. From there he could build west. His strategy was to use Southern front men and dummy corporations to buy up individual Southern roads.[30]

Scott's first attempt failed, both because of the federal unwillingness to subsidize the South and because he had potent rivals. Moncure Robinson and Alexander Boyd Andrews had already organized the Seaboard Inland

27. Beckert, *The Monied Metropolis*, 162–63.
28. David Sievert Lavender, *The Great Persuader* (Niwot: University Press of Colorado, 1998, 1970), 2–3.
29. *Philadelphia Sunday Morning News*, n.d. 1878, enclosure with Frazier to CPH, Nov. 6, 1878, in *Collis P. Huntington Papers, 1856–1901*, Microfilming Corporation of America (Syracuse, NY: Syracuse University Library), CPH Papers, ser. 1, r 15.
30. Nelson, *Iron Confederacies*, 72–81.

Air Line (so named in the sense of direct, i.e., the shortest distance between two points) to connect Georgia and South Carolina to the deep-water port at Portsmouth, Virginia. They recruited William Mahone, a Confederate war hero and newly minted Republican, who was creating a railroad network of his own, to mount a neo-Confederate attack on Scott. Mahone denounced Scott as the head of a Northern carpetbagging railroad company in league with Radical Republicans, which, in point of fact, Scott was.[31]

Mahone's accusations begun as a tactic in a corporate battle, became part of the political—and racial—war over Reconstruction. Assaults on Scott's corruption involved charges against black legislators, most of whom voted to subsidize him. White resentment over the railroads employing black and northern workers became attacks on the railroads themselves. It is no wonder that the eruption of Ku Klux Klan violence in the late 1860s and early 1870s centered on the railroads through interior North and South Carolina; they embodied everything many white Southerners hated. Allied with Radical Republican governments, the railroads were altering old trade relations, pushing property taxes upward, corrupting government, and giving new opportunities to black men.[32]

Scott was nothing if not resilient. By 1870 he was back in a very crowded Virginia field. Virginia had invested millions in the railroads that Huntington received for a mere promise to complete the line to the Ohio River within six years. Scott, Huntington, and Mahone could all afford to bribe and grant private favors to Virginia legislators since the public gifts they received in return were so large. By the time the giveaway was over, Virginia had lost $26 million.[33]

As in the West, subsidies produced railroads, albeit heavily indebted, indifferently constructed, and quite fragile; and railroads, as intended, expanded the range of cotton by freeing transportation from the rivers. The railroads fed the new deep-water ports necessary to accommodate large steamships, and they hauled the phosphate needed to grow cotton on the uplands. In the words of the Carroll County Times of Georgia in 1872, the railroads in spreading cotton had achieved "a considerable revolution" in the South. Cotton had always been a slave crop, but now it became a poor white man's crop as well as a black man's.[34]

31. Nelson, Iron Confederacies, 52–53, 79–89, 93–94.
32. Ibid., 84–94.
33. Thomas, 188; Nelson, 138–40.
34. Stanley Engerman, "Slavery and Its Consequences," in The Cambridge Economic History of the United States, 2: 356–60; Steven Hahn, The Roots of Southern Populism: Yeomen Farmers and the Transformation of the Georgia Upcountry, 1850–1890 (New York: Oxford University Press, 1983) 147, 159–62.

The Republicans succeeded in boosting cotton; they did not succeed in creating a prosperous free-labor South. Rising cotton prices in the early 1870s and the need to pay taxes induced upland farmers to plant cotton. The number of small farms, including those operated by black farmers, increased. In a sample of Georgia counties, however, the average black farmer controlled only 10 percent of the land his average white neighbor did, and it was worth 10 percent as much. And this reflected only the most successful black and white farmers who were able to gain or retain land. In Georgia, as elsewhere, farmers moved into tenancy and sharecropping. In the country as a whole farm sizes would rise during the Gilded Age, but they declined in the South.[35]

Across the Southern political spectrum, propagandists from Henry Grady, the Atlanta editor who was spokesman for the New South, to Tom Watson, who would become the most prominent Southern Populist, praised small farmers as the hope for the Southern future. It proved a tenuous hope. Expanding cotton cultivation in the Piedmont restricted an older way of life in which subsistence crops and security came first. In the South, a man with enough corn stored to feed family and livestock until the next harvest was regarded as happy and secure. He could pursue a safety-first strategy, making sure his family's subsistence needs were covered and producing cotton for the cash it would bring. The spread of cotton made this safety-first strategy harder to pursue. A rise in fence laws, trespass laws, lien laws, and controls over livestock curtailed access to the woods and old fields where small farmers used to graze animals, hunt, fish, and cut timber. Many of those woods and abandoned lands became cotton fields. Corn and hog production—the basis of Southern subsistence—declined by nearly half across the South in the late nineteenth century.[36]

A partial independence from the market in which farmers provided for their own sustenance or relied on local exchanges was vanishing, but it would be a mistake to think it gone entirely. Tenants might produce only one thing—cotton—but those who farmed their own land retained a more varied scheme of production. They reduced their corn and other crops, but they did not abandon them, and they continued to raise livestock, albeit in lesser numbers. They also made significant investments in farm technology. Some combined farming with blacksmithing, carpentry, logging, milling, and weaving to supplement their agricultural income.

35. Wright, 54; Lou Ferleger and John D. Metz, *Cultivating Success in the South: Farm Households in the Postbellum Era* (New York: Cambridge University Press, 2014), 25–29.
36. Ferleger and Metz, 35–36; Wright, 34–35, 48–49; Hahn, 141–42, 149–52, 163, 239–54.

Cotton was their risk crop; their other activities were hedges, a modification of the older safety-first strategy.[37]

Even when an initial boom in cotton prices fizzled as the South competed with India, Egypt, and Brazil, small farmers, sharecroppers, and tenants produced more cotton because cotton proved economically sticky. Once a farmer took it up, he had difficulty shaking it loose. Southern lands seemed to beg for cotton. The acidic soils of the South did not welcome wheat or even corn, which grew more abundantly elsewhere, but the South gave cotton all it required: 200 frost-free days annually, a temperature that rose above 77 degrees Fahrenheit for at least ninety days, and abundant rainfall well in excess of the 25 inches that the plant required. Until the advent of large-scale irrigation, no other place in the United States could meet those requirements.[38]

But more was involved than the suitability of the South for cotton; cotton had become the only road to credit. Once farmers started down the crop-lien road there were few exits. Creditors demanded cotton. Storeowners advanced consumer goods only with a lien on the customer's anticipated cotton crop; planters took liens on their tenants' and sharecroppers' cotton. The various lien holders battled in court when the crop was short and could not cover all debts. Storeowners who advanced goods on credit took their own merchandise on credit from wholesalers who sent their jobbers to every Southern crossroad store. Wholesalers, in turn, depended on credit advanced them by northern manufacturers or money borrowed from northern banks. Everything ran on cotton and credit. The Southern economy rose and fell with the worldwide demand for the crop. Rising cotton prices meant more cotton, but so too did falling prices, which necessitated more cotton to cover debts. Debt, credit, and cotton marched together across the South. The terror of tenant and small farmer alike was not being able to pay out and clear their balance with storeowners.[39]

Cotton once again reigned as king, and cotton exports had again become critical to the larger American economy, but cotton's kingdom remained a poor one. Some small farmers did well, operating shrewdly in the new environment. The Southern economy grew, and by the 1880s it was growing at the same rate as the North's. But by every measure, the average Southerner was poorer, was less educated, and had fewer oppor-

37. Ferleger and Metz, 57–91.
38. Wright, 34–38; Beckert, *Empire of Cotton*, 292–94; Hahn, 137–69; Eugene R. Dattel, *Cotton and Race in the Making of America: The Human Costs of Economic Power* (Chicago: Ivan R. Dee, 2009), 229–42; Engerman, "Slavery and Its Consequences," in *The Cambridge Economic History of the United States*, 2: 356–60.
39. Ayers, 13–15; Wright, 50, 110.

tunities than the average Northerner. The South became, as historian Gavin Wright has put it, "a low wage region in a high wage country." The burden fell most heavily on the freedpeople.[40]

Charles Chesnutt recorded part of the result. Chesnutt, later a successful writer, was a light-skinned, well-educated school teacher so devoted to ideas of home and self-improvement that in the 1870s he hand copied pages from A *Handbook of Home Improvement* to master middle-class standards of hygiene. He captured, quite unsympathetically, the toll that tenancy, sharecropping, and the relentless cheating and chiseling by white people intent on the racial subordination of blacks exacted from the freedpeople. He also recorded the often-fraught relations between the urban black elite and the country people because he shared the ambivalence of that elite toward most freedpeople. He grew discouraged and angry with the parents of the children he taught. Chesnutt complained of their ignorance, but their complaints about him registered the economic desperation of their lives and the relative privilege of Chesnutt. "You want us to pay you thirty or forty dollars a month for sitting in the shade," Chesnutt reported them telling him, "and that is as much as we can make in 2 or 3 months.... We all of [us] work on other people's, white people's, land, and sometimes get cheated out of all we make." Unable to persuade them to pay what he asked, Chesnutt denounced them as the "most bigoted, superstitious, hardest-headed people in the world! These folks downstairs believe in ghosts, luck, horse shoes, cloud-signs, witches, and all other kinds of nonsense, and all the argument in the world couldn't get it out of them." Chesnutt recorded his disgust with poor freedpeople, but he also noted how race and class curtailed their opportunities and created their poverty.[41]

Ultimately, the economic policies of the Southern Republican Reconstruction governments helped doom both those governments and Reconstruction itself in the South. Railroad subsidies meant debt, and debt meant increased tax burdens, which alienated the constituency Republicans hoped to lure into the party. New taxes added economic grievances to racism and created a toxic mix that fueled the political resistance to Reconstruction. Such policies hardly amounted to the only, or even the most important, factor weakening Reconstruction. The failure to curb terror was more critical, but Radical economic policies created

40. Wright, 7, 12, 55, 66–70, 76.
41. Allyson Hobbs, A *Chosen Exile: A History of Racial Passing in American Life* (Cambridge, MA: Harvard University Press, 2014), 115.

hostility within the very class—Southern yeoman farmers—that Republicans sought to attract and conciliate.[42]

III

Republicans intended Reconstruction to spread free labor, contract freedom, and prosperity into the South and West, but they presumed that these things had been secured in the North. Abundant signs in the wake of the Civil War indicated they were right. In 1865, when John Richards, a "foreman mechanic" who had redesigned the equipment and methods for producing woodworking machines for J. A. Fay's factory in Cincinnati, visited Providence, Rhode Island, the world of free labor was vibrant. Richards went out of his way to call at the works of J. R. Brown and Lucian Sharpe. He had no business to conduct with them. Brown and Sharpe made, among other things, measuring tools, and Richards wanted to talk shop, particularly about their use of precision English gear-cutting gauges. Brown and Sharpe received him courteously, gave him the information that he desired, and set aside their regular business to provide a tour of the shop.[43]

There was nothing unique about Richards's visit or the way that Brown and Sharpe received him. In the overlapping working-class and business culture of the North, craftspeople regularly shared processes, tools, and minor innovations. They also increasingly pursued inventions and patents, but even here the culture was collaborative. Charles Williams's machine shop on Court Street in Boston produced fire alarms and telegraph equipment, but he also did custom work for inventors. Thomas Edison worked on the telegraph at Williams's shop; Alexander Graham Bell perfected the telephone there, and Moses Farmer worked on the dynamo, an electrical generator that produced direct current. In Milwaukee inventors clustered at Charles Kleinsteuber's shop, where Carlos Glidden and Christopher Sholes worked on the typewriter.[44]

Richards, Browne, Sharpe, and Williams occupied the world of free labor that Republicans regarded as the North's core achievement and crowning glory. Many of the men who ran northern shops and small manufacturing firms had risen from the ranks of skilled workers, and initially

42. Foner, 375–77.
43. Philip Scranton, *Endless Novelty: Specialty Production and American Industrialization, 1865–1925* (Princeton, NJ: Princeton University Press, 1997), 27–33.
44. Steven W. Usselman, *Regulating Railroad Innovation: Business, Technology, and Politics in America, 1840–1920* (New York: Cambridge University Press, 2002), 63–68, 71–75; Scranton, 31–59; A. J. Millard, *Edison and the Business of Innovation* (Baltimore, MD: Johns Hopkins University Press, 1990), 25–26.

little social distance separated them from their employees. In smaller cities like Cincinnati and San Francisco, many businessmen maintained strong cross-class ties with skilled workers built on common trade identities, free labor Republicanism, and membership in the Masons, Odd Fellows, or other lodges. Workers still expected eventually to run shops of their own. At an 1870 meeting in Cincinnati of "manufacturers, mechanics and inventors" all gathered together as "practical working men." In Chicago, during and immediately after the war, many workingmen succeeded in establishing their own enterprises. Workmen sometimes called themselves engineers or mechanics, but they had learned their trades in private firms and workshops or the large armories run by the U.S. government.[45]

Mark Twain captured, and caricatured, the American mechanic in Hank Morgan, the lead character in *A Connecticut Yankee in King Arthur's Court*.

> I am an American...a Yankee of Yankees—and practical; yes, and nearly barren of sentiment, I suppose—or poetry, in other words. My father was a blacksmith, my uncle was a horse doctor, and I was both, along at first. Then I went over to the great arms factory and learned my real trade; learned all there was to it; learned to make everything: guns, revolvers, cannon, boilers, engines, all sorts of labor-saving machinery. Why I could make anything a body wanted—anything in the world, it didn't make any difference what; and if there wasn't any quick new-fangled way to make a thing, I could invent one....[46]

The "Yankee of Yankees" might, in Philadelphia, actually be a British or Irish immigrant, but the essentials did not vary much with ethnicity or nativity. These were practical men, enamored of new technologies, and they admired other practical men who got their hands dirty. They thought their ability to manage their firms depended on their grasp of constantly changing tools and problems of production. Their workers, in turn, prided themselves on their skill, knowledge, and independence. They expected their competence and their ideas of manliness to be respected.[47]

Many postwar Americans retained a faith that the new industrial economy, like the older economy of small farms, shops, and stores, could

45. Jeffrey Haydu, *Citizen Employers: Business Communities and Labor in Cincinnati and San Francisco, 1870–1916* (Ithaca, NY: ILR Press, 2008), 19, 27–31, 38–39.
46. Mark Twain, *A Connecticut Yankee in King Arthur's Court* (New York: Harper & Brothers, 1917, orig. ed. 1889), 5.
47. Scranton, 29–34, 73–74; Philip Scranton, *Proprietary Capitalism: The Textile Manufacture at Philadelphia, 1800–1885* (Cambridge: Cambridge University Press, 1983), 310–11, 337–49.

sustain free labor ideals of independence. In 1868 James Parton, a British immigrant and liberal journalist, chose Pittsburgh as the topic for an article in the *Atlantic Monthly*. He spent considerable time describing the coal mines critical to the city's growth. He was convinced that there was in free markets a harmony of interests between workers and owners, and the coal mines around Pittsburgh were his exhibit A. He argued that in the industrializing United States material progress would not degrade workers to European conditions. Even in the dark of the coal mines Parton found free labor in all its republican glory. In 1868 coal miners maintained old usages that made them more independent contractors than wage workers. Each had his own "room" in a mine, deciding how the seam was to be mined and how much coal he would dig each day. The miner

> begins work when he likes, works as fast as he likes, or as slow, and goes home when he likes. His "room" is his own against the world; when he has dug out of it his regular hundred bushels, which he usually accomplishes about three o'clock in the afternoon, he takes up his oil-bottle, and his dinner kettle, gets upon a load of coal, rides to daylight, and saunters home. . . . If he fancies to get rich, he can.

The miners were citizens, "proud, honest and orderly," and cherished their right to vote. They sent their children to school rather than into the mines. This was American free labor.[48]

Competitive small businesses also seemed evidence that free labor worked. Postwar manufacturing produced a tumultuous system of individual proprietorships, owned and managed by a single person; partnerships, which had two or more owners and managers; and unincorporated shareholder companies in which several shareholders, bound by written agreement, owned a company and could leave it by selling their shares. Publicly traded joint stock corporations also existed, but they were rare and exotic.

In aggregate these firms appeared to inhabit a Hobbesian world. From one decennial census to another, 60–80 percent of new firms in a manufacturing state like Pennsylvania disappeared, casualties of competition or lack of capital, or simply abandoned when partners quarreled or died. They might appear to be engaged in an all-against-all war, but from the inside they looked far stabler and more cooperative. The owners of smaller shops were often related to their workers, and the various companies sought out quite specific niches in the larger economy. Around Philadelphia

48. Christopher Jones, "A Landscape of Energy Abundance: Anthracite Coal Canals and the Roots of American Fossil Fuel Dependence, 1820–1860," *Environmental History* 15, no. 3 (2010): 449–84; James Parton, "Pittsburg" [*sic*], *Atlantic Monthly* 21 (1868): 17–36.

textile mills and small specialty manufacturers produced everything from carpets to new hardware to pianos. Custom manufacturers produced individually crafted goods for a specific task—a dynamo or a tailored suit, for example. Custom producers could, however, also be batch producers, manufacturing goods in a number of styles according to advance orders for products ranging from locomotives to pianos, jewelry, silverware, books, carpets, and styled fabrics. These firms emphasized quality over quantity and relied on skilled labor. Technique, style, and skill added value during manufacture. Into the 1890s, those firms that added the most value paid the highest wages.[49]

The great symbol of this world of striving mechanics, technical innovation, and new products was Thomas Edison. He epitomized American invention, and his greatest invention was Thomas Edison. He grew up in a world of shops, and he prospered in them, but he transformed the figure of the inventor into the solitary native American folk genius, a man who made his way in the world by remaking the world. He symbolized the possibilities of free labor even as he mythologized the way it worked. Edison's chosen persona was the Wizard of Menlo Park, an icon of individualism and a child of the small-town Midwest, who embodied values forged in rural America within an urban and increasingly immigrant country. Like Buffalo Bill, Edison proved far more complicated than anything his image could contain.

In the 1870s and beyond, as the currents of a modern America crossed, shifted, and eddied, obscuring a clear route to the future, Edison could appear to be a beacon, signaling the shores of a familiar world of free labor to people exhausted from beating against prevailing winds and tides. Raised in Ohio and Michigan in a family whose father was tainted by fraud and a relentless downward mobility, he never received an extensive formal education. His subsequent career, like Lincoln's, seemed to validate all the homilies of self-reliance, social mobility, and free labor.

Edison grew into a restless and an inveterate improver. He picked up telegraphy and thought of new ways to improve the telegraph. He tramped, moving from job to job. He valued independence and absorbed the craft culture of machine shops whose workmen admired ingenuity, improvement, and fellowship more than wealth. Edison wanted his own laboratory, where he would be free from the "damn capitalists" whose needs and investments shaped his work on the telegraph. He staffed the dream

49. Philip Scranton, "Conceptualizing Pennsylvania's Industrializations, 1850–1950," *Pennsylvania History* 61, no. 1 (1994): 9; Suresh Naidu and Noam Yuchtman, "Labor Market Institutions in the Gilded Age of American Economic History," Working Paper 22117, NBER (Cambridge: National Bureau of Economic Research, 2016), 7–8; this whole section depends heavily on the work of Scranton, *Endless Novelty*, 10, passim.

laboratory that he build in 1876 at Menlo Park, New Jersey, with, as an employee remembered, "learned men, cranks, enthusiasts, plain 'muckers' and absolutely insane men." Working alongside chemists with German Ph.D.s and a crew of craftsmen and machinists, some of them immigrants, he created an elaborately equipped invention factory whose goal was "a minor invention every ten days and a big thing every six months or so." What made Edison more than an improving mechanic found in thousands of American factories and shops was his desire to create entire systems that were new and unique.[50]

How could Americans not embrace the Edison of the 1870s as free labor came under siege? Edison prized the values and practices of the machine shop culture that had nurtured him, and they were simply a variant on older antebellum artisan values, which had fed into and helped inspire the free labor ideology of the Republicans. He cultivated an everyman persona, dressing in workman's clothing so he was "as dirty as any of the other workers and not much better dressed than a tramp." The Menlo Park factory was a loud, rowdy, and raucous place full of nightly singalongs around a large organ, gaming, practical jokes, and midnight feasts. Its informality and democratic atmosphere contrasted with the new factories and their posted rules, which workers despised. A story, perhaps apocryphal, circulated of the new employee who asked Edison about the rules of the lab. Edison replied, "Hell, there are no rules here. We're trying to accomplish something."[51]

But it was more than the atmosphere that made the lab seem a surviving fortress of free labor. Edison gave his employees control over and responsibility for their work. He held to the old craft belief that a person who had mastered a set of skills was best suited to decide how to apply them. On the railroads and in emerging factories, the demand of workers that, as skilled men and citizens, they should control the conditions of their work was perhaps the most fruitful site of conflict in American industry in the late nineteenth century. Edison not only indulged such beliefs, he incorporated them into his lab's practice. At Menlo Park the work was demanding and the employees were responsible for achieving outcomes, but how and when they went about the task and met deadlines was their responsibility. Edison was notoriously scornful of working by the clock. The lab's rhythms were those of inspiration and necessity. Men rose quickly if competent, and even if entry pay was relatively modest, they shared in profits from successful inventions. Although Edison could

50. Thomas Parke Hughes, *American Genesis: A Century of Invention and Technological Enthusiasm, 1870–1970* (New York: Viking, 1989), 24–30.
51. Millard, 22–26.

be demanding, sarcastic, and harsh if results were not forthcoming, most employees enjoyed working at the lab.[52]

The lab at Menlo Park and its successors were neither a workers' paradise nor a model for the transition from free labor to industrial production. For all the lab's camaraderie and egalitarianism, it was Edison's factory. He hired and fired. Edison could allow his workers autonomy and creativity in large part because they were producing inventions—single prototypes more similar to the creations of craftsmen than to thousands and eventually millions of identical products with interchangeable parts that flowed out of factories. Edison's employees were masters and inventors of machinery; factory workers were becoming mere accessories to machines.

When the Republicans published "The Workingman's Banner" to promote their presidential ticket, they glossed the differences between a shop and a small factory, but in doing so, they underestimated the changes taking place. Factories did differ from shops. They were not just larger, but they also imposed a distance between the owner, who no longer worked alongside his men and who often did not know them by name. Factories were more likely to adopt steam engines to power machines.

This happened gradually and unevenly, but it was clearly happening in the early 1870s. The number of factories in the United States, most of them in the Northeast, New England, and parts of the Midwest, had nearly doubled in the ten years since 1860. These factories vastly increased the number of workers involved in manufacturing. New York City alone had 130,000 manufacturing workers by 1873, but they did not eliminate smaller shops.[53]

Chicago and Boston revealed the complicated nature of an economy that continued to generate small producers but where larger producers were becoming more and more important. The total number of manufacturing firms in Chicago increased from 246 in 1850 to 1,355 in 1870, but where the top 5 percent of the firms in 1850 accounted for 6 percent of the industrial capital, they accounted for 39 percent in 1870. The amount of capital in manufacturing quadrupled between 1865 and 1873 to $400 million. Invested capital in terms of dollar per output increased 18 percent in the 1860s and 30 percent in the 1870s. Industry was becoming more capital-intensive, and the trend was accelerating in the 1870s as manufacturers switched to coal and steam, added machines, and built larger factories. Factories with fifty or more workers relied most heavily on steam-driven

52. Ibid., 31–42.
53. Amy Dru Stanley, *From Bondage to Contract: Wage Labor, Marriage, and the Market in the Age of Slave Emancipation* (Cambridge: Cambridge University Press, 1998), 63–64; Beckert, *The Monied Metropolis*, 145–46.

machines, and they employed more than half of Chicago's workers by 1870. In Boston even in the late 1870s more than half of the city's manufacturing firms employed six workers or fewer, but roughly two-thirds of workers labored in shops and factories of twenty people or more.[54]

In 1871, three years after writing about Pittsburgh, Parton wrote an account of a Philadelphia newspaper publisher for a volume entitled *Sketches of Men of Progress* in which he noted and exaggerated the changes in the economy. In Pittsburgh in 1868 he had reassured Americans that the new industrial economy changed nothing. In 1871 he claimed that it had changed everything. Parton conflated all industries under a single economic law that he called "a law of modern business, against which it was idle to complain." The law dictated that "a business establishment must now be immense or nothing. It must absorb or be absorbed. It must either be a great, resistless maelstrom of business, drawing countless wrecks into its vortex, or it must be itself a wreck, and contribute its quote to the all-engulfing prosperity of a rival." He thought he saw in this process "glorious promise for the future of our race in that irresistible tendency, which so many deplore, that is everywhere businesses of enormous proportions."[55]

Parton, as liberals were wont to do, collapsed a messy competitive present into a natural law with an inevitable outcome. His law of modern business, in which large fish inexorably swallow small fish, should have yielded large corporations in every industry, but this was not the case. Manufacturing had become an ecosystem with quite specific niches. The smaller specialized firms that typified manufacturing in Philadelphia did not simply represent an evolutionary stage of capitalism doomed to give way to more advanced corporations. The presence of corporations or very large firms in one part of an industry did not create advantages that allowed them to take over the entire industry. The Philadelphia textile industry survived and prospered despite the existence of much larger and highly capitalized corporations in Lowell, Massachusetts.[56]

Large firms had not yet become synonymous with corporations. Larger firms emerged in industries where they could pursue a strategy of replacing

54. John B. Jentz and Richard Schneirov, *Chicago in the Age of Capital: Class, Politics, and Democracy During the Civil War and Reconstruction* (Urbana: University of Illinois Press, 2012), 19–20; Stanley, 63–64; Matthew S. Jaremski, "National Banking's Role in U.S. Industrialization, 1850–1900," Working Paper no. 18789, NBER (2013), http://www.nber.org/papers/w18789.

55. *Sketches of Men of Progress*, ed. James Parton ([n.p.]: New York and Hartford Pub. Co., 1870), 75–76; Nancy Cohen, *The Reconstruction of American Liberalism, 1865–1914* (Chapel Hill: University of North Carolina Press, 2002), 107–9.

56. Scranton, "Conceptualizing Pennsylvania's Industrializations, 1850–1950," 9, 72–73; William G. Roy, *Socializing Capital: The Rise of the Large Industrial Corporation in America* (Princeton, NJ: Princeton University Press, 1997), 5, 22, 78–79, 97, 256–57.

skilled labor with capital in the form of machines run by less-skilled workers. They sold standardized goods at low margins in immense quantities. The mechanized flour mills revolutionizing the American diet, for example, added relatively little value to the wheat that passed through their rollers. They made money selling vast quantities of flour on a mass market.[57]

Competitive and dynamic, the economy was supposed to protect the primacy of small producers and prevent economic dependency. In the boom years that largely coincided with the first Grant administration, many politicians insisted that even with the rising scale of production this was the case. The "Galena Tanner" and the "Natick Shoemaker," however, did not convince everyone.

IV

A fundamental shift was transforming the economy: the rise of wage labor. As structural changes in the economy forced workers to accept wage labor not as a temporary state but a permanent condition, they resisted. Free labor depended on independence, and, as Lincoln had said, permanent wage labor signified "either a dependent nature which prefers it, or improvidence, folly, or singular misfortune," but as the 1860s turned into the 1870s wage labor was becoming not a transitory stage in life but the norm. In 1873 the Massachusetts Bureau of Statistics of Labor proclaimed that wage labor had become "a system more widely diffused than any form of religion, or of government, or indeed, of any language." Excluding farmers, wageworkers by 1870 outnumbered the self-employed. They did not sell the products of their minds and hands. They sold their hours and days.[58]

Contract freedom attempted to reconcile wage labor and independence. A wage earner remained free, his contract willingly negotiated. He owed his employer no more than the labor specified in it. The employer, in turn, owed the laborer only his wages. The market guaranteed freedom and independence. The combination of wage labor and contract freedom, however, remained full of tensions and contradictions, which even some liberal intellectuals such as Godkin acknowledged. Sounding like a working-class radical, Godkin wrote that wage work was as much a servile labor regime as slavery or serfdom. Writing anonymously in the *North*

---

57. This whole section depends heavily on the work of Philip Scranton, *Endless Novelty*.
58. Stanley, 60–62; Jentz, 82–83.

American Review, he proclaimed that it was ludicrous to see exchanges of labor in market as exemplars of freedom.[59]

> What I agree to do in order to escape from starvation, or to save my wife and children from starvation, or ignorance of my ability to do anything else, I agree to do under compulsion, just as much as if I agreed to do it with a pistol at my head; and the terms I make under such circumstances are not by any means the measure of my rights, even "under the laws of trade."[60]

In the early 1870s officials in the Massachusetts Bureau of Statistics of Labor began to link threats to the home and the wretched condition of the poor not to their moral failings or bad social influences but to the wage system. The consequences of low wages meant a man lost the benefits of home life. When a man could not support his wife, she was forced to labor, scrubbing floors or taking in laundry: "No cheerful smile greets a returning father whose six days earnings pay for but five days of meat." Poverty "kills love and all affection, all pride of home . . . nay emasculates home of all its quickening powers." Poor men sought solace in saloons or on the street while their wives "toiling at the wash-tub and iron board" performed the work of other families. To force wives to work for money was to deprive husbands of ownership of wives' labor and service.[61]

Contract freedom provided no solution. Wages sufficient to support a family and home could not be left to the market, since a wage insufficient to support a wife and children endangered the home and the republic. Even the most ardent liberal advocates of contract freedom recognized that workers deserved a wage that allowed a man to support his family. John Stuart Mill's *Principles of Political Economy* accepted the tenet that a worker's wages must support "himself, a wife, and a number of children." If a just wage had to support a worker's dependents, then it could not be left only to the free bargaining of individuals. Wages, in the words of the Boston minister Joseph Cook, must include the "cost of producing labor" if "our institutions are to endure," and that cost included "the expense of keeping wives at home to take care of little children."[62]

Such complaints reflected the assumption that the role of the economy was to produce homes and prosperity was necessary to sustain them.

---

59. Stanley, 73–83; Daniel T. Rodgers, *The Work Ethic in Industrial America: 1850–1920*, 2nd ed. (Chicago: University of Chicago Press, 2014), 30, 32.
60. Michael J. Sandel, *Democracy's Discontent: America in Search of a Public Philosophy* (Cambridge, MA: Belknap Press of Harvard University Press, 1996), 189–90.
61. Stanley, 148–55, quote 151.
62. Hendrik Hartog, *Man and Wife in America: A History* (Cambridge, MA: Harvard University Press, 2000), 101; Stanley, 138–48, 146–47.

When men did not earn enough to support wives and children, the economy was failing. These complaints also bared assumptions about the home. Men owned and had a right to their wives' labor and property. A home was a domestic space in which wives rendered services in exchange for support. When male workers could not adequately support a wife, they lacked homes even if they had wives. As the labor radical George McNeill would put it, the poor laborer "was a man without the rights of manhood...homeless, in the deep significance of the home."[63]

Few white married men had wives who worked for wages outside the home. In the late nineteenth century only about 3–5 percent of married white women entered the labor force, although a much higher percentage of single, widowed, and divorced women did so. Married women worked, but their work was not captured by economic statistics. Most did laundry, cared for children, cleaned houses, and cooked, but they earned no wage. In speaking of married men who could not support a wife, however, McNeill included more than those whose wives worked for wages. Wives who took in laundry or assisted their husbands in their labor did not count as wage workers, but neither were they supported in the sense that McNeill desired.[64]

The single women who left their paternal homes to work were considered women adrift, moving outside of the usual and accepted cultural categories, and their conditions very often were unenviable. In the winter of 1869 a writer for the Chicago Tribune applied the trope of homelessness to women, not men, deprived of a domestic space. He compared "the richly-dressed lady of the avenue" sweeping by "her thinly-clad sister of the alley" who was hurrying from her "fireless garret to perform her daily fourteen hours labor for a pittance too small to pay rent and purchase sufficient food." Worse off than she were the "houseless wanderers in our streets who in vain seek for employment," and below them were the "many among us to whose dire poverty is added sickness or, may be they are crippled from accident." The reporter chronicled the failure of the economy to sustain the homes needed for republican citizenship. The lower down the social order Americans proceeded, the less likely they were to find homes.[65]

Wage labor, women adrift, and workers whose incomes would not support homes all underlined problems with the operation of liberal contract freedom, but instead of abandoning free labor, workingpeople created

---

63. Ibid., 156–66, quote 166.
64. Walter Licht, Industrializing America in the Nineteenth Century (Baltimore, MD: Johns Hopkins University Press, 1995), 184.
65. Jentz, 13.

new versions. They sought to use the eight-hour day as a bridge between self-making and republican citizenship. At its heart, workers' demand for the eight-hour day involved a debate about the relationship between republican independence, home, and work. As the mayor of Chicago told a labor rally on May Day in 1867, eight hours of work had become more exhausting than ten or twelve hours had been earlier. The results affected them as citizens and family members as well as producers. Since the welfare of the republic depended on the ability of working people to cultivate their talents, the eight-hour movement's goal was to give laborers the time to "read, study, and acquire knowledge." The more knowledgeable workers became, the more productive they would be as producers and citizens. The struggle became part of a larger effort enunciated in the *Boston Daily Evening Voice*, that city's leading labor paper, at the end of the war: "All this talk about Republican equality and the rights of man is as water spilled upon sand, if the right of the laboring man to govern those affairs which pertain to his political, social, and moral standing in society be denied him."[66]

Playing on old ideals of improvement, progress, republican citizenship, and manhood, the workers' campaign for the eight-hour day initially seemed to sweep all before it. Both Republicans and Democrats, recognizing a new wage-earning constituency, responded. Legislatures endorsed the eight-hour day in Connecticut, California, New York, Pennsylvania, Wisconsin, Missouri, and Illinois. In 1867 Congress mandated an eight-hour day for federal workers.[67]

Early success proved deceptive. Except for federal workers, there was no mechanism in the bills to secure enforcement. The laws were statements of good intentions. Large factory owners and corporate managers predictably opposed the reform, but so did smaller entrepreneurs. Many of the owners of these smaller shops considered themselves as much producers as their workers, but the pressures of competition led them to stress their own interests as employers.[68]

In Chicago the city as well as the state government had enacted eight-hour-day laws, without providing mechanisms for enforcement or penalties

66. Richard Schneirov, *Labor and Urban Politics: Class Conflict and the Origins of Modern Liberalism in Chicago, 1864–97* (Urbana: University of Illinois Press, 1998), 32–36; David R. Roediger and Philip S. Foner, *Our Own Time: A History of American Labor and the Working Day* (New York: Greenwood, 1989), 101–19; Jentz, 81–82, 86–90.
67. David Montgomery, "Strikes in Nineteenth-Century America," *Social Science History* 4, no. 1 (1980): 94.
68. Adam-Max Tuchinsky, *Horace Greeley's New-York Tribune: Civil War-Era Socialism and the Crisis of Free Labor* (Ithaca, NY: Cornell University Press, 2009), 192–96; Jentz, 92–94.

for violating them. The issue ended up being decided on the streets. In May 1867 skilled workers turned to walkouts, demonstrations, marches, and moral suasion to induce employers to obey the law. Employers largely refused: in a nationalizing economy, they could not grant an eight-hour day and still compete with manufacturers outside Chicago who did not do so. In some wards mobs—often composed of teenage boys, who formed a substantial segment of the workforce, frequently providing from 15 to 20 percent of a family's income—closed down shops and factories not observing the law.[69]

The recalcitrance of the employers and the aggressiveness of workers brought liberals and labor reformers into conflict. Both Horace White, editor of the *Chicago Tribune*, and Charles Dana, editor of the *Chicago Republican*, would go on to become leading liberal New York newspaper editors, but in 1867 Dana's loyalties were still with Whiggish Radical Republicans. The differing positions of the two men on the eight-hour day exposed the ambiguities of free labor in an industrial society. Free labor still imagined autonomous individuals freely negotiating under conditions of equality, but with increasing numbers of people living hand to mouth and dependent on a daily wage, there was little autonomy, less negotiation, and no equality.

Dana supported the eight-hour day. His rationale went to the producerist core of free labor. *The Republican* thought "the creator of wealth to be of supreme importance rather than the product he creates." He supported the Republican neo-Whig economic program and had no issues with government intervention in the economy.[70]

White and the *Chicago Tribune* also embraced free labor, but White stressed contract freedom. He appealed to universal laws of political economy that workers had failed to understand. Assuming a harmony of interests between employer and employee, he assured workers that their employers would fairly divide the profits with them. Strikes were the product of shiftless workers, the advocates of mediocrity and idleness.[71]

Liberals believed that free labor had liberated all workingpeople. "Masters" had given way to employers who could not force employees to labor; creditors could no longer imprison debtors, and landlords could not seize property for failure to pay rent. Contract freedom worked to the advantage of all workers, white and black, but White spied a new danger. He regarded unions, which workers labeled "cooperation for mutual

---

69. Steven Mintz, *Huck's Raft: A History of American Childhood* (Cambridge, MA: Belknap Press of Harvard University Press, 2004), 136; Jentz, 100–101.

70. Jentz, 100–110.

71. Ibid., 94–97.

protection," as a form of coercion. White—and more critically employers and the courts—defined contract freedom as the right of an individual to exercise free choice and initiative without unnecessary governmental restraint or outside interference. The eight-hour law and labor unions embodied both. George McNeill of the National Labor Union scoffed at such arguments: "An empty stomach can make no contracts." Workers who "must sell to-day's labor to-day or never...assent but they do not consent, they submit, but they do not agree." If free labor did not yield a living wage, then there was no such thing as free labor.[72]

When violence erupted, both the *Chicago Tribune* and the *Republican* condemned it and demanded its suppression, although the latter continued to support the strike. White's *Tribune* grew hysterical at the threat to property and called for use of artillery against the "mob." Employers aided by the police broke the strike in June 1867. Irish and German workers lost faith in the Anglo-American reformers who had led it.[73]

The eight-hour movement extended well beyond Chicago, and it formed yet another wedge to fracture Radical Republicans. In Massachusetts Wendell Phillips, the prominent abolitionist, embraced the movement as a new struggle "to discover, define, and arrange the true and lasting relations between capital and labor in society." He wanted every American child to have "as far as possible, an equal chance with each other." Every man deserved "eight hours for sleep, eight hours for work, and eight hours for his soul." But other Massachusetts Radicals emphasized contract freedom and supposedly immutable social laws. Two different state commissions concluded that the hours of work should be a matter of individual contract and not subject to state intervention. Amasa Walker, Francis Amasa Walker's father, was a leading Massachusetts economist, and he proclaimed that economic laws—"above all human enactments"—rather than legislation would decide working hours.[74]

Free labor provided ideals of independence, citizenship, and manhood that workers were loath to surrender, but as long as it remained attached to ideas of contract freedom, it also provided their employers with a powerful weapon. When the workers demanded intervention by the state to secure working hours, they were asserting that competition and contract freedom were insufficient to produce just outcomes, independent citizens, and prosperous homes. They would have to accomplish collectively what

72. Cohen, 38–43; Jentz, 94–95.
73. Jentz, 106–10.
74. David A. Zonderman, *Uneasy Allies: Working for Labor Reform in Nineteenth-Century Boston* (Amherst: University of Massachusetts Press, 2011), 11–18, 95; Cohen, 35–38.

they could not secure individually. Failing that, they would have to appeal to the state and laws.

Competition lived at the ideological center of free labor, but by the 1870s both capitalists and workers grew leery of the costs of competition and less certain that it reliably yielded prosperity and progress. Workers had made real gains during the economic boom of the late 1860s. The inflation that had hurt them badly during the Civil War gave way to deflation that, although imposing real long-term costs on the economy, initially increased real wages and workers' buying power. Because this was not yet a fully national economy, wages in the Midwest and West remained significantly higher than in the Northeast while the cost of living remained lower in the Midwest. As the railroad network improved, however, firms competed at greater and greater distances. Wage cuts in one place put pressure on wages in another. Competition, which free-labor doctrines regarded as the source of equality and prosperity, seemed to be turning into a problem rather than providing a solution.[75]

White was correct that workers attempted to subvert competition by organizing. Between 1863 and 1867 nineteen new unions arose in Chicago. These unions were multiethnic, and their members considered themselves part of a permanent working class. They no longer anticipated, as Lincoln had, that wage labor formed a transitory stage in their lives. Most of these unions lasted into the 1870s. They grouped together in the Chicago Trades and Labor Assembly that alarmed men like White.[76]

Wages mattered to workers, but their independence and control over their work mattered even more. When Parton described the coal miner who "begins work when he likes, works as fast as he likes, or as slow, and goes home when he likes" and whose "'room' is his own against the world," he described how American workers thought work should proceed. This was what they meant by control over work. They were republican citizens and their independence should not vanish when they entered the workplace.

V

Free labor promised not simply prosperity, but a shared prosperity that rewarded those who worked. Yet at the very top and bottom of the economic scale, the rules did not seem to apply. Very little united Jay Cooke, Jay Gould, and John Henry—a steel-drivin' man—except railroads, a changing economy, and an ever more common perception that prosperity

75. Jentz, 19–24.
76. Ibid., 23–24.

had become detached from labor and that Republican intervention in the economy had bestowed great wealth on those who did not work for a living, while sometimes penalizing those who did.

Cooke, a Philadelphia banker and devout evangelical Christian, had helped save the Union; his fortune rested on the changing economy and the government's role in it. He had dispatched an army of salesmen to persuade small investors to buy U.S. bonds during the Civil War, selling bonds on the basis of patriotism and profit. The bonds made Cooke rich, and they proved a safe investment. His country and his investors were grateful. He became the most trusted banker in the United States.[77]

Cooke was a private banker, a financier, which was a type relatively rare before the Civil War but common after the war remade American banking. Foreign investment had dried up during the early years of the Civil War, and this, in turn, had helped spur both American capital accumulation and a class of American financiers. National banks provided capital for the growth of manufacturing, usually through loans, but as critical as national banks were, they played only a secondary role in funding corporations. The federal charters of the national banks deprived them of the legal flexibility they needed to float the huge bond issues that the railroads needed. Private investment banks, brokerage houses, and the stock and bond markets formed the necessary appendages of corporate capitalism. These institutions—the House of Cooke, Fisk & Hatch, J. S. Morgan & Co., J. & W. Seligman & Co., Lehman Brothers, and Kuhn, Loeb & Co.—had first arisen to serve the state: selling government bonds and making loans. Many were creations of the Civil War. As bond issues became larger, investment houses created syndicates to split the risks, buying railroad bonds below par, and then reselling them to investors in the United States and Europe at a markup.[78]

Private investment banks served as brokers for the sale of bond issues from the government and railroads, and around the banks, like seabirds circling fishing boats, hovered brokers and speculators, large and small, who dealt in the paper—stocks, bonds, treasury notes, greenbacks, and financial paper of all kind—that the system produced. Between 1864 and 1870 the number of bankers and brokers increased tenfold to about 1,800 in New York City, the country's financial capital. When at the end of the war the government cut back on borrowing and began to retire bonds and notes, it freed up a large amount of capital for other investment.[79]

77. White, 10–13.
78. Beckert, *The Monied Metropolis*, 243; Roy, 115–43.
79. Bensel, 248–51.

Because the United States remained largely an agricultural economy, the demand for money followed the cycles of planting and harvest. In winter and summer, state and regional banks, both to get higher interest and to meet the requirements of the law, made deposits in the national banks in New York City. The banks advanced the money to brokers and speculators on Wall Street as call loans, payable on demand. Between 1868 and 1878 call loans made up about one-third of the total loans at New York's national banks. In the spring and fall, the New York banks had to send money back to their correspondent banks, which retrieved their deposits to finance plantings and harvest.[80]

Spring and fall signaled dangerous times on New York financial markets. When money grew scarce, the brokers and speculators had to be able to sell securities to raise cash to meet their obligations. If stock and bond prices were falling when the banks called in their loans, panic ensued. Investors dumped securities, borrowers defaulted, and rumors of insolvency at the banks triggered bank runs by depositors. The result could become a financial death spiral for brokers, banks, and businesses in need of cash.[81] Keeping the money supply in balance and avoiding panics depended on the intervention of Treasury officials, which was one of the things liberals hated about it. It also meant that men like Cooke and Gould cultivated those officials as well as congressmen and the president. Their fortunes depended up on it.

After the war, Cooke continued to rely on his Washington connections, nurtured through his brother Henry—an effective lobbyist although a terrible banker. With the retirement of the federal debt, Cooke's government business steadily declined. So he turned to railroads. He tapped his old pool of investors for the Northern Pacific, and he continued to cultivate both the president and congressmen to get further aid for that railroad. He nurtured the political relationships with the Republicans, individually and collectively, that he had developed during the Civil War. Cooke's professional friendships mattered because his fortune depended on government business and government subsidies. The Republican National Committee tapped Cooke for funds for Grant's campaign in 1872, and Grant became an occasional guest at Cooke's Ogontz estate outside Philadelphia. The president, who had few close personal friends, spent far

80. Richard Sylla, "Federal Policy, Banking Market Structure, and Capital Mobilization in the United States, 1863–1913," *Journal of Economic History* 29, no. 4 (1969): 659–65; John A. James, *Money and Capital Markets in Postbellum America* (Princeton, NJ: Princeton University Press, 1978), 9–10, 25, 27–28, 60–62, 67–71, 97–104, 118–21, 125–48, 234–35, 242–43.
81. Bensel, 263–65; Sylla, 678–85; James, 63.

more time at the tables of Cooke and men like him than socializing with shoemakers.[82]

Gould also cultivated President Grant because he, too, had a great deal of interest in the government's monetary policy and its railroad subsidies. From the very beginning of the first administration, Gould had visited and entertained the Grants. He brought the president perilously close to a moral chasm.

Financiers such as Gould and Cooke—the investment bankers, brokers, and speculators of the postwar economy—were the people whom Americans referred to as capitalists. They distrusted them because they were alien to the world of free labor. They did not work with their hands; they did not make things. Capitalists justified the rewards they reaped by the risks that they took rather than the work they did. Without their willingness to risk their fortunes, so the argument went, there would be no progress, no jobs for workingpeople, and no prosperity.

In fact, capitalists, like everyone else in this society, sought to avoid risk as much as possible by deflecting it onto others or by hedging their bets. This was quite rational, but it created discord between their rhetorical justifications of their role in the economic system and its actual practice. Jay Gould, like Jay Cooke, or for that matter Collis P. Huntington and Tom Scott, abhorred risk. That is why they sought subsidies, influence over governmental policies, and insider information, which all tipped the playing field in their favor. They used any means, including the corruption of legislatures and judges, to gain such favors.

When Gould cultivated Grant, he was attempting to avoid a quite specific risk. In 1869 Gould and "Diamond Jim" Fisk launched a complicated gold corner. They were an odd pair. Gould was shy, retiring, and most comfortable among his orchids and family, while Fisk was in every way his opposite. Fisk would be shot dead in a New York hotel lobby in 1872, the casualty of a too-successful seduction. Because the United States retained greenbacks and Europe had gone to the gold standard, exchanging greenbacks for gold was essential to American foreign commerce. The exchange took place in the Gold Room in New York City, where merchants bought the gold they needed for transactions with countries on the gold standard. If Gould and Fisk cornered the supply of gold, they could hold merchants for ransom. Those involved in the import-export trade would have to choose between paying Gould an immense premium and bankruptcy. In the process, Gould threatened to derange American trade.[83]

82. White, 75, 81–82.
83. Maury Klein, *The Life and Legend of Jay Gould* (Baltimore, MD: Johns Hopkins University Press, 1986), 99–115; McFeely, 320–31.

The success of the scheme depended on the Treasury Department, since if the government sold gold, it would break the corner. To make sure the government stayed on the sidelines, Gould and Fisk recruited, first, President Grant's brother-in-law, then the always recruitable Orville Babcock—Grant's private secretary. And finally, they brought an assistant treasury secretary in charge of gold sales into their scheme. They may also have given Grant's wife, Julia, a share in the speculation. When Grant, whom Gould had convinced that a rise in the price of gold would help stimulate agricultural exports, thus promoting prosperity and improving the American balance of payments, discerned the real intent of the scheme, he had the Treasury intervene to break the corner. Grant, however, gave word to his sister of his intentions in an attempt to save her and her husband from ruin, and Gould thus learned of the president's decision to sell gold. He switched positions, selling rather than buying gold. He betrayed his collaborators. He probably came out ahead as the rapid rise and dramatic fall in the price of gold brought panic on Wall Street. Black Friday ruined thousands who lacked access to a relative of the president.[84]

Capitalists and government officials stood as godparents to corporations, which bore the marks of their origins as companies chartered by the government to fulfill public purposes. Many cities were corporations, and so were universities, canal companies, and the original Bank of the United States. All received charters giving them special rights in exchange for serving public purposes.

Before the Civil War, Americans had democratized corporations by making corporate charters readily available and curtailing the extraordinary benefits they enjoyed, but they had not completely stripped them of the combination of public purpose and special privilege. Governments chartered corporations to do specific things, and they could not go beyond their charters. The corporation had a legal identity separate from its stockholders. It was theoretically eternal, enduring even if its owners died or sold their shares. Corporations could raise funds through the sale of stock and bonds, and many states offered charters that gave stockholders limited liability: they would not be held responsible for the corporation's debts beyond their own investment. In exchange for all this, Americans believed that corporations had a greater obligation than other enterprises to serve a public good. They were different from normal businesses and were subject to regulations beyond normal businesses. Until the 1890s, the corporate form dominated only one sector of the American economy—railroads—

84. McFeely, 320–29; Klein, 80–81, 102–15.

which were considered common carriers, equally open to all, on public highways.[85]

As corporations and railroads became virtually synonymous in Gilded Age America, railroads became materially ubiquitous even as their corporate structure rendered them mysterious and opaque. Charles Francis Adams had captured this in 1869 when he wrote *Chapters of Erie* with his brother Henry. He pronounced the railroads "an enormous, an incalculable force practically let loose suddenly upon mankind; exercising all sorts of influences, social, moral, and political, precipitating upon us novel problems which demand immediate solution; banishing the old before the new is half matured to replace it.... Yet, with the curious hardness of a material age, we rarely regard this new power otherwise than as a money-getting and time-saving machine."[86]

As publicly traded firms whose stock was available on the New York Stock Exchange, railroads differed from other firms. In partnerships and proprietary firms, the value of the company depended on profits from the sale of its products or the appreciation of its assets, such as land or buildings. The value of corporations, too, depended in part on their profits and appreciation of assets. But since the chief assets of the railroads were paper bought and sold on financial markets, the ability to control and manipulate the value of that paper became a new way to make money, very large amounts of money. In the long run, the value of that paper depended on the profitability of the corporation, but in the short run insiders could profit from unprofitable companies. Rather than indicating a profitable corporation, rising stock values might indicate the diversion of borrowed money to dividends. This put money in the pockets of insiders who held the original stock even as it threatened the financial health of the company. It could not be sustained, but it did not have to be. If investors thought the dividends indicated a profitable corporation, they bid up the price of the stock, which insiders had acquired for a pittance. Insiders then sold, reaping a windfall. The new investors were left holding the bag for an unprofitable and indebted corporation.

Insiders had other ways to make money from unprofitable corporations. Corporations could also pay large fees to companies owned by insiders, or income could be drained off to other companies that insiders controlled, leaving the parent railroad even deeper in debt. Because insiders controlled information that influenced the price of a railroad's securities,

85. Maury Klein, *The Genesis of Industrial America, 1870–1920* (Cambridge: Cambridge University Press, 2007), 106–7; Roy, 41–77.
86. Charles Francis Adams, *Chapters of Erie and Other Essays*, ed. Henry Adams and Francis Amasa Walker (New York: H. Holt, 1886, orig. ed. 1869), 335.

they used this information to manipulate values. Those with inside information became a corporate class. They dominated Wall Street, the boards of corporations, and the banks.[87]

These were the secrets that allowed Gould as well as Huntington, Stanford, and their Associates to garner fortunes from railroads that had trouble paying their debts. Huntington later claimed that he and other builders of the Central Pacific had "profited very little by the building of the roads." Huntington thought that the people of California had failed to appreciate the selflessness of the Associates in working so hard for so little because Leland Stanford, Mark Hopkins, and Charles Crocker had taken out "something over five millions to build three dwelling houses for the communists and agrarians to look at" on Nob Hill in San Francisco.[88]

How people who had "profited little" could take out five million to construct mansions so large that they looked as if they could contain small villages seemed a puzzle, but Huntington was, perhaps inadvertently, making a significant point about railroad financiering. The Associates did not make most of their money from the Central Pacific or Southern Pacific railroads, at least not directly. They made money from the Contract and Finance Company, the Western Development Company, and the Pacific Improvement Company. San Francisco bankers knew money flowed through the railroads to these companies and on to the Associates. California was a state that held stockholders liable for unpaid corporate debts, but the process for collecting was onerous. Bankers who knew how the Central Pacific was run would not loan it money. As late as 1877, David Colton, the last man to become an Associate, found that San Francisco bankers would not advance funds to the Central Pacific and Southern Pacific without personal notes from the Associates guaranteeing the loan.[89]

In their size, complexity, financing, and opaqueness, the railroad corporations were something new under the American sun. They often had more employees than the states through which they built their lines. The Pennsylvania Railroad, the country's most powerful and best-run, operated slightly under a thousand miles of track in 1867, and the road's traffic

87. Roy, 98–109; White, 67–69.
88. Collis P. Huntington to W. W. Stow, Feb. 8, 1893 (misdated 1894), in *Collis P. Huntington Collection, 1856–1901*.
89. Colton to C. P. Huntington, May 23, 1877, in *The Octopus Speaks: The Colton Letters*, ed. David Douty Colton, Collis Potter Huntington, and Salvador A. Ramirez (Carlsbad, CA: Tentacled Press, 1992), 36.

and complexity made its organization closer to the military than previous forms of business.[90]

It was, however, a mistake to confuse size and power with efficiency. In theory, the Pennsylvania emphasized centralization, hierarchy, and bureaucracy; running it demanded detailed, and preferably accurate, information. Against the supposed invisible hand of the market, it deployed the visible hand of management. In practice, however, Tom Scott's Pennsylvania was rife with insider dealing and subordinate companies that siphoned off profits; most railroad corporations hardly provided models of efficiency. The railroads failed, and were resurrected, with great regularity.[91]

In the South the coming of railroads and corporations presented even more serious dangers. The railroads, originally denounced by Southern whites for providing opportunities for free black labor, led the way in restoring new forms of coerced labor. It is a testament to the power of American popular culture that the memory of John Henry persisted long past that of both Collis P. Huntington and Tom Scott. John Henry was black, but not a freedman. He came from New Jersey, apparently moving with the army as a soldier or laborer into Virginia. Huntington, as an old abolitionist, remained sensitive about black people, Southern violence, and railroads. Years later Huntington remembered himself as a crusader for racial justice. He claimed to have used railroad resources to prosecute the murderer of a black worker who was employed on the Chesapeake and Ohio extension into Kentucky.[92]

Huntington's story lies buried within the notes for a memoir that was never published, but the story of John Henry became widespread and lasting. Work and folk songs immortalized him as a "steel drivin' man" who raced a steam drill in building a tunnel. John Henry won the race but "died with a hammer in his hand."

Figuratively, the song was right. A steam drill killed the actual John Henry, but it was not a race, and Henry was not a giant of a man. He was 5 feet 1 inch tall, which was, as it turned out, a perfect height for men cutting tunnels through the Appalachian Mountains. Henry was a convict. Huntington leased Virginia convicts to work his railroads, including

90. Henry V. Poor, *Poor's Manual of Railroads*, ed. Henry V. Poor (New York: H. V. & H. W. Poor; [etc., etc.], 1868), 226–29.
91. Alfred D. Chandler, *The Visible Hand: The Managerial Revolution in American Business* (Cambridge, MA: Belknap Press, 1977), 104–21.
92. Collis P. Huntington as told to Charles Nordhoff, "'Autobiographical Sketch'," in *Collis P. Huntington Papers, 1856–1901*, 61.

tunnel work so dangerous that free workers quit or went on strike rather than do it.[93]

John Henry had been convicted of theft. The evidence against him was as hazy as the particulars of the crime. He was arrested under the Black Codes, which turned what had been misdemeanors into felonies. Henry was tried the same day in 1866 as a more famous man charged with far greater crimes: Jefferson Davis stood accused of treason, piracy, and complicity in the murder of five hundred soldiers at Andersonville Prison. Northerners, among them Horace Greeley and Cornelius Vanderbilt, put up Davis's bail. The most influential Northerners had lost their appetite for prosecuting him. They would either create a martyr or, if they failed to convict, cast doubt on the northern version of the war. The judge in the Davis proceeding suspended the trial indefinitely, and Davis went free. Henry, born in New Jersey and nineteen at the time of his arrest, received a sentence of ten years. Sending poor men to prison while the powerful walked fed a Gilded Age romanticization of criminals like Jesse James.[94]

John Henry turned out to have received a death sentence administered by Huntington's Chesapeake and Ohio. Reformers justified the leasing of convicts to corporations because it allowed better conditions than living in decrepit, overcrowded, and brutal Virginia prisons. Henry, and the more than two hundred other convicts contracted to the Chesapeake and Ohio, initially did unskilled work around the tunnels piercing the mountains. But in 1870 new steam drills on the Lewis Tunnel began to fail, and the convicts were thrown into the task of hand-drilling the holes for explosives and clearing debris in the tunnel. Henry probably died in 1873 after working the tunnel. The cause of death was silicosis, tuberculosis, or pneumonia, any or all of them brought on or exacerbated by the microscopic pieces of sandstone and other rocks that he and other workers inhaled after drills and explosions shattered the rocks. Everyone working the tunnel was probably dead within a few years. Nearly one hundred convicts either returned to the prison only for burial or died soon after their arrival. Roughly 80 percent were young black men. One of them was John Henry.[95]

Henry's death provided a stark reminder of the continuing limits on extending free labor in the South, and when the "Galena Tanner" and the

93. Scott Reynolds Nelson, *Steel Drivin' Man: John Henry, the Untold Story of an American Legend* (New York: Oxford University Press, 2006), 41–58.

94. Dattel, 227; Nelson, *Steel Drivin' Man*, 41–58; William Alan Blair, *With Malice toward Some: Treason and Loyalty in the Civil War Era* (Chapel Hill: University of North Carolina Press, 2014), 245–51; Richard White, "Outlaw Gangs of the Middle Border: American Social Bandits," *Western Historical Quarterly* 12, no. 4 (1981).

95. Nelson, *Steel Drivin' Man*, 41–58.

"Natick Shoemaker" ran for office, fissures in the ideal of free labor had already appeared in its heartland. Convict labor marked a clear continuance of unfree labor, but wage labor, though allowing workers to come and go as they chose, was not free in the sense that the proponents of free labor had once imagined. A new element and a deep new division had come to define American society.

7

Panic

In 1872 Ulysses S. Grant had demonstrated the depth and strength of the ethnocultural loyalties quickened by the Civil War; in 1874 he demonstrated their limits. When they ran against Grant, the Liberal Republicans had badly misjudged their own ideological appeal. More than that, they both overestimated the power of ideology in American politics and misunderstood how the Civil War and its aftermath had changed those politics. Liberal Republicans had expected one or both of the old parties to disappear in 1872, and they thought that voters would coalesce around their issues and positions. They were wrong about many things. This was one of them.[1]

The Liberal Republicans wanted an ideological party in an age when American political parties were not ideologically consistent. Both Democrats and Republicans comprised voters who spanned the ideological spectrum on economic and social issues. Debates over the tariff, the gold standard, corporate subsidies and regulation, and the dangers that disparities in wealth and power posed to the Republic were constant, usually intelligent, and widely followed, but positions on these issues were not strictly determined by party. Even the tariff, a signature issue of Northeastern Republicans, could not have been sustained after 1874 without Democratic votes.[2]

Issues were never the whole issue. The Republicans were for an activist federal government, a homogeneous citizenry with contract freedom guaranteed by the nation, and government stimulation of the economy. The Democrats remained the party of no: they wanted a small federal government, local control, and free trade. These broad general stances, however, were inflected by region, and they were only partly what made people

---

1. Andrew L. Slap, *The Doom of Reconstruction: The Liberal Republicans in the Civil War Era* (New York: Fordham University Press, 2006), 164–72.
2. See, for example, Philip J. Ethington, *The Public City: The Political Construction of Urban Life in San Francisco, 1850–1900* (Cambridge: Cambridge University Press, 1994), 249–65.

Democrats or Republicans. Issues could bring voters to the polls or keep them home, but usually they would not lead them to desert one party and vote for another. Politics remained as much about identity as issues.

Both parties depended on associations more primal than ideology or promises of honest governance. Nurtured by the blood of the Civil War and deep ethnic, religious, and regional loyalties, parties demanded a richer diet than principles could provide. The struggle between the Union and the Confederacy had invested words like *loyalty* and *treason* with emotional meanings that carried over into party politics. Native-born northern whites were heavily Republican, unless they had been Copperheads during the Civil War; native-born Southern whites were heavily Democratic, unless they had been Unionists or were small farmers who hated the planter class. African Americans were understandably Republican. Catholic immigrants, particularly the urban Irish, were Democrats. Protestant evangelicals were overwhelmingly Republican in the North, but their zeal for prohibition, Sabbatarian laws, and eradicating all but the English language in schools and public life could drive some nonevangelical Protestants, particularly Germans, to sit out elections or occasionally to vote for the Democrats. Permanently changing party was not easy. Once forged, and nourished through upbringing, association, and patronage, party loyalty formed part of a person's quotidian identity. Those who betrayed their party were regarded as lesser men or not men at all. Sen. Roscoe Conkling, a leading Republican Stalwart, hated the liberals as thoroughly as they despised him. He denigrated their manhood, calling them "the man-milliners, the dilettanti, and carpet knights of politics."[3]

Like muscles, party loyalties had to be regularly exercised to remain strong. Citizens publicly performed their loyalty in dramatic spectacles, from parades to tableaus to meetings designed to stimulate the turnout on which electoral victory depended. Voting was public. Each party printed its own easily identifiable ballots listing only its own candidates and distributed them to voters who deposited them at the polls. Unless suppressed by violence or laws intended to disenfranchise them, voters turned out in consistently high numbers in the late nineteenth century.[4]

3. Paul Kleppner, *The Third Electoral System, 1853–1892: Parties, Voters, and Political Cultures* (Chapel Hill: University of North Carolina Press, 1979), 148–197; Michael E. McGerr, *The Decline of Popular Politics: The American North, 1865–1928* (New York: Oxford University Press, 1986), 13–14; Richard Hofstadter, *The American Political Tradition* (New York: Knopf, 1948, Vintage Books ed. 1954), 173.

4. Jean H. Baker, *Affairs of Party: The Political Culture of Northern Democrats in the Mid-Nineteenth Century* (Ithaca, NY: Cornell University Press, 1983), 261–316; McGerr, 25–33, 64–65; Kleppner, 46–47; Ethington, 232–35.

National issues centered on Reconstruction roiled politics into the early 1870s, but parties and campaigns remained intensely local. The parties were alliances, and a party's success often depended on suppressing divisive issues, particularly those relating to liquor, religion, and public schools, that could blow them apart. National parties, in turn, consisted of aggregations of state parties, with only the weakest of central organizations to hold them together. In 1872 the Republican National Committee operated out of three small rooms in a New York City hotel. The charisma of presidential candidates did not unite the parties. American presidential candidates seemed to have buried charisma with Lincoln and would not disinter it until the end of the century. And even if presidential aspirants were more compelling figures, voters considered public campaigning by presidential candidates unseemly.[5]

It soon became apparent that Grant did not know what to do with the tremendous victory he won in 1872; he alienated many of his friends in an attempt to conciliate his enemies, both liberals and Southerners. As he awaited his second term, the president spent his time making appointments, both major and minor. He tried to accommodate party factions and balance state machines. His second cabinet was as undistinguished as his first and could not provide worthwhile advice even if Grant had been willing to listen to it. The Supreme Court was Grant's to remake, but his appointments, several of which failed either when candidates turned him down or the Senate refused to confirm them, were odd. Without any clear method or intent, he created a court that would help eviscerate the legislative base of Reconstruction. He mostly elevated mediocrities to the bench, although Morrison Remick Waite, who became Chief Justice (succeeding Salmon P. Chase, who died in 1873) was competent, even if little known outside of Republican Party circles.[6]

Grant dawdled even as political and economic storms gathered. Many of the 1872 elections in the South ended up disputed, with clear evidence of fraud and corruption involving Southern railroads and Republican politics. This was neither edifying nor surprising. The larger scandal, and the greater danger, was a belated inheritance from the Lincoln and Johnson administrations that had long lain dormant and dangerous.[7]

Charles Dana's *New York Sun* broke the Crédit Mobilier scandal in the midst of the presidential campaign of 1872. With the Republicans fighting

5. Stephen Skowronek, *Building a New American State: The Expansion of National Administrative Capacities, 1877–1920* (Cambridge: Cambridge University Press, 1982), 19–21, 26, 28–31; McGerr, 25–33.

6. William S. McFeely, *Grant: A Biography* (New York: Norton, 1981), 384–94.

7. Mark W. Summers, *The Ordeal of the Reunion: A New History of Reconstruction* (Chapel Hill: University of North Carolina Press, 2014), 327–35.

off rumors of corruption, it was not what the party needed. The *Sun* pro-claimed the Crédit Mobilier "The King of Frauds." It was the king be-cause it linked the private corruption of railroad corporations with public corruption: "Congressmen who have robbed the people and now support the national robber." The press never did get the financial details straight, but they did not have to: congressional attempts to quiet the scandal per-versely kept it alive. Reporters could concentrate on the cover-up as Congress was forced to investigate.[8]

The railroads had come to Congress offering stocks, bonds, and land, and politicians had swarmed like flies. The men running the Union Pacific had sold stock in the Crédit Mobilier, a construction and finance company used to funnel profits to insiders, at below-market prices to in-fluential politicians. The scandal implicated the leadership of the Union Pacific railroad, including Congressman Oakes Ames, and it snared Schuyler Colfax, the sitting vice president of the United States; Congressman James A. Garfield, James G. Blaine, the speaker of the House; and a bevy of leading senators and representatives. Some would be ruined; most would only be tainted. It took a heavy load of scandal to sink a Gilded Age politician.[9]

Among the frank, but not particularly wise, defenses offered by Oakes Ames was that the gifts of stock were not bribes because bribes were quid pro quo while the offers of a chance to buy into the Crédit Mobilier were exchanges between friends already willing to do each other favors. The stock could not possibly be a bribe, he argued, because its value was beneath the going price of a congressional vote. Ames was drawing a distinction essential to Gilded Age politics. The Union Pacific and other railroads distinguished between their friends and those they had to bribe. Those who received Crédit Mobilier stock already counted as friends. Friendship was the preferred way of phrasing connections between businessmen and politicians. To be a friend, it was not necessary to actually like someone; bonds of obligation and reciprocity were sufficient. Corporate leaders had many friends in the press, on the courts, and in other businesses, but above all they had politicians who were friends. On "being asked the secret of political success," John Morrissey, "prize fighter, professional gambler and member of Congress...replied 'Stick to your friends, and be free with your money.'" As a lawmaker told reporter George Alfred

8. Maury Klein, *Union Pacific* (Garden City, NY: Doubleday, 1987), 291; Richard White, *Railroaded: The Transcontinentals and the Making of Modern America* (New York: Norton, 2011), 63–64.

9. Ibid., 64–65.

Townsend, "measures lived or died on friendship." It was not only good to have friends; it was essential.[10]

Friendship was about reciprocity; it was unnecessary and insulting to offer a bribe to a friend. Ames's explanation of the differences between bribery and friendship in the exchange of private favors for public goods was not particularly helpful in restoring the public's faith in their representatives. Congress censured Ames, a Republican, for offering bribes and James Brooks, the Democratic floor leader, for taking one, but no one else was punished and no money was recovered. This made the scandal all the more lethal and long-lasting. How could Ames be punished for offering favors for support when no one but Brooks was punished for taking them?[11]

The scandals, however, would offer little sustenance to liberals; instead they nurtured another reform movement, antimonopolism, that would soon loom much larger than liberalism, with which it shared some common roots. In the early 1870s antimonopolism was just taking shape in the form of Grangerism. Merchants, more than farmers, pushed through the first of the railroad laws in the upper Mississippi Valley, but the laws regulating railroads were known as the Granger laws in part because the Grange—the Patrons of Husbandry—claimed them as their own and because liberals like Godkin were eager to portray western railroad regulation as an agrarian attack on property.[12]

The Grange began as a farmer's cooperative movement to raise the standards and prosperity of farmers, particularly in the West and South. Oliver H. Kelley, who worked for the U.S. Department of Agriculture, founded the organization in 1867. Strongest in the Republican heartland of Illinois, Iowa, Wisconsin, and Minnesota, the Grange grew steadily before ballooning in 1873, when 8,667 new chapters raised the total to 10,029 nationally. There were more than seven hundred thousand members. It was not a movement Republicans could dismiss, but the political danger seemed manageable.[13]

Grangers divided between a reformist wing and a more conservative one, but the Grange itself—containing Republicans, Democrats, and those who

---

10. This account is taken from my book *Railroaded*, 93–133; Mark W. Summers, *The Era of Good Stealings* (New York: Oxford University Press, 1993), 109.

11. White, 65–66.

12. Herbert Hovenkamp, *Enterprise and American Law, 1836–1937* (Cambridge, MA: Harvard University Press, 1991), 156–58; George H. Miller, *Railroads and the Granger Laws* (Madison: University of Wisconsin Press, 1971), 164–65.

13. Miller, passim, particularly 161–68; Thomas A. Woods, *Knights of the Plow: Oliver H. Kelley and the Origins of the Grange in Republican Ideology* (Ames: Iowa State University Press, 1991), 150–51.

urged the formation of a third party—was supposed to be nonpartisan. Although it became, in the words of a supporter, "a power which no party can afford to ignore," its adherents maintained their existing party loyalties. The Grange advocated education, cooperative purchasing, stores, grain elevators, and marketing to combat what it saw as railroad monopoly and unconscionable markups by manufacturers and middlemen, which resulted in a McCormick reaper that cost $45 being sold at retail for $217 in 1873.[14]

Ignatius Donnelly, a prominent Minnesota Republican who had served several terms in Congress, became a leader of the Grange's reformist wing, just as he would become a leader in later antimonopoly movements. He believed that the struggle between the North and South had yielded to "the struggle between the East and West": "It will not be a conflict of arms, but of ideas, a contest of interests—a struggle of intelligence—one side defending itself from the greed of the other."[15]

The Grangers gave liberals such as Godkin new nightmares, but the antimonopolism of the Grange had its own liberal roots. The Grangers, as farmers and consumers, were predictably antitariff, and initially some were hard-money men in favor of the gold standard. But Grangers never embraced laissez-faire. They demanded state regulation of railroads and grain elevators, and they attacked the banking system as favoring the East.[16]

The men who ran the railroads initially mocked the Grangers' demand for regulation, but gradually they came to dread them. The Central Pacific's chief lobbyist, Richard Franchot, wrote Huntington in 1870 that Congress was "very much demoralized on R.R. and as scary as the very devil and I should not be surprised any day they bolt like a drove of sheep." With the "country press…howling[,]…members are very weak kneed in regard to legislation in favor of great monopolies." Franchot later dismissed increasing congressional opposition to the railroads as a "spasm of virtue," but he was wrong. Three years later Mark Hopkins, one of the Associates of the Central Pacific, noted that things had not improved: "When we commenced, eleven years ago, Congress and Legislatures were gentle steeds. Bless me how they rear and tear now."[17]

14. The standard account of the Grangers remains Miller; Edward Winslow Martin (pseud. of James Dabney McCabe), *History of the Grange Movement; or, the Farmer's War against Monopolies…* (Chicago: National Publishing Co., 1874), 6; Woods, 160–64; Hal S. Barron, *Mixed Harvest: The Second Great Transformation in the Rural North, 1870–1930* (Chapel Hill: University of North Carolina Press, 1997), 109–11.
15. Woods, 148.
16. Ibid., 139–49.
17. Mark Hopkins to Collis P. Huntington, Feb. 4, 1873, in *Collis P. Huntington Papers, 1856–1901* (Sanford, NC: Microfilming Corporation of America, 1978–79), ser. 1, r. 5; White, 109–10.

By 1872 antimonopolists in Congress had halted the granting of new federal subsidies to railroad corporations, although efforts to obtain them persisted and states and localities continued to give aid. They also began a long struggle to scratch back land grants from those railroads that had not fulfilled the terms of their grants, and to ensure the repayment of the bonds advanced to the Pacific Railway. The Crédit Mobilier scandal, ironically, intensified the entwinement of railroad corporations with the government. The rise of antimonopoly made it all the more important for railroad corporations to have lobbyists in Congress to protect their interests. Railroad lobbies grew in size and sophistication. Private corporations cultivated influential friends, Roscoe Conkling and James G. Blaine being two of the most prominent. Railroads were not always hostile to antimonopolist reform. Congress had become a place for corporations to compete, and when reform threatened a particular railroad, its competitors very often used their lobbies to push that reform. In the 1870s Congress would become the site of spectacular legislative battles between Tom Scott's Texas and Pacific and the Southern Pacific, whose guiding genius was Collis P. Huntington.[18]

The Democrats had proved feeble opponents in 1872, but by 1873 it appeared the Republicans did not need enemies; they were perfectly capable of inflicting harm on themselves. With the Crédit Mobilier scandal already tarring Congress, outgoing congressmen in the Forty-second Congress voted an increase in government salaries. A rise in salaries, given the inflation of the Civil War years, was justified, but congressmen also voted themselves a retroactive raise, raising a public outcry. Scandal, public outrage, and the rise of antimonopolism, which threatened to divide the Republican Party along east-west lines, were not promising signs for Grant and the Republicans. Still, it appeared that Grant could ride out these storms. The election had demonstrated the deep support Republicans enjoyed in the northern electorate and the power of the black vote in the South. Grant had run on a record of peace and prosperity, and the relative peacefulness of the 1872 election and the country's continuing prosperity put a stiff wind at his back. He and the Republicans had reason to believe they could sail away from the approaching storms and let them dissipate.[19]

The Crédit Mobilier scandal produced two congressional investigating committees—one in the House and one in the Senate—that dominated American attention in the spring and summer of 1873 and never let the Grant administration find open water. Congress followed the pattern

18. White, 93–133.
19. Summers, *The Ordeal of the Reunion*, 316, 325, 336.

Henry Adams had described earlier in the investigation of Gould's gold corner: "took a quantity of evidence which it dared not probe, and refused to analyze." The trail died out "at the point where any member of the Administration became visible." The Crédit Mobilier investigations indicated how much was wrong, but Congress did little about it. The Crédit Mobilier only deepened Congress's disrepute.[20]

The Republican banker Jay Cooke watched the Crédit Mobilier unfold with genuine alarm. Cooke wanted Congress to guarantee Northern Pacific bonds just as it had guaranteed those of the Union Pacific and Central Pacific. The scandal ended any immediate possibility of that, but more critically it frayed the web of friendship that had served him well. Although it was sometimes hard to say who was lying in Congress, the contradictions, the accusations, and the denials made it clear someone was.[21]

Even at its worst, however, the Crédit Mobilier seemed only a tempest. It could harm political careers and end railroad subsidies, but that policy was already widely rejected. Its economic consequences seemed to threaten only such railroads as the Northern Pacific and Union Pacific, which deserved the pain. The prospect of across-the-board economic collapse posed a far greater danger.[22]

I

Greater storms were already brewing on far shores. American prosperity was linked more deeply to Europe than most Americans suspected. What happened on one side of the Atlantic would eventually wash up on the other. On May 9, 1873, the stock exchange in Vienna crashed. The financial carnage in Vienna spread to Berlin, because Germans had helped create the Austrian boom by investing gold that had flowed as reparations from Paris to Berlin following the Franco-Prussian War. Germany suffered when Austria went bust.[23]

Gold was one commodity circuit; wheat formed another. It connected Vienna to London and ultimately to New York and Chicago and the prairies beyond. The Austro-Hungarian economy depended on its exports of wheat to Britain. Around 1871, however, British grain purchases tilted toward North America as the immense investments Americans had made

20. White, 62–66, 82–83; Nelson, 167–68; Henry Adams, *The Education of Henry Adams: An Autobiography* (New York: Heritage Press, 1942, orig. ed. 1918), 252–53.
21. White, 65–77.
22. White, 65–66.
23. Scott Nelson, *A Nation of Deadbeats: An Uncommon History of America's Financial Disasters* (New York: Knopf, 2012), 161–63.

in railroads and western farms took effect. American wheat, produced by men such as Dick Garland, poured from the prairies into the grain elevators of Chicago, where it was loaded onto rail cars and carried by the great trunk lines to the eastern seaboard for export. Additional grain arrived in Europe from California by ship. As harvests increased and transportation costs fell, American wheat displaced more expensive grain from central and Eastern Europe. This endangered Austrian banks, which were heavily invested in the export trade in cattle and wheat that the Americans were undercutting.[24]

Few Americans outside of New York's financial markets initially noted the Austrian crash. More noticed the Bank of England's response. Uncertain where panic would strike next, the British sought both to curtail the reckless borrowing that had brought Austria to its knees and to increase the gold reserves of the Bank of England. The Old Lady of Threadneedle Street raised her discount rates—the amount charged other banks for short-term loans—thus effectively raising interest rates across Europe and North America. The discount rate jumped from 4 percent at the beginning of May to 9 percent by November.[25]

Investors were already worried about American railroads even before the Vienna crash. Nervous Europeans were bad for American railroads. Americans funded the bulk of their railroad expansion, but the British, as well as the Germans and Dutch, had also invested heavily. The Europeans were particularly enamored of western railroads, many of which were, as a British banking house noted, "wild cat enterprises...Railroads through deserts—beginning nowhere and ending nowhere." The bonded debt of American railroads had risen from $416 million in 1867 to $2.23 billion in 1874. Such numbers were deceptive. Many bonds sold at discount, leaving the railroads to repay a debt much larger than the money they received.[26]

---

24. Ibid., 161–63; William Cronon, *Nature's Metropolis: Chicago and the Great West* (New York: Norton, 1991), 97–147.
25. Nelson, 161–63.
26. *Historical Statistics of the United States, Earliest Times to the Present: Millennial Edition*, ed. Scott Sigmund Gartner, Susan B. Carter, Michael R. Haines, Alan L. Olmstead, Richard Sutch, and Gavin Wright (New York: Cambridge University Press, 2006), 4: 920, Railroad property investment..., table Df 891–900; White, 78–79; Standard, Oct. 24, 1874, *The Newspaper Cuttings Files of the Council of Foreign Bondholders in the Guildhall Library, London* (East Ardsley, UK: EP Microform, 1975), r. 219; National Car Builder, quoted in *Railway Age* (New York [etc.]: Simmons-Boardman Publishing Corp. [etc.]), 343; "Capital and Railroad Extension," *Bankers Magazine and Statistical Register* (American Antiquarian Society; Oct. 1876), 279; Ralston Lees & Waller to Mills, and Bell, Dec. 7, 1872, Lees & Waller to Bell, Dec. 9, 1872, in *William Chapman Ralston Correspondence, 1864–75* (Bancroft Library, UC Berkeley).

Financial numbers were often so many decoys deployed to lure actual dollars to their destruction. Railroad promoters manipulated numbers so that they proclaimed security and profit to the unwary when the investment in question provided neither. As long as investors reinvested the interest from the railroad bonds in new bonds, the railroads could use new investments to pay interest on existing loans. Once worried investors could get better and safer returns in England, however, money began to flow back across the Atlantic and trouble loomed. The situation looked serious in 1872. By 1873 it looked dire. As the usual financial stringency of the fall harvest season approached in the summer of 1873, Vienna seemed uncomfortably close to New York City. American railroads lacked the revenue to pay both expenses and interest, and without access to fresh capital, they would fall into receivership.[27]

The weakness of the railroads threatened the bankers who financed them. It particularly endangered Jay Cooke & Company, which had in 1870 taken on responsibility for financing the Northern Pacific Railroad. Cooke initially succeeded in enticing small investors to whom he had sold government bonds to put their money in Northern Pacific bonds. He also attracted such famous men as Horace Greeley and Henry Ward Beecher. But he failed to convince large European houses to market his bonds, and the feckless Northern Pacific had soon run up a debt with the House of Cooke far beyond what Cooke had told his partners and investors he would allow. Cooke had promised to limit his bank's advances to the railroad to $500,000, but by the summer of 1873 they had reached $7 million. The Northern Pacific was sucking him dry, and its unmarketable bonds constituted the only security for its loans.[28]

Cooke's problems were variants on the problems faced by virtually all Western and Southern railroads as well as many in the East and Midwest. In the spring of 1873 Huntington registered the strain. He could not sleep, consumed by a "nervous unrest." He was ready to unload the Central Pacific, but no one would buy.[29]

To meet their costs, some railroads resorted to short-term borrowing, but although this relieved immediate cash flow problems, it made them vulnerable to contraction in the money supply during the predictable autumn stringencies in the financial markets when the banks would call loans in or fail to renew them. Grant had relied on Secretary of the

27. White, 65–84.
28. Ibid., 56–57, 81–84; Sven Beckert, *The Monied Metropolis: New York City and the Consolidation of the American Bourgeoisie, 1850–1896* (Cambridge: Cambridge University Press, 2001), 152.
29. White, 81–82.

Treasury George Boutwell to see him through those crises, but now Boutwell had returned to the Senate.[30]

In 1873 William Richardson was secretary of the Treasury. Although Grant had just defeated the Liberal Republicans, who worshipped the gold standard, both he and Richardson were susceptible to pressure from the hard-money men, who blamed inflation and higher interest rates on the fiat currency. The debate over fiat currency dominated monetary policy, but while it took center stage, one of the more bizarre conspiracies in American history performed as a kind of sideshow.[31]

In January 1873 Congress voted to demonetize silver, except for minor coins. Only Senate and Treasury insiders and William Ralston, the California banker, noted the bill's passage. The United States would issue no more silver dollars, keeping only a trade dollar (often called "the China dollar") for commerce with silver-standard countries, which basically meant China. Silver would no longer be a legal standard within the United States; bimetallism was over. Largely ignored at the time, the law would eventually be damned as the "Crime of '73." It reverberated through American politics for the remainder of the century.

There was little opposition to the bill's passage since soft-money men regarded silver as just another form of specie and hard-money men wanted gold. Only later, when antimonopolists and soft-money advocates recognized silver as the inflationary option to the gold standard in a deflationary world, would they retrospectively demonize it and lay responsibility at the feet of Eastern and European bankers.[32]

There was a Crime of '73, but Eastern and European bankers were not the culprits. They actually wanted the United States to maintain its bimetallism. With the movement of Europe onto the gold standard, a large amount of European silver, no longer needed by European treasuries, as well as bullion from new discoveries flooded commodity markets, depressing the price of silver. Eastern bankers, who also held silver, feared a rapid fall in silver prices and wanted the U.S. Treasury to purchase silver and thus protect the value of their holdings. Like European bankers, the last thing they wanted was the demonetization of silver.[33]

30. Irwin Unger, *The Greenback Era: A Social and Political History of American Finance, 1865–1879* (Princeton, NJ: Princeton University Press, 1964), 164–65, 190–94, 213–15; Summers, *Ordeal of the Union*, 336.
31. Unger, 213–15.
32. Walter T. K. Nugent, *Money and American Society, 1865–1880* (New York: Free Press, 1968), 72–93; 140–71; Unger, 328–31.
33. Samuel DeCanio, *Democracy and the Origins of the American Regulatory State* (New Haven, CT: Yale University Press, 2015), 92–120.

Antimonopolists got the conspirators wrong. In 1873 William Ralston of the Bank of California and his colleagues controlled Nevada's Comstock Lode, whose mines provided much of American silver production. As Ralston watched Europe go onto the gold standard, he too recognized that demonetized European silver would rapidly drop in value, and if the U.S. Treasury provided a market, that silver would flood into the United States in amounts the Treasury could not absorb. Ralston's Bank of California was seriously overextended. Declining silver prices would provoke a run on Comstock mining stocks, which could destroy the bank. He accepted that U.S. silver prices would fall; he wanted to cushion the fall and create alternate markets for his silver.[34]

Ralston shared financial interests in the Comstock with Sen. William Stewart of Nevada, and he helped to finance Stewart's campaigns. He conspired with Stewart and a small group of senators to push the passage of the Coinage Act, which on the surface seemed a mortal blow to his interests. In fact, it struck a delicate and clever balance. The act demonetized silver, thus preventing a rush of European silver into American markets, but it also created a government market for American silver by authorizing silver trade dollars to be used in the China trade. These would be produced at the San Francisco Mint, giving Comstock silver an immense price advantage over silver that had to be shipped from Europe. The act killed two birds with one stone, discouraging European imports while creating a protected market for American silver. It gave Ralston a final gift by eliminating the coinage fee that those who sold gold and silver to the mint had to pay to get their bullion converted to coin.

Henry Linderman, who had headed the Philadelphia Mint and had great influence in the Treasury Department, essentially wrote the Coinage Act. Ralston paid him well for his efforts in drafting the bill and shepherding it through Congress. Most members of Congress regarded the bill as a relatively innocuous tidying up of currency issues. It attracted little opposition. It was all part of the "inwardness"—the word Americans commonly used to describe events different from what they appeared to be on the surface—of nineteenth-century politics. Ralston's lobbying success ultimately did him no good. The Panic of 1873 overwhelmed him. He drowned in San Francisco Bay in 1875, a possible suicide.[35]

The Panic of 1873 was the financial crisis that erupted in the United States in the fall. Secretary Richardson responded timidly. He released some greenbacks, but mostly he substituted gold standard homilies for the cash Cooke and other bankers and financiers were desperately trying to

34. DeCanio, 92–120.
35. Ibid., 92–120.

raise. "Confidence," Richardson said, "was to be entirely restored only by the slow cautious process of gaining better knowledge of true values... and by conducting business on a firmer basis, with less inflation and more regard to real soundness and intrinsic values."[36]

Panic in Europe, scandal in the United States, and a tightening money market left the Northern Pacific and other railroads adrift in stormy financial seas. The Crédit Mobilier affair made further subsidies unlikely and bond guarantees unimaginable. Only the most trusting and desperate would invest in railroads that insiders plundered, unless, of course, they planned to become plunderers, too. As attacks from rivals made it even harder for Jay Cooke to sell bonds, Cooke became a desperate man. His need to sustain the Northern Pacific Railroad led him to the Freedman's Bank.[37]

The Freedman's Bank was not a government institution, although some freedmen were led to believe that it was. It was a congressionally chartered savings bank promoted by men closely associated with the Freedmen's Bureau. It owed its growth to the government's refusal to redistribute land to the freedpeople. Agents of the bank and the Freedmen's Bureau had convinced many ex-slaves that by depositing their meager savings from military service, wages, or sharecropping in a Freedman's Bank, they could eventually buy land. Like their white working-class contemporaries, the freedpeople were great savers. The American saving rate was staggering, an estimated 24 percent of the gross national product by the 1870s. In all, approximately a hundred thousand freedpeople entrusted some $50 million to the bank between 1865 and 1874.[38]

Jay Cooke, a former abolitionist, became involved in the Freedman's Bank through his brother Henry. William Dean Howells had as a young man enjoyed working with Henry Cooke, whom he considered the "easiest of easy gentlemen." Cooke gave Howells very bad advice, which Howells considered good advice. (Making bad advice seem good was Henry Cooke's great talent.) "Never," he told Howells, "write anything you would be ashamed to read to a woman." Howells's "preference of decency" would mark his writing, and, as a result, much of the world he actually lived in vanished from his pages. What he refused to write about hurt his standing among his contemporaries. It hurts his reputation still.

36. White, 83–84.
37. Jonathan Levy, *Freaks of Fortune: The Emerging World of Capitalism and Risk in America* (Cambridge, MA: Harvard University Press, 2012), 126–36; White, 81–82.
38. Levy, 126–36; Robert E. Gallman, "Growth and Change," in *The Cambridge Economic History of the United States*, ed. Stanley L. Engerman and Robert E. Gallman (Cambridge: Cambridge University Press, 1996), 39–45.

Henry Cooke, as reluctant as he was to talk indecently, was more than ready to act indecently when his interests required.[39]

After Henry came onto the board of the Freedman's Bank, he played a major role in investing its deposits. Seeking returns higher than the going rate on government bonds, Henry secured a change in the charter, turning the savings bank into an investment bank, which could make riskier investments. He moved funds into transcontinental railroad bonds. The bank also made dubious loans to political insiders whose security was often virtually worthless but whose influence the Cookes valued. As Jay Cooke & Company ran into trouble, the Freedman's Bank purchased some of its worst assets. Eventually, Henry transferred Freedman's Bank deposits to Jay Cooke & Company, allowing his brother to pay less interest for the money than the interest the Freedman's Bank was paying to the depositors. Finally, Henry loaned Freedman's Bank funds to Jay Cooke & Company, taking the Northern Pacific bonds that his brother could not sell as collateral. Not for the last time, the poorest of Americans were about to fall victim to the greed, bad judgment, and ambition of the richest.[40]

On September 18, 1873—another Black Friday and only a few days after Jay Cooke had entertained Grant at his estate outside Philadelphia—the New York branch of Jay Cooke & Company shut its doors. The other branches followed, triggering the Panic of 1873. If Cooke could fail, anyone could. Depositors rushed to withdraw savings. On September 20, the New York Stock Exchange closed for the first time in its history. Banks called in loans, businesses collapsed, and the United States slid into a depression, which would last until 1879. At the end of September, Huntington of the Central Pacific, overwhelmed by work and worry, wrote simply: "I stay in my office not knowing just what to do." The federal response was tepid and inadequate: the Treasury bought bonds to inject greenbacks into the system and then began reissuing a limited number of greenbacks to inflate the currency. It proved too little, too late.[41]

As they had in good times, the railroads led the way in bad times. They carried the economy over a cliff. The press labeled the Panic of 1873 a railroad depression. Twenty-five railroads defaulted on their debts in the first few months after the crash. Seventy-one followed in 1874 and another twenty-five in 1875. By 1876 roughly half of the railroad companies had gone into receivership. Railroad stocks lost 60 percent of their value

39. William Dean Howells, *Years of My Youth, and Three Essays* (Bloomington: Indiana University Press, 1975), 125–26.
40. Levy, 139–44; White, 83.
41. *London Times*, Feb. 3, 1876, Newspaper Cutting Files, v. 6: 88, r. 221; White, 83–84.

between 1873 and 1878. By 1876 receivers appointed by the courts controlled half the railroad mileage in the country. American iron foundries, whose main market was the railways, also suffered. Half had closed within a little more than a year of the crash.[42]

The country was littered with bankrupt and derelict lines; others survived only through the mercy of creditors. Scott's Texas Pacific went into receivership, as did Huntington's Chesapeake and Ohio. Important New York banks realized that because bankers had hypothecated the Central Pacific's securities repeatedly, they were effectively worthless as collateral. It was better to strike a deal with the Central Pacific; otherwise the chain of debt would choke even more banks. Jay Gould scavenged the Union Pacific, saving it from bankruptcy and setting up what would eventually become one of his biggest financial killings.[43]

Reliable statistics on the scale of the downturn do not exist. It appears that the loss in industrial output—around 10 percent—may have been less than in both earlier and later depressions, and agricultural output may have declined little or not at all, but these numbers conceal a deeper problem that would plague the economy for the remainder of the century. Because farmers responded to lower prices by producing more, agricultural output did not shrink. But more crops on the market led to falling prices and deflation, which meant the farmers would pay back the cheap dollars they had borrowed with more expensive dollars. Here was fuel for agricultural rebellion. A similar situation confronted railroads and other industries with high fixed costs. Needing to pay back money they had borrowed and invested in plants and machinery, they continued to produce, even with prices falling. As the economist Arthur Hadley would later explain, in the case of railroads, the necessity to pay fixed costs meant that if a railroad took freight at $0.11 cents a ton that cost it $0.25 to handle, it lost $0.14 a ton. But if $0.15 of the $.25 cents it cost to haul the freight was fixed—interest and maintenance—then the railroad lost even more ($0.15) on a ton if it refused to take traffic at a loss. Output, and gross domestic product, could remain remarkably high even as incomes and profits fell and labor suffered.[44]

---

42. White, 85.
43. White, 82–85.
44. White, 82–87; Samuel Rezneck, "Distress, Relief, and Discontent in the United States During the Depression of 1873–78," *Journal of Political Economy* 58, no. 6 (1950): 495; Nicolas Barreyre, "The Politics of Economic Crises: The Panic of 1873, the End of Reconstruction, and the Realignment of American Politics," *Journal of the Gilded Age and Progressive Era* 10, no. 4 (2011): 408; Joseph Davis, "An Annual Index of U.S. Industrial Production: 1790–1915," *Quarterly Journal of Economics* 119, no. 4 (2004),

Financial numbers may have been deceptive, but the suffering was quite real. There were 5,183 bankruptcies in 1873, and the Panic did not really take hold until October. In 1878, the last full year of the depression by the usual measures, there were 10,478. The Society for Improving the Condition of the Poor estimated that 25 percent of New York City's workers were unemployed during the winter following the Panic. The next winter, their estimate was one-third. In his memoirs, Samuel Gompers, then a young immigrant cigar maker in New York City, remembered thousands walking the streets in search of work during a winter of appalling misery. The family of a man he worked with was reduced to eating their pet dog. Although some scholars think the depression eased as early as 1876, by standard measures it took until March 1879 for the economy to hit bottom and begin to rise. The sixty-five-month contraction was the longest in American history.[45]

Americans had entered a period of radical economic and political instability that they were ill prepared to understand. Although the signs of fundamental changes had appeared well before 1873, the economic rhythms of free labor had still seemed dominant in the years following war. Independent production on Northern and Western farms had thrived; workingmen had risen from wage labor to start small businesses, and retailing was still a domain of small shops and stores. Experts had noticed that the fastest-growing part of the population consisted of wageworkers, but this had not yet destroyed the general conception that the arc of a working life led to independence. When the Panic of 1873 struck, not only did many of these wageworkers lose their jobs, but independent producers also failed and were thrown into the ranks of laborers.

Unemployment was a relatively new phenomenon, an artifact of the rise of industrial America where large gains in productivity often came at the expense of economic security. The word *unemployment* took on its modern meaning of being without work and seeking a wage-paying job only within a dominant wage-labor system where the wageworkers lacked the opportunity to retreat to the countryside to engage in independent agricultural production during downturns. Unemployment, in the sense of being without work through no fault of one's own, marked a shift in

particularly 1203; Arthur Twining Hadley, *Railroad Transportation Its History and Its Laws* (New York: G. P. Putnam's Sons, 1886), 70–71.

45. Unger, 226–28; Economic Cycle Dating Committee of NBER, "Business Cycle Expansions and Contractions." NBER, http://www.nber.org/cycles.html; Davis; Rosanne Currarino, *The Labor Question in America: Economic Democracy in the Gilded Age* (Urbana: University of Illinois Press, 2011), 88–89; White, 82–83; Rezneck, 495–96; Alexander Keyssar, *Out of Work: The First Century of Unemployment in Massachusetts* (Cambridge: Cambridge University Press, 1986), 4–8; Barreyre, 407–8.

moral and social universes as well as economic. Americans had previously attributed lack of work to individual causes—laziness or disability—but unemployment involved a structural shift. People looking for employment could not find it, and they lacked access to land or other resources to employ themselves. Unemployment became the engine driving a train of social problems: homelessness, malnutrition, crime, and illness.[46]

In 1878 Massachusetts, the nation's bastion of wage labor, made a systematic attempt to determine the rate of unemployment. The state had three hundred thousand workers in manufacturing, and by 1875 70 percent of males and nearly all women employed outside the home worked for wages. Unable to cope with competition from the Midwest, the number of farmers plunged from 60 percent of the workforce in 1820 to 13 percent by 1870.[47]

Counting the unemployed had significant ideological implications. Carroll Wright, a disciple of Francis Walker and a leading statistician in his own right, led the effort, which found only twenty-two thousand unemployed in Massachusetts. He regarded the result as a refutation of the "croakers" who claimed three million unemployed in the United States and a quarter of a million in Massachusetts. But Wright's figures concealed as much as they revealed. He did not count women; nor did he count children under eighteen, a substantial part of the workforce. For Wright, not everyone thrown out of work by the depression qualified as unemployed. Those whom he considered not actively looking for work, not looking hard enough for work, or unwilling to accept cuts in wages did not count as unemployed. Neither did beggars or those too sick to work regularly. The goal in whittling down the number of unemployed was to buttress the belief that work and opportunity were still available for those who sought them.[48]

If Wright's figures were revised to include all workers thrown out of work during the depression of the 1870s, it would appear that the unemployment rate was more than 15 percent in 1878. More significantly, well above 30 percent of the workforce was unemployed for at least a hundred days during part of the year. Even in good times, seasonal unemployment was a reality for many workers. Regular spells of unemployment had become normal. They became markers of working-class identity.[49]

As workers came to expect extended layoffs—less frequent in good times, more frequent in bad—they sought remedies. They struggled to keep the wolf from the door. Workers accumulated savings for hard times

46. Keyssar, 1–8, 11–14, 17–18.
47. Ibid., 1–2, 14–16.
48. Ibid., 1–8, 15–16, 50.
49. Ibid., 37, 50–52, 62–69.

by putting children out to work, taking in boarders, and cutting consumption. In 1872, for example, Tim Harrington of Newburyport, Massachusetts, put his wife and children out to work and bought only the family's flour from his own salary, saving the rest. In effect, families like Harrington's mortgaged their children's future to create a safety net. All of this amounted to a kind of self-insurance against inevitable economic downturns, but, as a Massachusetts furniture polisher reported at the end of the depression, unemployment made saving difficult. To save $100 over the course of a year—the amount he considered necessary to accumulate a competence—a family of three had to earn $12 a week for fifty-two weeks. But if a man was "idle a couple of months, or sick: what is going to become of the family?"[50]

When they exhausted their savings, workers resorted to extended family and neighbors, and then to local merchants and landlords, who would advance them credit. Only when these failed would they seek aid, and then reluctantly, from churches, charities, Industrial Aid Societies, unions, and local relief committees. Workers looked for aid only when desperate, received aid only when deemed worthy, and got, at most, a pittance.[51]

When all else failed, families broke apart, sometimes temporarily, sometimes permanently. One of the distinguishing characteristics of the American working class was its mobility, but greater physical mobility no longer translated easily into increased social mobility. The data remain partial and localized, but it appears that both workers' ability to move to better jobs and the speed at which they did so declined between 1850 and 1880. In Newburyport, Massachusetts, the locale of one of the earliest and most influential studies, fewer than 5 percent of unskilled workers rose into the middle class, and only slightly more became skilled workers. Between 75 and 80 percent of them remained where they began, as unskilled laborers. These figures were worse for immigrants, who formed a rising proportion of unskilled labor, but social mobility for native-born workers, who dominated the ranks of the skilled, also declined. What the country did add were masses of men moving around the nation in the 1870s. Americans created a new meaning for an old word: tramp. It had meant a walking expedition, or during the Civil War a toilsome march, but now it meant someone "with no visible means of support."[52]

50. Stephan Thernstrom, *Poverty and Progress: Social Mobility in a Nineteenth Century City* (Cambridge, MA: Harvard University Press, 1964), 136; Keyssar, 143.
51. Keyssar, 143–66.
52. Thernstrom, 85–104; Todd DePastino, *Citizen Hobo: How a Century of Homelessness Shaped America* (Chicago: University of Chicago Press, 2003), 5, 15–17.

Tramps, unemployed men defined by their homelessness, became symbols of the changes sweeping the American economy. Some tramps were criminals; many found it necessary to beg; but during hard times the vast majority were workers, largely young men, who took to the roads in search of jobs. Their numbers swelled during the depression of the 1870s, fell when the depression ended, and rose once more when the economy faltered again between 1882 and 1885. In some trades tramping was a stage of life. Thomas Edison was, for a period, a tramp mechanic.[53]

The *New York Times* saw tramps as expressions of primal sloth and savagery or as relics of Civil War camp life, and the terms for tramps and bums came out of the war; but poets were more perceptive. The numbers of tramps struck Walt Whitman as an omen of American decline: "If the United States, like the countries of the Old World, are also to grow vast crops of poor, desperate, dissatisfied, nomadic, miserably-waged populations such as we see looming upon us of late years—steadily, even if slowly, eating into us like a cancer of lungs or stomach—then our republican experiment, notwithstanding all its surface successes, is at heart an unhealthy failure."[54]

Tramps were often met with fear and abuse, hounded out of towns, imprisoned for vagrancy, beaten by local authorities. But there was, particularly in the Midwest and West, a subset of tramps—hoboes—who were seasonal laborers integral to regional economies. These were the gandydancers, who laid and repaired railroad tracks from spring through fall; loggers; harvest hands; ice cutters; and more. Inured to a labor market that offered them only temporary and often dangerous work, they adjusted by working just enough to get the money they needed to survive the winter and begin the cycle again. For some, it was a stage of life. For others it became their life, which too often was rough, brutal, and short.[55]

The tramps, the urban unemployed, and business failures became visible social sores, the signs of an underlying disease that seemed to be destroying free labor's promise. With the onset of the depression in 1873, Americans had entered what economists have come to call the long depression of the late nineteenth century. It was marked by deflation,

53. DePastino, 5, 15–17; Rezneck, 495–96; A. J. Millard, *Edison and the Business of Innovation* (Baltimore, MD: Johns Hopkins University Press, 1990), 31.
54. Kenneth L. Kusmer, *Down and Out, on the Road: The Homeless in American History* (New York: Oxford University Press, 2002), 37–39; DePastino, 17–29; "The Tramp and Strike Question: Part of a Lecture proposed, (never deliver'd)," in Walt Whitman, *Complete Prose Works* (Philadelphia: David McKay, 1897), 330.
55. Kusmer, 40–45, 49–52; Frank Tobias Higbie, *Indispensable Outcasts: Hobo Workers and Community in the American Midwest, 1880–1930* (Urbana: University of Illinois Press, 2003), 1–10, 25–26; Keyssar, 130–42.

downward pressure on wages, declining returns on capital, and wild fluctuations in farm income. The combination of the inflation of the 1860s
and the depression of the 1870s registered statistically—although these
statistics are often indirectly derived and crude—in declines in per capita
real income between 1860 and 1880, with the losses during the Civil War
years and the depression years wiping out the gains of the postwar boom.
In 1880, at the end of the depression, unskilled workers were worse off
than they had been twenty years earlier at the beginning of the Civil War.
This was not the anticipated outcome of the triumph of free labor and
contract freedom.[56]

Statistics on nineteenth-century growth are shaky, but the most reliable indicate that even though the United States grew faster than Europe
between 1870 and 1913—with the most rapid and sustained growth
coming after 1897—its growth rate was very similar to those of other
British settler colonies: Canada, New Zealand, and Australia. The
American growth rate after 1870 was actually lower than it had been
between 1820 and 1870. In part the American economy was growing
because the United States was growing. Its population would double
from 31.4 million to 62.9 million in the thirty years following 1860. The
United States grew steadily but, at least compared with nations that industrialized in the twentieth and twenty-first centuries, unspectacularly
over the course of the nineteenth century. Growth in real GNP has been
estimated at about 4 percent over the course of the century. Much of it
arose from investment in capital goods: farms, factories, machines, and
railroads. This growth was far from even and between the end of the
Civil War and 1900 growth was far less than 4 percent, with the economy
often slipping into recession or depression.[57]

Because so much of the growth came from capital rather than consumer goods, the economy did not gain as much as it would have from
increased consumption. Nor did growth automatically yield greater profits for businesses. As prices fell and deflation took hold following the Civil
War, profit margins were tighter, and with their capital sunk into factories,
machinery, and infrastructure, businesses had less liquidity to confront

56. Higbie, 1–10, 25–26; DePastino, 19–23; Keyssar, 130–42; Louise Carroll Wade,
    Chicago's Pride: The Stockyards, Packingtown, and Environs in the Nineteenth Century
    (Urbana: University of Illinois Press, 1987), 115; Robert A. Margo, "Wages and Wage
    Inequality," in *Historical Statistics of the United States, Earliest Times to the Present:
    Millennial Edition*, 2–44.
57. Jeremy Atack, *A New Economic View of American History: From Colonial Times to
    1940*, ed. Peter Passell and Susan Lee, 2nd ed. (New York: Norton, 1994), 14–18.

crises. The squeeze on profits and the failure to sustain pools to raise prices led to attempts to cut labor costs to ensure profit, but this would be easier said than done.[58]

II

The political ramifications of the Panic of 1873 fell hardest on the Republican Party. The second Grant administration became synonymous with both scandal and economic failure. Investigators uncovered the Whiskey Ring and the Indian Ring, which involved fraudulent contracts on Indian reservations. There was more. John D. Sanborn, a protégé of Benjamin Butler, secured a contract to collect taxes due the government, but government investigators had already determined the amount due and collected the necessary evidence to secure payment. Sanborn merely secured the checks from the delinquent taxpayers, deducted more than half as his fee, and forwarded the rest to the treasury. Butler probably shared in the proceeds.[59]

The Panic of 1873 brought the Republicans to their knees, but given party loyalties, they might have survived all of this except for their reaction to the Panic. Much of the initial press reaction to Black Friday was sanguine. A speculative bubble, much like Gould's attempt to corner gold, had burst; things would soon be put right. When it became clear that the Panic would have serious effects, Americans debated what to do according to terms set by the 1860s. The issue was hard-money versus soft-money. The House of Representatives faced endless currency bills introduced by its members.[60]

Because the Republicans controlled Congress in the wake of the 1872 elections, the most important debate raged between gold-standard Republicans, mostly from the Northeast, and soft-money Republicans, largely from the Midwest, who had allies in greenback Democrats. The Forty-third Congress, which convened in December 1873, was the first to reflect the new demographic dominance of the Midwest. The nation's population growth had added fifty seats to the House, giving the Midwest

58. "U.S. Real Per Capita GDP from 1870–2001," blogspot.com, http://socialdemocracy 21stcentury.blogspot.com/2012/09/us-real-per-capita-gdp-from-18702001.html; Angus Maddison, ed., *The World Economy* (Paris: Development Centre of the Organisation for Economic Co-operation and Development, 2006), 187, Appendix A, table 1-e.
59. Summers, *The Era of Good Stealings*, 92–98, 184–91.
60. Barreyre, 409; Currarino, 17–18, 20.

the largest delegation. From 1876 into the early twentieth century, Ohio produced presidential candidates the way Georgia produced peaches.[61]

In early 1874 Congress passed the so-called Inflation Bill with comfortable Republican majorities. It was a modest victory for soft-money men, but it added only $64 million to the currency. The figure included the greenbacks that Richardson had already reissued, and most of the rest of the additional currency would be in banknotes. Liberals, bankers, eastern merchants, and the respectable Protestant clergy responded in horror. John Murray Forbes, president of the Chicago, Burlington and Quincy Railroad, got the American Social Science Association to publish a new weekly, the *Financial Record*, to proselytize for the gold standard and oppose the Inflation Bill. Its contributors included leading liberals such as Francis Walker and a young Yale professor, William Graham Sumner.[62]

When Grant vetoed the bill, the liberals rejoiced. Men who had spent years vilifying the president now praised him. Grant's principles were often at war with his politics and personal loyalties, and it was hard to tell which would triumph at any given moment. This time, his hard-money tendencies and desire to lure dissident liberals back to the Republican Party won out over the political appeal of soft money. Even though the Republicans passed additional legislation providing an even smaller addition to money supply, the veto was a political disaster.[63]

Rarely has an American political party suffered a defeat on the scale that the Republican Party did in the congressional elections of 1874. In the House they went from a 70 percent majority to a 37 percent minority in a single election. The Republicans lost in the South, but the more critical losses were in the Midwest and Mid-Atlantic states. Northern Republicans did not become Democrats; instead they voted for independents or stayed at home on Election Day. Republicans had not simply failed to meet the economic crisis, they had raised hopes only to have Grant dash them. Democrats could, and did, attack the Republicans as tools of rich Northeastern bankers and merchants. In the South, white Democrats laid economic disaster at the feet of the Republicans. The Senate served as a Republican firewall both because only a third of its seats were up for election in 1874 and because every new state of the West, though electing few representatives, had the same number of senators as the more populous states east of the 100th meridian. The states west of the Missouri River had twelve senators; in 1875 eleven were Republicans. The

61. Barreyre, 403–23.
62. Unger, 235–44; Barreyre, 414–15; Michael F. Holt, *By One Vote: The Disputed Presidential Election of 1876* (Lawrence: University Press of Kansas, 2008), 16–17.
63. Barreyre, 415ff.; Holt, 16; Unger, 240–44.

election ushered in an era of divided government and rough parity between the parties. Until 1897 the same party would control the House, the Senate, and the presidency for only four years.[64]

The defection of antimonopolists within the Republican Party hurt the Republicans in the North, particularly since they were simultaneously faced with the resurgence of the Democratic Redeemers in the South. Grant's veto drove many Illinois antimonopolists temporarily from the party; they voted for independents and a third party, the Greenbackers. Antimonopolists dominated the Illinois legislature without dominating either major party. The Republican *Chicago Tribune* compared the advocates of fiat currency to the Paris Commune; the *Illinois State Register*, the leading Democratic newspaper, described them as "Inflationists and Lunatics." But the "Inflationists and Lunatics" were, as hard-money men admitted, the majority of the American people.[65]

Antimonopolism was not inherently racist; there were black antimonopolists in the South and interracial antimonopoly movements would emerge, but antimonopolism was vulnerable to racial scapegoating. Western antimonopolists grew more Sinophobic in the 1870s in the face of Chinese immigration. They and northern antimonopolists in the Democratic Party became sympathetic to a virulently racist strain of antimonopolism that led white Southern farmers to ally with far more conservative Southern Redeemers on the basis of white supremacy. Antimonopolists within the Democratic Party buttressed their party's opposition to Reconstruction.

Henry George, emerging as the country's leading antimonopolist intellectual and a Democrat, demonstrated how this worked. George cast black men in the South and Chinese in the West as tools of the corporations and the rich, and as threats to white manhood. Campaigning for the Democrats in California in 1876, George drew the parallels.

> Imagine our Chinese population increased until it equaled or exceeded in number the whites. Imagine them all voters. Place in thought in the gubernatorial chair a canting hypocrite from the East, elected by Chinese votes, and holding office only to make as much out of it as he could before leaving the country. Fill up your legislature with Chinamen,

64. Barreyre, 415ff.; Unger, 240–44.
65. Holt, 16; Peter Argersinger, "The Transformation of American Politics: Political Institutions and Public Policy, 1865–1910," in *Contesting Democracy: Substance and Structure in American Political History, 1775–2000*, ed. Byron E. Shafer and Anthony J. Badger (Lawrence: University Press of Kansas, 2001), 121–24, 126–27; Gretchen Ritter, *Goldbugs and Greenbacks: The Antimonopoly Tradition and the Politics of Finance in America* (Cambridge: Cambridge University Press, 1997), 129–35, quotes 32.

Eastern adventurers, and whites from the Barbary Coast. Imagine Chinese militia, Chinese policemen, Chinese judges and Chinese school directors. Imagine the debt of the state run up at forty or fifty millions of dollars, every public fund squandered in the most shameless corruption.... Gentlemen do you think that California in this condition would be a peaceful state?[66]

George took the Redeemers' rhetoric of the South, substituted Chinese for black people, and let his audience draw their own conclusions.

By the time George made these analogies in 1876, the Southern attack on Reconstruction had regained its vigor after the setbacks of 1872. During the 1872 election both Southern Republicans and moderate Democrats, many of them ex-Whigs who advocated a "New Departure," had based their hopes on continued prosperity. They had accepted government intervention in the economy, aid to corporations, and the reality of black suffrage. Advocates of "New Departure" rejected the "White Line" policy of the white supremacists, who sought to make the Democratic Party a white man's party bent on uprooting the economic and political accomplishments of Reconstruction. The Panic of 1873 undercut both Republicans and moderate Democrats and fed a resurgent white supremacy. Prosperity faded as cotton prices fell nearly 50 percent between 1872 and 1877. Taxes on farmers, both large and small, felt particularly onerous, and farmers united in their demand for retrenchment in government and the overthrow of the Republicans.[67]

The Republican economic program became a liability, and Democrats abandoned the "New Departure." White supremacy became the glue that held the Democratic Party together. By the end of 1873 Tennessee, Georgia, and Virginia had reverted to complete Democratic control. In addition, resurgent Democrats had reclaimed parts of the state governments everywhere but in Arkansas, Louisiana, Mississippi, and South Carolina.[68]

Monopolists had their fingers up to the political winds. They had cooperated with the Radicals; now they supported the "redeemers." Tom Scott was always a pretty dependable guide to which way the wind was blowing; he adjusted his sails to capitalize on both a resurgent white supremacy in the South and the rise of antimonopolism there. Both could support his interests. Scott made peace with the Southern "redeemers."[69]

66. Henry George, "Speech Made in San Francisco During the 1876 Presidential Election," in *Henry George Papers* (New York: New York Public Library, n.d.), 66–67.
67. Michael Perman, *The Road to Redemption: Southern Politics, 1869–1879* (Chapel Hill: University of North Carolina Press, 1984), 228–31; Eric Foner, *Reconstruction: America's Unfinished Revolution, 1863–1877* (New York: Harper & Row, 1988), 535–36.
68. White, 120; Perman, 135–77; Foner, 547–48.
69. White, 120.

Scott had reorganized his railroad interests by creating the Southern Railway Security Company in 1871. It was a holding company, a relatively recent invention by which one corporation controlled the stock of many other corporations. A holding company made consolidation much easier since it did not require the time-consuming and difficult legal merger of the various roads, and a holding company bore none of the legal responsibilities to the public of a nineteenth-century corporation. The Southern Railway Security Company controlled a new railway system stretching from Baltimore to Atlanta. Bribing when necessary, illegally enticing traffic, buying out its constituent roads, and controlling newspapers and thus publicity, the Southern Railway Security Company slowly drove down its rival, the Seaboard Inland Air Line.[70]

Scott, once denounced as a carpetbagger, made the company a vehicle for white supremacy. He cultivated Democratic political allies by hiring Southern white labor and contracting black convicts, while limiting his use of free black labor. Southerners joined the boards of his railroads and helped Scott reorganize the Southern transportation system into a pump that drew cotton, tobacco, timber, and other raw materials from the South for northern and world markets. Scott's bargain with white supremacy did more for him than for the Southern economy. The South remained the poorest and most backward part of the United States for the remainder of the century.[71]

Scott, the monopolist, recruited men who ideologically should have been his enemies. Antimonopolists came into office opposed to corporate subsidies and full of regional resentments, but he knew that regional resentments could be played upon for the benefit of the Texas and Pacific. He moved away from the cultivation of individual lobbyists—strikers, as they were called—and created instead a modern congressional lobby under his direct control. He played on Southern resentment to work for the extension of federal credit to finish the Texas and Pacific. He made it a matter of justice for the South and a cure for the transcontinental monopoly held by the Central Pacific and the Union Pacific. Huntington, pushing the rival Southern Pacific from the west, organized his own lobby and raised the banner of antisubsidy to oppose Scott and attract Western antimonopolists. That Scott enlisted Southern antimonopolists on his side and that Huntington, a man who had reaped immense subsidies,

---

70. David Sievert Lavender, *The Great Persuader* (Niwot: University Press of Colorado, 1998, 1970), 253, 271; Scott Reynolds Nelson, *Iron Confederacies: Southern Railways, Klan Violence, and Reconstruction* (Chapel Hill: University of North Carolina Press, 1999), 140–63.
71. Nelson, *Iron Confederacies*, 138–78.

recruited northern and western antisubsidy congressmen spoke to the adaptability of American politics and the complexity of reform.[72]

The White Line strategy, however, also presented problems for the Democrats. In large swaths of the Deep South, Republicans could win with black votes alone. With free and honest elections, Louisiana, Mississippi, South Carolina, and Florida promised to remain largely Republican. The Democrats' solution was a return to violence. This time, however, the violence would be calibrated: enough to repress black people but not so much as to invite Northern intervention. The federal government had made the Democratic strategy possible by reducing its own capacity to suppress terror. The number of federal troops stationed in Louisiana had dropped to only 421 in 1872.[73]

The Red River Country became the flashpoint of racial conflict in Louisiana and in the nation. The black Henry Adams, discharged from the army and living in and around Shreveport, recorded the toll in almost pointillist detail. Individual outrages accumulated into a larger pattern of terror. Like other ex-soldiers, Adams was feared and hated by local whites for helping tenants with their contracts and standing up to white nightriders. Adams served on the Shreveport Louisiana grand jury in 1873 and helped form "the Council" or "the Committee," a secret intelligence-gathering body that functioned in the area. Its members used only their first names; their meetings were secret; and neither politicians nor preachers could belong. The committee kept a record of Southern violence in Louisiana and other states. Numbered, dated, with names and places, every entry was brief and matter-of-fact. The killings were sometimes black-on-black or white-on-white, but mostly white people murdered black people. The enumerated murders and beatings ran to 683.[74]

Strung together, parish by parish, the list of dead and maimed was almost Homeric. Caddo Parish:

> Donahoue, colored, was killed by a white man on Nick Marchu's place, in the year 1873. Miss Delia Young, beat and severly whipped by James Robinson (white) on Hayne's place…and also all her crop taken from her in the year 1872. Margaret Bates, badly whipped by John Brown, a white man on Levee Bend plantation, in the year 1873. Henry Hard (colored) killed by a white man, in the year 1874. Dick, a colored man,

72. White, 109–33.
73. Gregory Downs, *After Appomattox: Military Occupation and the Ends of War* (Cambridge, MA: Harvard University Press, 2015), 58–61, 69, 80–81, 86–87.
74. Nell Irvin Painter, *Exodusters: Black Migration to Kansas after Reconstruction* (New York: Knopf, 1976), 33–34, 71–81; Steven Hahn, *A Nation under Our Feet: Black Political Struggles in the Rural South, from Slavery to the Great Migration* (Cambridge, MA: Belknap Press of Harvard University Press, 2003), 122–23.

was killed by a white man in the year 1874. Fred, a colored man, killed by being burnt up at the stake, on Joe Bealey's place, in the year 1872.

And on, and on, and on. Henry Adams was a man brave beyond all reason, but with the eruption of the White Leagues in 1874, he lost faith that black people could live freely among white people in the South.[75]

The explosion came at Colfax, a new settlement named after Schuyler Colfax, Grant's vice president. It was the seat of Grant Parish (as counties are called in Louisiana), created after the Civil War and named for the president. Colfax embodied both the slave legacy of the Old South and the as-yet-not-fully-realized possibilities of the Reconstruction South. Located on the plantation of William Calhoun, Colfax in 1873 consisted of a steamboat landing, a courthouse, a school, a store, and some warehouses. Nearby were the cabins of an old slave quarters. Calhoun, who had developed a hunchback from a childhood accident, was the son of a man rumored to have been the inspiration for Simon Legree in *Uncle Tom's Cabin*. William Calhoun, however, had become a scalawag and a Republican officeholder. He lived with, and might have been married to, a mixed-race woman, Olivia Williams. They had children. Calhoun had sold land to freedmen and helped them establish a school. The freedmen around Colfax were assertive. There were ex-soldiers among them, and they had organized as part of the Louisiana militia.[76]

In the wake of the 1872 elections, competing groups of officeholders laid claim to the Colfax courthouse. In April 1873 the Radicals were in control when about 140 whites, well-armed and equipped with an artillery piece, marched on the town. Some were Confederate veterans, at least one was a Union veteran, and others had been too young to fight in the Civil War. The Knights of the White Camellia and a group called the "Old Time Ku Klux Klan" had helped organize the attackers, who had murdered blacks on their approach. The black defenders of Colfax were more numerous, but they were short of ammunition. On Easter Sunday the attackers overwhelmed them, set the courthouse on fire, and forced them to surrender. People on each side knew each other; what followed was personal as well as political. Whites lined up their prisoners and then called black men out of line by name, sometimes one, sometimes more. They shot some, slit the throats of others, and hanged a few. The total number killed in the fighting

75. U.S. Senate Select Committee, "Report and Testimony of the Select Committee of the United States Senate to Investigate the Causes of the Removal of the Negroes from the Southern States to the Northern States" (Washington, DC: U.S. GPO, 1880), 2: 193; Hahn, 319–20; Downs, 27, 78–79.

76. LeeAnna Keith, *The Colfax Massacre: The Untold Story of Black Power, White Terror, and the Death of Reconstruction* (New York: Oxford University Press, 2008), 27, 78–79.

and executed afterwards was somewhere between 70 and 165. It was hard to get an accurate count. Men were killed beyond the town; others ended up in anonymous graves. Militia reinforcements from New Orleans arrived too late to rescue the defenders, but they provided graphic accounts of the evidence of the executions. Among the dead was Alexander Tillman, a black framer of the 1868 Louisiana constitution.[77]

The Colfax Massacre became a rallying point for both sides. President Grant declared parts of Louisiana to be in a state of insurrection and imposed martial law. More elements of the Seventh Cavalry were sent to the South, but not in sufficient numbers to overawe the nightriders. The federal government, using the Enforcement Acts of 1870 and 1871, which had proved effective against the Klan, put nine of the perpetrators of the Colfax massacre on trial, but only three were convicted, and not for murder but the lesser charge of conspiracy.[78]

The collapse of the Republican economic program after the Panic of 1873 and the renewal of violence set the stage for the 1874 election in the South. In much of the upper South the Republicans hemorrhaged white voters, and this was enough for Democrats to carry the election. Elsewhere violence proved necessary. White supremacists organized White Leagues across the Louisiana. In Grant Parish the new newspaper was called the *Caucasian*. Whites murdered blacks and threatened and intimidated Republican officials, who resigned in many parishes. Henry Adams reported that the "Democrats would say to us that 'you all is trying to follow these carpet-baggers, scalawags, and negro leaders, and just as long as you to follow them we are going just to kill you as we did them.' They told us to our teeth. They told me so many a time." There were new confrontations on the Red River, and in New Orleans eight thousand armed men invaded the city in September 1874 to overthrow the Republican government headed by Gov. William Pitt Kellogg. At the Battle of Canal Street they overwhelmed the police; seized the city hall, statehouse, and arsenal; and forced Kellogg to retreat to the Custom House. This armed rebellion shocked Grant into action. Kellogg was saved by the arrival of six regiments of federal troops in the city. The Republicans were in charge of counting the vote, and their returning board threw out the returns from the violent parishes. With the troops in place, violence temporarily abated.[79]

77. Keith, 125–52.
78. Ibid., 125–52; Frank Joseph Wetta, *The Louisiana Scalawags: Politics, Race, and Terrorism During the Civil War and Reconstruction* (Baton Rouge: Louisiana State University Press, 2012), 141–42; Foner, 530–31, 550.
79. Perman, 159–60; James T. Otten, "The Wheeler Adjustment in Louisiana: National Republicans Begin to Reappraise Their Reconstruction Policy," *Louisiana History:*

The result was another disputed election in Louisiana. When the Democrats forcibly seized control of the state assembly, federal troops escorted five Democrats who had claimed contested seats out of the chamber. Grant, after warning Southerners not to test him, dispatched Philip Sheridan to investigate the violence, and Sheridan made himself as popular among white Louisianans as he had been among white Texans. He denounced the White Leagues as banditti and claimed twenty-five hundred political murders since the end of the war. Sheridan wanted habeas corpus suspended and nightriders tried before military tribunals. The black ex-soldier Henry Adams became a spy and a scout for the Seventh Cavalry in 1875. It was, he said, "a very dangerous business." Grant would not go as far as Sheridan, but he justified federal intervention in Louisiana. Some liberals in the North, including Godkin and the *Nation*, denounced Sheridan and defended the White Leagues. A meeting at Faneuil Hall in Boston compared the White League favorably to the founding fathers and shouted down Wendell Phillips's defense of Grant's actions. A Congressional delegation eventually negotiated the so-called Wheeler Settlement, which left Kellogg as governor but gave the Democrats the lower chamber of the legislature. Similar violence elsewhere led Julian Burrows of Michigan to complain in the House that Southern conservatives had "sheathed the bloody sword of open revolt only to draw the bloodier dagger of the assassin." An Alabama scalawag said the question had come to this: "Is this a 'government of the people, for the people, and by the people', or is it a government of a country which proposes to control all votes of the people by intimidation and violence?"[80]

After the 1874 elections, the Republicans held on only in Mississippi and South Carolina, and more precariously in Louisiana and Florida. Grant wanted an end to federal intervention, which he saw as imposing an unacceptable political cost on the Republicans. Referring to the problems in Louisiana, Grant told Republican leaders that "this nursing of monstrosities has nearly exhausted the life of the party."[81]

In regard to Reconstruction, the Republicans still had two advantages. Their appointees controlled the federal bench, and until the new Congress took office in 1875, they retained control over the House, Senate, and

The Journal of the Louisiana Historical Association 13, no. 4 (1972): 355–56; Foner, 526, 551; Keith, 111–50; Charles W. Calhoun, *Conceiving a New Republic: The Republican Party and the Southern Question, 1869–1900* (Lawrence: University Press of Kansas, 2006), 48–52; U.S. Senate, *Report and Testimony*, 2: 207; Wetta, 141–43.

80. Foner, 551–56; Keith, 117–18, 131–52; Calhoun, 60–69, 76; Painter, 79; Otten, 359–60; U.S. Senate, *Report and Testimony*, 2: 128; Perman, 159, 161.

81. Perman, 161–64; Calhoun, 55–78.

presidency. The courts, however, proved a weak reed. They not only did not prevent the dismantling of Reconstruction; they expedited it.

The Supreme Court decided its first Fourteenth Amendment case in the *Slaughterhouse* decision of 1873, handing down its decision the day after the Colfax Massacre. The case did not directly involve either black people or civil rights legislation, but it was critical to the larger issues of federalism and the federal government's authority to protect rights threatened by state actions. At issue was environmental and public health regulation based on the police powers of municipalities. In order to control pollution, the Louisiana legislature had created a corporation to run a central slaughterhouse for New Orleans; it required all of the city's butchers to use it. The butchers sued. They accused the city of creating a monopoly that deprived them of their right, protected under the Fourteenth Amendment, to pursue their profession.[82]

A dispute over monopoly and how to dispose of offal became central to the ability of the federal government to protect the rights of freedpeople because it resurrected in the courts the old dispute in Congress over the intention of the amendment. Did the Fourteenth Amendment guarantee only an equality of rights, which the states could curb and curtail as long they did so equally and reasonably? Or did it guarantee certain absolute rights that the federal government, the states, or other citizens could not abridge?[83]

Arguing the case for the butchers was John A. Campbell. Racist, able, bitterly opposed to the Reconstruction government of Louisiana, and an ex-associate justice of the U.S. Supreme Court who had concurred in the *Dred Scott* decision, he equated the butchers with slaves in that they had been deprived of the contract freedom that the Fourteenth Amendment was meant to protect. The amendment, he argued, guaranteed "that as man has a right to labor for himself, and not at the will, or under the constraint of another, [so] he should have the profits of his own industry." This protection applied to "persons of every class and category."[84]

The initial ruling by Justice Joseph Bradley, who was riding circuit, as U.S. Supreme Court justices still did following the Civil War, agreed with Campbell and spoke of the "sacred right of labor." This admittedly had to be subject to some restrictions, but Bradley denounced the quite legitimate

82. William E. Nelson, *The Fourteenth Amendment: From Political Principle to Judicial Doctrine* (Cambridge, MA: Harvard University Press, 1988), 148–65; Keith, 135; Ronald M. Labbe and Jonathan Lurie, *The Slaughterhouse Cases: Regulation, Reconstruction, and the Fourteenth Amendment (Abridged Edition)*, ed. Jonathan Lurie (Lawrence: University Press of Kansas, 2005), 1–11.
83. Labbe and Lurie, xiii, 7–8, 174–77; Nelson, 151–81.
84. Labbe and Lurie, 128–29, 134, 140.

public health concerns of New Orleans as a mere "pretense...too bald for a moment's consideration" to create "a monopoly of a very odious character." As with so many aspects of the case, Bradley's decision was a double-edged sword. On the one hand, it overturned a law passed by a legislature with strong black representation and limited longstanding police powers of the states and municipalities. On the other hand, it upheld a broad interpretation of the Fourteenth Amendment. The amendment guaranteed absolute rights of citizens, which held throughout the nation and which no state government could abridge. It gave citizens the right to use federal courts to get injunctive relief against state and local laws.[85]

The U.S. Supreme Court reversed Bradley in 1873. The majority five-to-four opinion in the *Slaughterhouse* cases delivered by Justice Samuel F. Miller began by concentrating on the matter at hand. Miller recognized the health problem posed by the slaughter of animals in New Orleans and upheld the right of the city to regulate it as a legitimate exercise of the police power. He could have stopped there, but since he knew that the minority opinions would address Fourteenth Amendment issues, he did too. He stated the obvious: the freeing of the slaves and the protection of their rights had motivated the Thirteenth, Fourteenth, and Fifteenth Amendments to the Constitution. This did not mean, however, that the guarantees in the amendments applied only to black men. They applied to all citizens.[86]

Miller then went further and drew a distinction between citizens of the United States and citizens of the states. He regarded Americans as having, in effect, two bundles of rights: one as citizens of a state and the other as American citizens. The protections of the amendments to the federal Constitution and federal civil rights laws applied only to state actions against the "privileges and immunities" belonging to citizens of the United States. Citizens had to rely on the states to protect their other rights. Miller did not enumerate what "privileges and immunities" belonged to citizens of the United States; he said nothing about the protections the amendments gave the ex-slaves. He simply ruled that the rights claimed by the butchers to pursue their profession without regulation were not among those protected by the Fourteenth Amendment and, in an aside, stated that since the Louisiana law involved no discrimination against black people, the equal protection clause did not apply. He argued that it was not the intent of Congress to have the federal government protect all the rights of citizens and to be the arbiter of all state restrictions on the freedom of their citizens. By his narrow interpretation of the

85. Ibid., 98–100; W. E. Nelson, 155–56.
86. Labbe and Lurie, 146–47.

amendment, including the equal protection clause, he left a large opening for the erosion of the protection of the freedpeople.[87]

Miller's decision was ultimately conservative. Except for the unspecified protections extended to black people, the Supreme Court thought that the Civil War had not significantly changed the fundamental nature of the Union. It sought to try to make the legal relationship between states and the federal government closer to what it had been before the war.[88]

Among the numerous ironies of the case was that Stephen Field, a Democrat, a Lincoln appointee to the Supreme Court, and a conservative, wrote a dissent that was a strong defense of federal power. Field opposed Reconstruction and cared little for the political rights of black men. He was, however, concerned with the rising antimonopoly movement and the beginning of calls for increased state regulation of the economy. He desired, as his later decisions showed, to buttress federal power in order to curb regulation by the states. Field argued that in creating a single slaughterhouse for New Orleans, the legislature had exceeded its police powers and created a monopoly that deprived the butchers of their rights. More critically, he rejected Miller's distinction between rights as a citizen of a state and of the United States. Instead he argued that it protected "the natural and inalienable rights that belonged to all citizens." Laws had to be "just, equal, and impartial." The states, he argued, could regulate federally protected rights, but those regulations had to be reasonable and equal.[89]

The Supreme Court eventually addressed the Colfax Massacre in *U.S. v. Cruikshank et al.* (1875). The federal government had used the Enforcement Acts to prosecute William Cruikshank and the other defendants who had killed the black militiamen at Colfax. The Enforcement Acts depended on the Fifteenth Amendment prohibition of denying or abridging the right to vote "by the United States or by any state on account of race, color, or previous condition of servitude." The government also accused the defendants of violating the First Amendment right of black people to assemble and their Second Amendment right to bear arms.

The court settled the question of three convictions under the Enforcement Acts by ruling that the prosecutors had not supplied enough evidence to prove that the killings were an attempt to suppress African American political rights protected under the Fifteenth Amendment. The government had presented a sloppy case, and a unanimous Court dismissed the indictment as insufficient for drawing up criminal charges under the

87. Labbe and Lurie, 149–55; W. E. Nelson, 162–64.
88. Labbe and Lurie, 155–56; W. E. Nelson, 161–62.
89. Labbe and Lurie, 156–59.

Enforcement Acts. It left open the possibility that a more careful indictment could have done so.[90]

The Supreme Court, however, went further, ruling on the meaning of
the First and Second Amendments, and by implication the entire Bill of
Rights, and the Fourteenth Amendment. The Fourteenth Amendment
specified that "No state shall make or enforce any law which shall abridge
the privileges or immunities of citizens of the United States; nor shall any
state deprive any person of life, liberty, or property, without due process of
law; nor deny to any person within its jurisdiction the equal protection of
the laws," but the court decided that this seemingly clear language gave no
new protections to the right of assembly or the right to bear arms. The Bill
of Rights, the justices declared, did not actually bestow the right of assembly, the right to bear arms, or other rights. The amendments only declared
that Congress could not abridge them. The rights to assemble and bear
arms were not among the "privileges and immunities" of citizens. Citizens
had protection only from congressional interference; any further protection depended on the states. The ruling vitiated the Fourteenth and
Fifteenth Amendments insofar as they applied to political rights.[91]

Cruickshank was part of a parade of disastrous decisions that ruled the
Reconstruction amendments did not protect freedmen from actions of
one citizen against another or from actions by the states. The right to vote
came from the states, and voters had to turn to states for protection. On
the same day in 1875, the Supreme Court ruled in *U.S. v. Reese* that attempts by county officials in Kentucky to prevent blacks from voting could
not be prosecuted under the Enforcement Acts. It ruled unconstitutional
sections 3 and 4 of the Enforcement Act of 1870. Those sections provided
for the federal prosecution of officials who stopped eligible voters from
exercising the franchise and of citizens who obstructed or intimidated
voters, but the court ruled that since these sections, unlike prior sections,
did not specifically mention race but only referred to the earlier sections,
they were too broad and fell outside the Fifteenth Amendment. Federal
protection for the freedpeople was crumbling.[92]

In 1875, led by Benjamin Butler in the House, the Republicans used
their large majority in the lame duck session of the outgoing Forty-third
Congress to pass a final civil rights bill. After Charles Sumner's death in
March 1874, Republicans had reintroduced a bill that he had originally
sponsored that moved beyond political equality toward a fuller social

90. Foner, 530–31.
91. Michael Kent Curtis, *No State Shall Abridge: The 14th Amendment and the Bill of
    Rights* (Durham, NC: Duke University Press, 1986), 178–80; Foner, 530–31.
92. Curtis, 178–80; Keith, 155–57.

equality by prohibiting racial discrimination in public accommodations. Opponents attacked it as a dangerous expansion of federal power that threatened the progress made in the South and would only feed the corruption of Southern governments. Newspapers publicized the bitter debates in Congress and created caricatures of lazy and dependent freedmen. A weakened version of the bill, stripped of its prohibition of segregation in schools, passed in the closing days of the session.[93]

Congress, however, failed to pass a more robust Enforcement Act. The Ku Klux Klan Act had expired in 1872, and this left the president without authority to suspend habeas corpus or declare martial law to repress anti-black violence. Republican congressional leadership feared the political costs were too high. The Civil Rights Act banned discrimination by hotels, theaters, and railroads, but it left enforcement up to individual litigation by black plaintiffs in the federal courts. The law was practically a dead letter even before the U.S. Supreme Court ruled it unconstitutional in 1883.[94]

In many ways the Civil Rights Act of 1875 was the last hurrah of Republican Radicals. Individual Radicals would remain active; there would be occasional attempts to enact "force bills" to implement the civil rights legislation of Reconstruction and secure freedmen their rights, but the splintering of the old Radicals into liberal Republicans, Stalwarts, and antimonopolists signaled that other issues had taken precedence and that new alliances were emerging.

The revolutionary optimism of 1865 had vanished. Politics looked different, but the loss of Stalwart Republican hegemony did not mean the ascent of liberal reformers. Liberals learned their lesson in 1872: they were not competitive in national elections. Their surprising influence over Grant and their successful defense of hard money in 1874 only underlined their electoral weakness when voters repudiated the Republicans in that year's election. They would concentrate on working within the two major parties and, increasingly, seek influence through the courts.

Antimonopolism was a rising force, but reform proved neither easy nor pretty. For the rest of the century, antimonopolists put railroads on the defensive. Western railroads fought to retain what they had already secured. Later investigations showed that forty of the more than seventy railroads that received land grants had failed to complete their lines in the time required by their grants. Yet failure to build the required railroads did not mean they had to return the land. The Supreme Court ruled in

---

93. Foner, 532–34; Perman, 139–42.
94. Foner, 533–34, 553–56; Calhoun, 71–79; Heather Cox Richardson, *The Death of Reconstruction: Race, Labor, and Politics in the Post–Civil War North, 1865–1901* (Cambridge, MA: Harvard University Press, 2001), 125–52.

Schulenberg v. Harriman in 1874 that the land belonged to the corporations until Congress passed specific acts forfeiting the grants. The railroads fought a congressional war of delay and attrition to protect their
grants and privileges. A railroad wanted to protect its own land grants, but
it was usually not averse to having its competitors' grants taken away. In
many congressional battles, reformers received aid from the lobbyists of
the rivals of the railroad under attack. By 1887 Congress had reclaimed a
total of 21,323,600 acres. Not until 1890 would Congress pass a general
forfeiture act, which restored all unearned grants to the United States, but
even then there were enough loopholes that tens of millions of acres of
lands that might have been recovered remained in railroad hands.[95]

The antimonopolists had more success in deploying government at the
local and state levels. There was a long common law tradition, which the
Slaughterhouse decision acknowledged, that allowed government to exercise
its police power in pursuit of *Salus populi*, the people's welfare. In *Thorpe v.
Rutland and Burlington Railroad* (1855) the court had held that the rights
given corporations by their charters were not absolute, but rather subject to
new regulations "with a view to the public protection, health, and safety."
Government could stipulate the quality of equipment, the levels of staffing,
the number and timing of trains, the training of workers, and more. All were
necessary for a "well-regulated society." Railroads complained, but in 1874
Chief Justice Edward Ryan of the Wisconsin Supreme Court countered that
railroad complaints about state regulation amounted to tantrums from the
"spoiled children of legislation" who, "after some quarter of a century of legislative favors lavishly showered upon them, unwisely mutiny against the first
serious legislative restraints they have met."[96]

Grant, his party decimated, held on. With his administration weakened
by turmoil in the South, his veto of the inflation bill, corruption, and the
ongoing depression, the president still hoped for an unprecedented third
term. Many suspected that his desire to avoid further intervention in the
South was a bid for Southern white support. The saddest thing about his
desire for a third term was that a man who had admitted he was unprepared
for the presidency feared leaving it because he was equally unprepared for
anything else.[97]

---

95. Much of what follows is from White, 109–33; Paul W. Gates, *History of Public Land
    Law Development* (Washington, DC: [for sale by the Superintendent of Documents,
    U.S. GPO], 1968), 381, 458–60.
96. Quoted in Peter Karsten, "Supervising the 'Spoiled Children of Legislation': Judicial
    Judgments Involving Quasi-Public Corporations in the Nineteenth Century," *American
    Journal of Legal History* 41, no. 3 (July 1997), 322.
97. Perman, 161; McFeely, 404; Calhoun, 54–57.

8

Beginning a Second Century

Louis Simonin was not the most astute Frenchman to write about the United States, but he was among the most opinionated. His own translator disavowed him, condemning views he found "highly reprehensible," but he published Simonin's pamphlet on the Centennial International Exposition of 1876 in Philadelphia because "large-hearted Americans were willing to forgive ingratitude." Even though crowds followed and jeered Turks, Egyptians, Chinese, Japanese, and even Spaniards visiting the Exposition, Americans cared what Northern Europeans, whom they considered equals and rivals, thought about displays of American progress.[1]

Philadelphia mounted the Exposition—the equivalent of a modern World's Fair—on the one hundredth anniversary of American Independence. Despite the depression and an inordinately hot summer, it proved a great success, attracting 9,799,392 visitors (perhaps more, since broken turnstiles failed to record the count on some busy days) to its seventy-four acres before it closed in the fall. Most came from the Northern and Western United States and made at least part of their journey over the Pennsylvania Railroad, which built new facilities to accommodate them.[2]

A European liberal, Simonin ended his pamphlet by lecturing the United States on the necessity for free trade, but his reaction to the Women's Pavilion demonstrated the gendered limits of liberalism. Simonin ridiculed the demonstrations mounted at the Exposition by Susan B. Anthony and Elizabeth Cady Stanton, probably the most consistent liberals in the women's movement. Anthony and Stanton had by 1875 become fixtures on the lyceum circuit, which carried anyone with enough

1. Louis Simonin, A French View of the Grand International Exposition of 1876 Being a Graphic Description, with Criticisms and Remarks, ed. Samuel H. Needles (Philadelphia: Glaxton, Remsen & Haffelfinger, 1877), 1, 13, 61; Robert W. Rydell, All the World's a Fair: Visions of Empire at American International Expositions, 1876–1916 (Chicago: University of Chicago Press, 1984), 14, 18–19, 21–22.
2. Rydell, 10–11; Albert J. Churella, The Pennsylvania Railroad (Philadelphia: University of Pennsylvania Press, 2013), 450–51.

fame or talent to draw a crowd on speaking tours across America. Their celebrity gave them an opportunity both to make a living and to propagate the cause for women's suffrage and equal rights. Simonin, however, predicted that the movement "will soon vanish like smoke." American women, he claimed, appreciated all too well their special status within the home.[3]

Simonin acted as a barometer of French attitudes and prejudices, approving and disapproving in turn Americans and their practices. He disparaged American men, particularly New Englanders, but praised "American ladies—elegant, well-formed, lively in manners, and as amiable as the men of their country are generally wanting in that virtue." Women were, however, also as garish and gaudy as other Americans and passionately fond of sandwiches, ice cream, and "iced, composite drinks" that they sucked through straws.[4]

Simonin sniffed at American popular culture. He noted the Exposition's bakery, where Americans made bad bread from good flour. He was astonished by the American love of processions and parades, their willingness to dress up in strange costumes, and the passion for titles. The profusion of Masons, Knights-Templars, and Odd Fellows in their regalia and the abundance of American judges and colonels amused, astonished, and irritated him in turn. But he rather envied the Americans' "artless patriotism," which had no European equivalent and produced extravagant Fourth of July celebrations across the North. He noted the American devotion to public education and their willingness to tax themselves to pay for it. New York alone spent as much on its public schools as all of France. He nicely marked the distinctive combination of American industry and religiosity by noting that the Singer sewing machine pavilion was near the Bible House, which printed bibles in "every known language and sold them at cost."[5]

To mark progress, it was necessary to emphasize the past so visitors could see the distance traveled. Simonin longed to see Western Indians, but he had to settle for Cherokees, Creeks, Iroquois, and the Indian artifacts that dominated the Smithsonian exhibit in the Government Building. The designers portrayed Indians and their works as the continent's barbaric past, the antithesis of the progressive American future. Simonin also lamented the absence of Southern states, but the South with its embrace of slavery was, like the Indians, consigned to the American past; the Exposition, as the California poet Joaquin Miller put it, was the future, its

3. Simonin, 31.
4. Ibid., 49.
5. Ibid., 24–25, 37, 52, 59, 62, 64–67.

displays "but the acorn from which shall grow the wide-spreading oak of a century's growth." Indians and Southerners were to be reconstructed and assimilated into the progress the Exposition displayed.[6]

I

The absence of Indians and Southerners marked the limits of the crusade for free labor and the unanticipated consequences of progress. Grant, partially out of spite, had turned to the Quakers to supervise some of the reservations. He chose them not because of their administrative accomplishments but rather because of their symbolic value. They were pacifists, and the myth of peaceful relations between Pennsylvania Quakers and the Indians had entered American culture long before.[7]

With what became known as the peace policy, Grant resorted to the old program of delegation, subsidy, and fee-based administration to achieve governmental ends. He turned the reservations over to Christian denominations to run and supervise. The most surprising thing about Grant's peace policy was that anyone thought the churches were any more capable of administering the reservations than the Indian Office.[8]

Congress pushed other changes in the early 1870s. As the Board of Indian Commissioners recommended, Congress abolished the treaty system, but not for the reasons given by the board and not with the results the commissioners wished. Treaty making ended because of the backlash to James Joy's attempts to use the Osage Indian treaty to transfer Indian land directly to his railroad. Joy had inadvertently united popular grievance with existing congressional rivalries. The Constitution reserved to the Senate the power of advice and consent on treaties, and the House had long resented being shut out. Since the House had to appropriate money for Indian Affairs and land purchases, it used its power of the purse to tack an amendment onto an appropriations bill in 1871 declaring that there would be no new treaties, although tribes would retain their status

6. Simonin, 56; W. D. Howells, "A Sennight of the Centennial," *Atlantic Monthly* (1876), 103.

7. Clyde A. Milner, *With Good Intentions: Quaker Work among the Pawnees, Otos, and Omahas in the 1870s* (Lincoln: University of Nebraska Press, 1982), 1–26; Francis Paul Prucha, *The Great Father: The United States Government and the American Indians* (Lincoln: University of Nebraska Press, 1984), 1: 480–83, 512–15.

8. Ibid., 1: 512–14; Francis Paul Prucha, *American Indian Policy in Crisis: Christian Reformers and the Indian, 1865–1900* (Norman: University of Oklahoma Press, 1976), 51–52; Paul Andrew Hutton, *Phil Sheridan and His Army* (Lincoln: University of Nebraska Press, 1985), 113–17, 186–200.

as semi-sovereign nations and existing treaties would be honored. The change was important, but agreements that were virtually identical to treaties and approved by both the House and Senate continued to be negotiated.[9]

By 1872 the peace policy was in full flower. Churches controlled seventy Indian agencies containing a quarter of a million people. Churchmen proved no more honest, vigorous, or competent than the old Indian agents. The widespread corruption of the Interior Department continued. Columbus Delano, the secretary of the Interior from 1870 to 1875 and an intimate of the Cookes, made that department a hothouse for scandal. Zachariah Chandler, who succeeded him and who benefited from the theft of Indian allotments in Michigan, was, if anything, worse.[10]

Evangelizing, "civilizing," and promoting the assimilation of Indians were hardly new; what distinguished Grant's peace policy was its urgency. What in earlier periods had seemed the work of generations by the 1870s had to be accomplished immediately. If the United States did not transform Indians, many Americans believed that they would vanish, ground up by the relentless advance of the American nation (and there were some Americans who were happy enough to see this happen).[11]

Commissioner of Indian Affairs Ely Parker became one of the victims of the convoluted struggle over Indian affairs. He never fully trusted the reformers of the Board of Indian Commissioners; nor did they trust him. An Indian intellectual and activist, he sought to operate within the constraints imposed by American power, and to use the tools of the larger society—treaties, schools, laws, churches, politics, and voluntary organizations—to allow Indians to maintain diminished but viable and distinctive communities within the larger nation. He failed. The Board of Indian Commissioners accused him of fraud—apparently falsely—and forced him to resign in 1871.[12]

9. H. Craig Miner, *The End of Indian Kansas: A Study of Cultural Revolution, 1854–1871*, ed. William E. Unrau (Lawrence: Regents Press of Kansas, 1978), 27–34, 121–32; Prucha, *The Great Father*, 527–34; Paul W. Gates, *Fifty Million Acres: Conflicts over Kansas Land Policy, 1854–1890* (New York: Atherton Press, 1966), 194–229.

10. Prucha, *American Indian Policy in Crisis*, 41–46, 58–60; Mark W. Summers, *The Era of Good Stealings* (New York: Oxford University Press, 1993), 196–97, 268–69; Elliott West, *The Last Indian War: The Nez Perce Story* (New York: Oxford University Press, 2009), 101–13.

11. Brian W. Dippie, *The Vanishing American: White Attitudes and U.S. Indian Policy* (Lawrence: University Press of Kansas, 1991), 10–11, 120–24.

12. C. Joseph Genetin-Pilawa, *Crooked Paths to Allotment: The Fight over Federal Indian Policy after the Civil War* (Chapel Hill: University of North Carolina Press, 2012), 73–90; Frederick E. Hoxie, *This Indian Country: American Indian Activists and the*

The seemingly ubiquitous Francis Walker succeeded him. Walker knew nothing about Indians, but his desire to remain in Washington to keep working on the *Statistical Atlas* led him to accept appointment as commissioner of Indian affairs. In 1873 he published "The Indian Question," a version of his annual report; it was one of the most chilling documents of the late nineteenth century. Full of statistics, calculations, and analyses of particular social and political examples and radiating confidence in human progress, it was quintessentially liberal. It appealed to a rational philanthropy and restraints on the state's ability to exercise violence, and yet it made the liberal reformer a frightening figure. Although the dispossession of the Indian was the currency of the age, Walker to his credit wanted to leave the Indians enough to establish prosperous homes. What was chilling was the price he demanded in exchange.[13]

The "modern Indian question," Walker explained, divided itself in two: first, "What shall be done with the Indian as an obstacle to national progress?" and second, "What shall be done with him when, and so far as, he ceases to oppose or obstruct the extension of railways and settlements?" In effect, the first question dealt with Indians as obstacles to white homemaking. The second question dealt with creating proper Indian homes.[14]

The first part of Walker's question was still playing out when he asked it. Although he thought that no more than sixty-four thousand Indians were actively resisting or likely to resist American expansion in 1873, Walker did not downplay the danger they posed. Quoting an estimate of Sherman and other generals, he wrote that the fighting that had followed Chivington's slaughter at Sand Creek in 1864 led to the withdrawal of eight thousand troops who would otherwise have been fighting the Confederacy. Hundreds of American soldiers and many border settlers lost their lives to kill fifteen or twenty warriors "at an expense of more than a million dollars apiece." The exactitude of the figures was less important than the conclusion that such Indian wars were unnecessary, "useless and expensive."[15]

Peace by whatever means necessary was Walker's answer to the first part of the Indian Question. Peace allowed the building of the railroads, and

_____

     Place They Made (New York: Penguin, 2012), 1–11, 119–238; Prucha, *American Indian Policy in Crisis*, 44.

13. Margo J. Anderson, *The American Census: A Social History* (New Haven, CT: Yale University Press, 1988), 78, 88–90; James Phinney Munroe, *A Life of Francis Amasa Walker* (New York: H. Holt, 1923), 110–27; F. A. Walker, "The Indian Question," *North American Review* 116, no. 239 (1873).

14. Walker, 337.

15. Elliott West, *The Contested Plains: Indians, Goldseekers, & the Rush to Colorado* (Lawrence: University Press of Kansas, 1998), 271–307; Walker, 353.

in stopping Indians from obstructing American progress, Walker's approach was instrumental. The Americans were — or rather "the Anglo-Saxon" was — civilized, the Indians "savage." They were "wild men," and as with wild beasts, the best policy was "what is easiest or safest" in a given situation. What to do with Indians once they were conquered was a moral problem, but conquering Indians was not. Indians had "no right to prevent the settling of this continent by a race which has not only the power to conquer but also the disposition to improve and adorn the land, which he has suffered to remain a wilderness."[16]

Walker, like Sherman and railroad executives, believed the railroad would provide the means of subduing the Indians. He thought, in the short run, the vulnerability of white settlers necessitated "temporizing with hostile savages," preserving for them large reservations and providing them with annuities as a way to protect both the railroads and settlers. But this was only a temporary solution. Within a few years, as Americans established homes, the most powerful Indian nations would be "thrown in entire helplessness on the mercy of the government." A "reasonable policy of concession" would hold in check the "whole body of dangerous Indians" until "the advance of population shall render them incapable of mischief." Temporarily feeding the Indians on large reservations was cheaper than fighting them. Keeping them on the reservations would be the job of the military; they would pursue any Indians who dared leave.[17]

The rest of Walker's article was prospective. Walker dismissed arguments that the Indians were doomed to disappear, were intractably savage, or would acquire only the faults of whites and none of their virtues, citing evidence that the large majority of Indians were "now either civilized or partially civilized." He put particular emphasis on the Cherokees — "entitled to be ranked among civilized communities" — as an example of a larger future success.[18]

Walker urged that the reservation policy be made "the general and permanent policy of the government... secluding Indians from whites for the good of both races." The alternative, he feared, would be racial mixing and a Western population that sprang from white fathers and Indian mothers. Rendered landless, the remaining Indians would be reduced to bands of what he called American gypsies, people without civic standing or permanent homes, camping on the borders of American settlements. The reservations Walker proposed were not, however, those guaranteed the tribes by treaty. There were too many of them and too inconveniently

16. Walker, 348, 77.
17. Ibid., 345–46, 347–54, 355.
18. Ibid., 358–62.

located; instead the Indians were to be concentrated. For the Great Plains, he imagined two reservations: the existing Indian Territory and a second on the northern plains. Within the bounds of these reservations, the government would protect Indians from white intrusion and liberally provide for them, but Indians would be prohibited from leaving. The government would exert "a rigid reformatory control," requiring them "to learn and practice the arts of industry." The government's right to do this sprang from the "supreme law of public safety" that allowed it to discipline paupers and imprison criminals. Walker could so cavalierly classify Indians with paupers and criminals—something the North had vehemently objected to when Southerners attempted to do much the same thing in the black codes of the South—because the Indians were not citizens and enjoyed none of the rights or privileges of citizenship.[19]

Walker presented the peace policy as a moral obligation and a form of philanthropy. The United States was honor-bound to recognize the Indians' status as "the original occupants and owners of substantially all the territory embraced within our limits." The advance of the Americans deprived them of their existing livelihood and cut them off from necessary resources. The Americans could not simply dispossess them. Walker stressed that Americans had incurred a debt and obligation to the Indians and that "Honor and interest urge the same imperative claim." Americans owed it to their own posterity to "do justice and show mercy to a race which has been impoverished that we might be made rich."[20]

To train Indians for contract freedom, the government would confine them and subject them to a regimen of industrial education and labor until they could demonstrate sufficient "civilization." If they tried to escape, they would be arrested and returned to reservations. Their education in freedom and civilization had devolved into coercion, whose rationale sounded much like the slaveholders' justifications for the slavery just ended in the South: the care and feeding of an inferior people who needed to be forced to labor and adopt Christian civilization. Some of that coercion would ironically come from black soldiers—whom the Lakotas called black Wasichu or black white men. Western Reconstruction had taken an odd turn, indeed.[21]

The people with the least say in answering the Indian Question were the Indians themselves. Most recognized that change was inevitable, but they did not see American dictation as inevitable. Walker praised the

19. Walker, 355, 376–77, 385–87.
20. Ibid., 388.
21. John G. Neihardt, *Black Elk Speaks* (Lincoln: University of Nebraska Press, 1979, orig. ed. 1932), 267.

Cherokees, but he did not consult them. Speaking of Indian Territory, John Beeson later identified the principal mistake of legislators and the American public as the belief "that the Indians of this territory are but savages, and that their country can be monopolized by railroad speculators and governed by the appointees of the president of the United States instead of those of their own selection." Beeson favored development. He just wanted development to take place under the governments of Indian nations and under Indian control. Where to the West the Plains tribes would embark on a path of gallant but futile resistance, the Cherokees, led by William Potter Ross, a Cherokee, and Beeson, would seek to wield their treaties as weapons and work through politics and the courts. This battle would continue long beyond the nineteenth century.[22]

Indians did not reject everything Americans offered or demanded. They had long borrowed from whites. Yet even the Cherokees, whom Walker praised, had ideals of landholding, property, matrilineal descent, and a clan system foreign to the American Protestant home. The Indians rarely desired the kind of homes that whites offered and black people were often denied.[23]

Walker's plan for peaceful coercion had failed by 1876. It had gone off the tracks along with progress in 1873. The Panic of 1873 littered the western prairies and plains with the wrecks of railroads, or as John Murray Forbes of the Chicago, Burlington and Quincy, put it, collections of rails, ties, bridges, and rolling stock "called railroads, many of them laid down in places where much of it was practically useless." The Northern Pacific, whose problems triggered the Panic, stalled in the Dakotas. The bankrupt Atchison, Topeka and Santa Fe was derelict in western Kansas, and the Texas Pacific was stuck in central Texas. These were roads without traffic or purpose, except to sell bonds and stock. As was often the case with the western railroads, failure was as transformative as success. The bankruptcy of the railroads spurred their attempts to get traffic, forced men who worked for them to seek other ways to make a living, and helped produce environmental disaster. The first step involved the doom of the bison, which Americans colloquially referred to as buffalo. The slaughter of the bison, in turn, aggravated the conflicts with the Plains Indians, which would cost Simonin his opportunity to see them in Philadelphia.[24]

22. John Beeson, "To the American Public," ed. Newberry Library, Graff 234 (Fort Gibson, Indian Territory, 1874); Hoxie, 99–141.
23. Prucha, *The Great Father*, 491–92; Prucha, *Indian Policy in Crisis*, 381–82; Hoxie, 141.
24. Richard White, *Railroaded: The Transcontinentals and the Making of Modern America* (New York: Norton, 2011), 83–87; Gerald Berk, *Alternative Tracks: The Constitution of American Industrial Order, 1865–1917* (Baltimore, MD: Johns Hopkins University Press, 1994), 38.

The massive herds of bison had been an ecological anomaly for millennia because it is unusual for one animal so thoroughly to dominate an area as large as the Great Plains. Bison had been a kind of weed species, its numbers and range expanding and contracting along with climatic cycles. Only with the introduction of the horse in the seventeenth century had the nomadic Indian cultures of the Great Plains begun to evolve into their classic form and more fully exploit the herds. In the early nineteenth century the combination of drought, disease, competition with horses for winter habitat, settlement along the eastern margins of their range, and hunting pressure had taken a heavy toll on the herds. The railroads delivered the coup de grâce.[25]

During the fall of 1873 the bodies of tens of thousands of bison stripped of their skins lay rotting and stinking along the banks of the Arkansas River. George Reighard and men like him had put them there. Reighard had hauled goods for the railroad and then hunted out of Dodge City on the Atchison, Topeka and Santa Fe. He killed the bison "for the hide and the money it would bring." Good hunters, if positioned downwind, could use a Sharp "big fifty" to drop bison, one after another, while the living grazed placidly alongside the dead. Asked years afterward whether he felt any pity for the animals, Reighard said no: "It was a business with me. I had my money invested in that outfit…I killed all I could."[26]

White hunters took about 4,374,000 from the herds south of the Platte River between 1872 and 1874, dwarfing the estimated Indian kill of a little more than a million animals during the same period. These bison would be turned into boots for European armies or machine belts attached to the steam engines of eastern factories. The hunters worked with frightening speed. By 1875 the Southern herd was for all practical purposes extinct. The smaller northern herd survived, protected by the Lakotas and the failure of the Northern Pacific to push into buffalo country.[27]

The slaughter of the buffalo was not part of some larger American imperial plan to subjugate Indians; nor did it necessarily doom Indian peoples, although it certainly hurt them. On the Southern Plains, the Comanches had already shifted to a pastoralism that relied on horses and cattle as well as bison. But buffalo had a religious and cultural significance

25. West, *The Contested Plains*, 69–72, 233–35; Andrew C. Isenberg, *The Destruction of the Bison: An Environmental History, 1750–1920* (Cambridge: Cambridge University Press, 2000), 1–122.
26. Richard White, "Animals and Enterprise," in *The Oxford History of the American West*, ed. Clyde A. Milner, Carol A. O'Connor, and Martha A. Sandweiss (New York: Oxford University Press, 1994), 237, 248–49; Isenberg, 131–36.
27. Isenberg, 130–40; West, *The Contested Plains*, 39–41, 69–70, 72–73.

for both nomads and agriculturalists on the Great Plains that led the tribes to hunt even after hunts became both meager and dangerous.[28]

The most powerful native groups fought to monopolize and control the remaining bison. On the Southern Plains the Comanches, along with their Kiowa and Southern Cheyenne allies, dominated. On the northern plains the Lakotas, the most westerly group of Sioux, along with their Arapaho and Northern Cheyenne allies, controlled the lands north of the Platte River.

The Comanches fell first. They had revived their fortunes during the Civil War, but in the early 1870s the army began to protect the Texan advance into Comancheria in central and western Texas. Between 1871 and 1875 the Southern Plains descended into chaos. Most Comanches and their allies used the reservations as supply depots, coming in only seasonally. Off the reservations, multitribal bands emerged, part of a long tradition of ethnic mixing. Raiders struck into Texas, carrying off cattle to trade to *comancheros*, Mexican American traders from New Mexico, and to Anglo liquor traders and horse thieves, who began operating within hunting grounds guaranteed to the Indians by treaty. In response, the American cavalry struck the Comanches and their allies hard in 1871 and 1872, driving them west into the Llano Estacado or onto the reservations.[29]

With the Indians returning to the reservations and violence diminishing in Texas, there seemed a real chance for peace if the Americans could observe the terms of the Medicine Lodge Treaty. Gen. John Pope thought military posts along the Arkansas River could both prevent Indians from raiding southward and be used to evict white hunters, liquor traders, and horse and cattle thieves from the Indians' hunting territories. Generals Sheridan and Sherman, however, wanted a military solution aimed at Indians rather than whites. The army did nothing to stop white buffalo hunters, who in 1873 and 1874 carried industrial slaughter onto Kiowa and Comanche hunting grounds. Taking matters in their own hands, the Comanches attacked the hunters at Adobe Walls. The hunters' rifles proved as lethal against the Indians as they had against the bison. The attack failed.[30]

American officials floundered in the midst of a crisis of their own making. The Quakers, in charge of the Comanches under the peace

---

28. Pekka Hämäläinen, *The Comanche Empire* (New Haven, CT: Yale University Press, 2008), 320; West, *The Contested Plains*, 39–41, 69–70, 72–73; Richard White, *The Roots of Dependency: Subsistence, Environment, and Social Change among the Choctaws, Pawnees, and Navajos* (Lincoln: University of Nebraska Press, 1983), 206–7.

29. Hämäläinen, 334–36.

30. Gary Clayton Anderson, *Ethnic Cleansing and the Indian: The Crime That Haunts America* (Norman: University of Oklahoma Press, 2014), 278–81; Hämäläinen, 335–36.

policy, proved indecisive and ineffective as they quarreled with the army. Army generals, meanwhile, fought among themselves. For Sheridan, the Indians had become racial enemies to be subdued and punished. In August 1874 soldiers who had moved onto the Indian agencies in violation of the peace policy tried to disarm a band of Kiowas and Comanches who had come to the Wichita Agency to collect annuities. They provoked a skirmish in which soldiers killed six or seven Indians. The Comanches, Cheyennes, and Kiowas fled to the west, where they joined bands that had never come into the agency. This was the Red River "War." That fall and early winter the army hunted down the refugees, burned their villages and supplies, captured or killed their horses, and accepted their surrender in family groups or small bands. The Indians' defeat was more economic than military. They could no longer sustain themselves.[31]

Sheridan and Sherman proved vindictive in victory. They wanted captives tried by military tribunals, and they wanted executions. The officer put in charge of prosecuting the prisoners could find no evidence that a "state of war" ever existed, and without a state of war military commissions had no authority. The army had precipitated the violence; the Indians had fled into territory promised to them by the treaty, and they had resisted when the soldiers pursued them. Sherman only partially backed down. The army exiled seventy-one Kiowa, Cheyenne, and Comanche captives to prison in Florida. Sherman wanted them imprisoned until they died. Grant backed him. This was the peace policy in action.[32]

The defeat of the Comanches in 1875 left only the Lakotas and their allies as an armed force capable of contesting the American advance. Their situation was similar to that on the southern plains with the Indians split between bands—Red Cloud's Oglalas and Spotted Tail's Brules— that had taken up fairly permanent residence at the agencies on the Great Sioux reservation and other groups that rarely came to the agencies. The Americans had negotiated a right of way for the Northern Pacific across the reservation, but the more westerly Lakota groups—Sitting Bull's Hunkpapas, the Sans Arc, those Oglalas who followed Crazy Horse, the Miniconjous, and the Sihásapa or Blackfoot Sioux—vowed to prevent the railroad from crossing their lands. They harassed the road's surveyors and clashed with the army in 1872 and again in 1873.[33]

31. Hämäläinen, 335–41; G. C. Anderson, 280–84.
32. G. C. Anderson, 285–87; Hämäläinen, 338–41.
33. G. C. Anderson, 289–309; Jeffrey Ostler, *The Plains Sioux and U.S. Colonialism from Lewis and Clark to Wounded Knee* (Cambridge: Cambridge University Press, 2004), 51–54.

In effect, the Lakotas created a dual policy. The Brules and Oglalas maintained peace with the Americans, but aggressively attacked the Pawnees, Crows, Arikaras, and other rivals for the dwindling bison herds. Those Lakotas who followed Sitting Bull obstructed the railroad, which would mean death to the bison, and they also attacked neighboring groups who sought access to the northern herds.[34]

The bankruptcy of the Northern Pacific, which brought construction to a halt, should have eased the crisis on the northern plains. It did not, because of divisions within the army that were similar to those on the southern plains. Colonel David Stanley was one of many officers angry over the abandonment of the Bozeman Trail and the resistance of the Lakotas to the Northern Pacific, but he had complicated attitudes toward the Lakotas. He sympathized with the agency Indians, yet regarded those Lakotas who stayed away from the agencies and threatened Indians willing to conciliate the whites as "a people who were practically and professedly assassins." He thought the best way to reduce Lakota resistance and force the Indians into the agencies was to deprive them of the land promised in the Fort Laramie Treaty and promote white settlement in the Black Hills, Powder River, and Yellowstone country, the last of the productive buffalo grounds. His desire to concentrate the Lakotas on smaller reservations or remove them to Indian Territory converged with the larger aims of the peace policy. Stanley commanded the 1873 expedition to protect surveyors. He also took geologists with him, but he was not necessarily searching for gold, and he found none.[35]

General Sheridan desired a military occupation of lands promised to the Lakotas, but he remained committed to enforcing the Fort Laramie Treaty until ordered to do otherwise. In 1874 he secured permission to send another exploring party into the Black Hills. Science became subservient to military strategy. Sheridan thought that war with the Lakotas was inevitable, and he had recalled portions of the Seventh Cavalry from the South to cow the Lakotas. He sent Custer into the Black Hills to find a site for a post to strengthen the army's position. It included ten companies of the Seventh Cavalry and a geologist. Custer dispatched messengers who announced a massive gold find. The expedition's geologist refuted the claim, but it had already set miners in motion.[36]

34. Richard White, "The Winning of the West: The Expansion of the Western Sioux in the Eighteenth and Nineteenth Centuries," *Journal of American History* 65, no. 2 (1978); G. C. Anderson, 292–93.
35. G. C. Anderson, 289–93; Catherine Franklin, "Black Hills and Bloodshed: The U.S. Army and the Invasion of Lakota Land, 1868–1876," *Montana: The Magazine of Western History* 63, no. 2 (2013): 31–32; Prucha, *American Indian Policy in Crisis*, 108–11.
36. Franklin, 34–35.

Sheridan ordered intruders banished from the Black Hills, and Generals Alfred Terry and George Crook sent soldiers to evict the miners. Terry supported American efforts to obtain the Black Hills, but he wanted the treaty enforced until then: "it is the greatest importance that any attempt to defy the law and to trample on the rights secured by the Sioux...should be met with the most vigorous manner at the very outset." He considered the Black Hills "absolutely closed to intruders." His troops removed the miners. Crook sympathized with the miners whom his troops evicted: "Their side of this story should be heard, as the settlers who develop our mines and open the frontier to civilization are the nation's wards no less than their more fortunate fellows, the Indians." Still, he evicted them.[37]

There was no need for war between Lakotas and Americans in 1875. Although the peace policy had often been an oxymoron, as illustrated by an ugly little war against the Modocs in California in 1873 that followed years of a genocidal assault on Indian peoples in northern California and southern Oregon, there were significant constituencies for peace among the Americans and the Lakotas. Spotted Tail and Red Cloud, complicated and sophisticated men, hated each other, but both feared war with the United States. The Lakotas under Sitting Bull, a less complicated and less sophisticated man at this stage of his life, were ready to resist the Americans, but if the Americans observed the Fort Laramie Treaty there should have been no Americans to resist. The treaty banned Americans from Lakota territory, and Crook and Terry had enforced the ban.[38]

The Americans squandered all of this by dispatching a third expedition under Richard Henry Dodge into the Black Hills in the summer of 1875. This time they did discover gold. Lieutenant John Bourke sent a private note to Sheridan, which indicates that by this time gold had become a central part of American policy: "The main purpose of the expedition, as I understand it, has been accomplished, in the discovery of gold." Crook and Terry, however, remained determined to keep Americans out of the Black Hills. Their troops scoured the region in 1875 and by November had once more emptied it of miners, but the government was wavering.[39]

Grant abandoned efforts to enforce the Fort Laramie Treaty. With Secretary of the Interior Chandler, both corrupt and incompetent, and with the press falsely reporting the region already occupied by miners, the government ordered the army to ease up on efforts to evict intruders, and

37. G. C. Anderson, 295–96, 298–301; Franklin, 36, 38.
38. Benjamin Madley, *An American Genocide: The United States and the California Indian Catastrophe* (New Haven, CT: Yale University Press, 2016), 333–35.
39. G. C. Anderson, 296–300; Franklin, 38–40.

Grant acquiesced. He sent the Allison Commission to demand the cession of the Black Hills. The Lakotas refused. Senator Allison recommended that Congress simply fix a price and legislate the sale without Lakota consent. In early December 1875, Chandler demanded all Indians leave the Yellowstone River Valley, where they had a perfect right to be, and return to their agencies. If they did not, they would be declared hostile. Even if the Indians had agreed to come in, they could not move in the deep snows and bitter cold of winter. In February the secretary of war ordered troops to force to them to return to their agencies.[40]

That the Grant administration, the proponent of the peace policy, wanted the army to move against the Lakotas in clear violation of the Fort Laramie Treaty while Grant refused to act forcefully in the South revealed much about how far the Republicans had retreated from their ambitions in 1865. The party had failed to secure the homogeneous citizenry it imagined in the South. It had not secured peace in the West. And the prosperity it had promised had turned to ashes. The bankruptcy of the western railroads created a brief opportunity for the Grant administration to actually pursue the peace that the peace policy promised, but the government squandered it. Railroads, desperate for revenue, encouraged the slaughter of the buffalo, which sparked warfare on the Great Plains, and the administration, at war with itself, ultimately allowed the invasion of the Black Hills, which brought resistance from the Lakotas.

The American campaign against the Lakotas ended attempts to establish encampments of the Plains Indians at the Philadelphia Exposition that Simonin had so eagerly anticipated, and the American attempt to force those Lakotas gathered under Sitting Bull and Crazy Horse into the agencies brought resistance that was splashed across the papers that year. In annual reports for 1874 and 1875 the commissioner of Indian affairs had ventured that there would never again be "a general Indian war" in the United States.[41]

In the spring of 1876 the Americans had a general Indian war on their hands. The Lakotas and their allies stymied and beat back American troops invading their country. Black Elk, a Lakota and a cousin of Crazy Horse, the brilliant Lakota war leader, was thirteen that spring, and years later he remembered the events of the American invasion with a vividness that came both from their drama and from a lifetime of recounting them. His aunt gave him a pistol and told him he was a man now. The Lakotas, Black Elk said, "were in their own country and doing no harm. They only

---

40. Prucha, *American Indian Policy in Crisis*, 170–71; G. C. Anderson, 297–300.
41. U.S. Office of Indian Affairs, "Annual Report of the Commissioner of Indian Affairs to the Secretary of the Interior for the Year 1875" (Washington, DC: U.S. GPO, 1875), 11.

wanted to be left alone." He said it as an old man recalling the simplicity of a thirteen-year-old, but what he said was true enough.[42]

The Lakotas, after defeating General Crook's column on the Rosebud, formed a large encampment on the river they called the Greasy Grass and the Americans the Little Bighorn. It was, Black Elk recalled, so large a village that you "could hardly count the teepees." There were probably about twelve hundred lodges in six separate tribal circles that extended three miles along the river. Together they numbered around two thousand warriors, along with numerous old men, women, and children. But Crook's column was not the only American force converging on the Lakotas. Gen. Alfred Terry was approaching from the east and Col. John Gibbon from the west. Terry sent George Armstrong Custer and about six hundred men of the Seventh Cavalry, a unit ubiquitous in Gilded Age conflicts, to find and attack the Indians. For the first time, all twelve companies of the regiment were together under Custer's command.[43]

On June 25, 1876, Custer struck the village on the Greasy Grass. "Hurrah, boys, we've got them," he supposedly told his men as he prepared the attack, but this was not the Washita. He sent Maj. Marcus Reno in from the south, while he swung north. The soldiers, Black Elk recalled, "came there to kill us."[44]

Black Elk heard the warning—"The chargers are coming!"—and caught sight of Major Reno's detachment descending on the southern end of the village where the Hunkpapas—one of the Lakota tribes—were camped. The soldiers "came out of the dust...on their big horses. They looked big and strong and tall." The Hunkpapas broke in confusion, but were rallied by Gall, another war leader. Black Elk described a valley dark "with dust and smoke and there were only shadows and many cries and hoofs and guns." From the dust he heard a great cry, "Crazy Horse is coming," and so he was, rallying the Lakotas to meet Custer, who was attacking from the north with his detachment of five companies of cavalry. The battle became a chaotic running fight: "Men and horses were all

42. Raymond J. DeMallie, ed., *The Sixth Grandfather: Black Elk's Teachings Given to John G. Neihardt* (Lincoln: University of Nebraska Press, 1984); for a carefully crafted evaluation of the Neihardt account of Black Elk, see Neihardt, *Black Elk Speaks*, 91–92.

43. Robert M. Utley, *The Indian Frontier of the American West, 1846–1890* (Albuquerque: University of New Mexico Press, 1984), 183–84; Neihardt, *Black Elk Speaks*, 105–6; T. J. Stiles, *Custer's Trials: A Life on the Frontier of a New America* (New York: Knopf, 2015), 441–47.

44. Neihardt, *Black Elk Speaks*, 105; Robert V. Hine and John Mack Faragher, *The American West: An Interpretive History* (New Haven, CT: Yale University Press, 2000), 254.

mixed up and fighting in the water, and it was like hail falling in the river." The Lakotas stripped and mutilated the dead soldiers where they fell. The Lakota artist Red Horse graphically captured the fight and mutilations in ledgerbook drawings he made in 1881. Cheyennes, who had lost relatives at Sand Creek years before, cut off the soldiers' hands and feet. Black Elk killed a dying soldier and scalped him. His mother "gave a big tremolo just for me when she saw my first scalp."[45]

Every man in the five companies with Custer died, and Reno's command barely escaped the same fate. The dead soldiers had been born in New York, Ohio, Pennsylvania, Michigan, and other northern states as well as a few border states, but some had come from France, England, Spain, Poland, Denmark, Scotland, Switzerland, and Canada. The numerous Irish- and German-born soldiers far outnumbered the few from the South. Before being soldiers they had been shoemakers, coopers, farmers, goldsmiths, clerks, and plasterers. They died alongside Crow and Arikara scouts. The Little Bighorn was a minor battle compared not only to the Civil War but to the losses American armies suffered against Indians in the wars of the early republic, but shocking because of its timing. Such defeats were, as the commissioner had claimed, the things of the past. Indians were supposedly no match for the army of a modern industrial nation. When news of the battle came during the Exposition, Americans greeted it with incredulity and outrage.[46]

By 1876, although it was still possible for Indians to win battles, it had become impossible for warriors to win a war against U.S. soldiers. The denouement of Custer's defeat played out over the next year. If summer belonged to warriors, winter still belonged to the army. Warriors had women and children who needed to be protected, and in the bitter cold, with declining bison, they were vulnerable targets if the soldiers could find them and destroy their food supplies and teepees. Thanks to Crow, Pawnee, Shoshone, Arikara, and even Lakota scouts, the army could find them. By the end of winter, the Lakotas and their Cheyenne allies had either surrendered or, like Sitting Bull, fled into Canada. The Lakotas' leading war leader, Crazy Horse, gave himself up, only to be bayoneted to death by white soldiers in September 1877.[47]

The impact of these wars was neither slight nor passing, but they registered more powerfully in culture than in policy. The American press turned warfare on the Great Plains into "Savage War," a trope they

45. Neihardt, *Black Elk Speaks*, 105–13; Utley, 184; Ostler, 62–63.
46. Friends of the Little Bighorn, "List of Soldiers, Oficers, and Civilians at the Little Bighorn," http://www.friendslittlebighorn.com/7th%20Cav%20Muster%20Rolls.htm.
47. Ostler, 66–105.

would use for the rest of the century to describe a country in the midst of bitter and bloody conflict. "Savage War" could be put to work to turn selected social conflicts—between workers and capital, immigrants and the native born, blacks and whites—into equivalents of the Indian wars, which were understood as conflicts between "savagery" and "civilization." Over the longer run Custer's defeat, like the Alamo, became an iconic American battle. On the surface, this seems quite odd. Why celebrate defeat, particularly catastrophic defeat, at the hands of what by any measure was a weaker foe? The answer was that such defeats provided justification for conquest. An invasion of Lakota lands became the noble defense of outnumbered white men against savage warriors. Americans, by this logic, did not invade Indian lands; they simply defended themselves against ruthless enemies. Their ultimate victory was not the work of invasion, conquest, and empire. It was the product of self-defense.[48]

No one exploited the opportunities of savage war more artfully than Buffalo Bill Cody. He had been performing on stage in Taunton, Massachusetts, when the conflict with the Lakotas commenced. He went west to join the Fifth Cavalry as head of scouts. Frank Grouard did the actual tracking, and he marked the complexity of the West and its cultural mixing. The son of a Mormon missionary and a Hawaiian woman, he had been captured by the Lakotas and for a while was one of them. Cody played to sharp divisions, and not the complicated mixtures Grouard represented. Dressed in a showman's vaquero outfit, Cody participated in a skirmish, killing a Cheyenne war leader named Yellow Hair. He scalped Yellow Hair, dramatically yelling, "First scalp for Custer," and took Yellow Hair's weapons and war paraphernalia. Yellow Hair was about to become a show business prop. Cody resigned from the army and embarked for the east as star of a new show, "The First Scalp for Custer." Wearing the same outfit, he killed Yellow Hair nightly on stage. He exhibited Yellow Hair's scalp, war bonnet, and weapons at the theatres until Boston authorities confiscated the scalp. When Cody created his traveling extravaganza, Buffalo Bill's Wild West, in the 1880s, he moved from using dead Indians as his props to recruiting live ones to reenact racial warfare before American and European audiences. Men who had fought Custer at the

48. Richard Slotkin, *The Fatal Environment: The Myth of the Frontier in the Age of Industrialization, 1800–1890* (New York: Atheneum, 1986), 53; Richard White, "Frederick Jackson Turner and Buffalo Bill," in James Grossman, ed., *The Frontier in American Culture: An Exhibition at the Newberry Library, August 26, 1994–January 7, 1995* (Chicago: The Newberry Library, 1994), 7–65.

Little Bighorn would reenact this and other fights in arenas with Buffalo Bill's Wild West.[49]

For the government, however, the war against the Lakotas changed little. In his report, Commissioner of Indian Affairs John Q. Smith in 1876 still spoke of Indian policy as a largely administrative problem, one in which Indians would have little say. It was not, he thought, in the best interests of either Indians or the United States to observe the treaties strictly. The United States would give Indians a "secure home" and "just and equitable laws," but this was a matter for the government, and not Indians, to decide. Public necessity was the supreme law. He noted the resistance of Sitting Bull's followers, but dismissed them as malcontents and desperadoes.[50]

II

The virtual absence of the South from the Exposition, like the absence of Indians, marked the continuation of a bloody struggle, but Grant, willing to commit troops in the West, did not commit them in the South even to save the Republican Party there. Mississippi, with its large black population, was a state that the Republicans should have been able to retain in fair elections, but since 1870 "White Men's Clubs" had dedicated themselves to the restoration of white supremacy. They believed black suffrage was "wrong in principle and disastrous in effect." Members vowed not to hire any black man who voted Republican, but their most effective tactic was violence. Whites created "dead books" that contained the names of black Republicans. By 1875 the murder of black people, particularly political leaders, had become routine. White militia occupied the towns and roads and kept black men from the polls. Gov. Adelbert Ames, Benjamin Butler's son-in-law, called for Grant to send federal troops. There was, he said, a counterrevolution under way; a race was being disenfranchised. They were "to be returned to a country of serfdom—an era of second slavery." Grant acknowledged federal responsibility, but his attorney general told Ames that the government was "tired of the[se] autumnal outbursts in the South." He would act only after Mississippi raised a militia to suppress the violence. Such an answer ignored the political realities in

49. Louis S. Warren, *Buffalo Bill's America: William Cody and the Wild West Show* (New York: Knopf, 2005), 117–22, 168–73.
50. U.S. Office of Indian Affairs, "Annual Report of the Commissioner of Indian Affairs to the Secretary of the Interior for the Year 1876" (Washington, DC: U.S. GPO, 1876), xi–xiv.

Mississippi, where well-armed whites threatened to wipe a black militia "from the face of the earth." Republicans feared that calling out the black militia would incite a race war. The ensuing election became known as the Revolution of 1875. In Yazoo County, with an overwhelming black majority, the Republicans received just seven votes. The new Democratic legislature impeached and removed the lieutenant governor. It also impeached Governor Ames, who resigned and fled the state.[51]

According to John R. Lynch, the only Mississippi Republican congressman to gain reelection in 1875, Grant told him that he decided not to send troops to Mississippi after Ohio Republicans warned him that doing so would cost the Republicans Ohio in 1876. Without Ohio, the Republicans' chances of retaining the presidency were nil. Action in Mississippi would also hurt Grant's chances to woo back the Liberal Republicans It was a straightforward political calculation.[52]

On July 8, 1876, roughly two weeks after the Battle of the Little Bighorn, hundreds of armed whites led by former Confederate Gen. Matthew C. Butler attacked the largely African American town of Hamburg, South Carolina. The precipitating cause was a quarrel between two local white farmers and the black militia of Hamburg. When the militia refused Butler's demand to disarm, the white mob, armed with a cannon, murdered the sheriff and besieged the armory. They hunted down the militia and summarily executed five freedmen in the "Dead Ring" near the town's railroad trestle.

According to testimony before the U.S. Senate, when a member of the crowd asked, "Well, now, what will we do with the rest?" the answer was "By God, let's pile them up like frogs and shoot them off." The mob did not execute the remaining militiamen, but the whites, many of them now drunk, broke into houses and stores, calling out the names of the executed men, and then telling their companions "he don't answer." This brought gales of laughter. So too did a corpse in the road. "By God, he is looking at the moon and don't wink his eyes," a member of the mob chortled. Alfred Minyard was still living when someone "cut off a big piece of meat from off his rump." The next morning Prince Rivers, a Union veteran and the town's African American mayor, convened a coroner's inquest. Rivers issued arrest warrants for eighty-seven white men, including Matthew Butler and Benjamin Tillman, a leader of the Red Shirts who set out to

51. William S. McFeely, *Grant: A Biography* (New York: Norton, 1981), 421–23; Eric Foner, *Reconstruction: America's Unfinished Revolution, 1863–1877* (New York: Harper & Row, 1988), 558–63.
52. Michael F. Holt, *By One Vote: The Disputed Presidential Election of 1876* (Lawrence: University Press of Kansas, 2008), 47.

violently suppress the black vote. The Democratic South Carolina legislature elected in 1876 made Butler a senator. Tillman was a future governor.[53]

Ultimately for Simonin, the absence of Indians and Southerners mattered much less than the evidence for Northern progress on display at the
Exposition. He recognized that Americans were creating an industrial
society whose possibilities threatened European economic dominance.
Although the United States was only ten years removed from a devastating Civil War and suffered the grip of a depression, Simonin accepted
that it had become an economic powerhouse. He feared that Americans
would soon learn to dispense with Europe, although Europeans could not
dispense with the United States so long as it fed and clothed them. He
warned the French, "Even our wines and brandies are not safe from their
attempts at imitation."[54]

Like virtually all other intellectuals who visited the Exposition, Simonin
condensed its meaning down to the 680-ton steam engine from the
George H. Corliss works in Providence, Rhode Island. The "walking-
beam" engine transformed the up-and-down motion of pistons into the
circular motion of a flywheel 30 feet in diameter. "Eight miles of shafting"
distributed its power to a hall full of "useful machines, all ingeniously
contrived," which spun silk, cut wood, made envelopes, rifled gun barrels,
embroidered cloth, and performed dozens of other tasks. They were not
wrong in seeing the engine's ability to enhance and replace human labor
as the message of Machinery Hall. The aged poet Walt Whitman sat
transfixed before the Corliss for half an hour.[55]

The opening ceremony of the Exposition presented the machine as a
product of human ingenuity that eliminated older human skills. With
simple instructions from the machine's designer, the president of the
United States and the emperor of Brazil could mount twin platforms and

53. U.S. Senate, South Carolina Committee, "'Testimony as to the Denial of the Elective
    Franchise in South Carolina at the Elections of 1875 and 1876' in Miscellaneous
    Documents of the Senate of the United States for the Second Session of the Forty-
    Fourth Congress," (Washington, DC: U.S. GPO, 1877), 712, 734; Stephen Budiansky,
    The Bloody Shirt: Terror after Appomattox (New York: Viking, 2008), 221–54; Foner,
    570–71.

54. Simonin, 61, 62, 68–69.

55. J. S. Ingram, *Centennial Exposition Described and Illustrated: Being a Concise and
    Graphic Description of This Grand Enterprise Commemorative of the First Centennary
    [sic] of American Independence* (Philadelphia: Hubbard Bros., 1876), 97, 157–90;
    Simonin, 18–22; John Maass, *The Glorious Enterprise: The Centennial Exhibition of
    1876 and H. J. Schwarzmann, Architect-in-Chief* ([Watkins Glen, NY:] published for
    the Institute for the Study of Universal History Through Arts and Artifacts, by the
    American Life Foundation, 1973), figs. 34, 35; Rydell, 15–16.

set the giant engine in motion. It, in turn, brought all the other machines in the hall to life.[56]

In Machinery Hall gears interlocked, machine belts hummed, and all seemed to run in harmony, which was the dominant message of the Exposition, but promoters also advanced a second, less harmonious message: the replacement of labor with machinery. Employers and those journalists sympathetic to them read this as the triumph of capital, and they drove that message home. The Philadelphia and Reading Coal and Iron Company, which dominated the anthracite coalfields, sponsored excursions for miners and their families to go to the Exposition. The *Philadelphia Inquirer* read an ideological lesson into such visits: a worker could see that if he did not progress beyond "his own comparatively worthless" life, he and his children would sink even lower. The machines on exhibit gave the workers their choice: improve or perish.[57]

In Machinery Hall, machines powered other machines, and the Exposition's designers purposely disguised both the labor and the nature inside the devices, rendering them invisible to visitors. They placed the boiler that powered the engine in a separate building, sparing visitors coal dust and sweating human workers. Miners had dug the coal that fed the boiler; railroad workers had transported that coal, the Corliss engine, and the machines that it ran. Loggers had cut the timber, harvested from American forests, and millworkers had planed it into the boards that carpenters had transformed into the platform that supported the machine. Other workers pumped and refined the oil that lubricated it. Intermediate industries manufactured the iron and steel necessary to produce the machines.[58]

Seen this way, the miners visiting Machinery Hall glimpsed not a future that had no need for them but rather a present for which their labor was essential. In the mines and factories, not everything ran so smoothly; there conflict reigned. Designed as a window onto a utopian American future, the Philadelphia Exposition could not quite disguise a disquietingly divisive and violent American present. Securing the resources that fed American industry yielded another variant on "savage" war.

In 1876 the Philadelphia and Reading was preparing to prosecute the Molly Maguires. The "Mollies" were Irish coal miners, saloonkeepers, and others associated with the miners who were accused of waging a campaign of terror against the owners of mines largely controlled by the

56. Rydell, 15.
57. Kevin Kenny, *Making Sense of the Molly Maguires* (New York: Oxford University Press, 1998), 242–44.
58. Livingston, 102.

Philadelphia and Reading, which was a creation of the Reading Railroad. The Reading had symbiotically brought together in one company the combination of coal, iron, and railroads necessary for the Corliss engine.

Coal and the men who mined it had proved intractable. Timber provided 73 percent of the nation's inanimate energy in the 1870s, compared to coal's 26 percent, but wood packed less energy per pound than coal and was more valuable for other uses. The lumber industry remained the nation's second-largest manufacturer in terms of value added at the end of the century, and Midwestern oaks, Wisconsin pine, and California redwoods were far more critical for railroad ties, bridges, stations, and other buildings than for fuel. In opening up the Western and Midwestern prairies, the railroads became a conduit for the timber that flowed south and west for new houses, fences, and barns. Coal consumption in the 1870s was concentrated in heavy industry and transportation, but it was on the way to becoming the country's dominant fuel. By the late 1870s the United States entered what has been called the paleotechnic: the age of coal, steam, and iron.[59]

Coal allowed cities to concentrate factories and homes in a density that organic energy sources could not support. Factories could operate more efficiently and workers could keep their homes warmer because of the high heat content of anthracite. For most urban residents, life with coal was far easier and preferable than life without it. Once committed to fossil fuels, Americans would find it impossible to change.[60]

In return anthracite exacted substantial environmental costs, but these were largely confined to mining communities. The mines deforested the hills, scarred the landscape with slag heaps, and polluted water supplies. Coal dust fouled houses and clothes. Like the bituminous mines farther West, anthracite areas became sacrifice zones, places ravaged to feed progress.[61]

In the abstract, the mine owners and workers in Schuylkill County in the heart of anthracite country shared the values of free labor and antimonopolism, but, as was happening across the country, the meanings they attached to them diverged. Antimonopolism and free labor came in

59. Harold G. Vatter, *The Drive to Industrial Maturity: The U. S. Economy, 1860–1914* (Westport, CT: Greenwood Press, 1975), 62; William Cronon, *Nature's Metropolis: Chicago and the Great West* (New York: Norton, 1991), 148–207; Lewis Mumford, borrowing from Patrick Geddes, popularized the term; Mumford, *Technics and Civilization* (Chicago: University of Chicago Press, 2010, orig. ed. 1934), 151ff.

60. Christopher Jones, "A Landscape of Energy Abundance: Anthracite Coal Canals and the Roots of American Fossil Fuel Dependence, 1820–1860," *Environmental History* 15, no. 3 (2010), 449–84.

61. Ibid.

multiple varieties. Workers demanded control over the conditions of their labor and a greater share of the proceeds. The operators countered worker demands with assertions of the right of independent producers to control their property and its products. A mine, to them, was no different from a farm, and a coal miner no different from a field hand whose ambition should be to acquire a farm of his own. Schuylkill mine operators could thus denounce corporations and fear their intrusion into the coal fields and, in nearly the same breath, denounce unions for limiting the operators' freedom.[62]

Mine operators claimed the right to determine the operations of the mine because they owned it. It was their property and fortune that were at risk. But in coal mining, risk included miners' lives as well as owners' property. Miners most often died alone or in small groups when slabs fell in the shafts or tunnels collapsed; but they also died in spectacular accidents, often from gas leaks. The 1869 explosion and fire at the Steuben Shaft operated by the Delaware, Lackawanna, and Western Railroad killed 110 miners. Men who didn't die beneath the earth often died of miner's asthma and black lung disease. Mining was dangerous everywhere, but miners in the anthracite region died at three times the rate they did in the coal mines of Great Britain. In Schuylkill County alone, between 1870 and 1875 556 miners died and 1,667 were injured. Miners sought to hedge the all-too-real risks through the burial and health benefits offered by their unions.[63]

The rhetorical devotion to free labor became a fraying bridge over a widening class divide. As a Pennsylvania state report on the anthracite region put it in the mid-1870s, "the line dividing...[workers] from the employing class, and their better paid and provided confidential servants as superintendents, store keepers, clerks, etc. was widened day by day, until they were as completely separated in feeling, habit of thought, purposes, interest and sympathy as if they were separate peoples in race and civilization."[64]

Competition made things worse by putting great pressure on both sides. Anthracite coal came from four roughly parallel fields in the Appalachians. The first or southern field lay about fifty miles northwest of Philadelphia in Schuylkill County. It was the most productive and the

62. Grace Palladino, *Another Civil War: Labor, Capital, and the State in the Anthracite Regions of Pennsylvania, 1840–68* (Urbana: University of Illinois Press, 1990), particularly 8–14; Clifton K. Yearley, *Enterprise and Anthracite: Economics and Democracy in Schuylkill County, 1820–1875* (Baltimore, MD: Johns Hopkins University Press, 1961), 15; Kenny, 120–22.
63. Kenny, 126–28.
64. Yearley, 174.

most distinctive, for the operators were largely small producers working on leased lands. The northern and western fields were dominated and owned by transportation corporations—first canals and then railroads.

Both workers and independent producers recognized the decline in their well-being and status during the late 1860s and 1870s. Anthracite production overshot demand, and coal prices were not high enough to guarantee profit or attract investment. The independent coal producers in the southern anthracite fields organized, hoping to regulate production and lower costs. They protested railroad rates, but they could not easily affect them. The cost most immediately under their control was labor. In 1869 mine owners formed the Anthracite Board of Trade of Schuylkill Country in order to cut wages. The workers organized in response, but the concerns of the Workingmen's Benevolent Association of St. Clair (WBA) went beyond wages. The union tried to implement the weak eight-hour law passed in Pennsylvania in 1868, and it secured legislation to improve mine safety. It also tried to curb production and raise coal prices. Although the WBA and the Board of Trade continued to battle each other, they agreed on a sliding scale under which workers' wages rose and fell with the price of coal. The result was a hostile but oddly symbiotic relationship between owners and miners, both of whom blamed the region's problems on the Philadelphia and Reading Railroad and on middlemen. The miners' recurrent strikes created scarcity and boosted the price of coal, but the miners sustained their wages only at the price of long periods of unemployment and a continued decline in their standard of living. The mine owners privately admitted that the union was the only organization capable of restricting production and increasing prices, which was the mine owners' goal.[65]

Franklin Gowen, head of the Philadelphia and Reading Railroad, sought to arrest this destructive spiral. Like many businessmen, he had little patience with liberal platitudes about laissez-faire. He believed that the day of the individual proprietor was gone in the coal industry; only combinations could succeed. In the early 1870s he began to buy coal lands and leases as they came on the market and then lease them back to individual operators. The Reading loaned money to improve the mines so as to produce cleaner, higher-quality coal. Gowen disavowed high coal prices; he wanted coal prices low enough to drive out competitors and allow expansion into new markets.[66]

65. Ibid., 175–91; Richard G. Healey, *The Pennsylvania Anthracite Coal Industry, 1860–1902: Economic Cycles, Business Decision-Making and Regional Dynamics* (Scranton, PA: University of Scranton Press, 2007), 220–24, 226; Kenny, 129.
66. Yearley, 197–211; Healey, 232–33.

These tactics failed, and with the anthracite railroads losing money on every ton they shipped, Gowen adopted a very different strategy. After unsuccessfully trying to enlist Tom Scott and the Pennsylvania Railroad, in 1873 he lured competing railroads—the Leigh Valley Road and the Lackawanna—into a cartel to divide up the market and maintain prices. The cartel set a base price $5 a ton in New York and successfully enforced it. Although the Reading accumulated a massive debt in gaining control of coal, the next two years were good ones for the cartel. The railroads argued the cartel was the only way to secure steady supplies and create the stability needed to attract capital.[67]

By the end of 1874, however, with the depression eating into the demand for coal, the cartel began to lose its ability to maintain its base price. Gowen turned on the union. The cartel announced wage cuts of 10–20 percent across the anthracite region. Gowen attacked the WBA in order to lower wages, and thus costs, and to end disruptions to the Reading's coal traffic caused by strikes. The WBA fought back in the Long Strike of 1875, which stretched through the first half of that year, but it fought against a powerful corporation and not numerous divided owners. Gowen's triumph destroyed the union. Its demise unleashed demons that had stalked the region since the Civil War.[68]

Gowen cast the union as murderers, criminals, and terrorists. He identified the WBA with the Molly Maguires, a shadowy descendant of anti-landlord groups in Ireland supposedly resurrected in the anthracite coalfields. Portraying the Molly Maguires as a secret conspiratorial terrorist organization was the work of an ex-Whig journalist, Benjamin Bannan, whose *Miner's Journal* was the voice of the remaining independent mine owners and operators. Bannan was a nativist, anti-Catholic, Republican, and ardent proponent of free labor, whose tenets he thought the Irish—with their drinking, clannishness, and Democratic politics—failed to observe.[69]

The Molly Maguires never existed as Bannan pictured them, but he did not invent them out of whole cloth. The Irish in the anthracite region did foment a collective violence aimed at achieving retributive justice against mine owners, police, and British miners. Ethnic and religious divisions between Welsh, Irish, German, and English workers complicated deep class conflicts.[70]

Bannan and Gowen combined the county's crime, the retributive justice of Irish mobs, and the quite real unrest among Irish coal miners into

67. Yearley, 197–211; Healey, 132, 232–33; Kenny, 141–43, 150–51.
68. Healey, 258–65; Yearley, 209–13, 236–48; Kenny, 168–81.
69. Kenny, 85–111, 143.
70. Palladino, 8–14; Kenny, 7–10.

a single violent mix and attributed it to the Molly Maguires. Gowen had served as district attorney in Schuylkill County during the Civil War and had been unable to secure convictions in the murders that had then plagued the region. He blamed them on the Molly Maguires, and he was not a man to forget. In a country awash in secret societies, it was easy to imagine a society so secret that no one could actually locate it. Identifying individual Molly Maguires became the handiwork of operatives employed by Allan Pinkerton, a Scots immigrant who parlayed his experience as head of the Union Intelligence Service during the Civil War into the creation of the Pinkerton Detective Agency. Pinkerton also became a novelist, and the line between his fictions and his accounts of his detectives ranged from fine to nonexistent.[71]

In 1873 an Irish immigrant Pinkerton operative, James McParlan, went undercover in the coalfields. He used his considerable skills as a dancer, a fighter, a drinker, and a talker to insinuate himself among a class of saloonkeepers, brawlers, and workers in Schuylkill's coal towns. He even briefly worked in the mines but quickly left, calling it the hardest work he had ever seen. Eventually, he joined the Ancient Order of Hibernians (AOH), a secret fraternal organization similar to other American fraternal orders that was often at odds with the Catholic Church.[72]

McParlan certainly discovered, and participated in, a world of faction fighting, brawling, and revenge killings that included murders countenanced by a clique of so-called body-masters within the AOH. McParlan claimed the Mollies had become for all practical purposes the Ancient Order of Hibernians, but he did not find the Workingmen's Benevolent Association to be associated with the violence. The union expelled those with criminal records. Gowen, however, persisted in the claim that the overlap in membership between the AOH and the WBA amounted to the Mollies controlling the union. The violence that rose with the defeat of the union—some of which had little to do with the labor struggles but were instead clashes and revenge killings involving the Welsh and Irish—became evidence that the union was a mask for terrorism. Trials beginning in 1876 and ending in 1878 yielded twenty executions.[73]

Prosecutors lumped in the innocent with the guilty because the real crime was leadership in the AOH and opposition to the mining companies.

71. Wayne G. Broehl, *The Molly Maguires* (Cambridge, MA: Harvard University Press, 1964), 86–87, 118, 152–79; Kenny, 74–75, 85–111.
72. Broehl, 94, 131; Kenny, 154–57.
73. Harold W. Aurand, *From the Molly Maguires to the United Mine Workers: The Social Ecology of an Industrial Union, 1869–1897* (Philadelphia: Temple University Press, 1971), 96–110; Kenny, 186–202, 213–76.

The defendants were Irish. The juries were German, some of whose members did not speak English. Key testimony was offered by men who traded fingering other defendants for amnesty and by McParlan, who certainly seemed to have acted as an *agent provocateur*. He dropped his cover and became the lead witness for the prosecution. As was typical of the period, Pennsylvania had delegated state power to private parties. In 1866 and 1867 mine owners had secured the right from the Pennsylvania legislature to form a special police force, the Coal and Iron Police, who were paid for by the coal industry but clothed with public authority while being free from the control of any local elected official. With the special police came a special court. As historian Harold Aurand put it, "A private corporation initiated the investigation through a private detective agency; a private police force arrested the alleged offenders; and coal company attorneys prosecuted them. The state provided only the courtroom and the hangman." The Coal and Iron Police and the Reading Railroad ruled the region.[74]

Gowen and collaborators clapped individualism and free labor, which the miners once welcomed as their legacy from the Civil War, onto the workers like a ball and chain. The railroads and mine owners could consolidate and cooperate, but not workers. They were sentenced to atomization in the name of individualism. With their union destroyed, they could now negotiate individually only with the Philadelphia and Reading Coal and Iron Company and its equivalents. Individually, they were no match for the company.

Gowen sowed the wind in the early 1870s and a decade later reaped the whirlwind. The Reading destroyed the WBA, and for all practical purposes ruled Schuylkill County, but to do so, it borrowed more than it could repay. A dividend-paying road at the beginning of the decade, it sank into receivership in the early 1880s. Gowen would try to come back, but he failed. A decade later he committed suicide.[75]

Pinkerton, the Philadelphia and Reading Coal and Iron Company, and popular writers made the Mollies into savages, which meant Indians. As F. P. Dewees said in 1877, "The Indians boasts [*sic*] of numerous scalps and of acts of savage butchery, but the scalps he shows are those of his enemies.... The 'Molly' commits his crimes against those with whom he has been in daily and apparently friendly intercourse...And yet the boast of the savage was not more exultant." In 1876 and 1877 savagery had become a particularly resonant metaphor, with western Indians waging war against Americans.[76]

74. Aurand, 24–26; Kenny, 213–44.
75. "Death of Franklin B. Gowen," *Railway World* (Dec. 21, 1889): 1206.
76. F. P. Dewees, *Molly Maguires: The Origin, Growth, and Character of the Organization* (New York: Burt Franklin, 1877), 124–25.

III

Continuing racial and sectional conflict, along with class conflict and the gendered exclusion of women from voting, all formed fault lines visible at the Exposition, but a final, less obvious division, also surfaced. Louis Simonin, who did not grasp the nuances of American Protestantism, missed it. When he praised the American public schools during his visit to the Exposition in 1877, presenting them as consensual institutions supported by both the citizens and the government, he neglected one of the great cultural controversies of the age: the place of religion in the public schools. He noted religion only in the controversies over the Sunday closing of the Exposition, and even then mistakenly identified evangelicalism with "narrow Puritan ideas."[77]

In the 1870s Grant and the Republicans increasingly focused on Catholicism as a danger that could unite both liberals and Stalwarts. Henry Ward Beecher regarded the Catholic Church as unsuited for the age and for a democratic United States. Its priesthood was "an aristocracy of the most intense character in a nation and an age peculiarly penetrated with the democratic spirit." Catholicism demanded submission and a suspension of reason in the face of its teachings on faith and morals, while Protestantism supposedly appealed to reason. Protestantism, Beecher declared, sought to develop an individual conscience, while Catholicism demanded a corporate conscience. Beecher confidently predicted Catholicism could not survive in its present form in the United States. But, at the same time, Beecher defended its right to exist and took a quite moderate position on the place of religion in the public schools.[78]

Catholic conservatives agreed with their enemies that the Church was out of step with a liberal republic, but they regarded this as a good thing. The Church proclaimed revelation in a country increasingly enamored with science and social science, and it demanded obedience to authority in a country whose authorities were supposed to reflect the popular will. During the Civil War, the Republican press had paired popery and slavery as "incompatible with the spirit of the age" and doomed to extinction. With the defeat of the slaveholding elite in the South, the Catholic Church was the country's only explicitly conservative

77. Simonin, 24–25, 44–46.
78. Henry Ward Beecher, "Progress of Thought in the Church," *North American Review* 135, no. 309 (1882): 104; John T. McGreevy, *Catholicism and American Freedom: A History* (New York: Norton, 2003), 116.

institution; it rejected contract freedom, individualism, liberty of conscience, and equality.[79]

The Catholic Church was neither as homogeneous as its enemies thought nor as homogeneous as Catholic conservatives wished it to be. The emigration of European liberals following the revolutions of 1848 had supplemented longstanding American Protestant antipathy to Catholicism. In both Europe and the United States the Church and liberals regarded each other as deadly enemies. Although their very existence seemed an oxymoron, some liberal Catholics wanted to prevent the United States from becoming a new theater in old European quarrels. Bishop John Ireland, eventually the most prominent Catholic liberal, had served as a Catholic chaplain during the Civil War, supported Reconstruction, and became a friend of African American Catholics.[80]

Attacking the Catholic Church attracted liberals while costing the Republicans little because the vast majority of Catholics were already Democrats. Liberals already regarded poor Catholics, particularly Irish Catholics, as both symbols of the excesses of democracy and as tools of the enemies of the republic.[81]

The Republicans targeted two linked issues that had agitated the nation since the antebellum era: public aid to sectarian schools and the teaching of religion in public schools. Protestants had originally fought out these issues among themselves, but the mass migration of Irish and German Catholics had given them new potency after the 1830s. At the end of the Civil War, Protestants largely agreed that there was to be no sectarian teaching in the public schools, but nonsectarian Protestantism in the form of Bible reading would be central to the curriculum. Protestants reasoned that the public schools were, as the *New York Times* put it in 1875, "the nursery of the Republic," and the Bible contained what the school reformer Horace Mann had called "universal" religious values critical to an education that would instill character and morality, producing sober, industrious, and righteous citizens. At the same time, since the First Amendment guaranteed freedom of religion and forbade the establishment of any particular religion, Protestants decided that the doctrines of no particular church would be taught in public schools and public funds would not go to support private religious schools. Funding religious schools would violate rights of conscience by forcing one person to pay for

79. Jon Gjerde and S. Deborah Kang, *Catholicism and the Shaping of Nineteenth-Century America* (Cambridge: Cambridge University Press, 2012), xiv–xvi, 11, 13; David M. Emmons, *Beyond the American Pale: The Irish in the West, 1845–1910* (Norman: University of Oklahoma Press, 2010), 49–51, 56–57; McGreevy, 33–37.

80. McGreevy, 75, 90–105; Emmons, 49–57.

81. McGreevy, 118–24.

another's religious instruction; it would lead both to sectarian competition for funds and to church control over public monies.[82]

This position gained overwhelming Protestant support as Catholics, whose school system rivaled the public schools in size in Cincinnati, San Francisco, and elsewhere, demanded public aid. Opponents of aid complained, as a speaker in Brooklyn put it in 1873, that it funded "a band of foreign priestly conspirators, with no sympathy for American Government, or its system of education, secretly plotting the destruction of both." Catholics countered by pointing to the number of students they educated and by claiming that the public schools, with their use of the Protestant King James Bible and public prayers were, in effect, Protestant schools.[83]

THE AMERICAN RIVER GANGES.

The crocodiles crawling ashore to devour children in this Thomas Nast cartoon, "The American River Ganges," are Catholic bishops in their miters. They seek to destroy the public schools, one of which is in ruins on the bluff, and to halt reading from the King James Bible in secular schools. The stout boy sheltering the children has the Bible tucked into his jacket, while simian Irishmen in the background lead what seem to be teachers toward the gallows. Nast composed this political cartoon in the midst of the fight for secular schools and over aid to parochial schools. *Harper's Weekly*, Sep. 30, 1871. Library of Congress, LC-USZ6-790.

82. Steven K. Green, *The Bible, the School, and the Constitution: The Clash That Shaped Modern Church-State Doctrine* (New York: Oxford University Press, 2012), 14–15, 21–22, 27–32, 44–46.
83. Green, 96, 107–8.

After the Civil War both Catholics and evangelical Protestants hardened their positions. The Civil War had led some evangelicals and many Calvinists, some of whom blamed the early defeats of Union troops during the Civil War on God's displeasure with Northern sins, to demand the country specifically identify itself as a Protestant republic. They denounced the North's toleration of slavery as a collective sin, but they also pointed to the absence of any mention of God in the Constitution. Because the Constitution failed to acknowledge that all political authority derived from God, said the theologian Horace Bushnell, it created "no feeling of authority, or even respect among the people." The leading Protestant journal, the *Independent*, accused Americans of worshipping the work of their own hands. The source of authority was not "We the People," but God, and the Constitution should acknowledge this. Catholic immigrants further threatened the country's identity as God's chosen nation for spreading Protestantism across the world.[84]

The result was the Christian Amendment of 1863. It proposed to change the Preamble of the Constitution to read (with changes in italics): "We, the People of the United States, *recognizing the being and attributes of Almighty God, the Divine Authority of the Holy Scriptures, the law of God as the paramount rule, and Jesus, the Messiah, the Savior and Lord of all,* in order to form a more perfect union. . . ." Among all but the Calvinists of the National Reform Association, the push for the amendment lost steam with Union victories, but proponents had raised a critical issue that would persist in continuing attempts to secure the amendment after the war. "Our nation is Christian—the Constitution is unchristian," Felix R. Brunot, a later head of the National Reform Association, declared. After the war, the goal of the amendment's proponents was to arouse the "Christian people of America" into a movement "to carry out the religious idea of government in all its practical applications." The program included Sabbath laws, the Bible in public schools, marriage and divorce laws that "conformed to the law of Christ," a purge of "immoral and irreligious men" from office, and confining voting to "moral men" and "fearers of God." Such ambitions alarmed not just Catholics, Jews, Seventh-Day Adventists, and freethinkers, but also many Protestants. Even Protestants who opposed the amendment, however, feared that immigration and intellectual developments such as Biblical criticism and Darwinism were eroding a consensus on Christian values.[85]

The Catholic hierarchy represented the other extreme in the postwar contest. The pope's 1864 Syllabus of Errors had condemned the separation

84. McGreevy, 112–18, Green, 139–40.
85. Green, 137–42.

of church and state and attacked education outside the control of the Catholic Church. Although not all Catholics concurred, American bishops and church publications denounced the public schools as either godless or sectarian and denied the state had any role in education. Removing the Bible from the public schools would not appease them, because they opposed secular schools as fully as Protestant schools. Protestants were correct in citing Catholic polemicists, who hated the public schools and proclaimed that they would rejoice only when "our school system shall be shivered to pieces."[86]

The schools became a cauldron containing the tensions generated by immigration. Cincinnati, where a "Bible War" raged from 1869 to 1873, formed the persistent center of the conflict. A religiously diverse city with a large German Catholic population, Cincinnati had a school board that in 1869, conceding to Catholic and Jewish objections, voted to prohibit "religious instruction and the reading of religious books including the Holy Bible" in the schools. This set in motion a political controversy that ultimately found its way to the Ohio Supreme Court. Both sides in the dispute abandoned the old consensus that Bible reading was moral but not religious. Each side agreed it was an act of Protestant devotion; they disagreed on whether such devotion in the schools was legitimate or constitutional. Although the school board lost in the lower court, sparking a powerful and influential dissent by Judge Alphonso Taft, who argued that the government had to show complete neutrality in regard to religion, it prevailed in the Ohio Supreme Court. In 1873 the Ohio Supreme Court rejected the argument that the United States was a "Christian nation." Justice John Welch wrote that "Legal Christianity is a solecism, a contradiction of terms" since if "Christianity is the law of the State, like every other law, it must have a sanction." The state would have to provide adequate penalties "to enforce obedience to all its requirements and precepts. No one seriously contends for any such doctrine in this country, or, I might almost say, in this age of the world." In other cities across the country, school boards also moved toward secular rather than nonsectarian schools.[87]

In September 1875, as violence raged across Mississippi, the usually taciturn Ulysses S. Grant gave the most reproduced speech of his presidency before the veterans of the Union Army of Tennessee in Davenport, Iowa. He urged that not one dollar be "appropriated to the support of any sectarian school." By sectarian Grant meant Catholic. He also warned, "If we are to have another contest in the future of our national existence,

86. Ibid., 99, 128.
87. Ibid., 93–135, Judge Welch quote 132.

I predict the dividing line will not be Mason and Dixon's but between patriotism and intelligence on the one side, and superstition, ambition and ignorance on the other." Grant drew the line between Catholic and Protestant to replace the line between Northerner and Southerner.[88]

A wave of proposals for constitutional amendments followed Grant's speech. The main thrust of all of them was to extend the First Amendment's ban on the establishment of religion to the states and to ban any state funding of sectarian schools. They varied significantly in their details, however. Grant's was the most far-reaching—ending exemptions from taxes for church property—but that of Sen. James J. Blaine of Maine, a leading contender for the Republican nomination for president, got the most notice. His amendment confined itself to extending the first amendment and prohibiting aid to sectarian schools. Democratic versions of the amendment stripped Congress of the power to enforce it, and a Republican Senate version replaced Blaine's amendment with one that would permit Bible reading in the schools.[89]

More was involved in this debate than fear of Catholics. Observers correctly noted that Grant's proposal would gore both Protestants, by eliminating Bible reading in the schools, and Catholics, by giving no funding to sectarian schools. Blaine certainly acted from political expedience, hoping to attract evangelical voters. Blaine was hardly anti-Catholic. His mother and daughters were Catholics, and his cousin, Mother Angela Gillespie, founded the Holy Cross Sisters. The debate over the various amendments got caught up in states' rights as well and divided the Protestant majority. None of the federal amendments passed, although many states would add similar amendments to their constitutions, and both issues would slowly fade following the election. In an increasingly diverse society, the public schools were moving from giving a nonsectarian Protestant education to providing a secular education.[90]

Catholics pulled back from their demands for public funding and in the 1880s set to work to strengthen and expand a parallel school system. Condemning the public school system, bishops said Catholic parents should not send their children to them without "sufficient cause." Poverty became de facto sufficient cause, but despite the working-class status of most Catholics, they paid parochial school tuitions in schools that depended on the unpaid labor of nuns. By the mid-1890s Catholics had

88. McGreevy, 91–93.
89. Green, 179–80, 187–94, 212–23.
90. Ibid., 179–80, 193–95, 201–23; Holt, 65–66.

created a network of four thousand schools that enrolled 755,038 students.[91]

In Ohio the gubernatorial candidate, ex-general Rutherford B. Hayes, saw anti-Catholicism as a way to unite Republicans fractured over the money question and the corruption of the Grant administration. Democrats had supported a bill in the Ohio legislature that allowed Roman Catholic priests access to Catholics in reform schools, prisons, orphanages, and asylums. Republicans used it as evidence of their subservience to the Catholic Church and claimed aid to Catholic schools formed the inevitable next step. Hayes saw a chance "to rebuke the Democracy by a defeat for subserviency to Roman Catholic demands." The tactic worked. A rejuvenated Republican base, whose turnout increased by 11 percent, gave Hayes a narrow victory.[92]

By 1875 the initial skirmishes between Protestants and Catholics over the schools had advanced to something close to a cultural war. More was involved in attacks on the Catholic Church than mere prejudice, although Republican tactics certainly played on prejudice. Less sanguine than Beecher about how American democracy would inevitably change the Catholic Church, opponents of the Church acted from a combination of real convictions about the danger a hierarchical church posed to American democracy and political opportunism. The ironic result of disputes between Protestants, who hoped to either convert or marginalize Catholics, and Catholics, who never doubted that theirs was the one true Church, was a pluralism that neither originally desired. Increasingly secular institutions arose not from tolerance and understanding, but through conflict and stalemate.[93]

Designed as a monument to American progress and harmony, the Exposition could not escape the conflicts of the country that produced it. It supplied abundant evidence of American achievement even as the nation struggled over who counted as Americans.

91. McGreevy, 114.
92. Holt, 60–65, 139–41.
93. McGreevy, 116.

Part II

The Quest for Prosperity

9

Years of Violence

In 1876 and 1877 the country trembled and fractured. Only a decade after the defeat of the Confederacy, a political crisis led sober men to talk of renewed civil war, while class divisions, long regarded as alien to the free labor system, became so deep and wide that people drew parallels to the Paris Commune.

The nation's centennial was also a presidential election year, which meant the Exposition came to an end as the campaign reached its culmination. In 1875 the Republicans had begun laying the groundwork for one of the more unlikely comebacks in American political history. They moved to revise their unpopular economic program, while the Catholic hierarchy and unrepentant ex-Confederates provided the Republicans with an opportunity to revitalize their base.

The Specie Payment Resumption Act of 1875 was the shaky centerpiece of the Republican attempt at economic revival. It was, as opponents proclaimed, a "Janus-faced measure," providing for both fractional silver coins—dimes, quarters, and half-dollars—and more bank notes, along with a smaller proportional reduction in greenbacks. It thus potentially expanded the currency while also providing redemption in gold of greenbacks on January 1, 1879. It was thus also a hard-money measure. Because the bill neither mandated an expansion of the currency nor provided for the acquisition of gold necessary to redeem banknotes and greenbacks, its ambiguity was its virtue. Grant signed it.[1]

Grant's signature did not make the law popular. Not only did supporters of a fiat currency, who the bill's supporters privately admitted were the majority of voters, despise it, but so too did many conservative businessmen. They thought that it put too much power in the hands of the secretary

---

1. Samuel DeCanio, "State Autonomy and American Political Development: How Mass Democracy Promoted State Power," *Studies in American Political Development* 19 (Fall 2005): 121–25; Michael F. Holt, *By One Vote: The Disputed Presidential Election of 1876* (Lawrence: University Press of Kansas, 2008), 23–25.

of the treasury. The bill threatened to become an albatross around the Republicans' neck, costing them the Midwest.[2]

Rutherford B. Hayes offered the Republicans a way of distracting voters from the Specie Payment Resumption Act by giving the Democrats a gaudy Roman albatross of their own. He had used anti-Catholicism to trump the gold standard in Ohio when he ran for governor in 1875; the same tactic could work in the presidential election. His gubernatorial victory allowed him to become the dark-horse candidate for the Republican presidential nomination.[3]

William Dean Howells, by then the influential editor of the *Atlantic*, grafted many things onto his Ohio Republican roots, but he never wholly abandoned them. Howells's wife, Elinor, was a relation of Hayes's wife, Lucy, and the owner of the *Atlantic* gave Howells a month off to write one of the candidate's campaign biographies, which reads like a book written by a man given a month off to write a book. In the 1870s Howells still tinged his novels with romanticism, which was a good thing since a campaign biography is not supposed to challenge its subject. Howells created a pedestrian Hayes, which probably reflected the persona that the new president wanted visible.[4]

James G. Blaine had been the Republican frontrunner. Many Republicans loved him. Robert Ingersoll, the nation's leading atheist and most eloquent orator, described him as "a plumed knight" who "threw his shining lance full and fair against the brazen forehead of every traitor to his country...." An equal number hated him as opportunistic and corrupt. His entanglement with railroad corruption and Tom Scott and then a stroke caused him to stumble and lose momentum. They created an opening for Hayes, as the governor of a state critical to Republican chances.[5]

The Democrats nominated the liberal Samuel Tilden of New York, who had won the governorship in the Democratic landslide of 1874. Carrying New York was as critical to them as carrying Ohio was to the Republicans. A lawyer whose work with the railroads had made him wealthy, Tilden, like Hayes, was intellectual and well read. He followed Democratic orthodoxy in wanting reconciliation between North and South. A hard-money man, whose liberalism derived from states' rights Democratic traditions, Tilden held Democratic loyalties but this did not make him a democrat. Although he had earlier worked closely with

2. Holt, 23–25.
3. DeCanio, 123–35; Holt, 60, 65, 139–44.
4. Kenneth Schuyler Lynn, *William Dean Howells: An American Life* (New York: Harcourt Brace Jovanovich, 1971), 195–96; William Alexander, *William Dean Howells: The Realist as Humanist* (New York: B. Franklin, 1981), 1–2.
5. DeCanio, 134; Holt, 75–77, 87–88.

Tweed, he had helped unseat him. He attempted to sideline Tammany in New York politics by appointing the Tilden Commission, of which E. L. Godkin was a prominent member. The commission recommended a property requirement for voters in New York City municipal elections, which would have disenfranchised up to 69 percent of New York City's voters. In the uproar that followed, Tilden backed away, but Tammany hated him. Personally cold, a hypochondriac who had withdrawn from Yale because the college's food disagreed with him, and a lifelong bachelor, Tilden did not take naturally to politics. He substituted money and organization for the common touch.[6]

The Democrats moved to diminish their vulnerabilities. The Catholic Church was a formidable burden, particularly in the face of Thomas Nast's wickedly effective anticlerical cartoons. The Democrats in the House tried to remove it from the election by passing a toothless constitutional amendment against aid to sectarian schools, while blocking Blaine's Senate version. Tilden could not effectively attack Grant's monetary policy without losing soft-money Midwestern Democrats; the Democrats attempted to straddle the issue by nominating Thomas Hendricks, a soft-money man, for vice president. The Republicans attacked the incoherence of the Democrats' position, which, to be fair, was scarcely less coherent than their own. The Democrats also created avoidable problems for themselves after taking control of Congress in 1875. They dismissed congressional employees, many of whom were disabled Union veterans, and replaced them with disabled Confederate veterans. The Republicans were already going to wave the bloody shirt, but the Democrats didn't have to hand it to them.[7]

The Republicans ran, as astute Democrats recognized they would, against "the Pope and Jeff Davis." The Republicans waved the bloody shirt and attacked what they claimed was a Catholic assault on the schools. Hayes, quite sincerely, feared a Democratic return to power as an annulment of the constitutional and legal changes that had followed the war. The question was, "Shall the ex-Rebels have the Government?" Rep. James Garfield of Ohio, one of Hayes's leading supporters, warned in a widely reprinted pamphlet that, with the South eager to overturn the results of Reconstruction, the North must maintain its memory of the War and sustain "the whole meaning...of the revolution through which we have passed and are still passing." The North had won the war, but as the South contested the peace, Northerners "could never relax their vigilance

6. Holt, 96–112; James J. Connolly, *An Elusive Unity: Urban Democracy and Machine Politics in Industrializing America* (Ithaca, NY: Cornell University Press, 2010), 49–52.
7. Holt, 68, 70, 102–18.

until the ideas for which they fought have become embodied in the enduring forms of individual life." Hayes advocated "peace" in the South, but only if the Southerners agreed to protect the rights of black citizens and the Constitution — "the parts that are new no less than the parts that are old." For good measure, the Republican denounced Tilden as a tool of the railroads and promised civil service reform. Tilden, in turn, denounced Republican corruption and also promised civil service reform. He blamed the Republicans for the depression and asserted that high taxes were responsible for the country's economic problems. The Democrats embraced opposition to Reconstruction and denounced military intervention in the South. Neither Tilden nor Hayes promised to do anything for the unemployed.[8]

Grant, the sitting president, vacillated about the South. Tilden and the Democrats cynically calculated that the slaughter of black people in the South would play to their advantage by forcing Republicans to send federal troops into the affected states, thus antagonizing a Northern electorate increasingly opposed to such military intervention. Grant feared they were right. When he finally did send troops into South Carolina, many Democrats considered the election won. Although not many of them sympathized with black people, Northern voters did not respond as Democrats hoped. Thomas Nast, whose early postwar political cartoons had trumpeted the black civil and political rights, had turned in a different direction by 1876. Perhaps his most famous cartoon — short of Santa Claus — established equivalence between the Irish immigrant North and the black South. Both were the "ignorant voters"; both were a burden on democracy.[9]

Election Day 1876 was the first attempt in American history to create a single day during which all the nation's voters would cast their ballots: the Tuesday after the first Monday in November in even numbered years. Because of some state constitutional provisions, the effort did not completely succeed, but it came close. Democrats violently repressed black voters in parts of the South, but among white voters the election of 1876 had the highest rate of participation to date in American history.[10]

Hayes cast the Democrats, particularly Catholics and Southerners, as the enemies of homogeneous citizenship. Having ridden his assault on

8. Holt, 70, 129–56; Eric Foner, *Reconstruction: America's Unfinished Revolution, 1863–1877* (New York: Harper & Row, 1988), 567–68; Charles W. Calhoun, *Conceiving a New Republic: The Republican Party and the Southern Question, 1869–1900* (Lawrence: University Press of Kansas, 2006), 98–103.

9. Holt, 150–51.

10. Ibid., 150–51, 166–67, 169.

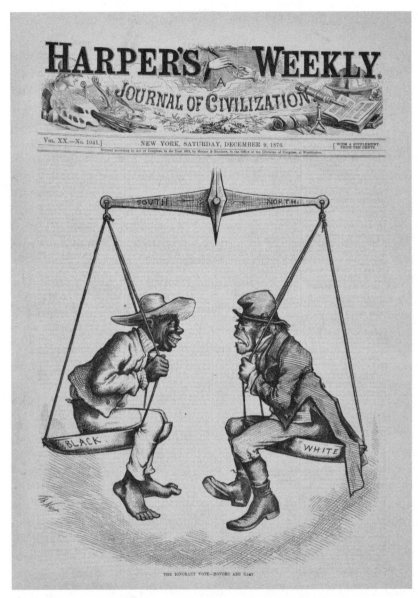

This famous cartoon by Thomas Nast captures the antidemocratic turn of liberals like Nast against both black suffrage and immigrant suffrage. Nast equates the two as "The Ignorant Vote." *Harper's Weekly*, Dec. 9, 1876. Library of Congress, LC-USZ62-57340.

sectarian schools to the governorship of Ohio and the Republican nomination, he bet that the horse had enough stamina to carry him to the White House. Hayes made himself the candidate of universal free public education, with no public aid to sectarian schools. The government, he declared, had no authority to interfere with religious sects, but it "is equally true that religious sects ought not to interfere with the government or political parties."[11]

Hayes also ran on two other issues: the money question, which he could not avoid, and civil service. He stood for "honest money," which meant a return to the gold standard. In a country undergoing serious price deflation, he worried about inflation; in a country where debtors were growing desperate, he advanced the interests of creditors. He framed civil service reform, too, as a matter of principle and morality, but there were also practical interests at stake. The power of appointment vested in the president under the Constitution had drifted into Congress, creating a patronage system that made office holding a reward "for services to party leaders." This, although he did not say so, buttressed the power of state machines such as Roscoe Conkling's in New York.[12]

Southern Democrats who had stayed home in 1872 flooded the polls in 1876. The Democrats also increased their total number of votes in the North, particularly in the four Northern states Tilden carried: New York, Indiana, New Jersey, and Connecticut. Hayes took Ohio and the Midwest except Indiana, but Tilden took New York, and his overwhelming margins in the white South garnered him roughly 250,000 more votes than Hayes. Hayes went to sleep on election night convinced that he had lost, since Tilden already had 184 of the 185 electoral votes he needed for victory.[13]

For the next week, Hayes continued to think that he had been beaten, but his operatives remained at work. They recognized that the election would come down to the disputed votes in the Southern states still under Republican rule: South Carolina, Louisiana, and Florida. They were determined to win these states where the votes had been cast but not yet approved by the "returning boards" in charge of validating the election results. In the contest for the electoral votes of these states, all that slithered through the corruption, failures, and disappointments of American politics during the previous decade rose to the surface. The Democrats had relied on fraud, violence, and coercion to suppress the black vote, and the Republicans marshaled fraud of their own and their control of the

11. William Dean Howells, *Sketch of the Life and Character of Rutherford B. Hayes* (New York: Hurd and Houghton, 1876), 152; Rutherford B. Hayes, "Inaugural Address of Rutherford B. Hayes," March 5, 1877, in *The Avalon Project: Documents in Law, History, and Diplomacy*, Yale University Law School, Lillian Goldman Law Library, http://avalon.law.yale.edu/19th_century/hayes.asp.

12. Howells, 121–24.

13. Holt, 152–76.

returning boards to count out the Democrats. Even the Democrats agreed that Hayes had carried South Carolina in a corrupt and violent election where there were more votes cast than adult males. Florida and Louisiana were much harder to determine. In Florida, first the courts and then the new Democratic legislature had intervened, resulting in three different counts, one for Hayes and two for Tilden. In Louisiana, the head of the electoral commission, with his eye on the main chance, tried to sell the results to the highest bidder, but although there is some evidence that both sides nibbled, they did not bite. The attempt failed. Both states gave their electoral votes to Hayes.[14]

When Hayes carried Florida, South Carolina, and Louisiana, he seemingly had snatched the victory from Tilden, but the Democrats challenged and invalidated one of the electors in Oregon, leaving the candidates stalemated at 184 Electoral College votes apiece. After the College met on December 6 to cast its votes, Congress still had to convene and count them. At this point the dispute became impossibly arcane because of the nebulous wording of the Twelfth Amendment. It provided for the counting of electoral votes, and the legal and constitutional status of congressional joint rules, which allowed challenges to the electoral votes. Were the rules constitutional? Were they even in force if, as was the case, the Senate had repealed them but the House had not? Would the election be decided by having the president of the Senate, Rep. Thomas Ferry of Michigan, count the votes, in which case Hayes would win? Or would it be thrown into the Democratic House, where Tilden would win?[15]

Amidst threats of violence, the business of the country sputtered to a halt. George McClellan, a Democrat and the first commander of the Army of the Potomac, conspired and blustered about raising troops to march on Washington, and Tilden's allies urged the candidate to act forcefully. These same allies did not consider him capable of forceful action. Even John Bigelow, Tilden's confidant, thought that "A man who must have a man rub him every morning & evening for an hour or so, who must take a clyster every morning to get passage... how could such a man be expected to [demand the presidency] and wind up perhaps at last in prison?" But the candidate unwilling to threaten resistance in December grew privately more strident as the crisis went on.[16]

---

14. Holt, 165–73.
15. Ibid., 204–10; Foner, 575–79; Blight, 135–39.
16. Gregory P. Downs, "The Mexicanization of American Politics: The United States' Transnational Path from Civil War to Stabilization," *American Historical Review* (2012): 399–402, quote 402. For full accounts of the crisis, Calhoun, 105–36; Holt, 204–43.

Never a man to avoid the muck if advantage beckoned, Tom Scott intervened. He wanted additional federal aid for the Texas and Pacific and promised to deliver Southern Democratic votes for Hayes in return for a promise to support subsidies for that railroad. It is unclear that he had the votes. Hayes did not think so, and he made no promises. More critically, newspapermen and lobbyists—the two were sometimes synonymous—promised to deliver Southern votes if Hayes swore not to use federal troops or marshals to enforce federal civil rights and voting rights laws.[17]

The negotiations came to naught as the two parties, realizing that the Republican Senate could stalemate the Democratic House and vice versa, struggled to create a Federal Electoral Commission drawn from the Supreme Court, Senate, and House to resolve the crisis. Each side bargained and bet, and the bet came down to a single man: Joseph Bradley, an associate justice of the Supreme Court. Everyone knew how the rest of the commission would vote. The contest turned on partisan loyalties. Each side abandoned its principles. The Republicans embraced state rights: the electoral votes were those, fairly or unfairly decided, ratified by the states. Congress could not challenge them. Democrats claimed Congress had the right and power to look beneath the vote and see if it was fair and just. The debate could be summarized in one quite simple Gilded Age exchange. "Fraud vitiates everything," the Democrat Jeremiah Black claimed. "No, it does not," the Republican Supreme Court Justice Stanley Matthews replied.[18]

Justice Bradley voted with the Republicans on every single issue in dispute. Hayes had 185 electoral votes. The Democrats still could have blocked him by refusing to convene the House in the joint session needed to ratify the results, but now the December compromise returned without the Texas and Pacific. Hayes would not enforce the civil rights laws in the South; he would not deploy federal troops; he would abandon the freedmen to the promises of Southern Democrats that they would recognize their political and civil equality. The Democrats retained their majority in the House. The Republicans kept the Senate.[19]

On March 1, 1877, Rutherford B. Hayes took the train from Columbus, Ohio, to Washington, D.C. The presidential party rode in Tom Scott's private car. The inauguration was only days ahead, yet no one was sure, when Hayes embarked, that he would actually be sworn in. While he was still on the train, he received word that the two houses had agreed on the

17. Allan Peskin, "Was There a Compromise of 1877?" *Journal of American History* 60, no. 1 (1973); Michael Les Benedict, "Southern Democrats in the Crisis of 1876–1877: A Reconsideration of Reunion and Reaction," *Journal of Southern History* 46, no. 4 (1980): 489–524.
18. Holt, 209–32, quote 228; Calhoun, 214–36.
19. Holt, 233–43.

results and his election was official. On March 5, 1877, Hayes was inaugurated. Grant left office under a shadow that shaped his revealing, odd, self-pitying, and very human final State of the Union message: "It is but reasonable to suppose errors of judgement [*sic*] must have occurred," he said, but he claimed his motives had been pure.[20]

I

If ever an American president stepped out of the frying pan and into the fire, it was Rutherford B. Hayes. Other elections had been closely contested, but none since the election of 1824 had threatened to tear apart the constitutional fabric as did the election of 1876. Lincoln's election had rent the Union, but no one doubted that Lincoln had been elected president. Many Democrats, and some Republicans, doubted Hayes's legitimacy even as he took office. Conkling, who hated Hayes, referred to him as "His Fraudulency" and "Rutherfraud B. Hayes."[21]

The wounds of Reconstruction gaped open behind Hayes; the signs of a long and ongoing depression appeared around him; and a year of upheaval and widespread violence across the North and West awaited him. These were not the fruits that the Republicans had expected from their policies in 1865.

Hayes disappointed Scott in not securing him a new subsidy for the Texas and Pacific, but not nearly so much as he disappointed the freedmen. Hayes had persuaded Grant not to pull all the troops out of the South because he did not want to vitiate the principle of federal supremacy and the central government's right to intervene in state affairs within the limits of the law. He thought the troops gave him the leverage to negotiate an arrangement on the South with the Democrats.[22]

Hayes needed the leverage in South Carolina and Louisiana. The election outcomes were disputed in both states, and the same returning boards that had given those states' electoral votes to Hayes also ruled that Republican governors—Daniel Chamberlain in South Carolina and

20. Charles Richard Williams, ed., *Diary and Letters of Rutherford Birchard Hayes, Nineteenth President of the United States* ([Columbus]: Ohio State Archaeological and Historical Society, 1922), 3: 424–26; Holt, 241–43; Foner, 580–83; William S. McFeely, *Grant: A Biography* (New York: Norton, 1981), 441–44; Ari Arthur Hoogenboom, *Rutherford B. Hayes: Warrior and President* (Lawrence: University Press of Kansas, 1995), 295.
21. David M. Jordan, *Roscoe Conkling of New York: Voice in the Senate* (Ithaca, NY: Cornell University Press, 1971), 280.
22. Hoogenboom, 295, 306.

Stephen Packard in Louisiana—had won the election. Because the Democrats refused to recognize their legitimacy, the governors' authority extended no further than the immediate vicinity of the statehouse, where federal troops protected them. Logically, Hayes seemed compelled to support the governors. As Blaine, said, if "Packard is not the legal governor," then "President Hayes has no title."[23]

Hayes, like Grant before him, appeased his enemies and disappointed his friends. Hayes did not act as though he was abandoning Reconstruction. In his inaugural address he repeated the notes Howells had hit in his campaign biography, giving a full-throated endorsement of the Republican goal of a homogeneous citizenry.

> Our government has been called a white man's government. Not so. It is not the government of any class or sect or nationality, or race. It is a government founded on the consent of the governed, and Mr. Broomall, of Pennsylvania, therefore properly calls it the 'government of the governed.' It is not the government of the native born, or of the foreign born, of the rich man, or of the poor man, of the white man or of the colored man—it is the government of the freeman. And when colored men were made citizens, soldiers, and freemen, by our consent and votes, we were estopped from denying them the right of suffrage.[24]

The "permanent pacification of the country upon such principles and by such measures as will secure the complete protection of all its citizens in the free enjoyment of their constitutional rights" remained the basis of public affairs. There had been a revolution in the labor system advancing "4,000,000 people from a condition of servitude to that of citizenship," and the South had borne the economic cost of that revolution. The South remained impoverished and "the inestimable blessing of wise, honest, and peaceful local self-government is not fully enjoyed." The national government retained both "a moral obligation" to "employ its constitutional power and influence to establish the rights of the people it has emancipated, and to protect them in the enjoyment of those rights when they are infringed and assailed." To this he added the "material development of that section of the country...now needs and deserves the considerate care of the National Government within the just limits prescribed by the Constitution and wise public economy."[25]

What Hayes said was not what Hayes did. After securing promises from the Democrats, including Sen. Matthew Butler, that they would respect black civil rights, Hayes in March withdrew the troops from the South

23. Hoogenboom, 304–15; Calhoun, 139–40.
24. Howells, 145.
25. Hayes, "Inaugural Address of Rutherford B. Hayes."

Carolina statehouse, thus effectively ending Chamberlain's governorship. His decision won the praise of white Southerners and northern liberals alike. In Louisiana a federal commission negotiated a settlement that yielded the same results. In neither state did the Democrats keep their promises. A South Carolina freedman saw the writing on the wall: "I am an unprotected freedman...O God Save the Colored People." Amos Akerman, Grant's old attorney general, thought the new president rewarded "lawlessness by letting the lawless have their way."[26]

The black Henry Adams recognized that an arrangement with the Democrats meant all was lost. In 1877 the committee he had helped organize in Shreveport sent a petition to Hayes telling the president what he did not want to hear: "the colored people of the South had been debarred from...the right to vote hold office and the privilege of education without molestation." They had been "oppressed, murdered, and disenfranchised on account of our race and color." Adams feared the Union soldiers had shed their blood in vain.[27]

Hayes thought he had cemented the gains of Reconstruction, and he basked in the approval that many Northerners gave to his policy of conciliation. Rather than preserve a black Republican Party that had just won elections, Hayes imagined a white Whiggish Republican Party in a conciliated South. Such a party was a chimera. Frederick Douglass claimed that he told Hayes this in a long conversation in Columbus, but Hayes made only symbolic concessions to the black Republicans whom he abandoned. He nominated Douglass as marshal of the District of Columbia, essentially the chief federal law enforcement officer in the capital, reporting directly to the attorney general.[28]

Historians customarily argue that Reconstruction died in 1877, but this was not completely true. The freedpeople did not cease political activity, and the Republicans continued to try to secure black suffrage in the

26. Hoogenboom, 305–15; Hans L. Trefousse, *Rutherford B. Hayes* (New York: Times Books, 2002), 91–92; Blight, 87–94, 135–39; Calhoun, 140–53.

27. U.S. Senate Select Committee, "Report and Testimony of the Select Committee of the United States Senate to Investigate the Causes of the Removal of the Negroes from the Southern States to the Northern States" (Washington, DC: U.S. GPO, 1880), 2: 156–57; Steven Hahn, *A Nation under Our Feet: Black Political Struggles in the Rural South, from Slavery to the Great Migration* (Cambridge, MA: Belknap Press of Harvard University Press, 2003), 319–20.

28. Mark W. Summers, *The Ordeal of the Reunion: A New History of Reconstruction* (Chapel Hill: University of North Carolina Press, 2014), 385–88; Hoogenboom, 306; David W. Blight, *Frederick Douglass* (New York: Simon & Schuster, forthcoming), chap. 26; Michael Perman, *The Road to Redemption: Southern Politics, 1869–1879* (Chapel Hill: University of North Carolina Press, 1984), 264–70; William McFeely, *Frederick Douglass* (New York: W.W. Norton, 1991), 289–93.

South. Reconstruction took a long time to die. Its deathwatch had begun when the Democrats captured the House in 1873, but death did not immediately ensue. With Democrats in control of the House, it became much harder to enforce existing civil rights legislation and impossible to pass new legislation, but sporadic attempts to resuscitate the patient would continue into the 1880s. The Republicans remained, from both principle and self-interest, determined to try to secure black suffrage.

Hayes, elected with a minority of votes in a disputed election, held a bad hand in 1877, but he made things worse by misplaying it. He believed that only governments that maintained "inviolate the rights of all" represented "true self-government," and he wanted to compel the South to observe the Fourteenth and Fifteenth Amendments. But Democratic control of the House of Representatives limited his options. The House had refused to appropriate funds for the army beyond July 1, 1877; the army, in any case, was small—twenty-five thousand men—and fully engaged in the West, warily watching both Indians and a Mexican Revolution that exacerbated troubles along the southern border.[29]

Hayes, like Grant before him, had miscalculated in his attempt to conciliate the South. He believed that Southerners would respect black suffrage. His Stalwart enemies, rightfully as it turned out, never trusted the South. In growing swaths of the South black voting rights melted away. After 1877 federal troops would for the rest of the nineteenth century never be deployed to protect the constitutional rights of black citizens.[30]

Reconstruction was not doomed to fail. Republicans had squandered their opportunity to bring prosperity to ordinary white people and black people. The corruption of the Republican governments and the high taxes for small landowners were not just Democratic slanders; they were Republican failures. This, coupled with the failure to counter terror, which the government could have done, ended Republican rule in the South. When the Republicans acted forcibly against terror, they prevailed. The decision not to do so killed their party figuratively and literally. Nor was the dismantling of the protections of the Reconstruction amendments inevitable. Grant's careless appointments to the Supreme Court yielded decisions only slightly less destructive than *Dred Scott*. A newly solid South meant that with Democratic Northern votes concentrated in key states—New York, New Jersey, Connecticut, and Indiana—the Democrats had attained parity with the Republicans.

29. Hoogenboom, 304–5; Calhoun, 161–66.
30. Holt, 210–36, 580–83; Foner, 105–36; Calhoun, 149–52; Wesley Hiers, "Party Matters: Racial Closure in the Nineteenth-Century United States," *Social Science History* 37, no. 2 (2013): 255–308.

Nationally, the Democrats had returned as the Party of No, defined by their opposition to the tariff, Reconstruction, and the interventionist federal government the Republicans had created. They capitalized on Hayes's willingness to compromise by disenfranchising black voters when necessary and by controlling their votes when possible, thus fortifying the Solid South. The partisan battlefield over Reconstruction moved from the South to Washington, D.C., where resurgent Democrats fought Republicans in a divided federal government.

The reticence of Hayes and Grant marked the waning power of the Radicals and the unwillingness of the party to define itself in terms of Reconstruction. The bloody shirt worked in 1876, but its effectiveness decreased over time. Not only the suppression of black citizens in the South but also the ambiguities of free labor in an industrial society sapped the old power of contract freedom and free labor. This left the Republicans with a program based on prosperity, which was not much of an asset in the midst of a depression.

The standoff the Republicans achieved in 1876 was far better than they had any reason to expect. After ten years of Republican rule, their record could very well have driven them from power entirely. The nation was in economic depression and had not resolved old divisions. The Indian problem refused to go away; the political compromise and the resolution of Southern Reconstruction proved no more than scab over a festering sore; Southern Democrats scratched that scab, hoping to weaken the Republicans further. Above all the new industrial republic erupted in conflict, disorder, fear, and anger. Workers—largely immigrants—demonstrated their power to disrupt the nation; their targets in this case were often railroad corporations, which to most Americans seemed as essential as they were dangerous. The year 1877 devolved into a series of violent clashes.

II

Gen. O. O. Howard did not mean to instigate the Nez Perce War in 1877 when he arbitrarily ignored the Nez Perce claims in Oregon, any more than Tom Scott intended to precipitate the Great Strike of 1877 when he escalated his battle with John D. Rockefeller of Standard Oil. The army that Hayes refused to deploy against Southern whites who murdered and subordinated Southern blacks saw plenty of action elsewhere in the summer of 1877, most spectacularly in the West.

President Grant in his final State of the Union message blamed the "avarice of the white man" for troubles with Lakotas in the Black Hills, and the same avarice created similar troubles with the Nez Perce. Nearly two-thirds of the Nez Perce in Idaho Territory and Oregon had refused to ratify the "steal treaty" of 1863, which had dramatically reduced their homeland. The Nez Perce had split into treaty and nontreaty bands. The latter returned to their lands, the most isolated of which lay along the beautiful and remote Wallowa Mountains in present-day northeastern Oregon. This was the home of the followers of Heinmot Tooyalakekt or Chief Joseph, who was a civil chief and not, as the Americans thought, a war leader.[31]

For a while, it appeared the United States would leave these bands alone, admit they were not subject to the treaty, and acknowledge their claim to the land. But then the government sent General Howard, the former head of the Freedmen's Bureau, to negotiate. Gen. George Crook's sardonic description of Howard's zeal, sanctimony, and obtuseness was accurate enough: "The Creator had placed him on earth to be the Moses to the Negro," and having performed that duty, "he felt satisfied his next mission was with the Indians." Howard initially favored allowing the Nez Perce to remain, but the army's humiliation at the hands of the Lakotas and Howard's own conviction, which was also the government's, that Indians had to be controlled and remade changed his opinion and his instructions. Howard ordered the Oregon Nez Perce to move to the reservation in Idaho Territory within thirty days—June 15, 1877—or face war. Most Nez Perce prepared to submit, but just before the deadline some young men took revenge for years of abuse. They initially killed selectively, singling out people who had murdered their relatives, set dogs upon them, or protected those who had beaten Indians. But once the violence started, anyone found with the guilty parties died, too. Howard dispatched troops. The first reports of the fighting began to appear in eastern newspapers in late June, even though the defeat of the Lakotas was supposed to have ended such violence in the West.[32]

In the stories Americans told themselves, refugees fled *to* the United States, not *from* it, but the Nez Perce, like Sitting Bull's people before them, saw Canada as their haven. They escaped the converging columns of Generals Miles and Howard, outwitting the soldiers when they could. They crossed impossible terrain while burdened with children and old people, and fought and defeated the soldiers when cornered. At the Battle of Big Hole in Idaho Territory, they repulsed the Americans, but American soldiers slaughtered dozens of Indian women and children. The Nez Perce sought to avoid further confrontations with the army by moving

31. Elliott West, *The Last Indian War: The Nez Perce Story* (New York: Oxford University Press, 2009), 69, 89–93, 106–7; Ulysses S. Grant, "Eighth Annual Message (December 5, 1876)" (Miller Center, University of Virginia, 2015).
32. West, 111–20; "The Hostilities in Idaho," *New York Times*, June 29, 1877.

OH! OH! HOWARD!
"I am still pursuing the Indians."—*Telegram from General O. O. Howard.*

This cartoon ridicules General O. O. Howard, the same man who headed the Freedmen's Bureau, for failing to catch the fleeing Nez Perce. The Oh! Oh! (or Uh! Oh!) refers to the Civil War nickname his soldiers gave him, which played on his initials to convey his lack of military success. The Nez Perce called him General Day-After-Tomorrow. *Puck*, Aug. 7, 1878. Library of Congress, LC-USZC2-1241.

through Yellowstone Park in Wyoming Territory. In 1872 President Grant had signed a bill creating the park, heavily promoted by Jay Cooke as a source of traffic for the Northern Pacific; it was to be "a pleasuring-ground for the benefit and enjoyment of the people." With the Northern Pacific moribund after 1873, the park remained remote though not impossible for tourists to reach. When the Nez Perce fled across the new park, two very different but connected Americas collided. The Nez Perce, resisting forced incorporation into American society, ran into a party of tourists, whose members were vacationing to escape the pressures of an industrializing society. Some young warriors saw the Cowan Party as targets for revenge, and they tried to take it. Miraculously, in a harrowing escape, all survived what historian Elliott West has called "the worst vacation in American history."[33]

33. West, 186–229, quote 221.

The Nez Perce pushed out of the park and into Montana, still eluding the army when they could, fighting when they could not. During the Civil War Howard's soldiers had, in a pun on his initials O. O., nicknamed him "General Oh! Oh! Howard." The Nez Perce simply called him "General Day-after-Tomorrow." He could not catch the Nez Perce, but Gen. Nelson Miles did. Against the advice of Poker Joe, one of the war leaders who had brilliantly led them through Montana, the Nez Perce stopped to rest just short of the Canadian border near the Milk River. Hunters had encountered bison, remnants of the fast-disappearing herds, and the Nez Perce were hungry. Miles attacked them while they rested at Bear's Paw. After all those months of flight and all the death, Canada and refuge were achingly near, but the United States grabbed the Nez Perce and surrounded them. About a third slipped out of the camp to join Sitting Bull's Lakota in Canada; the bulk of the Nez Perce under Chief Joseph surrendered on October 5, 1877. Joseph probably never gave the speech later attributed to him, but he did say something like what the Americans translated as "From where the sun now stands, I will fight no more."[34]

Taken for granted in the drama of the flight lurked a significant truth. The border mattered. It divided not the just the United States and Canada, but the homelands of Indian peoples. Over the rest of the century, the U.S. Army and the Royal Canadian Mounted Police made the border more and more impassable for native peoples, considered citizens of neither country but wards of one or the other. They harassed them and stopped them on journeys that had once been routine.[35]

The Americans showed no more generosity to the Nez Perce after the war than they had before it. General Sherman wanted to hang Joseph, treating him far more harshly than the United States had treated Jefferson Davis. Instead he just broke General Miles's promises to the Nez Perce and exiled them to Indian Territory. The Nez Perce paid a greater price for defending their homeland than the Confederates had for trying to destroy the Union. They endured a slow execution. Before their release eight years later, half of the captured Nez Perce died, including nearly all their young children.[36]

Indian violence was old violence, and although the flight of the Nez Perce gripped the public, for most of the summer it was both juxtaposed

---

34. Benjamin Hoy, "A Wall of Many Heights: The Uneven Enforcement of the Canadian–United States Border" (Stanford, CA: Stanford University Press, 2015), 242; West, 230–82.
35. Hoy, 206–8, 243–67.
36. West, 283–302.

against and overshadowed by a new violence that struck much closer to home. There were, as the newspapers phrased it, *two* "red" wars taking place in the country that summer.

Among the many casualties of the Panic of 1873 was Scott's Texas and Pacific Railway, but more critically the Panic had weakened the Pennsylvania Railroad, of which Scott became president in 1874. His attempts to resurrect the Texas and Pacific led to bitter battles with Collis P. Huntington of the Southern Pacific; his need to increase the revenues of the Pennsylvania led to war against John D. Rockefeller's Standard Oil. Scott was used to fighting other railroads, but now he had to confront industries that the railroads had made possible, a few of which had grown strong enough to defy him.[37]

In many ways the story of the Great Strike of 1877 was the story of how a conflict in the state of Pennsylvania went national. The national capital had long ago left Philadelphia for Washington, D.C., and the financial capital had shifted to New York, but Pennsylvania, with its coal, oil, and industry, remained the workshop of the nation. The Pennsylvania Railroad was the country's most powerful and best-run corporation, which, given the road's insider dealing, says much about American corporations.

Tom Scott was overextended following the Panic of 1873, and when overextended, he tended to double down on his bets. To rescue the Texas and Pacific, he badly needed help. He turned to Andrew Carnegie, who had once been his protégé and was now an increasingly powerful iron and steel manufacturer. In 1877 Carnegie had to confront a conflict between the values expressed in "pull," as the kind of business friendship that made both his and Scott's careers was called, and the efficiency, ruthless eradication of competition, and limitation of risk that made them adroit businessmen. When his mentor asked for help in keeping the Texas and Pacific afloat, Carnegie refused. He regarded the Texas and Pacific as a dangerous distraction; success came from focusing on a central business. He refused to throw good money after bad.[38]

Steel and oil were both core Pennsylvania businesses, and any major business in Pennsylvania involved Scott and the Pennsylvania Railroad. As a businessman, Rockefeller was in some ways Carnegie's twin, but Rockefeller's public persona was much different: quiet, familial, and secretive. He sprang from one of those Gothic pockets scattered across

37. Albert J. Churella, *The Pennsylvania Railroad* (Philadelphia: University of Pennsylvania Press, 2013), 389, 447, 471.
38. Pamela Walker Laird, *Pull: Networking and Success since Benjamin Franklin* (Cambridge, MA: Harvard University Press, 2006), 28–31, 35–36; David Nasaw, *Andrew Carnegie* (New York: Penguin Press, 2006), 151–54.

New England and the South that had fascinated American novelists since Poe. His father was a bigamist, probably a rapist, and a huckster who specialized in patent medicines. He deserted his family seasonally and eventually abandoned them altogether for his other, younger wife. John D. Rockefeller purposely molded himself into his father's opposite: monogamous, moralistic, disciplined, and devout. He retained only his father's love of money. From his earliest days, he combined his avarice with charity. If he did not tithe—giving away 10 percent—he came close. He adamantly believed that "God gave me my money." He regarded himself as God's steward.[39]

Rockefeller made his fortune in Cleveland, which along with Chicago, Milwaukee, Cincinnati, Minneapolis, and St. Louis made the Midwest the most dynamic and fastest-growing section of the United States. He began as a clerk, studied bookkeeping, and became a wholesaler, trading and speculating in commodities. He bought a substitute for doing military service in the Civil War and branched out into oil, which, refined into kerosene, was then rapidly replacing whale oil in lighting American homes. Rockefeller was not interested in drilling for oil, which was then confined largely to a relatively small area in western Pennsylvania. He invested in refineries.[40]

Rockefeller had no patience with the liberal pieties of laissez-faire; for him the problem of the age was excessive competition. Oilmen produced, and wasted, too much oil. The existing refineries were small and inefficient, but there were so many of them that they still glutted markets with kerosene, driving prices down. The economy needed order: pools to regulate production and prices and consolidation to yield larger and more efficient refineries. Rockefeller preached cooperation. Cooperation meant joining Standard Oil, which he founded in 1870. Rockefeller made many enemies and few friends, but he had a knack for absorbing the most able of his rivals into Standard Oil, which was ruthless, efficient, and only as scrupulous as it needed to be. His partner, Henry Flagler, was Presbyterian rather than Baptist, but he replicated Rockefeller's business Christianity. On his desk he kept a quote from the contemporary novel David Harum: "Do unto others as they would do unto you—and do it first."[41]

The key to Rockefeller's initial success was, unsurprisingly, the railroads. Oil was cheap; refineries were cheap; but transportation of oil to the refineries and of kerosene from the refineries to market was relatively

39. Ron Chernow, Titan: The Life of John D. Rockefeller, Sr. (New York: Random House, 1998), 3–44, 49–50, 54–55, 66, 88.
40. Ibid., 69–73.
41. Ibid., 78–80, 109–17, 131, 223–24.

expensive. Rockefeller sought his advantage in transportation. In Cleveland he had rail connections and, for part of the year, access to shipping through the Great Lakes to the Erie Canal. In 1868 Rockefeller obtained rebates—refunds of part of what he paid to ship freight—from the Erie Railroad, owned by Jay Gould, and Vanderbilt's New York Central. The railroads gained efficiencies of scale and guaranteed traffic by granting Standard Oil special privileges that antimonopolists denounced as a violation of the railroads' duties as common carriers.[42]

In 1872 Scott and Rockefeller jointly moved to control Pennsylvania oil. Scott had formed the South Improvement Company (SIC), a creature of what his enemies called the Tom Scott legislature: the Pennsylvania General Assembly. An anonymous legislator introduced the bill chartering the SIC, no roll call vote was recorded, and the proceedings of the General Assembly contained no record of its passage. The idea was to regulate production and traffic, stabilizing prices for the benefit of the trunk lines and participating refiners. The goal was to make the SIC an instrument for concentrating refining in Cleveland and Pittsburgh at the expense of refiners elsewhere. Ultimately the scheme failed, as oil producers instituted a boycott and independent refiners exerted enough political pressure to get the charter for the SIC canceled.[43]

The collapse of the SIC was only a setback in Rockefeller's campaign to reduce competition and centralize refining. He had used the threat of the SIC and the lack of oil resulting from the producers' boycott to absorb virtually all the rival refineries in Cleveland. Rockefeller gave his Cleveland rivals a choice: ruin, or sale to Standard Oil. They could take Standard Oil stock—which choice he urged—or cash, with his assessors determining the price. The ordering of an irrational industry came from the quite visible hand of Standard Oil, not the supposed invisible hand of the market.[44]

Dominating Cleveland was a major step, but other refiners in western Pennsylvania and the Northeast remained. Rockefeller organized rival refiners in pools, dividing the market and determining the prices between them, and trying to control production. Such pools were fragile, virtually always breaking apart and launching a new bout of competition. Rockefeller made sure to maintain his advantage with the railroads and

42. Ibid., 111–12; Chester McArthur Destler, "The Standard Oil, Child of the Erie Ring, 1868–1872. Six Contracts and a Letter," *Mississippi Valley Historical Review* 33, no. 1 (1946): 89–120; Churella, 360–62.
43. Chernow, 130–48; Churella, 363–69.
44. The phrase *visible hand* is Alfred Chandler's, from *The Visible Hand: The Managerial Revolution in American Business* (Cambridge, MA: Belknap Press, 1977); Chernow, 143–48, 154.

with pipelines that delivered oil to railheads. He built his own tank cars and took on his own insurance, getting further reductions in rates in return. He invested in newer and more efficient refineries and sought savings everywhere possible.[45]

For Rockefeller, the Panic of 1873 represented opportunity. Crude oil prices plummeted, and so did the price of kerosene. Cutting costs and dividends, Rockefeller moved systematically to acquire first his largest rivals and then the smaller ones in Pittsburgh, Philadelphia, and Oil City. He also established a foothold in New York. By 1875 he controlled all the major refining centers. He was not afraid to borrow. He built pipelines to control access to the railheads and depots.[46]

In 1876 a new oil field was discovered in Bradford, Pennsylvania. The cost of entry was low, production soared, and oil fell from four dollars a barrel in 1876 to seventy cents by 1878. Rockefeller, as was his wont, saw in plummeting prices an opening. Standard Oil expanded its pipelines into the new field, connected new wells for free, and constructed tanks to store the surplus. Production soon exceeded storage capacity, and oil ran into the ground. Rockefeller announced Standard Oil would accept oil only for immediate shipment and slashed the price offered by 20 percent. He gave priority to shipments to his own refineries, cutting off rival refiners. Despite a glut of oil, his rivals found their refineries running dry. When a Pennsylvania state investigation exonerated Rockefeller, the producers claimed Standard Oil had bribed the investigator. Standard Oil's profits soared as the producers faced collapse.[47]

Events escalated quickly and unpredictably. Rockefeller's expansion threatened the Pennsylvania Railroad's lucrative oil traffic. The Empire Line, one of the many Pennsylvania affiliates designed to siphon profits from the Pennsylvania and deposit them in the pockets of insiders, built competing pipelines to connect with the Pennsylvania and purchased refineries on the East Coast to compete with Rockefeller. This was war, not only between Standard Oil and Empire, but also between the Pennsylvania Railroad and the New York Central and the Erie, which also transported Standard Oil shipments. The independent oil producers, seeking protection from Standard Oil, sided with Empire, whose president, Colonel Joseph D. Potts, described the methods of Rockefeller's cartel—the Central Refiners Association—as resembling "the gentle fanning of the

45. Chernow, 149, 157–61, 170.
46. Ibid., 161–68, 170–72.
47. Ibid., 198–200.

vampire's wing, and it had the same end in view—the undisturbed abstraction of the victim's blood."[48]

The war came at a bad time for Scott. Investors in the Pennsylvania, who had organized a stockholder investigating committee in 1874, disliked the insider operations, which siphoned off revenue. Scott and his predecessor as president of the Pennsylvania Railroad, J. Edgar Thomson, tried to maintain dividends at 10 percent on the well-founded belief that well-fed stockholders tended to be less curious stockholders, but declining revenues after 1873 that came with the depression and competition made this harder and harder to do. To keep dividends up, the Pennsylvania cut wages, laid off employees, and increased the workweek to sixty hours without an equivalent raise in pay. The extended workweek and the earlier pay cuts amounted to a 20 percent decrease in wages, but this was not enough. The Pennsylvania had to cut dividends to 6 percent by May 1877 and planned another pay cut for June 1, 1877.[49]

The competitive struggles of the Pennsylvania and other large eastern railroads in the 1870s had driven them to form the Eastern Trunk Line Association led by Albert Fink. It was a giant pool with a strong bureaucracy that would allocate traffic and set rates. The other pool members had apparently also agreed to cut wages. Scott's war with Rockefeller threatened the association. By diverting all of Standard's shipments away from the Pennsylvania and demanding rebates from its rivals, Rockefeller had precipitated precisely the kind of rate war the Eastern Trunk Line Association was supposed to prevent. He shut down his Pittsburgh refineries and upped the output of his Cleveland refineries in order to starve the Pennsylvania of revenue. The Pennsylvania lost both market share and money.[50]

When Scott went forward with his wage cut, he set a timer on a bomb that he did not think would explode. What followed looked less like a conventional strike than a social revolution.[51]

III

In early July the violence that dominated American newspapers was the pursuit of the Nez Perce in the West. The North seemed quiet. In the East

48. Ibid., 200–201; Churella, 456–58.
49. Churella, 477–78.
50. Scott Nelson, A Nation of Deadbeats: An Uncommon History of America's Financial Disasters (New York: Knopf, 2012), 177–78; Churella, 457–58, 461–67, 476–79; Chernow, 200–201.
51. David O. Stowell, Streets, Railroads, and the Great Strike of 1877 (Chicago: University of Chicago Press, 1999) 1–11.

the Pennsylvania Railroad had easily managed both worker delegations and scattered walkouts, and so the other trunk lines implemented their wage cuts on July 1. Added to earlier decreases in pay, the new wage cuts, depending on a worker's job, amounted to a reduction of between 20 percent and 29 percent since 1873. Accompanying the wage cuts were drastic changes in work rules that put the organization and conduct of work under firmer managerial control. Besides the practical effects—less predictable schedules, deadheading (waiting without pay in a strange town for a new assignment), longer hours, less time with their families, and less job security—workers regarded the new rules as an attack on their dignity as men and citizens. They were expected to submit unquestioningly to orders of officials whom they had not chosen and often did not respect. Who controlled the conditions of work—the workers or management— became a central issue in 1877. Of the seven demands that the workers on the Pennsylvania presented to the company, only one concerned wages.[52]

The absence of immediate trouble masked the ticking of a time bomb. Workers on the Baltimore and Ohio became the first to walk out in response to the wage cuts. With a nice symmetry, John W. Garrett, the president of the road, approved a 10 percent dividend for stockholders the same day he cut wages by 10 percent. The strike began at Camden, Maryland, and quickly spread on July 14 to Martinsburg, West Virginia, an important division point, as the railroads called the towns where they located shops and switching yards. Trainmen declared a blockade on freight traffic until their wages were restored, though shopmen remained at work. By evening, a crowd had gathered in support of the trainmen. As would be the case in many towns and cities during the strike, most members of the crowd were not railroad workers. Some were wives and teenage children of railroad workers; most of the others were unemployed, workers in other industries, and even clerks and small businessmen. Here, as elsewhere, the strike was as much a community rebellion against the railroads as a work action. Initially, the local and even parts of the national press sympathized with the strikers. The *Missouri Republican* refused to condemn men who were forced to choose between "revolution and the abject submission to the heartless demand of capital." The railroad workers, who were stopping the passage of freight but not passenger trains, had to struggle to maintain control of the strike, sometimes escorting passenger trains through crowds that wanted to stop all traffic.[53]

---

52. Churella, 477–80, 488.

53. Stowell, 1–8, 99, 104, 113–14, 124–26; Philip Sheldon Foner, *The Great Labor Uprising of 1877* (New York: Monad Press, distributed by Pathfinder Press, 1977), 104; Michael A. Bellesiles, *1877: America's Year of Living Violently* (New York: New Press, 2010), 148–49; David O. Stowell, ed., *The Great Strikes of 1877* (Urbana: University of Illinois Press, 2008), 2–3, 86–87.

The strike on the Erie Railroad began when the receiver for that road, which was in bankruptcy, backed the divisional superintendent, who had fired all the members of a delegation that without the superintendent's permission had gone to New York and remonstrated over the wage cut: "The company will not make any concessions whatever [on this issue] to the men, and if it is necessary to close the road until the company's authority is re-established then the road will be closed." At stake, as a vice president of the Erie put it, "was the right of the company to operate its own property." The workers cast the dispute equally broadly; in the words of a strike leader, the railroads were trying to

> break the spirit of the men and any and all organizations they belonged to.... Many of the men belonged to Masonic and Odd Fellowship societies and also various societies associated with the Catholic church, so if the men had not the money to pay their dues, of course, they would have to withdraw from all those associations, from all fellowship for mutual aid with fellow men, leaving them a heterogeneous mass without civil or social aid.[54]

The first significant violence erupted at Martinsburg, and it set a pattern that recurred in other places. When the strikers shut down the Baltimore and Ohio and the local police proved incapable or unwilling to protect workers willing to move freight trains, the governor mobilized the local militia, who often sympathized with the strikers. At Martinsburg Governor Henry Matthews sent troops at the behest of John Garret, president of the B&O. A striker shot at a militiaman escorting a cattle train when the soldier tried to change a switch. The militiaman returned fire. Both were wounded, the striker fatally. At Martinsburg, the beginning of violence was also its end. Strikebreakers were not willing to attempt to move other trains, and with no trains moving and no further violence, the militia, sympathetic to the strikers, withdrew. The governor ordered militia in from Wheeling, but they too proved undependable. In a dramatic break from past practice, President Garrett demanded federal troops. The U.S. Army had not previously intervened in a labor dispute in the states, although it had been deployed in the territories. Using troops in a strike represented a more radical extension of federal power than using them to protect voters in the South, where there was specific legislation that sanctioned their use.

The loudest demands for troops came from railroad executives such as Garrett and Scott. They controlled so many state officials that they

---

54. Shelton Stromquist, "'Our Rights as Workingmen': Class Traditions and Collective Action in a Nineteenth-Century Railroad Town, Hornellsville, N.Y., 1869–82," in Stowell, ed., *The Great Strikes of 1877*, 68–69.

sometimes seemed to forget they were not elected officials themselves and could not ask the president for soldiers. Governors had to do that. To make their requests credible, the governors needed to demonstrate that the police and militia could no longer protect life and property. Since this was often not the case, railroad officials suggested other arguments. Scott claimed the free movement of trains was the equivalent of freedom of the seas and designated the strikers as pirates. Charles Francis Adams, Jr., of the Massachusetts Railroad Commission, equated a striking worker with a "public enemy" of the Commonwealth.[55]

President Hayes, having refused to deploy troops in the South, was hardly eager to use them to settle civil disputes in the North, but as would be his pattern during the first part of his presidency, he objected in principle only to yield in practice. Governor Matthews of West Virginia reported that "much property may be destroyed and . . . lives lost." Hayes accepted the mere possibility, and not the actuality, of violence as sufficient, proclaimed the strike "unlawful and insurrectionary proceedings," and dispatched troops, despite the lack of violence or property destruction since the initial shooting. The Baltimore and Ohio charged the government for the soldiers' fares to Martinsburg.[56]

In Pennsylvania, Scott enlisted both Philadelphia's mayor and the governor—who was vacationing with his family in another of Scott's private cars when the strike broke out—to ask for troops. Hayes initially confined the use of federal troops to protecting government property and keeping the peace, but Scott wanted the soldiers to suppress the strike and, if necessary, operate the trains. Hayes yielded, in part. When three federal judges ruled that workers striking against bankrupt railroads in the hands of federal receivers were in contempt of court, they opened a huge loophole for federal intervention. Bankruptcy proceedings became a tool to acquire the federal aid needed to crush strikes. Hayes stood firm on one thing. He refused Scott's demand that he raise seventy-five thousand volunteers to end the strike.[57]

For all the legal and symbolic significance of their use, federal troops played a relatively minor role in actually suppressing the strike. They spent July and August shuttling between one outbreak and another, often arriving after whatever violence had occurred was over. The contest re-

---

55. Thomas A. Scott, "The Recent Strikes," *North American Review* 125, no. 258 (1877), 351–62; Nancy Cohen, *The Reconstruction of American Liberalism, 1865–1914* (Chapel Hill: University of North Carolina Press, 2002), 126–27.
56. Bellesiles, 150; Hoogenboom, 326–27.
57. Hoogenboom, 327–33; Robert V. Bruce, *1877: Year of Violence* (Indianapolis: Bobbs-Merrill, 1959), 73, 279–80.

mained largely between the strikers and their supporters on the one hand and police, deputized volunteers, and militia on the other.

Although the strikers lacked national leadership or coordination, the strike appeared national because it was so widespread and news of the various outbreaks traveled so quickly. It marked how thoroughly the railway and telegraph network had reconstructed American space. Workers could move quickly from city to city by rail, and news of the various strikes moved even more quickly by wire. In July the strike jumped from Martinsburg to Baltimore and then to Pittsburgh and then throughout the Northeast, Midwest, and into the West. Only New England and the Deep South were spared.[58]

Workers used modern technologies as effectively as their employers. Railroad workers embodied the changing economy; they were demanding control over that change, not resisting it. In a kind of chain reaction, news of a strike in one place sparked eruptions in other towns, cities, and regions. The strike ignited social tensions that had been developing for a decade. Workers and their supporters resisted "monopolies": the railroad corporations that governed the conditions of their daily lives and work.

The strike seemed like a social revolution because it involved far more people than the railroad workers. Much of the violence came from those who, though not employed by the railroads, had seen their lives disrupted and endangered by them. Trains crisscrossed American cities at street level, the same streets in which the poor quite literally lived—working, scavenging for wood or coal, peddling, and buying goods. Children played, and worked, on these streets, and small businesses received and shipped goods on them and gained access to customers along them. Tracks down the middle of such streets or crossing over them on a level turned neighborhoods, as a South Side Chicago resident put it, into "a prolonged and perpetual switchyard," creating "terror and alarm" for those who used them.[59]

The injuries and deaths that came from working for the railroads and living alongside them generated deep resentment. In New York State alone during the 1870s, hundreds of workers and residents died every year, crushed by the trains or falling victim to runaway horses spooked by trains.

58. Stowell, *Streets, Railroads, and the Great Strike of 1877*, 70–115; Stromquist, "'Our Rights as Working Men'," in Stowell, ed., *The Great Strikes of 1877*, 56.

59. Stowell, *Streets, Railroads, and the Great Strike of 1877*, 6–8, 19–25, 36, 66–69; Christine Meisner Rosen, *The Limits of Power: Great Fires and the Process of City Growth in America* (Cambridge: Cambridge University Press, 1986), 168.

Children were killed trying to hitch rides on the cars. Crowds angry at the railroads joined the strikers and were often more militant and violent.[60]

Older ideals of independence and manhood fed the strike, but they could also, at least in some towns, prevent the emergence of class divisions. In 1877 Eugene Debs, a local official of the Brotherhood of Locomotive Firemen in Terre Haute, Indiana, and an aspiring Democratic politician, opposed the strike. Along with many other conservative workers, he thought of himself as sharing a common and harmonious world with employers, whom he regarded as fellow producers and fellow citizens. Most railroad workers in Terre Haute endorsed the strike, but they were clear that although they were striking against the Vandalia Railroad, their real enemy was the Pennsylvania Railroad and Tom Scott. They thought that "their fellow citizens of all classes" shared the same resentment against the Pennsylvania and supported the strike. In this they were wrong. Terre Haute employers did not welcome the strike, and federal troops cleared strikers from the depot they had occupied.[61]

Violence subsided for nearly a week following the shootings at Martinsburg, but on Friday July 20 Baltimore militia marched from their armory to protect the property of the B&O. Many militiamen had refused to muster; those who did faced an angry crowd that threatened and threw stones. Soldiers shot into the crowd, but instead of retreating, the rioters attacked the troops all along their march to Camden station. Half the militia, either fearful or in sympathy with the crowd, deserted. Only one soldier was badly injured, but a dozen citizens lay dead, including Patrick Gill, a forty-year-old Irish immigrant tinner; Thomas Byrne, a salesman at a clothing store; and Willie Hourand, a fifteen-year-old newsboy.[62]

In Pittsburgh the violence on July 20 was far worse. Railway workers, supported by numerous sympathizers, had stopped all freight movement through the city. The mayor hated the railroad officials, whom he regarded as "imperious and dictatorial." Businessmen resented the Pennsylvania Railroad's rate structure, which had long discriminated against Pittsburgh shippers. The depression had hit the city hard, and on July 19, the city, desperate for funds, had laid off half its police department. The local militia openly fraternized with the strikers, men who were their neighbors, friends, and co-workers. Militia officers, doubting the loyalty of their own troops, requested reinforcements from Philadelphia, and railroad officials

60. Mark Aldrich, *Death Rode the Rails: American Railroad Accidents and Safety, 1828–1965* (Baltimore, MD: Johns Hopkins University Press, 2006), 2–4; Stowell, *Streets, Railroads, and the Great Strike of 1877*, 25–35, 70–115.
61. Nick Salvatore, "Railroad Workers and the Great Strike of 1877: The View from a Small Midwest City," *Labor History* 21, no. 4 (1980): 522–45.
62. Bruce, 93–114; Bellesiles, 152–53; Stowell, ed., *The Great Strikes of 1877*, 3–4.

eagerly seconded them. The Philadelphia militia came by special train, and on July 20 they began to clear the tracks and railroad yards of strikers and their sympathizers, who included women and children. There were competing accounts of who precipitated the violence, but once militiamen with fixed bayonets moved on the crowd, fighting erupted. The soldiers fired, killing from ten to twenty people and wounding between thirty and seventy. The deaths, which a grand jury later described as "unauthorized, willful and wanton killing," enraged the city, and the crowds grew in response. The Pittsburgh militia threw down their arms and deserted, leaving the Philadelphians on their own. By Monday July 23, mobs had driven the militia from the railroad yards and looted and burned two thousand railroad cars and forty buildings. Rioters destroyed a three-mile stretch of Pennsylvania Railroad property and stopped firemen from quenching the flames. The violence halted only when there was little belonging to the Pennsylvania Railroad left to burn.[63]

In Baltimore and Pittsburgh the violence unleashed by the strike brought the by-now standard comparison from frightened liberals and employers: the Paris Commune of 1871. They imagined communist revolutionaries in league with workers and the dangerous classes in an assault on free labor and property. The strikers, the *Brooklyn Daily Eagle* wrote, refused "to recognize the right of every American to control his own labor and his own property." Henry Ward Beecher condemned strikers for "tyrannical opposition to all law and order." He insisted that a man with a family of five children needed no more than a dollar a day if he did not smoke or drink beer. "Is not a dollar a day enough to buy bread? Water costs nothing…the man who cannot live on bread and water is not fit to live." Even the *New York World*, controlled by Tom Scott, distanced itself from Beecher, calling his remarks "suicidal and the part of a lunatic." In an attempt to explain himself, Beecher preached that it was the intention of God for "the great to be great and the little to be little." The poor had to "reap the misfortunes of inferiority."[64]

When liberals denounced communist revolutionaries, they usually meant the Workingmen's Party of the United States, then only a year old and headquartered in Chicago. The party had but a few thousand members and arose from a temporary healing of sectarian disputes between Marxists—who favored the organization of trade unions to advance class struggle and thought political action premature—and the followers of

63. Stowell, ed., *The Great Strikes of 1877*, 5–7; Churella, 481–84, 485–86; Bruce, 121–27, 131–83.
64. Philip Sheldon Foner, 103–6; Nell Irvin Painter, *Standing at Armageddon: The United States, 1877–1919* (New York: Norton, 1987), 15–24; Bruce, 312–14.

Ferdinand Lassalle, who thought the organization of workers' cooperatives and political action were the route to a new society. The strike surprised the party as much as anyone else, but in Chicago, St. Louis, and San Francisco the Workingmen attempted to lead the strikers and their supporters.[65]

In Chicago, where the influence of socialism was growing particularly among German immigrants, both German workers and the anti-immigrant and antidemocratic Citizen's Association funded their own militias, making political conflicts there potentially deadly. When the strike hit Chicago on July 24, the socialists tried to expand it into a general strike. The most eloquent and unlikely socialist orator was Albert Parsons, a Texan and an ex-Confederate cavalryman who became a Radical Republican. Socialism was only another stop on his road to anarchism. He married a black woman, Lucy Parsons, who claimed to be Mexican but was probably an ex-slave and was nearly as eloquent as her husband. With the failure of Reconstruction in Texas, they had moved to Chicago. Albert Parsons denied that the United States was any longer different from Europe; it had fallen under the sway of despots. The strikers, he said, demanded "that they be permitted to live and that those men [in possession of the means of production] do not appropriate the life to themselves, and that they be not allowed to turn us upon the earth as vagrants and tramps."[66]

In many ways the Chicago strike followed the lines of the city's earlier eight-hour-day struggle. Bands of workers, many of them teenagers, who were a critical part of the workforce, marched to factories urging the workers there to strike and sometimes forcibly shutting them down. The mayor, who initially refused to have either the police or the militia take an active role in suppressing the railroad strike, faced pressure from the Citizen's Alliance to act more forcefully as the strike spread. The police, regarded as traitors by Irish workingpeople, attacked workers both in crowds and in peaceful meetings. Police violence provoked violence in response. And here the war against Indians in the West and workers in the city converged. Hayes ordered federal troops into Chicago from the West to conduct what the *Tribune* headlined as a "Red War." The "war," however, remained largely in the hands of the police, and it culminated in the Battle of Halsted Street Viaduct on July 26. Halsted was in a neighborhood of mostly Bohemian immigrants, but significant numbers of Irish and other workers, men and women, joined

65. Philip Sheldon Foner, 103–14.
66. Richard Schneirov, "Chicago's Great Upheaval of 1877: Class Polarization and Democratic Politics," in Stowell, ed., *The Great Strikes of 1877*, 78–82, 82–85; Michael Kazin, *American Dreamers: How the Left Changed a Nation* (New York: Knopf, 2011), 87–89.

the fighting. The violence in the city as a whole claimed thirty dead and about two hundred wounded. The vast majority of the casualties were workers. Eighteen police were wounded, none killed.[67]

Far to the west, news of the violence in the East riveted San Franciscans. The Central Pacific rescinded its 10 percent wage cut, but this did not quell the anger at the railroads nor mitigate the suffering brought by the depression. The *San Francisco Chronicle* declared that "the bedrock cause of the trouble [is] the general, bad, wasteful, tyrannical, insolent, plundering and corrupt management of the great railway corporations." In San Francisco, too, the Workingmen's Party took the initiative, calling a rally on July 23 attended by eight to ten thousand people. Despite speakers' attempts to keep the focus on monopoly, the crowd targeted the Chinese. Anti-Chinese politics were the warp in the railroad weave of antimonopoly politics in the West. The Workingmen's Party lost control, and a night of rioting and attacks on the Chinese followed. Many owners of small businesses forged alliances with organized workers to combat competition from larger businesses that employed lower-paid Chinese workers in their factories. Together they boycotted Chinese-made goods.[68]

In Chicago the attempt at a general strike had deteriorated into violence; in San Francisco, it had turned into anti-Chinese rioting; but in St. Louis, then a city of three hundred thousand, the general strike called by the Workingmen's Party briefly succeeded despite the presence of federal troops. The St. Louis and Southeastern was in the hands of a court-appointed receiver designated to run the railroad. He asked for federal troops, but when they arrived from Fort Leavenworth in Kansas, their commanding officer said, to the outrage of the receiver, that they were there to protect government and public property, and not "to quell the strikers or run the trains." As the general strike took shape, workers in other industries added demands for wage increases and the eight-hour day. But having paralyzed the city, the leaders of the strike vacillated and were at a loss as to what to do next. They disavowed and denounced the black workers whom they had just urged to join the strike. The strike had already lost its momentum at the end of June, when the police and militia forcibly broke it and arrested its leaders.[69]

The railroad strike, having taken so many local forms, petered out at the end of July. Neither largely peaceful general strikes nor furious mobs

67. In Chicago soldiers arrived in time to play an active role. Bellesiles, 167–69; Schneirov, 86–96.

68. Michael Kazin, "The July Days in San Francisco: Prelude to Kearneyism," in Stowell, ed., *The Great Strikes of 1877*, 136–38, 144–55; Jeffrey Haydu, *Citizen Employers: Business Communities and Labor in Cincinnati and San Francisco, 1870–1916* (Ithaca, NY: ILR Press, 2008), 67–71.

69. Bruce, 255, 257, 259–60; Philip Sheldon Foner, 157–87.

had been able to counter the organized violence that the local, state, and federal governments brought against them. Aftershocks in other industries continued into August, but by the end of the summer, the workers' uprising was over. It had terrified many employers and white-collar workers, and provoked virtual hysteria in the liberal bastions of the urban press.

The repression of the strike hardly signified an unalloyed triumph of corporate interests. The support strikers received in many towns and cities, stretching across class lines, forced the railroads to appeal for state militias and federal troops. Local political leaders elected with workers' votes were unwilling either to intervene against strikers or to ask for state aid. A strike in Paterson, New Jersey, among ribbon weavers—largely French, German, and English immigrants—that took place simultaneously with the Great Railroad Strike affected two thousand workers and shut the mills. The local government confined itself to keeping the peace, and because community support was solidly with the strikers, mill owners compromised. The result led some manufacturers to fund a private militia for use in future strikes.[70]

The lines between who had won and who had lost blurred in the aftermath of the Great Strike. The corporations and the government had suppressed the strike, but the railroads were reluctant to put any more pressure on wages. The lesson that President Robert Harris of the Burlington took from the strike was that "a reduction of pay to employes [sic] may be as expensive to the Co. as an increase of pay." Over the next several years many of the railroads restored all or part of the pay cuts. They were, however, unwilling to concede control over work. That struggle would continue. The cities that experienced the worst violence had clearly lost. Pittsburgh, sued by the Pennsylvania Railroad, had to pay the cost of the railroad property destroyed in the rioting, according to Pennsylvania law. City officials did so by issuing bonds. But the Pennsylvania, and particularly Scott, had also lost. The Pennsylvania had to cancel its dividends, and its stock fell to half of par. Scott surrendered to Standard Oil. He agreed to get out of the oil business and sell the Empire Line's assets to Rockefeller. The Pennsylvania's share of oil traffic had fallen from 52 to 30 percent.[71]

Charles Nordhoff, a leading journalist and a man hardly hostile to capital, thought the strike "finishes Tom Scott, and I shall not be sorry." He turned out to be close to right. In the fall of 1878 Scott suffered the first of

70. Herbert Gutman, "Class, Status, and Community Power in Nineteenth-Century American Industrial Cities: Paterson, New Jersey: A Case Study," in Gutman, *Work, Culture & Society in Industrializing America* (New York: Vintage Books, 1977, orig. ed. 1966), 242–46.

71. Perry K. Blatz, "Philadelphia, Pittsburgh, and the Pennsylvania Riot Damage Law, 1834–1880," *Pennsylvania History* 78, no. 4 (Autumn 2011); Churella, 458, 489; Bruce, 301–3.

what would be a series of strokes. By then his attempt to build the Texas and Pacific was in shambles, and his own lobbying was stymied by the equally effective lobbying of Huntington and his associates in the rival Southern Pacific Railroad. Huntington was determined to deny Scott his subsidies, and deny him he did. Sick and depressed, Scott, like so many other rich Americans during the Gilded Age, departed on a tour of Europe and the Middle East. In May 1879 his young son and namesake died at the age of thirteen. Jay Gould bought out Scott's interest in the Texas and Pacific and took up his quarrels with the Southern Pacific. Scott resigned as president of the Pennsylvania in 1880. In 1882 the man who had once seemed to be everywhere and in control of nearly everything in Gilded Age America died. He was 57.[72]

IV

It is hard to imagine a more disastrous beginning to a presidency than what Rutherford B. Hayes had experienced in 1877, but he was someone who thought that attracting opposition from nearly every direction meant that he was right. The president represented an odd ideological mix. In many respects he was a liberal, but not consistently enough to win the loyalty of Godkin, whose cracked scheme to deny Hayes the presidency during the election crisis cost the *Nation* half its declining number of subscribers. Hayes had been a free trader in Congress, but as president he accepted the tariff for revenue and protection, alienating those for whom free trade was essential to liberalism. Hayes's liberalism ran toward hard money and civil service reform, but other hard-money men hated him. Roscoe Conkling and James G. Blaine, both in that category, detested civil service reform, which threatened the political machines that sustained their power. They were also appalled by Hayes's Southern policy.[73]

What appeared to be half-measures and indecision to others, Hayes regarded as moderation. His wife, Lucy, was a noted temperance advocate. The couple banned liquor at the White House, earning Lucy the nickname of Lemonade Lucy. But when she refused to denounce a claret punch being served at a dinner in their honor in Philadelphia, the Lucy Hayes Temperance Society of Washington condemned her and changed its name. James A. Garfield, watching the president flounder in big things and small, thought

72. Hoogenboom, 334; Bruce, 300–301; Richard White, *Railroaded: The Transcontinentals and the Making of Modern America* (New York: Norton, 2011), 129–30; Churella, 491.
73. William Martin Armstrong, *E. L. Godkin: A Biography* (Albany: State University of New York Press, 1978), 138–39, 141; Calhoun, 144–59; Hoogenboom, 306, 352–56, 362, 435.

that the "impression is deepening that he is not large enough for the place he holds" and that his election "has been an almost fatal blow to his party."[74]

The failure of Congress to pass appropriations for the army forced Hayes to call a special session in the fall of 1877. He not only did not get the appropriations—the Democrats would fund neither the army nor the civil service without riders repealing the civil rights laws—but also got much that he did not desire. Congress checked the federal power he had deployed to help the railroads. In 1877 the Democrats proposed a bill to prevent the use of federal troops as a *posse comitatus*, a civil force. They aimed to cripple civil rights enforcement. The bill failed, but antimonopolist Republicans and Democrats substituted a bill that allowed their use only when "expressly authorized by the Constitution." This permitted the use of the army to protect suffrage rights and to protect the mails and enforce court orders, but not to intervene otherwise in labor disputes or to enforce revenue laws aimed at bootleggers.[75]

Without appropriations to fund much of the government, Hayes simultaneously found himself at war with the Republican Stalwarts over control over appointments. Congress had, civil service reformers contended, violated the Constitution's separation of powers by taking over the executive's right to appoint officials, draining power from the presidency. Political appointees gave their loyalty to state and local party machines rather than the nation and contributed their time and part of their salaries to the parties to which they owed their offices. The foot soldiers in this patronage army were the postmasters, who would number roughly fifty thousand by the mid-1880s. When Hayes vowed to stop federal office holders from also taking political positions; appointed the Jay Commission, which recommended staff reductions in the New York Collector of Customs office; and tried to replace Conkling's collector, Chester A. Arthur, with his own appointee, it meant war.[76]

In taking on the customs offices, Hayes wanted to break the Stalwart machines, which opposed him and which capitalized on the American

74. Hoogenboom, 359–63.
75. Ibid., 352, 392.
76. Peter Argersinger, "The Transformation of American Politics: Political Institutions and Public Policy, 1865–1910," in *Contesting Democracy: Substance and Structure in American Political History, 1775–2000*, ed. Byron E. Shafer and Anthony J. Badger (Lawrence: University Press of Kansas, 2001), 119–20; "1885 Annual Report of the Postmaster General," ed. Post Office Department (Washington, DC: U.S. GPO, 1885), 229–30; Daniel P. Carpenter, *The Forging of Bureaucratic Autonomy: Reputations, Networks, and Policy Innovation in Executive Agencies, 1862–1928* (Princeton, NJ: Princeton University Press, 2001), 41–44; Ira M. Rutkow, *James A. Garfield* (New York: Times Books, 2006), 56–57.

system of fee-based governance. Arthur was actually quite competent. He had improved the procedures of the New York Customs Office and eliminated much of the outright bribery of officials. Arthur remained, however, a loyal functionary of the Conkling machine. He had proved a master of the so-called moiety system (a key element of fee-based governance), which entitled government officials to 50 percent of the penalty on goods undervalued for import, and used it to enrich himself, his subordinates, and his sponsors. In a famous 1872 case, the import house of Phelps, Dodge and Company was assessed a penalty of $271,000 on a shipment that turned out to have been undervalued by only $6,000 and that represented a revenue loss to the government of a mere $1,600. Half the $271,00 went to government officials, including Arthur, and the officials, in turn, paid significant legal fees to Conkling and Ben Butler. The scandal was bad enough to end the moiety system, but plenty of other opportunities for gain remained.[77]

Fee-based governance represented an administrative strategy that was no less "modern" than the bureaucracies that came to define European states. It used fees, bounties, subsidies, and contracts with private individuals or corporations to enforce laws and implement public policy. In the immediate wake of the Civil War, what might superficially look like a bureaucracy in the General Land Office, the Office of Indian Affairs, or the Treasury Department really amounted to a collection of agents who lived on the fees they collected and the economic opportunities their jobs presented. Where fees and bounties did not suffice, the federal government routinely delegated governmental functions to corporations, churches, and a variety of other independent actors. The net result was an unwieldy and inefficient system that required few taxes but was ubiquitous and often intrusive.[78]

Fee-based governance assumed that officials would forgo self-interest and follow the rules and laws designed to control their fees, but the system was purposefully weighted to serve those seeking favors. Anyone who required a government service paid a fee; those who violated a law or code paid a penalty. Governments offered bounties or fees for collecting taxes, arresting criminals, killing predators, seizing enemy vessels in times of war, and performing services. Government subcontracted or subsidized services from supervising Indian agencies to building necessary infrastructure. Political machines preferred fee-based appointments since the men

---

77. Jordan, 209–11.
78. Nicholas R. Parrillo, *Against the Profit Motive: The Salary Revolution in American Government, 1780–1940* (New Haven, CT: Yale University Press, 2013), 21–23, 120, 183–86.

they appointed had to make mandatory political contributions, often a percentage of the office's income, to the party. Fee-based offices, being the most lucrative, yielded the greater kickbacks.[79]

Three very different figures, Chester A. Arthur, Grover Cleveland, and Wyatt Earp, demonstrated the pervasiveness of fee-based government and how it worked. As the Collector of Customs for the Port of New York, Arthur controlled one of the most lucrative offices in the country. In the 1870s the collector's salary and fees alone amounted to $50,000, equal to the salary of the president. He supervised a staff that earned another $2 million. The Republican Party of New York regularly assessed 3 percent of that $2 million, with other contributions added as elections demanded.[80]

Democrats were just as adept at using the system. Grover Cleveland began his political career as sheriff of Erie County, New York, in 1870. Because of the fees he collected, being sheriff proved much more lucrative than his own legal practice. He went on to become mayor of Buffalo and governor of New York. He eventually would be elected president.[81]

Fee-based governance grew as the country expanded. Wyatt Earp became famous as a figure of the mythic West. He stood as the face of law and order against the disorder embodied in outlaws like Jesse James and Billy the Kid. In fact, Earp was a specialist in violence, and he and his associates sought opportunity on either side of the law. The most lucrative opportunities, as Earp knew, often involved public office.[82]

Earp was a chameleon. He began his career as a pimp, probably a horse thief, an embezzler, an enforcer at bordellos, and a gambler; he then became a deputy marshal and a deputy sheriff in Wichita and Dodge City, Kansas. He well recognized how many opportunities the government's reliance on fee-based services presented.[83]

Deputy marshals gained their income from fees. In 1866 the principal chief of the Choctaws had complained that in pursuit of criminals seeking shelter in Indian Territory, deputy marshals "annoyed and harassed"

79. Parrillo, 17, 21, 135–37, 145–46, 162–63, 169–71, 380 n. 24.
80. Carpenter, 41–44; Rutkow, 56–57.
81. Charles W. Calhoun, *Minority Victory: Gilded Age Politics and the Front Porch Campaign of 1888* (Lawrence: University Press of Kansas, 2008), 23; Alyn Brodsky, *Grover Cleveland: A Study in Character* (New York: St. Martin's Press, 2000), 30–31; Richard E. Welch, *The Presidencies of Grover Cleveland* (Lawrence: University Press of Kansas, 1988), 24.
82. Jonathan Obert, "The Six-Shooter Marketplace: 19th-Century Gunfighting as Violence Expertise," *Studies in American Political Development* 28, no. 1 (April 2014): 49–79.
83. Andrew C. Isenberg, *Wyatt Earp: A Vigilante Life* (New York: Farrar, Straus and Giroux, 2013), 84, 88–89, 92–96, 162–67.

the Choctaws by "going about our country with an armed force and arresting numbers of our citizens for offenses alleged to have been committed."
The arrests were, he alleged, without cause, "the main inducement with
the assistant marshals being to make fees thereby."[84]

When the Earp brothers moved to the boomtown of Tombstone,
Arizona, in 1879, Wyatt began a stint of law enforcement that ultimately
led to his becoming the town's chief of police, a deputy to his brother
Virgil when he was chief of police, and a deputy sheriff for Pima County.
Between 1879 and 1882, Wyatt was also a deputy U.S. marshal. He aspired
to become the sheriff for Pima County. The office was a political plum;
the sheriff kept 10 percent of all the fees and taxes he collected, and with
the Southern Pacific running through the county, the office was worth
tens of thousands of dollars annually.[85]

Imagine thousands of Wyatt Earps, and the problems, and opportunities,
of American governance during this period become clear. Many American
officials who got paid little could make a lot, which was one reason so many
men and women aspired to what seemed like such minor offices and why
political machines so valued the ability to bestow them. Land office receivers
and registers received a fee for every transaction, and postmasters were entitled to a percentage of the stamps they sold at all but the largest post offices.
Public prosecutors received a fee, sometimes for each case brought, sometimes only for convictions. They could institute cases on the complaint of
citizens and get paid for doing so. The complicated regulations that governed the taxes Congress had imposed on tobacco and liquor to finance the
Civil War and continued afterward created fines for any violation of the
regulations, which penalized home consumption as much as production for
sale. The percentage of the penalties that went to prosecutors and agents, as
well as the bounties offered to catch violators, gave officials an incentive to
attack practices that might otherwise have been ignored. Fees and bounties
fueled the war between moonshiners and revenuers, and it also made federal
marshals and prosecutors an intrusive presence in thousands of communities. In the North, judges and clerks received a fee paid by the applicant for
every immigrant receiving citizenship, which in the larger cities amounted
to handy sums. Fee-based governance made holding government office a
profit center even for the honest.[86]

The consequences of the system went further. With more and more
intangible wealth—bank accounts, bonds, and stocks—easily hidden, fee-
based governance threatened to turn the country into a snitch nation, by

84. Parrillo, 119–20; Isenberg, 56–169, quote 62.
85. Isenberg, 135–37.
86. Parrillo, 120–22, 133–34, 240–41, 255, 257–58, 274–76.

offering bounties to tax ferrets for the violators they reported. Instead of reforming an antiquated tax system, the government offered bounties on tax evaders. It did so even as it doled out cash to private parties to carry the mail, provide the goods for fulfilling Indian treaties, and supply army posts, without effectively monitoring those who received the contracts.[87]

In replacing Arthur, Hayes did not try to change fee-based governance; he wanted to capture it for his allies. The system combined great legal authority, limited administrative control, and wondrous corruption. It depended on bounties, fees, and licensed coercion. It contributed to the declining legitimacy of institutions. There was much to reform, but Hayes was only trying to get rid of Conkling's men and substitute his own. New York was not particularly corrupt, only especially lucrative. The Illinois legislature gave street railway companies ninety-nine-year leases in 1865 and over the vehement objections of Chicago's citizens, granted the railroads Chicago's downtown lakefront in 1869. In the early 1890s, Chicago aldermen controlled contracts to scavengers to clean city streets, and in return they got kickbacks and votes. The aldermen were little concerned with the quality or frequency of street cleaning so long as they received their boodle. Across the country, contracts, subsidies, and remunerative offices provided the kickbacks that funded political parties and politicians. In the immediate wake of the Civil War, this was usually the Republican Party, which was why Republican officials only reluctantly sought reform.[88]

When Hayes attacked the source of his power, Conkling struck back at the president and the men whom he liked to call the "snivel service reformers" who backed the president. Conkling, appealing to the tradition of senatorial privilege that gave senators veto power over appointments in their own states, blocked Hayes's initial attempt to remove Arthur and replace him with Theodore Roosevelt Sr., Conkling's enemy and father of the future president. Hayes, in turn, suspended Arthur when the Senate was out of session, and with the aid of the Democrats he replaced him in 1878. This made reform seem more a matter of personal animus against Conkling than principle, particularly when he appointed known spoilsmen as collectors of customs at other ports and allowed federal employees to contribute to election campaigns.[89]

87. Parrillo, 129–40, 169–72, 191–206, 244–52, 284–85.
88. Nicholas Parrillo does not regard facilitative payments and the liberality of officials in granting common resources as corrupt per se; they were a technique designed to achieve a certain end. Ibid., 21, 33–35, 226–52; Robin L. Einhorn, *Property Rules: Political Economy in Chicago, 1833–1872* (Chicago: University of Chicago Press, 1991), 210–13, 227, 229; Louise W. Knight, *Citizen: Jane Addams and the Struggle for Democracy* (Chicago: University of Chicago Press, 2005), 297–99.
89. Hoogenboom, 351–56, 362–63, 370–71; Jordan, 279–87, 292–300.

The battle over Arthur amounted to only one front in Hayes's conflict with the Stalwarts. As the Stalwarts predicted, Hayes's Southern policy created a series of catastrophes for the Republicans and black voters. Even before 1876, new Democratic governments had begun to call constitutional conventions. The conventions did not focus on officially eliminating the black civil rights Southerners had promised Hayes they would protect. In principle the conventions left civil rights untouched, even as state governments constricted them in practice. Instead, the conventions concentrated on the Republican programs of internal improvements, education, and active government. Democrats struck particularly at debt and taxation and curtailed government powers. On this the agrarian and Bourbon wings of the Democratic government could unite. In North Carolina there was no official repudiation of the debt, but the state paid only twelve cents on the dollar. In other states the government did repudiate large amounts of debt, particularly railroad bonds. Most states imposed severe limits on taxation. By 1890 the Southern states had repudiated $116 million in debt and avoided paying another $150 million in interest payments.[90]

Hayes had promised Southern blacks that they would have "all the protection the law will give," but in the midterm elections of 1878 they received no protection at all. Hayes admitted the election was marred by fraud, intimidation, and "violence of the most atrocious character." Fraud and violence gave the Democrats sweeping victories in the South, and they also made gains in the North. The seventy-three representatives to the House elected from the old Confederacy included only three Republicans, and none from those states with a majority black population. James G. Blaine denounced the results as "a violent perversion of the whole theory of republican government." The new Congress lacked "the consent of the governed." The Republicans lost the Senate and failed to regain the House. The only silver lining was that the total Republican vote in the North would have carried enough states to give it the presidency, had it been a presidential year.[91]

The resurgent Democrats proved Hayes's political salvation: they overplayed their hand. In 1878 the House appointed the Potter Commission in an attempt to investigate Republican fraud and overturn the election of 1876. The commission only served to unite the fractious congressional Republicans and divide the Democrats. Republicans and moderate Democrats passed a resolution confirming the election results and condemning attempts to upend them. Ultimately Congress adjourned after

90. Perman, 193–220.
91. Calhoun, *Conceiving a New Republic*, 156–59; Hoogenboom, 374–77.

an all-night session that turned into a drunken debacle. Hayes was disgusted.[92]

In control of Congress, the Democrats once again used the power of the purse to deny the government funding unless Hayes and the Republicans repealed civil rights legislation. They particularly opposed federal marshals who could be used to protect black voters in the South and often acted against immigrant voters in the cities. Democrats were a white man's party and from the end of the Civil War to the end of the century, no Democratic congressman or senator voted for a piece of civil rights legislation. When in 1879 the Democrats refused to fund the government, Hayes saw an advantage and seized it.[93]

Most presidents had used the veto sparingly, but for Hayes it was one of his few weapons, and he unsheathed it frequently. Hayes vetoed the appropriation bills with the Democratic riders repealing Reconstruction measures. He then vetoed the separate repeal bills they sent him. The Democrats lacked the votes to overturn his vetoes. The Democrats made Hayes, a minor Civil War general, seem the embodiment of Union lines holding firm against rebels and their sympathizers. Hayes framed his actions as opposing an "unconstitutional and revolutionary attempt" by the Democrats to eliminate the constitutional "independence of the Executive" and to corrupt elections. The minority Republicans remained united against the Democrats and demanded the enforcement of voting laws in the South.[94]

The Republicans maintained their support, as ineffectual as it was on the ground, for black civil rights and suffrage from both conviction and self-interest. The courts sustained their position on the legality of Reconstruction civil rights legislation, which they had narrowed in earlier decisions. In March 1880 in *Ex parte Siebold*, the Supreme Court incensed Democrats by ruling that "if Congress has the power to make regulations it must have the power to enforce them."[95]

The war Hayes waged with the Democrats and his factional quarrels with Conkling and Blaine obscured the quickening of antimonopolism, which obtained its early victories in the states. The laws passed in the Upper Midwest to regulate railroads and middlemen yielded the so-called Granger Cases, covering state regulatory powers over railroads and middlemen,

92. Hoogenboom, 365–68.
93. J. Morgan Kousser, "The Voting Rights Act and the Two Reconstructions," in *Controversies in Minority Voting: The Voting Rights Act in Perspective*, ed. Bernard Grofman and Chandler Davidson (Washington, DC: Brookings Institution, 1992), 149; Peter H. Argersinger, "New Perspectives on Election Fraud in the Gilded Age," *Political Science Quarterly* 100, no. 4 (1985): 680–86.
94. Calhoun, *Conceiving a New Republic*, 158–68; Hoogenboom, 393–402.
95. Calhoun, *Conceiving a New Republic*, 2–5, 171–72; Hiers, 280.

which came to the Supreme Court in 1877. The Court validated the well-established police power of local and state governments and their right to restrain corporations and other businesses in pursuit of the ideal of a well-regulated society. The decisions were, in part, a triumph of *Salus populi* or public welfare, but in *Munn v. Illinois* (1877), the Supreme Court went beyond arguments resting on public safety. It qualified the due process clause regarding property in the Fourteenth Amendment by marking the railroads as a specific class of property "clothed with a public interest" and holding monopoly power, in the sense that the public had no realistic choice but to make use of the services railroads provided. The court countenanced state regulation of railroad rates and grain warehouse rates in the public interest. Fundamental to these cases was a recognition of the failure of competition. Businesses, critical to the operation of many other businesses, had either colluded to fix rates or had a monopoly power allowing them to eliminate competition. By threatening competition, monopolies limited individual liberties and the whole edifice of free labor. The court implicitly recognized that pure markets did not exist; markets operated within specific sets of political rules. In the Granger Cases, the court tried to set the parameters of legitimate rule making.[96]

In 1878 antimonopolist Greenbackers elected fifteen congressmen, threatening the Southern Democrats as well as Republicans. All the Democrats in the South were racist, but the Bourbons, the faction strongest among the old elite, were reactionaries, while their opponents, some of them ex-Republicans who had returned to the white man's party, were agrarians upset at the misdistribution of wealth and taxes. In those Southern states where freedmen could still exercise their suffrage, there was the possibility of an alliance between the Republicans, black and white, and the agrarian wing of the Democratic Party. Such a possibility emerged in Virginia.[97]

Redeemer governments in the South had nearly uniformly renounced much of the Reconstruction Era state debts, just as Reconstruction governments had usually renounced antebellum government debts. When conservatives redeemed Virginia, the legislature had, however, decided to fund most of the antebellum state government's debt, which meant that the members of the old plantation elite and investors who had bought the debt at steep discounts reaped a windfall at the expense of taxpayers. The Virginia Bourbons declared the debt a matter of honor and used it as a

96. Herbert Hovenkamp, *Enterprise and American Law, 1836–1937* (Cambridge, MA: Harvard University Press, 1991), 274; George H. Miller, *Railroads and the Granger Laws* (Madison: University of Wisconsin Press, 1971), 172–93, particularly 188–89.
97. Hahn, 364–400.

way to cripple government and common schools. In lieu of interest, the legislature issued coupons to bondholders and accepted those coupons for taxes. By 1878 nearly half the state's taxes were paid in the coupons, leaving the government strapped for cash. The Bourbons opposed public schools and used the lack of revenue to defund them and to institute poll taxes, which made it difficult for the poor, black or white, to vote.[98]

Devotion to free public schools and anger at the poll tax provided a bridge over the racial divide. Those opposed to these policies—urban black workers, white immigrants in Virginia's cities, western white farmers, and black tenants and sharecroppers—became known as Readjusters because they wanted to readjust the debt. William Mahone, ex-Confederate general and railroad entrepreneur, became the unlikely face of a rebellion uniting white Democrats in the western half of the state and black and white Republicans in the southeast. The Readjusters emerged in 1877 within the Democratic Party. Mahone never intended to challenge white supremacy, but it was the only way to defeat the Bourbon Democrats.[99]

In 1879 the Readjusters became a separate party in an integrated convention. Although the majority of blacks continued to vote Republican, a coalition of white Readjusters and black Republicans took control of the Virginia legislature in 1879. They elected Mahone to the U.S. Senate, but he was not sworn in until 1881. When Readjusters and Republicans ran separate candidates in the 1880 elections for Congress, however, they both lost.[100]

Antimonopolist reform existed alongside liberal reforms that Hayes enacted. Stalwarts hated Carl Schurz for his role in the Greeley campaign in 1872 and his support of civil service reform, and they hated him even more when Hayes appointed him secretary of interior. Schurz intended to bring liberalism, honest administration, and free labor to the Interior Department. He worked to clean up some of the worst frauds in the Indian Service and the General Land Office. Religion had failed to check corruption, and he gradually divorced the churches from administration of the reservations. Helped by the impeachment of Secretary of War William Belknap for malfeasance in office in 1876, Schurz thwarted another attempt to transfer the Indian Office to the War Department.[101]

98. Jane Elizabeth Dailey, *Before Jim Crow: The Politics of Race in Postemancipation Virginia* (Chapel Hill: University of North Carolina Press, 2000), 28–29.
99. Ibid., 32–44, 48, 53.
100. Ibid., 45–47, 55–57.
101. Francis Paul Prucha, *The Great Father: The United States Government and the American Indians* (Lincoln: University of Nebraska Press, 1984), 526–27, 558, 588–89; Hans L. Trefousse, *Carl Schurz: A Biography* (Knoxville: University of Tennessee Press, 1982), 237, 244.

Schurz's success did not necessarily benefit Indians. When violence erupted in Colorado between whites and the White River Utes in 1879, Schurz and Ouray, the Ute leader, prevented a wider war, but the price for the Utes was the loss of their White River reservation. Coloradans wanted Indians out of the new state, and Schurz consented to what amounted to the ethnic cleansing of Colorado, with the Uncompahgre and Southern Utes retaining only a small reservation in southwestern Colorado.[102]

Himself a German immigrant, Schurz in effect treated the Indians in a way he would never have allowed Germans to be treated. He advocated eliminating their language and traditions. They were to be assimilated; Indian children were to be educated to possess "civilized ideas, wants, and aspirations." All communal practices would be abolished. The Indians' common lands would be divided in severalty so that they would be independent farmers and herders living in monogamous nuclear families. Any "excess" lands were to be sold and the money used to relieve the government of the costs of providing for them. Once the process was completed, the Indians would become American citizens, no different from any other. Even as the idea of a homogeneous citizenship fell into ruins in the South, Republicans worked to extend it to Indians, who, unlike the ex-slaves, did not desire it.[103]

V

Four years of conflict and economic depression took their toll on Hayes. He claimed the presidency was a burden that he longed to shed, but it did not seem particularly burdensome when he entertained William Dean Howells. Howells and his wife visited the White House for six days in the spring of 1880. Hayes escorted his guests around the capital. "We saw them as constantly as if they were private persons," Howells told his father. On Saturday they visited Mount Vernon; Monday they went to the Capitol and Arlington. Tuesday they took a carriage ride around the city, and Wednesday they took a cruise on a steam yacht down the Potomac. Even in the midst of political battle, nineteenth-century presidents had time on their hands.[104]

---

102. Prucha, 543–44.
103. Ibid., 595.
104. W. D. Howells to W. C. Howells, May 17, 1880, William Dean Howells, *Selected Letters*, ed. George Warren Arms (Boston: Twayne, 1979), 2: 253; Lynn, 195.

Late in 1880, soon to be free of the burden of the presidency and party leadership, Hayes addressed students at Hampton Institute in Virginia, founded for the education of Southern freedpeople. Freedpeople had hoped for an education that would establish their equality, but the education Hampton offered did not challenge social inequities or white power. Hampton became famous as a trade school, though its original emphasis was to train teachers for segregated black schools in the South.[105]

One of the teachers at Hampton was a former student, Booker T. Washington, who had been born a slave. He had arrived at the school in 1872 with fifty cents in his pocket. When he returned as a teacher in 1879, his charges included Indian children, whom Lieutenant Richard Henry Pratt, later the founder of Carlisle Indian Institute, had gathered from the "corrupting and demoralizing surroundings" of the reservations to develop capacities that he thought equal to those of whites. Pratt had brought them to Hampton despite "the prejudices" of agency officials (including Pratt), against "Hampton Institute, as a colored institution." Washington was likely in Hayes's audience.[106]

Hayes, reluctant to disavow his disastrous policy of conciliation, lectured on the limits nature placed on reform. For all his avowals of political equality, he was clear that blacks were not entitled to social equality: "We would not undertake to violate the laws of nature, we do not wish to change the purpose of God in making these differences of nature. We are willing to have these elements of our population separate as the fingers are, but we require to see them united for every good work, for national defense, one, as the hand." Years later, Booker T. Washington would famously invoke the same metaphor.[107]

Washington left Hampton in 1881 to take charge of Tuskegee Normal School in Alabama, and he and that school would soon become synonymous. Tuskegee was an impressive accomplishment, with most of the money coming from Washington's assiduous fundraising and the labor of

105. James D. Anderson, *The Education of Blacks in the South, 1860–1935* (Chapel Hill: University of North Carolina Press, 1988), 33–34.
106. Everett Arthur Gilcreast, *Richard Henry Pratt and American Indian Policy, 1877–1906: A Study of the Assimilation Movement* (New Haven, CT: Yale University Press, 1967), 24–38.
107. Calhoun, *Conceiving a New Republic*, 137–68; Robert J. Norrell, *Up from History: The Life of Booker T. Washington* (Cambridge, MA: Belknap Press of Harvard University Press, 2009), 29–40; Hiers, 287–94; Richard Henry Pratt, "Report of Lieut. R. H. Pratt, Special Agent to Collect Indian Youths to Be Educated at Hampton Institute, Va.," ed. 45 Congress House Executive Document No. 1, 3 Session, serial 1850 (1878); Eugene R. Dattel, *Cotton and Race in the Making of America: The Human Costs of Economic Power* (Chicago: Ivan R. Dee, 2009), 264.

the students. Tuskegee, like Hampton, embraced black self-help, the cultivation of white goodwill in both the North and South during an age where it was in desperately short supply, and social separation. Tuskegee grew as the relocation of responsibility for black education moved from the public sphere to the private. It reflected a politics of lowered expectations. Ambitions for a homogeneous citizenry and full equality in the South had yielded to a system that regarded existing social relations and black inferiority as natural and thus unalterable.

Hayes entered office with the Republican vision of the United States inspired by the great democratic triumph of the Civil War, which was grounded on free labor and a homogeneous citizenry, weakened but still intact, but during his administration that goal slipped away. Homogeneous citizenship, which originally had been inclusionary, narrowed once more to mean rights for white men only, and there were pressures to narrow it further to white Protestant men. Where efforts at homogeneous citizenship persisted, they grew more coercive. Indians found their families, religions, cultural practices, economies, governments, and territories under attack, all in the name of preparing them for future assimilation as Americans. The free labor vision of a nation of small producers, their efforts aided by government, was yielding a world in which large producers, some of them organized as corporations, dominated crucial parts of the economy. The rise of antimonopolists in both parties signaled that many Americans regarded monopoly and privilege, rather than competition and general equality, as defining the new economy.

10

The Party of Prosperity

In the midst of political retreat on Reconstruction and economic depression, the Republicans regrouped, staking their future on the claim to be the party of prosperity. Hayes, with his emphasis on "honest money" and his evocation of the home, tried to give prosperity a moral content, even though it lacked the moral grandeur that had inspired the Greater Reconstruction's call for the eradication of slavery's legacy and the elevation of freedpeople to equal citizenship.

Politics rather than any grand ideology such as free labor drove the emphasis on prosperity. Hayes may not even have recognized the larger economic and social ramifications of the changes to which he contributed. The program involved old issues: the tariff, the gold standard, the regulation of railroads and interstate commerce. These issues individually divided the Republicans, but collectively they created something larger than the pieces. Republicans claimed that the sum of their policies would ensure a prosperous United States.

Hayes promised prosperity in order to save his floundering presidency. He toured the country, proclaiming a coming economic revival, but virtually every piece of evidence that he offered was either a sign of depression or had contributed to the depression. Interest rates had fallen, but interest rates often fall in hard times, and, in any case, they remained relatively high. The public debt had declined, but the lack of public spending, which had helped reduce the debt, contributed to the depression. Inflation had declined, but deflation had become the fertile source of antimonopolist complaints. Agricultural exports continued to be strong, but it was because farmers produced more to make up for low prices. Angry farmers desired inflationary measures. Hayes pledged that the gold standard would usher the country back into the promised land of prosperity.[1]

Republican political economy evolved piecemeal in response to necessity, events, and opportunity. Its distinct pieces made it particularly well

1. Ari Arthur Hoogenboom, *Rutherford B. Hayes: Warrior and President* (Lawrence: University Press of Kansas, 1995), 372–73.

suited to a tripartite government. Congress took responsibility for the tariff, a key issue for those Republicans who were ex-Whigs. It provided the main source of the nation's revenue and protected key industries. It also demonstrated the realities of national borders, making them effective dams in the flow of trade. The president and the executive branch monitored and administered the money supply, which, with resumption in 1879, made gold the basis of the nation's currency. This was foundational for the liberals. The states and localities had clear powers to regulate economic matters within their boundaries, but Congress sought to maintain its authority over interstate commerce. Federal courts increasingly intervened to strike down state regulations that affected interstate commerce. The courts created what amounted to a de facto, largely unregulated, national market.[2]

The emergence of the solid Democratic South solidified the Republican position. Republicans exacted an economic price for Southern whites' political success, but the Republican goal was neither punishment nor revenge. With the party's Southern voting base diminished or demolished, Republicans had little chance to carry elections over much of the South and so nothing to lose from imposing policies that benefited the North at the expense of the South. Taxing Southern consumers and farmers, who were overwhelmingly Democrats, to subsidize northern industrialists and workers, who were largely Republicans, made political sense. So did implementing a gold standard that helped the Northeast while harming the South. What complicated matters was that the tariff and the gold standard also hurt the agricultural Midwest and the West, areas the Republicans would have to carry to control the federal government. Compensating for this would demand considerable political maneuvering.

There was a soft-money majority in Congress during the Hayes administration, although on monetary policy Hayes had the support of Conkling, Blaine, and most northeastern Republicans. With the Resumption Act's approaching deadline of January 1, 1879, for making greenbacks redeemable in gold, Secretary of Treasury John Sherman had arranged for a $77 million bond sale to build up the necessary gold reserves, but the Great Strike and antimonopolist agitation had undermined investor confidence. The bonds sold slowly. In the House, antimonopolists, who preferred greenbacks, allied with less radical soft-money representatives to pass the Bland Bill, which required unlimited coinage of silver at a ratio of 16:1 with gold. This was inflationary since the market price of silver was less

---

2. I have taken this argument from Richard Franklin Bensel, *The Political Economy of American Industrialization, 1877–1900* (Cambridge: Cambridge University Press, 2000), 4–11, and passim.

than the price the Treasury would offer, ensuring that silver would flow into the Treasury and increase the money supply. The House also voted to repeal the Resumption Act, but the Senate did not concur. During the next regular session of Congress, the Senate amended the Bland Bill to give the president discretion over how much silver would be coined. Hayes vetoed this bill—the Bland-Allison Act—but Congress passed it over his veto. Senate amendments to the bill made it a largely meaningless victory for those who favored a fiat currency; Hayes minted only the minimum amount of silver dollars and, with the Resumption Act still in place, demonstrated the power that the executive branch wielded over the money supply. Secretary Sherman borrowed $50 million in gold from a consortium of European bankers to keep progress toward the gold standard on track. The greenbacks were doomed and continued deflation was all but inevitable. Hayes credited the serendipitous return of prosperity in 1879 to the gold standard. But if gold was the cure, why had Great Britain, which had adopted the gold standard long before the United States, endured the same economic downturn?[3]

Liberals, at their simplest, thought of the gold standard as self-regulating, but the country's monetary system could not run on autopilot. The Treasury Department had to monitor trade, the tariff, and the national banks to make sure that it always had enough gold to redeem paper currency and silver coins when presented. To fail to do so would, in effect, be to take the country off the gold standard. Given the difficulty of the task and the efforts of opponents to subvert the system, the country often hovered on the brink of default.[4]

Opponents of the gold standard, particularly those in favor of bimetallism—the antebellum practice of having both gold and silver serve as the basis for currency—did all they could to undercut the system. Here the Bland-Allison Act did have an effect. Every month the government, according to law, bought and minted $2 million in silver dollars, and every month it issued those dollars only to have the vast majority quickly come back to the Treasury in exchange for paper or gold. Carrying around silver dollars—popularly known as a "stove-lid currency"—was inconvenient. As a result, silver flowed into the Treasury, and notes backed by gold reserves flowed out. The unwanted silver coins piled up. By 1880 the Treasury held thirty-two thousand ordinary nail kegs full of silver dollars in its vaults. The situation only got worse. By 1885 the government had coined a little more than two hundred million silver dollars, with only one-quarter in circulation. The Treasury had to rent space and build new

3. Bensel, 370, 377–78, 382–83; Hoogenboom, 356–60.
4. Bensel, 367–70.

vaults to hold the excess. If someone had *stolen* all of the silver dollars, it would have saved the government money. The government purchase of silver worked largely to subsidize western mines.[5]

By limiting the money supply in a growing economy, the gold standard led to deflation, which transferred wealth from debtors to creditors and hurt producers, particularly in the South and West. Between 1865 and 1897 prices fell at about 1 percent a year, and the consumer price index declined from 196 to 100, according to retrospective calculations (1860 = 100). Wealthy creditors gained premiums beyond interest payments since deflation meant that the dollars paid to them in interest, and ultimately in the repayment of principal, were always more valuable than the earlier dollars they had lent. The monetary system transferred wealth from the debtor West and South to the East, whose banks and investors controlled the money that was lent. The gold standard also allowed a much smoother integration of New York and London capital markets.[6]

A policy that hurt the majority of states and the majority of the population survived in a democratic system because, once instituted and centered in the executive branch, it proved hard to dislodge. So long as a gold standard Republican or Democrat occupied the presidency, the policy could not be overthrown without the two-thirds majority necessary to override a presidential veto. Winning the presidency, not controlling Congress, became the key to monetary politics.[7]

Republican control of the tariff proved more complicated. Basic tariff policy was the legacy of the Morrill Tariff of the Civil War. Except for taxes on tobacco and alcohol, which continued to produce about a third of all federal revenue, the tariff had replaced excise taxes, which were a direct tax on consumption and extremely unpopular, as the major source of federal revenue.[8]

The original aims of the Morrill Tariff were to raise revenue to pay for the Civil War debt and to protect "infant" core industries, particularly the iron and steel industry, cotton goods, and manufactures. Duties usually ran to 40 or 50 percent of the value of the goods, but could run as high as

5. Ibid., 382, 391–92.
6. Douglas W. Steeples, *Democracy in Desperation: The Depression of 1893*, ed. David O. Whitten (Westport, CT: Greenwood Press, 1998), 29; Table Cc1-2—Consumer price indexes, for all items: 1774–2003, in *Historical Statistics of the United States, Earliest Times to the Present: Millennial Edition*, ed. Scott Sigmund Gartner, Susan B. Carter, Michael R. Haines, Alan L. Olmstead, Richard Sutch, and Gavin Wright (New York: Cambridge University Press, 2006); Bensel, 356–57.
7. Bensel, 366–67.
8. W. Elliot Brownlee, *Federal Taxation in America: A Short History*. Woodrow Wilson Center Series (Cambridge: Cambridge University Press, 2004), 36–38.

100 percent. Raising the rates to where imports could not compete made the rates prohibitive, and such rates could benefit more than the protected industry. Protecting iron and steel, for example, meant indirectly subsidizing iron ore, coal, and coke, all of which the steel industry consumed in vast quantities. Prohibitive rates, of course, yielded no revenue at all, thus impeding debt reduction. To compensate, Congress relied on other commodities for revenue. The American demand for sugar was so strong that domestic producers could not fill it; the sugar tariff acted to raise prices for domestic producers while still allowing imports. Sugar yielded more tariff income than any other commodity.[9]

The price difference attributable to the tariff on a given transaction for any single consumer might be small, but the cumulative effect for aggregated consumers was large. Tens of millions of people paying a little more on every purchase created a fund that benefited a very small set of producers concentrated in one part of the country. These producers claimed the tariff also raised their workers' wages, but this was not so easy to demonstrate, particularly during a period of tumultuous labor unrest. Not only liberal free traders but also Southern, Western, and Midwestern farmers disliked the tariff, which taxed them to subsidize Eastern industrialists.[10]

The tariff created both political problems and opportunities for the Republicans. The chief problem was that the House wrote tariff legislation, and with the large majority of Democrats advocating free trade, their control of the House after 1874 represented a threat to Republican interests whenever the tariff had to be revised in the face of changing economic circumstances. The Republicans adjusted by elaborating the tariff. The core protection for iron, steel, and selected manufacturing remained and formed the trunk of the tariff Christmas tree, but Congress created numerous branches that individual congressmen decorated with endless duties and special rules as favors for local constituencies. These made up the tariff's tinsel and ornaments, and they served to shore up political support in the House. The star crowning the tree was the tariff on wool, which brought necessary Western support. Raising the price of wool hurt carpet manufacturers, and so they were granted higher rates to protect them from foreign imports. As the House decorated the tree, it lost economic coherence, but the gaudy pastiche was beautiful to the eyes of Republican beholders. Its political function became as important as its

9. David Nasaw, *Andrew Carnegie* (New York: Penguin Press, 2006), 141, 148; Brownlee, 37; Bensel, 457, 489.
10. Bensel, 458, 462–63, 466–67.

economic function. The byzantine and ornate tariff schedule offered many constituencies compensation for their pain.[11]

Without a final brilliant touch, however, the tariff would have probably been an untenable political liability for the Republicans. It not only raised consumer prices, it generated a surplus that gathered in the treasury, exacerbating the inadequate money supply. Henry Blair, a senator from New Hampshire and an ardent protectionist, had a solution. By spending the surplus the tariff generated to create a federal welfare system, he diminished the surplus, expanded the realm of the federal government, and created powerful constituencies that would serve to sustain both the tariff and the Republicans. The Arrears Act, signed by President Hayes in 1879, proved to be one of the more unheralded pieces of legislation in American history. It expanded a U.S. pension system designed to take care of the dependents of Union Army soldiers killed during the war as well as disabled soldiers. The expenditures of the Bureau of Pensions had peaked in the mid-1870s and gone into decline. The Arrears Act stimulated new growth, and President Hayes linked expenditures under the act to the home: "Look at the good done. In every county of the North are small but comfortable homes built by the soldier out of his arrearage pay."[12]

By making pension payments retroactive to the date of a soldier's discharge, or in the case of dependents from the date of a soldier's death rather than the date of an approved application, the Arrears Act created a windfall for veterans and their families. All recipients would receive a check for the "arrears" owed them, and anyone filing for a new pension before July 1880 would also receive a payment covering the period from the date of his discharge. The average first payment including arrears in 1881 was roughly $1,000, at a time when the annual earnings of nonfarm employees were about $400. Between 1879 and 1881, total disbursements for pensions roughly doubled and then rose even more steeply during the 1880s. Civil War pensions became the leading expenditure of the U.S. government. Republicans used it to justify high tariff rates.[13]

The Arrears Act created a conundrum for Democrats, who wanted to use mounting surpluses from tariffs to reduce the tariff rates. As was intended, the act split Northern and Southern Democrats. The vast majority of Southern whites would get nothing, but the pensions would benefit a

11. Brownlee, 36–38; Bensel, 488, 490–92.
12. Theda Skocpol, *Protecting Soldiers and Mothers: The Political Origins of Social Policy in the United States* (Cambridge, MA: Belknap Press of Harvard University Press, 1995), 116.
13. Daniel P. Carpenter, *The Forging of Bureaucratic Autonomy: Reputations, Networks, and Policy Innovation in Executive Agencies, 1862–1928* (Princeton, NJ: Princeton University Press, 2001), 50, 59–60; Skocpol, 114–23.

wide swath of northern veterans, many of whom lived in rural areas and whose votes the Republicans needed. The Pension Bureau became a bulwark of the Republican Party. W. W. Dudley, the commissioner of the Bureau of Pensions, worked closely with the Union veterans' organization, the Grand Army of the Republic (GAR), to recruit new applicants, particularly in the electorally critical states of Illinois, Indiana, New York, Ohio, and Pennsylvania. In 1879 the Democrats controlled the House and could have blocked the act, but this would have amounted to swallowing a poison pill. Northern Democrats almost unanimously voted for the act, to refute, as an Illinois Democratic congressman put it, "every accusation against the [D]emocratic party of want of regard for the interest of the soldier."[14]

By linking pensions to the tariff, the Republicans protected an unpopular policy by making it the chief support of a popular policy. The Arrears Act rejuvenated the GAR, which had devolved into a disorganized fraternal organization with a membership of only 26,899 in 1876. It resurrected itself in the 1880s as a veterans' organization that packed a potent political punch. When at the end of the decade the GAR lobbied for a universal pension system for all Civil War veterans and their dependents, they were also indirectly lobbying for a high tariff, which was the only way to provide the taxes to pay for the program.[15]

The last piece of the economic program—the creation of national markets—was left to the courts, staffed by Republican appointees. The Hayes administration did not directly bring about this change. Hayes simply added to the Republican appointments to the courts. Between 1881 and 1887 the entire Supreme Court was composed of justices appointed by Republican presidents. The rules—or lack thereof—governing the national market emerged gradually, and the ultimate impact of the court's decisions increased as the century wore on.

As the Granger Cases demonstrated, the courts still held the door open to considerable market regulations by the states at the end of the 1870s. Into the 1880s, the states' right to regulate railroads as established in *Munn* did not appear to be in immediate danger. Supreme Court Justice Stephen Field, however, was attacking *Munn* in a series of influential minority opinions. At his most extreme, Field argued that any interference in a business's practices could amount to confiscation and would be declared unconstitutional. By the end of the decade, the momentum had turned. The courts struck down state legislation governing the railroads on the

14. Skocpol, 115–24.
15. Ibid., 124–28; Stuart McConnell, *Glorious Contentment: The Grand Army of the Republic, 1865–1900* (Chapel Hill: University of North Carolina Press, 1992), 15–32; Bensel, 462, 486.

grounds that state laws violated either federal control over interstate commerce or the due process clause of the Fourteenth Amendment. The appointments made by Hayes and other Republican presidents created the conditions for a legal revolution, which limited the authority of Congress to regulate the economy.[16]

I

That American governance, and even democracy itself, had failed following the Civil War became the theme of the white Henry Adams. In the 1870s Adams had clung to a sense that American politics was a vocation, a calling, and not a business. It *should* produce men like his presidential grandfather and great-grandfather; he just no longer believed it *would*. On April Fools Day 1880 he anonymously published a novel, *Democracy*, which he had actually finished in 1876. In an era full of great novels, it was a slight work, but revealing.[17]

Democracy, like so many of the novels of the period, was both a *Bildungsroman*—a story of an education—and a *roman à clef*, whose leading characters were modeled on well-known Washington figures. Madeline Lee—or Mrs. Lightfoot Lee—was a Philadelphian, the widow of a Virginian, who comes to Washington "bent on getting to the heart of the great American mystery of democracy and government," but she was really a fictional amalgam of Henry and Clover Adams. She imagined that she could use Sen. Silas Ratcliffe, one of her several suitors, to purify the republic. Madeleine Lee's sister, Sophie, was supposedly modeled after Fanny Chapman, Carl Schurz's lover and the sister of a Massachusetts neighbor of the Adams.[18]

Guessing who wrote *Democracy* became a kind of genteel international parlor game. Adams took great pleasure in the failed efforts of critics and readers, including his brother Charles Francis Adams, to identify the

16. Herbert Hovenkamp, *Enterprise and American Law, 1836–1937* (Cambridge, MA: Harvard University Press, 1991), 112–13, 126, 128–30, 160; George H. Miller, *Railroads and the Granger Laws* (Madison: University of Wisconsin Press, 1971), 172–93, particularly 188–89; Paul Kens, *Justice Stephen Field: Shaping Liberty from the Gold Rush to the Gilded Age* (Lawrence: University Press of Kansas, 1997), 258–59; Bensel, 329–36, 344–49.
17. John P. Diggins, *The Promise of Pragmatism: Modernism and the Crisis of Knowledge and Authority* (Chicago: University of Chicago Press, 1994), 22–23, 29–30, 65, 67; Henry Adams, *Democracy* (New York: Signet, 1961, orig. ed. 1880).
18. Natalie Dykstra, *Clover Adams: A Gilded and Heartbreaking Life* (Boston: Houghton Mifflin Harcourt, 2012), 117–20; Adams, 17.

author. Figuring out who was the inspiration for Senator Ratcliffe was a Washington political preoccupation. There were just too many Gilded Age senators who could have been a senator who "talked about virtue and vice as a man who is colorblind talks about red and green." Charles Sumner may have been the original inspiration for Ratcliffe, but Sen. James Blaine with good reason thought he was Ratcliffe and that *Democracy's* author sought to block his quest for the presidency. Blaine decided that Clarence King was the author and cut off relations with him.[19]

Like Ratcliffe—and Blaine—Roscoe Conkling, the senator from New York, was corrupt and a presidential aspirant. He provided yet another prototype for the fictional Senator Ratcliffe. If Adams blended Blaine and Conkling into one character, he showed a nice touch. Conkling, whom his admirers described as an Adonis, never forgave Blaine for attacking his "haughty disdain, his grandiloquent swell, his majestic, super eminent, overpowering, turkey-gobbler strut."[20]

Roscoe Conkling embodied the problems with writing satires in the Gilded Age when satires diluted an already outrageous reality rather than exaggerating it. Conkling's escapades gave a taste of the politics that Adams despised. In 1879 Conkling was the paramour of Kate Chase Sprague, daughter of the late Chief Justice Salmon Chase. She was a famous beauty, courted by John Hay, a Washington hostess, and a well-informed insider whom Hay and others consulted for political advice. She was also the abused wife of an ex-senator, William Sprague, who had lost a considerable portion of his family fortune in the Panic of 1873.[21]

William Sprague drank, squandered his remaining money, chased the female servants, and kept mistresses, one of whom wrote a thinly disguised book about her affair with him. Kate Sprague retreated to Europe and then returned to Washington; she spent such money as she could get from her husband, and she began an increasingly public affair with Conkling. The romance enraged William, who in drunken spite dragged out and burned their expensive furniture on the lawn of his estate and threatened to throw his wife out a second-story window. It all hit the newspapers in the summer of 1879 when he unexpectedly returned home from a trip and found that Conkling was his wife's guest at the Spragues' summer

19. Patricia O'Toole, *The Five of Hearts: An Intimate Portrait of Henry Adams and His Friends, 1880–1918* (New York: C. N. Potter, 1990), 120–22; Edward Chalfant, *Better in Darkness: A Biography of Henry Adams: His Second Life, 1862–1891* (Hamden, CT: Archon Books, 1994), 128–29, 328–29; Adams, *Democracy*, 182.

20. David M. Jordan, *Roscoe Conkling of New York: Voice in the Senate* (Ithaca, NY: Cornell University Press, 1971), 80.

21. Peg A. Lamphier, *Kate Chase and William Sprague: Politics and Gender in a Civil War Marriage* (Lincoln: University of Nebraska Press, 2003), 25, 120–33, 150–52.

home in Narragansett, Rhode Island. Sprague drove him out and threatened him with a shotgun. Conkling attempted a cover-up, which went badly. He cared far more about his reputation than he did about Kate Sprague, and he left her to deal with the consequences.[22]

In *Democracy* Mrs. Lightfoot Lee's grandiloquent denunciation of Ratcliffe could have applied to a range of American political figures. "I have degraded myself," the text ran, "by discussing with you the question whether I should marry a man who by his own confession has betrayed the highest trusts that could be placed in him, who has taken money for his votes as a Senator, and who is now in public office by means of successful fraud of his own, when in justice he should be in a State's prison." But her real disappointment was in her fellow countrymen, "nine out of ten" of whom "would say I had made a mistake." "Democracy," she said, "has shaken my nerves to pieces."[23]

In Adams's view, the American public got pretty much the government it deserved. Cynical, funny, well-informed, and dyspeptic, Adams traced the sad and ridiculous arc of American decline from civic duty and the great cause of the Civil War to a squalid pursuit of wealth and office.[24]

As a political weapon, *Democracy* lost impact because in 1880 it was hard to distinguish the degrees of corruption among the Republican rivals for the nomination. Adams, a Liberal Republican who had supported Tilden in 1876 and approved of Hayes's reforms, probably presumed a Tilden-Blaine contest, which was what most knowledgeable observers assumed. Hayes had enjoyed being president about as much as his Democratic and Stalwart enemies took pleasure in having him as president. He declined to run for a second term.[25]

Republicans divided. Blaine led a Republican faction, the Half-Breeds, who broke with the Stalwarts over civil service reform. The Stalwarts, led by Conkling, hated Blaine nearly as much as liberals like Adams did. The availability of the nomination gave both Conkling and Blaine a chance to prance and preen. Conkling talked of giving Ulysses S. Grant a third term, although Conkling's preferred candidate was, as always, Roscoe Conkling. If the Stalwarts had their way, the approaching 1880 electoral campaign would offer a choice between two of the best-known quantities in American politics: Ulysses Grant and Samuel Tilden.[26]

Grant denied he wanted a third term, but he was available if drafted by the convention. Tainted by scandal and tarred by the economic depression,

22. Ibid., 130–83; Jordan, 313; Hoogenboom, 408.
23. Adams, *Democracy*, 188–91.
24. Diggins, 29–30; Chalfant, 398–99, 411–13, 475–76.
25. Chalfant, 329.
26. Hoogenboom, 423–31.

he adopted a brilliant campaign tactic: he left the country. In May 1877 he and his wife, Julia, who probably wanted to return to the White House more than her husband did, departed on a two-year grand tour whose ocean breezes Grant hoped would dissipate the aroma of scandal and failure that clung to him like his cigar smoke. Leaving the country did not involve disappearing from public view. Grant took John Russell Young of the *New York Herald* along with him. Even in the Gilded Age, reporters were not a usual accouterment of family vacations, even very Grand Tours. Young sent home regular dispatches, keeping the American public informed of Grant's travels. He later gathered them into a two-volume illustrated memorial to the trip—*Around the World with General Grant*—that was published the year before the presidential election.[27]

Young's account mixed innumerable receptions, banquets, and speeches with a Victorian travelogue that gave Grant's relentless sightseeing the atmosphere of a military campaign. It demonstrated, if nothing else, the ex-president's power of endurance. Young slanted his accounts to appeal to a Republican constituency. He liked Protestant countries, particularly Great Britain and Prussia. They were modern, expansive, and, whatever their faults, progressive. Catholic Europe was often beautiful but full of signs of an ancient and decayed civilization. Like Russia, North Africa, the Near East, India, China, and Japan, it was most often just old and irritating.

When Young described the sights, the Grants disappeared for pages at a time, but Ulysses Grant was very much the center of the carefully edited "conversations" sprinkled throughout the volume. Here Grant shed the garments of a failed president and reappeared as the republican warrior hero. Both Young in his dispatches and Grant in his speeches and conversations reminded American audiences that when Europeans praised and welcomed the ex-president, they were really praising the United States.[28]

Young never lost sight of Grant's political rehabilitation. The ex-general reminisced about the war, reminding readers of his distinguished military career and service to his country. Whenever possible, Young associated Grant with Lincoln. Grant defended his presidency in terms that perhaps only Conkling did not find astonishing. He said that he had met just six men in public life who had been "dishonest of absolute moral certainty," although

27. William S. McFeely, *Grant: A Biography* (New York: Norton, 1981), 455–74; John Russell Young, *Around the World with General Grant: A Narrative of the Visit of General U. S. Grant, Ex-President of the United States, to Various Countries in Europe, Asia, and Africa, in 1877, 1878, 1879. To Which Are Added Certain Conversations with General Grant on Questions Connected with American Politics and History*, 2 vols. (New York: American News Co., 1879).

28. Young, 1: 26–27, 30–31, 74–75, 254–57, 365, 396–97, 408–9, 425–53, 622; for Grant in Asia, see 2: 149–444.

a cynic could have thought that he had appointed at least that many to his own cabinet. He claimed that government under the Republicans had been "honestly and economically managed, [and] that our civil service is as good as any in the world that I have seen." He attacked reformers and praised Conkling's "great character and genius." Conkling would, Grant thought, have been a better candidate than Hayes in 1876.[29]

While Grant traveled, the country fragmented, and that fragmentation became both Grant's great political asset and a potent danger. As a politician, Grant mirrored his military preferences. He needed clear enemies, and given a choice, he attacked. His chosen enemies were familiar ones: Southern Democrats, immigrant workers, and Catholics. If anyone wondered how Grant would have reacted to the Great Strike of 1877, they could read his sanguinary conversation with Bismarck. Grant and the Prussian chancellor agreed that the only solution to anarchism, socialism, and disorder was blood in the streets.[30]

Grant preferred enemies whom he could classify in the Civil War's terms of traitors and patriots. "Since the war," he told Young, "the Democratic Party has always been against the country." White Southerners had created "a South only solid through the disfranchisement of the negroes." Northern Democrats were largely "a foreign element…which has not been long enough with us to acquire…education or experience. Neither has any love for the Union."[31]

Having identified a disloyal Democratic constituency, Grant attacked. He outlined a Stalwart program: order in the North with little sympathy for strikers or industrial reform, and order in the South with a renewed effort to protect black suffrage. He advocated hard money and opposed civil service reform. The country's fragmentation gave Grant his enemies and the basis of his political program, but its increasing complexity while he toured the world made his political task more difficult. Relatively minor distractions during Grant's presidency—Chinese immigration, Mormon polygamy, and the rise of antimonopoly politics—had grown into major sources of conflict.[32]

As long as he was abroad, Grant could avoid the new issues and hammer on the old. His political mistake was coming home too soon. He and Julia had planned to continue on to Australia and return in the summer of 1880 just before the Republican convention, but they found there was no direct steamship service to Australia from Japan, so they returned to San Francisco in September 1879 "to the thunder of the batteries of Angel

29. Ibid., 2: 263–67, 274, 279–308, 355–58, 452–57.
30. Ibid., 1: 414–15, 581.
31. Ibid., 2: 269–70.
32. Charles W. Calhoun, *Conceiving a New Republic: The Republican Party and the Southern Question, 1869–1900* (Lawrence: University Press of Kansas, 2006), 169–74.

Island, Black Point and Alcatraz" and the "Anglo-Saxon cheer ringing out from thousands of voices."[33]

When the *San Francisco Chronicle* interviewed Grant, one of the first questions was about the Chinese. Chinese immigration had begun during the Gold Rush and continued to flow in the 1870s. More than 22,000 Chinese—largely from Guangdong Province—had entered the United States in 1876, and nearly 10,000 came in 1879. By 1880 there were roughly 105,000 Chinese in the American West. Because they were overwhelmingly male, they formed a disproportionate percentage of wage laborers. Only 4.5 percent of the Chinese population was women, and roughly 25 percent of the work force of California was Chinese.[34]

Grant had been well received in China, and he would meet separately with an American Chinese delegation, but he dodged the "Chinese question" as being "entirely new to me." It really wasn't. As president, Grant had signed the Page Law of 1875, which was a Republican attempt to stop the Democrats from bludgeoning them with the Chinese issue. It passed in federal form a California law ruled unconstitutional by the Supreme Court banning the immigration of Chinese women sold into slavery. Its intention was to severely restrict the immigration of all Chinese women. Grant certainly knew of the success California Democrats had achieved in bending the laws and amendments barring slavery into a way to regulate and try to ban the Chinese on the grounds that they were unfree laborers, which they were not. The linked issues of antimonopoly and Sinophobia posed problems for Grant.[35]

Free labor began as an argument for equal rights and homogeneous citizenship, but it became an argument for exclusion. Free labor demanded self-ownership and freedom of contract; Sinophobes on the West Coast claimed that the Chinese were incapable of either. They were supposedly not only degraded, semislaves, but they could never be anything else. They were as much threats to free labor and white manhood as chattel slaves had been before the Civil War.[36]

33. Young, 2: 628.
34. *Historical Statistics of the United States Colonial Times to 1970*, Bicentennial ed. (Washington: U.S. Dept. of Commerce, Bureau of the Census, 1975), Table Ad136-148—Immigrants, by country of last residence—Asia: 1820–1997; Beth Lew-Williams, *The Chinese Must Go: Racial Violence and the Making of the Alien in America* (Cambridge, MA: Harvard University Press, forthcoming) 22, 37; Roseanne Currarnino, *The Labor Question in America: Economic Democracy in the Gilded Age* (Urbana: University of Illinois Press, 2011), 41.
35. "Home Again! The Safe Return of the Illustrious Soldier," *San Francisco Chronicle*, Sep. 21, 1879; Stacey L. Smith, *Freedom's Frontier: California and the Struggle over Unfree Labor, Emancipation, and Reconstruction* (Chapel Hill: University of North Carolina Press, 2014), 206–18.
36. Moon-Ho Jung, *Coolies and Cane: Race, Labor, and Sugar in the Age of Emancipation* (Baltimore, MD: Johns Hopkins University Press, 2006), 4–13, 67–68.

The "Chinese Question" dominated Western politics not just because Californians were racist (although they were) and not just because Chinese in shoe making, cigar making, and laundries worked for lower wages than whites (which they did), but because whites, both immigrant and native-born, had rhetorically turned the Chinese into "coolies." Coolies were indentured laborers, which Chinese immigrants were not, but by portraying them as such, Sinophobes made them the tools employers would use to reduce white workers to slavery. They were part of a system that Henry George denounced in a speech on July 4, 1877, as slavery since it took from a worker "all the fruits of his labor, except a bare living."[37]

Sinophobia differed from generic American racism in predicting that the "inferior" race would triumph in a contest with whites. In the providential racist thinking that had become conventional by midcentury, Indians were destined to be displaced by a superior race; people of African descent were destined to be slaves or disappear because they could not stand in direct competition with whites; Mexicans, derided as a mixed race, could not stand against "Anglo-Saxons." But unless banned from the continent, the Chinese would displace white Americans. This was the theme of Pierton W. Dooner's 1880 novel *The Last Day of the Republic*, which portrayed the Chinese as an invading army destined to occupy California. The Chinese would triumph because they worked for wages that no white man supporting a home and family would, or could, accept.[38]

For Grant to have no opinion on the Chinese in California seemed to most Californians the equivalent of having no opinion on the devil. The connections between Sinophobia and antimonopoly politics made his position worse. He had made his opposition to the Great Strike of 1877 very clear, but in California support for that strike, hatred of the Central Pacific Railroad, and Sinophobia all merged into a single stream. Grant was rowing against the current.

Denis Kearney, an Irish immigrant drayman—a small businessman rather than a wageworker—had entered politics around the Strike of 1877 and had used the Chinese issue to gain control of the anti-coolie clubs at the heart of San Francisco's Democratic Party. He turned them into the basis for a new Workingmen's Party that spread outward from San Francisco. Kearney's hatred of the Chinese was vicious and murderous,

37. Michael Kazin, "The July Days in San Francisco: Prelude to Kearneyism," in *The Great Strikes of 1877*, ed. David O. Stowell (Urbana: University of Illinois Press, 2008), 140; Joshua Paddison, *American Heathens: Religion, Race, and Reconstruction in California* (Berkeley: published for the Huntington–USC Institute on California and the West by University of California Press, 2012), 5, 19–20, 35, 46–52, 88–92, 151; Jung, 4–13; Currarino, 36–59.
38. Lew-Williams, 25–33.

but he also saw anti-Chinese agitation as a way to attack monopoly and corruption. The Workingmen's slogan became "The Chinese must go."[39]

The Workingmen serendipitously rose just as California prepared for a new constitutional convention in 1878. The Republicans and Democrats, terrified of the Workingmen's strength, united to present joint tickets to run against them wherever the new party was strongest. On paper the two established parties controlled a solid majority of delegates in the constitutional convention, but in practice many of the non-Workingmen delegates from the interior were agrarians: antimonopolist and anti-Chinese. The convention created a railroad commission, but it lacked teeth, while the new constitution stipulated that "no native of China, no idiot, insane person, or person convicted of any infamous crime" be allowed to vote in the state. This prohibition duplicated the federal ban on Chinese voting because they were not "free white persons" under the 1790 immigration act. Nor under Article XIX could any "Chinese or Mongolian" be employed on public works except as punishment for a crime. There was no real opposition to these clauses, but Article XIX was of dubious constitutionality and the state could not prohibit Chinese immigration. That came under federal purview.[40]

The Workingmen's Party collapsed soon after the constitutional convention, but the constitution was adapted in May 1879, just before Grant's return. The marriage of antimonopolism and racism that the Workingmen had engineered endured, and it presented problems for Republicans like Grant even as most Workingmen, beliefs intact, returned to the Democrats. Republicans split over antimonopolism, but California Republicans were as Sinophobic as the Democrats. An 1879 referendum asking California voter opinion on Chinese exclusion favored exclusion by a vote of 150,000 to 900. Sinophobia had gone mainstream. It had become part of what historian Joshua Paddison has called white Christian nationalism.[41]

Grant hoped to leave the Chinese question behind him once he left the Pacific Coast, but the issue became national. Californians had turned to Washington in their effort to restrict Chinese immigration. In 1879 President Hayes vetoed a bill limiting the number of Chinese any ship could carry on the grounds that it violated the Burlingame Treaty with China and threatened the activities of Protestant missionaries and American merchants in that country. That same year, however, the U.S. minister to China was quietly instructed to begin negotiations to revise the treaty.[42]

39. Alexander Saxton, The Indispensable Enemy: Labor and the Anti-Chinese Movement in California (Berkeley: University of California Press, 1995), 116–21.
40. Richard White, Railroaded: The Transcontinentals and the Making of Modern America (New York: Norton, 2011), 299; Saxton, The Indispensable Enemy, 116–32.
41. Lew-Williams, 40; Saxton, The Indispensable Enemy, 138–56; Paddison, 139–56.
42. Lew-Williams, 40–41; Saxton, The Indispensable Enemy, 123–37.

Nor could Grant leave antimonopoly behind. Antimonopolists distrusted both Grant and Conkling since both were embedded in a politics of friendship that connected them specifically with the Central Pacific and Southern Pacific railroads and generally with the men who controlled railroad corporations. Conkling often deployed his congressional influence for the benefit of his railroad friends. Oliver Ames of the Union Pacific wrote in 1874 that Conkling "has always been in the interest of the Central Pacific and ready at all times to work for whatever they wanted," which was one reason Huntington thought him "decidedly the greatest man in the United States Senate." Such friendship was corrupt, but it was not bribery. Quid pro quo and prearrangement were unnecessary. Huntington once asked Leland Stanford to "arrange something out of which he [Conkling] could make some money (something handsome). You will have to be very careful how you do it, as he is very sensitive, but, of course, like the rest of us, has to eat and drink." Such arrangements were common. When J. N. Dolph was elected to the Senate from Oregon in 1882, he asked for, and got, reassurances from Henry Villard of the Northern Pacific that his "interests will be properly taken care of." Villard also assured him that "I shall take good care that your identification with our interests shall not embarrass you in the least as senator."[43]

Grant was less obviously a friend of the railroads during his presidency, but after he left office he accepted the favors of rich men bestowed in the name of a grateful nation. Wealthy men bought him houses, subscribed funds for him to invest, and created business opportunities. He joined Huntington and Jay Gould in building Mexican railroads. The rich, in fact, were more grateful than the nation. In resigning from the army to run for president, Grant had forfeited his military pension, and ex-presidents had no pension. The Democrats in Congress petulantly blocked the restoration of the military pension he had lost on becoming president. The Senate eventually passed a bill, but President Arthur said he would veto it if it reached his desk because he had already vetoed similar pension bills. Arthur offered a separate nonmilitary pension, but Grant refused it as charity.[44]

The anti-Chinese agitation and the rise of antimonopoly were difficult issues for Grant or the Stalwarts to avoid since they involved matters of corruption and rising class tensions, but the new divisions went beyond that. They involved the renewed power of evangelical reform. Traveling east on the Pacific Railway from California took Grant through Utah, where another issue that had seemed minor during his presidency had

43. White, 101–2, 116–17.
44. Ibid., 216; Adam Badeau, *Grant in Peace: From Appomattox to Mount McGregor* (Philadelphia: S. S. Scranton & Co., 1887), 431–32; McFeely, 264–65, 488.

exploded onto the national stage. In 1874 Ulysses and Julia Grant had gone to a lecture by Ann Eliza Young, "wife number 19," of Brigham Young during her tour of the United States. In divorcing Brigham Young, she became known as the "Rebel of the Harem." Brigham Young had married at least fifty-five wives, some of whom were in their teens and others had not obtained divorces from their gentile husbands. Sixteen of these wives had given birth to his fifty-eight children.[45]

The Mormons, like the Chinese, fell afoul of prevailing American notions of home and family, but initially they seemed better able to protect themselves. Congress had failed to pass antipolygamy legislation before the Civil War, partially because the South regarded such legislation against a "peculiar institution" as a precedent for laws against slavery. The Republicans did equate the two. Slavery and polygamy formed the "twin relics of barbarism" denounced in the Republican platform. Congress traditionally left such moral legislation to states and municipalities, but the Republicans had passed the Morrill antipolygamy bill in 1862. Mormon control over courts and marriage records in Utah, however, rendered it a dead letter. It seemed that the Mormons' identity as white and their status as citizens would grant them protection that the Chinese and Indians could not muster. But the Mormons demonstrated that whiteness did not always provide the magic key to qualifying as American. The Mormons were both white and suspect. Polygamy with its threat to the home was too great a burden for them to bear.[46]

II

The reformer's assault on polygamy demonstrated the bridgehead reform maintained in what might otherwise seem corrupt and debased politics. Reformers did not depend on political parties alone. Reform lodged itself in voluntary organizations, from the New York Society for the Suppression of Vice to the Woman's Christian Temperance Union, the Grange, and the Knights of Labor. These organizations, however, went well beyond moral suasion. Reformers turned to Congress and legislatures to secure their ends.

In the late 1870s Mormons had attracted the opposition of evangelical Christians, who had considerable influence in Congress. When the

45. Sarah Barringer Gordon, *The Mormon Question: Polygamy and Constitutional Conflict in Nineteenth-Century America* (Chapel Hill: University of North Carolina Press, 2002), 110.

46. Stephen Eliot Smith, "Barbarians within the Gates: Congressional Debates on Mormon Polygamy, 1850–79," *Journal of Church and State* 51, no. 4 (2010): 604–5; Gordon, 81–83, 112–16.

Christian lobby—as the loose alliance of representatives of Protestant evangelical groups in Washington was called—joined with the Republican Party to renew the fight against polygamy, the issue pushed the Mormons, and Democrats, into a corner.

The attack on polygamy made Utah, a poor, thinly populated, and distant territory, into an unlikely focal point of political controversy. The Mormons, who had sought to escape the reach of the United States, found themselves reeled back in by the completion of the transcontinental railroad and the telegraph. Mining attracted more gentiles—as the Mormons called non-Mormons—to Utah, and unflattering accounts of the territory proliferated. Protestant women in Utah, exposed directly to plural marriage, attacked polygamy as antithetical to the Protestant home: "degrading to man and woman, a curse to children and destruction to the sacred relations of family, upon which the civilization of nations depends." Christian missionaries demanded the "Christian Reconstruction of Utah," the overthrow of Mormon political power, and "the establishment of a Christian commonwealth."[47]

Protestants reduced polygamy to male lust and female slavery, but Mormons justified the practice by appealing both to the Old Testament example and as a "new dispensation," part of the revelations given to the church's founder, Joseph Smith. Some men were called to take additional wives in order to produce more patriarchs from among the souls waiting for embodiment. These patriarchs—"Lords of Creation"—ruled over polygamous homes in this life and would rule over eternal worlds in the afterlife. A man who took multiple wives was a man rising in the church and in Utah. A wife had to consent for her husband to take new wives, but if she refused for selfish reasons, she would be "damned." Her marriage would not endure for "time and eternity."[48]

Marriage in the United States, however, was a civil contract. Altering forms of marriage meant altering basic components of republican society and the nation itself. Mormons regarded polygamy as an affirmation of their faith and its doctrines, but to outsiders women's consent to plural marriage was not real consent, and polygamy reduced marriage to a command made by men to women to "receive, conceive, bear, and bring forth in the name of Israel's God." It reflected an older patriarchy and mocked evolving American ideas of companionate marriage and female control

47. David Prior, "Civilization, Republic, Nation: Contested Keywords, Northern Republicans, and the Forgotten Reconstruction of Mormon Utah," *Civil War History* 56, no. 3 (2010): 289–301; Gaines M. Foster, *Moral Reconstruction: Christian Lobbyists and the Federal Legislation of Morality, 1865–1920* (Chapel Hill: University of North Carolina Press, 2002), 54–57.
48. Turner, 377; Gordon, 22–27, 92–93.

over the home. Asking whether Utah *could* alter marriage—which was separate from questions about whether it *should* do so—involved the First Amendment guarantee of religious freedom and resurrected the old doctrine of states' rights and the right of local communities to govern their own practices.[49]

Much was thus at stake in the battle over polygamy. In 1874 Congress passed the Poland Act, named after its sponsor, which moved prosecutions from the Mormon-controlled probate courts into the federal courts, despite the opposition of the powerful Central Pacific Railroad lobby, which sought to protect its allies, Young and the Mormon Church. Democrats, such as Sen. Thomas F. Bayard of Delaware, who saw the Poland Act as an extension of Reconstruction, opposed it. "I am so sick and tired of bayonet rule and bayonet threats in this country," Bayard complained. "This country is to-day passing away from the theory of being supported by the hearts of the people, and it is becoming a mere Government of coercion, and this bill is a suggestion of it." Grant had signed the Poland Act of 1874, but he had also removed Thomas McKean, a federal judge who acted too aggressively against Brigham Young. This being the Gilded Age, it was hard to be sure why McKean was removed. It could have been his actions against Young; it could have been because he faced accusations of corruption; and it could have been because he had censured a brother-in-law of Supreme Court Justice Stephen Field, who then demanded McKean's removal. Once the Democrats controlled the House, there would be no more anti-polygamy legislation passed during the 1870s.[50]

The Republicans, however, persisted. Their 1876 platform renewed the attack on polygamy as the surviving relic of barbarism. Utah was hardly the threat to the Union that the South had been, but Utah's ideological salience made it loom large. Like Catholics, Mormons belonged to a hierarchical church whose leaders claimed access to divine revelation and thus the authority to direct their followers in faith and morals. Most Protestants had been unwilling to sanction the Christian Amendment to the Constitution proposed during the Civil War because it violated the principle of the separation of church and state, and they now objected to a territory that flaunted that separation. They believed that Mormons, like Catholics, posed a danger to the republic when the faithful followed the dictates of their church in political matters and blurred the lines between church governance and secular governance.

49. Gordon, 65–71, 91–93.
50. Smith, "Barbarians within the Gates," 612–16; Gordon, 111–14; Thomas G. Alexander, "Federal Authority Versus Polygamic Theocracy: James B. Mckean and the Mormons, 1870–75," *Dialogue: A Journal of Mormon Thought* 1, no. 3 (1966): 85–100; Foster, 54–57.

The cultural battle that pitted the Christian lobby and Protestant women's groups against the Mormons abounded in ironies. The Mormon Church had made religious doctrine into secular practice in Utah, which was what—using different doctrines—the Christian Amendment had imagined for the country as a whole. Utah was a democracy, but, as the Mormon leadership proclaimed, it was a "Theo-Democracy—the voice of the people consenting to the voice of God." Mormons argued that the purpose of democratic processes was to sanction the laws of God as interpreted by the church leadership. Utah observed God's laws as revealed to the Mormons. This certainly bore a family resemblance to the intent of the Christian Amendment. The observation of a Utah gentile, recorded by Mark Twain in *Roughing It*, remained only slightly exaggerated in the 1870s: "There is a batch of governors, and judges, and other officials here, shipped from Washington, and they maintain the semblance of a republican form of government—but the petrified truth is that Utah is an absolute monarchy and Brigham Young is king!" Young, the "American Moses," stood as a "law giver," although he held no federal or state office.[51]

The role played by women in the attack on polygamy added to the ironies. Protestant women attacked plural marriage as a form of slavery since Mormon women lived under conditions that denied them true consent. Yet not only did Mormon women overwhelmingly defend plural marriage, but Utah in 1870 also gave women what many of them sought elsewhere in the country: the vote. Since Mormon women backed church candidates, some women who advocated suffrage found themselves arguing that Mormon women should be stripped of the suffrage they had obtained because they used it to sustain polygamy. For many women, monogamous marriage trumped suffrage.[52]

The Republicans turned to the courts. The Mormon leadership had selected George Reynolds to serve as the defendant in a test case, and early in 1879, when Grant was still abroad, the Supreme Court outlawed polygamy in *Reynolds v. United States*. Amidst a series of decisions limiting the reach of the federal government in the Reconstruction South, *Reynolds* was an affirmation of federal authority to limit and regulate local practices that, lawyers for the Mormons had argued, the Constitution left to the states and territories. The government stressed polygamy as slavery's analogue; the appellants cited the *Dred Scott* decision as a precedent for

51. Gordon, 91–96; Mark Twain, *Roughing It* (New York: New American Library, 1962), 96. For biographies of Brigham Young, see Leonard J. Arrington, *Brigham Young: American Moses* (New York: Knopf, 1985); John G. Turner, *Brigham Young, Pioneer Prophet* (Cambridge, MA: Belknap Press of Harvard University Press, 2012).
52. Gordon, 97–98, 168–71.

the unconstitutionality of the Morrill Act. This did not prove particularly wise or helpful. In justifying federal regulation of marriage, the court had a clear path to follow. The Republican promise of contract freedom and a homogeneous citizenry translated easily into a standard marriage contract for all U.S. citizens. The form of the marriage contract could not be delegated to religious authorities. The Court ruled that antipolygamy legislation did not violate the First Amendment because that amendment protected only belief and not actions. The Court argued by analogy, citing all kinds of other practices that might be justified under freedom of religion, from "Hindu widows hurl[ing] themselves on the funeral pyres of their husbands" to "East Islanders...expos[ing] their newborn babies...." Polygamy, the justices decided, led to barbarism and despotism; monogamy was the republican form of marriage. Implicit in the limitations placed on Mormon religious practices was the conviction that Protestant Christian practices were normative and protected by the Constitution.[53]

Antipolygamy formed only one target of the Christian lobby in the 1870s and 1880s, and only one of the demands it made on the federal government. In the 1870s religious reformers sought to expand the moral authority of the federal government and institute a kind of moral reconstruction, predictably centered on the home. Anthony Comstock located other dangers in pornography, birth control, and free love. In doing so, he achieved the lobby's first national success.[54]

As leader of the New York Society for the Suppression of Vice, Comstock traced lust back to "obscene literature and articles of indecent and immoral use," including "books, pamphlets, leaflets, songs, pictures, and these articles in rubber, wax, and other materials—all designed and cunningly calculated to excite the imagination and inflame the passions of the youth into whose hands they may come." He then enumerated the consequences. They induced "evil thoughts," which were "an introduction to every debasing practice." First boys would masturbate, then they would resort to prostitutes, and then they would seduce. Pornography thus threatened children, home, family, and the reproduction of the republic. Masturbation and pornography were not private vices but public dangers that must be suppressed. Suppression was Comstock's life work, and it demanded being always on the alert. He even succeeded in getting a new edition of Walt Whitman's *Leaves of Grass* banned as pornography.[55]

53. Gordon, 119–45.
54. Foster, 30–31.
55. Nicola Kay Beisel, *Imperiled Innocents: Anthony Comstock and Family Reproduction in Victorian America* (Princeton, NJ: Princeton University Press, 1997), 3–8, 53–57, 167; Carpenter, 85.

Comstock was simply the best-known figure, and the one most easily satirized, in a larger purity crusade. Josiah and Deborah Leeds, who worked out of Philadelphia, began their careers with censoring billboard advertisements for the Centennial Exposition in 1876 and expanded their efforts to theater, art, ballet, the *Police Gazette*, and social dancing. Their goal was to prevent vice by striking at its causes. If government had to intervene to enforce proper social habits, then censorship was necessary.[56]

Moral reformers acquiesced to, and even demanded, increases in federal and state power to protect the home, in part because once the reforms were in place, the power of enforcement was delegated to the reformers. Francis Willard eventually advocated a cabinet-level Department of Recreation, which would enforce laws on the "decency...of all public spectacles." Local committees, composed of both men and women, would censor all local amusements. Local governments had long regulated personal behavior. What distinguished the efforts of the 1870s and 1880s was that they had gone national in scale. Comstock was a fanatic, but his cause attracted support because it embraced larger nineteenth-century worries over threats to the home, the family, and a Protestant nation. Sex was private, thus any public discussion or expression was by definition obscene. Lust and impurity—like Catholics, strong drink, and Mormons—menaced a Protestant nation. Individual freedoms mattered less than preservation of home and family.[57]

Frances Willard was not a fanatic, but she too formed part of the Christian lobby and was far more formidable than Comstock. The Woman's Christian Temperance Union was overwhelmingly Protestant, and no one made the home as intimidating a weapon as did Protestant women. When Mormon polygamists attempted to portray themselves as white men defending the home, evangelical women cast them as archaic and blundering patriarchs who threatened women and the republic.

The WCTU was a voluntary organization that provided a maternal gateway to politics. Superficially, Willard's emphasis on home and Christianity should have put her in the same camp as liberal critics of women's rights such as William Dean Howells, who thought the emphasis on women's rights and women's achievements at the Philadelphia Exposition subverted their proper domestic role. "Those accustomed to think of women as the wives, mothers, and sisters of men," he wrote, "will be puzzled to

56. David Jay Pivar, *Purity Crusade: Sexual Morality and Social Control, 1868–1900* (Westport, CT: Greenwood Press, 1973), 109–10, 161, 237.

57. Alison M. Parker, *Purifying America: Women, Cultural Reform, and Pro-Censorship Activism, 1873–1933* (Urbana: University of Illinois Press, 1997), 3–5, 126–27; John D'Emilio and Estelle Freedman, *Intimate Matters: A History of Sexuality in America* (New York: Harper & Row, 1988), 159–63.

know why the ladies wished to separate their work from that of the rest of the human race, and those who imagine an antagonism between the sexes must regret, in the interest of what is called the cause of woman, that the Pavilion is so inadequately representative of her distinctive achievement." Willard took domesticity in a very different direction, although not at the Exposition. Annie Wittenmyer, the first head of the WCTU, persuaded her not to join with Susan B. Anthony in promoting women's suffrage there.[58]

Willard believed in the equality of women and their ability to compete with men, but she also believed in women's higher nature and in separate women's organizations as havens for cultivating women's talents. Women, she wrote in 1886, possessed higher spiritual power, "more open to the 'skyey influences' of the oncoming age. Already, [h]alf of the world's wisdom, more than half its purity, and nearly all its gentleness are today to be set down on woman's credit side." She imagined a new woman.[59]

Willard's religiosity, her advocacy of temperance, and her embrace of a separate female nature and sphere — no matter how expansive — separated her from some of the women who had dominated the women's movement in the wake of the Civil War, but her personal charm and sense of female solidarity nonetheless turned many of these women into friends. Willard became entranced with Anna Dickinson, whose fame was beginning to recede in the mid-1870s as Willard's star rose. Dickinson did much to teach Willard how to dominate a platform and win over an audience, but Dickinson's feminism did not include temperance or evangelical religion, and Willard disapproved of Dickinson's decision to become an actress. Willard had more luck with Susan B. Anthony. They agreed on temperance, though Anthony did not share Willard's desire for total prohibition. They also agreed on women's suffrage, differing however in their arguments. Anthony stressed natural rights, while Willard emphasized home protection.[60]

Willard's relationship with Elizabeth Cady Stanton was particularly revealing of the tensions within the women's movement during the Gilded Age. While dean of women at Northwestern, Willard had instituted special rules to create a protected sphere for female undergraduates. Stanton

58. W. D. Howells, "A Sennight of the Centennial," *Atlantic Monthly* (July 1876): 101; Ruth Birgitta Anderson Bordin, *Woman and Temperance: The Quest for Power and Liberty, 1873–1900* (Philadelphia: Temple University Press, 1981), 60–61.

59. Frances E. Willard, *How to Win: A Book for Girls in the Ideal of "the New Woman" According to the Woman's Christian Temperance Union*, ed. Carolyn De Swarte Gifford (New York: Garland, 1987), 50.

60. Ruth Birgitta Anderson Bordin, *Frances Willard: A Biography* (Chapel Hill: University of North Carolina Press, 1986), 83–86, 98–99, 101.

had attacked her, demanding equality for men and women. Willard never really forgave Stanton.[61]

Willard sought to ride Protestant currents of reform. Except for the lead she took later in the WCTU's turn to labor reform, "Christian Socialism," and international reform efforts, her role was to direct the abundant energies of her members. The WCTU became a school for women's politics. Willard's famous slogan, "Do Everything," initially referred to tactics and methods, but it gradually included the causes embraced by the WCTU. The causes grew every year. The WCTU pushed school reform, particularly free kindergarten, day nurseries for the children of working women, and federal aid to education. The organization embraced "Social Evil Reform," which ranged from Sabbatarian laws, seeking federal prohibitions on interstate train travel, the movement of the mails, and all interstate commerce on Sundays, to censoring "impure" and "obscene" literature, and promoting "pure literature." Willard and the WCTU participated in the antipolygamy campaign and defended the "beloved Home Religion." The organization campaigned to tighten divorce laws because divorce threatened home and family. It advocated stronger laws against rape; attacked prostitution, demanding the prosecution of male patrons; and agitated to raise the laws governing the age of consent, which were as low as ten in twenty states and seven in one state. The WCTU by the end of the decade advocated the eight-hour day and labor reform. It did not confine itself to the United States, but tried to project reform around the world.[62]

Only superficially did reform politics as practiced by the Christian lobby seem entirely the realm of voluntary organizations and individual reform. Evangelical reformers did not change society the way Protestant churches claimed to save souls: one voluntary conversion at a time. As the WCTU's formidable legislative agenda showed, there was often only the most permeable of membranes between voluntary organizations and the state.

Comstock waged his most important battles in Washington, D.C., and the federal government delegated his real power to him. He lobbied Congress in 1873, setting up shop in the vice president's office in the Senate to display his collection of confiscated pornography for the education of the senators. Congress, with a critical intervention by James G. Blaine, responded by passing the Comstock Act in 1873, greatly expanding federal supervision of American sexuality. It made the U.S. Post Office

---

61. Ibid., 101–2.
62. Parker, 6–9, 27, 33–34; Gordon, 230; Foster, 40–47, 93; Ian R. Tyrrell, *Reforming the World: The Creation of America's Moral Empire* (Princeton, NJ: Princeton University Press, 2010), 3–9, 27, 75; Bordin, *Frances Willard*, 130–48.

Frances E Willard

Frances Willard's genius was in recognizing the political power women could gain from agitating, petitioning, and demonstrating to protect the home. These twinned pictures from the 1880s show Willard holding a petition (this page, courtesy of the Frances E. Willard Memorial Library and Archives) and the Woman's Christian Temperance Union's *Home Protection Manual*, 1879 (opposite page). Willard made "home protection" the core of the WCTU program.

HOME PROTECTION MANUAL:

CONTAINING AN ARGUMENT

FOR THE

TEMPERANCE BALLOT FOR WOMAN,

AND HOW TO OBTAIN IT, AS A MEANS OF

HOME PROTECTION;

ALSO

CONSTITUTION AND PLAN OF WORK FOR STATE AND LOCAL W. C. T. UNIONS.

By FRANCES E. WILLARD,

PRESIDENT OF ILLINOIS W. C. T. U.

PRICE 15 CENTS.

PUBLISHED AT "THE INDEPENDENT" OFFICE,

BROADWAY, NEW YORK,

1879.

and the courts a kind of morals police in charge of American censorship. The act banned "obscene, lewd and lascivious" materials in any form from the mails, including contraceptives, abortifacients, and information about how to obtain or use them. A judge in any district court could order the seizure of obscene materials. The initial law was relatively ineffective, but as revised in 1876, postmasters could bar commercial materials and publications. When Robert Ingersoll secured a petition with fifty thousand signatures to repeal the Comstock Law, Congress refused to do so. In any contest featuring an atheist — even a prominent Republican atheist — allied with those favoring free love, Protestant moralists were going to win. Comstock continued to lobby, and Congress continued to strengthen the law in the 1880s and 1890s, giving postal inspectors the right to open envelopes in search of obscene materials.[63]

The Christian reformers' demand for laws increased the authority of government without enlarging its administrative capacity. Instead the government delegated enforcement to private parties. Willard's suggestion of local volunteer committees for her proposed Department of Recreation was typical, as was Grant's delegation of Indian administration to the churches. Comstock easily adapted himself to fee-based governance and the delegation of powers. The New York Society for the Suppression of Vice was a private organization that took on public powers. The postmaster general appointed Comstock as a special agent to enforce the law with the society paying his salary. There was nothing unusual in this kind of delegation. As cities passed laws against cruelty to animals, San Francisco delegated police powers to the San Francisco Society for the Prevention of Cruelty to Animals. Its agents had the right to arrest and prosecute, and the fines that resulted went to the society.[64]

This expansion of federal, state, and local power, without an expansion of administrative capacity, often delegated authority to petty tyrants. At the end of his career, Comstock credited himself with more than thirty-six hundred arrests, and the destruction of 73,608 pounds of books, 877,412 obscene pictures, 8,495 photographic negatives, and 98,563 articles that encouraged immorality. He even tabulated the 6,436 indecent playing

63. Parker, 2–5, 60; Comstock's positions were not synonomous with those of the WCTU, 39–40; Beisel, 36–103; Carpenter, 88; Foster, 50–57.
64. Janet M. Davis, *The Gospel of Kindness: Animal Welfare and the Making of Modern America* (New York: Oxford University Press, 2016), 86–90; Foster, 53–54; Andrew Robichaud, *The Animal City: Remaking Human and Animal Lives in America, 1820–1910* (Stanford, CA: Stanford University Press, 2015), 11, 169, 189–94.

cards he destroyed, as well as the 8,502 boxes of pills and powders sold to induce abortions.[65]

The WCTU had a more complicated relation with government than the New York Society for the Suppression of Vice. With its local chapters, national lobby, and vigorous leadership, the WCTU could simultaneously push national measures and advance locally and incrementally with local or state temperance ordinances and censorship. The WCTU's program of "Do Everything" allowed it to elaborate on its basic agenda and enlist its members in programs of education and surveillance. The WCTU grouped drunkenness, animal cruelty, and family violence under a single Department of Mercy. It collaborated with other reform organizations, among them the National Association of Colored Women, the Audubon Society, and the Woman's Foreign Mission Society; mobilized its own membership for surveillance, publicity campaigns, and education; and sought laws against cruelty to animals, vivisection, or animal experimentation as well as cruelty to children.[66]

The operations of the WCTU, the New York Society for the Suppression of Vice, and other voluntary organizations demonstrate the futility of distinguishing too starkly between on the one hand an American tradition in which voluntary organizations take on social welfare functions and the home and family bear responsibility for producing citizens, and on the other a European tradition where such matters increasingly become the domain of the state. Beginning in the late 1870s and through the 1880s, attempts at social reform and social regulation intertwined the private and the public, the voluntary and the coercive, and the home and the state. Voluntary organizations could spur an increase in federal authority and stimulate the beginnings of institutionally autonomous government bureaucracies. Margaret Dye Ellis, who became the national superintendent of legislation for the WCTU in Washington, D.C., explained that it had learned that prayers alone could not close saloons: "We found that there must be law back of sentiment and sentiment back of law."[67]

Reform operated on a political terrain that continued to make it difficult to classify political issues by party. Neither party had become ideologically homogeneous. Grant's Stalwart program of order in the North, with little sympathy for strikers or industrial reform, order in the South with a renewed effort to protect black suffrage, hard money, and opposition to civil service reform, alienated Republican antimonopolists in the

65. Jerry L. Mashaw, "Federal Administration and Administrative Law in the Gilded Age," *Yale Law Journal* 119, no. 7 (2010): 1449.
66. Davis, 50–80, Bordin, 131–34; Turner, 94.
67. Parker, 31–32; Foster, 39.

West and Midwest. Nor did it really address the concerns of the Christian lobby, while it rebuffed both Republican Liberals and Half-Breeds.[68]

III

Liberals found themselves in a quandary as the 1880 election approached. Henry and Clover Adams, who had been abroad since the fall of 1879, opposed both Blaine and Grant. William Dean Howells believed Hayes had squandered his presidency. He thought the Republicans had no chance except for Grant, but he also thought that "his re-election would be almost a confession that popular government was near its end among us: when in time of peace only one man can save us, we're hardly worth saving."[69]

The echoes of 1877 had not fully faded. In 1878 Jonathan Baxter Harrison, yet another Ohioan, an ex-abolitionist, journalist, and Unitarian clergyman, published three widely noted articles for Howells in the *Atlantic*. The longest, "Dangerous Tendencies in American Life," appeared in the October issue. Howells incorporated Harrison's articles into his own fiction as he moved toward literary realism. John Hay did likewise.[70]

Howells relied on Grant to stand against the dangerous tendencies enumerated by Harrison, who became part of the circle around Charles Eliot Norton, the country's leading liberal intellectual and Harvard professor. Harrison discerned beneath the Strike of 1877 "the earlier stages of a war upon property, and upon everything that satisfies what are called the higher wants of life." Universal suffrage had been a mistake, one too late to correct, and American democracy had yielded "a great and successful movement for the propagation of uneducated thought, the spectacle of the untaught classes and disorganizing forces of the time taking possession of the printing-press, of rostrum, and of the ballot, and attacking

68. Calhoun, 169–74.
69. Chalfant, 399–400; W. D. Howells to W. C. Howells, June 16, 1878, W. D. Howells to Hayes, Mar. 16, 1879, in William Dean Howells, *Selected Letters*, ed. George Warren Arms (Boston: Twayne, 1979), 201–2, 220.
70. William Alexander, *William Dean Howells: The Realist as Humanist* (New York: B. Franklin, 1981), 11, 15; Jonathan Baxter Harrison, "Certain Dangerous Tendencies in American Life," *Atlantic Monthly* 42, no. 252 (1878): 389–403; Kenneth Schuyler Lynn, *William Dean Howells: An American Life* (New York: Harcourt Brace Jovanovich, 1971), 273–75, 277–78; W. D. Howells to Charles Norton, Sep. 4, 1878, in Howells, *Selected Letters*, 2: 205, n. 2, n. 3.

modern society with its own weapons. It is a wide-spread revolt against civilization."[71]

Harrison based a second article on interviews with thirty-four native-born Protestant workmen who belonged to "the Nationals," a political movement that Harrison inflated into a looming threat to the nation. In fact, the Nationals were the ephemeral product of currency and labor reformers who met in Toledo in 1878. The party's platform demanded a fiat currency (greenbacks), reduction in hours of labor, the end of contract prison labor, the creation of a bureau of industrial statistics, and a halt to the importation of "servile labor."[72]

Harrison saw in a minor party with common antimonopolist demands a threat to the republic and civilized life itself. He identified the reformers with spiritualism, and he made spiritualism a symbol of a country that was breaking free from organized religion and rational thought. The Nationals, Harrison said, used "very largely the methods of thought of uncivilized or prehistoric men," and this made them even more dangerous because the vast majority of the country shared this mode of thinking. Where his article "Dangerous Tendencies" had often been abstract and general, Harrison was quite particular about what individual Nationals wanted. They advocated nationalizing the railroads, telegraphs, and banks. They desired postal savings banks and demanded an end to Chinese immigration; they wanted term limits on elected officials, graduated income tax, and fiat currency. Some wanted a proportional representation by class in Congress and legislatures. They supported a protective tariff. They thought the present order was flawed and unjust, and they advanced a series of specific measures—some more practical than others—to fix it.[73]

That such modest reforms, some of which were already in place and others of which would be enacted either in the United States or elsewhere, inspired such horror was revealing. Harrison wrote of the Nationals, "If their undertaking could succeed, we should have wealth without labor, and a system of morals without self-restraint; and instead of the orderly empire of law we should have 'mob-voiced lawlessness,' anarchy uttered or ordained by the people." Howells thought the opinions of the Nationals "astonishing, disheartening and alarming. If those fellows get the upper hand, good-by, Liberty! We shall be ground down by the dullest and stupidest despotism that ever was." Harrison and Howells were appalled by

71. Harrison, 392–93, 402.
72. John R. Commons, *History of Labour in the United States*, ed. David J. Saposs et al. (New York: Macmillan, 1918), 2: 244–45; Jonathan Baxter Harrison, "The Nationals: Their Origin and Their Aims," *Atlantic Monthly* 42, no. 253 (1878): 521–30.
73. Harrison, "The Nationals," 521–30.

the Nationals' specific reforms, but it was their willingness to redesign the social and political order that alarmed them even more. These working-men and reformers were, in fact, only tinkering with a set of laws and practices that gave advantages to some groups while hurting others, but outraged liberals saw them taking an axe to the "moral order of the universe." They were trifling with "the constitution of things, by the laws of an order which man did not make and cannot change." Harrison wanted Americans to reject "empty theories of millennial progress" and return to "manly self-reliance and intelligent recognition of the real conditions of human life in this world."[74]

A more important embodiment of Harrison's and Howells's fears was the Noble and Holy Order of the Knights of Labor, in part a labor union; in part a fraternal organization like the Masons, the Ancient Order of Hibernians, and the Odd Fellows; and yet another of the voluntary organizations that blossomed in the late 1870s. The Knights had originated in Philadelphia in 1869 as a secret order with the attendant rituals and regalia that so fascinated American men. There was reason for labor unions to mimic the fraternal organizations to which many of their members belonged, since these organizations had proved larger, more successful, and longer-lasting than labor unions. Secrecy also seemed a necessity when employers often fired men for union membership.[75]

The Knights grew slowly until Terence Powderly became their Grand Master in 1879. The child of Irish immigrants who had settled in the Pennsylvania coal country, Powderly had become a railroad mechanic. He took pride and joy in his work. He also possessed the Gilded Age's adoration of home. He married Hannah Dever, the daughter of a mine-worker, in 1872. He aspired to rise in the world: "onward and upward," he wrote in his diary. He forswore alcohol and joined the Catholic temperance organization, the Father Matthew Total Abstinence and Benevolent Union. Unlike the overwhelming majority of Irish workers, he became a Republican, but he was also a union man. The two were hardly antithetical. His own loss of work and the suffering he witnessed as a tramp during the depression of the 1870s both intensified his loyalty to workers and weakened his attachment to the Republicans, who drew heavily on the loyalty of anti-Catholic Welsh Protestants in the coal country. Powderly's

---

74. W. D. Howells to Charles Norton, Sep. 4, 1878, in Howells, *Selected Letters*, 2: 205 n. 2, n. 3; Harrison, "The Nationals," 529; Harrison, "Certain Dangerous Tendencies in American Life," 401.

75. Kim Voss, *The Making of American Exceptionalism: The Knights of Labor and Class Formation in the Nineteenth Century* (Ithaca, NY: Cornell University Press, 1993), 1–3, 74; Robert E. Weir, *Beyond Labor's Veil: The Culture of the Knights of Labor* (University Park: Pennsylvania State University, 1996), 22–30.

own politics shifted toward antimonopoly. He supported the Greenback Party in 1876, the same year he joined the Knights of Labor. He found labor solidarity was not easily achieved among Irish Catholics and anti-Catholic Welsh miners.[76]

The Great Strike of 1877 alarmed Powderly as much as Harrison. In Scranton it had spawned a violent coal miners' strike that was repressed by a private militia. As Grant and Bismarck recommended, blood did run in the streets. Powderly counted the costs of the strike, and assessed the disproportionate counterviolence that violence by workers could unleash. He did not reject strikes completely, but he thought that they should be used only rarely and when there were no alternatives. Since Powderly also retained the Knights' opposition to direct political involvement, he seemingly began his career as a labor leader by surrendering workers' two greatest weapons: their power to withhold labor and to vote collectively. It appeared that the only tools he retained were mediation, arbitration, and cooperative enterprises such as the coal mine the Knights operated in Cannellburg, Indiana. It and similar enterprises failed.[77]

In practice Powderly proved more pragmatic. When he thought it necessary, he supported strikes even against long odds. And Powderly was right in thinking an organization that contained Irish Democrats, Welsh Republicans, and third-party antimonopolists would break apart if it tried to offer candidates for election. Powderly, however, hardly forsook politics. He believed that unless workers captured local government, its repressive powers would be used against them. He envisioned a municipal economy geared toward the needs of its working people: city-owned gasworks, a revamped tax structure, and more public works. Here again voluntary organization was an avenue to government action. Powderly, as much as the liberals in the American Social Science Association, thought government policy toward labor should be guided by accurate statistics (one of the Knights' officers was Grand Statistician) gathered by the government. Powderly pressed for an appointment as head of a new Bureau of Labor Statistics in 1884. Although the Knights might not endorse or offer candidates, they would lobby Congress for reforms and present their members with information as to how their representatives acted and voted.[78]

76. Craig Phelan, *Grand Master Workman: Terence Powderly and the Knights of Labor* (Westport, CT: Greenwood Press, 2000), 11–33; M. Elizabeth Sanders, *Roots of Reform: Farmers, Workers, and the American State, 1877–1917* (Chicago: University of Chicago Press, 1999), 35–37.

77. Ibid., 25–28, 57–61; Sanders, 44–45.

78. Phelan, 27–29; Edward T. James, "T. V. Powderly, a Political Profile," *Pennnsylvania Magazine of History and Biography* 99, no. 4 (1975): 448–49.

Powderly achieved local political success in Scranton, Pennsylvania. The Pennsylvania Knights did not offer candidates, but instead after their regular meetings those members interested in politics reconvened into separate Committees on Progress. These committees, in turn, created a Greenback-Labor Party that swept Luzerne County elections in 1877 and elected Powderly mayor of Scranton in 1878. Although both the Knights, infiltrated by spies, and the Greenback-Labor Party faltered in Scranton, Powderly would be repeatedly reelected.[79]

Grant, so astute as a general in assessing his enemies and position, could grasp neither the political terrain nor the armies arrayed on it in 1880. He did not know what to make of the Knights, or the emerging WCTU, or the Christian lobby. The ability of voluntary organizations to drive politics baffled him. His antilabor positions cost him support among antimonopolist workingmen. His identification with the Stalwarts allied him with political machines whose basis in patronage politics was coming under attack.

In both the Democratic and the Republican parties, the challenge for candidates was to avoid issues that could divide the party and emphasize issues that drew distinctions with the opposing party. When Howells wrote Rutherford B. Hayes's campaign biography for the 1876 election, the candidate had instructed Howells not to commit him on "religion, temperance, or free trade. Silence is the only safety." That task was even more complex in 1880. A successful Republican candidate had to unite Stalwarts, Half-Breeds, liberals, and antimonopolists. Creating a national party paradoxically meant tailoring messages to local constituencies. A successful Democrat had to bridge the gap between Northerners and Southerners; Catholics and Protestants; and liberals, conservatives, and antimonopolists.[80]

These tricky politics proved too much for the frontrunners, Grant and Tilden. Grant's absence *had* made the heart grow fonder, however a slightly longer absence and better political advice would have helped. Grant conducted a triumphal tour across the country, but it lasted too long. The audience tired. He was no longer news, and as he attended banquets and sought the support of local politicians along the way, the public began to see him not as the old warrior whom they might have to draft to serve the republic but as a failed president too eager to return to office. So he left again. He went to Cuba and Mexico and returned close to the time of the Republican Convention in June. The tactic really didn't work. "Grant returns...again" didn't have the same ring. His chances of

79. Phelan, 27–31, 64–65, 103–5.
80. Hayes to W. D. Howells, Aug. 5, 1876, in Howells, *Selected Letters*, 136 n. 2.

a third term diminished as voters remembered his actual record. He had only fitfully defended black suffrage while in office, and largely abandoned the freedmen at the end of his second term. Why would he protect them now? A third term was unprecedented, and this made it even harder to explain why it should go to a man whose administration was marred by constant scandal. Grant had real political strength, but so too did the equally flawed James G. Blaine. The result was a deadlocked party approaching the Republican convention.[81]

For all his flaws, Grant remained a national hero. James G. Blaine and Roscoe Conkling were decidedly unheroic creatures of the Gilded Age: vain, corrupt, venomous, and greedy. Their only real principles were the tattered remnants of the old Radical vision. Both ultimately backed the right of the government to use force to combat violent attempts to deprive citizens of their lawful suffrage. Grant's support remained solid until the end, while Blaine's melted away; but neither got the nomination. Grant, rejecting his wife's entreaties that he appear at the convention, failed to reach the numerical threshold for the nomination. The Republicans picked a dark horse, James Garfield of Ohio, on the twenty-sixth ballot. He had a reputation for indecision. Tarred by the Crédit Mobilier scandal, he could, in the party of Grant, Blaine, and Conkling, still appear to walk among the righteous.[82]

Garfield professed not to have desired the nomination, but most observers doubted him. He was another Midwesterner, born in Ohio to a poor family, and an intellectual in love with books. He had come to the Western Reserve Eclectic Institute in 1851 as a student and janitor. The next year he was an assistant professor. After spending two years as a student at Williams College, he returned to Eclectic and soon became the school's president. He was twenty-six. Free labor seemed but common sense, with achievements like his.[83]

William Dean Howells knew Garfield, as he seemed to know virtually everyone. He told of sitting on the man's porch in Hiram, Ohio, around 1870. It was evening, and Howells started telling Garfield a story about the New England poets—then already elderly—whom he published in the *Atlantic*. Garfield stopped him, ran out into his yard, and hallooed the neighbors sitting on their porches: "He's telling about Holmes, and Longfellow, and Lowell, and Whittier." The neighbors came and listened

81. Young, 2: 628. Calhoun, 169–71; McFeely, 476–83.
82. Calhoun, 171–72; Ira M. Rutkow, *James A. Garfield* (New York: Times Books, 2006), 48–56; McFeely, 482–83; White, 64.
83. Allan Peskin, *Garfield: A Biography* (Kent, OH: Kent State University Press, 1978), 23–25, 30–34, 45–46, 49; Candice Millard, *Destiny of the Republic: A Tale of Madness, Medicine, and the Murder of a President* (New York: Doubleday, 2011), 22–23.

to Howells while the whippoorwills flew and sang in the evening air. There still existed a strong tradition of vernacular intellectualism in the Midwest that provided the crowds for the touring lectures, the lyceums, and later the Chautauquas.[84]

Garfield did more than listen that night. Small Midwestern towns like Hiram were full of men who had fought in the war. And Garfield, because the cool of this summer evening roused the memory of the cool of another summer evening at the beginning of the Civil War, told a story of riding into the valley of the Kanawha with his command. He saw on approaching a meadow men lying in sleep, until he suddenly realized they were not sleeping but dead. At "the sight of these dead men whom other men had killed, something went out of him, the habit of his life-time, that never came back again: the sense of the sacredness of life, and the impossibility of destroying it." That story, too, told something of the Midwest and of the memories that shaped elections.[85]

Despite his intimacy with presidents, and the bookishness of the presidents that he knew, Howells felt that the cultural world that gave him stature and brought neighbors to Garfield's porch to hear of New England poets was in decline. He thought younger men took little interest in literature; the audience for fiction seemed increasingly feminine.[86]

The fight for the Democratic nomination was less dramatic than the battle between Grant and Blaine, but the outcome was equally surprising. "Honest John Kelly" of Tammany Hall had initially supported Tilden as governor of New York but broke with him over state patronage. Kelly declared that if the Democrats nominated Tilden, New York City's Democratic machine would sit out the election. A Democrat who could not run strongly in New York City had no chance of carrying the state, and without New York, the Democrats were doomed in 1880. The Democrats dropped Tilden and, in another attempt to shake their taint of treason, nominated Winfield Scott Hancock, who had commanded a Union Army corps at Gettysburg. He had sided with President Johnson on Reconstruction and undone the policies of his predecessor, Phil Sheridan, in Texas and Louisiana. In the end, it appeared that both the Democrats and the Republicans had found their nominees by rummaging through the political bag of old Civil War generals.[87]

84. William Dean Howells, *Years of My Youth, and Three Essays* (Bloomington: Indiana University Press, 1975), 175–76.
85. Ibid., 176–77.
86. Lynn, 225–26.
87. Steven P. Erie, *Rainbow's End: Irish-Americans and the Dilemmas of Urban Machine Politics, 1840–1985* (Berkeley: University of California Press, 1988), 39; Jordan, 295.

The Democrats relied on their near-complete control of the Southern states—and a Solid South necessitated that the Republicans secure an almost solid North and West to retain the presidency and win back the Senate and House. Ethnoculturally, the two major parties remained distinct and hostile to each other. Midwesterners with Southern roots, Catholics, and liberals in the Northeast allowed the Democrats to remain competitive in Indiana, Ohio, New Jersey, New York, and Connecticut. The Republican majority depended on mobilizing their constituency since poor turnout spelled doom. Waving the bloody shirt and recalling the Civil War worked less well with every passing year.

After accepting the nomination, Garfield attempted to unite the party by making Chester A. Arthur, Conkling's close associate and the man whom Hayes had removed from the New York Custom House, his vice-presidential nominee. Conkling, furious at seeing his ally moving above him, demanded that Arthur reject the offer. Arthur, never expecting to rise to such heights, accepted it, but he was never loyal to Garfield.[88]

Howells and his circle were pleased with Garfield's nomination, which Howells thought a mark of the "goodness and good sense of the country." Writing from Arlington, Massachusetts, he congratulated the nominee on behalf of "this part of Ohio." Visited by Samuel Clemens and Charles Dudley Warner, both "hot Republicans," Howells and his friends exulted in Garfield's impending victory. Howells used his connections with Garfield, as he had with Hayes, to arrange diplomatic appointments for relatives and writers.[89]

Wade Hampton of South Carolina promised to deliver a Solid South to the Democrats, and he did. "Their machinery is now so perfect," John Hay wrote, "that even murder, the cheapest of all political methods in the South, will hardly be necessary this year." Hancock carried the entire South, as well as California and Nevada, where Sinophobia and antimonopoly were strong, but the Republicans countered with a strategy of a solid North. Rhetorically, the Republicans ran a campaign based on the sanctity of the ballot and the promise of universal manhood suffrage. Their greatest orator, Robert Ingersoll, proclaimed that "Unless we see to it that every man who has a right to vote votes, and unless we see that every honest vote is counted, the days of the Republic are numbered." Practically, as P. B. S. Pinchback, briefly the Republican governor of Louisiana, pointed out, the Republicans failed to protect Southern black voters,

88. Rutkow, 56.
89. W. D. Howells to W. C. Howells, June 30, 1880, in Howells, *Selected Letters*, 2: 257.

although as the Readjusters in Virginia showed, possibilities still remained for black-white alliances across party and color lines.[90]

In the North the Republicans unpacked the bloody shirt, patched up their own quarrels over civil service, and dressed the tariff in the clothes of prosperity. Garfield carried the North and the election. The Republicans gained the Senate and the House, however, only by making alliances with antimonopolists. Although the Democrats won a plurality in the House, the Greenbackers and Republicans together had a slim majority, and together they elected a Republican speaker. In the Senate, the Republicans picked up seats, but the result was a tie, broken when Senator Mahone, elected as a Readjuster, caucused with the Republicans. In return, he was given control of Republican patronage in Virginia. The Republicans rhetorically clung to free labor and the idea of a homogeneous citizenry, at least in the South, but the campaign was for all practical purposes a requiem for both.[91]

90. Calhoun, 178, 179, 181–85.
91. Ibid., 178–79, 181–85, 187.

11

People in Motion

In 1877 the American journalist William Rideing tracked the emigration of an English immigrant named Giles and his family. Giles was almost certainly a fabrication, but less a fiction than a composite portrait. He was a reader of "America letters," advertisements from steamship companies posted in the local English pubs. Discouraged by lack of prospects at home and attracted by cheap advertised fares on Liverpool steamers, which then carried half the immigrants to the United States, he decided to emigrate. The majority of the embarking passengers, Rideing wrote, were English, Irish, and Scots, but also "bearded Russians and Poles, uncleanly Italians" (Rideing did not like Italians), and a considerable number of Germans who migrated through Liverpool rather than Hamburg or Bremen. Some of the passengers were "respectable," rural laborers like Giles, but there were also "sinister men and loose women." In the 1870s British laborers were more likely to be skilled than unskilled. The unskilled dominated in the years the American economy was booming. The migrants had "contract tickets" specifying the fare and the provisions they would be served, but they needed to provide their own bedding and utensils. Interpreters and emigration agents treated them all brusquely and rudely. Before the voyage began, they were mustered and examined by agents of the shipping company for infectious disease. By the late 1870s mortality among the immigrants had dropped drastically, seldom exceeding "one and two-thirds percent, and in some instances...no greater than one-eighth percent," but that still meant that roughly fifteen to eighteen of the thirteen hundred steerage passengers on Giles ship would not survive a voyage of a week to two weeks.[1]

Steerage, the cheapest accommodations in the lower decks, was cold, dark, and foul, and it grew fouler as the voyage proceeded: "Neither officers nor men consider them worthy of the least respect, and treat them as

---

1. Brinley Thomas, *Migration and Economic Growth* (Cambridge: Cambridge University Press, 1954), 64–65; Willam Rideing, "The Immigrant's Progress," *Scribner's Monthly* (1877): 577–88.

a drove of cattle." Four tiers of bunks lined each side of compartments ten feet tall. "Poles, Germans, English and French are thrown together without discrimination," Rideing wrote. "A cleanly, thrifty English or German woman is berthed next to a filthy Italian woman." Mrs. Giles had "a dreadful hag" in the berth next to her. In the crowded quarters, the passengers could feel the vessel quiver and the steam engines throb. The food was abundant, but the quality variable. Dirty stewards served it in filthy rusted pots, and the passengers reached in with utensils or hands to serve themselves.

Conditions bearable in good weather became hellish in bad. The vomit, urine, feces, and waste of the passengers confined to steerage accumulated by the hour. As the ship rolled, terrified passengers—most of whom had never been at sea—wailed, cursed, prayed, and screamed. When the storm passed, sailors refused to enter the compartments to clean them until fortified with rum. Filthy passengers were hosed down on deck. Rideing was sympathetic to Giles, but he thought the Italians born to filth and not bothered by it.

After such a voyage, Castle Garden, where newcomers embarked for inspection in New York, could seem like heaven. The immigrants were still browbeaten and cursed as they were loaded onto the barges to take them to shore, but Castle Garden had begun as a summer resort and still retained a pleasant air. It had partially burned down in 1876 but was quickly rebuilt. The immigrants were not destitute. Rideing estimated that the average passenger possessed $100 in cash and $50 more in property. But their main asset was their capacity for labor. He reminded his readers that the value of their labor and the property they brought added $400 million annually to the American economy. Once inspected and passed, the immigrants received messages and remittances left for them from relatives, and they could use the telegraph office and post office at Castle Garden to write to relatives or friends. They could change their money at a broker's office without the danger from swindlers. The railroad companies had agents in the building to gather passengers with tickets and guide them to the trains that would take them to their ultimate destinations. These were emigrant trains; they resembled the steerage without bunks. The least lucky were those who resorted to the boarding houses, which although licensed and cheap, were notorious for their dangers and filthiness.[2]

Foreign immigration linked with internal migration. Four years earlier, in 1873, a group of Indianapolis investors, who had prospered after the

2. Rideing, 577–88; Vincent J. Cannato, *American Passage: The History of Ellis Island* (New York: Harper, 2009), 30–49; Edwin G. Burrows and Mike Wallace, *Gotham: A History of New York City to 1898* (New York: Oxford University Press, 1999), 738–39.

Civil War, read Charles Nordhoff's *California: For Health, Pleasure and Residence*. After considering, and ruling out, investing in Texas and Louisiana, they formed the "California Colony of Indiana." They sent Daniel Berry on the Pacific Railway to look for land. Berry became enamored with a well-watered 2,800-acre tract in the San Gabriel Valley. The area was ideal for fruit, and Berry suggested they buy it at ten dollars an acre. He, as many did, fell in love with Southern California. When his wagon broke down he described the men who helped him fix it: two ex-lawyers with Harvard educations who now ran vineyards, the nephew of Edward Atkinson, "the great Free-trader," who now ran sheep, and an ex-Nebraska state senator. He explained that the "aristocracy here work and raise fruit." They also speculated in land.

The Panic of 1873 crushed the original plans for the California Colony of Indiana, but Berry was too smitten to give up. He gathered another group of investors and put $50,000 into land improvements. In 1874 they named the place "Pasadena," which they claimed was an Indian name for "Key of the Valley." They began selling off land to Indiana migrants who planted oranges. Within a few years, as the economy recovered, they had built forty houses and planted tens of thousands of trees. Berry went into real estate, selling "Lands of Every Description and City Property... Money Loaned and Colony Lands selected." Pasadena flourished. Charlotte Perkins Gilman, who visited there in the winter of 1885–86 to cure her neurasthenia, wrote of traveling "down the Great inland plain of California, over the Mojave Desert, and to heaven."[3]

These stories of movement tend to be told separately in U.S. history, segregating immigration from abroad and internal migration within the United States. In the nineteenth-century popular imagination, foreigners were alien and exotic. Americans watching them come ashore at Castle Gardens, and later at Ellis Island, often mistook immigrants for "traditional" peasants uprooted from a timeless past and thrust into the modern United States. They regarded them as essentially different from men like Berry.

But migration both from abroad and within the United States is better understood as a single complicated movement in which travel within and across borders combined wrenching change, dislocation, and dispossession, as well as opportunity. That Giles moved out of discouragement and his ship reeked of desperation did not mean that there was not also hope. That Berry was giddy with opportunity did not change the fact that his earnest boosterism reflected the necessity of persuading others that change

---

3. Charlotte Perkins Gilman, *The Living of Charlotte Perkins Gilman: An Autobiography* (New York: Harper & Row, 1975, orig. ed. 1935), 93; Walter T. K. Nugent, *Into the West: The Story of Its People* (New York: Knopf, 1999), 89–92.

would prove beneficial. Giles and Berry may have been at opposite ends of a spectrum, but it was still a single spectrum.

The starkest difference between Giles's movements and Berry's was that one crossed national boundaries and the other did not. But even that difference was not so stark. The same changes that uprooted Giles and his fellow passengers—English, Irish, Scots, Russians, Poles, Italians, and Germans—pushed internal migration within Europe as well as emigration abroad and spurred movements within the United States. And American internal migration looked decidedly less internal, when studied closely. A quarter-century earlier, Pasadena had not been part of the United States, and most of the lands Americans settled in the West had to be wrested from semi-sovereign Indian nations. When migrants faced west, they saw, in effect, foreign countries within their own country. They saw Indian Country.

I

As Hamlin Garland recognized, a great stirring took place during the Gilded Age. Americans and immigrants went west, and even more of them went into cities. The mean center of the country's population, located in western Ohio in 1870, moved 58 miles farther west, close to the place where Indiana, Ohio, and Kentucky meet, in 1880. It moved 48 miles west into eastern Indiana in 1890, and then only 15 miles farther west toward central Indiana in 1900. The shifts indicated the clustering of the country's population in the Northeast and Midwest.

America grew continuously more urban as people moved into towns and cities. A little more than a quarter of the country's population counted as urban in 1870; nearly 40 percent did in 1900. The West and Midwest nearly mirrored these figures. The Northeast, with two-thirds of its population in urban areas, far exceeded them. The South remained the least urban area of the country, but its people too moved into towns and cities.[4]

4. Edward L. Ayers, *The Promise of the New South: Life after Reconstruction* (New York: Oxford University Press, 1992), 55; Michael B. Haines, "Population Characteristics," *Historical Statistics of the United States, Earliest Times to the Present: Millennial Edition*, ed. Scott Sigmund Gartner, Susan B. Carter, Michael R. Haines, Alan L. Olmstead, Richard Sutch, and Gavin Wright (New York: Cambridge University Press, 2006); Robert J. Gordon, *The Rise and Fall of American Growth: The U.S. Standard of Living since the Civil War* (Princeton, NJ: Princeton University Press, 2016), 98; "Growth Characteristics of Large American Cities, 1790–1890," in David Ward, *Cities and Immigrants: A Geography of Change in Nineteenth-Century America* (New York: Oxford University Press, 1971), 16–17.

Immigrants moved along a set of informal networks that helped them arrange passage and assisted in finding them work when they arrived. Many only paused in port cities. Most quickly left New York City, the leading debarkation site, but enough remained to make the city a place of immigrants and their children. Only about 55,000 of the roughly 1.5 million Germans (more than 25 percent of all migrants) entering the United States during the 1880s stayed in New York, but this, combined with earlier immigration, made it the third-largest German-speaking city in the world, after Berlin and Vienna. The Irish-born in New York and Brooklyn also increased in the 1880s, even though their percentage of the total population fell. Taken together, the Irish-born and those of Irish extraction composed 40 percent of the city's population in the mid-1880s.[5]

The movement of immigrants toward family, old neighbors, or simply former countrymen mixed the streams of immigrants with internal migrants. Foreign immigrants, however, precipitated out at particular places, creating clusters of people who were related, or had the same origins in Europe, Canada, Asia, or Latin America. They often worked in similar jobs for similar companies. Polish workers in Pittsburgh; Irish in Butte, Montana; and French Canadians in New Hampshire or Rhode Island textile mills recruited relatives and helped place them in jobs. Many jobs became the domains of certain ethnic groups—Jewish and Italian garment workers in New York or Mexican railroad section gangs in the Southwest.[6]

This migration of wageworkers concentrated in the East and Midwest, but it extended into the West. Butte fed on copper and silver, and in the mid-1880s the place employed 2,500 men in its underground mines, smelters, reduction works, and railroads. Silver remained Montana's leading metal, but copper—concentrated in the "richest hill on earth"—was rising quickly. By 1890 Butte, which dominated Silver Bow County, had 10,723 occupants, and 45 percent of the county was foreign-born. Dublin Gulch wound down from the surrounding hills into the city. Cornishmen and Welsh—both of whom hated the Irish—occupied Meaderville. The suburbs of Dog Town, Chicken Flats, Busterville, Butchertown, and Seldom Seen surrounded Butte. Chippewa, Cree, and Métis refugees from Canada occupied a squalid encampment near the city dump. All these groups lived in one of the world's most dangerous, ravaged, and toxic landscapes. The mines and the silicosis and other lung diseases they

5. Burrows and Wallace, 1111–12.
6. Thomas J. Archdeacon, *Becoming American: An Ethnic History* (New York: Free Press, 1983), 94–97; John E. Bodnar, *The Transplanted: A History of Immigrants in Urban America* (Bloomington: Indiana University Press, 1985), 57–71.

produced were dangerous enough, but smoke from the smelters killed surrounding vegetation and during inversions thickened the air with arsenic and sulfur so that lamps were lit midday and pedestrians could not see across the street.[7]

Most immigrants became wage laborers, but some from northern Europe became part of a much smaller, if much mythologized, migration of farmers into the western reaches of the Middle Border and Far West. Texas, Kansas, Nebraska, and Dakota Territory boomed. Berry grew rhapsodic over California, but that state grew comparatively slowly. California did not overtake Kansas and Minnesota in total population until the twentieth century. Between 1870 and 1900, nearly every measure of American agriculture—the number of farms, improved acreage, the production of wheat, corn, cattle, and swine—doubled or more than doubled. The countryside continued to gain population, even if it grew less rapidly than the metropoles. The percentage of Americans living on farms fell from 43.8 percent in 1880 to 39.3 percent in 1890.[8]

Americans mythologized the movement of population onto uncultivated lands as quintessentially American. The number of people going into the cities, however, far exceeded the pioneers near or beyond the 100th meridian. The urban immigrants were creating the American future. In 1890 the collective population of Chicago, New York, and Brooklyn exceeded the 2.8 million people who lived in the states and territories lying wholly west of the 100th meridian, and even then, the Far West was increasingly urban. A quarter of California's population lived in San Francisco in 1890. Subtract San Francisco's population from the West's total, and New York and Brooklyn alone came within a couple hundred thousand people of the population of the Rocky Mountains, Southwest, and Pacific Coast combined.[9]

Americans noted western migration with pride, but worried as cities grew to a size and importance unprecedented in American history. Their

7. Michael P. Malone, *The Battle for Butte: Mining and Politics on the Northern Frontier, 1864–1906* (Seattle: University of Washington Press, 1981), 30–34, 61–68. For results, Timothy J. LeCain, *Mass Destruction: The Men and Giant Mines That Wired America and Scarred the Planet* (New Brunswick, NJ: Rutgers University Press, 2009), 171 ff..

8. Table Da28-92—Farm population, by region and state: 1890–1969, and Table Da14-27—Farms–number, population, land, and value of property: 1850–1997 [Census years], in *Historical Statistics of the United States*; David B. Danbom, *Born in the Country: A History of Rural America*, 2nd ed. (Baltimore, MD: Johns Hopkins University Press, 2006), 131–33.

9. Table Aa22-35—Selected population characteristics-median age, sex ratio, annual growth rate, and number, by race, urban residence, and nativity: 1790–2000, in *Historical Statistics of the United States, Earliest Times to the Present*.

fears were compounded as the cities became disproportionately immigrant. Roughly 61 percent of the foreign-born, nearly twice the percentage
of native-born, lived in urban places by 1890. They were particularly noticeable in New York City, Philadelphia, and Chicago.[10]

Immigration contributed to a rapidly rising population even as the
American birth rate as a whole fell by 40 percent between 1800 and 1900.
The 50,155,783 people in the United States in 1880 ballooned to 62,947,714
by 1890, with immigrants contributing nearly one-third (30.9 percent) of
the growth. In all, 9,249,547 people, or 14.8 percent of the U.S. population, had been born abroad by 1890, with roughly eight out of nine immigrants born in Europe. This has remained the peak percentage ever
since.[11]

A high percentage of immigrants moved into the Middle Border and
West, making them the states and territories with the largest percentage of
immigrants. By 1890 44.6 percent of the population of North Dakota was
of foreign birth; in South Dakota the figure was 27.7 percent. California
had 30.3 percent and Washington had 25.8 percent. In the Mountain
West, Montana, Arizona, and Nevada all had over 30 percent, while
Idaho, Wyoming, Colorado, and Utah all had over 20 percent, roughly
the same percentage as New York and Illinois and greater than
Pennsylvania. As in the East, Germans, Irish, and English remained the
largest immigrant groups in the early 1880s, but significant numbers of

10. Michael Haines, "Population Characteristics," Table Ad707-710 — Percentage of for-
    eign- and native-born persons living in urban and rural locations: 1890–1990; Table
    Ad696-706 — Geographic concentration of the foreign-born population, top three
    states and the South: 1850–1990, in ibid. In New York, Pennsylvania, and Illinois re-
    spectively, the foreign born composed 26.2 percent, 16.1 percent, and 22 percent of the
    population in 1890.

11. Table 14 — Nativity of the Population, for Regions, Divisions, and States: 1850 to
    2000, in Campbell Gibson and Kay Jung, "Historical Census Statistics of the Foreign-
    Born Population of the United States: 1850–2000, Working Paper No. 81," ed. U.S.
    Bureau of the Census Population Division (Washington, DC: U.S. Census Bureau,
    February 2006); "Foreign-Born Population and Percentage of Total Population, for
    the United States: 1850 to 2010," in U.S. Census Bureau, "The Foreign-Born
    Population in the United States," https://www.census.gov/newsroom/pdf/cspan_fb_
    slides.pdf; Robert J. Gordon, *The Rise and Fall of American Growth: The U.S.
    Standard of Living since the Civil War* (Princeton, NJ: Princeton University Press,
    2016), 34–35. In Haines, Table Aa1-5 — Population, population density, and land area:
    1790–2000; Table Ab52-117 — Total fertility rate and birth rate, by race and age: 1800–
    1998; Table Ac-B — Net migration of the native-born population, by region, race, and
    major time period: 1850–1990; Table Aa15-21 — Components of population growth, by
    decade: 1790–2000; and Table Ad354-443 — Foreign-born population, by country of
    birth: 1850–1990.

Immigration to the United States, 1820–2015

Persons Obtaining Lawful Permanent Resident Status

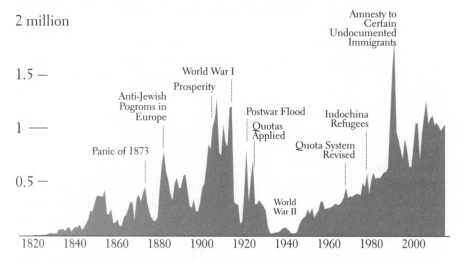

Source: 2015 Yearbook of Immigration Statistics, Department of Homeland Security.

Mexicans and Chinese distinguished the West's demographic mix from the East. Some Mexicans could become foreign-born without moving. American boundaries moved; they did not.[12]

The growth of cities and the movement west masked declining geographical mobility among native-born Americans. Native-born whites were less likely to leave the state of their birth after 1880. Where roughly half of white males aged fifty to fifty-nine in the years between 1850 and 1880 lived outside the state of their birth, the percentage plunged after 1880 and would fall below 40 percent by the early twentieth century. Still the sheer growth in the number of Americans meant an increase in the number of migrants, and even those who did not leave the state where they were born were liable to move into a town or city.[13]

12. Elliott Robert Barkan, *From All Points: America's Immigrant West, 1870s–1952* (Bloomington: Indiana University Press, 2007), 44–59, 463; Table 14—Nativity of the Population, for Regions, Divisions, and States: 1850 to 2000, in Gibson and Jung. In Haines, Table Ad707-710—Percentage of foreign- and native-born persons living in urban and rural locations: 1890–1990; and Table Ad696-706—Geographic concentration of the foreign-born population, top three states and the South: 1850–1990, in *Historical Statistics of the United States.*

13. Patricia Kelly Hall and Steven Ruggles, "'Restless in the Midst of Their Prosperity': New Evidence on the Internal Migration of Americans, 1850–2000," *Journal of American History* 91, no. 3 (2004): 836–39, fig. 3, fig. 4, fig. 5.

The long-distance movement of the foreign-born and the shorter-distance movements of the native-born reflected the availability of economic opportunity rather than any predisposition of a group to move. Like the United States, the countries that the immigrants left were part of an emerging, interconnected capitalist economy and a demographic revolution of rapidly rising populations. And like the United States, these countries were deeply divided over immigration, encouraging, or even expelling, some populations while trying to retain others.[14]

Industrialization, the mechanization of agriculture, steamships, and railroads were parts of transnational developments altering Europe and large parts of Asia and setting people in motion. The American economy demanded labor, and it extracted people from Europe both by attracting them to the United States with higher wages and by undercutting their existing ways of life, thus setting them in motion. Inexpensive grain pouring off American farms cost Austro-Hungarian farmers their markets, deprived them of their livelihoods, and gave them reason to move to the United States and elsewhere. Commercial agriculture in Central Europe led to consolidated landholdings that drove more peasants from the land; new factories undercut craft production. People married earlier, and more of their children survived to adulthood, thus straining the ability of small farmers to provide their sons with land and craftsmen to provide their sons with trades. They could not continue as they had.[15]

A menu of migratory options existed in both Europe and the United States. A nearby industrial town, city, or region that offered work could absorb the displaced and remove the necessity for longer-range moves. This first move, however, could lead to others, as dissatisfaction with the work or living conditions drove migrants to seek other alternatives and even emigrate. Scandinavians who migrated to the United States usually had made an earlier migration from the countryside to a town or city. A lack of nearby options sometimes made emigration abroad the first step rather than the last, as was often the case in the Austro-Hungarian Empire. Unlike Europeans, Americans usually found sufficient opportunity within their expansive country.[16]

14. Tara Zahra, The Great Departure: Mass Migration from Eastern Europe and the Making of the Free World (New York: Norton, 2016), 23–63; Bodnar, 43–45.
15. Scott Nelson, A Nation of Deadbeats: An Uncommon History of America's Financial Disasters (New York: Knopf, 2012), 159–64; Bodnar, 4–6, 23–24, 34–35; Kerby A. Miller, Emigrants and Exiles: Ireland and the Irish Exodus to North America (New York: Oxford University Press, 1985), 355–70, 380–89, 397–403.
16. Bodnar, 1, 9–10, 34–37, 43–45; Annemarie Steidl, Engelbert Stockhammer, and Hermann Zeitlhofer, "Relations among Internal, Continental, and Transatlantic Migration in Late Imperial Austria," Social Science History 31 (Spring 2007): 76–77, 82–83, 87.

The distribution of migrants was splotchy—large numbers left some areas, few left others—and the pattern shifted over time both among nations and within nations. In 1880 more than 70,000 immigrants to the United States came from Great Britain and an equal number came from Ireland. Some 80,000 more came from Germany, including German Austrians. Scandinavians, who had begun to appear in the United States in the 1860s and early 1870s, would reach 100,000 in 1882, surpassing those from Great Britain and Ireland. They remained well below the 250,000 Germans entering the United States that year. Initially Czechs from Bohemia, who already had established a presence in the United States, dominated the rising migration from the Austro-Hungarian Empire, but Austro-Hungarian immigration became less heavily Bohemian as the 1880s proceeded. Between 1876 and 1910 7–8 percent (of the 1910 population figure) had left Austria-Hungary for foreign destinations.[17]

Germans formed the largest body of immigrants coming into the United States for most of the nineteenth century, but those who came after the Civil War were not from the same parts of Germany; nor were they members of the same social classes as the earlier arrivals. By the late 1870s German migrants were poorer peasants, their landless children, and farm laborers from northeastern Germany rather than the small landowners from southwest Germany who came before the war. Irish immigration after 1870s increasingly came from the south and west of Ireland. They were more heavily Catholic, less Anglicized, more likely to speak Irish, and poorer, with fewer skills and less capital than earlier immigrants. They were also overwhelmingly young, single, and, more than ever, female.[18]

In a sense, immigration was contagious, affecting many in one place but few in others. Some were immune. Most of the rich had no incentive to leave, and the very poor lacked the means to do so. Those with declining opportunities and enough education to be literate were among the most likely to emigrate. They could, like Giles, read the immigration brochures circulated by American labor contractors, states, railroads, and

17. *Historical Statistics of the United States Colonial Times to 1970, Bicentennial ed.* (Washington, DC: U.S. Department of Commerce, Bureau of the Census, 1975), Table Ad106-120—Immigrants, by country of last residence-Europe: 1820–1997; Adolph Jensen, "Migration Statistics of Denmark, Norway, and Sweden," in *International Migrations, Volume II: Interpretations*, ed. Walter F. Willcox (NBER, 1931); Zahra, 25; Steidl et al., 76–77, 83.

18. Bodnar, 2–3, 8–9, 13, 18, 20, 23–24, 34–37, 43–45, 52–53; Steidl et al., 82; Hasia R. Diner, *Erin's Daughters in America: Irish Immigrant Women in the Nineteenth Century* (Baltimore, MD: Johns Hopkins University Press, 1983), 32–34; Miller, 349–51.

land companies and American letters written to relatives and neighbors describing opportunities and conditions and promising or providing aid. As immigration rose at the end of the century, worries over lessening numbers of conscripts for European armies, the loss of cheap labor, and concerns over the abuse of emigrants led to attacks, much of it anti-Semitic, on, and prosecution of, immigration agents in Eastern Europe.[19]

Americans, then and now, tended to regard the most atypical migrations of the nineteenth century—those caused by famine in Ireland before the Civil War, the failed revolutions of 1848, and the Russian pogroms that began in 1881 with the assassination of Czar Alexander II—as representative. Most immigrants were not fleeing persecution or famine; they chose to come, although their choice was shaped by circumstances. They wanted a better life and left regions that offered them little hope of one. Their arrivals tracked (although calculations are not precise) the rise and fall of the American economy. There were no direct measures of GDP in the nineteenth century, making calculations of the gross national product (GNP) more reliable. The economy grew from a GNP calculated in 1860 dollars of $1.1 billion in 1869 to $13.7 billion in 1896, but it did not grow evenly. The broad patterns are clear, but the annual variations are less reliable.[20]

Annual immigration figures are more accurate, but they too have their limits. Passenger lists at major ports such as New York and San Francisco are pretty dependable, but they missed those immigrants who simply passed over the Canadian and Mexican borders, which in 1880 were unguarded over thousands of miles. And, until 1908, officials did not count, and thus did not subtract, returning migrants from the totals. These could be migrants who came temporarily just for work, or those who found only misery or failure, or they could have been successful and were returning home to invest in a farm or business. In any case, their

19. Zahra, 23–63; Bodnar, 23, 52–53; Miller, 356–58, 405.
20. The GDP measures final purchases made by households, business, and government. It lumps together consumption, investment, government spending, and net exports. The related Gross National Product (GNP) adds the proceeds from American investments abroad and subtracts outflows from foreign investments in the United States. These are twentieth-century inventions calculated retroactively from partial data. They are useful as a broad measure across decades. The standard historical calculations come with a caveat from their author, regularly ignored, that the estimates "were not constructed for analysis as an annual series," which means we cannot use them as reliable measures for any given year. Bureau of Economic Analysis, "GDP: One of the Great Inventions of the Twentieth Century," *Survey of Current Business* (January 2000): 158–60; Paul W. Rhode, "Gallman's Annual Output Series for the United States, 1834–1909," *National Bureau of Economic Research Working Papers Series*, Working Paper 8860, April 2002.

future was not in the United States. When counted in the early twentieth century, their numbers were substantial, for many groups amounting to a third or more of the migrants, a number in line with the returns from other nations in the Western hemisphere. Long-distance labor migrations and the availability of steamships could move people back to Europe and Asia as well as to North America. Many immigrants did not regard their moves as permanent.[21]

The statistics on the economy and on migration display the same pattern of a slump during the crisis of the 1870s, a boom in the late 1870s and early 1880s, and then downturns in the mid-1880s and early 1890s. In 1873 402,000 immigrants entered the United States, but with the depression the numbers dropped precipitously, bottoming out at 71,000 in 1877. By 1880 immigration had rebounded, and roughly 424,000 foreigners, the vast majority from Europe, entered the country.[22]

The correlation between economic cycles and immigration, though quite real, can also mislead by making immigration seem simply a function of the labor market, when the labor market, like the economy as a whole, was not independent of legal and political structures. Free labor and contract freedom remained cultural ideals rather than actual descriptions of the labor conditions immigrants confronted. The most obvious sign of this was the paucity of immigrants in the South and controversies over contract and servile labor, which erupted across the country in the 1870s and 1880s.

II

There were internal barriers to migration more significant than national boundaries. As in so many other things, the South stood apart. Its citizens moved, but they largely sloshed back and forth within its boundaries. Relatively few outsiders entered the region. The borders of the old Confederacy might as well have been a dam, so effectively did they turn aside immigrants and hold Southerners within the confines of Dixie. The percentage of foreign-born in the South actually fell between 1860 and 1900. By 1910 only 2 percent of the Southern population had been born

---

21. Archdeacon, 115–19; Günter Moltmann, "American-German Return Migration in the Nineteenth and Early Twentieth Centuries," *Central European History* 13, no. 4 (1980): 378–81.
22. *Historical Statistics of the United States Colonial Times to 1970*, Table Ad21-24—Net immigration, various estimates: 1870–1957.

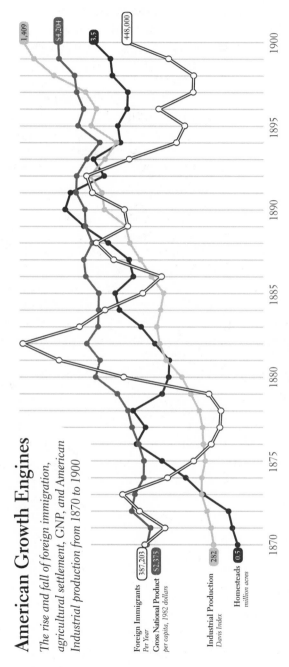

American Growth Engines

*The rise and fall of foreign immigration,
agricultural settlement, GNP, and American
Industrial production from 1870 to 1900*

Foreign Immigrants
Per Year — 387,203 ... 1,409

Gross National Product — $2,375 ... $4,204
per capita, 1982 dollars

Industrial Production — 282 ... 3.5
Davis Index

Homesteads — 0.5 ... 448,000
million acres

1870   1875   1880   1885   1890   1895   1900

Sources: Treasury Department, Bureau of Statistics (1867–1895), Immigration and Naturalization Service (1892–1900) (Immigration); Nathan S. Balke and Robert J. Gordon, "The Estimation of Prewar Gross National Product: Methodology and New Evidence," *Journal of Political Economy,* 1989 (Gross National Product); Joseph H. Davis, "An Annual Index of U.S. Industrial Production, 1790–1915," *Quarterly Journal of Economics,* 2004 (Industrial Production); U.S. Department of the Interior, 1868–1940 (Homesteads).

outside the United States, compared with 14.7 percent for the country as a whole.[23]

Immigrants avoided the South because of low wages, sharecropping, tenancy, and the pervasive poverty they yielded. Although a national labor market was developing, it evolved only gradually in the late nineteenth century and did not extend to the South, where wages, particularly pay for unskilled workers, lagged far behind the Midwest, Northeast, and West. Low wages persisted despite the growth of the Southern economy. Cotton production rose, and rose again, even as prices fell. The tobacco, lumber, and textile industries, and even iron, grew rapidly in the 1880s. Southern rates of economic growth were respectable, equaling or exceeding those of the North, but in large part this was because they started from a disastrously low base.[24]

By the mid-1880s boosters, the most prominent of whom was Henry Grady of Atlanta, proclaimed a "New South," a region that shared the dynamic capitalism of the North, but their claims were exaggerated at best and false at worst. The South lacked the class of inventive mechanics and machinists so abundant in the North, and its refusal to invest in education put Southern workers at a disadvantage. Industries such as iron, lumber, and textiles that employed immigrant labor in the North depended on native low-wage labor, black and white, in the South. Most were low-end operations, manufacturing cheap products while the North claimed the most lucrative markets. Southern industries were less highly capitalized and had less value added per worker than similar industries outside the South.[25]

Textiles and timber, in different ways, set Southerners in motion. Southern textiles grew steadily after 1870 but most rapidly in the 1890s, when Southern coal production allowed mills powered by steam engines to be placed across the South. Mill towns attracted rural white families, particularly those with teenage daughters and smaller children to work in

23. Joshua L. Rosenbloom, "Was There a National Labor Market at the End of the Nineteenth Century? New Evidence on Earnings in Manufacturing," *Journal of Economic History* 56, no. 3 (1996): 650–51; Ayers, 24–25; Gavin Wright, *Old South, New South: Revolutions in the Southern Economy since the Civil War* (New York: Basic Books, 1986), 75–78; Moon-Ho Jung, *Coolies and Cane: Race, Labor, and Sugar in the Age of Emancipation* (Baltimore, MD: Johns Hopkins University Press, 2006), 107–80.

24. Joshua L. Rosenbloom, "One Market or Many? Labor Market Integration in the Late Nineteenth-Century United States," *Journal of Economic History* 50 (1990): 93–96; Wright, 61–64; Rosenbloom, "Was There a National Labor Market at the End of the Nineteenth Century?"; Ayers, 15, 21–22.

25. Wright, 68–77, 160–63, 172–77; Monica Prasad, *The Land of Too Much: American Abundance and the Paradox of Poverty* (Cambridge, MA: Harvard University Press, 2012), 65; Rosenbloom; "One Market or Many?" 93–96.

the mills. Cotton mills were the preserve of whites, but white workers earned from 30 to 50 percent less than northern workers. Easier access to capital, new machinery, and skilled operatives gave the North an advantage that offset the low wages of the South until the end of the century.[26]

The iron and coal industries also relied on native labor in the South. In the 1880s Birmingham, Alabama, located in the midst of both coal and iron ore deposits, overtook Chattanooga, Tennessee, as the center of the Southern iron industry. As the more modern and highly financed northern mills moved into steel, Birmingham produced cheap pig iron used chiefly in pipes for new water and gas lines. Relying on poorly paid black workers, Birmingham turned inferior coal and inferior iron ore into an inferior metal. Southern iron and steel mills' productivity fell further and further behind that of northern mills.[27]

In the South, as in the North, population shifted westward and into cities, but Southerners did not usually leave the South. A Southern labor migration, sometimes spurred by labor agents, disproportionately involved young black men seeking work beyond sharecropping and farm labor in the 1880s and 1890s. They moved into the lumber and turpentine industries, where conditions were harsh and the work hard and dangerous, but that paid better than farm labor. Louisiana and Texas attracted large numbers of migrants, both black and white. Southerners leaving the farms were most likely to go to smaller towns and regional cities. In the Old Confederacy, only New Orleans and the border state cities of Baltimore and Louisville ranked in the top twenty cities in the 1880s.[28]

The failure of Southerners to leave the South was not wholly a matter of choice. In the 1870s South Carolina, northern Florida, Texas, Georgia, northern Louisiana, and the delta counties of Arkansas, Mississippi, and Tennessee—all areas of the cotton South that had suffered the most from terrorism and economic repression—were hotbeds of black emigration. Some sought to emigrate to Liberia. Others wanted a region carved out for them within the South. Still others looked west, particularly to Kansas. Their departure, however, threatened the existing order and was resisted not just by landowners and employers, but also by established black ministers and Republican leaders—the "representative colored men." Many of them, like Frederick Douglass, lived in the North or in the smaller Southern bastions where blacks retained political influence. The debate about immigration deeply split black leaders, for what seemed at stake was less tactics than the whole meaning of the past fifteen years.

26. Ayers, 114–17; Wright, 130–35.
27. Wright, 165–72; Ayers, 59, 100–111.
28. Ayers, 123–31, 150; Wright, 65.

Migration meant Reconstruction had been a failure, and escape was the only hope. This Douglass was unwilling to admit, and his opposition prompted Charleton H. Tandy, who led relief efforts for the Kansas migrants, to denounce Douglass as a "fawning sycophant, who deserted his own people and toadied to those in power."[29]

Henry Turner, a missionary for the African Methodist Episcopal Church, once a Radical politician and an ardent proponent of black manhood, became the most effective advocate of emigration to Liberia in the middle and late 1870s. Turner succeeded in purchasing a ship, but measles en route and tropical diseases on arrival decimated the colonists. Many of the survivors sought to return to the United States.[30]

The destinations of black emigration varied and shifted, but the goal remained the same. Freedmen wanted a place where their children could attend school and their wives could be free from labor in the fields. Many observers thought that women, as much as or more than men, drove the emigration. In 1879 Kansas came into focus as a land of freedom, in part because of the efforts of Benjamin "Pap" Singleton, a freedman from Nashville. Henry Adams remained open to several destinations, including Kansas, because freedom mattered more than the place it might be secured. As he explained, "It is not that we think the soil climate or temperature of Kansas is more congenial to us—but it is the idea, the thought, that pervades our breast that 'at least we will be free,' free from oppression, free from tyranny, free from bulldozing, murderous southern whites."[31]

By 1880 attempts of black people to leave the South had become alarming enough for the U.S. Senate to investigate and subsequently publish "The Causes of the Removal of the Negroes from the Southern States to the Northern States." The Democrats controlled the Senate and named three of the committee's five members; one, Zebulon Vance, was an ex-Confederate. In questioning black witnesses, some of whom testified at the risk of their lives, the Democrats hectored, ridiculed, and conde-

29. Heather Cox Richardson, *The Death of Reconstruction: Race, Labor, and Politics in the Post–Civil War North, 1865–1901* (Cambridge, MA: Harvard University Press, 2001), 168–82; Steven Hahn, *A Nation under Our Feet: Black Political Struggles in the Rural South, from Slavery to the Great Migration* (Cambridge, MA: Belknap Press of Harvard University Press, 2003), 320–34, 341–45; Nell Irvin Painter, *Exodusters: Black Migration to Kansas after Reconstruction* (New York: Knopf, 1976), 22–30; David W. Blight, *Frederick Douglass* (New York: Simon & Schuster), chap. 26.
30. James T. Campbell, *Middle Passages: African American Journeys to Africa, 1787–2005* (New York: Penguin Press, 2006), 107–13.
31. Painter, 108–17; Hahn, 335–37, 340–41.

scended. The two Republicans were more sympathetic. They subpoenaed the black Henry Adams. Dignified, polite, direct, and eloquent, he proved more than a match for the committee. His testimony about the persecution of black people and the despair that drove them to emigrate was among the most powerful ever delivered to Congress. He made those questioning him seem lesser men, as indeed they were.[32]

Ultimately, the excitement of 1879–80 yielded relatively few migrants. Those going to Liberia numbered in the hundreds. The migrants to Kansas, who became known as the Exodusters, amounted to perhaps 20,000 to 25,000 people. The same conditions that created the desire to migrate inhibited actual migration. Poverty constrained the movement of poor black families, just as it limited the movement of the very poor in Europe and poor white families in the United States. Migration demanded money to fund the trip, to acquire a farm, or, if homesteaders, to provide the tools and animals necessary to stock a farm and to sustain a family until the farm became productive. Blacks also faced the intimidation of landowners who feared the loss of tenants and laborers. They found their crops confiscated before sale, their leaders arrested, and their meetings broken up. Nightriders assaulted them and their families on the way to the Mississippi River or in camps. Steamboat companies, intimidated by threats of boycott by whites or by vigilantes, refused to pick up the travelers and transport them.[33]

Only a relatively small number of black people moved into the West outside of Texas. Black migrants established a series of towns in Kansas and, later, in Oklahoma, and there were smaller populations elsewhere. The migration yielded attempts at black colonization in Mexico in the 1880s and 1890s, led by William Ellis, a freedman, who remade himself by passing as Mexican and then Cuban, and eventually recruited colonists from Georgia and Alabama. The colony failed, but Ellis would eventually become rich in Mexico.[34]

---

32. Adams testimony is in volume 2, beginning on page 101, U.S. Congress, Senate, Select Committee to Investigate the Causes of the Removal of the Negroes from the Southern States to the Northern States, *Report and Testimony of the Select Committee of the United States Senate to Investigate the Causes of the Removal of the Negroes from the Southern States to the Northern States: In Three Parts* (Washington, DC: U.S. GPO, 1880).

33. Painter, 184–201; Hahn, 355–63.

34. For blacks in the West, see Quintard Taylor, *In Search of the Racial Frontier: African Americans in the American West, 1528–1990* (New York: Norton, 1998); Karl Jacoby, *The Strange Career of William Ellis: The Texas Slave Who Became a Mexican Millionaire* (New York: Norton, 2016), 60–119; Albert Broussard, Quintard Taylor, and Lawrence Brooks De Graaf, eds., *Seeking El Dorado: African Americans in California* (Los Angeles: Autry Museum of Western Heritage, 2001).

Low Southern wages compared with those in the North and West impeded immigration, and one of the things that secured a low-wage labor regime was coerced labor. The South quite consciously and deliberately turned its judicial system into an engine to generate servile labor, of the most deadly sort.

Fee-based governance and pervasive racism gave Southern sheriffs and deputy sheriffs strong incentive to arrest black people for misdemeanors. The fines assessed for misdemeanors, largely property crimes, provided money for the sheriffs, and when poor defendants could not pay the fees, officials obtained the money by leasing out the convicted. The Southern practice of assessing penalties for nonpayment of debts and assigning forced labor if the defendant failed to pay provided similar fees for court officials, and more prisoners for leasing. The system had the added advantage of providing local revenue to keep down taxes.[35]

Convicts—90 percent of whom would be black as the system endured into the twentieth century—worked on railroads, in the turpentine industry, and in the mines. Employers rented them for less than eight cents a day, supplying them with food and clothing. The conditions were horrific. Convict laborers could not strike, and their presence inhibited strikes by free workers. By the 1880s every Southern state except Virginia, where the Readjusters ended the practice, was wedded to the convict lease system. The companies that leased their labor took responsibility for the prisoners, whom they could whip or kill if they tried to escape. Those who leased the prisoners expected large numbers to die. As a Southern leasee reported in 1880s, "Before the war, we owned the negroes. If a man had a good negro he could afford to keep him. . . . But these convicts, we don't own 'em. One dies, get another."[36]

The death rates among convict laborers were appalling. In Mississippi the death rate between 1880 and 1885 averaged 11 percent. It was about the same in Arkansas in the mid-1880s. In Louisiana in 1881 it was 14 percent; in Mississippi in 1887, 16 percent. Of the roughly eleven hundred prisoners brought to the Slope No. 2 mine run by the Pratt Mining Company of Alabama in 1888–89, only forty had prior criminal records. More than 10

35. Alex Lichtenstein, *Twice the Work of Free Labor: The Political Economy of Convict Labor in the New South* (London: Verso, 1995), 70–71; Douglas A. Blackmon, *Slavery by Another Name: The Re-Enslavement of Black People in America from the Civil War to World War II* (New York: Doubleday, 2008), 61–67.
36. Washington, New Mexico, and Nebraska also leased out prisoners. Rebecca M. McLennan, *The Crisis of Imprisonment: Protest, Politics, and the Making of the American Penal State, 1776–1941* (New York: Cambridge University Press, 2008), 104–5, 110; Matthew J. Mancini, *One Dies, Get Another: Convict Leasing in the American South, 1866–1928* (Columbia: University of South Carolina Press, 1996), 1–3; Lichtenstein, 60.

percent of them died that year; many were teenagers. By comparison, the death rate, including infant mortality, in New Orleans was 2 percent. In northern penitentiaries the 1885 death rates were much lower: 1.08 percent in Ohio and 0.76 percent in Iowa. Those Southern prisoners who survived lived under dreadful conditions, poorly sheltered and clothed and ill fed to the point of scurvy and dysentery.[37]

The Northern prison system, too, leased convicts to private employers, but the North differed from the South in that Northern states built penitentiaries and kept felons within them. After the Panic of 1873 northern states turned to larger employers. By 1887, forty-five thousand prisoners, 80 percent of them in the North, labored for profit-making corporations. Employers often preferred prisoners to immigrants because they were more easily disciplined. The employers paid bounties — supplementing guards' wages — and the guards used corporeal punishment on prisoners accused of "slacking, disobedience, and poor workmanship." The prisoners were whipped on their bare buttocks, strung up by their thumbs, or plunged into ice baths on the orders from company overseers and foremen.[38]

The Northern system remained strong in the 1870s and 1880s but ultimately broke down from a combination of prison rebellions, union opposition, and moral revulsion from voters. Manufacturers worked captive labor to the point of exhaustion, and although prisoners did not die in the same numbers as in the South, they suffered injury and illness at higher rates than free labor. They had no legal recourse when injured. Judges held that by virtue of their crime, they were responsible for whatever injuries befell them within a servile labor system that depended on torture. As manufacturing processes grew more complicated and coordinated, prisoners gained leverage. Individuals or small groups could create bottlenecks that brought production to a halt. Unions ratcheted up their opposition to an arrangement that made a travesty of free labor and was used to break unions. In 1883 voters in New York, which had pioneered large-scale prison labor, voted to abolish the system by a margin of nearly two to one. It was the beginning of the end for use of prisoners for profit in the North.[39]

The convict lease system formed the most glaring example of the persistence of servile labor in a free labor country, but it was, workers

37. Mancini, 66–67, 139; Blackmon, 56–57, 90–92, 96–97.
38. Nicholas R. Parrillo, *Against the Profit Motive: The Salary Revolution in American Government, 1780–1940* (New Haven, CT: Yale University Press, 2013), 300–306; McLennan, 87–89, 97–101, 108–9, 113–16, 125–32.
39. McLennan, 121–25, 135, 172; Parrillo, 303–6.

contended, not the only example. What counted as coerced labor and what to do about it became central political questions in the Gilded Age and directly linked to immigration. The accusation that the Chinese were coolies—servile labor brought in by employers to drive down the wages of free labor—had been prevalent in the West since the California Gold Rush. The Chinese were indebted, usually to the Six Companies that arranged their passage and often found them employment, but they were free laborers able to quit when they chose.

By the late 1870s, labor contractors and employers were recruiting immigrants in both Europe and Asia. Some were destined for the western United States as gang laborers on the railroads or as workers in the mines. They came with a job awaiting them, but with the cost of their transportation deducted from their wages. Like the Chinese the workers were free, if exploited, and they could and did break their contracts, but contract labor undercut American wage rates and aroused the ire of American workers in general and the Knights of Labor in particular. Organized labor fought to outlaw the practice.[40]

Early efforts to ban Chinese immigration ran up against the Burlingame Treaty with China, which guaranteed Chinese immigrants and travelers access to the United States, but in 1880 the United States succeeded in renegotiating it. The new treaty still protected the movement of Chinese businessmen, tourists, students, and scholars, but it permitted limitations on the migration of laborers, although those workers already in the country would be allowed to return.[41]

Sen. John F. Miller of California introduced a bill creating a twenty-year prohibition on new Chinese workers entering the country. It passed both houses of Congress in 1882, but the president vetoed it, influenced by railroads and other large employers of the Chinese. The veto badly embarrassed Western Republicans. It produced a League of Deliverance in California, designed to drive the Chinese out by ostracism and boycott if possible, and by force if necessary. When presented with a bill reducing the length of immigration restriction to ten years, the president signed it in May 1882. It banned the immigration of Chinese workers, skilled or unskilled, from all ports and forbade the courts from naturalizing Chinese.[42]

Labor achieved further success against contract labor with the Foran Act of 1885, which prohibited "the importation and migration of foreigners

40. Bodnar, 58; Gunther Peck, *Reinventing Free Labor: Padrones and Immigration Workers in the North American West, 1880–1930* (New York: Cambridge University Press, 2000), 50–55, 82–93.
41. Alexander Saxton, *The Indispensable Enemy: Labor and the Anti-Chinese Movement in California* (Berkeley: University of California Press, 1995), 110, 116, 132, 172.
42. Ibid., 172–78.

and aliens under contract or agreement to perform labor in the United States." It made no attempt to distinguish between voluntary and involuntary labor; it cut the Gordian knot by prohibiting all contract labor. It represented one of the triumphs of the Knights of Labor and ended the equation of contract freedom with free labor. Ultimately the act, which proved devilishly hard to enforce until the United States gained greater administrative control of its northern and southern borders, had greater ideological than practical effect. Even after its passage, labor contractors brought Greek, Serbian, Croatian, and Slovenian miners to Utah, and Japanese laborers to the Pacific Northwest.[43]

III

Contract labor loomed so large in the vast expanses of the interior West because it proved so hard to attract both workers and farmers into the region. In 1881, when John Wesley Powell became head of the U.S. Geological Survey, he was nationally famous for exploring the Grand Canyon and regionally infamous for publishing his *Report on the Lands of the Arid Region of the United States* in 1878. He did not question that the arid regions should be turned over to non-Indians for improvement. He had no particular reverence for wild nature; he thought that water was too valuable to remain in natural drainages in the arid region. It needed to be diverted for irrigation and livestock. Where he differed from the other improvers was in his belief that the Jeffersonian grid and its 160-acre homesteads were worse than useless in the arid regions. He proposed substituting what he considered scientific settlement, marked by irrigation districts and much larger pasturage homesteads. He used a word gaining currency and about to gain much more: cooperation. This, he said, was the key to successful settlement.[44]

Powell's advice was anathema to boosters. Under his plan, there would be fewer farms and thus fewer towns. To boosters who marched under the banner of more, Powell was misguided, delusional, dictatorial, and undemocratic. They mustered their own science, one that would promote the dense settlement of the West. It was not precipitation, they insisted, that increased crop yields; it was farming that produced rain. They summarized their findings in the phrase "rain follows the plow." Samuel Aughey, who had an appointment as professor of natural science at the University of

43. Peck, 33–34, 55–56, 84–90.
44. Donald Worster, *A River Running West: The Life of John Wesley Powell* (New York: Oxford University Press, 2001), 342–60.

Nebraska, admitted in 1880 that the statistics on rainfall west of the 100th meridian did not yet provide evidence of sufficient moisture to grow crops, but he was confident that they soon would. Aughey had been a member of Ferdinand Hayden's survey team, and Hayden, whom Powell dismissed as a charlatan, accepted and promoted the idea. Charles Francis Adams and Sidney Dillon, both presidents of the Union Pacific, publicized claims of changing climate in popular national publications into the 1890s.[45]

More than wishful thinking prompted opposition to Powell. His proposal would put into the hands of experts decisions that had been left to individual citizens. It embodied the liberal tension between contract freedom and individualism, on the one hand, and expertise and bureaucracy, on the other. That the land system was inefficient, fraudulent, and corrupt mattered less to boosters and many western settlers than that it seemed democratic. Fear of monopoly ran deep, and it was easy to portray Powell as encouraging it.[46]

In any case, it appeared that Aughey might be right. Not only do wet years follow dry on the Great Plains, but there are also spatial variations on large and small scales. A thunderstorm could soak one township or county and miss another. The southern plains could be wet and the northern plains dry. An unusual amount of rainfall drenched the southern plains in the late 1870s, and this coincided with a rush of settlement. Settlers could plausibly see themselves as the agents of climate change.[47]

The delusion that rain followed the plow took strongest hold in western Kansas, which enjoyed an exceptionally wet year in 1877 and adequate rains in 1878. Boosters proclaimed a trend. Farmers turned confidently to wheat. The number of homestead entries filed at the land offices skyrocketed, as did timber culture entries.[48]

The settlers pushing out of the prairies and into the Great Plains included both immigrants and the native-born. As with the Indiana Colony in Pasadena, migrants often came as organized groups, who bought blocks

45. Charles Francis Adams, "The Rainfall on the Plains," *The Nation* 44 (Nov. 24, 1887): 417; Richard White, *"It's Your Misfortune and None of My Own": A History of the American West* (Norman: University of Oklahoma Press, 1991), 132–33, 135; David M. Emmons, *Garden in the Grasslands: Boomer Literature of the Central Great Plains* (Lincoln: University of Nebraska Press, 1971), 131–41; Worster, 359–61, 365; Sidney Dillon, "The West and the Railroads," *North American Review* 152 (April 1891): 444–47; Samuel Aughey, *Sketches of the Physical Geography and Geology of Nebraksa* (Omaha, NE: Daily Republican Book and Job Office, 1880), 35, 36, 41–47.
46. Worster, 366–70.
47. Cary J. Mock, "Rainfall in the Garden of the United States Great Plains, 1870–79," *Climatic Change* 44 (2000): 184, 187–88, 191.
48. Craig Miner, *West of Wichita: Settling the High Plains of Kansas, 1865–1890* (Lawrence: University Press of Kansas, 1986), 119–23.

of land, often from the railroads, creating communities of people from a single place. Massachusetts, Wisconsin, and Pennsylvania provided colonists, but others were made up of Swedes and German-Russians from the Volga. Some of the German-Russians were Catholics, but most were Mennonites. They had settled in Russia more than a century before and were emigrating to escape the Czar's draft. Agents of western railroads — the Atchison, Topeka and Santa Fe and the Kansas Pacific — had solicited their emigration to Kansas in the mid-1870s.[49]

The German Russians had money to buy land and were exceptional farmers, but the men in their sheepskin coats, which blossomed out like a skirt around their legs and their high boots decorated with embroidered flowers, attracted unfriendly attention. They gathered in groups, as a Hays, Kansas, editor wrote, "jabbering about this and that no one knows what." They were, he contended, "filthy," eating with their hands and seldom changing clothes. He claimed to be able to smell them within twenty rods. They were, in an ultimate insult, "nearer... the aborigines, in the mode of life than any other class of people we have chanced to fall in with."[50]

The German Russians were strangers in a strange land, but they were more familiar with vast grasslands, brutal winters, and hot summers than most of their American neighbors. A young girl from Ohio remembered being "burned brown as a penny" from riding in an open wagon on the trip to the family's claim. Between fear of snakes and the conviction that a cowboy would steal her croquet set at the first opportunity, she got no sleep. The first reaction of migrants to the plains could be awe at their grandeur and, particularly in the spring, their beauty. Or it could be a catalog of emptiness: "no roads,... nor trees, nor houses." The sum of this initial nothingness was homesickness until dugouts and sodhouses yielded to frame houses, and Kansas became home.[51]

The rains lessened in 1879 and a drought lasting until 1882 commenced. The editor of *The Osborne County Farmer* remembered that during these years it seemed that the "heaven above our heads was as brass, and the earth beneath our feet was as iron." Western Kansas struggled to hold population. When Mrs. Lucena Mercier wrote the governor from Trego County, her township only held two families from the original settlers. The others had all departed. Her husband had gone to New Mexico in search of work, leaving her with five children, including an infant, who were living on corn meal mixed with water. "I beg you to help me some

49. Ibid., 67–68, 80–88.
50. Ibid., 88–91.
51. Ibid., 135–37.

way, that my little ones may not have worse privations to endure than they have already endured. I ask of you in the name of all you hold most dear, not to throw this aside and forget it, for no one can realize the terrors of such a situation until placed as I am here." At the governor's urging, the legislature funded relief for those who tried to hold on.[52]

In this case aid came from the state, but disasters, when severe enough, created avenues for expansion of federal powers under the general welfare clause of the Constitution. Following longstanding practice, which became more common with the destitution in the South following the Civil War, the government intervened. When the Mississippi overflowed in 1874, 1882, and 1884, the federal government provided aid. When grasshoppers ravaged western farmers in 1874, 1875, 1877, and 1878, the federal government provided aid. Great fires, yellow fever epidemics, tornados, and flooding all produced federal aid. When citizens suffered through no fault of their own, it became a justification for federal intervention.[53]

Even as the rains ceased on the southern plains, they came to the northern plains. In the late 1870s and early 1880s, the Dakotas boomed. Among the boomers migrating to Dakota Territory were Dick Garland and his family. Hamlin Garland later described his migration in Son of the Middle Border, a memoir, which like all memoirs, turned actual people into literary characters, whose lives the author plotted to reveal lessons that arose not from immediate experience but from the writer's later thought and rumination.[54]

In Garland's telling it was an insect, the chinch bug, that set the family in motion. Chinch bugs prospered because farmers had created a near monoculture of wheat. With farmers providing food beyond chinch bugs' wildest dreams, their populations exploded. In the fall of 1880 the bugs created "a season of disgust and disappointment," devouring grain and filling "our stables, granaries, and even our kitchens with their ill-smelling crawling bodies." The next year they came again in "added billions" ... "innumerable as the sands of the sea." The wheat turned yellow, Dick Garland's wheat buying business failed, and Garland "turned his face toward the free lands of the farther west. He became again the pioneer."[55]

52. Miner, 128–30, 144.
53. Michele Landis Dauber, The Sympathetic State: Disaster Relief and the Origins of the American Welfare State (Chicago: University of Chicago Press, 2013), 17–47.
54. Gilbert Courtland Fite, The Farmers' Frontier, 1865–1900 (New York: Holt, Rinehart and Winston, 1966), 98–100; Miner, 124–31; Hamlin Garland, A Son of the Middle Border (New York: Grosset & Dunlap, 1928).
55. Allan G. Bogue, From Prairie to Corn Belt: Farming on the Illinois and Iowa Prairies in the Nineteenth Century (Chicago: University of Chicago Press, 1963), 125–26; Garland, 229–30.

His wife did not want to go. The Garlands could have switched crops, as others did. And, as Garland wrote, "each of our lives was knit into these hedges and rooted in the fields and yet, notwithstanding all this, in response to some powerful yearning call, my father was about to set out for the fifth time into the still more remote and untrodden west." Home's hold did not prove strong enough. His "face...again alight with the hope of the borderman," he took the train and staked out a homestead in Ordway, Brown County, Dakota Territory in the James River Valley.[56]

The twenty-one-year-old Hamlin Garland joined his family in 1881. He moved beyond the "Jim River Valley," where his father and grandfather settled, and staked a preemption claim, which allowed the claimant first right of purchase on the unsurveyed public domain. He, like most of the settlers in what would become South Dakota, stayed east of the 100th meridian. The Great Sioux Reservation blocked progress farther west. Nonetheless, the farmers were moving into a harsh and unforgiving environment in the subhumid short grass plains just east of the line of 20 inches of rainfall. He was part of "an exodus, a stampede." It seemed that everyone who could sell out had gone west or was going. "Norwegians, Swedes, Danes, Scotchmen, Englishmen and Russians all mingled in this flood of land-seekers rolling toward the sundown plain, where a fat-soiled valley had been set aside by good Uncle Sam for the enrichment of every man. Such elation, such hopefulness could not fail to involve an excitable youth like myself."[57]

Garland, like many other land seekers, including female schoolteachers who filed preemptions near him, planned to flip their claims for a profit. He marked his preemption with "three boards set together in a tripod and was used as a monument, a sign of occupancy." This "'straddlebug' defended a claim against the next comer."[58]

The Harris family also moved from Iowa to the Dakotas in the early 1880s. They rented out their Delaware County, Iowa, farm and joined the Dakota boomers for traditional American reasons. The son, Frank, had married and had a growing family. They needed additional land for him and his children. Jamestown, Dakota Territory, where they went to look for land, had grown from 200 people to 2,000, most of them land seekers filling not only hotels but also huts and old stables. Every night men slept on the floor of the railroad depot.[59]

56. Garland, 229–30, 238; Robert F. Gish, "Hamlin Garland's Dakota: History and Story," *South Dakota History* 9 (1979).

57. Garland, 237, 301.

58. Ibid., 303, 306.

59. Paula Nelson, "'All Well and Hard at Work,' the Harris Family Letters," *North Dakota History* 57 (Spring 1990): 25–26.

The Harrises described the same ethnic mix in the migration as Garland, but they also described how the migrants self-segregated. Elizabeth Harris wrote her sister Julia that they would settle "eighteen miles southwest of Grand Rapids in the county of Dickey…The settlement will be mostly Americans, the Swedes and Germans go on to Bismarck and Glendive." No one, she reported, "has ever lived in this part of the state but savages and wild beasts …" The Harrises lived in a combination dugout and shanty, fourteen by eighteen feet, and were relieved when they found a cat to thin out the field mice that invaded their one-room home. The family claimed 480 acres of land along with that one room and was hoping for more.[60]

The enthusiasm of Dick Garland and the Harrises seemed justified as the settlers enjoyed a string of unusually wet years between 1878 and 1885. The Red River Valley boomed, and settlement extended out along the line of the Northern Pacific past the 100th meridian to Bismarck. Settlers in Dakota Territory as a whole entered 41,321,472 acres, an area as large as Iowa, under the public land laws during the 1880s. Entries peaked in 1884 when settlers claimed 11,082,818 acres. Dakota was, boosters declared, "the sole remaining section of paradise in the western world," and paradise yielded wheat in abundance. Settlers reported working a homestead into a $10,000 estate in five years. The railroads brought in plows, drills, harrows, and self-binders by the carload; farmers confidently went into debt to buy them and expand their acreage. They stocked their farms with livestock. Faulk County, like Dickey County, grew rapidly, jumping from 4 to 3,120 people (700 more than it would have in 2010) between 1880 and 1885. As long as the rains came, anything seemed possible.[61]

In retrospect Hamlin Garland cast the settlement of the Dakotas as a slowly developing tragedy, although one that originated in hope. He emphasized the beauty of the spring during which hope was born, then the "flare of horizontal heat" that came with the summer, the withering gardens, the women complaining of loneliness, and the lack of shade. And finally, there was "Winter! No man knows what winter means until he has lived through one in a pine-board shanty on a Dakota plain with only buffalo bones for fuel." Winter on the Great Plains brought blizzards, 70-mile-an-hour winds that swirled the snow into whiteouts with temperatures dropping to 40 below. Garland wrote that it "permanently chilled my enthusiasm for pioneering the plain," but it did not quell the enthusiasm of

60. P. Nelson, 25–32.
61. Fite, 98–107.

his father and men like him. Their hope, if not always the hopes of their wives, revived with each spring.[62]

Elizabeth Harris maintained her hope in the 1880s. She recognized that her own and surrounding families were replacing Indians –the "savages"—but she had to reassure relatives who, in the American way, thought the native people the United States had killed and dispossessed were threats to the safety of American families when the opposite was the case. In reassuring them, Harris pointed to a fundamental difference between Indians and white migrants. The whites could move easily and freely; Indians could not They needed permits and passes to leave the reservation. And going off the reservation even with passes opened them up to lethal attacks by whites. [63]

On the reservations conditions were often deadly. Between 15 and 25 percent of the Piegans starved and died on their Montana reservation during the winter of 1882 and 1883. It was hardly noticed. Indians discerned things that whites did not. They knew that Western boundaries could be firm for Indians while porous for whites. Reservations and Indian Territory were supposed to be havens for Indians, a remnant of their land not subject to white entry, but they were subject to constant pressure from whites who wanted them opened up for white settlement, or for their resources—from grass to minerals—to be made available for white use. Indians, on the other hand, found their movements restricted.[64]

In 1879 President Rutherford Hayes accompanied Gen. William T. Sherman into western Kansas. They gave speeches at Larned, Kansas, where Sherman remarked that he was glad to see the Indians gone and added, "I don't care where they are gone to." The crowd laughed. Kansas had largely emptied itself of Indians earlier in the decade, but they had briefly returned the year before.[65]

Like their relatives the Southern Cheyennes, the Northern Cheyennes of Montana had been dispossessed and banished to Indian Territory. There, as one said later, "we were sickly and dying…and no one will speak our names when we are gone." Better to flee and try to return to Montana. In September of 1878, 353 Northern Cheyenne led by Dull Knife and Little Wolf crossed the Kansas border. Soldiers pursued them, and the initial sympathy for them in Kansas quickly evaporated. For years

62. Garland, 309–12.
63. P. Nelson, 32–33.
64. Benjamin Hoy, "A Wall of Many Heights: The Uneven Enforcement of the Canadian-United States Border" (Stanford, CA: Stanford University, 2015), 386, 203–355.
65. Miner, 119–23.

Sherman and General Sheridan had conjured the specter of Indian war-riors as the bearers of horrific violence, men who raped and killed without provocation. In Kansas the Northern Cheyennes briefly became those Indians; the racial war whites had proclaimed became actual. In a bloody passage of several weeks, the Cheyennes killed 41 settlers and committed 25 rapes, the youngest against a girl of 8. They fought and defeated the soldiers sent to stop them. The Northern Cheyennes hated whites for good reason, and they made that hatred ferocious and palpable. White settlers now suffered as the Cheyennes had suffered. Little Wolf would make it to Montana. Dull Knife's band would not. In January 1879, during an escape attempt from Fort Robinson, Nebraska, where they were con-fined—the same post where Crazy Horse had died—the army killed 64 of them, including all but six of their warriors. Not until 1883 did the govern-ment agree to allow the remaining Northern Cheyennes to leave Indian Territory.[66]

The Poncas' attempt to return home ultimately proved more successful. The northern prairies and plains had once been Ponca Indian country, but the Poncas, like the Cheyennes, had fallen victim to the government's consolidation policy. The government had forced them to move south to Indian Territory in 1877 under armed guard. As Standing Bear, one of their chiefs, recounted: "They took our reapers, mowers, hay rakes, spades, ploughs, bedsteads, stoves cupboards, everything we had on our farms." The trip south became a parade of horrors. Among the many dead were two of Standing Bear's children. Indian Territory was worse. Their horses and cattle died and so did 158 more Poncas, including Standing Bear's son, whom he promised he would take north and bury in their old home along the Niobrara River in northern Nebraska.[67]

Standing Bear was good to his word. He and a small band of followers fled north. They reached the Omaha reservation in Nebraska, and Carl Schurz, Hayes's secretary of interior, ordered them arrested and returned. The officer delegated to do so was Gen. George Crook. He sympathized with Standing Bear and leaked the story to Henry Tibbles, who had been first a follower of John Brown in Kansas, then a scout on the plains, then an itinerant preacher, before becoming a newspaperman. Tibbles made Standing Bear a *cause célèbre* when he arranged for a lawyer to file a habeas corpus brief on the Poncas' behalf. A judge declared Standing

66. Miner, 109–18; Francis Paul Prucha, *American Indian Policy in Crisis: Christian Reformers and the Indian, 1865–1900* (Norman: University of Oklahoma Press 1976), 120–23.

67. Prucha, 113–18; Peter Nabokov, ed., *Native American Testimony: From Prophecy to the Present, 1492–1992* (New York: Viking, 1991), 168–69.

Bear a person under the Fourteenth Amendment and ordered Crook to free him. Tibbles and Suzanne La Flesche, an Omaha with a Ponca grandmother, toured with Standing Bear. They attracted considerable sympathy and engaged Schurz in a public quarrel that did not reflect well on either Schurz or the administration. Tibbles and LaFlesche would marry, and in 1880 a government commission allowed the Poncas under Standing Bear to return to the Niobrara. Although a majority of the tribe remained in Indian Territory, the government indemnified them for their losses. The government, in a sign of things to come, granted both groups land in severalty—that is, individual ownership.[68]

Indians learned to muster American law as well as their treaties, and they learned to use the Americans' language of home against their persecutors, but they still had to appeal to American tribunals and American authority for justice. The choices still belonged to the government, even if the postwar policy of consolidating the tribes in Indian Territory was falling apart. Sara Winnemucca knew this when she met with President Hayes.[69]

In 1880 Rutherford Hayes again traveled west, becoming the first sitting president to visit the Far West when he took the Pacific Railway to San Francisco. From there much of the travel was by stagecoach, steamboat, and horse-drawn army ambulance. He returned through New Mexico, connecting finally with the Atchison, Topeka and Santa Fe Railway, which was still building west. The trip's two-month duration emphasized the vastness of the country; it also showed how easily Washington could do without the president.[70]

Much of Hayes's journey went through what had recently been Indian country and demonstrated how different the conditions of movement and residence were for Indians and whites. He told an audience, which included Indians, at an Oregon Indian school, "We have displaced them and are now completing that work." Hayes believed Indians would "become part of the great American family," but until then, the government would determine what was best for them. Winnemucca, a Paiute, made a plea that her people, confined to the Yakima reservation, be allowed to return to their homes farther south. The plea reduced Hayes's wife, Lucy, to tears, but the president refused.[71]

68. Prucha, 114–19.

69. This is the theme of Frederick E. Hoxie, *This Indian Country: American Indian Activists and the Place They Made* (New York: Penguin, 2012), 143–81.

70. Ari Arthur Hoogenboom, *Rutherford B. Hayes: Warrior and President* (Lawrence: University Press of Kansas, 1995), 441–46.

71. Ibid., 443.

Winnemucca's speech was sincere and artful; she intended to play on Lucy Hayes's emotions. Over an eventful life she perfected turning the home against the Americans. She was a Paiute headman's daughter, who learned to appeal to white audiences. She donned what can loosely be described as her Indian princess garb for the camera and for white audiences. In a kind of self-fashioning familiar to Buffalo Bill Cody, she made herself into something that existed only in nineteenth-century Victorian imaginations: an Indian princess. She disputed both a division of time that gave Paiutes the past and whites the future and the racial division of Nevada's space that gave whites homes and pretty much anything else they wanted. She reversed the narrative that made Indians threats to white homes; she portrayed whites as threats to Indian homes.[72]

Sara Winnemucca made herself an Indian reformer who often praised the U.S. Army and was at odds with white Indian reformers, who endorsed the peace policy. She attacked Christians and Christianity as hypocritical and corrupt in taking Paiute land without Paiute consent. Reformers retaliated by attacking her and defending the peace policy.[73]

Winnemucca intended her *My Life Among the Piutes* to give her standing as both a Paiute and a Victorian woman. Like the female Christian reformers she both appealed to and criticized, the book defended female virtue, wielded domesticity as a weapon, and extended women's realm into public politics. She swung back and forth between emphasizing her status as "the chieftain's weary daughter" and her status as a woman who moved into male realms. She cried often and endlessly, but she also rode alone or in the company of other women across dangerous terrain in war. She cared for children; she faced down men.[74]

Where Cody featured Indian attack and white defense of the home, Winnemucca made her story the story of white rape and pillage and made her hero the Indian woman. She made the domestic space Indian space and put Indian women in constant danger from white men. She turned Cody's scouts, cowboys, and settlers into rapists and cowards; none of them could be trusted. The white men who could be trusted were soldiers, whom Winnemucca made friends of the Indians, and men who married Indian women and entered Indian domestic circles. Winnemucca

---

72. Hoxie, 143–78; Richard White, "The West Is Rarely What It Seems," in *Faces of the Frontier: Photographic Portraits from the American West, 1845–1924*, ed. Frank H. Goodyear III (Norman: University of Oklahoma Press, in cooperation with the National Portrait Gallery, Smithsonian Institution, 2009), 21–32.
73. Hoxie, 165–66; Sara Winnemucca Hopkins, *Life among the Piutes: Their Wrongs and Claims* (Boston: G. P. Putnam and Sons and by the Author, 1883), 52, 87, 90, 209–10, 267.
74. Hopkins, 12, 34, 22, 23, 24, 26, 29, 70, 77, 82–86, 101, 104, 120, 151, 168–69.

did all this in Victorian prose aimed at the sympathy of a largely white, feminine audience that was predisposed in many ways to accept versions of predatory male behavior.[75]

In 1879 Chief Joseph went to Washington to plead the case of his people, the most famous victims of the policy of concentration and confinement. The struggle would take years, but in 1885 118 Nez Perce from Oklahoma were allowed to return to the Lapwai reservation in Idaho. It proved a bittersweet victory; threats by whites against 150 others meant they were exiled, again, to the Colville Reservation in Washington Territory. Joseph was among them.[76]

In the face of Indian deaths, resistance, and scandal the policy of consolidation became largely a dead letter in the 1880s, but reducing Indian landholdings to open up lands for white settlement remained very much alive. The associated policy of distributing Indian lands to tribal members under severalty was on the rise.[77]

Reservations that restricted Indian movements also had the ironic effect of protecting American settlers against themselves, at least temporarily. Reservations blocked access to large tracts of arid land that, with first the belief in rain following the plow and then later irrigation, increasingly aroused the desire of American farmers. The movement west of the 100th meridian became one of the greatest social and environmental miscalculations in American history, one that would play out far beyond the nineteenth century. There were warnings of disaster, but boosters drowned them out. It was easy to be convinced that the very scale of the transformations taking place indicated their inevitability and ultimate success. When plows turned up the grasslands, the men who guided them seemed but part of what Americans regarded as the natural finishing of the landscape, the turning of a wilderness into farmland. They misread the landscape as well as the climate. The landscape was not an untouched wilderness. It had been shaped by centuries of Indian burning, pastoralism, and, in some places, agriculture, but to new settlers the lack of fenced fields, houses, and barns marked a landscape that could not have been the product of human intervention and labor.[78]

75. I develop this argument more fully in White, "The West Is Rarely What It Seems"; Hopkins, 84, 92, 102, 198, 239.

76. Prucha, 123–28.

77. Ibid., 128–31.

78. Elliott West, *The Contested Plains: Indians, Goldseekers, & the Rush to Colorado* (Lawrence: University Press of Kansas, 1998), 84–90; Richard White, *The Roots of Dependency: Subsistence, Environment, and Social Change among the Choctaws, Pawnees, and Navajos* (Lincoln: University of Nebraska Press, 1988), 157–77.

There was a second, less noticed, parallel movement into lands that were too wet rather than too dry. For all the environmental destructiveness of this settlement, it proved more economically successful. Draining the wetlands of the Midwest, Mississippi Valley, and California created prime farmland that formed a counterpoint to the movement onto arid lands. Because of the abundance of wetlands, the malaria that killed Standing Bear's son in Indian Territory was endemic in the Mississippi Valley and its tributaries as well as in the Central Valley of California. Health as well as profit seemed to depend on transforming these environments.[79]

Settlers recognized the association of malaria, dysentery, and other diseases with standing water, although they would not understand the vectors such as the anopheles mosquito for malaria until the end of the century. Their explanation was miasma. The exact definition of miasma was vague. It was a vapor whose palpable signs were dampness, foul odors, and haziness. Victorians believed that human bodies, particularly female bodies, were permeable, so easily affected by their surroundings that they virtually became a part of them. Humans breathed the miasma that arose from decaying matter and stagnant water; it penetrated their bodies when they ate and drank or when they touched each other. As a result, humans sickened and died. This was why swamps and wetlands were regarded as deadly. Into the 1880s the Sacramento and San Joaquin Valleys of California had reputations of being sickly landscapes, particularly dangerous to whites. White settlement depended on draining the landscape.[80]

Indiana and Illinois held a good chunk of the 64 million acres—roughly the equivalent of Oregon—designated as swampland in eight Midwestern states. The federal government donated swamplands to the states, which, in turn, could sell them on terms that would finance their drainage and improvement, but the law left large loopholes for misuse and fraud. Substantial amounts of land went to speculators, who improved very little of it.[81]

79. Linda Lorraine Nash, *Inescapable Ecologies: A History of Environment, Disease, and Knowledge* (Berkeley: University of California Press, 2006), 20–23, 74–77; Conevery Bolton Valenčius, *The Health of the Country: How American Settlers Understood Themselves and Their Land* (New York: Basic Books, 2002), 79–81.
80. Harold L. Platt, *Shock Cities: The Environmental Transformation and Reform of Manchester and Chicago* (Chicago: University of Chicago Press, 2005), 178–89, 306–7, 379–81; Nash, 11, 24–27, 64–74; Valenčius, 53–84, 114–32.
81. Ann Vileisis, *Discovering the Unknown Landscape: A History of America's Wetlands* (Washington, DC: Island Press, 1997), 76–91.

Draining of the wetlands following the Civil War depended on technical innovations, limits on the property rights that stood in the way of improvement, and on what John Wesley Powell called cooperation. The technical tools were horse-drawn digging machines that cut four-foot trenches at a single pass, and steam-powered tile-making machines to make the tiles that lined them. The technology improved again in the 1880s, and by 1890 steam-driven machines could cut 1,320 to 1,650 feet of 4½-foot trench in a day. By 1882, Indiana farmers had laid 30,000 miles of drainage tiles.[82]

Legal tools were necessary because when the farmer, the state, or the federal government drained wetlands or built levees, the water had to go somewhere, usually onto or through neighboring properties. Developing wetlands meant modifying the common law rights of neighboring property owners. The drainage districts—yet another expansion of government authority to facilitate development—demanded the cooperation and association of the landowners within them. The districts had the power to tax to pay for improvements and rights of eminent domain to create the necessary infrastructure.[83]

The federal government played its part in accelerating drainage in the West and the South. The increased power of congressional Democrats after 1874 meant a growing share of federal subsidies to the South. Democrats secured the Mississippi River Commission in 1879, which subsidized the levees that rose on the Mississippi to replace and extend those ruined during the Civil War. In the Sacramento–San Joaquin Delta of California swampland legislation allowed speculators to amass, often fraudulently, huge acreages, where they employed Chinese laborers at low wages. They built levees under conditions other workers refused to tolerate. The delta, like most of California, was seasonally arid; its freshwater came largely from mountain runoff. Californians failed to find the means to irrigate dry land on a large scale in the 1870s, but they paradoxically succeeded in irrigating wetlands. The first step was to build levees and dikes to separate land from water. The tidal action provided for what amounted to natural irrigation. High tides raised the level of freshwater in the Delta, allowing farmers to open their irrigation gates and water their fields. Low tides allowed them to drain their fields. But what seemed an ingenious system that worked with natural cycles was, in fact, an intervention that created a complex productive system liable to collapse without the addition of constant labor and capital. After 1884, federal legislation made the maintenance of this impossibly convoluted system—dredging

82. Ibid., 124–27.
83. Ibid., 76–90; Bogue, 41.

the rivers, repairing the main levees, and building them up—the work of the Army Corps of Engineers.[84]

The human migrations sweeping across the country had profound repercussions for other species. Nearly all that was left of the bison herds were the bones gathered in immense piles by railroad tracks to be shipped and ground into fertilizer. Intentionally and unintentionally, often under the guiding hand of federal legislation, some of the most common landscapes in North America began to dwindle and disappear, and with them went what had been some of the continent's most common species. The early accounts of passenger pigeons, which ranged the woodlands of the eastern part of the continent from Quebec to Texas, later seemed the stuff of fantasy. Alexander Wilson described a flock along the Ohio River early in the century that he initially mistook "for a tornado, about to overwhelm the house and everyone around in destruction." It took the birds five hours to pass over. He estimated that they stretched for 240 miles and that the flock contained two billion birds. In 1831 John Jay Audubon claimed he had seen a roosting ground in Kentucky that stretched over forty miles. There were still billions in the 1870s; by the 1890s there were dozens, and then in 1914 when the last bird died in captivity, there were none. Americans overhunted the birds, and destroyed the forests and the wetlands and marshes that supported the last vast tracts of hardwood forests along the flyways until the flocks, which depended on a critical mass, declined to the point where they ceased to reproduce. They were only the most spectacular case of decline. Overhunting for the hat and feather trades pushed many other birds along the same path toward extinction.[85]

Hamlin Garland detected a "haunting sadness in the settlement of the grasslands and the coming of the inexorable plow. They prophesied the death of all wild creatures and assured the devastation of the beautiful, the destruction of all the signs and seasons of the sod." He did not think other settlers shared the feeling. Most probably did not. Even John Muir, reflecting at a distance on the eradication of the bison and the settling of the prairies and plains, thought "we need not go mourning the buffaloes.

84. Vileisis, 131; Christopher Morris, *The Big Muddy: An Environmental History of the Mississippi and Its Peoples from Hernando De Soto to Hurricane Katrina* (New York: Oxford University Press, 2012), 151–60; Donald J. Pisani, *From the Family Farm to Agribusiness: The Irrigation Crusade in California and the West, 1850–1931* (Berkeley: University of California Press, 1984), 129–53; Matthew Morse Booker, *Down by the Bay: San Francisco's History between the Tides* (Berkeley: University of California Press, 2013), 86–100.

85. Jennifer Price, *Flight Maps: Adventures with Nature in Modern America* (New York: Basic Books, 1999), 1–109, particularly 1–7.

In the nature of things they had to give place to better cattle, though the change might have been made without barbarous wickedness."[86]

In good times, when the economy boomed and when the rains fell, setting millions of people in motion, most migrants never doubted that their movement was synonymous with progress. When the economy declined, when drought struck, they were less certain that the benefits were worth the cost and more likely to consider what had been lost as well as what had been gained.

---

86. Garland, 303, 306; Donald Worster, *A Passion for Nature: The Life of John Muir* (New York: Oxford University Press, 2008), 288.

12

Liberal Orthodoxy and Radical Opinions

In early 1881, making appointments, large and small, consumed the newly elected president, James Garfield. William Dean Howells, hearing rumors that Garfield was about to appoint him ambassador to Switzerland, wrote both to decline the appointment and to solicit the consulship at Montreal for his father. Garfield had greater concerns. He was engaged in the battle between Stalwarts, led by Roscoe Conkling, and Half-Breeds, whose leader, James G. Blaine, became his secretary of state. At stake was party patronage, particularly the lucrative position of collector of customs at the Port of New York. The machinations were convoluted, sordid, and occasionally comic. To protest Garfield's denial of his control over New York patronage, Conkling resigned his U.S. Senate seat and persuaded Sen. Thomas Platt, a New York politician open to payments from both Conkling's friend Collis P. Huntington and Jay Gould, to resign also. Both expected to be immediately reelected by the New York legislature, demonstrating to Garfield and to Conkling's many enemies his control over the state machinery. Platt, however, got caught in bed with another man's wife, derailing his reelection.[1]

Charles Guiteau was also seeking office in the spring of 1881. He was a traveling evangelist. He lived on borrowed money and promises, and he sought powerful friends. He wanted a political appointment as minister to Austria or as a consul (preferably in Paris)—the kind of appointment that Howells procured for his friends and relatives. He was sure that Garfield was blocking him despite his imagined service to the party, and he

---

1. W. D. Howells to Victoria Howells, Apr. 10, 1881, in William Dean Howells, *Selected Letters*, ed. George Warren Arms (Boston: Twayne, 1979), 2: 278–79; Candice Millard, *Destiny of the Republic: A Tale of Madness, Medicine, and the Murder of a President* (New York: Doubleday, 2011), 79–84, 108–12; Ari Hoogenboom, *Outlawing the Spoils: A History of the Civil Service Reform Movmeent 1865–1883* (Urbana: University of Illinois Press, 1968), 203–8.

decided the Stalwarts would reward him if he killed Garfield. He also believed God was guiding him.[2]

Guiteau shot Garfield on July 2, 1881, in the Baltimore and Potomac Railroad station on B Street in Washington, D.C., a building that an appalled Garfield had called "a nuisance which ought long since to have been abated." Garfield was going on vacation, in an age when presidents traveled on public conveyances without protection. He was walking through the station, talking with Blaine, when Guiteau came up from behind and fired.[3]

The wounded president was taken to the White House. One of Guiteau's bullets remained in his body, but the doctors could not locate it. Andrew Jackson had carried a bullet in his body through his two terms in the White House; if lodged in fatty tissue, as Garfield's was, a bullet need not be fatal, but the doctors' failure to find it made them all the more determined to locate it. Alexander Graham Bell, the inventor of the telephone, thought he could help by employing a machine using sound waves. He tried and failed. The doctors continued to seek the elusive bullet.[4]

Their probing took place in an unsanitary White House with instruments and hands that had not been fully sterilized. The White House was infested with rats and afflicted with a plumbing system that left the soil in the basement saturated with excrement; this, to be fair, did not make it worse than many hospitals. The knowledge to prevent infection was readily available and widely accepted in Europe, where Joseph Lister had demonstrated that sanitizing operating equipment and operating rooms with his "antiseptic surgery" prevented infection and saved lives. Garfield's physician, Willard Bliss, had attended the wounded Lincoln and was called in by Robert Lincoln, Abraham Lincoln's son and a member of Garfield's cabinet. Bliss rejected Lister's methods. He quarreled with, subverted, and excluded other physicians. New knowledge and new inventions were not enough to change the world, as James Garfield was about to find out. They had to be accepted, systematized, and disseminated. The nation spent the summer of 1881 absorbed by the struggle of the president to recover.[5]

The Gilded Age shaped Guiteau's delusions, the assassination, and the president's convalescence. Guiteau imagined his shooting of Garfield would aid Conkling, and once he escaped being lynched, he confidently

2. Millard, 91–97, 104–8, 113–24.
3. Ibid., 125–32.
4. Ibid., 150–52.
5. Ibid., 14–17, 138, 140, 156–62, 176–77, 186–90.

expected the grateful Stalwarts to free him from Washington's jail, whose accommodations he had inspected beforehand. But Garfield's shooting was the crowning blow to Conkling's ambitions and career. A shooting by an avowed Stalwart, even a crazy one, could not help his cause, and his resignation had already proved a terrible mistake and boon to his enemies. His reelection was probably doomed even before Guiteau shot Garfield. The New York Legislature had deadlocked in the same way the 1880 Republican convention had deadlocked, and Conkling finally lost his bid for reelection to the Senate in July. If Garfield died, it would be Chester A. Arthur, Conkling's creature, who would become president even though Arthur had not and did not aspire to the presidency. William Dean Howells felt only "shame" at the thought of Arthur being president.[6]

It took Dr. Bliss most of the summer to kill Garfield. His incessant probing tortured and infected the president. Garfield finally insisted on being transported to the New Jersey shore in September, and a special train took him there. Dr. Bliss remained confident to the end. Garfield died on the evening of September 19, 1881. James Garfield had been a minor Civil War general, who had become a Republican politician from a major state, Ohio. He had a minor role in a major scandal, the Crédit Mobilier. He died a minor president, whose term in office was short and inconsequential but contained the seed of major changes. A crazy man had killed him, and a nation went crazy with grief and wanted revenge. Guiteau's official defense was insanity, but he was sane enough to circulate a statement saying that the doctors were the real killers. The jury, in a trial that Henry and Clover Adams attended, rejected the insanity defense. Guiteau was hanged on June 30, 1882. By then Arthur had been president of the United States for more than seven months. Arthur dismissed Blaine from the cabinet. "No harm he can ever do," Henry Adams wrote Godkin about Arthur, "will equal the good of ejecting Blaine."[7]

Horatio Alger offered an unintentionally revealing summary of Garfield's life and the significance of his death. His biography of Garfield, written in two weeks as Garfield lay dying, was, like so much of Alger's own life and writings, an exercise in denial. Alger insisted that in the decade and half between Lincoln's assassination and Garfield's nothing fundamental had changed in the United States. *From Canal Boy to President* began with a barefoot four-year-old Garfield emerging from a

6. Millard, 164–69; W. D. Howells to W. C. Howells, July 3, 1881, in Howells, *Selected Letters*, 2: 287; David M. Jordan, *Roscoe Conkling of New York: Voice in the Senate* (Ithaca, NY: Cornell University Press, 1971), 393–409.

7. Edward Chalfant, *Better in Darkness: A Biography of Henry Adams: His Second Life, 1862–1891* (Hamden, CT: Archon Books, 1994), 426–28; Millard, 195–96, 204–5, 212–14, 224–29, 238–46.

log cabin. It ended with Garfield dead by an assassin's bullet. In between was the story of his work and his rise to the White House. It was a "romance" of a rise from "humble beginnings" full of lessons that Alger, with his customary didacticism, drew out for his "young readers." He crammed a minor president into the mold of a major one.[8]

Alger contended that what was true in 1865 remained true in 1881. Garfield was but another version of Lincoln, the once and future king. But Lincoln was dead; Garfield was dead; and it looked as though the promised world of free labor and contract freedom were if not dead then afflicted with a wound as fatal as Garfield's. And like the president, free labor would not go easily. In the Knights, the WCTU, the Grange, and other reform groups the old ideals lived, but they were taking new form and demanding new actions by the government to ensure their realization. What could seem a retreat from government was nothing of the sort. Howells left the country for a long European sojourn at the beginning of 1882; when he returned to the United States from Europe in the summer of 1883, he "found America changed even in the year I was gone; it had grown more American." Howells's "crimson opinions"—and his ideas were growing more radical—seemed only "dull purple in politics and religion." The radical opinions in the United States drew on deep currents of American republicanism and evangelical Protestantism, but young American intellectuals studying in Europe were mixing them with ideas borrowed from European reformers.[9]

Howell's opinions appeared "crimson" when he looked either to his earlier opinions or to his old liberal associates, whose faith in both liberal politics and a philosophy most famously expounded by Herbert Spencer sailed on through ever stormier seas. He seemed "dull purple," when he looked at the younger intellectuals and reformers who, like Frances Willard, advocated a "practical Christianity" and a "social gospel," or at Henry George, the most widely read American intellectual of the age.

As Howells struggled to find his footing, adjusting his earlier opinions to a country changing fast around him, he sometimes appeared lost or contradictory, but this is precisely what made him a useful guide through a tumultuous decade. He had grown concerned and conservative in the wake of the Great Strike of 1877; then he reversed direction. In 1878 he wrote that his life "has been too much given to the merely artistic and to worldly ambition . . . My morality has been a hand to mouth affair."[10]

---

8. Horatio Alger, *From Canal Boy to President, or the Boyhood and Manhood of James A. Garfield* (Boston: DeWolfe, Fiske & Co., 1881), 297, 307–8.
9. W. D. Howells to Edmund Gosse, Dec. 9, 1883, in Howells, *Selected Letters*, 3: 85–86.
10. W. D. Howells to W. C. Howells, July 21, 1878, in ibid., 2: 203.

Howells's prejudices were constantly at war with his sympathies. It may have been Jonathan Harrison's articles on working people in the *Atlantic Monthly* following the Great Strike of 1877 that prompted Howells to start visiting the Boston Police Court. Such visits initially seem to have confirmed his biases. In the article he published about the courts in 1882, the Irish were conventionally drunk, violent, and, usually, stupid. Blacks were comic. The poor were ignorant. "They were, indeed, like children those poor offenders, and had a sort of innocent simplicity in their wickedness." The courts were overwhelmed, but just. Howells's sympathies went to those who seemed potential candidates for his fictions: they dressed well, were articulate, seemed down on their luck, and were paying for their mistakes. Howells thought the courts and police were "all a mere suppression of symptoms in the vicious classes, not a cure." In the House of Correction the convicted would "go from bad to worse." Howells thought the "Black Maria," a term that later gave way to Paddy Wagon for the Irish it transported to jails and prisons, might be more profitably "driven out to some wide, open space, where the explosion could do no harm to the vicinity, and so when the horses and driver had removed to a safe distance — But this is perhaps pessimism."[11]

Such pessimism rose like miasma from liberalism, but the gloom lifted with Howells's growing distance from his liberal fellows. The heyday of liberalism was past; its great figures were aging and influential largely among more conservative Americans. Classical liberalism was metamorphosing into modern conservatism.

Younger men who remained faithful to the old creed found themselves challenged; they grew irritable. The visit of Herbert Spencer to the United States captured liberalism's precarious intellectual condition and its rising association with wealth and privilege. Spencer was a British social philosopher who fought in a grand cause — the acceptance of the great scientific theory of the age, Charles Darwin's account of biological evolution — but Spencer's own version of evolution was eclectic and, like that of most American evolutionists, not strictly Darwinian. He naturalized his liberalism through analogies with biological evolution. He turned what had been a radical attack on privilege into a conservative defense of liberal societies that protected individual and property rights and whose utility appeared over the long run rather than the short. Spencer did not so much praise the existing order as warn that social reform inevitably infringed on

11. William Dean Howells, "Police Report," *Atlantic Monthly* 49 (January 1882): 1–17.

property and individual rights and was dangerous and unnecessary. Change would come at its own pace.[12]

Spencer invented the catchy phrase "survival of the fittest" before Darwin published *Origin of the Species* and grafted it to Darwin's theory of evolution. Unlike Darwin, Spencer promised that evolution was progressive and that progress—material and moral—was inevitable. The existing order and its faults were just so much scenery on the road to a better world. That road could not be altered by fiat, although state action could block and slow progress. Spencer condemned the tariff and any public aid to the poor; he also opposed public education and the post office. Earlier nineteenth-century liberals had been activists, collectively opposing an existing order of inherited privilege and slavery; Spencerian liberalism became passive, a bulwark against tampering with evolutionary "laws." Earlier liberals had opposed claims that God ordained an existing monarchical and feudal social order. Spencerian liberals crowned nature; it determined social outcomes. The older liberal advocacy of human freedom, most visible in the attack on slavery, yielded to a set of restraints on collective action. Individuals should pursue their interests while natural laws systematically weeded out the biologically unfit. In a December 1881 after-dinner speech at Delmonico's, the New York restaurant synonymous with Gilded Age excess, Spencer advised American businessmen to relax, pay less attention to the "gospel of work," and attend to the gospel of relaxation.[13]

Spencer's American followers, who thought him a prophet, paid the great man to tour the United States. He would turn sixty-two in 1882, and he had many years to live, but he and his reputation were already in decline. Most of Spencer's American disciples—Carl Schurz, E. L. Godkin, and Henry Ward Beecher—were also aging and fusty, although Schurz would get second acts in the debates over civil service and the acquisition of the Philippines. They were, for the most part, intellectual equivalents of the Grand Army of the Republic, veterans of a great struggle, ever less

12. I am profitably informed by Weinstein without sharing his enthusiasm for, or his rehabilitation of, Spencer. David Weinstein, "Herbert Spencer," in *The Stanford Encyclopedia of Philosophy*, ed. Edward N. Zalta (Stanford, CA: Stanford University Press, 2012); T. J. Jackson Lears, *No Place of Grace: Antimodernism and the Transformation of American Culture, 1880–1920* (New York: Pantheon Books, 1981), 20–22.

13. Richard Hofstadter, *Social Darwinism in American Thought* (Boston: Beacon Press, 1992), 31–50; for the tour, Barry Werth, *Banquet at Delmonico's: Great Minds, the Gilded Age, and the Triumph of Evolution in America* (New York: Random House, 2009), 279–81; Ronald L. Numbers, *Darwinism Comes to America* (Cambridge, MA: Harvard University Press, 1998), 69; Lears, 20–23, 52.

nimble on their feet and afraid that the changes they had once sponsored had escaped their control. They represented an American past rather than a future. Henry Ward Beecher, who cut his teeth on abolition, had long since adapted his sunny Christianity to comforting the comfortable.

Edward Youmans, the editor of *Popular Mechanics*, which had serialized Spencer's *The Study of Sociology*, arranged the tour. It was not an easy task. Spencer was grouchy, self-centered, and demanding. He refused to give interviews and then complained when newspapers mangled his opinions and appeared a little uncertain of his identity, in one case confusing him with Oscar Wilde, who was also touring the United States. Spencer eventually consented to a kind of call-and-response interview with Youmans on his impressions of the country. Among other things, the interview went to race: the "eventual mixture of the allied varieties of the Aryan race forming the population [of the United States] will produce a finer type of man than has hitherto existed." Such theories were not uncommon.[14]

How little hold Spencer had over the rising generation of American intellectuals, academics, and reformers was apparent in the pages of Howells's old magazine, the *Atlantic*. William James, the brother of Henry James, was a faculty member at Harvard, moving over the course of his career between medicine and physiology, psychology, and philosophy. In 1880 in an *Atlantic* article, James objected to Spencer's "evolutionary view of history."[15]

James's views were of their time, centered on a now-outmoded argument for "great men," but they can just as easily be read as an argument for contingency in history and a premonition of James's evolving philosophy of pragmatism. James condemned Spencer's "science" as a "metaphysic creed." His "sociological method is identical with that of one who would invoke the zodiac to account for the fall of the sparrow." James, like Spencer, praised Darwin, but he praised Darwin's refusal to venture into things he could not explain and to concentrate on what he could. James argued that environments influenced but did not determine: "Societies of men are just like individuals, in that both at any given moment offer ambiguous potentialities of development." He deplored as "folly" Spencerian appeals to "'laws of history' as something inevitable, which science has

14. Harold C. Livesay, *Andrew Carnegie and the Rise of Big Business* (Boston: Little, Brown, 1975); Werth, xix–xxx, 259–62, quote xxv.
15. William James, "Great Men, Great Thoughts, and the Environment," *Atlantic Monthly* (October 1880): 441–59.

only to discover, and which any one can then foretell and observe, but do nothing to alter or avert."[16]

James, in contrast, had already begun to move toward his more fully developed theory of free will encompassed in his "will to believe." What distinguished human beings was their ability to sort out and assemble elements from inchoate perceptions and sensations into ideas and beliefs: "My experience is what I agree to attend. Only those items which I notice shape my mind—without selective interest, experience is in utter chaos." In forging ideas and actions, volition and willpower were what mattered. Human beings chose the elements of their "empirical selves" that they would develop. James did not regard the will to believe as wishful thinking; instead he pragmatically tested it against the world, regarding the truth of ideas and beliefs according to how they produced enlightened action and how successful the behavior they prompted proved to be. This became the core of the philosophy of pragmatism.[17]

Spencer's American followers embraced the "metaphysic creed" that James attacked. John Fiske was an historian and philosopher who celebrated the ascendancy of an English "race." His 1879 lecture "The Manifest Destiny of the English Race" was, in the words of an admirer, a "logical application of the doctrine of Evolution to the developing interest of humanity" and a comprehensive view of "America's place in universal history." Andrew Carnegie, something of an outlier among the acolytes, was approaching fifty in 1882, and he had latched onto Spencer to justify his own amazing fortune—which owed more to the tariff than the survival of the fittest—as a contribution to human progress.[18]

William Graham Sumner, a professor of economics and sociology at Yale, deeply admired Spencer. He had studied in Europe but in preparation for the ministry, and, like Francis Amasa Walker, whom he hated, lacked the advance training of the younger academics and reformers who came to challenge him. He was now an anachronism, though a powerful one, in a new intellectual world.

Sumner's thought evolved over the course of the Gilded Age. Beginning with a mix of Calvinism and the classical political economy of David Ricardo and Adam Smith, he forged a robust defense of Lockean individualism. Later alarmed by the way workers and antimonopolists used free labor to attack industrial capitalism, he recalibrated. He came to regard

16. Ibid.
17. Jeffrey P. Sklansky, *The Soul's Economy: Market Society and Selfhood in American Thought, 1820–1920* (Chapel Hill: University of North Carolina Press, 2002), 140–51.
18. John Spencer Clark, *The Life and Letters of John Fiske*, vol. 2 (Boston and New York: Houghton Mifflin, 1917), 109–10; Livesay, 148–52.

the gains of liberalism, which he equated with civilization, as under constant threat. The Paris Commune and the Great Strike of 1877 horrified him, and he denounced equality as "the equality of swine...no other equality is realizable in the material culture of man on earth." He redefined liberty. It was not a natural right; liberty, like property, was something a person acquired, and like property, not all acquired it equally. The poor, by failing to acquire property, failed to acquire liberty. They made themselves a burden on society, appropriating the earnings of tax-paying citizens. Society was justified in restricting their freedoms. Liberty was the product of "cooperation and organization," and capital accumulation was the epitome of modern cooperation and civilization. The market rewarded society's best members, and its laws ensured the growth of civilization through their progress. Government should not interfere with those laws. "At bottom," he wrote, "there are two chief things with which government has to deal. They are the property of men and the honor of women."[19]

Sumner was extreme even among Spencerian intellectuals in his fear of socialism, antipathy toward the poor, disdain for popular government, zeal for individualism, and identification of capitalism with civilization and progress. He popularized the idea that the new social order of capitalism was natural and necessary. He thought that the intellectual challenge of the age was to reconcile the autonomous individual of classical liberalism with the interdependent society of industrialism.[20]

Sumner's problem was a real one, but Sumner's solution—what the historian Richard Hofstadter later called Social Darwinism—far from defining the age became an outlier. Hofstadter mistook a liberal army in retreat for conquerors and then described Sumner's extreme minority opinion as in the vanguard. Liberals retained relevance in the 1880s, but most were not Social Darwinists. Their opponents ridiculed them as Mugwumps, self-important and supposedly aloof from party politics. They were leaders without followers. Liberals ensconced themselves in the judiciary and, far less reliably, in the executive; their power in Congress, never substantial, was receding.

Liberals made Howells look crimson, but this worried him less than the new academics and reformers, the men and women who made him seem purple. They, like Howells, traveled to and from Europe, but they traveled to different parts and brought back different ideas.

19. Nancy Cohen, *The Reconstruction of American Liberalism, 1865–1914* (Chapel Hill: University of North Carolina Press, 2002), 148–52; Brian Balogh, *A Government out of Sight: The Mystery of National Authority in Nineteenth-Century America* (Cambridge: Cambridge University Press, 2009), 311–12; Sklansky, 112–13, 118–19, 124–27, 130–31.
20. Sklansky, 112–13.

Howells's European sojourn formed part of the customary trail of American literati and tourists. He and his family tended to move in a cocoon of Americans. As a critic, he had already wounded English writers, and they did not seek him out the way they sought out Henry James or Mark Twain. After leaving London, he published articles on Twain and James in the *Century* that contrasted emerging American literary realism favorably with the British pantheon: Trollope, Richardson, Fielding, Thackeray, and even Dickens. The British literati now hated him. Hay assured him that "They may scream and dance all they like but there is no man in England who can hold a lance with you or James."[21]

The younger American intellectuals came to Europe to study. They were convinced that Americans and Europeans confronted common problems of industrial modernity, and the Americans might learn something, particularly from the Germans. The Americans who flocked to Germany were less well known than the intellectuals and writers who visited Great Britain. They were closer to the American artists who went to Paris than to the American tourists who also came there. They had to work to gain access to the networks emerging among European reformers, but they attained entrée to new thinking in the emerging academic disciplines, particularly economics. Even as laissez-faire made inroads into France, Germans remained skeptical, regarding free trade as "English economics" or "Manchester economics," less an elucidation of universal laws than a set of prescriptions designed to help English manufacturers. American students who arrived in the 1870s could see that laissez-faire liberalism was under attack in Great Britain as well as Germany. Richard T. Ely and Simon Patten found themselves drawn to the economic seminars of the German critics, who reversed the polarity of laissez-faire. The free choices of individuals in the market were not moral acts, and there was no invisible hand guiding them to a larger good. Society acting through the state needed to impart morality to an economy that, if left unchecked, rewarded greed and spawned disorder and injustice.[22]

---

21. Martha A. Sandweiss, *Passing Strange: A Gilded Age Tale of Love and Deception across the Color Line* (New York: Penguin Press, 2009), 111; J. Hay to W. D. Howells, Mar. 26, 1883, in John Hay, *John Hay–Howells Letters: The Correspondence of John Milton Hay and William Dean Howells, 1861–1905*, ed. William Dean Howells, George Monteiro, and Brenda Murphy (Boston: Twayne, 1980), 68–69; Kenneth Schuyler Lynn, *William Dean Howells; an American Life* (New York: Harcourt Brace Jovanovich, 1971), 268–72.

22. Daniel T. Rodgers, *Atlantic Crossings: Social Politics in a Progressive Age* (Cambridge, MA: Belknap Press of Harvard University Press, 1998), 62–63, 77–78, 82–84, 88–91; David G. McCullough, *The Greater Journey: Americans in Paris* (New York: Simon & Schuster, 2011); Roseanne Currarino, *The Labor Question in America: Economic Democracy in the Gilded Age* (Urbana: University of Illinois Press, 2011), 63–66.

German professors told their American students that humans were social animals shaped by the very traditions and institutions that they created. True human life was not the private life embraced in the American worship of the home, but rather the public life and entertainments that evangelical Americans so distrusted. Social welfare was not the responsibility of the family, but rather of society as a whole. In the 1880s, even as Bismarck attacked socialists, he simultaneously adopted state social insurance schemes and protectionism. American feelings about this active state were mixed. The benign face of the German state was in the clean streets; the dark side was worrisomely visible in the ubiquitous police, the standing army, the antidemocratic stances of German professors, and the restrictions on what could be thought and said. It was not as if Europe introduced them to state intervention and regulation—that already existed at home—but it provided them with new ways to think about it. They returned to the United States with a wider sense of the world and new vocabularies for talking about events in their own country.[23]

By the early 1880s, these young Americans with German Ph.Ds. were making their way into the American universities where the modern disciplines were taking shape. Ely returned with a degree from Heidelberg and began teaching economics at Johns Hopkins, the first American university with a modern graduate program. He and his fellow travelers dramatically broadened the earlier and more parochial concerns of American intellectual life, but, particularly in Ely's case, they worked through established channels.[24]

Ely, Simon Patten, John Bates Clark, Edwin R. A. Seligman, and others became the "ethical economists" of the 1880s, heavily influenced by the Germans. Herbert Baxter Adams came home with a German history Ph.D. to teach at Johns Hopkins. Although they all retained the liberals' elite sensibilities and distrust of authoritarian states, they nonetheless rejected the older political economy. They saw many economic "laws" as the products of particular national histories; there was nothing either universal or inevitable about them. Better ways could be found for creating a democratic and ethical economy. Most remained leery of workers and their organizations and rejected a Marxian communism, but they accepted the legitimacy of workers' complaints and even embraced what Clark, who became the leading economist of the period, called a "true socialism," which in its "economic republicanism" and praise of independence and cooperation sounded like the Knights of Labor. They often

23. Rodgers, 88–90, 95–98.
24. Ibid., 97–99; Benjamin G. Rader, "Richard T. Ely: Lay Spokesman for the Social Gospel," *Journal of American History* 53, no. 1 (1966): 61–74.

mocked individualism and were unwilling to follow the older liberals such as Godkin and Sumner in their march toward reactionary politics. They treated individualism, contract freedom, and laissez-faire as a set of anachronisms utterly out of step with modern conditions. What had seemed like solutions in 1865 had become the problems.[25]

The new professors—particularly in economics and the emerging disciplines of political science and sociology, and then, later, in history—established a connection between the growing tumult on the streets and the workplace and the classroom. Ely wrote in 1884: "This younger political economy no longer permits [economic] science to be used as a tool in the hands of the greedy and the avaricious for keeping down and oppressing the laboring classes. It does not acknowledge laissez-faire as an excuse for doing nothing while people starve, nor allow the all-sufficiency of competition as a plea for grinding the poor." He disavowed revolution, advising workers to "*Educate, Organize, Wait.* Christ and all Christly people are with you for the right." In part because he feared the growth of anarchism and Marxist socialism, he vowed to use his education "to benefit those who suffer."[26]

Many reformers embraced socialism, but they used the term in a quite particular, non-Marxian way in the 1880s. Socialism involved an appreciation and a celebration of "society" and a rejection of atomistic individualism. If socialism meant anarchism or Marxism, the younger economists opposed it, but to the extent it meant only a kind of antithesis of individualism and an advocacy of cooperation, they too embraced it. They believed, as Ely put it, that government was "the agency through which we must work."[27]

When they founded the American Economic Association in 1885, younger economists saw its mission as including economic science, a "system of social ethics," and "practical Christianity." They wanted to abandon classical economics, which proceeded from a set of presumptions about human nature and human society, and systematically attempt to investigate, measure, and understand actual economic behavior. By

25. James Livingston, *Pragmatism and the Political Economy of Cultural Revolution, 1850–1940* (Chapel Hill: University of North Carolina Press, 1994), 53–54; Cohen, 159–60. For wider international reform, Thomas Bender, *A Nation among Nations: America's Place in World History* (New York: Hill and Wang, 2006), 246–54.

26. Rader, 64; James T. Kloppenberg, *Uncertain Victory: Social Democracy and Progressivism in European and American Thought, 1870–1920* (New York: Oxford University Press, 1986), 250–51, 265; Charles Howard Hopkins, *The Rise of the Social Gospel in American Protestantism, 1865–1915* (New Haven, CT: Yale Universiy Press, 1940), 68–69; Rodgers, 98–99.

27. Rodgers, 98–101.

the late 1880s, Ely thought the United States faced a "spectacular crisis" that offered a golden opportunity for Protestant churches. "The Church must gain leadership," he wrote. "The spirit of Christ should be infused into the social movement under consideration and the social forces which are producing this upheaval should become mighty ethical forces." Ely sought to apply Christian social teachings to industrial society not just through the churches but professionally. He wanted the AEA to be an "association of the younger progressive elements and the platform must be broad, yet it must not include men of the [William Graham] Sumner type."[28]

I

Like Howells, Henry George had journeyed to Europe in 1882. When George published his enormously influential *Progress and Poverty* in 1879, he asked a simple question: Why had not the "enormous increase in the power of producing wealth" made "real poverty a thing of the past"? Instead, from "all parts of the civilized world come complaints of industrial depression; of labor condemned to involuntary idleness; of capital massed and wasting; of pecuniary distress among business men; of want and suffering and anxiety among the working classes." George claimed that where "population is densest, wealth greatest, and the machinery of production and exchange most highly developed—we find the deepest poverty, the sharpest struggle for existence, and the most of enforced idleness." Then for over five hundred more pages, George analyzed the problem.[29]

George claimed the existing debate had become locked in a choice between two unnuanced positions. Radicals asserted that the existence of great poverty alongside vast accumulations of capital signified "the aggressions of capital on labor." Defenders of the emerging industrial order argued that capital aided labor and made it more productive. They saw nothing unjust in vast differences of wealth; it was "but the reward of industry, intelligence, and thrift; and poverty but the punishment of indolence, ignorance, and imprudence."[30]

28. Donald Cedric White, *The Social Gospel: Religion and Reform in Changing America*, ed. Charles Howard Hopkins (Philadelphia: Temple University Press, 1976), 26–30; Hopkins, *The Rise of the Social Gospel in American Protestantism*, 77–78, 171–83; Kloppenberg, 283; Rader, 65–67.
29. Henry George, *Progress and Poverty* (New York: Robert Schalkenbach Foundation, 1942, orig. ed. 1879), 3, 5, 6.
30. Ibid., 194.

George changed the debate. His answer to his own question allowed him to praise capitalists while demanding such radical reform that his enemies denounced him as a socialist. He was not, although he could praise the ideals of socialism. John Dewey, who received his Ph.D. from Johns Hopkins in 1884 and became another of the young intellectuals and social reformers challenging the old tenets of liberalism, thought that George's writings probably had a greater American circulation "than almost all other books on political economy put together." Dewey considered him one of the relatively few original social philosophers that the world had produced. Although George's roots were liberal, he infuriated orthodox liberals. *Progress and Poverty* was a sustained attack on Thomas Malthus and the idea that mass poverty was inevitable as a rising population pushed against scarce resources.[31]

At the heart of George's argument was a redefinition of capital and a resurrection of the old liberal hostility to a landed aristocracy. Instead of dividing the world between labor and capital, George divided it between land and labor. By land he meant "all natural opportunities or forces," including coal, minerals, petroleum, and any other natural resources existing separate from human labor. In terms of urban land, he really meant space. By labor he meant "all human exertion." Labor and capital—preserved manifestations of labor—were but "different forms of the same thing—human exertion." Both were social, flowing from relations of exchange and consumption.[32]

Having melded capital and labor, George did not see any inevitable conflict between them. He thought capitalists useful and returns on capital justified. He opposed strikes and a personal income tax, but he condemned monopoly, which was capital in large masses and "frequently wielded to corrupt, to rob, and to destroy." Monopoly derived from a far

---

31. Ibid., 91, 99–100, 480–81; Sklansky, 112–16, 119–24; Tamara Venit Shelton, A *Squatter's Republic: Land and the Politics of Monopoly in California and the Nation, 1850–1900* (Berkeley: University of California Press, 2013), 75–76, 88–96; for the most recent account of George, see Edward T. O'Donnell, *Henry George and the Crisis of Inequality: Progress and Poverty in the Gilded Age* (New York: Columbia University Press, 2015), particularly 42–63; Edward J. Rose, *Henry George* (New York: Twayne, 1968), 63, 65–73.

32. Christopher William England, "Land and Liberty: Henry George, the Single Tax Movement, and the Origins of 20th Century Liberalism" (Ph.D. diss., Georgetown University, 2015), 8, 64, 76–77; John L. Thomas, *Alternative America: Henry George, Edward Bellamy, Henry Demarest Lloyd and the Adversary Tradition* (Cambridge, MA: Belknap Press, 1983), 58–82, 102–30, 173–201; Sklansky, 123–24; Shelton, 100–101; George, *Progress and Poverty* 162, 198.

more fundamental problem: the ownership of land, which was "the source of all wealth and... the field of all labor."[33]

By not counting land and natural resources as capital, George differed from most economists, then and now, who have understood capital, as the twenty-first century economist Thomas Piketty summarized it, to include all "non-human assets that can be owned and exchanged on some market." Under this definition, capital consisted of all economic assets except human labor, unless the human laborers were owned and bought and sold as slaves. Capital not only could increase or decrease in amount, it could also shift in kind. A major consequence of industrialization was that agricultural land, though still important, formed a decreasing portion of capital, while buildings—both factories and housing in the new cities— other infrastructure, and financial instruments, particularly bonds, had become more valuable than land by roughly 1880.[34]

In more conventional economic terms, George wanted to remove the tax on labor and working capital—houses and factories, domestic live-stock, machinery—while heavily taxing land and resources such as coal, oil, forests, and minerals. George regarded the ownership of land as the root of all evil because it would always yield "the ownership of men" who needed access to land and resources to live. Without access to land and resources, "nominally free laborers are forced by their competition with each other to pay as rent all their earning above a bare living, or to sell their labor for wages which give them a bare living." This was, he said, slavery, defining it as "compelling men to work, yet taking from them all the produce of their labor except what suffices for a bare living." He linked his reforms to antislavery: "if chattel slavery be unjust, then is private property in land unjust." George did not advocate the state pur-chase or confiscation of land; he would simply arrange the tax system "to confiscate rent," the unearned increment that came from the owner-ship of land.[35]

George argued that unlike all other forms of capital—machines, facto-ries, and buildings—land did not depreciate or lose its utility. Rising pop-ulation would only make it more valuable, without any labor invested by its owners. Those who owned land got an unearned increment in the form of its rental value; ideally the state would own all the land and lease it to citizens as they needed it. But with most land already in private

33. England, 3–4; George, *Progress and Poverty*, 188–89, 191–93; Rose, 75.
34. Thomas Piketty, *Capital in the Twenty-First Century*, trans. Arthur Goldhammer (Cambridge, MA: Belknap Press, Harvard University Press, 2014), 46–47, 116–17, 160.
35. Sklansky, 115–16; George, *Progress and Poverty* 190, 328–29, 347, 405–6, 413–14, 425, 438–40.

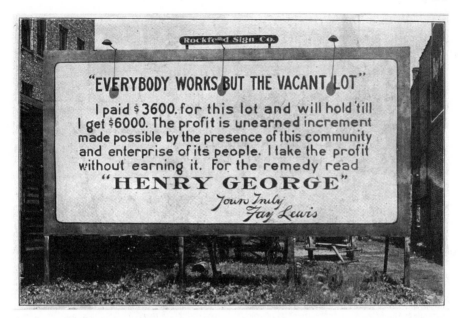

"EVERYBODY WORKS BUT THE VACANT LOT"

I paid $3600, for this lot and will hold 'till I get $6000. The profit is unearned increment made possible by the presence of this community and enterprise of its people. I take the profit without earning it. For the remedy read "HENRY GEORGE"

Yours Truly
Fay Lewis

This billboard encapsulates Henry George's argument that the American economy rewarded speculation in resources—land, minerals and other natural resources—that should be available to those willing to use them while taxing labor and productive property. The lot increased in value even though its owner did nothing to improve it. George's solution was a single tax that would heavily tax undeveloped resources in private ownership. The New York Public Library Digital Collections. ID 1160280.

hands, he proposed a tax—the single tax—that would assess landowners the rental value of their land minus improvements. The tax would be set at rates that forced those who held land or other resources for speculation or pleasure to sell it to those who would put it into production. It was a "use it or lose it" tax. All other taxes would be eliminated. Improvements would not be taxed, so that a working farm would be taxed only at "the value of the bare land." The result would be a redistribution of wealth as both capital and labor gained access to productive resources. The reform would eliminate "the dangerous classes," who were "the very rich and the very poor."[36]

George appealed to the ameliorative and optimistic spirit that had fueled liberal and evangelical reform before the Civil War, but he also linked American reform to a transnational land reform, particularly in

36. England, 3–5, 25–29; Sklansky, 115–16; George, *Progress and Poverty*, 405–6, 413–14, 425, 438–40, 447–53.

Great Britain and the British Empire. Poverty, George insisted, was not the slow sorting of the fit from the unfit or a result of the moral failings of the poor. Quite particular and alterable human causes produced vice and misery: "ignorance and rapacity,...bad government, unjust laws or destructive warfare." Given its capacities, he proclaimed, the "earth as a whole is yet most sparsely populated."[37]

Progress and Poverty resonated with both the old free-labor ideology and emerging antimonopolism. George's prose swung between pedantry and aphorism, but when its rhetoric soared, it captured the times: "Is it a light thing that labor should be robbed of its earnings while greed rolls in wealth?" If his prescription were followed, George wrote, "Society would...approach the ideal of Jeffersonian democracy, the promised land of Herbert Spencer, the abolition of government. But of government only as a directing and repressive power. It would at the same time, and in the same degree, become possible for it to realize the dream of socialism." He saw his program as the logical extension and encouragement of an earlier America. In an argument that anticipated Frederick Jackson Turner, George attributed the superiority of existing American "conditions and institutions" to abundant, cheap, and fertile land that was open to immigrants. But the "republic has entered upon a new era, an era in which the monopoly of the land will tell with accelerating effect."[38]

The claim that old American conditions were disappearing, and with them the best of American society, was at the heart of antimonopolism, and it gave *Progress and Poverty* its power. The country could neither go backward nor go on in the old ways. George balanced his optimism about the possibility of change against the looming catastrophe that threatened. If nothing were done to decelerate "the tendency to the unequal distribution of wealth and power," then the propensity of the "rich to become very much richer, the poor to become more helpless and hopeless, and the middle class to be swept away" would bring American decline. The "transformation of popular government of the vilest and most degrading kind, which must inevitably result from the unequal distribution of wealth, is not a thing of the future. It has already begun in the United States, and is rapidly going on under our eyes."[39]

George's message echoed in the immigrant labor press. In 1877 the *New York Labor Standard*, edited by an Irish socialist, lamented: "There

37. David Thomas Brundage, *Irish Nationalists in America: The Politics of Exile, 1798–1998* (New York: Oxford University Press, 2016), 114–16, 125–26; George, *Progress and Poverty* 106, 110.
38. England, 71; George, *Progress and Poverty*, 77, 390–91, 455–56, 495, 507–8, 514, 517, 551.
39. George, *Progress and Poverty*, 528, 533.

was a time when the United States was the workingman's country,... the land of promise for the workingman.... We are now in an old country." Nearly a decade later the *Detroit Labor Leaf* used nearly identical language: "America used to be the land of promise to the poor.... The Golden Age is indeed over—the Age of Iron has taken its place. The iron law of necessity has taken the place of the golden rule."[40]

George closed *Progress and Poverty* with one of those roaring perorations of which Gilded Age America was so fond: "In permitting the monopolization of the opportunities which nature freely offers to all, we have ignored the fundamental law of justice." But the single tax promised the world "equality in the distribution of wealth and power; we shall abolish poverty; tame the ruthless passions of greed; dry up the springs of vice and misery; light in dark places the lamp of knowledge; give new vigor to invention and fresh impulse to discovery; substitute political strength for political weakness; and make tyranny and anarchy impossible."[41]

If a reader accepted George's premises, his analysis seemed logical, closely reasoned, and easily translated into a political program. For George, everything was built upon "those which procure wealth directly from nature." Poverty existed in the midst of progress because with burgeoning population the returns that should go to capital and labor instead went as an unearned increment to rent. The analysis appealed to a nation with an agrarian tradition, in which labor in the earth was fundamental and which deeply distrusted wealth that seemed to flow from mere exchanges of paper; but it was also quixotic, reductionist, and full of unintended consequences. It promised to force owners to expand production to maintain ownership of their land even when there was no market for what they produced. It reduced the natural world to a set of resources, and in this it was not so different from either corporate capitalism or later Progressive conservationists.[42]

Henry George originally admired Herbert Spencer, who, in an earlier incarnation, had attacked private ownership of land, but Spencer had renounced such views. George came to regard him as a shoddy fatalist living comfortably among mass suffering. Sumner predictably denounced and dismissed *Poverty and Progress* even though his analysis of industrial society, if not his judgment of it, shared much with George.[43]

40. Herbert G. Gutman, "Work, Culture, and Society in Industrializing America, 1815–1919," *American Historical Review* 78, no. 3 (1973): 568.
41. George, *Progress and Poverty* 545.
42. Ibid., 212, 243, 250.
43. Rose, 85; Hillel Steiner, "Land, Liberty, and the Early Herbert Spencer," in *Herbert Spencer: Critical Assessments*, ed. John Offer (London: Taylor & Francis, 2000), 4: 210–14; Sklansky, 105–36.

Compared to their reception of Henry George, most British intellectuals had curtsied and scraped before Howells, but British reformers welcomed George. The American Land League, Irish Americans dedicated to Irish independence and land reform, had already embraced him, and he enthusiastically endorsed Irish land reformer and Irish reformers. "In the Irish Land League cause," he declared, "the best men were the women." George visited Ireland and toured Great Britain as a whole in 1881–82 and 1883–84. It was not just the tenancy and mass misery of Ireland that made George relevant. In a nation where only 360 people owned one-quarter of the land in all of England and Wales, and 350 landowners had possessed two-thirds of Scotland in 1873, George could hardly be ignored. The respectable press far more often attacked and vilified George than it praised him, but he realized vilification was a sign that the British had to take him seriously. Denunciation provided publicity for his ideas, and he drew large, often adoring, crowds. Sidney Webb, who was a socialist, credited George, who was not, with reinvigorating British socialism.[44]

Howells's ability to feel both crimson and dull purple on his return to the United States reflected the ferment in American politics and religion and the cracking of liberal orthodoxy's hold on respectable opinion. Popular radicals like George, Christian reformers who embraced the Social Gospel, the new social scientists in expanding American universities, all made men like Godkin seem old-fashioned and intellectuals like Sumner isolated and besieged. The liberal tide was ebbing faster and faster.

III

Howells agonized over the industrial United States that greeted him on his return for quite personal as well as intellectual and moral reasons. In 1880 Howells's sixteen-year-old daughter, Winnie—vibrant, charming, attractive, and the apple of her father's eye—had fallen ill in the way so many Gilded Age women, and men, fell ill. She quite suddenly could not cross a room unaided. She had to drop out of school. Winnie became sick the same year that George Miller Beard published *American Nervousness*. He created a new word—"neurasthenia"—to describe what he thought was a new phenomenon, "lack of nerve force." Its symptoms were baffling and various, a desire for excitement and stimulation coupled with fears that ranged from fears of being alone to fears of being afraid, to "fear of everything." Charlotte Perkins Gilman, whose story "The Yellow Wall-

44. Rodgers, 35–36, 70–71; Brundage, 114–19; Rose, 86–89, 97–109.

Paper" captured the disease, was also its victim. It consisted, she wrote in her *Autobiography*, "of every painful sensation, shame, fear, remorse, a blind oppressive confusion, utter weakness, a steady brain-ache that fills the conscious mind with crowding image of distress." The end and defining result was the paralysis of the will that afflicted Winnie.[45]

The cause, doctors agreed, was modern life itself: its barrage of information, noise, and distraction, its luxuries, and its constant demands. It unmanned men and defeminized women, leaving both men and women "overcivilized": nervous, artificial, weak, and detached from real emotion and vital experience. The introspection of Reformation Protestantism, once devoted to monitoring the soul and the chances of salvation, had turned morbid and transmuted into mere self-obsession. Gilman noted the significant aspect of her own case. She was, in effect, allergic to the home. Although she loved her husband and child, she "saw the stark fact—that I was well while away and sick while at home."[46]

Neurasthenia seemed to denote a failure of character. Character mattered to Victorians, and it mattered to Howells, in his writing, his politics, and his life, even though his thinking about character was contradictory. As a literary critic and novelist, he connected characters with "character." Good fiction showed how the fates of a novel's characters grew from their character and revealed the working of immutable moral law. Such immutable laws meant history did not matter except as local color. Historical facts, as one of his characters said, "oughtn't to matter" because moral law was the same at all times and all places. History didn't change the essential things: human nature and moral law. Everyone, everywhere, at all times marched to the same drummer. Yet as an emerging realist, Howells believed that characters—recognizable human beings, real people—should drive fiction. The plot should unfold from their everyday struggles in recognizable times and places. Howells carefully captured the tumultuous contemporary history of the Gilded Age because writers had to get particular historical worlds right to make their characters' lives and struggles real. The tension between Howells the realist, who wanted to portray his society accurately and fully, and Howells the wavering liberal, for whom morality was a matter of immutable law, became visible in his writing.[47]

45. W. D. Howells to Anne H. Frechette, Aug. 14, 1881, in Howells, *Selected Letters*, 2: 293. Lynn, 252; Charlotte Perkins Gilman, *"The Yellow Wall-Paper" by Charlotte Perkins Gilman: A Dual-Text Critical Edition*, ed. Shawn St. Jean (Athens: Ohio University Press, 2006), 90; Lears, 50; Charlotte Perkins Gilman, *The Living of Charlotte Perkins Gilman: An Autobiography* (Madison: University of Wisconsin Press, 1990, orig. ed. 1935), 90.
46. Gilman, *The Living of Charlotte Perkins Gilman*, 95; Lears, 48–50.
47. Livingston, 134–37.

Howells held his life to the standards of his fiction; he felt obligated to display character, and this would make his crimson opinions redder and redder as the decade wore on. Small things nagged at him when they revealed his lack of character. In 1884 "shabby motives" led him to call the police to evict people sitting on his back fence to get a better view of rowers racing on the Back Bay. He condemned himself for, in a small way, upholding the rights of property against the small pleasures of ordinary people.[48]

For J. P. Morgan, the New York banker escaping the shadow of his father in the 1880s, upholding the rights of property was nothing to be ashamed of; it was a mark of character. At the end of the era, Morgan said that the basis of the whole financial system was character. Character was not morality. A man of character might be dissipated, lie, cheat, steal, and either order or condone deeds punishable by time in a penitentiary, but he did not do those things to his friends. Friendship depended on character; friends were loyal and keepers of bargains (whenever possible). They did not talk outside of school. This was why Collis P. Huntington could consider his political friend Roscoe Conkling a man of character, even as he asked Conkling to give him public goods in exchange for private favors. Character existed in a network of friends who judged it and sustained it. Having character meant being someone whom J. P. Morgan could trust.[49]

Morgan's idea of character repulsed Howells, but in the early 1880s Howells himself could have been mistaken for a Boston banker; he still seemed the kind of conventional figure whom Morgan could trust. When called on to translate his evolving beliefs into politics, he lingered in Cambridge to be able to vote against Ben Butler, who was seeking a second term as governor of Massachusetts on the Democratic ticket in 1883. Butler, pursuing his own idiosyncratic, opportunistic, and corrupt version of reform politics, would run on the Greenback ticket for president in 1884.[50]

By the mid-1880s, despite the social ferment and new ideas, intelligent men still thought American politics could be reduced to a simple matter of character. Liberals, in particular, bereft of other ways of ordering

48. William Alexander, *William Dean Howells, the Realist as Humanist* (New York: B. Franklin, 1981), 31–44.

49. Susie Pak, *Gentlemen Bankers: The World of J. P. Morgan* (Cambridge, MA: Harvard University Press, 2013), 1–16; R. White, 102–3, 166–17; Sven Beckert, *The Monied Metropolis: New York City and the Consolidation of the American Bourgeoisie, 1850–1896* (Cambridge, MA: Cambridge University Press, 2001), 237–72.

50. W. D. Howells to W. C. Howells, Nov. 4, 1883, in Howells, *Selected Letters*, 3: 80, 81.

American politics, fell back on character. In 1884 national politics had reached low tide. The epic efforts to reconstruct the South and West according to the old free labor vision had largely ended. The economy had suffered through its second major postwar downturn. For more than a decade, recession and depression had been far more prevalent than prosperity. Both Civil War generations—those already mature when the war began and those who reached adulthood with the war—were aging. Even most whites who survived the ravages of early childhood would barely see sixty. Black life spans were far shorter. Civil War veterans retained great moral authority, and they regularly wielded it against younger men untested in battle, but that moral authority did not elevate politics. Scandal and corruption had proved pervasive and nearly constant.

Seen through the newspapers, American life seemed to unfold like the kind of bad Victorian novel Howells had come to detest, but could not quite shake, full of suffering and redemption. Ulysses S. Grant remained the face of the older Civil War generation. The years since the war had largely been a study in his weaknesses and limits, and in 1884 these became tragic. Grant and his wife, Julia, did not just want to be rich; they thought they deserved to be rich. Grant had always been susceptible to the flattery of the wealthy and was a little uncertain about the sources of the vast new fortunes that arose even in the midst of depression. In the early 1880s, through the gifts of rich admirers and investments, the Grants thought they had at last achieved their desire. Outside of their homes, the Grants' wealth, like most new wealth, was paper: stocks, bonds, and promissory notes.

The Grants' fortune arose largely through the firm of Ward & Grant. Ferdinand Ward, the son of a minister, hailed from upstate New York. His inattentive partner was Grant's son Buck, who had made money in western mining speculations using his father's political connections and the geological knowledge of Ward's brother. Ward was running what would later be called a Ponzi scheme; in an economy with falling returns on investment, he delivered dividends and annuities that seemed too good to be true. They were.[51]

Ward had hung the horns of a Texas Longhorn in his Wall Street office to symbolize the bull market that would carry him and clients to prosperity. It was not the wisest choice of symbols. Ward imitated the methods of western cattlemen, and he would reap similar results. He hypothecated the same securities repeatedly to secure multiple loans and then used

51. Geoffrey C. Ward, *A Disposition to Be Rich: How a Small-Town Pastor's Son Ruined an American President, Brought on a Wall Street Crash, and Made Himself the Best-Hated Man in the United States* (New York: Knopf, 2012), 146–69.

some to pay interest on others. The debt ballooned, but as long the interest and dividends were paid, only Ward showed much interest in how the money was secured. He depended on new loans and new investors. He joined Grant's poker games, and the other players, including Conkling, invested with Ward & Grant. Thomas Nast, the cartoonist who had championed Grant, invested his life savings. Some of these investors were politically sophisticated, but they combined financial ignorance with the almost painfully innocent greed of the Grants. Others sensed what was going on but thought they could calculate when to get out.

In May 1884, the whole scheme collapsed. Ward & Grant failed; the Marine National Bank, a key instrument in Ward's duplicity, shut its doors. Ulysses S. Grant considered himself a millionaire the morning of the crash. By evening the $80 he had in his pocket and the $130 Julia had with her represented all their liquid assets. He kept his houses, and William Vanderbilt would forgive a large loan, but otherwise he had lost nearly everything. Ferdinand Ward fled, was caught, tried, and imprisoned.[52]

In the summer of 1884, Grant's omnipresent cigars caught up with him. The taciturn general bit into a peach, swallowed, and screamed in pain. He had throat cancer and was dying, but he retained the fierce determination that had seen him through the Civil War. Grant made his last year his finest hour since the war's conclusion. He set out to write his memoirs— *The Personal Memoirs of U. S. Grant*—in order to provide for his family after he died. With the help of Mark Twain, who published them, he did so. His *Memoirs*—whose conclusion begins, "The cause of the great War of the Rebellion against the United States will have to be attributed to slavery"—remain one of the finest memoirs of the Civil War. In July 1885 he wrote a kind of literary memorandum to himself: "I think I am a verb instead of a personal pronoun. A verb is anything that signifies to be, to do, or to suffer. I signify all three." Fortunately, he ran out of time to write about his presidency. On July 23, 1885, with his family around him, he died. Twain, as well as Julia Grant, did very well by the *Memoirs*.[53]

Both Mark Twain and Henry James were close friends with Howells, and Grant became the most unlikely member of a literary renaissance sparked by writers whose best work came with middle age. Twain published *Huckleberry Finn*, Howells published *The Rise of Silas Lapham*, and Henry James published *The Bostonians*. All embraced a naturalism that represented bold steps away from sentimental fiction. The *Century*, which descended from the older *Scribner's Monthly*, serialized Twain,

---

52. R. White, 479; Ward, 168–223, 169–71.
53. William S. McFeely, *Grant: A Biography* (New York: Norton, 1981), 495–517; Ron Powers, *Mark Twain: A Life* (New York: Free Press, 2005), 500–504.

Howells, and James in 1884 and early 1885. Its editor, Richard Watson Gilder, was forty and part of the younger Civil War generation, and his magazine in its sweep and circulation of about 130,000 in the 1880s dwarfed the *Atlantic Monthly*, from which Howells had resigned.[54]

Grant and Howells converged in another way. Grant's last days would be about character, and they aptly converged with the theme of Howells's *The Rise of Silas Lapham*. It detailed the rise of a Yankee businessman, his fall, and moral redemption. It was typical of Howell's fiction, at once closely observed and yet willing to suppress much of what might disturb his Brahmin neighbors and friends. In the book version he deleted passages that some *Century* readers and his editor had found objectionable. In the end, Lapham did not fall victim to his ambitions, actions, and vices; they were aberrations. He had character, and it saved him. But his salvation was the problem. Howells very much admired Leo Tolstoy, and his admiration sprang in part from Tolstoy's refusal in *Anna Karenina* to redeem or rescue his eponymous character. This Howells could not or would bring himself to do in *Silas Lapham*. In Russian novels, figures like Lapham met their doom, the product of their own flaws and actions. Lapham escaped, and because of his escape, the book's ending failed. Character seemed but an excuse to avoid the severity and tragedies of life.[55]

The *Century*, for all its embrace of the new, was also a literary haven for liberals such as Wayne MacVeagh. He was a leading Republican liberal and the man who had headed the commission that turned Louisiana over to the Democrats in 1877. His activities touched both the black Henry Adams, whom his commission doomed and betrayed, as well as the patrician Henry Adams, who was MacVeagh's friend. MacVeagh became Garfield's attorney general, serving with James G. Blaine in Garfield's brief cabinet. In the March 1884 issue of the *Century* he wrote an article, "The Next Presidency." Looked at from one angle, it was a collection of liberal homilies. Looked at from another, it accurately recognized the ebbing passions of the Civil War. Looked at from yet another, it was deeply obtuse, mistaking what was the eye of a hurricane for the passing of the storm. Most significantly, MacVeagh, like other liberals, misunderstood American governance.[56]

---

54. Powers, 486–87.
55. Alexander, 34–44; "Editor's Study," April 1886, in William Dean Howells, *Editor's Study*, ed. James W. Simpson (Troy, NY: Whitston, 1983), 16–20; William Dean Howells, *The Rise of Silas Lapham* (New York: Signet, 1963, orig. edition, 1885).
56. Chalfant, 478–79; Wayne MacVeagh, "The Next Presidency," *The Century* 27, no. 5 (1884): 670–77.

MacVeagh thought that voters were apathetic about the coming election because there were no great issues left in American politics, and government had little relevance to their lives. Municipal government, he proclaimed, was simply a matter of character and administration, which meant taking it away from the parties and the machines and handing it over to experts. The disenfranchisement of the freedmen was not a cause of concern because nobody could seriously believe that "the civil government of great industrial States, such as the Southern states are rapidly becoming could be widely intrusted to the least intelligent of their people." With the country supposedly resolved on civil service reform, voters should ignore party platforms and old loyalties and vote on the basis of the past careers and personal characteristics of the nominee. In a statement that seemed to come hurtling out of the early republic, he declared that the president "must not have sought the nomination, nor must he have shown after his nomination what [Yale] President Woolsey so aptly called 'a most uncommon anxiety' for his election, for he must be without friends to reward, and without enemies to punish." He "must be not only an honest man, but he must be a cause of honesty in others."[57]

Honesty was a serious issue. Recognizing corruption proved easy enough—it became a national sport, a source of amusement and disgust—but figuring out how to attack it proved more difficult. Even though he wrote one of era's most famous political satires, his novel *Democracy*, Henry Adams complained that "the grossest satires on the American Senator and politician never failed to excite the laughter and applause of every audience. Rich and poor joined in throwing contempt on their own representatives." As Adams noted, "society laughed a vacant and meaningless derision over its own failure." At the end of the period, Mark Twain wrote, "that there is no distinctly native American criminal class except Congress." He would add, "The political and commercial morals of the United States are not merely food for laughter, they are an entire banquet."[58]

When as MacVeagh said there was no issue except honesty, he and other Mugwumps and liberals meant that there was no real issue except civil service reform. He located dishonesty in political machines and

57. Chalfant, 478–79; MacVeagh, 670–77.
58. Henry Adams, *The Education of Henry Adams: An Autobiography* (New York: Heritage Press, 1942, orig. ed. 1918), 253–54; Mark Twain, *Following the Equator, a Journey around the World* (New York: Harper & Bros., 1906), 98; Twain, *Mark Twain in Eruption: Hitherto Unpublished Pages About Men and Events*, ed. Bernard Augustine De Voto, 3rd ed. (New York: Harper, 1940), 81.

patronage rather than in the fee-based nature of the offices themselves. If appointment to office — whether fee-based or salaried — could be wrested away from politicians and be made subject to exams, then the result would be an efficient, streamlined bureaucracy whose members would have secure tenure so long as they performed their jobs well. As with the gold standard and free trade, liberals sought a single overarching reform to produce a minimal, but efficient and expert, government, removed from the direct control of elected officials. That reform was the Pendleton Civil Service Act of 1883.[59]

The Pendleton Act enjoyed bipartisan support. The tight elections of 1876 and 1880 and the prospect of a Democratic administration had given Republicans incentive to agree to civil service reform, which might protect at least some of their office holders from immediate dismissal. The system had, in any case, become unwieldy, demanding the time of Congress despite the actual control of offices being in the hands of local machines. The assassination of Garfield had made public pressure irresistible. The Pendleton Act created a salaried Civil Service Commission to replace the old U.S. Civil Service Commission, which had been defunded in the Grant administration. It was to craft exams for the selection of officials in certain classified government positions. The Pendleton Act also prohibited contributions from office holders, thus choking off a key conduit of patronage.[60]

The results were not what reformers intended. Rarely has a law so failed to achieve its stated objectives while creating a set of unanticipated consequences. The Pendleton Act initially affected only a relatively few "classified" federal appointments — about 10 percent — which were merit-based and required successful passage of an exam. It, however, did expand relatively quickly. Within five years of passage, half of federal appointments

59. Jerry L. Mashaw, *Creating the Administrative Constitution: The Lost One Hundred Years of American Administrative Law* (New Haven, CT: Yale University Press, 2012), 236–38.

60. Ronald N. Johnson, *The Federal Civil Service System and the Problem of Bureaucracy: The Economics and Politics of Institutional Change*, ed. Gary D. Libecap (Chicago: University of Chicago Press, 1994), 12–29; Charts, "Removals By Year" and "Types of Removal," in Scott C. James, "Patronage Regimes and American Party Development from 'the Age of Jackson' to the Progressive Era," *British Journal of Political Science* 36 (2006), 39–60; Mashaw, 238–40; "Federal Administration and Administrative Law in the Gilded Age," *Yale Law Journal* 119, no. 7 (2010): 1389–92; "Transcript of Pendleton Act: An Act to Regulate and Improve the Civil Service of the United States," ed. National Archives and Records Administration (1883), https://www.ourdocuments.gov/doc.php?doc=48; Ari Hoogenboom, *Outlawing the Spoils: A History of the Civil Service Reform Movement 1865–1883* (Urbana: University of Illinois Press, 1968), 236–52.

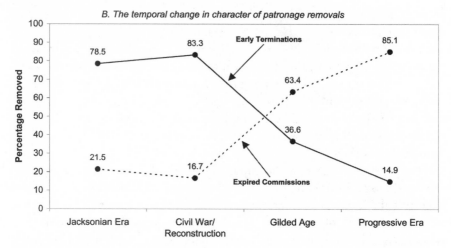

This Graph of Temporal Change in Character of Patronage Removal Across Four Periods shows the minimal effect civil service legislation had in halting the patronage system. Political opponents were still removed from office, but instead of being fired, they were let go when their commissions expired. The results were the same. From Scott C. James, "Patronage Regimes and American Party Development from 'The Age of Jackson' to the Progressive Era," *British Journal of Political Science* 36, no. 1 (2006): 10.

outside the Post Office fell within the scope of the act, although not until the twentieth century would 80 percent of federal appointees achieve civil service status. The act had a loophole that allowed bureau and division chiefs to hire whomever they wanted for positions above the test-passing line. The act thus transferred political power as well as social power to those chiefs. Nor did patronage vanish; it took up residence in new places. The states did not immediately follow Congress's lead; most did not begin to institute civil service until the twentieth century.[61]

The ultimate goal of the Pendleton Act was to create a bureaucracy separate from partisan governments whose members would enjoy uninterrupted tenure in their offices so long as they performed their duties, but the act utterly failed to achieve this during the late nineteenth and early twentieth centuries, except in the smaller technical and professional agencies. Instead, it created a nonpartisan gloss on a persistent partisan system. Presidents continued to replace members of the opposing party with members of their own; they just did it differently. After the passage of the Pendleton Act, removal from office did not appreciably decline in

61. Nicholas R. Parrillo, *Against the Profit Motive: The Salary Revolution in American Government, 1780–1940* (New Haven, CT: Yale University Press, 2013), 379 n. 24.

periods of party turnover; indeed it sometimes increased. Before the Pendleton Act new presidents had dismissed officials from office as soon as their own terms began; after the passage of the act they did not resort to early terminations. Instead they waited until officials' terms expired and then replaced them. Since most terms ran for four years, commencing with the beginning of a new administration, the net result was that officials served a few months longer than they would have without the act. Presidents could, however, use the act to protect holders of new offices, whom they appointed late in their administration. Their successors would be stuck with them until the appointee's term of office expired.[62]

The relative ineffectuality of the act extended its reach. Not reappointing office holders achieved the same results as firing them. And since the act could be turned to actually enhancing the protection given some patronage employees, there was little sense in spending political capital opposing an act that had popular support. More and more offices came under the act without changing the pattern of partisan dismissal.[63]

The Pendleton Act did change the financing of political campaigns. With federal officials prohibited from contributing to political campaigns, a major source of financing for the national parties dried up. There is no denying the corruption of the old system, but turning to corporate and wealthy donors hardly seemed a turn for the better.

The Pendleton Act failed, but reformers launched a grinding piecemeal assault on what was a larger problem: fee-based governance. Popular opposition to fee-based governance arose not from hostility to patronage but instead from anger at corruption, favoritism, and abuse of power. Reformers regarded lawful fees as the inevitable gateway to unlawful fees and exactions. Fee-hunting officials abused their offices and raised the cost of services. Even when they were not overtly dishonest, they paid attention largely to those parts of their job with the most lucrative fees. The cure was to replace fees with salaries, and efforts to do so began well before the Pendleton Act and continued well after it. Reform took place at the local, state, and federal levels.[64]

62. Mashaw, "Federal Administration and Administrative Law in the Gilded Age," *Yale Law Journal* 119 (2010): 1389–92; Mashaw, *Creating the Administrative Constitution*, 239–40; Charts, "Removals by Year" and "Types of Removal," in James, 48–50; Daniel P. Carpenter, *The Forging of Bureaucratic Autonomy: Reputations, Networks, and Policy Innovation in Executive Agencies, 1862–1928* (Princeton, NJ: Princeton University Press, 2001), 95; Johnson, 12–29.

63. Johnson, 12–29; Mashaw, "Federal Administration and Administrative Law in the Gilded Age," 1389–92; James, 39–60.

64. Parrillo, 18, 117, 183–294.

The attack on corruption and fee-based governance did not create the equivalent of Europe's centralized, hierarchical bureaucracies insulated from the popular will, but changes in administrative law and practice did gradually create much more bureaucratic autonomy. Between 1862 and 1888, Congress created as many new bureaus and departments as had existed in the country's previous history. The list of major additions were impressive: the Department of Agriculture, created in 1862 and raised to cabinet rank in 1889; the Department of Justice (1870); and a Department of Labor, without cabinet rank, in 1888. In addition there was a Department of Education (1867), subsequently abolished and its functions moved to the Interior Department. Congress staffed these departments and new bureaus with salaried personnel. The country doubled its population between 1861 and 1891, but the number of people employed by the government quadrupled. These departments could not dictate their allocations, but they by and large did control the disposition of the funds that Congress gave them.[65]

These new bureaus eventually fell within the Pendleton Act without being products of the act. They created internal procedures that allowed them to function as bureaucracies. They gathered data, supervised state-sponsored activities, and formulated rules about them. They had discretion over how they spent their funds, and they were also in charge of formulating the rules to enforce broad powers, which stretched from auditing railroad accounts to stopping the spread of communicable animal diseases such as Texas fever, to banning any substance "made in imitation or semblance of butter" that might threaten public health. Disputes over pensions, land claims, customs duties, and more were adjudicated within government agencies and created new categories of administrative law. The Pension Bureau was not able to get salaried surgeons to rule on disability cases, but it did succeed in tightening up the process of examinations. All of this created significant administrative discretion, which the courts upheld as early as 1868 in *Gaines v. Thompson*.[66]

The Post Office and USDA demonstrated that there was no single route to bureaucratic autonomy. Beginning in the 1880s, the USDA gradually moved from an agency that existed to distribute seeds to farmers to one that regarded itself as composed of scientists responsible not just for

65. Mashaw, *Creating the Administrative Constitution*, 232–33, 240, 256–77; Mashaw, "Federal Administration and Administrative Law in the Gilded Age," 1375–78, 1395–97, 1459; Peter Zavodnyik, *The Rise of the Federal Colossus: The Growth of Federal Power from Lincoln to F.D.R.* (Santa Barbara, CA: Praeger, 2011), 147, 321, Balogh, 314.

66. Mashaw, *Creating the Administrative Constitution*, 240–44, 254–55; Mashaw, "Federal Administration and Administrative Law in the Gilded Age," 1398–99, 1416–17, 1430–39.

research but for forging policy based on that research. Its strength came from expertise and from the creation of networks that gave skilled bureaucrats connections and reputations that made them hard to ignore. The process was uneven and would suffer setbacks. Still, by the 1890s the Chemistry Division studied and then attacked food adulteration, and both the Division of Forestry and the Biological Survey became the domain of scientists who carved out semi-independent domains. The Railway Mail Service began inside the Post Office in the 1860s and 1870s and achieved considerable professional autonomy. In the 1890s, the Post Office built on the success of the Railway Mail Service and centralized its operations, created a corps of postal inspectors, and began to generate its own programs and reforms, the most sweeping of which—rural free delivery—began in 1896. When regulatory legislation and this new administrative capacity converged, a far more powerful government would result.[67]

IV

MacVeagh was wrong about the direction of governance, wrong about the issue in the election of 1884 being honesty and character, and most spectacularly wrong about the indifference of the public. When the parties produced their nominees and the campaign began, it seemed that MacVeagh had been describing another country. To the surprise of virtually everyone (including Chester A. Arthur), Arthur had turned out, at least by Gilded Age standards, to be a reasonably competent president. He signed the Pendleton Act knowing that it gave him cover as a reformer. He had modified the tariff in a compromise that created the "Mongrel Tariff," and assented to laws restricting Chinese immigration. The reforms were modest. They were meant to defuse issues that threatened the Republican Party, and this, particularly in the West, they for the moment achieved.

Arthur reasonably thought that his success in protecting the Republicans would make him the Republican nominee for president, but instead the party chose Blaine, still leader of the Half-Breeds and master of the minutiae of American politics. He had been out of office since Arthur had accepted his resignation as secretary of state following Garfield's assassination. It was a mark of both his political ability and the corruption of the Gilded Age that Blaine's well-known and eager involvement in the railroad scandals of the 1860s and 1870s did not bar him from consideration for the presidency. His ardent enemies took Blaine's denials of guilt as

67. Carpenter, 76–83, 94–103, 179–211.

lies, as they were, and his equally ardent friends accepted them. "James G. Blaine's audacity, good humor, horror of rebel brigadiers, and contempt for reformers," E. L. Godkin wrote, "made his nomination sooner or later inevitable." New blood—Henry Cabot Lodge of Massachusetts, Theodore Roosevelt of New York, and William McKinley of Ohio—were at the Republican convention, but this was still the Republican Party of the receding Civil War generations. In 1884 Blaine's year came at last. The ebbing tide had exposed the detritus of the last twenty years, and Blaine bulked largest among the wrecks.[68]

Blaine pushed men like MacVeagh toward the Democrats, who nominated Grover Cleveland. Among his rivals for the nomination was Stephen Field. Field was a Californian and a Supreme Court justice widely hated in California. Field, while riding circuit had already ruled on the cases that would eventually make up *Santa Clara County v. Southern Pacific Railroad Company* (1886). Antimonopolists regarded him as a thoroughly corrupt tool of the railroads, and there are good reasons to believe this, but he was also the most influential interpreter of the Fourteenth Amendment. Field brought the Fourteenth Amendment to the defense of corporate personhood, but in a much more limited way than later courts would interpret it. His intent seems to have been to expand the power of the Supreme Court to strike down what he considered invasions of liberty, particularly freedom of contract, by state governments. He did not extend the due process and privileges and immunities clauses to corporate persons.[69]

Field would rather have been president than a justice of the Supreme Court, but California antimonopolists killed his presidential ambitions in 1884. He hated them in turn, regarding them as "agrarian and communistic" and desiring "to break down all associated capital by loading it with unequal and oppressive burdens." The Supreme Court's ruling and later interpretations, or misinterpretations, of Field's ruling lay in the future, but antimonopolists recognized that by weakening the distinctions between corporate persons and natural persons he had created a dangerously slippery slope. California Governor George Stoneman objected that the conflation of corporate persons with actual living and breathing citizens was both illogical and unjust. He argued that the state had a right

68. George H. Mayer, *The Republican Party, 1854–1964* (New York: Oxford University Press, 1964), 207–9; Lewis L. Gould, *Grand Old Party: A History of the Republicans* (New York: Random House, 2003), 99–100.

69. Ruth Bloch and Naomi R. Lamoreaux, "Corporations and the Fourteenth Amendment," paper in author's possession, 9–10; Paul Kens, *Justice Stephen Field: Shaping Liberty from the Gold Rush to the Gilded Age* (Lawrence: University Press of Kansas, 1997), 242–46.

to distinguish between "the natural person…who is part of the Government" and the "artificial person, which is but a creature of the Government."[70]

Cleveland, a man celebrated for his honesty, easily shoved Field aside, but an election MacVeagh believed would be based on character soon became comic. Cleveland had, or accepted that he very likely might have, fathered a son out of wedlock. He initially supported the child and the mother, but then arranged to have the boy adopted. This led to the Republican campaign chant: "Ma, Ma, where's my Pa?" The Democrats resurrected Blaine's corrupt dealing with the railroads. Joseph Pulitzer used his cartoonists to caricature Blaine week after week on the *New York World's* front page. When MacVeagh said there were no real issues but honesty, this was not what he had in mind. Henry Adams, who hated Blaine, came to enjoy the campaign: "When I am not angry, I can do nothing but laugh."[71]

Most liberals were not laughing. Appalled by the candidates, they had surplus anger to devote to each other. Some — Howells, King, and Hay, for example — remained loyal to the Republicans and were bitter at their friends (Godkin, Schurz, MacVeagh, the Adams brothers) who supported Cleveland. Clarence King privately denounced the Adamses, Henry and Clover, for being "fastidious moralists" who were foisting a "grovelling ignoramus" on the country. Howells wrote that he would vote "for a man *accused* of bribery," but he would not "vote for a man *guilty* of what society sends a woman to hell for." Howells was nearly a caricature of Victorians in regard to sex; he used to hide copies of Emile Zola's novels to keep them from his children. His reaction to Cleveland greatly amused Mark Twain: "To see grown men, apparently in their right mind, seriously arguing against a bachelor's fitness for President because he has had private intercourse with a consenting widow!"[72]

Usually a quarrel among liberals had little effect on a national election, but by 1884 the parties were exquisitely balanced. The Republicans were brittle and quarrelsome; the inability to protect black Southern voters had crippled their chances for national popular majorities. Although they maintained pluralities in every region of the North and West, they lost overwhelmingly in the South. In key Northern states, their margins were

70. Kens, 242–46; R. Hal Williams, *Democratic Party and California Politics, 1880–1896* (Stanford, CA: Stanford University Press, 1973), 31–41.
71. Charles W. Calhoun, *Minority Victory: Gilded Age Politics and the Front Porch Campaign of 1888* (Lawrence: University Press of Kansas, 2008), 23–24; Chalfant, 483–84.
72. Chalfant, 484; Hay to Howells, Sep., 16, 1884, in Hay, *John Hay–Howells Letters*, 82; Lynn, 278–79; W. D. Howells to Thomas Perry, Aug. 15, 1884, W. D. Howells to W. C. Howells, Nov. 9, 1884, in Howells, *Selected Letters*, 3: 107–8, 113.

slim enough that they were vulnerable to defections or lowered turnouts. In 1884, even liberal intellectuals mattered, particularly in New York.[73]

President Arthur's and the Republicans' endorsement of the anti-Chinese legislation helped restore California and Nevada to the GOP. Carrying the West maintained the Republican majority in the Senate, just as the Democrats' hold on the South gave them control of the House. The presidential election would come down to New Jersey, Connecticut, Indiana, and New York. Both parties waged what was the last of the full-fledged national "hurrah" campaigns, which were less about issues than stimulating party, ethnic, sectional, and religious loyalties and ensuring turnout. Ultimately, the candidate who won New York would carry the election.[74]

The Republicans were vulnerable in New York, and Blaine initially cultivated the Irish vote knowing that detaching even a small number of Catholic Irish could make the difference in the election. Cleveland's rocky relations with Tammany, which endeared him to liberals, made this seem possible, but Honest John Kelly was not about to cut off his nose to spite his face. Sending Cleveland to Washington was preferable to having him in Albany. In support of Cleveland, Godkin, who by 1884 also edited the *New York Post*, adopted a tactic used against Greeley in 1872. Blaine, over the course of a long career, had made many contradictory statements on many things. Godkin took to printing them in adjoining columns.[75]

Blaine, for all his cultivation of the Irish, suffered a fit of inattention when, at a meeting with Protestant clergy, he let pass a denunciation of the Democrats as the party of "Rum, Romanism, and Rebellion." The Democrats seized on it. Blaine did himself no favors by the same day attending a dinner with his millionaire backers, including the usually reclusive Jay Gould, at Delmonico's. Pulitzer, himself a millionaire, festooned the *World's* front page with a cartoon, "The Royal Feast of Belshazzar Blaine and the Money Kings." In the foreground, a poor family begged for

73. Paul Kleppner, *The Third Electoral System, 1853–1892: Parties, Voters, and Political Cultures* (Chapel Hill: University of North Carolina Press, 1979), 298–99; in 1884, however, Blaine made a credible showing in West Virginia, Virginia, and Tennessee; Charles W. Calhoun, *Conceiving a New Republic: The Republican Party and the Southern Question, 1869–1900* (Lawrence: University Press of Kansas, 2006), 207; Mayer, 211.

74. Daniel Klinghard, *The Nationalization of American Political Parties, 1880–1896* (Cambridge: Cambridge University Press, 2010), 49–57; Mayer, 209–10.

75. Mayer, 208–12; Chalfant, 479, 483–84; Steven K. Green, *The Second Disestablishment: Church and State in Nineteenth-Century America* (New York: Oxford University Press, 2010), 296; Mark W. Summers, *Party Games: Getting, Keeping, and Using Power in Gilded Age Politics* (Chapel Hill: University of North Carolina Press, 2004), 205–6.

THE ROYAL FEAST OF BELSHAZZAR BLAINE AND THE MONEY KINGS.

Walt McDougall's cartoon "The Royal Feast of Belshazzar Blaine and the Money Kings," appeared in Joseph Pulitzer's *New York World* on October 30, 1884. It skewered the Republican presidential candidate, James G. Blaine, for attending a lavish banquet with plutocrats at Delmonico's, the famous New York City restaurant. A poor family begs for scraps. The Ohio State University Billy Ireland Cartoon Library and Museum.

food. "Mammon's Homage," the headline read. Pulitzer identified the leading men at the banquet—Gould, Carnegie, John Jacob Astor, Chauncey Depew, H. M. Flagler, D. O. Mills, Cyrus Field, and the rest—with Wall Street, with New York and California banks, with monopoly, and with inequity. They were reigning figures of American finance and corporate capitalism.[76]

The menu, which became a campaign document circulated by the Democrats, was actually relatively restrained for Delmonico's, certainly less extravagant than the dinner for the Democratic nominee Winfield Scott Hancock in 1880. American cooking no longer, as Europeans reported earlier in the century, offended every sense but hearing. In New York, at least, Americans were open to trying different cuisines, but chefs at Delmonico's did not just bring French cooking to the United States; they garnished it with American excess. Blaine's banquet proceeded relentlessly from oysters, through seafood soups, hors d'oeuvres, three kinds of fish, beef, sorbet, fowl, and desserts. It was certainly restrained compared with the artificial lakes and swimming swans that sometimes graced society dinners at the restaurant. Even the diners looked avian, with the

76. "The Royal Feast of Belshazzar," *New York World*, Oct. 31, 1884; Mayer, 211–12.

women adorned in their feathers and the tuxedoed male diners looking like so many cigar-smoking penguins.[77]

The course before dessert captured the age. The Ortolan is a small bunting, similar to a finch. The songbirds weigh less than an ounce, but when confined to a lightless box they will gorge on millet, grapes, and figs, increasing in size until they are four ounces of fat. Chefs drowned them in Armagnac, roasted them, and flambéed them. Diners ate them, innards and all.[78]

Cleveland carried New York by less than a thousand votes, and with it the election. The margin was so slight that analysts could plausibly credit his defeat to any—or all—of several causes. It could have been Conkling, who refused to campaign for Blaine, saying that although he was a lawyer, he did not "engage in criminal practice." Oneida County, the core of Conkling's constituency, had a two-thousand-vote Republican majority in 1880. In 1884, it went for Cleveland. But it could have been Pulitzer's cartoons or the Republican alienation of New York Catholics. The Democrats controlled the White House for the first time since the Civil War.[79]

Howells thought that with Cleveland's victory "A great cycle has come to a close; the rule of the best in politics for a quarter of a century is ended. Now we shall have the worst again." It was an astonishing opinion, both in its judgment on the last twenty years and its prediction that substituting a Democratic president for a series of largely ineffectual Republican presidents with a continuing divided Congress amounted to transformative change. The "best" of the Republican Party had been its insistence on protecting the rights of the freedpeople, but Blaine had refused to make repression in the South a campaign issue. He did so only after he had lost. "The course of affairs in the South," he declared, "has crushed out the political power of more than six million American citizens and has transferred by violence to others." This was certainly true, but it was not the ground on which the Republicans had fought.[80]

Cleveland was poorly prepared for the White House. Horace White, who had moved from Chicago and was editor of the *New York Evening Post*, interviewed him and found his grasp of national issues "extremely defective." The *New York Tribune's* Charles Nordhoff thought he was

77. Harvey A. Levenstein, *Revolution at the Table: The Transformation of the American Diet* (New York: Oxford University Press, 1988), 11–12, 14.

78. "Ortolans," in "The American Menu," http://www.theamericanmenu.com/2012/03/ortolans.html.

79. Jordan, 420–21; Calhoun, 207.

80. W. D. Howells to W. C. Howells, Nov. 9, 1884, in Howells, *Selected Letters*, 3: 113; Lynn, 278–79; Chalfant, 484; Calhoun, *Conceiving a New Republic*; 203–8.

"curiously ignorant of federal questions and politics." Vague promises of good government had won him office, but he would have to transform promises into policy and, Nordhoff wrote, he was "bound to have a troublesome time."[81]

Grover Cleveland was a liberal elected with the support of Mugwump Republicans, and his election made liberalism seem far more vigorous than it was. Liberalism looked antique and virtually incoherent in the nation's factories and cities, but it still retained life in Washington. Cleveland was for economy, honesty, efficiency, the gold standard, and tariff reduction. He saw the West as the hope of free labor and promised to make sure it was reserved for actual settlers, while Indians would be set on the road to "education and civilization...with a view to their ultimate citizenship." He promised to protect "the freedmen in their rights," a promise that reassured Frederick Douglass, but by the 1880s any promise made to the freedmen by Democrats was empty. There would not be a single Democratic vote for a civil rights bill for the rest of the century. Cleveland regarded black people, particularly Southern black people, as lazy and thriftless.[82]

V

In 1884 Howells voted for Blaine, an awkward vote for a man so devoted to character. Howells's politics still took a back seat to his writing and criticism, and his writing and criticism, he feared, took a back seat to his zeal for making the money necessary to support his house on the Back Bay near Oliver Wendell Holmes, Sr.; his desire to finance his ailing daughter Winnie's social debut in Boston society; and his need to help his aging father. His ideas on what literature should do had become ever clearer. He agreed with his friend Henry James that the main object of the novel was to represent life. Howells praised "simple naked humanness" in fiction, but James noted Howells's limits. His love of the "common, the immediate, the familiar and vulgar elements of life" made him unable to engage fully with the "surprising and incongruous." He was most at home in "the moderate, the optimistic, the domestic, and the democratic."[83]

81. Calhoun, *Minority Victory*, 32.
82. Richard E. Welch, *The Presidencies of Grover Cleveland* (Lawrence: University Press of Kansas, 1988), 48, 66–69.
83. W. D. Howells to John Hay, July 30, 1883, W. D. Howells to W. C. Howells, Nov. 4, 1883, W. D. Howells to E. W. Howe, Apr. 4, 1884, W. D. Howells to J. W. De Forest, Sep. 2, 1887, in Howells, *Selected Letters*, 3: 74–75, footnote 5, 80–81, 96, 195; Alexander, 61–62.

But Howells was becoming a man who, in his own words, "won't and can't keep on doing what's been done already." In 1886 he published *The Minister's Charge* and was dismayed by how quickly his critics took to "the genteel ground," attacking him for writing about common people with common lives. As he wrote Henry James, they reproached him "for introducing [them] to low company." He took it as a response to his "frankness about our civilization," the very thing James had wondered if Howells was capable of mustering. The attacks, which Howells thought approached personal defamation, demonstrated how easy it was to shock the newspaper reviewers and genteel readers. He took it as a mark of how the "very, very little culture and elegance with which our refined people have overlaid themselves seems to have hardened their hearts against the common people: they seem to despise and hate them." Howells criticized a liberal cultural project that had enshrined as gentility and good taste the very mediocrity and self-satisfaction that it was supposed to displace.[84]

Howells struck hard at the romance, delicacy, and uplift of the genteel project, and he scorned its refusal to deal with the realities that confronted the nation. His changing politics became part of his literary criticism. In January 1886 he had begun a monthly column, the "Editor's Study," for *Harper's Weekly*. The magazine paid him well for it. He had come late to reading Leo Tolstoy and Fyodor Dostoyevsky, but he now became their American champion and an ardent advocate of the literary realism they represented. His praise of Tolstoy's *Anna Karenina* encapsulated his gospel: "As you read on you say, not, 'This is like life,' but, 'This is life.'" The goal of the novel was "the True." But Tolstoy, he wrote privately, made Howells's own "pleasure in possession all spoiled." Tolstoy lived by an unchanging Christian moral law. He showed Howells "the utter selfishness and insufficiency of my past life," but he could not see how Tolstoy's solution—simple life in the country among the peasants—helped "except that it makes all poor alike, and saves one's self from remorse."[85]

Howells was turning fifty, and that seemed old to him. He did not "plan so largely" as he used to. His sister had just died of malaria, but his daughter Winnie, living with the neurasthenia that doctors could neither decipher nor cure, swung between hopeful improvement and heartbreaking decline. He had considerable expectations for his other two children, but life no longer seemed as rosy and expansive as it once did.[86]

84. Livingston, 134–37; W. D. Howells to H. James, Dec. 25. 1886, W. D. Howells to George Curtis, Feb. 27, 1887, in Howells, *Selected Letters*, 3: 174, 183.
85. "Editor's Study," April 1886, in *Editor's Study*, 16–20; W. D. Howells to W. C. Howells, Apr. 17, 1887, in *Selected Letters*, 3: 186.
86. W. D. Howells to H. James, Dec. 25. 1886, in ibid., 3: 174–76.

13

Dying for Progress

Nineteenth-century Americans were a sickly people. The decline of virtually every measure of physical well-being was at the heart of a largely urban Gilded Age environmental crisis that people recognized but could neither name nor fully understand. By the most basic standards—life span, infant death rate, and bodily stature, which reflected childhood health and nutrition—American life grew worse over the course of the nineteenth century. Although economists have insisted that real wages were rising during most of the Gilded Age, a people who celebrated their progress were, in fact, going backwards—growing shorter and dying earlier—until the 1890s. Real improvement would come largely in the twentieth century.[1]

The crisis began well before the Civil War and initially affected both rural and urban Americans; in the late nineteenth century it coincided with increasing urbanization. In the Gilded Age people living in most rural areas outside the South were comparatively healthier and lived longer lives, but in the cities the crisis intensified, producing a facsimile of war with a series of epidemic invasions and eruptions as well as a steady annual carnage that took a particular toll on the nation's infants and children. The diseases came through the air, in the water, and via insects. The losses were not simply an ancient and predictable toll. This was a decline from previous American standards, which were deteriorating toward those of Great Britain and France, slightly better by some criteria, worse by others.[2]

---

1. For basic data, Dora L. Costa, "Health and the Economy in the United States from 1750 to the Present," *Journal of Economic Literature* 53, no. 3 (2015): 507–13; Roderick Floud, Robert W. Fogel, Bernard Harris, and Sok Chul Hong, *The Changing Body: Health, Nutrition, and Human Development in the Western World since 1700* (Cambridge: Cambridge University Press, 2011), 297–98; the approach to this chapter is inspired by Mark Fiege, *The Republic of Nature: An Environmental History of the United States* (Seattle: University of Washington Press, 2012).

2. The crisis was not confined to the United States. Richard J. Evans, *Death in Hamburg: Society and Politics in the Cholera Years, 1830–1910* (Oxford: Clarendon Press, 1987), 110; Daniel Scott Smith, "Differential Mortality in the United States before 1900," *Journal of Interdisciplinary History* 13, no. 4 (1983): table 4, 758; Costa, 530–33.

Life Expectancy and Average Height

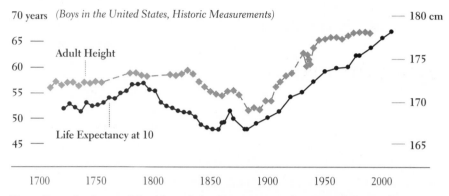

From Dora L. Costa, "Health and the Economy in the United States from 1750 to the Present," *Journal of Economic Literature* 53, no. 3 (2015): 507–13.

If economic growth translated directly into well-being, the crisis should not have happened. According to a crude economic logic, health is in large part a product of adequate nutrition and housing, which depend on income. As wealth rises, health and well-being should also rise. People should live longer and grow larger and stronger, and more of their children should survive to adulthood. Over most of the nineteenth century, despite a rising per capita income, this did not happen in the United States.[3]

Three major indexes take the measure of a calamity that afflicted human beings as well as their surroundings: average life expectancy at birth, average number of years left for a person who reached ten and twenty, and measures of adult height. All trended in the direction of trouble. These developments were not simply the result of shorter, sicker immigrants entering the country. Scholars have derived the basic data on height from sources that measured only the native-born.[4]

3. For discussion of early work on this, see Samuel H. Preston and Michael R. Haines, *Fatal Years: Child Mortality in Late Nineteenth-Century America* (Princeton, NJ: Princeton University Press, 1991), 51; for current theories, Costa, 507–13; Floud et al., 297–98; for real wages, Jeffrey G. Williamson, *Late Nineteenth-Century American Development: A General Equilibrium History* (London and New York: Cambridge University Press, 1974), 78, 98.

4. Nineteenth-century Americans saw parts of the picture, but no one could grasp its entirety because much of what is known about the crisis is retrospective: the product of historical statistics painstakingly culled from incomplete records. Historians who know how numbers are collected never put full faith in historical statistics. They are directions received thirdhand, their origins suspect. They are creatures of the suppositions needed to create them and the models that fill their gaps. Their sources have often been repurposed, surrogates for information not gathered. They are best treated

The average life expectancy of a white man dropped from the 1790s until the last decade of the nineteenth century. A slight uptick at midcentury proved fleeting; nor was it certain that the smaller rise in 1890 would be permanent. A clear trend toward longer lifespans for white men was not visible until the turn of the century. It would be well into the twentieth century before white American men achieved the average lifespans of late eighteenth-century New England men. Black men lagged far behind. What this added up to was that an average white ten-year-old American boy in 1880, born at the beginning of the Gilded Age and living through it, could expect to die at age forty-eight. His height would be 5 feet, 5 inches. He would be shorter and have a briefer life than his Revolutionary forebears.[5]

Ten-year-olds in 1880 were among the lucky ones since they had lived through early childhood, which were the most dangerous years. During the Gilded Age, the average American lifespan at birth was shorter than at twenty because so many children died in early childhood that a person reaching twenty had on average more years to live than an average baby did at birth. Infant mortality worsened after 1880 in many cities. In Pittsburgh it rose from 17.1 percent in 1875 to 20.3 percent in 1900. Between 1850 and 1890 the chances of an American white child dying before the age of five were often between 25 percent and 30 percent, with a sharp bump upward in 1880, the figure falling to around 20 percent by 1890. Existing figures for black children indicate they died in far greater numbers than white ones in comparable situations. Even Massachusetts, which was healthier than most regions and kept the best statistics, had an infant death rate of 118 per 1,000 in 1857, which would be exceeded every year except 1858 until 1912, peaking at 194 in 1872. Dramatic declines in childhood mortality awaited the twentieth century.[6]

Disease played the greatest role in the crisis, but over the course of time the leading killers changed. For most of the century tuberculosis was the

---

with skepticism. When these statistics all point in a similar direction, they are worthy of some attention. Floud et al., 298–99; J. David Hacker, "Decennial Life Tables for the White Population of the United States, 1790–1900," *Historical Methods* 43, no. 2 (April 2010), 45–79; Barry Muchnick, "Publics of Nature: Communities of Environmental Citizenship in the Progressive Era," paper at American Society for Environmental History (Seattle, 2016).

5. Table 1, in Michael R. Haines, "Estimated Life Tables for the United States," *Historical Methods* 31, no. 4 (1998): 154–55; Floud et al., 321; Hacker, 52, 55–56, 65; Costa, 503.
6. Robert J. Gordon, *The Rise and Fall of American Growth: The U.S. Standard of Living since the Civil War* (Princeton, NJ: Princeton University Press, 2016), 207–13; Costa, 515–16; S. J. Kleinberg, *The Shadow of the Mills: Working-Class Families in Pittsburgh, 1870–1907* (Pittsburgh, PA: University of Pittsburgh Press, 1989), 106–8.

great destroyer. Before the Civil War tuberculosis had been known as consumption, a name derived from how the victim wasted away as the disease slowly consumed the body. It accounted for one in five deaths before the Civil War, but the death rate from consumption had begun to decline by the 1880s, perhaps because the bacteria that caused the disease were mutating into less deadly forms. Then in 1882 Robert Koch discovered the cause of consumption: the tubercle bacillus. Doctors changed the name to tuberculosis. Koch's discovery did not produce a cure, but it did reveal how the disease was communicated, what conditions contributed to its survival, and how to prevent it.[7]

As tuberculosis declined, water-borne and insect-transmitted diseases became the most lethal killers. Malaria was endemic across the Midwest, while yellow fever epidemics plagued the Southern coasts, advancing up the Atlantic seaboard and the Mississippi Valley. Cholera epidemics struck repeatedly, spread through contaminated water. Bacterial diseases such as dysentery and other diarrheal diseases were less spectacular but more consistent killers.[8]

The crisis involved more than mortality; the economy grew, but Americans shrank. Figures on height are confined largely to white native-born males, thus ruling out distortions from the arrival of possibly shorter immigrants. The numbers have yielded the so-called antebellum puzzle: why mean male height declined by about an inch from 1830 until 1870 despite the rise in real per capita GDP at a rate of 1.2 percent over the same period. The decline among American-born males reached its nadir in the 1880s. Since height depends on nutrition and health during early childhood, disease or poor nutrition or both are likely to blame.[9]

A final set of numbers indicates the differential effects of whatever was causing this decline in well-being. A comparison of figures derived from passport records with those for the general population reveals that passport holders were consistently taller than the population as a whole. Since passports were preponderantly issued to people from the middle and upper classes, it appears that they—like aristocrats in European records—were

---

7. Sheila M. Rothman, *Living in the Shadow of Death: Tuberculosis and the Social Experience of Illness in American History* (Baltimore: Johns Hopkins University Press, 1995), 13–18, 131.

8. Costa, 503, 548.

9. Angus Deaton, *The Great Escape: Health, Wealth, and the Origins of Inequality* (Princeton, NJ: Princeton University Press, 2013), 141–47, 156–58; Dora L. Costa and Richard Steckel, "Long-Term Trends in Health, Welfare, and Economic Growth in the United States," in *Health and Welfare During Industrialization*, ed. Richard Steckel and Roderick Floud (Chicago: University of Chicago Press), 50; Costa, 545; Hacker, 52–53, 56; Gordon, 83–84.

largely exempt from the conditions driving height, and lifespan, down. When the figures are sorted further to find differences between rural and urban passport holders, those outside the cities showed a height advantage.[10]

After 1870 the rural death rate began to improve, much more so in the North than the South and among whites rather than blacks, but improvement had yet to arrive in the cities. As the economic historian Robert Gordon has summarized the data, "There was no improvement in either mortality rates or life expectancy before 1870, and in most data series there was no improvement before 1890." For black people and urban dwellers, particularly poor and immigrant urban dwellers, the crises continued into the twentieth century. This was the country Henry George described and came to know first hand in New York in the 1880s: a land of pervasive poverty in the midst of progress. It gave the lie to the image of the United States as a good poor man's country. What may have been true in a largely rural United States no longer held true in a rapidly urbanizing nation.[11]

I

Americans knew that their built environment was killing and stunting them, but they did not know how. They phrased the cause in terms of filth and miasma. In 1854 John Snow, a London physician, made a simple but brilliant discovery that revealed how cholera spread. He had traced a London cholera outbreak to a specific well and pump in Broad Street. The removal of the pump handle curtailed the outbreak, confirming the disease spread when the feces and vomit of its victims contaminated water supplies.[12]

10. Marco Sunder, "The Height Gap in 19th-Century America: Net-Nutritional Advantage of the Elite Increased at the Onset of Modern Economic Growth," *Economics & Human Biology* 11, no. 3 (2013): 245–58.

11. Gordon, 209; Katherine G. Morrissey, *Mental Territories: Mapping the Inland Empire* (Ithaca, NY: Cornell University Press, 1997), 32; Edward T. O'Donnell, *Henry George and the Crisis of Inequality: Progress and Poverty in the Gilded Age* (New York: Columbia University Press, 2015), 76–80.

12. For the best biography of Snow and a detailed account of cholera, Peter Vinten-Johansen, Howard Brody, Nigel Paneth, Stephen Rachman, and Michael Rip, *Cholera, Chloroform, and the Science of Medicine: A Life of John Snow* (New York: Oxford University Press, 2003); Harold L. Platt, *Shock Cities: The Environmental Transformation and Reform of Manchester and Chicago* (Chicago: University of Chicago Press, 2005), 188–89.

Recognizing the connection between feces and cholera did not mean understanding how excrement communicated disease. Americans and Europeans assimilated Snow's discovery into the existing theory of miasma. Most would continue to believe in miasma for the rest of the century, even after the bacteriological revolution of the 1880s, which introduced germ theory. As late as 1892, the *Chicago Tribune* emphasized that "Cholera is born of filth. It lives upon filth. It is spread by filth. The first duty of cities, therefore, is to clean up."[13]

For Victorians, miasma in the cities sprang from the same causes as miasma in swamp. Rotting garbage, vegetation, and corpses produced the same ubiquitous vapor that entered bodies and caused disease. The smells, haziness, and dampness that they took as signs of miasma were real, but miasma itself remained utterly imaginary, even as British sanitarians used it to propose a set of quite sensible reforms. Edwin Chadwick, a British Benthamite wedded to the utilitarian principle of the greatest good for the greatest number, began his career as a student of the British Poor Laws. He had little sympathy for the poor, but rather than seeing poverty as the cause of disease, he regarded poor health as a quite preventable cause of poverty. Though he did his major work in London in the 1840s and 1850s, his influence spread to the United States.[14]

Chadwick envisioned a sanitary city. At its heart were four elements. First was the belief that health depended on sanitation, and that sanitation depended on a hydraulic infrastructure that would bring pure water into the city and carry effluents out. Second was centralized public control over the new system, and third was the need for substantial investment in the infrastructure. Finally, the new system had to cover as much of the city as possible. Everyone, even if unequally, was endangered in a sickly city. At its simplest, the Chadwickian system involved flushing wastes out and pumping clean water in.[15]

American Chadwickians embraced engineering as a way to render the four classical elements—earth, air, fire, and water—that encapsulated the crisis beneficial rather than harmful. Their new hydraulic systems would clean up contaminated soil and water while also providing the means to stop the catastrophic fires that ravaged American cities. They would construct buildings that could withstand such fires as occurred. There was

13. Platt, 381.
14. Martin V. Melosi, *The Sanitary City: Urban Infrastructure in America from Colonial Times to the Present* (Baltimore, MD: Johns Hopkins University Press, 2000), 44–67.
15. Ted Steinberg, *Gotham Unbound: The Ecological History of Greater New York* (New York: Simon & Schuster 2014), 117; Melosi, 48.

little they could do about the air, except escape it, because the combination of coal, fire, and steam that pumped their water, fueled their industry, powered their trains, and heated their buildings also polluted their air.

As engineers and public health reformers, usually called sanitarians, assumed the task of improving the cities, their numbers grew. Only 512 civil and mechanical engineers lived in the United States during the Civil War, but in 1867 there were enough civil engineers for them to organized their own professional organization, the American Society of Civil Engineers. By 1880 civil engineers alone numbered 8,261, and that rose to well over 100,000 in the early twentieth century.[16]

Engineers epitomized the ambiguities and ambitions of a new professional class most visible in the cities. They were particularly skilled workers, but still workers under the direction of others. They could not control what was to be done, although they hoped to control how it was done. Although in many ways socially and politically conservative, engineers in their writings and journals saw their profession as creating a future for the betterment of the majority, and not just a few. One of the most promising routes to social responsibility was employment by cities, municipalities, and private corporations that were constructing new urban water and sewage systems. Urban waterworks doubled in the 1870s. Per capita consumption increased from about two or three gallons a day to as much as one hundred gallons a day for drinking, bathing, cooking, and sanitation. By 1880 a basic modern water infrastructure was in place in most cities.[17]

Ellis Sylvester Chesbrough became one of the leading engineers and sanitarians of his generation. He learned both in in Boston, where he began and ended his career, and again in Chicago, which lured him from Boston in 1850 and made him city engineer, that making experts a part of urban governance did not make governance any less political.

Chesbrough had a flair for the dramatic. During the Civil War he designed the system that drew water into Chicago from Lake Michigan. To ensure that it was pure, he placed the water intake crib two miles out from shore. Men worked beneath the lake, constructing the tunnel that connected the intake to Chicago's celebrated Water Tower and its Pumping Station, which, in the style of the time, resembled a late medieval fortress. On its completion in 1867, Chesbrough asked three reporters to accompany him on an inspection tour. Many people had traveled by boat atop the lake, but no one had ever taken a boat beneath it. He and

16. Melosi, 69–71; Edwin T. Layton, *The Revolt of the Engineers Social Responsibility and the American Engineering Profession* (Baltimore, MD: Johns Hopkins University Press, 1986), 3, 5–9.
17. Melosi, 73–75; Layton, 56–58.

the reporters embarked in a rowboat, propelling themselves by grasping the tunnel walls. The lamps they carried went out, which rendered inspection rather problematic. Still, they went on until the tunnel grew too narrow for the boat, which swamped. Wet, dizzy, and cold, feeling their way in total darkness, the four men sang "The Star Spangled Banner" to keep their spirits up as they waded a mile back to their starting point at the crib. Chesbrough ruled the inspection sufficient.[18]

Chesbrough regarded Lake Michigan as "a fountain inexhaustible, lying at our very feet, requiring us only to provide a means for drawing from its boundless resources." Chicago's early sewers, however, discharged via the Chicago River into Lake Michigan and turned the fountain, at least near shore, into the city's latrine. Chicagoans, who valued "trade and barter" over "healthfulness," had built on a swamp and then deposited a cargo of excrement and garbage. Chesbrough's tunnel provided the remedy.[19]

Constructing and calibrating waterworks and sewers depended on raising capital, either publicly or privately. As William Hyde, who worked for the Southern Pacific phrased it to Mark Hopkins, one of the owners of that road, engineering was but the servant of investment. In this respect city engineers were no different from the engineers building railroads. Sewers demanded capital. They also involved complicated politics. Although the sewers might stay within city boundaries, the rivers, lakes, and oceans they emptied into moved across political boundaries, demanding coordination beyond individual cities and towns. Capital, politics, and property all shaped engineering for Chesbrough.[20]

II

The urban environmental crisis bared the weaknesses of liberal individualism. Under an older Jacksonian political economy a commonsense, and common-law, approach had reigned: those who benefited from improvements should pay for them, and those who created nuisances had to remove them. In 1866 New York's new Board of Health ordered the removal of rotting garbage, fetid water, overflowing cesspools and outhouses, and decaying animal corpses. By April 1866, the board had issued 7,600

18. Carl S. Smith, *City Water, City Life: Water and the Infrastructure of Ideas in Urbanizing Philadelphia, Boston, and Chicago* (Chicago: University of Chicago Press, 2013), 42–50, 136.
19. Platt, 188–89; C. S. Smith, 136.
20. Richard White, *Railroaded: The Transcontinentals and the Making of Modern America* (New York: Norton, 2011), 88.

orders against nuisances as "dangers to life and detrimental to health." It mandated the removal of 160,000 tons of manure from vacant lots and had 6,481 privies disinfected. All of these privies, vacant lots, and cesspools had individual owners, and the city held them responsible. This impressive burst of activity made New York more pleasant, but it did not address the causes of cholera.[21]

Nuisance doctrines proved even less useful in securing preemptive measures. Political doctrines and environmental realities did not align. Jacksonians regarded society as consisting of segmented interests. If property owners in a certain district wanted improvements along a street—such as paving, sewers, or water pipes—and would pay for it, the city would contract for the project and assess those taxpayers who benefited from it. The next street got no benefits.[22]

Even before the Civil War, the need for pumps, reservoirs and sewers that served the whole city made it hard to segment public works. There was a democracy of defecation. For all their advantages, the rich could not avoid contamination by the feces of the poor. Polluted water and germs on the hands of their servants penetrated their residences. Like feces and urine, neither fire nor disease respected property boundaries. Water and sewer systems had to cover and protect everyone. Cities were like ships; they sailed, and sank, as a whole.

Chicago's politicians confronted the limits of nuisance doctrines when they attacked the pollution of the Chicago River. The common law classed pollution as a nuisance, and local governments could abate nuisances by forcing the people responsible for them to cease their activities and provide remedies. The cost fell on the perpetrators, not the public. But when powerful polluters refused to clean up, Chicago confronted the plutocracy of pollution.[23]

Meat packing ranked as Chicago's largest industry following the Civil War, producing a quarter of the city's manufacturing output by 1868. Five large firms produced half of Chicago's pork, then the city's leading product. The packers dumped blood, offal, and manure into the Chicago River, despite an ordinance prohibiting them from doing so. They protested that

21. Charles E. Rosenberg, *The Cholera Years: The United States in 1832, 1849, and 1866* (Chicago: University of Chicago Press, 1987), 189–94, 199–205, 210–11; "New York and the Cholera," *The Nation* 2, no. 28 (1866): 40–41.
22. Terrence J. McDonald, *The Parameters of Urban Fiscal Policy: Socio-Economic Change and Political Culture in San Francisco, 1860–1906* (Berkeley: University of California Press, 1986), 40; Robin L. Einhorn, *Property Rules: Political Economy in Chicago, 1833–1872* (Chicago: University of Chicago Press, 1991), 76–78, 91, 99–103.
23. Einhorn, 134–43, 206–16.

to do otherwise would increase their costs, put them at a disadvantage against competitors elsewhere, and force them out of Chicago.[24]

The packers made the Chicago River a sewer, but with the slaughter-houses refusing to pay and threatening to leave the city, the old common-law solution seemed impossible. The river near the original slaughterhouses was a foul, fetid, smelly, and dangerous place where only the poorest residents lived. It was both unfair and impossible to make this a neighborhood problem and create a special tax assessment to force those residents bordering the river to clean it up.[25]

The city accepted cleaning up the river as a public responsibility. In doing so, it created an enlarged "public" interest and used that interest to challenge segmented governance, but public interest doctrines had weaknesses of their own. They made environmental problems a means of redistributing wealth upward. To clean up the river, the city took money from the pockets of all Chicago taxpayers instead of only from the pockets of the packers, who had caused the problem and made money in the process. The packers gained wealth; most other Chicago residents lost it.[26]

The very scale of the large slaughterhouses, which allowed them to force the city to socialize environmental cleanup, also gave them advantages against smaller competitors. Famous for using every part of the pig but the oink, the great packinghouses of Chicago—Swift and Company, Philip Armour and Company—could undersell independent butchers on meat while making money off what to butchers would only be waste: hides, bones, entrails, hearts, tails, blood, fat, hooves, and feet. These by-products became shoes, fertilizer, handles for cutlery, oleomargarine, glue, and more. Refrigerated railcars allowed the Chicago firms to ship chilled beef across much of the nation, penetrating what had been safe markets for local butchers. By 1883–84 the number of refrigerated cattle carcasses for the first time surpassed the number of live animals shipped from the stockyards. A by-product of the by-products was a decline in the amount of offal and waste dumped into the Chicago River, even if the aggregate remained staggering.[27]

Environmental improvements and corporate advantages combined in 1865 when the railroads and the big packinghouses in Chicago combined to create the 320-acre Union Stockyards, a "bovine city" just outside the city limits on the Southwest Side. Unloading livestock from the

24. Einhorn, 205–9.
25. Ibid., 210–14.
26. Ibid., 210–15.
27. William Cronon, *Nature's Metropolis: Chicago and the Great West* (New York: Norton, 1991), 233–35, 249–57.

railroads at the new yards eliminated the need to move cattle and pigs through the streets of the city, a real gain for public health and safety. The big meat packers having opposed attempts to make them take responsibility for slaughterhouse wastes switched positions and supported stricter environmental and health regulations within Chicago's limits. They hoped these laws would both drive independent butchers out of business and force other packers to move into the yards, where they would share the expenses.[28]

Unable to eliminate pollution, Chicago took measures to export it. In 1871 the city government passed Chicago's problems on to its downstate neighbors by pumping waste and water from the South Branch of the Chicago River through the Illinois and Michigan Canal instead of allowing it to flow into Lake Michigan. The project did not prove a complete success. When at the end of the century Chicago finally reversed the flow of the Chicago River and built its sanitary canal to push its wastes away from Lake Michigan, it achieved a decades-old ambition.[29]

The clean water that flushed away wastes was also necessary to prevent the other great scourge of American cities, fire. Fire both fueled the Gilded Age industrial city and presented its greatest threat. In combination, water and fire powered the steam engines that drove the great pumps bringing water into the city and the pumps that pushed the wastes into the Illinois and Michigan canal.

In the fall of 1871, fires on a scale that strained the imagination struck the Midwest. On October 8, fires burning around Peshtigo, Wisconsin, exploded into an inferno that consumed not only the cutover of slash and stumps from logged-over white pineland but also forests, farms, and towns. Before it was over, it killed up to fifteen hundred people. The fire was little remembered because simultaneously the Great Chicago Fire destroyed most of the largest city in the Midwest.[30]

---

28. Louise Carroll Wade, *Chicago's Pride: The Stockyards, Packingtown, and Environs in the Nineteenth Century* (Urbana: University of Illinois Press, 1987), 47–57, 68–69, 98–99, 177; Cronon, 282–84; Stephanie W. Greenberg, "Industrial Location and Ethnic Residential Patterns in an Industrializing City: Philadelphia, 1880," in Theodore Hershberg, ed., *Philadelphia: Work, Space, Family, and Group Experience in the Nineteenth Century: Essays toward an Interdisciplinary History of the City.* Philadelphia Social History Project (New York: Oxford University Press, 1981), 204–29.

29. Einhorn, 206–16, C. S. Smith, 236; Cronon, 249–50.

30. The classic description of the connection between rural and urban development is Cronon, for Peshtigo, 202; Vernon R. Carstensen, *Farms or Forests: Evolution of State Land Policy for Northern Wisconsin* (Madison: University of Wisconsin, Department of Argricultural Journalism, 1958).

More than chronology linked these fires. The same dry weather and strong winds that had settled over the region fueled both, but beyond that, Chicago was the lumber emporium of the country. Loggers and sawmill workers turned trees to lumber, and the lumber came to the great yards along the Chicago River for sale either in the western prairies or in Chicago and other cities. When Chicago went up in flames, some of the houses that burned were probably made of lumber from around Peshtigo; part of the lumber stacked around the Chicago River was almost certainly from there.[31]

The Chicago Fire started in Catherine and Patrick O'Leary's barn on the southwest side of Chicago. Like New York, Chicago was very much an animal city, and the cow that supposedly kicked over the lantern was not an unusual resident. The fire spread to working-class bungalows, built from the cheap lumber of the Wisconsin and Michigan pine forests. Chicago and other cities were, as historian Stephen Pyne has pointed out, "wildland fuels...rearranged in form."[32]

Gale-force winds whipped the flames and drove them northeast toward the industrial district, where vast piles of lumber shipped in from the forests to the north, coal heaps, and wooden warehouses provided, as one commentator noted, "everything that would make a good fire." The fire breached the south branch of the Chicago River. It had become so hot that firefighters could not stand before it. It hit the shanties in Conley's Patch with full force before people could flee, and a disproportionate number of the fire's approximately three hundred victims perished there and in similar districts. It enveloped the municipal gasworks, creating a spectacular explosion and knocking out the city's streetlights. By the time the fire reached the central business district, it had become a firestorm, generating its own wind and weather. The "fireproof" downtown of brick and stone collapsed as the mortar in the buildings melted and dissolved. The blaze pushed relentlessly north, jumping the main branch of the Chicago River. Residents could only flee. The fire had disabled the waterworks and the city's pumping station, depriving firemen of the ability to fight it. After twenty-hours, it burned itself out on Chicago's northern boundary, four and a half miles from the O'Learys' barn. It had run out of fuel. The fire covered twenty-one hundred acres, destroyed eighteen

31. Cronon, 202.
32. For the cow and other stories current at the time, Elaine Lewinnek, *The Working Man's Reward: Chicago's Early Suburbs and the Roots of American Sprawl* (New York: Oxford University Press, 2014), 34–35; Stephen J. Pyne, *Fire in America: A Cultural History of Wildland and Rural Fire* (Princeton, NJ: Princeton University Press, 1982), 457.

thousand buildings, and left about seventy-five thousand people—one quarter of the city's population—homeless.[33]

In destroying cities, nineteenth-century fires simultaneously presented opportunities. They swept away decades of haphazard growth and offered possibilities to begin again. Despite annihilating real property—buildings and roads—the property in land that Henry George decried remained intact. Fire could not touch property lines, and property restrained possibilities. As conflagrations destroyed large sections of Chicago, Boston, San Francisco, and other cities following the Civil War, dreamers sometimes imagined smaller versions of Haussmann's Paris, but the resistance of property owners, large and small, to taxes and alteration of their holdings derailed grand plans. Although change followed fires, it mainly served those who sought to create commercial districts. The Chicago fire freed Fifth Avenue (later Wells Street) in Chicago of "frame shanties, brothels, 'jew clothiers,' and cheap boardinghouses" and added it to the business district. Traffic congestion, crowding, and high rents, however, remained pervasive in the rebuilt cities.[34]

In the wake of the Great Chicago Fire, business interests and the city's political machines recognized that the fire and the continuing threat of disease endangered Chicago's future. The water system had failed to protect the city, but pure and abundant water still remained the prophylactic guarding against conflagrations and epidemics. Essential elements of the old water system remained intact. The miraculous survival of the Water Tower made it a symbol of Chicago's resilience and a reminder of the need for even more robust waterworks.

But as Chesbrough knew, technology could not be separated from political economy. Questions of infrastructure raised questions of taxes. Preventing future fires raised issues of building codes and property rights framed in explicit class terms. Housing inevitably led to questions of the home, the basic cultural frame in which Americans understood change. As the controversies spun out, it was easy to forget that they were at root environmental: how to prevent the cities from burning up and their inhabitants from dying of disease.

The Great Chicago Fire produced an immediate struggle for political advantage. Chicago's elite reformers dismissed the aldermen as "bummers," a term resonant of Sherman's scavengers on the march through Georgia, who could not be trusted with the recovery of the city. In order

33. The account of the fire is drawn from Karen Sawislak, *Smoldering City: Chicagoans and the Great Fire, 1871–1874* (Chicago: University of Chicago Press, 1995).

34. Lewinnek, 61; Christine Meisner Rosen, *The Limits of Power: Great Fires and the Process of City Growth in America* (Cambridge: Cambridge University Press, 1986), 11.

to keep relief funds and donations out of the aldermen's hands, Roswell Mason, the city's reform mayor and a leading businessman, embraced the Chicago Relief and Aid Society. CRAS—the acronym was fitting—had as its leading lights the industrialist George Pullman and Marshall Field (of Field's department store). They embraced "scientific charity"; their goal was to help the "deserving poor," while refusing aid "to anyone who could help themselves."[35]

Within weeks CRAS proved capable of both aiding and disciplining the city. Joseph Medill, publisher of the *Chicago Tribune,* recognized that workers needed emergency housing and food or they would decamp and move elsewhere, but Medill and CRAS did not want relief to be so generous that the workers would have no incentive to rejoin the labor market immediately. CRAS would be the iron fist of free labor, fostering independence by refusing aid that created dependence. Reformers gave CRAS a stranglehold over the city's charities that it would not relinquish once the emergency had passed. This evolution of charity was typical of the nation as a whole. Similarly, Mayor Mason distrusted the police commissioners as being too susceptible to influence on the part of the aldermen. He declared martial law, and the ubiquitous Phil Sheridan arrived. The general deployed regulars, raised a volunteer regiment, and dismissed as untrustworthy the militia sent by the governor, who was outraged.[36]

In the election that immediately followed, fear of fire led the dazed city to elect a "Fireproof" ticket headed by Joseph Medill, who attacked the "alarming deterioration of integrity of municipal administration" and rampant "vice and dishonesty." He promised retrenchment, denounced borrowing, and vowed no public works "except by general taxation," by which he meant no special assessments against business interests. All this looked like a limited-government program, but he also extended Chicago's fire limit laws to prohibit the construction of any wooden building within Chicago's city limits. Medill and the CRAS reformers were of two minds about this. They shared with the city's workers a devotion to the individual home and thought of property holding as the basis of social stability. CRAS offered substantial aid to workers who had lost homes and built 8,033 small wooden cottages on the city's outskirts. But Medill also felt he had to pacify eastern investors and insurance companies, who were reluctant to invest in or insure a combustible Chicago. He demanded building codes that would prohibit the cottages of the poor inside the city while not

35. Lewinnek, 40; Rosen, 177–248; Sawislak, 78–93; Einhorn, 231–35.
36. David Montgomery, *Citizen Worker: The Experience of Workers in the United States with Democracy and the Free Market During the Nineteenth Century* (Cambridge: Cambridge University Press, 1993), 78; Sawislak, 49–63, 88–106; Einhorn, 234–36.

This photograph of the Smithsonian and Capitol captures Washington, D.C., on the verge of Reconstruction. Brady National Photographic Art Gallery (Washington, DC), ca. 1860–ca. 1865. National Archives and Record 529074.

This appears to be a photograph of crowds outside Grace Cathedral in New York City gathered for Lincoln's funeral cortege on April 25, 1865. It was taken from the window of Matthew Brady's studio. Matthew Brady / National Archives, NARA 526373.

Illinois Street in Springfield during the 1850s contained the law office of Abraham Lincoln and William Herndon. Library of Congress, LC-USZ62-12416.

This is a street view of Abraham Lincoln's home in Springfield, Illinois, draped in mourning. Library of Congress, LC-DIG-stereo-1s04301.

This Matthew Brady photograph of the Grand Review of the Army in May 1865 shows the Nineteenth Army Corps passing on Pennsylvania Avenue near the Treasury. Library of Congress, LC-DIG-cwpb-02945.

"Home Again," a sentimental celebration of the Union veteran coming home from the war. Library of Congress, LC-DIG-pga-01172.

Private George W. Warner of Company B, Twentieth Connecticut Infantry Regiment, was wounded at Gettysburg on July 3, 1863, and lost both his arms. The photograph is a very unsentimental reminder of the human cost of the war. Library of Congress, LC-DIG-ppmsca-40166.

The mustering out of victorious black soldiers at Little Rock, Arkansas, celebrates community and family as much as the soldiers themselves. *Harper's Weekly*, May 19, 1866. Library of Congress, LC-USZ62-138382.

Thomas Nast contrasts the deaths and degradation of Union prisoners at Andersonville with the comparative ease of the captured Jefferson Davis. Library of Congress, LC-DIG-ppmsca-05574.

This photograph of the Freedmen's school at Edisto Island, South Carolina, was one of many taken of the schools established for freedpeople. The schools and teachers would become targets of white attacks. Library of Congress, LC-DIG-ppmsca-11194.

This 1866 photograph of the destroyed Atlanta roundhouse, with steam engines and train cars in place, was part of a genre showing the South in ruins following the war. Library of Congress, LC-DIG-ppmsca-18960.

Southerners, as well as many Northerners, denounced distributions to freedpeople as fostering dependency, but in some areas such as upcountry Alabama the main recipients of aid in the immediate aftermath of the war were white people. *Harper's Weekly,* Aug. 11, 1866. Library of Congress, LC-USZ62-111069.

The abolition of slavery was not the same thing as the abolition of coerced labor, as this illustration of a freedman being auctioned off to pay his fine, at Monticello, Florida, shows. *Frank Leslie's Illustrated Newspaper,* Jan. 19, 1867. Library of Congress, LC-USZ62-117139.

California refused to ratify the Fourteenth Amendment. Opponents claimed, as in this cartoon, that the black vote would soon result in the Chinese vote, and the Indian vote. The man leading the chimpanzee equates all of them with apes. George Gorham was the Union Party candidate for governor and opposed the anti-Chinese movement. UC Berkeley, Bancroft Library.

Thomas Nast's cartoon "Uncle Sam's Thanksgiving Dinner" seems more like a multicultural illustration of the twenty-first century than a reflection of the United States of the 1870s. It captures the fading hopes for a homogeneous citizenry in the sense of a single set of rights for people of diverse origins. *Harper's Weekly,* Nov. 20, 1869. UC Berkeley, Bancroft Library.

The Wasp was a West Coast magazine that combined liberalism, nativism, conservative antimonopoly, and Sinophobia. In "Uncle Sam's Christmas Dinner" in 1881 the cartoonist mocks Nast's "Uncle Sam's Thanksgiving Dinner." He depicts immigrants and nonwhites as unfit for citizenship. The difference between Nast's Thanksgiving and this cartoon encapsulates the changes in the country's attitudes over the intervening dozen years. UC Berkeley, Bancroft Library.

This Alfred A. Hart photograph, "End of the track, on Humboldt Plains," shows a Chinese track crew building the Central Pacific across Nevada. Nevada would actually lose population following the completion of the transcontinental. It would be years before there was substantial transcontinental traffic. Courtesy of the Department of Special Collections, Stanford University Libraries.

This group gathered at Fort Sanders, Wyoming, in July 1868 included Generals Philip Sheridan, John Gibbon, U. S. Grant, William T. Sherman, W. S. Harney, and Joseph H. Potter, the commander of the post. They were meeting in regard to the Union Pacific Railroad. Without the aid given by the army, the transcontinentals could not have been built across the Great Plains. Library of Congress, LC-DIG-ppmsca-34094.

This Chicago, Burlington and Quincy Railroad brochure from the late 1870s advertises Nebraska land in Danish. Brochures such as this one show the railroads did not *follow* settlement; they *solicited* it as a way to sell land granted them by the government and to obtain traffic to carry. Photo courtesy of the Newberry Library, Chicago.

In this Thomas Nast cartoon, "Every Dog (No Distinction in Color) Has His Day," an Indian points out that whites have pushed Indians out of their homelands even as they excluded Chinese, who they feared would push them out. *Harper's Weekly*, Feb. 8, 1879. The Ohio State University Billy Ireland Cartoon Library and Museum.

The bloody fighting in New York City during the Orange Riot of July 12, 1871, reminded liberals of the Paris Commune. It fostered a fear and an analogy that would remain for the rest of the century. *Frank Leslie's Illustrated Newspaper*, July 29, 1871. Library of Congress, LC-USZ62-120337.

Office seekers besiege a congressman. Their goal was not so much salaries as the right to perform services for fees, which made office holding a source of profit. *Harper's Weekly*, Apr. 17, 1869. Library of Congress, LC-USZ62-99132.

Thomas Nast never fully lost his hopes for Reconstruction. Here he laments the restoration of "white man's government" over the South. "The Union as it was / The lost cause / Worse than slavery." *Harper's Weekly*, Oct. 24, 1874. Library of Congress, LC-USZ62-128619.

In 1876, in the midst of depression and on the verge of a contested election, Americans could still celebrate technological progress at the Centennial Exposition in Philadelphia. Here President Grant and Dom Pedro, the emperor of Brazil, start the Corliss Engine. *Harper's Weekly*, May 27, 1876. Library of Congress, LC-USZ62-96109.

This is one of a series of remarkable drawings by Red Horse, a Minneconjou Lakota (1822–1907), of the defeat of Custer. National Anthropological Archives, Smithsonian Institution, NAA INV 08569200.

The people the popular press often labeled rioters were a combination of strikers, other workers, and residents of towns and cities who had deep animosity toward the railroads. Here a crowd stops a train carrying troops at Corning, New York, in July 1877 during a strike against the Erie Railroad. *Frank Leslie's Weekly*, Aug. 11, 1877. Art & Picture Collection, The New York Public Library, Astor, Lenox, and Tilden Foundations.

Whether the War Department, symbolized by General Philip Sheridan, or the Interior Department, symbolized by Carl Schurz, was to supervise Indian policy was a lasting Gilded Age controversy. Thomas Nast, "The new Indian war Now, no sarcastic innuendoes, but let us have a square fight." *Harper's Weekly*, Dec. 21, 1878. Library of Congress, LC-USZ62-55403.

A veteran wearing a Civil War–era forage cap labeled "U.S. Pensioner" scoops coins out of a bowl labeled "U.S. Treasury." Civil War pensions created the first U.S. welfare system. "The Insatiable Glutton." *Puck*, Dec. 20, 1882.

This photograph by Solomon D. Butcher shows the machinery and labor deployed near Berwyn, Custer County, Nebraska, in 1887. Western wheat flooded European and American markets. Nebraska State Historical Society, nbhips 12401.

Cholera, yellow fever, and smallpox formed only a portion of the environmental crisis afflicting American cities. "At the Gates: Our Safety Depends on Official Vigilance." *Harper's Weekly,* Sep. 5, 1885. National Library of Medicine.

The Croton Reservoir, pictured in this 1879 photograph at the present site of the New York Public Library on Fifth Avenue, was part of the attempt to bring clean water to the city. It did not immediately allay the city's environmental crisis. Courtesy of New York Public Library Digital Collections, http://digitalcollections.nypl.org/items/510d47da-ea38-a3d9-e040-e00a18064a99.

A diagram of how Chicago brought in clean water from Lake Michigan. Frontispiece from *The Great Chicago Lake Tunnel* (Chicago: Jack Wing, 1867).

An alley in Packingtown in Chicago showing the tenements there at the end of the century. From Robert Hunter, *Tenement Conditions in Chicago: Report by the Investigating Committee of the City Homes Association* (Chicago: City Homes Association, 1901).

An illustration of the chaos at Haymarket after the bomb was thrown. The crowd, more observers than participants in the violence, become murderous rioters in this drawing. Portraits of the dead policemen line the top of the page. *Frank Leslie's Illustrated Newspaper*, May 15, 1886. Library of Congress, LC-DIG-ds-04514.

This antitariff cartoon claims that rich industrialists use the tariff to enrich themselves while terrifying workers, who fear their wages will be cut if they have to compete with lower-priced European products. "The Free-Trade Bugaboo," *Puck*, May 5, 1886. Special Collections and Archives, Georgia State University Library.

This classic portrayal by Samuel Ehrhart shows the Robber Barons as creatures of government policies: war, the tariff, and laws creating monopolies. *Puck*, Nov. 26, 1889. "History Repeats Itself—The Robber Barons of the Middle Ages and the Robber Barons of To-day." Special Collections and Archives, Georgia State University Library.

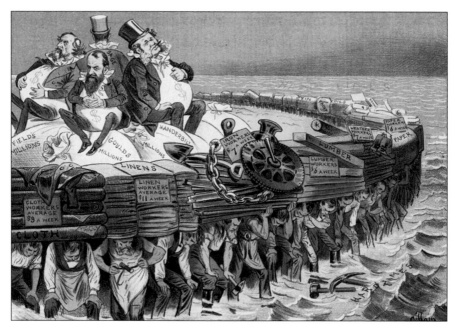

Another attack on monopoly. Jay Gould, Cyrus Field, Russell Sage, and Cornelius Vanderbilt (who had died in 1877) rest comfortably with their millions on the backs of workers and tradesmen. "The protectors of our industries." *Puck*, Feb. 7, 1883. Library of Congress, LC-USZC4-310.

This photograph by Solomon D. Butcher of branding on the Cal Snyder Ranch near the Middle Loup River at Milburn, Nebraska, in 1888 is notable for the presence of women and children, who would not have been on the large corporate ranches farther west. Nebraska State Historical Society, nbhips 12082.

Within the cartoon:

CARNEGIE

HOMESTEAD ||| MILLS.
⇒ PROTECTED ⇐
— BY THE —
McKINLEY TARIFF
AND A
PINKERTON ARMY.

☞ WANTED ☜
4000 FOREIGN
PAUPER
LABORERS

NOTICE ║ TO PROTECTED
AMERICAN WORKMEN.
ON & AFTER THIS DATE
WAGES REDUCED 30 %
YOUR LOVING EMPLOYER CARNEGIE.

"The Tariff is doing its own talking."—McKinley.—Chicago Herald.

This antimonopoly cartoon portrays the tariff as a fraud. It is a gift to Andrew Carnegie who, instead of keeping wages high, as promised, brings in poor European workers and cuts wages, enforcing his decrees with the Pinkertons. *Greencastle Democrat*, July 16, 1892.

The March 1888 blizzard that shut down New York City and led to the death of Roscoe Conkling. Here a horse-car sits abandoned in front of the Hotel Martin, 17–19 University Place, corner of Ninth Street, from Samuel Meredith Strong, *The Great Blizzard of 1888* (Brooklyn, ca. 1938). Courtesy of the New York Academy of Medicine Library.

William Louis Sonntag, Jr., in "Bowery at Night" captures the area in 1895 at the end of its reign as New York's theater district. Museum of the City of New York 32.275.2.

Strikers have set fire to the barge that brought three hundred Pinkerton detectives to Homestead Works on July 7, 1892, after a daylong battle. The Pinkertons surrendered and were forced to run a gauntlet of workmen and their families. Courtesy of The Frick Collection / Frick Art Reference Library Archives.

This photograph shows the east side of the 11100 block of Champlain Avenue in Pullman, looking south toward Market Hall in about 1883. At this point it was regarded as a model town and an inspiration to reformers. Collection of the Pullman State Historic Site.

Workers leave the Pullman Palace Car Works, 1893. This picture originally appeared in a promotional booklet celebrating Pullman's labor policies. A year later Pullman's policies helped launch a wave of violent strikes that swept over the Midwest and West. From *The Story of Pullman* (1893).

Most of the violence in Chicago did not involve striking Pullman railroad workers but instead mobs of the unemployed. "Police Driving Back the Mob From a Train Blocked by Obstructions on Track Near Forty-Third Street." *Harper's Weekly*, July 21, 1894.

A classic antimonopoly cartoon depicting the inequities of the Gilded Age that, like many others, employs medieval analogies. The shield is labeled "Corruption of the Legislature," the lance "Subsidized Press." A barefoot man labeled "Labor" rides an emaciated horse labeled "Poverty" and carries a sledgehammer labeled "Strike." Cyrus W. Field, William H. Vanderbilt, John Roach, Jay Gould, and Russell Sage are sitting in stands labeled "Reserved for Capitalists." "The tournament of today—a set-to between labor and monopoly." *Puck*, Aug. 1, 1883. Library of Congress, LC-DIG-ppmsca-28412.

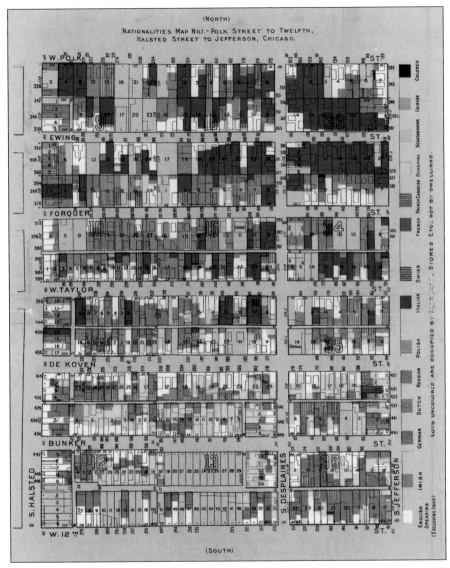

This and other stunning Hull House maps reveal not only how immigrants distributed themselves in Chicago but also how middle-class Chicagoans categorized the poor. Nationalities Map No. 1—Polk Street to Twelfth, Halsted Street to Jefferson, Chicago. From Hull-House Residents, *Hull-House Maps and Papers: A Presentation of Nationalities and Wages in a Congested District of Chicago, together with comments and essays on problems growing out of social conditions* (New York: Thomas Y. Crowell & Co., 1895).

Today, only a small part of the original Hull House remains on the campus of the University of Illinois at Chicago. The site was near of some of the most dramatic events of Gilded Age Chicago. From *American Review of Reviews*, July–December 1909.

The famous White City at the Columbian Exposition, which captivated not only ordinary Americans but also American intellectuals. From C. D. Arnold, *Official Views of the World's Columbian Exposition* (1893).

A cartoon dismissing William Jennings Bryan and his supporters as a rabble of eccentrics and cranks. "In battle array,—and there's not much doubt about the result." *Puck*, Sep. 30, 1896. Library of Congress, LC-DIG-ppmsca-28845.

Zaida Ben Yusuf photographed William Dean Howells at the end of the Gilded Age. Library of Congress, LC-DIG-ppmsca-15877.

This is the St. Gaudens statue of Abraham Lincoln in Lincoln Park, Chicago, that Jane Addams went to for inspiration and wrote about in her *Twenty Years at Hull-House*. Andrew Horne (CC BY-SA 3.0, http://creativecommons.org/licenses/by-sa/3.0), via Wikimedia Commons.

restricting the wood used in the houses of the well-to-do. He appealed to wealthy Chicagoans who, having "erected $100,000 marble fronts," did not want "$500 tinder-boxes beside them."[37]

Medill's plans threatened the interests of the stablest elements of Chicago's working class. Twenty percent of skilled workers and 17 percent of the unskilled owned homes. These were the small and inexpensive wooden cottages, clustered two or three on a lot, that had fueled the fire. The small house inhabited by the O'Learys, which miraculously survived the blaze, was typical. It was a double cottage, with the O'Learys and their five children crowded into the rear half and the front rented to another family. The house and its neighbors were firetraps, but they were also all a working-class family could afford. To eliminate new wooden houses would be to eliminate the possibility of homeownership for the vast majority of workers within the city's limits. These workers organized and protested, and bummers led the protests. Like the workers, they were mostly German American and Irish American. In the 1870s Chicago was, in the phrase of the time, a "foreign" city with about a third of the city being German in origin, 20 percent Irish, large numbers of Scandinavians, and a scattering of other immigrants. The *Illinois Staats-Zeitung* posed the issue as a contest over a measure "that makes the rich richer and the poor poorer." This was true. When the protests turned violent, the grand jury brought no indictments. The city retreated and allowed the construction of wooden houses in the German and Scandinavian sections of the burned-over North Side.[38]

As workers flooded into Chicago to help reconstruct the city, the devotion to the home briefly seemed to trump class and ethnic divisions in the city. Members of the home-owning German, Scandinavian, and Irish working class allied with evangelical Republicans, who followed Medill on the need to suppress crime and disorder. They feared the drinking and brawling of young, single, male workers. The coalition soon dissolved. Medill's evangelical allies believed liquor was at the root of disorder and pushed for a strict enforcement of Sunday closure laws. This would require the police to shut saloons and beer gardens, the common resorts of Irish and German workers, on the Sabbath. When Medill acceded in the fall of 1872, class and ethnocultural conflict reemerged. German-born Chicagoans, who had led the push against the fire limits, denounced the

37. Lewinnek, 40–53; Sawislak, 121–29, 136–48; John B. Jentz, *Chicago in the Age of Capital: Class, Politics, and Democracy During the Civil War and Reconstruction*, ed. Richard Schneirov (Urbana: University of Illinois Press, 2012), 137–54, 179–80; Einhorn, 235–37.
38. Jentz, 135–36; 148–54; Einhorn, 236–39; Lewinnek, 22–23, 53–56; Montgomery, 78; Sawislak, 43–46, 140–59.

Sunday closure laws, which they regarded as a threat to their status in the community just as the fire limit was a threat to their property.[39]

Anton Hesing, who had led the campaign against the fire limits, defended "industrious, honest, thrifty, sober men" who lived

> in a small home with his family, in a room 7 by 9. He cannot invite anyone to visit him because the room doesn't permit it....Then comes Sunday. In the morning he goes to church...when he comes back he yearns to go out in the fresh air with his wife and child, to look up acquaintances and discuss the events of the week, politics and religion — and to seek out the one diversion that this life offers him. These people have the same right to live here [i.e., Chicago] as those who live in palaces, and who on Sunday stretch out on soft couch cushions, lazy and doing nothing.

The *Chicago Tribune* denounced the protests as communism.[40]

Hesing was a Republican and a bummer who would later go to jail in the Whiskey Ring scandal, but he spoke for his constituency. He and Irish American Democratic leaders formed an alliance in 1873, which toppled Medill and the reformers. They embraced an ethnic Chicago. Although corrupt and not necessarily averse to redistributing a certain amount of income upward, they protected ethnic voters who elected them from the evangelical Republican temperance reformers. They reclaimed the police force, which had under Medill increasingly become the domain of the native-born, and they handed out the small favors immigrants often needed to survive. Their triumph proved short-lived. Economic collapse and threats to the built environment trumped them. The Panic of 1873 and a second major fire on the South Side, which threatened the rebuilt downtown, recast Chicago's politics and disrupted the bummers' control. The second fire brought an extension of the fire limits, and CRAS refused to allow the city to dispense aid to help the unemployed. These policies drove workingmen beyond the existing city limits. Small wooden houses did not disappear; they just moved to the suburbs, along with many of Chicago's industries.[41]

Political battles over housing easily morphed into fights over water and sewage. The business reformers wanted fire protection. This required a water system covering the entire city so that a fire could be stopped before it reached critical mass. They did not, however, want either urban debt or high taxes. The result in Chicago, and elsewhere, was a grand political accommodation. Liberalized city charters allowed cities to pay for public

39. Jentz, 141–42, 145, 147; Sawislak, 218–49.
40. Lewinnek, 53–58; Jentz, 150–53.
41. Lewinnek, 57–59, 62; Jentz, 117, 132, 138.

improvements through increases in bonded debt to finance the pumping stations, aqueducts, underground pipes, and sewers; in return business secured a legal limitation on the maximum size of the city's municipal debt and taxes. As long as the politicians maintained low taxes, business-men would not monitor the conduct of local government. The new system awkwardly grafted together a public interest solution—infrastructure covering the whole city—and a Jacksonian solution that maintained aspects of segmented governance. The city would charge individual users both significant hook-up fees to connect and then annual fees for water and sewage. These fees would pay the interest and debt on the bonds. This hybrid solution reduced the system's efficacy since poorer residents often could not afford to connect, but it allowed the cities to build and expand.[42]

Chicago's politicians accepted the compromise because the water system leaked water but gushed money. The city's Department of Public Works, created in 1875, became the center of a so-called pump house gang. The fee structure produced revenues far above the cost of maintaining the system. Aldermen did not use the profits to provide universal access; instead they used it as a source of patronage jobs, and to create a special surplus fund. By 1883 the system was generating a surplus of $20 million; by the end of the decade the surplus had risen to $30 million. The profit ratio was immense, more than 400 percent by the 1890s. But as long as taxes were low and big users received favored rates, businessmen were quiet. Middle-class homeowners did not recognize the enormous subsidies they were providing to both business and politicians. Water, too, distributed income upward. Businesses used far more water than households but paid proportionately lower fees, and the fee system was so opaque that it left room for negotiation and bribes. Chicago's level of water consumption was one of the highest in the nation, despite the system's partial exclusion of the poorest Chicagoans, who still resorted to public pumps.[43]

This system reached perfection with the election of Carter Harrison as Democratic mayor. Harrison and the city council, particularly the powerful Finance Committee, guaranteed low taxes, leaving the capitalists free to concentrate on making money. In 1885 Chicago ranked last among the nation's thirteen largest cities in per capita taxes. Public water systems did not arise everywhere; sometimes, as in San Francisco, the system was a private monopoly that gave kickbacks to politicians, but the low tax principle was the same. Versions of the compromise appeared across the country. When Honest John Kelly consolidated control of Tammany Hall

---

42. Jentz, 186–90, 237; C. S. Smith, 100; Dominic A. Pacyga, *Chicago: A Biography* (Chicago: University of Chicago Press, 2009), 85–86.
43. Platt, 161–62, 171–72, 178–89, 379–81; Rosen, 125, 170–74.

in the 1870s, he concluded an uneasy peace with businessmen, the Swallowtails, then headed by Samuel Tilden, who had tried and failed to disenfranchise Kelly's electorate.[44]

III

Even when contained and domesticated, fire created smoke, but how much and what kind depended on the fuel. In this, and so many other things, cities remained rooted in the natural world. Chicago, like Pittsburgh, used bituminous coal, the region's blessing and its curse. The coal seams around Pittsburgh alone, James Parton proclaimed in 1868, were worth all of the gold produced by California's mines for a thousand years. Sitting beside the rivers and "half a dozen railroads," the coal summoned iron and copper to Pittsburgh for smelting, since minerals could more cheaply be brought to coal than coal could come to them.[45]

Pittsburgh seemed an American Manchester. That British city, with its dark satanic mills, had emerged as the Victorian era's conflicted symbol of industrialization. No city in the world had the same ability to simultaneously appall and amaze. When Alexis de Tocqueville brilliantly described Manchester, his metaphors were organic and environmental but hardly pastoral: "From this foul drain, the greatest stream of human industry flows out to fertilize the whole world. From this filthy sewer, pure gold flows." It was what Americans feared they were replicating. Pittsburgh was, visitors thought, "hell with the lid off."[46]

If Pittsburgh was hellish, then Parton and the city's citizens seemed Pollyannas in hell. Angels rather than Satan reigned. Pittsburgh's smoke and filth formed his leitmotif, but he emphasized the "legitimate triumphs of skill, fortitude, and patience." Its residents claimed to be happy with their lot. They converted "the products of the Pennsylvania hills and mountains…into wealth" and distributed them across the world. The "better uses" that Americans had found for the land along the Alleghany and Monongahela rivers had "played havoc with the striking beauties of the landscape."[47]

44. Melosi, 119–23; Rosen, 48–49; Steven P. Erie, *Rainbow's End: Irish-Americans and the Dilemmas of Urban Machine Politics, 1840–1985* (Berkeley: University of California Press, 1988), 29, 45–47, 54–56; Platt, 174–75; Edwin G. Burrows and Mike Wallace, *Gotham: A History of New York City to 1898* (New York: Oxford University Press, 1999), 1027–28; Kleinberg, 85–87; Jentz, 236–37.
45. James Parton, "Pittsburg [sic]," *Atlantic Monthly* (January 1868): 17–36.
46. Parton, 22; De Tocqueville, quote in Platt, 7; Kleinberg, 3.
47. Parton, 17–22.

Parton quite literally inspected Pittsburgh in the dark: in the summer "every street appears to end in a huge black cloud, and there is everywhere the ominous darkness that creeps over the scene when a storm is approaching." In November he could not tell when the sun had risen, and the gas lamps had to burn even at midday. Everywhere there was smoke—smoke from factories, smoke from coke ovens, smoke from stoves and furnaces. This caused obvious problems and health problems unrecognized until later. Women passed "their lives in an unending, ineffectual struggle with the omnipresent black." Neither men nor women paid much attention to dress; there was no point amidst the "ever-falling soot." The legal problem was that it was virtually impossible to connect a particular piece of soot to a particular polluter, thus rendering nuisance law ineffectual.[48]

In dealing with the smoke Parton was sardonic, but what sounded like satire repeated the actual opinions of some Pittsburghers. The smoke had "its inconveniences," but it combated miasma. Inhabitants credited it with killing the malaria they believed arose from wetlands. It saved eyesight by cutting down the glare. Far from being an evil, the smoke was a blessing and the residents of Pittsburgh claimed to live longer than anyone in the world. Above all, it was a mark of prosperity. Parton noted, however, that as the smoke grew worse, residents who could afford to do so moved farther and farther away from the city proper to avoid the damage it did. Those who lived near the mills did so amidst smoke, a deafening roar, and occasional explosions.[49]

Smoke from bituminous coal was similarly the flag of Chicago's prosperity. Hamlin Garland remembered his first visit in the 1880s, when he saw from the train windows "a huge smoke-cloud which embraced the whole eastern horizon, for this, I was told, was the soaring banner of the great and gloomy inland metropolis." Not everyone celebrated such signs of prosperity. President Hayes wrote in his diary of "the age of petroleum, of coal, of iron, of railways, of great fortunes suddenly acquired: smoke and dust covering, concealing or destroying the beauty of the landscape. Coarse, hard, material things." Smoke abatement took root, particularly among women's clubs, but made little progress until the twentieth century.[50]

48. Ibid., 17.
49. Ibid., 18–22; Kleinberg, 72; Frank Uekoetter, *The Age of Smoke: Environmental Policy in Germany and the United States, 1880–1970* (Pittsburgh: University of Pittsburgh Press, 2009), 27–28.
50. Cronon, 9; R. Dale Grinder, "The Battle for Clean Air: The Smoke Problem in Post-Civil War America," in *Pollution and Reform in American Cities, 1870–1930*, ed. Martin V. Melosi (Austin: University of Texas Press, 1980), 84–85, 89–93; Uekoetter, 20–31; Peter Thorsheim, *Inventing Pollution: Coal, Smoke, and Culture in Britain since 1800* (Athens: Ohio University Press, 2006), 2, 10–18.

Smoke looked somewhat different in the East because the coal was different. Philadelphia, New York, and Boston used anthracite, which, though more expensive, had a greater energy density and burned more cleanly than bituminous coal. William Dean Howells, then living in Cambridge, wrote his sister in Ohio, who had never seen an anthracite fire, that its "jolly, malignant looking heat—a sort of merry devil...makes the room very warm without asking to be sawed or split or even allowed the poor boon of making everything black about it." Anthracite confined its most visible environmental costs to mining communities: deforested hills, a landscape scarred with slag heaps, and polluted water supplies, houses, and clothes fouled with coal dust.[51]

Chicago's rich and poor alike drowned in smoke and breathed polluted air, but expanding the hydrological infrastructure created a more segregated social environment because the poorest housing was still the least likely to be hooked up to sewage systems and to have direct access to clean water. As Chicago expanded, taking in surrounding areas, it extended the existing pattern of areas with adequate access to water and sewers and areas without such access.

The movement of Irish and German wageworkers into Chicago's suburbs in pursuit of small lots and small houses reflected a common desire among immigrant workers for property and independence, but it came at a cost. The Irish, both in Massachusetts mill towns and in Chicago, were more likely to sacrifice education for their children and consumption for their families in order to maximize the number of wage earners, aggregate their wages, and acquire title to a home. Wages for skilled workers in Chicago packinghouses remained relatively high in the 1870s and into the 1880s, and this gave some workers the opportunity to buy small lots and cheap wooden-frame cottages. The Irish and the Germans built near the stockyards in New Town and the Back of the Yards in the Town of Lake. Together these districts became known as Packingtown.[52]

Built on swampy ground, Packingtown initially lacked virtually all the elements of the new urban infrastructure: paved streets, sidewalks, sewers, pure water, and indoor plumbing. Homeowners delayed paying the fees necessary to connect to the water and sewage systems while landlords, who

51. W. D. Howells to Victoria M. Howells, Dec. 8, 1867, in William Dean Howells, *Selected Letters*, ed. George Warren Arms (Boston: Twayne, 1979), 1: 288; Christopher Jones, "A Landscape of Energy Abundance: Anthracite Coal Canals and the Roots of American Fossil Fuel Dependence, 1820–1860," *Environmental History* 15, no. 3 (2010): 461–63, 470–72.

52. Lewinnek, 68–74; Wade, 144–60, 270; Stephan Thernstrom, *Poverty and Progress; Social Mobility in a Nineteenth Century City* (Cambridge, MA: Harvard University Press, 1964), 155–57, 99–201.

erected buildings for families that did not purchase land, often simply refused to pay. Everywhere there were garbage dumps, mud, and a pervasive stench from the stockyards. A study conducted at the end of the century described "outside insanitary conditions as bad as any in the world. Indescribable accumulations of filth and rubbish, together with the absence of sewerage, makes the surrounding conditions of every dilapidated frame cottage abominably insanitary."[53]

Only a few miles away in Hyde Park, situated alongside Lake Michigan just south of Chicago, one could have been on a different planet. Hyde Park had everything Packingtown lacked: parks, large private homes with indoor plumbing, sewers, and rail commuter connections to downtown. To protect itself, Hyde Park used a public agency, the South Park Commission, to create a *cordon sanitaire* that isolated their residents from working-class communities. Nuisance laws in the right hands could still prove formidable, and Hyde Park employed nuisance abatement laws to keep out fertilizer factories and other unwanted industries, forcing them back into Packingtown.[54]

When Ellis Chesbrough returned to Boston in 1875, he confronted the limits of the wealthy and prosperous to insulate themselves from unhealthy conditions. He came as a consultant to remedy the collapse of sanitation in that city. His engineering skills could only ameliorate the situation, not correct it. Boston's sewer system was less a single system than a collection of projects designed to favor wealthy neighborhoods, but as Boston expanded and suburbanized, the local elite found they were unable to wall themselves off from larger urban failures.[55]

The development of street railways in Boston allowed artisans, small shopkeepers, and the best-paid clerks and salespeople to move into suburbs, which thickened and grew denser with smaller lots and cheaper buildings. Small-scale developers, building a few houses at a time, as well as individual lot buyers provided affordable housing. This usually did not involve a graduation to homeownership. In Boston's near suburbs most people rented; only 25 percent owned their own homes.[56]

53. Robert Hunter, *Tenement Conditions in Chicago* (Chicago: City Homes Association, 1901), 12.

54. Platt, 167–69.

55. For background, Michael Rawson, *Eden on the Charles: The Making of Boston* (Cambridge, MA: Harvard University Press, 2010), 75–232; Sarah S. Elkind, *Bay Cities and Water Politics: The Battle for Resources in Boston and Oakland* (Lawrence: University Press of Kansas, 1998), 49–57.

56. Sam Bass Warner, *Streetcar Suburbs: The Process of Growth in Boston, 1870–1900*, 2nd ed. (Cambridge, MA: Harvard University Press, 1978), 26.

Once the process was under way, Boston's elite suburbs, unlike Hyde Park, fell before the invaders. The well-to-do staged a gradual retreat outward in the 1880s and 1890s, as artisans with comparatively high wages and the growing number of white-collar workers moved beyond the city. The populations of Roxbury, Dorchester, and West Roxbury boomed in the 1880s. In the 1870s Lucy Stone, the head of the American Woman Suffrage Association, her daughter Alice, and husband Henry Blackwell lived on Pope's Hill in Dorchester in a seventeen-room house with 160 trees, an orchard, gardens, and a cow. Alice's diaries nicely capture the suburban life of a privileged and precocious upper-middle-class girl. It was a world fading even as she recorded it. The population of Dorchester, along with Roxbury and West Roxbury, increased from 60,000 to 227,000 between 1870 and 1900. It was a sign of both their own rapid growth and the stagnation of California following the arrival of the transcontinental railroad that the increase in population of these three Boston suburbs roughly equaled that of San Francisco, the largest city on the West Coast, during the same period. By one estimate, twice the number of families moved into the city of Boston between 1880 and 1890 as had lived there in 1880. The population, however, grew only modestly because a nearly equal number moved out, many to the suburbs.[57]

Over time the near suburbs came to resemble the cities. Originally small amenities—street trees, access to parks, and miniscule backyards—had set them apart. But the small rowhouses on pinched lots and suburban three-deckers in Roxbury seemed indistinguishable from urban houses and tenements. The city sucked the new suburbs back in: Dorchester, Roxbury, and West Roxbury became part of Boston, just as Hyde Park and Packingtown were annexed to Chicago in the late 1880s and Queens, much of the Bronx, and Brooklyn, already a major city in its own right, became part of New York City in the late 1890s.[58]

The search for health and comfort could also bring people back into the cities, but this was more unusual. In the early 1880s, the Howells returned to Boston, driven there by Winnie's mysterious sickness and Howells's own poor health. They wanted easier access to doctors. By 1884 Howells, like his hero in The Rise of Silas Lapham, lived "on the water

---

57. Warner, 35–37; Alice Stone Blackwell, Growing up in Boston's Gilded Age: The Journal of Alice Stone Blackwell, 1872–1874, ed. Marlene Merrill (New Haven, CT: Yale University Press, 1990), 6–12, passim; Stephan Thernstrom, The Other Bostonians: Poverty and Progress in the American Metropolis, 1880–1970 (Cambridge, MA: Harvard University 1973), 13–21.

58. John R. Stilgoe, Borderland: Origins of the American Suburb, 1820–1939 (New Haven, CT: Yale University Press, 1988), 151–61; Warner, 35–37, 44, 56–58, 79, 86–88, 93–100, 103–4.

side of Beacon," formed by the filling in of the Back Bay with earth from Beacon Hill. He marveled to find himself living in what had become Boston's haven for the well-to-do. Watching sunsets over the Back Bay, he joked that the sun "goes down over Cambridge with as much apparent interest as if he were a Harvard graduate." This creation of new land from old represented a kind of environmental change particularly prevalent in West Coast cities such as San Francisco and Seattle.[59]

The outward march of cities, the growth of suburbs, and the development of new regions such as the Back Bay provided, at least temporarily, more fresh air, space, and sunlight, but they also increased pressure on the ecological networks that served both city and suburbs. When Ellis Chesbrough returned to Boston, the city was soaking in its and its neighbors' wastes as the rivers, currents, and tidal action, supposed to carry sewage away, instead drove it back on shore and pushed it up pipes and into streets and basements.

Part of the problem was faulty design. In 1875 physicians reported sewers that terminated against stone walls. In other cases the sewer gases vented in the streets. And, as in Chicago, many houses did not connect to the sewer system at all. A medical journal reported: "The soil upon which the larger portion of the city stands is fairly saturated with sewage, which slowly oozes into a bank of dock mud which forms almost a complete circle around us." Physicians attributing disease to miasma from "decomposing matter" argued that improved sewage was necessary to rescue the city from "twenty millions of gallons of sewage...discharged daily at different points, completely skirting the city and polluting the atmosphere throughout most of its length and breadth."[60]

Chesbrough's solution was the so-called Main Drain, a single system designed to capture the entire city's wastes and pipe them out to Moon Island, where they would be released only on outgoing tides. The remedy was still dump and dilute, but the dumping would take place farther away from the city. The Main Drain was completed in 1884, but it adopted only part of Chesbrough's solution. He recognized that the expansion of the

59. Stilgoe, 151–61; Warner, 17, 26, 35–37, 53, 56–57, 64, 79, 86–88, 93–100, 103–4; W.D. Howells to H. James, Aug. 22, 1884, *Selected Letters*, 3: 108–9; Matthew Morse Booker, *Down by the Bay: San Francisco's History between the Tides* (Berkeley: University of California Press, 2013), 43–61; Matthew W. Klingle, *Emerald City: An Environmental History of Seattle* (New Haven, CT: Yale University Press, 2007), 44–118.
60. J. Collins Warren, and Thomas Dwight Jr., "The City Sewers," *Boston Medical and Surgical Journal* 93 (July–December 1875): 111; "Health of Boston," in *Annual Report of the State Board of Health of Massachusetts* (Boston: Wright & Potter, 1876), 496–98, 506.

suburbs meant that Boston would still receive its neighbors' wastes even if it successfully disposed of its own. The scale of the solution had to be municipal, extending beyond Boston's boundaries. Neither Boston nor its neighbors, however, were willing to do this; nor did they have a political mechanism for doing so. The environmental crisis continued to demand expansions of government powers, and it could not be remedied until those powers increased. As with so many other things, the environmental improvements initiated during the Gilded Age would not bear fruit until the Progressive Era.[61]

IV

New York, the nation's largest city, revealed how complicated the connections among humans, other species, natural systems, the built environment, capital, property, and governance had become. Every response to the crisis seemed to create an array of new problems.

New York had begun providing the rudiments of the Chadwickian system of pure water to promote health, fight fire, and remove waste even before the Civil War. In the 1830s voters authorized the Croton Aqueduct, which tapped the Croton River and emptied into the Croton Reservoir on Fifth Avenue, where the New York Public Library now stands. The system was completed in 1842.[62]

Implementing such reforms transformed urban ecology of nineteenth-century cities, where animals remained ubiquitous and vital to the city's functioning. Horses pulled the omnibuses basic to the city's transportation network as well as wagons. Expensive trotting horses of the rich raced on the roads at the city's edge. Horses lived, and died, on the streets. In 1880 the city removed nearly ten thousand dead horses. Pigs roamed the city, scavenging garbage, excrement, and household wastes, which they turned into flesh that the poor consumed. Many urban households kept a cow or two for milk; others were grouped in urban dairies. Antebellum cities had existed within a closed ecological loop, one Chadwick had hoped to retain by turning human and animal excrement into fertilizer. In antebellum New York City manure, as well as human excrement—night soil—had found a ready market on Long Island, where farmers used it to fertilize the hay and oats that they resold

---

61. Elkind, 49–57.
62. Burrows and Wallace, 625–28, 1229–30; David Soll, "City, Region, and in Between: New York City's Water Supply and the Insights of Regional History," *Journal of Urban History* 38, no. 2 (2012): 297–98, 300–303; Melosi, 83–84; Steinberg, 155–59.

to urban buyers to feed their horses and other animals. Waste as fertilizer flowed out, and food flowed in.[63]

After the Civil War the sheer magnitude of urban growth overwhelmed New York and other organic cities. New York's population in 1860 was 813,669; in 1890 it was 1,515,301, while neighboring Brooklyn grew from 266,661 to 806,343. Chicago rose from 112,172 in 1860 to 1,099,850 in 1890, Philadelphia from 565,529 to 1,046,964, and Boston from 177,840 to 448,477. The farms on Long Island receded farther from the city, making transport difficult, and with the number of city horses at more than 800,000 and growing on the eve of the Civil War, the city produced more manure than could be profitably exported or sold. Gilded Age cities could not do without horses, which remained a major source of motive power. Each urban horse deposited from fifteen to thirty pounds of manure daily into the streets. In the early twentieth century there were still 82,000 horses in Chicago, producing 600,000 tons of manure each year.[64]

Pigs, animals that eliminated wastes as well as producing them, lost their place in the city. In the 1850s New York, for good reason, had declared war on pigs—the great urban scavengers, but also mean, aggressive, and sometimes dangerous animals. After the Civil War they were driven north of Eighty-sixth Street. More people and fewer pigs meant urban streets accumulated the filth that pigs had devoured.[65]

Cattle continued to crowd into the cities, but urban residence became increasingly dangerous for them and for the humans who consumed their meat and milk. Dairies concentrated cows near breweries and distilleries, where they could eat the spent grain—swill—left at the end of the distilling process. This proved profitable, but it left the cows badly nourished

63. Joel A. Tarr, *The Search for the Ultimate Sink: Urban Pollution in Historical Perspective* (Akron, OH: University of Akron Press, 1996), 327. The same was true of European cities like Hamburg, but on a smaller scale; Evans, 110–20. As animal cities, see Catherine McNeur, *Taming Manhattan: Environmental Battles in the Antebellum City* (Cambridge, MA: Harvard University Press, 2014); Steinberg, 136–51, 167–71; Andrew Robichaud, *The Animal City: Remaking Human and Animal Lives in America, 1820–1910* (Stanford, CA: Stanford University Press, 2015).

64. Table 9 and table 12, in Campbell Gibson, "Population of the 100 Largest Cities and Other Urban Places in the United States: 1790 to 1990," ed. U.S. Bureau of the Census Population Division (Washington, DC, 1998); Elkind, 48; Martin Melosi, "Refuse Pollution and Municipal Reform: The Waste Problem in America, 1880–1917," in Melosi, 106; Bonnie Yochelson and Daniel J. Czitrom, *Rediscovering Jacob Riis: Exposure Journalism and Photography in Turn-of-the-Century New York* (New York: New Press, 2007), 15; Tarr, 323–33; Rosen, 177–78.

65. Steinberg, 112, 122; McNeur, 6–44, 134–74; McNeur, "The 'Swinish Multitude': Controversies over Hogs in Antebellum New York," *Journal of Urban History* 37, no. 5 (2011): 639–60.

and sickly, and they produced pale blue milk, which was mixed with chalk, molasses, flour, starch, plaster of Paris, sugar, and other substances until it resembled ordinary milk in texture and color.[66]

Milk from urban dairies contributed to the soaring infant death rate in New York and other cities. A staple of the urban poor, milk carried "tuberculosis, typhoid, scarlet fever, diphtheria, and streptococcal germs." The diseases came from sick cows, and dairy operators exacerbated the problem by diluting their milk with impure water. As late as 1902, however, the New York Public Health Commission found that more than half of the nearly four thousand samples of milk they tested had been adulterated. Dairy operators left the adulterated milk exposed to contamination from germs carried by flies and vermin. Improvement in the milk supply began about 1890, but dramatic changes came only in the early twentieth century with pasteurization, regular testing of cows, and refrigeration. The improvements correlated with a decline in the infant death rate.[67]

The density of animals and humans in the Gilded Age city turned the accumulating organic wastes they produced into a pressing urban problem. After the closed loop was broken, cities became so many spigots spewing sewage, garbage, smoke, and other pollutants onto surrounding water and land. Newly abundant water in cities exacerbated pollution. Before the 1870s, virtually all human waste went into cesspools, which owners paid private haulers to empty. What the night men did not haul moved into the soil. As access to farms decreased, New York's night men dumped much of the night soil into the rivers and harbor surrounding Manhattan. Those buildings and streets connected to the new sewer systems had their wastes conveyed directly to the rivers and harbor.[68]

The medium-term effect of the new sewer systems was paradoxical. Sewers, because of the cost of connecting to them, did not eliminate cesspools and privies, but once engineers solved the technical difficulties that had allowed sewer gases to vent back into houses, wealthy and middle-class householders adopted water closets—indoor flush toilets—in businesses and the homes. Water and feces from these toilets, as well as water used every day in household tasks, poured into cesspools in those houses unconnected to the sewers, rapidly filling them, and increasing the wastes that drained into the soil. When homes and businesses

66. Robichaud, 17–65; Burrows and Wallace, 786; for an account of the solution to the urban dairy problem, see Kendra Smith-Howard, *Pure and Modern Milk: An Environmental History since 1900* (New York: Oxford University Press, 2014).

67. Gordon, 81–82, 209, 220.

68. Steinberg, 116–18, 122; Tarr, 113.

connected to sewers, the waste moving into the soil decreased, but the amount flowing into the creeks, rivers, lakes, bays, and ocean increased.[69]

A boring made in 1879 at the West Thirteenth Street outfall in New York City illustrated the scale of the pollution. The drill passed through 175 feet of sewage and sludge before it found the bottom of the harbor. The combination of nitrogen from the decaying wastes of urban areas and phosphorus that entered the rivers with the deforestation of the Hudson River Valley produced eutrophication. The declining level of oxygen in urban waters meant many could not sustain life. As the amount of sediments and eutrophication increased, urban fisheries declined, eliminating another cheap and common source of food for the poor. A reporter thought in 1869 that "New York without oysters would cease to be New York." Some oyster beds around the city survived, but since oysters were filter feeders, they turned toxic and their consumption became dangerous for anyone.[70]

Pouring sewage into the rivers and harbor was supposed to dilute it and make it disappear, but tides flowed in as well as out. Writing of Coney Island, which became New York City's beach resort, a reporter noted in 1880 that it was "not pleasant when you are tumbling in the surf to have a decayed cabbage stalk or the carcass of a dead cat strike you full in the face." Irrefutable statements were rare in the Gilded Age press, but this was one of them.[71]

The waste that reached Coney Island had traveled through the sewer system, but much garbage remained on the streets. The filth in the poorer neighborhoods was most notable. When writing A Hazard of New Fortunes in the late 1880s, William Dean Howells incorporated a tour of Greenwich Village, then a New York slum, into the novel.

> Some of the streets were filthier than others; there was at least a choice; there were boxes and barrels of kitchen offal on all sidewalks, but not everywhere manure heaps.... One Sunday morning, before the winter was quite gone, the sight of the frozen refuse melting in heaps, and particularly the loathsome edges of the rotting ice near the gutters with the strata of wastepaper and straw litter, and eggshells and orange peel, potato skins, and cigar stumps made him unhappy.[72]

69. Tarr, 114–22; Rosen, 30; Platt, 160–61.
70. Steinberg, 118–25.
71. Ibid., 123.
72. William Dean Howells, A Hazard of New Fortunes (1890, reprint New York: New American Library ed., 1965), 260.

A largely unregulated private real estate market drove urban expansion and produced extremes: ever more lavish and garish mansions of the rich lining broad avenues, on the one hand, and crowded tenements without sufficient space, light, or amenities along narrow streets on the other. Property owners and developers found it easy to coexist with the new municipal agencies that managed water and sewage. The cities provided services property owners could use at their discretion and opened up public spaces at low cost for private developments, while at the same time placing few effective controls on the use of private property.

The vertical landscape of the streets—underground, on the ground, and in the air above the streets—illustrated how public policies created an urban infrastructure at little cost to developers, while providing a windfall to property owners. When in the 1880s Thomas Edison, America's most famous inventor, moved from Menlo Park, New Jersey, to New York City to build his Pearl Street generating station in an attempt to electrify New York, he proclaimed himself "a business man. I'm a regular contractor of electric lighting plants and I am going to take a long vacation in the matter of invention." He recognized the opportunities that the expansion of cities and their need for infrastructure presented, and the limited space available for that infrastructure.[73]

Edison decided to place his wires below the ground. As he laid several miles of conduits, neither he nor his workmen were lonely. He met C. E. Emery of the New York Steam Heating Company "at all hours of the night, I looking after my tubes and he after his pipes." The company's pipes brought steam from central plants to heat the new buildings, which otherwise would need large boilers and face the problem of moving coal through the crowded city. This was a problem Chicago did not solve until it built extensive tunnels for moving coal and other goods from the railways to downtown, early in the twentieth century.[74]

Edison could build at night because gaslight had already changed American cities, with the number of streetlights growing rapidly, particularly after 1860. Light, too, marked class. When the sun set, the affluent areas of the city still sparkled. The slums and poorer areas remained dark.[75]

73. A. J. Millard, *Edison and the Business of Innovation* (Baltimore, MD: Johns Hopkins University Press, 1990), 3.
74. Burrows and Wallace, 1052–53; Thomas A. Edison, *The Papers of Thomas A. Edison*, ed. Reese Jenkins (Baltimore, MD: Johns Hopkins University Press, 1989), 817–18; "Infrastructure," in *The Encyclopedia of Chicago*, ed. James R. Grossman, Ann Durkin Keating, and Janice L. Reiff (Chicago: University of Chicago Press, 2004), 413–14.
75. Peter C. Baldwin, *In the Watches of the Night: Life in the Nocturnal City, 1820–1930* (Chicago: University of Chicago Press, 2012), 18–19.

On the streets themselves, people mingled with fleets of vehicles that carried them and their goods. Unlike trains, horse-drawn streetcars allowed access all along the line. They stopped for women, but they only slowed for men and boys, who had to jump on and off. In cities such as Pittsburgh and San Francisco, hills restricted the utility of the horse cars, and only the introduction of cable cars and electric trolleys allowed expansion of the transit system. In 1887 Richmond, Virginia, opened the first lines for electric streetcars, which ran twice as fast and carried three times as many passengers as horse cars, and by the late 1880s and early 1890s electric streetcars were in Boston, Chicago (which also used cable cars), Brooklyn, and other cities. Marshall Field put his department store on State Street in Chicago for the same reason Macy's located on Herald Square in Manhattan: these were the central streetcar hubs.[76]

The urban infrastructure also soared above the streets. Overhead wires strung along poles webbed the air above Broadway in New York City and South La Salle Street in Chicago. "The sky," one English visitor to New York wrote in 1881, was "obscured by countless threads of wire" that belonged to telegraph and telephone companies, providing high-cost services for a limited clientele. They became a fixture in cities, large and small. Even the mining boomtown of Tombstone, Arizona, had its telegraph and telephone wires. Electric companies in the 1880s, most franchised affairs with limited customers, strung high-voltage wires in major cities rather than going underground as Edison had done. Electric streetcar lines contributed more overhead high-voltage wires, which mingled and crossed with telephone wires, telegraph wires, and wires for stock tickers. The gruesome death of a Western Union lineman, whose body dangled over the streets of Manhattan for an hour with blue flames shooting from his mouth, symbolized the danger they presented. Even indirect contact with the wires was dangerous. If a telephone wire crossed a high-voltage power line, a person picking up the telephone could be electrocuted.[77]

By 1885 thirty-two companies were reported to have wires running along New York's streets. At the densest point, a 96-foot-tall pole in New

76. Francis G. Couvares, *The Remaking of Pittsburgh: Class and Culture in an Industrializing City 1877–1919* (Albany: State University of New York Press, 1984), 32–33; Burrows and Wallace, 1098–99; Gordon, 147; Warner, 28, 34, 49, 53, 57, 76, 88–90.
77. Burrows and Wallace, 1068; Richard R. John, *Network Nation: Inventing American Telecommunications* (Cambridge, MA: Belknap Press of Harvard University Press, 2010), 222; Andrew C. Isenberg, *Wyatt Earp: A Vigilante Life* (New York: Farrar, Straus & Giroux, 2013), 120–21.

York held a hundred separate wires. In New York during the 1880s, the danger prompted successful efforts to force many of the wires underground. Underground or aboveground, the lines still ran along public streets, and companies needed permission to use them. It was a privilege they often paid for in bribes and kickbacks to aldermen and city councilmen. The public got little recompense.[78]

New technologies were not immediately transformative. In creating the incandescent light bulb, his most famous invention, Edison succeeded where others had failed by recognizing how to correct the weak point— the filament—in existing designs. But to create indoor electrical lighting, he had to design not just a bulb but also an entire lighting system, from generation to transmission. This is what brought him to New York City in 1881, but despite Edison's hopes, his Pearl Street Station and his incandescent bulb proved quite marginal to the city in the 1880s and 1890s. The Pearl Street Station produced a direct rather than alternating current, which was at once expensive and unable to travel far from the generating station.[79]

Only the well-to-do could afford Edison's electricity. Discouraged, Edison complained his light bulb had proved a "cumbersome invention." Like so much that he did, the station remained a marvelous novelty rather than a profitable business. He had no way of calculating the cost of production, and since the system lacked meters, he could not gauge consumption. He could, however, sell franchises in American and European cities. Edison's electric light turned into an accouterment of a narrow set of fashionable urban spaces: theaters, restaurants, banks, office buildings, hotels, and high-end stores. It became a toy of the rich, and when Mrs. Cornelius Vanderbilt came to Alva Vanderbilt's "Ball of the Century" in 1882 dressed as an electric light bulb in satin trimmed with diamonds, she unintentionally captured the new technology perfectly. In New York, Pearl Street had just 710 customers and lit only 16,377 lamps in 1888. It was a piece of conspicuous consumption.[80]

78. John, 221–23.
79. Thomas Parke Hughes, *Networks of Power: Electrification in Western Society, 1880–1930* (Baltimore, MD: Johns Hopkins University Press, 1983), 31–38; Hughes, *American Genesis: A Century of Invention and Technological Enthusiasm, 1870–1970* (New York: Viking, 1989), 73–75.
80. Hughes, *Networks of Power*, 38–46; Steven W. Usselman, "From Novelty to Utility: George Westinghouse and the Business of Innovation During the Age of Edison," *Business History Review* 66, no. 2 (1992): 264–66; Roger L. DiSilvestro, *Theodore Roosevelt in the Badlands: A Young Politician's Quest for Recovery in the American West* (New York: Walker, 2011), 103; Hughes, *American Genesis*, 73–74.

Those outside the range of a power station had to rely on individual plants in private homes and offices. J. P. Morgan, already a leading New York banker, installed a system in his new Madison Avenue mansion. It lit three hundred lamps, but the machinery initially shook the house, and its noise and smoke disturbed the neighbors. An engineer had to be on duty between 3:00 and 11:00 p.m., when the system ran. In 1883 faulty wiring set Morgan's library on fire, and the whole system was plagued with "frequent short circuits and many breakdowns." Morgan's son-in-law was not impressed. The plant "was not in favor, either in the family or with the neighbors."[81]

The impact of the electric light came largely during the next century, through the efforts of others. George Westinghouse also made his mark as an inventor, but he never loomed as large in American culture. Westinghouse flowed with the currents of the late nineteenth century, rather than fighting against them. He was an engineer and a Union veteran. What the Civil War had taught him was the value of discipline, hierarchy, and subordination in running large organizations. Edison's fame rested on expensive consumer goods; Westinghouse capitalized on the Gilded Age economy's emphasis on producer goods. He cultivated the market for marginal improvements in established technologies rather than creating transformative novelties. Westinghouse prospered by improving railroad brakes. He understood the corporate needs for uniformity, predictability, and control.[82]

Westinghouse invented his automatic railroad air brake in 1869. As with Edison's incandescent bulb, "invent" is a deceptive word. Virtually all the inventions of the period arose from the tinkering culture of American shops and factories. There were numerous versions of most devices. Attaching a single inventor to any of them and awarding a patent often involved seemingly endless litigation. Westinghouse became a fearsome litigant. His lawyers successfully took on the railroad corporations, which despised patents and patent holders. The railroads would purchase new inventions or get a license to manufacture them, modify them, and then claim them as their own. Westinghouse blocked their tactics. He refused to license the manufacture of his brakes. He did not just litigate; he persuaded the railroads that the new braking system would work only if the brakes on all cars were uniform and part of a single system. He

81. J. Pierpont Morgan to Sherburne Eaton, Dec. 27, 1882, and notes, in Edison, *The Papers of Thomas A. Edison*, 6: 750–51.
82. Steven W. Usselman; *Regulating Railroad Innovation: Business, Technology, and Politics in America, 1840–1920* (New York: Cambridge University Press, 2002), 131, 133–34, 137, 138–39, 159–60.

convinced the public that new brakes were critical to public safety, putting pressure on the railroads to adopt them. They did so for passenger trains; it would take federal legislation to make them mandatory for freight trains nearly a quarter of a century later.[83]

Westinghouse's use of the patent revealed the ambiguities of innovation. The number of patents issued in the late nineteenth century swelled dramatically, but this was not necessarily a sign that Americans were becoming more inventive. It meant that the old system of tinkering and what amounted to a kind of nineteenth-century open-source innovation was giving way to a system where some successful inventors secured monopoly rights over what were often common ideas. The results could stifle as well as protect invention. The vacuum brake was a dangerous rival to Westinghouse's air brake, but by securing patents to vacuum brakes and buying out rivals, he blocked competition and secured a monopoly for his airbrakes. He preserved his fortune.[84]

When, in the 1890s, Edison's direct current and Westinghouse's alternating current clashed head to head, it was no contest. Westinghouse won, but by then Edison had triumphed as a cultural figure. Edison's greatest invention remained Thomas Edison, "The Wizard of Menlo Park."[85]

In New York, and by the 1890s in Chicago, the elevated railroads formed the most substantial part of the aerial architecture of the city. New York's "L" began in the 1870s, stalled during the depression following 1873, and renewed their growth with new state charters in 1878. They formed a circus of speculation, stock manipulation, financial instability, court battles in front of corrupt judges, and constant political controversy. All of this was Jay Gould's home country, and he and his associates had by 1881 largely secured control of the Manhattan Elevated Railroad, a holding company that controlled the city's elevated lines.[86]

William Dean Howells's fictional Mr. and Mrs. March in A Hazard of New Fortunes reveled in the "L roads." "They kill the streets and avenues," Mr. March admitted, "but at least they partially hide them, and that is some comfort; and they do triumph over their prostrate forms with a savage exultation that is intoxicating. Those bends in the L that you get at the corner of Washington Square, and just below the Cooper Institute — they're

83. Usselman; "From Novelty to Utility," 251–304; Usselman, *Regulating Railroad Innovation*, 133–34, 137–39, 159–60.
84. Usselman, *Regulating Railroad Innovation*, 135–37.
85. Usselman, "From Novelty to Utility," 267; Hughes, *American Genesis*, 91.
86. Maury Klein, *The Life and Legend of Jay Gould* (Baltimore, MD: Johns Hopkins University Press, 1986), 276, 282–91, 308–10, 330–31, 387–91, 474–75.

the gayest things in the world. Perfectly atrocious, of course, but incomparably picturesque! And the whole city is so."[87]

The fictional Marches joined actual millions on the elevated railways. The Manhattan Elevated carried 75.6 million people in 1881. By 1884 ridership numbered 96.7 million. The Brooklyn Bridge opened in 1883, but not until 1885 could riders on the "Ls" transfer to a cable car running across the bridge and connect with new Brooklyn Elevated Company trains. By 1886 the system carried 115 million passengers a year, at a nickel a head. They traveled in a rush of noise, smoke, and cinders on trains that were a constant affront to the ears, noses, and eyes of everyone near them. Residents who had trains thundering by and above their windows filed nuisance suits, which the railroads fought with grim determination. Passengers complained of the crowds, the inconvenience, the accidents, and the delays, but once in place, the city could not function without the trains. By 1891 they conveyed 197 million people a year, contributing a large share of the million people who flowed into and out of Manhattan each day.[88]

The "Ls" reached into the sky, but they did not loom above Chicago and New York's skyline because the cities grew upward as well as outward. This, too, was connected to political economy and had environmental consequences. Thomas Edison stated the logic succinctly when he moved to New York. Edison wrote that he had little idea of the cost of New York real estate when he began construction of the Pearl Street Station. He built on the "worst, dilapidated, deserted street there was," and 50 feet of street frontage cost him $155,000, nearly eight times what he expected to pay. "Then I was compelled to change my plans and go upward in...the air where real estate was cheap. I...built my station of structural iron work, running it up high."[89]

By the 1880s "skyscraper" had moved from describing the highest sail on masted vessels to designating tall buildings. They were the real estate market's response to rising land values and the concentration of new urban businesses, which needed to house significant amounts of records and large numbers of office workers at a single site. It was cheaper to build up than out.[90]

Corporations made the New York their headquarters even when, like Standard Oil and American Tobacco, they had originated elsewhere.

87. Howells, 54.
88. Burrows and Wallace, 1053–56, 1058; Klein, 474–75.
89. Burrows and Wallace, 670, 1050–53; Rosen, 36–38, 44–45; Edison, *The Papers of Thomas A. Edison*, 820.
90. The *Oxford English Dictionary* gives early uses of the word. Burrows and Wallace, 1050–52.

Along with banks, they acted as magnets, attracting large law firms and insurance companies that also required centralized office space. As an article in the *Building News* in 1883 entitled "Sky Building in New York" put it, capitalists "discovered there was plenty of room in the air and that by doubling the height of its buildings the same result would be reached as if the island had been stretched to twice its present width."[91]

New technologies allowed the buildings to rise. The safety elevator, invented by Elisha Otis in 1852, moved people and things from floor to floor without undue labor. Pipes brought steam from central plants to heat the new buildings. In New York, buildings sprouted water towers on their roofs to create the necessary pressure for running water and sprinklers to suppress fires. The buildings had become too large for fire ladders and fire hoses to reach their upper stories, and the new water systems offered them protection. But the most critical innovation was the use of iron and steel in revolutionary new designs cloaked by stone and brick exteriors. Instead of having thick weight-bearing masonry walls, these buildings used cage or skeleton construction, which permitted thin walls, providing more floor space, larger windows, and thus more interior light. Pittsburgh steel and iron makers recognized that the market for their products had dramatically expanded. It had also moved beyond their ability to supply it. Cleveland, already a port for Lake Superior iron ore on its way to Pittsburgh, began to combine that ore with Pennsylvania coal to develop its own steel and iron industries.[92]

By the end of the century, there were three hundred buildings nine stories or taller in New York, and in 1889 Joseph Pulitzer, the New York newspaper publisher, had begun to build what was then the tallest office building on the planet, in order to house his *New York World*. He replaced French's Hotel on Park Row and Frankfurt Streets with a 345-foot, fifteen-story tower complete with a gilded dome supposedly visible from forty miles at sea. Edison provided the dynamo to light the building's eighty-five hundred bulbs.[93]

Not New York but rather Chicago gave birth to the American skyscraper. The city's immense growth—nearly doubling every decade—produced more than a million residents by 1890 and powered it past Philadelphia,

91. James McGrath Morris, *Pulitzer: A Life in Politics, Print, and Power* (New York: Harper, 2010), 278–79, 286–87; Burrows and Wallace, 670, 1050–53.
92. Burrows and Wallace, 670, 1050–52; Harold C. Livesay, "From Steeples to Smokestacks: The Birth of the Modern Corporation in Cleveland," in Thomas F. Campbell and Edward M. Miggins, eds., *The Birth of Modern Cleveland 1865–1930* (Cleveland, OH: Western Reserve Historical Society, 1988), 57–58.
93. Burrows and Wallace, 1051–52.

making it the nation's second-largest city. With downtown real estate values at a premium, Chicago architects borrowed from the French, who were the leaders in iron construction. The 1889 Eiffel Tower was the equivalent of an eighty-one-story building and would be the tallest structure in the world for decades. Louis Sullivan, who came to Chicago in 1873 and joined his partner, Dankmar Adler, in 1881, perfected the possibilities of the iron- and steel-framed building.[94]

Sullivan's buildings suited the business needs of a rapidly growing city, but they were also beautiful. In his use of steel and iron he achieved an amazing delicacy that emphasized interior curves and adopted designs of the emerging *art nouveau*. He made the industrial seem organic as cast-iron leaves and flowers climbed up among geometric forms. Sullivan and Adler created a distinctive American urban architecture, but one that faced resistance from conservative architects, and many property owners.[95]

Particularly on their upper floors, skyscrapers allowed their occupants to be *in* but not *of* the city, whose noise and tumult, as one New Yorker complained, made life "an everlasting concussion of the brain." They were cut off from street noise yet had abundant light and expansive views. In the nineteenth-century city, the street poured into offices; the apple lady, the bootblack, the book agents, and other salesmen intruded into offices and work. In skyscrapers an elevator operator could act as a gatekeeper, blocking visitors' access to higher stories unless they made a tedious climb up the stairs. Skyscrapers liberated the dwellers on their upper stories, but they darkened the streets and cut off light from the smaller buildings beneath them. The skyscrapers made the privileges of capital manifest in steel.[96]

In their light, quiet, and isolation, the upper floors of an office building could not have been further from the other distinctive urban building: the tenement. A *Harper's Weekly* series on "Tenement Life in New York" in 1879 began: "Half a million men, women, and children are living in the tenement-houses of New York today, many of them in a manner that would almost disgrace heathendom itself." The journalist deplored "the utter wretchedness and misery, the vice and crime, that may be found

94. Pacyga, 131–32; David Garrard Lowe, "The First Chicago School," in *The Encyclopedia of Chicago*, ed. James R. Grossman, Ann Durkin Keating, and Janice L. Reiff (Chicago: University of Chicago Press, 2004), 28–29.
95. Rosen, 27–28; Pacyga, 133–34; Lowe, 28–29.
96. "Our High Buildings," *Chicago Daily Inter-Ocean* (Dec. 30, 1888): 10; Pacyga, 134; Helen Campbell, "The Tenement House Question," *Sunday Afternoon: A Monthly Magazine for the Household* (April 1879): 318.

within a stone's-throw of our City Hall, and even within an arm's-length of many of our churches."[97]

The nineteenth-century tenement was also a product of increasing density and rising urban land values, as well as little effective public regulation over what a landlord could do with his property. Not all the poor lived in tenements, although the percentage went up between 1870 and 1900, but most of the poor lived among crowding and the unavoidable filth of the new industrial cities. By the 1890s the worker's cottage—usually no more than 400 to 800 square feet—survived in Chicago and other cities, but largely in dilapidated form, divided up into small rooms and crowded behind larger four- or five-story buildings. New York and Boston limited the height of these new buildings and the amount of a lot they could cover, but numerous exceptions were granted and conditions remained appalling. Landlords in Chicago covered virtually every inch of their urban lots with housing for the poor.[98]

The worst tenements actually started out as an attempt to create model housing. The design for the dumbbell tenement won a contest sponsored by the *Plumber and Sanitary Engineer*, a monthly journal. In New York the dumbbells numbered five or six stories, four apartments on a floor with a narrow airshaft in the center for air and light. The name, as the diagram shows, derived from the building's shape. In 1888 the *American Magazine* described them as "great prison like structures." The narrow courtyard in the middle was a "damp foul-smelling place...had the foul fiend designed these great barracks, they could not have been more villainously arranged to avoid any chance of ventilation." The chief marks of the urban environmental crisis were fire and disease, and the tenements nurtured both. In the case of fire, they were death traps, and the sanitation was terrible.[99]

A five-story dumbbell housed from eighteen to twenty families, who in turn took in boarders and lodgers, so the building could contain from 100 to 150 people. At their most crowded, they offered about two square yards of floor space per inhabitant. Privies were usually in the basement, and water did not go beyond the first floor. By the 1890s the New York Tenement Commission regarded it as "the one hopeless form of tenement construction.... It cannot be well ventilated; it cannot be well lighted; it is not safe in case of fire.... Direct light is only possible for the rooms at the front and

97. Yochelson and Czitrom, 32–77; "Tenement Life in New York," *Harper's Weekly* (Mar. 22, 1879): 226–27.
98. Kleinberg, 67–75; Hunter, 21–24.
99. Moses Rischin, *The Promised City: New York's Jews, 1870–1914* (Ithaca, NY: Cornell University Press, 1962), 82–83.

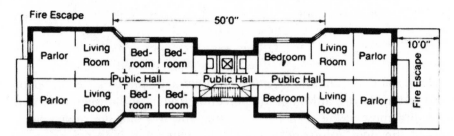

This is James Ware's design of the ubiquitous dumbbell tenement. The winner of a design contest for affordable housing for the poor, it became synonymous with poverty, filth, and urban squalor. From *The Plumbing and Sanitation Engineer* (1879).

rear. The air must pass through other rooms or tiny shafts, and cannot but be contaminated before it reaches them." About sixty thousand new tenements, the large majority of them dumbbells, were constructed in greater New York between 1880 and 1900. The tenements drove people (including children) into the streets, particularly in the summer to escape the heat and the crowding, but not the smell. In the summer every parked dray or wagon was in danger of being made into a privy. The summer stench was "perfectly horrible."[100]

Dumbbell tenements became the fetid heart of the urban environmental crisis. In them disease and death festered and spread throughout the rest of the urban body. At the end of the century, after years of agitation and legislation, only 306 of the 255,033 people who fell under the New York Tenement House Committee's inspection had "access to bath-rooms in the houses in which they live." In one building, inspectors found that a sink that a fishmonger used to wash his fish provided water for a baker and was also used by the building's tenants as a urinal.[101]

Tenements bred disease, but they also grew money. They allowed landlords to get maximum revenue from the city's most undesirable buildings, in part because they were located near where the poor worked. In the late nineteenth century the old walking city was not yet dead, but it was becoming more and more confined to the poorest classes. Unskilled and semiskilled workers labored ten to twelve hours a day or more for wages that barely covered their rent and subsistence. Whether it be garment factories in New York or the stockyards and slaughterhouses in Chicago,

100. Yochelson and Czitrom, 40; Hunter, 43–46; Rischin, 83.
101. Yochelson and Czitrom, 23–26, 29–30, 40, David Huyssen, *Progressive Inequality: Rich and Poor in New York, 1890–1920* (Cambridge, MA: Harvard University Press, 2014), 40.

or the factories and workshops of Philadelphia, tenements clustered around places of employment so that the poor could save fares and walk to work. Workers might live farther from their jobs than they had before the war, but they still remained within walking distance.[102]

Tenement landlords were often immigrants themselves, the so-called cockroach capitalists, who saved, borrowed from small immigrant banks, and hired immigrant contractors. Immigrant storekeepers leased space, and tenants took in boarders. They made tenements both hothouses of entrepreneurship and sinks of misery. Evasion of housing laws was an essential part the business plan of housing owners and managers.[103]

Tenements concentrated all the maladies of the poor: infant mortality, disease, and their declining stature and health. The working life of their residents and the conditions in which they lived contributed to the problems that made poor children die young and stunted those who survived. Although human manifestations of the environmental crisis were related to nutrition and disease, precise cause-and-effect connections are difficult to make. Average caloric intake for Americans seems to have fallen, and the cost of food seems to have risen between 1840 and 1870, but they had held steady before 1840. The availability of food improved after 1870, so scarcity and hunger alone cannot explain the decline in measures of well-being across most of the period.[104]

The quality of food seems to have mattered as much as its abundance. Roughly 40–45 percent of American disposable income went to food in the late nineteenth century, and poor people spent the highest percentage of their income on subsistence. They could not afford to be picky. Until the 1890s and the growth of refrigeration, the poor had no place to store food, and they had little ready cash. As a result they bought food daily and in small quantities and always paid a premium. With little space to cook in crowded and often stifling apartments and little time after long hours of labor, workers, like workers elsewhere since the beginning of the industrial revolution, depended on bread and sweets as sources of cheap calories. They were loath to discard food even when it was in danger of spoiling.[105]

102. Theodore Hershberg, "The 'Journey-to-Work': An Empirical Investigation of Work, Residence and Transportation, Philadelphia, 1850 and 1880," in Hershberg, *Philadelphia*, 135–47; Greenberg, 129–46, 160–61, 211–14; Warner, 18–34.

103. Jared Day, *Urban Castles: Tenement Housing and Landlord Activism in New York City, 1890–1943* (New York: Columbia University Press, 1999), 31–56; Yochelson and Czitrom, 43–44.

104. Gordon, 63–64, 71; Floud et al., 315–17, 320.

105. Katherine Leonard Turner, *How the Other Half Ate: A History of Working Class Meals at the Turn of the Century* (Berkeley: University of California Press, 2014), 56–58, 59–70; Gordon, 37–42, 62–66.

Ice may have been the crucial element in reversing declines in American stature and nutrition. The rapid spread of refrigeration increased consumption of ice by a factor of five between 1880 and 1914. The sale of chilled beef by Chicago packinghouses, the development of canning, and the shipping of fresh winter vegetables to Eastern and Midwestern cities from the South and West all also potentially contributed to improving the diet and nutrition of urban workers, but simple iceboxes in residences probably did even more good. Refrigeration reduced spoilage, particularly of dairy products and meat, and decreased food-borne disease. Ice can claim credit for perhaps 50 percent of the improvement in nutrition in the 1890s, and with it the beginning of the rise in average height.[106]

Other conditions in tenements proved hard to change. Koch's discovery that light killed the tubercle bacillus and that the pest spread easily in close, dirty, and dark quarters could be used to inhibit its spread among the middling classes and in rural areas, but it did little good in tenements and on Indian reservations. Tuberculosis became a disease of the poor. By the end of the nineteenth century, the disease accounted for only one in eight American deaths, but the decline was not even. On the upper West Side of New York in 1890, the death rate from tuberculosis was 49 per 100,000. A few miles away in the tenements of the lower Manhattan, it was 776.[107]

Tuberculosis provided both more evidence that personal choice and the market were not going to solve the urban environmental crisis and that the authority and tools of the new municipal agencies were still too limited. In many ways, the public bodies sanitarians created remained prisoners of their origins. They were designed to attack corrupt political machines rather than the abuses of private landowners and landlords. Very often they wielded more power against poor tenants than against the landlords who exploited them.[108]

In 1866, when New York City was preparing for an anticipated cholera epidemic, reformers had attacked filth by attacking Tammany. E. L. Godkin's *Nation* argued that it was necessary to take public health out of the hands of politicians and place it in the hands of independent experts. Citing statistics that showed New York's death rate as 50 percent higher than London's and its infant mortality rate twice as high, the magazine attributed its sickliness to the politicization of health. It was misplaced democracy,

106. Lee A. Craig, Barry Goodwin, and Thomas Grennes, "The Effect of Mechanical Refrigeration on Nutrition in the United States," *Social Science History* 28, no. 2 (2004): 325–36; Turner, 32–34; Gordon, 70–71.
107. Rothman, 131, 184.
108. Day, 31–56; Yochelson and Czitrom, 63–65, 74.

the *Nation* argued, to leave public health in the control of elected officials rather than giving control to professionals. The magazine argued it was like taking a watch to a blacksmith for repair, or, in a more loaded metaphor, asking a hod carrier (an unskilled worker who carried bricks to bricklayers and was usually Irish) to act as a physician. A pending bill in the New York legislature to create a Metropolitan Sanitary District and Board of Health would remove public health from the purview of Tammany. With the epidemic looming, the bill passed.[109]

The Boards of Health did not become the bastions of expertise that reformers had promised; nor did they possess the powers necessary to attack environmental problems. Most of the members of these boards lacked either medical training or sanitation expertise. In New York a Tenement House Act (1879) and a New York Tenement House Commission (1884) granted additional power to the Board of Health, but efforts at enforcement brought bitter opposition from immigrant landlords, who regarded all regulation as attacks on their property rights. Commissioners could punish recalcitrant landlords by shutting down their buildings and evicting their tenants, but this obviously provided few incentives for the poor to report problems or cooperate with inspectors. In practice, enforcement was lax, exceptions were the norm, and judicial hostility was nearly constant. Appeals to a Christian capitalism of modest profit and model tenements had even less of an impact. Women, seizing on sanitation as an extension of their domestic responsibilities, proved most successful in pushing reform, but it would be a long fight. By 1884 Felix Adler, the founder of the Society for Ethical Culture, was demanding even greater state action to restrict the rights of property. Adler, the son of a Reform rabbi whom historian Moses Rischin dubbed New York's first advocate of "social Christianity," emphasized, "Deed not Creed."[110]

The urban infrastructure designed to overcome the environmental crisis of the cities had succeeded only in part. Municipal tax policy passed the burden of the crisis to taxpayers as a whole while reserving the benefits, and profits, of the proposed solutions for the wealthiest. The poor derived the least benefit from the infrastructure of sanitation and clean water in the cities. As late as 1893, 53 percent of the families in New York City, 70 percent of those in Philadelphia, 73 percent in Chicago, and 88 percent in Baltimore had access only to an outdoor privy. Although the percentages differed drastically from place to place, in 1900 just one-third of American homes had indoor running water.[111]

109. Rosenberg, 189–94, 199–205, 210–11; "New York and the Cholera," 40–41.
110. Yochelson and Czitrom, 26, 37–39, 40–44, 60–61, 74; Melosi, "Refuse Pollution and Municpal Reform," 105–14; Rischin, 201–2.
111. Gordon, 45, 114.

The failure to spread the benefits of the new infrastructure to the poor became evident in their homes. Dark, dank, and filthy, tenements were as antithetical to American ideas of the home as they were hospitable to tuberculosis, typhoid, dysentery, and other waterborne diseases. At a Cooper Institute meeting on the tenement problem in 1879, Parke Godwin, the editor of the *New York Post*, touched the heart of the danger: "These are the homes of the people. The homes! God forgive us for such prostitution of the blessed word home! As you and I know it, it has no meaning there." The home was supposed to be "the resort of peace and joy and love, the center of the sweetest and tenderest ties, the educator of the young, and through them far more the educator of the old; the source of whatever is noble and manly and truthful in human character, diffusing its gentle influences outward over all society..."; but these "rayless holes in the wall" were where "intemperance is nursed, where crime is cradled, where pale-eyed famine and flushed fever lodge, where the instincts of innocent childhood are stifled..." and on and on in the swelling lists the Victorians loved so well. Jacob Riis, the most famous housing reform advocate of the era, was more succinct. Tenements were the "murder of the home." All the emotional power of the home could not overcome the political economy that free labor had unintentionally created.[112]

---

112. "Tenement Life in New York," 226–27; Yochelson and Czitrom, 61, 74.

14

The Great Upheaval

In 1886 more than six hundred thousand American workers walked out of shops, factories, and work sites. There were fourteen hundred separate strikes affecting 11,562 businesses. Employers locked out still more. The strikes peaked on May Day, May 1, with a national strike for the eight-hour day; collectively they became what the economist and labor historian Selig Perlman later called the Great Upheaval. The size, extent, organization, and expanse of the strikes far exceeded those of 1877. This was not the spontaneous walkout of largely unorganized workers. Labor organizations of a size the country had never seen before coordinated, or tried to coordinate, most of them.[1]

To the alarm and discomfort of its cautious national leader, General Master Workman Terrence Powderly, the Knights of Labor formed the vanguard. An organization with 110,000 members in 1885, it numbered 729,000 by July 1, 1886, forming roughly fifteen thousand assemblies scattered across the country.[2]

The Knights grew because they had defeated Jay Gould, one of the most hated men in the country, and because they had renounced their vows of secrecy in deference to the Catholic Church's ban on membership in secret societies. But they also grew because they had helped mobilize the West against the Chinese in what amounted to an American

---

1. For comparison, there were only 471 strikes in 1881. James R. Green, *Death in the Haymarket: A Story of Chicago, the First Labor Movement and the Bombing That Divided Gilded Age America* (New York: Pantheon Books, 2006), 145; James J. Connolly, *An Elusive Unity: Urban Democracy and Machine Politics in Industrializing America* (Ithaca, NY: Cornell University Press, 2010), 90.
2. Eric Arnesen, "American Workers and the Labor Movement in the Late Nineteenth Century," in *The Gilded Age: Perspectives on the Origins of Modern America*, ed. Charles W. Calhoun, 2nd ed. (Lanham, MD: Rowman & Littlefield, 2007), 61; Melton Alonza McLaurin, *The Knights of Labor in the South* (Westport, CT: Greenwood Press, 1978), 53–55; Kim Voss, *The Making of American Exceptionalism: The Knights of Labor and Class Formation in the Nineteenth Century* (Ithaca, NY: Cornell University Press, 1993), 75–79; Richard White, *Railroaded: The Transcontinentals and the Making of Modern America* (New York: Norton, 2011), 289.

pogrom, and because they were preparing to expand into the South. Together, these developments had made them the most powerful labor organization in the country.

On the surface, the Knights seemed unchanged. They retained all their American men's club paraphernalia of oaths and offices. They still opposed the wage system and believed in a cooperative economy. They continued to be an antimonopolist reform group as well as a labor union that welcomed nonwageworkers so long as they were producers. Antimonopolists used "producer" to describe people who lived off their own labor, as opposed to bankers, landlords, speculators, and investors, who lived off the labor of others; and as opposed also to supposedly servile workers, who were the tools of corporations. Perched in between were small merchants and lawyers. The Knights cared less about class than about labor and independence.[3]

European socialists watching the sudden growth of the Knights were impressed, confused, and amused. Friedrich Engels, the coauthor with Karl Marx of *The Communist Manifesto*, regarded the organization, beliefs, and actions of the Knights of Labor as an "American paradox." Their "immense association" represented "all shades of individual and local opinion within the working class." Their constitution was authoritarian but "impracticable." What united them was "the instinctive feeling that the very fact of clubbing together for their common cause makes them a very great power in the country; a truly American paradox clothing the most democratic and even rebellious spirit behind an apparent, but really powerless despotism." He concluded, "Whatever their shortcomings and little absurdities, whatever their platform and constitution, here they are, the work of practically the whole class of American wage-workers, the only national bond that holds them together, that makes their strength felt to themselves not less than their enemies, and fills them with proud hope of future victories."[4]

In regarding the Knights as the expression of "practically the whole class of American wage-workers," Engels proved astute. The Knights organized black as well as white workers, women as well as men, and unskilled as well as skilled. They confined their membership neither to

3. Rosanne Currarino, *The Labor Question in America: Economic Democracy in the Gilded Age* (Urbana: University of Illinois Press, 2011), 13–16.
4. Robert E. Weir, *Beyond Labor's Veil: The Culture of the Knights of Labor* (University Park: Pennsylvania State University, 1996), xv, 11–12; For Marx and Engels's views, R. Laurence Moore, *European Socialists and the American Promised Land* (New York: Oxford University Press, 1970), 3–24; Richard Jules Oestreicher, *Solidarity and Fragmentation: Working People and Class Consciousness in Detroit, 1875–1900* (Urbana: University of Illinois Press, 1986), 13–25.

whites nor to men, but the Knights were not open to everyone. Whom the Knights included and whom they excluded said much about them. Their victory over Gould gained them members, but so did their attacks on the Chinese.

Look to the Midwest, East, and South, and the Knights seemed the vanguard of at least a limited racial equality; look to the West and they appeared very different. At various times, the Knights distrusted Italians, Finns, Hungarians, and more, but the one racial or ethnic group they banned from the organization was the Chinese. The Chinese were largely wage laborers like themselves, but the Knights thought them quite different from other immigrants or freedpeople. They regarded them not as workers but as coolies, virtual semislaves who undermined free labor. Their attacks on the Chinese had as much to do with their popularity, particularly in the West, as did their resistance to Gould. Both sowed the ground for the Great Upheaval.[5]

The Knights considered the Chinese tools of the corporations. Restrictions on immigration still left a large Chinese population in the western United States, and Chinese workers who emigrated back home or into Mexico or Canada retained the right to return. Americans had no real control over their southern or northern borders, and Chinese immigrants continued to pass across both. The incapacity of the federal government to enforce its immigration ban fertilized continuing resentment against the Chinese.[6]

The solidarity the Knights preached in the West depended on workers' identity as white men rather than as wage earners. As Joseph Buchanan, the leading Western Knight, put it, the Chinese made him alter his belief from the brotherhood of man to "The Brotherhood of Man, Limited." In February 1885 a town official in Eureka, California, died when he unwittingly wandered into a gunfight between Chinese. White citizens drove out the entire Chinese population, numbering in the hundreds, in retaliation. Their expulsion from neighboring Arcata followed. Then there was nothing for six months.[7]

When widespread violence erupted in the autumn of 1885, the Knights were at the center of it. It began in Rock Springs, Wyoming, where Chinese, employed by labor contractors, worked in the mines owned by the Union Pacific Railroad alongside white miners, the majority of whom were European immigrants. A work rule that whites thought favored the

---

5. Beth Lew-Williams, *The Chinese Must Go: Racial Violence and the Making of the Alien in America* (Cambridge, MA: Harvard University Press, forthcoming), 133–34, 145; Currarino, 36–59.
6. Lew-Williams, 48, 108–11; White, 304–5.
7. White, 301; Lew-Williams, 98.

Chinese and endangered the safety of all miners triggered a fight between Chinese miners and white miners. Things escalated quickly. Officially, the Knights played no role and condemned the violence, but their desire to banish the Chinese was clear. A mob burned down the Chinese quarter with some of the inhabitants inside, shot others, and drove survivors into the desert. Roughly fifty Chinese died. Public sympathy lay with the white miners, as officials reported to Charles Francis Adams, then the president of the Union Pacific, that the "Chinese Question was the most prominent topic west of the Missouri River."[8]

News of Rock Springs triggered violence elsewhere. By the spring of 1886, 150 western communities had expelled, or attempted to expel, the Chinese. In Washington Territory Daniel Cronin, an organizer for the Knights, made anti-Chinese agitation a tool for a wider attack on corporations and monopolies in order "to free the laboring man from the shackles that he now bears." The expulsions amounted to a kind of ethnic cleansing, designed to drive people out rather than to kill them. Sinophobes initially relied on boycotts and threats rather than the violence, but they escalated into vigilante actions, which often had the acquiescence of local authorities.[9]

Absence of lethal violence did not mean the absence of force. In Tacoma, no murders took place, but mobs burned down the city's Chinatown, evicted the Chinese, and beat some of them. The vigilantes considered their actions as extralegal—enforcing the law when officials failed to do so—rather than illegal. They claimed their actions secured the intent of anti-Chinese legislation, which the government lacked the administrative capacity to enforce. In Seattle federal troops and the state militia supported the Loyal League, which was drawn from the local elite and largely favored "cheap labor," temporarily preventing the expulsion of the Chinese. Some members of the Loyal League regarded the violence as a socialist uprising, and they saw their victory over the anti-Chinese vigilantes in Seattle quickly morph into defeat. Most of the terrorized Chinese accepted a negotiated settlement to abandon the city. Those indicted for the mob actions were acquitted. The violence of 1885–86 strengthened the Sinophobes' hand, and they drove home their political advantage. Territorial Governor Watson Squire of Washington, who had called on federal troops to protect the Chinese, recognized that this was not a stance helpful to his political future. With the eventual admission of Washington as a state, Squire would be elected to the U.S. Senate on an anti-Chinese platform. All over the West the Chinese became more segregated,

8. Craig Storti, *Incident at Bitter Creek: The Story of the Rock Springs Chinese Massacre* (Ames: Iowa State University Press, 1991), 108–21; White, 307, 310–11.
9. Lew-Williams, 98–133.

retreating into large Chinatowns—particularly in San Francisco—where numbers brought protection.[10]

The corporations also retreated. In 1885 Charles Francis Adams emphasized the link between corporate battles with the Knights of Labor and their fight against the anti-Chinese movement in the West: both conflicts were "between law and order, civilization and Christianity on the one hand, and massacre and riot, socialism and communism on the others." He quickly decided, however, that this was a battle he preferred not to fight. He reasoned that railroads were "commercial enterprises; they are not humanitarian, philanthropic, or political." Change would come gradually, but for now the Union Pacific was held in "odium" in Wyoming, and for that matter in the West, and this imposed a heavy burden. In neighboring Colorado, the legislature was full of Knights and their sympathizers ready to regulate railroads. He thought the best course was to adapt to the political reality. He would, however, move to replace white miners with machinery and Chinese.[11]

Many white businessmen across the West voiced more sympathy for the Knights than the businesses that employed Chinese workers. In San Francisco most merchants and manufacturers, though wary of organized labor, saw monopolies, particularly the Southern Pacific Railroad, as a threat to the public good. They regarded themselves and the Knights as part of single mass of white proprietors and craftsmen. Like the Knights, they framed the issue racially. The California Knights declared the Chinese to be the tools of monopolies and "a menace to free labor and free men." White Westerners, they said, had no choice but to act in self-defense and expel an inassimilable people.[12]

In the East, Midwest, and South the Knights did not draw such stark racial lines. The Knights regarded black workers as their legal, if not yet social, equals, who had assimilated the core cultural values of home and republican manhood. In upholding the legal equality of black people, they appealed to the federal government and the federal constitution over the opposition of "redeemer" Democratic state governments in the South. They attracted black members but often did precious little to help them.

---

10. Lew-Williams, 105, 107–8, 112, 127–55, 170–81; Terence Vincent Powderly, *Thirty Years of Labor, 1859–1889* (New York: A. M. Kelley, 1967), 162, 213, 216–17; White, 301–2; Tamara Venit Shelton, *A Squatter's Republic: Land and the Politics of Monopoly in California and the Nation, 1850–1900* (Berkeley: University of California Press, 2013), 108–12, 118–20.

11. White, 314–15.

12. Jeffrey Haydu, *Citizen Employers: Business Communities and Labor in Cincinnati and San Francisco, 1870–1916* (Ithaca, NY: ILR Press, 2008), 16–17, and passim.

I

The Knights were the largest and most unusual labor organization in the United States, but by the 1880s most big American cities also contained Central Labor Councils or Central Labor Unions formed from affiliated unions of skilled workers, some of whom belonged to the Knights as well. The Knights and the Councils occupied a rather large swath of ideological terrain. Both contained socialists as well as the more conservative "brotherhoods." Both drew heavily from native-born and Irish workers, but in Chicago and other cities they also contained more radical German and Bohemian workers.[13]

Anarchists and socialists formed the far left of the labor movement. In Chicago, where Joseph Buchanan would move from Denver and which became the center of the Great Upheaval, "bomb talking," which was shorthand for terrorist threats, and the romance of dynamite had become common both among German anarchists such as August Spies and native-born anarchists such as the ever-more-radical Albert and Lucy Parsons, who had become the unlikely Romeo and Juliet of the Left.[14]

The numbers of anarchists and socialists remained small—they drew most heavily from German and Bohemian immigrants—but they were loud, provocative, and the favorite whipping boys of conservatives and a fearful bourgeoisie, whose own rhetoric could be just as bloody. Their political year began with celebrations of the formation of the Paris Commune. In 1879 the anarchist parade in Chicago drew forty thousand people. Few Irish were anarchists, but the bombing of the British Houses of Parliament and Westminster Hall in early 1885 by the Clan Na Gael, which drew significant support from Irish American workers, augmented the fears sowed by anarchist rhetoric. German immigrants made up most of the Socialist Party.[15]

On the most conservative edge of the movement was the so-called aristocracy of labor. Peter M. Arthur, the head of the Brotherhood of Locomotive Engineers, proclaimed labor's and capital's interests to be

---

13. For the formation of the Central Labor Union in New York, Edward T. O'Donnell, *Henry George and the Crisis of Inequality: Progress and Poverty in the Gilded Age* (New York: Columbia University Press, 2015), 119–21; Richard Schneirov, *Labor and Urban Politics: Class Conflict and the Origins of Modern Liberalism in Chicago, 1864–97* (Urbana: University of Illinois Press, 1998), 174–78; Bruce C. Nelson, *Beyond the Martyrs: A Social History of Chicago's Anarchists, 1870–1900* (New Brunswick, NJ: Rutgers University Press, 1988), 44–48.
14. Nelson, 47–51; Green, 53–59.
15. Green, 132–33, 140–45; Schneirov, 122–23, 173–79.

identical. The brotherhood depended on a monopoly of craft skill and canny negotiating over work rules to maintain its power.[16]

The plethora of organizations made a united labor movement unlikely, but it still improved on the paucity of organizations in the Great Strike of 1877. Nor did the divisions retard militancy. Between 1880 and the end of the century, the United States had three times the strike activity of France. Most strikes were over wages, but strikes by skilled workers were more likely to be about work rules and control over work. Control over work sounds abstract, but very often it was a matter of life and death.[17]

The unwillingness of employers to invest money in technologies or practices that would increase safety at the expense of profit was a constant source of contention between workers and management. Competition, as the economist Henry Carter Adams observed about the carnage tolerated in industry, forced "the moral sentiment pervading any trade down to the level of that which characterizes the worst man who can maintain himself in it." At stake in the struggle over the conditions of work was worker safety and well being.[18]

By the end of the 1880s national politicians and state commissions were proclaiming that the "destruction of human life is much greater in the peaceful pursuits of industry than in war." Compared with the Civil War with its vast carnage, this was demonstrably untrue, but it was not so exaggerated when compared with other American wars. Industrial accidents annually produced greater casualties, although not higher death rates, than Americans experienced in the American Revolution, the War of 1812, the Mexican American War, and the Indian Wars. Mining, railroad work, construction, and labor in the steel and iron mills produced a toll of dead and injured to make it seem that the nation was producing "an army of cripples."[19]

War, with its loss of life and injuries, was the metaphor of first resort, but in terms of death rates a better metaphor would have been childbirth. Industrial death rates hovered around those of women in childbirth. To

---

16. White, 344, 416.
17. David Montgomery, "Strikes in Nineteenth-Century America," *Social Science History* 4, no. 1 (1980): 86, 89–93, 97–98; James Livingston, *Pragmatism and the Political Economy of Cultural Revolution, 1850–1940* (Chapel Hill: University of North Carolina Press, 1994), 90.
18. John Fabian Witt, *The Accidental Republic: Crippled Workingmen, Destitute Widows, and the Remaking of American Law* (Cambridge, MA: Harvard University Press, 2004), 31.
19. "America's Wars," Office of Public Affairs, Department of Veterans Affairs, http://www.va.gov/opa/publications/factsheets/fs_americas_wars.pdf; Mark Aldrich, *Death Rode the Rails: American Railroad Accidents and Safety, 1828–1965* (Baltimore, MD: Johns Hopkins University Press, 2006), 97–180; Witt, 23–26.

maintain family and home, working men had paradoxically entered the zone of risk long endured by women. Deaths in childbirth were higher than anywhere else in the industrialized world, hovering at or above seven deaths per thousand births for American women as a whole. The death rate for black women was nearly twice as high. Although in 1890 accidental deaths of men between the ages of fifteen and forty-five were five times those of women in the same age cohort, because of deaths in childbirth women still led riskier lives. Badly trained doctors and unsanitary conditions that led to puerperal fever produced the carnage.[20]

Statistics are woefully incomplete, but between 1850 and 1880 the likelihood that American males between ten and fifty would die from accidental death rose by two-thirds, from 7 percent to 12 percent of total deaths. In 1860 railroad accidents accounted for fewer than 1 percent of the deaths among this male cohort; in 1890 the figure jumped to 3 percent. The dangers of work rose in every industrial country in the late nineteenth century, but they rose faster and higher in the United States, where work was more dangerous than elsewhere and far more dangerous than it would be a century later.[21]

Mining has always been hazardous, and although some new technologies made mining safer, what technology gave with one hand, it took back with the other. Machine drills, electric lights with their wires and cables in wet mines, dynamite, steam, and electrical lifts removed old dangers, added new ones, and allowed mines to go deeper into more and more risky places. Fatalities in hard rock mines in Colorado, Idaho, Montana, and South Dakota were twice those of the United Kingdom and Germany, which ranged around three deaths annually per thousand miners. If only underground miners were counted, the death rate was about six per thousand in Colorado. Annual death rates from accidents in the mines didn't even capture the main danger: miner's consumption or phthisis, which was an artifact of the machine drill and the fine particles it produced. Compared with an explosion, a fire, a fall, or a mine collapse, it killed slowly.[22]

20. The death rates were certainly even higher, given that the statistics were partial and came from the more medically advanced North and not from the South, which when statistics were collected had higher rates. Irvine Loudon, *Death in Childbirth: An International Study of Maternal Care and Maternal Mortality, 1800–1950* (Oxford: Clarendon Press, 1992), 152–54, 286–97, 366–74; Witt, 37.
21. Aldrich, 103–5, 114, 120; Witt, 23–26.
22. Witt, 25–26; table Ba4726-4741—Injuries and fatalities in mining, quarrying, and related industries: 1870–1970, in *Historical Statistics of the United States, Earliest Times to the Present: Millennial Edition*, ed. Scott Sigmund Gartner, Susan B. Carter, Michael R. Haines, Alan L. Olmstead, Richard Sutch, and Gavin Wright (New York: Cambridge University Press, 2006); Thomas G. Andrews, *Killing for Coal: America's*

Railroads, the symbol of the new age, provided the most dangerous work of all. American railroad men had a death rate of more than eight per thousand in the 1890s. This was not simply the nature of railroads; Americans were twice as likely to die on the job as those working on British railroads. Among trainmen—those on the moving trains—the rate was between nine and eleven deaths per thousand, still below the death rate of black women in childbirth. The casualties came less from spectacular accidents than the incidents of everyday work: coupling and uncoupling cars, making up trains, and setting handbrakes on freight trains, which involved men making their way over the tops of moving box cars in all kinds of weather. By 1893, the year that Congress enacted the first national safety legislation, 1,567 trainmen died and 18,877 were injured annually.[23]

The daily struggles over who decided how work would proceed went to the heart of workers' safety and self-identity as men. Miners, who could read the dangers of a badly ventilated mine, wanted to determine when and how they should work. Railroad workers wanted to determine when it was safe to run a train and how to run it. Unions demanded state regulation of mines, compulsory mine inspections, and the mandatory adoption of safety equipment like automatic couplers on railroad cars. All of these became the sources of long and grueling fights.[24]

Organized workers were fighting to set the rules of the game. They were often successful. Although statistics suggest that the success rate fell following the Great Upheaval, the sides remained relatively evenly matched. Between 1886 and 1889, workers won 44 percent of the strikes and compromised on 13 percent.[25]

Deflation made the 1880s particularly volatile. On the one hand, deflation meant that if workers could simply maintain existing wages, they would earn more because the dollar was growing more valuable and their purchasing power was thus increasing. But deflation and competition also

Deadliest Labor War (Cambridge, MA: Harvard University Press, 2008), 146; Mark Wyman, *Hard Rock Epic: Western Miners and the Industrial Revolution, 1860–1910* (Berkeley: University of California Press, 1979), 84–117.

23. White, 285–87; I have given a lower estimate than Witt, 26–27. See also Aldrich; Marc Linder, "Fatal Subtraction: Statistical MIA on the Industrial Battlefield," *Journal of Legislation* 20, no. 2 (1994): 104–5, 108; Aldrich, 317–18, 327–29.

24. Wyman, 180–81, 187–89; Steven W. Usselman, *Regulating Railroad Innovation: Business, Technology, and Politics in America, 1840–1920* (New York: Cambridge University Press, 2002), 121–23; Aldrich, 104–12, 181–215.

25. Livingston, 90; Herbert G. Gutman, "Work, Culture, and Society in Industrializing America, 1815–1919," *American Historical Review* 78, no. 3 (1973): 566; John R. Commons, *History of Labour in the United States*, ed. David J. Saposs et al. (New York: Macmillan, 1918), 2: 360–61; Montgomery, 86, 89–93, 97–98.

increased the pressure that employers put on their wages. Convinced of the possibility of better conditions, workers felt threatened by the status quo of long hours, frequent unemployment, the burden of disease, a declining life span, and relentless pressure on wages. To many Americans who identified with neither "Labor" nor "Capital," the explosion of strikes indicated that the country was moving toward conditions they associated with Europe.

The fluidity of American social conditions gave many people who were neither workers nor large employers a stake in the outcome of the strikes erupting across the country. The free-labor ideal imagined social mobility as unidirectional, with wage work merely a stage in life, but in actual experience people moved down as well as up. Men and women who had worked for wages took up farming or opened small businesses: stores, saloons, shops, and boardinghouses. When these enterprises failed, the proprietors fell back into the ranks of wage earners. From census to census, people might bounce between the ranks of the working class and the ranks of small proprietors, without changing their beliefs, associations, or loyalties.[26]

Wageworkers thus had allies beyond the labor movement. Many small proprietors sympathized with laborers, who were their friends, neighbors, and relatives. Particularly in towns and smaller cities, skilled workers were a known quantity to their neighbors: men with families and homes, who often held local office. Like the Knights, farmers and small proprietors tended to divide society between producers and nonproducers rather than capital and labor. Within the large and fluctuating mass of "producers"— farmers, skilled workers, and small proprietors—the American capacity to distrust those above and below them, the nonproducers, ran strong. Such attitudes made Gould, who epitomized men who grew wealthy without productive labor, an ideal enemy. After the failed and bitter strike against his Western Union in 1882, a machinist testified before Congress that "Jay Gould never earned a great deal, but he owns a terrible lot." This was a belief held beyond the ranks of workers. Collis P. Huntington described Gould as a vulture, "as usual lighting down upon one thing [or] another and sucking some portion of its lifeblood, and then taking wing again for some other carcass."[27]

When the Knights under the leadership of Joseph Buchanan defeated Gould, they won sympathizers and supporters beyond the working class.

26. Nick Salvatore, *Eugene V. Debs: Citizen and Socialist* (Urbana: University of Illinois Press, 1982), 48; Herbert Gutman, "Class, Status, and Community Power in Nineteenth-Century American Industrial Cities," in *Work, Culture and Society in Industrializing America* (New York: Vintage Books, 1977, orig. ed. 1966), 234–92.

27. Livingston, 44–45; White, 196.

Buchanan, was, like Henry George, a printer turned journalist and a virulent Sinophobe. He became an eclectic radical: nominally anarchist and more practically a socialist who believed workers could exercise influence both in the workplace and through the ballot box. He had won strikes against the Union Pacific, and when early in 1885 Gould cut wages on the Wabash and Missouri, Kansas and Texas, and Missouri Pacific, Buchanan and the Knights forced Gould to rescind the cuts. This more than any other single event brought a rush of members to the Knights.[28]

Powderly had no desire to confront Gould in 1886, but circumstances forced his hand after Gould broke an agreement negotiated by Buchanan. Gould and his managers had kept their promises to the most powerful workers, the trainmen, whose skills made them difficult to replace. But they refused to restore pay cuts to section hands and yardmen, as they had pledged. When Gould failed to live up to his bargain, Powderly participated in negotiations with Gould's Southwest system, but by then the Knights were struggling with both bitter internal divisions and new members who launched strikes the Knights were ill-prepared to sustain. Stretched thin, Powderly did not stand up well to the pressure. He fell sick in November 1885, thought he was going crazy in December, and tendered his resignation as Grand Master Workman. But he stayed on. By March 1886 requests for charters for new assemblies were rolling in at about fifty per day and overwhelmed the board. Powderly and the central committee issued a "Go Slow" circular asking for a suspension of all organizing for forty days with no new strikes or boycotts. This was not auspicious.[29]

It was a mark of Powderly's ineffective leadership that things not only speeded up, but the Knights embarked on a massive strike. When the Knights went out on strike against Gould's Southwest System, which covered forty-one hundred miles of track and stretched over five states and Indian Territory, Powderly learned about it in the newspapers. Gould had set an elaborate trap. Key leaders of the Knights recognized it, but they could not control their membership, angry at Gould's refusal to keep the terms that had ended the earlier strike against his railroads. As in so many strikes, the precipitating cause seemed trivial and arcane to outsiders but a matter of high principle to the strikers themselves. The Knights working for Gould refused to countenance his refusal to keep his bargain with the

28. White, 288–89; Joshua D. Wolff, *Western Union and the Creation of the American Corporate Order, 1845–1893* (New York: Cambridge University Press, 2013), 271–72; John P. Enyeart, *The Quest for "Just and Pure Law": Rocky Mountain Workers and American Social Democracy, 1870–1924* (Stanford, CA: Stanford University Press, 2009), 25–28, 48–50.

29. Craig Phelan, *Grand Master Workman: Terence Powderly and the Knights of Labor* (Westport, CT: Greenwood Press, 2000), 172–76.

lowest-paid workers, and then, as a final provocation, the Texas and Pacific fired a local Knights assembly leader after he left work with the permission of his foreman to attend a district meeting of the Knights. This was the bait that the Knights took.

Martin Irons would be unfairly blamed for leading the Knights into a strike that paralyzed a good section of the nation over the firing of a single worker, but in fact he tried to prevent the walkout. He recognized that Gould's strategy was to split the Knights, separating the most skilled from the rest. More critically, Gould would not fight the Knights in 1886 on the same losing ground that he had in 1885, when the strikers had considerable local support; he would bring the state and federal courts in on his side. Gould had run a key portion of his Southwest System, the Texas and Pacific, into receivership. It had failed to meet its payments on bonds, but those bonds were due to other roads in the Gould system. Gould, in effect, sued Gould to place the Texas and Pacific in receivership. In receivership its employees became federal employees responsible to court-appointed receivers, one of whom was ex-governor John C. Brown of Texas, known as "Gould's political whip for the Southwest." The court deputized railroad officials, "making interference with the work of deputies interference with the laws of the United States" and making such interference contempt of court. Railroads in receivership claimed the right to abrogate labor agreements and to appeal to the courts for the armed force to combat strikes that resulted. Receivership allowed Gould blandly to tell Powderly that "the contest is not between your order and me, but between your order and the laws of the land."[30]

Joseph Buchanan saw no hope for the second Southwest strike. His logic was impeccable. A successful railroad strike depended on stopping trains from running, and without the support of the trainmen this could not happen, at least quickly enough to make a difference, unless the strikers used force to halt them. If they used force, they would meet counterforce. They could defeat deputies, Pinkertons, and railroad detectives. Fighting for wife and children — "Betty and the babies" — they might even prove a match for the militia. But taking on roads in receivership meant drawing in the federal government and federal troops. Workers were no match for the army. And, as they escalated the violence, the workers

30. Theresa Case, *The Great Southwest Railroad Strike and Free Labor* (College Station: Texas A&M Press, 2010), 163; "Correspondence between Officers of the Missouri Pacific Railway Co. and Members of the Knights of Labor of America [Railway Pamphlets]," ([S.l.]), v. 109, Stanford University Library; Missouri Commissioner of Labor Statistics, *The Official History of the Great Strike of 1886 on the Southwestern Railway System* (n.p.: Commissioner of Labor Statistics and Inspection, Missouri, n.d.), 13–14.

would, as Gould said, make the contest not against monopoly but against the government. That was revolution, and workers unwilling to vote for revolution would be unlikely to fight for one.[31]

Receivership provided the critical element in the conflict; without it, the federal government had less authority to intervene. The *Posse Comitatus* Act of 1878, passed in the wake of 1877 strikes, had taken away, for the moment, the president's ability to deploy the U.S. Army in cases of civil unrest except when such use was expressly allowed by the Constitution or an act of Congress. It thus created a greater reliance on state militias to supplement the police and private guards.[32]

States were not necessarily in a position to take up the slack. Militias had languished in the wake of the Civil War. They had nearly disappeared in parts of the Midwest and West, and the redeemer governments of the South had quickly extinguished the Reconstruction militias. Following the Great Strike of 1877, fear of civil disorder had led to new National Guard units in the Midwest that relied on smaller, better-financed, better-disciplined, better-armed volunteer groups recruited largely from the middle classes. In the 1880s the creation of National Guard units was most pronounced in the industrial states of the Northeast, particularly in New York and Massachusetts. The armories of New York City were designed to overawe the working classes, but the state also funded twenty-six armories outside the city. In 1887, in response to the Great Upheaval the federal government doubled the appropriations to equip National Guard units, but the amount was still a modest $400,000.[33]

Governors eventually used the Guard to quell civil disorder 328 times between 1886 and 1895. The Guard most often confronted strikers in the industrial states of Illinois, Pennsylvania, Ohio, and New York, but even here governors were reluctant to use soldiers. Although workers came to see guardsmen as the tools of employers, the reorganized National Guard units were not a strikebreaking force over most of the country, and they sometimes sympathized with the strikers.[34]

Gould recognized that the most critical interventions in labor unrest would come from the least democratic sector of the government: the courts, particularly the federal courts. The ability of corporations and

---

31. Case, 165–66; White, 339–40.
32. D. Laurie Clayton, "Filling the Breach: Military Aid to the Civil Power in the Trans-Mississippi West," *Western Historical Quarterly* 25, no. 2 (1994): 156–62.
33. Jerry M. Cooper, *The Rise of the National Guard: The Evolution of the American Militia, 1865–1920* (Lincoln: University of Nebraska Press, 1997), 23–43, 49–53, 57–58.
34. David Montgomery, *Citizen Worker: The Experience of Workers in the United States with Democracy and the Free Market During the Nineteenth Century* (Cambridge: Cambridge University Press, 1993), 95–96; Cooper, 44–64.

large employers to gain more and more influence over the courts and the ability of those courts to deploy force in support of private companies shifted the balance of power between workers and employers. Gould gambled that the courts would be on his side, and he was right.[35]

Gradually, and with much internal conflict, the courts were interpreting free labor only as a worker's property right in his labor. It was thus both a "natural" right and subject to the constraints on property rights embodied in considerations of *Salus populi*. Workers could withhold their labor in strikes or boycotts, but not if such actions infringed on the rights of other workers, harmed public welfare, disrupted the rules of the market, or illegally diluted the value of an employer's property. Judges drew on Stephen Field's earlier dissent in the *Slaughterhouse* cases (1873) defining free labor as the right to pursue a calling without restraint. Congress had intended the Fourteenth Amendment to ensure that states did not interfere in the exercise of civil liberties guaranteed by the Constitution. Through substantive due process, judges sought to use the amendment to enshrine freedom of contract, open competition, and laissez-faire in the Constitution even though none of these things had been part of the document. The courts made the amendment a means for ruling on the constitutionality of regulatory legislation that applied to business and labor by evaluating their substantive effect. Any attempt to limit competition was an attempt at monopoly, which was anathema to a liberal judiciary.[36]

By making free labor virtually identical with substantive due process, the courts potentially made licensing laws, strikes, boycotts, the closed shop, and even some public health regulations the legal equivalents of slavery. Attempts by workers to organize a strike or boycott became a conspiracy against the rights of other workers who did not strike to pursue a calling as well as a violation of the new "right" of capital to a fair expected return on investment.[37]

The legal formalists who enshrined substantive due process did not operate in isolation; they had political allies who shared their interpretation of free labor. In 1887 Republican Sen. Henry Teller of Colorado provided an unadulterated version of this interpretation. No worker, Teller

35. Suresh Naidu and Noam Yuchtman, "Labor Market Institutions in the Gilded Age of American Economic History," in Working Paper 22117, NBER (Cambridge: National Bureau of Economic Research, 2016), 3; Karen Orren, *Belated Feudalism: Labor, the Law, and Liberal Development in the United States* (Cambridge: Cambridge University Press, 1991), 122–54; Case, 135, 182–84
36. William E. Forbath, *Law and the Shaping of the American Labor Movement* (Cambridge, MA: Harvard University Press, 1991), 38–39.
37. Herbert Hovenkamp, *Enterprise and American Law, 1836–1937* (Cambridge, MA: Harvard University Press, 1991), 17–18, 171–82.

proclaimed, should surrender his right to sell his labor, because the "difference between a slave and a freeman consists mainly of the fact that a freeman may dispose of his labor...on the terms fixed by himself." What "the American laborer needs is individualism, freedom from the control of others," and neither "legislation, the rules of guilds, associations, trade unions or other conditions" should interfere. Echoing Lincoln, Teller claimed that the laborer of today was the capitalist of tomorrow. Judges increasingly regarded a strike, by definition, as a violation of natural law and public welfare and issued injunctions to stop them.[38]

When the Great Southwest Strike erupted in March 1886, the rank and file, both black and white, drove it forward. They were convinced that the Knights had no choice but to defend the 1885 agreement or lose all credibility and effectiveness. They believed that their only chance for victory was challenging the Southwest System as a whole, because all the roads had violated the agreement. They thought that the Knights on other connecting roads would refuse to handle the Southwest System's cars. Gould and his general manager, for their part, portrayed the strike as an unreasonable reaction to the firing of a single worker by a railroad, the Texas and Pacific, that the court rather than Gould controlled. The Southwest System was, Gould claimed, the victim rather than the instigator of the dispute. At the time of the walkout, Knights District Assembly 101, which called the strike, had no money in its treasury and had not notified Powderly or the national union of their actions.[39]

Gould's tactics, as planned, hived off the most-skilled workers. Although many individual trainmen supported them, the Knights lacked the backing of the railroad brotherhoods: the engineers, brakemen, conductors, and firemen who actually operated the trains. The strikers, not trusting the engineers and the firemen to honor the strike, had seized and disabled engines and occupied roundhouses to stop the trains from moving.[40]

Nor did the Knights garner the same kind of community support that they had mustered in 1885. How a community and local and state government broke—for the company or for the workers—often determined the fate of strike. In the strikes of 1885, state governments had largely remained neutral, and when local governments intervened, they often did so on the side of the strikers. In any large strike, critical decisions came early. Would the local police allow employers to arm scabs—a term derived from the

---

38. Hovenkamp, 96–101, 223; Melvin Dubofsky,"The Federal Judiciary, Free Labor, and Equal Rights," in *The Pullman Strike and the Crisis of the 1890s: Essays on Labor and Politics* (Urbana: University of Illinois Press, 1999), 161–64.
39. White, 336–39; Case, 151–67.
40. Case, 168–84; White, 339–41.

old English term for slut and applied to strikebreakers—or bring in armed guards of their own, usually hired from the Pinkerton Detective Agency, to protect their property and the workers they recruited? Or would they disarm Pinkertons and scabs and deputize the striking workers to keep order? The decision depended on whether workingmen and their sympathizers held local office. Hatred of a "monopoly" ran across class lines and often put local officials on the side of local residents. Similar considerations came into play at the state level.[41]

In 1886 Midwestern businessmen usually arrayed themselves against workers, but not from any sympathy for corporations. In Cincinnati, for example, businessmen came to oppose union labor, even as they denied the existence of class. They appealed to a recalibrated republicanism that stressed citizenship, the public welfare, and good government in a manner that made these things identical to their interests. The Knights needed to counter such formulations, but, distrustful of the press, they had not given the public their version of the story, thus allowing Gould to cast the narrative of the strike. The union's aggressiveness and failure to produce a compelling explanation of the strike did not turn small-town businessmen into supporters of Gould, but it did make them less likely to support the strikers, particularly as the strike cut them off from commerce. They viewed both the Knights and the railroad as powerful outside organizations disrupting local life.[42]

The courts turned the tide of the Southwestern strike. In Texas the court overseeing the receivership of the Texas and Pacific ruled the strike illegal and authorized the use of federal marshals to suppress it. More unexpectedly, in mid-March the federal courts in Missouri issued injunctions against the strikers, ordering them to vacate railroad property. This pushed the conflict into the streets. Gould and his railroads could muster money, guns, and lawyers; the Knights could not.[43]

The combination of armed men in the employ of the railroads and angry strikers and their supporters who were determined to maintain the strike and stop the trains proved lethal. Many strikers upheld the right of

41. Shelton Stromquist, A Generation of Boomers: The Pattern of Railroad Conflict in Nineteenth-Century America (Urbana: University of Illinois Press, 1987), 174–87; Connolly, 89; Herbert Gutman, "Workers Search for Power: Labor in the Gilded Age," in The Gilded Age: A Reappraisal, ed. H. Wayne Morgan (Syracuse, NY: Syracuse University Press, 1963). For scab, this is the etymology listed in the Oxford English Dictionary.
42. Haydu, 16–17, and passim; Case, 168–84; Michael J. Cassity, "Modernization and Social Crisis: The Knights of Labor and a Midwest Community, 1885–86," Journal of American History 66, no. 1 (1979): 41–61; White, 339–41.
43. Case, 182–84.

individuals to work and depended on persuasion to stop them, but others believed that only communal violence could counter the violence of the railroads, their deputies, and their gunmen. The strikers relied on force of numbers to intimidate strikebreakers, but faced with the injunctions and the presence of armed guards, some turned to arson, the disabling of trains, and the stoning of crews. By the end of March 1886, pitched battles had erupted in Fort Worth, St. Louis, and East St. Louis, Illinois. Opponents portrayed the strikers as dangerous mobs; the strikers pointed to deputized gunmen who fired into crowds containing women and children. In either case, the strikers were up against the armed force of the state as militia joined police and deputized gunmen. By April, barring a miracle, the strike was doomed. The courts had taken over public policy.[44]

II

The Great Southwest Strike was the largest strike in the nation, but Chicago became the center of the Great Upheaval. The labor unrest there involved all the elements agitating working people in the mid-1880s: the surge of new members into the Knights (who embodied, more than any other union, the noble, if sometimes disastrous, stance that an injury to one was an injury to all), the contest over control of work, the dangers and deskilling involved in the spread of mechanization, and a renewed push for the eight-hour day. All had become political.

Chicago politics took a critical turn just as the Great Upheaval gathered momentum. In 1885 Mayor Carter Harrison's ability to win working-class votes and keep the social peace collapsed. Frances Willard and the WCTU played a role. A reinvigorated temperance campaign signaled the return of the evangelical middle class to Chicago politics. And even though the WCTU and its allies failed to win the temperance legislation they desired in the city, they did obtain a licensing bill from the state, which served to shut down many of the city's smaller saloons, raised the price of alcohol, and gave Chicago a shot of new tax revenue. Harrison's opposition to restrictions on liquor and other sumptuary legislation that regulated personal expenditures on moral grounds, as well as his geniality and charm, had secured him German and Irish Catholic votes. The

44. Case, 181–83, 195–208; Ruth Allen, *The Great Southwest Strike*, University of Texas Publication 4214 (Austin: University of Texas Press, 1942), 71–91; Missouri Commissioner of Labor Statistics, 7, 25, 28–35, 43–55, 57–62; for increase in worker violence, 81–87, 101–4.

licensing bill took sumptuary legislation out of his hands and cost him a rallying point that held together his coalition. It could not have happened at a worse time. Accusations of fraud against the Democratic Machine cost him German liberal votes and made him vulnerable to pressure from the elite Citizens' League. Businessmen successfully pressed the city to use the new liquor revenue to hire more police. Police presence per capita in Chicago increased from one for every 1,033 residents to one for every 549 in the 1880s. The city exemplified a national trend.[45]

The police, disproportionately Irish Catholic and working-class, did not naturally side with employers, but Harrison, eager to stave off the resurgent Citizens League, put men sympathetic to business in command. Foremost among them was Capt. John Bonfield, Irish but Republican and able but brutal. Bonfield rose to prominence by violently breaking a streetcar strike that had paralyzed the city in 1885. The company, as widely hated by its customers as by its workers, had precipitated the strike by firing men for belonging to a union. Crowds initially blocked the tracks, stopping trains run by scabs and occasionally pelting them and the police with stones. On July 3 Bonfield unleashed the police to clear the streets. He led by example in cracking the skull of a seventy-year-old man. A teenage girl, vendors selling vegetables and newspapers, and ditch diggers fixing a gas main, as well as strikers, felt the clubs. The police clubbed anyone slow to move—including children—and attacked those who called them rats. They arrested hundreds more. Harrison defended Bonfield, accepting his claim that clubs today prevented gunfire tomorrow. It marked a turn away from a police force that had often been reluctant to interfere in confrontations between strikers and scabs. Harrison's support for Bonfield vitiated, but did not end, his alliance with labor since the mayor also forced some concessions from the company.[46]

The willingness of police to act violently also arose from divisions within the working class itself. At issue was religion, but the division was neither sectarian nor ethnic. There was a thriving native-born agnosticism in Chicago; it was, after all, the home base of the "Great Agnostic," Robert Ingersoll, who was both popular in the Midwest and a leading Republican politician. But just as prominent were immigrant freethinkers, agnostics, and atheists associated with socialism and anarchism. Although some anarchists, like Spies, mined the Bible as a revolutionary text, more disdained religion. Only a small number, perhaps 5 percent, of the immigrant workers in Chicago were freethinkers and atheists, but they were

---

45. Green, 119–22; Schneirov, 162–68; Montgomery, *Citizen Worker*, 70–71.
46. Timothy Messer-Kruse, *The Haymarket Conspiracy: Transatlantic Anarchist Networks* (Urbana: University of Illinois Press, 2012), 138–39; Schneirov, 168–73; Nelson, 184–85.

loud and visible. Anarchists mocked religious holidays and the clergy, enraging Catholic policemen.[47]

Both Evangelicals and Catholics recognized their weakness within the working class. In 1890 those unaffiliated with organized religion— 43 percent of Chicago's population—outnumbered those who were Catholic (30 percent), Protestant (23 percent), and Jewish (3 percent). The unaffiliated were disproportionately working-class. The churches had little or no chance of converting anarchists, but in 1885–86 they attempted a religious revival to win over the far more numerous workers who were alienated from organized religion but not freethinkers. Chicago was the headquarters of Dwight Moody, the country's leading Protestant evangelist, and Moody "confidently expected…such a revival…as Chicago has not experienced for years." Moody's revival in January was followed by those of Sam Jones and Sam Small, the "Two Soul-Saving Sams." Although the newspapers reported a large number of working people at both revivals, the revivalists spoke only English and their successes seemed overwhelmingly middle-class. Catholics more successfully targeted working-class parishes since their priests spoke multiple languages. Powderly, who remained a devout Catholic, did not oppose the revivals. The Knights sought to get religious sanction for labor reform. Chicago's anarchists ridiculed both the revivals and the Knights' attempts to accommodate them. This division was typical of two very different labor movements.[48]

Labor demonstrations and strikes roiled Chicago in the winter and spring of 1886. The Central Labor Union staged some, and the Knights led others. To outsiders the wave of strikes and working-class marches and meetings in the spring of 1886 seemed a single uprising, but it consisted of two streams. The first centered on the Knights, who reported 22,592 Chicago area members in July 1886, and on skilled workers organized in the city's Trades and Labor Assembly, which in March had fifty unions and roughly 20,000 members. These unions tended to be English-speaking and made up of the native-born or Irish Catholic immigrants. The second stream centered on the Central Labor Union (CLU). It included German and Bohemian workers, many of them very recent immigrants and some of them anarchists and revolutionary socialists. They were dissatisfied with the inability of the brotherhoods to counter mechanization and deskilling and restive under the leadership of English-speaking skilled workers. Like the Knights, they advocated the organization

47. Bruce C. Nelson, "Revival and Upheaval: Religion, Irreligion, and Chicago's Working Class in 1886," *Journal of Social History* 25, no. 2 (1991): 233–42.
48. Green, 110–12; Nelson, "Revival and Upheaval," 242–45.

of the unskilled as well as the skilled. The CLU had twenty-four unions, among them the eleven largest unions in the city, and 20,000 members. Engels grew frustrated with these German socialists as being unable to move beyond being rigid sectarians and to organize a wider working class.[49]

The rival factions often wanted nothing to do with each other. The two groups spoke different languages, sang different songs, hoisted different banners, and even flew different flags. Both displayed the stars and stripes, but in the immigrant demonstrations the American flags were outnumbered by the red flag of socialism. The red flag stood for the revolution that the radicals advocated in the place of unions, but the content of the revolution remained vague. Despite their aptitude for arcane ideological quarrels, the lines between anarchists, socialists, and communists were not clearly drawn in the 1880s. Those calling themselves anarchists, for example, were not necessarily followers of the Russians Mikhail Bakunin and Peter Kropotkin, whose competing versions of anarchism came to epitomize the movement. Most anarchists embraced neither bomb talk nor propaganda of the deed, as terrorism was called. Their enemies collapsed the radical rainbow into a single hue, and the radicals themselves were not particularly clear about what divided one group from another. In 1882 Johann Most, a leading Chicago anarchist, illustrated why it was easy to be confused: "I follow four commandments. Thou shalt deny God and love Truth; therefore I am an atheist. Thou shalt oppose tyranny and seek liberty; therefore I am a republican. Thou shalt repudiate property and champion equality; therefore I am a communist. Thou shalt hate oppression and foment revolution; therefore I am a revolutionary. Long live the social revolution!"[50]

In this formulation only the atheism was clear. Republicanism blended American and European variants into a not fully coherent whole. If socialism meant the abolition of the wage system and cooperative production, then not only anarchists and communists but also the Knights were socialists. If it meant the abolition of all private property, then far fewer were socialists. Revolution was an incendiary phrase, but it had American roots since the nation was born in a revolution and sponsored revolutions elsewhere.[51]

49. Green, 109–11; Messer-Kruse, 140, 145–49; Carl S. Smith, *Urban Disorder and the Shape of Belief: The Great Chicago Fire, the Haymarket Bomb, and the Model Town of Pullman* (Chicago: University of Chicago Press, 1995), 111; Schneirov, 173–79; Moore, 17; Nelson, *Beyond the Martyrs*, 27–33, 48–51, 182.
50. Messer-Kruse, 149–52; Nelson, *Beyond the Martyrs*, 156.
51. Nelson, *Beyond the Martyrs*, 156–73.

The anarchists united in the International Working People's Association (IWPA), which embraced social revolution and praised the Paris Commune. A portion of them had lost all hope that the system could be reformed short of revolutionary means, and they placed no faith in any reform that stopped short of voluntary association in cooperative enterprises. They regarded union attempts to gain wage hikes and retain control over work as silly and useless at best and as diverting workers from revolutionary action at worst. Roughly twenty-eight hundred active anarchists and seven newspapers with a circulation of thirty thousand made Chicago a center of anarchism, which developed its own subculture and traditions. The typical anarchist was a skilled, relatively recently arrived, German worker employed in a small shop, not a factory, but there were some native-born anarchists, most notably Albert and Lucy Parsons.[52]

Despite their small numbers and hostility to trade unions, anarchists achieved considerable influence in the Central Labor Union (CLU). August Spies, who in 1884 became editor of the *Arbeiter-Zeitung*, the most influential German paper in Chicago, emerged as the city's leading anarchist. Like the flamboyant, eccentric, and slightly cracked San Franciscan Burnette Haskell (who in the mid-1880s was an associate and friend of Joseph Buchanan), Spies wanted to revolutionize existing unions. He succeeded better than Haskell, who tried to infiltrate and transform the Western Knights. Haskell admitted that he had failed, denouncing the Knights as "densely ignorant, cowardly, and selfish," the tools of politicians, "church people and masons." The Knights were, he concluded, useless. He tried to replace them with his own organization, the International Workingmen's Association, but it existed largely in his imagination. Albert Parsons also joined the Knights of Labor. He differed from the majority of anarchists, who distrusted efforts that aimed at anything short of revolution. He was more like Buchanan and many socialists, who held membership in the Knights, other unions, and socialist parties, but men like Buchanan and Parsons could not heal divisions. In 1885 the Chicago Trades and Labor Assembly tried to ban anarchists and socialists from the Labor Day parade.[53]

The Chicago anarchists were in the right place at the right time; all the forces driving the Great Upheaval came together in their city. Under pressure from the efficiencies and capital investments of Carnegie in

52. Ibid., 81–84, 100–101; Messer-Kruse, 5–7, 86–99.
53. Green, 109–11; Nelson, *Beyond the Martyrs*, 42–43, 46–47; Joseph Buchanan would try to create an umbrella union under the same name. Messer-Kruse, 140–50; Schneirov, 171, 173–74, 177; Philip J. Ethington, *The Public City: The Political Construction of Urban Life in San Francisco, 1850–1900* (Cambridge: Cambridge University Press, 1994), 321–22; Smith, 111.

Pittsburgh, the Union Iron and Steel Company had cut wages and forced a strike, which workers won. In the nail industry, overproduction led to falling prices, followed by attempts to cut wages, and then a strike and boycott that endured into 1886. When box makers rushed to cut costs, they encountered worker resistance and a strike. But the action that got the most notice was at McCormick Harvester, where skilled iron molders and metal workers had successfully struck in 1885. The company had brought in Pinkertons; McCormick's Irish workers, who held a deep animosity to Pinkertons because of the Molly Maguires, had attacked them and assaulted strikebreakers. Molders represented one of the last strongholds of skilled labor in the plant. Work that had employed 2,145 men in the early 1870s now required only 600. After the molders' victory, the company began systematically firing the skilled union men. This led to a second strike and a demand for their rehiring, as well as wage increases for unskilled workers. The company responded by once more bringing in strikebreakers under the protection of Pinkertons.[54]

To support the McCormick strikers and the Maxwell boxcutters, the local Knights assemblies called for boycotts. A boycott linked workers' consumption to workers' production and was an effective tactic against any business that depended on a working-class clientele. On the West Coast it became a staple of the anti-Chinese movement, and in 1886 the Typographical Union deployed the boycott to win a closed shop from the anti-union San Francisco *Morning Call* and *Evening Post*. It was less effective against companies like McCormick and Maxwell, which manufactured producer goods.[55]

The call for boycotts came at virtually the same time that Powderly issued his "go slow" circular, advising against strikes and boycotts, and suspending the organization of new assemblies. The boycotts produced a rush of new members, most of them unskilled, into the Knights, and enthusiasm for new strikes to support a growing movement for an eight-hour day mounted.[56]

The rationale for the eight-hour day had evolved considerably by 1886. It had originated in free-labor beliefs in republican manhood and the worker as citizen: workers needed leisure to be fathers and husbands, to be informed citizens, and to educate themselves to be more productive workers. By the 1880s this rationale was overshadowed by a more complicated and paradoxical justification: by working less, workers would earn more. Mary Steward, the wife of Ira Steward, a leader of the earlier

54. Green, 105–7, 116–18; Schneirov, 189–91.
55. Ethington, 304.
56. Phelan, 187–90; Schneirov, 192–94.

eight-hour movement, put this into a couplet: "Whether you work by the piece or by the day / Decreasing the hours increases the pay." Ira Steward and other working-class leaders turned the logic of their employers against them. Workers were, as George McNeill put it in 1887, "merchants of time," and their employers were consumers of time. McNeill and the Knights agreed with Marx, who argued that just as the "capitalist maintains his rights as purchaser when he tries to make the working day as long as possible, the laborer maintains his right as seller when he wishes to reduce the workers' day." Pushing the logic further, workers argued that by making labor scarce they would increase its value. More than that, they argued that in market societies it ultimately would be consumption rather than production that would lift wages. The cost of living, and the higher "American standard," necessitated higher wages. By increasing workers' leisure, the eight-hour day would raise their wants, and by allowing higher wages to fulfill those wants, aggregate demand would go up, thus smoothing out the boom-bust economy, which regularly collapsed under inadequate demand.[57]

So confident in this logic were the advocates of the eight-hour day that they demanded only eight hours of wages for eight hours of work, agreeing, in effect, to a cut in pay. Less pay for less work would, Steward hoped, diminish opposition from employers, who feared giving an advantage to competitors who did not concede the eight-hour day. The loss of income would be temporary. The reduction in the workday would, he believed, improve the demand for workers, and the greater demand for labor would then allow workers, particularly skilled workers, to obtain pay raises, which would restore their old wages. Workers' higher consumption would do the rest.[58]

Many industries had fourteen- and even fifteen-hour days, but worker enthusiasm for the eight-hour day still took the leading labor organizations by surprise, and they did not initially endorse it. The anarchists continued to regard eight hours as a meaningless reform since it did nothing to overthrow capitalism. But newly unionized workers, particularly the unskilled, embraced the idea. The Chicago Trades and Labor Assembly, representing largely skilled workers, was not enthusiastic about a movement that in the short run would cut their pay, but in January 1886 the bricklayers union won an eight-hour day in Chicago, and the Trades'

57. Lawrence B. Glickman, A *Living Wage: American Workers and the Making of Consumer Society* (Ithaca, NY: Cornell University Press, 1997), 99–105; David R. Roediger, *Our Own Time: A History of American Labor and the Working Day*, ed. Philip Sheldon Foner (New York: Greenwood, 1989), 129–31, 152–53.
58. Glickman, 104–5; Schneirov, 186–87.

Assembly gradually backed the movement. Faced with a revolt by members, the CLU shifted its position by early 1886. The anarchists also endorsed the movement, although their support was only tactical. They hoped employers would resist the eight-hour day, thus precipitating a conflict, potentially violent, which would lead to revolution. As the movement grew, it transmuted again, away from Steward's idea, and spawned a large faction that called for an eight-hour day without a reduction in pay.[59]

By April little pretense of labor unity remained in Chicago; instead the two streams of the labor movement sponsored two parallel campaigns for the eight-hour day. The Knights and the Trades Assembly met in the Cavalry Armory. More conciliatory than confrontational, they asked for an eight-hour day with eight hours' pay. Later in the month, the CLU and the anarchist IWPA mobilized from ten to fifteen thousand marchers and eight bands in a march through downtown. Their speakers were multilingual; they sang the "Marseilles" where the Knights had sung "My Country 'Tis of Thee." The red flag was everywhere, and they demanded the eight-hour day with no reduction in pay. August Spies urged wageworkers to arm so that they could meet repressive force with revolutionary force.[60]

To the alarm of some anarchists, employers in Chicago began to yield at the end of April: brick makers, boot and shoe manufacturers, some of the smaller packinghouses, foundries, picture frame manufactures, and more granted the eight-hour day. In the nation as a whole, forty-seven thousand workers gained the eight-hour day, some with and some without a reduction in pay. The leaders of Chicago's eight-hour movement feared that the anarchists would use their influence on the CLU unions to subvert this success since the anarchists thought employer concessions drained the movement of its revolutionary potential. The Knights, in turn, denounced the CLU "as a body of outlawed anarchists who falsly [sic] claimed to be...leaders in the eight-hour movement." Leaders of the movement called for a national general strike for the eight-hour day on May Day 1886.[61]

The enthusiasm of Chicago's workers for the eight-hour movement was on display on Saturday, May 1, with widespread work stoppages across the city: Bohemian lumber shovers; Jewish garment workers, most of them women and girls; native-born dry goods clerks, again most of them women;

59. Nelson, *Beyond the Martyrs*, 178–79; Messer-Kruse, 149–50, 158–61. For many workers, eight hours was not just about wages or uplift, but for the freedom to spend their leisure as they wished; Roy Rosenzweig, *Eight Hours for What We Will: Workers and Leisure in an Industrial City, 1870–1920* (Cambridge: Cambridge University Press, 1983); Roediger, 131–34.
60. Messer-Kruse, 151–52, 154–55, 157, 163; Nelson, *Beyond the Martyrs*, 182–83.
61. Messer-Kruse, 165–67; Nelson, *Beyond the Martyrs*, 183–84; Green, 156.

railroad workers, and more joined the general strike. The mood was bois-
terous and celebratory. The Knights held an eight-hour ball.[62]

By then the national tide had turned against labor. When attempts by
the governors of Kansas and Missouri to get Gould to arbitrate the
Southwest Strike failed, the governors condemned the strike. Powderly
met with Gould and thought he had secured an agreement to arbitrate,
but Gould repudiated it since injunctions from the federal and state
courts had strengthened his hand. The courts forbade strikers from trying
to persuade, even peaceably, other workers to strike. They arrested and
fined leaders who did. The courts permitted the railroads to recruit
gunmen, who were often deputized to act against the strikers. The Knights
denounced the "golden spectacles" that Gould placed upon the courts
allowing them to see "but the rights of wealth."[63]

Monday, May 3, 1886, proved a dark day in Chicago. First, Chicago's
Knights received word that Powderly had capitulated to Gould in the
Southwest strike, and Chicago's railroads and other large employers hardened their stance against strikers. The strike at McCormick's Reaper Works
had already turned into a guerrilla war between workers and the police,
under Bonfield and the Pinkertons guarding what the strikers called Fort
McCormick. The police attacked picket lines, and strikers harassed and
sometimes attacked strikebreakers as they entered and left the plant. On
May 3, Spies was addressing a meeting of striking Bohemian and German
lumber shovers within sight of the McCormick factory. When strikebreakers
left the factory under police escort, striking McCormick workers rushed to
meet them, fighting broke out, and the police opened fire. They killed six
workers. Armed workers fired back. Spies, who had initially tried to restrain
the workers, and then unsuccessfully urged the lumber shovers to go to the
aid of the McCormick strikers, would be blamed by the virulently anti-labor
Tribune for instigating the violence. The paper turned the two hundred strikers involved in the initial brawl into ten thousand and made them "fighting
drunk." Spies, enraged by what he saw, rushed back to the *Arbeiter-Zeitung*
office and quickly produced a circular: "Workingmen, to Arms. Your masters
sent out their bloodhounds—the police—they killed six of your brothers at
McCormick's this afternoon." It echoed earlier anarchist calls for workers to
arm themselves, just as businessmen armed their militias. The Chicago
Commercial Club had bought a Gatling gun for a militia company they had
funded. The *Chicago Mail* said Spies and Albert Parsons should be driven
from the city.[64]

62. Green, 160–66.
63. Case, 181–83, 188–89, 192.
64. Green, 167–71; Messer-Kruse, 174–76.

Neither side had a monopoly on bloodthirsty rhetoric, but business had readier access to the means of violence. Illinois had in 1879 outlawed the Lehr- und Wehr-Verein, the workers' military and drill societies, when it prohibited any marching and drilling by armed bodies of men except the authorized militia, now organized into a National Guard, and federal troops. The Lehr- und Wehr-Verein defied the ban. Ideally, the task of preventing and suppressing violence would have been in the hands of the police, but workers saw the police under Bonfield as an agent of employers and far readier to use violence than to suppress it.[65]

The revolutionary anarchists, who had lamented the restraint of the workers during April, decided to instigate the violence that the workers had avoided. They were holding a secret meeting at Thomas Grief's saloon, readying plans to attack police stations, when news of the killings at McCormick's arrived. With the outbreak of violence, they tabled their plans. There were no assaults on police stations and no mustering of their armed militias. Instead, they called for a rally at the Haymarket at Randolph Street and Desplaines. When the original flyers for the meeting were printed, they told workingmen to "arm yourselves and appear in full force." Neither Spies nor Parsons attended this meeting, and Spies later said that when he saw the fliers, he demanded the words urging the workers to arm be removed and new ones printed. A few hundred of the original fliers, however, circulated.[66]

On May 4 the strikes continued and employer resistance hardened. The rally at the Haymarket was poorly organized and smaller than anticipated; roughly three thousand attended. Bonfield commanded a heavy police presence. Spies spoke, as did Albert Parsons, who brought his wife, Lucy. Accounts that he also brought his children, clearly an act of a man not expecting trouble, were disputed. Mayor Harrison was in attendance to monitor the situation and to control the police. By 10:00 p.m. it had begun to rain. Nothing happened. Harrison thought the speeches tame and told Bonfield to disperse his reserves. With a tip of his hat to crowd, the mayor rode off to his home. Parsons and his family had already left. Roughly fifteen minutes later, with the crowd down to five hundred people, the last speaker, Samuel Fielden, said that the law was framed and enforced by the oppressors of labor. Workers should "Throttle it. Kill it. Stop it. . . ." This was enough to bring in the police.[67]

65. Montgomery, *Citizen Worker*, 98–100; Nelson, *Beyond the Martyrs*, 184–86.
66. Nelson, *Beyond the Martyrs*, 185; Messer-Kruse, 172–73.
67. Timothy Messer-Kruse, *The Trial of the Haymarket Anarchists: Terrorism and Justice in the Gilded Age* (New York: Palgrave Macmillan, 2011), 89–91; Green, 180–81.

Nearly everyone agreed on what happened next: a bomb sailed from the crowd and exploded amidst the advancing phalanx of officers. Then the stories diverge into police accounts, workers' accounts, and accounts from a few uninvolved bystanders. The police said they came under fire from the anarchists. The workers and bystanders said that all the firing was by the police, who panicked, shooting not only into the fleeing crowd but also into their own ranks. Seven police died as well as at least five, possibly more, workers. Dozens of police and workers were wounded.[68]

The bomb blast echoed for a decade or more. Its immediate result produced what Brand Whitlock, a Chicago reporter, called "one of the strangest frenzies of fear that ever distracted a whole community." The anarchists wanted to bring Chicago to the brink of revolution, but all the bomber succeeded in doing was to make the city's upper and middle classes believe that the city's workers were on the verge of armed revolt and to countenance virtually any repressive act and the suspension of civil liberties. Richard Ely, the economist and advocate of the Social Gospel, would call it "a period of police terrorism." The arrest of anarchist leaders and their subsequent trial became a *cause célèbre*.[69]

The trial united neither Chicago's workers nor the nation's. The divisions that the Great Upheaval revealed became even more apparent as the strikes failed and a wave of state repression rolled over the country. For all the Knights' dreams of unity, they had incorporated skilled and unskilled, native-born and immigrant, Catholic, Jewish, and Protestant without unifying them. Nor had the Knights been able to avoid their own destructive rivalries with the skilled brotherhoods on their right and the anarchists on their left. Powderly had never had faith in strikes, and now he and the Knights had to cope with the results of their failures.

III

In the wake of Haymarket, in September 1886, William Dean Howells published perhaps his most quoted "Editor's Study" columns in *Harper's*. He praised the novelist Fyodor Dostoyevsky but cautioned that the Russian's work was to be appreciated "only in its place." Its "profoundly tragic" note and the author's socialism were unsuitable for the United States. Howells thought that American novelists should "concern themselves with the more smiling aspects of life, which are the more American, and to seek the universal in the individual rather than the social interests."

68. Green, 179–84.
69. Ibid., 184–91.

In a country where "journeymen carpenters and plumbers strike for four dollars a day the sum of hunger and cold is certainly very small, and the wrong from class to class is almost inappreciable." It would be wrong to boast, but "the race here enjoys conditions in which most of the ills that have darkened its annals may be averted by honest work and unselfish behavior."[70]

Howells wrote the column in July, before the conclusion of the trial of the eight anarchists, including August Spies and Albert Parsons, for the Haymarket bombing. None of them was accused of throwing the bomb, although one of them, Louis Lingg, twenty-two years old and a recent immigrant, had manufactured the bomb thrown at Haymarket. The bomb thrower was probably a man named Rudolph Schnaubelt, whom police interrogated and released. He escaped. No one was tried for murder; the prosecutor accused the defendants only of conspiring to kill police officers at the Haymarket. The prosecutor himself worried about a conspiracy charge attached to a murder for which no one had been accused. He thought a conviction for conspiracy demanded proof that the conspirators aided and abetted the actual bomber.[71]

Capital trials for conspiracy were unusual but not unprecedented in the nineteenth century, and rules for the admissibility of evidence had not evolved to their present form. As in most trials, the witnesses for both the prosecution and the defense were sometimes confused and not always credible. Still, Lingg did manufacture bombs, several of the defendants had attended meetings to plan revolutionary violence and attacks on the police, and all of the defendants had mustered bloodthirsty rhetoric and armed themselves. Except for Lingg's activities, however, none of this amounted to proof that they planned the bombing or aided the bomber. The trial provided clear evidence that the anarchists were failed revolutionaries; it did not prove that, with the exception of Lingg, they aided or abetted whoever threw the bomb. The Chicago anarchists were convicted of conspiracy in August, and seven of the eight defendants were sentenced to death. They were to die for what they said, not for what they did. Their execution, as Parsons said, would be "judicial murder." In their unsuccessful appeal, their attorney, in what became a common analogy, said that hanging them would be the equivalent of hanging the abolitionists who had sympathized with John Brown. In the wake of Haymarket, Illinois passed a

---

70. "Editor's Study," September 1886, William Dean Howells, *Editor's Study*, ed. James W. Simpson (Troy, NY: Whitston, 1983), 40–41.

71. The most recent and most complete account is in Messer-Kruse, *The Trial of the Haymarket Anarchists*.

conspiracy law making anyone who advocated revolution guilty of criminal conspiracy, and, if a court found a life was taken as a result, guilty of murder. They had written the verdict into state law.[72]

The conviction of the anarchists provided the catalyst that prompted Howells to forge his own personal discontent, his worries about American society, and his crusade for literary realism into an engine that smashed his own "smiling aspects of life." A new Howells was emerging, one who thought the verdict "hysterical and unjust," but initially he concentrated, and then only privately, on the "impolicy" of hanging the Chicago anarchists.[73]

The denial of anarchists' legal appeals and Howells's own inability to win over influential liberals, particularly James Lowell; George W. Curtis, his editor at *Harper's*; and Whitelaw Reid, the editor of the *New York Tribune*, toughened his opinions. The man who in September 1886 thought American workers could banish most of the ills of life with hard work and honest behavior visited, apparently for the first time, the Lowell cotton and carpet mills in February 1887 with his wife, Elinor. The mills were "as humanely managed as such things can be," but they made the Howellses "feel that civilization was all wrong in regard to the labor that suffers in them. I felt so helpless about it, too, realizing the misery it must cost to undo such a mistake. But it is slavery."[74]

Howells became the most noted and surprising advocate of clemency for the Haymarket convicts. He opposed "punishing men for their frantic opinions, for a crime they were not shown to have committed." There was strong sympathy for the convicted among workers, but not all labor leaders joined the campaign for clemency. Samuel Gompers did, but Terence Powderly defended the verdict. Many workers never forgave Powderly.[75]

Hundreds of thousands of people signed a clemency petition to Gov. Richard Oglesby, but they were largely drowned by the demands of the press for executions. Oglesby, an old Radical Republican, was troubled by the trial, saying that if there had been such a law during the antislavery agitation, "all of us abolitionists would have been hanged a long time

72. Green, 230–54; for Brown, 245.
73. Alfred Kazin, *On Native Ground* (Garden City, NY: Doubleday, 1956, orig. ed. 1942), 3–4; Messer-Kruse, *The Trial of the Haymarket Anarchists*, 155; William Alexander, *William Dean Howells, the Realist as Humanist* (New York: B. Franklin, 1981), 83; "Editor's Study," September 1886, Howells, *Editor's Study*, 40–41.
74. W. D. Howells to W. C. Howells, Feb. 20, 1887, W. D. Howells to Editor, Nov. 4, 1887, in William Dean Howells, *Selected Letters*, ed. George Warren Arms (Boston: Twayne, 1979), 3: 182, 199.
75. Green, 230–54.

ago." But Oglesby thought the law required the condemned men to ask for clemency, and four of the seven condemned refused to do so on the grounds they had not committed the crime. In the end, the governor pardoned the two who asked for mercy. Lingg, unrepentant until the end, escaped the hangman; he committed suicide in his cell. The other four were hanged on November 11, 1887. The fall was supposed to break their necks, but instead they strangled slowly at the end of the ropes before 250 newspapermen and selected witnesses.[76]

With the execution of the anarchists the older divisions between Howells and his liberal friends over partisan politics seemed "trivial...in this lurid light." He wrote a blistering and eloquent letter to the *New York Tribune*, which had joined other papers in celebration of the execution of the anarchists, men who died, Howells wrote, *"in the prime of the freest Republic the world has ever known for their opinions' sake."* By the logic that justified their execution, the whole New England and Radical Republican Pantheon—"Emerson, Parker, and Howe, Giddings and Wade, Sumner and Greeley and all who encouraged the war against slavery in Kansas," as well as Wendell Phillips and Henry David Thoreau, "whose sympathy inflamed Brown to homicidal insurrection at Harper's Ferry"—deserved to be convicted and executed. He never sent the letter, but preserved it in his files.[77]

By the beginning of 1888 Howells was writing to Hamlin Garland about Henry George's single tax, but he could not bring himself to see "confiscation in any direction as a good thing." He didn't "know yet what is best; but I am reading and thinking about questions that carry me beyond myself and miserable literary idolatries of the past. . . . I am still the slave of selfishness, but I no longer am content to be so." He told his father that he thought the future and "our safety and happiness" lay with socialism, but "the Socialists offer us nothing definite or practical to take hold of." Like much of the country, Howells was growing convinced of the insufficiency of the existing order but was not yet certain of what kind of world was struggling to be born.[78]

Howells despaired of a system that his friend John Hay continued to defend. Hay had in many ways anticipated how the liberals would interpret the Haymarket trial. For them it was just an extension of 1877, and the anarchists needed to be suppressed. Hay published *The Bread-Winners*, a

76. Edward J. Rose, *Henry George* (New York: Twayne, 1968), 124; Green, 247–73.
77. W. D. Howells to F. F. Browne, Nov. 11, 1887, in Howells, *Selected Letters*, 3: 200; W. D. Howells to Editor, Nov. 12, 1887, ibid., 3: 201–6.
78. W. D. Howells to Hamlin Garland, Jan. 15, 1888, W. D. Howells to W. C. Howells, Jan. 22, 1888, ibid., 3: 214–16.

novel equal parts melodrama and romance, in 1883, setting it in imaginary Buffland. It fictionalized Hay's anger over the strikes of 1877. He thought those strikes revealed the "shameful truth" of a "government...utterly helpless and powerless in the face of an unarmed rebellion of foreign workingmen, mostly Irish."[79]

In Hay's Buffland, modeled on Cleveland, the prosperous either neglected politics or, as with the book's hero, pursued reform ineptly and without undue exertion. Hay's characters were stereotypes, who spoke in clichés. The dialogue ran to "Now, my beauty, you will be mine," and "I would rather love her without hope than be loved by any other woman in the world." The book was, in the words of Hay's first biographer, "a polemic...in defense of Property."[80]

The Bread-Winners accepted the United States as a sharply divided class society united only by a universal love of money. Hay had married into money, a lot of money, when in 1874 he wed Clara Stone, whom he described as "a very estimable young person—large, handsome and good." She was the daughter of Amasa Stone, a man who like Andrew Carnegie had begun to make his fortune by building railroad bridges and compounded it by investments in railroads, Western Union, and Standard Oil. Clara was pious—"fragrant with the odors of Presbyterian sanctity," as Mark Twain put it—and literary without being a writer. As time went on, she spent her time on church, her children, and consumption. Hay moved to Cleveland in 1876, where his father-in-law presented him with a Euclid Avenue mansion next to his own as a wedding present. That same year a railroad bridge over Ashtabula Gorge on Stone's Lake Shore and Michigan Southern Railway collapsed. Final counts varied, but roughly 92 of the 159 passengers in a train passing over the bridge died. Stone had chosen the design against his engineer's advice; the I-beams that buckled came from Stone's Cleveland Rolling Mill, and the bridge had not been regularly inspected. The stoves in the cars were not self-extinguishing, as required by state law, and many of the passengers burned to death.[81]

79. John Hay to Amasa Stone, July 24, 1877, in William Roscoe Thayer, *The Life and Letters of John Hay* (Boston: Houghton Mifflin, 1915), 2: 1–2.

80. John Hay, *The Bread-Winners* (New York: Harper & Brothers, 1884), 164, 288; Thayer, 2: 15.

81. Patricia O'Toole, *The Five of Hearts: An Intimate Portrait of Henry Adams and His Friends, 1880–1918* (New York: C. N. Potter, 1990), 49–58; Jan Cigliano, *Showplace of America: Cleveland's Euclid Avenue, 1850–1910* (Kent, OH: Kent State University Press, 1991), 74–78, 117–25; John Taliaferro, *All the Great Prizes: The Life of John Hay from Lincoln to Roosevelt* (New York: Simon & Schuster, 2013), 172.

The tragedy had repercussions. The state investigated. The railroad's chief engineer and Stone both answered questions. The engineer then went home and put a bullet through his brain. A coroner's jury blamed the railroad, and specifically its executive officer, Stone, for the accident. The railroad paid heavy damages, and Howells, then editor at *Harper's*, condemned the railroad for naked greed. Hay passionately defended his father-in-law; Howells recanted, praising the "high character" of the railroad's officials. Stone, as was the habit of the American rich in personal or professional crisis, decamped for Europe. While his father-in-law was in Europe, Hay managed his affairs. Amasa Stone could not escape Ashtabula. In 1883, the year Hay published *The Bread-Winners*, Stone would climb into a bathtub in his Euclid Avenue mansion and put a bullet through his heart.[82]

Buffland's fictional Algonquin Avenue was Cleveland's actual Euclid Avenue, and it was as distinct from Lincoln's Springfield as could be imagined. Algonquin Avenue was "three miles long" and had "hardly a shabby house in it, while for a mile or two the houses on one side...are unusually fine, large and costly. They are all surrounded with well-kept gardens and separated from the street by velvet lawns." Euclid Avenue, lined with American elms, was slightly longer and grander, reaching its peak in the years after the Civil War and maintaining its stature until the end of the century. Cleveland's elite lived along this "Millionaire Row." John D. Rockefeller lived there in one of the street's more modest houses before he moved farther out into the suburbs.[83]

The houses with their arches, towers, and mansard roofs grew ever larger, grander, odder, and more fanciful as the century aged. In the 1870s the architecture was a collision of chateaus, English country houses, churches, and city halls, which left individual houses with mismatched pieces of each. Later residents settled on imitations of English manor houses and Romanesque mansions. The mansion of Sylvester Everett, a banker and railroad man, was a Romanesque palace with round and polygonal towers, four-foot-thick outer walls, thirty-five rooms, forty fireplaces, stained glass windows with the image of Richard the Lion-Hearted, and Japanese- and Scandinavian-themed bedrooms. Only visiting American presidents supposedly used its ebony guest room. Everett built a special windowless and soundproof room for his young wife, Alice, who was terrified of thunderstorms.[84]

82. Taliaferro, 173–74; O'Toole, 49–58.
83. Cigliano, 1–4; Ron Chernow, *Titan: The Life of John D. Rockefeller, Sr.* (New York: Random House, 1998), 119–20, 183–84; Hay, 7–8.
84. Cigliano, 101–84, esp. 158–63.

In *The Bread-Winners* Algonquin Avenue was the manifestation of the superiority of the propertied class and the target of working-class anger and envy. Hay's working class seemed to spring from bad breeding, ignorance, and misplaced ambition. There was a scene in which the hero, Arthur Farnham, his love, and her mother examine and converse about his recently acquired objets d'art, while utterly ignoring the presence of a worker repairing woodwork in the library. This was a world in which the aesthete and the consumer, not the worker and producer, held the higher status.[85]

The Bread-Winners was a fantasy of privilege that became, in part, real. Hay imagined how the Strike of 1877 should have been handled. Farnham mustered members of his old regiment, whom he armed at personal expense, had them deputized, and easily dispersed the mob. Except for lack of worker resistance, this was not so different from Pinkertons and the company of the new Illinois National Guard, armed and equipped by Chicago merchants and industrialists. In both fantasy and reality, patrician forms of white manhood took center stage, and with them a longing, which would grow ever stronger, for the clarity, virtue, and manliness of the Civil War. This sense of the military as the ideal expression of republican virtue had old and deep roots, and it would take both conservative and radical versions in the years to come. In a democracy that distrusted a standing military and largely despised its existing immigrant and black army, the supposed selflessness and courage of Civil War soldiers became an ideal shared across the political spectrum.[86]

Hay, as the ex-personal secretary of Lincoln, was as close to the great hero of the Republic as any man could be. He portrayed a heroic Lincoln and a country that mastered a crisis. He was still writing, along with John Nicolay, their biography of Lincoln when *The Bread-Winners* appeared. The two books marked how much Hay and the country were changing. In his novel, Hay made working people the dupes of demagogues, charlatans, and criminals, who played on resentments that sprang from the poor's own failings. To be fair, Hay was also hard on the rich. The poor were a threat only because the rich were so obsessed with accumulation and consumption that they were blind to danger. The only memorable sentence in the book was: "The rich and intelligent kept on making money, building fine houses, and bringing up children to hate politics as

---

85. Hay, 94–95; Livingston, 48.
86. This is one of the prominent themes in T. J. Jackson Lears, *Rebirth of a Nation: The Making of Modern America, 1877–1920* (New York: Harper, 2009).

they did, and in fine to fatten themselves as sheep which should be mutton whenever the butcher was ready."[87]

In Hay's *Lincoln* the old free-labor vision persisted, but in *The Bread-Winners* Hay agreed with Clarence King that the battle was between "real Americans" and the "rabble." If this was the ultimate legacy of the liberal version of free labor, Howells was unwilling to embrace it.[88]

87. Hay, 246–47; Nancy Cohen, *The Reconstruction of American Liberalism, 1865–1914* (Chapel Hill: University of North Carolina Press, 2002), 160.

88. "Howells's Review of *Abraham Lincoln: A History*," in John Hay, *John Hay–Howells Letters: The Correspondence of John Milton Hay and William Dean Howells, 1861–1905,* ed. William Dean Howells, George Monteiro, and Brenda Murphy (Boston: Twayne, 1980), 141.

15

Reform

No matter how impassioned their rhetoric nor how harrowing the fears of their enemies, the anarchists' revolution was utterly chimerical. What remained was reform. Reformers pushed against the bonds of the status quo, but when they broke those bonds their own lack of common purpose became all too apparent. They scattered, pursuing different targets. All complained about corruption, but the types of corruption they emphasized differed. Most complained about the advantages given the few over the many. All agreed that the spirit, if not the form, of older values had to infuse new social institutions and practices. Groups that had originally invested their hopes in voluntary associations, economic cooperation, and moral suasion recognized that their aims could only be achieved politically. Laws had to change.

Changing the laws demanded political alliances and either influence within the established parties or new parties. Reformers expanded their repertoires beyond direct action and propagandizing to lobbying and supporting individual candidates. To attempt anything larger—to do what antislavery crusaders had done, and gain control of a major political party, or form one that could contain a significant chunk of the electorate—seemed beyond them. No major reform party took shape; smaller parties formed to push particular reforms. The Greenbackers and Prohibitionists more often influenced elections by draining off votes from one major party candidate or another than by electing their own candidates, although they occasionally provided swing votes in Congress or legislatures. Reformers continued to work through the two major parties, backing candidates in elections at the local, state, and federal levels and trying to hold them accountable. Reformers of all stripes—but especially evangelicals—made American elections more and more unpredictable.

By the late 1880s evangelicals, antimonopolists, labor, agrarian, and even liberals seeking civil service reform had achieved impressive, but piecemeal, political success. Evangelical reformers had enlisted the federal government to try to turn Mormons and Indians into Protestant Americans, and more than ever they took aim at Catholics and immigrants. Anthony

Comstock regulated the content of what passed through the mails. The Knights of Labor had successfully agitated for Chinese immigration restriction and the prohibition of contract labor. Antimonopolists successfully pressed their case against "monopolies," particularly railroads, even if the resulting legislation was often ineffectual. The WCTU had lobbied for and secured local option laws and the teaching of "scientific temperance in public school." Frances Willard, however, aspired to nothing less than total prohibition and ceaselessly pushed for it. In 1881 Kansas, despite its cow towns and cowboys, stitched prohibition into its constitution, and in 1882 Iowa followed suit. The Iowa Supreme Court nullified the amendment, but in 1884 the Republican legislature in Iowa passed a prohibition law that stood.[1]

The combination of evangelicalism and antimonopolism within the Iowa legislature illustrated the possibilities of coalitions of reformers as well as its dangers. Members of successful coalitions had to put aside what divided them, but victory usually reminded them of their disagreements. In the 1880s Republican reformers had carried Iowa with the slogan of "a schoolhouse on every hill and no saloon in the valley." The Republican governor of Iowa, William Larrabee, became a leading temperance reformer and already was a strong antimonopolist. Iowa secured both prohibition and a reasonably effective railroad commission.[2]

Temperance did not always involve nativism, but it often did. Willard grew more tolerant over the course of her career, but in the mid-1870s she had argued for women's suffrage so "that Woman, who is truest to God and our country by instinct and education, should have a voice at the polls where the Sabbath and the Bible are now attacked by the infidel foreign population of our country." When temperance and nativism overlapped, the combination could prove lethal to not only temperance but also antimonopoly.[3]

1. Ruth Birgitta Anderson Bordin, Woman and Temperance: The Quest for Power and Liberty, 1873–1900 (Philadelphia: Temple University Press, 1981), 55–56, 135; Frances E. Willard, Do Everything: A Handbook for the World's White Ribboners (Chicago: White Ribbon Co., 1895); The Ideal of "the New Woman" According to the Woman's Christian Temperance Union, ed. Carolyn De Swarte Gifford (New York: Garland, 1987), 40–45; Richard J. Jensen, The Winning of the Midwest: Social and Political Conflict, 1888–1896 (Chicago: University of Chicago Press, 1971), 89–115.
2. Richard White, Railroaded: The Transcontinentals and the Making of Modern America (New York: Norton, 2011), 177–78; Benjamin F. Gue, History of Iowa from the Earliest Times to the Beginning of the Twentieth Century, Volume IV: Iowa Biography (New York: Century History, 1903), 4: 181; Jensen, 89–104.
3. Bordin, 57, 87–88; Ruth Birgitta Anderson Bordin, Frances Willard: A Biography (Chapel Hill: University of North Carolina Press, 1986), 98, 103.

Iowa reformers claimed prohibition reduced crime and nurtured schools and savings, but Catholic workers in Dubuque defied the law, and so did German Lutheran farmers, who were part of the Republican coalition. The legislature responded to resistance with stricter enforcement, enraging German Lutherans, a group not associated with protest and civil disobedience. Reform thus weakened the Republican majority necessary to maintain the reforms.[4]

Iowa encapsulated the reformers' dilemma. They had to form coalitions to capture the existing parties, but these coalitions seemed inherently unstable. As the WCTU moved from temperance to prohibition and linked prohibition to women's suffrage, the association of the two, and the identification of prohibition with the Republican Party, alarmed both nonevangelical reformers and Republican Party regulars. Many suffragists wanted women's suffrage kept as a separate issue and opposed Willard's abandonment of the Republicans for the Prohibition Party in the 1880s. They feared that the association of suffrage with prohibition would cost them Catholic, Democratic, and working-class votes.[5]

Willard came to recognize the difficulties her alliance with the Prohibition Party created. She had anticipated that it would replace the Greenbackers as the country's most important minor party and hold the balance of power in key elections. It did not, and the connection of prohibition and women's suffrage, as her critics predicted, hurt the drive for the vote. Suffragists blamed premature prohibition measures in the new western states for the defeat of women's suffrage in that region in the 1880s. They thought Willard's continuing efforts to secure both would kill the chances of women's suffrage in the remaining states of the West and Middle Border. And outside of local and school board elections, success did prove elusive. Wyoming and Utah granted women suffrage as territories, and both kept it when admitted as states in the 1890s. Colorado and Idaho also passed amendments allowing women's suffrage, but almost everywhere else suffragists suffered defeats until the twentieth century.[6]

4. Jensen, 96–98.
5. Bordin, *Frances Willard*, 135–37.
6. Virginia Scharff, "Broadening the Battlefield: Conflict, Contingency, and the Mystery of Woman Suffrage in Wyoming, 1869," in Adam Arenson and Andrew R. Graybill, eds., *Civil War Wests: Testing the Limits of the United States* (Berkeley: University of California Press, 2015), 202–23; Sally G. McMillen, *Lucy Stone: An Unapologetic Life* (New York: Oxford University Press, 2015), 206–7; Henry B. Blackwell to Frances Willard, Aug. 26, 1889, in *Frances E. Willard Papers*, ed. Frances Willard Historical Association (Evanston, IL: Frances E. Willard Memorial Library and Archives); for WCTU and suffrage, Bordin, *Woman and Temperance*, 120–21.

The tumult of 1885 and 1886 propelled Willard into reform's deeper waters. Her early allies had been Prohibitionists and business reformers in cities such as Chicago, but she moved away from them and became part of a group—including the Social Gospel minister Washington Gladden, the liberal statistician Carroll D. Wright, and the economist Richard Ely—that sought to establish a new reform journal addressing the full range of reform causes. She corresponded with Frances Cleveland, the young wife of the president, who initially asked that their correspondence about temperance be kept private since temperance was hardly a favorite Democratic issue.[7]

Willard also made contact with Terence Powderly of the Knights of Labor. As Willard realized, if any labor organization had the power to link evangelical reform and working-class reform, it was the Knights. Powderly was a Catholic and a temperance man; his original success in building the Knights had involved linking Catholic Irish with English and Welsh Protestants. He struggled, even if ineptly and only partially, to link black and white workers and male and female workers. He was an antimonopolist who supported Henry George's demands for land reform.

Willard's interest in the Knights alarmed her usual allies. Lucy Stone wrote Willard during the Great Upheaval that "I watch with fear and trembling your approaches to the Knights of Labor," who carried, Stone thought, the disruption of all business as the heart of their creed. Stone, who had refused to join Elizabeth Cady Stanton and Susan B. Anthony in race baiting when blacks obtained suffrage before women, had few inhibitions about protecting her own class interests. She told Willard of the problems of the Batcheller firm, shoe manufacturers in Massachusetts "on the friendliest terms with their help," until the Knights appeared and forced the workers to strike because of the discharge of "boys who had to be and deserved to be discharged." A. H. Batcheller vowed never to employ Knights again and to break the union. The Knights were, Stone wrote, "a menace to business integrity and to national prosperity, don't you see?"[8]

Batcheller's labor problems were actually the result, not the cause, of the firm's difficulties. In a competitive, rapidly mechanizing industry, the firm did not keep up. Changes in the shoe market and the organization of the firm not only rewarded innovation, they demanded it. Batcheller had grown old, feeble, and inattentive. His firm borrowed heavily and went

---

7. Joseph Cook to Frances Willard, Dec. 15, 1886, T. V. Powderly to Frances Willard, Dec. 12, 1886; Frances F. Cleveland to Frances Willard, June 17, 1886, in *Frances Willard Papers*.
8. Lucy Stone to Frances Willard, Mar. 28, 1887, in ibid.

into receivership in 1889. Stone reduced a story illustrative of the competitive pressures that helped produce the Great Upheaval to one of benevolent employers, evil agitators, and duped workers.[9]

Stone was typical of liberals horrified at the new reformers. The influence of great liberal Protestant ministers, men like Henry Ward Beecher, who died in 1887, yielded to the broadening scope of newer evangelical reform. Willard, Josiah Strong, and even Ely were far more typical of American evangelical Protestants, who clearly hearkened to the message of the Social Gospel.

In the universities, liberals were in full retreat, particularly as the new German- educated scholars returned and took up teaching posts. First the ethical economists and then, more critically, the marginalists attacked the dominant liberal tradition of classical economy. The marginalists vitiated David Ricardo, rejected the labor theory of value, modified Adam Smith, and inserted all kinds of exceptions and caveats to supposedly universal economic laws. They turned the center of analysis from production to consumption and routed their opponents in economics department after department across the country.

The new "ethical economists" won scholarly battles, but they were vulnerable to political pressure. Boards of trustees and the aging liberal intellectuals tried to suppress them. When Ely praised the Knights of Labor, a review of his book in the *Nation* declared that "Dr. Ely seems to us to be seriously out of place in a university chair." Godkin tried to have him fired from Johns Hopkins. Ely survived, but as Henry Carter Adams wrote to Clark, "Plutocracy is in the saddle and is bound to unhorse everybody who does not ride behind."[10]

Henry Carter Adams was an Iowan who had lost both his liberal and Congregationalist faith and, having studied with Walker at Johns Hopkins, went to Germany for his Ph.D. There he was reborn in a new faith: "I only know that English Economy has served & is serving as an opiate to the consciences of men who are trampling their fellow men in the dirt— The slavery question is not yet worked out." On his return, Adams took a position at Cornell and attacked the narrow liberal conceptions of liberty that he had once embraced.[11]

Plutocracy did unhorse Adams. After he defended the Knights of Labor, mocked contract freedom, and suggested that the Knights presented a

---

9. Ross Thomson, *The Path to Mechanized Shoe Production in the United States* (Chapel Hill: University of North Carolina Press, 1989), 236; "The Batcheller Failure," *Boston Evening Transcript*, July 31, 1889.

10. Nancy Cohen, *The Reconstruction of American Liberalism, 1865–1914* (Chapel Hill: University of North Carolina Press, 2002), 168–69.

11. Ibid., 156–59.

road to democratic control over industrial production, he was dismissed from Cornell. Russell Sage, one of the attendees at the 1884 Blaine banquet, a close associate of Jay Gould, and a member of the Cornell Board of Trustees, led the attack on Adams, denouncing him as either a socialist or a communist and unfit to teach at an American university. In order to secure an appointment at the University of Michigan, Adams condemned the Haymarket anarchists and defended their conviction. He disavowed his praise of the Knights and denied his sympathies with socialism. He had proven himself craven enough for tenure, and secured the appointment. But he did not abandon all his former opinions; in 1887 he was also appointed the chief statistician of the new Interstate Commerce Commission, which he pushed toward active regulation until thwarted by the courts.[12]

On the ICC Adams would serve under Thomas Cooley, a man whom he earlier might have despised but whom he could now meet in the middle. A rapidly changing world had overtaken the ethical economists, but they negotiated it better than their liberal adversaries. Haymarket scared them; the Great Upheaval scared them; anarchists scared them. They glimpsed the possibility of social change, to which they would not only be largely irrelevant but which would threaten their own positions in a society that, for all its faults, they still saw as enabling economic and political progress. They also identified the new outbreaks of working-class anger and radicalism with these immigrants, whom they thought inferior. Frightened by militant workers and new immigrants, threatened within the universities in which they made their careers, the ethical economists and allied academics retreated, but did not fully capitulate. Boards of trustees might crack down on Henry Carter Adams, but it was his and his colleagues' ideas, not the ideas of liberal trustees, that triumphed in the classroom. William Graham Sumner might banish Francis Amasa Walker from Yale for attacking Ricardo, but Walker landed as president of MIT, and by the end of the century Sumner had been effectively exiled from academic economics, shifting his disciplinary home to sociology, which itself became largely hostile to liberals.

I

In the aftermath of the Great Upheaval, workers turned toward politics. Many of them thought that the lesson of the repression of strikes during the Great Upheaval was that economic justice required political success.

12. Ibid., 171–75.

Between 1886 and 1888 workers ran their own tickets in 189 cities and towns. They did not intend to substitute politics for union activity. Indeed, without strong unions to mobilize workers as voters, political action usually failed. Workers' parties, however, proved hard to sustain, although several, particularly in the West, endured over a number of election cycles. Even when successful, they dominated only local elections; because they depended largely on working-class votes, they had trouble gaining traction in larger arenas.[13]

Henry George's 1886 candidacy for the office of mayor of New York emerged as the most ambitious of the workers' tickets as well as an attempt to forge a wider reform coalition. George was already the country's most famous antimonopolist. Although not overtly religious, he had strong evangelical tendencies and sympathies; he also had a Catholic wife. When New York's Central Labor Union (CLU), with more than two hundred affiliated unions and a membership of 180,000, drafted him to run for mayor in 1886, he insisted on evidence of the backing of the United Labor Party's membership. The CLU presented him with petitions containing 34,000 signatures. He accepted the nomination at a mass meeting at Cooper Union. Frank Ferrell, a prominent black member of the Knights of Labor, nominated him. The CLU's Irish and German workers knew George well through his writing and his association with the radical wing of the Irish Land League and contacts with prominent English radicals. He was already a member of the Knights of Labor when he joined the CLU. George seemed to unite in his own person the various strains of reform needed for victory. Even Samuel Gompers, who would later disavow labor politics, was swept up in a campaign that everyone involved thought full of portents for reform. George's single tax advocacy resonated in New York. Although half of Manhattan remained undeveloped, the city had the world's highest density, exorbitant rents, blatant inequality, and conditions that made it a center of the environmental crisis afflicting the nation.[14]

13. James J. Connolly, *An Elusive Unity: Urban Democracy and Machine Politics in Industrializing America* (Ithaca, NY: Cornell University Press, 2010), 88–89; David Montgomery, *Citizen Worker: The Experience of Workers in the United States with Democracy and the Free Market During the Nineteenth Century* (Cambridge: Cambridge University Press, 1993), 153–54; Leon Fink, *Workingmen's Democracy: The Knights of Labor and American Politics* (Urbana: University of Illinois Press, 1983), 25–26; Harold C. Livesay, *Samuel Gompers and Organized Labor in America*, ed. Oscar Handlin (Boston: Little, Brown, 1978), 65.
14. Christopher William England, "Land and Liberty: Henry George, the Single Tax Movement, and the Origins of 20th Century Liberalism," Ph.D. dissertation, Georgetown University, 2015, 85; Edward T. O'Donnell, *Henry George and the Crisis*

Even more than the man, the moment seemed right. The Great Upheaval had enraged New York workers, already angry with landlords, and they vented their anger against Tammany, the courts, and their employers. In New York the Great Upheaval centered on a bitter and violent strike that spread outward from the Dry Dock Horsecar Line to all of New York's and Brooklyn's streetcar lines. These streetcar strikes featured villainous employers straight from nineteenth-century melodramas. "Deacon" Richardson, an ardent Brooklyn Baptist, owned the Dry Dock Horsecar Line, whose workers labored up to sixteen hours a day. He imposed numerous fines and docked their pay. They demanded a raise to two dollars a day. Richardson refused. The police had to muster 750 men (25 percent of the city's force) to allow one car to complete a four-mile round trip. When all the streetcars in the city went on strike, Richardson caved, giving into the key demands and agreeing to arbitration on the others.[15]

A connected strike followed against the Broadway Railroad Surface Line of the aptly named Jacob Sharp. Police again intervened against workers, who in this and other strikes resorted to boycotts. In suppressing the boycotts, the courts convicted five CLU organizers of conspiracy and extortion and sent them to Sing Sing prison. Workers regarded the convictions as direct attacks not only on their interests but also on their rights as citizens.[16]

The strike against Sharp failed, but a Gilded Age version of "it takes a thief to catch a thief" brought Sharp down. Roscoe Conkling served as counsel of a New York state senate committee investigating Sharp and his relation to New York's aldermen. The committee discovered that Sharp had bribed the entire Board of Aldermen—Tammany men, rival County Democrats, and Republicans—to obtain an extension of his lucrative franchise. Sharp ended up in jail, and the legislature voided his railway charter, but only a few of the aldermen served prison sentences. Taken together, these events drove home the advantages accruing to workers if they controlled the city's politics and made a compelling case for independent political action. Workers refashioned older republican language

---

of Inequality: Progress and Poverty in the Gilded Age, 79–80, 104–25, 130–34 152–53, 203, 211.

15. O'Donnell, 174–76.

16. Ibid., 187–97; Montgomery, 151–52; John R. McKivigan and Thomas J. Robertson, "The Irish American Worker in Transition, 1877–1914: A Test Case"; David Brundage, "'In Time of Peace, Prepare for War': Key Themes in the Social Thought of New York's Irish Nationalists, 1890–1916," both in The New York Irish, ed. Ronald H. Bayor and Timothy J. Meagher (Baltimore, MD: Johns Hopkins University Press, 1996), 305–10, 322–25; Connolly, 91–92.

to claim that government had become a corrupt bargain between the wealthy and political bosses. They vowed to take the city back, arguing that economic change could come only through political action.[17]

To win, George had to push a reform platform wide enough to contain the working class and ethnic voters who usually went to Tammany and to attract some voters from New York's middling classes. The difficulties he faced in forging such a coalition were symbolized by a man who had become a public champion of immigrant and working-class New York: Joseph Pulitzer. George expected and received the opposition of the existing parties and of the mass-circulation press of the city. The opposition of the city's largest paper, Pulitzer's *World*, was, however, not a foregone conclusion, even though Pulitzer was an ardent Democrat. A Jewish immigrant from Hungary and a Union veteran, Pulitzer had made his fortune with the *St. Louis Post Dispatch*. In 1883 he bought the money-losing *New York World*, which he described as a mummified corpse, from Jay Gould. He considered Gould a financial and political vampire, but this was business; he paid a premium for the paper and then borrowed most of the purchase price from Gould. If Pulitzer failed to resurrect this corpse, he was doomed. He increased the *World's* circulation from about 15,000 to 153,000 in two years. By 1888 it had nearly doubled again to 300,000. He geared the publication—lavishly illustrated, simply but vividly written, sensationalist, and reform-minded—to an immigrant, urban audience. As Charles and Mary Beard summarized the paper's journalism under Pulitzer, "It exploited to the utmost limit the tragedy and comedy of contemporary life, in all its component elements of sex, society, crime, perversion, love, romance, and emotion generally." He covered Irish Nationalist struggles that involved George and detailed the horrors of Russian pogroms. In 1889, after the publication of Jules Verne's *Around the World in Eighty Days*, he would send his reporter Nelly Bly to beat the novel's record. He published her telegraphed reports, until she returned seventy-two days later. Matthew Arnold coined the term *new journalism* to describe the popular press and denounced papers like the *World* as "feather-brained."[18]

Pulitzer attracted an eclectic set of friends and allies, and George certainly fell within his spectrum of possibilities. Liberals despised Pulitzer,

17. Edwin G. Burrows and Mike Wallace, *Gotham: A History of New York City to 1898* (New York: Oxford University Press, 1999), 1098–1100; O'Donnell, 185–88; David M. Jordan, *Roscoe Conkling of New York: Voice in the Senate* (Ithaca, NY: Cornell University Press, 1971), 423.

18. James McGrath Morris, *Pulitzer: A Life in Politics, Print, and Power* (New York: Harper, 2010), 203–6, 240–43, 282; Burrows and Wallace, 1051–52; Charles and Mary Beard, *The Rise of American Civilization* (New York: Macmillan, 1930), 462.

and his enemies attacked him as "Jewseph" Pulitzer, but the publisher, briefly and unhappily a Democratic congressman in 1884, counted Jefferson Davis as a friend and employed Roscoe Conkling as his lawyer. If any paper could be expected to support George, it was the *World*. Ultimately Pulitzer proved a loyal Democrat, while George was a disloyal Democrat threatening to overthrow the city's Democratic Party.[19]

George spoke day and night across the city and recruited hundreds of surrogates—some of them middle-class reformers, including William Dean Howells—to speak for him. Tammany had offered George a congressional seat if he refused the nomination of the United Labor Party. They told him he could not win; they would count him out, but they recognized that his candidacy would "raise hell," which they would rather avoid. Raising hell was, however, both George's preference and specialty. Although George focused on the Single Tax as a solution to the ruinous rents of New York City, he ran unabashedly as a working-class candidate. His platform embraced the key union demands of shorter working hours, higher pay, the laborer's control over the condition of work, government ownership of railroads and telegraph, the end of police interference with "peaceful assemblages," and eradicating corruption.[20]

Henry George was hardly hostile to capitalism, but he denounced a system in which "Most of us—99% at least—must pay the other 1 per cent by week or month or quarter for the privilege of staying here and working like slaves." Vacant land remained on Manhattan, but "nowhere else in the civilized world are men and women and children packed together so closely." Ordinary New Yorkers suffered while "a few individuals" reaped the benefits of rising rents and land values produced by the growing population. George was the only candidate to address—at least indirectly—the city's environmental crisis. Charles Wingate, a journalist turned "sanitary engineer," who had despaired of private charity and moral uplift ameliorating New York's tenement and environmental problems, supported him.[21]

George's candidacy created alarm at what the Union League Club called the "present revolt of the working men of this city." Implicit in the statement was that there was an identifiable group to revolt against. And there was. By 1886 American and European observers wrote of plutocracy

19. Morris, 223, 246, 269–71; George Juergens, *Joseph Pulitzer and the New York World* (Princeton, NJ: Princeton University Press, 1966), 12–13.

20. Edward J. Rose, *Henry George* (New York: Twayne, 1968), 120–21; Burrows and Wallace, 1098–1101, 1105–6; O'Donnell, 204–8, 27; Connolly, 85–86.

21. O'Donnell, 211, 224, 228–29; Bonnie Yochelson and Daniel J. Czitrom, *Rediscovering Jacob Riis: Exposure Journalism and Photography in Turn-of-the-Century New York* (New York: New Press, 2007), 78–80.

and an "aristocracy of wealth." The very wealthy were among the men of property—a much larger group who formed a bourgeoisie in the European sense—who feared George and mobilized against him. They had emerged and consolidated in New York in reaction to that city's assertive working class. This bourgeoisie—merchants, manufacturers, builders, investors, and the professionals who served them—self-consciously conceived of themselves as men of property, recognizing, like George and his adherents, that property in New York had become concentrated in a small minority of residents.[22]

In American popular usage, "men of property" had become synonymous with capitalists, but George distinguished among New York's rich by the source of their wealth. He had no objection to merchants, manufacturers, or even capitalists who invested in productive enterprises. He tried to distinguish them from *rentiers*, who grew rich simply by owing land and resources, but by the time of his campaign such distinctions were increasingly fruitless, not just because sources of income ran together but also because as the new elite coalesced into a coherent social class, how a person obtained wealth mattered less than wealth itself.

Just prior to the Civil War, John Jacob Astor and, more impressively, Cornelius Vanderbilt had created the nation's first great fortunes, piling up individual wealth on a scale as unprecedented as the size of their mansions. Until the 1880s such fortunes remained unusual, their holders more freaks of nature than people to be emulated. As late as 1877 Lydia Maria Child thought the Vanderbilts and the Stewarts—a wealthy New York merchant family—"did not constitute a class, there are too few of them." It was the people beneath them, what she labeled a "genteel class," who were growing more numerous.[23]

A decade later the Astors, Stewarts, and Vanderbilts were no longer alone. The railroads, the rise of manufacturing, and the financial market created vast new fortunes. The consolidation of industries into larger holdings added lesser fortunes as those whom men like Rockefeller or Carnegie bought out found themselves with more than sufficient money on which to live and no further need to labor. This was no longer a mere competence. They could afford considerable extravagance. These *arrivistes* peopled the novels of Howells and later Edith Wharton. They also

22. Sven Beckert, *The Monied Metropolis: New York City and the Consolidation of the American Bourgeoisie, 1850–1896* (Cambridge: Cambridge University Press, 2001), 170–79.
23. Ibid., 156; Stuart M. Blumin, *The Emergence of the Middle Class: Social Experience in the American City, 1760–1900* (Cambridge: Cambridge University Press, 1989), 288–89; For Vanderbilt, T. J. Stiles, *The First Tycoon: The Epic Life of Cornelius Vanderbilt* (New York: Knopf, 2009).

became the subjects of Frederick Townsend Martin's *The Passing of the Idle Rich*, a book he wrote in the early twentieth century looking back at the invasion of New York society by the nouveau riche.[24]

Martin's book was a lament for the world of free labor and the American home, lost, so he thought, during the Gilded Age. He chronicled a descent in which "the Bible is no longer read,...religion has lost its hold,...the Constitution and laws are trampled upon by the rich and powerful, and are no longer held sacred by the poor and weak." Martin wrote as "a rich man," but he longed for the days when "great fortunes were very rare," and when it was "the harvest time of Opportunity in the land."[25]

Shrewd, funny, and with a telling eye for the foibles of a class that he both lived among and despised, Martin recalled the *arrivistes'* assault on New York's old money, which was "pleased to call itself the Aristocracy of America." The nouveau riche formed "an army better provisioned, better armed with wealth, than any other army that had ever assaulted the citadels of Society." The assault gathered steam as the century neared its close. This was an army "of men who do not work," but who held enormous amounts of property. It was this army that organized in opposition to George.[26]

Martin's new rich concentrated in New York, but they dwelled too in Chicago, Pittsburgh, and San Francisco. The funniest parts of the book were simply accounts of their extravagances, from pet monkeys fed on silver plates to dinner parties where the oyster of each guest was graced with a black pearl. American millionaires treated Europe as a giant rummage sale. In a classic burst of Gilded Age invective, A. A. Cohen, a San Francisco businessman, described Charles Crocker of the Central Pacific Railroad as "a living, breathing, waddling monument of the triumph of vulgarity, viciousness, and dishonesty." The vulgarity counted as heavily against him as his viciousness and dishonesty.[27]

The explosion of bad taste created opportunities for social arbiters to consolidate the interests of the bourgeoisie around something more than

---

24. Frederick Townsend Martin, *The Passing of the Idle Rich* (Garden City, NY: Doubleday, Page, 1911).
25. Ibid., 15, 61, 92.
26. Ibid., 80, 89.
27. Ibid., 23–58; Harvey A. Levenstein, *Revolution at the Table: The Transformation of the American Diet* (New York: Oxford University Press, 1988), 14; James Livingston, *Pragmatism and the Political Economy of Cultural Revolution, 1850–1940* (Chapel Hill: University of North Carolina Press, 1994), 46–49; *Central Pacific Railroad Company Vs. Alfred A. Cohen, Argument of Mr. Cohen, the Defendant...* (1876), Huntington Library, 67742, p. 49 (1876).

property. Class formation involved more than common economic interests, and knitting New York's bourgeoisie into a coherent class required cultural and social work to overcome the differences among them. Social arbiters created a self-conscious class with similar educations, similar tastes, common entertainments, and common networks. The rich sent their children to the same private schools and to Harvard and Yale. The families of merchants, financiers, and industrialists intermarried. The old New York families both confirmed and abdicated their social authority by opening up, with varying amounts of grace and resistance, balls, the opera, and the whole New York social season to the newly wealthy. The Metropolitan Opera House, the New York Metropolitan Museum of Art, and the New York Philharmonic did subtle political work, setting the standards for taste and art and creating a common cultural identity for the new bourgeoisie.[28]

When Frederick Martin claimed that "the class I represent cares nothing for politics," but only for "its own interests," he was not entirely correct. But he was correct enough. In an emergency they were willing to abandon the Republican Party, to which most belonged. The candidate the New York elite abandoned was Theodore Roosevelt. He was one of them, but he was also the antithesis of this idle rich, which was why Martin admired him. Roosevelt shared with Martin and many others of their class a deep cultural anxiety, but he fought to overcome it. Workers presented a challenge not only to the economic interests of the bourgeoisie but also to their manhood. Once supposedly inured to hardship through vigorous living in the outdoors, American men of the middling and upper classes, so the story went, had declined into a neurasthenic mass of urban "brain workers." In 1889 William Blaikie, an ex-Harvard athlete, published "How to Get Strong and Stay So" in Harper's Weekly, which captured the anxiety that sent men and women to bicycles, gyms, and barbells all over the country.[29]

Roosevelt was fanatical about fitness and could get nearly hysterical about the dangers workers, and for that matter western antimonopolists, presented, but he also was willing to enter into coalitions with labor and evangelical reformers. While an assemblyman, he had cooperated with Samuel Gompers. When he wrote about machine politics in the Century, he did so with a characteristic mix of manly bluster, nostalgia for an earlier America, and hardheaded acceptance of the realities of the new

28. Beckert, 239–40, 246–48, 255–56.
29. Martin, 149–50; O'Donnell, 212–13; Beckert, 255–56, 277–79; T. J. Jackson Lears, *Rebirth of a Nation: The Making of Modern America, 1877–1920* (New York: Harper, 2009), 28.

United States. Roosevelt expressed an admiration for Tammany's organization, if not its voters. Roosevelt had moved from a social world where men had first names like Chauncey, Poultney, and Emlen to the New York Assembly, where members had last names like Murphy, Shanley, Higgins, and Gideon. Gideon he described as "a Jew from New York who has been a bailiff and is now a liquor seller." He dismissed the bulk of the Democrats in the Assembly as "vicious, stupid-looking scoundrels," and his catalogue of them produced a liberal's collective portrait of the Democratic politician: "a decided looseness of ideas as regards the 8th Commandment," "either dumb or an idiot—probably both," and an "unutterably coarse and low brute...formerly a prize fighter...is more than suspected of having begun his life as a pickpocket." By the time he ran for mayor and had seen the "idiots," "brutes," and thieves outmaneuver and outwit him, his views were more sober. He recognized politics as a business, even if he did not think it should be, and he knew that businessmen were as devoted to class interests as workers. He expressed his opinions in an article on New York politics published the month of the election, and thus written well before it. The frankness of the article was an admission that his candidacy was doomed. He had already booked passage to England, where he would remarry. His larger political ambitions remained. He intended, he said, "to be one of the governing class."[30]

In abandoning Roosevelt, New York's Republican elite made him a footnote to the campaign. They joined both Tammany and the Democratic Swallowtails—the prosperous and largely Protestant opposition to Tammany within the Democratic Party whose derisive nickname came from the tails of their formal dress coats—to defeat George. They backed Democrat Abram Hewitt, the son-in-law of Peter Cooper—a rich antislavery industrialist and reformer who had run as the Greenback candidate for president in 1876. Cooper was known as a friend of labor and the founder of the Cooper Union, the educational institution where George accepted the nomination. Affection for him helped his son-in-law. Hewitt was a man whom Tammany would normally oppose, but 1886 was not a normal election. With much of its constituency turning to George, Tammany could not win without forging a new coalition that went beyond the usual business interests that profited from the machine to include liberal Democrats and Republicans.[31]

30. David G. McCullough, *Mornings on Horseback* (New York: Simon and Schuster, 1981), 252–55; Theodore Roosevelt, *Theodore Roosevelt: An Autobiography* (New York: Scribner, 1920), 56; "Machine Politics in New York City," *The Century* 33, no. 1 (1886): 74–83.
31. Martin, 149–50; O'Donnell, 212–16; Beckert, 255–56, 277–79; Burrows and Wallace, 1104–5.

Hewitt believed that the dogmas of free labor still held in an industrial society. He thought "self-help is the remedy for all the evils of which men complain," but he did not infuse his beliefs with the class rage that characterized many of his wealthy contemporaries. He did not oppose unions on principle; he had helped publicize the abuses that had prompted the Strike of 1877. George spoke against class rule and for the "people," but Hewitt, a wealthy man whose election depended on the defection of elite voters and their allies to him, accused both George and Roosevelt of running class campaigns. The Labor Party was, he said, attempting "to organize one class of our citizens against all other classes." And with Haymarket still fresh, he denounced the party as a collection of "anarchists, nihilists, communists, [and] socialists." He reached further back to touch the core fear of the propertied classes in North America and Europe. George's proposals would revive "the atrocities of the Commune." As for Roosevelt, Hewitt dismissed him as the millionaires' candidate.[32]

The election culminated in George's appeal to workers and Tammany's appeal to the Catholic Church. Tens of thousands of Union Labor Party supporters paraded into Union Square under banners that read THE WORKERS OF THE CITY ARE NOT ANARCHISTS! THE SPIRIT OF '76 STILL LIVES and HONEST LABOR AGAINST THIEVING LANDLORDS AND POLITICIANS. Tammany countered by mobilizing the Catholic hierarchy, which had already tried to stop the immensely popular Father Edward McGlynn from supporting George. McGlynn had defied Archbishop Michael Corrigan, saying that he had not surrendered his "rights and duties as a citizen" when he became a priest. Corrigan suspended him from his parish duties, and just prior to the election, in concert with Tammany, the diocese released a statement asserting the overwhelming opposition of the Catholic clergy to George. Tammany distributed it the Sunday before the election at the doors of the parish churches.[33]

As sometimes happens in American elections, the least historically significant candidate won. In an election replete with the usual frauds Hewitt received 90,552 votes. George got 68,110 votes and Roosevelt 60,435, about 20,000 below the normal Republican vote. George ran strongly among working-class Irish and German Catholics, and he did particularly well among the growing number of Jewish immigrants. He claimed, probably with good reason, that Tammany counted out many of his votes, adding

32. Burrows and Wallace, 1104–5; O'Donnell, 209, 213; Beckert, 278.
33. David Brundage, *Irish Nationalists in America: The Politics of Exile, 1798–1998* (New York: Oxford University Press, 2016), 118–19, 125–26; O'Donnell, 228–33; Burrows and Wallace, 1105–6.

them to the Democratic total. Tammany obtained the middle-class Catholic vote and, with the help of the Church, the vote of the poorest and most recent Irish immigrants. Hewitt's victory margin came from the Swallowtails and Republicans.[34]

George had lost, but virtually everyone involved saw his campaign as a victory and a harbinger of workers' power. Pulitzer's *World* thought it an "extraordinary thing for a man without political backing, without a machine, without money or newspaper support" to have polled so many votes. George, never a man to diminish his own accomplishments, thought the election was a "Bunker Hill." Workers had "lit a fire that will never go out." He prepared for a larger statewide campaign the next year.[35]

Hewitt proved a terrible mayor. His proposals to fund public improvements and provide jobs ended up tangled in controversy. He broke with Richard Croker, the Tammany boss who had supported him, and he turned against not only labor but also immigrants. He refused to review the St. Patrick's Day parade and prohibited the flying of the shamrock flag at City Hall on the day of the parade. "America should be governed by Americans," he said. In the next election, Hewitt failed to secure the Democratic nomination. The Swallowtails ran him as an independent. He lost badly.[36]

George's strong showing was not the only encouraging sign for labor's turn to politics. In what became known as the Bay View Massacre, Wisconsin's governor had sent militia into the streets of Milwaukee against the advice of local officials during the eight-hour strikes. A Polish militia unit fired on largely Polish crowds, who had escaped the control of the Knights and the Central Labor Union in that city. The militia killed five people, including a child on his way to school and an old man standing in his garden. Authorities reacted by rounding up anarchists, socialists, and the entire district executive board of the Knights of Labor. The eight-hour strike collapsed, but when the trial of the Knight's leader, Robert Schilling, ended in a hung jury, he announced he would "gain revenge— by the ballot." And he did. The Knights and German and Polish immigrants formed the core of the Wisconsin People's Party. It showed little strength outside of Milwaukee and a few other cities, but over the opposition of the Catholic Church, it swept the Milwaukee city and county

34. Burrows and Wallace, 1106; Chris McNickle, *To Be Mayor of New York: Ethnic Politics in the City* (New York: Columbia University Press, 1993), 12; O'Donnell, 234–39; Peter H. Argersinger, *Structure, Process, and Party: Essays in American Political History* (Armonk, NY: Sharpe, 1992), 109.
35. Burrows and Wallace, 1106.
36. Ibid., 1107–8.

government and elected a congressman. The new district attorney dropped the remaining charges against Schilling and the Knights.[37]

In Chicago a Union Labor Party brought together Knights and socialists and carried 25 percent of the city vote for county offices. It elected seven candidates to state office and nearly elected a congressman. In a stinging rebuke to the Democrats who had controlled Chicago during the strike, it took away enough votes to give Cook County to the Republicans. In Cincinnati, too, worker anger at the repression of the eight-hour movement produced a successful labor ticket in 1886. In the wake of the Southwest strike, labor slates dominated Kansas City, Kansas, and lasted throughout the decade. A workers' ticket in Denver proved less successful.[38]

In the Midwest the emergence of labor tickets complicated the efforts of reformers to maintain functioning alliances. Iowa was illustrative of their problems. Already beset with the tensions created by the success of prohibition and railroad regulation, Iowa reformers also had to deal with the rapid rise, and equally rapid fall, of successful labor/antimonopolist tickets. In 1886 a Knights of Labor ticket overthrew the local business elite and carried Clinton, Iowa. The victory proved short-lived, because the next year Irish Catholic workers, who had supported the labor ticket, abandoned it, sending Clinton's antimonopolist mayor down in defeat. Henry F. Bowers, who had been instrumental in the antimonopolist victory, blamed the defection on a priest who had urged his parishioners to vote against the incumbent. In response, Bowers helped found the American Protective Association in 1887; he initially grounded the organization in antimonopoly, but when he took it national in 1890, he reinvented it as an awakening of Protestant America against subversion by the Catholic Church.[39]

Bowers was a type that the American political system had coughed up before and would cough up again. His success in spreading nativism and anti-Catholicism deeper into the reform movement weakened the chances of forging a broad alliance. Bowers tapped into a reservoir of distrust of Catholics and immigrants nurtured by the controversies over public and

37. Fink, 189–99.
38. Richard Schneirov, *Labor and Urban Politics: Class Conflict and the Origins of Modern Liberalism in Chicago, 1864–97* (Urbana: University of Illinois Press, 1998), 216–18; John P. Enyeart, *The Quest for "Just and Pure Law": Rocky Mountain Workers and American Social Democracy, 1870–1924* (Stanford, CA: Stanford University Press, 2009), 77–82; Fink, 126–35, 222–23.
39. Nick Salvatore, *Eugene V. Debs: Citizen and Socialist* (Urbana: University of Illinois Press, 1982), 106–7, 111; John Higham, *Strangers in the Land: Patterns of American Nativism, 1860–1925*, 2nd ed. (New Brunswick, NJ: Rutgers University Press, 1988), 62–63, 80–87.

parochial schools, the threat of cheap labor, and the often blatantly reactionary and antidemocratic bent of the Catholic hierarchy.[40]

When Bowers turned xenophobic, he skillfully told origin stories grounded in the quotidian institutions of American life: schools, political parties, and fraternal organizations like the Masons. Bowers spun a personal tale that he cast as a national story. His experience stood in for an assault on everything native-born Protestant Americans valued about their country: its opportunities, its freedom from the old hierarchies and autocracy of Europe, and the ability of voters to come together to effect change. He believed that he had been thwarted during his childhood by a powerful, conspiratorial, and vindictive Catholic Church. He summoned memories to validate things that had never happened, not an uncommon trait in memoirs. Sensitive about his lack of formal schooling, Bowers claimed that as a child in Baltimore the Catholic Church had denied him an education by forcing the closure of the public schools. Bowers's mother had homeschooled him, but this was not because the public schools had shut down. In fact, they had been expanding.[41]

By 1893 the APA had enrolled more than a million members. It was paradoxically nativist, stressing the Anglo-Saxon Protestant roots of the country, without being against all immigrants. It was particularly strong among British and Canadian immigrants, who brought to the United States their existing attachments to the anti-Catholic Orange order. APA newspapers printed forged papal encyclicals calling for a Catholic uprising and fed its adherents a steady diet of familiar tales of nuns imprisoned in convents, but APA speakers were capable of adding new technologies to old conspiracies. They alleged that there was a secret cable to relay messages between the White House and Baltimore's Archbishop Gibbons.[42]

Such stories attracted the credulous, but the Catholic Church provided plenty of ammunition to the APA. The efforts of the church and Catholic politicians to undermine public schools were quite real, as Florence Kelley discovered in Chicago. Despite a state compulsory education law, in 1892 there were 2,957 seats available for 6,976 schoolchildren in Chicago's nineteenth ward. Kelley led a campaign for new schools, which was fought tooth and nail by Alderman John Powers, an Irish Catholic who opposed public education and sought to promote

40. Salvatore, 102, 104, 105.
41. Jo Ann Manfra, "Hometown Politics and the American Protective Association, 1887–1890," *Annals of Iowa* 55 (Spring 1996): 138–66.
42. Higham, 67–72; Jensen, 286–87; Manfra, 138–47, 151–52, 163–64.

parochial schools. Powers blocked Kelley's first effort, but a new school was built in 1893.[43]

The fissures that opened in Clinton, Iowa, and Bowers's reaction to them were symptomatic of reform's problems. When evangelicals pushed for temperance, women's suffrage, social purity, and English language education, they reinforced the ethnocultural political divisions that reformers needed to bridge to create majority alliances. Yet evangelicals could not give up these measures; they were, as Josiah Strong emphasized, the core of their attempt to redeem and reform America.

No evangelical reformer and intellectual, with perhaps the exception of Frances Willard, loomed larger than Josiah Strong in the last decades of the late nineteenth century. In a very different fashion from Henry George, he took on the ideological task of turning widespread discontent into a coherent political program. Strong's *Our Country, Its Possible Future and Its Present Crisis* appeared in 1885 just before the Great Upheaval. Strong saw God's hand at work in American society, which was not unusual, but God had laid his hand on new places. In the "Battle Hymn of the Republic," God marched with the Union armies through the South, but *Our Country* barely mentioned slavery, citing its abolition only as a mark of human progress, even though he wrote while the division between blacks and whites was deepening and becoming codified as Jim Crow, the social separation by law of black and white people. *Our Country* demonstrated the shift in the American conversation about race away from the advancement of black people to meditations on the racial destiny of Anglo-Saxons and the threat to it.[44]

Strong rode few ideas as hard as progress, but then progress was the country's favorite horse. Strong had no doubt about its breeding: its parents were "first, a pure, spiritual Christianity, and second, civil liberty." The more Strong wrote, the heavier the load progress carried. Progress was in his first sentence, and he elaborated it from the first chapter on. Like other Americans, he saw progress in the exploitation of American resources, the production of wealth, and the increase in things. "The material progress of the United States," he declared, was "wholly without a parallel in the history of the world," but he also connected material with social and religious progress. He lauded the telegraph, steam power, and the increase in invention largely because steam power eradicated space

43. John T. McGreevy, *Catholicism and American Freedom: A History* (New York: Norton, 2003), 123–24; Louise W. Knight, *Citizen: Jane Addams and the Struggle for Democracy* (Chicago: University of Chicago Press, 2005), 243–44.

44. Josiah Strong, *Our Country* (Cambridge, MA: Belknap Press of Harvard University Press, 1963), 13, 205, 213–18.

and the telegraph and popular press "brought minds into contact," opening them up to Christianity, the spread of liberal ideas of individualism, and the increased valuation of human life.[45]

By making progress more than material well-being and rapid change, Strong represented a formidable American intellectual tradition. He recognized progress by the baggage it carried: temperance, Sabbatarianism, democracy, Protestant but nonsectarian schools, and the "honor" granted to womanhood. The obstacles to progress appeared in the growth of the Catholic Church, liquor consumption, divorce, socialism, and the dominance of those "American barons and lords of labor" who had "developed a despotism vastly more oppressive and more exasperating than that against which the thirteen colonies rebelled."[46]

Strong organized *Our Country* so as to make it less a celebration than a warning. In addressing a series of perils to progress—Romanism, Socialism, Mormonism, Wealth, and the City—he reflected the Gilded Age sensibilities. Edward Bellamy's *Looking Backward* used the same technique even if his progress and perils were different from Strong's. Other Americans, too, tended to frame heavens that resided just beyond more-immediate hells. Fears of declension and loss could never quite erase the convictions of ultimate progress. Articulate Americans, William Dean Howells and Jane Addams, the founder of Chicago's Hull House, swung between giddy enthusiasm for the future and near despair over their country. In this they, too, reflected the age.

Strong attempted to do more than reflect the age; he tried to explain it. He wanted to elucidate why the United States had emerged as the home of progress and Americans as the people assigned to overcome challenges to it. He drew his answers from a hodgepodge of mystical geographies, popular Darwinism, evangelical Christianity, and contemporary medical science. All reflected the assumptions of the period. The very idea of progress meant that the present was better than the past. Anglo-Saxons formed, Strong thought, the most recent race, and "Time's noblest offspring is the last." Natural selection had created Anglo-Saxons and made them the most fit.[47]

Space had conspired with time and race to make the United States the modern home of progress. Strong appealed to a geographical mysticism to which Americans had long been partial, which made the middle latitudes of the northern hemisphere the latitudes of progress. Since the territory of

45. Ibid., 13–18, 117–18, 201.
46. Ibid., 13–18, 59–88, 117–18, 124, 150, 167–69, 184.
47. Ibid., 208–10.

the United States was the last to be populated by a superior race, it must be there that a higher civilization would flower.[48]

Strong ignored, was ignorant of, or creatively interpreted data that subverted his racial triumphalism. Unaware that Americans were growing smaller, he proclaimed them taller and celebrated this as a sign of their fitness. He embraced George Beard's idea of American nervousness and turned it into a sign of a "refined nervous organization" that would yield the highest civilization. Even immigrants, who by and large he regarded as inferior, would, if not allowed to overwhelm the nation's Anglo-Saxon core, create a kind of hybrid vigor in a new Aryan race.[49]

This convergence of elements in the late-nineteenth-century United States, Strong concluded, could not be an accident; it was part of God's plan. God was "training the Anglo-Saxon race for an hour sure to come in the world's future." The moment of a final contest between the races was at hand, and God was schooling Anglo-Saxons for victory and conquest. Strong's God was an evangelical one, not Calvinist, and Anglo-Saxons had to choose their destiny. God had given them capacities—their skill at creating wealth, their "genius for colonizing"—that, if properly used would lead Americans to spread across the world, and other races would not only have no choice other than submitting but would also be happy to do so. Strong spiced his racism with religion to explain why Americans would make the right choice. All civilizations had their vices, and Anglo-Saxons would succumb to their own materialism without the "salt" of Christianity. He regarded popular government as providential and irreversible, but without Christianity, it could decline into anarchism.[50]

The removal of religion from the public schools, Mormonism, intemperance, socialism, economic inequality, the growth of cities, and the exhaustion of the supply of arable public lands together constituted "a mighty emergency" not just for the country, but for the world because America had to become "God's right arm in his battle with the world's ignorance and oppression and sin." The United States was the "elect nation...the chosen people" destined to lead "in the final conflicts of Christianity for the possession of the world." The elect did not include all Americans. Strong regarded most urban workers—immigrant, Catholic, potentially socialist—not as allies but as obstacles in the fight for reform, which Christian reformers already imagined as a worldwide battle. Willard and the WCTU had spread the temperance crusade abroad, where it merged with Protestant missionary efforts. Suffragists learned

48. Strong, 208.
49. Ibid., 119–21, 208–13.
50. Ibid., 154–55, 213–18.

to frame the claim for women's suffrage as springing not from citizenship but from whiteness and civilization. Like Willard, they often questioned the wisdom of having given the vote to black men and Catholic immigrants.[51]

Strong operated from similar assumptions. He recognized that immigration brought "unquestioned benefits," but it also "furnishes the soil which feeds the life of several of the most noxious growths of our civilization." Strong portrayed the "typical immigrant" as a "European peasant, whose horizon has been narrow, whose moral and religious training has been meager or false, and whose ideas of life are low." They were disproportionately paupers and criminals. They debauched the Sabbath and promoted liquor. Many were Mormon and Catholic; others were socialists. He portrayed them as rabble, and "there is no more serious menace to our civilization than our rabble-ruled cities." They might be citizens, but they were not Americans, and "their appetites and prejudices constitute a very paradise for demagogues." There was "a dead-line of ignorance and vice in every republic, and when it is touched by the average citizen, free institutions perish." The United States was in danger of reaching that line.[52]

Strong and George shared many of the same evangelical and free-labor impulses; both rooted their antimonopolism in an older liberalism even as they moved away from many individualist assumptions, but where George turned east and sought an alliance with workers and immigrants, Strong turned west and summoned the evangelical middle class to the work of conquest and redemption. Strong proclaimed that the fate of the world depended on the United States, and that the fate of the United States depended on the West. If Americans seized the opportunities God offered, they would achieve the racial destiny of Anglo-Saxon domination and the Christian conversion of the world. But if they failed, the late nineteenth century would culminate in catastrophe and decline.[53]

The anti-Catholic and anti-immigrant leanings of Evangelical reformers like Strong weakened the chances for broad reform coalitions, but so too did the decline of the Knights, with whom Willard sought to partner. The Great Upheaval had badly weakened the Knights, and their attempt to organize in the South inflicted additional wounds. Amidst the fallout from Haymarket, the Knights turned to the South,

51. Ian R. Tyrrell, *Reforming the World: The Creation of America's Moral Empire* (Princeton, NJ: Princeton University Press, 2010), 75–97; Strong, passim, and 252–54; Allison L. Sneider, *Suffragists in an Imperial Age: U.S. Expansion and the Woman Question, 1870–1929* (New York: Oxford University Press, 2008), 5–10.

52. Strong, 41–58; quotes 52, 53, 55, 56.

53. Ibid., 13.

FRANK LESLIE'S ILLUSTRATED NEWSPAPER

No. 1,621.—Vol. LXIII.]   NEW YORK—FOR THE WEEK ENDING OCTOBER 16, 1886.   [PRICE, 10 CENTS.

GENERAL FITZHUGH LEE.

VIRGINIA.—TENTH ANNUAL CONVENTION OF THE KNIGHTS OF LABOR, AT RICHMOND—FRANK J. FARRELL, COLORED DELEGATE OF DISTRICT ASSEMBLY NO. 49, INTRODUCING GENERAL MASTER WORKMAN POWDERLY TO THE CONVENTION. FROM A SKETCH BY JOSEPH BECKER.—SEE PAGE 134.

At the tenth annual convention of the Knights of Labor, in Richmond, Virginia. Frank J. Farrell, "colored delegate of District Assembly No. 49," introduced General Master Workman Powderly to the convention. Under Powderly the Knights were relatively egalitarian in regard to black people, while demanding exclusion of the Chinese. From a sketch by Joseph Becker. *Frank Leslie's Illustrated Newspaper*, Oct. 16, 1886. Library of Congress, LC-USZ62-120765.

where they tackled the divisions between white and black workers and launched a major organizational campaign.

In October 1886, during the last months of the Great Upheaval, a remarkable scene unfolded in Richmond, Virginia, where the Knights held an integrated convention in a segregated city. Frank Ferrell, a black delegate from New York District Assembly 49 and the man who nominated Henry George for mayor of New York, was one of roughly sixty thousand black Knights. When their Richmond hotel refused to give Ferrell a room, the entire delegation abandoned the facility in solidarity.[54]

Powderly, eager to recruit black members in the South, invited Ferrell to introduce him on the platform. Through the Clan na Gael and the American Land League, Powderly had absorbed Patrick Ford's ultimately unsuccessful attempts to graft the Irish struggle in Ireland and America to the struggle to secure rights for freedpeople. In his speech, Ferrell behaved like an orthodox Knight, refusing to make sharp distinctions between economy, politics, and social life. He spoke of the Knights' "efforts to improve the condition of humanity." Among the objectives he listed were "the abolition of those distinctions which are maintained by creed or color." These were "superstitions."

Ferrell had unbottled the genie, and Powderly, whose sympathies were always at war with what passed as his pragmatism, tried to stuff it back in. He vitiated the symbolism and power of Ferrell's introduction by retreating to a conventional distinction between legal and social equality, which, he said, "cannot be regulated by law. The sanctity of the fireside circle cannot be invaded by those who are not welcome."[55]

But the distinction was a hopeless and dangerous one. Ferrell had been excluded from a hotel, not a home, and that night he and his fellow members from District Assembly 49 attempted to integrate a Richmond theater, which drew an armed mob of whites to the theater the next night. Whites claimed their abhorrence of social equality came from their desire

54. For caution about the numbers, Joseph Gerteis, *Class and the Color Line: Interracial Class Coalition in the Knights of Labor and the Populist Movement* (Durham, NC: Duke University Press, 2007), 41–42; Melton Alonza McLaurin, *The Knights of Labor in the South* (Westport, CT: Greenwood Press, 1978), 132–35, 138–39, 141–43; for District Assembly 49, O'Donnell, 151–53.

55. Eric Arnesen, "American Workers and the Labor Movement in the Late Nineteenth Century," in Charles W. Calhoun, *The Gilded Age: Essays on the Origins of Modern America* (Wilmington, DE: SR Books, 1996), 48; Terence Vincent Powderly, *Thirty Years of Labor, 1859–1889* (New York: Kelley, 1967), 61; Brundage, *Irish Nationalists in America*, 120–22; Joseph Gerteis, "The Possession of Civic Virtue: Movement Narratives of Race and Class in the Knights of Labor," *American Journal of Sociology* 108, no. 3 (2002): 598–601.

to protect the sanctity of the home, but hotels and theaters were private businesses soliciting a public clientele. Was this defense of the "fireside circle"? What exactly was Powderly talking about? These incidents electrified blacks and horrified whites. Angry whites in the South knew that social equality—equal access to schools, businesses, and transportation— was a corollary of political equality, and they were not about to accept it. The Southern press attacked the Knights for breaking down necessary barriers between the races.[56]

As so often happened, the appeal of the Knights was deeper than their ability to support those they organized, and in the South they faced particularly formidable obstacles. Much wage labor in the South was in extractive industries, with the lumber industry providing more jobs than any other Southern industry. Northern lumbermen, recognizing the impending shortage of white pine from overharvesting in the upper Midwest, came to the South, which had twice as much pine as the rest of the nation combined. Southern yellow pine captured much of the trans-Mississippi market once held by white pine. But forest jobs and sawmills lasted only as long as the timber. The industry and its workforce, much of it black, were transient. Work in the woods and mills was dangerous and low-paying, but for many young men it proved preferable to sharecropping. Once the forest was cut, the industry moved on; in most places, it spawned no meaningful lasting local development. The isolation of the lumber camps and the transience of the workers made it a tough industry to organize.[57]

Southern manufacturing was significant, but except in the manufacture of cigarettes it lagged behind the North in capital invested and technical proficiency. James Buchanan Duke, a Confederate veteran and a farmer, had prospered marketing tobacco in the 1870s, and when he moved into manufacturing cigarettes, he originally attracted skilled immigrant workers to North Carolina to roll them. A skilled worker, however, could roll only four cigarettes a minute, and in 1885 Duke gambled on the Bonsak rolling machine, while simultaneously setting up distribution centers in major cities to market his mass-produced cigarettes. By 1890 he had combined with his four leading competitors to create the American Tobacco Company, a modern, mechanized, integrated corporation. In its attention to cost and detail, American Tobacco resembled Carnegie Steel more than other Southern enterprises. Duke concentrated

56. McLaurin, 132–35, 138–39, 141–43.
57. Gavin Wright, *Old South, New South: Revolutions in the Southern Economy since the Civil War* (New York: Basic Books, 1986), 159–62; William Cronon, *Nature's Metropolis: Chicago and the Great West* (New York: Norton, 1991), 196–97; Edward L. Ayers, *The Promise of the New South: Life after Reconstruction* (New York: Oxford University Press, 1992), 123–31.

production into six factories, and by 1898 they were producing 3.78 billion cigarettes annually. Unskilled labor, usually black in the South, was still necessary for preparing the tobacco, but the machines did the production. Even as the price of cigarettes declined, American Tobacco's profits rose, ranging from 42 percent to 56 percent in the 1890s. It diversified its production with factories in the North as well as in Durham. The headquarters moved to New York. Having an addictive product paid.[58]

The Knights concentrated on two segregated industries: textiles and sugar production. The textile industry depended on the labor of white women and children. In the Southern textile mills, badly paid women and children constituted roughly two-thirds of the work force during the 1880s. The harvesting of sugar cane and the production of sugar were both hard and brutal work that depended on largely black labor.[59]

Powderly continued to oppose strikes as anything but a last resort, but the combination of desperately poor Southern workers eager to better their condition pitted against recalcitrant and increasingly organized and emboldened employers made strikes inevitable. In 1886 white textile workers in Augusta, Georgia, struck, and employers responded with a lockout and evictions from company housing. The Knights provided little aid, and what came was too late. The manufacturers took no chances. They used race baiting, accusing the Knights of favoring social equality and claiming they would promote the replacement of white workers with black. By November the strike was defeated, and the Knights were no longer a threat in the Southern textile industry.[60]

That same fall attempts to organize largely black sugarcane workers in Louisiana fell short, but efforts continued during 1887 in preparation for the next harvest season. The region had a history of organized black resistance to planters. Roughly ten thousand sugarcane workers declared themselves Knights, demanded collective bargaining rights, and struck for a daily wage of $1.25. When white employers brought in strikebreakers, hostile crowds, both men and women, met them at the railroad station. Employers prevailed on the governor to mobilize the militia, which evicted strikers and installed strikebreakers on the plantations. When the militia withdrew, a white vigilante force took over, and a shooting triggered an assault on strikers in the town of Thibodaux. The vigilantes moved systematically through the town, hunting down and executing strike leaders and strikers. Mary Pugh, a white woman who observed the

---

58. Ayers, 106–7; Alfred D. Chandler, *The Visible Hand: The Managerial Revolution in American Business* (Cambridge, MA: Belknap Press, 1977), 382–91.
59. McLaurin, 14–22, 26–27, 36–37.
60. Ibid., 69–73.

killings and whose sons took part in them, recognized the conflict as race war. She was "sick with horror of it. But I know it had to be else we would all have been murdered before a great while. I think this will settle the question of who is to rule, the nigger or the white man? For the next 50 years but it has been *well done*. . . ." The vigilantes killed dozens and injured a hundred or more. It was the end of the Knights in the sugar country. No one was prosecuted, let alone convicted.[61]

II

Despite the barriers race, religion, and ethnicity presented to interregional reform alliances, a powerful antimonopoly movement formed nonetheless. The fragmentation of the old ethnocultural alliances holding the Democrats and the Republicans together, coupled with deep anger at corruption and inequality, fed a still-inchoate demand for reform.

Antimonopoly had gestated within the land question so central to Henry George and the single tax, but it went well beyond land issues and, for that matter, beyond George. The attacks against western railroad land grants began in the 1870s, but the main focus of antimonopoly reform was on railroad rates. Except for the struggle over the federal land grants, the major legislative efforts to control railroads had been largely left to the states, despite the seemingly quixotic efforts of John H. Reagan, the ex-postmaster general of the Confederacy and a congressman from Texas to provide for federal regulation. In the 1870s Reagan had sought regulation in order to aid Tom Scott, who had promised to extend the Texas, and Pacific into Reagan's congressional district. Reagan designed his legislation to punish Scott's rivals for thwarting the Texas and Pacific in much the same way that Scott had aided the California Railroad Commission to punish the Southern Pacific. Reagan's outrage at the "unjust discrimination of the common carriers" was thus initially politically self-interested. A thorough racist, he did not consider the Southern demands that railroads segregate their black passengers "unjust discrimination." He was concerned with freight rates. Republican control of the Senate meant that Reagan's bills went there to die. Failure did not moderate him. He denounced the railroads and those protecting them for seeking to reduce the people "to serfdom, poverty and vassalage." The rise of an "aristocracy of wealth with monopolies and perpetuities which are forbidden and

---

61. Rebecca Scott, "'Stubborn and Disposed to Stand Their Ground': Black Militia, Sugar Workers, and the Dynamics of Collective Action in the Louisiana Sugar Bowl, 1863–67," *Slavery and Abolition* 20, no. 1 (2003): 103–19; McLaurin, 74–75.

denounced by all our constitutions" endangered the republic, "breaking down…all the bulwarks of civil liberty." Monopoly would destroy American manhood itself and with it "that personal freedom and independence which is the pride of every American citizen." Americans would cease to be citizens and become subjects.[62]

During the 1880s an antimonopoly majority—a combination of Democrats and Republicans—customarily ruled the House, and Reagan took himself and his cause to the Senate, which had consistently rejected regulation. In 1886 the passage of federal railroad regulation in some form seemed inevitable. In January of that year the Senate Select Committee on Interstate Commerce reported that "upon no public question are the people so nearly unanimous as upon the proposition that Congress should undertake in some way the regulation of interstate commerce." When in October the Supreme Court in *Wabash, St. Louis & Pacific Ry. Co. v. Illinois* ruled that state regulation of interstate commerce was unconstitutional, it was clear that Congress would pass a bill of some kind.[63]

Most of the great trunk lines that carried interstate commerce were not necessarily averse to regulation; they just wanted it to serve their interests, and they sought to have their practices sanctioned by law and enforced by government regulation. The more honest among them admitted the truth of much of what antimonopolists said. The financiers who sat atop most corporations did loot and pillage, but there was a set of emerging corporate leaders who despised them as either buccaneers or troglodytes, men whose power and interests had expanded far beyond their capacities. Charles Francis Adams purposely set himself apart from his contemporary tycoons, who had the "peculiarities of self-made men." They could neither organize nor delegate: "Their minds all run to extreme simplicity, and to the primary relations of employer and employe [sic]." The systems had outgrown them, and their employees regarded them as "capitalists having no interest whatever in them or the property except to draw money from them and it."[64]

Adams styled himself a manager actively engaged in making the Union Pacific Railroad an efficient and profitable enterprise. Lecturing to undergraduates at Harvard College in 1886, he told them that the organization was now everything: "The individual withers, and the whole is more and more." He viewed his task as president to be keeping the whole operating in harmony. Adams placed his hopes in middle management; he wanted

---

62. White, 356–57; Samuel DeCanio, *Democracy and the Origins of the American Regulatory State* (New Haven, CT: Yale University Press, 2014), 149–79.
63. White, 356–57; DeCanio, 149–79.
64. White, 357–58.

men who took the long view and were honest, patient, cautious, careful, and peaceful. Quarrels did not pay.[65]

The actual corporation proved somewhat different from the one Adams described to Harvard students. It was one thing to draw up organizational charts and accounting procedures; it was quite another to have them function as planned. A task seemingly as simple as confining the dividends paid to investors to money earned as profits proved difficult. The standard accounting forms for railroads in 1879 calculated profits simply as the difference between income and expenses. There was no modern calculation of depreciation, only the costs of actual repairs and replacements, and there was no calculation of the rate of return on capital assets and no way to calculate the capital actually invested in the road. Calculating and distributing profits was hard, but skimming off value was comparatively easy. This involved manipulating stock and bond issues and prices, draining off dividends and assets into the pockets of insiders, and mortgaging companies to the hilt and then selling them to unsuspecting buyers.[66]

The rational middle managers Adams desired also proved hard to find. Actual managers often replicated the faults of the financiers who controlled the roads. In private, Adams derided the Union Pacific as "the worst school for railroad management that the country now possesses." Inefficiency and fraud were everywhere, the legacy of Gould's control of the road, Adams believed. "Like master, like man," he wrote. "The large operations of Messrs. Gould and [Russell] Sage in the stock market just as certainly led to a system of peculation and jobbery throughout the organization in its subordinate parts as an example of sharp dealing and dishonesty leads to more sharp dealing and dishonesty." Even worse was the willingness of the middle managers, like the financiers, to take risks with money that was not their own, not so much from greed as from manhood. Adams blamed "nine quarrels out of ten, costing large sums of money" on "subordinates," who, as a rule had "no sense of the responsibility of their positions." He complained to Jay Gould that

> the average railroad official is...so jealous of what he is pleased to call the prestige or honor of the company to which he belongs that he is always ready to involve it in complications which may cost it millions, either through competition or false competition rather than see it bear the loss which may not amount to ten thousand dollars. About nine

---

65. "Railroad Management: A Lecture to Harvard Students by Charles Francis Adams, Jr.," *New York Times* (Mar. 17, 1886): 5; White, 244–45.
66. Chandler, 112–15.

tenths of the railroad misfortunes of the country, so far as my experience goes, may be traced to this fruitful source.

The average railroad manager had "no judgment, less discretion, and less conscience." Harmony, peace, and rationality were works in progress. Manliness reigned.[67]

Explaining the economy through classical economics—David Ricardo, Adam Smith, and Thomas Malthus—was like citing a wizard in a fairy tale to explain how a locomotive worked. Liberals conceived of the market as a collection of rational actors pursuing their own interests. All had equal access to information and an equal choice to participate or not participate. Every transaction was separate from all that preceded or followed. These were the foundational ideas of free labor and laissez faire. They had arisen in opposition to slavery and feudalism, and had done effective work against them, but they seemed virtually irrelevant in the new industrial economy. Where the liberal market was supposed to be transparent, equitable, and made up of separate transactions between individuals, the actual market was opaque, was inequitable, and consisted of connected transactions between entities of vastly different influence and power.

The leaders of the new economy were as impatient with inherited prescriptions as were the new generation of academic economists. Organized capital, the world with investment bankers and corporate leaders at the top, paid little attention to homilies about competition, individualism, laissez-faire, and the invisible hand. There were some, like Charles E. Perkins of the Burlington, who clung to laissez-faire, but John D. Rockefeller, Andrew Carnegie, Collis Huntington, J. P. Morgan, Charles Francis Adams, and Marcus Hanna actively worked to eliminate competition, which they saw as ultimately damaging, and to insert a quite visible hand into the working of the economy. There was, however, a considerable difference between their attempts to order the economy and their success in doing so.

The sentiment grew in the late 1880s among the more advanced capitalists that the industrial economy was as likely to devour them as enrich them, while among workers there was an even more acute sense that teeth were already gnawing at their bones. Herbert Spencer might be sanguine about the ultimate beneficence of this economy, but few of its actual participants were.

Charles Francis Adams played a central role from the 1870s onward in organizing railroad corporations, the dominant corporate form, to reduce and manage competition. Before becoming president of the Union Pacific, he had joined Albert Fink in running the Eastern Trunk Line

67. White, 244–51.

Association, founded in 1877; it was a giant railroad cartel embracing the great eastern trunk lines of the Pennsylvania, the New York Central, the Baltimore and Ohio, and the Erie. The idea was to pool traffic, set common rates, and arbitrate disputes, and, in effect, to regulate competition. It was part of a larger trend of standardization and consolidation that created the standard time zones (1883) and the standard gauge (1886) to ease schedule making and the movement of cars from line to line. Pools blossomed across the country in the 1880s, but most withered quickly. They had no legal means of enforcement. When members cheated, kept false books, gave rebates to preferred customers under the table, and did all the other things that made the railroad business a byword for chicanery and corruption, the pool could do nothing beyond expelling them, which, of course, ended the pool. Companies with little compunction about cheating their customers did not hesitate to cheat each other. "Our method of doing business," wrote Adams, "is founded upon lying, cheating, and stealing: all bad things."[68]

Adams regarded government regulation as the necessary means for decreasing competition. Adams and Fink realized that unless the government legalized and enforced the pools, they could not succeed. The issue by 1886 was thus not government regulation, but rather the form it would take. Politically, the core differences were embodied in the Reagan Bill, which would rely on local courts for enforcement, and the Cullom Bill, supported by many railroad men, which would rely on an appointed expert commission of the kind orthodox liberals loved and antimonopolists loathed as "salaried apologists for the railroads."[69]

Economically the differences were contained in two influential books. In 1886 James Hudson published *The Railroads and the Republic*, a book that antimonopolists like Reagan embraced and Adams, who hated many things, despised. Hudson summarized the complaints of more conservative antimonopolists. Railroad rates, along with virtually all other prices, were falling in the 1880s, but the decline of overall rates was not the issue. The essence of the complaints, as the Senate Select Committee on Interstate Commerce reported, was "the practice of discrimination in one form or another." The "great desideratum is to secure equality."[70]

Discrimination became a key word in the antimonopolist vocabulary because it affected the material interest of millions and basic notions of republican equity. When railroads charged different rates, all other things being

68. White, 174–78, 355-65, quote 359.
69. White, 355–59.
70. White, 327–29; James F. Hudson, *The Railways and the Republic* (New York: Harper & Brothers, 1886).

equal, to one shipper and his competitor, when they offered different rates in different towns, and when they charged different rates for different forms of a similar product—wheat and flour—they discriminated against the citizens of the republic that gave them life. Hudson excoriated the injustice and its consequences. "When railroads charged more to some shippers than to others and more per mile from one place to another," then "the equality of all persons is denied by the discriminations of the corporations which the government has created." Wealth was "not distributed among all classes according to their industry or prudence, but is concentrated among those who enjoy the favor of the railway power; and general independence and self respect are made impossible." This undercut a "nation of intelligent, self-respecting and self-governing freemen," and the result would be "little better than national suicide." Hudson's panacea was competition.[71]

But Adams and many other corporate leaders regarded competition as the problem and thought that discrimination was necessary if the railroads were to function. For railroads, the longer the haul the lower the cost per ton because the cargo required less handling and because expensive equipment did not sit idle. To be able to move bulk commodities such as wheat, corn, coal, and minerals, it was necessary to discriminate between short hauls and long hauls and charge rates accordingly. Some shippers would suffer and others would gain, but, the railroads argued, the public interest would benefit.[72]

In 1885 Charles Francis Adams had endorsed a new book, *Railroad Transportation*, by Arthur Twining Hadley, a young professor at Yale. Hadley proposed an amendment to laissez-faire and the liberal gospel. Competition did not provide the best outcome in every industry. There were certain industries, particularly railroads, where competition produced inefficiency and ruin. The immense initial costs of building railroads resulted in "sunk capital" nearly impossible to extricate, and made the duplication of routes a species of insanity. Ensuing competition either drove all to ruin or produced what it was supposed to prevent: monopoly. It was best to recognize the inevitable outcome and provide for cooperation and regulation. The only alternative was the organization of existing railroads into a few massive systems that would absorb or eliminate smaller roads. Like Adams, J. P. Morgan regarded competition as inefficient; he preferred that bankers encourage syndicates to underwrite loans to finance larger, merged railroads.[73]

71. White, 327–28; Hovenkamp, 144; Hudson, 9, 107–24, 135–38.
72. Hovenkamp, 134–37, 141–67.
73. Arthur Twining Hadley, *Railroad Transportation: Its History and Its Laws* (New York: G. P. Putnam's Sons, 1886), passim, particularly 67–74; Susie Pak, *Gentlemen Bankers:*

The divisions over the reform bills varied by region and party. The Democrats—and the South, Border States, and Midwest—favored the Reagan bill; Northeastern Republicans and Democrats favored the Cullom bill, but Midwestern Republicans were less enthusiastic. The Interstate Commerce Act of 1887, produced by a conference committee, cobbled together parts of both bills into a nearly unworkable amalgam. Reagan's specific prohibitions against rebates and rate discrimination, which privileged long hauls over short hauls, were gone, and the bill produced the commission he loathed. But Reagan did get a provision requiring the public posting of freight rates, a reform so basic that the necessity for legislation to secure it says much about nineteenth-century railroads. Reagan also deprived the railroads of what they most wanted; pools would be illegal. In these two respects, the bill promoted competition. The vagueness of the statute's language, however, was, as a cynical Adams wrote, "big with litigation for the courts and fees for the lawyers." Still, even Adams thought, a bad bill was better than no bill at all since the "current system is so bad, so rotten, so corrupt, that it cannot long continue." The even more cynical Huntington reasoned that the bill outlawed pools "but there is, I suppose, a way of dividing up the traffic that is just as good as a pool."[74]

Adams and Huntington, however, underestimated the ICC and Charles Cooley, the liberal judicial theorist whom Adams dismissed as "a second rate Judge, somewhat past the period of usefulness, and long since wholly past the period of growth." Adams often mixed arrogance and insight. In this case, he was just arrogant. Cooley's experience since the 1860s with railroad corporations and the rise of wage labor had drawn him further and further away from his famous *Treatise on the Constitutional Limitations Which Rest Upon the Legislative Power of the States of the American Union* (1868), dedicated to protecting individual rights to property and toward a reformist stance aimed at social equity, which would flower in Progressivism. He grew more dismayed about the judicial conclusions that Stephen Field and other liberal judges drew from his *Treatise*, and increasingly sympathetic to the regulation of corporations. He brought in Herbert Baxter Adams, who was skeptical of the ability of competition to promote either equity or efficiency in the railroad industry, as the chief statistician of the ICC. Influenced by Herbert Baxter Adams and his own son, the social psychologist Charles Cooley, he focused the ICC on the

The World of J. P. Morgan (Cambridge, MA: Harvard University Press, 2013), 15; White, 329–31.

74. Keith T. Poole and Howard Rosenthal, "The Enduring Nineteenth-Century Battle for Economic Regulation: The Interstate Commerce Act Revisited," *Journal of Law and Economics* 36, no. 2 (Oct. 1993): 846; White, 355–59.

fair distribution of transportation and its benefits. He still desired the broad opportunity and economic decentralization that had prompted his earlier beliefs, but he now saw government regulation as the best way to achieve them in a world of powerful railroad corporations. The Supreme Court would gut both his efforts and the ICC, but he had pointed the commission toward a destination it would reach two decades later.[75]

Where antimonopoly reformers aligned most closely with a major party was on the tariff. Here antimonopolists of every stripe were closest to the Democrats, to the Mugwumps, and to their own liberal roots. Tariff reform was particularly tempting because there was a relatively efficient administrative system in place to enforce any changes reformers made.[76]

In December 1887 President Cleveland elevated the stakes of reform by taking on the tariff. Gilded Age presidents did not deliver their annual messages to Congress in person. Instead they sent a written message, which was usually tedious and anodyne. Cleveland's message was neither. He warned of a coming financial crisis that would be triggered by the mounting surplus in the Treasury, and he blamed the tariff.[77]

Cleveland used the Treasury surplus to give tariff reform urgency. The surplus was locking money up in the Treasury during a period of deflation, but the president had previously seemed both unaware and unconcerned about this. He had significantly contributed to the growing surplus by vetoing bills designed to reduce it because he opposed increased pensions for veterans. His decision to act on the tariff combined ideology and political calculation. He believed that the protective tariff allowed the government to manipulate trade, rewarding some interests and hurting others, which violated his liberal convictions of limited government and market freedom. Attacking the tariff also put him in league with antimonopolists, not his natural allies, who thought it an unnecessary and unfair tax that produced "immense profits" for a few while punishing the mass of consumers with higher prices. Combining the surplus with tariff reform seemed a good campaign tactic.[78]

75. William Forbath, "Politics, State Building and the Courts, 1870–1920," in *The Cambridge History of Law in America*, ed. Michael Grossberg and Christopher Tomlins, three vols. (New York: Cambridge University Press, 2008), 660, 665, 668–70; White, 365; Jeffrey P. Sklansky, *The Soul's Economy: Market Society and Selfhood in American Thought, 1820–1920* (Chapel Hill: University of North Carolina Press, 2002), 205–17.

76. Charles W. Calhoun, *Minority Victory: Gilded Age Politics and the Front Porch Campaign of 1888* (Lawrence: University Press of Kansas, 2008), 15–16.

77. Joanne R. Reitano, *The Tariff Question in the Gilded Age: The Great Debate of 1888* (University Park: Pennsylvania State University Press, 1994), 8–9.

78. Ibid., 8–9, 14, 43–44; Daniel Klinghard, *The Nationalization of American Political Parties, 1880–1896* (Cambridge: Cambridge University Press, 2010), 164–70.

Cleveland probably did not anticipate how enthusiastically reform Democrats dressed liberal arguments against the tariff in the clothes of antimonopoly, economic equality, workers' rights, and the dangers of economic concentration. To listen to the Democratic advocates of tariff reform, it would be easy to think the entire party had stampeded into the antimonopoly camp. Saul Lanham of Texas proclaimed that "no man or set of men has the right in this country to be legislated into wealth." The tariff was the "mother of trusts," a triumph of avarice over liberty; it concentrated wealth while the people were "sinking lower and lower in want, wretchedness, degradation and squalor." It created conditions where "the millions own nothing and the few own millions."[79]

House Democrats introduced the Mills Bill, which the Republicans branded a free-trade measure, but which was really a relatively moderate tariff reform designed to lower import duties on key commodities. The bill passed the House and died in the Senate, but not before spurring a debate that would continue into the presidential campaign of 1888. The debate quickly spilled over into a much broader discussion of the industrial economy.

The surplus was not the ground on which the Republicans wanted to fight tariff issues. They tried using familiar tactics by pitting reform against reform, but their preferred reforms—spending the surplus on social welfare programs—was blocked by Cleveland's veto of increased pensions and the failure to pass a program of educational aid sponsored by Henry Blair. The Blair Education Bill aimed to reduce the high rate of illiteracy in the United States, particularly in the South, and the failure to fund Southern common schools adequately. School spending provided one of the starker measures of the difference between North and South. In 1880 the sixteen former slave states spent roughly $12 million on education. The former free states appropriated more than five times as much. In North Carolina the state spent 87 cents per child. Only five states spent $2.00 or more per student to educate their children. Average northern spending per child ranged from a low of $4.65 in Wisconsin to $18.47 in Massachusetts, with only two other states spending below $5.00 per student. The results were predictable. Although the percentage of illiterates in the country fell from 20 percent to 17 percent between 1870 and 1880, the total number rose from 5.7 million to 6.2 million. They were concentrated in the South, which had 65 percent of the country's illiterates. In the South as a whole, 37 percent of the population was illiterate, with a high of 54 percent in South Carolina. Much of this was a legacy of slavery, since the rate of illiteracy among black people was 75 percent.[80]

79. Reitano, 69–76.
80. Allen J. Going, "The South and the Blair Education Bill," *Mississippi Valley Historical Review* 44, no. 2 (1957): 268–71.

The Republicans cleverly crafted the bill to hive off Southern Democrats. Because the formula for federal aid to schools in the Blair Bill was tied to the rate of illiteracy, the large majority of the initial appropriation of $10 million would go to the South, thus in a way balancing the disproportionate amount of pension funds that went North. Although the bill got strong Southern backing, support was not universal. Proponents of the New South, recognizing the drag illiteracy placed on the economy and confident of their ability to control the appropriations, by and large favored federal aid. Opponents, however, denounced the bill as unconstitutional, defended state's rights and common schools, and condemned the bill as a Reconstruction measure—a federal intervention aimed at helping black people. Northern Democrats recognized that the bill was a way to maintain high tariffs and opposed it. In the 1880s the bill won in the Senate, but remained bottled up in the Democratic House.[81]

The Blair Bill created odd bedfellows. Willard, who regarded Christianity and education as the "father and mother of all reforms" and the foundation of the "Christian American home," was a strong advocate of the bill. Opponents were a mixed bag. Secular liberals, Southern Bourbons, and Catholics united in opposition. The liberals feared corruption, and the Catholic hierarchy feared even greater Protestant influence on the schools; both thought control of the schools should remain local. Blair blasted Catholics on the Senate floor and urged the deportation of Jesuits from the United States. He came to lump together an "unrepentant Southern aristocracy" and a "Jesuitical opposition." The Blair Bill never became law. The discrepancy between the North and South remained, but the number of children in school still almost tripled from seven million in 1870 to nearly twenty million by 1915. Total expenditures rose almost tenfold from the $63 million spent in 1870. The number of high schools went up 750 percent between 1880 and 1900, but still in 1920 only 16 percent of seventeen-year-olds graduated from high school, with more girls attending than boys and more native-born children than immigrants.[82]

The Republicans had to fight tariff reform elsewhere, and they retreated to their preferred ground: they were the party of prosperity, and the tariff was the source of high American wages, at least compared to Europe. They equated even modest tariff reform with free trade, a doctrine of both the slave South and Great Britain, the great enemies of free

81. Ibid.
82. Steven Mintz, *Huck's Raft: A History of American Childhood* (Cambridge, MA: Belknap Press of Harvard University Press, 2004), 174, 197, 204–5; Frances E. Willard, "The White Cross in Education," *Minnesota White Ribboner: Purity in the Home and God in Government*, July 15, 1890; Going, 271–90.

labor. The Republicans accused Democrats of not being interested in attacking monopolies but only in replacing American monopolists with British monopolists. They challenged the Democrats to produce legislation that would dismantle monopolies and trusts.[83]

The debate on the tariff had taken a surprising turn; it had become a discussion of American industrialism and the dangers of concentrated wealth. Politicians raised these concerns because they touched a nerve and captured the spirit of the times. President Cleveland had warned in his inaugural address that "corporations, which should be carefully restrained creatures of the law and servants of the people, are fast becoming the people's masters." In this he was no different from former President Hayes. Although horrified by labor violence and an advocate of repression, Hayes thought "excessive wealth in the hands of the few means extreme poverty, ignorance, vice and wretchedness as the lot of the many." He framed the problem as how "to rid our country of the conflict between wealth and poverty without destroying either society or civilization, or liberty and free government." Excessive wealth was "the evil" to be eradicated. Neither Cleveland nor Hayes was being duplicitous. The fear and distrust of corporations and inequality remained widespread.[84]

The social turmoil of the late 1880s manifested itself in the streets and workplaces of the nation, but it had spilled quickly into electoral politics from municipalities to Congress. It yielded a vibrant and strong reform politics, yet those very politics reflected the fractured ground of reform. Class lines, deep divisions between Catholics and Protestants, strong distrust among many of the native-born and between immigrants and children of immigrants, and a racial chasm Reconstruction had failed to bridge meant that one reform often stood against another. Reformers tried to form alliances to bridge the gaps between them; many succeeded briefly, but none for long. Existing ethnocultural politics and party loyalties divided reformers, but the opposite also became truer than ever. Reform alliances across party lines, no matter how fragile, began to take on a salience that threatened the old logic of the parties and the loyalty of their partisans. National politics were becoming unstable. It appeared that the existing parties could not govern.

83. Reitano, 78–82, 95–96, 103.
84. Alyn Brodsky, *Grover Cleveland: A Study in Character* (New York: St. Martin's Press, 2000), 168; Ari Arthur Hoogenboom, *Rutherford B. Hayes: Warrior and President* (Lawrence: University Press of Kansas, 1995), 494–95.

16

Westward the Course of Reform

The valence of westering has changed over the course of American history. In the colonial and early national period, moving into the borderlands and beyond had been a journey into the heart of darkness. The people who went there became suspect as "white Indians," as savage as the existing inhabitants. Then, over the course of the nineteenth century, westering had become pioneering. In the post–Civil War West, settlers became bearers of civilization and nature awaited not conquest but finishing to the final state for which God intended it.[1]

Clarence King celebrated the pioneer as the quintessential American in the autumn of 1886 when the *Century* magazine published his "Biographers of Lincoln," a puff piece for John Hay and John Nicolay's *Abraham Lincoln: A History*, which was about to be excerpted by that magazine. Hay and Nicolay had been Lincoln's secretaries during the Civil War, and King's article was both fawning and peculiar. Hay was King's friend, and so King predictably praised the authors, but where they made slavery the cause of the Civil War and that conflict the central event of American history, he demurred. King offered an interpretation in which the divisions between North and South faded and the Civil War became but a dramatic incident. The true division of the country, as King phrased it, was between "genuine Americans" and the "rabble." Genuine Americans had appeared only in the generation born after the Revolution; they were "the product of a new life" and had cast off European habits. "From that day to this [the country's] whole history may be summed up as the subjugation of the continent, the elaboration of democracy, and the rebellion."[2]

1. Richard White, "Frederick Jackson Turner and Buffalo Bill," *The Frontier in American Culture: An Exhibition at the Newberry Library, August 26, 1994–January 7, 1995*, ed. James R. Grossman (Berkeley: University of California Press, 1994), 19–24.
2. Clarence King, "The Biographers of Lincoln," *The Century* 32 (October 1886): 861; Joshua Zeitz, *Lincoln's Boys: John Hay, John Nicolay, and the War for Lincoln's Image* (New York: Penguin, 2014), 6–7, 307–8.

King signaled a cultural shift in which the Civil War became but an aberration from a larger history of westward expansion. Americans had wrested the continent "from barbarism," through a "dominating resolve to found new homes where the conditions of nature were favorable to instant comfort and not too distant wealth." Now, in the declining years of the century, the occupation of the continent was complete. This "vast ACT OF POSSESSION is far the most impressive feature of our history." There was nothing "so wonderful as the great Westward march of homemakers." It was "out of this great migration that the true, hardy American people have sprung; it was out of it that Lincoln came." King echoed on a higher plane the evolving popular entertainments of Buffalo Bill Cody, who in the mid-1880s made the "Attack on the Settler's Cabin" into the centerpiece of his Wild West. For Cody as much as King, the West was about homemaking.[3]

King hit on the great Gilded Age theme of homemaking, but just as John Gast before him, he fudged the considerable differences of American expansion before and after the Civil War. He ignored the new legal framework that the government had put in place during and immediately after the war and the administrative framework taking shape in the last years of the century. The Homestead Act, its allied land laws, and the Mining Act of 1872 were all expressions of government-sponsored free labor. The acts aimed to transfer public resources into the hands of small, independent producers, who presumably would compete on a free market. To be sure, resources in larger amounts also moved to corporations, particularly railroads, but the rationale was to provide the infrastructure necessary for free labor and contract freedom to thrive.

By the 1880s the Republican program produced a West that many found perplexing, as full of danger and disappointment as promise. Western development sometimes seemed more like a runaway train than an engine powering lasting growth. The Republicans had subsidized railroads the West did not need. These roads carried more wheat than the country wanted or export markets could absorb, more cattle than the country needed, and minerals that it often did not need at all. Instead of a pastoral paradise of small producers, the West became a region of bankrupt railroads, wasted capital, and angry workers and farmers. Since much of what the West produced in the 1880s could be produced elsewhere, overproduction and competition put intense pressure on the small farmers and the workers who were supposed to be the beneficiaries of Republican development.

3. King, 861; Louis S. Warren, *Buffalo Bill's America: William Cody and the Wild West Show* (New York: Knopf, 2005), 30–32.

Millions of small farmers did make homes, but they existed alongside vast holdings derived from Spanish and Mexican land grants, speculative holdings amassed from the manipulation of U.S. land laws or from railroad land grants that the railroads could not or would not sell. Large cattle companies, most owned by foreign or Eastern investors, commandeered public lands, fenced them in, and closed them to competitors. Timber companies manipulated land laws to create their own fiefdoms or simply harvested timber from public lands. The mining laws formulated with prospectors in mind became tools to create large mining corporations whose workers came to hate the companies that employed them. Without reform, the West could never fully be King's and Cody's land of homes.[4]

When Josiah Strong sounded the alarm over the West in *Our Country*, he gave voice to widespread worry and discontent. Strong's West was vast, its resources inexhaustible, and its apparent aridity and barrenness a somnolence from which the region would awaken with the presence of irrigation and American enterprise. It was an infant destined to outgrow and dominate the East, *if* reformers could save it from being strangled in the cradle.[5]

All the dangers confronting the nation were magnified in the West. Instead of a middling society of independent producers, Strong feared that the "two extremes of society—the dangerously rich and the dangerously poor," of which the "former are much more to be feared than the latter"—were arising there. The "striking centralization of capital" and the reckless gambling spirit of Westerners underlined the dangers. Strong regarded the public domain as at least a temporary antidote if it went to small producers, particularly farmers, whom he thought immune to socialism, but the public domain would soon vanish. Those who settled it would create the social foundations for those who would follow, and thus it was critical that proper people—which was to say not Catholics, Mormons, or "pagans"—settle it in a proper way.[6]

Strong's stress on the public domain and its proper settlement echoed the reforms coming out of both Democratic and Republican adminis-

---

4. Richard White, *"It's Your Misfortune and None of My Own": A History of the American West* (Norman: University of Oklahoma Press, 1991), 258–68, 280–96. This is the theme of Tamara Venit Shelton, *A Squatter's Republic: Land and the Politics of Monopoly in California and the Nation, 1850–1900* (Berkeley: University of California Press, 2013), and the formulation in Robert J. Steinfeld, *The Invention of Free Labor: The Employment Relation in English and American Law and Culture, 1350–1870* (Chapel Hill: University of North Carolina Press, 1991), 187.

5. Josiah Strong, *Our Country* (Cambridge, MA: Belknap Press of Harvard University Press, 1963), 27–40.

6. Ibid., 150–51, 165, 168–70.

trations in the late 1880s. Antimonopolists continued to press their war of attrition against western railroad corporations that had not fulfilled the terms of their land grants. Congress, the Department of the Interior, and the General Land Office launched an assault on cattle and timber companies encroaching on the public domain. Because politics and business were thoroughly intermeshed, this struggle involved more than a simple contest between reformers and corporations, or government and business. What hurt one company often helped another, and some western railroad companies were more than happy to support reforms that stripped their rivals of subsidies if those reforms did not affect them. In the 1880s special forfeiture acts reclaimed 28 million acres in Arizona and New Mexico from the Atlantic and Pacific and the Texas and Pacific.

The rush to build railroads, delays in the surveys, and the lavishness of the subsidies created a morass of overlapping claims that the government found hard to clear up. Settlers and railroads often claimed the same land, and the lieu lands given to railroads to compensate for lands already alienated within their grants created new conflicts with other settlers. The railroads could use these indemnity grants to blackmail settlers with incomplete titles on legitimate claims "at every point and in every stage," so that pioneering could become a slog through the courts. It sometimes became easier for settlers to just pay the railroad for the land.[7]

The federal government could push reform in the West more directly than elsewhere in the country because it had greater authority in the territories than in the states. It owned the public lands, and could also act with an impunity on Indian reservations that it could not employ elsewhere. So long as it relied on fee-based governance and the delegation of powers to private parties, federal administrative capacity continued to lag far behind the government's legal powers. It was no accident that some of the first bureaucracies took shape in the West: the National Forest Service, the Bureau of Indian Affairs (which gradually took modern form as the older Indian Service sank beneath its long heritage of fraud and corruption), and the U.S. Geological Service. Mythologized as the heartland of individualism, the West became the kindergarten of the modern American state.

---

7. Paul W. Gates, *History of Public Land Law Development* (Washington, DC: [for sale by the Superintendent of Documents, U.S. GPO], 1968), 457, 460; Richard White, *Railroaded: The Transcontinentals and the Making of Modern America* (New York: Norton, 2011), 130–31.

I

Cows and the men who chased them later became symbols of a supposed American West of individualism and self-reliance. When Owen Wister, a Philadelphian and friend of Theodore Roosevelt's, romanticized the American cowboy and cattleman in his novel *The Virginian* (1902), he had his hero say that "back East you can be middling and get along. But if you go to try a thing on in this Western country, you've got to do it well." This might have been the most astonishing line written about the nineteenth-century West, a land where the federal government repeatedly intervened to correct mistakes, many of them its own and others made by its citizens, and bail out Western failure. Nowhere was this truer than in the cattle industry.[8]

In the 1880s the Western open-range cattle industry became both a cautionary tale of Republican development policies and a sign of the possibilities for reform. There is probably no greater irony than the emergence of the cowboy as the epitome of American individualism, because cattle raising quickly became corporate. Cowboys became corporate employees in a heavily subsidized industry whose disastrous failure demonstrated the limits of corporate organization and fed the reforms in land policy that emanated from Washington.

The Western cattle industry flourished in the 1860s and 1870s because the Civil War had been hard on cattle. Where there had been 749 cattle for every thousand people in the United States in 1860, the Civil War, largely through destruction of livestock in the South, had cut the number to 509 in 1870. Only in 1890, when it reached 809 per thousand, would cattle per capita rise above the 1860 level. Simultaneously, the great anthrax epidemic of the mid-nineteenth century decimated European herds and put Great Britain in the market for North American beef. Texas meanwhile had three million beef cattle in 1870.[9]

Texas longhorns were probably the three million worst-quality beef cattle on the continent, "eight pounds of hamburger on 800 pounds of bone and horn." They neither fattened well nor were particularly palatable. But they had evolved to tolerate human neglect and to survive on the open ranges of South Texas. And they were fecund. Sufficient grass and benign weather allowed Texas cattle to increase to more than five

8. Owen Wister, *The Virginian: A Horseman of the Plains* (New York: Heritage Press, 1951, orig. ed. 1902), 348–49.
9. Mark Fiege, *The Republic of Nature: An Environmental History of the United States* (Seattle: University of Washington Press, 2012), 206–7; White, *Railroaded*, 466–67.

million by 1880, a number nearly as large as the two next-largest cattle-producing states, Iowa and Missouri, combined.[10]

Ticks and Texas fever kept the longhorns from market. Two species of the protozoan *Babesia* caused splenetic or Texas fever, and Texas longhorns carried both of them. Having evolved to live with Texas fever, longhorns had a mild case when young and were thereafter resistant. When longhorns moved, the disease went with them. They did not transmit the disease to other cattle directly. Ticks fed on the longhorns, absorbed the disease, dropped off, and laid eggs, and when the young ticks hatched, they, too, carried Texas fever. If other cattle passed along the same trail as the longhorns or shared a pasture, stockyard, or railroad car with them, they were likely to pick up the ticks and get infected. Unlike the longhorns, local stock died. Although farmers did not know how the disease spread, they quickly and correctly associated it with Texas cattle. Angry, armed farmers and state quarantine laws meant that Texas cattle could not walk to market or move to farms where they might fatten on corn. Texas cattle had to move toward railheads outside agricultural districts so as not to endanger far more valuable domestic stock.[11]

The ticks produced the famous long drive. Longhorns walked the seven hundred or more miles from southern and central Texas to Kansas, going through Indian Territory, in order to get to the railroads that had pushed their lines onto lands with few white people and were desperate for traffic. Beginning in 1867, cattle towns—Abilene, Ellsworth, Wichita, Dodge City, and Caldwell—grew up alongside the Atchison, Topeka and Santa Fe, the Kansas Pacific, and connecting lines. Although each in turn yielded to a rival farther west when farmers arrived, their initial lifeblood was cattle. The towns that came to epitomize the Wild West were creations of a tick.[12]

The long drive survived better railroad connections to Texas because going north turned out to have unanticipated advantages for cattle and cattlemen. When dealers held the longhorns until after the first hard freeze or overwintered them in Kansas, the cold killed the ticks, making the Texas cattle far less likely to infect domestic stock. Holding cattle on the central and northern Great Plains had a second, unplanned, advantage: they put on weight more quickly than they did in Texas. The industry became specialized, with Texas becoming a bovine nursery and the grasslands to the North a place for young steers to fatten for market. The pattern was in place by 1871 when buyers at Abilene purchased 190,000

10. White, *"It's Your Misfortune and None of My Own,"* 220; White, *Railroaded*, 467.
11. For a fuller discussion and citations, see White, *Railroaded*, 467–69.
12. Robert R. Dykstra, *The Cattle Towns* (New York: Knopf, 1968), 38–39, 55, 60–73.

head, but the railroads shipped only 40,000 from the town. The movement of cattle onto the Great Plains intensified in the 1880s. Roughly 200,000 head of cattle changed hands at Dodge City in 1882, but less than a third of them went to market by rail. Some stayed in Kansas; others went farther north.[13]

Cattle grazed among the ghosts of bison. Silas Bent informed the Cattle Growers' Convention in St. Louis in 1884 that bison had "infested" the Great Plains, and their elimination prepared the ground for the open-range cattle industry. Americans consumed slightly less meat per capita in 1900 than in 1870, but a greater percentage of the meat was beef. Yet beef never replaced pork on the country's table. In 1870 Americans consumed 131 pounds of pork per capita, compared to 62 pounds of beef. In 1900 they consumed 83 pounds of pork to 78 pounds of beef.[14]

Texas cattle gave an initial boost to beef consumption. Beef from longhorns was tough, but it was cheap; the grass on the public lands, and for that matter railroad lands, was free. Always desperate for things to carry, the railroads touted the Great Plains as a place where cattle effectively cared for themselves. It spawned a separate genre of boosterism pretty much summed up by the title of Gen. James S. Brisbin's *Beef Bonanza or How to Get Rich on the Plains*. In the late 1870s and early 1880s cattle raising spread steadily north.[15]

Drovers also brought stock eastward from the ranges of Oregon, Washington, and Idaho. These were descendants of cattle that had originally gone west along the Oregon Trail or come up from California. By the mid-1880s, the railroads were hauling so many "pilgrims," or barnyard stock, from the Midwest into the Great Plains that trainloads of cattle going west nearly equaled the trainloads of cattle going east. Some of these cattle were "improved," but often only in comparison to longhorns.

13. David Galenson, "The End of the Chisholm Trail," *Journal of Economic History* 34, no. 2 (1974): 350–64; Margaret Walsh, *The Rise of the Midwestern Meat Packing Industry* (Lexington: University Press of Kentucky, 1982), 77; Ernest Staples Osgood, *The Day of the Cattleman* (Chicago: University of Chicago Press, 1957), 90; White, *Railroaded*, 468–71; Dykstra, 79.

14. White, *Railroaded*, 466–70; Herbert O. Brayer, "The Influence of British Capital on the Western Range-Cattle Industry," *Journal of Economic History* 9 (1949): 87–92; Robert J. Gordon, *The Rise and Fall of American Growth: The U.S. Standard of Living since the Civil War* (Princeton, NJ: Princeton University Press, 2016), 67.

15. James S. Brisbin, *The Beef Bonanza; or, How to Get Rich on the Plains, Being a Description of Cattle-Growing, Sheep-Farming, Horse-Raising, and Dairying in the West* (Norman: University of Oklahoma Press, 1959); White, *Railroaded*, 468–71; White, "Animals and Enterprise," in *The Oxford History of the American West*, ed. Carol A. O'Connor, Clyde A. Milner II, and Martha A. Sandweiss (New York: Oxford University Press, 1994), 257–58.

They were, as one purchaser put it, "a crooked lot, half starved milk calves classed as yearlings and there was scarcely a good one even among the older cattle." In the explosion of hyperbole about endless grass and swelling herds of cattle, it was easy to lose sight of the reality that, outside of California and Texas, there were always far fewer cattle both in total numbers and per acre on the western ranges than on the lands east of the 98th meridian.[16]

By the 1880s cattle companies and corporations, created by Eastern and British investors, dominated the western ranges. Some of these investors followed their cattle into the West. Theodore Roosevelt, to the extent that he was typical of anything, played to type. He owned no land; he grazed his cattle on the public domain, which he fenced as if he owned it. He knew little of the West and less about stockraising, but as a very young and very patrician New Yorker a pair of nearly unbearable personal tragedies sent him West. His wife, having just given birth, died of kidney disease on the same day and in the same house that his mother, Martha Roosevelt, died of typhoid, a bacterial disease usually transmitted through water contaminated with human feces. Martha Roosevelt, who was known for her obsession with cleanliness, probably contracted it through vegetables washed in polluted water. Leaving his infant daughter to his sisters, Roosevelt had resigned from the New York Assembly and moved to Dakota Territory. Roosevelt's experience connected an emerging environmental crisis on the Great Plains with the urban environmental crisis.[17]

Like other wealthy Easterners, he played cowboy—complete with a silver mounted Bowie knife from Tiffany's and alligator boots—but he turned his experiences as a failed rancher into an account of manly self-fashioning, beating barroom bullies, and hunting down rustlers. He admired what he would later call the "barbarian virtues" of courage, stoicism, and endurance as antidote to "over-sentimentality...softness,...washiness and mushiness."[18]

16. J. Orin Oliphant, "The Eastward Movement of Cattle from the Oregon Country," *Agricultural History* 20 (January 1946): 24–38; Osgood, 93, 97; White, *Railroaded*, 470–71; John Clay, *My Life on the Range* (New York: Antiquarian Press, 1961), 91–92, 129–39.

17. David G. McCullough, *Mornings on Horseback* (New York: Simon and Schuster, 1981), 283; Roger L. DiSilvestro, *Theodore Roosevelt in the Badlands: A Young Politician's Quest for Recovery in the American West* (New York: Walker, 2011), 61.

18. Matthew Frye Jacobson, *Barbarian Virtues: The United States Encounters Foreign Peoples at Home and Abroad, 1878–1917* (New York: Hill and Wang, 2000), 3–5; DiSilvestro, 63–67, 90, 235–40; Edwin G. Burrows and Mike Wallace, *Gotham: A History of New York City to 1898* (New York: Oxford University Press, 1999), 1102–3; T. J. Jackson Lears, *Rebirth of a Nation: The Making of Modern America, 1877–1920* (New York: Harper, 2009), 36–37; McCullough, 282–24, 320–23, 344–45.

Roosevelt romanticized the cattle industry. He later recalled that we "knew toil and hardship and hunger and thirst...but we felt the beat of the hardy life in our veins, and ours was the glory of work and the joy of living," but he was a toy cowboy. He was a tourist on his own ranch, and although he worked the roundup at least once, he did not do it year after year. George Shafer, who grew up on a ranch and later became governor of North Dakota, knew the hardships of the work all too well. He would have none of the romance of rich men. He thought it no wonder that "nearly every cowboy is a...physical wreck at the age of thirty-five years."[19]

Like the railroads, cattle raising was an industry. That it was badly organized did not mean that it was not highly structured and controlled, with all kinds of regulations and claims to privileged appropriation of grass and water. It was virtually impossible to participate effectively without belonging to the cattlemen's or stockgrowers' associations that appeared quickly on the northern plains. They not only regulated roundups and the distribution of stray cattle but also protected from summer use areas set aside for winter grazing. The stockgrowers' association in the Dakotas, organized in part by Roosevelt, came into being almost as soon as the range cattle industry did.[20]

British and Scottish investors alone pumped $34 million worth of capital (declared book value) into the western livestock industry in the United States during the last quarter of the nineteenth century. What attracted investors was an industry heavily subsidized by the federal government, a set of economic calculations too good to be true, and promises made by promoters that amounted to little more than a modern Ponzi scheme. John Clay was a Scotsman who spent much of his adult life in the cattle business. "It was," Clay remembered, "a crude business at the beginning, and it remained so until the end."[21]

The subsidies, as with the railroads, were enormous. The federal government had opened up the public domain by evicting Indians, whom

19. Elwyn B. Robinson, *History of North Dakota* (Lincoln: University of Nebraska Press, 1982), 189–90, 193.
20. Harold E. Briggs, "Development and Decline of Open Range Ranching in the Northwest," *Mississippi Valley Historical Review* 20, no. 4 (1934): 523–25; Daniel Belgrad, "'Power's Larger Meaning': The Johnson County War as Political Violence in an Environmental Context," *Western Historical Quarterly* 33, no. 2 (2002): 172–73. Osgood, 114–24, 130–37, 140, 149–52, 181–88, 190–91; David Breen, *The Canadian Prairie West and the Ranching Frontier, 1874–1924* (Toronto: University of Toronto Press, 1983), 32–38; Robinson, 188–90. Numerous writers refer to the plains as a tragedy of the commons and then provide evidence for how it was regulated and apportioned.
21. Osgood, 97; Clay, 20–25, 91–92, 129–39; Brayer, 90–92.

Roosevelt despised, and whose removal he saw as both inevitable and commendable. He characterized their life as "but a few degrees less meaningless, squalid, and ferocious than that of the wild beasts with whom they held joint ownership." The federal government provided Roosevelt and other cattlemen with free land, and nature provided the grass and water that the cattle consumed. The federal government and states subsidized the railroads that promoted cattle-raising and hauled cattle to market. For all practical purposes, the "producer" in this industry was the product itself, for cows and steers got precious little help from humans in surviving on the Great Plains. Their owners branded them, gathered them when ready for shipping, and sent them off to market.[22]

A fairly simple set of calculations made profits seem inevitable. Cattlemen calculated the price of maintaining a steer at between $0.75 and $1.25 a year. When stockmen reported that they could sell a four-year-old Wyoming steer for between $25 to $45, with costs—exclusive of capital and transportation—being between $3 and $6 a steer, how could they lose?[23]

If corporate reports were to be believed (always a dangerous thing to do in the Gilded Age), investors were not losing. Anglo-American cattle corporations produced dividends of 15–30 percent between 1881 and 1883. The dividends, as it turned out, actually came from new investments and loans, not profits from cattle. The corporations actually had little idea how many head they owned because actual cattle were hard to find during roundups. So to estimate their herds, cattle companies created a book count. Book-count cattle existed only in a ledger. In an age that was perfecting actuarial tables and life insurance policies, there was nothing remarkable about making educated guesses based on the average survival and reproduction of large numbers of cattle, but men seeking investors do not make good actuaries.[24]

In the book counts, the West was a land of perpetual spring and toothless wolves. Real cattle died, had accidents, and failed to calve. Book-count cattle reproduced at a dependable annual rate, usually 70 percent. Book-count calves matured and begat more book-count calves. Western cattle corporations borrowed on their book-count cattle, which were immune to the vagaries of Western life. As a Cheyenne saloon keeper told a group of disconsolate cattlemen drinking at his bar while a blizzard

22. Jacobson, 3–5; DiSilvestro, 63–67, 90, 235–40; Lears, 36–37; McCullough, 282–84, 320–23, 344–45.
23. Brayer, 94; White, *Railroaded*, 472; Osgood, 129; Briggs, 526–27.
24. White, *Railroaded*, 473.

raged outside, "Cheer up boys, whatever happens the books won't freeze."[25]

For John Clay, it all became a single story repeated by cattle company after cattle company, "one pyramid upon another of reckless mismanagement and extravagance, of criminal neglect, expounding...the old adage that 'Fools rush in where angels fear to tread.'" That the steers, cows, and calves at the annual roundup did not match the book count didn't matter. If there were not enough four-year-olds to ship, then they could be supplemented with three-year-olds or cattle purchased from others, preferably with stock certificates or borrowed money. Credit in the cash-starved West was expensive; "normal interest" was 10 percent compounded every three or six months in 1883. All of this created debt and a deficiency of cattle for the next year, but that was next year's worry.[26]

By the mid-1880s more cattle roamed the Great Plains than the grasslands could maintain in years of drought and harsh winters. The present "manner of wintering stock," wrote the agent for the Cheyenne and Arapaho Indians, who were leasing lands to cattlemen in the Indian Territory in 1884, "is nothing less than slow starvation, a test of stored flesh and vitality against the hard storms until the grass comes again. The skeleton frames of last winter's dead dot the prairies within view of the agency with sickening frequency." He thought it was "only a question of time when all stock must be provided with feed during the severe winter weather." During the spring roundup, slow starvation gave way to what amounted to torture of weakened cattle as cattlemen "work extremely hard, work their horses harder, and nearly kill their cattle to separate their various brands." The agent would prove prophetic.[27]

The arrival of cheap longhorns acted as a spur to farmers in Missouri, Illinois, Iowa, Kansas, and Nebraska to improve their own livestock. The production of shorthorn cattle boomed in the late 1860s and 1870s. The shorthorns put on weight much more quickly than the longhorns and produced better beef, which brought a premium price. As the grasslands of the Midwest and Middle Border went under the plow and yielded corn and wheat, the cattle industry began to take on a new form. The prairie farms produced improved stock, which moved west to replace the longhorns. They fed on grass for a season or two before being shipped back to farms to fatten on corn.[28]

25. White, *Railroaded*, 473–74; Clay, 35, 104–5, 116, 158–67, 171, 172, 206.
26. Clay, 129–40, 171.
27. "Report of Agent, Cheyenne and Arapaho Indians," ed. 48th Cong. Senate Executive Document 16, 2nd Session, 21 (Washington, DC: U.S. GPO).
28. Allan G. Bogue, *From Prairie to Corn Belt: Farming on the Illinois and Iowa Prairies in the Nineteenth Century* (Chicago: University of Chicago Press, 1963), 89–102.

By the end of the 1880s the cattle companies were reeling, the victims, as John Clay put it, of "three great streams of ill luck, mismanagement, [and] greed," which merged to produce catastrophe. It was only a matter of time before drought, part of longstanding climatic patterns on the grasslands, cut down forage available to the excessive number of cattle dumped on the plains. The particularly harsh winter of 1886–87 on the northern plains had cut down the stressed and weakened herds like the grim reaper. The blizzards came so fast and so hard that it seemed like a two-month storm. Temperatures fell to 40 degrees below zero. Cowboys could do little but wait for spring, count the carcasses, and gather the emaciated cattle that had survived for sale on a glutted market that had little demand for more beef. This was the "Great Die-Up," and all of it was predictable.[29]

Having subsidized the railroad corporations that made the western cattle industry possible and allowed the looting of the public domain by cattlemen, the federal government shut its large Western barn door only after the Great Die-Up. The open-range cattle industry had ceased to depend on the open range, as the cattle corporations built fences around public domain land they did not own. In the late 1880s the government took action against 375 enclosures containing 6.4 million acres of land. The fences came down, but most prominent cattlemen escaped indictment. The cattle corporations had lost their dominance, but as the industry turned to improved stock and winter feeding, smaller ranchers were better able to complete. Still, by controlling water sources—usually through the use of illegal dummy entrymen who pretended to be bona fide settlers—cattle companies could still monopolize some grazing lands by denying competitors access to water.[30]

In the late 1880s and early 1890s, both Democrats and Republicans tried to bring order and honesty to land policy. William A. J. Sparks, a Democrat, became what seemed at the time an oxymoron: an honest head of the General Land Office. Sparks attacked abuses of swampland acts by speculators in California, who acquired much of the best farmland in the state for a pittance. He attacked timber theft by lumber companies. Congress and some Western states passed bills, spurred by the fear of Irish landlord practices, which Henry George denounced were spreading to the West, to ban alien ownership. By 1890 Benjamin Harrison's commissioner of the General Land Office, a Republican, would write with more

29. White, *Railroaded*, 479–80; White, "*It's Your Misfortune and None of My Own*," 224–25.
30. White, "*It's Your Misfortune and None of My Own*," 272–73; Gates, 467–68; White, *Railroaded*, 480–82.

credibility than was possible earlier, "The great object of the Government is to dispose of the public lands to actual settlers only—to bona fide tillers of the soil. . . ."[31]

II

What counted as public land was not always easy to determine without litigation. Potentially the public domain included lands granted to those railroads that had failed to fulfill the condition of the grant. It also potentially included some of the Spanish and Mexican land grants in the Southwest. The Board of California Land Commissioners had ruled on the grants in that state, but in New Mexico and Colorado questions about the validity of land grants dragged on well after the Civil War.

Antimonopoly reformers recognized that the old Spanish and Mexican land grants tore giant holes in the fabric of the American land system. Delivering this land into the hands of Americans proceeded without much difficulty, but getting access for small freeholders remained far harder. Despite their considerable flaws, most of the original grants stood up against legal assault, though the victories of the original holders in California usually proved so costly that the owners had to sell or surrender the land to their American lawyers to pay their bills. This did not necessarily lead to dismemberment; the grants just became the property of American and foreign investors.[32]

Lucien Maxwell became rich by marrying well; his wife brought to the marriage a much-disputed land grant of 1.75 million acres in New Mexico and Colorado, or in the conventional measurement of the West, two and a half Rhode Islands. Maxwell ran it as a *patron* of a modern hacienda. *Nuevo mexicano* settlers, who had migrated in from the Rio Grande Valley, lived on the grant, as did Apaches, part of whose homeland it contained. The settlers formed a subordinated work force, products of the long history of peonage in New Mexico, but one with clearly understood use rights to the land. They could farm, hunt, gather, graze animals, and take timber. In 1869, Maxwell sold the grant to European investors, and the hacienda became the Maxwell Land Grant Cattle Company. The settlers moved from being *peones* to free laborers, but in doing so they lost their existing use rights and instead sold their labor directly on the market.

---

31. Gates, 459–62.
32. Shelton; Leonard Pitt, *The Decline of the Californios: A Social History of the Spanish-Speaking Californians, 1846–1890* (Berkeley: University of California Press, 1998), 37–73.

The new investors also denied Jicarilla Apaches their existing rights. This set off a series of complicated conflicts that lasted through the 1870s and 1880s. White miners and other Anglos also opposed the land company, but they and *nuevo mexicanos* often fought each other.[33]

The struggle over the Maxwell Grant demonstrated once again that free labor could prove a double-edged sword for workers and small producers. Residents of the grant appealed to antimonopoly, and land reformers challenged the extent and legality of the original grant, portraying the investors as men trying to monopolize the public domain and to deprive Anglo settlers and *nuevo mexicanos* of home and homestead. The investors, in turn, enlisted the aid of the Santa Fe Ring, a New Mexican manifestation of the corrupt Gilded Age Republican machines that wielded power in many states and territories, and appealed to rights of property and the sanctity of contract. The surveyor general of New Mexico had extraordinary power in determining the boundaries of Mexican and Spanish land grants, and this made the office lucrative. In the 1880s the legal struggle over the validity of the grant and the social struggles between, and among, the residents of the grant merged into a combination of gunfights and litigation. Corruption, gunfights, and litigation pretty much defined New Mexican politics in the 1870s and 1880s, which repeatedly degenerated into a series of county "wars" that spawned, among other desperados, William Bonney, also known as Billy the Kid. In 1887 the Supreme Court confirmed the company's right to its land in Colorado and New Mexico. Internally contradictory, legally incoherent, and historically inaccurate, the decision in *U.S. v. Maxwell Land Grant* condoned a corporate land grab of stunning proportions.[34]

The federal government had far more consistent success in stripping lands from Indians and adding them to the public domain than it did in halting corporate plundering. Most Indians lived on unceded lands guaranteed them by treaty. Their possession of those lands, however, denied white farmers, but not necessarily white cattlemen, access. Indians found themselves in the sights of free labor, and when reformers squeezed the rhetorical trigger, they fell.

33. María E. Montoya, *Translating Property: The Maxwell Land Grant and the Conflict over Land in the American West, 1840–1900* (Berkeley: University of California Press, 2002), 72–75, 85, 96–113; Stacey L. Smith, "Emancipating Peons, Excluding Coolies: Reconstructing Coercion in the American West," in *The World the Civil War Made*, ed. Gregory P. Downs and Kate Masur (Chapel Hill: University of North Carolina Press, 2015), 46–58; Howard R. Lamar, *The Far Southwest: 1846–1912: A Territorial History* (New York: Norton, 1970), 136–70, 182–85.

34. Montoya, 72–75, 85, 96–113; Homer F. Socolofsky, "Benjamin Harrison and the American West," *Great Plains Quarterly* 5 (Fall 1985): 256; Lamar, 136–70, 182–85.

Even after the passage of the Fourteenth Amendment, Indians retained their anomalous position under American law. They lived as semi-sovereign wards of the government with separate treaty rights in territory claimed by the United States. The Fourteenth Amendment did not make them citizens or initially grant them common Constitutional protections. When a band of Ho-Chunks attempting to retain their residence in Wisconsin tried to use the Fourteenth Amendment to claim such protections and resist removal, they failed.[35]

American officials, not Indians, determined the form and content of wardship. In 1883 in *ex parte Crow Dog*, a case arising from the murder of Spotted Tail, the leading chief of the Brulé division of the Lakotas, the Supreme Court delivered what turned out to be a Pyrrhic victory for Indian self-governance. The court found that the United States government did not have jurisdiction in crimes that an Indian committed against another Indian. Two years later Congress passed the Major Crimes Act, giving the United States jurisdiction over seven major crimes in Indian Country. Opponents challenged its constitutionality, but the Supreme Court upheld it in *U.S. v. Kagama* (1886). The court cited the plenary power of Congress since the tribes were wards of the nation and dependent on the United States. Wardship trumped sovereignty. Eventually, in *Lone Wolf v. Hitchcock* (1903) the Supreme Court went further, ruling that treaties could not stop Congress from exercising its plenary powers. It could unilaterally void explicit treaty promises.[36]

Indian reformers—the so-called Friends of the Indian—urged on the government's efforts to subvert treaty rights. The Indian Rights Association (IRA), the country's major reform organization devoted to Indian policy, formed the vanguard of the reformers' assault abuses of Indians and Indian rights. Evangelicals dominated the IRA. Beginning in 1883, Indian reformers met annually at a resort on Lake Mohonk in upstate New York. They proclaimed themselves "the conscience of the American people on

35. Stephen Kantrowitz, "'Not Quite Constitutionalized': The Meanings of 'Civilization' and the Limits of Native American Citizenship," in Downs and Masur, 75–105; William Forbath, "Politics, State Building and the Courts, 1870–1920," in *The Cambridge History of Law in America*, three vols., ed. Michael Grossberg and Christopher Tomlins (New York: Cambridge University Press, 2008), 683–88; Francis Paul Prucha, *The Great Father: The United States Government and the American Indians* (Lincoln: University of Nebraska Press, 1984), 2: 775–76.

36. C. Joseph Genetin-Pilawa, *Crooked Paths to Allotment: The Fight over Federal Indian Policy after the Civil War* (Chapel Hill: University of North Carolina Press, 2012), 24–25; Prucha, *American Indian Policy in Crisis: Christian Reformers and the Indian, 1865–1900* (Norman: University of Oklahoma Press 1976), 333–34; Prucha, *Great Father*, 775–76.

the Indian question." The Indians' own judgment could not be trusted. The people who were native to the country became strangers in their own land. "Friends of the Indian" did not admire Indians. They were not technically racist, since they considered Indians the potential equal of whites, but they considered most actual Indians to be woefully deficient. Liberal free-labor ideas survived in near purity in the formulation of Indian policy in the West. Indian peoples, to the extent that they remained communal, sometimes polygamous, and (outside the Pacific Northwest, Indian Territory, and the Midwest) at the margins of the markets, served as a perfect counterpoint to free-labor values. For what they considered the Indians' own good, reformers planned to toss them into a political cauldron to be recast as autonomous individuals who enjoyed contract freedom and created homes based on monogamous marriage.[37]

Even some other "friends of the Indian" thought Richard Henry Pratt, who founded Carlisle Indian School in 1879, an "honest lunatic." He may have been, but only because he pushed Indian reform to its logical conclusion. The goal of Carlisle became "to kill the Indian and save the man." If the United States could absorb five million immigrants in the 1880s, Pratt asked, why couldn't it eradicate native culture and absorb 250,000 Indians without a trace? With friends like these, Indians hardly needed enemies, but they had them anyway.[38]

For all its hubris, the Indian Rights Association accurately discerned a crisis in Indian Country. The dramatic decline of Indian populations to less than a quarter million people—fewer than the estimated number of Indians who had lived in California alone at the founding of the United States—fed the perception that Indians were on the road to ultimate extinction. But the crisis hardly mandated the solution reformers proposed. Reformers attacked everything that legally and politically differentiated Indians from other Americans. They treated the lands remaining to the Indians—their great asset—as a liability, which, for their own good, would have to be redistributed to whites. Indians would receive a portion of their land in severalty (or individual ownership) with the "surplus" restored to the public domain and sold to whites. Government and missionaries would suppress Indian religions and substitute Christianity. They would educate—and indoctrinate—Indian children in boarding and reservation

37. Prucha, *American Indian Policy in Crisis*, 143–62, quote 153.
38. Richard Henry Pratt, "The Advantages of Mingling Indians with Whites," in *Americanizing the American Indians: Writings by the "Friends of the Indian" 1880–1900* (Cambridge, MA: Harvard University Press, 1973), 260–71; Prucha, *American Indian Policy in Crisis*, 132–49, 272–83; Brian W. Dippie, *The Vanishing American: White Attitudes and U.S. Indian Policy* (Lawrence: University Press of Kansas, 1991), 113–21.

schools. Indian communities would be stripped of governing authority and their leaders replaced with government appointed agents. The agents' authority would remain supreme until Indians emerged as rights-bearing individuals, no different from other citizens.[39]

The IRA faced opposition from a second group of reformers. In 1885 Thomas Bland helped form the National Indian Defense Association, an organization with significant Indian membership. Bland was pragmatic and historical where the IRA was ideological. Like working-class intellectuals who sought to reformulate free-labor ideology and adapt it to industrial America, he tried to reframe it in regard to Indians. He pointed out that the allotment in land in severalty among Indian peoples had proved a disaster everywhere it had been tried. He instead proposed mimicking the policy in Indian Territory, where the Cherokees, Choctaws, Creeks, Chickasaws, and Seminoles had been given "patents in fee," in which the community rather than individuals held title to the land. He pointed out that "those five tribes still own and occupy the lands then secured to them . . . and they have solved the problem of civilization for themselves in their own way." Indians like other peoples had been changing for centuries; the real issue was who would determine how social transformation proceeded.[40]

Momentum, however, lay with the Indian Rights Association. In 1886 Sen. Henry Dawes of Massachusetts introduced the Dawes Severalty Bill, which became the General Allotment Act. Predictably, he made the home the act's justification: "The home is the central force of civilization, and next to religion, the most powerful of all its agencies. Now this home is what the Severalty Act attempts to supply." Dawes drew heavily on the work of Alice Fletcher, who had turned her initial fascination with Standing Bear's and Suzanne La Flesche's 1879 tour on behalf of the Poncas into a study of ethnology, particularly of Indian women. She became the country's most prominent female Indian reformer as well as a leader in the Association for the Advancement of Women. Convinced that private property, the nuclear family, and gendered labor modeled on the American home provided the key to Indian advancement, she had in 1883 accepted appointment as the special agent for the allotment of the Omaha Reservation. Francis La

39. Genetin-Pilawa, 135–49; for boarding schools, see David Wallace Adams, *Education for Extinction: American Indians and the Boarding School Experience 1875–1928* (Lawrence: University of Kansas Press, 1995); and Margaret D. Jacobs, *White Mother to a Dark Race: Settler Colonialism, Maternalism, and the Removal of Indigenous Children in the American West and Australia, 1880–1940* (Lincoln: University of Nebraska Press, 2009); Dippie, 152–55.
40. Genetin-Pilawa, 124–28.

Flesche, Susan's half-brother, was her interpreter. At the invitation of the Senate, she created a nearly seven-hundred-page compendium of U.S. policies that helped shape the Dawes bill, which she enthusiastically backed.[41]

Henry Dawes considered himself a realist. He believed whites were going to seize Indian lands one way or another; he would save something for the Indians. Dawes's realism was less blind than blindfolded. Allotment had been tried well before 1887, and, as Bland pointed out, it had proven to be a disaster. In Michigan the allotment of Odawa and Chippewa reservations had led to merciless and remorseless fraud, aided and abetted by government officials, both elected and appointed. The impoverishment of Indians had been nearly complete.[42]

In 1887, over the objections of Bland and many Indians, Congress passed the General Allotment Act that allowed distribution of tribal lands in severalty, with the exception of Indian Territory and Iroquois country, without Indian consent. Reformers proclaimed the act the equivalent of the Magna Carta, the Declaration of Independence, and the Emancipation Proclamation all rolled into one. It recognized, they said, Indian manhood. Secretary of the Interior L. Q. C. Lamar, an ex-Confederate from Mississippi, presented the law as the only escape available to Indians "from the dire alternative of impending extirpation." In a century of disasters for Indian peoples, the General Allotment Act ranked among the greatest. In 1881 Indians held 155 million acres of land; by 1890 the total had fallen to 104 million. By 1900, when Merrill E. Gates praised the act at the Lake Mohonk Conference as "a mighty pulverizing engine for breaking up the tribal mass," the total was down to 77 million.[43]

---

41. Henry Dawes, "The New Indian Law," *Friends Intelligencer* 44 (July 23, 1887): 474; Louise Michele Newman, *White Women's Rights: The Racial Origins of Feminism in the United States* (New York: Oxford University Press, 1999), 121–28. Fletcher had a long relationship, unusual even by Victorian standards, with Francis, who was many years her junior and whom she considered adopting. La Flesche lived with Fletcher in Washington, D.C., from 1884 until her death in 1923, even as he briefly married and Fletcher shared a long, live-in relationship with Jane Gay. Both Fletcher's relationship with Gay and La Flesche's marriage crumbled in 1906. La Flesche and Fletcher endured. In Victorian America, sex very often did not signal intimacy, and intimacy did not necessarily involve sex; Prucha, *American Indian Policy in Crisis*, 170–87.

42. Newman, 126–27.

43. Genetin-Pilawa, 134–43; Jeffrey Ostler, *The Plains Sioux and U.S. Colonialism from Lewis and Clark to Wounded Knee* (Cambridge: Cambridge University Press, 2004), 203–12; Prucha, *American Indian Policy in Crisis*, 248–57.

III

Farmers and miners were the original beneficiaries of free-labor policies in the West, but by the late 1880s they were in open revolt against the political system originally designed to aid them. Although they welcomed attacks on corporations, Indians, and large land grants, farmers and western miners demanded measures that went well beyond a world of small producers and competition.

The Mining Act of 1872 encapsulated the problems with free-labor ideology in the West. The law was both harmful and obsolete at the moment of its enactment. It took a set of practices created for prospectors and miners able to compete and mine surface gold with relatively little skill and capital, and applied it to conditions in which refractory ores demanded large amounts of capital for mining and smelting. Prospectors remained, but they were less independent producers than bounty hunters who could discover and claim mining sites and sell them to capitalists for development. The world of the Forty-Niners had quickly evolved into a world of industrial mining and wage work. As the first public lands commission reported to President Hayes in 1880, "while 20 acres of... mineral land on the Comstock lode at $5 per acre are sold for $100..., as in the case of the Consolidated Virginia and California mines, [they] may yield more than $60,000,000."[44]

Mining was quite literally a search for stardust and the remnants of ancient swamps. Precious metals—gold and silver—were the last products of dying supergiant stars with seventy times the mass of Earth's sun. The same stars had produced copper as they aged. These minerals became parts of planets formed from the dust and detritus of the exploded stars. Earth's geological processes concentrated the minerals in amounts that humans could exploit.[45]

Railroads and laborers brought the collected stardust of the Rockies together with coal—the fossilized vegetation of the Late Cretaceous Era, approximately seventy million years ago—with dramatic consequences. The first smelters depended on wood turned into charcoal, but along with the timber needed for bracing the mines, the resulting drain on the forests proved too much for them to bear. Corporations initially received what seemed a carte blanche to pollute and destroy forests, rivers, and surrounding farms. The damage inflicted on rivers flowing from the Sierra Nevada to the San Francisco Bay by hydraulic miners was curtailed only

44. White, "It's Your Misfortune and None of My Own," 398.
45. Timothy J. LeCain, Mass Destruction: The Men and Giant Mines That Wired America and Scarred the Planet (New Brunswick, NJ: Rutgers University Press, 2009), 32–34.

with *Woodruff v. North Bloomfield* (1884) and the Caminetti Act of 1893. On the Comstock Lode of Nevada an estimated 600 million feet of timber went underground to support the mines while the mining towns consumed two million cords of firewood. The journalist "Dan De Quille" described the Comstock Lode as "the tomb of the forests of the Sierras." The gains were private; the costs were public.[46]

Because forests could not sustain the load and wood provided less energy than coal, the smelters turned to coke, produced from coal, for energy to separate minerals from the ore. The Union Pacific controlled the Wyoming coal lands; the Denver and Rio Grande Railway dominated those of Colorado. By the 1880s it had become apparent that it was cheaper to bring ore downhill to coal than to haul coal uphill to ore, and large and more-efficient smelters in Denver and Pueblo began to displace the smelters built near the Colorado mines. Some coal, however, continued to move uphill to power the hoists, fans, pumps, and steam drills that allowed the miners to go deeper and deeper underground. Burning coal blanketed Leadville and other mining towns with "noxious black and yellow" smoke, but it also spared the forests from being stripped bare.[47]

The United States was not unusually well endowed with resources, but American laws and policies spurred the development of what the country did possess. The Mining Act of 1872 was only the first step. With the creation of the U.S. Topographical Engineers and the U.S. Geological Survey, the government systematically searched for minerals and made them available for development. Subsidized railroads provided an additional spur to expansion. Mining had preceded the railroads, but without the rails hard-rock mining was confined to the richest and most easily worked deposits of precious metals. Renewed building came at the end of the long depression following the Panic of 1873. It resulted in the completion of the Southern Pacific (1883), then the Northern Pacific (1883), the Atchison, Topeka and Santa Fe on leased lines in 1883 and on its own lines in 1887, and the Atlantic and Pacific (1885). The Oregon Short Line, a subsidiary of the Union Pacific, broke through the Rockies and reached Portland in 1884. The abundance of mines meant that no matter how many failed, the remainder would turn out more silver than anyone needed.[48]

46. White, *"It's Your Misfortune and None of My Own,"* 234–35, 398.
47. Thomas G. Andrews, *Killing for Coal: America's Deadliest Labor War* (Cambridge, MA: Harvard University Press, 2008), 29–31, 53–54, 62–63, 74, 75–78.
48. Lorena M. Parlee, "Porfirio Diaz, Railroads, and Development in Northern Mexico: A Study of Government Policy toward the Central and Nacional Railroads, 1876–1910"

Mining amounted to a form of gambling. The worst Western mining corporations rivaled the cattle companies in the extravagance of their claims, the looseness of their finances, and their propensity for swindle and fraud. They became the punch line of the old Western joke that the definition of a mine was "a hole in the ground with a liar on top." For every productive mine, many others absorbed cash and gave only paper in return.[49]

As with other forms of gambling, it was always best to stack the deck, and Western mine owners struggled to do so, but the effort was a complicated one involving both the American and Mexican governments, mining and smelting companies, and the railroads. Mineral deposits extended into Mexico and up into Canada, but it was the Mexican mines that proved most critical in the 1880s and 1890s. American railroads and American capital did not confine themselves to the United States. The Atchison, Topeka and Santa Fe, which arrived in El Paso, Texas, in 1881, controlled the Mexican Central, which was building south from El Paso and north from Mexico City. The Mexican Central's most lucrative traffic moved between Northern Mexico and the United States, and that cargo included ore from the Sierra Mojada in Coahuila whose high lead content, yield a valuable by-product and increased the yields of the "dry" (i.e., low lead) silver ores of Colorado and Arizona when these were mixed with Mexican ores. In order to secure longer hauls, the rail roads set rates lower for imports and exports between the United States and Mexico than for the transportation of commodities within Mexico. This rate structure, created connections between Sierra Mojada and smelters in Kansas, Texas, Colorado, and Missouri.[50]

(Ph.D. diss., University of California, San Diego, 1981), 5; White, *Railroaded*, 186–224; Paul A. David and Gavin Wright, "Increasing Returns and the Genesis of American Resource Abundance," *Industrial and Corporate Change* 6, no. 2 (1997): 204–9, 226–34.

49. Joseph E. King, *A Mine to Make a Mine: Financing the Colorado Mining Industry, 1859–1902* (College Station: Texas A&M University Press, 1977), 171–80; Geoffrey C. Ward, *A Disposition to Be Rich: How a Small-Town Pastor's Son Ruined an American President, Brought on a Wall Street Crash, and Made Himself the Best-Hated Man in the United States* (New York: Knopf, 2012), 154.

50. Arturo Grunstein Dicter, "Competencia O Monopolio? Regulación Y Desarrollo Ferrocarrilero En Mexico, 1885–1911," *Ferrocarriles Y Vida Económica En México, 1850–1950: Del Surgimiento Tardío Al Decaimiento Precoz.* (México: El Colegio Mexiquense, 1996), 170–71; Marvin D. Bernstein, *The Mexican Mining Industry, 1890–1950: A Study of the Interaction of Politics, Economics, and Technology* (Albany: State University of New York, 1964), 21–22; Sandra Kuntz Ficker, *Empresa Extranjera Y Mercado Interno: El Ferrocarril Central Mexicano, 1880–1907* (México, D.F.: Colegio de México, 1995), 77–78; James W. Malcolmson, "The Sierra Mojada,

Mexico invited U.S. investment through a new mining code in 1884 and the Tax Law of 1887 and encouraged the export of ores. The result was that by 1900 virtually all the mines of the region would be in American hands. In 1887 the Consolidated Kansas City Smelting and Refining Company constructed a smelter at El Paso, Texas, a site that combined American jurisdiction with access to rich Mexican ore and inexpensive Mexican labor. The production of the Sierra Mojada mines quadrupled, but the local smelters shut down.[51]

The moves by the railroads, American investors in Mexican mines, and Mexico threatened the interests of other American capitalists and all American miners. They sought the aid of Congress to turn the border into a barrier that could stop imports of Mexican silver. In 1889 lead interests used U.S. labor law to get the U.S. customs authority to rule that the Mexican ore was produced by "pauper labor." Then in 1890 the McKinley Tariff slapped prohibitory duties on the lead content of the ore. Only the El Paso smelter, whose border location lowered its transportation costs, continued to smelt Mexican ores in any quantity. American mines were largely freed of Mexican competition.[52]

The tariff gave a particular boost to American mines that also had "wet" silver ores containing significant amounts of lead. By 1880 Leadville, with 14,820 inhabitants, was the second-biggest city in Colorado behind Denver, with 35,000, which said as much about the comparative lack of Coloradans as about the size of Leadville. One-third of the residents were immigrants: Irish, Cornish, Canadians, and Germans. Leadville was, as a

Coahuila, Mexico and Its Ore-Deposits," in *Transactions of the American Institute of Mining Engineers* (New York: American Institute of Mining, Metallurgical, and Petroleum Engineers, 1902), 102–3; Juan de la Torre, *Historia y Descripción del Ferrocarril Nacional Mexicano: Reseña Histórica de Esa Via Férrea desde 1853...* (Mexico: I Cumplido), 1888), 14–15; for rate structure in general, John H. Coatsworth, *Growth against Development: The Economic Impact of Railroads in Porfirian Mexico* (DeKalb: Northern Illinois University Press, 1981), 27.

51. Malcolmson, 102–14; Fred Wilbur Powell, *The Railroads of Mexico* (Boston: Stratford, 1921), 163–64; Kuntz Ficker, 46–56; Parlee, 188; Bernstein, 18–19, 21–22; Edward S. Meade, "The Fall in the Price of Silver since 1873," *Journal of Political Economy* 5 (June 1897): 323.

52. Malcolmson, 102–3; Parlee, 188–91; "Trade and Commerce of Paso Del Norte," ed. Reports from the Consuls of the United States, House Miscellaneous Document (Washington, DC: U.S. GPO, 1889), 755–56; Bernstein, 22; James E. Fell, *Ores to Metals: The Rocky Mountain Smelting Industry* (Boulder: University Press of Colorado, 2009), 194–97. For El Paso and the smelter, see Monica Perales, *Smeltertown: Making and Remembering a Southwest Border Community* (Chapel Hill: University of North Carolina Press, 2010), 21–57.

traveler noted in Colorado, part of an "organized system of capitalists or corporations... The poor man, instead of working for himself is a day laborer for hire." Mining meant industrial labor, and in the West, as in the East, industrial labor attracted a disproportionate number of immigrants. The coal mines of Colorado by the early 1880s similarly combined skilled Cornish miners with Irish, Mexicans and New Mexicans, Italians, and few Scandinavians.[53]

By giving American silver an advantage, the tariff united mine owners and workers in its support, as did policies advocating free silver and those providing for Treasury purchases of silver. But the tariff benefited workers only if mine owners used higher prices to raise American wages. Mine owners instead cut wages and tried to take control over the conditions of work, thus making the mines bastions of unionism. Wage cuts in Utah, Colorado, and Montana gave rise in 1893 to the Western Federation of Miners, one of the most militant unions in the country. Butte, Montana, emerged as the "Gibraltar of Unionism." The unions embraced largely Irish, native-born, and British miners. Cripple Creek, Colorado, for example, became a "white man's camp" where native-born and Northern European miners drove out Slavs, Italians, Mexicans, Chinese, and Japanese. In Butte there were deep divisions between the Irish, Cornish, and Eastern Europeans.[54]

The technological sophistication of Butte's mines underlined their modernity. Anaconda Copper, the most powerful of the mining corporations in the West, dominated Butte. Copper quickly became more critical to the new industrial society than silver. The country already mined vast amounts of copper in the Upper Peninsula of Michigan, where Alexander Agassiz, the son of the famous Harvard scientist, had made the Calumet and Hecla the most productive copper mines in the country. This copper was far purer and closer to markets than anything in the West, seemingly limiting the value of Montana and Arizona copper.[55]

53. Mark Wyman, *Hard Rock Epic: Western Miners and the Industrial Revolution, 1860–1910* (Berkeley: University of California Press, 1979), 41–51; Andrews, 59–61, 75–78, 102–3; Rodman W. Paul, *Mining Frontiers of the Far West, 1848–1880* (New York: Holt, Rinehart and Winston, 1963), 128–29, 132, 148, 158–59.

54. Elizabeth Jameson, *All That Glitters: Class, Conflict, and Community in Cripple Creek* (Urbana: University of Illinois Press, 1998), 140–42; White, *"It's Your Misfortune and None of My Own,"* 288–93; Michael P. Malone, *The Battle for Butte: Mining and Politics on the Northern Frontier, 1864–1906* (Seattle: University of Washington Press, 1981), 24–36.

55. Angus Murdoch, *Boom Copper: The Story of the First U.S. Mining Boom* (New York: Macmillan, 1943), 141–50.

Marcus Daly had found copper in Butte while looking for silver, and the devilish complexity of ores and smelting paradoxically gave him an opportunity. Daly persuaded his partners—George Hearst, who had made fortunes in the Comstock Lode, the Emma Mine in Utah, and the Homestake Mine in the Black Hills; and Hearst's associates, the brothers-in-law James Haggin and Lloyd Tevis—that its very impurity would allow Anaconda copper to compete with Michigan copper. Western copper ores contained gold and silver, and selling these by-products would allow Anaconda to undercut Michigan's advantages. A huge investment, however, proved necessary to create the infrastructure necessary to produce copper. The partners had to create concentration works, a smelter, and expensive technological control over a complicated underground—and underwater (for the mine lay beneath aquifers)—environment. They could succeed only if the demand for copper continued to increase. It did.[56]

In the 1880s the market for copper both as a component of the common alloys of bronze and brass and, in its pure form, as wire exploded. Telegraph companies, electric utility companies, telephone companies, and trolley companies all demanded copper wire. American copper production increased fivefold from 378 million pounds in 1868 to 1.9 billion pounds in 1910.[57]

Butte grew with the demand for copper. Already in the mid-1880s Butte employed twenty-five hundred men in its underground mines, smelters, reduction works, and railroads. Silver remained Montana's leading metal, but copper, concentrated in the "richest hill on earth," was rising quickly.[58]

IV

Miners enlisted in Western antimonopolism, but farmers formed the movement's political core. They organized around the Farmers' Alliance. In its first incarnation the Farmers' Alliance arose in central Texas's Lampasas County in the mid-1870s. This organization, which targeted horse and cattle thieves, smacked of Western vigilantism, and

56. LeCain, 39–51; Malone, 15–29; Paul, 146–47.
57. LeCain, 28–32, 68; May N. Stone, "The Plumbing Paradox: American Attitudes toward Late Nineteenth-Century Domestic Sanitary Arrangements," *Winterthur Portfolio* 14, no. 3 (1979): 297.
58. Malone, 30–34, 61–68.

when it faded, it was succeeded by more complicated and ambitious groups in Parker, Wise, and Jack counties, part of the Cross Timbers region of north central Texas. The Cross Timbers form a dagger of land stretching north into Oklahoma, and here large cattle companies had presaged later abuses on the federal lands. Texas was not a federal public land state. It had entered the Union as an independent nation and thus retained control of all of its lands, but its government had granted large tracts to railroads and sold millions of acres to Eastern and European investors. As they would farther west, the cattlemen mustered a new technology, the barbed wire fence, to cordon off vast swaths of land they sometimes owned and sometimes merely commandeered. The fences created barriers patrolled by armed line riders that forced travelers and nearby farmers to go miles out of their way. They formed an obstacle to agricultural development at a time and in a place where cotton and wheat farming were replacing cattle raising and subsistence farming.[59]

In central Texas farmers bested ranchers, but when cotton farming spread with the railroads across eastern and central Texas, it bred the same discontents that it had spawned in the upland South. By 1882, 140 suballiances had grouped themselves into a Texas state alliance, but rapid growth came only in 1884, when S. O. Daws created a system of lecturers to advance the Alliance gospel. The Texas Alliance adopted a full-blown antimonopolist platform calling for an alliance of farmers with "the industrial classes...now suffering at the hands of arrogant capitalists and powerful corporations." They demanded a return to a fiat currency, changes in the system of national banks, the creation of a Bureau of Labor Statistics, a mechanic's lien law, laws to force corporations to pay workers in money and not in goods or credit at a company store, an end to prison labor, and an interstate commerce law. In these demands they largely echoed the Knights of Labor.[60]

The Texas Alliance flourished under the leadership of Charles W. Macune, who was neither a farmer nor a native Texan. A physician, a Democrat, and a racist, Macune redefined the Alliance as a business organization, albeit an antimonopolist business organization. Farmers, as

59. Richard V. Francaviglia, *The Cast Iron Forest: A Natural and Cultural History of the North American Cross Timbers* (Austin: University of Texas Press, 1998), 136–61; Ralph Smith, "The Farmer's Alliance in Texas, 1875–1900: A Revolt against Bourbon and Bourgeois Democracy," *Southwestern Historical Quarterly* 48, no. 3 (1945): 346–69.
60. Charles Postel, *The Populist Vision* (New York: Oxford University Press, 2007), 19; M. Elizabeth Sanders, *Roots of Reform: Farmers, Workers, and the American State, 1877–1917* (Chicago: University of Chicago Press, 1999), 120.

Nelson Dunning, a publicist for the Alliance, put it, would organize "for the same reason that our enemies do." They would protect their businesses for "individual benefits through combined efforts." Macune had national ambitions for the Texas Alliance, which he merged with similar Southern farmers' organizations such as the Arkansas Wheel, the Louisiana Farmers' Union, and the North Carolina Farmer's Association, whose leader, Colonel Leonidas Polk, edited the *Progressive Farmer*. By 1887, he had moved to Washington, D.C., as head of the National Farmers' Alliance and Industrial Union (the Southern Alliance) to achieve them.[61]

So long as the Alliance remained a largely Southern organization, it did not pose much of a threat to Republicans, but they grew nervous as it expanded into the north and west. The Alliance created local organizations capable of mobilizing large numbers of farmers, farmers' wives, and sympathizers for education, uplift, and economic organization. It rallied scattered supporters for large meetings in country towns and supported a network of newspapers. The Kansas Alliance formed the Kansas Alliance and Exchange Company to centralize the marketing of crops from that state's farmers and to purchase their supplies. Cooperative endeavors proved particularly successful among California fruit growers, while Minnesota, the Dakotas, and Illinois all had thriving movements based on antimonopoly and cooperation. Discontented Western farmers remained Republican during the 1880s, but they were restive.[62]

A union between Western farmers and Southern farmers was not easily forged. Western farmers, though hardly racial egalitarians, did not subscribe to a white supremacy they associated with the Klan and a racial order embodied in emerging Jim Crow. Their largely Republican loyalties clashed with the Democratic loyalties of Southern farmers. The unity of farmers on economic issues remained tenuous. An important attempt to strengthen it came when the Northern and Southern wings of the Farmers' Alliance met with other reformers in St. Louis in 1889 to create a national reform organization. The attempt failed, but more radical elements of the Northern Alliance did join the Southerners in the National Farmers' Alliance and Industrial Union.[63]

61. Sanders, 120–21; Postel, 33–37.
62. Postel, viii, 4–6, 62–67, 77, 121–23, 287; Lawrence Goodwyn, *The Populist Moment: A Short History of the Agrarian Revolt in America* (New York: Oxford University Press, 1978), 74–89, 110–15; Richard J. Orsi, *Sunset Limited: The Southern Pacific Railroad and the Development of the American West, 1850–1930* (Berkeley: University of California Press, 2005), 325–26.
63. Sanders, 122–27; Ruth Birgitta Anderson Bordin, *Frances Willard: A Biography* (Chapel Hill: University of North Carolina Press, 1986), 175.

Miners and farmers, like cattlemen and lumberjacks, worked in nature, but nature played a role in Western reform that went beyond access to resources and battles over their production. In part, the work of these Westerners could be easily assimilated into the standard narratives of development and finishing that underlay the free-labor West. But there was a second reform narrative that cast both nature and humans in a different role.

In a world where more and more Americans did not know nature through their work, Western nature had a new role to play. Nature would keep native-born Americans "true" and "hardy." By the 1880s the fear of softness and weakness among middle-class men provoked a movement to restore manliness, vigor, and strength—in a word, character. Not work but leisure would lead men back into nature, particularly Western nature; they would seek recreation and health rather than wealth. The rehabilitation of sick and weak men turned into an unlikely secondary path for conservation and wilderness preservation. If nature and manly activities, particularly hunting, restored weak, effete, and exhausted men, then it became critical to preserve the nature and game animals critical to curing the neurasthenic. Civilization paradoxically demanded wilderness. The Boone and Crockett Club was only the most famous of the elite associations devoted to manliness and conservation. To preserve game and manhood, hunting had to be done right, and the Boone and Crockett Club became part of a campaign against commercial "pothunters," Indian hunters who did not observe game laws, and immigrant hunters. Conservation, like the industrial world that inspired it, could look like class war.[64]

John Muir, who came to know the Yosemite Valley in California during the 1870s and a wider West thereafter, became a regular contributor to California's *Overland Monthly* in the 1870s and also a popular regional lecturer, but he had spent much of the 1880s as an orchardist, resuming his wilderness writing only late in the decade. He underwent his own rebirth as John of the Mountains, lobbying to protect wilderness in general and Yosemite in particular. He drew on nature's curative powers. The Western mountains could be dangerous, but they

---

64. For differing views on these developments, see Louis S. Warren, *The Hunter's Game: Poachers and Conservationists in Twentieth-Century America* (New Haven, CT: Yale University Press, 1997); Karl Jacoby, *Crimes against Nature: Squatters, Poachers, Thieves, and the Hidden History of American Conservation* (Berkeley: University of California Press, 2001); John F. Reiger, *American Sportsmen and the Origins of Conservation*, 3rd, rev., and expanded ed. (Corvallis: Oregon State University Press, 2001).

were "decent, delightful, even divine, places to die in, compared with the doleful chambers of civilization. Few places in this world are more dangerous than home." The mountains "will kill care, save you from deadly apathy, set you free, and call forth every faculty into vigorous, enthusiastic action...for every unfortunate they kill, they cure a thousand."[65]

In the 1880s Muir began a cultural mapping of California and the West whose repercussions would roll through the twentieth century. He saw his enterprise as recording a reality, but he was creating one. He did not disavow development or finishing; he embraced both of them, but he also divided the world into the wild, the pastoral, and cities, which he regarded as the purely human, a place from which nature had been banished. His goal in delineating "the wild" was to protect it from human beings. Muir came to think of the wildest and best places as those that contained glaciers, because in the shadow of glaciers nature was newest and freshest, and the processes of its creation the most apparent. This land was sacred and not to be defaced by human use. Its epitome was the high country around his beloved Yosemite. It was to be a place where humans only visited and a site for leisure, self-discovery, and religious experiences. In Yosemite, and elsewhere, this meant that Indians had to be banished.[66]

Descending from the high country into the foothills and valleys, Muir reconciled himself, sometimes with regret, to human labor of the proper sort. This was the pastoral landscape where human labor ideally finished nature, in the sense of producing its final state. Muir, in effect, provided the blueprint for the modern Western American landscape: wild and preserved higher up, a more fruitful landscape in the hills, valleys, and plains, and then supposedly a space devoid of nature in the cities. It was less an accurate description than a prescription, and one whose legacy is with us still.

The key landscape by the 1880s, particularly in California, was not Muir's wilderness, but the orchards, where he spent much of his working life. Remaking the West into a garden landscape resonated across the Pacific, so that New Zealand and Australia sometimes seemed doppelgangers of the United States as the regions exchanged ideas, people, plants, insects, and technologies. The goal, as in so many of the endeavors

---

65. John Muir, "The Mountains of California," in *Nature Writings* (New York: Library of America, 1997), 363–64, 842–45. The best biography is Donald Worster, *A Passion for Nature: The Life of John Muir* (New York: Oxford University Press, 2008).
66. Muir, 372–73.

of the period, was to produce a landscape of small irrigated farms and orchards that would nurture Anglo-Saxon homes, as opposed to the vast
wheat and cattle ranches that depended on Mexicans and Chinese laborers, who were cast as enemies of the white home.[67]

67. Ian R. Tyrrell, *True Gardens of the Gods: Californian-Australian Environmental Reform,*
     1860–1930 (Berkeley: University of California Press, 1999), 13, 36–55, 61, 103, 106–8,
     113–14, 130, 133–34, 136–38, 161–62.

17

The Center Fails to Hold

Josiah Strong proclaimed the "closing years of the nineteenth century" to be a moment "second in importance to that only which must always remain first; viz., the birth of Christ." In these "extraordinary times the destinies of mankind, for centuries to come" depended on the next twenty years of American history. If extraordinary times demanded extraordinary men, American voters in 1888 could be excused for thinking they had wandered into the wrong election.[1]

The tariff took center stage in 1888. The style of the campaign replicated what had come before, but the issues were more narrowly focused. The issue involved far more than duties on a bewildering set of commodities; it carried the burden of arguments over economic equity and morality. Both parties cast the election as a clear-cut choice between protection and tariff reform, but while using the tariff to emphasize the differences between the parties, both the Democrats and Republicans had to bridge the differences between their own antimonopolist and regular wings. The Democrats linked the tariff to special privilege and monopoly, unleashing the ferocious rhetoric of antimonopolist congressmen onto the campaign trail. Advocates of tariff reform told voters, in the words of the *Indianapolis Sentinel*, that a vote for Republicans was a vote for "cheap whisky and tobacco, dear clothing and food and shelter, the indefinite perpetuation of war taxes in time of peace, for the benefit, not of the public treasury, but of monopoly." Republicans, for their part, framed the campaign as a battle for "industrial independence," higher wages, and worker well-being to

---

1. Josiah Strong, *Our Country* (Cambridge, MA: Belknap Press of Harvard University Press, 1963), 13; James Bryce, *The American Commonwealth* (London: Macmillan, 1888), 1: 62, 65, 71, 73–75, 79–80; Mark W. Summers, *Party Games: Getting, Keeping, and Using Power in Gilded Age Politics* (Chapel Hill: University of North Carolina Press, 2004), 4–5.

bridge their own deepening division between their antimonopolist wing and the regulars who sympathized with capital.[2]

Ultimately the election had a weight and importance greater than either the candidates or the tariff, but this would be apparent only retrospectively. In 1888 the political system tipped, lost its balance, and would not right itself for nearly a decade. When it did recover, it would be different: less democratic, more centralized, and more dependent on corporate funding. The parties that mustered their forces in 1888 were still the old coalitions resting on deep ethnocultural loyalties, but these coalitions were fraying. Newer issues and urgent reformers pressed forward, challenging the ability of the parties to graft evangelical and economic reform onto the old ethnocultural roots.[3]

Grover Cleveland's renomination was virtually ensured since he was the only successful Democratic presidential candidate since the Civil War. Benjamin Harrison's nomination, however, depended on the reticence of James G. Blaine, who possessed much of Ulysses Grant's popularity, many of his faults, and nowhere near his accomplishments. In 1888 Blaine left the country, taking a lesser version of Grant's world tour of 1880. He limited his journey to Europe. He consorted with the wealthy and sent pronouncements home. A high-tariff man, Blaine departed in June on a coaching trip with Andrew Carnegie to Cluny castle in Scotland, which was not actually a castle but an 11,000 acre Highland estate fully staffed with servants. Reporters, a member of the party reported, trailed them "by rail, horseback, and tricycle." Blaine said he was not a candidate but hinted that although refusing to run for the president was good for him, it was not necessarily good for the Republican Party or the United States. He seemed more than open to a draft since he had a powerful organization working to deadlock the convention. Carnegie was less reticent. He sent messages assuring the convention that Blaine would accept the nomination if drafted. Blaine then said he wouldn't, but few believed him.[4]

2. Charles W. Calhoun, *Minority Victory: Gilded Age Politics and the Front Porch Campaign of 1888* (Lawrence: University Press of Kansas, 2008), 109–11, 147–55; Joanne R. Reitano, *The Tariff Question in the Gilded Age: The Great Debate of 1888* (University Park: Pennsylvania State University Press, 1994), 123; Michael E. McGerr, *The Decline of Popular Politics: The American North, 1865–1928* (New York: Oxford University Press, 1986), 78.

3. Calhoun, 126–29, 131; McGerr, 69, 78, 80–84.

4. David Nasaw, *Andrew Carnegie* (New York: Penguin Press, 2006), 326–27; Calhoun, 56–58, 73–80, 97–98, 102–08; Daniel Klinghard, *The Nationalization of American Political Parties, 1880–1896* (Cambridge: Cambridge University Press, 2010), 171; Summers, 3–6.

Blaine's enemies had always said that he was false and duplicitous, but his most cutting enemy, Roscoe Conkling, had fallen silent. He died as a result of the Blizzard of '88. On March 12, with winds reaching seventy-five miles an hour, temperatures plunging to zero, and more than sixteen inches of snow, the storm completely shut down New York City. Live electrical wires dangled in streets, which drifts rendered nearly impassable. Those cab drivers still available raised their fares, which, although he was not a man known for undervaluing his own services, outraged Conkling. He refused to pay $50 for a cab to his club. He walked. It took him three hours, and on arrival he collapsed. He initially seemed none the worse for the experience, but he had contracted an ear infection. Among his physicians was Dr. D. Hayes Agnew, who had also treated Garfield after he had been shot. Agnew did no better with Conkling. The patient came down with bronchitis. On April 18 his heart failed. Robert Ingersoll, who surely knew better, eulogized Conkling's "independence,... courage, and... absolute integrity."[5]

Indirection had not worked for Grant, and it did not work for Blaine. The fight for the nomination became a battle of Midwesterners. William Tecumseh Sherman's brother, Sen. John Sherman of Ohio, took the early lead. His warmth and charm had earned Sherman the nickname the "Ohio Icicle," and his early advantage melted away. Benjamin Harrison, born in Ohio but now of Indiana, won the Republican nomination on the eighth ballot. The Democrats rejoiced. He had Alabama Sen. James L. Pugh said, "more ways to make people dislike him than any man I ever met in Congress." Sen. Matthew Butler of South Carolina thought, "If we can't beat Harrison, we can't beat anybody."[6]

Harrison was the scion of a political dynasty, but it was probably until that time the most undistinguished dynasty in American history. His great-grandfather had signed the Declaration of Independence, and then rested on his laurels. In the presidential campaign of 1840 his grandfather, William Henry Harrison, had been the Tippecanoe of "Tippecanoe and Tyler, too," who had attacked Tecumseh's brother the Prophet at Tippecanoe or Prophetstown, launching the western portion of the War of 1812. It was an odd coincidence that his grandson was now seeking the nomination against the brother of the country's most famous general, named for Tecumseh. In 1840 the Whigs had needed a Westerner to counter the Jacksonians. They had settled on Harrison, who won the

5. David M. Jordan, *Roscoe Conkling of New York: Voice in the Senate* (Ithaca, NY: Cornell University Press, 1971), 426–31.
6. Thomas Adams Upchurch, *Legislating Racism: The Billion Dollar Congress and the Birth of Jim Crow* (Lexington: University Press of Kentucky, 2004), 17–18.

election but caught pneumonia at his inauguration and died after serving a little more than a month. Benjamin Harrison's father had done little of note.

Benjamin Harrison did not lack talents. He was a formidable public speaker, and Rutherford B. Hayes, who advised him, thought him a man of ability. In his front porch campaign, Harrison gave daily speeches not from his porch but from a dais erected in a park in front of his Indianapolis house. The decision to stay home was calculated. "There is a great risk of meeting a fool at home," Harrison said, "but the candidate who travels cannot escape him." He did not want to be in attendance if supporters offered "Rum, Romanism, and Rebellion" speeches. Delegations came to him; stenographers recorded his speeches, and the Associated Press distributed them. Both sides moved closer to waging so-called educational campaigns, dependent more on mass mailings than massive rallies of the party faithful.[7]

Although the Democrats had launched the battle over the tariff, the Republicans put them on the defensive by equating tariff reform with the liberal nostrum of free trade that would remove all duties on imports. Cleveland mostly seemed confused, simultaneously attacking and retreating. A New Jersey congressman put Cleveland's problem succinctly: "He argues free trade and declares he is not a free trader. It is like a drunken man protesting that he is sober." Too often the Democrats played defense, and as a California Democrat put it, "defensive wars do not generally win in politics."[8]

In November 1888 Cleveland took a majority of the popular vote, but Harrison carried the electoral vote 233–168. Turnouts exceeded 90 percent in the hotly contested states of Indiana, New York, and New Jersey. As usual, the election came down to Indiana and New York. Harrison carried both of them. He won in New York by 14, 373 votes (1.1 percent of those cast) and Indiana by 2, 376 votes. Cleveland's margin in Connecticut was only 336 votes. Overall, Harrison carried the North and West and ran surprisingly well in those Border States where blacks retained the vote. Republicans added some Southerners, including three black congressmen, to their House delegation. The Mugwumps largely deserted Cleveland, disappointed in what they regarded as his lukewarm actions on civil service. The Democrats attempted to carry the West by attacking the Chinese, but the Republicans were beating that horse just as hard.[9]

7. Calhoun, 87–108, 132–34; McGerr, 77–91.
8. Calhoun, 140, 146.
9. Ibid., 178–80.

Accusations of fraud were rampant. That the majority of voters cast their ballots from deep loyalty to their party, that most of those who sold their votes would have voted for that candidate anyway, and that there may have been less fraud than usual did not really settle the role of fraud when the election in New York and Indiana was so close. Harrison attributed his victory to "Providence." The Republican boss, Sen. Matthew Quay of Pennsylvania, sneered that Harrison "ought to know that Providence hadn't a damn thing to do with it." Harrison would "never know how close a number of men were compelled to approach the gates of the penitentiary to make him President."[10]

The defeat of Cleveland, despite his majority of the popular vote, was not the blot on democracy that it seemed because there were far larger blemishes. Given the suppression of the Republican black vote in the South, it was hard to argue that Harrison was truly a minority president. Three black-majority Southern states—South Carolina, Mississippi, and Louisiana—sent only 311,674 voters to the polls to determine twenty-six electoral votes. Their electoral votes were based on the total population, black and white, but in reality only white votes counted. Illinois cast nearly twice as many votes, but had only twenty-two electoral votes. Ohio cast more than 839,000 votes for only twenty-three electors. Southern fraud and violence ensured that every white vote in the South was worth two Northern votes in presidential elections.[11]

Radical Republicans had designed the Fourteenth Amendment to punish any state that denied the vote to male citizens not involved in rebellion against the country by reducing its representation, but Congress never imposed the penalties. As a result, by 1888 Southern white voters had a disproportionate representation not only in the Electoral College but also in the House of Representatives. Seven states of the Deep South—Alabama, Arkansas, Florida, Georgia, Louisiana, Mississippi, and South Carolina—sent forty-five members to the House. Averaged together, this was a representative for every 19,200 voters. California, Kansas, Minnesota, Nebraska, New Hampshire, Oregon, and Wisconsin had only thirty-three members, or an average of 47,200 voters per member.[12]

Racial discrimination, and the exclusion of women from the vote, formed the greatest stains on democracy, but they were not the only ones. Gerrymandering remained ubiquitous, and it undercut equal representation.

---

10. Richard Hofstadter, *The American Political Tradition* (New York: Knopf 1948, Vintage Books ed., 1954), 172; Calhoun, 174–78; Summers, 9–12.
11. Calhoun, 179–80; Summers, 12–14, 30.
12. Calhoun, 178–80; R. Hal Williams, *Years of Decision: American Politics in the 1890s* (New York: Wiley, 1978), 30.

In Wisconsin the population of state legislative districts in 1887 ranged from 6,226 to 35,388, making a vote in the least populous district worth 5.68 times that in the largest district. An observer noted that Democrats in Kansas drew up to 40 percent of the vote, but they "have no more hope of being represented in the Congress at Washington than if they had no vote at all." The Democrats gerrymandered just as adroitly. In Indiana, a state usually almost evenly divided between the two parties, the Democratic legislature of 1884 had crafted districts with such exquisite care that Republicans calculated they yielded Democratic majorities in 105 of 150 districts in the state legislature and 11 of 13 congressional districts if the Democrats mobilized their vote. Benjamin Harrison drew the parallel between Democrats in Indiana and those in the South: the Indiana gerrymander was as effective "as the shotgun policy of Mississippi and the tissue ballot system of South Carolina combined." Democrats were everywhere undemocratic. The goal in neither Kansas nor Indiana was to protect incumbents; most legislators rotated in office serving only a term or two, and it was to protect parties, which were the beating heart of the American political system.[13]

By turning the task of determining the popular will over to private organizations—the political parties—the United States had created both a means to integrate the politics of the nation and an open invitation for fraud and corruption. The foundational documents of the world's leading democracy said precious little about conducting elections. The Constitution made no provision for funding elections, and states were reluctant to do so. By failing to provide a mechanism for funding and conducting the constant elections that the democracy demanded, the Constitution had created a vacuum that the parties had occupied.[14]

The parties made elections possible by printing ballots, organizing voters, and bringing them to the polls. They bound innumerable local elections into a national system, and created common political identities in a decentralized and often discordant and divided nation. Parties provided the large numbers of men and women necessary to conduct campaigns and recruit voters, and they needed large amounts of money to enable them to do so. To raise that money they conducted politics as a business. Parties bestowed offices and favors on supporters, who then kicked back a percentage of the proceeds from those offices to the party.

13. Peter H. Argersinger, *Representation and Inequality in Late Nineteenth-Century America: The Politics of Apportionment* (New York: Cambridge University Press, 2015), 17–18, 21–26, 34–41.
14. Gary Gerstle, *Liberty and Coercion: The Paradox of American Government from the Founding to the Present* (Princeton, NJ: Princeton University Press, 2015), 151–53, 154–61.

Officeholders also had access to valuable information and the power to aid "friends" needing public favors. The friends reciprocated. Until the Pendleton Act of 1883, parties relied largely on money paid in by office holders and job seekers. The resulting system was both democratic—the United States conducted more elections and enfranchised more voters than any nation in the world—and incredibly corrupt.[15]

By the 1880s, the state political machines created to conduct elections and wage campaigns had grown immense. The New York Republican machine, run first by Roscoe Conkling and then by Thomas Platt, needed to support ten to thirteen thousand regulars at an estimated $20 million a year. The Pennsylvania Republican machine under Matthew Quay was even larger. They made the electoral system work, but at a considerable price. Attempts to curtail one type of graft usually resulted only in turning the parties to other sources of income. Getting elected and deriving the necessary revenue for running and winning elections mattered much more to most politicians than any particular policy agenda.[16]

An unintended effect of the Pendleton Act was that the prohibition of contributions by federal workers to campaigns amplified the reliance of the parties on corporate money and larger donors. A Republican official called on the party to "put the manufacturers of Pennsylvania under the fire and fry all the fat out of them." And they did. The Republicans raised far more money than the Democrats and used it more efficiently. They cast the election as a clear-cut choice between protection and free trade. By framing the campaign as a battle for "industrial independence," they bridged the deepening division between their own antimonopolist wing, which dominated much of the Republican Party in the Upper Midwest, particularly in Iowa, where Gov. William Larrabee had taken the lead on railroad regulation, and men like Blaine and Harrison, who sympathized with capital.[17]

I

William Dean Howells voted for Benjamin Harrison, but he did so at the same time he read socialist writers and attended socialist meetings and those of the Bellamy Clubs, whose members wanted to nationalize the nation's "industries, resources, and distribution." The irony of Howells,

15. Gerstle, 154–66; Ari Hoogenboom, *Outlawing the Spoils: A History of the Civil Service Reform Movmeent 1865–1883* (Urbana: University of Illinois Press, 1968), 224–29.
16. Calhoun, 126–29; Gerstle, 164–73; Mutch, 16–17.
17. Summers, 8–9; Calhoun, 126–29, 131, 147; Mutch, 16–17; Reitano, 123.

one of the best American writers, attending clubs inspired by a very bad American novel, Edward Bellamy's *Looking Backward*, only added to the irony of his talking socialist and voting for Harrison.[18]

Looking Backward encapsulated the conditions with which Americans were struggling, and which, no matter how indirectly, were reflected in the debate over the tariff. In the novel, Julian West, like Howells a member of the Boston bourgeoisie, went to sleep in the turmoil and conflict of nineteenth-century Boston and awoke a century later in a utopian Boston. Serious American ideas shone through a stilted story and didactic dialogue. Dr. Leete, speaking at the dawn of the twenty-first century, explained that the misery of the late nineteenth century arose from "that incapacity for cooperation which followed from the individualism on which your social system was founded." Bellamy adopted the Knights of Labor's insistence on the abolition of wage labor and their conviction that the rights of American citizens extended to the workplace. He coupled this with the assertions, echoing both vanguard antimonopolists and industrialists such as John D. Rockefeller and Charles Francis Adams, that large-scale organizations were more efficient and more productive and that cooperation would inevitably triumph over competition. He glossed the whole with a pervasive nostalgia for the democratic army of the Civil War as the ideal form of social organization. The result was a society that had finally completed the American Revolution by democratizing and socializing industry. The trusts had been consolidated in one "Great Trust" controlled by the people. No revolutionary violence had been necessary. Every person had a competence, although none was rich.[19]

Later readers would mistake Bellamy's novel as Marxist, but it was very much of its American time. He celebrated home, family, work, freedom, and equality in the tradition of free labor, but he had detached it from competition. Life was pleasant, easy, and cultured. Bellamy ignored the other problems of American society. The urban environment had somehow become clean and healthy; rural areas got scant reference. Frances Willard much admired Bellamy's utopia, which lifted the domestic burden from women, but it did not alter gender roles, and racial and ethnic tensions seem to have vanished along with black people and Catholics.[20]

18. W. D. Howells to W. C. Howells, Jan. 22, 1888, and July 8, 1888, in William Dean Howells, *Selected Letters*, ed. George Warren Arms (Boston: Twayne, 1979), 3: 216, 226–27.
19. Edward Bellamy, *Looking Backward* (Boston: Houghton Mifflin, 1888, Riverside ed., 1966), 34–35, 56, quote 73.
20. Ruth Birgitta Anderson Bordin, *Frances Willard: A Biography* (Chapel Hill: University of North Carolina Press, 1986), 145–49.

Howells's attraction both to Bellamy's Nationalists and to socialism and his vote for Harrison told much about the relation between American politics and society. Howells's idea of socialism, like Dr. Leete's, was largely an endorsement of cooperation and a rejection of individualism. Socialism, as Howells understood it, was "not a positive but a comparative thing; it is a question of more less in what we have already, and not a question of absolute difference. Every citizen of a civilized State is a socialist." If anyone believed "that the postal department, the public schools, the insane asylums, the almshouse are good things; and that when a railroad management has muddled away in hopeless ruin the money of all who trusted it, a Railroad Receiver is a good thing," then that person embraced socialism. Howells believed "that the postal savings-banks, as they have them in England; and national life-insurance as they have them in Germany are good things." He would push American "socialism" only a little further.[21]

Howells's radicalism indicated that the Republican success in the election of 1888 might not be as complete as it seemed. The Republican Party remained diverse, and tariff reform would hardly be enough either to satisfy all its members or to address a social and economic crisis that voters regarded as dire. Republicans controlled the presidency and both houses of Congress for the first time since 1874, but their narrow margins—seven in the House and two in the Senate—meant that the desertion of a few members on any vote could stalemate them. The situation indicated caution, but Republicans leaders chose to treat the election as a mandate. They would revise the tariff, but upward. They would change the rules in the House of Representatives to make their narrow margin effective. They would pass new legislation to increase their numbers in Congress and the Electoral College, and they would add other reforms to keep their anti-monopolist members from deserting them on key votes.[22]

In the House the Republicans had a man up to the task of making a slim majority into a tool for party dominance. Thomas Reed of Maine, soon to be dubbed Czar Reed by the Democrats, changed procedural rules and practices. Democrats had blocked action by refusing to vote, thus denying the Republicans a quorum, but Reed simply counted nonvoting Democrats as present to create the necessary quorum. He controlled committee assignments with an iron hand, punished rebellion, and rewarded loyalty. Maintaining party discipline, the Republicans pushed bills through the

21. Howells to Editor of the *New York Sun*, Nov. 23, 1888, in Howells, *Selected Letters*, 3: 236–38.
22. George H. Mayer, *The Republican Party, 1854–1964* (New York: Oxford University Press, 1964), 221–22.

House. Known for his wit as well as his ruthlessness, Reed used both. When a Democrat, objecting to one of his measures and paraphrasing Henry Clay, said he would rather be right than president, Reed replied, "The gentleman need not be disturbed, he will never be either."[23]

The Senate, operating under different rules and with an even more tenuous Republican majority, presented a more difficult task to which the West promised the solution. Republicans threw the political doors open to western territories that had been denied statehood in the years of divided government. Most were still vast expanses with few people, but the Republicans countered the Democrats' structural advantage in the House, which came from disenfranchising black voters to create the Solid South, with their own ability to elect senators by the acre. Following Harrison's victory, Cleveland and the lame duck Democrats recognized the inevitable and agreed to admit Montana, Washington, North Dakota, and South Dakota (1889) in the hope that Montana at least would vote Democratic. In 1890 the Republicans also admitted Idaho and Wyoming. Montana didn't go Democratic.

Republicans got twelve new senators but, since these new states had few voters, only five new Republican representatives. In the West, as in the South, small numbers of voters elected a disproportionate number of representatives. Wyoming and Idaho, with about a hundred thousand people, had four senators and two representatives; the two hundred thousand people in New York's First Congressional District had one representative. The substantial body of new senators west of the Missouri buttressed the Republican majority but strained its tenuous unity. The Republicans, like the Democrats, remained an alliance of state parties, and the state parties were an alliance of local interests, only gradually becoming national in the 1880s and 1890s. As Richard Croker of Tammany Hall pointed out, the parties voted for the same national candidate only once every four years; at other times they pursued much more insular interests. The parties were supposed to agree on "fundamental doctrines," but the rise of "Silver Republicans," who were eager to abandon the gold standard, threw into question what fundamental doctrines the Republicans agreed on.[24]

---

23. Lewis L. Gould, *Grand Old Party: A History of the Republicans* (New York: Random House, 2003), 106–7; H. Wayne Morgan, ed. *The Gilded Age: A Reappraisal* (Syracuse, NY: Syracuse University Press, 1963), 181; Williams, 22–23; Mayer, 223–24.

24. Heather Cox Richardson, *To Make Men Free: A History of the Republican Party* (New York: Basic Books, 2014), 124–27; Peter H. Argersinger, "The Transformation of American Politics, 1865–1910," in *Contesting Democracy: Substance and Structure in American Political History, 1775–2000,* ed. Byron E. Shafer and Anthony J. Badger (Lawrence: University Press of Kansas, 2001), 124–25; Calhoun, 180–81; Klinghard, 49–51.

Using the West to buttress their hold on the Senate, the Republicans looked south to weaken the Democrats in the House. The Lodge Bill sprang from a principled unwillingness to see the gains of the Civil War evaporate with the repression of black voters, but also from a cold-blooded assessment of political advantage. Without black Republican voters, the South would remain solid for the Democrats, all but ensuring their control of the House should they make inroads in the North.

The Harrison administration backed the Lodge Bill, but it did not promise blacks the full range of rights due them. The bill only dealt with congressional elections, not state or local elections. It allowed federal judges, upon petition of citizens, to appoint supervisors to observe and report on elections and make their own vote tallies. A federal board of canvassers would decide disputed elections, and if challenged, a federal judge would determine the victor. The House could overturn the decision of a federal judge.[25]

Southern Democrats initially were not much worried about the Lodge Bill. Sen. John Morgan of Alabama thought that Northerners would "prefer to leave the negro to work out his own salvation, rather than lose money. Money, my dear friend, is the real power in American politics at this day. I am glad to have its shelter, just now, when it is the most efficient barrier to the new descent upon the South." Henry Grady, editor of the *Atlanta Constitution*, was less crass, but he had persuaded liberals that a New South was arising amidst the reconciliation of the Blue and Gray. Why spoil it by attempting to secure votes for black men? In an 1888 Dallas speech he declared, "the truth above all others is that the white race must dominate forever."[26]

Morgan underestimated the lingering strength of the older Radical Republican vision and the desire of Republicans to break the Democrats' hold on the South. Henry Cabot Lodge had no patience with the nostalgic rewriting of the history of the Civil War. As he later said, "No good is ever done by falsifying the past. There was a right and a wrong in the Civil War.... The North was right and the right won." Charles Hill of Illinois declared the Democrats' suppression of the vote and fraud "a species of treason." If tolerated, "this great Republic will totter and fall." Benjamin Harrison told the Grand Army of the Republic that the "free ballot,

25. Charles W. Calhoun, *Conceiving a New Republic: The Republican Party and the Southern Question, 1869–1900* (Lawrence: University Press of Kansas, 2006), 239–40; Williams, 29–31.
26. Charles Postel, *The Populist Vision* (New York: Oxford University Press, 2007), 175; Philip Klinker with Roger Smith, *Unsteady March: The Rise and Decline of Racial Equality in America* (Chicago: University of Chicago Press, 2002), 93; Williams, 28–29.

honestly expressed and fairly counted is the main safeguard of our institutions, and its suppression under any circumstances cannot be tolerated."[27]

Democrats dubbed the Lodge Bill the "force bill" and saw in it, as an Arkansas newspaper put it, the "gleam of a half-concealed bayonet," but the bill did not mention enforcement by the army, which in any case did not have sufficient soldiers to protect black voters. Republicans protested that calling a measure designed to stop the suppression of votes by fraud and violence a "force bill" was "senseless" since it "transfers the settlement of a great public question from the shotgun to the court." Southern Democrats remained defiant. John Hemphill of South Carolina said whites would not be "overridden and down-trodden by a race whom God never intended should rule over us."[28]

Frances Willard indicated how lukewarm the enthusiasm of the northern electorate was for any strong measures to ensure black civil rights. The child of abolitionists, she seemed distant from men like John Hemphill in her relatively wide sympathies and openness to a variety of reforms. Like Josiah Strong, however, Willard connected reform with Anglo-Saxons and white evangelical Protestants and corruption with liquor, blacks, Mormons, and immigrants. By 1890 she was far more interested in extending the WCTU into the white South than in securing the rights of freedpeople, whom she consigned to the category of "ignorant" voters who were tools of the liquor interests. An ardent proponent of votes for women, she was not enthusiastic about universal suffrage and sought to limit the votes of black and immigrant men. She opposed the Lodge Bill, telling the *Voice*, a leading temperance journal, "we have wronged the South" with the Fifteenth Amendment and wronged "ourselves by putting no safeguard on the ballot-box at the North that would sift out alien illiterates." She stressed the supposedly ineradicable differences between blacks and whites, and she urged ambitious young blacks to return to Africa and control their own destiny. Anglo-Saxons, she predicted, would not stand for the rule of ignorance and immorality embodied in black and immigrant suffrage.[29]

Still, with Harrison's support, Reed's newly disciplined House passed the Lodge Bill on a party line vote. No Democrats voted for it. It moved on to the Senate, where its fate illustrated the delicacy of the Republicans' position. Democrat senators could filibuster the bill threatening the

27. Williams, 28–29.
28. Calhoun, *Conceiving a New Republic*, 222–23, 227, 234–35, 240, 242–43, 249, 250, 254; Williams, 30–31; Edward L. Ayers, *The Promise of the New South: Life after Reconstruction* (New York: Oxford University Press, 1992), 50.
29. Edward J. Blum, *Reforging the White Republic: Race, Religion, and American Nationalism, 1865–1898* (Baton Rouge: Louisiana State University Press, 2005), 201–2.

passage to the tariff, which remained the Republican priority. As critically, the new Western senators—virtually all of them both Sinophobes and antimonopolists of one degree or another—had little sympathy for any bill protecting the rights of nonwhites. They would need inducements to vote for either the tariff, which also passed the House in 1889, or the Lodge Bill. The Republicans decided to give priority to passing a new tariff and the additional reforms necessary to secure Western votes.[30]

Harrison played a large, but not always helpful, role in honing Republican strategy in the Fifty-first Congress of 1889–90. He met with Reed, Sherman, and others in the White House to coordinate and advance his party's agenda. More conventionally, he united party factions by including their leaders in his cabinet. Unfortunately, given Harrison's self-righteousness and a personality that Reed likened to being in the chill of a "dripping cave," the more closely the president worked with party leaders, the more he alienated them. The Pendleton Civil Service Act had done little to weaken patronage, which remained central to governing. Harrison appointed a supervisor of personnel in the postal department who purged the local post offices of Democrats, firing a Democratic postmaster every three minutes. Patronage was supposed to win friends within one's own party, but Reed complained that although he "never had but two personal enemies in my life…One of these Mr. Harrison has pardoned out of the penitentiary and the other he just appointed Collector of the Port of Portland." Appointing Blaine secretary of state predictably offended the Mugwumps, and then Harrison went on to offend Blaine.[31]

Ultimately, Republican control of the Fifty-first Congress and the priority they put on the tariff proved that sometimes in American politics nothing fails like success. Republicans had courted the American public by convincing them that the Democrats would institute free trade by lowering the tariff. They then convinced themselves that their victory meant Americans wanted dramatically higher tariffs and shaped their legislative agenda around that. In fashioning Congress into a comparatively well-honed and efficient piece of legislative machinery, the Republicans had no idea that they were creating a political suicide machine.

On paper, the Republicans' legislative agenda was ambitious and coherent. With the Lodge Bill, the party reached backward to try to reclaim its great achievement of black suffrage and the older free-labor vision of a homogeneous citizenship with uniform rights protected by the federal government. In pushing for a strengthened tariff, they embraced a newer vision of the United States as an industrial nation, which an active federal

30. Calhoun, Conceiving a New Republic, 255–59.
31. Williams, 59–60; Mayer, 221–22.

government would protect and nurture. Recognizing the need to secure antimonopolist support, they would offer measures that at least gestured toward currency reform and regulation of the trusts. The tariff remained the sun around which all the others revolved.[32]

What emerged from innumerable hearings, conferences, and debates in 1889 and 1890 was the McKinley Tariff, principally sponsored by William McKinley, a rising Republican congressman from Ohio. It was the most protectionist in American history, raising duties by an average of 48 percent. It protected not only infant industries but also industries not yet born. Congress, for example, shielded the manufacturing of tinplate, necessary for tin cans, even though the industry hardly existed in the United States. Tin cans were doubly blessed. The U.S. Army had stripped the Black Hills, which contained tin mines, from the Lakotas, and now the tariff would protect those who mined and manufactured that tin. To placate consumers, who would see the price of canned food and other items rise, Congress eliminated the duties on sugar.[33]

Republicans were well aware that the tariff could cost them votes unless they were careful. Recognizing the power of the tariff to alienate farmers, the Republicans tinkered with it to create a tool for expanding agricultural markets abroad. In an important innovation, the McKinley Tariff gave Secretary of State Blaine the power to negotiate reciprocal agreements with foreign countries. Other nations would receive favored status with lower duties on their products in return for opening markets for American goods, particularly farm products. Falling farm income reflected the intense competition that American agricultural exports were up against in European markets, and the Republicans sought to create new ones.[34]

The federal budget surplus, which had instigated the tariff debate, presented both a problem and an opportunity. During the fiscal year ending on June 30, 1889, the tariff provided 60 percent of federal revenue. Most of the rest came from taxes on tobacco and alcohol, for total revenue of $387 million. Of this sum, $87 million was surplus, unspent by the government. The rates on many commodities under the new McKinley Tariff would be so high as to bar their entry, thus reducing revenue by an estimated $86 million. The Republicans regarded this as a good thing since it partially took care of the problem of the growing Treasury surplus. To

32. Williams, 25–28.
33. Ibid., 25–28, 40; Jeremy Atack, *A New Economic View of American History: From Colonial Times to 1940*, ed. Peter Passell and Susan Lee, 2nd ed. (New York: Norton, 1994), 500; Reitano, 129–30.
34. Williams, 25–28.

further reduce the surplus, the Republicans passed the Dependent Pension Act of 1890, making any veteran who had served ninety days eligible for a pension if at any time he could not perform manual labor. With further tinkering and administrative rulings, it became a de facto pension to all Union veterans, who served a core Republican constituency. There would be 966,012 pensioners by 1893. Between 1890 and 1907 the United States would spend $1 billion for pensions under the act. Congress also raised spending on the navy and the army and spent money on rivers and harbors. These amounts were hardly exorbitant. The American military remained small. The U.S. Army had twenty-eight thousand soldiers at a time when Germany had more than half a million men under arms.[35]

The debate over the tariff and the budget reflected a country grown large and industrial; if the government remained administratively ineffective, it was also increasingly powerful and pervasive. Congress reached a psychological milestone that shocked many Americans: actual expenditures went up only modestly but the budget containing ongoing obligations for pensions and public improvements was now supposedly $1 billion, and Democrats branded it the Billion Dollar Congress, a label that would stick even though actual federal expenditures, though rising between 1890 and 1892, do not seem to have remotely approached a billion dollars.[36]

With both the McKinley Tariff and the Lodge Bill awaiting votes in the Senate, the fracturing of the Republican coalition became real. A fight over whether to put off a vote on the Lodge Bill until the next session badly split the Republicans. Ultimately, the Republicans postponed the vote in order to ensure they obtained a vote on the tariff, which passed only a month before the elections in 1890. Blaine's honesty may have

35. Table Ea584–587—Federal government finances—revenue, expenditure, and debt: 1789–1939, in *Historical Statistics of the United States, Earliest Times to the Present: Millennial Edition*, ed. Scott Sigmund Gartner, Susan B. Carter, Michael R. Haines, Alan L. Olmstead, Richard Sutch, and Gavin Wright (New York: Cambridge University Press, 2006); Theda Skocpol, *Protecting Soldiers and Mothers: The Political Origins of Social Policy in the United States* (Cambridge, MA: Belknap Press of Harvard University Press, 1995), 110–13; "Strength of German Army," http://www .germanhistorydocs.ghi-dc.org/sub_document.cfm?document_id=795; Thomas B. Reed and W. S. Holman, "Spending Public Money," *North American Review* 154, no. 424 (1892): 319–35; Calhoun, *Minority Victory*, 185; Stuart McConnell, *Glorious Contentment: The Grand Army of the Republic, 1865–1900* (Chapel Hill: University of North Carolina Press, 1992), 147–65; Williams, 31, 41.
36. Table Ea636–643—Federal government expenditure, by major function: 1789–1970, in *Historical Statistics of the United States, Earliest Times to the Present: Millennial Edition*; Williams, 41.

been suspect, but his political judgment rarely faltered. He warned the Republicans against passing the tariff so close to the election.[37]

In making their control of the Senate depend on relatively few voters in the West, the Republicans had created a monster, one that bestrode the Senate in 1890. The 1888 campaign had demonstrated how the tariff was open to attack as a gift to monopolies and trusts, which meant the Republicans had to show voters that the party was not a tool of corporations. Republicans claimed, and many believed, that the tariff would raise workers' wages in the industrial Northeast and Midwest, but they had to go beyond this to appease farmers and Western soft-money men who had sent antimonopolists to the Senate. Farmers west of the Mississippi produced wheat and cotton, the nation's two leading exports. Both crops faced significant competition and falling prices on world markets, and because of the tariff farmers' incomes in the years of peak rural discontent declined faster than the cost of what they consumed.[38]

The first concession that the Republicans made to antimonopolists was the Sherman Antitrust Act, one of two bills that bore John Sherman's name in the Fifty-first Congress. Where Bellamy's *Looking Backward* reflected advanced antimonopoly thinking, the Sherman Act literally looked backward. It reflected a strain of antimonopoly that saw the competitive market as the guarantor of an equitable society and a guard against economic consolidation. The act outlawed "every contract, combination in the form of trust or otherwise, or conspiracy in restraint of trade or commerce among the several states or with foreign nations," but it never defined a trust. It struck another blow against railroad pools, but it actually encouraged consolidation since a corporation that absorbed its rivals did not have to form pools with them. Corporations were already moving to a new device, the holding company, to escape the restraints imposed by state laws, and the Sherman Antitrust Act accelerated that movement. That no one voted against the bill in the House, and only one opposing vote was cast in the Senate, when it passed on July 2, 1890, demonstrated how little immediate danger the act posed to corporations.[39]

37. Calhoun, *Conceiving a New Republic*, 244–51; Williams, *Years of Decision*, 39–45.
38. Williamson notes that industrial and agricultural prices declined in tandem between 1870 and 1905, but he does not note that they fail to do so in the peak years of agricultural discontent. Jeffrey G. Williamson, *Late Nineteenth-Century American Development: A General Equilibrium History* (New York: Cambridge University Press, 1974), 148–50. For closer correlation, see Atack, 500; Table Ee1–21—Balance of international payments: 1790–1998, in *Historical Statistics of the United States, Earliest Times to the Present: Millennial Edition*.
39. Atack, 488–89.

Antimonopolists in the Senate demanded more than symbolic legislation; they also wanted monetary reform. With declining silver prices, Western mines shut down, creating reasons for Western miners to hate the gold standard. Because farmers were borrowers, deflation hurt them twice. It made money scarce, and it also made the money they eventually paid to creditors more valuable than the money they had borrowed. Deflation, by definition, meant the dollar rose in value over time. Until they got monetary reform, opponents of the gold standard blocked the McKinley Tariff. In June 1890, to the shock of Harrison and the goldbugs, antimonopolists in the Senate passed a bill providing for the free coinage of silver; if it became law, the bill would repeal the gold standard. Harrison, of course, could veto the bill even if it passed the House, but the silverites would then block tariff legislation. The goldbugs' concession was the Sherman Silver Purchase Act, which also passed in July 1890. It repealed and replaced the Bland Allison Act.

The Sherman Silver Purchase Act, looked at one way, was just another largely symbolic gesture with minimal immediate effect. Senator Stewart of Nevada, who had worked with William Ralston to demonetize silver, had resurrected his political career and returned to the Senate in 1887 by denouncing demonetization, proving himself as accomplished a political chameleon as anyone who ever graced the U.S. Senate. As president of the American Bimetallic League, he claimed to be rectifying the Crime of '73, the very measure he had helped pass.[40]

Senator Sherman, an ardent defender of the gold standard, compromised with Stewart to advance the larger Republican program. The Sherman Silver Purchase Act increased the amount of silver that the U.S. Treasury would purchase, thus subsidizing Western silver mines. Yet it did not require that this silver be used to augment the amount of currency. The issue of silver notes—currency, as distinct from unwieldy coins—would proceed at the discretion of the secretary of the Treasury, who, of course, would be a hard-money man so long as the president remained one. The Treasury Department did not issue silver notes, and currency remained redeemable in gold. But the act had the potential to be more than symbolic. If soft-money men could gain the presidency, the country could adopt bimetallism without any further legislation. Soft-money men accepted the compromise as placing them a step closer to their goal.[41]

40. Samuel DeCanio, "Populism, Paranoia, and the Politics of Free Silver," *Studies in American Political Development* (2011): 17–25.
41. Atack, 500–501.

The Lodge Bill, meanwhile, remained stranded in the Senate, and Democrats in the South had already begun erecting a firewall against further federal interventions. In the Senate debate over the Lodge Bill, Republicans repeatedly cited the new constitution Mississippi had adopted in 1890 as a glaring example of Southern repression. Mississippi imposed a poll tax and a literacy test, both designed to eliminate black voters who were overwhelmingly poor, disproportionately illiterate, and consigned to a segregated school system. Since the illiteracy rate in the South was higher than anywhere in the country, the literacy test was cleverly arranged to eliminate black voters, not white. It read: "Every elector shall…be able to read any section of the constitution of this State; or he shall be able to understand the same when read to him, or give a reasonable interpretation thereof." A registrar could thus pick and choose voters. A white voter might be illiterate, but a clerk could read him Section 8: "All persons resident in this State, citizens of the United States, are hereby declared citizens of the State of Mississippi," and, unless a complete fool, he could vote. A black voter might be literate, but the registrar could ask him to interpret Section 111, which began "All lands comprising a single tract sold in pursuance of decree of court, or execution, shall be first offered in subdivisions not exceeding one hundred and sixty acres, or one-quarter section, and then offered as an entirety, and the price bid for the latter shall control only when it shall exceed the aggregate of the bids for the same in subdivisions as aforesaid…." Unless the prospective voter was a lawyer, he was probably not going to be able to vote. To further ensure that literacy tests did not disenfranchise existing white voters, a grandfather clause exempted from the test all those whose grandfathers could vote. This included most whites and no blacks. Would the Lodge Bill change any of this? The bill's advocates admitted it would not. It would protect only those already registered to vote from fraud and violence in federal elections. White Southerners were institutionalizing racial inequality, making fraud and violence less necessary, and the Supreme Court would validate their efforts in *Williams v. Mississippi* in 1898. The Republicans had, in effect, traded the West for the South.[42]

II

The vagaries of American politics were sometimes hard to predict, but there was always the certainty that no matter where American politicians

42. John Ray Skates, "The Mississippi Constitution of 1890 as Originally Adopted," Mississippi Historical Society, http://mshistory.k12.ms.us/index.php?id=270, particularly sections 8, 111, 207, 242, 243, 244; Upchurch, 151–66.

wandered, it would not turn out well for Indians. Indian policy gave the Harrison administration an opportunity to firm up its own fractured coalition by appealing to evangelicals, liberal reformers, Western antimonopolists, and boosters eager to break up Indian reservations. There was a price, but one Republicans were willing to pay. To gain Republican advantage, Harrison turned what had been a bipartisan policy into an ethnocultural quarrel. In 1889 the president named Thomas Jefferson Morgan, a Baptist minister and an educational reformer who had led a black regiment in the Civil War, as commissioner of Indian affairs. Morgan had devoted his career to using the public schools to acculturate as well as educate immigrants for, as the title of a book he wrote put it, *Patriotic Citizenship*. He easily translated such concerns into Indian policy. The reformers at the Lake Mohonk Conference had already pledged "to remove at once the National dishonor of supporting ignorant and barbaric peoples in the heart of a Christian civilization." The Indian Rights Association argued that only by dismantling native societies "can they [Indians] be preserved as individuals from ultimate destruction." The price of survival for Indians would be ceasing to be recognizably Indian.[43]

Morgan declared that "the tribal relations should be broken up, socialism destroyed, and the family and autonomy of the individual substituted." Indians would have to "conform to 'the white man's ways,' peaceably if they will, forcibly if they must." He planned to create a national system of Indian schools modeled on the public schools, which endeared him to Indian reformers but alienated Catholics who controlled many existing reservation schools. Morgan's schools would be nonsectarian but definitely Protestant, and he brought the controversies that raged in the battles over public schools into Indian policy. Catholics counterattacked, and Morgan became embroiled in the larger ethnocultural controversies of the nation.[44]

Opening Indian lands to white farmers went more smoothly. Both Indian Territory and the Great Sioux Reservation presented tempting targets. The railroads and the boomers—Democratic Texas cotton farmers to the south and Republican Kansas wheat farmers to the north—had long been pressing for the opening of new lands. The Dawes Act had exempted Indian Territory from allotment, but Harrison moved where Cleveland had held back.

43. Francis Paul Prucha, *American Indian Policy in Crisis: Christian Reformers and the Indian, 1865–1900* (Norman: University of Oklahoma Press 1976), 292–301.
44. Prucha, 292–317; "Fifty-Eighth Annual Report of the Commissioner of Indian Affairs to the Secretary of Interior" (Washington, DC: U.S. GPO, 1889), 3–4.

Oklahoma Land Openings
By Conveyance, 1889–1906

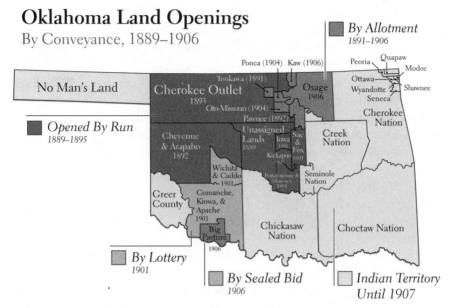

Source: Oklahoma Historical Society.

Indian Territory was a complicated place. East of the 98th meridian it largely encompassed lands settled by the so-called Five Civilized Tribes — the Choctaws, Creeks, Cherokees, Chickasaws, and Seminoles — driven from the Southeast. After the Civil War, the government had forced them to agree both to the incorporation of their ex-slaves as tribal members and to the settlement of refugee tribes from the Middle Border, such as the Osage and Pawnees, on part of their old territory. Lands west of the 98th meridian had gone to Indians defeated in the wars on the Southern Plains: Comanches, Kiowas, Cheyennes, and Arapahos. The Cherokees also controlled the Cherokee Outlet west of the 96th Meridian. It adjoined an administrative anomaly, the "no man's land" to the west. Cherokees leased their western lands to white cattlemen; the payments were the major source of revenue for the Cherokee Nation.[45]

Cherokee relations with cattlemen were often difficult, but they were almost fraternal compared with the Indians' problems with white squatters, boomers, and outlaws. The boomers were as much promoters and developers as settlers. They urged the opening up of Indian Territory to white settlement, and in anticipation they sold rights to claims that they, acting as vigilantes, promised to enforce. They were thus doubly illegal, selling

---

45. William T. Hagan, *Taking Indian Lands: The Cherokee (Jerome) Commission, 1889–1893* (Norman: University of Oklahoma Press, 2003), 1–21.

rights to land they did not own and promising the exercise of force to protect those rights. In the 1880s boomers regularly invaded Indian Territory, and cavalrymen, often black, just as regularly expelled them. Outlaws who fled to Indian Territory to escape the jurisdiction of neighboring states and territories established more permanent residence. The more that white intruders disrupted and threatened Indian Territory, the more that the boomers' supporters in Congress declared the Indians incapable of self-government. The *Cherokee Advocate*, the tribal newspaper, replied, "We have two National colleges, male and female...over 100 public schools. We have Cherokees among us, graduates from the best colleges in the United States, Harvard, Princeton, Andover, Dartmouth, Yale, Ann Arbor and tens of others of lesser fame. No man or woman who has ever been among the Cherokees goes home saying that we are not able to govern."[46]

The initial struggle focused on the Cherokee Outlet and the Unassigned Lands, which had originally been acquired by the United States from the Chickasaws and Seminoles to resettle other tribes. Senator Stewart of Nevada cast the struggle as one of white homesteaders desperate for land. He claimed the Cherokees were "the richest people in the United States"; half of them were "white men who have...married squaws." Indian Territory had become a battle between "barbarism and civilization...between cattle barons and the people." The Cherokees resisted. With the help of cattlemen, they stalled legislation stripping them of their lands in Congress, but only at the price of negotiating with a commission for their sale.[47]

The Unassigned Lands, which had acquired the name Oklahoma, proved to be the greatest chink in the Indians' armor. In 1889, soon after taking office, Harrison signed an Indian appropriation bill declaring "Oklahoma"—located on the 98th meridian surrounding present-day Oklahoma City—part of the public domain and open for homesteading. To distribute the land, the government sanctioned one of the silliest ideas ever to pass an American Congress: on April 22, 1889, roughly fifty thousand people seeking land lined up on the borders of Oklahoma and raced to stake their claims. The U.S. Army and U.S. deputy marshals were supposed to police the race. With no discernible irony, William Willard Howard, a reporter from *Harper's Weekly*, thought the land rush both

---

46. Prucha, 373–85; Roy Gittinger, *The Formation of the State of Oklahoma, 1803–1906* (Norman: University of Oklahoma Press, 1939), 118–37; W. David Baird and Danney Goble, *Oklahoma: A History* (Norman: University of Oklahoma Press, 2008), 141–45; Hagan, 10–11.
47. Hagan, 11–17.

"one of the most noteworthy events of Western Civilization" and "merely a particularly lively town-site speculation."[48]

The Oklahoma Land Rush stood as yet another monument to the vexing contradiction that the federal government commanded great power even as it lacked reliable administrative capacity. Stealing the land was relatively easy but distributing it was hard. Too few soldiers patrolled the borders of Oklahoma, and too many deputies. The deputies depended on fees for apprehending those who tried to sneak into Oklahoma before the race, but this was dwarfed by the money they could make by sneaking in themselves, filing claims, and then selling them. And so instead of stopping the illegal claimants called the sooners, they joined them. Howard reported that it was deputies who laid out many of the lots in Guthrie and Oklahoma City. Men on fast horses who obeyed the rules found the land they desired already claimed by men on foot or in wagons with ox teams who had arrived long before them. Howard thought that 90 percent of the claims, and all the best land, had been taken by sooners.[49]

The results were predictable: fraud, some violence, and endless legal disputes. As Howard wrote, Rome wasn't built in a day, but Guthrie, Oklahoma, was—or at least its streets were laid out and ten thousand people populated it. Litigation over the instant town and other claims would go on for years, but since Congress had neglected to provide government for Oklahoma, and would not do so until the following year, in the short run the settlers were left to work things out as best they could.[50]

The Cherokees feared they saw their own future in the creation of Oklahoma, and they continued to fight the cession of the Cherokee Outlet. In language recycled since Andrew Jackson had used it in the Removal controversy, the Cherokee Commission appointed by Harrison claimed the Cherokee government spoke for white men, while the commissioners spoke for the "real Cherokees" who wanted to sell the Outlet. In 1890 President Harrison broke the back of Cherokee resistance by ordering the eviction of white cattlemen from the Cherokee Outlet, thus threatening to bankrupt the Cherokee Nation. The chipping away of Indian Territory had begun.[51]

The attack on the northern tribes proceeded much more rapidly. Stretching from the Missouri River to the western boundary of Dakota

48. William Willard Howard, "The Rush to Oklahoma," *Harper's Weekly* (May 18, 1889): 391–94.

49. Ibid.

50. Howard reported little initial violence. John Thompson, *Closing the Frontier: Radical Response in Oklahoma, 1889–1923* (Norman: University of Oklahoma Press, 1986), 48–58; Prucha, 384–86.

51. Prucha, 386–87.

Territory, the Great Sioux Reservation was a smaller twin of Indian Territory. Following the Sioux War, the reservation had already had its far western lands, including the Black Hills, sheared off in violation of the Treaty of 1868. Sen. Henry Dawes, the architect of the Dawes Severalty Act, called for the cession of half the land that remained.[52]

Like reformers in Oklahoma, Dawes used the old Jacksonian language of "rich" Indians abusing "poor" ordinary Indians to give dispossession an antimonopolist tinge. He accused Red Cloud, who opposed his bills, of being "for the old order of things, when chiefs ruled and made themselves rich out of the Indians." Red Cloud, however, was neither rich nor a bastion of the old order. The aging war leader had become a quite sophisticated and modern opponent of the Indian Office, frustrating Agent Valentine McGillycuddy, whose own interpreter described the agent as "overbearing," "revengeful," "tyrannous," and "haughty."[53]

In 1888 Congress passed the Sioux Bill, but with a significant caveat: the government would have to obtain the consent of three-quarters of the Sioux, as required in previous treaties to the cession of roughly half their remaining lands. The government had failed to do so in the past, and it failed again in 1888 when Richard Henry Pratt headed a commission to gain a cession. In 1889 Harrison sent out a commission headed by Gen. George Crook to try once more. The commission employed both carrot and stick. Commissioners told the Sioux to stop "growling about the past," and agents told them that if they rejected the agreement Congress might "open the reservation without requiring the consent of the Indians." Crook raised the price to be paid for the land; he gave feasts, tolerated social dances, and promised improved rations, services, and protection of remaining reservation lands. But it was ultimately coercion that won consent. A leading Sioux chief, Gall, said he signed "after learning the Government could take our lands for nothing if it wanted to." High Hawk said the Indians feared that those who did not sign would be disarmed and deprived of rations. And even as Crook promised more rations, the Indian Office was preparing to cut beef rations by 25 percent. In 1890 the president declared the ceded areas of the Sioux reservation open to white settlement.[54]

52. Prucha, 170–87.
53. C. Joseph Genetin-Pilawa, *Crooked Paths to Allotment: The Fight over Federal Indian Policy after the Civil War* (Chapel Hill: University of North Carolina Press, 2012), 130–33, quote 142; Jeffrey Ostler, *The Plains Sioux and U.S. Colonialism from Lewis and Clark to Wounded Knee* (Cambridge: Cambridge University Press, 2004), 203–12; Prucha, *Great Father*, 587–88.
54. Ostler, 221–33.

In 1889 and 1890, two of the four horseman of the Apocalypse—pestilence and famine—arrived at Pine Ridge and the other Lakota reservations. Agriculture west of the 100th meridian was always a gamble, and the gamble often failed. The cut in rations and crop failure meant the Lakotas went hungry. Disease came hard on the heels of famine. Whooping cough and influenza took a heartbreaking toll on Indian children.[55]

Hope arrived in a message from the west that the Lakotas might evade the third horseman: war. The message came from Wovoka, who drew on a tradition of millennialism while responding to deteriorating economic conditions in Nevada that were an exaggerated version of those all over the West.[56]

Wovoka, a ranch hand in Nevada also known as Jack Wilson, was a Paiute Indian. Americans, often without even bothering with treaties, had stripped the Paiutes, whom they dismissed as nearly subhuman "Diggers," of nearly everything except their language, beliefs, kin, and remarkable resilience. Many Paiutes, with their economy in shambles, had retreated into towns and wage labor. As with Mexican Americans in the Southwest and blacks in the South, the best-paying jobs were closed to them, but so long as Nevada prospered from silver mining and cattle ranching they could find work. When silver prices fell in the 1880s, and as drought struck and cattle raising suffered, Nevada too declined. It had sixty-two thousand residents in 1880; by 1890 there were about forty-seven thousand, and the population would continue to fall through the remainder of the century.[57]

Nevada in the 1880s appeared to be drying up and blowing away. A state stripped of white people might seem a good thing for Indians, but not if the Indians were working people and whites were their employers. They could not easily revert to old ways in an overgrazed and ravaged landscape in the midst of a drought. Jack Wilson became a famous man because he promised to make it rain. But his rainmaking was only his first response to economic crisis; like Midwestern evangelicals, he linked religion to the coming of a reformed and much better world.[58]

Americans heard of the mysterious prophet but did not realize it was Jack Wilson, although he never concealed his identity. Whites often missed the most obvious things about Indians. Like many Indian religious

55. Ibid., 238–61.
56. Louis S. Warren, "Wage Work in the Sacred Circle: The Ghost Dance as Modern Religion," *Western Historical Quarterly* 46, no. 2 (Summer 2015): 152.
57. Warren, 148–50, 152–54, 157; for the Paiutes and Shoshones in Nevada, see Ned Blackhawk, *Violence over the Land: Indians and Empires in the Early American West* (Cambridge, MA: Harvard University Press, 2006).
58. Richard White, *Railroaded: The Transcontinentals and the Making of Modern America* (New York: Norton, 2011), 496–98; Warren, 148–66.

figures before him, he had a vision that drew on both native elements—in this case the prophet religion long present in the Great Basin, interior Pacific Northwest, and California—and Christianity. He told his followers to dance a special ritual dance. And if they danced, the world would be regenerated, their dead would return, and whites would vanish. The dance and the promise gave the religion its name, the Ghost Dance religion, but the dance and the resurrection of the dead was only part of what he told them. Wovoka also said that until this happened they should work for whites, cease to fight, and attend white churches. "We must work," he preached, "when the white man asks us." When Indians debated how they should act while awaiting a Messiah and a transformed world, they were not particularly unusual in nineteenth-century America.[59]

As news of Wovoka's vision and his message spread—often through the mails, for by now Indians educated in American schools were literate and had a common language in English—delegates from across the West came to him. There were Ghost Dancers in the Cheyenne, Arapaho, and Comanche settlements. Lakotas, riding the trains west and joining Indians from other tribes, came to see Wovoka. They heard his message and carried it home.[60]

Wovoka advocated peace, and he told his followers to love one another. Short Bull was both a Lakota holy man and a teamster, who had journeyed partially by horse and partially by train, to visit the prophet. He and the other Lakotas did not alter Wovoka's message. The Lakotas were to dance, to work, and to get along with whites and with each other. Wovoka combined a promise of future deliverance with self-help and accommodation until the moment of deliverance arrived. Spiritual power and not armed resistance would deliver them from whites. What the Lakotas did not count on was that the whites themselves would, in effect, identify Wovoka with the fourth horseman—the Antichrist—and move to suppress the Ghost Dance.[61]

Parts of Wovoka's message resonated with existing Lakota religious beliefs, and other parts did not. Not surprisingly, the message split the Lakotas. Some bands feared the Ghost Dance would invite government repression; other bands, such as Sitting Bull's, with a history of resistance to government measures, welcomed it even though Sitting Bull himself seems to have done so strategically without fully believing. About

59. Warren, 147–48, 159, 162; for background to Ghost Dance, see Gregory E. Smoak, *Ghost Dances and Identity: Prophetic Religion and American Indian Ethnogenesis in the Nineteenth Century* (Berkeley: University of California Press, 2006).
60. Ostler, 243–58; Warren, 159–61; White, 496–98.
61. Warren, 153–59; Ostler, 238–61.

one-quarter to one-third of the Lakotas danced. Large numbers, including Red Cloud, stayed on the sidelines to see what developed. Had the government let the dance alone, the result most likely would have been what happened at other reservations touched by the Ghost Dance: it would have turned into a new sect or merged with existing ones. Millennial religions among both Indians and non-Indians have ways of coping with the failure of the millennium to arrive. The government, however, did not leave the dance alone.[62]

During the fall of 1890, as the election campaign between the Democrats and Republicans unfolded across the United States, the Lakotas danced. The dancing and the upcoming election intertwined. The Republicans, looking toward retaining their majority in the 1890 midterm, behaved normally. They gave patronage appointments to those who they thought would be most helpful in retaining Republican South Dakota. The only twist was Harrison's stepping back from direct involvement in the appointments, leaving the process to what the Republicans called "home rule," which gave state politicians rather than federal politicians the key role.[63]

The process yielded Daniel Royer as the agent for Pine Ridge. According to one of his many critics, the new agent owed his appointment to his ability "to control votes in a county convention." As ex-agent McGillycuddy remarked, only a fool would have appointed Royer to "superintend six men building a wood shed let alone handling six thousand Indians." Gen. Nelson Miles, who had just taken command of the Department of the Missouri, was initially sanguine about the Ghost Dance, even as Royer and other agents began urging military intervention. By the time reports of the dancing reached Harrison, they had been distilled down, in the words of Harrison, to "the coming of an Indian Messiah and the return of the dead Indian warriors for a crusade upon whites." Wovoka had already written Harrison, offering to make it rain in exchange for Harrison recognizing his (Wovoka's) authority over the West, while he would recognize Harrison's dominion over the East. Harrison ordered an investigation and then ignored its conclusion, which was to let the Ghost Dance take its course. Instead, he dispatched troops to support the agents and "to prevent

62. William K. Powers, *Oglala Religion* (Lincoln: University of Nebraska Press, 1975), 202; Raymond DeMallie, "The Lakota Ghost Dance: An Ethnohistorical Account," *Pacific Historical Review*, no. 51 (November 1982): 385–405; Ostler, 264–74, 278–79.

63. Jon Lauck, *Prairie Republic: The Political Culture of Dakota Territory, 1879–1889* (Norman: University of Oklahoma Press, 2010), 95–97; Heather Cox Richardson, *Wounded Knee: Party Politics and the Road to an American Massacre* (New York: Basic Books, 2010), 169.

any outbreak that may put in peril the lives and homes of settlers in adjoining states."[64]

Part of the Ghost Dance's appeal was that it would, as one of its leaders said, allow the Indians "to be Indians again." The Ghost Dance was slow and stately; it involved men and women, who regularly toppled into trances and had visions of their dead and the world Wovoka promised. Among the dancers were Christians, Indians educated at Carlisle and other schools, and those who had taken up farming. The agents cut off rations to the dancers, and they sent out the Indian Police, who were other Lakotas, to stop the dances. All such efforts failed, but they led some of the dancers to take up arms to defend the dance.[65]

The Ghost Dance collided with American politics at the intersection of patronage, military ambitions, and the extraordinary beliefs American officials held about Indians. Harrison was channeling his grandfather, William Henry Harrison, who had launched a supposedly preventive show of force against another Indian prophet long before. But there was nothing in the agents' reports about a threat to settlements and no credible evidence of any threat. Nor were there signs that surrounding whites felt threatened until a series of robberies and confrontations in December. Until then Indians worried settlers on the arid plains much less than did drought, hot winds, and dying crops. Although Harrison may have thought he was forestalling violence, he was instigating it.[66]

General Miles reversed his position. He proclaimed he needed more troops and was threatened with a general Indian War by a "doomed race," but one never as well armed and equipped as they were now. A "hungry, wild, mad horde of savages" was about to overrun the Dakotas, Montana, Nebraska, Wyoming, Utah, Colorado, Idaho, and Nevada. He thought the "most serious Indian war of our history was imminent." Agent Royce reported the "Indians are dancing in the snow & are wild & crazy," but the pronouncements of Miles, Royce, and Harrison were to all appearances far crazier.[67]

There was a method behind this madness. Miles's experience in the Nez Perce War should have taught him some lessons about the tragedies of unnecessary Indian wars, but he had both military and presidential ambitions. He wanted to achieve the old dream of army control over Indian affairs and to stop the drawing down of troops in the West.

64. Richardson, *Wounded Knee*, 170–71; Ostler, 290–93; Jerome A. Greene, *American Carnage: Wounded Knee, 1890* (Norman: University of Oklahoma Press, 2014), 96–97; Warren, 157.

65. Ostler, 276–88; Warren, 162.

66. Greene, 160–61; Ostler, 293–300.

67. Ostler, 294, 302ff.

Suppressing the most serious Indian threat in American history would further all these goals, and it would be particularly easy to do if there were no actual threat. The movement of troops and Miles's statement created the panic among settlers that had not existed previously, and things began to spin out of control.[68]

The arrival of the troops terrified both the Indians and the settlers. Miles's attempts to take over the management of Indian Affairs from the agents by recruiting Buffalo Bill Cody to negotiate with Sitting Bull ended up only precipitating an attempt by Agent James McLaughlin to send the Indian Police—the Ceska Maza (Metal Breasts)—to arrest Sitting Bull. The result was a wild shootout that left eight members of Sitting Bull's band and six policemen dead. Among the dead was Sitting Bull.[69]

Sitting Bull's people fled, with some joining Big Foot's band, which had embraced the Ghost Dance. After botched negotiations, Big Foot started toward the agency at Pine Ridge in fear of the soldiers. He thought he would be safe there. It seemed the trouble might be contained. The Ghost Dancers in the Bad Lands agreed to stop dancing, at least for now, and come into the agencies. With Big Foot and his band on their way to Pine Ridge, the conflict seemed defused. Miles, however, fixated on Big Foot, who was by then very sick with pneumonia, as a dangerous and cunning man whose band had to be disarmed and kept under guard. It was like sending a posse to capture a fugitive who was desperate to turn himself in.[70]

Soldiers of the Seventh Cavalry, Custer's old regiment, surrounded Big Foot's band before they reached Pine Ridge and escorted them to the soldiers' camp at Wounded Knee Creek. Roughly five hundred soldiers surrounded the 120 or so Lakota men and boys and demanded that they surrender their weapons. As when the fleeing Nez Perce encountered tourists in Yosemite, incongruous elements converged. The Jesuits had a mission at Pine Ridge, and Fr. Francis Craft, a Jesuit, moved among Big Foot's people seeking to avert a tragedy. He talked with the Lakotas, passing out cigarettes (almost certainly a product of James Buchanan Duke's factories). Soldiers too distributed them, apparently to women. The distribution of tobacco in its most modern form did not allay distrust. The Lakotas were unwillingly to surrender weapons.[71]

When the army's search produced relatively few weapons, the soldiers began to ransack the Indians' camp. They began to search the gathered

68. Ibid., 294, 301–12.
69. Greene, 176–84.
70. Ostler, 326–31.
71. Greene, 224–30.

men and boys. At that point the accounts grow contradictory and confused. One man, who was deaf, resisted. A struggle erupted. Someone fired a gun. The surrounded Indians surged forward; those with guns opened fire; those without them were desperate to reclaim weapons to defend themselves and their families. Knives flashed; men fought; the soldiers' firing became general. The Indians had no chance. Eighty-three of the men and older boys in Big Foot's band died, most within the first ten minutes of fighting. Women and children fled in a confusion of dust and smoke. Hotchkiss guns with explosive shells opened up on them. The slaughter went on for hours among the wailing and death songs. When it was over, 170 to 200 women and children were dead or mortally wounded. One soldier found a woman to whom he had given cigarettes. Her legs were gone. Some of the wounded had been executed on the spot. Roughly three-quarters of Big Foot's band died at Wounded Knee. Thirty-three soldiers either died or expired later from their wounds. Many of them died in their own crossfire.[72]

Neither the press nor Indian reformers had much sympathy for the Indians. Americans saw the encounter through the lens of race war. Fifteen years earlier, the year of Custer's defeat, William Dean Howells had visited the Smithsonian's Indian exhibit at the Centennial International Exposition in Philadelphia. Howells thought the Exposition revealed the Indians as "hideous demons." Their malignity could hardly "inspire any emotion softer than abhorrence." Howells made a labored joke that the moldy flour and rotten beef that officials delivered to them at their agencies was too good for them.[73]

Howells's opinions about many things had changed between 1876 and 1891, but not about Indians. In his "Editor's Study" column in January 1891, he reviewed Lizzie Custer's reminiscence of the 1876 Custer campaign. He condemned "the grotesque and cruel absurdity of our Indian policy," but it was hardly out of sympathy with Indians. Howells praised soldiers, particularly the soldiers of the Seventh Cavalry, echoing Ruskin and also Bellamy, in thinking "the army should ever serve us as the norm of the civil state" and exalted Custer, who "ought to be known to every grateful American." The Sioux were "butchers," and the Cheyennes were "idiotic murderers." The United States, Howells complained, indulged

72. Ostler, 343–48; Greene, 215–46; Jerome Greene, "The Medals of Wounded Knee," *Nebraska History* 75 (1994): 200.

73. David W. Grua, *Surviving Wounded Knee: The Lakotas and the Politics of Memory* (New York: Oxford University Press, 2016), 28–29; W. D. Howells, "A Sennight of the Centennial," *Atlantic* Monthly 38 (July 1876): 103.

Indians, and he longed for the day that "the Indians should have ever been treated otherwise than in severalty."[74]

Frances Willard, for her part, thought the "winter's tragedy" would have been avoided if Alice Fletcher and other women Indian reforms had "been given power over our bewildered Indians." But Fletcher had been given power; she had been instrumental in instituting the severalty policy that Howells praised and that had helped bring on the tragedy.[75]

General Miles, who bore considerable responsibility for what happened, would rise to become the commanding general of the U.S. Army, but he also changed his mind about Wounded Knee. He eventually described the fight as a "massacre . . . unjustifiable and worthy of the severest condemnation," but by then twenty soldiers at Wounded Knee received the Medal of Honor, a laurel not as great as it would later become. The army arrested leading Ghost Dancers and imprisoned them at Fort Sheridan, near Chicago, which was originally erected to have troops available following the Haymarket bombing. They were out of prison by spring, and Short Bull, Kicking Bear, and other prisoners joined more than one hundred Lakotas in Buffalo Bill's Wild West when it sailed for Antwerp on April 1, 1891, on a European tour.[76]

None of this surprised Ely Parker, the Seneca who was once Grant's adjutant in the Civil War and then his commissioner of Indian affairs. Parker had retreated into obscurity as allotment and the dismantling of Indian Territory quickened. Employed as a police clerk in New York City, he could only watch as assimilation policies he had once championed did their damage. They became in his eyes just another episode in a long history of dispossession. At the end of the 1880s, he wrote that "Black deception, damnable frauds, and persistent oppression have been its characteristics. . . . All other methods of dispossessing the Indians of every vested and hereditary right having failed, compulsion must now be resorted to, a certain death to the poor Indian." He particularly condemned the evangelical reformers who advocated allotments to which the "Indians, as a body, are deadly opposed." He no longer even granted the reformers good intentions: "It is very evident to my mind that all schemes to apparently serve the Indians are only plausible pleas put out to hoodwink the civilized world that everything possible has been done to save this race from annihilation and to

74. "Editor's Study," January 1891, William Dean Howells, *Editor's Study*, ed. James W. Simpson (Troy, NY: Whitston, 1983), 293–94.

75. Louise Michele Newman, *White Women's Rights: The Racial Origins of Feminism in the United States* (New York: Oxford University Press, 1999), 116.

76. Ostler, 353–54, 360; Warren, "Sacred Circle," 159; Greene, "Medals of Wounded Knee," 200–208; Louis S. Warren, *Buffalo Bill's America: William Cody and the Wild West Show* (New York: Knopf, 2005), 381–85.

Indian Lands in January 1891

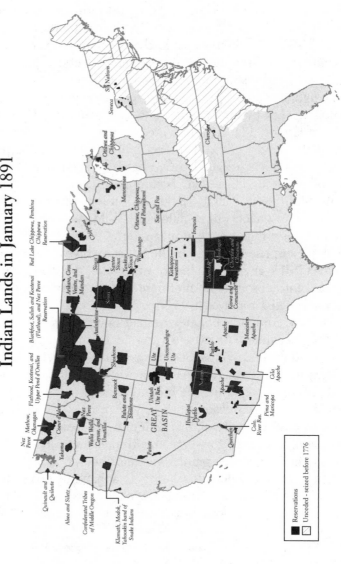

Quinault and
Quilente

Aleea and Siletz

Confederated Tribes
of Middle Oregon

Klamath, Modok,
Yahooskin band of
Snake Indians

Nez   Methow,
Perce   Okanagan

Yakima

Coeur d'Alene

Nez
Perce

Walla Walla,
Cayuse, and
Umatilla

Flathead, Kootenai, and
Upper Pend d'Oreilles

Blackfoot, Salish and Kootenai
(Flathead), and Nez Perce
Reservation

Red Lake Chippewa, Pembina
Chippewa
Reservation

Assiniboine

Shoshone

Bannock

Paiute and
Shoshone

Paiute

GREAT
BASIN

Uintah
Ute Res.

Uncompahgre
Ute

Ute

Arikara, Gros
Ventre, and
Mandan

Sioux

Santee
Sioux

Yankton
Sioux

Winnebago

Sioux

Kickapoo—
Potawatomi

Ottawa, Chippewa,
and Potawatomi

Sac and Fox

Menominee

Chippewa

Ottawa and
Chippewa

Seneca

Six Nations

Iroquois

Cherokee

Cherokee

Creek

Seminole

Choctaw and
Chickasaw

Kiowa and
Comanche

Pueblo

Apache

Mescalero
Apache

Navajo

Apache

Hualapai
Pueblo

Gila
Apache

Pima and
Maricopa

Colo.
River Res.

Quechan

Reservations

Uncceded – seized before 1776

wipe out the stain on the American name for its treatment of the aboriginal population."[77]

The 1890 census would announce the end of the frontier—in the sense of a clearly demarcated line of settlement—and Frederick Jackson Turner would use the census to memorialize it, but the claim was the product of a kind of ideological mapping. The underlying census data showed no such thing as a vanishing frontier line, and the "frontier" would reappear in the 1900 census. The belief in data and statistics as transparent and unforgiving had driven the American Social Science Association, which had lent important support to Francis Walker's effort to improve and elaborate the census, but ultimately the data were not transparent, they had to be represented, and the representations could be ideological. There was real angst over the changing nature of the country, and this would be loaded onto the idea of a vanished frontier, but real worry rode an imaginary horse.[78]

III

The 1890 election was over by the time the Seventh Cavalry opened fire at Wounded Knee. The Lakotas died by the dozens; the Republicans were only figuratively slaughtered. Like the Seventh Cavalry, their casualties were a result of friendly fire as much as hostile. They had not passed the Lodge Bill to secure black votes in the South; the reforms evangelical Republicans secured in the Midwest rent state coalitions. The party failed to win over antimonopolist farmers in the West. Most of all, Republicans were impaled on the centerpiece of their program: the tariff.

The tariff alienated the Middle Border and West, where opening up Indian lands and the two Sherman acts proved too weak a tea to satisfy antimonopolist farmers. Although both parties again played the Sinophobia card, the Republicans held the weaker hand since Harrison had in 1882 initially opposed Chinese immigration restriction.[79]

The Farmers' Alliance became a major problem for the Republicans in the Middle Border and West. It emerged at the center of an attempt to create a broad reform coalition whose foundation was antimonopolism.

77. Francis Paul Prucha, *The Great Father: The United States Government and the American Indians* (Lincoln: University of Nebraska Press, 1984), 2: 752–53; Prucha, *American Indian Policy in Crisis*, 391–99; Hoxie, 176–77.

78. Benjamin M. Schmidt, "Reconstructing the Map" (talk at Spatial History Lab, Stanford University, May 2015).

79. Homer F. Socolofsky, "Benjamin Harrison and the American West," *Great Plains Quarterly* V (Fall 1985): 255–56.

Both Terence Powderly and Frances Willard had attended an 1889 convention of reformers in St. Louis. Willard was there as a Prohibitionist. That party had adopted her Home Protection program, but she was losing faith in the Prohibitionists' efficacy. Powderly arrived as the best-known national labor leader, but his organization was crumbling rapidly everywhere but in the West. The Texas Alliance and the Knights of Labor had cooperated in the Great Southwest Strike, and they now issued a common set of demands, one that stressed antimonopoly issues much more than purely labor issues. Most were familiar reforms: the abolition of national banks and the restoration of a greenback currency whose amount would be calculated to facilitate the business of the country; free and unlimited coinage of silver; government ownership of telegraph and railway lines; an end to alien land ownership; and equitable taxation.[80]

The Southern Alliance retained its nonpartisan stance following the St. Louis meeting, but in the fall of 1889 Alliance farmers in Cowley County, Kansas, broke with the Republican Party to run a victorious nonpartisan slate. Both Republican reformers and party stalwarts recognized the danger. Harry Blackwell, Willard's associate at the *Woman's Journal*, went into near panic over Willard's sympathy for the movement. "For Heaven's sake," he wrote, "do not let our last & only hope for our day and generation be lost by a premature & suicidal Third party agitation!" Blackwell was not being alarmist. The antimonopoly triumph in Cowley County marked the beginning of what would become the Populist Party. The Populists would back women's suffrage, but Blackwell argued that the Republicans were the only realistic hope for women's suffrage. Encouraging third parties would weaken the Republicans and ensure that women's suffrage "is killed for a generation to come unless we save Kansas and Wyoming."[81]

The Republicans' problems with antimonopolists and evangelical reformers surfaced all across the Middle Border and the Midwest in 1890. The Kansas People's Party ran a separate ticket, and independent antimonopolist tickets appeared elsewhere in the Middle Border. A different set of dangers appeared on the other side of the Missouri. Iowa was a state

80. Alison M. Parker, *Articulating Rights: Nineteenth-Century American Women on Race, Reform, and the State* (DeKalb: Northern Illinois University Press, 2010), 158–62; Craig Phelan, *Grand Master Workman: Terence Powderly and the Knights of Labor* (Westport, CT: Greenwood Press, 2000), 248–50; Bordin, 178–83; Lawrence Goodwyn, *Democratic Promise: The Populist Moment in America* (New York: Oxford University Press, 1976), 162–65.

81. Bordin, 175; Harry Blackwell to Willard, Aug. 26, 1889, in *Frances Willard Papers*, ed. Frances Willard Historical Association (Evanston, IL: Frances E. Willard Memorial Library and Archives).

usually so reliably Republican that Jonathan Dolliver, a Republican politician, had once quipped that "Iowa will go Democratic when hell goes Methodist," but prohibition pushed through by evangelical Republicans was changing that. The signs of trouble had appeared in the state election in 1889, when Democrats campaigned for local option, which gave localities a choice on whether to allow liquor sales, instead of total prohibition. They had also run against the proposed McKinley Tariff. The Democrats elected the governor and made gains in the legislature, and the Republican vote fell all across the ticket.[82]

In the dependably Republican states of Wisconsin and Illinois, laws restricting liquor also played a role in the resurgence of the Democrats, but the key issue was the schools. The Edwards law in Illinois and the Bennett law in Wisconsin demanded mandatory schooling and an end to child labor, but they attached these popular reforms to requirements that core subjects in private schools as well as public be taught only in English. The Democrats accused the Republicans of paternalism. They not only mobilized Catholics but also turned German and Scandinavian Lutherans against the Republicans. To all these groups, as well as German and Scandinavian freethinkers, this was a campaign in defense of home, family, and the mother tongue. To native-born evangelicals it was a battle to save the homeland. The Wisconsin Methodist Conference, in words that seemed to echo Josiah Strong, called it: "a question of domestic or foreign domination. Shall there be one or many nationalities on our soil? Shall Roman Catholicism and Lutheranism maintain foreign ideas, customs and languages to the exclusion of what is distinctively American?"[83]

The Republicans were finding it difficult to appease reformers, both antimonopolist and evangelical, while maintaining the ethnocultural alliance that formed their base, but their main problem across the North remained the tariff. Whatever the tariff's promised benefits, they had not yet been realized, while merchants, seeing an opportunity, raised prices on a wide range of goods alarming voters. The Democrats presented themselves as defenders of American consumers. The Republicans sloughed off large numbers of voters. Some went to the Democrats, Populists, or Independent slates; others simply stayed home. In 1890 Democrats gained five Congressional seats in Iowa, six congressional seats in Wisconsin, and seven in Illinois. William McKinley, the architect of the tariff, lost his seat

82. Richard J. Jensen, *The Winning of the Midwest: Social and Political Conflict, 1888–1896* (Chicago: University of Chicago Press, 1971), quote 136.
83. Williams, 46; Johnson Brigham, "The Iowa Experiment," *The Century* (October 1889): 957–58; Jensen, 94–114.

in Ohio, and Republicans suffered even in the industrial Midwest and Northeast.[84]

In Kansas the People's Party won control of the legislature and elected five of seven congressmen. In 1891 the new Kansas legislature ended the political career of J. J. Ingalls, who had soared with Republican free labor and floated back to earth in the years of Republican dominance. Charles Francis Adams left a memorable account of Ingalls, then president pro tempore of the Senate, soliciting a bribe from him for a fellow senator. The People's Party legislature ended his career. In Nebraska the People's Party elected two of three congressmen and won the legislature. Nationally, local tickets that grew out of the Farmers' Alliance elected nine congressmen, all but one—Thomas Watson from Georgia—at the expense of the Republicans.[85]

The contours of a coherent set of antimonopolist demands and politics were emerging, although older sectional divisions persisted. Even as alliance members split from the Republican Party to run surprisingly successful Populist or independent tickets, the Southern Alliance largely continued to operate from within the Democratic Party. This made the Western Populists vulnerable to Republican accusations that Populism was only the stalking dog for Democrats who benefited from Republican losses. The fledgling Populists had to go national or die.

The 1890 elections brought 238 Democrats and 86 Republicans to the House of Representatives. The Republicans retained the Senate only because just a third of the seats in that body were up for election. It was the greatest midterm reversal in American history. Among the new congressmen were men who would have long careers. There were antimonopolist Democrats as well as Republicans, and those who ran on independent tickets backed by the Farmers' Alliance. Nebraska had elected one Democratic congressman in its entire history before 1890, when it elected its second, William Jennings Bryan. Bryan played up his antimonopolist credentials. He attacked trusts, the tariff, and the gold standard. Although a devout Presbyterian and evangelical, he learned from the Republican mistakes in neighboring Iowa. He kept his private temperance beliefs out of the election. He drank soda water but bought voters beer. As an orator, he came to realize that he could move an audience as he chose. As a

84. Jensen, 122–41.
85. White, 354–55, 370; Jeffrey Ostler, *Prairie Populism: The Fate of Agrarian Radicalism in Kansas, Nebraska, and Iowa, 1880–1892* (Lawrence: University Press of Kansas, 1993), 120–33.

Northern Democrat, he could trounce his Republican opponent in a normally Republican state—and this made him a figure to watch.[86]

Tom Watson, the new congressman from Georgia, also rode antimonopolism into office, but he did so in a particularly Southern way. Devoted to the Lost Cause, as every aspiring white Southern politician had to be, Watson was also an Independent disgusted by both the Bourbon dominance of the Democratic Party in the South and Henry Grady's vision of the New South, which he regarded as "claptrap." He sympathized with the Farmers' Alliance without ever joining it, and with the agrarian South and its sharecroppers, tenants, and small farmers. He could turn that sympathy into effective political speech.

> Here is a tenant—I do not know, or care, whether he is white or black, I know his story. He starts in and pays $25 for a mule, 1,000 pounds of cotton for rent, and two bales for supplies. By the time he pays for that mule, and the store account, and the guano, he has not enough money left to buy a bottle of laudanum, and not enough cotton to stuff his old lady's ear.... Thousands of your Georgia homes are going to decay. I have witnessed it, and it makes my heart ache with sadness.[87]

Black farmers were not yet entirely outside the range of his, or alliance, sympathies (although by the end of his career he was as virulent a racist as anyone in the country), but his heart was with white farmers. "The fight is upon you," he told audiences composed of Confederate veterans, "not bloody as then,—but as bitter; not with men who come to free your slaves, but who come to make slaves of you." Watson's victory reminded the Democrats that even as the rise of the Populists helped them in the North, it potentially threatened them in the South.[88]

In the North, Howells registered a common disgust with the GOP. His fellow Republicans, he thought, were their own worst enemies, with men like Senator Quay corrupting Pennsylvania for Harrison while working against the Lodge Bill. The Republicans had given a great gift to manufacturers, but those manufacturers refused to raise their employees' wages,

86. Gould, 110, gives slightly different results for the election, 235 Democrats and 88 Republicans. The results in the text come from "Party Divisions of the House of Representatives," http://history.house.gov/Institution/Party-Divisions/Party-Divisions/. Jensen, 141–42, gives the party breakdown as 236 Democrats and 87 Republicans; Michael Kazin, *A Godly Hero: The Life of William Jennings Bryan* (New York: Anchor Books, 2007), 24–28.

87. C. Vann Woodward, *Tom Watson: Agrarian Rebel* (New York: Oxford University Press, 1963), 122–47, quote 31.

88. Joseph Gerteis, *Class and the Color Line: Interracial Class Coalition in the Knights of Labor and the Populist Movement* (Durham, NC: Duke University Press, 2007), 141–49; Woodward, quote 135, 135–47.

driving workers from the party. Yet he believed the Democrats' success would prove temporary. They would, he was sure, abuse their victory and be driven from office. Convinced that a "plutocracy" was "fastening its grasp upon the country," he depended on others to save it. He looked forward to the "decay of the old parties, and the growth of a new one that will mean true equality and real freedom." He did not intend this as a call to the barricades. He and his close friend Mark Twain remained "theoretical socialists, and practical aristocrats."[89]

Howells had more personal and pressing worries. His daughter Winnie—"a sad problem"—and his son's enrollment at Harvard drained him emotionally and financially. By November 1888 the Howells had embarked on another expensive treatment, a last best hope for Winnie. The only other choice seemed "dementia and death." The diagnosis was hysteria; the cure was force-feeding. Winnie died that March from heart failure. Her autopsy found an unspecified organic malady.[90]

Her death temporarily exiled Howells's disgust and disappointment with American politics to a rarely visited place. The Harrison administration had two years to run, but the president was at the mercy of his enemies, and he hardly had any friends. Politics had become both unstable and oddly predictable. The Republicans had won in 1888 by taking advantage of Democrats' miscalculations over the tariff. The Democrats had won in 1890 by taking advantage of Republican miscalculations about the tariff. They stood to win by an even larger margin in 1892. The tariff mattered in its own right, but it mattered mostly because it had become shorthand for the benefits and inequities of an industrial economy. The steel industry ranked among the foremost beneficiaries of the tariff, and Andrew Carnegie had clawed his way to the top of that industry. He became the face of the tariff, which would not prove beneficial to the Republicans.

89. Howells to Charles D. Warner, Jan. 17, 1890, W. D. Howells to W. C. Howells, Feb. 2, 1890, and Nov. 9, 1890, in Howells, *Selected Letters*, 3: 271, 296.
90. W. C. Howells to W. D. Howells, Feb. 26, 1888, and Apr. 1, 1888, W. D. Howells to W. C. Howells, Nov. 18, 1888; W. D. Howells to W. C. Howells, Mar. 4, 1889, W. C. Howells to W. D. Howells, Mar. 10, 1889, W. D. Howells to S. W. Mitchell, Mar. 7, 1889, in ibid., 3: 218, 221, 235, 246–48.

18

The Poetry of a Pound of Steel

During the 1880s Andrew Carnegie lived with his mother at the Windsor Hotel—"a mountain of cherry bricks and mortar"—on Forty-sixth Street and Fifth Avenue in New York City. It had large apartments, lavish accommodations, and "dudes": an American type who were somewhere between the Parisian *flâneurs* and the English mashers. They were identifiable by their extravagant clothes, their usually unwanted attention to women, and their sometimes welcome attention to each other. The Windsor served the same purpose for elite businessmen that Washington's Willard Hotel had served for lobbyists and politicians during the Civil War. Leland Stanford and George Westinghouse lived there when they were in New York City. Jay Gould's mansion was nearby on Fifth Avenue, and he spent occasional afternoons in the lobby, reading newspapers and meeting with brokers and associates. The Carnegies had their own table in the dining room, and the genial Carnegie was happy to mingle with other plutocrats, but he did not want to be numbered among the philistines.[1]

Carnegie balanced his ability to make money with a serious engagement with ideas. This set him apart from other tycoons. His success in steel illustrated how American industry worked, the competitive pressures that shaped it, and the government programs that favored it. His own carefully cultivated image as the poor and grateful immigrant who pulled himself up by the bootstraps served to enshrine him along with Edison as symbols of the success of individualism and free labor. His writings demonstrated a real engagement with the problems of great wealth among pressing poverty. In thinking about income distribution, he stumbled clumsily into one of the great changes in the American economy, as questions of production yielded to questions of consumption, as production shifted from capital goods to consumer goods, and as issues of abundance

1. Maury Klein, *The Life and Legend of Jay Gould* (Baltimore, MD: Johns Hopkins University Press, 1986), 454; Kenneth D. Rose, *Unspeakable Awfulness: America through the Eyes of European Travelers, 1865–1900* (New York: Routledge, 2014), 82.

replaced convictions of scarcity. He offered solutions forged in one industrial world for another very different world, and this laggard vision paradoxically shaped philanthropy.

Carnegie aspired to be a sage and not just a plutocrat. He collected intellectuals, particularly aging British liberals such as Herbert Spencer, William Gladstone, Matthew Arnold, and the poet Edwin Arnold. Carnegie liked to pontificate, and as he grew older it became increasingly hard to shut him up; he could drive the British to distraction with his praise of the United States and its opportunities. He appears to have sincerely believed this even though he had for decades neglected to become an American citizen, doing so only in 1885 when he finally abandoned hope of becoming a British MP. Citizenship did not cause him to spend less time in Great Britain, where he built a lavish Scottish estate. The English novelist William Black nicknamed him "The Star Spangled Scotsman," but British intellectuals still liked him better than they liked the United States. When Carnegie brought Spencer to Pittsburgh and lauded the city as an example of evolutionary progress, Spencer said "Six months' residence here would justify suicide." Edwin Arnold found the combination of Carnegie's enthusiasm and the actual United States too much. He told his doctor that if he did not get out, he would die. Arnold canceled his lecture tour and fled to Japan.[2]

Some British liberals—James Bryce was certainly one—shared Carnegie's views about America, but no British intellectual loved the United States the way Henry James loved England. Bryce qualified as an eminent Victorian: a mountain climber, historian, Oxford don, Member of Parliament, and later British ambassador to the United States. He had begun visiting in the 1870s. He was not impressed with the sophistication and culture of the nation but rather its hopefulness and its "abounding strength and vitality." American liberals such as Godkin influenced his influential account of the United States, *American Commonwealth*, and received it enthusiastically.[3]

William Dean Howells dined with Carnegie and Edwin Arnold (who dyed his beard purple) in February 1892, before Arnold decamped. They ate, predictably, at Delmonico's "amidst the pretty and fashionable women who crowd the place." Carnegie had "a sort of queer pig face, shrewd, and humorous and set. He told Scotch stories and laid down the law." Howells liked him but "would rather not be one of his hands." A few weeks later

2. David Nasaw, *Andrew Carnegie* (New York: Penguin Press, 2006), 264, 330–31; Harold C. Livesay, *Andrew Carnegie and the Rise of Big Business* (Boston: Little, Brown, 1975), 123–28.
3. James J. Connolly, *An Elusive Unity: Urban Democracy and Machine Politics in Industrializing America* (Ithaca, NY: Cornell University Press, 2010), 78–79; James Bryce, *The American Commonwealth* (London: Macmillan, 1888), 10.

Howells, as editor of the *Cosmopolitan*, asked for an article from Carnegie, "The Poetry of a Pound of Steel." He flattered Carnegie, but he did not get the article. The timing was bad; Carnegie had provoked trouble with his workers, on strike at his mill at Homestead, Pennsylvania. There was not much poetry left in steel.[4]

The road to Homestead stretched over nearly two decades. It traced the successes and failures of the American economy and the strengths, and considerable limits, of the men who sought to control and profit from it. Carnegie's mills made iron and steel, things out of which other people made other things, which were the drivers of American economic growth. Workers turned steel into railroads: engines, bridges, and above all tracks. They turned steel into the new buildings rising in American cities. In short, they turned steel into the infrastructure on which American business depended. Producer goods like steel and iron, along with primary goods, particularly agricultural, rather than consumer goods, had driven American growth since the Civil War. The great American fortunes came from railroads, iron and steel, oil, and finance.

By the late 1880s Carnegie's fortune ranked among the greatest. Like John D. Rockefeller, he had absorbed the lessons of the new industrial economy and ruthlessly eliminated competition, but where Rockefeller harbored the illusion that God had given him his money, Carnegie cultivated an even greater one: he thought his success was the product of evolution. He should have known that it was the product of Tom Scott.

A poor Scottish immigrant, Carnegie became a telegraph operator and then studied bookkeeping. They made his self-presentation as the epitome of the self-made man credible, but Carnegie was initially something more common: a creature of the insider politics of the Gilded Age. Just as J. Edgar Thomson, the president of the Pennsylvania Railroad, made Scott's career, so Tom Scott made the early career of Andrew Carnegie. Carnegie learned that success in nineteenth-century America involved connections—what Americans would come to call pull.[5]

Thomson and Scott taught Carnegie how to make connections pay. If sleeping car companies wanted to sell sleeping cars to the Pennsylvania Railroad, Thomson and Scott got a kickback, and they made sure their protégé, the young but well-connected Carnegie, did too. Like Rockefeller,

4. W. D. Howells to W. C. Howells, Feb. 7, 1892, and W. D. Howells to Andrew Carnegie, Feb. 26, 1892, in William Dean Howells, *Selected Letters*, ed. George Warren Arms (Boston: Twayne, 1979), 4: 12, 15.

5. Nasaw, 55–59; Pamela Walker Laird, *Pull: Networking and Success since Benjamin Franklin* (Cambridge, MA: Harvard University Press, 2006), 28–31, 35–36.

Carnegie avoided military service during the Civil War. Both men began to build their fortunes through investments in the oil industry, but Carnegie also continued to profit from businesses that contracted with the Pennsylvania Railroad.[6]

Carnegie steered iron purchase for the Pennsylvania's expansion to his (and Thomson's) Keystone Bridge Company. After the Civil War, Thomson, Carnegie, and Scott granted themselves a franchise for a new telegraph company that would have the right to string its wires along the Pennsylvania right-of-way. They paid nothing for the franchise and sold the company at a profit to another company in which they retained a minority interest. This company then hired yet another Carnegie company to construct the telegraph. It was how business was done.[7]

Carnegie branched out in the years after the war, selling bonds and speculating in stock. He later claimed that he "never bought or sold a share of stock speculatively in my life," but that was a lie. He did so for years and did so profitably. He sold paper in the Davenport and St. Paul Railroad; the Missouri, Iowa, and Nebraska; and the Keokuk Bridge Company. Carnegie sold many of the bonds on railroads promoted by Tom Scott, and he sold them in the United States and Europe. He worked with Junius Morgan and Company, the leading American investment bank in London, and Drexel and Company in the United States.[8]

By 1873 Carnegie had shifted his interest to the steel business. He had made his first foray into steel, investing in new technologies for steel rails, in the 1860s. Both Carnegie and the technologies proved unsuccessful, but in 1872 he returned to steel, becoming a partner in a Pittsburgh mill. By then he was thirty-seven years old, affable, entertaining, and shrewd. Both he and steel making were advancing rapidly. The new Bessemer conversion process and similar techniques that purged the impurities from iron and turned it into its much stronger and less brittle form— steel—allowed manufacturers to produce the metal on a large scale. Carnegie's mill became part of the American Bessemer Association, which, by controlling the American patents, controlled access to the American steel market. Another prominent member of the association was the Pennsylvania Steel Company, controlled by Thomson, Scott, and the Pennsylvania Railroad. When Congress imposed a $28 per ton tariff on steel, the British lost their price advantage. Carnegie later said that it

6. Albert J. Churella, *The Pennsylvania Railroad* (Philadelphia: University of Pennsylvania Press, 2013), 212–14, 383, 407–12, 417; Nasaw, 61–62, 85.
7. Steven W. Usselman, *Regulating Railroad Innovation: Business, Technology, and Politics in America, 1840–1920* (New York: Cambridge University Press, 2002), 80–81; Livesay, 62–64.
8. Livesay, 61–72, 95–96.

was the tariff more than anything else that brought him into the steel business.[9]

In becoming a steelmaker, Carnegie abandoned neither the friendships nor the connections that had served him so well. He located his new steel works on a site twelve miles south of Pittsburgh and named them after Edgar Thomson. Flattery was always part of Carnegie's repertoire. He depended on the Pennsylvania Railroad for contracts, but he had no intention of depending solely on its goodwill. His mill had access to the Baltimore and Ohio as well as the Pennsylvania. The new mill also fronted the Monongahela River, which provided river transportation for coal and coke. Carnegie's advice to aspiring businessmen was, "Put all your good eggs in one basket, and then watch the basket."[10]

Scott had taught Carnegie how necessary pull, connections, and insider dealing were to making money, but he had also shown him how necessary speed, organization, and efficiency were to the Pennsylvania Railroad's success. Carnegie brought the lessons of cost accounting, organization, and integration that he had learned from Scott and Thomson to manufacturing. Speed, lower unit costs, and volume translated into greater efficiency and potentially greater profit. Most of the ironworks around Pittsburgh in the 1870s were proprietorships employing two hundred to three hundred workers. By this scale, the Edgar Thomson works were mammoth. They were located on a 106-acre site, ran twenty-four hours a day, and employed a continuous-process method of making steel. Although incorporated under Pennsylvania law, Carnegie Steel was not a joint stock corporation. It was a partnership with Carnegie as the dominant partner.[11]

Carnegie recognized that reducing the competition that plagued the iron makers was critical to the new steel industry. For all practical purposes the market for steel initially consisted of the railroads. As late as 1882, steel rails composed 90 percent of steel production. The new steel rails lasted much longer than iron rails, and their strength allowed the railroad companies to run bigger, faster, and longer trains. Once the tariff eliminated British steel, and the steel companies' control of patents limited new entries into the field, the major companies formed pools to allot production. The Pennsylvania Railroad did not object to the premium that the tariffs and the pools placed on steel rails. The railroads owned some of the steel

9. Ibid., 83–90; Nasaw, 100–102, 141; Usselman, 77–84.
10. Thomas J. Misa, *A Nation of Steel: The Making of Modern America, 1865–1925* (Baltimore, MD: Johns Hopkins University Press, 1995), 23; Nasaw, 137.
11. Livesay, 83–90; Maury Klein, *The Genesis of Industrial America, 1870–1920* (Cambridge: Cambridge University Press, 2007), 110–11; Walter Licht, *Industrializing America: The Nineteenth Century* (Baltimore, MD: John Hopkins University Press, 1995), 111; Misa, 23; Nasaw, 173–75.

mills and sought to profit from the ore and coal they transported to virtually all of them. This was a lucrative business, and they had no wish to disrupt it. Carnegie got the lion's share of sales because within this closed system he had the largest works. He ruthlessly cut costs. His goal was a small profit on unit sales with a large profit resulting from sales volume. His great opportunities came not during good times but bad. As railroad construction collapsed and iron and steel mills closed following the Panic of 1873, smaller producers went under. Carnegie opened his Edgar Thomson Mill in 1875 and expanded production. His goal was to increase his market share and keep his works running. The profits would come when the economy improved. The price of steel rails would drop from $160 a ton in 1875 to $17 a ton in 1898, but Carnegie still made a fortune.[12]

Carnegie's life changed dramatically in the late 1880s. The key event was the death of his mother, when he was nearly fifty-one years old. He had redeemed her hard life, but she dominated him, refusing to allow him to marry, and he had, as a result, strung along Louise Whitfield, whom he met in 1880. She was twenty-three years his junior, three inches taller than his five foot three, and considered Carnegie's mother the most unpleasant person she had ever met. She was also ambivalent about marriage. In 1886 Carnegie's brother and partner, Tom, died of pneumonia, his health weakened by heavy drinking. Carnegie, sick with typhoid fever, kept the news from his mother, who was dying in the next room. When shortly afterward she expired, the doctors refused to tell Carnegie, whom they did not think would live. He did live and married Louise in 1887. She replaced his mother in his household, and he replaced his brother, Tom, in his business with Henry Clay Frick, who had already made a fortune in manufacturing coke for steel production. Carnegie brought Frick in as a partner.[13]

In nearly every trait but ability and ruthlessness, Henry Clay Frick, a descendant of Pennsylvania Mennonites, differed from Carnegie. Where Carnegie was congenial, Frick was dour; where Carnegie charmed, Frick glowered. Where Carnegie at least claimed beneficence, Frick threatened and carried through on his threats. His great-granddaughter described him "taciturn, brusque...and guarded." His dominant emotion was anger; his first instinct was distrust. The deaths of two of his children hardened him even more. The day after his young son and namesake was buried, he was at work, answering mail.[14]

12. Nasaw, 169–71, 174–75; Usselman, 89–91; David Brody, *Steelworkers in America; the Nonunion Era* (Cambridge, MA: Harvard University Press, 1960), 4–5; Misa, 21; Klein, *The Genesis of Industrial America, 1870–1920*, 110–11.
13. Livesay, 124–28; Nasaw, 204–5, 233–34, 241–46, 284–87, 296.
14. Leon Wolff, *Lockout, the Story of the Homestead Strike of 1892: A Study of Violence, Unionism and the Carnegie Steel Empire* (New York: Harper & Row, 1965), 21–27; Nasaw, 210, 396, 443–44.

Carnegie became acquainted with Frick after the latter gained control of the coke industry, which produced the fuel necessary for iron production. He raised the price and made it stick. Carnegie bought a half interest in Frick's firm, and, as it turned out, a full interest in Frick. It was his greatest acquisition. A preternaturally able executive and ruthless foe of labor, he restored Carnegie's edge. When Carnegie fell behind in implementing new technologies, Frick bought the companies that possessed those technologies. Like Carnegie, he cut costs by eliminating unnecessary steps, keeping his factories running, and minimizing labor and fuel costs. Carnegie Steel's factories were tremendously productive and extravagantly dangerous places.[15]

Unlike Frick, Captain "Bill" Jones had mitigated Carnegie's worse tendencies, and he might even have mitigated Frick's, had he lived. The son of a Welsh immigrant who had begun his career as a machinist, Jones joined Carnegie Steel to manage the Edgar Thompson Works. Jones regarded low wages as counterproductive, believing that "low wages does not always imply cheap labor. Good wages and good workmen I know to be cheap labor." Jones did not bully men or dictate to them, but he did manipulate them in order to control work. He wanted to "steer clear as far as we can of Englishmen, who are great sticklers for high wages, small production, and strikes." He preferred an ethnically mixed workforce of Germans, Scotsmen, Irish, Swedes, a few Welshmen, and "Buckwheat— young American country boys." By mixing these groups in work crews, he avoided the ethnic disputes that plagued the coal mines. Jones persuaded Carnegie to put his mills on three eight-hour shifts instead of two twelve-hour shifts, but the experiment failed when competitors refused to follow his example. When Jones was in charge, Carnegie's workers enjoyed steady employment and a living wage, until, like many of his men, Jones died working steel. A blast furnace explosion killed him in September 1889.[16]

I

By the 1890s, Carnegie had publicly distanced himself from the everyday running of his company. He presented himself as the businessman philosopher who had changed his responsibility from producing wealth to dispersing it for the benefit of society. He claimed that he, too, was a

---

15. Wolff, 21–27; Livesay, 130–32.
16. Jones's methods were more subtle, but he too was committed to taking the control of work away from the employees. Paul Krause, *The Battle for Homestead, 1880–1892: Politics, Culture, and Steel* (Pittsburgh, PA: University of Pittsburgh Press, 1992), 71–72, 75–76, 141–44; Livesay, 98–99, 132–33, 134–35.

workingman; he granted the legitimacy of unions and attacked strike-breaking. Or at least this is what he said. His actions were somewhat different. He systematically undermined unions, increasingly pushed for reduced wages, and ultimately demanded ironclad contracts that would prohibit his employees from unionizing. When employees resisted, he resorted to lockouts, scabs, and Pinkertons.[17]

Carnegie's workers died and were injured in shocking numbers; they worked twelve-hour days in brutal conditions, six and eventually seven days a week. They worked amidst open furnaces, molten iron and steel, unstable stacks of beams and ingots, and exploding machinery. In the summer, the mills themselves might as well have been furnaces. Until he brought in Frick, however, Carnegie did not have a reputation as a terrible employer. That bar was set pretty high. Carnegie initially paid wages higher than most of his competitors, but he and Frick worked to correct that.[18]

As in so many industries, new technological processes were undermining the control of skilled workers. The Bessemer and related processes replaced iron with steel and cut the power of the molders, who channeled and shaped the molten iron. "In every direction," one iron maker reported, "our customers are calling for steel, and we must satisfy them or see them go elsewhere." The puddlers who made iron were industrial chefs whose furnaces served as so many ovens; their cooking determined the quality of the product. Steel making also demanded skill, but that skill, and its rewards, lodged in many fewer heads and hands. In the new Phoenix steel mill, for example, the two melters and the chemist who supervised them controlled production and earned ten times the daily wage of a manual laborer. Other workers were now more easily dismissed and replaced, making it easier for Carnegie to attack the unions. Former members of the Iron Molders' Union migrated into the Amalgamated Association of Iron and Steel Workers (AAISW) and the Knights of Labor, but their status and power declined while their resentment increased.[19]

Carnegie's mill at Homestead was initially an exception. It had originated as an attempt by rival steel makers to escape the monopoly the Bessemer patent holders had established, and to do so they created an idiosyncratic and hybrid plant whose operation depended on skilled workers familiar with its peculiarities. When in 1882 its owners tried to institute

17. Krause, 233–41, 246–50.
18. Livesay, 132–33; S. J. Kleinberg, *The Shadow of the Mills: Working-Class Families in Pittsburgh, 1870–1907* (Pittsburgh, PA: University of Pittsburgh Press, 1989), 27–28; Krause, 221.
19. Misa, 54–57. David Montgomery, *The Fall of the House of Labor: The Workplace, the State, and American Labor Activism, 1865–1925* (Cambridge: Cambridge University Press, 1987), 9–32; Nasaw, 326; Kleinberg, 5–9, 20–21, Krause, 141–44.

ironclad contracts under which workers promised not to unionize, the AAISW went on strike. The workers cast the strike in the classic form of worker republicanism: to sign an ironclad contract would be to "sign away our rights as freeborn American citizens." For management, the issue boiled down to rights of property: "It has become an issue between some workmen and ourselves as to whether we shall be allowed to run our business or whether they will run it for us."[20]

The strike demonstrated that Homestead's owners could not run their business without skilled workers. Production plummeted. The mill lost customers due to inferior products, and Homestead missed contracts, opening the owners to lawsuits. The mill owners were unable to protect the scabs they hired, who were subject to abuse and sporadic violence. Workers dominated the community, and strikers became deputy policemen. Eventually, the owners turned to the county, but this too proved ineffective. The disorder, though real, never mounted to a level that required the militia, and thus the owners could not muster the necessary state aid to break the strike. After nearly three months, the owners conceded. Carnegie bought the mill in 1883.[21]

The workers' ability to control the conditions of their own labor and their monopoly of knowledge were their great strength; but scabs—"black sheep," as they were called in Pennsylvania—were their Achilles heel. In the early 1880s the AAISW was open to only about one-third of the workers in the plant, and some skilled workers in other plants whose unions had been broken were tempted to take work there. They were not numerous enough to break the strike, but their presence marked future dangers, which grew even more pronounced as the relentless mechanization of steel making and divisions between puddlers and finishers weakened the AAISW. The union struck the steel industry eleven times between 1882 and 1885, but Homestead was the only strike that it won.[22]

In 1888 Carnegie broke the Knights of Labor at the Edgar Thomson works, locking out the workers, bringing in Pinkertons, and taking employees back individually only after they agreed to wage reductions, a twelve-hour day, and an ironclad contract. East European workers—whom other workers lumped together as "Hungarians" or Huns and who were not members of the Knights—returned first. The Knights denounced them as "buzzards of labor," but Knights, their union broken, followed.[23]

20. Krause, 165–78, quotes, 178.
21. Ibid., 178–92, 212.
22. Ibid., 182, 199–200; Kleinberg, 11–12; Montgomery, 25–26, 31–34.
23. Krause, 208–9, 215–17.

By 1889 Homestead was the last steel union stronghold in the Pittsburgh area. It was also a political stronghold for workers, who in 1888 had elected Beeswax Taylor as burgess, as the mayor's office was called. Beeswax Taylor, whose nickname came from his saying that work in English mills in his youth had sucked all the honey out of life, leaving him and other workers only with the wax, combined in his sometime eccentric person much of the complexity of American working-class life. He was an old English Chartist, but his American experience convinced him that the Chartist dream of the vote for the workingmen being enough to change society was misguided. He became an advocate of the cooperative common-wealth embraced by the Knights and Bellamy, but he also helped to found the American Federation of Labor (AFL). That, like Terence Powderly, he proved at various times a successful businessman did not in the least dilute his enthusiasm for unions and cooperation. As a politician, he ran for burgess on a workers' ticket, but nationally, like Andrew Carnegie, he remained a Republican, a strong supporter of Benjamin Harrison, and an eager supplicant for a patronage appointment. He accepted the Republican argument that the tariff, by protecting American markets, would protect American wages.[24]

Republican politics worked out much better for Carnegie than for Taylor, who did not get his patronage appointment. The tariff buttressed steel prices against foreign competition, but domestic competition and new production processes steadily drove down the price of steel rails. Carnegie turned to open-hearth furnaces at Homestead in 1886 and moved into structural steel and armor plate for the U.S. Navy. The navy provided one means for the Republicans to spend down the treasury sur-plus. Spurred by Alfred Thayer Mahan's *The Influence of Sea Power Upon History*, published in 1890, Congress embarked on the construction of steel-plated battleships. Carnegie was, and would remain, opposed to war, but not to making money off of preparing for it. He successfully lobbied the Harrison administration for contracts to provide steel armor for the battleships, including the USS *Maine*. The plate would be manufactured at Homestead. Pleased with the potential for profit, he also enlisted Secretary of State James G. Blaine to help him sell armored plate to Russia.[25]

Homestead expanded beyond its original ninety acres to accommodate the new production; it could do so because Carnegie's political contacts were local as well as national. He bribed Pittsburgh officials to sell him the city poor farm, insane asylum, and poorhouse, all of which abutted

24. My interpretation here differs from that of Krause, 253–63.
25. Nasaw, 377–89; Krause, 281–85.

Homestead. The residents went elsewhere. By 1892 the Homestead mills employed four thousand workers. As he expanded, Carnegie demanded wage concessions by his workers, particularly a sliding scale that tied their wages to the price of steel rather than to Carnegie's profits. To tie employee wages to a product steadily and dramatically falling in price was like tying stones to workers and pushing them overboard. Carnegie could profit despite falling prices because of reduced costs and increased output, but workers, some already working twelve-hour days seven days a week, could not realistically increase their own hours of labor. They could decrease their costs only by having their families live on less.[26]

Carnegie tried to break the union in 1889. He locked the workers out and succeeded in winning wage concessions with a sliding scale above a base wage, but both the Amalgamated and the Knights remained. Carnegie was so furious that his negotiator, William Abbott, had settled without breaking the unions that he turned to Abbott's rival within the company, Henry Clay Frick, to take over active management. A new contract would be negotiated in 1892, and Carnegie's goal was to bring the wages at Homestead in line with nonunion mills. To protect themselves, the local Homestead lodges of the AAISW, against the rules of the national union, began to welcome unskilled as well as skilled workers. These unskilled workers were the largely Eastern European immigrants whom the Knights earlier regarded as the equivalent of the Chinese and their very existence a threat to American standards of living. Within Homestead, however, the mostly Catholic Slovak workers merged relatively easily with English, German, Irish, and native-born workers and maintained solidarity.[27]

Everyone knew a fight was coming in 1892. Negotiations for the contract at Homestead began in January under the supervision of Frick. Carnegie went to Scotland. Frick built what his workers called Fort Frick: an eleven-foot fence topped with barbed wire and portholes that encircled the steel works. Frick was not interested in an accommodation. On June 28 he locked out the workers. On July 1, Carnegie consolidated all of his and his partners' properties into Carnegie Steel. It was privately held and capitalized at $25 million, well under its actual value. He made Frick chairman.[28]

26. Nasaw, 379–83; Krause, 94–95, 104, 232, 235–48, 274–81. The sliding scale originally was a proposal by the puddlers in the 1860s intended for the iron rather than steel markets when the puddlers had much greater control over production. In the steel industry it became a weapon against workers.
27. Nasaw, 363–64, 367–72; Paul Kahan, *The Homestead Strike: Labor, Violence, and American Industry* (New York: Routledge, 2014), 54, 59–60; Krause, 220–26, 321–22.
28. Krause, 211–14, 235–42; Nasaw, 385–92, 396; Kahan, 63.

The strike evolved at the cadenced pace of a medieval siege; the only—and quite critical—uncertainty was the level of violence it would provoke and whether it would be sufficient to induce the state to intervene. Frick could keep the workers out of the mill, but the workers could keep scabs from entering since they needed to proceed through the town of Homestead. Beeswax Taylor was no longer burgess, but an equally pro-union man was, and the town united against Frick. The easiest way into the mill was by the Monongahela River, which bordered Homestead, and to prevent access the union posted scouts to warn of an approach by water.

When Frick procured two barges and a tug to pull them and loaded them with three hundred Pinkertons, most of whom were newly enlisted and did not know where they were going or why, the union tracked the barges. Workers were not surprised when the tug ran them ashore outside the Homestead Mill on July 6, 1892. A mobilized town as full of angry women as of angry men confronted the Pinkertons. Both sides were armed. When the Pinkertons tried to force their way ashore, they and the defenders took casualties. Among the first workers to go down with what proved a fatal wound was George Rutter, who had been wounded nearly thirty years before at Gettysburg. When a second attempt by the Pinkertons to reach the mill failed, they found themselves trapped in the barges. The tug had carried away casualties and was unable to return. Most of the Pinkerton recruits had little stomach for the fight.[29]

Throughout the day workers, enraged by the invasion and the casualties they suffered and urged on by the women of the town, thought of ever more inventive ways to destroy the barges and the Pinkertons. They set a lumber barge on fire and tried to float it into the Pinkertons' barges. They tried to ignite an oil slick. They fired cannons and used dynamite. They sent a flat car loaded with burning barrels of oil down the tracks to the docks. All failed but terrified the men in the barges.[30]

Politics initially favored the workers. Town officials sympathized with them and blamed the Pinkertons for provoking the violence. The town deputized workers. The company appealed to the county sheriff, but he was torn. He refused to deputize the Pinkertons; instead he deputized businessmen, but they were few and ineffective. The Democratic governor, Robert Pattison, feared the loss of workers' votes, but Pennsylvania's byzantine politics had saddled him with a political debt to the Republican boss of Allegheny County, whose desire to defeat his own party's nominee, his archrival Matthew Quay, had secured Pattison his election. Pattison

29. Nasaw, 415–21; Krause, 15–24.
30. Krause, 24–25.

refused to intervene until satisfied that the sheriff had exhausted all the means to enforce the laws.[31]

On the evening of July 6, the Pinkertons mutinied, hoisted the white flag, and surrendered. What followed was the most widely reported part of the strike. Although the workers had assured them of their safety, and received in return the sheriff's promise that the Pinkertons would be arrested and tried, neither promise held. The Pinkertons ran a gauntlet of workers, their wives, and children, who beat the disarmed guards bloody and screamed for their deaths. None died, but only an armed guard of union men saved the lives of some of them. The press, following the tropes of the time, relished, sensationalized, and condemned the "savagery" and "barbarity" of the crowd, whom they also likened to a pack of wolves. Once transported to Pittsburgh, the Pinkertons were freed.[32]

The surrender of the Pinkertons on July 6 proved a costly victory for the workers. On July 10, Governor Pattison ordered eighty-five hundred militia to Homestead, and they took possession of the mill on July 12. Gen. George R. Snowden, who commanded them, considered the workers communists and his task to be suppressing them and breaking the strike. Scabs began to arrive on July 13, and although union men persuaded them to leave, more—black and white—followed. The arrival of black strikebreakers set off violent racial conflicts inside the mills between black and white strikebreakers and later, in November, produced a riot as whites attacked the homes of black workers. The mills resumed steel production with nonunion workers.[33]

The strike continued against ever-lengthening odds. The mainstream press trumpeted the rights of property and Carnegie's right to employ whomever he chose in his mills. Pulitzer's World initially came out in support of the strikers, attacking Carnegie and the tariff, but Pulitzer was, like Carnegie, traveling in Europe, and when he learned of his editor's stance in his absence, he was furious. "Workers," he said, "must submit to the law. They must not resist the authority of the State. They must not make war upon the community." The days of the World as a reform paper and Pulitzer as a reformer were fading fast. But Pulitzer did not much differ from some of the advocates of the Social Gospel, who, like Washington Gladden, condemned the Homestead strikers.[34]

31. Nasaw, 392–93; Krause, 22, 24–33.
32. Krause, 13–14, 35–38, 322–26; Nasaw, 422–23.
33. Montgomery, 38–41.
34. Jacob Henry Dorn, Washington Gladden, Prophet of the Social Gospel (Columbus: Ohio State University Press, 1967), 222; Krause, 33–41, 319; James McGrath Morris, Pulitzer: A Life in Politics, Print, and Power (New York: Harper, 2010), 296–98.

The workers' position was most fully presented in an "Address to the Public" by the strike's Advisory Committee: " 'the right of employers to manage their business to suit themselves,' is causing to mean [sic] in effect nothing less than the right to manage the country to suit themselves." The workers, they contended, had devoted years of their lives and labor to the mill in the expectation of continued employment. Their rights in it were as strong as Carnegie's, and they wanted from Congress and the legislature a "distinct assertion of the principle that the public has an interest in concerns such as Homestead." They were not demanding something revolutionary, but instead the control of work and the workplace embedded in an existing code of mutualism. They found what they considered to be their rights denounced as "imaginary" and their efforts to secure them as revolution and insurrection. The public interest in steel production and the passage of laws to aid it had often been heard in Congress in tariff debates, but the public's interest in getting a living wage and reasonable hours in return was heard far more rarely.[35]

The state of Pennsylvania indicted strike leaders and some strikers for murder, riot, and conspiracy. It was an overreach; most juries would not convict, but the trials drained the union coffers and put workers on the defensive. The anarchists, who rarely missed an opportunity to make a bad situation worse, garnered public sympathy for Frick by trying to assassinate him. In the summer of 1892, Andrew Berkman and Emma Goldman were operating an ice cream parlor in Worcester, Massachusetts. They were hoping to use the profits to return to Russia to join the anarchist movement there, which was their "long-cherished dream." Homestead diverted them. The international class struggle, they decided, had come to the United States. Berkman, whom the press described as a "Russian Hebrew Nihilist," shot and stabbed Henry Clay Frick, but failed to kill him. Although wounded, Frick helped subdue Berkman, had the bullets extracted in his office without anesthetic, and finished his work before departing in an ambulance.[36]

Frick implied the assassination attempt was the work of the AAISW, which it was not, but few in Homestead regretted the shooting. The burgess of Homestead said that Frick had "sent a lot of thugs and cut-throats into the peaceful village of Homestead...and they murdered my friends and fellow citizens." When news reached Homestead of the attack on Frick, a state militiaman, W. L. Iams, shouted out his approval. His commander

---

35. Montgomery, 38–39; Krause, 347–55.
36. Roy Rosenzweig, *Eight Hours for What We Will: Workers and Leisure in an Industrial City, 1870–1920* (Cambridge: Cambridge University Press, 1983), 9; Krause, 4, 271, 296, 329, 331, 345, 349, 354–55; Nasaw, 436–37.

had him hanged by his thumbs until he passed out, but he refused to recant. He was accused of treason and drummed out of the encampment. Frick showed no more remorse for what had happened at Homestead than the workers showed for what had happened to him. He urged the state of Pennsylvania to try the strike leaders for treason.[37]

The union held out through the summer and into the fall, far longer than Frick and Carnegie expected. The two thousand new workers could not bring the mills close to full production, and Homestead hemorrhaged money. But Frick believed that the wage cuts would allow the company to make it back. By October the troops were gone from Homestead, but only in mid-November did the union vote to call off the strike. The men would return under company terms, which meant their unions were dead. The company hired spies in the plant and town to root out any attempt to organize, and fired those involved. On receiving the news that the strike was over, Carnegie, who was traveling in Italy, cabled: "First happy morning since July. Congratulations all around."[38]

Carnegie could not so easily escape Homestead. The European papers had been full of news of the strike, and the American papers detailed the suffering in Homestead as winter came on. "The mass of Public Sentiment," Carnegie admitted, "is not with us about Homestead on the direct issue of the adjustment of the [wage] scale." By 1893 Carnegie had decided that silence was the best policy; he and Frick refused to talk about Homestead and threatened to fire any worker who talked to the press.[39]

The reformist press, evolving into its muckraking phase, proved persistent. Hamlin Garland visited Homestead, "infamously historic already" in 1894, and sneaked into the plant. He described a "squalid and unlovely town" of unkempt buildings in a sea of yellow mud. Its people were brutalized and demoralized, "American only in the sense in which they represent the American idea of business." Inside the factory, where machines screamed and thundered and molten metal glowed in "pits like the mouth of hell," the smell was terrible, and the heat was worse. For the workers it was "a dog's life. Now those men work twelve hours, and sleep and eat out ten more. You can see a man don't have much time for anything else." The work "brutalizes a man. You can't help it...you become more and more a machine, and pleasures are few and far between." The twelve-hour day only worsened the strain. For this work, a furnace man got $2.25 for a twelve-hour shift and unskilled labor $1.40. Most workers got less than

37. Krause, 354–57.
38. Nasaw, 455–56, 465.
39. Nasaw, 458–59, 465.

$2.00, and wages were dropping. There were no old men. If death or injury did not claim them, they quit before fifty.[40]

Escaping injury was a matter of attentiveness and luck, but on a twelve-hour day in a loud and hot mill, attentiveness waned with the hours. Workers needed luck, and new workers needed it most of all. As wages sank, more and more of Carnegie's workers were southern and eastern Europeans. Between 1907 and 1910, 25 percent of the recent immigrants employed in Carnegie's South Works—3,723 in all—were killed or seriously injured. The company eliminated breaks in the workday that the unions had once secured; it apportioned work and set work rules as it saw fit. The death rate from accidents in Pittsburgh's iron and steel mills nearly doubled between 1870 and 1900. The system was disastrous for workers, who became the equivalent of cannon fodder, but for Carnegie the profits were, in his words, "prodigious."[41]

II

Frick suppressed the strike at Homestead, while Carnegie pursued philanthropy. In 1889 Carnegie published "Wealth" in the *North American Review*. It would become more famous under its British title "The Gospel of Wealth." He advocated the dispersal of great fortunes, including his own, for the public benefit. It is hard to imagine as slight a piece of work as "The Gospel of Wealth," written by anyone else at any other time in American history, achieving significant influence. It repeated liberal homilies at a time when they were going out of fashion and brushed aside any objections to the way the world worked with appeals to immutable laws. Carnegie's wealth and career gave the essay its authority, and his essay justified his career. He was a man who, in his beginnings and his wise choice of patrons, could have been an Alger hero. But he knew that if examined closely his career of insider dealing, private benefit from public policy, and capitalizing on the inventions of others did not justify itself; the "Gospel of Wealth" legitimated his life work by promising that he would give his fortune away before he died, and by urging others to follow his example.

---

40. Nasaw, 461; Hamlin Garland, "Homestead and Its Perilous Trades: Impressions of a Visit," *McClure's Magazine* 3 (June 1894): 3–20.
41. Montgomery, 40–41; Herbert Gutman, "Work, Culture, and Society in Industrializing America, 1815–1919," in *Work, Culture & Society in Industrializing America* (New York: Vintage Books, 1977, orig. ed. 1966), 30; Kleinberg, 28–33. These are years for which we have statistics; there is no reason to suspect conditions were better earlier.

In disposing of his wealth, Carnegie also sought to justify the existing social order. He acknowledged that he lived in a time of growing class conflict, when great fortunes like his own were coming under attack as the plunder of a privileged few. Antimonopolists argued that these fortunes depended less on ability than on influence, pull, inside information, and the favors of powerful political and social friends unavailable to citizens at large. Procuring such wealth reduced ordinary people to conditions of dependence and made life worse for the vast majority of Americans. Carnegie had two tasks. First, he had to justify these fortunes as the deserved rewards of those who ranked among Spencer's fit, and second, he had to show that they benefited society at large by providing a road to improvement and independence.

"The problem of our age," Carnegie began, "is the proper administration of wealth." What followed were a series of clichés about the rise of humans from savagery, the rising scale and competitiveness of modern society, and how wealth ensured the "progress of the race." The prime examples that he chose for this progress, however, were not those of productive forces but rather of consumption: it was better that "the houses of some should be homes for all that is highest and best in literature and arts, and for all the refinements of civilization, rather than none that be so." He did not pause to explain or justify any of this because the change, "for good or ill," had come and it was beyond the power of anyone to alter it.[42]

The great danger modern society presented was the rise of classes— "Rigid Castes"—whose hostility sprang not from real wrongs or clashing interests but from "mutual ignorance" and the necessities of the "law of competition," which forced employers to drive down wages. Competition imposed a great price, but it also brought "our wonderful material benefits" and "cheap comforts and luxuries." Many of Carnegie's contemporaries, from John D. Rockefeller to the Knights of Labor, argued that competition was the problem; Carnegie, pursuing his "say what you will" style of argument, did not try to refute them. He simply stated that the law of competition could not be evaded. He was hardly alone in recognizing that the combination of intense competition and deflation cut into profits and led employers to replace men with machines and to pay the lowest rates possible; although it "may sometimes [be] hard for the individual, it is best for the race, because it ensures the survival of the fittest in every department."[43]

42. Andrew Carnegie, "Wealth," *North American Review* 148, no. 391 (1889): 653–57.
43. James Livingston, *Origins of the Federal Reserve System: Money, Class, and Corporate Capitalism, 1890–1913* (Ithaca, NY: Cornell University Press, 1986), 35–40, 59–61; Carnegie, 653–57.

Everything that antimonopolists criticized—"great inequality of environment, the concentration of business, industrial and commercial, in the hands of a few, and the law of competition between these"—Carnegie praised as "essential for the future progress of the race." It was the rare talent for "organization and management" that brought men to the top, and according to yet another unwritten law "as certain as any of the others," such men must soon acquire more wealth than they could spend upon themselves. This law was "as beneficial for the race as the others." To attack the present conditions of things, as socialists and anarchists did, was to attack "the foundation upon which civilization itself rests," which was the "sacredness of property." Over any foreseeable future, Carnegie thought, it was impossible to change human nature. "Individualism, Private Property, the Law of Accumulation of Wealth, and the Law of Competition" were "the highest results of human experience, the soil in which society has produced the best fruit." The results might be unequal and unjust, but they were still "the best and most valuable of all that humanity has yet accomplished."[44]

Carnegie distinguished great fortunes from the older idea of a competence, the moderate sums that took many years to acquire and were "required for the comfortable maintenance and education of families." The question was what to do with these fortunes. Carnegie examined and rejected the two usual modes: leaving it to a person's descendants, or leaving it to trustees who would dedicate it to public purposes. Leaving anything beyond a moderate income to heirs worked for neither their benefit nor that of society. And if wealth was to be given to the community, why wait until death, particularly when the possessor—by virtue of his "superior wisdom, experience, and ability to administer"—could act as "trustee for his poorer brethren"? The proper use of the great fortunes was "the reconciliation of the rich and poor." The rich were those who would judge what was best for the poor. To encourage the disbursement of great fortunes, Carnegie praised heavy taxes on the estates of the deceased—"death duties."[45]

Unlike Howells, who admired Tolstoy, Carnegie advocated a more flexible moral standard. He proposed not an imitation of Christ, as he said Tolstoy tried, but a new method that recognized "the changed conditions under which we live." This was the new gospel, the Gospel of Wealth that threw out the old beatitudes and denigrated charity. In effect, it imagined a Christ fit for the Gilded Age, a tycoon, amassing a fortune and dispersing it all, but only to the worthy poor, "those who desire to improve."[46]

44. Carnegie, 653–57.
45. Ibid.
46. Ibid., 657–64.

What was most interesting in this was less Carnegie's attempt to make Christ an acolyte of Herbert Spencer and to make Christianity a version of an already antique liberalism, but rather his reticence, compared with men like Rockefeller and Charles Francis Adams, to acknowledge publicly how fortunes were acquired. Carnegie knew his own fortune owed much to the tariff, which he assiduously labored to keep high; but he wrote as if tariffs, subsidies, and insider dealing were the fruits of evolution. His praise of Senator Leland Stanford, who founded Stanford University, as an example of how to disperse a fortune, ignored both how the fortune originated—like Carnegie's, in public subsidies—and that the federal government was preparing to sue to retrieve the unpaid loans, which threatened to close the new university. It also presumed that Stanford's wealth attested to his competence, to which few who knew Stanford would swear.[47]

How the "Gospel of Wealth" worked out for steel workers became clear in Braddock, the site of Carnegie's Edgar Thomson works, where Carnegie had broken the union in 1888. The next year Carnegie gave Braddock a library. At the dedication he addressed the citizens as "fellow workmen," assured them that "the interests of Capital and Labor are one," and claimed that his workers now made more under his new contract. Technically they did, since they now had to work twelve-hour days instead of eight hours.[48]

Carnegie imposed work rules that deprived his employees of virtually all their leisure; then he built a library and lectured them on how to spend time they did not have. He owned their days, but declared the meager time they had left between work and sleep or their bursts of unemployment to be "the key to...progress in all the virtues." Mill officers dominated the library board, and the professional staff agreed that "the library has the right to control the character of the reading, it has a right to direct the reader to the desired information." Workers predictably scorned Carnegie, and when he built a library at Homestead, they despised his library too. As one said, "Conditions at the mill, overtime work, and the fact that the men are not readers" meant they did not use the library when it established extensions in the mills. Union glassblowers mocked Carnegie's claim that the library was "Free to the People." Taxes had to sustain what workers regarded as Carnegie's monument to himself. It, like

47. Richard White, *Railroaded: The Transcontinentals and the Making of Modern America* (New York: Norton, 2011), 80, 350–51, 378–79, 404; Charles Francis Adams, *An Autobiography, 1835–1915, with a Memorial Address Delivered November 17, 1915, by Henry Cabot Lodge* (Boston: Houghton Mifflin, 1916), 190.
48. Krause, 231–33.

the Pinkertons, was "a challenge to the manhood of free American laborers."[49]

III

Carnegie and his workers were fighting a battle over the control of production that they all could understand. It was an important battle, one that in the midst of a brutally competitive economy they all feared losing. The Knights of Labor had as their announced goal in the 1880s the overthrow of the wage system. They were very much descendants of an older republicanism that appealed to independent manhood, citizenship, and the worker as producer, but producerist ideas seemed to lead at best to steady rearguard actions in defense of often arcane work rules and, at worst defeat. The Knights had failed to solve the conundrum that the old reformer Lyman Abbott had outlined in 1879: "politically America is a democracy; industrially America is an aristocracy." The worker might make political laws, but "he is under industrial laws. At the ballot box he is a king; in the factory he is a servant, sometimes a slave." This was the core of what was known as the labor question: how to reconcile the democratic promise of the nation with the profoundly undemocratic organization of industry. What always haunted American leftists was the possibility that the achievement of democratic rights before industrialization had vitiated the struggle to attain industrial rights and power. Democracy, later analysts contended, had actually inoculated American capitalism against strong working-class parties, such as arose in Europe and which were devoted to both industrial and political rights.[50]

The lords of the factories, however, sat uneasily on their thrones. Like the liberal intellectuals Edward Atkinson and David Wells, Carnegie and Frick thought that the labor movement was winning and unions' ability to maintain wages and control work endangered a capitalism that they equated

49. Krause, 331; Francis G. Couvares, *The Remaking of Pittsburgh: Class and Culture in an Industrializing City 1877–1919* (Albany: State University of New York Press, 1984), 112, 115–16.

50. Rosanne Currarino, *The Labor Question in America: Economic Democracy in the Gilded Age* (Urbana: University of Illinois Press, 2011), 2–4, 14–16; Mark Hendrickson, *American Labor and Economic Citizenship: New Capitalism from World War I to the Great Depression* (New York: Cambridge University Press, 2013), 16–17; Louis Hartz, *The Liberal Tradition in America: An Interpretation of American Political Thought since the Revolution* (New York: Harcourt, Brace, 1955), 89–94; Karen Orren, *Belated Feudalism: Labor, the Law, and Liberal Development in the United States* (Cambridge: Cambridge University Press, 1991), 110–17.

with progress. But if the labor movement was winning, it did not look that way to workers. Real wages of skilled workers might be rising because of deflation, but many of the skilled jobs were vanishing, being replaced by unskilled and semiskilled work. American workers labored long hours when employed and suffered sporadic layoffs that taxed their resources. Unskilled workers often lived in abject poverty. For many immigrant workers, American industry was better than the conditions they had left; for others it became a motive for returning home. In industry after industry, mechanization hammered at workers' control while employers attacked their unions.

Samuel Gompers and the AFL recognized the gravity of the defeat at Homestead, but Gompers did not fully recognize its causes or implications. He naïvely thought that, had Carnegie been present, there would have been no strike, and he believed centralizing power in the AFL could help prevent further defeats. The dangers, long hours, and lowered pay of Homestead were, however, manifestations of deeper changes. Workers were rapidly losing the ability to set the hours and pace of their work and to determine how tasks were to be done. They had entered a world where fences around factories restricted movements, time clocks monitored hours, and long lists of rules — enforced by fines or dismissal — determined how work was to be performed. In the 1890s, employers began to realize the fruits of their labors to mechanize industry, deskill work, discipline workers, and break unions. Real wages, which rose in the 1880s, stagnated for much of the 1890s. The elite among workers, earning $800 to $1,000 annually, were prosperous, but the bulk of skilled and semiskilled workers had a standard of living later workers would associate with poverty. They had sufficient food but often inferior shelter and little disposable income; they lived in the shadow of unemployment and disaster. The bottom quarter of workers lived in virtual destitution.[51]

Pressed by deflation, falling profit margins, and competition, employers had since the 1870s used machines to replace skilled workers, but like Gompers most Americans were as far from being Luddites as could be imagined. There was no antimachinery campaign as there was in England. Although John Ruskin and William Morris, advocates of a crafts revival in Great Britain, had influence in the United States, it was as advocates of

51. Calculations of real wages were (and remain) a source of controversy in the early twentieth century: Hendrickson, 10; Samuel Gompers, *Seventy Years of Life and Labor: An Autobiography* (Ithaca, NY: ILR Press, 1984, orig. ed. 1925), 105–6; Robert J. Gordon, *The Rise and Fall of American Growth: The U.S. Standard of Living since the Civil War* (Princeton, NJ: Princeton University Press, 2016), 278–79, 281; Daniel T. Rodgers, *The Work Ethic in Industrial America: 1850–1920*, 2nd ed. (Chicago: University of Chicago Press, 2014), 27–29.

an Arts and Crafts movement stripped of the political content that it had in Europe. In the United States, Arts and Crafts as it developed in the 1890s was Tiffany lamps and windows and Craftsman houses. The reactionary aspects of the movement became part of a middle-class and elite reaction against modernism, and not a working-class revolt.[52]

Workers did oppose a more insidious turn: engineers began to engineer workers themselves. Frederick Taylor would gain his greatest fame in the twentieth century, but he began his career in the 1880s. Taylor's advanced education was spotty. He was accepted by but never attended Harvard; he received an engineering degree from Stevens Institute of Technology but neither attended classes nor paid tuition. He rose through family connections. At Midvale Steel he began as a laborer and foreman, worked hard, learned quickly, rose rapidly, and entered wholeheartedly into the battle over control of work on the shop floor.[53]

Taylor regarded the "Midvale fight" as the beginning of scientific management and made it a center of his talks after he became famous. He dramatized a common struggle of the time: the demand of employers for greater output and the insistence of workers for control over work. At Midvale, however, the struggle did not take place between organized labor (his machinists were unorganized) and a business owner or entrepreneur. Taylor had joined an influential new organization, the American Society of Mechanical Engineers. He was only a foreman, but he decided to take control of a shop that was, as he later recalled, "really run by the workmen, and not the bosses."[54]

When Taylor fired or demoted the recalcitrant and rewarded new employees whom he hired, workers resorted to "soldiering," working at a slower pace over at least portions of a long day. When necessary, they engaged in sabotage. The fight continued over three years, between 1878 and 1880. Instituting a speed-up and a fine system that made workers pay for broken tools, Taylor triumphed by securing what he called "a fair day's work" through a "scientific" piecework system. His account elevated a quotidian struggle into a symbolic incident. His more famous innovations of time motion studies and careful tracking of output came later during the 1880s. Calculating the optimal output formed part of a new bureaucratization of work that accelerated the growth of white-collar professions.

52. T. J. Jackson Lears, *No Place of Grace: Antimodernism and the Transformation of American Culture, 1880–1920* (New York: Pantheon Books, 1981), 60–65; Rodgers, 66–81.

53. Montgomery, 178–79; Rodgers, 53–57; Daniel Nelson, *Frederick W. Taylor and the Rise of Scientific Management* (Madison: University of Wisconsin Press, 1980), 24, 26, 29–46.

54. Nelson, 33–35; Montgomery, 178–91.

Determining output demanded accountants, managers, and clerks. In the 1890s, Taylor took it a step further. He not only calculated maximum output; he determined exactly how workers should perform the tasks at hand. He recognized that his early success came from his being unlike other foremen. He had social connections with the owners, and did not live among his workers and was immune from harassment, ostracism, and threats that he would have faced in a working-class neighborhood.[55]

Much of Taylor's system remained guesswork posing as calculation, but he presented it as science, and as a self-publicist Taylor rivaled Buffalo Bill, Thomas Edison, and Andrew Carnegie. In a well-run factory every man had "to become one of a train of gear wheels." He wanted "to take all the important decisions... out of the hands of the workmen," but he insisted that his system was the first to recognize their true individuality, which now consisted simply and solely of fixing individual rewards to individual output. Taylor valued kindness to workers and respect for their skills, but in a mark of how much free labor had changed, obedience and efficiency became the marks of the individual. Workers were not to think; they were not to alter one iota of what they were told to do.[56]

Everywhere workers looked in the 1890s, what they regarded as their rights and manhood seemed under challenge. They were watched, counted, and tracked. A different Pinkerton, William Pinkerton, a Western railroad worker and union man, bitterly assailed the keeping of personal records on workers. An employment form was a hive of dangers. The worker's name? It allowed employers to check union affiliation and strike activity. Previous employment? It was a way to see if he had been blacklisted or had work infractions. His age? Most railroads refused to hire anyone over thirty-eight for skilled positions outside of laborer. A skilled workman who left or lost a job after thirty-eight would most likely sink back into the ranks of unskilled laborers. His health or injuries? Another reason not to hire him. All deprived him of the ability to support home and family.[57]

Carnegie mounted a two-pronged attack on workers. Homestead represented an ongoing battle over control of production; the "Gospel of Wealth" represented an attempt to regulate their consumption and leisure. Carnegie, in effect, doubly countered the movement for the eight-hour day—"eight hours, for work, eight hours for sleep, eight hours for what you will"—by first extending the hours of work and then by trying to

55. Rodgers, 53–57; Montgomery, 189–90; Nelson, 33–35, 38–46, 123.
56. Nelson, 38–46; Rodgers, 53–57.
57. William Pinkerton, *His Personal Record: Stories of Railroad Life* (Kansas City, MO: Pinkerton Publishing, 1904), 60–61, 268.

substitute guided uplift, encapsulated in his libraries, for the inappropriate leisure of the worker's "what you will." In his attempt to shape working-class leisure and consumption, Carnegie had allies among evangelical reformers.

A sharp distinction between leisure and consumption was relatively new. It arose with the separation of home and male work, the changing nature of work, the American sanctification of the home and its domestic space, and the rise of temperance in particular and evangelical reform in general. In the workshops of antebellum America, work went on amidst gambling, socializing, singing, storytelling, debating, and drinking. Men wandered in and out of the workplace. As employers, particularly in the new factories of the Gilded Age, took greater control of work, they, as buyers of their workers' time, succeeded in banning drinking and limiting socializing.[58]

Male social life and drinking gravitated to a new, largely working-class institution, the saloon. By the 1890s Carnegie's twelve-hour day was unusual. In Massachusetts the usual workday had shrunk to ten hours. The gradual decline of the working day and the limited space available to workers in their tenements and small houses, which left workers no room to entertain or meet friends at home, made the saloon a preferred site for male camaraderie. And in an age of brutal work, which took its toll on muscles and joints, workers ached at the end of the day. They drank. The efforts of temperance workers to reduce drinking actually drove working-men into the saloon. As the temperance movement obtained stricter license requirements, regulations forced the smaller liquor dealers out of business. Particularly among the Irish, women, often widows, sold liquor from their kitchens. They could not meet the new licensing requirements, but larger saloons could. Saloons existed as a reverse image of most factories: all-male spaces but largely devoted to leisure rather than work. The division was not clean. Many saloons attracted patrons from specific trades, and workers used them to seek employment.[59]

By the end of the century, the saloon had emerged as the bête noire of the evangelical middle classes. There was no denying the social problems that came from drink. Reformers denounced it as the site of vicious habits as men gambled and drank, spending money they should have saved or devoted to their families. Saloons were notoriously associated with political machines and bosses. In the eyes of both the evangelical middle class and Protestant nativists, the saloon and all its vices were the domain of the

58. Rosenzweig, 35.
59. Ibid., 36–46, 53, 55–57; Elliott West, *The Saloon on the Rocky Mountain Mining Frontier* (Lincoln: University of Nebraska Press, 1979), 73–96.

immigrant working classes, at once signs and causes of their inferiority. A nativist rhyme in Worcester, Massachusetts, captured the idea:

> The Irish and the Dutch, they don't amount to much.
> For the Micks have their whiskey and the Germans guzzle the beer.
> And all we Americans wish they had never come here.[60]

Such sentiments reflected more than prejudice. Reformers recognized that the saloon—with its male camaraderie, collective public life of treating, gambling, singing, and billiards—stood in opposition to the virtues of liberal individualism, thrift, self-denial, and the private and domestic values of the home. In the 1890s the temperance movement fell into disarray, weakened by the failure of prohibition in Iowa. It gained a new focus with the rise of the Anti-Saloon League, first in Ohio in 1893 and then nationally in 1895. It concentrated its attack on the saloon, but its goal was national prohibition.[61]

The most basic thing about the saloon remained its function as a commercial establishment devoted to selling liquor. Whiskey and beer were consumer goods, even if luxuries, more like food and clothing than the steel produced in Carnegie's mills. Drink, food, tobacco, and clothing had formed the basics of the consumer economy since the beginning of the century. Cheap cotton clothing had set industrial capitalism in motion and remained important even as capital goods dominated the economy. The great meat packinghouses, central to Chicago's economy, produced food for mass consumption, as did the flour pouring from Minneapolis mills. The American tobacco company pioneered mechanized production.[62]

The new department stores indicated a wider impending shift from producer to consumer goods, but the change came gradually. Marshall Field, while maintaining a thriving wholesale business, opened his flagship retail store on State Street in Chicago in 1893. Aaron Ward launched Montgomery Ward as a wholesale mail-order business aimed at Grange members and cutting out the middlemen. His business model depended on railroads and the post office, and he dominated the business until the 1890s, when Richard Sears founded his eponymous company.[63]

60. Rosenzweig, 49–50.
61. Ibid., 60–62; K. Austin Kerr, "Organizing for Reform: The Anti-Saloon League and Innovation in Politics," *American Quarterly* 32, no. 1 (1980): 37–53.
62. Alfred D. Chandler, *The Visible Hand: The Managerial Revolution in American Business* (Cambridge, MA: Belknap Press, 1977); Gordon, 37–43; Sven Beckert, *Empire of Cotton: A Global History* (New York: Knopf, 2014), 74–82.
63. William Cronon, *Nature's Metropolis: Chicago and the Great West* (New York: Norton, 1991), 310–40; Gordon, 90–91; Gavin Wright, "The Origins of American Industrial Success, 1879–1940," *American Economic Review* 80, no. 4 (1990): 335–40.

Most Americans still could not consume much because they did not earn much. In 1870 they spent virtually all they earned on food, clothing, and shelter. According to statistics from Massachusetts, the average person spent about $3.80 per week, or $197 a year; in 2010 dollars this was equivalent to $54 per week, with more than 50 percent going to perishable goods, largely food, and 25 percent going to rent. This basic pattern did not change much over the course of the century, but consumption gradually shifted as families moved from purchasing dry goods and producing clothes at home to purchasing ready-made clothing. The purchase of goods outside of this triad came largely among the middle classes: people who could afford to purchase homes, which cost from $3,000 to $10,000, furnish them, and employ servants. Successful farmers, skilled workers, and foremen, who formed the so-called labor aristocracy, consumed at a lower level.[64]

Consumer goods that would shape the twentieth century became available in the nineteenth, but they did not reach mass markets. Like Edison's light bulb, many new inventions got off to a halting start. Ingenuity and novelty rather than immediate utility characterized many new consumer products. Alexander Graham Bell, who had failed to locate the bullet in President Garfield, was a Canadian immigrant who came to Boston as a teacher of the deaf. His attempts to understand acoustics led to experiments that yielded the telephone. He introduced it at the Centennial Exposition of 1876 to a resounding journalistic silence. William Dean Howells never mentioned it in his account of the exposition.[65]

In the 1880s the telephone occupied a narrow and exclusive niche, despite its ability to create new experiences and possibilities in the world. Mark Twain wrote a piece for Howells's *Atlantic Monthly* in 1880 whose humor played on a situation where he could hear only one part of a telephone conversation between his wife and a friend. People had eavesdropped since the first conversation, but they had always been able to hear both parties. Now, unless they listened in on a party line, they could hear only one. A dialogue became a comically fractured monologue.[66]

Twain's wife had made a personal call, and that was unusual, because few Americans used the telephone, and those who did were usually businessmen, physicians, and servants in large cities placing orders. Companies discouraged subscribers from making frequent calls, which had to be

64. Gordon, 36–37, 43–44, 63, 86–92.
65. Richard R. John, *Network Nation: Inventing American Telecommunications* (Cambridge, MA: Belknap Press of Harvard University Press, 2010), 163–64, 200.
66. Ibid.; Mark Twain, "A Telephonic Conversation," *Atlantic Monthly* 45, no. 272 (1880): 841–43.

patched together by operators on lines with limited capacity. The system earned a profit because even though volume was low, charges were high. In 1881 William Forbes was in the midst of creating American Bell. It did not provide telephone service but instead was a holding company that controlled patents and licensed operating companies and manufacturers. American Telephone and Telegraph was its wholly owned subsidiary. American Bell won the battle over patents, which continued into the 1890s, creating a monopoly and profit.[67]

The telephone remained far less important than the telegraph for conveying information, but it played a critical role in stimulating other inventions. It spurred Edison to try to improve the phonograph. In an 1878 article in the *North American Review* he made extravagant claims for that machine; the possibilities were in his words "so illimitable and the probabilities...so numerous" that they were impossible to fully describe. In the twentieth century, it would become ubiquitous as a means of consuming music, but he conceived of it as a way for users to *produce* sound, not consume it. It would "perfect the telephone" and revolutionize telegraphy by allowing callers to create a transcript of conversations. It would render the ephemeral—human speech—permanent and confidential, allowing businesspeople to maintain privacy and dispense not only with telegraph operators, who leaked messages, but also with clerks and stenographers.[68]

The phonograph did none of these things. Edison did little with the machine for ten years, allowing Alexander Graham Bell to design a superior prototype. When after ten years new patents destroyed Edison's monopoly, he tried to develop it as a kind of dictaphone, but he could not create a stable design. Eventually, he licensed his patents to a new company that combined them with the Bell patents, and the licensees finally achieved success by creating phonographs that sold captured sound rather than recording it.[69]

Edison's misjudgment about the phonograph proved characteristic. He often failed to predict the practical results of his early inventions, but he excelled at turning the inventions into tools of self-promotion. This was both calculated and reflective of the man himself. In his early years he ran his laboratory for intellectual enjoyment and to satisfy his curiosity. He

67. John, 219–20, 227–30.
68. Ibid., 219–20; Thomas A. Edison, "The Phonograph and Its Future," *North American Review* 126, no. 262 (1878): 527–36.
69. A. J. Millard, *Edison and the Business of Innovation* (Baltimore, MD: Johns Hopkins University Press, 1990), 63–87; Steven W. Usselman, "From Novelty to Utility: George Westinghouse and the Business of Innovation During the Age of Edison," *Business History Review* 66, no. 2 (1992): 261–63.

initially cared more about accumulating patents than money. For all of his fame, his most famous early inventions — except for his improvements on the telegraph — seemed little more than exotic toys for the emerging urban bourgeoisie.[70]

Consumption became more political as well as economic. Because workers consumed locally, sites of working-class consumption were vulnerable to organized action. Bakeries (a huge proportion of working people's diets was bread in one form or another), saloons, cheap theaters, the penny press, and other businesses catering to working-class clientele were vulnerable to boycotts.[71]

The boycott was an old American practice. American revolutionaries boycotted British tea, white Southerners boycotted carpetbaggers during Reconstruction, and the Knights of Labor and its allies boycotted businesses employing Chinese in the West. By the Great Upheaval of the 1880s, the practice had traveled to Ireland, acquired new connotations, and returned with an Irish name. The literally thousands of boycotts of businesses in the 1880s had become public ostracism, which created an imagined community of consumers who exercised power through their collective consumption. In a world of widening markets and the mass circulation of newspapers and magazines, it could spread beyond a single target to take in those who patronized or supplied the boycotted business. Advocates praised it as democratized consumption. *Harper's Weekly* attacked it as an un-American conspiracy against freedom and a form of "terrorism," but opponents had a difficult time explaining how boycotts could be un-American when the American Revolution had begun with boycotts.[72]

The courts hit boycotts hard in the 1880s, jailing their organizers for conspiracy, but in the early 1890s the practice infiltrated the consumers' unions and consumers' leagues that had arrived from across the Atlantic. It became the domain of women, who were claiming consumption as their own and using organized consumption to shape society. The National

70. For Edison's methods, Thomas Parke Hughes, *Networks of Power: Electrification in Western Society, 1880–1930* (Baltimore, MD: Johns Hopkins University Press, 1983), 26–28; Usselman, 256–57.

71. Katherine Leonard Turner, *How the Other Half Ate: A History of Working Class Meals at the Turn of the Century* (Berkeley: University of California Press, 2014), 3, 60–70.

72. Lawrence B. Glickman, *Buying Power: A History of Consumer Activism in America* (Chicago: University of Chicago Press, 2009), 115–51. Charles Boycott was the agent of an English landlord who found himself cut off from all social intercourse by the tenants on his estate and by most merchants and residents in the surrounding countryside. Those who violated Boycott's ostracism were threatened with violence and isolation of their own. The practice took on the name *boycott*.

Consumer League would not emerge until the end of the 1890s, but its leading figures, such as Florence Kelley, had already become convinced that consumption was a public act, not private.[73]

Consumption also became more subtly political as new consumer products arose to exploit changing popular tastes. These products also depended on the new infrastructure that the American mix of public law, public services, and private production created. Coca-Cola exemplified how all these factors played into the rise of what became an iconic American consumer product.

A rough history of American consumption can be seen through the evolution of the word *coke*. Until the early twentieth century, when Americans heard "coke" they thought of the fuel, distilled from coal and essential to steel making, that earned Henry Frick his first fortune. But coke became slang for a soft drink, Coca-Cola, which emerged in Atlanta in 1886. Like Pillsbury Flour and Quaker Flour, two brand names created earlier, and mass retailers like Sears and Roebuck and Montgomery Ward, which were expanding in the 1890s, Coke depended on the new late-nineteenth-century infrastructure that companies such as Carnegie Steel helped create, on the national markets that railroads moving on steel rails enabled, and on mass advertising and brand names made possible by the penny press, the post office, and the telegraph.[74]

Coca-Cola began as something old—a patent medicine—and became something new. In the days before strict licensing requirements, drug stores often also sold liquor, and many patent medicines were, for all practical purposes, alcoholic drinks laced with other ingredients. Coca-Cola originated in that world of disreputable consumption.

John Stith Pemberton had not intended to create a new product when he developed Coca-Cola; he was trying to steal an existing one. Shot and slashed during the Confederate defense of Columbus, Georgia, a few days after Lee's surrender, Pemberton suffered painful stomach problems for the remainder of his life. He took morphine and became an addict, as well as a pharmacist and a concoctor of patent medicines. His businesses rose and fell with the larger economy, until this casualty of the Old South invented the most famous product of the New South.[75]

In the 1880s, as Carnegie consolidated his control over steel, Pemberton was seeking something that could make him money; he decided to copy

73. Ibid., 155–62, 178–80.
74. Kathleen G. Donohue, *Freedom from Want: American Liberalism and the Idea of the Consumer* (Baltimore, MD: Johns Hopkins University Press, 2003), 14; Bartow Elmore, *Citizen Coke: The Making of Coca-Cola Capitalism* (New York: Norton, 2015), 18–27.
75. Elmore, 17–20.

rather than invent. He chose to imitate Vin Mariani, a French mixture of Bordeaux wine and cocaine that claimed to cut pain, improve energy, and promote wakefulness, all of which it probably did. Edison, who reputedly rarely slept beyond catnaps, endorsed it. So did Pope Leo XIII and Ulysses S. Grant, who understandably found comfort in a mixture of wine and cocaine as he died of cancer. Pemberton differentiated his drink from the original by adding kola, or cola, nut powder, but the key was the combination of alcohol and cocaine, which worked as well in the South as it had in Europe and the North. Success did not last. The problem wasn't cocaine, but alcohol. Atlanta banned alcohol sales in saloons in 1885, and Pemberton saw the writing on the wall. He changed his formula.[76]

The new formula emphasized sugar (a lot of sugar), caffeine (a lot of caffeine), and only small amounts of cocaine, a drug that would commandeer the name *coke* in popular language later in the twentieth century. Pemberton marketed Coca-Cola as a temperance drink. Making a virtue of necessity since he did not have the wagons, horses, employees, or money to ship the finished product, he condensed it into a syrup; soda fountain operators had only to add carbonated water. A glass of Coke was just five cents. Campbell Soup followed the same formula in condensing soup, cutting costs, and also reaching a mass market in the 1890s.[77]

The business did not take off, however, until Asa Candler bought it. Candler used the rail network, subsidized by government, to distribute the syrup; he relied on soda fountains, and then, unwilling and unable to bottle the product himself, on franchisees who put up the capital and took the risks for bottling Coca-Cola, agreeing to buy the syrup from the parent company. Bottlers were willing to assume the risk because the improvements in municipal water supplies allowed them to get abundant cheap water to mix with their syrup. What Candler invested in was advertising. By 1890 Coca-Cola was available across the South; by 1895 it had spread across the nation. By the early twentieth century it was not only a national brand, but also a model of how to produce a cheap, mass-distributed, consumer product through a franchising system that passed most of the risk on to the franchisees.[78]

The new American infrastructure connected Carnegie and Candler; one provided the steel that built it; the other was dependent on it. Both

76. Elmore, 20–22.
77. Daniel Sidorick, *Condensed Capitalism: Campbell Soup and the Pursuit of Cheap Production in the Twentieth Century* (Ithaca, NY: ILR Press, 2009), 17–18; Elmore, 21–24.
78. Elmore, 24–32.

were trying to shape American leisure and consumption, but here they moved in different directions. Carnegie thought of himself as a guide into the future. In making the wealthy into the arbiters of what the poor should consume, however, "The Gospel of Wealth" fitted poorly with the world of mass consumption symbolized by Coca-Cola. And in applying relentless pressure to lower wages, Carnegie retarded the consumption that Candler depended on.

With his determination to shape working-class consumption as well as production, Carnegie came to symbolize both the power and the arrogance of the wealthy. Whether they bought beer or Coca-Cola, workers did not want either their leisure or their compensation to be determined by men like Carnegie and Frick. As the constitution of the Iron Molders' Union declared, "The welfare of a community depends on the purchasing power of its members."[79]

Samuel Gompers may have been deceived about the good intentions of Carnegie at Homestead, but more than any other labor leader he recognized the wisdom of the Iron Molders, and that labor's struggle was moving from production to consumption. Gompers's parents were Dutch Jews who immigrated to London, where he was born, and then to the United States. An agnostic in religion, he was a fervent believer in trade unionism. In the United States he joined the Order of Foresters and the Odd Fellows, and he read Marx. He embraced Marxian socialism and abandoned it; but he always kept his class consciousness.[80]

To harness consumption for the labor movement, Gompers had to rescue it from its critics, both inside and outside the labor movement. They embraced thrift and self-denial and regarded working-class consumption as wasteful, profligate, irresponsible, and immoral. They blamed poverty on drink, diversions, and bad values rather than low wages.

Josiah Strong veered from his concerns about the rich and misdistribution of wealth to anxiety over workers, as luxuries were "cheapened and brought within the reach of an ever-widening circle." Americans were softening, growing languid and "tropical." Strong typified a kind of moral panic about working-class consumption. Critics grew alarmed at cheap amusements such as those emerging after 1895 at Coney Island, whose nickel fares attracted the immigrant working class. Young unmarried men and women formed the majority of those seeking "evening pleasures," commercial entertainments such as the amusement parks, theaters, dancehalls,

79. Currarino, 93.
80. Michael Kazin, *American Dreamers: How the Left Changed a Nation* (New York: Knopf, 2011), 94–97; Harold C. Livesay, *Samuel Gompers and Organized Labor in America* (Boston: Little, Brown, 1978), 8–22, 36–37.

and shows that drew audiences of both sexes. They flocked to the circuses and Wild West Shows that drew both middle- and working-class audiences. More time and more money would only lead to depraved tastes and wastes.[81]

Gompers embraced the living wage as a source of uplift as well as prosperity. Higher wages would increase consumption, and that would stimulate the economy. He fought back against those who condemned workers' consumption as the growth of the immoral, the enervating, and the tawdry. Gompers insisted that by creating new wants and demands, higher pay and shorter hours would make workingmen better, not worse. He told an audience in Louisville, Kentucky, in 1890: "A man who works eight hours a day has sixteen hours a day left. He must do something with them.... When his friend visits him he wants to have, probably, a pretty picture on the wall, or perhaps a piano or organ in his parlor; and he wishes everything about him to be bright and attractive." He emphasized the parlor, not the saloon.[82]

Gompers became a walking advertisement for popular consumption. He purposely dressed well, and his own love of music was so intense that he once spent the family savings on a violin that he could not play. He learned. Gompers believed that "liberty can be neither exercised nor enjoyed by those who are in poverty." This became the AFL's controversial doctrine of "more." *More* expanded for Gompers so that by the end of the 1890s it meant "better homes, better surroundings, higher education, higher aspirations, nobler thoughts, more human feelings, all the human instincts that go to make up a manhood that shall be free and independent and loving and noble and true and sympathetic. We want more."[83]

Refocusing American unionism on wages and consumption rather than on control over work represented a philosophical shift as well as a tactical one. For different reasons but in a parallel way to academic economists, Gompers was rejecting central premises of classical laissez-faire economics. "The first economic theory that came under my eyes," Gompers later remembered, "was not calculated to make me think highly of economists. My mind intuitively rejected the iron law of wages, the immutable law of supply and demand, and similar so-called natural laws." The iron law of wages sprang from Ricardo's wage fund theory, which

81. John F. Kasson, *Amusing the Million: Coney Island at the Turn of the Century* (New York: Hill & Wang, 1978), 37–43; Josiah Strong, *Our Country* (Cambridge, MA: Belknap Press of Harvard University Press, 1963), 166–67; Montgomery, 142–43; Donohue, 47–50, 68–70; Estelle Freedman and John D'Emilio, *Intimate Matters: A History of Sexuality in America* (New York: Harper & Row, 1988), 194–95.
82. Currarino, 87–94, quote 93.
83. Donohue, 27–29; Currarino, 87–94.

held that wages came from previously accumulated capital. At any given time, the amount was finite and had to be divided among existing laborers. To raise the wages of some workers necessarily meant decreasing the wages of others. When capital decreased, as it did during a depression, wages necessarily had to fall. As Gompers recognized, coupled with Malthusian theories and rising population this meant wages had to retreat back to near subsistence.[84]

Gompers suspected that the popularity of such views arose more from employers' self-interest than natural laws, and on this he agreed with Francis Amasa Walker. Walker struck the crippling blow against the wage fund theory. The idea that nothing could alter the distribution of income between labor and capital provoked his scorn. He curtly dismissed it as a "most comfortable doctrine surely, and one which made it a positive pleasure to conduct a quarterly review in times when the laboring classes were discontented and mutinous." Walker argued that increasing numbers of workers need not force wages down; more workers meant more production, and potentially higher profits. And better productivity—through either technology or higher worker efficiency—meant even more profits. Employers estimated their profits from their greater production, and this determined wages. Employers might resort to the doctrine to justify lower wages, but it was not how they ran their businesses in practice.[85]

The new economists, a generation younger than Walker, pushed the attack on classical economics and laissez-faire. Led by John Bates Clark, they were embracing marginal utility theory and turning classical economic theory into neoclassicism. Marginalism shifted the emphasis of economic analysis from production to consumption, focusing on how consumers determined the value of a product. Clark retained an atomistic version of choice and society, but Simon Patten, Henry Carter Adams, and Edwin Seligman all disputed individualism. These economists thought consumption was social and believed that changes in patterns of consumption could change society itself. Seligman thought value came not from the direct relationship of humans to things but rather from relationships of humans to each other. Humans noted what other humans did and what other humans desired. In an industrial society, what people

84. Lawrence B. Glickman, *A Living Wage: American Workers and the Making of Consumer Society* (Ithaca, NY: Cornell University Press, 1997), 1–5, 11–15, 18–27, 61–64, 71–77; David Montgomery, *Beyond Equality: Labor and the Radical Republicans, 1862–1872, with a Bibliographical Afterword*, Illini books ed. (Urbana: University of Illinois Press, 1981), 25–30.

85. Nancy Cohen, *The Reconstruction of American Liberalism, 1865–1914* (Chapel Hill: University of North Carolina Press, 2002), 151–53; Glickman, *A Living Wage*, 57; Currarino, 66–67.

wanted and what people consumed was far more complicated than meeting immediate needs.[86]

The new economists moved away from philosophical abstractions such as freedom of contract to what they regarded as testable economic hypotheses. In the words of historian Herbert Hovenkamp, they believed no one could prove that an economic "right" such as "an employer has right to pay any wage he and his employees agree on" actually existed. They argued for efficiency and believed that statements such as "minimum wage laws provide more efficient use of economic resources" were testable, verifiable, and "more plausible than doctrines like liberty of contract."[87]

Some of the new economists became Gompers's equivocal, sometimes unwilling, and usually unreliable allies. Simon Patten, for example, insisted the characteristic of the new industrial economy was abundance and not scarcity, and he advocated a higher standard of living for workers, but not higher wages because that would reduce profits. Patten believed higher profits would create more jobs, whose benefits would trickle down to workers.[88]

Rough intellectual convergence did not translate into political support for labor or antimonopoly. Most academic social scientists held back as labor and vanguard antimonopolists pressed forward in the 1890s, urging on cooperativist and state-based solutions to the long economic and social crisis. The academics, by and large, were not willing to join the assault, but neither were they willing to accept a set of liberal doctrines and social arrangements that they had spent their careers in overthrowing. Instead, they fashioned a new position, which emphasized consumption over production, corporations and large-scale production over competition, and bureaucratic expertise over democratic control. It was a position that some of the older liberals, whom antimonopolists had opposed, could also embrace. It jettisoned laissez-faire, reduced the scope of individualism, and abandoned small government, but it left private property, capitalism, natural rights, and elite rule within a restricted democratic framework intact. Thomas Cooley, Carroll Wright, Andrew White, and other liberals would find common ground with many of the former ethical economists. The compromise would provide part of the intellectual and ideological

86. Jeffrey P. Sklansky, *The Soul's Economy: Market Society and Selfhood in American Thought, 1820–1920* (Chapel Hill: University of North Carolina Press, 2002), 181–88; Currarino, 79–85.
87. Herbert Hovenkamp, *Enterprise and American Law, 1836–1937* (Cambridge, MA: Harvard University Press, 1991), 170–72, 174–76, 192.
88. Donohue, 47–50.

underpinnings of twentieth-century Progressivism and a new liberalism. It would also, eventually, have room for the living wage.[89]

Gompers received indirect philosophical and moral support from other academics. William James defended the virtue and necessity of increased consumption by arguing that a "starvation of objects" blocked healthy growth and development. James compared the "accomplished gentleman with the poor artisan or tradesman of a city." During the adolescence of the gentleman, "objects appropriate to his growing interests, bodily and mental were offered as fast as the interests awoke," equipping him "at every angle to meet the world." But for the poor youth, "no such golden opportunities were hung, and in his manhood no desires for most of them exist.... Perversions are too often the fruit of his unnatural upbringing." More consumption would strangle vice, not feed it.[90]

William James's larger intellectual influence embraced a circle that included practical men like Gompers and academics like Walker and his younger colleagues. James shared with these men an unwillingness to reason deductively from foundational truths, whether received truth from the Bible, from Adam Smith, David Ricardo, Thomas Malthus, or from the natural laws the Spencerians saw as inalterable. But James, John Dewey, and Charles Peirce went further in producing the radically empirical philosophy of pragmatism, which was willing to dispense with truth in the sense of penetrating the inner nature of things, and instead pursue the relations and connections between things. Reality changed with history, and truth was simply the beliefs that at any given time worked, in the sense of having predictable results in the world. Dewey, teaching at the University of Chicago in the 1890s and active in social reform, was already thinking of the human mind more as a "problem-solving tool for adjusting to an unstable environment" than as a "logical faculty for defining truth." He sought not truth but "warranted assertability": propositions that could be observed and verified.[91]

These subtler intellectual shifts were easily lost in the tumult of the times. Their demands for a new intellectual and economic order were sometimes shocking and unfamiliar. Their accounts of how the world

89. Although I do not think that the ethical economists were defeated in the way that she does, this analysis owes much to Nancy Cohen, 11, 14–15, 179, 208, 210, 228–30.
90. Donohue, 47–50; Sklansky, 149–50.
91. John P. Diggins, *The Promise of Pragmatism: Modernism and the Crisis of Knowledge and Authority* (Chicago: University of Chicago Press, 1994), 12–13, 229; James T. Kloppenberg, *Uncertain Victory: Social Democracy and Progressivism in European and American Thought, 1870–1920* (New York: Oxford University Press, 1986), 43–45. For an account of the rise of pragmatism and its influence, see Louis Menand, *The Metaphysical Club: A Story of Ideas in America* (New York: Farrar, Straus & Giroux, 2001).

would change were as yet inchoate and unclear, compared with Carnegie's philanthropic simplicities and appeals to the guiding hand of an evolutionary elite who could be distinguished by their great wealth. But far more than Carnegie, they had tapped a subterranean river that would burst to the surface in the next century.

Part III

The Crisis Arrives

19

The Other Half

In 1888 Jacob A. Riis, a Danish immigrant and a journalist, began giving a lantern slide lecture that he entitled "The Other Half: How It Lives and Dies in New York." He portrayed a world that Samuel Gompers knew well and that Gompers hoped would disappear with the success of his doctrine of "more." The photographs he showed—then taken by others—were a safe form of a slumming, a kind of social voyeurism, to which Riis contributed a running patter of ethnic jokes. His popular entertainment had a serious intent: he wanted to reveal to more comfortable New Yorkers "how the other half lives." In New York the other half were immigrants, largely Catholics and Jews from Eastern and Southern Europe; Riis targeted a Protestant and native-born audience. He desired reforms that would protect and expand the home, which remained by nearly universal consensus the core institution of American society. In revealing how immigration was changing New York, he sought to show Americans how they should deal with social problems.

Riis expanded his lecture into an article in *Scribner's* in 1889 and then into a book, *How the Other Half Lives: Studies Among the Tenements of New York*, published in 1890. All the elements of Riis's book—concern over the tenements, the dangerous classes, the "murder of the home"—were already familiar. They were the kind of topics that had interested the American Social Science Association, and they flourished among Social Gospel reformers and popular journalists. What set Riis apart was his style. He combined human-interest stories, ethnic stereotypes, statistical data, and a blunt investigatory approach that upended the myths and solved the mysteries of the city. He started taking his own photographs, but he never considered himself a photographer.[1]

In his life as well as his writings, Riis captured the ambiguities of the new, urban, industrial America. Like Edison, he had been a tramp working

1. Jacob A. Riis, *How the Other Half Lives* (New York: Hill & Wang, 1957, orig. ed. 1890), 1–2; Bonnie Yochelson and Daniel J. Czitrom, *Rediscovering Jacob Riis: Exposure Journalism and Photography in Turn-of-the-Century New York* (New York: New Press, 2007), xiii–xix, 86–105, 123–26, 132, 146–50, 154–60.

in the shipyards, lumber mills, factories, and icehouses of the Northeast and the Midwest. He had sold books on commission. He had been desperately poor, lonely, and lovesick. He dismissed socialism as "nonsense," embraced self-improvement, opposed unions, and distrusted working-class amusements from the saloon to the theater. He had become a journalist in 1874, about the same time he converted to Methodism. A police reporter on the *New York Tribune* from 1877 until 1890, he supplemented his salary with freelance work published in Denmark; some of it was translated and syndicated in American newspapers. Riis was successful enough to go back to Denmark, marry his longtime sweetheart, and return to New York City.[2]

In reporting on the immigrant poor of New York, Riis covered the sometimes seamy and tragic end of their lives—the 150 bodies pulled annually from the city's rivers, the suicides, and the 10 percent of the city's dead who found their final resting place as paupers in potter's field—and he documented the equally pathetic beginnings of foundlings abandoned on the streets. He portrayed the tenements and their dwellers as the sources rather than the victims of problems: the seedbed of epidemics, the "nurseries of pauperism and crime," the "scum of forty thousand human wrecks to the island asylums and workhouses year by year," "a round half million beggars to prey upon our charities," and "a standing army of ten thousand tramps." He wrote about the armed and the intoxicated. He publicized Chief of Detectives Thomas Byrnes, who, like Riis, was fascinated by photography and used it to create the "Rogues Gallery": sixteen hundred photographs of criminals that, when displayed, became a tourist attraction. The tenements were a cancer, and Riis traced their spread through the city, touching "family life with deadly moral contagion. This is their crime." The lack of privacy made true homes impossible.[3]

Riis treated social problems as an amalgam of nature and nurture, or, in nineteenth-century terms, "race" and "surroundings." He wrote that it was "the surroundings that make the difference." Housing, sanitation, dress, and food, as well as education and child rearing—the elements of the larger environmental crisis, which he detailed without recognizing— all counted as surroundings. Riis described and pictured them in vivid detail. He led his readers through the debris of a tenement fire, where lay the dead, partially dressed bodies of Jewish immigrants who had jumped to escape the flames, and where a "half-grown girl with a baby in her arms" wandered aimlessly. When a doctor took her arm to lead her

2. Roy Lubove, *The Progressives and the Slums; Tenement House Reform in New York City, 1890–1917* (Westport, CT: Greenwood Press, 1974), 55–58; Yochelson, 1–15, 82–86.
3. Riis, 3; Yochelson and Czitrom, 14–17, 106–9, 116.

This famous 1889 photograph of "Lodgers in Bayard Street Tenement, Five Cents a Spot," used by Jacob Riis in *How the Other Half Lives*, captures the dirt and crowding of immigrant life in New York City. These men paid a nickel each for a place to sleep. Paying by the night was an extreme version of lodgers who often rented quarters from immigrant families. Jacob A. (Jacob August) Riis (1849–1914) / Museum of the City of New York. 90.13.4.158.

away, he found the baby was dead, as were the girl's parents. Her "reason had fled."[4]

Yet nature—not the germs that killed, the water that carried them, or the contaminated food, but rather nature as race—often overwhelmed nurture in Riis. Race determined people's attributes, and those attributes determined the rankings of races. Race was a flexible category—sometimes determined by skin color, sometimes phenotype, sometimes ancestry, and even religion—but once people fell into a racial category, it described the "normal" range of their emotions, intelligence, thriftiness, cleanliness, sexual behaviors, and more. "The one thing you shall vainly ask for," Riis wrote, "in the chief city of America is a distinctly American community," blacks apparently not counting as Americans. Among immigrants,

4. Riis, 84–85; Yochelson and Czitrom, 69–70, 97.

the highest-ranking race was the Germans, but all this meant was that they were the least deficient since immigrants were the sum of their deficiencies. Although Riis recognized the burdens anti-Semitism put on Jews, he still scorned them ("Money is their God"). He similarly recognized the problems that the *padrone* system of contract labor inflicted on Italians, but it only convinced him of their limits ("learn slowly, if at all"). At the bottom, predictably, were the Chinese and the Irish, who for Riis embodied all the social evils of New York: drink, violence, pauperism, begging, corruption, and crime. A person who failed to conform to racial stereotypes did not escape them; he or she reinforced them. This would mean being calm for an Italian, extravagant for a Jew, and sober for an Irishman.[5]

Riis's analysis was at war with itself. With his background in Christian philanthropy, he accepted and embodied the distinction between the deserving and the undeserving poor. His emphasis on surroundings, however, stressed how the conditions in the tenements inevitably ground down their residents. His highlighting of the harm done to children undercut the distinctions between deserving and undeserving. In this he echoed Charles Loring Brace, who as head of the New York Children's Aid Society had been sending children west for resettlement from New York since the 1850s. This often did not end well. How, except among the strictest Calvinists, could small children be responsible for their fate? His solution was "Philanthropy plus 5%," an existing slogan that emphasized a kind of Christian social investment for a profit. It assumed capitalism, which already made the tenements the most lucrative and destructive investment in the city, would cure its own ills. It had already failed to do so in New York; it would soon fail in George Pullman's model town outside Chicago. But more than that, it cut against the powerful emerging trend of Gilded Age social analysis, both conservative and radical, which saw social conditions rather than character as crucial in explaining how the world worked. In explaining poverty, Riis, like Washington Gladden and other Social Gospelers, bounced, often uncritically, between the environment, capitalism, and immigration on the one hand, and the decline of manliness and independence on the other.[6]

5. Yochelson and Czitrom, 110–13; Matthew Frye Jacobson, *Whiteness of a Different Color: European Immigrants and the Alchemy of Race* (Cambridge, MA: Harvard University Press, 1998), 41–62, 79–81; Riis, 15, 38, 79.
6. Riis, 4; Washington Gladden, "Present-Day Papers: The Problem of Poverty," *The Century* (December 1892): 245–57; Robert Hamlett Bremner, *From the Depths: The Discovery of Poverty in the United States* (New York: New York University Press, 1956), 83–85; Yochelson and Czitrom, 82–86, 117–18; Steven Mintz, *Huck's Raft: A History of American Childhood* (Cambridge, MA: Belknap Press of Harvard University Press, 2004), 164–66; David Huyssen, *Progressive Inequality: Rich and Poor in New York, 1890–1920* (Cambridge, MA: Harvard University Press, 2014), 64–70.

Riis's work had consequences. In 1894 Governor Roswell Flower appointed Richard Watson Gilder, the editor of the *Century*, to New York's Tenement House Committee, responsible for making "a careful examination into the tenement house of the city of New York" and their effects "on the health education, savings, and morals of those who live in such habitations." Gilder was an influential intellectual, as well as a poet whose major literary asset was owning a magazine. Like Riis, he was a devout Christian and a reformer. As chair of the Tenement House Committee, he inherited legislation regulating the construction and maintenance of tenements and a belief that controlling physical space was the key to shaping the lives of those within that space. He also inherited a lack of regulatory authority and administrative capacity to enforce those laws. When faced with violations, the committee's only recourse was to evict the tenants, thus victimizing the victims and forcing them into the streets.[7]

The committee's investigators intruded on the poor, examined them, and reported on them. They had the ability to alienate the poor, but they lacked much ability to help them. They did not doubt that the poor lied to them, and they placed the pattern of lies within ethnic stereotypes that could have come straight from *How the Other Half Lives*. Investigators saw the material facts of the tenements with their own eyes and regarded them as undeniable. Many immigrants were unable to afford tenement rents without taking in boarders so the already crowded quarters swelled with humanity. Investigators reported that an accurate account of residents could be gotten only at midnight, when the cots and blankets came out. On a hot summer's nights — "the time of greatest suffering among the poor" — the count would have to include the roofs, fire escapes, and streets.[8]

I

What began as concern over immigrants began to look more like panic in the 1890s. Anti-Catholic propagandists and nativists in the American Protective Association fed it, but far more potent fuel came from leading intellectuals and social scientists. Their thinking about immigrants, cities, and American society revealed the changing contours of American social thought.

By the 1890s, Francis Walker was president of the Massachusetts Institute of Technology, long removed from his government work in the Census Bureau and the Indian Bureau. Like so many others, he was

7. Lubove, 88–100; Huyssen, 12–13, 21, 47, 50.
8. Riis, 124; Rischin, 83–85; Lubove, 94–98; Huyssen, 23–26, 29, 40, 80–81.

poised halfway between the older liberalism and those who had rebelled against it. Unlike William Graham Sumner, his career had been based on recognition of a role for government intervention; his critique of what he termed the "hypothetical school" of classical economics had earned him Sumner's ire and led to his being hounded out of Yale. But he emerged on the winning side. He became president of the American Statistical Association in 1882 and the American Economic Association in 1886. He enjoyed the support of the younger German-educated social scientists, but he never wandered far from the liberal tree.[9]

Just as liberalism had been an admirable engine for smashing slavery and the claims of European monarchists, so pragmatism, in both the loose and the strict sense, became a powerful tool for dismantling liberalism's foundational beliefs. But just as it proved hard for liberals to be consistently liberal, so it was difficult for pragmatists to remain consistently pragmatic. Walker and the new social scientists, who were influenced by the tendencies that produced pragmatism without necessarily being pragmatists themselves, found it hard to discard absolutes. Appeals to history and indeterminate change could still shelter racial dogmas. Appeals to experience disguised ideology.

Walker the quasi-liberal reformer and Walker the social scientist were both visible when he turned his attention to immigration in the 1890s. He entered into the fray over interpreting the results of the 1890 census, which astonished and frustrated Americans because there should have been more Americans. Walker defended the count. What the critics ignored, he contended, was the falling birth rate among the native-born. He contended that the increasing number of immigrants contributed to fewer births among native-born Americans: "Vast hordes of foreigners began to arrive upon our shores, drawn from the degraded peasantries of Europe, accustomed to a far lower standard of living, with habits strange and repulsive to our people. This, again, caused the native population more and more to shrink within themselves, creating an increasing reluctance to bring forth sons and daughters to compete in the market for labor." He called this phenomenon the displacement principle.[10]

9. Mary O. Furner, *Advocacy and Objectivity: A Crisis in the Professionalization of American Social Science, 1865–1905* (Lexington: published for the Organization of American Historians [by] University Press of Kentucky, 1975), 45–48, 79; James Phinney Munroe, *A Life of Francis Amasa Walker* (New York: Holt, 1923), 305–7, 311.
10. Bernard Newton, *The Economics of Francis Amasa Walker: American Economics in Transition* (New York: Kelley, 1968), 143–50; Francis Amasa Walker, *Discussions in Economics and Statistics: Statistics, National Growth, Social Economics* (New York: Holt, 1899), 121–24; Walker, "The Great Count of 1890," *Forum* 11 (1891): 416.

This was an argument that Walker would amplify and repeat until his death in 1897. It contrasted with his evaluation of black Americans. He saw their declining proportion of the population as a sign of their limitations to thrive outside the semitropical South and an inability to compete with whites. The logical corollary would seem to be that native-born whites could not compete with immigrants, but Walker instead employed a version of the old anti-Chinese argument. Native-born Americans would have gladly done the work immigrants performed, no matter how dangerous and low-paying, if there had been no immigrants present. The new immigration, he thought, had become a race to the bottom as Italians replaced Irish and then Jews replaced Italians. The result would only be a continuing deterioration of wages and the American standard of living. "It is much to be doubted," he wrote, "whether any material growth which is be secured only by the degradation of our citizenship is a national gain, even from the most materialistic point of view."[11]

Where once the United States had attracted the able and industrious, now it supposedly got the dregs of Europe. Steam had cut the costs of transportation, and agents planned the trips for even the most feckless. Walker complained that "so broad and smooth is the channel, there is no reason why every foul and stagnant pool of population in Europe, which no breath of intellectual or industrial life has stirred for ages, should not be decanted upon our soil." In Walker's analysis, the poor of Southern and Eastern Europe were loosened by a kind of social gravity that drained them from Europe, channeled them onto trains and steamships, and deposited them in the United States. "Such vast masses of peasantry, degraded below our utmost conceptions," was a cause for alarm. They were "beaten men from beaten races, representing the worst failures in the struggle for existence."[12]

For evidence, Walker abandoned the census numbers and turned to anecdote: Riis's description of "the police driving from the garbage dumps the miserable beings who try to burrow in these depths of unutterable filth and slime in order that they may eat and sleep there! Was it in cement like this the foundations of our republic were laid?" Walker made desperation into choice, but poverty was only a chrysalis. These "beaten men," these "miserable beings," reemerged as a political threat to the republic, providing members for the "socialistic mob" that knew "no restraint upon their own passions but the club of the policeman or the bayonet of the soldier."

11.   Francis A. Walker, "Restriction of Immigration," *Atlantic Monthly* (June 1896); 822–29; "The Colored Race in the United States," *Forum* 11 (July 1891): 501–9, also in Walker, *Discussions in Economics and Statistics*, 125–37.
12.   Walker, "Restriction of Immigration," 822–29.

Americans had the duty of self-protection, and they had to protect a system that was the envy of the world. The country needed to confront its problems without the aggravation of "some millions of Hungarians, Bohemians, Poles, south Italians and Russian Jews."[13]

The "beaten races" were the "new immigrants," a collective identity constructed by Walker and other intellectuals. A Russian Jew and a Sicilian, after all, failed to recognize their kinship. The United States did receive the largest number of these new immigrants, but Canada, Argentina, Brazil, New Zealand, and Australia were also immigrant nations, even though they drew from a narrower set of groups with Australia embarking on a "White Australia" policy in the 1890s. In the demographic revolution, lower mortality arrived before declining fertility and population pressure forced Jews, Italians, and Poles to seek alternative ways to make a living inside or outside Europe. In the case of Poles, many of whom were incorporated into Bismarck's Germany, or Jews living in the Pale of the Russian Empire, active persecution gave further impetus to a migration already under way. In Southern Italy, landlords squeezed poor peasants, producing first social rebellion and then emigration. Many came to the United States.[14]

Whether going to Stamford, Connecticut, or Chicago, the new immigrants, like the old, participated in chain migrations, going to places where they had relatives or old neighbors. Emigration was not spread evenly across the old country, and immigrants did not settle evenly in the United States. Statistics from the early twentieth century showed that most Southern Italian immigrants intended to stay for only a few years; the majority returned to Italy. The Italians and Greeks returned more often than other immigrants, but a significant percentage of many groups returned home. "Antonio C.," the pseudonym for a migrant born in Sambuca, Italy, in 1889, came to the United States as a child in 1891, but his father had first migrated to Brooklyn in 1880, went back to Italy to marry in 1884, and then returned to Brooklyn with his wife and children. Antonio had three aunts and uncles around him in Brooklyn, among the three hundred people from Sambuca living near his parent's apartment,

13. Walker, "Restriction of Immigration," 822–29.
14. Dino Cinel, *From Italy to San Francisco: The Immigrant Experience* (Stanford, CA: Stanford University Press, 1982), 1–3. Cinel should be used with caution; see http://historynewsnetwork.org/article/1420. John Higham, *Strangers in the Land: Patterns of American Nativism, 1860–1925*, 2nd ed. (New Brunswick, NJ: Rutgers University Press, 1988), 94–96, 101; Archdeacon, 122–28; Donna R. Gabaccia, *Militants and Migrants: Rural Sicilians Become American Workers* (New Brunswick, NJ: Rutgers University Press, 1988), 17–36, 55–75.

who were only a part of the predominantly western Sicilian population surrounding Hopkins Street.[15]

Though the old immigration had consisted of skilled workers and farmers as well as unskilled workers, the new immigrants only rarely farmed in the United States and were overwhelmingly unskilled. Those workers without skills accounted for more than 80 percent of the immigrants by the turn of the century. Earlier German immigrants to a city like Poughkeepsie, New York, had been artisans. They had prospered in an economy full of small enterprises and had been able to own shops and achieve a modicum of independence, but their sons joined more recent immigrants as unskilled workers in the factories. Unskilled jobs were most abundant in the industrial Northeast, so this was where immigrants concentrated. Specific industries often relied on certain ethnic groups for their labor force.[16]

Conditions had changed, and nativists argued the changing conditions meant that the United States had to restrict immigration, and in this, nativist thinking paralleled that of many European nationalists, imperialists, and conservatives. Initially in the latter half of the nineteenth century, European countries relaxed their restrictions on emigration. In Russia violent pogroms drove out Jews, and even in the absence of violence Russia encouraged Jewish emigration and then taxed the emigrants. In the 1880s, Great Britain tried to dump the poorest Irish on American shores. In Asia, Japan relaxed its restrictions on emigration. By the 1890s, however, Austria-Hungary feared the loss of conscripts for its armies and cheap labor for its mines and estates. Anti-Semites blamed Jewish travel and immigration agents for tricking and cheating immigrants, sometimes putting them on trial to discourage both emigrants and those who facilitated their passage. Complete bans would come later.[17]

15. Gabaccia, 76; Susan J. Matt, *Homesickness: An American History* (Oxford: Oxford University Press, 2011), 145; MacDonald and MacDonald, 82–85.

16. Matthew Frye Jacobson, *Barbarian Virtues: The United States Encounters Foreign Peoples at Home and Abroad, 1878–1917* (New York: Hill and Wang, 2000), 67–69; Clyde Griffen and Sally Griffen, *Natives and Newcomers: The Ordering of Opportunity in Mid-Nineteenth-Century Poughkeepsie* (Cambridge, MA: Harvard University Press, 1978), 170–84, 260; MacDonald and MacDonald, 84–85; Archdeacon, 132–36, 140–41, 152–53; David R. Roediger and Elizabeth D. Esch, *The Production of Difference: Race and the Management of Labor in U.S. History* (New York: Oxford University Press, 2012), 11–15.

17. Hidetaka Hirota, "Officials, the Federal Government, and the Formation of American Immigration Policy," *Journal of American History* 99, no. 4 (March 2013): 1092, 1099–1103; Tara Zahra, *The Great Departure: Mass Migration from Eastern Europe and the Making of the Free World* (New York: Norton, 2016), 30–32, 36–39, 55–56; Andrea Geiger, *Subverting Exclusion: Transpacific Encounters with Race, Caste, and Borders, 1885–1928* (New Haven, CT: Yale University Press, 2011), 40–43.

As the leading destination for immigrants, the United States became the focus for both North American and European concerns over migration. Many Americans doubted both the country's ability to absorb immigrants and whether the new immigrants were absorbable.

The public lands were, Walker thought, largely exhausted; agricultural prices were falling; farming was becoming mechanized. There was no guarantee that even the skilled and industrious could find work, and he thought that the need for unskilled labor would evaporate. Nor did the United States have the means to handle the resulting discontent: "We have not the machinery; we have not the army, we have not the police, we have not the traditions and instincts...."[18]

Whether one agreed or disagreed with Walker, part of his analysis was based on observable phenomena. In the 1890s real wages were falling. The birth rate among native-born Americans was in decline. Immigration had gone up, and the sources had changed to Eastern and Southern Europe. Steamships and economics of shipping had so reduced rates that Italian workers could get to New York more cheaply than to Germany.[19]

The remainder of Walker's analysis was, however, deeply ideological. Just as liberals had blamed the supposed racial deficiencies of black people for the failure of Reconstruction and blamed political corruption on immigrants, Walker blamed the racial deficiencies of immigrants for the growing social and economic problems that Riis described. That a small number of desperately poor during the 1890s sought food and shelter in garbage dumps was, for example, true, but that they did so because they were "beaten men from beaten races" depended on an ideology that created, classified, and ranked races. His evidence that foreign immigrants composed the "socialistic mobs" conflated socialists and mobs and came from talking to a New England minister who mingled with a Boston crowd rather than any empirical data. Eugene Debs became the actual face of American socialism. He was a child of immigrants to be sure, but far more a child of the Midwest.[20]

Walker's observation that the decline of American birth rates correlated with the rise in immigration did not demonstrate cause and effect. The first step in making such a case would have been to show that birth rates in other industrialized countries that did not take in immigrants in the same numbers as the United States were not declining. But declining birth rates

18. Walker, "Restriction of Immigration," 822–29.
19. Hirota, 1092, 1099–1103; Aristide R. Zolberg, A Nation by Design: Immigration Policy in the Fashioning of America (New York: Russell Sage Foundation, 2006), 202–5.
20. For ideology, Jacobson, Whiteness of a Different Color: European Immigrants and the Alchemy of Race (Cambridge, MA: Harvard University Press, 1999), 71–72; Nick Salvatore, Eugene V. Debs: Citizen and Socialist (Urbana: University of Illinois Press, 1982), 1–87, 232–35.

in the United States were part of a larger demographic transition of declining mortality and, after a lag, declining fertility, which began in Europe about 1800. Scholars have suggested an array of economic, social, and cultural factors as the cause of the transition. Walker, in any case, was not as interested in the empirical problem of declining fertility and rising immigration as in the ideological problem: the arrival of supposedly inferior races in the United States. The racial concerns that had driven his Indian policy drove his and others' enthusiasm for immigration restriction.[21]

Walker was not alone in massaging evidence to bolster his desired conclusions. Edward Bemis went much further when in an influential 1890 article he used the 1880 census to claim 50 percent of the white population in the United States was of foreign birth or parentage. He manipulated his categories to exaggerate the number of immigrants and their children, who in 1890 made up only a third of the white population.[22]

Henry Cabot Lodge was a congressman from Massachusetts in the early 1890s, and he too demonstrated how complicated data could be simplified and politicized. Lodge, who had a Ph.D. in history from Harvard, used 1890 census figures to show the disproportionate number of immigrants in penitentiaries and almshouses. His figures appear to be accurate, but his analysis was crude. He did not control for age, or urban-rural residence, or the prevalence of almshouses and prisons in various areas; nor was he aware that the crime rate between the 1870s and the early 1890s was falling despite the rising numbers of immigrants. A relationship between immigration and crime was not imaginary, but it was far more complicated than Lodge knew. Studies of antebellum Pennsylvania, for example, have found members of the old immigrant groups had committed more crimes than the native-born. This correlation between immigration and crime, however, held only for violent crime and not for property crimes.[23]

21. Zolberg, 207–14; John C. Caldwell, "Mass Education as a Determinant of the Timing of Fertility Decline," *Population and Development Review* 6, no. 2 (1980): 225–55; Jacobson, *Barbarian Virtues*, 90–94; Ron Lesthaeghe, "A Century of Demographic and Cultural Change in Western Europe: An Exploration of Underlying Dimensions," *Population and Development Review* 9, no. 3 (1983): 413–15; Newton, 146–47; Timothy J. Hatton and Jeffrey G. Williamson, "What Drove the Mass Migrations from Europe in the Late Nineteenth Century?" NBER Working Paper Series on Historical Factors in Long Run Growth, (Cambridge, MA: National Bureau of Economic Research, 1992).
22. Zolberg, 208–9.
23. Henry Cabot Lodge, "The Census and Immigration," *Century Illustrated Magazine* (September 1893): 737–39; John A Garraty, *Henry Cabot Lodge: A Biography* (New York: Knopf, 1965), 37–39; Howard Bodenhorn et al., "Immigration: America's Nineteenth Century 'Law and Order Problem'?" NBER Working Paper Series (Cambridge, MA: National Bureau of Economic Research, August 2010), 2–42.

Gilded Age New York—the ground zero for the new immigration—was a violent city, but it was growing less violent as immigration climbed after 1870. There was no popular panic over murder; nor was its decline due to draconian measures to suppress it. At least in the years before 1870, juries in New York City were reluctant to convict, and even more reluctant to execute, people for murder. Most convicted murderers got very light sentences with a good chance of pardon or commutation. There were disproportionate numbers of immigrants in prison, which might have been due to their criminality, but it also might have been because immigrants were more likely to be convicted and sentenced to prison and their sentences were not commuted. In any case, explaining why there were so many immigrants in prison demanded going beyond the supposed criminality of the newer immigrants.[24]

The new academic disciplines were being established in the late nineteenth century, but there seemed to be no new discipline that did not worry about immigrants. Political scientists certainly did. John Burgess of Columbia University, one of the founders of that field, came of age during the Civil War and grounded his beliefs in a classic liberal combination of Hegelian idealism, nationalism, and laissez-faire. He regarded the nation as a transcendent ideal that rose from the racial genius of a people, and he declared that the racial genius of the American commonwealth was Aryan and specifically Teutonic, since only the "race-proud Teutons" had resisted intermixture and the tainting of their Aryan blood. Polluting the United States with non-Aryans was a "sin against American civilization." Only those non-Aryans who had been "Aryanized in spirit" should be allowed to become citizens since only Aryans were capable of democratic government. Everywhere Burgess looked, he saw danger to the Aryan genius of American governance: socialism, European immigration, the spreading scope of government, the extension of suffrage to the unworthy, and last but not least, his younger colleagues in political science both at Columbia and elsewhere, who he thought were infected by socialism.[25]

Burgess certainly distrusted E. A. Ross, a young sociologist and a Midwest Presbyterian who embraced the Social Gospel in the 1880s and antimonopolism in the 1890s, but their thinking on immigrants was not very different. Ross would eventually provide one of the intellectual

24. Eric H. Monkkonen, *Police in Urban America, 1860–1920* (Cambridge: Cambridge University Press, 1981), 76–78; Monkkonen, *Crime, Justice, History* (Columbus: Ohio State University Press, 2002), 90–93; Monkkonen, *Murder in New York City* (Berkeley: University of California Press, 2000), 149–50.
25. Michael H. Frisch, "Urban Theorists, Urban Reform, and American Political Culture in the Progressive Period," *Political Science Quarterly* 97, no. 2 (1982): 295–303; John W. Burgess, "The Ideal of the American Commonwealth," ibid., 10, no. 3 (1895), 404–25.

bridges to twentieth-century Progressivism. For him, society was not a struggle between individuals but rather between social groups, particularly between the "big group" and the "sect or clan." There was not, as William Graham Sumner believed, any simple ethical principle or social law, some universal set of values, that determined rights or justice; there were competing beliefs and principles. Laissez-faire was impossible. Society could not simply stand back in the midst of the struggle. As society grew more complex, the individual confronted forces beyond personal control, and the state took on a larger role. "The more a state helps the citizen when he cannot help himself," Ross would later write, "protecting him from disease, foes, criminals, rivals abroad and monopolists at home, the more he will look to it for guidance."[26]

Ross embraced racial thinking. He became ever more convinced of the dangers immigrants posed to the Aryan stock, which he, like Burgess, identified with American democracy. In the 1890s, Ross was still elaborating his views on race and racial superiority. Races were not fixed, but they were at any given time distinct and slow to change. Ross agreed with Walker, and for that matter Theodore Roosevelt and Frances Willard, that white Americans of Anglo-Saxon stock had emerged as the world's superior race, and he thought they were in danger of committing "race suicide" as the "inferior" races outbred them. This would become a common view among later Progressives. In its extreme form, it would show up during the early twentieth century in Madison Grant's *Passing of the Great Race*, but there were hints of it in Theodore Roosevelt's speech on "National Duties" in 1901: "The willfully idle man, like the willfully barren woman, has no place in a sane, healthy, and vigorous community."[27]

Ross made race, which was not yet distinguished from ethnicity, the foundation for social groups. Like Frederick Jackson Turner, the historian who first rose to prominence in the 1890s and who was later Ross's colleague at the University of Wisconsin, he celebrated the supposed American genius for governance, drawing heavily on frontier communities, particularly in California, for examples. When Ross listed dangers to democracy and community in his 1901 book *Social Control*, they came largely from European immigration: the "fanatic and sectary, zealot and

26. Furner, 307–9; Edward A. Ross, *Social Control: A Survey of the Foundations of Order* (New York: Macmillan, 1916, orig. ed. 1901), 52, 55–56, 82–83.

27. Furner, 308–9; Theodore Roosevelt, "National Duties: Address at the Minnesota State Fair" (1901), in *The Strenuous Life: Essays and Addresses by Theodore Roosevelt* (New York: Century Company, 1905), available at http://www.theodore-roosevelt .com/images/research/txtspeeches/678.pdf; Ian R. Tyrrell, *Reforming the World: The Creation of America's Moral Empire* (Princeton, NJ: Princeton University Press, 2010), 33; Jacobson, *Whiteness of a Different Color*, 81–82.

partisan, as well as from the egoist. Society must muzzle Jesuit and Mafiote [members of the Mafia], conspirator and anarchist, as well as the man of prey." Only the man of prey—by which Ross meant men like Jay Gould—was an American type.[28]

In the 1890s Ross's racial views were not particularly controversial at Stanford, where he then taught; they fitted well with those of Stanford President David Starr Jordan. Ross's economic views were a different matter. In an age when rich people were founding colleges and universities—the University of Chicago, Stanford, Rice, Vanderbilt, and Carnegie Mellon—and sat on the boards of existing universities, his opposition to the gold standard and his attacks on corporations caused him problems. Stanford was still only a minor college funded by a railroad fortune. Jane Stanford ran the university as if she owned it, which in a sense she did. When she dismissed Ross, she divided the Stanford faculty; most signed a proclamation supporting her, but many resigned. The American Economic Association treated the dispute as a matter of academic freedom, issuing a report stating that he had been fired for his opinions. William Graham Sumner refused to sign it. The case became a national scandal and ultimately burnished Ross's reputation as much as it tarnished Stanford's.[29]

Immigrants did not cause the crisis over objectivity and advocacy in the 1880s and 1890s, but they did provide much of the raw material for the disputes that fed it. Bemis, Lodge, Walker, Burgess, Ross, and others panicked over the new immigration and claimed objective research justified it, but the future they projected would not arrive. The new immigration would have less of a demographic impact than the older immigration. During the peak years of the new immigration (1899–1924), Southern and Eastern European immigrants—particularly Jews, Poles, and Italians—formed the largest groups, but large numbers of Germans, Irish, Scandinavians, and British continued to come. Although the number of immigrants went up, the American population was much larger in 1890 than it had been before Civil War. This diluted the impact of the new immigrants. The 2.8 million immigrants of the 1850s had equaled 12.1 percent of the population in 1850; the 5.2 million immigrants of the 1880s had amounted to 10.8 percent and the 3.7 million immigrants of 1890s would be only 5.8 percent. And the ease of access that Walker cited as a cause for the growth in immigration also made return to homelands easier. Millions

28. Jacobson, *Barbarian Virtues*, 64–65, 73–75; Philip J. Ethington, *The Public City: The Political Construction of Urban Life in San Francisco, 1850–1900* (Cambridge: Cambridge University Press, 1994), 345–52; Ross, 52.

29. Ethington, 349–54; Furner, 230–50; Edward A. Ross, "The Causes of Race Superiority," *Annals of the American Academy of Political and Social Science* 18 (1901): 67–89.

would settle and raise families in the United States, but millions more were "sojourners," single male laborers who came intending to earn money to establish themselves and their families in the home country and then return. Reliable statistics are sketchy, but roughly one in every three immigrants would go back home after 1890.[30]

Politics, however, proceeds on perception, and the panic over immigration drove demands for its restriction. Advocates of the tariff feared cheap goods; restrictionists feared cheap labor. Americans recognized the value of immigrant labor, but this labor could not be detached from the exotic, clamoring, sometimes desperate bodies of these workers, nor from the religious and social beliefs they brought with them. Not only nativists feared for their country; Irish and British working-class immigrants in the Midwestern coal towns favored immigration restriction to protect them from "the fatal competition of low priced labor."[31]

The precedents for federal restriction of immigration were already in place in 1890, but legislating a broad program proved difficult. In *Henderson vs. Mayor of New York* in 1876 the Supreme Court struck down head taxes—per capita taxes on immigrants—that New York and Louisiana placed on immigrants and put control over immigration into federal hands. Passing legislation through Congress, however, proved difficult as steamship companies successfully opposed legislation that would have both restricted their business and forced them to finance facilities for the reception and inspection of immigrants. When an act finally passed in 1882, it levied a fifty-cent head tax and provided for the deportation of "immoral women," convicts, mental defectives, and persons likely to become a public charge. In addition, there were the racial restrictions already placed on Chinese immigration and the ban on contract labor in the Foran Act of 1885. Congress would add to this list in 1891. If immigrants felt they had been unfairly treated, they had no appeal to the courts, only to administrators in the executive branch. All these laws were, however, unenforceable without improved federal administrative capacity. Not only did Congress model the new immigration law after state acts grounded in anti-European nativism, but in the 1880s the federal government delegated much of the enforcement to states, particularly New York State.[32]

30. Archdeacon, 113–19.
31. Richard J. Jensen, *The Winning of the Midwest: Social and Political Conflict, 1888–1896* (Chicago: University of Chicago Press, 1971), 259–61.
32. Hirota, 1092–94, 1099–1101, 1107–8; Zolberg, 189–98, 223–24; Vincent J. Cannato, *American Passage: The History of Ellis Island* (New York: Harper, 2009), 61–62; Archdeacon, 144–46; Erika Lee, *At America's Gates: Chinese Immigration During the Exclusion Era, 1882–1943* (Chapel Hill: University of North Carolina Press, 2003), 41–46.

Only in March 1891 did Congress create a new superintendent of immigration located with the Treasury Department to supervise permanent inspection stations, but in Massachusetts the State Board of Lunacy and Charity reported that the change had yielded "no practical change of administration." Change came gradually. Chief among the inspection stations was Ellis Island, which opened in New York in 1892. It became the port of entry for about 80 percent of the immigrants coming to the United States thereafter and was designed to sift the wheat from the chaff, separating out and deporting those immigrants who fell into the undesirable categories. The first immigrant to disembark at Ellis Island was Annie Moore from County Cork, Ireland, who came with her two younger brothers to meet her father, who already resided in New York. Hers was a familiar figure after decades of Irish immigration, but most of the passengers on the *Nevada*, the ship that brought her, were Russian Jews. They were the changing face of immigration.[33]

American impediments to immigration remained mild compared with those enacted in Europe. Even the most basic measures restrictionists introduced to Congress—a literacy law proposed in 1888 and endorsed by Rep. Henry Cabot Lodge in 1891, went nowhere. The Immigration Restriction League (IRL), organized by Boston Brahmins in 1894, cooperated with Lodge and operated much like the American Social Science Association. Its membership was small, but it produced reams of studies to be distributed to the popular press. The IRL advocated restriction rather than exclusion. Although it did not advocate restricting immigrants "on the ground of race, religion, or creed," the measures advocated—a great increase in the head tax and a literacy test—would have significantly curtailed Eastern and Southern European immigration.[34]

Both American business and labor remained divided over restriction. The opinion of the *New York Journal of Commerce* that "men, like cows, are expensive to raise and a gift of either should be gladly received" remained common among businessmen. Industrialists, largely Republican, needed the unskilled labor of immigrants. But unions also split, with Powderly and the Knights favoring restriction and much of the AFL (but not Samuel Gompers) opposing it. American unions hated contract labor, which recruited and transported foreign workers to take American jobs, but many members of these unions were themselves immigrants who sought to have family members and ex-neighbors join them.[35]

33. Cannato, 57–62; Hirota, 1106; Archdeacon, 145–46.
34. Higham, 101–5; Cannato, 95–105; Zolberg, 199–201, 206, 211–12; Jacobson, *Barbarian Virtues*, 7, 200.
35. Zolberg, 217–18, 222; Cannato, 109–17; Higham, 70–72.

With elements in both political parties hostile to immigration, with liberal intellectuals and social scientists condemning it in the press, and with labor equivocal, immigrants needed friends. They found them among urban Democratic politicians, coreligionists, and those Americans whose families had come earlier from the places immigrants had just left. The Roman Catholic Church and organized Judaism proved effective in protecting immigrants, and the immigrants themselves turned self-help organizations into political organizations to protect their interests. By the end of the decade, Italian, Irish, German, and Jewish groups had created the Immigration Protective League.[36]

Immigration policy was the domain of the federal government, but immigrant politics took place on the local and state levels. Democratic politicians were not going to consent to policies that would eliminate their own political base. Tammany had thrived by manufacturing voters from new immigrants and continued to do so, even though the pace of naturalization slowed. As Henry George had found to his dismay, the more recent and vulnerable the immigrant, the more likely the immigrant voter would support the machine. Democratic efforts to secure immigrant votes brought a Republican backlash. When the Republicans gained control of the New York Constitutional Convention in 1894, they passed a set of reforms designed to limit the immigrant vote. Even seemingly straightforward good government reforms such as the secret or Australian ballot also served as a kind of literacy test, disproportionately affecting immigrants since voters could not simply hand in a prerecorded paper ballot. Other measures specifically targeted immigrants. One obliged naturalized citizens to wait ninety days before voting, and it required in-person voter registration, but only in cities with a population of more than five thousand, where immigrants congregated. Such restrictions on the franchise were not unusual. Michigan rescinded voting rights for noncitizens, which had existed for years as a way to attract population.[37]

II

In the short run, immigration brought the greatest changes to those institutions that worked to protect it. Immigrants transformed American

36. Higham, 70–72; Zolberg, 216–23.
37. Richard L. McCormick, *From Realignment to Reform: Political Change in New York State, 1893–1910* (Ithaca, NY: Cornell University Press, 1981), 52–54; Alexander Keyssar, *The Right to Vote: The Contested History of Democracy in the United States* (New York: Basic Books, 2000), 136–46; Steven P. Erie, *Rainbow's End: Irish-Americans and the Dilemmas of Urban Machine Politics, 1840–1985* (Berkeley: University of California Press, 1988), 51–53.

Judaism, American Catholicism, political machines, popular entertainments, and eventually the character of the nation as a whole.

The most dramatic changes took place in American Judaism. The first Jewish immigrants had been German Jews, who assimilated fairly easily into American society. In New York, as well as in Cincinnati, Chicago, and San Francisco (where there were sixteen thousand Jews by the 1870s), they had become prominent members of the business classes, active politically, and leading reformers. Anti-Semitism shut certain doors—elite clubs, for example—but when denied access to Protestant institutions, Jews formed parallel ones. German Jewish merchants concentrated in "dry and fancy goods" and clothing manufacture; some of the wealthiest controlled emerging investment banking houses (the Speyers, Wormsers, and Seligmans, as well as Kuhn, Loeb and Company). These banking houses were to a large extent kinship groups: partners were born or married into them. Even the most successful, however, did not reach the highest tier of American wealth, which included the Rockefellers, Carnegies, Astors, Goulds, and Vanderbilts. The House of Morgan often collaborated with the Jewish bankers in syndicates and avoided public expressions of anti-Semitism, but J. P. Morgan and his associates were old-stock Protestants, whose social network excluded Jews. By the turn of the century, Morgan designated his firm and the Baring Brothers as the only "white firms in New York."[38]

The trickle of Jewish emigration from Germany, however, became a stream from lands farther east as roughly two hundred thousand Eastern European Jews arrived in the United States during the 1880s. They were culturally and economically quite distinct from German Jews, who greeted the newcomers with considerable ambivalence. Ultimately German Jews, alarmed by rising anti-Semitism, aided the emigrants, but they also insisted that, as the *Jewish Messenger* put it, "they must be Americanized in spite of themselves in the mode to be prescribed by their friends and benefactors."[39]

---

38. Phyllis Dillon and Andrew Godley, "The Evolution of the Jewish Garment Industry," in *Chosen Capital: The Jewish Encounter with American Capitalism*, ed. Rebecca Kobrin and Jonathan Sarna (New Brunswick, NJ: Rutgers University Press, 2012), 42–50; Susie Pak, *Gentlemen Bankers: The World of J. P. Morgan* (Cambridge, MA: Harvard University Press 2013), 4–11, 48–49, 80–83, 91.
39. Hasia R. Diner, *A New Promised Land: A History of Jews in America* (New York: Oxford University Press, 2003), 43–44; Edwin G. Burrows and Mike Wallace, *Gotham: A History of New York City to 1898* (New York: Oxford University Press, 1999), 1113–15; Irving Howe, *World of Our Fathers* (New York: New York University Press, 2005, orig. ed. 1976), 230.

Americanization involved religious as well as secular changes. Reform Judaism, driven by the same motives as liberal, Americanized Catholicism, had made considerable gains among German Jews. Reform rabbis in Pittsburgh declared that Jews were no longer a nation "but a religious community" and that the ancient dietary laws were no longer necessary for being an observant Jew. The movement from Orthodox to Reform Judaism, however, was not clear-cut. Many congregations vacillated between Orthodox and Reform rabbis. In the late 1870s a revival among young Jews in Philadelphia spawned an effort to bring Jews back "to the ancient faith." It was the beginning of Conservative Judaism, an attempt, in the words of one founder, to reconcile "proclivities...toward reform Judaism and...[a] disposition toward orthodoxy." Like Reform Judaism, it proved mutable and continued to evolve.[40]

Some of the new Jewish immigrants arriving in the United States were Sephardim from the Mediterranean, but most were Ashkenazi from Eastern Europe, and their arrival distressed some Orthodox Eastern European rabbis as much as it did native-born Americans. In the words of one, the United States (which to many immigrants was the *medinah* or golden land) was a "*trefa* [food forbidden by the dietary laws] land where even the stones are impure." As the rabbis feared, many immigrants came from those already slipping the bonds of piety, and the United States would tempt others to do so. There were immigrants who spent their days in a cycle of prayer and study, but they became a minority in American cities.[41]

Emma Lazarus had captured the hopes of German Jews for the Ashkenazi before the waves of Eastern European immigration really had begun, and she countered Walker's theories of the beaten races before he enunciated them. She was Sephardim on her father's side and German Jewish on her mother's, and she had written a poem as part of an effort to finance a pedestal for the Statue of Liberty in New York Harbor. Her poem caught the transformative possibilities of the United States.

> Give me your tired, your poor,
> Your huddled masses yearning to breathe free,
> The wretched refuse of your teeming shore,
> Send these, the homeless, tempest-tost to me
> I lift my lamp beside the golden door.[42]

40. Diner, 46–47; Jonathan D. Sarna, *American Judaism: A History* (New Haven, CT: Yale University Press, 2004), 99–100, 144–59.
41. Diner, 46–47; Ellen Eisenberg, Ava Kahn, and William Toll, *Jews of the Pacific Coast: Reinventing Community on America's Edge* (Seattle: University of Washington Press, 2009), 76; Rischin, 145–48.
42. Diner, 41–42.

Eastern European Jews varied considerably in their desire to be transformed, and the recalcitrants threatened to change everything for German American Jews. In their appearance and opinion, German Jews tended to be indistinguishable from other Americans; the Eastern Europeans were overwhelmingly poor and working-class, dressed differently, wore their beards untrimmed and their hair in sidelocks, and spoke Yiddish, which seemed a "piggish jargon." Russian Jews in particular seemed hopelessly exotic. The *Hebrew Standard* thought German Judaism closer to Christianity than "the Judaism of these miserable darkened Hebrews." The newspapers of the newer immigrants, which proliferated from the 1880s onward, were "socialistic," their practices barbarous, and their rapidly expanding theater melodramatic and parochial. There are differing accounts of the derivation of the slur, but German Jews dismissed the Eastern Europeans as "kikes."[43]

Still, although always condescending, often resentful, and sometimes insulting, Western European Jews settled into ambivalence and took responsibility for aiding the new immigrants. The Hebrew Immigrant Aid Society, the Independent Order of B'nai B'rith, the Baron de Hirsch Fund, and the Union of American Hebrew congregations fed the hungry and helped the newcomers obtain employment, even as they tried to remake the Eastern Europeans into what they regarded as model Americanized Jews. The immigrants needed the aid and resented the scorn and condescension that sometimes accompanied it. When they were able, they opened benevolent institutions of their own.[44]

The first wave of immigrants concentrated on the Lower East Side of New York, where pushcart peddlers turned Hester Street into an open-air market. Jewish dietary restrictions produced an abundance of butchers and bakers; the tendency of Jews to avoid saloons and liquor multiplied purveyors of soda water. In the 1890s and into the twentieth century, Eastern European Jews replaced German Jews in the garment industry, which was being dominated by the production of ready-made clothing. They usually owned small shops or were the middlemen, the sweaters,

---

43. Riis, 77; Burrows and Wallace, 1114. One derivation comes from the Yiddish word for circle, *kikel*, which many illiterate Jews used to make their mark or documents; the other derives from the last names of Eastern European Jews, which often ended in "kik." Leo Rosten, *The Joys of Yiddish* (New York: McGraw Hill, 1968), 180; Rischin, *The Promised City*, 96–98.

44. Diner, 52–53; Rischin, *The Promised City*, 103–8; Sarna, 157, 256; John E. Bodnar, *The Transplanted: A History of Immigrants in Urban America* (Bloomington: Indiana University Press, 1985), 124; Eisenberg et al., 76; Moses Rischin, "The Jewish Experience in America," in *Jews of the American West*, ed. Moses Rischin and John Livingston (Detroit: Wayne State University Press, 1991), 26–47.

who coordinated production and sale. Immigrants, both Jewish and Italian, worked in sweatshops under miserable conditions that fed labor activism. Some immigrants came from among the men and women swept up first in the brief liberal opening in Russian society that allowed them higher educations and, when this window closed, in the socialist politics spreading across Russia and Europe. They carried their radicalism to the United States, and the sweatshops of the garment industry fertilized it.[45]

The Jewish radical vote and labor vote were significant, but most Jews stayed within Republican and Democratic organizations. The Eighth Assembly District, called "De Ate," centered on the Bowery, the Broadway of the working class. It remained bitterly contested between Martin Engel ("kosher chicken czar and Tammany district leader") and "Stitch" McCarthy (born Sam Rothberg). Engel operated out of his live chicken market and slaughterhouse; McCarthy worked from his saloon. Only after 1892 did the Democratic advantage become more secure as Tammany solidified its hold on new immigrants, but immigration issues, minor in other parts of the country, could always swing votes on the Lower East Side.[46]

Eastern European and Southern European Catholic immigrants destabilized the American Catholic Church as thoroughly as the Eastern European Jewish immigrant shook American Judaism. The immigrants provided useful to the conservative, or ultramontane, elements of the Catholic hierarchy at war with the liberal bishops and clergy who sought an "American Catholicism" that reconciled the Church with American democracy and nationalism. The flood of new Catholics who did not speak English, and thus had difficulty fitting into the geographical parishes dominated by Irish Catholic and German clergy, allowed the creation of special new parishes—so-called national parishes—organized by nationality and language. Here immigrant priests could supervise immigrant Catholics largely separate from other American Catholics. This fragmented church made "American Catholicism" harder to achieve even as the number of Catholics in the United States grew dramatically.[47]

Protestants saw proliferating numbers of Catholics and not their internal divisions, and Protestant resentment contributed to a Catholic vision of a church under siege. Like Orthodox Jews, immigrant Catholics seemed extravagantly religious, but unlike Jews they were often more religious in the United States than they had been in Europe. Compared to urban Protestants, they attended church far more regularly. In 1890 Catholics constituted 68 percent of the churchgoers in New York and

45. Riis, 77; Rischin, *The Promised City*, 55–68, 96–98, 159–68.
46. Rischin, *The Promised City*, 222–28.
47. Archdeacon, 153–55.

Chicago and 56 percent in Cleveland. In Boston, the heartland of American Puritanism, 76 percent of the regular congregants were Catholic.[48]

Rome condoned the unions that the conservative bishops distrusted, but otherwise it largely supported the bishops. The Catholic Church as a church of immigrants was also a working-class church, and in the late 1880s and early 1890s the Church turned to the "social question." In 1891 Pope Leo XIII issued the encyclical *Rerum Novarum*, denouncing the "misery and wretchedness" affecting the working classes and permitting both unions and government intervention on behalf of the poor and working classes. Closer to the ground, whether in orphanages and hospitals staffed by nuns or in parish pulpits, Catholic clergy proved sympathetic to the living wage and skeptical of laissez-faire. A Catholic lecturer in 1889 complained, "It will not do to attribute the condition of the poor to themselves—to their improvidence, idleness, and intemperance."[49]

This attack on the abuses of capitalism was an expression of an older European conservatism that opposed both American and European liberalism. The pope and conservative bishops attacked individualism, emphasized the reciprocal duties between hierarchical social classes, and identified the family, not the individual, as the core unit of society. *Rerum Novarum* said nothing about political liberty or democracy. The other shoe dropped in 1897, when Leo XIII issued *Testem benevolentiae*, which declared heretical many of the ideas associated with Catholic "Americanism" with its embrace of democracy, progress, individualism, and liberalism.[50]

Catholic, and to a lesser extent Jewish, voters were the mainstays of political machines. *Political machine* was a term Mugwump reformers popularized, and they equated it with spoils politics in general, but by the 1880s it had become the ambiguous metaphor for urban political organizations. Reformers sometimes portrayed machines as running by themselves and bosses as mere parasites who harvested their benefits. But they also presented machines as intricate constructions needing constant care and modification. In either case, they connected machines with the working class and immigrants. Urban politicians often rejected the metaphor entirely; they referred to themselves as "the Organization."[51]

48. John T. McGreevy, *Catholicism and American Freedom: A History* (New York: Norton, 2003), 128.
49. McGreevy, 127–30.
50. Archdeacon, 153–55.
51. James J. Connolly, *An Elusive Unity: Urban Democracy and Machine Politics in Industrializing America* (Ithaca, NY: Cornell University Press, 2010), 64–69.

Organization better conveyed how urban politics worked. The foundations of the organization were in neighborhoods and wards, whose aldermen or city council members were drawn largely from among small businessmen. The alderman might or might not be the local boss, but the organization was, in effect, a coalition of bosses. Even when a single party dominated a ward, there was usually competition—occasionally violent—between factions within a dominant party. The successful boss provided access to political power aggregated at the city level.[52]

The most lucrative part of being an alderman lay in the council's power to grant franchises, which were a great source of corruption and political funds, but most of an alderman's time was spent securing far less lucrative favors for constituents: jobs, permits, licenses, and more. This was the administrative power that city governments retained. The jobs they commanded were important but limited because the public sector remained small. In New York in the 1880s Tammany controlled only forty thousand jobs in a labor force that approached a million, and these were overwhelmingly low-paying blue-collar jobs. The bosses supplemented these with jobs obtained from those holding franchises from the city who had to be attentive to politicians' requests. Aldermen also sought public works projects—street paving, lampposts, and gas or water mains—that would provide amenities for constituents. Aldermen scratched each other's backs and did not interfere in each other's wards.[53]

This system was corrupt—public goods were constantly exchanged for private favors—but politicians distinguished between varieties of corruption. Reformers portrayed political machines as criminal organizations, linked with crime and prostitution, and made up of men with shady pasts and dubious presents. E. L. Godkin returned to the battle against Tammany in the 1890s, but only when it did not threaten President Cleveland. Godkin publicized his claims with *Tammany Biographies*, published in the *New York Evening Post*. Tammany was, he declared, made up largely of "illiterate or ignorant men, who have never followed any regular calling." The biographies of the various district leaders, police justices, police commissioners, and aldermen gave the particulars with varying degrees of accuracy: murders, brawls, gambling, bribes, saloon keeping, and running brothels. The goal of the publication was to deliver the city from "this extraordinary menace to both liberty and property," but

52. Ibid., 65; Jon C. Teaford, *The Unheralded Triumph: City Government in America, 1870–1900* (Baltimore, MD: Johns Hopkins University Press, 1984), 24–40, 174–87.
53. Erie, 2–4, 12, 29–30, 58–61; Teaford, 25–32, 155.

he regarded Tammany as simply a symptom of an "immense democracy, mostly ignorant," that was fed by immigration.[54]

The Reverend Charles Parkhurst was even more sensational and successful in denouncing Tammany than was Godkin. He charged Tammany and the police with being a "lying, perjured, rum-soaked and libidinous lot." When hauled before a grand jury to produce evidence, he could provide only newspaper stories. Humiliated, he hired a private detective to guide him, disguised himself, and set out to find his evidence. His instructions to the detective were simple: after every visit—to dance halls, saloons, opium dens, and other locales—he said "Show me something worse." He began at a Cherry Street dance hall where a nineteen-year-old girl greeted him with "Hey whiskers, going to ball me off?" He called it quits at Scotch Ann's Golden Rule Pleasure Club, whose basement was filled with cubicles, each containing a young boy with heavy make-up and the mannerisms of a young girl. That was enough. Parkhurst's exploration of vice led to a state investigation and the defeat of Tammany in the 1894 election by a nonpartisan ticket.[55]

Tammany might scoff at good government reformers, but corruption mattered. When Parkhurst proclaimed that he had supposed the police "existed for the purpose of repressing crime, [but] it began to dawn upon me...[that] its principal object...was to protect and foster crime and make capital out it," more people than upper-class liberals listened. Independent Democrats, Republicans, and nonpartisans joined rival Democratic clubs in a fusion ticket. Germans deserted Tammany in droves.[56]

One result of the election was that Theodore Roosevelt became president of the four-member police commission of New York City, and Jacob Riis became his unofficial guide. Roosevelt was a native of a city that was largely unknown to him. "I loved him from the day I first saw him," Riis remembered. Like Parkhurst, Roosevelt discovered vice and corruption and believed in strict enforcement of the laws; unlike the other moral reformers, he had no interest in political "nonpartisanship." He remained a committed, if independent, Republican. Roosevelt also learned that the moral reform that motivated evangelical reformers like Parkhurst, Willard, and Comstock came at a political and social price. Roosevelt

---

54. William Martin Armstrong, *E. L. Godkin: A Biography* (Albany: State University of New York Press, 1978), 193–95; *Tammany Biographies* (New York: New York Evening Post, 1894), 3–4; Connolly, 83–85.
55. Burrows and Wallace, 1167–69. For a full account of the scandal, see Daniel J. Czitrom, *New York Exposed: How a Gilded Age Police Scandal Shocked the Nation and Launched the Progressive Era* (New York: Oxford University Press, 2016).
56. McCormick, 46–50.

pushed Sunday closure of saloons both as a political tactic to hurt Tammany and as a way to break police corruption. He was right: saloon-keepers routinely bribed police to ignore Sunday openings. But Sunday closure deeply angered a working-class male constituency, especially German Americans, for whom a Sunday in a saloon or family beer garden was one of their few pleasures, and they would help return Tammany to office in 1897. The state Republican machine understandably regarded Roosevelt's campaign as detrimental to the party's larger interests.[57]

Among the politicians listed in the 1894 edition of the New York Post's *Tammany Biographies* was George Washington Plunkitt. When he was in the New York State Senate in the 1880s, reformers thought Plunkitt "thoroughly bad," but his sins were comparatively venial. Unlike other Tammany politicians, he had not killed anybody nor bitten anyone's ear off. He was, *Tammany Biographies* declared, "in politics as a business. He has no hesitation in using his position for his private gain in the way of assisting his contracts or real estate speculations." Private gain still took precedence over public service. When Plunkitt controlled street cleaning in New York, he cleaned up, but the streets remained filthy.[58]

Plunkitt was a more typical Tammany politician than Godkin's thugs. He did not deny that he made money from politics, but he was sensitive to the *Post*'s and Parkhurst's contention that Tammany was a collection of criminals who grew rich from protection money and bribes. That was what he called "dishonest graft." He rose through "honest graft." Honest graft worked the way corporations worked: it exploited insider information, used public policy for private gain, and relied on "friendship." Plunkitt happily admitted what his critics contended; consciously echoing the *Tammany Biographies*, he claimed, "If my worst enemy was given the job of writin' my epitaph when I'm gone, he couldn't do more than write: 'George W. Plunkitt. He Seen His Opportunities, and He Took 'Em.'" Tammany took care of itself by taking care of its friends. That was, he said, good politics and honest graft.[59]

Plunkitt had done well. Born poor in a shantytown in what later became Central Park, he rose from a cart driver to a butcher's boy, and later became a butcher. By the early twentieth century, he was a millionaire

57. Thank you to Daniel Czitrom for help on this. Kathleen Dalton, "Theodore Roosevelt: A Strenuous Life" (New York: Knopf, 2002), 149–61; Lubove, 64; McCormick, 95.
58. *Tammany Biographies*, 15–16.
59. William L. Riordon, *Plunkitt of Tammany Hall* (New York: McClure, Phillips, 1905), 7–10.

through city contracts and lucrative investments, relying on inside information about city projects that would raise property values.[60]

Plunkitt's sensitivity about "dishonest graft" thus involved his pocketbook as much as his pride. When reformers successfully made such charges, it cost the machine votes and Plunkitt money. In 1894 and 1901 Tammany lost the election to reform tickets. It would recover because, Plunkitt contended, the people, by which he meant the immigrant public, ultimately understood honest graft and friendship. Friendship would never hurt Tammany since "every good man looks after his friends.... If I have a good thing to hand out in private life, I give it to a friend. Why shouldn't I do the same in public life?" Machines sought friends by giving aid and favors, many of them public, in exchange for the votes that gave them the power to pursue honest graft.[61]

The difference between Republican and Democratic machines in New York was in their friends and the level at which they operated. Thomas Platt was an old lieutenant of Conkling and an "easy boss," who ran the Republican state machine on the basis of consultation, rural votes, and railroad, utility, and insurance money. The votes were open; the money was secret. Platt and his cohorts got lucrative government contracts and freely used political connections to help their own and their associates' businesses. He used Republican legislative victories in the mid-1890s to squeeze Tammany by diminishing municipal powers when New York City and Brooklyn combined, and by regulating and taxing liquor. The liquor industry had been a source of Tammany's strength; when it moved under state regulation, the taxes went to state coffers, which Republicans controlled. The corruption of the Republican machine angered reformers as much as the corruption of Tammany did, but it, and Platt's involvement, would be fully revealed only with Charles Evans Hughes's investigation of the life insurance industry after the turn of the century. Those who smelled rats eventually found them.[62]

Neither Republican nor Democratic political machines were social welfare organizations, although they could be mistaken for them in hindsight. They were usually far more conservative than the voters who supported them; machine politicians had no ambitions to overturn the existing order of things. They were often fiscally conservative. In part they had to be, since legislatures restricted the ability of cities to borrow. In New

60. Riordan, iii–vi, 3–11, 154, 170.
61. Ibid., 8–9.
62. McCormick, 69–72, 78, 89–94, 198–203; Richard McCormick, "Prelude to Progressivism: The Transformation of New York State Politics, 1890–1910," *New York History* 59, no. 3 (1978): 253–76.

York and San Francisco, the machines allied with local business groups that sought low taxes. They were, for a price, just as likely to protect landlords who exploited their tenants against code violations "as to seek protection for the tenants. Often they would do both. Machine politicians were, as Henry George knew, also quick to sell themselves as bulwarks against radicals and socialists.[63]

William Riordon, a New York newspaperman, wrote a day-in-the-life account of Plunkitt. He rendered him as vaudeville Irishman complete with dialect, although Plunkitt was Protestant and native-born. Riordon did, however, accurately demonstrate the machine's appeal to the immigrant poor and why its activities could be mistaken for social welfare. Plunkitt's day began at 2:00 in the morning, when a bartender awoke him to go bail out a saloonkeeper. He did so and went back to bed, but was awakened by fire engines at 6:00 a.m. Fires were "considered great vote-getters." He and his district captains gathered up the tenants and found them food, clothing, and temporary quarters. The morning was a tour of courts, helping indiscriminately the "worthy" and "unworthy" poor. He bailed out drunks and intervened on behalf of widows about to be thrown out on the streets. He spent the late morning arranging jobs for constituents. At 3:00 in the afternoon he was at an Italian funeral, followed by a Jewish funeral; he "went conspicuously to the front both in the Catholic church and the synagogue." After dinner he presided over a meeting of election district captains. When the meeting adjourned, he went to a church fair: "Kissed the little one, flattered their mothers, and took their fathers out for something down at the corner." The day closed with Plunkitt buying tickets for a church excursion and a baseball game. He handled the complaints of pushcart peddlers, before attending "a Hebrew wedding reception and dance. Had previously sent a handsome wedding present to the bride." At midnight he was in bed.[64]

Jane Addams, who founded the famous Chicago settlement Hull House, battled men like Plunkitt, but she granted them a grudging respect. Her account of Johnny Powers, a ward boss in Chicago, was condescending but sympathetic. The successful politician, she wrote, "must be a good man according to the standards of his constituents. He must not attempt to hold up a morality beyond them, nor must he attempt to reform or change the standard." The standard was generosity: "Any one who has

63. Connolly, 157–58; for argument of social safety net, see Terry Golway, *Machine Made: Tammany Hall and the Creation of Modern American Politics* (New York: Norton, 2014), xviii–xx; William Issel and Robert W. Cherny, *San Francisco, 1865–1932: Politics, Power, and Urban Development* (Berkeley: University of California Press, 1986), 130–32; Riordon, iii–vi, 3–11, 154, 170.
64. Riordon, 8–9.

lived among poorer people cannot fail to be impressed with their constant kindness to each other: that unfailing response to the needs and distresses of their neighbors." If men like Powers and Plunkitt acted appropriately, their constituents were not likely to question their motives or be concerned with the larger costs to the city. Addams echoed Plunkitt: a man should stand by his friends. Her account of the nineteenth ward in Chicago was a mirror of Riordon's account of Plunkitt's New York, down to the widows, the weddings, the funerals, the church bazaars, the jobs, and the gifts at Christmas. Honesty and candidates from the "better element" usually had little chance against this.[65]

The Reverend Charles Parkhurst denounced the boss as "the most sagaciously devised scheme ever originated for the purpose of crushing out, weakening, and drying up the individual all manly personality," but immigrant voters did not judge bosses so harshly. When reformers succeeded, if only briefly, in ousting the boss, they found their constituents expected them to act like the boss. As one wrote, "The Alderman is, next to the Tammany Hall district leader, supposed to be the principal comforter of the afflicted and the aid of the undeserving unfortunates within his district."[66]

III

In what became one of the enduring tropes of American popular culture, immigrant parents—Jewish, Italian, more rarely Irish or German—complained that their sons were bums more interested in baseball, or boxing, or sneaking off to whatever circus or entertainment was available than in studying or working. Abraham Cahan, a Russian Jewish immigrant and journalist, captured it precisely. Writing in Yiddish in the *Jewish Daily Forward* at the turn of the century, he responded to a father who complained about his teenage son's love of baseball: "They run after a leather ball like children. I want my boy to grow up to be a *mensh*, not a wild American runner. But he cries his head off." Let him play, Cahan replied. "Let us not so raise the children that they should grow up foreigners in their own birthplace." A few years earlier, when Cahan published his novella *Yekl*, set in the Lower East Side, he stated his case more forcefully. When challenged over his enthusiasm for boxing and baseball, the title character, who had changed his name to Jake, retorted, "Once I live in

65. Connolly, 172–77; Jane Addams, "Why the Ward Boss Rules," *Outlook* 57 (Apr. 2, 1898): 879–82.
66. *Outlook* 50 (Dec. 8, 1894): 973; Teaford, 27–30.

America, I want to know that I live in America." "Here," he said, "a Jew is as good as a Gentile."[67]

That a Jew being as good as a gentile involved play—sometimes bloody play—and that nationality somehow connected to adults participating in and watching what both immigrants and native-born Americans of an earlier generation thought of as children's games was a relatively new phenomenon. Mark Twain's 1876 evocation of an antebellum childhood in *Tom Sawyer* was full of games, animals, imaginary play, and highly anticipated entertainments, but only some of the entertainments involved adults, and no one mistook them for uplift.[68]

At the end of the Civil War, the words *sport* and *sporting* usually indicated something untoward. They referred to the activities of working-class toughs or dissolute rich men and the women, often prostitutes, who consorted with them. Sport was connected with gambling and saloons. The sporting life brought to mind pool, billiards, cockfighting, dogfighting, rat baiting, prizefighting, hunting, and horse racing. By the end of the century, how people played, whom they played with, and who watched them play had become markers of a rapidly changing society. Sport, particularly amidst the middle and upper classes, became a way to cultivate manliness, to overcome neurasthenia, and to demonstrate the will and character that earlier generations had supposedly developed through war or hunting in the wild.[69]

In 1876, William Dean Howells reported his son John's and daughter Winnie's enthusiasm for baseball. They went "to all the matches, and our table talk is a jargon of 'hot balls,' 'hot grounders,' 'second bases,' 'pitchers,' 'catches,' 'licks,' and I don't know what else. It amuses me, who never cared a straw for any sort of game, except marbles." After Winnie had fallen sick and the doctors diagnosed neurasthenia, the first resort was to the gymnasium, from which Howells hoped for "great good."[70]

---

67. Peter Levine, *Ellis Island to Ebbets Field Sport and the American Jewish Experience* (New York: Oxford University Press, 1992), 87–88. Cahan helped found the paper and edited it for years; Diner, 57.

68. Mark Twain, *The Adventures of Tom Sawyer*, Author's National Edition: The Writings of Mark Twain (New York: Harper & Brothers, 1903, orig. ed. 1875).

69. For sporting life, see Paul E. Johnson, *Sam Patch, the Famous Jumper* (New York: Hill and Wang, 2003), 134–42; Elliott J. Gorn, *The Manly Art: Bare-Knuckle Prize Fighting in America*, updated ed. (Ithaca, NY: Cornell University Press, 2010), 102–3, 130–31, 192–94.

70. W. D. Howells to W. C. Howells, June 2, 1878, and W. D. Howells to W. C. Howells, Dec. 5, 1880, in William Dean Howells, *Selected Letters*, ed. George Warren Arms (Boston: Twayne, 1979), 2: 201, 270.

Howells as a novelist and critic was all too aware of the tension between entertainment and uplift; the necessity of the novel to entertain could sap its duty to educate. But the idea of adding uplift and education to sport and popular entertainments could seem less a parallel development than a parody. Yet this is precisely what promoters of sports and entertainments proposed. In a piece of unsolicited fan mail to Buffalo Bill Cody, Mark Twain pronounced the Wild West "purely and distinctly American." It revealed a truer and vanishing America. By the 1880s Albert Spalding— who moved easily from player to manager to president of the Chicago White Stockings—had managed to anoint baseball, by then a largely urban game, as the "national pastime," redolent of a rural past and reeking of American virtue.[71]

Spalding was hardly alone; in 1889 Walter Camp praised baseball as quintessentially American and presented it as a "good wholesome sport" that should be played by every boy. Camp, a persistent defender and promoter of American sports, was better known for his marketing of football as an antidote to softening and emasculation. He was a business executive, sports writer, and coach at Yale who standardized the rules for football. In one of those developments too good to be true, he married the half-sister of his professor at Yale, William Graham Sumner. Sumner, as devoted as anyone in America to the survival of the fittest, had acquired a relation who turned sport into a manifestation of fitness. Baseball, Camp wrote, would free the American boy from the "taint of dissipation" and bind him by "his honor to his captain and to his fellows." It had, Camp explained a little optimistically, escaped from being linked to the saloon and gambling. It not only avoided evil; it promoted good. Spalding simply listed baseball's contributions more or less alphabetically: "American Courage, Confidence, Combativeness; American Dash, Discipline, Determination; American Energy, Eagerness, Enthusiasm; American Pluck, Persistency, Permanence; American Spirit, Sagacity, Success; American Vim, vigor, virility."[72]

71. T. J. Jackson Lears, *Rebirth of a Nation: The Making of Modern America, 1877–1920* (New York: Harper, 2009), 28; T. J. Lears, *No Place of Grace: Antimoderism and the Transformation of American Culture, 1880–1920* (New York: Pantheon Books, 1981), 107–8; Steven A. Riess, "Sport and the Redefinition of American Middle-Class Maculinity, 1840–1890," in *Major Problems in American Sport History: Documents and Essays*, ed. Steven A. Riess, 2nd ed. (Stamford, CT: Cengage, 2015), 194–203; Louis S. Warren, *Buffalo Bill's America: William Cody and the Wild West Show* (New York: Knopf, 2005), 294–95.

72. Julie Des Jardins, *Walter Camp: Football and the Modern Man* (New York: Oxford University Press, 2015), 37, 42, 63, 73, 83, 86; Walter Camp, "Base-Ball—for the Spectator," *The Century* (October 1889): 831–37; Levine, *Spalding*, 43–45, 98–99.

Buffalo Bill Cody's Wild West even more spectacularly combined sport, entertainment, and uplift. With its rough riders (first Indians, scouts, cowboys and vaqueros, and then horsemen from around the globe) and its marksmen (Buffalo Bill himself, and later the famous Annie Oakley), it speeded the transition of horsemanship and marksmanship associated with war and the hunt into sport and entertainment. Cody proclaimed them a form of patriotic education.[73]

Cody and Spalding made the Wild West and baseball into missionary endeavors spreading American culture and virtue. They celebrated the democratic tendencies Godkin despised. "The genius of our institutions," Spalding declared, "is democratic, and baseball is a democratic game." In 1889 immigrants coming into New York harbor could have seen Buffalo Bill's Wild West departing on a European tour that would last until 1892, and that same year other immigrants would have entered New York harbor alongside the ship carrying Albert Spalding's Chicago White Stockings, who were returning from their world tour of 1888–89.[74]

Baseball may have been a more democratic game than other American sports in terms of its inclusiveness and mass appeal, but it did not take much looking to find that, like the ballot, it was not available to all. Spalding did not ask Moses Fleetwood Walker, a black player for the Toledo Mud Hens, for testimonials on the democratic appeal of baseball. Spalding's Chicago White Stockings refused to play Toledo if Walker took the field. Walker was soon exiled to the new Negro League. Louis Sokalexis, a Penobscot Indian, did play professional baseball for the Cleveland Spiders, which later became the Cleveland Indians. He went about his business amid a cacophony of war whoops and insults. He was, according to an 1897 account, "hooted at and howled at by the thimble-brained brigade of the bleachers." Ball players' terms of employment shredded ideas of free labor. Team owners instituted the reserve clause, which prohibited teams from trying to hire other teams' players. Players could not be bought and sold, but their contracts could be. Spalding sold "King" Kelly's contract, which, in effect, meant selling Kelly (the star of the White Stockings and the best-known player in the country), to Boston in 1887 after the White Stockings lost the championship series to St. Louis. Kelly—and much of the rest of the team—had been drinking, leaving them "in no condition to play the Browns." In 1887 Spalding made the team take temperance pledges.[75]

73. Warren, 126–28, 224–26, 239–51.
74. Ibid., 344–57; Thomas W. Zeiler, *Ambassadors in Pinstripes: The Spalding World Baseball Tour and the Birth of the American Empire* (Lanham, MD: Rowman & Littlefield, 2006), 73–192; Levine, *Spalding*, 99–109.
75. Jeffrey P. Powers-Beck, *The American Indian Integration of Baseball* (Lincoln: University of Nebraska Press, 2004), 23–24; Levine, *Spalding*, 30–31, 40–43, 47, 52–54.

In its racial relations, employment of immigrants and children of immigrants, temperance pledges, and labor relations, baseball mirrored for better and worse the increasingly diverse, urban, and industrial society that produced it. To defeat defections to other leagues and punish bad behavior, Spalding's National League added the blacklist to the reserve clause. Baseball players, most of whom came from the working class and many of whom were Irish and German, made their own attempt at cooperative commonwealth with the creation of an independent Players' League in 1890. Among the insurgents was Kelly. The result was the Brotherhood War, with Brotherhood being the common name for organized skilled workers—and defeat of the players. Spalding was the architect of their defeat. American baseball looked a lot like American business, and for that matter like American politics. Tammany politicians were early team owners in New York, controlling, among others, the New York Giants.[76]

Those Americans who denied the existence of social class in America were wise to ignore sport, which traced the boundaries of social class, and the transgressions across those boundaries, with some precision. In important ways, sport formed a line of defense within the American social elite between "society" and the nouveau riche. As J. P. Morgan said, "You can do business with anyone, but you can go sailing only with a gentleman." Money gave people the leisure and space to play, but that play acquired social cachet by taking place in a whole set of new institutions. To play golf and tennis, the rich established country clubs. To play in the city, they created exclusive urban athletic clubs. To go boating, they established yacht clubs. They raced their trotters on the edge of the city, but more and more they raced them and thoroughbreds on elaborate tracks under rules and conditions that they controlled. Access to such venues was limited. The Howellses were invited to the Rockaway Hunt Club to watch a game of polo. They were, he wrote, "a set of horsey, rather tiresome rich people," who would find out soon enough that the Howellses were "not their sort."[77]

August Belmont understood this. He cared about both horses and social class. "Racing," he said, "is for the rich." Belmont was a German Jewish immigrant, the agent of the Rothschilds, who had married the daughter

76. Riess, *City Games*, 86–87, 103–4; Levine, *Spalding*, 49–69; Harold Seymour, *Baseball: The Early Years* (New York: Oxford University Press, 1960), 86–87, 92–93, 106–11, 130–31.

77. Pak, 86–87; Donald Mrozek, "Sporting Life as Consumption, Fashion, and Display— The Pastimes of the Rich at the Turn of the Century," in Riess, *Major Problems in American Sport History*, 189; W. D. Howells to A. Howells, May 31, 1896, in Howells, *Selected Letters*, 4: 127–28; Riess, *City Games*, 54–60; Katherine Carmines Mooney, *Race Horse Men: How Slavery and Freedom Were Made at the Racetrack* (Cambridge, MA: Harvard University Press, 2014), 136.

of Commodore Matthew Perry, converted to Christianity, and served as Democratic National Chairman following the Civil War. He had worked toward reconciliation of the Northern and Southern elites, and he found in his and the Southerners' mutual enthusiasm for horse racing a means to do so.[78]

Rich men's knowledge and ownership of horses gave them status, but there were limits. Belmont's status depended not only on his wealth but also on his marriage and conversion. Although as head of the Democratic Party he consorted with Tammany politicians, he was not one of them; still, their mutual interests included horses as well as politics. Saratoga Race Track was a joint venture of Tammany's John Morrisey, ex-prize-fighter and political fixer, and men such as Cornelius Vanderbilt, but the social lines did not disappear. Richard Croker, the Tammany boss, proved successful enough as a horse owner to win the Epsom Derby in England, but this did not make Croker a gentleman. A definitive moment in elite anti-Semitism came in Saratoga in 1877 when the Grand Union Hotel refused admittance to a leading German Jewish banker, Joseph Seligman, and his family because they were "Israelites" whose presence offended a Christian clientele. That the Seligmans had close connections with the Republican Party and that Joseph's brother was an old friend of Ulysses S. Grant did not matter. In 1893 New York's Union Club rejected Joseph's nephew for membership.[79]

Sports still patrolled the boundaries. The boxes of the new racetracks were for the rich, but there were grandstands for those spectators with insufficient money to own horses yet still enough money and sufficient time to make their way to the tracks at the edges of the city or at summer resorts like Saratoga to watch the races. Working-class gamblers, who had neither the time nor the resources to go the track, placed bets with bookmakers in saloons.[80]

Until the 1890s, however, racing was unusual in allowing racial integration at its lower and middle ranks. In the antebellum South the best riders and trainers had been slaves, and once freed they, alongside a new generation, continued to ride and train horses during the Gilded Age, creating a tight and prosperous community centered on Lexington, Kentucky. At least a dozen of the jockeys in the first Kentucky Derby in 1875 were black, but their status became part of the larger contest of Reconstruction. Black men might be the best trainers and jockeys, but white men owned the horses and controlled the tracks, as Isaac Murphy, the country's leading

78. Mooney, 158–61.
79. Diner, 38; Jacobson, *Whiteness of a Different Color*, 163–66; Mooney, 134–35.
80. Riess, *City Games*, 54–55, 60, 73, 209–12.

jockey, found out. Murphy was too good; he became too threatening. Slandered, kept from the best horses, sick from the constant need to keep off weight, he was dead at thirty-five. With the triumph of Jim Crow, black jockeys and trainers largely disappeared in the North as well as the South.[81]

Elite sports elided over into middle-class sports, spurred by a growing concern over the perceived feminization of American culture. "Sissy," "mollycoddle," and "pussy foot" all entered the language as terms for unmanly men. Football, boxing, and hunting were all meant to restore manliness. Football was a game played by rich men's sons and by the middling classes; it differed from many earlier games in being, like baseball, a team sport demanding organization, coordination, and direction, the very qualities typical of the new economy. Playing organized football usually meant attending a prep school or college. By and large the poor did not go to college, although Indian boarding schools such as Carlisle served as a surrogate and spawned famous football teams. Like racing, football was at once a sport and a major social event.[82]

When the sports of the rich and middling classes intruded on the poor, they could make social tensions manifest. Cycling, which became immensely popular in the 1890s, was one of the few sports open to both women and men, but it was always a middle- and upper-class preoccupation. Six-day bicycle races at Madison Square Garden attracted working-class spectators, but because it demanded the purchase of a bicycle and a place to ride it, cycling largely excluded the urban poor, black and white. When urban cyclists rode to work on Wall Street, crossing through immigrant neighborhoods, they annoyed pedestrians and often hit children. Residents responded by creating obstacles in the streets and pelting cyclists with stones and garbage.[83]

The opposite was also true: when the activities of the poor intruded on the spaces claimed by the rich, they faced resistance and suppression. In the late nineteenth century, hunting became a sport, whose rules were determined by rich and middle-class sportsmen. Game was declining and conservation laws were necessary to preserve it, but these laws imposed the greatest burdens on those—Indians, poorer whites and blacks, and rural residents—who hunted for food or as a living. Rich men hunted to cultivate their manhood, not to feed their families. They enunciated the rules of a fair hunt, limited their kill, defined which animals qualified as

81. Mooney, 164, 173–235.
82. Gorn, 192–94; Riess, *City Games*, 55–58; Gail Bederman, *Manliness and Civilization: A Cultural History of Gender and Race in the United States, 1880–1917* (Chicago: University of Chicago Press, 1995), 1–5, 15–19.
83. Riess, *City Games*, 62–65.

game animals, established seasons, and sought to preserve habitat to have enough game to kill. They used the state to suppress the activities of those who ignored these standards.[84]

Immigrant athletes initially played the games of their home countries, but like the character Yekl, they, and especially their children, took to American games. Immigrant sports clustered either around ethnic clubs like the German Turnvereins and Bohemian sokol halls, which often featured gymnasiums, or Irish sports organized by fraternal and political organizations like the Irish Clan Na Gael. By the 1890s, old-country athletics were yielding to American sports, and Irish Social and Athletic Clubs, often associated with gangs or politicians, were appearing in urban areas. The Young Men's Hebrew Association, modeled after the YMCA, promoted "muscular Judaism," and its gyms and athletic activities were a feature of German Jewish life.[85]

Boxing, an affectation of Theodore Roosevelt's, straddled the boundaries of respectability. "Scientific" sparring and later boxing under the Marquis of Queensbury rules was legitimate; prizefighting, particularly bareknuckle fighting, was becoming illegal. Professional prizefighting under the new rules became an overwhelmingly immigrant, and to a lesser extent black, sport. These fighters learned their skills in the streets as self or community defense against rival groups or gangs, and then perfected them in rundown gyms. The best prizefighters in the 1880s and 1890s were Irish. John L. Sullivan, the heavyweight champion from 1882 to 1892, legitimized the Queensbury rules and became the most famous American athlete of his era. He carried working-class toughness of the streets into the new world of professional sports. He symbolized a paradoxical heroic self-indulgence, until his bouts of intense training could no longer balance his high living and carousing. By the turn of the century, there would be Jewish champions; other ethnic groups followed.[86]

When George Washington Plunkitt bought the tickets to support a local baseball team, it was a small gesture that pointed to a larger pattern: in popular culture the things often regarded as the most quintessentially American were most enthusiastically adopted by the children of immigrants. Baseball was the sport where the tangled ethnic, racial, and social

84. John F. Reiger, *American Sportsmen and the Origins of Conservation*, 3rd, rev., & expanded ed. (Corvallis: Oregon State University Press, 2001); Karl Jacoby, *Crimes against Nature: Squatters, Poachers, Thieves, and the Hidden History of American Conservation* (Berkeley: University of California Press, 2001), 1–148; Louis S. Warren, *The Hunter's Game: Poachers and Conservationists in Twentieth-Century America* (New Haven, CT: Yale University Press, 1997), 48–105, and passim.

85. Riess, *City Games*, 94–100.

86. Ibid., 109–13; Gorn, 196–206, 222.

tensions of urban American played out most obviously. Like virtually all other team sports, it was a male game, but it had a wide geographic and social reach. Indians enthusiastically adopted it. It was played along the Mexican border and spread across it. But mostly, particularly in its professional form, it was an urban game played and watched by all social classes, who could, at least for the moment, claim a larger identity through the team and the place it represented.[87]

When immigrant fathers looked at baseball or the Wild West and saw childishness, they missed an essential part of both. These games were businesses that reeked of the very American modernity that both attracted and repelled the immigrants themselves. Albert Goodwill Spalding parlayed his athletic career into creating what became a famous sporting goods company. A son of the Midwest, who always said the right things about baseball as a tool for promoting character, he knew it was also a way to rise in the world.[88]

Buffalo Bill Cody embraced a capitalist modernity as well. The Wild West employed wage laborers and depended on modern advertising and steam transport in order to portray a vanished world that lacked all these things. Cody and his troupe traveled by special train. They created a tent city, often around a park—sometimes a park of their own creation—and used generators to stage nighttime shows under electric lights. The Wild West's encampments were transient modern cities—the opposite of tenements—that won praise for their sanitation and for their health.[89]

Within the tent city, particularly by the 1890s, was a world as diverse as the immigrant neighborhoods. The Wild West featured Indians, but it also contained Mexican vaqueros and band members who, like some of the cowboys, were children of immigrants. By 1894, when Cody played a six-month stand in Brooklyn, the Wild West had adopted a new format. It was now the Wild West and Congress of Rough Riders of the World. The show included Cossack, Gaucho, Gypsy, German, English, Arab, and Turkmen riders, a kind of mounted equivalent of the ethnic display of Brooklyn and New York.[90]

Abraham Cahan recognized the larger contours of sport and entertainment. Later in the 1890s, when Cody again played New York, Cahan interviewed both Buffalo Bill in English and his Cossacks in Russian. A Jewish immigrant, whose coreligionists suffered attacks from the Cossacks

87. Riess, City Games, 65–68; Alan M. Klein, Baseball on the Border: A Tale of Two Laredos (Princeton, NJ: Princeton University Press, 1997), 32–46; Powers-Beck, 7–10, 12–30.
88. Levine, Ellis Island, 5–6, 8–9, 13, 21, 26.
89. Warren, Buffalo Bill's America, 417, 442–47, 437–45, 452.
90. Ibid., 422–32, 432–37.

in Russia, interviewing a Cossack performing with the Wild West was star-
tling; however, the Cossacks turned out not to be Cossacks at all but rather
Georgians, who, like Russian Jews, were subjects of the Russian empire.
The Georgians were not impressed with American cowboys. The American
riders were "pretty good," the leader of the Georgians admitted, but "there
is no fire in them, and nothing sweet either, even if they know their
business."[91]

Buffalo Bill certainly knew his business, and Cahan both knew that
Cody knew it and realized what a complicated business it was. Cody was
in the business of popular entertainment, and he was good at it; still, he
also always refused to attach the word *show* to his entertainment, insisting
it was educational. The education was supposed to be in Americanism—
the conquest of savagery, the spread of the home—and the audience
American families. The audience, however, turned out to be international
as the show traveled, and, in a sense, international even at home as he
attracted immigrants. The audience was, however, never passive, and the
show could not be simply didactic. And this made popular culture a complicated business.

In popular culture, religion, politics, and ever more aspects of American
life, immigrants began to transform institutions that were supposed to
transform them. They did not turn them into versions of an old world; nor
did they intend to do so. Those who pined for an older world could, and
often did, return to it. Instead, immigrants created a more complicated
American world.

91. Abraham Cahan, ed., "We Are Not Cossacks," in *Grandma Never Lived in America:
The New Journalism of Abraham Cahan* (Bloomington: Indiana University Press,
1985), 424–27.

20

Dystopian and Utopian America

Lizzie Borden was born in Fall River, Massachusetts, in 1860, and still lived there in the 1890s. Over the course of her lifetime, Fall River had become the largest cotton milling center on the continent. Every morning Irish, French Canadian, and Portuguese workers streamed through the streets and into the mills, where they worked their ten hours in the heat of the summer and the cold of the winter, amid constant noise and dust. More than 55 percent of the workers in the mills were children.

The Bordens, reputedly among the richest families in Fall River, did not share in these hardships. The workers were Catholics; the Bordens were members of the Congregational Church. Lizzie belonged to the WCTU and served as secretary-treasurer of the local Christian Endeavor Society. She had traveled in Europe. But her life and that of her sister did not match their father's wealth. They lived not in the Hill District, the home of wealthy Yankees, but on Second Street, surrounded by middle-class Irish. Andrew Borden was if not a miser then a mean man who kept every dollar close. His own father had fallen in the world, and he did not intend to tumble. Lizzie's stepmother, Abby, was neither beautiful nor well-born, and her stepdaughters resented her, feared she would diminish their inheritance, and blamed her for their own unhappiness.[1]

Lizzie Borden was thirty-two, unmarried, and still living in her father's house under her parents' control, with a life confined to carrying out respectable good works. Whatever moral authority she mustered had yielded neither economic nor political influence. Unlike Frances Willard, or Borden's contemporary Jane Addams, she had not dared to claim a wider authority. She had not shed her desire for comfort and social prominence. There were signs of disorder as well as discontent. She had, among local

---

1. Joseph A. Conforti, *Lizzie Borden on Trial: Murder, Ethnicity, and Gender* (Lawrence: University Press of Kansas, 2015), 6–22, 23–42, 44–50; Cara W Robertson, "Representing Miss Lizzie: Cultural Convictions in the Trial of Lizzie Borden," *Yale Journal of Law and Humanities* (1996): 367–68.

merchants, the reputation as a kleptomaniac. The merchants billed her father, who paid.[2]

On August 4, 1892, in the middle of the day, someone used an axe to murder Abby Borden and then, an hour later, Andrew, after he had returned home to take a nap. Only Lizzie and an Irish maid—Bridget Sullivan, who like 60 percent of Irish-born women in the United States was a domestic servant—were at home. The murders took place in separate rooms, and neither Sullivan nor Lizzie reported an intruder. The first suspects named by Bridget were, like her, immigrants, a Portuguese laborer and a Swede, but they had alibis. Lizzie was indicted for murder three weeks after the crime, spawning the children's rhyme:

> Lizzie Borden took an ax,
> Gave her mother forty whacks,
> When she saw what she had done,
> She gave her father forty-one.[3]

The trial began in June 1893. That summer the Fall River mills, in a sign of growing economic turmoil, laid off seven thousand workers. The WCTU supported Lizzie. Women reformers demanded a female jury, a jury of her peers. An ex-governor of Massachusetts served as her attorney. The trial turned on womanhood and femininity. The prosecution portrayed the accused as unfeminine, not a true woman and thus a potential murderer; the defense emphasized her dependence, her submissiveness, her true womanhood, and her Christianity. Her attorneys invoked all the tropes of female disability to rescue her. They got statements she made after her arrest excluded as mere hysteria; they explained away her odd behavior and flecks of blood on her clothes by citing menstruation. She did not conform to contemporary ideas of criminal types, most of which were male and none of which included members of the WCTU. How could a loving daughter transform into "the most consummate criminal we have read of in all our history or works of fiction"? It took an all-male jury less than an hour to acquit her, to the applause of spectators. Even hysteria—the conventional diagnosis for unhappy and disruptive women—did not encompass murder. Lizzie Borden was not a member of the "dangerous classes," and the working people of Fall River (some of whom were) thought she got away with murder. Lizzie sold her parents' house, bought a house that she

---

2. Conforti, 33–41; Robertson, 369–72, 375; Louise W. Knight, *Citizen: Jane Addams and the Struggle for Democracy* (Chicago: University of Chicago Press, 2005), 226–37.

3. Conforti, 18–19; Ann Schofield, "Lizzie Borden Took an Axe: History, Feminism and American Culture," *American Studies* 34, no. 1 (1993): 98; Steven Mintz, *Huck's Raft: A History of American Childhood* (Cambridge, MA: Belknap Press of Harvard University Press, 2004), 144; Robertson, 357–60.

believed she deserved in the Hill District, and changed her name to Lizbeth. The WCTU gave way to a life of theaters and champagne suppers. She broke with her sister and was ostracized by Fall River society. She would go on to have a longer life in American popular culture than virtually any figure of the 1890s except perhaps Buffalo Bill. But where Buffalo Bill's fame rested on saving the home from "savages," Lizzie Borden's notoriety rested on the fear that the home might be producing them.[4]

I

Theodore Dreiser sent his fictional Caroline Meeber to Chicago from Wisconsin in the summer of 1889. *Sister Carrie* told of a girl leaving home and going adrift in a city that lacked true homes. But in the novel Dreiser also created a character who became a home wrecker in part by embracing the individualism that allowed men to destroy homes.

Dreiser framed Carrie's possibilities with Victorian simplicity: "When a girl leaves her home at eighteen, she does one of two things. Either she falls into saving hands and becomes better, or she rapidly assumes the cosmopolitan standards of virtue and becomes worse. Of an intermediate balance, under the circumstances, there is no possibility. The city has its cunning wiles...."[5]

In Chicago and New York, Dreiser's characters had houses and apartments. They were constantly going home, but they lacked homes. "A lovely home atmosphere is one of the flowers of the world," Dreiser wrote, "... nothing more delicate, nothing more calculated to make strong and just the natures cradled and nourished within it." It cultivated the "mystic chords, which bind and thrill the heart of the nation," but "Hurstwood's residence could scarcely be said to be infused with this home spirit."[6]

Sister Carrie traced the hardships of working women's lives—the low pay, the miserable conditions, the lack of recourse in the face of misfortune—and capitalized on the suspicions that young working women were "bad." Employers often paid their female employees below-subsistence wages, regarding their pay as a mere supplement to a male wage earner's income. Women without enough to live on had to do something. The something was, in some cases, prostitution, but prostitution, though paying twice

---

4. R. Hal Williams, *Realigning America: McKinley, Bryan, and the Remarkable Election of 1896* (Lawrence: University Press of Kansas, 2010), 33; Robertson, 351–56, 375–76, 378–416; Schofield, 98–99.
5. Theodore Dreiser, *Sister Carrie* (New York: Bantam Books Classic, 1958, orig. ed. 1900), 1.
6. Ibid., 67.

as much as factory work, was dangerous, and the city also provided other kinds of less dangerous sexual service jobs in cabarets, dance halls, and theaters where attractive women could attract a male clientele. Masseuses, chorus girls, actresses, and later taxi dancers—whom men paid to dance with them—all earned much higher wages than most working women, without actually selling their bodies.[7]

Concerns over women adrift surfaced both in pulp fiction and in social reform. A subgenre of dime novels portrayed young women facing challenges and crises, but the heroines were overmatched. They waited for male rescue and marriage. If they succumbed to temptation, they perished. Reformers shared the novelists' fear that young workingwomen were a step short of a life of vice and degradation. One of the goals of the Young Women's Christian Association, as its Chicago branch declared, "was to seek out women taking up their residence in Chicago and endeavor to bring them under moral and religious influences." The YWCA established an employment bureau and boarding house, which would duplicate "the comforts and blessings of a Christian home." By 1875 the YWCA already had twenty-eight branches. For all the vast, wrenching, and exciting changes in American cities, in the end, the answer to any and every problem seemed to be the home.[8]

Dreiser acknowledged and subverted the pieties of the home. Carrie had little lasting desire for a home. He matter-of-factly gave the details. She preferred Chicago to Columbia City and dreaded returning to her parents' home there. Her sister's house was dour and dreary. She wanted to have a good time and coveted nice things. She could embrace domesticity only as an actress, which she became. When she married Hurstwood after he left his wife, their home in New York depressed and confined her.[9]

Dreiser refused to make Carrie a victim. She ends up exploited by men, but she exploited them in turn. She used them, abandoned them, and succeeded in the theater. Men torn from the home ultimately longed for it, but found, like Hurstwood, only a pauper's grave. Dreiser granted Carrie success, but not happiness. In that, at least, he was true to the pulp fiction genre he otherwise rose far above.

Dreiser also denied Carrie insight, but in this she was little different from his male characters. Their limits made Carrie and her lovers useful vehicles for examining what Dreiser took to be the realities of American progress and the American condition. His characters, men and women,

7. Joanne J. Meyerowitz, *Women Adrift: Independent Wage Earners in Chicago, 1880–1930* (Chicago: University of Chicago Press, 1988), 33–37, 39–41.
8. Ibid., 46–47, 50, 56–60.
9. Dreiser, 11, 40, 41, 56 150, 243, 321.

were individualists looking toward their own gain and desire. He made Carrie a creature of American progress. It was her "longing for that which is better" that caused her to err.[10]

Almost uniformly shallow and narrow, living in a low-ceilinged world, Dreiser's characters lacked Josiah Strong's Christian measures of progress. They put their faith in material things, but Dreiser would not allow their individualism to be sufficient even for this. He suggested that a "man's fortune or material progress is very much the same as his bodily growth." First he grows stronger, and then, inevitably, he declines. The only protection against decline is social; it could be "conserved by the growth of a community or of a state." Left only to his own efforts, an individual's progress and fortune "would pass as his strength and will." This is what happened to Hurstwood.[11]

Carrie ends up dissatisfied with what she has gained, but she did not long for domesticity. Ultimately Carrie pursues beauty, but this was, Dreiser suggested, for her a hopeless pursuit. She could never really distinguish beauty from pleasure, a pursuit of "that radiance of delight which tints the distant hilltops of the world."[12]

Dreiser made Carrie a sensational representative of the large group of young women living outside of families in the city. Many of these women were poor, but it was not just their poverty that was alarming; it was the way they severed the connection between women and conventional ideas of the home. As the century progressed, a rising number of urban renters were women who, as they sought employment outside the home, often lived apart from their families. Such young women concentrated in the cities because the needlework, factory work, office work, teaching positions, and sales work that gave them employment were largely urban. Disproportionally native-born, female migrants came because cities offered better opportunities than rural areas or small towns. They were dissatisfied with the norms of patriarchal families for sometimes gritty and elemental reasons. They resented having to turn over their wages to their fathers, and they sometimes fell victim to violations of the patriarchal standards: assault from fathers, stepfathers, or other male relatives.[13]

Self-supporting women were "women adrift." Like male tramps, they were workers detached from the home and thus defined as dangerous. Landlords preferred men as boarders or renters. They complained that female boarders used the bathroom too often and were more likely to cook

10. Dreiser, 398.
11. Ibid., 261–62.
12. Ibid., 398.
13. Meyerowitz, 4–16, 29.

or do laundry in their rooms, but they also suspected that their female lodgers and renters were "bad" — sexually promiscuous and not respectable. To escape surveillance, judgments, and complaints, single women began to rent apartments communally by the end of the century.[14]

Jane Addams and educated, middle-class women like her shared many of the dissatisfactions that brought working-class women into the city and that drove Lizzie Borden to murder. In 1889 Addams co-founded Hull House on Halstead Street in Chicago's West Side, just blocks from where Mrs. O'Leary's cow had ignited the Chicago fire. Settlement houses were an American phenomenon that like so many other reforms initially replicated European models. Addams was one of many American visitors to Toynbee Hall in London's East End. Like their British cousins, American settlement workers had Social Gospel roots and emphasized culture and uplift, but unlike the British they went further. In 1891–92 ten new settlement houses had opened in Chicago, Boston, New York, and Philadelphia alone. They blended social gospel with social science to create a nondenominational Christian cooperativism, but in its early years Hull House was marked by an attempt to bring high culture to the masses. In 1892 it offered immigrants thirty-one classes, ranging from Greek art to Shakespeare and English literature. Both John Dewey, a young professor at John D. Rockefeller's new University of Chicago, and Samuel Gompers gave talks at Hull House.[15]

The blood of both workers and police had flowed on Halsted Street. A few miles south of Hull House ran the viaduct that was the site of a vicious battle during the Great Railroad Strike of 1877; less than a mile north was Haymarket. Unpaved, with its numerous wooden houses unconnected to the city's sewer system, Halsted was a street of mud, manure, human excrement, garbage, and animal carcasses as well as blood. Addams organized local boys into a "Columbian guards" during the World's Fair summer to battle the filth of the streets with short-handled shovels, but only winter tamed the smell.[16]

The people who lived on Halstead changed as new waves of immigrants washed into Chicago. Large numbers of Irish, twenty thousand in Holy Family Parish alone, dwelled near Hull House, but the color-coded

14. Ibid., 25–27, 74–80.
15. Daniel T. Rodgers, *Atlantic Crossings: Social Politics in a Progressive Age* (Cambridge, MA: Belknap Press of Harvard University Press, 1998), 64–65; Carl S. Smith, *Urban Disorder and the Shape of Belief: The Great Chicago Fire, the Haymarket Bomb, and the Model Town of Pullman* (Chicago: University of Chicago Press, 1995), 222; Knight, 236–39, 248, 256–59.
16. Jane Addams, *Twenty Years at Hull-House* (New York: Macmillan, 1911), 444–45; Knight, 199–200.

maps compiled under the direction of Florence Kelley in 1893 revealed an immigrant Near West Side that was made up not of homogeneous ghettos—except for black people "wedged in Plymouth Place and Clark Street"—but rather clusters, sometimes varying from building to building, of Italians, Bohemians, Russians, Poles, Syrians, Scandinavians, and more. The classifications, eighteen in all, reflected less how immigrant and native poor saw themselves than how the residents of Hull House saw them. The colors on the map labeled as "nationalities" represented mixtures of race, country of birth, language, and religion. The mapmakers, for example, used the color white to represent English-speaking peoples, and included English, English-speaking Canadians, Scots, and native-born Americans—except black Americans—whether they were born of native or immigrant parents. In the case of black people, race trumped nationality and language.[17]

The maps also sketched the neighborhoods in terms of income and classified the buildings by use. Whole blocks of Clark Street between Twelfth and Polk were largely brothels. Buildings where families earned more than $20 a week (the highest classification) often abutted those where families made less than $10.[18]

The press described Hull House as a charity, and Addams and her early associates as secular nuns or missionaries, but she regarded her work as an exercise in social democracy as well as the Christian charity embraced by the Social Gospel. Political democracy and the vote had proven insufficient in an industrial society, and the churches had lost the spirit of primitive Christianity with its imperative to love all men. The settlement house movement would restore both and would liberate not only the immigrants it served, but also the young men and especially the women who worked there. She thought of her work as using a female-dominated cooperative home to restore republican values to the city. She believed that:

> The social organism has broken down through large districts of our great cities. Many of the people living there are very poor, the majority of them without leisure or energy for anything but the gain of subsistence. They move often from one wretched lodging to another. They live for the moment side by side, many of them without knowledge of each other,

17. *Hull-House Maps and Papers: A Presentation of Nationalities and Wages in a Congested District of Chicago, Together with Comments and Essays on Problems Growing out of the Social Conditions*, ed. Rima Lunin Schultz (Urbana: University of Illinois Press, 2007), 19–20.
18. Ibid., map no. 2, map no. 4a.

without fellowship, without local tradition or public spirit, without social organization of any kind.[19]

Hull House would not impose organization from above but instead would create it in cooperation with the immigrant poor.

The residents of the Hull House intended to bring progress to immigrants, but Addams thought the educated young middle-class women, and a few men, who staffed the settlement houses would gain as much as the poor did. Young educated women had thus far accomplished "little toward the solution of this social problem, and...bear the brunt of being cultivated into unnourished, over-sensitive lives." They had been "shut off from the common labor by which they live and which is a great source of moral and physical health." The common labor of young residents ranged from teaching and social work to lobbying and organizing.[20]

Women, in particular, would benefit from settlement work. Addams, the daughter of a well-to-do and prominent Illinois Republican family, wrote:

> I have seen young girls suffer and grow sensibly lowered in vitality in the first years after they leave school. In our attempt then to give a girl pleasure and freedom from care we succeed, for the most part, in making her pitifully miserable. She finds "life" so different from what she expected it to be. She is besotted with innocent little ambitions and does not understand this apparent waste of herself, this elaborate preparation, if no work is provided for her.

Addams was, in effect, speaking of herself; Hull House provided the work.[21]

Settlement work involved a struggle—a tragic one, as Addams saw it— between generations. Parents who had been raised believing that women had no role outside the domestic sphere confronted daughters who made a claim to, as one scholar has put it, "individuality, independence, and...public life." As Addams phrased it, when parents "in the name of love" asserted the "family claim," conflict and bitterness often resulted.[22]

Jane Addams never married, but neither did she forsake the home. She imagined Hull House as an extension of the home. She sustained long, loving relationships with other women, which her Gilded Age

19. Victoria Brown, "Advocate for Democracy: Jane Addams and the Pullman Strike," in *The Pullman Strike and the Crisis of the 1890s: Essays on Labor and Politics*, ed. Richard Schneirov, Shelton Stromquist, and Nick Salvatore (Urbana: University of Illinois Press, 1999), 130–35; Jane Addams, "A New Impulse to an Old Gospel," *The Forum* (November 1892): 345–58.
20. Brown, 130–35; Addams, "A New Impulse to an Old Gospel," 346–50.
21. Addams, "A New Impulse to an Old Gospel," 351.
22. Brown, 138.

This photograph of children of immigrants playing in the nursery of Hull House in Chicago underlines the identity of the settlement house as literally a home. Jane Addams Collection, Swarthmore College Peace Collection (DG 001).

contemporaries termed "Boston marriages." She was part of a generation of women born between 1860 and 1900 who wed at the lowest rates in American history. This cut across class lines as working-class and immigrant women also chafed at parental control over their lives and earnings. Of those born between 1865 and 1874, 11 percent never married, and many more lost their husbands to disease or accident.[23]

Florence Kelley, next to Jane Addams the most famous resident of Hull House, was, like Sister Carrie, willing to leave men who failed her. Kelley arrived at Hull House with her three children as a refugee from an abusive marriage; she had become, but was no longer, a Marxist devoted to the class struggle. She did much to steer Hull House toward social reform. When the volatile Kelley and the imperturbable Julia Lathrop—another

23. David Montgomery, *The Fall of the House of Labor: The Workplace, the State, and American Labor Activism, 1865–1925* (Cambridge: Cambridge University Press, 1987), 140–41; John D'Emilio and Estelle Freedman, *Intimate Matters: A History of Sexuality in America* (New York: Harper & Row, 1988), 191–94; Knight, 216–18.

Hull House resident, who was a lawyer, a more moderate reformer, and like Kelley the daughter of a congressman—clashed, they produced some of the most brilliant intellectual conversation of the Gilded Age.[24]

II

The South did not stand outside reforms that swirled at the intersection of gender, race, and class. Despite all the violence and repression of Reconstruction and its aftermath, the South in 1890 still held possibilities that extended beyond black subordination. North Carolina, a complicated Southern state, possessed a strong residual Republican Party, white in the old Unionist western part of the state and black in the eastern part. Bourbon Redeemers dominated the Democratic Party, but the state also had a striving middle class, both black and white, and increasingly restive farmers. The black middle class, prosperous, often professional, and self-confident, educated both its sons and daughters. Although being squeezed by white discrimination, which bridled at black success—especially material success visible in carriages, comfortable homes, fine clothes, and servants—middle-class black North Carolinians retained a confidence in an American progress that would give them a brighter and more prosperous future. Particularly in cities like Wilmington and towns like New Bern, their success and their confidence remained on full display.[25]

The success middle-class blacks desired for themselves and their children did not extend to far more numerous poor black workers excluded from segregated southern industries. Sarah Dudley Pettey, a leading spokeswoman for the striving North Carolina black middle class, highlighted the multiple fissures of American society when she praised black strikebreakers at Homestead as pioneers for a black industrial future. Like Booker T. Washington in a speech at the Cotton States and International Exposition in Atlanta in 1895, she offered black workers as an alternative to striking immigrants. Pettey and other middle-class blacks, however, bridled at Washington's willingness to confine virtually all black education to vocational education. She accepted class barriers; she resisted racial barriers. The South that middle-class black North Carolinians imagined would reward the "Best People," both black and white.[26]

24. Knight, 229–32, 233–36, 256.
25. Glenda Elizabeth Gilmore, *Gender and Jim Crow: Women and the Politics of White Supremacy in North Carolina, 1896–1920* (Chapel Hill: University of North Carolina Press, 1996), 1–21, 32–33, 42–43.
26. Ibid., 21–27.

In the early 1890s, North Carolina represented one possibility for the South, but the odds against political accommodation, particularly in the Deep South, remained long. Ella Gertrude Thomas, the beautiful Georgia belle who struggled to deal with the changes brought by the Civil War in the late 1860s, was still struggling in the 1880s and 1890s. Her family, its properties mortgaged to the hilt and besieged by debtors, sank into genteel poverty. Her husband, a devotee of the Lost Cause, remained ineffectual. He apparently drank. She taught school and wrote.[27]

In the 1880s she became a reformer. She joined the WCTU and thought that temperance benefited black women as well as white. She denounced domestic abuse and the treatment of women in prison. By the end of the 1890s she was the president of the Georgia Women's Suffrage Association. She wrote articles promoting women's education and denouncing domestic violence. She had supported the Blair Bill with its promise for improved black education in the South. Her reforms included black people, but she went only so far. She joined the United Daughters of the Confederacy, accepted Jim Crow, and appears never to have written publicly about lynching.[28]

Lynching and Jim Crow were, as white Southerners saw it, the centerpieces of Southern reform and race relations. In 1890 Louisiana had imposed Jim Crow with a Separate Car Act, which segregated railroad cars by race. The act outraged all black people, but it particularly offended the large, prosperous, and well-educated mixed-race community in New Orleans. One of the many difficulties in defining race and imposing segregation was that racial origins were not always apparent, and this was particularly the case as much of the South moved toward the one-drop rule: any African ancestry defined a person as black. Homer Plessy was one-eighth Afro-American, as prosperous blacks were coming to call themselves, and he agreed to serve as the litigant challenging the Separate Car Act as a violation of the Fourteenth Amendment. In appearance, he seemed white, so much so that he traveled undisturbed in the all-white first-class car until his frustrated legal team had to notify the conductor and the railway company that he was black and have him ejected. At issue was whether the Jim Crow law violated both the privileges and immunities and the equal protection clauses of the Fourteenth Amendment.[29]

27. Carolyn Newton Curry, *Suffer and Grow Strong: The Life of Ella Gertrude Clanton Thomas, 1834–1907* (Macon, GA: Mercer University Press, 2015), 137–50; Ella Gertrude Clanton Thomas, *The Secret Eye: The Journal of Ella Gertrude Clanton Thomas, 1848–1889*, ed. Virginia Ingraham Burr (Chapel Hill: University of North Carolina Press, 1990), 447–52.
28. Curry, 151–54, 176–80, 186–90, 193–96, 198; Thomas, Epilogue, 447–54.
29. Allyson Hobbs, *A Chosen Exile: A History of Racial Passing in American Life* (Cambridge, MA: Harvard University Press, 2014), 12.

Plessy's lawyer, Albion Tourgée, a novelist, old Radical, and carpetbagger, took a bold chance in the way he challenged the law in *Plessy v. Ferguson*, which came before the Supreme Court in 1896. With the Supreme Court increasingly relying on Stephen Field's dissent in the *Slaughterhouse* case to turn the Fourteenth Amendment into a tool to defend property, Tourgée defined whiteness as property, which had "an actual pecuniary value." It was an inheritance, "the most valuable sort of property, being the master-key that unlocks the golden door of opportunity." Plessy, the descendant of white men, had a clear "reputation" of being white since whites did not recognize him as black. He thus had been stripped of his property, which should be protected under the Fourteenth Amendment. Tourgée argued that most white people "would prefer death to life in the United States as a colored person."[30]

Tourgée's argument revealed the turn that the Fourteenth Amendment had taken. An amendment aimed at securing racial equality had become instead armor for property and freedom of contract. This led a black man who could pass as white to claim a property in whiteness in order to gain the protection from racial discrimination the amendment had originally been intended to prevent. His best route seemed to be to claim that he had been denied the opportunity to pursue his calling. Tourgée and Plessy made a clever and very sad argument, and they lost.[31]

In *Plessy v. Ferguson* (1896), the Supreme Court upheld the distinction between legal equality and social equality. The judges appealed to a set of precedents used to justify the separation of blacks and whites in schools. Blacks and whites, the court argued, were biologically different, with the skin colors designating dissimilar temperaments. This was established by nature, not law, and the prejudice against black people was so deeply rooted and popularly held that no law could change it. The state could not force white people to associate with black people, but it could and must ensure that the facilities offered to both races were equal. It thus established the separate-but-equal doctrine, enshrining Jim Crow for generations to come.[32]

As for Plessy's contention that whiteness was property, the court agreed. It was, and a white man could not be deprived of it without compensation.

30. For a full account of the case, Mark Elliott, *Color-Blind Justice: Albion Tourgée and the Quest for Racial Equality from the Civil War to Plessy V. Ferguson* (New York: Oxford University Press, 2006), 263–94; Hobbs, 12–13.
31. These were literally the wages of whiteness that David Roediger details, in *The Wages of Whiteness: Race and the Making of the American Working Class* (London: Verso, 1991); Hobbs, 12–13.
32. William E. Nelson, *The Fourteenth Amendment: From Political Principle to Judicial Doctrine* (Cambridge, MA: Harvard University Press, 1988), 185–87.

If a white man was "assigned to a colored coach, he may have his action for damages against the company for being deprived of his so-called property. Upon the other hand, if he be a colored man and be so assigned, he has been deprived of no property, since he is not lawfully entitled to the reputation of being a white man." Plessy was not a white man; he was deprived of nothing. A colored man's reputation as such was worth nothing. The court could not have been clearer.[33]

Plessy underlined how tenuous a hold the black middle class had on status and respect. Homer Plessy's education, his standing, his money, even his skin color offered no protection against public discrimination. He was black. This was all that mattered. In the South, race—no matter how legally defined and no matter how contradictory from one state to another—trumped class. It also trumped gender. Women who defied Jim Crow would be forcibly removed from segregated facilities.

Ida Wells had her first confrontation with Jim Crow in the late 1880s. In 1883, she had filed suit against the Chesapeake and Ohio, Huntington's road, after she had been forcibly ejected from the white ladies' car despite having bought a first-class ticket. She did not go easily, biting and scratching the conductor, who, with the help of white passengers, dragged her out of the car. Wells challenged the Jim Crow system of legal segregation taking hold all over the South. She sued and won in the lower courts, but then lost decisively on appeal.[34]

Wells was a Victorian mix of rectitude and fierce rebellion against the murderous inequities of the South, and her tongue and her actions did not endear her to everyone in Memphis's black community. Early in her career, she commended Booker T. Washington for his denunciation of the lax standards for the black ministry, and she denounced both ministers and teachers who did not meet her standards. Ministers denounced her in turn. Her criticism of the black leaders drew blood, but they were tepid compared to her attack on lynching and its white perpetrators.

Lynching—the execution of accused criminals by mobs or posses without official legal sanction—was an old American practice, but only in the 1880s and 1890s did it become almost exclusively associated with the South. Before the 1880s lynching was most common in the West. Western vigilantes claimed that they intervened only when the legal system had broken down, and this claim virtually defined the practice. Most such claims were false. Western vigilantes killed men already convicted of crimes to save

33. *Plessy V. Ferguson*, 163 *U.S.* 537, Justia, U.S. Supreme Court, 163 (1896).
34. Paula Giddings, *Ida: A Sword among Lions—Ida B. Wells and the Campaign against Lynching* (New York: Amistad, 2008), 60–68.

the cost of imprisonment or execution, and they exiled and sometimes executed political rivals and members of threatening social groups. A narrative of lynching as a heroic response to intolerable disorder was far stronger than the facts that sustained it. Lynching's justification remained intact even as the victims became overwhelmingly black and the practice became concentrated in the South.[35]

When whites lynched a black man in Georgetown, Kentucky, after he had killed a white man who had "intimate relations" with his wife, arsonists torched parts of the town. Wells wrote an editorial praising the arsonists for demonstrating that black people could not be killed with impunity.[36]

In March 1892 three friends of Wells—men who had opened a cooperative grocery store across the street from a white-owned store—were lynched. The incident had begun with two boys, one black and one white, fighting over a game of marbles, but it escalated into an adult brawl. There were threats of violence all around. Black residents were eager to remove the white store—"a low gambling den"—and the white storeowner wanted his black rivals gone. When the county sheriff and his deputies met at the white store and invaded the black store, they were met with gunfire from black men, who were expecting a mob attack, which wounded three white men. A second white mob later entered the jail, dragged out three prisoners, murdered them, and mutilated the bodies.[37]

Wells was not in Memphis when the lynching occurred, but when she returned she wrote an editorial attacking not just the mob but white Memphis, "a town which will neither protect our lives and property, nor give us a fair trial in the courts, but takes us out and murders us in cold blood when accused by white persons." Lynching was not self-protection; it was murder. Wells advocated migration west into Oklahoma Territory, ironically into lands President Harrison had seized from Indians.[38]

35. Lisa Arellano, *Vigilantes and Lynch Mobs: Narratives of Community and Nation* (Philadelphia: Temple University Press, 2012), 1–109; for a memorable and chilling account of lynching and racial violence in early Los Angeles, John Mack Faragher, *Eternity Street: Violence and Justice in Frontier Los Angeles* (New York: Norton, 2016); Richard Maxwell Brown, *Strain of Violence: Historical Studies of American Violence and Vigilantism* (New York: Oxford University Press, 1975), 150–58.
36. Giddings, 172–74.
37. Ibid., 176–83; David Squires, "Ida B. Wells and Lynch Law," *American Quarterly* 67, no. 1 (2015): 141–53.
38. Squires, 141–53; Giddings, 188–89.

Wells became the nation's chief cataloguer of lynchings, but more than that she filled in the empty spaces of Josiah Strong's account of Anglo-Saxon domination and demonstrated how white Americans established that domination and repulsed what they regarded as threats to it. She discovered that no matter what the original reasons for the mob violence, newspapers turned them into stories of the rape of a white woman by a black man. Wells showed that in some cases the rape accusations disguised consensual sex, and in most other cases the original reasons for the lynchings had nothing to do with rape at all. Accusations of rape were, she wrote, "an old racket." Her attacks struck at the core of the mythic South: the purity of Southern womanhood and homes threatened by black men. Memphis papers attacked her "obscene intimations," and a mob destroyed her press and threatened to kill anyone who tried to resume publishing. Wells fled to New York, where she published *Southern Horrors: Lynch Law in All Its Phases* in 1892. She recognized that whereas lynching revolved around real events and claimed real victims, those events took shape and people died as part of a narrative of regional stories. Over the course of her life, she framed a counternarrative of lynching as a criminal and shameful act that would help undo it.[39]

The number of Southern lynchings had first mounted in the early 1880s, but in these years more whites than blacks were still lynched nationally. When the number of Southern victims peaked again in the early 1890s, blacks accounted for the overwhelming number of victims. Between 78 and 161 black men and boys died at the hands of mobs every year during the 1890s. The victims were most likely to be young black men, who, like young white men, were moving across the South in search of work. Such labor migrations—and lynchings—were most common on the Gulf Plain between Florida and Texas and in the cotton upland South from Texas to Mississippi. Whites feared what they called "strange niggers," who came to cotton plantations and lumber camps. Later compilations of lynchings bore out Wells's analysis. Between 1882 and 1946 fewer than a quarter of the cases initially involved even accusations of attempted rape or rape, let alone actual rape.[40]

Lynchings were more than executions; they were public spectacles, even entertainments, that often took place before large crowds. White

39. Arellano, 17–18, 111–32; Ida B. Wells-Barnett, *Southern Horrors: Lynch Law in All Its Phases* (New York: New York Age Print, 1892), 10–18, 111–32; Squires, 92.
40. Equal Justice Initiative, "Lynching in America: Confronting the Legacy of Racial Terror," (Montgomery, AL: Equal Justice Initiative, 2015); "Lynching Statistics," Charles Chesnutt digital Archives, http://www.chesnuttarchive.org/classroom/lynchingstat.html; Arellano, 11–12; Edward L. Ayers, *The Promise of the New South: Life after Reconstruction* (New York: Oxford University Press, 1992), 156–59.

men tortured black men, dismembering, castrating, and burning them. Photographers memorialized the murders. The photographs, turned into postcards, sold widely. As Wells asserted, rape had become a racial weapon; the mere accusation against a black man amounted to a death sentence.

Wells took on Northerners as well as Southerners, challenging Frances Willard, as well as Dwight Moody, for accommodating segregation and tolerating lynching in their pursuit of evangelical reform and progress. Willard's interest in middle-class black women lagged far behind her interest in recruiting Southern white women like Ella Thomas to WCTU. She was sensitive to claims of rape since she was simultaneously pressing issues of social purity—calling for stronger laws against rape and luring women into prostitution—and demanding laws that would make the age of consent sixteen. Willard contended that she did not have an "atom of race prejudice," but in urging equality for women one of her favorite slogans was "A white life for two." It had a double meaning. White, as in the white ribbon campaign, was the WCTU's slogan for sexual purity and its crusade against prostitution, but white in the late nineteenth century had unavoidable racial connotations that Willard emphasized in other contexts. In a newspaper interview she had attacked black suffrage, referring to "great dark-faced mobs whose rallying cry is better whiskey," and who threatened the "safety of women, of childhood, of the home." Wells wanted the WCTU to condemn lynching, and in 1893 it did, but Willard vitiated the resolution by arguing in a speech that lynching was the result of the rape of white women by black men and justifying lynch mobs as a kind of home protection. She claimed drink enflamed the passions of black men.[41]

When Ida Wells attended the WCTU convention in 1894, Willard attacked her for slandering Southern white women by saying that not all accusations of rape were true. The WCTU resolution of 1894, although lamenting lynching, indicated that it could not be banished until "the unspeakable outrages which have so often provoked such lawlessness shall be banished from the world, and childhood, maidenhood, and womanhood

41. Ruth Birgitta Anderson Bordin, *Frances Willard: A Biography* (Chapel Hill: University of North Carolina Press, 1986), 216–17; Giddings, 266–67; Louise Michele Newman, *White Women's Rights: The Racial Origins of Feminism in the United States* (New York: Oxford University Press, 1999), 66–68; Alison M. Parker, *Articulating Rights: Nineteenth-Century American Women on Race, Reform, and the State* (DeKalb: Northern Illinois University Press, 2010), 169–73; Gilmore, 56–57; Ian R. Tyrrell, *Reforming the World: The Creation of America's Moral Empire* (Princeton, NJ: Princeton University Press, 2010), 168–74; Shawn Leigh Alexander, *An Army of Lions: The Civil Rights Struggle before the NAACP* (Philadelphia: University of Pennsylvania Press, 2012), 23–97.

shall no more be the victims of atrocities worse than death." Wells struck back by going international. With the help of British allies, she delivered withering attacks on Willard and American evangelicals who refused to challenge lynching. Wells and the British forced Willard and the WCTU to retreat, but Wells's victory only embittered most American whites against her. The *New York Times* echoed the South, declaring her "a slanderous and nasty minded mulatress."[42]

Willard's stance on lynching, condemning the practice but denouncing the supposed cause even more harshly, indicated the difficulties facing attempts at reform across racial lines, particularly when Southerners could appeal to the home; but attempts persisted. The court's validation of Jim Crow did not mean that it immediately became the rule across the South, or for that matter that the black vote was everywhere suppressed; that became the political work of white supremacy, which involved the elimination of independent black voters and constitutional and legal changes. In black majority or near-black-majority states in the Deep South, the devices pioneered in the Mississippi Constitution of 1890 would for all practical purposes quickly eliminate black voting. In other states, blacks could vote so long as whites controlled their ballots, but in states like North Carolina black voters could still forge an alliance with white Republicans, who were a fading force, or Populists, a rising one in the early 1890s.

The embrace of the WCTU by Northern Carolina black women such as Sarah Dudley Pettey formed an important aspect of continuing attempts to bridge the racial divide. In the late 1880s separate black and white chapters cooperated under a statewide biracial WCTU. Black temperance advocates saw a chance to build a "female consciousness" in which white women would recognize the realities of black middle-class life and drop racist stereotypes of uniform black inferiority. White women had a different vision. Black women were to be junior, and inferior, partners in a common campaign of uplift aimed largely at men. The partnership was tense, unequal, and flawed, but it endured, surviving the public clash between Wells and Willard.[43]

III

In a country awash in news of the organized murders of black people, industrial strife, and cultural panic over women, the home, immigration, and Catholicism, politicians reacted warily. The Republicans had been

42. Tyrrell, 172–75; Parker, 171–73.
43. Gilmore, 45–59.

badly burned by intervening in social issues in the Midwest; they had scant desire to try again as the 1892 election cycle approached. The Democrats, knowing the election was theirs to lose, were cautious. They recognized that the tariff remained an albatross around the Republican Party's neck. Far from being a problem for the Democrats, lynching carried little political cost with their Southern base. It reinforced their standing as a white man's party and defender of Southern home and womanhood.

Only the Populists were willing to embrace a wide package of reform, but Southern racism posed grave problems for them. When in 1891 the Colored Alliance sponsored a cotton pickers' strike, the white Farmers' Alliance suppressed it with as much zeal as more conservative farmers. The strike ended with the lynching of its organizers and largely finished the Colored Alliance. White Alliance men who had once ridden with the Klan showed they were capable of riding with them again. They were far readier to reconcile the "Anglo-Saxon" North and South than black and white Southerners.[44]

When the Southern Alliance reinforced racial subordination, Republican accusations that it, like the Klan before it, served simply as a wing of the Democratic Party sounded credible. In Kansas and across much of the West and Middle Border, Alliance members had split from the Republican Party and run Populist or independent tickets, but in most of the South, the Alliance continued to operate from within the Democratic Party. Western Populists were vulnerable to Republican accusations that Populism was only a stalking dog for Democrats, who benefited from Republican losses. The Populists had to go national or die.

Creating a national party proved difficult. At the St. Louis Industrial Conference convened in February 1892, reformers—Greenbackers, Prohibitionists, advocates of universal suffrage, Knights of Labor, and members of the northern Alliance—created a provisional national party committee. Unity quickly faded. Evangelical reformers pushed moral reforms, but Alliance leaders were quite aware of the disasters that moral reform had inflicted on the Republicans in 1888 and 1890. They wanted to keep the focus on economic reform rather than embrace the full spectrum of evangelical cultural politics. The Prohibition Party balked and refused to authorize its delegation until the farmers' movement adopted prohibition. Willard came as a Prohibitionist, but abstained from the Prohibitionist abstention and stayed as a delegate of the WCTU. She tried to get the meeting to endorse antisaloon and universal suffrage planks, but

44. Charles Postel, *The Populist Vision* (New York: Oxford University Press, 2007), 173–84, 188, 203; Marek D. Steedman, *Jim Crow Citizenship: Liberalism and the Southern Defense of Racial Hierarchy* (New York: Routledge, 2012), 103–4.

both failed. Mary Elizabeth Lease of Kansas—"Queen Mary of the Alliance" and perhaps its leading orator—denounced demands for prohibition and women's suffrage as absurd. The key was economic reform. Always resilient, Willard urged the Prohibitionists to support any People's Party candidate who personally endorsed prohibition.[45]

The St. Louis conference ended up far more sectional than national. The opening address urged "the great West, the great South, and the great Northwest (the Middle Border and Midwest) to link their hands and hearts together and march to the ballot box and take possession of the government and restore it to the principles of our fathers and run it in the interests of the people." Ignatius Donnelly, a sometime congressman, sometime novelist, and longtime antimonopolist from Minnesota, issued a full-throated denunciation of the nation's current condition and demanded reform in what would become the preamble of the People's Party platform. It captured the dystopian side of the American vision.

> We meet in the midst of a nation brought to the verge of moral, political, and material ruin. Corruption dominates the ballot box, the legislatures, the Congress and touches even the ermine of the bench. The people are demoralized.... The newspapers are subsidized or muzzled; public opinion silenced; business prostrate, our homes covered with mortgages, labor impoverished and the land concentrating in the hands of capitalists. The urban workmen are denied the right of organization for self-protection; imported pauperized labor beats down their wages; a hireling standing army, unrecognized by our laws is established to shoot them down, and they are rapidly disintegrating to European conditions. The fruits of the toil of millions are boldly stolen to build up colossal fortunes, unprecedented in the history of the world, while their possessors despise the republic and endanger liberty. From the same prolific womb of government injustice we breed two great classes—paupers and millionaires.

The existing parties, Donnelly declared, would concentrate on "a sham battle over the tariff, so that corporations, national banks, rings, trusts, 'watered stocks,' the demonetization of silver, and the oppression of usurers, may all be lost sight of."[46]

The St. Louis convention created the Populist Party, but the party's first convention had to wait until July in Omaha, and here the tensions between Western Populists and Southern Alliance members still loyal to the Democratic Party came to a head. Before they even convened, the

---

45. M. Elizabeth Sanders, *Roots of Reform: Farmers, Workers, and the American State, 1877–1917* (Chicago: University of Chicago Press, 1999), 127–30; Bordin, 182–83; Postel, 95.
46. Lawrence Goodwyn, *Democratic Promise: The Populist Moment in America* (New York: Oxford University Press, 1976), 264–66.

Populists suffered two devastating blows. Leonidas L. Polk of North Carolina, the leading Southern advocate of a third party, died, and Southern Alliance leaders voted 21 to 16 not to endorse the People's Party, preferring to stick with the antimonopoly wing of the Democrats. North Carolina sustained an independent Populism, but it did not represent the South. Over much of the region, race, as the Democrats intended, trumped economic grievance. White Alliance farmers hated the Southern Bourbons, who largely controlled the Democratic Party, but they also hated and feared black people. The Populists nominated James B. Weaver, an Iowan, ex–Civil War general, and old Greenbacker, who had sterling antimonopolist credentials but little prior connection to the Farmers' Alliance.[47]

The preamble of the Populist platform reflected the Populists' anger, but the planks captured their essential moderation. They identified the country's problems as deflation, monopoly, the misdistribution of wealth, and corruption. All sapped the nation's vigor, but all could be reformed and the country restored. The Populists were not revolutionaries, and many policies they recommended would become staples of American political practice.

The Populists proved catholic in their cures. Adamantly against the gold standard and the deflation it brought, they advocated all the leading nostrums, demanding greenbacks, the free and unlimited coinage of silver at a ratio 16:1, and, at their most innovative, a subtreasury system that would inject an estimated half-billion dollars of new treasury notes into the money supply. To combat the misdistribution of wealth, they demanded a graduated income tax, an end to corporate subsidies, an eight-hour day, and more restrictions on immigrant contract labor. To fight monopoly, the Populists proposed the nationalization of the railroads and telegraph and telephone systems. These sounded more radical than they were. The country already had a national postal system, which was regarded as a model of efficiency. Congress had already come very close to nationalizing the telegraph system, and telephones were viewed as simply an extension of the telegraph. Nationalizing railroads had widespread support and essentially prefigured the modern highway system. The government would own the roads and regulate and tax those who used them. To reform politics, they wanted the Australian or secret ballot, the direct election of senators, and the implementation of the initiative and referendum. The country adopted many of these reforms over the next two decades.[48]

---

47. Postel, 13; Goodwyn, 270–72; Paul Kleppner, *The Third Electoral System, 1953–1892* (Chapel Hill: University of North Carolina Press, 1979), 299–303.
48. Richard R. John, *Network Nation: Inventing American Telecommunications* (Cambridge, MA: Belknap Press of Harvard University Press, 2010), 121–23; Goodwyn, 167–68.

The Populists were conflicted in their simultaneous distrust of govern-ment and their granting the federal government new powers and obliga-tions. They wanted to limit the president to a single term and demanded that "all State and national revenues shall be limited to the necessary ex-penses of the government, economically and honestly administered," thus eliminating the surplus. At the same time, besides advocating the nation-alization of critical infrastructure, they desired "postal savings banks be established by the government for the safe deposit of the earnings of the people and to facilitate exchange." They wanted a monopoly of organized force vested in the government and the outlawing of the Pinkertons and other private police forces.

The Populists implicitly admitted that cooperation as advocated by the Farmers' Alliance and Knights of Labor could not change society without government intervention. Politics would have to secure what the cooper-ative crusade could not. Alliance cooperatives had achieved some suc-cess, but only when existing businesses saw opportunities in advancing them. The California Fruit Growers Exchange, which became Sunkist, united small farmers and large corporate farms in that state because the Southern Pacific Railroad aided and cooperated with it and other grow-ers' exchanges. In the South, Kansas, and Nebraska, where the Alliance attained its greatest strength, vested business interests had usually bitterly opposed the cooperatives, which, stymied by the crop-lien system and boycotts by manufacturers and wholesalers, had largely failed. Here gov-ernment intervention was necessary.[49]

Populists made the subtreasury a signature reform because they be-lieved it would deal a deathblow to the Southern crop-lien system, stabi-lize farm prices, and inflate the currency. Even so, it too demanded not only government intervention but also political action from a movement that had sought to be nonpartisan. Charles Macune had introduced the subtreasury plan in 1889. The government would build warehouses, or sub-treasuries, in the major agricultural counties of the nation. Farmers could deposit their crops there so they would not have to sell at harvest, when prices were lowest. They could borrow 80 percent of the value of their crops and receive certificates of deposit by paying 2 percent interest. The certificates of deposit would be negotiable, circulating at prevailing market prices. The certificates would, in effect, function as treasury notes based not on gold or silver but on agricultural commodities; they could, however,

49. Postel, 112–33; Jeffrey Ostler, *Prairie Populism: The Fate of Agrarian Radicalism in Kansas, Nebraska, and Iowa, 1880–1892* (Lawrence: University Press of Kansas, 1993), 94–97. Richard Orsi, *Sunset Limited: The Southern Pacific Railroad and the Development of the American West, 1850–1930* (Berkeley: University of California Press, 2005), 325–27.

circulate for only a year. Macune did not stay in the Populist Party; he returned to the Democrats, who did not endorse the subtreasury.[50]

Once the Democrats secured the allegiance of the Southern Farmers' Alliance, the 1892 national election was over. The Democrats had merely to hold some of their previous gains in the Midwest, hope the Populists weakened the Republicans in the West, and await the results. By and large, this is what happened.

In most of the South, the Republicans had become insignificant; only in North Carolina did a Populist-Republican alliance prove fruitful, eventually yielding a Populist senator. Democrats in Georgia counted out Tom Watson, the only sitting Populist congressman, and he lost his seat. Watson complained that the whole Democratic appeal in the South boiled down to one word: "nigger." Its appeal kept many white Southern Farmers' Alliance members in the Democratic Party. Although they made gains on the local level, Populists carried only 15.8 percent of the presidential vote in the old Confederacy. Weaver and Mary Elizabeth Lease, whose racial views were as extreme as any in the South, campaigned in Georgia, but Southern crowds shouted her down for being a woman who took a public role and pelted Weaver, who had been a Union officer in the Reconstruction South, with so many eggs, that, Lease said, he was a walking omelet.[51]

In the short run, the Democrats' fear of losing white votes created, as odd as it seemed, a heightened dependence on blacks. In those parts of the South where the end of Reconstruction had not led to complete black disenfranchisement, black votes turned into "dead votes." Blacks could vote, if they voted for Democrats in support of the planters whose land they sharecropped, of the merchants to whom they were in debt, or for the benefit of the men who employed them. The rise of the Populists potentially threatened this system. Populism created a white constituency in favor of fair counts and fair elections. Bourbon Democrats had turned the tools Southern whites had forged to defeat Republicans and black people against white Populists. Populists—white men who had themselves killed and intimidated black men and endorsed electoral fraud—now often faced violence, intimidation, and fraud and sought to reverse them.[52]

---

50. Goodwyn, 166–69; Sanders, 125–27.
51. Postel, 99, 100, 182–83, 187–203; C. Vann Woodward, *Tom Watson: Agrarian Rebel* (New York: Oxford University Press, 1963), 370; Goodwyn, 324–30; George H. Mayer, *The Republican Party, 1854–1964* (New York: Oxford University Press, 1964), 236–37; Sanders, 133–34; Paul Kleppner, *Continuity and Change Electoral Politics, 1893–1928* (New York: Greenwood Press, 1987), 61–62.
52. Steedman, 70–77; Richard M. Valelly, *The Two Reconstructions: The Struggle for Black Enfranchisement* (Chicago: University of Chicago Press, 2004), 53; Postel, 188, 192, 196, 200.

Everywhere the Republicans looked in 1892, they saw liabilities. Andrew Carnegie became a particular problem. He was a leading Republican donor, a friend of James G. Blaine, an enthusiastic backer of the McKinley Tariff, and an ardent supporter of the gold standard. He had Frick send a $5,000 check to McKinley following a speech against silver. Carnegie had, however, horrified too many Republican voters with his actions at Homestead to be an asset. Rutherford B. Hayes attributed Republican weakness to the defection of laborers, who "saw the capitalists going to Europe to spend the fortunes acquired in America." Everything the Democrats had claimed about the tariff seemed luridly and spectacularly true: large companies had their markets protected while they cut workers' wages, working people paid more for necessities from thinner paychecks. The Republicans had tried, ineptly, to have their vice-presidential candidate, Whitelaw Reid, mediate the Homestead strike, but Reid, who had taken over Greeley's *New York Tribune*, was in 1892 locked in a strike with the typographical union that was hurting the Republicans in New York. Carnegie and Frick had refused to make any concessions.[53]

The Republicans renominated Benjamin Harrison, in part because their only alternative was Blaine, whose late and quixotic attempt at the nomination went nowhere. Harrison and Cleveland faced off in a rematch of the 1888 election. Their second meeting served only to underline James Bryce's interpretation of nineteenth-century presidential politics, in *The American Commonwealth*, that "eminent men" did not rise in American politics, both because the ablest men were not attracted to public life and because congressional politics gave little chance for distinction. The most famous congressmen, men such as Blaine and Roscoe Conkling, made too many enemies to be viable candidates for the presidency. Safe candidates were those who would not anger partisans in their own parties or who could help carry a key swing state. To the parties, a candidate who would be a bad president was preferable to someone who would be a good president but a bad candidate. In any case, Bryce thought the country did not need brilliant presidents. Their power was limited and, with the country at peace, their duties relatively few.

53. David Nasaw, *Andrew Carnegie* (New York: Penguin Press, 2006), 376; Mayer, 235; Ari Arthur Hoogenboom, *Rutherford B. Hayes: Warrior and President* (Lawrence: University Press of Kansas, 1995), 525; Paul Krause, *The Battle for Homestead, 1880–1892: Politics, Culture, and Steel* (Pittsburgh, PA: University of Pittsburgh Press, 1992), 344.

The United States could afford mediocrities. The 1890s would challenge that assessment.[54]

Cleveland's 1887 opposition to the tariff reaped him large if belated rewards in 1892. He learned to be a new kind of candidate, one who posed as the national voice of the people and not as the representative of regional bosses and machines. The old doctrines of individualism and self-reliance seemed ever more archaic, but the national parties recognized that the old ethnic, religious, and sectional ties, which were the foundation of postwar political loyalties, were also fraying. The best tactic seemed appeals to individual voters' self-interest, which might shear some away from older loyalties. Educational campaigns sought to convince as well as mobilize voters by persuasively, coherently, and consistently stating and disseminating a single policy. This demanded centralization and money. The Republican and Democratic national committees grew stronger and state and local organizations weaker. Those who funded them rose in influence. Presidential campaign expenses that totaled $300,000 in 1872 rose to just over $4 million in 1892.[55]

Henry Adams noticed the growing importance of money and thought it gave the Republicans the advantage; he underestimated the ability of the Democrats to learn and compete. Cleveland apparently raised more money than Harrison in 1892. The Democratic National Committee functioned as a political publishing house, reinforcing the connections between the tariff and the strike at Homestead. The Republicans had long trumpeted the steel industry as the fruits of a tariff that brought benefits to capital and labor alike, and those words came back to haunt them. At Madison Square Garden in New York, Cleveland told his listeners and the nation, "Scenes are enacted in the very abiding place of high protection that mock the hopes of toil, and demonstrate the falsity that protection is a boon to toilers."[56]

Other strikes underscored the lessons of Homestead and undercut the Republicans' appeal to labor. Silver miners in Coeur d'Alene, Idaho, coal miners at Coal Creek, Tennessee, railroad workers in Buffalo, New York, all walked out. Three governors had to call out their state militias. Harrison

54. Lewis L. Gould, *Grand Old Party: A History of the Republicans* (New York: Random House, 2003), 111–12; James Bryce, *The American Commonwealth* (London: Macmillan, 1897, orig. ed. 1888), 1: 78–85.
55. Robert E. Mutch, *Buying the Vote: A History of Campaign Finance Reform* (New York: Oxford, 2014), 17–18; Daniel Klinghard, *The Nationalization of American Political Parties, 1880–1896* (Cambridge: Cambridge University Press, 2010), 108–23, 176–77.
56. H. Adams to John Hay, Nov. 12, 1892, in *The Letters of Henry Adams*, ed. J. C. Levenson (Cambridge, MA: Belknap Press, 1982), 4: 78–79; R. Hal Williams, *Years of Decision: American Politics in the 1890s* (New York: Wiley, 1978), 64–65.

The 1892 Presidential Election

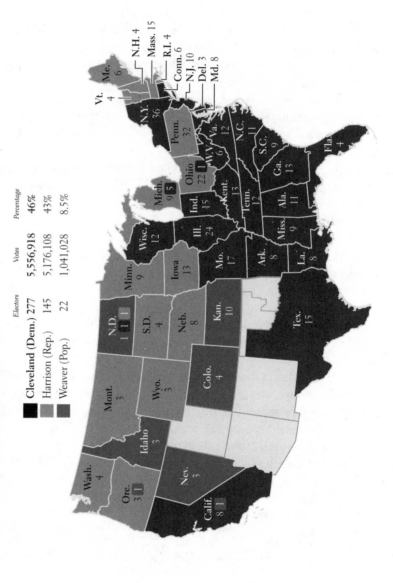

	Electors	Votes	Percentage
■ Cleveland (Dem.)	277	5,556,918	46%
■ Harrison (Rep.)	145	5,176,108	43%
■ Weaver (Pop.)	22	1,041,028	8.5%

Wash. 4

Ore. 3 1

Calif. 8 1

Nev. 3

Idaho 3

Mont. 3

Wyo. 3

Colo. 4

N.D. 1 1 1

S.D. 4

Neb. 8

Kan. 10

Minn. 9

Iowa 13

Tex. 15

Mo. 17

Ark. 8

La. 8

Wisc. 12

Ill. 24

Mich. 9 5

Ind. 15

Ohio 22 1

Kent. 13

Tenn. 12

Miss. 9

Ala. 11

Ga. 13

Fla. 4

S.C. 9

N.C. 11

W.Va. 6

Penn. 32

N.Y. 36

Vt. 4

Me. 6

N.H. 4

Mass. 15

R.I. 4

Conn. 6

N.J. 10

Del. 3

Md. 8

could not stay above the fray; he sent federal troops to Idaho, where the miners had considerable local support, to enforce federal injunctions and to ensure the free passage of the U.S. mail. Democrats took advantage of the growing class divisions, fishing for workers' votes.[57]

Nationally, Cleveland doubled Harrison's electoral vote and won by a plurality of four hundred thousand votes. The Republicans regained some of their losses in the House, but the Democrats still retained a ninety-four-vote majority and gained a new majority of six in the Senate. Henry Adams, who regarded the contest as one between "two stuffed prophets," reacted reasonably and cynically. Those who benefited most from the tariff had apparently failed to pony up sufficiently. "Is it possible," he asked Hay, "… that our Republican manufacturers after pocketing the swag, refused to disgorge? If so, they'll catch it." For the first time since 1856, the Democrats controlled all three branches of government.[58]

William Dean Howells had also remained unimpressed with either major party or candidate. He wrote his father that the "Republican Party is a lie in defamation of its past. It promises nothing in the way of economic and social reform, and it is only less corrupt than the scoundrelly democracy. The only live and honest party is the People's Party."[59]

The Populists could not overcome the political demography of the nation. Most of the nation's voting age population, 62.5 percent, lived outside the West, South, and the western extreme of the Middle Border. With the Democrats deflecting the Populist threat in the South, the party had no hope. They captured only 8.5 percent of the national vote.

As a regional party centered in the West and South, the Populists lacked significant appeal for immigrant workers in the Northeast and Midwest. They couldn't even attract Henry George, whose devotion to free trade had led him to campaign for Cleveland in 1888 and endorse him again, to Cleveland's discomfort, in 1892. George hoped that with the revenue from the tariff gone, the government would move toward the single tax. The Populists often fused with antimonopolist Democrats in the West and Middle Border to offer joint tickets that allowed them to carry the usually Republican states of Kansas, Colorado, and Nevada, and the new states of

57. Melvyn Dubofsky, "The Origins of Western Working Class Radicalism, 1890–1905," *Labor History* 7, no. 2 (1966): 138.

58. Mayer, 231–38; H. Adams to John Hay, Nov. 12, 1892, in *The Letters of Henry Adams*, 4: 78–79; Gould, 112–13; Edward T. O'Donnell, *Henry George and the Crisis of Inequality: Progress and Poverty in the Gilded Age* (New York: Columbia University Press, 2015), 277–78; Sanders, 135; Hoogenboom, 525; Williams, *Years of Decision* 68.

59. W. D. Howells to W. C. Howells, Nov. 6, 1892, in William Dean Howells, *Selected Letters*, ed. George Warren Arms (Boston: Twayne, 1979), 4: 29.

Idaho and North Dakota. In the Rocky Mountain States, the Populist reform agenda mattered less than the potent silver issue.[60]

Populism never became synonymous with antimonopolism. Southern Alliance farmers remained antimonopolists even if they remained loyal to the Democrats. The ability of antimonopolists to capture the established parties in Iowa, Minnesota, and Wisconsin worked against Populism. Why jeopardize those gains in order to join a new national party? The Populists found it easiest to lure voters in those states where conservative Republicans had blocked reform.[61]

The triumph of the Democrats in 1892 election proved deceptive. Their total voted declined from their 1890 high-water mark; the Republicans increased their percentage of the popular vote across the North. The Democratic advantage in the Midwestern states of Illinois, Indiana, Wisconsin, and Missouri fell from 2.2 percent to 0.7 percent of the vote. The Republican losses to the Populists in the West overshadowed the pathetic showing of Cleveland in these areas, although the Democrats seem to have purposely allowed their voters to vote for Weaver to weaken Harrison. Even in Kansas, the flashpoint for the People's Party, the Republicans had cause for optimism. The majority for the Populist state ticket in Kansas fell to only 5,000 votes out of 320,000 cast, a sign that Populist protest might be easier to galvanize than sustain.[62]

IV

Homestead and the other strikes of 1892, the rise of lynching and Jim Crow, the wild pendulum swings of politics that hinted at a confused and desperate electorate, and the preamble of the Populist platform all pointed to the dystopian fears that informed Bellamy's and Strong's vision. But utopian dreams were also taking shape.

Carrie Meeber's Chicago had begun preparing for the Columbian Exposition to commemorate the four-hundredth anniversary of the arrival of Columbus in the New World in 1889, even before Congress in 1890 made the city the official site of the celebration. The exposition had its

60. Paul Kleppner, *The Third Electoral System*, 299, 302–4; Kleppner, *Continuity and Change in Electoral Politics, 1893–1928*, 59–63; Goodwyn, 317–20; Christopher William England, "Land and Liberty: Henry George, the Single Tax Movement, and the Origins of 20th Century Liberalism" (Ph.D diss., Georgetown University, 2015), 136–40; Ostler, 6–11.
61. Ostler, 6–11.
62. Kleppner, *Continuity and Change in Electoral Politics, 1893–1928*, 59–62; Klinghard, 178; Goodwyn, 317–20; Kleppner, *The Third Electoral System, 1853–1892*, 299, 302–3.

public dedication on Columbus Day, October 12, 1892. Francis Bellamy, a minister, Christian socialist, cousin of Edward Bellamy, and the editor of *Youth's Companion*, suggested setting aside Columbus Day as a national holiday (which would not happen until the 1930s). He composed the Pledge of Allegiance to the flag of the United States and "the Republic for which it stands" to commemorate the holiday and the fair. His original version did not contain the phrase "under God," which was added in the 1950s. The exposition proper did not open until 1893, when it ran for 184 days, but preparations for it had already created a building boom in Chicago. Both the fair and the boom became enmeshed in the country's class tensions. Cooperation between Chicago's capitalist boosters and labor unions had foundered on the failure to secure the eight-hour day, union labor, and a minimum wage. The arrival of visitors gave Chicago a second economic boost. Railroads carried thirty-five million passengers to Chicago during the fair; the Pullman Palace Car Company thrived on the sale of new cars to the railroads. More than twenty-seven million people visited the White City, the shimmering array of water, alabaster buildings— most of which were temporary and made of steel skeletons covered with a mixture of jute and plaster—and electric lights. Something like 120,000 incandescent lamps and 7,000 arc lamps shone along Lake Michigan.[63]

All of that was the business of the exposition, but Chicago, which had grown in sixty years from a Potawatomi village to a city of a million plus, wanted the fair to demonstrate that it was more than a city of commerce and that there was more to American progress than wealth. The city hoped to outdo the Paris Exposition of 1889 and impress and silence New York, whose citizens contended that a Chicago Fair could only be provincial, an overgrown county fair. The homogeneous Beaux Arts design was intended to emphasize the unity of the nation one generation after the Civil War and the harmony of an ever more diverse population. It was not a lesson people would long associate with Chicago.[64]

63. Kevin M. Kruse, *One Nation under God: How Corporate America Invented Christian America* (New York: Basic Books, 2015), 100–101; Stanley Buder, *Pullman: An Experiment in Industrial Order and Community Planning, 1880–1930* (New York: Oxford University Press, 1967), 147–49; Wim de Wit, "Building an Illusion," in Wim de Wit, James Gilbert, Robert W. Rydell, Neil Harris, and Chicago Historical Society, *Grand Illusions: Chicago's World's Fair of 1893* (Chicago: Chicago Historical Society, 1993), 110; Robert W. Rydell, *All the World's a Fair: Visions of Empire at American International Expositions, 1876–1916* (Chicago: University of Chicago Press, 1984), 40, 46; Richard Schneirov, *Labor and Urban Politics: Class Conflict and the Origins of Modern Liberalism in Chicago, 1864–97* (Urbana: University of Illinois Press, 1998), 284–88, 332–33.
64. William Cronon, *Nature's Metropolis: Chicago and the Great West* (New York: Norton, 1991), 341–42; Wim de Wit, "Building an Illusion," 43–47, 51, 58; Rydell, 68.

The Beaux Arts White City, which helped give rise to the City Beautiful movement of the early twentieth century, disgusted Louis Sullivan, who had done so much to give Chicago the most innovative architecture in the nation and who loved its brawny vitality. Sullivan designed the Transportation Building, which broke from the neoclassical design of the Court of Honor and the historical recreations of much of the remainder of the Fair's aesthetic. Sullivan thought the damage that the fair caused to American architecture would "last for a half a century from its date, if not longer. It has penetrated deep into the constitution of the American mind, effecting there lesions significant of dementia."[65]

Chicago society women played an important role in the exposition, but they operated under the auspices of men and the prevailing modes of domesticity. Bertha Palmer, the wife of the owner of Chicago's Palmer House, headed a Board of Lady Managers appointed by male exposition directors. Susan B. Anthony protested. She did not want women on a separate board appointed by men, but Frances Willard of the WCTU agreed to join the board, and Palmer, to neutralize critics, organized a Congress of Representative Women to meet at the fair. Willard, sick and mourning her mother's death, was seeking to recover her own health in Europe. She had turned more and more to international efforts and was largely absent from the fair. Susan B. Anthony, Lucy Stone, and Elizabeth Cady Stanton spoke at the Congress, as did Jane Addams.[66]

Critics saw the Woman's Building as a symbol of the marginalization of women. Erected at the border between the White City and the Midway Plaisance, the building seemed to mark women as not really part of the White City. The center of the Plaisance was engineer George Ferris's Wheel—the equivalent of the Paris Fair's Eiffel Tower—which lifted visitors 260 feet above the ground. The Ferris Wheel symbolized modernity, but the Plaisance, which was nearly a mile long and six hundred yards wide, also displayed those peoples classified by Americans as primitive. There, as Howells recorded, were "the Samoan or Dahomeyan in his hut, the Bedouin and the Lap in their camps; the delicate Javanese in his bamboo cottage, [and] the American Indian in his teepee." The exhibit of

65. Neil Harris, "Memory and the White City," in Wim de Wit, James Gilbert, Robert W. Rydell, Neil Harris, and Chicago Historical Society, *Grand Illusions: Chicago's World's Fair of 1893* (Chicago: Chicago Historical Society, 1993), 3–32, quote 15.

66. Tyrrell, 2–64, passim; Knight, 270–71; Robert Rydell, "A Cultural Frankenstein? The Chicago World's Columbian Exposition of 1893," in de Wit et al., 151–57; Anna Gordon, Apr. 18, May 17, and May 22, 1893, and see also Willard, Aug. 5, Aug. 6, Sep. 9, Sep. 25, 1893, in Frances E. Willard, *Writing out My Heart: Selections from the Journal of Frances E. Willard, 1855*, ed. Carolyn De Swarte Gifford (Urbana: University of Illinois Press, 1995), 372–73.

The Ferris Wheel at the 1893 Columbian Exposition was the American response to the Eiffel Tower built for the 1889 Paris Exposition. It was the tallest structure at the Exposition and its single greatest attraction. From C. D. Arnold, *Official Views of the World's Columbian Exposition* (1893).

the world's "childlike races" mimicked one of the most popular parts of the Paris Fair. The exhibits aspired to be ethnological, embodying social evolution and demonstrating how far the United States had progressed since Columbus discovered the New World.[67]

Ida B. Wells published a small book, *The Reason Why the Colored American Is Not in the World's Columbian Exposition: The Afro-American Contribution to the Columbian Literature*, which highlighted the absence of black Americans. She wrote most of the book, but Frederick Douglass provided a preface. There was much, Douglass wrote, that black Americans could celebrate about their own progress over the past forty years, but they had a duty, he proclaimed in rising to his old eloquence, "of plain speaking of wrongs and outrages endured, and of rights withheld, and withheld in flagrant contradiction to boasted American Republican liberty and civilization." The spirit of American slavery still haunted the nation.

67. Letter 2, William Dean Howells, "Letters of an Altrurian Traveller, 1893–94," *Cosmopolitan* 16 (1893): 20–27; Rydell, "A Cultural Frankenstein?" 157; Rydell, *All the World's a Fair*, 40–43, 49–50, 55–58, 60, 63–68.

Although "Americans are a great and magnanimous people and this great exposition adds greatly to their honor and renown... in the pride of their success they have cause for repentance as well as complaisance, and for shame as well as for glory, and hence we send forth this volume to be read of all men." Wells followed with chapters on class legislation that stripped black people of their nominal rights, on the convict lease system, and on lynching. "Three human beings were burned alive in civilized America during the first six months of this year (1893)," Wells wrote. "Over one hundred have been lynched in this half year. They were hanged, then cut, shot and burned." She left it to others to detail black achievements and progress.[68]

The book helped inspire a "Colored American Day" at the Exposition, which predictably divided the black community. Douglass recognized the limited nature of the fair's acknowledgment, but nonetheless thought it an opportunity. His only official position at the fair was as manager of the Haitian pavilion. He gave a speech. Wells saw the "Colored Day" as condescending and insufficient. She advocated a boycott, but later apologized to Douglass, whose own speech was heckled by whites.[69]

The critics of the fair found themselves harping from the margins. For the mass of visitors to the exposition, protests disturbed neither their visits nor their enjoyment; Chicago had succeeded spectacularly. What astonished Henry Adams on his first visit to the fair was precisely what was supposed to astonish him: it was about much more than business. Adams was a man certain that he knew his generation and its limits. He despaired of the incapacity of his age to "rise to the creation of new art, or the appreciation of the old," but in Chicago he claimed to see both and was "for the moment stunned by the shock." Men he thought he knew well had surpassed themselves. The renowned landscape architect Frederick Law Olmstead had designed the fairground, and Richard Morris Hunt, Charles McKim, and Stanford White, leaders in the movement to graft an imperial classical architecture onto American design, were among the architects. The sculptor Augustus Saint-Gaudens was one of the artists. Daniel H. Burnham, the Chicago architect and urban

68. Giddings, 268–80; Christopher Robert Reed, *All the World Is Here! The Black Presence at White City* (Bloomington: Indiana University Press, 2000), 20–23, 26–31; Thomas C. Holt, *Children of Fire: A History of African Americans* (New York: Hill and Wang, 2010), 194–96; Ida B. Wells-Barnett, ed. *The Reason Why the Colored American Is Not in the World's Columbian Exposition: The Afro-American's Contribution to Columbian Literature* (Urbana: University of Illinois Press, 1999; reprint, 1999), 185; William McFeely, *Frederick Douglass* (New York: W.W. Norton, 1991), 367–69.
69. Rydell, *All the World's a Fair*, 52–53; Reed, 30–33, 133–39; McFeely, Douglass, 371–72.

designer, had overseen the whole project. Chicago had lavished millions "to produce something that the Greeks might have delighted to see and Venice would have envied, but which certainly was not business." In a revealing turn, the mark of American greatness would be its success in mimicking European art.[70]

By his second visit to the fair in September with his brothers and their families, Adams was cackling at the "madness of the times." The Panic of 1893 had struck, and his brothers, hit hard, had to borrow to stay afloat. It was more than his anti-Semitism that led Adams to marvel at the "lunatic gold-bug" and to volunteer to help if "a Rothschild or a Harcourt is by hazard, to be hung up to a lamppost." Conservative in his own investments, he had largely escaped the crisis, but it had "ended up making me a flat-footed Populist and an advocate of fiat-money." At the fair, he stepped away from the financial panic to take a more detached stance, "puzzled to understand the final impression left on the average mind of the ignorant rich and the intelligent poor." Entranced by the "lowest fakes of the Midway... fireworks and electric fountains" and enamored of the Ferris Wheel, he claimed not to understand the "astounding, confused, bewildering mass of art and industry" but thought it reflected the "same chaos in my own mind." He thought visitors would think the fair an education, although of "the education I know little... but the amusement was not to be denied."[71]

Adams wandered the fair's nearly two square miles: sand dunes and swamp transformed into firm land interspersed with lakes and lagoons replete with fake Venetian gondolas and actual Venetian gondoliers (although Howells complained that they were dressed as if in an opera). Americans indulged their enthusiasm for turning food into sculpture. There was a replica of the Venus de Milo made of chocolate and a statue of a horse and rider made of prunes. Adams arrived too late for the August ball of the Midway Freaks. In his *Education*, he recalled that the fair had inspired him to ask, "for the first time whether the American people knew where they were driving." Adams certainly did not know, and he "decided that the American people probably knew no more than he did," but he

70. Wim de Wit, "Building an Illusion," in de Wit et al., 43–47, 51, 58; H. Adams to Franklin MacVeagh, May 26, 1893, in *The Letters of Henry Adams*, 4: 102–4.
71. Edward Chalfant, *Improvement of the World: A Biography of Henry Adams, His Last Life, 1891–1918* (North Haven, CT: Archon Books, 2001), 40–43; H. Adams to W. MacVeagh, Sep. 6, 1893, H. Adams to J. Hay, Sep. 8, 1893, H. Adams to Elizabeth Cameron, Oct. 8, 1893, and H. Adams to Lucy Baxter, Oct. 18, 1893, in *The Letters of Henry Adams*, 4: 124–25, 4: 131–33; *The Education of Henry Adams: An Autobiography* (New York: Heritage Press, 1942, orig. ed. 1918), 320.

vowed to find out. "Chicago was the first expression of American thought as a unity; one must start there."[72]

Howells also visited the fair that September. Sickness had delayed his trip; he had skipped the Congress of Literature, another of the exposition's convocations. When he did arrive, he stayed with Burnham, the mastermind of the exposition. At the fair, he and his family were "in rapture and despair." He uncharacteristically gushed to the New York Sun, "There never was and may never be again anything so beautiful." He thought the fair the "outcome of a socialistic impulse," by which he meant social rather than individual, and cooperative rather than selfish. "There was no niggardly competition," he said, "but instead emulation toward the highest and best." Chicago's public spirit impressed him. Howells was thrilled that a democracy gave art "as good a chance as it has been given in any despotism."[73]

The exposition was a world's fair with a wide representation of foreign countries, but American visitors regarded it as their own, a sentiment Howells gently mocked in his Letters from an Altrurian Traveller. The fair city was, his fictional traveler thought, a little piece of the equally fictional Altruria and the opposite of the "egotistic civilization" exemplified by New York. It was constructed for art, not money; it was cooperative, not individualistic; and it was spurred by generosity rather than selfishness. It was un-American in that it expressed design, although very American in the speed and scale of its construction.[74]

The themes of the exposition—art, race, and education—spilled beyond the midway and even the fair. Buffalo Bill's Wild West set up next to the fairgrounds. Its core story remained racial conquest. Like the hundreds of railroad circuses with which the Wild West competed, Buffalo Bill exhibited exotic peoples as entertainment. The Wild West sold three million tickets in 1893.[75]

In July 1893 the new American Historical Association convened as the World's Congress of Historians; its vice president, Henry Adams, was away traveling in Europe. A young University of Wisconsin history professor, Frederick Jackson Turner, presented a paper, "The Significance of the Frontier in American History," which went largely unnoticed at the time. He marked "the closing of a great historic moment," the end of the American

72. Adams, Education, 320; Louis S. Warren, Buffalo Bill's America: William Cody and the Wild West Show (New York: Knopf, 2005), 419–20.
73. "Mr. Howells Sees the Fair," New York Sun, Oct. 22, 1893, 9; W. D. Howells to E. Howells, Sep. 20, 1893, in Howells, Selected Letters, 4: 51, note 3; Cronon, 341–42.
74. W. D. Howells to Elinor Howells, Sep. 20, 1893, in Howells, Selected Letters, 4: 50–51; Letter 2, "Letters of an Altrurian Traveller, 1893–94," 20–27; Rydell, "A Cultural Frankenstein?" 157.
75. Warren, 418.

frontier, and in this he was not that different from Buffalo Bill. Their core difference was that Buffalo Bill marked American homemaking in the West as a violent conquest, while Turner claimed it had been a largely peaceful movement.[76]

Turner reinforced the exposition's theme of progress, but in a paradoxical way. The United States achieved its vigor, on display in the White City, by retreating to the primitive along a successive set of frontiers. Chicago had once been the frontier, and its transformation encapsulated Turner's version of American history. Turner, like Clarence King, turned the American focus away from the Civil War and put it on westering as the formative American experience. He did not appeal so much to evidence, of which he presented little, as to a set of stories of the kind enshrined in the Midwestern mugbooks that captured the progress of both individual lives and the nation in the journeys from log cabins to finished farms. In the guise of presenting a new interpretation, he reinforced existing stories.[77]

Turner's homemaking and Buffalo Bill's violence both intended to set the United States apart from the European empires against which Americans still defined themselves. On Turner's frontier, Indians were not so much absent as peripheral; they had no central role in the story. In what amounted to an aside, he spoke of Indians as a "common danger" that kept alive "the power of resistance to aggression." He expected his audience to assume, as he did, that in the battle for the continent Indians were aggressors. Buffalo Bill made explicit what Turner left implicit. He gave an inverted story of conquest full of Indian killers and white victims. In the Wild West Indians attacked—the settler's cabin, the emigrant train, the Deadwood Mail Coach, and Custer. Whites simply defended themselves, and in defending themselves somehow managed to win the continent.[78]

In November 1893, six months after it had opened, the fair and the White City closed. In Howells's *Letters from an Altrurian Traveller*, a visitor—a Boston banker—had wondered "what will become of all the poor fellows who are concerned in the government of the Fair City when they have to return to earth?" The fictional banker was more correct than Howells knew when he saw difficulty for workers. They were about to move from utopia to dystopia.[79]

76. Richard White, *The Frontier in American Culture: An Exhibition at the Newberry Library, August 26, 1994–January 7, 1995*, ed. Patricia Nelson Limerick and James R. Grossman (Berkeley: University of California Press, 1994), 25–27.
77. Ibid., 24–27.
78. Ibid., 26–27.
79. Howells, "Letters of an Altrurian Traveller, 1893–94," 231.

When the fair closed, its employees merged with the workers who had flocked to Chicago to join local craftsmen in building it and the annual migration of tramps, the itinerant workingmen who wintered in the city. There was no work. By late August, ten thousand men had appeared to ask for jobs at the stockyards. Carter Harrison, who had had been reelected for a fifth term as mayor, was aware of the emerging crisis. After Haymarket, he had rebuilt his ties with Chicago's labor movement. He arranged for the employment of hundreds on the Chicago Ship and Sanitary Canal, part of Chicago's attempt to mitigate its ongoing environmental crisis. It was hardly enough. By late September, half the workers in the building trades were unemployed. On the last special day of the fair, October 28, Harrison was assassinated by a disgruntled office seeker.[80]

Both politicians and ordinary Americans struggled to comprehend the wrenching changes convulsing the country. They thought in terms of familiar categories and issues, which meant they filtered them through the home and the allied concepts of manhood and womanhood. Home remained the most capacious of American institutions and values. Jacob Riis had portrayed tenements as the murder of the home. Young women like Jane Addams established settlement houses among immigrants to create model homes. White Southerners justified lynchings, which became a horrifying norm in that region as a defense of women and the home. Northerners worried about single women as both home wreckers and victims who would never achieve their "natural" goal of creating homes. The home remained the gravitational center of American thinking.

The home had never seemed so endangered.

---

80. Knight, 284–85; Dominic A. Pacyga, *Chicago: A Biography* (Chicago: University of Chicago Press, 2009), 143; Schneirov, 332–33.

21

The Great Depression

The 1892 election cast doubt on the ability of Republican businessmen to control politics, and if plutocrats were in control of the economy and the country, they may have been the last to know it. Charles Francis Adams had spent the late 1880s trying to rescue the derelict, corrupt, and almost comically mismanaged Union Pacific Railroad, whose construction in the 1860s had given rise to the Crédit Mobilier scandal. Adams had come to believe that the railroads were a natural monopoly. Only consolidation, with or without government regulation, could enable them to run efficiently and profitably. He thought the Sherman Antitrust Act a quaint reflection of a lost world. Like Bellamy, and for that matter John D. Rockefeller, he believed consolidation and cooperation (this last a word of great amplitude in the Gilded Age) were the future. Yet the railroads failed to either consolidate sufficiently or cooperate effectively. The trunk lines established the Interstate Commerce Railway Association in order to divide freight and maintain rates, but it died in late 1890 at the hands of the very corporations that formed it. Adams considered himself a sophisticated and cynical man, and the failure of both invisible and visible hands in the railroad business did not surprise him, but in 1890 the collapse of Baring Brothers did.[1]

Baring Brothers and Company was a British bank with extensive investments in American transcontinental railroads, among them the Union Pacific and the Atchison, Topeka and Santa Fe. London remained the center of world capital, and Baring Brothers invested far beyond the western United States. The firm committed heavily to Argentina, whose wheat, overbuilt railroads, immigration, and wars to wrest the land from native peoples made it a doppelganger of the American West. Whether they fully realized it or not, Americans were part of a world capitalist

---

1. James Livingston, *Origins of the Federal Reserve System: Money, Class, and Corporate Capitalism, 1890–1913* (Ithaca, NY: Cornell University Press, 1986), 33–48; Richard White, *Railroaded: The Transcontinentals and the Making of Modern America* (New York: Norton, 2011), 372–78, 384–88.

system, which they did not control. In mid-November 1890 rumors circulated of an impending Baring Brothers' failure, which would cut off critical financing for important American railroads. William Dean Howells, who owned stock in the Atchison, Topeka and Santa Fe Railroad, watched its price drop precipitously. He had bought it at $1.13 a share. It was worth $0.24 on November 16.[2]

Charles Francis Adams had a closer view and a much larger stake in what Howells called a "calamity." In 1889 Argentina began to have trouble meeting the interest on its public and private loans. The situation grew worse in 1890, and foreign investment dried up. The Baring Brothers found themselves saddled with nonnegotiable paper and borrowers who could not pay. Desperate for money to pay their own creditors, the bank ceased making loans in the United States and tried to call in the obligations it had. The crisis spooked European investors. They quite accurately recognized the obvious parallels between Argentina and the United States, but they quite inaccurately thought that the Sherman Silver Purchase Act had teeth, so fear of devalued dollars amplified their panic. Shrewd insight and ignorance of the intricacies of American governance combined, and they began liquidating their investments. Capital took flight back across the Atlantic. A crisis that had begun in Argentina and ricocheted to Great Britain quickly struck the United States. "Assuredly," Adams wrote, "this is a complex world."[3]

The railroads suffered. Unable to sell bonds, they had to borrow more and more heavily. The securities they offered for collateral were dropping rapidly in value, which prompted margin calls for additional collateral. Wall Street bears smelled blood and attacked, further driving down prices for stocks and bonds. The railroads could not live without substantial inflows of capital. Adams did not realize how bad it was until the Baring Brothers refused him an essential loan, and he found that the bank—and with it the Union Pacific—was on the verge of collapse. At that point Adams knew "the game was up."[4]

The Bank of England stepped in to rescue Baring Brothers and stem the panic in London, but no one stepped in to rescue Charles Francis Adams. With so much blood on the water, everyone knew that the nineteenth century's great white shark of finance, Jay Gould, would strike, but no one knew where. Howells reported rumors that he would take over the Atchison, Topeka and Santa Fe at rock bottom prices, but his target was

2. White, 381–82; W. D. Howells to W. C. Howells, Nov. 16, 1890, in William Dean Howells, *Selected Letters*, ed. George Warren Arms (Boston: Twayne, 1979), 3: 297–98.
3. White, 381–82, 388.
4. Ibid., 388–89.

the Union Pacific. Adams used a different metaphor. "Gould, Sage, and the pirate band were scrambling on deck," he wrote. He had no choice but to surrender, and Gould took control of the Union Pacific. Gould, of course, phrased the raid as a rescue; no one else would touch the Union Pacific. Gould's loans and investments were the only way to save it from bankruptcy—at least for the moment.[5]

For Howells it was "not the Barings that have failed but our whole economic system... no one really knows what rascality is plotting in the darkness, and things must of course go from bad to very much worse before any radical reform comes." This crisis would end, but he knew it would really only be a pause: "It will begin again, sooner or later, for that is in the constitution of things as they now are."[6]

Howells was right. The brief panic of 1890 was only a harbinger of things to come.

I

Mandates had a way of souring quickly in the Gilded Age. Grover Cleveland began his second term with the kind of single-party dominance not seen since the Grant Administration. The Republicans hated him: "that fat and fatuous freak," John Hay called him. The Democrats had returned to power promising tariff reform, a devotion to the gold standard, and, of course, prosperity. Prosperity went off the tracks first. The Gilded Age remained an economic roller coaster, and the small dip that dislodged Adams in 1890 signaled the vulnerability of the gold standard economy, whose productive capacity exceeded consumption, with falling prices for agricultural staples and falling returns on capital.[7]

The economy had grown so large and so complicated that American farmers, bankers, and businessmen were unable fully to comprehend it. Railroad leaders knew that their firms, the largest group of corporations in the country, representing $10 billion in capital, depended on money borrowed through bond sales or direct loans. They recognized that American railroads were overbuilt; most consisted of either lines in disastrous competition with each other or lines built into unremunerative territories. First the failure and then the outlawing of pools exacerbated competition

5. Ibid., 388–90.
6. W. D. Howells to W. C. Howells, Nov. 16, 1890, in Howells, *Selected Letters*, 3: 297.
7. John Taliaferro, *All the Great Prizes: The Life of John Hay from Lincoln to Roosevelt* (New York: Simon & Schuster, 2013), 281–82; James L. Livingston, *Pragmatism and the Political Economy of Cultural Revolution* (Chapel Hill: University of North Carolina Press, 1994), 41–43.

and constrained railroad revenues. Without further borrowing, the revenues on many railroads were not sufficient to make interest payments and pay back loans as they came due. Railroad debt, a gun aimed at the larger economy, was always loaded and events that reduced access to credit could pull the trigger.[8]

Bankers recognized that the gun was most likely to go off in the spring or fall, when money flowed out of New York, the center of the financial system, into rural banks to finance harvest and planting. This depleted New York bank reserves, leaving them vulnerable to any further shocks. New York bankers, particularly private investment bankers who floated bond issues and arranged the loans connecting railroads to credit, knew these shocks could come from anywhere. The credit system was international. A significant part of the money in Western and Southern railroads came from European investors. They made their investments in gold-based currencies, and the possibility that the United States might abandon the gold standard and move to a "debased" currency, either bimetallism or greenbacks, alarmed them. European fears about the security of investments in the United States could, if strong enough, as they had been in 1890, lead to a withdrawal of money and trigger a financial panic.[9]

European skittishness about American investments and European downturns, which forced bondholders to liquidate American investments, were only two of the hands reaching for the trigger. Even graver problems lay with the gold standard and federal policies that served to make money scarce and expensive. A more abundant and more flexible money supply could help stay financial panics, nipping many of them in the bud and limiting their duration. Because the United States lacked a central bank, there was no governmental institution that could provide liquidity to extend credit in times of crisis. The Civil War mechanism of the national banks issuing notes after depositing federal government bonds with the comptroller of the currency had broken down. Government credit was so

8. Douglas W. Steeples, *Democracy in Desperation: The Depression of 1893*, ed. David O. Whitten (Westport, CT: Greenwood Press, 1998), 17; White, 372–91, and passim; Livingston, *Origins*, 50–51.

9. Christopher Hanes and Paul W. Rhode, "Harvests and Financial Crises in Gold Standard America," *Journal of Economic History* 73, no. 1 (March 2013): 201–2; White, *Railroaded*, 80–81; Mira Wilkins, "Foreign Investment in the U.S. Economy before 1914," *Annals of the American Academy of Political and Social Science* 516, no. 1 (1991): 12–15; Scott Reynolds Nelson, *Iron Confederacies: Southern Railways, Klan Violence, and Reconstruction* (Chapel Hill: University of North Carolina Press, 1999), 147–48; Gretchen Ritter, *Goldbugs and Greenbacks: The Antimonopoly Tradition and the Politics of Finance in America* (Cambridge: Cambridge University Press, 1997), 154–56; Elmus Wicker, *Banking Panics of the Gilded Age* (Cambridge: Cambridge University Press, 2000), 57–82.

strong that the market value of U.S. bonds exceeded their face value, cutting the profit of using them to issue bank notes and reducing the national banknotes in circulation by 55 percent between 1882 and 1891. The need for more money in circulation was one of the reasons the surplus that was locked in the federal treasury had become a campaign issue in 1888. It was also a primary reason for the campaign for bimetallism and the passage of the Sherman Silver Purchase Act. More moderate advocates of the gold standard thought it could be solved by giving banks more flexibility to issue notes in time of crisis.[10]

The remedies available did not prove adequate. The surplus declined as the government spent money and redeemed government bonds early, but the economy continued to grow, rendering the impact of the money put back in circulation temporary. The fundamental problem remained: since the money supply depended on the gold supply, the gold standard provided insufficient currency and thus contributed to deflation. American gold reserves in 1893 looked like sand draining from the top of an hourglass. By the time Cleveland took office, the gold in the Treasury had fallen to $100 million, the minimum amount regarded as necessary to redeem outstanding government notes and obligations, and it continued to fall.[11]

American farmers had the capacity to mitigate panics, but only to a degree. Waves of wheat and cotton rolled across the Atlantic, and gold, or gold-backed currencies, flowed westward in return. Cotton and wheat dwarfed other American exports, and if the American balance of payments had depended simply on the difference between imports and exports, the United States would have run a surplus in the early 1890s. That surplus, however, was more than offset by money sent abroad as interest on European investments. Still, the payments for American harvests provided a powerful annual boost to the amount of money in circulation. The nature of the economy meant much of this money became concentrated in New York and available for investment.[12]

Wheat and cotton affected the financial system in different ways and degrees. Production of wheat depended on independent Midwestern and Western farmers, who needed a great deal of cash to produce and ship it. The revenue from wheat exports was quickly reabsorbed into the larger

10. Ritter, 155–56; Livingston, *Origins*, 73–74, 78.
11. Livingston, *Origins*, 83–84; Horace Samuel Merrill, *Bourbon Leader: Grover Cleveland and the Democratic Party* (Boston: Little, Brown, 1957), 174–83.
12. Table Ee1-21—Balance of international payments: 1790–1998, in *Historical Statistics of the United States, Earliest Times to the Present: Millennial Edition*, ed. Scott Sigmund Gartner, Susan B. Carter, Michael R. Haines, Alan L. Olmstead, Richard Sutch, and Gavin Wright (New York: Cambridge University Press, 2006.); Steeples, 27–29.

Commodity Exports, 1879–1900

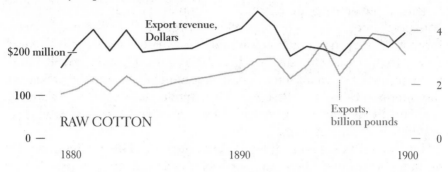

Sources: U.S. Department of the Treasury, Bureau of Statistics, Monthly Summary of Commerce and Finance, Statistical Abstract of the United States.

economy. Farmers bought farm equipment, hired labor, paid elevators to store their crop, and paid railroads to haul it. They mortgaged farms— more than 40 percent of the farms in many states in the West and Middle Border—and bought land to expand their operations.[13]

Cotton exports generated more revenue, and less of it was spent on producing, moving, and financing the crop. Southern farmers did have to spend on fertilizer—phosphate from inside and guano from outside the United States—but sharecroppers and tenants did not spend money on the sophisticated farm equipment of northern farmers. This did not mean that money remained in the hands of producers. Because of the crop-lien system, Southern sharecroppers and tenants had to dispose of their crops immediately at low prices, which fell further in the 1890s. Profits went to plantation owners, furnishing merchants, shipping companies, and the various agents—usually in New York—who financed, sold, and insured the crop.

13. Steeples, 16–17, 22; Hanes and Rhode, 202–3, 232.

A good cotton harvest thus pumped a disproportionate amount of money into New York banks, which supplied an important source of cash to the private banks, investment houses, speculators, and brokers. When flush with cash, the financial and credit system was far more likely to operate relatively smoothly. When, as in 1892, a poor cotton harvest diminished reserves, there was a danger the whole system would freeze up.[14]

There is no need to accept cotton as the sole cause of financial panics to argue that poor cotton harvests put tremendous additional pressure on the U.S. financial system. With so many enterprises saddled with debt, Henry Adams looked for "a big smash. Our bladder has been blown up till it must burst someday; perhaps better now than later...." In 1892–93 the combination of Europeans liquidating investments and a poor cotton harvest caused gold reserves to fall dramatically, credit to become more expensive, and investment to decline. Immense pressure came to bear on the overbuilt railroad system.[15]

In February 1893 the Philadelphia and Reading Railroad collapsed. The *Banker's Magazine* noted, a little late, that it and other corporations were so shoddily managed as to make their shares "the worst gambling stocks ever listed." Goldbugs said the problem was deteriorating confidence among European investors that the United States would remain on the gold standard. Believing that the Sherman Silver Purchase Act was the source of the panic, both outgoing President Harrison and incoming President Cleveland demanded its repeal. Cleveland brought Henry Villard, who since leaving the American Social Science Association had become a financier and was then a man en route to wrecking the Northern Pacific Railroad for the second time in a decade, to lecture the new cabinet on the need for hard money. Villard helped set in motion events that would nearly destroy the Democratic Party, which was deeply divided over silver. The first attempt at repeal in March—introduced by Republican Sen. John Sherman, the act's original sponsor—failed.[16]

On May 5, full-scale panic hit the New York Stock Exchange, and all over the country banks faced runs as depositors demanded cash. Starved

14. Hanes and Rhode, 202–6, 224–25, 234; Gavin Wright, *Old South, New South: Revolutions in the Southern Economy since the Civil War* (New York: Basic Books, 1986), 56, 59, 116.

15. David O. Whitten, "The Depression of 1893," *EH.net* (2015), http://eh.net/encyclopedia /the-depression-of-1893/; H. Adams to J. Hay, Nov. 7, 1892, in *The Letters of Henry Adams*, ed. J. C. Levenson (Cambridge, MA: Belknap Press, 1982), 4: 78; Steeples, 23–24, 28–29, 31–32.

16. Merrill, 174–83; Livingston, 83–84; White, 388–89, 391–93, 396–97; R. Hal Williams, *Realigning America: McKinley, Bryan, and the Remarkable Election of 1896* (Lawrence: University Press of Kansas, 2010), 32–36; Steeples, 32–33.

for capital, the national banks between May and October reduced their outstanding loans by nearly 15 percent, more than twice the reduction during the Panic of 1873. Virtually all private banks, state banks, and national banks were under siege. New York banks raised the cost of credit and through the use of clearinghouse certificates extended credit to each other, which temporarily stilled the panic. Cleveland—who in June discovered he had cancer, hid his illness, and in a secret operation had much of his jaw removed—called for a special session of Congress. If Cleveland had died, Adlai Stevenson, a free-silver man, would have become president. The special session did not restore confidence. The Erie Railroad failed, and stocks plunged again. Western and Southern banks continued to collapse. Credit dried up, and in California farmers could not borrow either to harvest or to ship their crops. Only in August did the second wave of the Panic subside. Cleveland brought patronage and party discipline to bear on the Democrats, but he never broke resistance to repeal in his own party. Republican senators provided the margin of victory. More Democrats voted for free silver than for repeal, but the real division was regional rather than partisan. The West and the South were for silver. Congress finally repealed the Sherman Silver Purchase Act at the end of October.[17]

Repeal was supposed to restore confidence and, with it, the economy; instead, more failures followed. In 1893 alone 360 national and state banks—343 in the Midwest, South, and West—shut their doors, with an eventual loss of roughly $42 million. The iron industry suffered the worst year in its history; textile mills closed, and railroads steamed into the abyss, unable to meet their interest payments or repay their loans. In all, 119 railroads went into receivership in 1893, including Henry Villard's Northern Pacific; the Atchison, Topeka and Santa Fe; and the Union Pacific. Furious investors hoped to indict Villard; banks sued him. He sailed for Europe. By 1895, 25 percent of the country's railroads were in receivership. Total business failures mounted to more than fifteen thousand.[18]

Gold continued to drain from the country. This depression—which until the 1930s would be known as the Great Depression—meant that tax revenue, particularly from the tariff, declined. With little new gold flowing into the Treasury, the government tried to prevent the collapse of the gold standard by issuing bonds, which purchasers paid for in gold. In

17. Livingston, 72; Steeples, 33–37; Michael Kazin, A Godly Hero: The Life of William Jennings Bryan (New York: Anchor Books, 2007), 38; Williams, 31, 33–34.
18. Herbert Hovenkamp, Enterprise and American Law, 1836–1937 (Cambridge, MA: Harvard University Press, 1991), 148; Livingston, 72, 80; White, 391–93, 396–97; Steeples, 36–38.

January 1894, with the gold reserves down to $69.76 million, the Treasury issued $50 million in bonds. This proved to be only a temporary stopgap, and reserves fell to $52.19 million in August, necessitating further bond sales. Cleveland's monomaniacal focus on gold had made silver a potent symbolic issue.[19]

II

Because of the boost the Columbian Exposition gave to Chicago, the city felt the impact of the Panic of 1893 later than most of the country did. George Pullman, one of Chicago's leading industrialists, had done well by the exposition. Many of those attending traveled in his Pullman cars.

Andrew Carnegie, in his *Triumphant Democracy*, labeled Pullman a "typical American" for his modest origins, great ambitions, and ultimate success. Pullman was not only a man who rose with Chicago; he literally raised Chicago out of its low-lying swamp by creating a company to jack buildings up to the new street levels. He made his serious money building railroad cars, the eponymous and ornate sleepers and dining cars that he leased to railroads. He did not attempt to compete in terms of cost; he offered higher quality. He had used the cars included in the Lincoln funeral train on its last stage from Chicago to Springfield as a venue to publicize his company. He staffed them with their own crews: white conductors and black cooks and porters. By the standards of the time, these were some of the best jobs open to black men. In the 1870s Pullman expanded into the day coach market, offering a parlor car for an extra fee. He improved his cars constantly, adding electric lights to replace dangerous oil lamps, steam heat circulating under the car floors, and the vestibule car, which allowed passengers to move easily from one car to the next. By 1893 the company had more than fourteen thousand employees, and three out of every four miles of American railroads ran cars leased from the Pullman system, even though the high rates had attracted attention from state legislatures and Congress.[20]

19. Livingston, 84–86; R. Hal Williams, *Years of Decision: American Politics in the 1890s* (New York: John Wiley and Sons, 1978), 83–84.

20. Stanley Buder, *Pullman: An Experiment in Industrial Order and Community Planning, 1880–1930* (New York: Oxford University Press, 1967), 3, 5, 11–14, 17–24, 28–30; Carl S. Smith, *Urban Disorder and the Shape of Belief: The Great Chicago Fire, the Haymarket Bomb, and the Model Town of Pullman* (Chicago: University of Chicago Press, 1995), 182; Almont Lindsey, *The Pullman Strike: The Story of a Unique Experiment and of a Great Labor Upheaval* (Chicago: University of Illinois Press, 1942), 25.

Pullman enjoyed and displayed his success. He and his wife, Harriet Sanger, had built a mansion on Prairie Avenue near that of Marshall Field, "Chicago's Merchant Prince." The house had its own library, theater, and music room. He entertained lavishly. When his daughters made their social debut in 1893, a thousand guests attended the reception at his home. He had, of course, other homes, including his summer estate Fairhaven at Long Branch, New Jersey, from which he commuted to New York, staying overnight, when necessary, at the Windsor Hotel.[21]

How the Panic affected Pullman mattered more than how it affected other Chicago industrialists because he had sought to distinguish himself from other industrialists. He imagined himself a reformer, if a particularly hardheaded reformer, who stripped reform of all sentiment and made it pay. He was active in the YMCA and temperance organizations, in part because he had seen drunken young men taking part in the disturbances around the Great Strike of 1877. He believed in vocational education for workers as a partial cure for the "labor problem," but he became convinced that the real solution was an improved environment that would yield "clean, contented, sober, educated, and happy" workers.[22]

In 1880 Pullman bought four thousand acres at Calumet, outside Chicago. Despite the failures of the model tenement movement, he accepted its premise that social justice and the welfare of the poor could be accomplished, along with an attractive return on investment. His new town, named, of course, after himself, would be an un-Chicago. It was to have decent housing, parks, clean streets, universal running water and sewage, and good schools. It would have facilities for meeting and entertainment. Above all, it would be "beautiful and harmonious." It would not have saloons or brothels or other "baneful" influences. It would not have entertainments or meetings that George Pullman thought inappropriate; nor would it have a popularly elected government that could limit the way he ran the town. It was "the simplest business proposition...we are landlords and employers. That is all there is of it." The town's beauty and improvements would be charged to the workers, who could only rent, not own. Pullman sought a 6 percent return on investment; he appears to have achieved 4.5 percent. In addition to producing railroad cars, he intended to produce better workers, who were "elevated and refined" by their surroundings.[23]

Their surroundings were impressive. The company laid out the houses and apartments in a grid along macadamized streets lined with elms,

21. Buder, 28–30.
22. Smith, 183–84; Buder, 32–37, 40.
23. Smith, 193–200; Buder, 38–45, 49–72, 89–91.

maples, and lindens. Sidewalks separated the streets and front lawns. There were a few detached and semidetached houses, but most workers lived in two-to-five-family buildings, all made of brick and all roughly the same size. On the eastern edge of the town were ten tenements. These rose three stories and were crowded three to a block. The tenements enjoyed high demand because their rents stayed relatively low, costing roughly a fifth of the residents' earnings, compared to about a third for private homes. The company retained the right to inspect the houses at its own discretion. By 1893, the population reached 12,600.[24]

Visitors and journalists praised both George Pullman and Pullman—the "most perfect city in the world," according to one London newspaper—but the people who paid a premium for the privilege of living there were more muted. Women more than men appreciated Pullman's amenities. Men resented the town's dullness and their long hours at work. They chafed at Pullman's control. They did not regard the town as home. People rapidly moved in and out. Women told Richard Ely, the economist and Social Gospeler, that they felt they were "living in a great hotel." Pullman's buildings were better, but his rents were higher than in Chicago and were high in terms of the wages he paid. To buy homes or to find cheaper rents, workers moved to Roseland and Kensington, which grew up nearby. They also sought to escape the constant surveillance of a

This photograph from the roof of the Arcade Building gives a bird's-eye view of George Pullman's model town. It captures the orderliness and ambition of the endeavor. Collection of the Pullman State Historic Site.

24. Buder, 70–78, 86–89.

company town, where Pullman's agents told them how to dress, how to behave, and how to keep house.[25]

Pullman's workers had not been plucked from the slums; they were unlikely to come from neighborhoods around Hull House on Halsted Street. His factory in the 1880s employed about 75 percent skilled workers, selected by personnel departments that sought to weed out those who drank, gambled, or had previously been discharged for cause. Male employees outnumbered women 3,752 to 1,945, and most were northern European immigrants: Swedes, Germans, English, and Dutch. Pullman avoided Irish, regarding them as preferring politics to "honest work." He sought families, but the town swelled with single men, who boarded with families or lived in boarding houses that operators rented from the company.[26]

Pullman really did intend to govern his town as "a man governs his house, his store, or his workshop." The theater in the Arcade at the center of the town put on only plays that Pullman "could invite his family to enjoy with the utmost propriety." Only the bar in the hotel, whose luxury and prices intimidated workers, sold liquor. He allowed one church, the elegant Greenstone church, which was supposed to house all denominations and return a 6 percent profit to Pullman, until the town's workers insisted on separate congregations and accommodations. Eventually Pullman agreed to lease land outside the town to the churches.[27]

An agent, employed by Pullman, managed the town, which was part of Hyde Park Township, and then, after 1889, part of Chicago. Neither Hyde Park nor Chicago exerted much control over Pullman, and company executives ran for township and city offices as Pullman's proxies. He desired, and got, low taxes and minimal interference from outside; the only local elections were for the school board.[28]

Pullman could not seal off his town from the country's labor troubles. Albert Parsons spoke in nearby Kensington; the Knights of Labor signed up workers, who went out on the eight-hour strike of May 1, 1886. Pullman contributed to the unrest by putting relentless pressure on wages, moving to piecework, and halting payments to men injured in the factories unless they could prove it was not due to their own negligence. Between 1887 and 1893 no large conflicts erupted, but tensions, especially over control of work and arbitrary foremen, simmered.[29]

25. W. T. Stead, *Chicago To-Day: The Labour War in America* (New York: Arno Press, 1969), 122–25; Buder, 72–73, 81–83, 88–89, 94–97; Smith, 186–93, 203–8.
26. Buder, 77–82.
27. Ibid., 61–69.
28. Ibid., 102–3, 107–17.
29. Ibid., 138–43.

The assassination of Mayor Carter Harrison came on the day William Stead, a journalist, British reformer, and advocate of the Social Gospel, arrived in the United States. His articles on child prostitution had helped spark the WCTU's movement for "social purity," as the battle against prostitution was called. A week later, he arrived in Chicago and began describing a world far removed from the fair. Stead was another sign of the internationalizing of reform. The WCTU had become an international organization, promoting temperance, women's rights, and social purity, but it was not alone in promoting American versions of applied Christianity around the globe; the YMCA, the Good Templars, and the United Society for Christian Endeavor did the same. Stead enthused over American reform. Nearly a decade after his arrival in Chicago, he would publish *The Americanization of the World*. He lauded the WCTU for teaching women to "recognize their capacity to serve the State in the promotion of all that tends to preserve the purity and sanctity of the home"; this was one of the America's contributions to the "betterment of the World."[30]

Stead came to Chicago with little knowledge of the city, but with a brazenness that either charmed or dismayed, a keen-eyed attention to detail and personality, and a style of investigative journalism that would within a few years be called muckraking. His moral certainty sprang from his embrace of the Social Gospel. Within a few months, he had used the tramps, who inundated Chicago in the winter of 1893, to batter Chicago's self-satisfaction produced by the Columbian Exposition. In December he called a meeting, which he entitled "If Christ Came to Chicago," and invited businessmen, reformers, newspapermen, labor leaders, and the social elite. His subsequent book with the same title became a bestseller.

Stead concluded that Christ would not be happy with Chicago; he might even prefer Czarist Russia, which Stead said treated its poor less harshly. Stead enraged those who had no intention of taking criticism from a preachy Englishman, and in their rage they supplied him with ammunition. A Chicago paper editorialized that Chicagoans knew how to deal with tramps, and Stead did not: "The toe of a boot by day and a cold stone floor by night—these be the leading courses in the curriculum by which we would educate into self-respect such tramps as are capable of it. The tramp is a pariah and we ought to keep him such." Stead happily quoted the paper, which made his case for him.[31]

30. Ian R. Tyrrell, *Reforming the World: The Creation of America's Moral Empire* (Princeton, NJ: Princeton University Press, 2010), 1–5, 13–14, 194–95; Tyrrell, *Woman's World/Woman's Empire: The Woman's Christian Temperance Union in International Perspective, 1880–1930* (Chapel Hill: University of North Carolina Press, 1991), 5, 168, 187.

31. William Thomas Stead, *If Christ Came to Chicago* (Chicago: Laird & Lee, 1894), 34; Richard Schneirov, *Labor and Urban Politics: Class Conflict and the Origins of Modern Liberalism in Chicago, 1864–97* (Urbana: University of Illinois Press, 1998), 332–33.

Stead talked to tramps and prostitutes and told stories that combined sentiment and sordid detail in the way Victorians loved. He hinted at sex, was explicit about suffering, and allowed readers to see the underside of Chicago. "Like the frogs in the Egyptian plague," he wrote, "you could not escape from the tramps, go where you would. In the city they wandered through the streets seeking work and finding none." At night they came together in great herds; "nocturnal camps of the homeless nomads of the civilization were all in the center of the city." He described the Harrison Street police station, where tramps were allowed to sleep in the corridors between the cells, and Chicago's City Hall, which opened its doors to tramps at night. He evoked a haze of tobacco smoke floating over sea of tobacco juice, spit, and phlegm. He described the reek of dirty bodies and armies of lice crawling from person to person. Harrison Street jail was a bedlam of drunks, whores, and criminals, with the tramps thrown among them. Stead demanded Chicago see the tramp as Christ's brother and the harlot as Christ's sister. He criticized the churches for failing to recognize "Christ the citizen," and "by insisting so exclusively upon the other life [they] have banished him from his own world, and by the substitution of Divine Worship for Human Service have largely undone the work of the Incarnation." Stead described and he prescribed, often putting the prescriptions in the mouths of his characters. Attack the indecent saloons—those that were fronts for gambling and sporting houses—and reform will succeed; attack all saloons, and it will fail. He detailed the corruption of political machines, but he also used them as a club against the churches. The machines embraced the "fundamental principle of human brotherhood," albeit for their own benefit, while the churches neglected their duty.[32]

As he came to know the city, Stead distinguished among the rich the way social reformers distinguished among the poor, dividing them into the very unworthy, the not quite so unworthy, and the merely rich. The predatory rich such as Charles Yerkes, the streetcar magnate, plundered the public. The "idle, frivolous, and vicious rich," who were born into wealth, imagined it as their due and had no sense of public obligation. At the very pinnacle of wealth Stead placed the "holy trinity" of Chicago: Marshall Field, Philip Armour, and George Pullman.[33]

Stead thought Armour, Field, and Pullman were honest men who helped create a corrupt city. Field and Armour were narrowly able and, within certain bounds, generous, but they fed corruption because they were unwilling to participate in what they could not control and because they so effectively protected what was theirs. The rich starved the city for funds by

32. Stead, *Chicago to-Day*, 12–17; Stead, *If Christ Came to Chicago*, 17–23, 52, 68.
33. Stead, *If Christ Came to Chicago* 107, 111–13.

keeping so much of its property off the tax rolls. They had no sense of public obligation; for them life did not go much beyond accumulating money.[34]

Stead, however, thought Pullman a "man of a different make" and the town of Pullman a great success of which "not only Chicago but America does well to be proud." The success, however, came at a price because it flew in the face of "the fundamental principles of American institutions." Stead desired "municipal socialism"—the cooperative efforts of an entire community under democratic control—but at Pullman he discovered "paternal despotism." Having a town and its residents under the control and oversight of a single man was "a little bit too much."[35]

Stead had his own contradictions. He wrote in the name of the American "Democratic idea," but he was less a democrat than a man who imagined himself as goading the rich, the wise, and the well-born to better the conditions of those below them. Stead acknowledged the common humanity of the rich and poor, but he was, like many advocates of the Social Gospel, ultimately more interested in a Christian stewardship than democratic governance. He was more like Pullman than he thought.[36]

It was typical of Stead that he claimed the Civic Federation of Chicago, a forerunner of Progressivism, as the fruit of his meetings, even though it sprang from the older wellspring of liberal reform. The federation differed from earlier Chicago reform organizations in the large number of women involved, its embrace of the Social Gospel, and its readiness to ally with labor, but the liberal businessmen Franklin MacVeagh and Lyman Gage remained key figures. Jane Addams served on the original board. Trade union men rose to prominence in the Civic Federation, but not trade union women.[37]

III

Trade union leaders could find common ground with civic reformers, and there was a time in Eugene Debs's life—a long time—when he would have admired George Pullman. By 1893, however, Debs had ceased to be the young man in Terre Haute, Indiana, who had opposed the Great Strike of 1877. Few Americans had embraced free labor as ardently as Debs, and few lives had traced the vicissitudes of free labor as delicately as did Debs. An ambitious American individualist, tied to the emerging middle classes

34. Ibid., 90–94.
35. Ibid., 85–90; Stead, *Chicago to-Day*, 120–22.
36. Stead, *If Christ Came to Chicago*, 72–73, 85, 87–97.
37. Schneirov, 334–35; Louise W. Knight, *Citizen: Jane Addams and the Struggle for Democracy* (Chicago: University of Chicago Press, 2005), 299–303.

by marriage and blood, and an ardent republican (although politically a Democrat) devoted to the ameliorative possibilities of American democracy, he had imagined his hometown as Lincoln's Springfield. Like Pullman, he had believed that, as producers, employers and workers shared the same interests and the line between them remained permeable. He had regarded the Knights as too radical and remained loyal to the conservative railroad brotherhoods of skilled workers. The anarchists of Haymarket shocked and appalled him. No one had believed in the sacred republican trinity of home, citizen, and white manhood more ardently than Debs.[38]

Debs never abandoned his ambition, his producerism, or his republicanism, but as the country changed, his politics changed. He served as a human seismograph, registering the shifts in the thinking of native-born Protestant working men. In the 1880s he admired Samuel Gompers, the Jewish immigrant head of the AFL, even when he disagreed with him, but he equated Southern European Catholic and Eastern European Jewish immigrants with the Chinese: "The Dago works for small pay and lives far more like a savage or a wild beast than the Chinese." Italians undercut the pay of American workers, and "Italy has millions of them to spare and they are coming." When the London Board of Guardians announced a program to speed the movement of Russian-Jewish immigrants to the United States, Debs denounced the immigrants as "criminals and paupers." Nor did he criticize the emergence of Jim Crow or try to break the racist culture of the railroad brotherhoods that he led.[39]

Despite being a child of Alsatian immigrants whose Protestant father had been disinherited for marrying his Catholic mother, Debs's attitudes initially mirrored those of Henry F. Bowers of the anti-Catholic American Protective Association (APA), but Debs did not follow Bowers into the netherworld of anti-Catholicism. He condemned the APA in the 1890s. Bowers regarded religion as the fault line of American society; Debs increasingly thought it was class. He kept his old emphasis on workers as both citizens and producers, but he now stressed solidarity, and mutual dependence rather than independence, while denouncing attempts to turn working people against each other. He saw American rights as under attack from increasingly powerful corporations, and workers had a duty to defend those rights.[40]

38. Nick Salvatore, *Eugene V. Debs: Citizen and Socialist* (Urbana: University of Illinois Press, 1982), 45, 48–50, 52, 59–61, 62, 64, 68.
39. Ibid., 104.
40. Ibid., 106–7.

By 1890 Debs, criticizing the sense of "caste" that weakened labor, had withdrawn from the Brotherhood of Fireman. In 1892 he helped organize a new industrial union, the American Railroad Union, which would replace a federation of craft unions with a single entity that would include all railroad workers, skilled and unskilled. The ambitions of the ARU were nearly as sweeping as those of the Knights. "If organized labor has any mission in the world," Debs proclaimed, "it is to help those who cannot help themselves." The ARU held its first board meeting in February 1893.[41]

Like the Knights of Labor, the ARU's greatest weakness was its rapid success. In 1893 two of the original transcontinentals, the Union Pacific and the Northern Pacific, and a new one, the Great Northern, conspired to cut wages and change work rules. The older transcontinentals were in their usual condition, saddled with debt, overbuilt, and disastrously managed. Most of their long western trunk lines between the 100th meridian and the Pacific Coast were a burden to them. The Great Northern was a different beast. Finished just before the onset of the depression of 1893, it too faced an immediate crisis of lack of traffic beyond the 100th meridian, but it was a much-better-built road with lower grades and a far more manageable debt burden. East of the 100th meridian it tapped the American breadbasket, and it could haul traffic for much less than its rivals. Whatever the faults and peculiarities of James J. Hill, who ran it, he was an experienced railroad man and a skilled manager glad to use the public subsidies he had inherited from roads he absorbed.[42]

With a newly organized union and hostile federal courts, Debs did not want a strike, but a strike was forced on him by the seemingly incongruent combination of the weakness of the railroads and their aggressiveness. As Gould had shown, railroads in receivership could abrogate their contracts with their workers, and both the Northern Pacific and the Union Pacific had slid into receivership. But even without receivership, as the Great Burlington Strike of 1888 had shown, judges could wield injunctions to break strikes. In 1893 a federal judge appointed the existing executives, the men who had managed the road into bankruptcy, as receivers of the Northern Pacific and Union Pacific. They cut wages, and more critically, they attacked work rules and the brotherhoods' control over work.[43]

41. Schneirov, 336; Salvatore, 110.
42. For a full, if hagiographic, account of Hill, see Albro Martin, *James J. Hill and the Opening of the Northwest* (St. Paul: Minnesota Historical Society Press, 1991); White, 422–29.
43. William E. Forbath, *Law and the Shaping of the American Labor Movement* (Cambridge, MA: Harvard University Press, 1991), 69–71; White, 423–24.

Fearing a strike, the receivers of the Northern Pacific and Union Pacific went to court to secure injunctions that forbade organized workers from even consulting their leaders. Lawyers for the brotherhoods succeeded in modifying these injunctions, but then federal judge Elmer S. Dundy issued a new one prohibiting Union Pacific workers from so much as meeting to discuss the wage cuts, let alone striking. It was an expansion of earlier injunctions that used the Sherman Antitrust Act to break strikes. Debs denounced this as "a deathblow to human liberty." He said there was "no difference between American and Russian slavery except that the former masquerades in a shroud of sovereign citizenship." Although Debs thought the corporations and the courts "synonymous nowadays," the federal courts were not uniformly against the strikes. Judge Henry Caldwell overruled Dundy and told the receivers to abide by existing agreements. Caldwell's decision hardly decided the larger issues.[44]

With the Union Pacific and Northern Pacific tangled up in court, Hill cut wages, following Gould's playbook by hitting his most vulnerable workers the hardest with reductions of 20–36 percent. He did not touch dividends. When the brotherhoods failed to roll back the cuts, the workers called on the ARU. Hill refused to recognize it and fired ARU members. The union struck, with Debs telling the workers that if they acted as men, "they would not want for the support of courageous manly men." He appealed to the citizens of towns along the Great Northern route for support against "this unholy massacre of our rights." In a West full of antimonopoly sentiment, he got it. When attempts to get the government to intervene failed, Hill agreed to arbitrate. Debs bested him. The arbiters, led by William Pillsbury of Pillsbury Flour, gave the ARU 97 percent of its demands.[45]

The ARU became the workers' new hope in the nation's largest industry. ARU organizers followed the tracks west in 1894, creating new locals as they went. The members were wildly enthusiastic, militant, but barely organized, a near-precise replica of the Knights in 1886. The ARU organizers had turned the railroad tracks into a fuse; Pullman lit it.[46]

Pullman had always insisted that his town was a business enterprise and not a charity, and he proved true to his word. As orders fell, Pullman cut wages, cut hours, and cut workers. While reducing pay, he did not reduce rents or the prices he charged for gas and water. And the corporation

44. White, 425–26; Salvatore, 118–21.
45. White, 421–22, 426–29; Debs to Frank X. Holl, Apr. 16, 1894, in *Letters of Eugene V. Debs, Volume 1, 1874–1912*, ed. Robert Constantine (Urbana: University of Illinois Press, 1990) 1: 58.
46. White, 421–22.

continued to pay dividends. In 1894 he took contracts at a loss to keep men at work, and he used this as a reason not to restore wages, even though workers absorbed a disproportionate amount of the losses. By the spring of 1894, the wages of one car builder had dropped from $2.26 to $0.91. His case was extreme, but those still working by April 1894 had seen their pay reduced by 28 percent. When the hardest-hit workers went to collect their pay, they received checks barely more than what they owed in rent. In extreme cases, their rent exceeded their income, and they owed Pullman money. He did not evict them, but they fell into arrears. When Jane Addams offered to arbitrate rents, Pullman refused.[47]

The ARU's charter was so broad that the small spur the railroads ran into Pullman allowed the organization of ARU locals in the factory. On May 11, after an initial meeting where Pullman laid off members of the ARU negotiating committee, 90 percent of the workers walked out. He laid off the remainder. Debs, too, tried to arrange arbitration. Pullman once again refused. In Chicago, sympathy for the workers cut across class lines and included middle-class reformers and local Democratic politicians, but Pullman, despite the entreaties of the Chicago Civic Federation, still refused to arbitrate. The company waited for an inevitable victory in a war of attrition.[48]

On June 12, the ARU convened its first national convention in Chicago, and Eugene Debs changed the equation, but not in the way he wanted. He urged caution and the necessity of avoiding conflicts that the union could not win, but he also unleashed the lofty rhetoric for which he was known: "When men accept degrading conditions and wear collars and fetters without resistance, when a man surrenders his honest convictions, his loyalty to principle, he ceases to be a man." Debs had once rejected the Knights, but his language harkened back to theirs: "an injury to one is the concern of all." Swayed by his eloquence, workers ignored Debs's insistence on caution. The ARU voted to back the Pullman strike by refusing to handle any Pullman cars. The powerful General Managers' Association, which represented the twenty-four railroads centering or terminating in Chicago, countered by announcing that any worker who enforced the boycott would be fired. On June 26, the workers began detaching the cars; the railroads fired workers, and other workers walked out, demanding their reinstatement. Who walked out and when, and who

47. Buder, 147–67; Knight, 312–14; Salvatore, 126–27; Nell Irvin Painter, *Standing at Armageddon: The United States, 1877–1919* (New York: Norton, 1987), 121–22; Schneirov, 337–38.

48. Salvatore, 127–30; Ray Ginger, *Altgeld's America, 1890–1905* (Chicago: Quadrangle Press, 1958), 155; Buder, 155–62.

returned and when, became a complicated dance. Some engineers, fire-men, and conductors sided with the ARU; others, loyal to the brotherhoods, remained on the job, but what had been an isolated strike became a na-tional strike, with its primary focus west of Chicago. By June 29, 125,000 workers were on strike and twenty railroads were tied up. Two-thirds of the nation—from Ohio to California—was affected.[49]

The railroads claimed they were innocent victims of a quarrel with Pullman, but they organized aggressively not only to break the strike but also to crush the ARU. From Chicago west, the strike in June and early July was largely peaceful, proved effective, and garnered public sympathy. When the strike shut down Chicago and crippled the Northern Pacific, the railroads appealed to the courts. In Minnesota and North Dakota, judges ruled that the bankrupt Northern Pacific did not even need an in-junction to summon marshals; strikers' interference with receivers was cause enough. In Montana, however, federal courts refused to intervene. Many federal officials in New Mexico, Colorado, and California were unsympathetic to the railroads. But the strike would not be decided on the ground; it would be decided in Washington by the Cleveland admin-istration, particularly by Attorney General Richard Olney.[50]

Olney was not an ogre, although he certainly could play the role. He had ostracized his own daughter for attending her father-in-law's funeral against his wishes, and he had arranged for the execution of a cow that wandered onto his tennis court. He was a laissez-faire liberal who had made his money as a railroad attorney for subsidized railroads. He became general counsel of the Chicago, Burlington, and Quincy, and Cleveland had made him his attorney general in 1893. Even after taking office, Olney remained on the Burlington's payroll and seems also to have been paid by the Atchison, Topeka and Santa Fe. He had, however, refused to inter-vene in the Great Northern strike, perhaps because the Burlington hated James J. Hill. As late as the spring of 1894 he was leery of federal interven-tion in labor disputes and thought that workers had good reason to think the present organization of society was stacked against them. With the outbreak of the Pullman strike, his deeper sympathies and fears surfaced. He thought that the strike, "if successful, would seriously impair the sta-bility of our institutions and the entire organization of society as now constituted."[51]

49. Painter, 123–24; Buder, 168–77; Carroll Davidson Wright, *Report on the Chicago Strike of June–July 1894* (Clifton, NJ: A. M. Kelley, 1972, orig. ed. 1895), xxvii, xxxii–xxxviii; Salvatore, 127–28; White, 429–50; Ginger, 155–57.
50. White, 429–42.
51. White, 417–18, 439–43. Pullman shared Olney's fears; Stanley Buder, *Capitalizing on Change: A Social History of American Business* (Chapel Hill: University of North Carolina Press, 2009), 179.

As the nation's great railroad hub, Chicago became the center of the struggle. The vast bulk of the railroad traffic from Chicago and elsewhere was freight, and since freight trains did not haul Pullman cars, there was no need for most of the nation's traffic to become involved in the strike. Not using Pullman cars on passenger trains would contractually cost the railroads money, but they could have left them off trains if they chose. For owners as well as workers, however, principles were at stake. John W. Kendrick of the Northern Pacific stated it in the usual way: it was a question of "whether the roads shall be absolutely controlled by the labor element, or by the managers, and the owners." Kendrick didn't mention that the managers and owners of the Northern Pacific had already driven it into the ground and it was under the control of the federal courts.[52]

Olney acted in full cooperation and consultation with the General Managers' Association in Chicago. As the commission investigating the strike later noted, the association represented an illegal "usurpation of power not granted" in corporate charters. It was "an illustration of the persistent and shrewdly devised plans of corporations to overreach their limitations and usurp indirectly powers and rights not contemplated in their charters and not obtainable from the people or their legislators." Olney used an earlier legal opinion that any train of any kind carrying a mail car was a mail train; interfering with it was thus a violation of U.S. law. The decision forced often-reluctant federal marshals to act when strikers blocked any train with both a Pullman and a mail car. The railroads refused to run any mail trains without Pullmans. Olney allowed the railroads to hire thousands of deputy marshals to enforce the decision.[53]

The federal government used the mail to break the boycott, but the General Managers' Association wanted the strike, which continued, crushed. On June 30, Olney appointed Edwin Walker, a railroad attorney who was the partner of a member of the association's legal committee, as special assistant to the U.S. attorney. Clarence Darrow, then both a rising radical lawyer in Chicago and a lawyer for the Chicago and Northwestern, complained that it was the equivalent of appointing "the attorney for the American Railway Union to represent the United States." Using the Sherman Antitrust Act and the Interstate Commerce Act, measures aimed at controlling the railroads, the government got injunctions against the ARU and its leaders forbidding them from advocating the boycott. They could neither write nor talk about it.[54]

52. White, 431, 440–44.
53. Ginger, 157–62; White, 417–18, 427–28, 431.
54. White, 440–41, for the strike as a whole, 429–50; Wright, xxvii–xxxi; Ginger, 158–59; Schneirov, 338–39; Buder, *Pullman* 183–86.

In effect, the federal government, in ways it refused to do any longer in the South and with far less legal justification or necessity, intervened to push aside local authorities. Under Mayor John Hopkins, the police remained neutral, and many were sympathetic to the strikers. Olney replaced local law enforcement and state militias, whose soldiers were often related to strikers and also sympathized with them, with deputy marshals, most of them appointed and paid for by the railroads, and federal troops. Both the secretary of war and the army chief of staff opposed sending troops to Chicago, but Olney claimed, without evidence, that this was the only way to move the mail. There had been little violence before Cleveland intervened, but the president's orders and the arrival of federal deputy marshals and troops precipitated the violence they were supposed to prevent. The U.S. marshal in Chicago reported that police and the five thousand deputy marshals deployed in Chicago were insufficient. On July 4, federal troops arrived. The painter Frederic Remington accompanied soldiers from the Seventh Cavalry; immigrant soldiers were taunted in largely immigrant neighborhoods. Remington, who was not the most reliable of observers, wrote of a soldier moving through "a seething mass of smells, stale beer and bad language" and absorbing abuse in "Hungarian, or Pollack, or whatever this stuff is." The soldier supposedly told Remington, "Say, do you know them things ain't human."[55]

Illinois Governor John Altgeld and Mayor Hopkins were incensed, even though the boycott was taking its toll on Chicago. Stopping trains meant stopping the shipments of coal on which Chicago's factories and its water supply depended. Without coal to power pumps, Chicago could not draw pure water from the inputs in Lake Michigan. Altgeld and Hopkins, both Democrats like Cleveland, insisted the situation was under control. Altgeld argued that the president had no constitutional authority under Article IV of the Constitution to send troops; neither the governor nor the legislature had requested them. He denounced "military government." Four other governors also protested. Cleveland justified his action on the grounds of the necessity to protect federal property, to prevent obstruction of the mails, to prevent interference with interstate commerce, and to enforce the decrees of the federal courts.[56]

The arrival of federal troops further fueled the conflict. On July 5 mobs—containing few strikers—destroyed railroad property in the Union Stockyards and forced police and soldiers to retreat. That night arsonists burned many of the empty buildings of the Columbian Exposition. On

55. Frederic Remington, "Chicago Under the Mob," Harper's Weekly (July 21, 1894): 680–81; Buder, 183–84; Lamont, 169–73; Ginger, 159.
56. Wright, xliv; Buder, Pullman, 184–86; Ginger, 159–61.

July 6, mobs blocked the tracks and burned dozens of railroad cars. By and large, neither the Pullman strikers nor railroad workers took part in the riot. When the authorities killed six members of the mob, the suddenly sanguinary Judge William Howard Taft thought it "hardly enough to make an impression." He was wrong; the violence died out nearly as quickly as it arose, and by July 7, the army was in control of the streets. Between the army, the militia, deputy sheriffs and marshals, and the Chicago Police, authorities commanded more than fourteen thousand armed men. Debs hoped for a general strike, but Gompers and the AFL declined to do more than offer sympathy. In the West, ARU strongholds in California and Montana, which operated nearly independently of Debs, fell as violence alienated the public and militia sympathetic to the strikes gave way to federal troops.[57]

The government targeted Debs. On July 2 the federal court had issued an injunction, which enjoined Debs and other officials from compelling or persuading railroad employees to refuse or fail to perform their duties. As the special commission that was formed to investigate the strike later concluded, it was very questionable "whether courts have jurisdiction to enjoin citizens from 'persuading' each other in industrial or other matters of common interest." On July 10, a federal grand jury indicted Debs for conspiracy to obstruct the mails, and he was immediately arrested. Other arrests followed. Engineers who refused to board an engine and switchmen who refused to throw a switch found themselves in jail. Debs got out on bail, but on July 17 he was accused of contempt of court and rearrested. He refused bail out of solidarity with imprisoned strikers, but eventually he posted bail to prepare for his trial. The judge delayed the trial until September so Edwin Walker, who was coordinating the prosecution for the government and the General Managers, could go on vacation.[58]

The defendants faced two trials: one for contempt of court and one for conspiracy. In the contempt trial, there was no jury. Clarence Darrow was one of the defense attorneys, and the judge admitted that the Sherman Antitrust Act under which the contempt citation was issued was "directed wholly against trusts and not at any organization of labor in any form," but he argued it was the court's duty to interpret the law and decide what combinations acted in restraint of trade. He sentenced Debs to six months. Lyman Trumbull, the eighty-one-year-old abolitionist, handled the appeal. Olney, who had come to hate Debs, argued for the government. He

57. Buder, *Pullman*, 183–84; Schneirov, 339–40; Stead, *Chicago To-Day*, 241–42; Forbath, 75; Ginger, 159–61; White, 441–50; Wright, xx; Lindsey, 218–35.
58. Wright, xix, xlv–xlvi; Buder, *Pullman*, 183–87; Salvatore, 131–40; Lindsey, 239–70, 277–85.

claimed that the government had to have broad powers to use courts of equity to act in the public interest. The Supreme Court ruled resoundingly in the government's favor, creating a new doctrine without the slightest legislative cover that the government had the power to halt labor disputes if they interfered with interstate commerce.

Governor Altgeld, convinced no jury would have convicted Debs, denounced the decision as government by injunction. The conspiracy trial indicated that he was right. The defense was winning when a jury member fell ill; rather than convene a new jury, the government abandoned the prosecution. Debs's conviction for contempt was part of a growing array of decisions that protected business and property at the expense of labor.[59]

Jane Addams, rebuffed in her attempts to mediate, remained fascinated by the drama at Pullman. In an 1896 speech entitled "A Modern Lear," she compared Pullman to King Lear. "This older tragedy," she said, "implied maladjustment between individuals; the forces of the tragedy were personal and passionate. This modern tragedy [Pullman] in its inception is a maladjustment between two large bodies of men, an employing company and a mass of employes [sic]. It deals not with personal relationships, but with industrial relationships."[60]

Pullman never backed down. Personally and professionally, he had become a man intent on getting his own way. He forced his daughter to break her engagement because she had failed to ask his permission; when she asked, he relented. In 1896 Pullman's daughter married. The Rockefellers and Carnegies attended. So did the widows of Grant, Blaine, and Sheridan, along with three Supreme Court justices. By then, the Illinois attorney general had sued to force him to divest himself of his town. Pullman died of a heart attack at sixty-six in 1897. Afraid that the many who hated him might take revenge on his body, Pullman had arranged to have his casket encased in steel and concrete. The suit went forward. In 1898, the Illinois Supreme Court ruled the company's charter gave it no right to own the town of Pullman and that company towns were "opposed to good public policy and incompatible with the theory and spirit of our institutions."[61]

Robert Todd Lincoln, the martyred president's son, provided the final irony and the marker of changing times when he became president of the Pullman Palace Car Company. Abraham Lincoln remained the great symbol of free labor; his son took over a company that in the name of contract freedom managed to be both paternalist and hated by laborers.[62]

59. Salvatore, 137–38; Lindsey, 277–85; Wright, xxxix–xli.
60. Knight, 320–32; Jane Addams, "A Modern Lear," *Survey* 29 (Nov. 2, 1912): 131–37. Addams composed this much earlier.
61. Ginger, 164; Buder, *Pullman*, 200–201, 208–9, 212–13.
62. Buder, *Pullman*, 211–12.

Manufacturing poor men was not supposed to be the outcome of free labor, but the industrialists Pullman and Carnegie—who most vocally proclaimed themselves the benefactors of labor—instigated bloody struggles with their own workers. Both earned the hatred of the men they employed. They became the symbols of an economy and a politics where the rising tide might lift the largest boats, while swamping the small vessels all around them.

IV

The courts that moved so resolutely against labor in the 1890s proved far gentler with corporations, whose leaders had as great a sense of economic crisis as Debs did. Until the 1890s corporations, which became virtually synonymous with monopoly, dominated only the railroads and the oil refining industry. There were large firms in other industries, but they tended to be partnerships of one kind or another, or other forms of privately held companies. In the 1890s, following the onset of the depression, American business began a great merger movement, creating the large corporations that would dominate the economy thereafter. It was the result of business weakness as much as strength; it indicated the growing potency of reform, not its feebleness.[63]

In the 1880s, industries were often divided between smaller companies that manufactured limited quantities of specialized high-end goods and a few larger companies that produced large quantities of cheap mass-produced goods. Specialized manufacturers sought to maintain prices rather than

Manufacturing Mergers Per Year
1895–1904

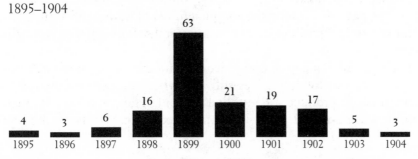

Source: Naomi R. Lamoreaux, *The Great Merger Movement in American Business, 1895–1904*.

63. Naomi R. Lamoreaux, *The Great Merger Movement in American Business, 1895–1904* (Cambridge: Cambridge University Press, 1985), 2–5.

output. They responded to downturns by cutting production. The larger companies with greater sunk capital sought to maintain output.[64]

The reasons for the different responses were structural. The higher fixed costs of the large companies—interest and depreciation charges on capital—meant they often could not respond to depression simply by cutting their variable costs, laying off workers, ceasing to buy raw materials, and awaiting better times. Their fixed costs remained, and if they could not pay them they slid into bankruptcy. They needed volume and income to pay interest and make repairs. As with the railroads, selling at a loss was better than not selling at all. Their goal was to "run full."[65]

The increase in the number of large manufacturers in the late 1880s and 1890s changed the dynamics of many industries. Larger companies arose with new and expensive manufacturing processes—the Bessemer process in steel, the Bonsack machine for making cigarettes. They also arose, with new products—the bicycle and barbed wire—or within markets protected by the tariff, such as tinplate and steel, or with such new mineral discoveries as those in oil, copper, and precious metals. As the firms grew larger and became more capital-intensive, they often sought vertical integration, which allowed them to control supply and marketing as well as manufacturing. Standard Oil was the pioneer and epitome of such developments.[66]

Those firms that had managed to exert significant control over their industry in the 1880s had great advantage over those that arose later. Carnegie Steel and Standard Oil had managed to control enough patents, achieve sufficient economies of scale, and restrict access to market to dominate a particular industry or a section of it. They could and did manipulate prices. In most industries, however, the larger firms still faced bitter price competition. This was the case in paper manufacturing and tinplate manufacturing. In these industries a relatively few large firms—about nine among the manufacturers of newsprint—engaged in competition that produced a downward spiral of falling prices and falling profits.[67]

Pools provided a partial corrective to competition in some established industries. Even though prices still fell, when the pool calculated correctly it could produce a controlled descent. The price cuts stimulated consumption and the pool eliminated excess capacity. Pools, however,

64. Lamoreaux, 15–16.
65. Ibid., 27–37, 87 ff.
66. Ibid., 29–30, 32, 91–93.
67. Ibid., 27–39, 120–36.

often failed to hold, and there was no legal mechanism to make members abide by their terms.[68]

In newer industries, such as the wire nail industry, made up of firms created in the late 1880s and early 1890s, there were much higher debt loads. These firms, particularly when they had trouble securing further financing, were more likely to increase production and cut prices to meet fixed costs and generate cash. They hoped to capture a growing share of expanding markets. When markets contracted after the Panic of 1893, firms found this strategy suicidal. They resorted to gentlemen's agreements, trade associations, and pools to stabilize price and divide the markets. Because of their debts and competition for market share, however, pools failed them, much as they had failed the railroads.[69]

These evenly matched firms in capital-intensive industries devoted to mass-produced goods became the preferred site of the merger movement. Rapid growth, competition, and high fixed costs encouraged consolidation. Although there is no denying the larger role of salaried managers in these enterprises, a drive for efficiency did not produce consolidation. Nor were these mergers the products of farsighted entrepreneurs or the inevitable result of technological advances. Consolidation did not necessarily lead to more efficient production; nor did it occur in all industries. Mergers resulted from attempts to eliminate competition. To maintain the advantages mergers created, these firms had to create and maintain high barriers to entry for new competitors.[70]

The particular circumstances of the 1890s explain why consolidation occurred, but they do not explain how it occurred. Finding the preferred means of consolidation took time. The long and contradictory history of judicial interpretations of the Sherman Antitrust Act extended well into the twentieth century, but the courts progressively, if not consistently, prohibited pools, price fixing, and acts in restraint of trade. Nor were courts always willing to validate all the techniques used in mergers. Congress could have solved the legal issues and established a clear basis for regulation with a federal incorporation law, which would have limited what corporations could do. Instead, by leaving incorporation to the states and

68. Ibid., 76–86.
69. Ibid., 62–76.
70. Ibid., 152–58, 188–94; Brian Balogh, A Government out of Sight: The Mystery of National Authority in Nineteenth-Century America (Cambridge: Cambridge University Press, 2009), 333–39; William G. Roy, Socializing Capital: The Rise of the Large Industrial Corporation in America (Princeton, NJ: Princeton University Press, 1997), 202–20; the argument for efficiency and functionalism is most powerfully stated by Alfred D. Chandler, The Visible Hand: The Managerial Revolution in American Business (Cambridge, MA: Belknap Press, 1977), 1–12.

attempting to regulate competition between firms, it left open a giant loophole in antitrust legislation. Corporations could not cooperate in restraint of trade, but they could find ways to merge and grow larger and larger.[71]

The eventual solution was the holding company, when New Jersey—the "Traitor State"—permitted corporations to purchase and hold the shares of other corporations. In 1889 the American Cotton Oil Company pioneered the corporate future when it organized as a New Jersey holding company. As the state modified and amended the act, it allowed New Jersey corporations to turn themselves into multistate holding companies, formed with only nominal paid-in capital, which could then use their stock to acquire other corporations. New Jersey subverted the ability of other states to control corporations, and the holding company seemed to fall outside the scope of the Sherman Antitrust Act. The struggle to contain holding companies would take place largely in the twentieth century.[72]

The financial houses of New York provided the final element in the merger movement. They were already critical to the functioning of the railroads, but the demand for financing for the mergers and the growth of the stock and bond markets both enlarged their roles and changed it. J. P. Morgan had been active in the failed attempts to organize the railroad pools. It taught him the limits of pools.[73]

The House of Morgan, usually operating through syndicates of bankers and large capitalists such as Rockefeller, played a central role in many of the mergers as the financial houses moved beyond railroads and government securities into industry. In the late 1890s and early twentieth century Morgan attended the birth of General Electric, International Harvester, and U.S. Steel. These were largely twentieth-century stories, but their roots were in the 1890s. Internal development of a limited partnership firm like Carnegie Steel, which ruthlessly drove down costs and seized on new technologies, gave way to U.S. Steel, which expanded horizontally, growing by acquisitions rather than through technological innovation. Morgan did not just help to assemble the capital necessary to bring them about; he also took a direct role in the governance of the new corporations and holding companies, seeking to ensure competent management and to forestall the ruthless competition of the 1890s, which Morgan had always thought wasteful and inefficient. The banking houses did not

71. Hovenkamp, 242–43.
72. Roy, 199–203; Hovenkamp, 241–51, 258–63.
73. White, 363, 365, 391; Jean Strouse, *Morgan: American Financier* (New York: Random House, 1999), 245–49, 260–61.

create the merger movement, but their ability to supply capital facilitated and quickened it. Morgan placed his own men on the board.[74]

The move toward centralization and consolidation was not an inevitable development, part of the natural order of things; it was historical, the result of accumulating human actions, networks, laws, and institutions. It was the work of the courts, the work of markets shaped by human hands, the work of corporations, the work of government, and the work of the networks that tied them all together.[75]

By the mid-1890s, the great crisis of the industrial economy had arrived and the outlines of a newer corporate economy had appeared. The liberal Republicans who had imagined an economy based on contract freedom and competition had to a degree gotten what they wished for. And the Republican Whigs who had wanted government subsidies and protection for American industry had also succeeded. Both groups had ultimately agreed on the gold standard, and that, too, they had achieved.

Neither group had imagined the results of their combined success. On the one hand, they had created an economy of undeniable productivity and an industrial infrastructure continental in scale, but this economy had not produced the republican society they desired. Contract freedom had yielded a world of dependence and wage labor rather than independence. Competition had yielded a chaotic economy of boom and bust and surplus production that markets could not absorb. Businessmen sought to escape competition, and failing that, to control costs. This created a relentless downward pressure on wages, exacerbated by the persistent deflation produced by the gold standard. The greatest rewards went not to those who labored to produce goods, but to those who controlled access to capital, and control seemed to many to be the fruits of corrupt webs of political friendship, pull, and governmental favors.

To increasing numbers of Americans, a dangerous inequality formed the rotten fruit of a system that had escaped their control. Larger and larger firms dominated the economy by the 1890s, wielding a power that seemed to match those of the governments that often enabled and abetted them. The economy produced the "dangerous classes," the very rich and the very poor. The country seemed European in an inequality that the eradication of slavery had supposedly eliminated. By the standard markers

74. Walter Licht, *Industrializing America: The Nineteenth Century* (Baltimore, MD: Johns Hopkins University Press, 1995), 146–47, 160–61; Roy, 250–51, 262, 272, 280–81; Susie Pak, *Gentlemen Bankers: The World of J. P. Morgan* (Cambridge, MA: Harvard University Press 2013), 14–15, 17–18.

75. Balogh, 314–15.

of health and well-being, life had grown worse, not better, for most Americans.

With the Great Depression of 1893, these concerns took on a new immediacy. The great economic machine, both industrial and agricultural, shivered and seemed about to fly to pieces, and neither party seemed up to the crisis.

22

Things Fall Apart

Mark Hanna considered George Pullman a "damn fool," as he did any employer "who refused to talk with his men." Hanna was from Cleveland, a rich man who had made his money in coal, iron ore, shipping, and railroads. Although Democratic cartoonists, particularly those working for William Randolph Hearst, parodied him as Dollar Mark, he was a relatively moderate Republican. He had no desire to emulate Pullman, or for that matter Carnegie, both of whom professed sympathy for workers while crushing them. Hanna imagined a harmony between business interests and the public interest, but he was not a reformer. He thought traditional Republican policies of the tariff and hard money would yield general prosperity.[1]

To understand the Republican Party that emerged from the debacle of 1892, it is necessary to understand Mark Hanna and his devotion to William McKinley, but it is also necessary to hold them in the same frame as Hazen Pingree, the mayor of Detroit. They represented different strains of resurgent Republican politics.

A Civil War soldier who had been imprisoned at Andersonville, Pingree became a shoe manufacturer. He entered politics late as the candidate in 1890 of liberal good-government Republicans seeking to defeat the Irish-dominated Democratic immigrant machine in Detroit. Pingree blended often antithetical reform movements—antimonopoly, labor, and liberal good government—in a manner that would become more common with Progressivism during the next century. He exploited divisions between the Germans, Poles, and Irish to win election and the first of his four terms as

---

1. Stanley Buder, *Pullman: An Experiment in Industrial Order and Community Planning, 1880–1930* (New York: Oxford University Press, 1967), 199–200; Herbert David Croly, *Marcus Alonzo Hanna: His Life and Work* (New York: Macmillan, 1912), 86–88, 95, 115; David Montgomery, *Citizen Worker: The Experience of Workers in the United States with Democracy and the Free Market During the Nineteenth Century* (Cambridge: Cambridge University Press, 1993), 157; R. Hal Williams, *Years of Decision: American Politics in the 1890s* (New York: Wiley, 1978), 100–101.

mayor. Initially, he was devoted to using expertise, rooting out boodle, and paving Detroit's wretched roads with concrete and asphalt.[2]

The violently destructive Detroit street railway strike of 1891 set Pingree in a new direction. All classes reviled the Detroit City Railway Company for its poor service, arrogance, and corruption. Pingree refused to call in the state militia and demanded and got arbitration. Settling the strike proved to be the first battle in a war against the company and its successors. Pingree blocked franchise renewal, promoted competition, forced electrification and lower fares, and pushed the system toward municipal ownership. He simultaneously battled General Electric and obtained city-owned electric power for Detroit. He waged a "gas war" that broke the gas monopoly in Detroit, drastically reducing prices. He alienated much of the Republican elite that had originally supported him, but endeared himself to Detroit's working class.[3]

The Depression of 1893 further estranged Pingree from his wealthier supporters. He financed relief measures equalizing real estate taxes that favored the wealthy and put the personal property tax on a fairer basis, saying, "I believe that our wealthy citizens, many of whom have accumulated the fortunes which they now enjoy through the sweat and toil of the laboring classes, owe a duty to those who have created their wealth." He targeted railroads and shipping interests that had largely evaded municipal taxes. He created public works jobs, opened up empty lots for cultivation by the poor, and harassed churches and the rich to do more to stave off the crisis. He threatened the tax-free status of the churches, which he thought did little to help the poor. He wanted more than charity, regarding it as the handmaiden of "economic oppression: and no substitute for justice." Threats of manufacturers to leave the city forced him to compromise, but he obtained partial reform. In 1895, Pingree said the vast wealth that accumulated in the midst of human misery was "more dangerous to the liberties of our republic than if all the Anarchists, Socialists, and Nihilists of Europe were let loose on our shores." Endowing universities or building libraries, he declared, changed nothing. Populists, socialists, Single Taxers, and advocates of municipal ownership moved into his administration.[4]

Hanna more closely resembled Pingree's original upper-crust supporters than he did the Detroit mayor. Whereas Pingree, the capitalist, grew critical of the abuses of capitalism and the need to constrain it, Hanna

---

2. Melvin G. Holli, *Reform in Detroit: Hazen S. Pingree and Urban Politics* (New York: Oxford University Press, 1969), 4, 11, 17–21.

3. Ibid., 40–55, 74–94, 101–12.

4. Ibid., 56–62, 68–73.

never lost faith in capitalism's expansive possibilities. He could not, how-ever, afford to hate Pingree, as the mayor's original silk stocking Republican supporters did. Pingree was the most popular Republican in Michigan. To elect McKinley president, Hanna needed Pingree and men like him. Compared to that, ideology was a small thing. And, besides, the two men shared a set of pragmatic beliefs and mutual enemies. Both believed in centralization and both scorned the "bosses" who controlled politics.[5]

Hanna gained a reputation as a puppet master, the man who controlled McKinley and the Republicans, but he admired, almost adored, McKinley, along with other men he had supported earlier. He eagerly enlisted in John Sherman's doomed presidential ambitions before he became enamored with McKinley. McKinley's tariff had certainly helped Hanna's interests, but there was more than financial benefit involved in their relationship. McKinley's wife, Ida, was epileptic, and tragedy had touched the couple in the loss of two young children. Ida became a semi-invalid, reclusive and dependent, and McKinley often cocooned himself in a darkened room, sitting with her for hours. Genial and friendly with many, conscious of his image and full of avuncular advice about clean living, he let few get close. Hanna was one of the few.[6]

Although no one thought McKinley deep, well read, or well informed (outside of Republican politics), he was intellectually open and willing to work with men who disagreed with him. McKinley's defeat in the Republican debacle of 1890 had not shaken Hanna's support, and that support mattered. As tactics of political mobilization shifted from locally based "army" campaigns, with their mass rallies to energize loyal voters, to more centralized educational campaigns, which demanded national organization and money, fundraisers and managers like Hanna replaced older bosses for whom they were sometimes mistaken.[7]

McKinley had rebounded quickly from his 1890 defeat. He won elec-tion as governor of Ohio in 1891, but the combination of the Panic of 1893 and his own carelessness, misjudgment, and devotion to friends nearly undid him. Robert Walker, a wealthy businessman, had helped McKinley in his early campaigns. The McKinley Tariff's nurturing of the tinplate industry had tempted him to go into tin. McKinley had cosigned loans for

5. R. Hal Williams, *Realigning America: McKinley, Bryan, and the Remarkable Election of 1896* (Lawrence: University Press of Kansas, 2010), 53–55; Holli, 194–95; H. Wayne Morgan, *William McKinley and His America*, rev. ed. (Kent, OH: Kent State University Press, 2003), 141–45.

6. Morgan, 45, 234–37; George H. Mayer, *The Republican Party, 1854–1964* (New York: Oxford University Press, 1964), 245–47; Williams, 50–53.

7. Michael E. McGerr, *The Decline of Popular Politics: The American North, 1865–1928* (New York: Oxford University Press, 1986), 144–45, 181; Williams, 55, 134–40.

him, without (or so McKinley claimed) paying much attention to the total amount. When Walker failed in the Panic, McKinley was liable for $100,000, far more money than he possessed.[8]

McKinley's debt cast yet another light on the friendship that greased the wheels of both American politics and business. That the governor of Ohio cosigned for loans to a businessman whose business depended on the tariff that the governor had helped enact when in Congress was how political friendship worked in the United States. It smacked of the favoritism, cronyism, and inequity that the Populists and antimonopolists decried. But a $100,000 debt (a very sizable sum in 1893), which was beyond McKinley's means to repay, actually convinced many voters of his honesty. They expected politicians to have enriched themselves, and McKinley had not. He initially refused to accept help, but reconsidered as gifts poured in. Small contributions showed popular support, but they did little to erase the debt. Hanna came to his rescue. He persuaded political and business "friends" of McKinley—some of whom barely knew him—that it was in their interest to help. Hanna himself, of course, subscribed money. So did John Hay, using the ample fortune his marriage had brought him. Henry Clay Frick contributed, as did Philip Armour and George Pullman. The banks that held McKinley's cosigned notes agreed to discount them. The loan was repaid.[9]

Hanna recognized the political dangers of rich men coming to the aid of a sitting governor. McKinley insisted that he would accept funds only from those with "proper motives," but such phrases could be ambiguous. When McKinley wrote Hay privately asking, "How can I ever repay you & other dear friends?" he raised a question pregnant with political meaning. If he would take money only from those who expected nothing in return, his question to Hay was either rhetorical or mysterious.[10]

There was a code to such things, although neither good government Mugwumps nor antimonopolists subscribed to it, and McKinley certainly did not want to accept it, at least publicly. William Allen White, then a young conservative Kansas newspaperman who would become a leading Progressive, described the Kansas Republican code in the 1890s. Most likely the Ohio Republican code mirrored it. Both resembled Tweed's honest graft. Among its tenets were:

8. Morgan, 129–33; Williams, 51.
9. Morgan, 130–34; John Taliaferro, *All the Great Prizes: The Life of John Hay from Lincoln to Roosevelt* (New York: Simon & Schuster, 2013), 281–82, 298–99.
10. Ibid., 281–82, 298–99.

A man may take money if he earns it.

He is dishonest if he takes money from both sides or if, taking money from one side, he deserts for any cause to the other.

If a man really has principles, he must not take money even to do what he was going to do anyway.

A scoundrel is a man who swindles his friends. It is, however, permissible to cheat your enemies.

By the lights of such a code, McKinley was an honest man. He won re-election in 1893 in a landslide.[11]

As governor in the midst of the strikes that wracked the country in 1893 and 1894, McKinley managed to maintain significant labor support even as he dispatched the National Guard. He walked a fine line, claiming that he used the Guard to suppress violence rather than to break strikes. Unlike Cleveland at Pullman, he did not dispatch troops until requested by local authorities whose resources were exhausted.[12]

The great coal strike of 1894 had presented him with a considerable challenge. The coal industry grew with the railroads and American industrial expansion. Ferociously competitive, operators flooded the market with coal at falling prices. The price of coal in Illinois fell nearly 50 percent between 1888 and 1892. Owners shut down seasonally, but if they shut down for longer periods, they risked greater losses than they did by selling coal at a loss. Coal owners had to pay interest on borrowed funds whether the mines operated or not. Some money coming in was better than none. They tried to scratch back money from workers through company stores selling to captive customers at large markups and payment in scrip redeemable only at those stores. Mostly they cut wages. The 97 cents per ton an Illinois coal miner earned in 1880 had plunged to 80 cents in the mid-1890s, and miners often worked only half a year. Although just a minority of miners—mostly Irish and British—joined unions, they fought back, and strikes plagued the industry. Between 1887 and 1897, 116 coal strikes hit the mines in Illinois; there were 32 strikes in Indiana and 111 in Ohio. Mine owners recruited Eastern and Southern European immigrants to work at lower wages, exacerbating deep ethnic tensions in the mines.[13]

The industry badly needed rationalization. In 1894 the workers tried to impose it, in a strike that most owners did not oppose. In spring the United

11. Morgan, 132–33, 134; William Allen White, *The Autobiography of William Allen White*, 2nd ed. (Lawrence: University Press of Kansas, 1970, orig. ed. 1946), 102–3.

12. Morgan, 134–35.

13. Richard J. Jensen, *The Winning of the Midwest: Social and Political Conflict, 1888–1896* (Chicago: University of Chicago Press, 1971), 238–45, 252–53.

Mine Workers, whose membership numbered only 20,000, induced some 170,000 miners in Pennsylvania and the Midwest to walk out. They sought to create scarcity, which would force prices to rise to a level adequate to restore wages. Miners tried to create the rough equivalent of a railroad pool, with workers rather than managers limiting output to control prices. As the *Chicago Tribune* understood, this wasn't so much a strike of workers against owners as a joint attempt by workers and owners "to get higher wages for the one and larger profits for the other." The effort would succeed only if all participated. If scabs allowed some mine owners to take advantage of rising prices and produce coal, the strike would fail.[14]

The 1894 strike shut down production in Pennsylvania and the Midwest and nearly paralyzed large swaths of the American economy, but mines in Virginia and West Virginia continued to produce. With Southern coal flowing north, some miners violently blocked trains carrying the "scab" coal. The Irish and British miners blamed the new immigrants for the violence. Public support for the strike ebbed. When county sheriffs in Ohio requested aid in keeping the peace, McKinley called up the militia. Even the pro-labor and antimonopolist Democratic governor of Illinois, John Peter Altgeld, sent militia into coal country, but he refused to allow them to guard the mines.[15]

During his second term, Grover Cleveland fashioned himself into the Andrew Johnson of the 1890s: a man spectacularly unsuited by temperament and belief for his time and his place. In his first term, Cleveland had established himself as a politician happiest when saying no. He vetoed more bills, most of them pension bills, than any president before him. During his second term, while presiding over the most severe economic downturn of the nineteenth century, he worried mainly about the danger of government paternalism, walking backward into the future undoing what the Republicans had done. He pushed the repeal of election laws protecting black voters. He tried to reform the McKinley Tariff. Nearly everything that had seemed a virtue to his supporters during his first term became a vice or a sign of hypocrisy in his second. He stood for small government and honesty, invoking both to justify his inaction in the midst of crisis. Desiring to project a public image of principled determination, he misled key congressional allies and then denounced them publicly, after privately agreeing to their actions. He catastrophically miscalculated political priorities and postponed action on the tariff, which his party had made the centerpiece of reform, in order to repeal the Sherman Silver Purchase Act. A powerful segment of his party opposed such a repeal.[16]

Tariff reform produced a debacle. The Democrats had thrown out the new rules that had allowed Reed to turn the House, with only a small majority, into a Republican juggernaut. Under the restored old rules, the large Democratic majority melted into an undisciplined and quarrelsome mass that bogged down the Wilson-Gorman bill, seeking to lower and reform the tariff. The Democrats failed to produce quorums or unite their members. Reed, who had retained his seat, enjoyed the spectacle, mocking the Democrats who had once mocked him as Czar Reed. It took until February 1894 to move the Wilson-Gorman bill from the House, and then it stalled again in the Senate, where senators—including Democrats—sought to protect their home industries, and Western senators demanded that it include an income tax. The bill was delayed in conference committee in the midst of the Pullman Strike. Cleveland denounced his own party's bill, saying "our abandonment of the cause of the principles upon which it rests means party perfidy and party dishonor." The Senate managers were outraged. Senator Gorman accused Cleveland of deception and deceit: "All the amendments" had been "as well known to [the President] as to me."[17]

Cleveland sulked and backed down. Democrats had spent their political careers fighting for tariff reform, and when despondent House Democrats accepted the Senate bill, they looked, Reed said, "like a grain field devastated by a hailstorm." Cleveland refused to sign the bill, letting it become law without his signature. He had made both himself and the Democrats the object of ridicule. "For solemn stupidity, for the wisdom of unwisdom," a Republican wrote, "he takes the cake." By 1894, two years after his triumphal return to the presidency, Cleveland was widely despised and isolated from a vast swath of his own party, which was losing its taste for the old Democratic doctrines of localism and limited government.[18]

The man who led the revolt against him was William Jennings Bryan, the young congressman from Nebraska elected in the Democratic landslide of 1890. Bryan had made his name attacking the tariff. Winning reelection with alliance support in 1892, he defended free silver in strikingly class terms: "The poor man is called a socialist if he believes that the

16. Williams, 31, 35–36; R. Hal. Williams, *Years of Decision: American Politics in the 1890s* (New York: Wiley, 1978), 91.

17. Williams, *Years of Decision*, 90–92; Williams, *Realigning America*, 31, 35–36.

18. Williams, *Realigning America*, 41–42; Alyn Brodsky, *Grover Cleveland: A Study in Character* (New York: St. Martin's Press, 2000), 322–31; Williams, *Years of Decision*, 90–93.

wealth of the rich should be divided among the poor, but the rich man is called a financier if he devises a plan by which the pittance of the poorest can be converted to his use." Seeing the hopelessness of the Democrats' chances in 1894 and coming from what was normally a tight district, he chose to sit out the election. He ran instead for Senate, hoping that a coalition of Democrats and Populists in the legislature would elect him, but the legislature had a Republican majority.[19]

I

In the absence of other systematic data, Massachusetts can reasonably act as a proxy for American unemployment during the depression of the mid-1890s. There was probably an uptick in employment in 1895, but the chorus of numbers in Massachusetts still sang misery. In Fall River the incidence of unemployment, the percentage of workers unemployed at some time during the year, was 85 percent in 1895 among the millworkers. The annual unemployment rate, the average number of unemployed as a percentage of the labor force, was 21.4 percent. The incidence of unemployment was lowest among paper workers in Holyoke and plumbers in Boston, with unemployment frequency of about 21 percent and unemployment rates of 9–10 percent over the course of the year. Mill workers in Lawrence had an unemployment frequency of nearly 18 percent and an unemployment rate of 8.2 percent.[20]

The fragmentary data from other sections of the country all pointed in the same direction. In Ohio, monthly factory reports tracked a decline of 26 percent in employment between April and October 1893. Chicago's carpenters lost an astonishing 80 percent of their work that summer, while the meat packers reduced their work force by 25 percent. On the West Coast, half the skilled workers in San Francisco were without jobs. The fortunate retained their jobs, but wages often fell 20 percent or even more. The Michigan Commissioner of Labor reported that the 2,066 factories inspected by the state had dismissed 43.6 percent of their workers at the

19. Michael Kazin, *A Godly Hero: The Life of William Jennings Bryan* (New York: Anchor Books, 2007), 39, 41–43.
20. Assessing the impact of the depression of 1893–1897 is challenging in the absence of systematic measures of unemployment or wages. It fell between the interstices of the decennial censuses, so only figures from the Massachusetts census of 1895 exist. But since the data for Massachusetts largely mirror those from other industrial states in 1890 and 1900, its census can reasonably act as a proxy for the industrial states. Alexander Keyssar, *Out of Work: The First Century of Unemployment in Massachusetts* (Cambridge: Cambridge University Press, 1986), 300–303, 307, 312–19.

end of 1893. Those who retained their jobs had wages cut by 10 percent. Estimates at the start of the depression put Detroit's unemployment at 33 percent, with Germans and Poles drawing more than half the poor relief. In Montana and Utah, 25 percent of workers were unemployed on January 1, 1894. In 1894, estimates of the unemployed ranged from 3,000 in Atlanta to 62,500 in Philadelphia. The mines in the Iron Range closed. When Michigan and Wisconsin timber workers struck in response to wage cuts, the owners locked them out and shut their mills. Chauncey Depew, the railroad attorney, businessman, and political fixer for the Vanderbilt interests in New York, thought the Panic had touched more people than any previous downturn. The unemployed swarmed freight trains looking for rides to places where there might be work. Tramps broke into Iowa schoolhouses, desperate for shelter.[21]

The only thing softening the blow was that the economy had already conditioned workers to endure a quota of misery. The general insecurity of wage work and its rising incidence in American society made the depression only a more intense version of what many workers already knew. In the generally prosperous years of 1890 and 1900, when the federal census measured unemployment, 15–20 percent of workers in industrial states lacked work at some time during the year. The average duration of unemployment ranged between three and four months.[22]

The impact of joblessness varied. A skilled worker with a previously steady job history and employed daughters or sons had resources to fall back on, but a younger worker with small children and scant savings had little or nothing. Aid from outside the family did not amount to much. Communities in Massachusetts had their Overseers of the Poor; some unions gave benefits. Some churches and private charities gave aid. Detroit, Boston, and other cities had work relief programs, but an investigating committee concluded that workers received what amounted to the equivalent of a week's wages when often they had been unemployed for months. During winters the unemployed welcomed snowstorms because they opened up temporary jobs to clear streets and railroad lines. The reformer Josephine Shaw Lowell, ex-head of the Board of Charities in New York, objected to such fragmentary public aid. She wanted regular relief work, so long as it was "continuous, hard, and underpaid."[23]

21. Carlos Schwantes, *Coxey's Army: An American Odyssey* (Lincoln: University of Nebraska Press, 1985), 13–14; Holli, 63–69; Richard White, *Railroaded: The Transcontinentals and the Making of Modern America* (New York: Norton, 2011), 422–24; Kleppner, *Continuity and Change*, 98, 102.
22. Keyssar, 47, 53–57, 300–301, 307, 314.
23. Ibid., 152, 155–66; Kleppner, 99.

Most workers never received aid from any source whatsoever. The New York legislature passed a relief measure to provide the unemployed with jobs, but the Democratic governor, Roswell P. Flower, vetoed it, proclaiming that in "America the people support the government; it is not the province of the government to support the people."[24]

To survive, workers, as they had done for years, combined savings, credit extended by landlords, local merchants, and kin with the labor of their children, unmarried daughters, and income from renting to boarders. As men lost work, women sought it, taking in laundry or doing domestic labor and other work they would have normally shunned.[25]

The extent of the suffering, the worsening desperation of working people, and the growing belief of many Americans that government had a responsibility to intervene in economic crises combined to explain the otherwise inexplicable Jacob Coxey. The United States was still the country Mark Twain took so much pained delight in, and it produced figures hard to imagine until they had actually emerged. Coxey, a successful Ohio businessman, combined the enthusiasms of many successful men, such as a passion for racehorses, with ideas popular among Midwestern reformers. His devotion to monetary reform verged on fanaticism: he named his youngest son Legal Tender. Much of the press mocked him, but he fascinated their readers. Many ordinary Americans took him quite seriously.[26]

In 1891 Coxey conceived the idea of a giant public works program to lessen unemployment. By 1893 he was promoting a $500 million appropriation by Congress to improve the country's horrendous roads as well as to construct public buildings and other infrastructure. The AFL endorsed the idea. A bill promoting it was introduced in Congress. Coxey proposed financing the project with noninterest-bearing bonds issued by local governments and bought by the United States with fiat money. Coxey would thus kill two birds with one stone: he would reduce unemployment by restoring the greenback and combating deflation.[27]

By later standards, the project was unremarkable. American roads appalled everyone who ever rode a wheeled vehicle. The bicycling craze had given impetus to a good-roads movement, originally spurred by the need of farmers to get their crops to the railroads. Congressional loans to local governments would create much-needed infrastructure. Congress

24. Kleppner, 99.
25. Keyssar, 155–66.
26. Benjamin F. Alexander, *Coxey's Army: Popular Protest in the Gilded Age* (Baltimore, MD: Johns Hopkins University Press, 2015), 3; Schwantes, 36–37, 40–41.
27. Alexander, 3, 45–46; Schwantes, 32, 37.

had already provided lavish aid to corporations; why couldn't it aid farm- ers, workers, and local governments? Wages would prime the pump to bring the nation out of the depression. But in a Congress dominated by small-government Democrats, Coxey's proposal had no chance.[28]

The program, in any case, had trouble emerging from the shadow of the men advancing it, both Coxey and his right-hand man, the even more eccentric, but quite shrewd, Carl Browne of California. Browne had con- siderable experience in public protest. He had been a lieutenant of Denis Kearney in the San Francisco anti-Chinese agitation of the 1870s with its parades and sandlot meetings. In Chicago in 1893 he marched with un- employed workmen demanding work. Browne took a common local tactic and made it national, proposing a march of the unemployed on Washington—a petition in boots—to induce Congress to pass Coxey's legislation. He planned to arrive on May Day 1894.[29]

The prospect of angry workingmen converging on Washington alarmed the Cleveland administration, but the popular press characterized the march as less a revolution than a circus coming to town. A theosophist who believed in reincarnation, Browne thought himself a partial reincar- nation of Christ and considered Coxey a partial reincarnation of Andrew Jackson. Browne often dressed in a buckskin suit, which gave him the appearance of an antimonopoly Buffalo Bill. He traveled in what looked like a medicine show wagon from which he unfurled incomprehensible illustrations that he had created for his free silver lectures. At various times, he did sell patent medicines, including "Carl's California Cure," concocted by "Carl Browne, Man's mightiest microbe master."[30]

Browne made himself a difficult man to ignore, but he turned out to be only a ringmaster. He had an entire circus, or actually multiple circuses since the contingent that marched from Coxey's Massillon farm amounted to only one of many. The army had a band and a bugler. It had Oklahoma Sam, a cowboy and trick rider from Coxey's Oklahoma ranch. It had Honoré Jaxon, who claimed to be Métis from Canada who had fought in the Riel Rebellion. He had fought in the Riel Rebellion, and he dressed like a Métis, but like Clarence King, he passed across racial and ethnic lines. He was the child of English immigrants, with a college education from the University of Toronto. And the army had "the Great Unknown," a man of mystery who spoke with a slight accent, walked with a limp everyone assumed to be a war wound, drilled Coxey's recruits, and preached social rebellion. The "Great Unknown" was A. P. B. Bozzaro of

28. Alexander, 42–43; Williams, *Years of Decision*, 88–89.
29. Alexander, 40, 44–50.
30. Schwantes, 25–26, 28, 32, 36–38, 40, 80.

Chicago, but this was almost certainly an alias. He, too, dabbled in spiritualism and patent medicine, dressing alternately as an Indian and a cowboy. Coxey referred to his marchers as Commonwealers, but in the press they were Coxey's Army.[31]

Coxey had predicted that 100,000 men would trek from Ohio, but at its departure the army consisted of about 122 marchers (there were various estimates), an unknown number of whom were undercover agents sent by the Pittsburgh police and the Secret Service. The march also attracted 44 reporters, which was its great achievement. As W. T. Stead understood, publicity was Browne's genius. By attracting vast press coverage, the marchers became, in a common analogy of the time, the "sandwich men" of poverty, mimicking the urban hawkers who carried sandwich boards draped back and front across their bodies. Coxey's men advertised a larger cause. They encountered an upwelling of support along the lines of march and contributions to the marchers that alarmed those who mocked them. Attorney General Richard Olney worried more about Coxey than he did the simultaneous strikes by the American Railway Union that same spring.[32]

The roads that Coxey wanted the unemployed to fix threatened to stop his army from getting anywhere near Washington. Marchers bogged down in the mud and sinkholes that were the normal misery of travel in late winter and spring. The frustration and delays prompted leadership quarrels between the "Great Unknown" and Browne. Coxey was often absent on business, but ultimately he rescued Browne from the Army's rebellion and expelled the "Great Unknown," who moved ahead of the march soliciting funds and pocketing the proceeds.[33]

By the time the army tramped out of the Alleghenies and began to pick up new recruits, other contingents had mobilized, largely in the West. Coxey's recruits always came largely from the West and Midwest. Marchers gathered in Los Angeles, San Francisco, Portland, Denver, Tacoma, and Butte, spurred to move on quickly by local authorities but often the beneficiaries of spontaneous support from citizens. The vast empty distances of the West meant marchers from the West Coast and in the Rockies could not literally march. Instead they jumped on freight trains, of which there were relatively few over much of the area. The Southern Pacific responded by purposely stranding the Los Angeles contingent in the Texas desert, to the outrage of Texas's antimonopolist Gov. James (Big Jim) Hogg. When the railroads refused passage or demanded full fares to carry

31. Schwantes, 42–43, 72–73; Alexander, 40–42.
32. Schwantes, 44–46, 49–60, 162; W. T. Stead, *Chicago To-Day: The Labour War in America* (New York: Arno Press & New York Times, 1969, orig. ed., 1894), 23.
33. Ibid., 60–70, 146.

stranded Coxeyites, the marchers began seizing and running trains. Ultimately, they hijacked more than fifty of them. In other cases the railroads hauled the marchers forward to be rid of them. Seizing trains allowed the federal government to intervene, and Olney authorized troops to arrest the Butte contingent.[34]

Given the number of troops massed for the defense of Washington, it seemed the Army of Northern Virginia had returned to threaten the Union. The troops and police far outnumbered the marchers since most of the Westerners were either under arrest or still en route. The march ended with a whimper on May 1, 1894, when Coxey and Browne were arrested for violating the Capitol Grounds Act, which prohibited demonstrations in front of the Capitol. The government prosecuted the marchers for damaging shrubs and lawns and carrying banners. Mobilizing the (real) army to keep people off the grass made the Cleveland administration, already unpopular, a target of national ridicule. Coxey abandoned his army and returned to Ohio to run, unsuccessfully, for Congress as a Populist.[35]

The national press, most of whose eastern members accepted the gold standard as the received word of God, focused on the eccentricities of Coxey and his coterie, but Coxey's policy ideas were not outlandish. Many would eventually become law and were already becoming public policy even as they were ridiculed. The proposals of the Western marchers were particularly revealing. The Kellyites out of San Francisco—one of whose members was Jack London, the future author—stressed the building of irrigation ditches rather than roads. They built on not only an old and enduring belief in the power of the public domain to ensure American prosperity and equality but also a growing belief in the duty of the government to intervene in the economy to help ordinary Americans.[36]

Plenty of land remained in the public domain, but what the marchers recognized was that without federal investment it would provide neither jobs nor farms to many people. Free land alone attracted relatively few, especially in the arid region beyond the 100th meridian. In 1890, Mississippi had more farms than the eleven far western states and territories combined, and Ohio had twice as many, even though those eleven states contained roughly 40 percent of the land area of the nation. Homestead entries, which had peaked at 61,000 in 1886, fell steadily until 1892. They rose and then plateaued between 1892 and 1894 before plunging to 33,000 in 1897. Homesteading fell during the 1890s for the same

34. Ibid., 83–165, 195.
35. Alexander, 74–75, 98–106; Schwantes, 182–83.
36. Schwantes, 116, 276–77.

reason that immigration fell: economic depression. Immigration, which stood at 644,000 in 1892, sank to 244,000 people in 1897, a year when an estimated 139,000 immigrants were returning home.[37]

The Coxeyites argued that the arid and lightly populated West would not be irrigated without government programs and government aid. Without irrigation, the West would not be farmed. Rain had not followed the plow. The boom in privately financed Western irrigation between 1887 and 1893 had turned to bust. Irrigation demanded capital that private investors were unwilling to provide, but with federal aid irrigated agriculture was possible.[38]

Irrigation also demanded preservation of the mountain forests to conserve the winter snowpack and gradually release the spring snowmelt. The Harrison administration had provided for federal forest reserves in an act barely noticed at the time: the 1891 General Revisions Act, which had begun as an attempt to reform the notoriously corrupt Timber Culture and Desert Land acts. The Prussian born Bernhard Fernow, head of the U.S. Department of Agriculture's Forestry Division, had advocated the forestry provisions of the act, but he realized that legislation alone was not enough. Successful management demanded administrative capacity. Even the Cleveland administrations had quietly recognized this, authorizing hydrographic studies that presumed federal funding in 1888. The Carey Act of 1894, however, used the old technique of land grants to the states to finance irrigation projects. Francis Newlands, a Nevada congressman who would later sponsor legislation for federal funding of reclamation, became active in the National Irrigation Service in the early 1890s. The legal structure for the Coxeyite program was already quietly taking shape in the West. The Commonwealers were more prescient than

37. Fred A. Shannon, "The Homestead Act and the Labor Surplus," *American Historical Review* 41, no. 4 (1936): 638–39; Table Cf71–78 — Vacant lands and disposal of public lands: 1802–2001, in *Historical Statistics of the United States, Earliest Times to the Present: Millennial Edition,,* ed. Scott Sigmund Gartner, Susan B. Carter, Michael R. Haines, Alan L. Olmstead, Richard Sutch, and Gavin Wright (New York: Cambridge University Press, 2006). Homesteading wasn't dead; entries would reach their all-time high, nearly one hundred thousand, in 1910; Timothy J. Hatton and Jeffrey G. Williamson, "What Drove the Mass Migrations from Europe in the Late Nineteenth Century?" in *NBER Working Paper Series on Historical Factors in Long Run Growth,* ed. National Bureau of Economic Research (1992).

38. Donald J. Pisani, *Water, Land, and Law in the West* (Lawrence: University Press of Kansas, 1996), 92–101; Pisani, *From the Family Farm to Agribusiness: The Irrigation Crusade in California and the West, 1850–1931* (Berkeley: University of California Press, 1984), 259–82.

their critics and had a keener idea of what was actually happening on arid lands.[39]

By the eve of the election of 1894, the conditions of 1892 had dramatically reversed themselves. The old Democratic Party was badly wounded everywhere except the South—a victim of the depression, its own carelessness, local corruption, and irrelevance. Even in the South it remained unclear if the Bourbons would retain control of the party, and if the party would retain the allegiance of rural whites. The Populists still hoped to supplant the Democrats and achieve the gains that had eluded them in 1892.[40]

The Republicans expected to take control of Congress in 1894, and their prospects looked promising. Many leading Democrats refused to run in 1894. Those who did, like the antimonopolist governor John Peter Altgeld in Illinois, asked voters to distinguish between antimonopoly Democrats, whom he likened to the apostles, and Cleveland, who, of course, was Judas. McKinley, preparing for a presidential run in 1896, campaigned widely for Republican candidates. He and other Republican speakers hammered on the Democrats' inability to govern.[41]

In 1894 the electoral pendulum made yet another of the era's characteristically dramatic swings. The Democrats lost 125 seats; the Republicans gained 130. Twenty-four states sent no Democrats to Congress; six others sent one each. A single Democratic congressman came from all of New England: John F. Fitzgerald, who would be the grandfather of John F. Kennedy. Even the South sent a few Republicans to Congress. The Republicans also gained control of the Senate, 44–34.[42]

The Populists tasted disappointment once again. They increased their national vote by 42 percent and, thanks to Eugene Debs, made some inroads among workers, but they elected only nine congressmen and four senators. Many of their luminaries lost: Ignatius Donnelly in Minnesota, Governor Davis H. Waite in Colorado, and Tom Watson in Georgia. States the Populists had carried in 1892—Kansas, Colorado, Idaho, and

39. Pisani, *From the Family Farm to Agribusiness*, 259–82; Michael McCarthy, *Hour of Trial: The Conservation Conflict in Colorado and the West, 1891–1907* (Norman: University of Oklahoma Press, 1977), 11–18; Daniel P. Carpenter, *The Forging of Bureaucratic Autonomy: Reputations, Networks, and Policy Innovation in Executive Agencies, 1862–1928* (Princeton, NJ: Princeton University Press, 2001), 205–7; Samuel P. Hays, *Conservation and the Gospel of Efficiency: The Progressive Conservation Movement, 1890–1920* (New York: Atheneum, 1975, orig. ed. 1959), 9–13.
40. Jensen, 230–31; Kleppner, *Continuity and Change*, 25–31.
41. Williams, *Years of Decision*, 93–94.
42. These figures on gains and losses differ slightly from those given by Williams, 94. I used the figures given by the U.S. House of Representatives History site.

North Dakota—reverted to the Republicans. Discontented voters had gone to the Republicans more than to the Populists. In the wake of the elections, Cleveland resembled a harpooned whale; whatever power he had was exhausted and the Republicans could haul him in and dispose of him when his term expired.[43]

The continuing violent swings between Democrats and Republicans coupled with the rise of the Populists disguised a significant and consistent drift toward centralization and increased federal power. With Cleveland Democrats discredited, it seemed that no matter which way elections turned—whether toward the Republicans, or the Populists, or the emerging Bryan Democrats—the federal government would grow more powerful and more interventionist. The process was already under way with the slow rejection of fee-based governance and the growth of fledgling bureaucracies in the Post Office and the USDA.

What rendered this process far less smooth and made it seem contradictory and inconsistent was the simultaneous expansion of the third branch of government, the courts. The extension of judicial authority launched a battle between the branches of the government, which involved power, ideology, and the very nature of governance. The clash between the legislative and judicial branches created an ideological whitewater as antimonopoly, labor, and evangelical reforms passed by Congress and the legislatures encountered judicial resistance. The contest was less over big government versus small government than which branch of government, the legislative or the judicial, would dominate and which definition of free labor would prevail. By the 1880s the original ideology of free labor had split into separate streams that clashed and roiled. Labor republicanism focused on the need to "engraft republican principles" onto work and the economy, while liberal judges emphasized freedom of contract and competition.[44]

II

Using the venerable language of independence, citizenship, and constitutional freedom, labor republicanism emphasized the autonomy of workers, their right to shape the conditions of their own work, and to negotiate

43. Williams, *Years of Decision*, 94–95.
44. William E. Forbath, "The Ambiguities of Free Labor: Labor and the Law in the Gilded Age," *Wisconsin Law Review* no. 4 (July 1985): 767–817, especially 768–69; Brian Balogh, *A Government out of Sight: The Mystery of National Authority in Nineteenth-Century America* (Cambridge: Cambridge University Press, 2009), 314–15; Forbath, *Law and the Shaping of the American Labor Movement* (Cambridge, MA: Harvard University Press, 1991), 38–40.

equitable returns on their labor. Most still wanted to regard themselves as producers who determined how work would proceed, but they thought that the changing scale and organization of industrial production threatened their rights as both freemen and citizens. The most militant among them wanted to restrict the role of employers to buying material and machines and selling the finished product. This would be the domain of capital. The existing wage system could only be at best a tenuous compromise since, when workers sold labor for wages, the exchange yielded subordination and degradation rather than freedom. The ultimate goal of reform — receding further and further into the future by the 1890s — was cooperative ownership; until that far-off glorious day, labor reformers sought to limit the workday and restrict employers' dictation. Freedom of contract had become an illusion.[45]

Other reformers shared this strain of free-labor republicanism, which survived the Gilded Age in diluted form. Walter Rauschenbusch, a leading minister in the Social Gospel movement, wrote in 1913 that when a minority held "all the opportunities of livelihood in its arbitrary control," while the majority lacked both property and "an assured means of even working for living," then freedom was denied and not secured. Cooperation rather than individualism was the key to freedom.[46]

Labor reformers and antimonopolists achieved considerable success in legislatures and Congress. They passed regulatory legislation that curtailed sweatshops and banned manufacturing in tenements. They passed laws that required payment to workers in cash rather than scrip, banned contract labor, mandated shorter workdays, outlawed the contracting of prison labor to private employers, created an array of health and safety requirements, and regulated railroads. Judges, however, struck down much of this legislation, invalidating more than sixty labor laws alone between 1880 and 1900.[47]

Judges embraced a very different version of free labor, one that rested on unadulterated contract freedom. Stephen J. Field's dissenting opinion in the *Slaughterhouse* case had done much to change the judicial rules of the game, and influential treatises by liberal judges and scholars had done the rest. Field's dissent upheld the power of the federal government under the Fourteenth Amendment to enforce a uniform set of rights for all citizens. He went further in expanding these rights into areas

---

45. Forbath, "The Ambiguities of Free Labor," 800–11, 816–17.
46. Walter Rauschenbusch, *Christianizing the Social Order* (New York: Macmillan, 1913), 350; James T. Kloppenberg, *Uncertain Victory: Social Democracy and Progressivism in European and American Thought, 1870–1920* (New York: Oxford University Press, 1986), 279.
47. Forbath, *Law and the Shaping of the American Labor Movement*, 37–38.

not mentioned in the Constitution or the amendment itself. For Field, the Fourteenth Amendment included the right to pursue a lawful calling "without other restraint than such as equally affects all persons." The state could not create limits of access without sanctioning monopolies. Publicly, Field professed the old liberal fear of monopoly, but privately he was a great friend and admirer of the railroad corporations, which had become the embodiment of monopoly power and whose favors he accepted.[48]

Stephen Field and his brother, David Dudley Field, a leading corporate attorney, embodied the contradictions of liberal free labor. They appealed to the old values of independence and equal competition, but both either worked for or took favors from corporations, whose success depended on suppressing the independence of their employees and, as far as possible, eliminating competition. Corporations did not hesitate to appeal to a strong government. Stephen Field tried in vain to uphold the powers of the federal government against the states in *Slaughterhouse*, but he did not believe those expanded powers could be safely lodged in representative government, which he deeply distrusted. Instead, he thought that the judiciary was the best guardian of liberty. Judges would act as the arbiter of the permissible. Field and other liberal judges appropriated the democratic language of Jacksonianism, which had sought to protect the many from the few, and turned it into a legal vocabulary that protected the few from the many. Turning people into commodities was impermissible, but turning people's labor into a commodity—a piece of property to be bought and sold—was the source of progress. Freedom became the protection of property. Rarely has a minority opinion been so influential.[49]

In inscribing his version of free labor in the Fourteenth Amendment, Field cited Adam Smith, a person notably uninvolved in either that amendment or the Constitution, and conflated republican free labor with classical political economy. The republican concept of free labor had arisen in an artisanal and agricultural economy that imagined the republican citizen as an independent producer entitled to the fruits of his labor. Field hollowed this concept out enough to cram in Smith's idea of freedom as the sale of labor and to enshrine free labor as contract freedom

48. Forbath, "The Ambiguities of Free Labor," 773–74; R. White, 170, 352, 418.
49. William E. Forbath, "Politics, State Building, and the Courts, 1870–1920," in *The Cambridge History of Law in America*, ed. Michael Grossberg and Christopher Tomlins, three vols. (New York: Cambridge University Press, 2008), 645–47; Forbath, "The Ambiguities of Free Labor," 784–85, 791–95.

into the Constitution. Judges could gauge the permissibility of regulations and laws by their substantive effect on such freedom.[50]

Substantive due process, as used in the Gilded Age, was largely the work of Thomas Cooley, the same man who headed the ICC. He wrote his *A Treatise on the Constitutional Limitations Which Rest Upon the Legislative Power of the States of the Union* (1868) just as the postbellum American economy began its transition to large factories and wage labor. Cooley had followed a common liberal trajectory, from Jacksonian Democrat to Free Soiler to Republican abolitionist. He maintained a fear of "discrimination by the state," but the concern he had once voiced for slaves he now voiced for a "sacred right" to private property that trumped popular sovereignty. He contended that the due process clauses of the state constitutions imposed "substantive" limits on the power of legislatures to interfere with private property rights, which existed in the common law prior to the Constitution. These sacred property rights limited popular sovereignty. Very much an old Jacksonian, Cooley condemned a range of laws that he thought discriminated against some and favored others. He condemned public subsidies to private corporations, laws that segregated students by race, and laws that created maximum hours for labor. All were class legislation. Legislatures could not "take property from one person and transfer it to another." They could only interfere with property rights for "the needs of government." By *property* he and other liberal judges meant not only real property, but also anything that had value, or potential value, in the marketplace. This concept of property proved wonderfully plastic, expanding to include gains anticipated in the future.[51]

Cooley's intent was to rein in the police power of the states. The Constitution did not grant police powers to Congress; these remained in possession of the states. The roots of state governments were more republican than liberal: the people's safety and welfare always ranked higher than any individual right. The states were not smaller, regional units of the federal government. They did not have the same limits placed on their powers to truncate individual rights. The federal government could not abridge the rights enumerated in the Bill of Rights, but within the

50. Richard Posner, "Legal Formalism, Legal Realism, and the Interpretation of Statutes and the Constitution," *Case Western Reserve Law Review* 37, no. 2 (1986–87): 180–82; Paul Kens, *Justice Stephen Field: Shaping Liberty from the Gold Rush to the Gilded Age* (Lawrence: University Press of Kansas, 1997), 166, 246–49; Forbath, "The Ambiguities of Free Labor," 779–82; Hovenkamp, 226–34.

51. Forbath, "Politics, State Building, and the Courts, 1870–1920," 648–49; Forbath, "The Ambiguities of Free Labor," 793–94; Jeffrey Sklansky, *The Soul's Economy: Market and Selfhood in American Thought, 1820–1920* (Chapel Hill: University of North Carolina Press, 2002), 207, 209–15.

limits of the Thirteenth, Fourteenth, and Fifteenth amendments state governments still could do so because the states' powers arose from different principles. This was why Cooley's treatise focused on the states and not the federal government, but reining in one kind of government power involved a concomitant expansion of another kind of government power. It would be the courts, not the legislatures elected by the people, that would decide what was permissible, and their standards would not necessarily be either statutory or constitutional law.[52]

By rendering freedom as the ability to dispose of "property"—either labor or capital—liberal judges cast restraints on property as potential attacks on freedom. Depending on the judge or the circumstances, anything that restricted contract freedom—whether licensing laws, certain kinds of public health regulations, strikes, boycotts, or the closed shop—became the legal equivalents of slavery. Such restrictions violated either the rights of workers to pursue a calling or the freedom of citizens to use property as they saw fit. Old protections against seizure of property without due process morphed into the "right" of capital to a fair expected return on investment.[53]

Christopher Tiedeman's *Unwritten Constitution of the United States*, which appeared in 1890, revealed the extensive superstructure that liberals built on Field's and Cooley's foundations. Tiedeman extended the argument to the Constitution and marked the expansion of an increasingly strident, defensive, and defiant liberalism. Together Field's decisions and the treatises formed the core texts of what came to be called substantive due process.[54]

The Unwritten Constitution of the United States revealed the ambition and sweep of substantive due process and the justification for judge-made law. Tiedeman encouraged judges to dig beneath the law to discern that "the same social forces which create and develop the ethics of a nation create and develop its law." The "substantive law is essentially nothing more than the moral rules commonly and habitually obeyed by the masses, whose enforcement by the courts is required for the moral good." Judges determined what counted as the moral rules of society. For Tiedeman, a natural right was what judges thought people believed to be a natural right, and such rights became the basis of law and part of the

---

52. William Forbath, "Politics, State Building, and the Courts, 1870–1920," 648–49; Forbath, "The Ambiguities of Free Labor," 793–94; Hovenkamp, 28–32, 80, 137; Sklansky, *The Soul's Economy*, 207, 209–15.
53. Forbath, *Law and the Shaping of the American Labor Movement*, 75–76; Hovenkamp, 17–18, 171; Forbath, "The Ambiguities of Free Labor," 792–93.
54. Forbath, "The Ambiguities of Free Labor," 792–94.

"unwritten" as well as the written Constitution. The actual Constitution, he argued, was just the skeleton; the flesh and blood was the "unwritten Constitution," which was in practice largely the work of the Supreme Court. Tiedeman was no originalist; he admitted that the Constitution changed with the times. He argued that changes elucidated by judges reflected the evolving morality of the nation.[55]

As long as laissez-faire "controlled public opinion," the courts could confine themselves to the formal provisions of the Constitution. But now, "under the stress of economical relations, the clashing of private interests, the conflicts of labor and capital, the old superstition that government has the power to banish evil from the earth" had resurfaced, endangering "all these so-called natural rights." The dangers? "Many trades and occupations are being prohibited because some are damaged incidentally by their prosecution, and many ordinary pursuits are made government monopolies." Socialists and communists alarmed "the conservative classes," who feared a tyranny "more unreasoning than any before experienced by man, — the absolutism of a democratic majority." Under such conditions, Tiedeman applauded the courts for seizing on natural rights "as an authority for them to lay their interdict upon all legislative acts, which interfere with individual's natural rights, even though these acts do not violate any special provision of the Constitution."[56]

By the 1890s liberal judges' expansive approach to the law had achieved breathtaking reach. By embracing classical economic theory, they applied the doctrine of substantive due process to enshrine a set of economic laws that no democratic government could overturn; they transformed metaphorical natural law into a body of actual law created by the judiciary. They treated freedom of contract, open competition, and laissez-faire as part of the Constitution. Judges justified their legal opinions by citing the laws of nature and the "laws" of the market, although neither was to be found on the statute books or in common law.[57]

Substantive due process did not triumph overnight; it had to contend not only with labor republicanism but also with the lingering strength of *Salus populi* and state police powers and the limits they placed on individual rights. When the Supreme Court in *Munn v. Illinois* (1877) upheld railroad regulations, and denied judicial review of the reasonableness of

55. Christopher G. Tiedeman, *The Unwritten Constitution of the United States: A Philosophical Inquiry into the Fundamentals of American Constitutional Law* (New York: G. P. Putnam's Sons, 1890), 15, 44–45, 71–72, 74–76.
56. Ibid., 74–81.
57. Hovenkamp, 1, 17–19, 171.

the rates state commissions established, Field had again dissented. He was not yet in the majority; regulatory legislation prevailed.[58]

In re Jacobs (1885) was the first of *Slaughterhouse's* children. The New York Court of Appeals overturned an 1884 law that used the police power of the state to prohibit the manufacture of cigars in tenement sweatshops in the name of public health. Samuel Gompers described the conditions that prompted the law in his 1883 testimony before the Senate Committee upon the relations between labor and capital. Employers rented tenements and sublet them, placing families in apartments with one room and one bedroom. The largest rooms were 12 feet by 9 feet, with ceilings about 8 feet high. They supplied each family with tobacco, which the husband, wife, and, usually, the children rolled into cigars. The rooms were full of drying tobacco. The children worked, played, and ate amidst it. Gompers described the conditions as "the most miserable ... that I have seen at any time in my life." Nearly two thousand families in New York City lived this way. The cigar manufacturers made money from renting the rooms and more money from the manufacture of cigars. The New York *Staats Zeitung* denounced manufacturers making money "at the expense of the health, morals, and manliness of his workingmen, and the system thereby becomes an aggravated nuisance. The system is not only a pecuniary injury to a great many; to enrich a few it is a social as well as an economical evil."

Gompers had promoted a law banning the system. Theodore Roosevelt, then a young Republican Assemblyman who was shocked by the conditions that Gompers showed him, had guided the bill through the New York legislature. It seemed a classic example of regulation in the name of *Salus populi*, but this was not how the New York Appeals Court saw it. The court rejected both the initial law and a subsequent one as exceeding the legitimate police powers of the state and undercutting contract freedom and free labor. With *in re Jacobs* the court defended sweatshop labor by treating the tenement as if it were a log cabin, the immigrant families

58. William M. Wiecek, *The Lost World of Classical Legal Thought: Law and Ideology in America, 1886–1937* (New York: Oxford University Press, 1998), 64–112; Forbath, "Politics, State Building, and the Courts, 1870–1920," 667; Forbath, *Law and the Shaping of the American Labor Movement,* 38–40; Novak, 127–28; R. White, 422–26; Dubofsky, "The Federal Judiciary, Free Labor, and Equal Rights," 162–63; Nick Salvatore, *Eugene V. Debs: Citizen and Socialist* (Urbana: University of Illinois Press, 1982), 118–19. Testimony of Samuel Gompers: John A Garraty, ed. *Labor and Capital in the Gilded Age: Testimony Taken by the Senate Committee Upon the Relations between Labor and Capital — 1883* (Boston: Little, Brown, 1968), 7–13; Harold C. Livesay, *Samuel Gompers and Organized Labor in America,* ed. Oscar Handlin (Boston: Little, Brown, 1978), 59–60.

as so many urban pioneers, and the cigar maker as an artisan "who carr[ies] on a perfectly lawful trade in his own home." The law deprived the sweated worker of "his property" and "his personal liberty," forcing him from his own "shop" into a factory where he would be at the mercy of his employer. Much like Horatio Alger, the court acted as if industrialism had changed nothing essential and the economy still consisted of open competition between small independent producers.[59]

Jacobs launched what became a bitter battle over the right of the states to regulate the conditions of work. The most crushing defeat of such attempts would not come until 1905, when the Supreme Court ruled in *Lochner v. New York* that the due process clause of the Fourteenth Amendment contained an implicit guarantee of "liberty of contract." The state could not regulate the number of hours bakers worked.[60]

In the 1880s and 1890s, labor reformers continued to win victories in state legislatures, only to lose them in the courts. In *Godcharles v. Wigeman* Pennsylvania courts struck down laws forbidding paying workers in scrip redeemable only at company stores. The law, the court said, violated the workers and employers' freedom of contract and placed on both "the badge of slavery." In addition, the legislation violated the substantive due process rights of the employers to use their property as they pleased.[61]

In some cases, the Supreme Court did not even bother to refer to statutory law to punish labor unions. *In re Debs* (1895), for example, the Supreme Court had given the executive the power to protect interstate commerce from labor disputes even though Congress had never passed any law authorizing such action.[62]

As the courts also took aim at work actions by organized labor, they attacked the very idea of unions. In upholding the conviction of an engineer who refused to move a train, Judge William Howard Taft decided in *Toledo, Ann Arbor Rwy Co. v. Pennsylvania Co.* (1893) that a legal act performed by an individual worker—quitting work—became illegal as part of a combination. The Supreme Court confirmed the decision in *ex parte Lennon* (1897). Taft ruled that any strike against railroads or other common carriers was harmful to the public and illegal, whether it involved coercion or not.[63]

---

59. Kathleen Dalton, *Theodore Roosevelt : A Strenuous Life* (New York: Knopf, 2002), 82–83; Forbath, *Law and the Shaping of the American Labor Movement*, 39–40.
60. Forbath, "Politics, State Building, and the Courts, 1870–1920," 649.
61. Forbath, "The Ambiguities of Free Labor," 795–800.
62. Hovenkamp, 173.
63. Ibid., 207–14, 231–32; Forbath, "Politics, State Building, and the Courts, 1870–1920," 675–77; Forbath, *Law and the Shaping of the American Labor Movement*, 69–73.

III

Judges regarded their decisions involving freedom of contract as even-handed, striking down any effort to prevent people from following their calling no matter whose ox was gored. The courts invalidated laws regulating hours, conditions of work, even many laws protecting women and children, but they also invalidated laws that tried to create licensing and education barriers to entry to professions. All these laws, they argued, made the market less efficient and thus in the long run hurt public welfare.[64]

Evaluating laws by their contribution to market freedom gave judges considerable leeway in deciding which regulations the courts would sanction and which regulations they would invalidate. In the name of restraining government, the courts were establishing broad new government powers. They overruled local authorities and popularly elected legislatures. As the judges expanded federal jurisdiction, challenges no longer arose only when defendants tested convictions as unconstitutional. Plaintiffs could file suits for injunctive relief. This became a feature of "government by injunction" deployed so effectively against labor. To enforce injunctions, judges could muster the armed force of the state.[65]

Judges insisted that corporations were different from unions and had to be measured by another standard. Liberal legal theorists appealed to the advantages of economies of scale, which added to the country's wealth. Unions, they contended, only created instability and inefficiency and restricted access to employment. This judicial ground remained contested, but at least until 1897, the courts tolerated business agreements not to compete. Sometimes the court ruled that the trusts in question, such as the Sugar Trust, might control national markets, but so long as their manufacturing centers largely remained within a single state they did not fall within federal purview. At other times courts argued that the trusts expressed a natural law "which is supreme over man-made laws," and federal statutes should not contradict natural law or interfere with its expression. The courts did consistently forbid agreements they thought stopped outsiders from entering a business. Congress engendered some of this contest and confusion by leaving legislation ambiguous and allowing the courts to settle its meaning by appealing to the common law's rule of reason.[66]

64. Balogh, 327–29; Hovenkamp, 176–82, 199–204.
65. Forbath, "Politics, State Building, and the Courts, 1870–1920," 675–76; Balogh, 318–19; Hovenkamp, 174–75, 199–204.
66. Forbath, "Politics, State Building, and the Courts, 1870–1920," 659–63; Richard Franklin Bensel, *The Political Economy of American Industrialization, 1877–1900* (Cambridge: Cambridge University Press, 2000), 344; Hovenkamp, 146–48, 210, 218–19, 268–95, 327.

The judicial imposition of liberal free labor and contract freedom in regard to workers and their unions had a large and surprising caveat. The courts continued to appeal to common law doctrines of "masters" and "servants," which flew in the face of freedom of contract. The contradictions gave judges even greater leeway to pick and choose among doctrines so that workers and their unions often faced "tails I win, heads you lose" situations. On the one hand, the courts granted workers property in their labor, but on the other, they also granted employers a property interest in their employees' labor. Actions by workers that deprived employers of this labor illegally stripped them of property. The courts assumed that companies were entitled to their "servants"' loyalty and obedience; actions by workers that threatened this entitlement could be ruled illegal. The courts sanctioned the employers' right to petition the courts to unleash state violence against workers' organizing efforts.[67]

The courts moved beyond common law to use statutory laws, passed to restrain corporations, against striking workers, who, judges said, were acting as part of combinations in restraint of trade. The Sherman Antitrust Act became virtually a dead letter against corporations for much of the 1890s, but unions, which were not the original concern of the legislation, became its targets. The courts could empty laws of content and fill them with new meaning. Of the thirteen decisions invoking antitrust law between 1890 and 1897, twelve involved labor unions. Ten came during the Pullman Strike. The Sherman Antitrust Act swiftly became a fecund source of the injunctions that crippled labor. Even *U.S. v. Trans-Missouri Freight Association*, 166 U.S. 290 (1897), which overturned the Interstate Commerce Commission's agreement to maximum and minimum rates fixed by railroads and provided bad news for railroad trusts, proved to be even worse for unions. By ruling that any agreement in constraint of trade was illegal, it opened the door to an even more expansive attack on unions. All strikes, ipso facto, could be accused of restraining trade. The list of forbidden labor activities would grow into the twentieth century.[68]

The courts similarly altered the ICC. Given the federal courts' devotion to competition and freedom of contract, it was surprising that the judges did not strike it down outright. Instead, they converted it into a source of judicial power. Charles Cooley was the first head of the agency, but by the 1890s he had become alarmed at the liberal judicial leviathan that he had helped create. He appointed the economist Henry C. Adams as chief statistician. Although no longer a radical, Adams remained an enemy of judicial liberalism and laissez-faire. Together Cooley and Adams sought to forge the ICC into an administrative agency that arbitrated

67. Forbath, "Politics, State Building, and the Courts, 1870–1920," 674.
68. Hovenkamp, 146–48, 207–11, 218–19, 229, 231–32, 280–83, 289–93, 327; Bensel, 341–43.

disputes, secured due process, and determined facts. The courts refused to allow it. They largely stripped the commission of administrative power, narrowly construed its authority, and took over much of its function.[69]

Still not all regulations fell. The courts condoned regulations that covered "an externality" outside the control of the market. They also upheld, often quite arbitrarily, some restrictions on hours of labor based on health and safety. As late as 1898 in *Holden v. Hardy*, the Supreme Court would uphold the constitutionality of Utah legislation mandating an eight-hour day for miners, ruling that the states had "the power to so amend their laws as to make them conform to the wishes of the citizen as they may deem best for the public welfare." Judges let stand a great array of legislation regulating property rights, from land use to fire regulations, to building codes.[70]

Taken as a whole, the decisions of the liberal judges contributed to a remarkable expansion of government power in the 1890s and into the twentieth century. The courts did so with and without the cooperation of Congress. Where legislative bodies legitimated their power by appealing to elections and the will of the people, the judges appealed to the Constitution, natural law, classical economics, the common law, and what judges decided to be the true interests of the people. Judges and courts became basic sites of state building, performing functions in the United States that bureaucracies undertook in other countries. The Supreme Court overturned old practices and clear precedents. Critics argued that judges commandeered authority belonging to other branches of the government. Contrary to existing precedents, the U.S. Supreme Court in *Pollock v. Farmers' Loan & Trust Co.* (1895) ruled unconstitutional the newly passed federal income tax because it was a direct tax requiring an impossible state-by-state apportionment. Opponents regarded the decision as judicial encroachment on the taxing power that the Constitution vested in Congress. Judicial imperialism and the claims of substantive due process grew so extreme that even Cooley rebelled.[71]

The wide array of interpretative tools employed by the court made some important decisions so opaque that it was hard to discern how the

69. Forbath, "Politics, State Building, and the Courts, 1870–1920," 665, 669–76; James W. Ely, *Railroads and American Law* (Lawrence: University Press of Kansas, 2001), 93–95.
70. William E. Nelson, *The Fourteenth Amendment: From Political Principle to Judicial Doctrine* (Cambridge, MA: Harvard University Press, 1988), 197–98; Hovenkamp, 176–82, 199–204, 293–95.
71. Morton J. Horwitz, *The Transformation of American Law, 1870–1960: The Crisis of Legal Orthodoxy* (New York: Oxford University Press, 1992), 19–27; William E. Forbath, "Courting the State," presented at Harvard Faculty Workshop (2010), 3–6; Forbath, "Politics, State Building, and the Courts, 1870–1920," 669–70, 673–74.

judges reached their conclusions. The court's decision in *Santa Clara v. Southern Pacific* (1886) had been a victory for the railroads since it embraced the idea of corporate personhood. In *Santa Clara* the Supreme Court had, without discussion or argument, ruled that in regard to the assessment of taxes the equal protection clause applied to corporations in California. The decision itself, however, said nothing about the status of corporations as persons. That came in a preface to the decision by the court reporter, and it did not articulate what personhood might involve.[72]

In his original circuit court decision, Field claimed the differential taxes California counties placed on the Southern Pacific were illegal because they violated the rights of the corporation's natural person stockholders. He did not rule that railroads could escape state regulations that differed from regulations applied to other persons in the state; nor did he say that railroads chartered in one state were immune from regulation in another.[73]

Into the twentieth century, corporate personhood did not present much of an obstacle to reform and regulation. The Supreme Court upheld state regulation of corporations, which had no rights beyond those specifically granted in the charters creating them. The court maintained the distinction between corporations as artificial persons and the rights of citizens, who were natural persons. But gradually, without clear reasoning or justification, the limited nature of the decision expanded and would continue to grow larger in compass.[74]

The courts ground down labor republicanism and antimonopolism, but they could not quell opposition to substantive due process. In the mid-1890s Oliver Wendell Holmes, Jr., the son of the New England physician, poet, and intellectual who had once been William Dean Howells's neighbor, was a justice of the Supreme Judicial Court of Massachusetts. He was beginning to question the premises of not only judicial liberalism but also natural rights theories of law and absolute rights of property. He had come to regard law as a social construction. The "life of the law," Holmes declared, "has not been logic: it has been experience." By experience Holmes did not mean the custom enshrined in the common law; he meant history. In an 1896 dissent, he argued that "the most superficial reading of industrial history" revealed "that free competition means combination, and the organization of the world, now going on so fast, means

72. Kens, 243–45; R. White, 170.
73. Ruth Bloch and Naomi R. Lamoreaux, "Corporations and the Fourteenth Amendment," http://economics.yale.edu/sites/default/files/files/Faculty/Lamoreaux/corporations-14th.pdf.
74. Ibid., 11–22, 28.

an ever increasing might and scope of combination. It seems to me futile to set our faces against this tendency. Whether beneficial on the whole, as I think it is, or detrimental, it is inevitable." As Holmes emerged as a leading critic of the liberal judiciary, he hardly embraced labor. He, too, could rule that an illegal conspiracy occurred even when the people involved were cooperating to commit an act that was not illegal in and of itself. The irony of the judicial imperialism forged in the late nineteenth century was that it created tools, precedents, and processes that could be turned to very different purposes later.[75]

The liberal enshrinement of classical economics in the law took place just as a rising generation of economists shredded the old doctrines. The intellectual battle between the old liberals and the generation of scholars that had risen out of the German graduate schools had been going on since the 1880s. By the 1890s, the liberals and classical economists had lost the intellectual battle, though their ideas were still regnant on the bench. Judges appealed to economic theory already deemed antique and abandoned by most economists. William Graham Sumner had retreated into sociology. The courts opened the gates of the judicial fortress, beckoned the politically defeated in, and guarded them with a set of aging, discredited, and rejected beliefs that now rested mostly on judicial authority.[76]

75. Horwitz, 125ff., quotes, 129, 134; Hovenkamp, 231–32.
76. For an account of this struggle, see Nancy Cohen, *The Reconstruction of American Liberalism, 1865–1914* (Chapel Hill: University of North Carolina Press, 2002), particularly 110ff.; Hovenkamp, 174–75, 222–23, 271; Amy Dru Stanley, *From Bondage to Contract: Wage Labor, Marriage, and the Market in the Age of Slave Emancipation* (Cambridge: Cambridge University Press, 1998), 60–97.

23

An Era Ends

The presidential campaign of 1896 was the last of the nineteenth century, the last in which a leading contender for the nomination was a veteran of the Civil War, and the first since 1876 to take place in the middle of an economic depression. William McKinley, the frontrunner for the Republican nomination, had served in the Twenty-third Ohio under Lt. Col. Rutherford B. Hayes. The deep legacies of the war remained, but the issues of 1866—racial equality, the protection of black rights in the South, and Indian policy—were receding from the national stage, though they had by no means wholly disappeared.[1]

The people who had dominated that stage, were, however, disappearing. In the early 1890s the generation that had either embraced free labor or grasped at its astonishing, if elusive, opportunities began to fall by the wayside—some dead, some exhausted and discouraged, some merely no longer relevant. In 1892 Jay Gould was very rich, very sick, and very reviled. He was the face of American financial capitalism, and one of several faces Americans put on monopoly.

Gould's last years had been marked by defeats and Pyrrhic victories. Having bested Charles Francis Adams for control of the Union Pacific Railroad, he found that the fruit of his victory rotted in his hands. Gould's attempt with J. P. Morgan to organize yet another cartel of Western trunk lines to manage rates and competition had failed. He retained control of the profitable New York "El," the Manhattan Railroad, but could not get permission to add a third track, which would have ruined Battery Park, wrecked Broadway, and in the words of the Pulitzer's *World*, "shut out the air and sunlight from thousands of downtown residents."[2]

Fresh air and sunlight were critical to the control of tuberculosis, and Gould was dying of it. He could not sleep and could barely eat. His daughter

1. R. Hal Williams, *Realigning America: McKinley, Bryan, and the Remarkable Election of 1896* (Lawrence: University Press of Kansas, 2010), 50.
2. Maury Klein, *The Life and Legend of Jay Gould* (Baltimore, MD: Johns Hopkins University Press, 1986), 459–61, 473–75.

read Twain, Dickens, and Scott aloud to him. While she slept, a servant watched as Gould often paced in front of his Fifth Avenue mansion across from the Windsor Hotel and its sidewalk dudes. In early December 1892, a month after the presidential election, he died at home in his bedroom.[3]

A generation was heading for the exits. Unlike Gould, most would not be remembered for long after they were gone, unless they had attached their names to institutions that survived them. Leland Stanford, praised by Carnegie for founding a university in 1885, died in the early summer of 1893. He left his estate, which the United States would sue in an attempt to recover the debts owed by the Central Pacific Railroad, to found a university named after his dead son. Joseph Pulitzer survived, but he had become blind and bitter, withdrawing from active management of the *New York World*, whose influence faded with the rise of an even richer and more flamboyant newspaper owner, William Randolph Hearst.[4]

In 1889 Benjamin Harrison had appointed Frederick Douglass minister to Haiti, but although Douglass remained vigorous, his opportunities in Jim Crow America were limited. He published a new and updated version of his famous autobiography in 1892. It said nothing of the lynchings then beginning to add a new set of Southern outrages and horrors to decades of outrages and horrors. Douglass was the past. Ida B. Wells, Booker T. Washington, and W. E. B. Dubois were the future.[5]

In 1892 Elizabeth Cady Stanton delivered a speech, the "Solitude of Self," at the woman suffrage convention, showing that, in her at least, the old liberal stream flowed undiluted. She proclaimed "the individuality of each human soul; our Protestant idea, the right of individual conscience and judgement [*sic*]: our republican idea, individual citizenship." The self-sovereignty of women as well as men, and not social relations of any kind, was paramount. A woman "as an individual must rely on herself." She turned to her reinterpretation of biblical texts: *The Woman's Bible*, a feminist critique of Christian doctrine and its subordination of women. She declared that women must be liberated from their superstitions before suffrage would be of any benefit to them. Frances Willard, convinced that the Social Gospel was a force for good in the world, disavowed the book without disavowing Stanton's work for women. There was a general stampede of suffrage leaders away from Stanton, but Susan B. Anthony stood by her.[6]

3. Klein, 476–80.
4. James McGrath Morris, *Pulitzer: A Life in Politics, Print, and Power* (New York: Harper, 2010), 269–304.
5. William S. McFeely, *Frederick Douglass* (New York: Norton, 1991), 334–58, 360.
6. Ruth Birgitta Anderson Bordin, *Frances Willard: A Biography* (Chapel Hill: University of North Carolina Press, 1986), 172–74; Lori D. Ginzberg, *Elizabeth Cady Stanton: An American Life* (New York: Hill and Wang, 2009), 169–79.

Willard drifted toward Christian socialism, which she described as "Gospel Socialism." In early 1892 she chaired a meeting at Chicago's all-male reformist Sunset Club on the topic "How Would You Uplift the Masses?" As an ally of the Knights, she expressed discomfort with middle-class uplift. She wondered if the question should not be reversed and announced that the "masses send us word that they are rising, and ten years from now I don't think [tonight's] question will be germane."[7]

Willard's own socialism was hardly revolutionary. It sprang from evangelicalism, a distaste for materialism, and a desire for cooperation, not conflict, between the classes: "In every Christian there exists a socialist: and in every socialist a Christian." Among those on the panel was Jane Addams, the co-founder of Hull House, who was still evolving as a young reformer. She was not yet willing to condemn the status quo as unjust. In the audience was Florence Kelley, also a Hull House resident, who was certain that the social order was unjust and determined to do something about it.[8]

Henry Adams seemed one of the more unlikely Americans to drift away from liberal verities, but the death of his wife, Clover, had demoralized him and, he realized, unmoored him. He remained productive, writing his *History of the United States of America during the Administrations of Thomas Jefferson and James Madison*, but he was now a middle-aged man in love with Lizzie Cameron, the much younger, bored, unhappy, and beautiful wife of J. Donald Cameron, the rich and not particularly able Republican senator from Pennsylvania. Adams traveled the world, but was drawn back to Lizzie and a relationship that he realized would never be consummated and that rendered him ridiculous. With his renunciation of her as anything more than a friend, he took a further step to detach himself from Gilded Age society. He had already begun writing his *Education*. With his customary irony, he began describing himself as a "conservative anarchist" and wrote a speech for Senator Cameron denouncing the gold standard.[9]

Lizzie Cameron was the niece of William Tecumseh Sherman, who died in February 1891, the same year as Sara Winnemucca, whose brief fame had passed. Rutherford B. Hayes, who had dismissed Winnemucca's

7. Louise W. Knight, *Citizen: Jane Addams and the Struggle for Democracy* (Chicago: University of Chicago Press, 2005), 240–42.
8. Ian R. Tyrrell, *Woman's World/Woman's Empire: The Woman's Christian Temperance Union in International Perspective, 1880–1830* (Chapel Hill: University of North Carolina Press, 1991), 243–45; Knight, 240–42.
9. Edward Chalfant, *Improvement of the World: A Biography of Henry Adams, His Last Life, 1891–1918* (North Haven, CT: Archon Books, 2001), 60–61; Chalfant, *Better in Darkness: A Biography of Henry Adams: His Second Life, 1862–1891* (Hamden, CT: Archon Books, 1994), 586, 637–41.

eloquent pleas for her people, had grown more and more worried that the United States was devolving into a plutocracy, but he was old and ready to join his beloved late wife, Lucy. In January 1893 he did. James G. Blaine, who had never for a moment worried about plutocracy, died soon after. John Hay was a pallbearer.[10]

Clarence King had by 1891 embarked on a double life, one as Clarence King, successful scientist and failed businessman, and one as James Todd, a Pullman porter and light-skinned black man. He invented Todd to marry a freedwoman, Ada Copeland, who lived in Brooklyn. He had a family with her, and neither she nor their children knew of his existence as King. His supposed traveling life as a Pullman porter explained his lengthy absences. To support himself and his family, he borrowed increasing sums of money from Hay.[11]

The century was closing with a mad and seemingly destructive rush. A new generation bemoaned the failures and limits of the generation whose lodestar had been free labor. Henry Cabot Lodge and Theodore Roosevelt were rising in a Republican Party that was unaccustomed to being in the minority. In the Democratic Party, a young congressman from Nebraska, William Jennings Bryan, had learned to ride the tide of antimonopoly. It was not at all certain that anyone could begin to control the changes sweeping the nation, but it was clear that these men were eager to attempt it, even if they hardly seemed ready to their contemporaries.

Mrs. Schuyler Van Rensselaer, a leading art and architecture critic and a member of a prominent New York family, mapped the changes, coding them by colors that signified not race but rather gender and class in New York City. In February 1895 she wrote an article for the *Century* entitled "People in New York." New York, she claimed, allowed a person to "see things that are worth seeing, and cannot be seen elsewhere." Manhattan had a specific spatial pattern. Moving from south to north, there were places for making money, places for spending money, and places of residence. Color marked every domain. The crowds downtown were "unusually black . . . the customary wear of men." Only briefly would they be brightened by "hundreds of girls named for their little clicking machines," the typewriter girls who labored among men. After Canal

10. Ari Arthur Hoogenboom, *Rutherford B. Hayes: Warrior and President* (Lawrence: University Press of Kansas, 1995), 493, 525, 531–33; Frederick Hoxie, *This Indian Country and the Place They Made* (New York: Penguin Press, 2012), 173; John Taliaferro, *All the Great Prizes: The Life of John Hay from Lincoln to Roosevelt* (New York: Simon & Schuster, 2013), 281.

11. This is the story wonderfully told in Martha A. Sandweiss, *Passing Strange: A Gilded Age Tale of Love and Deception across the Color Line* (New York: Penguin Press, 2009).

Street "petticoats become more and more numerous," dominating beyond Fourteenth Street. Men made money; women spent it. Van Rensselaer judged origins by dress. Dowdiness suggested the suburbs; dismal shabbiness and naïve attempts to copy fashion cheaply signified the poor and young workingwomen. By European standards, even the well-to-do overdressed with colors too bright and materials too costly for the streets. Although New Yorkers walked more than Europeans, the very richest were not pedestrians. To see them "one must visit Central Park of a pleasant afternoon."[12]

She thought New Yorkers, although hardly polite, were more polite than Europeans. They were glad to return kindness for kindness, brusqueness for brusqueness. The city lacked European types as well as European manners. Its servants were not servile; there were no soldiers; its dudes were fewer and younger; dowagers remained scarce. She claimed the most defining types were the American girl and the young matron, defined by "money, good taste, unaggressive self-content, and that highly finished physical bearing which in the vernacular is called style."[13]

Only toward the end of her survey did she touch directly on class, "the extremes of riches and poverty…bitterly expressed by the contrast by what have been called Upper and Nether New York." She thought they existed in such extremes nowhere else but London, but she should have gotten out more. They existed in Chicago, San Francisco, Boston, New Orleans, and in other American cities and the countryside, particularly the Southern countryside. Mrs. Schuyler Van Rensselaer, which was how she usually referred to herself, seemed to go off down the liberal road attributing poverty and vice to the faults of the poor. She claimed that "half the drunkenness in New York came from wastefulness and bad cooking in the homes of the poor," but she stopped. The poor, she insisted, sought work, but could not find it. They lived hand-to-mouth, and a day's wages bought "a day's hard fare." The average wage of workingwomen, some supporting men and children, was sixty cents a day, for which many, such as seamstresses, worked from four in the morning to eleven at night. "Where," she asked, "lies the real responsibility for the wretchedness of Nether New York?"[14]

Not everyone viewed the plight of the poor this way. The *Century* remained a voice of the respectable classes, and the mayor of Indianapolis wrote its editor in 1895 declaring "trampism [to be] the greatest curse this country has ever known, with the possible exceptions of human slavery

12. Mrs. Schuyler Van Rensselaer, "People in New York," *Century* (Feb. 1895): 534–48.
13. Ibid.
14. Ibid.

and alcoholism." He urged the return of the whipping post. He made no mention of hard times; tramps created themselves.[15]

In 1895 Eugene Debs celebrated his fortieth birthday in the Woodstock jail, serving his contempt sentence. He would eventually present his time there as the mythic center of his political life. Here his eyes were opened; here he embraced the class struggle. Here Victor Berger, the Socialist leader from Milwaukee, brought him Marx's *Das Kapital*. But Debs's socialism was not, in 1895, nor later, Marx's socialism, and in 1895 he was not a socialist at all. In jail he rejected a socialism "that measures everyone in the same mold," but instead desired a system that allowed every man to have "the opportunity to advance to the fullest limits of his abilities." Through 1895 he refused to adopt the label *socialist*. He had, however, come to scorn the competitive system. He demanded its overthrow, but his revolutionary ideal remained the American Revolution. His values remained the old Protestant values, and Lincoln remained his hero. But the world of Lincoln, he recognized, had vanished; big business had so changed the economic system that the old virtues brought no reward.[16]

What Debs thought mattered; his popularity only increased in the wake of Pullman. When he returned to Chicago after his release from jail, a crowd of more than a hundred thousand turned out in the pouring November rain to greet him. He addressed the crowd by appealing to the "spirit of '76" and the values of the Declaration of Independence. The country and its government had been hijacked. "What," Debs asked, "is to be done?" He did not make a revolutionary appeal. He advocated politics and the power that the people possessed: the ballot. How Debs would use his immense popularity became a political question for 1896.[17]

I

What was to be done was a political question, but it was also a philosophical one. William Dean Howells took it seriously. He sympathized with the Populists, and he flirted with socialism even as he continued to vote Republican. Like many Americans, he never full aligned his votes and his sympathies.

Between 1894 and 1896, Howells published three essays on the themes of liberty, equality, and fraternity. As attempts to rethink democratic

15. C. S. Denny, "The Whipping-Post for Tramps," *Century* (March 1895): 794.
16. Nick Salvatore, *Eugene V. Debs: Citizen and Socialist* (Urbana: University of Illinois Press, 1982), 147–53.
17. Ibid., 147–60.

values, American republicanism, and the ideas of the great Enlightenment revolutions in terms of an industrial society, they deserve attention even though they went off, he wrote sardonically, "like wet fireworks." That popular magazines would publish such essays by a thoughtful American writer revealed the extent to which the crisis had led to a questioning of existing values.[18]

Howells organized the first essay around equality; he entitled it "Are We a Plutocracy?" He took for granted the growing inequality of wealth in the United States; he was interested in a more abstract question. Did the general desire for wealth among all classes and the organization of the economy to fulfill such desires make the United States a plutocracy rather than a democracy? He presumed that a country could not have two sets of values, one that applied to the economy and the other to politics. He thought that the values of capitalism and democracy were antithetical, and that Americans needed to choose between them. His logic resembled that of Samuel Gompers, who said, "There never yet existed coincident with each other autocracy in the shop and democracy in political life."[19]

Howells, however, differed from Gompers because he thought that nearly all Americans, rich and poor, could be labeled plutocrats since they assented to the current economic system. "Whether he gets rich or not...," Howells wrote, "the man who pays wages with the hope of profit to himself is a plutocrat, and the man who takes wages upon such terms, believing them right, is in principle a plutocrat; for both approve of the gain of money which is not earned, and agree to the sole arrangement by which the great fortunes are won or the worship of wealth is perpetuated." This was an intellectual's pretension.[20]

Democratic values had not penetrated industry, but plutocratic values had invaded politics despite the expansion of suffrage. "If votes are bought and sold," the essay argued, "the spirit of money-making, of plutocracy, arrives in our politics all the same; and if there is a change in the motive of those who seek public office, if men have come to desire it for the profit rather than the honor, we are more plutocratic than we were when we were less democratic." The failure of American democracy registered in the people's assent to a plutocracy: "If we have a plutocracy, it may be

---

18. W. D. Howells to Walter Page, May 14, 1896, in William Dean Howells, *Selected Letters*, ed. George Warren Arms (Boston: Twayne, 1979), 4: 127.

19. David Montgomery, *Citizen Worker: The Experience of Workers in the United States with Democracy and the Free Market During the Nineteenth Century* (Cambridge: Cambridge University Press, 1993), 159; W. D. Howells, "Are We a Plutocracy?" *North American Review* 158, no. 447 (1894).

20. Howells, "Are We a Plutocracy?" 185–86.

partly because the rich want it, but it is infinitely more because the poor choose it or allow it."[21]

Howells's second essay, "The Nature of Liberty," appeared in the *Forum* in 1895. He renounced his own liberalism of the Civil War years, when he had regarded, while consul in Venice, poor Italians as touchingly naïve in thinking that freedom would bring them "security from want and from the fear of want." He now realized that it was his own ideas of abstract liberty and complete individualism that had been flawed. The "dream of infinite and immutable liberty," he said, "is the hallucination of the Anarchist, that is, of the Individualist gone mad. The moment liberty in this meaning was achieved we should have the rule, not of the wisest, not of the best, not even of the most, but of the strongest, and no liberty at all."[22]

In a nod to new conditions, Howells thought freedom had to yield a common good and not just individual good, and that the common good had to include a guarantee of the means of a livelihood, for without this there could be no independence, on which freedom rested: "Till a man is independent he is not free."[23]

Howells recalled the demands of freed slaves, who in 1865 asked for forty acres and a mule because they realized that freedom without independence was empty. He had been among those who mocked this demand, writing in the *Nation* that all the state owed a man was a fair start in life. He did not think this way any longer. He "thought it much less comical to give our acres, not by forties but by millions to certain railroad companies. Now that turns out to have been a great joke, too, and we are laughing again, but on the wrong side of our mouths." He now proclaimed that "liberty and poverty are incompatible." Opportunity was only a phase of liberty; "safety is another." Freedom from want and fear were essential: "Liberty cannot stop short of it without ceasing to be."[24]

The final essay, "Who Are Our Brethren?" concerned fraternity. The average American thought the idea of a universal brotherhood dismaying and onerous, but without it, Howells argued, neither liberty nor equality would matter. The idea that those suffering were paying the price for their own faults was no longer tenable. Although he did not phrase it in terms of the urban environmental crisis, he recognized that "In this age a man denies the claim of humanity with much greater risk to himself than

21. Howells, "Are We a Plutocracy?" 190–91, 193.
22. William Dean Howells, "The Nature of Liberty," *Forum* (December 1895), 403.
23. Ibid., 407.
24. Kenneth Schuyler Lynn, *William Dean Howells: An American Life* (New York: Harcourt Brace Jovanovich, 1971), 131; Howells, "The Nature of Liberty," 402–3.

formerly." Howells did not claim fraternity was natural. He deemed it supernatural, by which he meant social. It was necessary for freedom and equality in a mass society.[25]

Howells's changing politics, however, were hardly politics at all. He asked not for a political movement but rather a change in American consciousness. Until then, no meaningful transformation could take place.

II

Howells talked about liberty, equality, and fraternity; in 1895 and 1896 the Republicans and Democrats talked about gold and silver. All of them were, in a sense, talking about the same thing. In the so-called battle of the standards, silver stood for equality and fraternity; gold stood for liberty in the old liberal sense of sanctity of property.

Technically, the United States was bimetallist since silver coins still circulated, but it was a de facto gold standard nation since its currency and bonds were redeemable in gold and the Treasury always paid out in gold. The gold continued to drain away. The combination of American depression and the growing strength of bimetallists in Congress led European investors to liquidate their American holdings and to withdraw their money in gold. Cleveland's original bond sale had restored gold to the depleted Treasury, but confidence had not returned and a second sale had been necessary. In January 1895 gold was once again flowing out faster than it came in, and the Treasury held only $31 million in reserves, well below the desired $100 million minimum. In late January the Treasury informed Cleveland that there had to be another bond sale or the country was in danger of default.[26]

Default—which simply meant abandoning the gold standard—was precisely what many in Congress wanted. Cleveland proposed legislation incorporating a series of monetary reforms that would slow the flow of gold from the Treasury. In the Congress, these reforms became the Spencer Bill, which would make sure that the paper currency, once exchanged for gold, would be retired and not simply reissued and thus become available for yet another exchange for gold. It would also authorize a new bond issue at 3 percent. Banks holding these bonds could issue new

25. Howells, "Who Are Our Brethren?" 933.
26. Richard Franklin Bensel, The Political Economy of American Industrialization, 1877–1900 (Cambridge: Cambridge University Press, 2000), 408–9, 414–16; R. Hal Williams, Years of Decision: American Politics in the 1890s (New York: John Wiley and Sons, 1978), 83–84; Alyn Brodsky, Grover Cleveland: A Study in Character (New York: St. Martin's Press, 2000), 357–61, 381–88.

bank notes to replace the retired currency. These proposals had virtually no chance of passage.[27]

Stymied in Congress, Cleveland used an old Civil War law as authority for a bond sale, and in early February 1895 he turned to J. P. Morgan and August Belmont, the nation's leading bankers, to negotiate it. Cleveland's devotion to the gold standard put him over a barrel. He had no time for a public bond offering. The bankers would have to provide the gold up front and then market the bonds, and they demanded a hefty premium for doing so. Cleveland twisted and turned, balking at their demands. Supposedly during the talks, there was a dramatic telephone call telling him there was only $9 million dollars left in the New York subtreasury. Morgan informed the president that he knew of a $10 million dollar draft to be presented that day. It would throw the nation into default. Cleveland broke, reportedly saying, "What suggestions have you to make, Mr. Morgan?"[28]

Mr. Morgan's suggestions saved the nation from default and netted Morgan and the House of Rothschild, whom Belmont represented, a hefty profit. The bankers secured pledges from other banks to halt gold withdrawals, and they disposed of the bonds easily and quickly. The Rothschilds' involvement ensured a wave of anti-Semitic abuse, but the *New York World* hit the key charge: the Cleveland administration had "gratuitously given to the syndicate in a secret conference" what amounted to a $5 million bonus with little risk on their part, "and it will be paid out of the public treasury." The *World* actually underestimated the profit.[29]

Cleveland's bond sales escalated the battle of the standards. By the 1890s the depression and the rise of first the Farmers' Alliance and then the Populists had provided new recruits for the opposition to the gold standard, but that opposition had also fragmented. In the 1870s the Greenbackers had offered a single and quite sophisticated argument in favor of fiat currency, but in the 1890s financial reformers offered a menu of reforms. Those arguing for fiat currency resting on government credit and providing economic flexibility were a minority drowned out by bimetallists, who were divided into three groups: free silver advocates, agricultural bimetallists, and international bimetallists. Their critiques focused on the gold standard, but in practice they extended to the National Banking System and to the methods for extending agricultural credit.[30]

27. For operation of the gold standard, Bensel, 366–72; Brodsky, 360–61.
28. Bensel, 416–17; Richard E. Welch, *The Presidencies of Grover Cleveland* (Lawrence: University Press of Kansas, 1988), 126–27; Brodsky, 362–63.
29. Bensel, 414–18; Brodsky, 363–65.
30. Gretchen Ritter outlines the various positions in *Goldbugs and Greenbacks*, 152–207.

All of the groups seeking reform agreed on the basic problems with the gold standard. First of all, it was deflationary, providing neither an adequate money supply nor a flexible one, which contributed to financial panics and deflation. Second, it removed control of the financial system from the United States to London, the seat of the international economy and capital of the world's creditor nation, Great Britain. Third, coupled with the National Banking System, it concentrated money and credit in the Northeast, leaving the West and South starved for funds.[31]

The solutions, however, differed, sometimes quite dramatically. The Greenbackers, having lost the battle over fiat currency to the goldbugs, now combined their solution with other schemes. The most plausible was the Populist proposal for subtreasuries, to issue low-interest notes against crop deposits, which could circulate as currency but would have to be redeemed within a year. This would create a flexible monetary supply tied to the farmer's need for money and credit, but it still amounted to a roundabout solution to the problem of fiat currency and an inadequate banking system.[32]

But even in combination with other measures, fiat currency lost ground to the various proposals for silver. One of the most compelling criticisms of the gold standard was that it wrote ancient superstition into modern financial systems by claiming the intrinsic value of gold and its "natural" status as money, but silver advocates essentially attacked the nearly religious worship of gold by proposing another metallic deity—silver—which could also claim ancient lineage. Its advantage over gold was that in the late nineteenth century it was much more abundant.

The abundance of silver raised the issue of how much silver should be turned into money, and at what ratio to gold. This divided the bimetallists into factions. Free Silver advocates, particularly strong among Western silver mine owners and miners, favored monetizing all of it at a ratio of 16 ounces of silver to an ounce of gold. With the market price of silver running at half what the Treasury would pay for it, the effect would have been a bonanza for mine owners. It would also, under Gresham's law ("cheaper money drives out dearer money"), lead to cheaper silver being turned into currency and then presented to the Treasury for more expensive gold, thus putting the United States on a de facto silver standard. Agricultural bimetallists were more restrained. They feared silver monometallism as much as gold, so they favored turning silver to gold at market prices—a ratio of 32:1. The most conservative group of bimetallists— Francis Walker and Brooks Adams, the brother of Henry and Charles

31. Ibid., 185–98.
32. Ibid., 186–87; Charles Postel, *The Populist Vision* (New York: Oxford University Press, 2007), 153–55.

Francis, among them — wanted an international agreement that would set the value of silver and create an international bimetallic system. Critics contended such an agreement was impossible.[33]

Advocates of the gold standard had the advantages of not only position — they controlled the presidency, the Treasury, and the banks — but also of defending a single position against divided adversaries. They admitted to some flaws in the existing financial system and proposed remedies. They recognized that the National Banking System favored the Northeast, and they wanted to legalize branch banking to allow more banks in the West and South. They recognized that because the national banks could issue bank notes only on the basis of government bonds, there was a retraction of the currency when those bonds were scarce or expensive. They proposed switching to an asset-based system, which would create more elasticity by allowing banks to issue notes on the basis of the capital they held. But their ameliorative reforms only went so far. They did little to address the lack of agricultural credit. This deficit came, in part, from the inability of national banks to make loans based on real estate — the main asset of most farmers — or to address the abuses of mortgage companies and the crop-lien system.[34]

The result was a debate that yielded some light, as Americans focused on basic economic issues, but it generated even more heat, as the arguments became couched in ideology and culture. Gold and silver stood for more than money; they became icons of deep beliefs and ways to talk about civilization, morality, progress, and "inferior" and "superior" races.

Gold-standard advocates, who increasingly tended to be more conservative Republicans, associated gold with stability, natural values, a harmony of interests, prosperity, civilization, the white race, expertise, and American participation in the international economy. Where silverites denounced gold as the tool of international bankers and Great Britain, goldbugs praised it as the medium of international commerce. Gold, they said, unites, while silver divides. Silver, they claimed, was the standard of "barbarian" nations like China and the republics of South America. When opponents attacked the gold standard as arbitrary and deflationary, proponents defended it as natural and as a bar to inflation. When opponents blamed gold for panics and depressions, defenders claimed these were natural economic cycles that no financial system could cure.[35]

33. Ritter, 160–61, 183–85.
34. Ibid., 158–65.
35. For how discussions of money became intertwined with race, see Michael O'Malley, *Face Value: The Entwined Histories of Money & Race in America* (Chicago: University of Chicago Press, 2012). For cultural values and monetary values, Walter T. K. Nugent, *Money and American Society, 1865–1880* (New York: Free Press, 1968), 33–43, 263–75; Ritter, 124–29, 135–36, 151–58, 162–72.

Advocates for the gold standard had long regarded gold with a religious fervor, and their beliefs only intensified as they came under attack. Edward Atkinson argued that the law could not change nature, and "mankind recognized the superior value bestowed on gold by nature." Gold determined the value of money, and money had to be kept from democratic control. Financial matters were too arcane to be left to democratic votes; they had to be the realm of experts. Goldbugs found it more effective to attack than defend, and they denounced their opponents as radicals, communards, barbarians, and ignoramuses. They regarded the silverites as scofflaws seeking to escape their just debts.[36]

Silverites showed equal enthusiasm for attacking gold. They denounced gold Republicans as members of a party of Gold and Greed, condemning the "rapacious greed and tyrannical power of gold." Gold made "the rich richer, and the poor poorer." It was the currency of monopoly. It rewarded speculation and demeaned labor, and with Cleveland's bond policy, it drove the nation into debt to reward bankers. Silver, as the alternative to gold, was the currency of nationalism, republicanism, and the producing classes, while gold was the currency of British domination. Arguments against gold sometimes acquired a tinge of anti-Semitism, but anti-Semitism was the language of almost any nineteenth-century discussion of money and banking, and the Populists, the leading critics of the gold standard, were remarkably tolerant in this respect.[37]

In 1895 William H. Harvey's *Coin's Financial School*, a silverite tract, was selling five thousand copies a day, and free-silver organizations distributed tens of thousands more for free. In part, Harvey's arguments rehashed old conspiracy theories, and in part they resorted to mumbo jumbo worthy of goldbugs, but the fictional young Coin easily answered both the most basic and the most abstruse questions posed to him by Chicago newspapermen, bankers, and businessmen. Coin's lessons, flawed as they were, spoke to the seriousness of the public discussion, although the illustrations made the point for those who wearied of the explanations. Coin's most telling criticism of the gold standard for most readers was that it did not work.

> Anything can be proved by theoretical reasoning. In the practical appli-
> cation of a theory is the proof of its strength. The gold standard, now
> fitted to a shivering world, is squeezing the life out of it. The men of
> the country, the backbone of the republic, on whose strong arms the life
> of the nation may depend, are delivering over their property to their

---

36. Nugent, 33–43, 263–75; Ritter, 162–76.
37. Ritter, 171, 180–84, 191–93; Walter Nugent, *The Tolerant Populists: Kansas Populism and Nativism*, 2nd ed. (Chicago: University of Chicago Press, 2013), 82–86.

creditors and going into beggary. This is the test proof of the beneficence of monometallism.[38]

III

When Debs asked, "What is to be done?" part of the answer was easy, and
Populists, Republicans, and most Democrats agreed on it: disavow Grover
Cleveland and, as far as possible, prevent him from doing any more damage.
So complete was the disaster of the Cleveland administration that the election should have been no contest at all. The events of the preceding four
years had seemingly killed the chances of Democrats as the party of small
government. Most members of Cleveland's party treated him like an animated corpse, slowly decaying in the White House. He was an unpleasant
and unfortunate reminder of the days not long before, when the party had
lived and breathed. Henry George, who had campaigned for him, now denounced him as "more dangerous to the Republic than any of his predeces-
sors." The Democrats could not remove him, so most avoided him. The
presidential election seemed simply about the Republicans replacing
Cleveland with whomever they chose.[39]

By the end of 1895, it had become clear that the Republican choice
would most likely be William McKinley. He had been campaigning since
1894, when he gave 371 speeches in three hundred cities and reached a
total audience of an estimated two million people. Mark Hanna, his manager, had been calling in political debts, organizing the South, which although solidly Democratic still sent delegates to the Republican convention, and working patiently and assiduously to assemble the necessary
delegates. Thomas Reed, reelected speaker of the House, seemed McKinley's
strongest rival, but he failed to navigate between the silver Republicans of
the West and the goldbugs of the East. Speaking of his own chances for
the nomination, he, as usual, failed to resist wit when silence would have
served him better: "The Republicans might do worse, and they probably
will," he said.[40]

38. Lawrence Goodwyn, *Democratic Promise: The Populist Moment in America* (New
    York: Oxford University Press, 1976), 452–53; William H. Harvey, *Coin's Financial
    School* (Chicago: Coin Publishing, 1894), quote, 83.
39. Christopher William England, "Land and Liberty: Henry George, the Single Tax
    Movement, and the Origins of 20th Century Liberalism" (Ph.D. diss., Georgetown
    University, 2015), 146; Williams, *Years of Decision*, 95–96; Daniel Klinghard, *The
    Nationalization of American Political Parties, 1880–1896* (Cambridge: Cambridge
    University Press, 2010), 181–82; Williams, *Realigning America*, 63, 67, 71–72, 74, 80.
40. Klinghard, 221–25; H. Wayne Morgan, *William McKinley and His America* (Kent, OH:
    Kent State University Press, 2003), 152–59; Williams, *Realigning America*, 48–49, 159.

Mark Hanna, who had come to detest the Republican bosses only when they opposed him, could not have dreamed up better opponents than McKinley's two remaining obstacles to the nomination: Matthew Quay of Pennsylvania and the Easy Boss, Thomas Platt of New York. Quay was erudite, sophisticated, and corrupt. He defined politics as "the art of taking money from the few and votes from the many under the pretext of protecting one from the other." He took in a lot of money. Assessments on the salaries of patronage employees, fees to hold lucrative offices, payments from banks that held state funds, percentages of profits from those state funds the banks invested, payments for access, and more brought in the money necessary to run an elaborate Republican machine. Usually he was better at keeping his mouth shut; he was renowned for "knowing how to keep silent in sixteen different languages." He was also a master of information. He knew what opponents, and his own legislators, did not want him to know, and he knew how to use the information. The cards he kept on individual legislators were known as Quay's coffins. They could end careers. Platt possessed no erudition and no charisma, and he was almost as incapable of conducting a conversation as of giving a speech. But he was as calculating and shrewd as Quay. Platt and Quay wanted anyone but McKinley, whom they knew they could not control. When Reed faltered, they had no credible alternative, and Hanna had already embraced them as the enemy. It was a campaign of "McKinley against the Bosses" and "the People against the Bosses."[41]

McKinley's job was simply not to lose, and it was hard to imagine circumstances in which, if nominated, he could lose. The hardening lines on the gold standard initially formed a problem for him since he had been a mild bimetallist. He promised to work for an international bimetallist agreement while maintaining "our present standard." But ridiculed for trying to straddle the fence, he came out for gold in early 1896 without ruling out eventual bimetallism. The Republican platform echoed his position: a gold standard unless there was an international agreement on bimetallism. Although the gold standard framed the refrain of the coming campaign, McKinley really only hummed along. He cared mostly about the tariff.[42]

The Midwestern catastrophes of the late 1880s and early 1890s had inoculated the Republicans against the dangers in that critical region. They had moved to tamp down the evangelical reforms—particularly prohibition and legislation mandating English language instruction in the schools—that

41. Gary Gerstle, *Liberty and Coercion: The Paradox of American Government from the Founding to the Present* (Princeton. NJ: Princeton University Press, 2015), 165, 168–69; Morgan, 153–56; Williams, *Realigning America*, 48–50, 55–56.
42. Williams, *Realigning America*, 59–61, 139; Herbert David Croly, *Marcus Alonzo Hanna: His Life and Work* (New York: Macmillan, 1912), 175–89.

had divided their base and cost them control of the Upper Midwest. They used the depression to make the Democrats a punching bag, and every blow landed. They accused the Democrats of being incapable of governing, and that, by and large, was true. They accused Cleveland of failing to respond to the depression and restore prosperity. Restoring prosperity was beyond any president, but Cleveland had done little to relieve the nation's suffering. The Democrats in 1892 had accused the Republicans of being hostile to labor, and the tariff of being the tool of callous employers. The Republicans reversed the accusation. Now the Democrats were hostile to labor, and the tariff was the route to prosperity. Outside of the machine-dominated wards of the cities and a few states like Illinois controlled by pro-labor Democrats, it was hard to see why workers would vote for Democrats. Labor hated Cleveland for Pullman and its aftermath. Debs, who had left the Democratic Party, was labor's hero.[43]

Across the Mississippi, angry Western farmers framed the coming election as a choice between Populists and Republicans. Farmers in the West and South producing cotton and wheat had reason to be angry and desperate. Cotton prices in Georgia in 1894 were less than half their 1881 high, and wheat prices in the Midwest and West fell by two-thirds from their postwar high even as the cost of agricultural credit rose. Republican success in 1894, however, and their own antimonopolist wing east of the Missouri and on the West Coast gave the Grand Old Party, as Republicans had begun calling themselves, reasons for optimism. The Democrats had only the South, and even there the Populist revolt, although it had few real gains so far, showed signs, as in North Carolina, of threatening Democratic control.[44]

The Populists knew they had to expand their base beyond the core that came to them from the Farmers' Alliance. In some places, they showed signs of doing so. In 1894 William U'Ren united the Oregon Farmers' Alliance, the Grange, Portland Federated Trades, Portland Central Labor Council, and the Knights of Labor to create the Joint Committee on Direct Legislation. The committee denounced the legislature as the "representatives of the monied and monopolistic classes." U'Ren had led a

43. Theodore Roosevelt, "The Issues of 1896" Century (November 1895): 68–72; Williams, Years of Decision, 95–96; Williams, Realigning America, 42–43; Bensel, 285.
44. Robert Klepper, "The Economic Bases for Agrarian Protest Movements in the United States, 1870–1900," Journal of Economic History 34, no. 1 (1974): 283–85; Klepper, The Economic Bases for Agrarian Protest Movements in the United States, 1870–1900, Dissertations in American Economic History (New York: Arno Press, 1978), 73–74, 82–83; Charles Postel, The Populist Vision (New York: Oxford University Press, 2007), 104, M. Elizabeth Sanders, Roots of Reform: Farmers, Workers, and the American State, 1877–1917 (Chicago: University of Chicago Press, 1999), 101–4.

hardscrabble life working as a laborer, attending night school to become a lawyer, and working for a while as an editor in Tin Cup, Colorado. Already asthmatic, he came down with tuberculosis. The doctors sent him to Hawaii, where, as he recounted, "I went to Honolulu to die," but instead he read George's *Progress and Poverty* and vowed to live to bring about the Single Tax and political democracy. By 1894 he was secretary of the Oregon Populist Party and pressing for direct legislation: the initiative, referendum, and recall.[45]

Eugene Debs stood as the real wild card for the Populists; he had declared himself a Populist in 1896 and launched a national speaking tour. His program was vague. He regarded technological change and increasing unemployment as inevitable, and neither trade unions nor strikes could provide a solution. The core problems remained the wage system itself, corporate control of resources, and growing inequality. The ballot provided the means to the end, but what that end would look like remained hazy since Debs continued to reject socialism while endorsing an elusive cooperative commonwealth—one that neither the Knights nor the Farmers' Alliance had been able to secure. It appeared that Debs did not have a compelling answer to his own question of "What is to be done?" Still, the "middle of the road" faction of the Populists, who wanted to remain an independent party rather than fuse with the Democrats to stop the resurgent Republicans, embraced Debs as their great hope.[46]

With Hanna having secured delegates for McKinley and thoroughly undermined opposition within the party, the Republican convention in June proved as anticlimactic as Hanna intended. Twenty-three Western silver Republicans provided the only drama, tearfully walking out over the gold-standard plank to the jeers—including Hanna's—of the mass of delegates. On the wall of the St. Louis convention hall hung a large banner: "Republicanism is Prosperity." It announced the theme of the McKinley campaign. The candidate was "the Advance Agent of Prosperity" and would guarantee workers "the Full Dinner Pail."[47]

If there was ever any doubt about the Republican line of attack in 1896, Joseph Foraker eliminated it when he nominated McKinley. Foraker was Hanna's and McKinley's enemy in Ohio, but McKinley had agreed to back him for the Senate in exchange for Foraker's support. In nominating McKinley, he symbolized Republican unity; the Republican campaign

45. Robert D. Johnston, *The Radical Middle Class: Populist Democracy and the Question of Capitalism in Progressive Era Portland, Oregon* (Princeton, NJ: Princeton University Press, 2003), 122–25, 129–30.
46. Salvatore, 155–57.
47. Williams, *Realigning America*, 59–64.

This campaign poster was what led Theodore Roosevelt to say that Republicans advertised William McKinley like a patent medicine in the campaign of 1896. McKinley was the advance agent of prosperity, and despite all their failures, the Republicans clung to their identity as the party of prosperity, pinning the depression of the 1890s on the Democrats. Courtesy of the McKinley Replica Birthplace Home, Niles, Ohio.

would saddle the Democrats with Grover Cleveland, whose administration had been "one stupendous disaster." It had achieved an equality nobody desired: everyone, the rich and poor, Democrat and Republican, Northerner and Southerner, the just and unjust, all had suffered. Foraker proclaimed the silver lining: "Over against this fearful penalty we can set down one great blessed compensatory result. It has destroyed the Democratic party. The proud columns that swept the country in triumph in 1892 are broken and hopeless in 1896."[48]

Broken and hopeless the Democrats appeared to be, until something remarkable happened. The leading contender for the Democratic nomination, a rather dubious prize, was the aptly named silverite Sen. Richard Bland. Democratic dissidents—now a majority of the party—latched onto silver, not least because it disassociated the Democrats from Cleveland. In the state conventions, Cleveland used his influence to try to hold the party to gold. He failed. Delegates in the conventions denounced him. But Bland, "artless as a child" in the words of an associate, did nothing to secure the nomination. He waited for a call that would not come. The silverites fractured among numerous candidates, and William Jennings Bryan, the young Nebraska politician, saw his opportunity.[49]

Bryan had emerged as a leading spokesman for silver in 1893 when he opposed Cleveland's successful effort to repeal the Sherman Silver Purchase Act. He had cast silver in class terms then, and he continued to do so. "The Democratic Party," he claimed in 1896, "cannot serve God and Mammon; it cannot serve plutocracy and at the same time defend the rights of the masses." Bryan wanted to bring the scattered free-silver forces—Republicans and Populists as well as Democrats—together, and he had become a favored speaker before silver clubs across the country. His main weapon was his voice, "deep and powerfully musical" and "clear as a cathedral bell." Few who heard it ever forgot it or its power. He controlled its cadences like an actor, and he could project it so that his wife reported she once heard it perfectly although sitting in a hotel room three blocks from where he was speaking. His demeanor matched his speech; it radiated strength, youth, and vigor. When he cited Scripture, he appealed to evangelicals; when he denounced inequity and inequality, he captured antimonopolists; and even his opponents, like William Allen White, the Kansas Republican editor, found his "magnificent earnestness" to be "hypnotic."[50]

48. Croly, 138–39; Williams, *Realigning America*, 63.
49. Michael Kazin, *A Godly Hero: The Life of William Jennings Bryan* (New York: Anchor Books, 2007), 53; Williams, *Realigning America*, 68–69, 72–76.
50. Klinghard, 184–85; Kazin, 48–49, 52–53.

The Democratic convention in Chicago turned out to be as chaotic as the Republican convention was orchestrated. The battles over the platform and the seating of competing delegations resulted in the predictable rout of the goldbugs, but they insisted on a debate over a minority report endorsing the gold standard. The Democrats met in the cavernous Chicago Coliseum, which covered five and a half acres and was better suited to hosting Buffalo Bill's Wild West (which it had) than a convention where speakers struggled to be heard because of its size and miserable acoustics. The agreement for the debate over the minority report had Sen. Ben Tillman, involved in the slaughter of black Republicans in Hamburg, South Carolina, and a bitter and unrepentant racist as well as an antimonopolist and silverite, speaking first. Three Democratic goldbugs followed, with William Jennings Bryan speaking last.[51]

The audience expected drama, and they got it. Tillman predictably attacked gold and monopoly, but he also recklessly attacked the Northeast and defended secession. His speech provoked hisses and threatened to derail the silverites' momentum. Luckily, the three goldbugs were tedious and their doctrine unpopular. William Jennings Bryan seized the moment, giving one of the most famous speeches in American history. He came, he said, to speak "in defense of a cause as holy as the cause of liberty—the cause of humanity." He had his audience, and he did not let go. He had been countering gold-standard arguments for years, and his opponents had presented him with the usual targets, but he was not interested in making arguments. He was interested in mobilizing the convention for action. He demanded equity between small-town Americans, farmers, and small businessmen and an end to favoritism to "the few financial magnates who, in a back room, corner the money of the world." The audience cheered him on. He demanded free silver as a declaration of independence from British financial power.[52]

Then came the grand peroration. Bryan stepped forward, toward the audience. "Having behind us the producing masses of this nation and the world, supported by the commercial interests, the laboring interests and toilers everywhere," and then, stepping back, he extended his arms away from his body and delivered the final phrase, "we will answer their demand for a gold standard by saying to them: You shall not press down upon the brow of labor this crown of thorns, you shall not crucify mankind

51. Williams, *Realigning America*, 78–80; Kazin, 56–57.
52. Williams, *Realigning America*, 83–85; Kazin, 59–61; William Jennings Bryan, "Cross of Gold Speech," American Social History Project/Center for Media and Learning (Graduate Center, CUNY), and the Roy Rosenzweig Center for History and New Media (George Mason), http://historymatters.gmu.edu/d/5354/.

upon a cross of gold." He had used the phrase before, but never with the Christ-like pose he struck and held. There was, at first, total silence, and then the hall exploded with, as the *New York World* reported, "hills and valleys of shrieking men and women." The delegates nominated Bryan on the fifth ballot. The gold Democrats withdrew; they ran their own ticket, which Hanna secretly subsidized to draw votes from Bryan. They became the equivalent of the Western silver Republicans, who backed Bryan.[53]

The Populists were more important than either the silver Republicans or the gold Democrats; if they ran a separate ticket, they would doom Bryan by splitting the Western and Southern antimonopolist vote. The middle-of-the road Populists, particularly strong in the South, were willing to do exactly that, arguing that free silver alone was a mere panacea and not a solution to the crisis facing the country. The Democrats had not, with the exception of condemning the Supreme Court for ruling the income tax unconstitutional, adopted the broad array of reforms—nationalization of railroads and telegraph, the subtreasury system, electoral reforms, and more—urged by the Populists. The middle-of-the-roaders wanted the Populists to retain a strong antimonopoly program and continue to build the movement and the party. They hoped to enlist Eugene Debs as their candidate, but he refused to be drafted, and when Bryan was nominated Debs supported him. Among the Populists, fusionists opposed the middle-of-the roaders and were surprised and pleased by Bryan's nomination and the Democrats' embrace of free silver. They saw the election as antimonopoly's great chance and were willing to take free silver and Bryan's rhetorical devotion to the producing classes as the equivalent of half-a-loaf. Once in office, they could proceed with other reforms.[54]

The Populists met in late July in St. Louis after both major party conventions. Populist delegates were different from delegates to other conventions. There were more women among them. Many of the delegates were poor, some so poor that they slept in parks and walked to the convention site to save trolley fare. Some were shoeless; others took off their shoes when in the convention to save leather. They were soldiers in a cause that to them was much greater than a single election.[55]

Bryan's nomination put pressure on the fault lines of the Populist Party; it was no wonder it shattered. The fusionists were pragmatists, but what

53. Williams, *Realigning America*, 85–90; Kazin, 61–63.
54. The classic, if quite loaded, framing of the split among Populists comes from Lawrence Goodwyn. He pits a "shadow movement" dominated by office seekers against the "cooperative movement" culture of true agrarian Populists. Goodwyn, 426–36, 461–62; Williams, *Realigning America*, 110–14.
55. Williams, *Realigning America*, 114.

seemed pragmatism in the West looked like suicide or worse in the South. In the West, the Populists had forged fusion tickets in state after state since their inception. Fusion had brought success and office; purity had, to be sure, secured enthusiasm and votes but often not placed Populists in office, as the antimonopoly vote was split between parties. With no strong candidate of their own, the Populists would hemorrhage voters to Bryan in any case, so why not endorse him? In the South, however, fusion was different. There the Populists had defined themselves in opposition to the Democrats, who had sought to suppress them and disenfranchise them. When they fused, it was with Republicans. The bitter split between Populists and Bourbon Democrats, and the violence that had ensued, made it hard to go back. Tom Watson, with whom the Democrats had repeatedly resorted to fraud to count him out, bridled at fusion. The Democrats "say we must fuse, but their idea of fusion is that we play minnow while they play trout; we play June bug while they play duck; we play Jonah while they play the whale."[56]

The fusionists controlled the Populist convention, but not enough to prevent it from ending in utter confusion. The fusionists secured the nomination of Bryan, but the middle-of-the-roaders insisted on nominating Tom Watson for vice president. Watson first rejected and then accepted the nomination. Bryan insisted that the Populists take the whole Democratic ticket, including vice-presidential nominee Arthur Sewall, or withdraw his own name from nomination. The fusionists refused to acknowledge or read Bryan's message to the convention; the convention nominated him despite his withdrawal. Democratic Party chair James K. Jones told the Populists, "Mr. Sewall will, of course, remain on the ticket, and Mr. Watson can do what he likes." Bryan got Populist support, but this allowed the Republicans to portray him as the leader of what amounted to a political version of Coxey's Army: a collection of radicals, anarchists, cranks, and fanatics.[57]

By the mid-1890s Frances Willard was spending much of her time in England. She distanced herself from the Prohibition Party, which had abandoned her platform of wide reform to become a single-issue party. She did not take a position on the 1896 election, instead offering kind words for both candidates. Her own ambitions for a broad reform coalition had not reached fruition.[58]

56. Goodwyn, 458–59, 465–69; Postel, 271–74; Williams, *Realigning America*, 113–14.
57. Sanders, 140; Williams, *Realigning America*, 116–19; Goodwyn, 477–92.
58. For her international efforts, see Tyrrell, 106–7; Bordin, 221–37.

The Bryan nomination and the wholehearted Democratic commitment to free silver surprised Hanna, who specialized in not being surprised. He had planned to take a vacation and then to fight the election
on the tariff and prosperity. He expected to win "without half trying."
Instead, he faced a crusade and a Democratic Party that repudiated its
own president. To combat Bryan, he took personal charge of the campaign and mobilized resources that the Democrats could not match.
McKinley, for his part, recognized that he could not compete with Bryan
on the stump and refused to try. He persuaded Hanna to wage a front
porch campaign with Republican delegations coming to the candidate.
Although his tactics differed, his campaign appealed as directly to the
voters as did Bryan's. An estimated three thousand delegations and 750,000
people came to Canton, Ohio, to see McKinley. Hanna dispatched a
corps of fourteen hundred speakers, paying their expenses and pouring
them into the states most in danger of flipping to Bryan. The Republicans
flooded the country with literature; they mailed a hundred million documents from Chicago alone. Republicans produced roughly 275 separate
pamphlets issued in numerous languages as the Republicans targeted the
immigrant vote. They rang the same theme over and over again: McKinley
was "the Advance Agent for Prosperity." As Theodore Roosevelt observed,
"Hanna advertised McKinley as if he were a patent medicine."[59]

That was one side of Theodore Roosevelt, observant, wry, and shrewd,
but he could never quite quell his tendency to mingle the shrewd and the
hysterical. He, like many other Republicans, condemned Bryan and
the Populists as social revolutionaries, and to stop their "subversion," he
proposed putting twelve of their leaders against a wall and "shooting them
dead." Bryanites, to be sure, could match such rhetoric. The favorite song
of the delegates to the Populist convention had been "We'll Shoot the
Goldbugs, Every One." There were, to be sure, pragmatic assessments of
chances and issues, the continued movement toward mass educational
campaigns rather than the old local "army" campaigns, and a reliance on
corporate money and large donors. But very often both campaigns veered
off toward a kind of hysteria.[60]

The two parties had real and serious differences. Each side was capable
of recognizing that the election had great stakes. A democratic industrial
society had roused to sort itself out in new ways. Bryan had delivered his
position in one of the less-often quoted sections of his Cross of Gold
speech: "There are two ideas of government. There are those who believe

59. Croly, 209–11, 213–18; Kazin, 68; Klinghard, 228–29; Williams, *Realigning America*,
    129–39.
60. Williams, *Realigning America*, 115; Postel, 269.

that if you just legislate to make the well-to-do prosperous, their prosperity will leak through on those below. The Democratic idea has been that if you legislate to make the masses prosperous, their prosperity will find its way up and through every class that rests upon it." This had, in fact, not been the Democratic idea, as Cleveland could testify, but Bryan proposed to make it the Democratic idea.[61]

McKinley countered by accusing Bryan of waging a class campaign, which he was, and arguing that such divisions were un-American, which they clearly were not, or why would Bryan have such appeal? McKinley proposed nothing sweeping or stirring in response; nor did he have to do so. Bryan had to climb out of the deep hole Cleveland had dug for the Democrats. McKinley only had to remind Americans of a world before Cleveland. Many did not have such fond memories of that world, the one Bellamy had portrayed in *Looking Backward*, but compared with the depression it appeared rosy enough. McKinley spoke for "financial honor," prosperity, and protectionism, and disparaged any talk of inequality or class difference. The interests of capital and labor, employer and employed were the same.[62]

Hanna's efforts to counter Bryan and disseminate the Republican message demanded money, a lot of money. Hanna assessed banks at 0.25 percent of their capital. Standard Oil forked over $250,000. The audited accounts of the Republican Campaign Committee yielded contributions of $3.5 million, with popular estimates much higher. About $3 million of that came from New York. In 1892, the Republican committee had raised $1.5 million. With the exception of William Randolph Hearst's New York *Journal* and the St. Louis *Post-Dispatch*, no major Northeastern or Midwestern newspaper, not even Pulitzer's *World*, backed Bryan. Hearst pilloried and taunted Hanna as the business paymaster for the Republican Party, tempting Hanna to sue for libel. Hanna did not, realizing this was precisely what Hearst wanted him to do. But Hearst, by backing the underdog, ridiculing the wealthy and powerful, and being forthright and entertaining, stole from Pulitzer's own playbook and bested him in the newspapers wars of New York.[63]

Bryan countered Republican money, literature, newspapers, and surrogates with his best available weapon: his oratory. The Democratic Party apparatus, controlled by Cleveland until the convention, was in shambles. Bryan tried to mobilize silver clubs on his behalf and to take the campaign directly to the people. He could not be everywhere, but he

61. Bryan, "Cross of Gold Speech."
62. Williams, *Realigning America*, 140–41; Morgan, 178–79.
63. Croly, 218–22, 224–25; Morris, *Pulitzer*, 326–28; Kazin, 72.

seemed to be. He took four extended railroad trips, the first on his departure from Chicago speaking on his way back to Nebraska. The second and third trips, stretching from August 2 to October 31 with only a three-day break between them, were epic. The first carried him from Lincoln to New York and back. He gave 145 speeches, averaging five a day. The second trip, from September 11 to October 31, stretched over fifty days, covering the upper South, Midwest, and Middle Border with a foray into New England. It revealed how important the Midwest was to the election. If Bryan could tap antimonopolist sentiment there, he could win.[64]

A Democratic victory in the Midwest seemed possible in the late summer, with both workers and farmers expressing enthusiasm for Bryan and silver. The Republicans were worried. The Midwest, however, was a steep hill for the Democrats to climb, and the legacy of Cleveland was a weight they could not shake. The Republicans had disavowed their advocacy of total prohibition and embraced licensing and local option. Freeing themselves of this burden allowed them to focus their attacks on the Democrats and the depression. The Democrats in Iowa, faced with a deeply unpopular Cleveland administration, could not afford to disavow the president because they depended on him for national patronage. The result was that Bryan would have only a few months to resuscitate a deeply divided and unpopular party.[65]

Hanna rushed literature and speakers into the Midwest, reinforcing the connection between the Democrats and the depression, and emphasizing the danger free silver posed for wage earners. Proponents of silver claimed that inflation and easier money would bring prosperity and jobs; Republicans stressed that inflation would erode workers' wages. Deflation had badly hurt the economy, yet it had been one of the few safeguards for skilled workers. As long as they could prevent wage cuts, their wages would rise in real terms. It was not enough, but why discard one of the few weapons they possessed? On the relatively rare occasions when Bryan addressed working-class audiences in the East and Midwest, he did not stress free

64. Williams, *Realigning America*, 107–9; Nathan Sanderson, "William Jennings Bryan's Railroad Campaign in 1896," *Railroads and the Making of Modern America*, http://railroads.unl.edu/views/item/bryan_speech; Klinghard, 186–87; Jeffrey Ostler, *Prairie Populism: The Fate of Agrarian Radicalism in Kansas, Nebraska, and Iowa, 1880–1892* (Lawrence: University Press of Kansas, 1993), 175–76, 178–79.

65. Williams, *Realigning America*, 97–99; Peter H. Argersinger, *Representation and Inequality in Late Nineteenth-Century America: The Politics of Apportionment* (New York: Cambridge University Press, 2015), 195–96; Ostler, 176; Paul Kleppner, *Continuity and Change in Electoral Politics, 1893–1928* (Westport, CT: Greenwood Press, 1987), 78–81.

silver. Bryan's evangelical rhetoric worked well among farmers and small-town Americans, but it just raised alarms among Catholic and Jewish workers. Working-class urban Democrats did not desert the party, but Bryan needed more. He needed them to respond to him as they had responded to Henry George. There was no sign that this happened.[66]

As the election neared, Republican fears eased as antimonopoly Republicans in the Midwest remained loyal to their party. Poor harvests and scarcity in Russia, India, and Australia caused wheat prices to rise, and wavering farmers in the Midwest had an additional reason to reject free silver, which Democrats claimed was the only way to raise commodity prices.[67]

At the end of October Hanna deployed a final tactic, playing a new variation of the patriot card and the home card against the Democrats. He called for a national flag day on Saturday, October 31, the weekend before national elections. He called on voters to "unfurl your flags, show your colors and vote for the protection of your families." Enormous turnouts in New York City, Chicago, and San Francisco elated the Republicans, who were already confident from the results of early state elections, which showed no surprise movement toward the Democrats.[68]

William Dean Howells watched the parade in New York. The "gold men had a magnificent day for their parade," which was "enormous . . . but perfectly dull — just commonplace, prosperous people in hordes." Howells was dubious about free silver, yet he was even more dubious about the Republican Party, which "now contains *all* the monopolies that have corrupted and oppressed the people." Howells did not vote. He had missed the registration deadline — a reform that was not supposed to affect people like him but that was inhibiting turnout, as it was designed to do, and would continue to do so. Even he hedged his opinion. He would vote for Bryan "if there was no question of free silver." Free silver, of course, had become the main question. Still, he thought Bryan might win: "His supporters are mostly poor men, who in the cities dare not avow themselves."[69]

Employers did try to coerce workers, who in rallies in Northeastern and Midwestern cities had shown enthusiasm for Bryan. At a Cleveland counter rally to the Republican flag day, marchers covered their faces. They carried a banner saying "We cover our faces for fear of losing our jobs." There is no doubt employers threatened economic retribution —

66. Williams, *Realigning America*, 134–36, 153; Kazin, 69.
67. Williams, *Realigning America*, 142–43.
68. Ibid., 143–45.
69. W. D. Howells to Aurelia H. Howells, Nov. 1, 1896, in Howells, *Selected Letters*, 4: 133.

closing factories, laying off workers, and more—in the case of a Bryan victory, but such threats were not new, and given the high turnout and the secret ballot in most of the North probably not particularly effective. Urban workers had their own reasons for showing little enthusiasm for a largely agrarian, free-silver, and evangelical campaign.[70]

The campaign had stirred the nation. Despite the new registration laws and suppression of black votes in the South, the turnout was tremendous. In the bitterly contested Midwest—Indiana, Iowa, Michigan, Ohio, and Illinois—95 percent of the eligible voters turned out. McKinley gained the largest percentage of the popular vote, 51 percent, since Grant. He swept the Midwest and even gained North Dakota in the Middle Border. He carried California and Oregon and took four border states. He dominated the cities, even New York City. He took 271 electoral votes to Bryan's 176.[71]

As in many American campaigns, a switch of a relatively small number of votes in key states could have changed the outcome. If Bryan had drawn a little under twenty thousand extra votes spread over six states—California, Delaware, Indiana, Kentucky, Oregon, and West Virginia—he would have carried the electoral vote. But this provided him with little solace. He had lost the popular vote badly, and he had lost the electoral vote. In the Midwest, where he staked his hopes for victory, he had not carried a single state.[72]

IV

In and of itself, the Republican triumph in 1896 could seem merely another violent swing of the pendulum, in which angry voters had rejected the party in power. But this election was different. As the middle-of-the-road Populists had warned, loading the hope for a "producer's republic" onto a Bryan candidacy meant taking a tremendous chance. The Populists as a separate party did not disappear, but they were thereafter a shadow of themselves. They had no strong organization, and the reform press on which they depended dwindled. Eugene Debs became a socialist, and part of the hopes of antimonopoly followed him there. Reform was hardly dead. What had died was the transformative dreams of the Knights, the Farmers' Alliance, and Populists.[73]

---

70. Sanders, 143–46, 155; Williams, *Realigning America*, 150–51; Kazin, 76–78.
71. Williams, *Realigning America*, 149–50.
72. Sanders, 146–47; Kazin, 78–79.
73. Kazin, 79; I accept the persistence of antimonopoly reform, and thus agree with Sanders, 1.

The 1896 Presidential Election

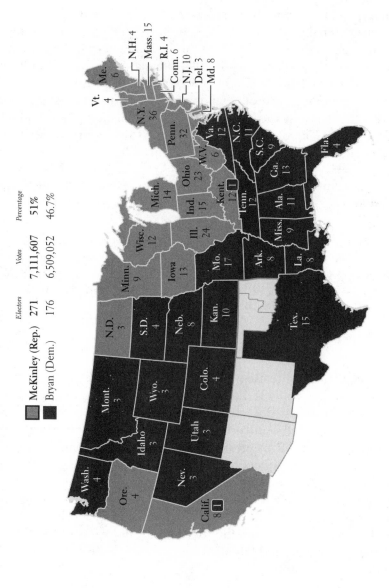

	Electors	Votes	Percentage
■ McKinley (Rep.)	271	7,111,607	51%
■ Bryan (Dem.)	176	6,509,052	46.7%

Wash. 4
Ore. 4
Calif. 8 ①
Nev. 3
Idaho 3
Utah 3
Mont. 3
Wyo. 3
Colo. 4
N.D. 3
S.D. 4
Neb. 8
Kan. 10
Tex. 15
Minn. 9
Iowa 13
Mo. 17
Ark. 8
La. 8
Wisc. 12
Ill. 24
Ind. 15
Mich. 14
Ohio 23
Kent. 12
Tenn. 12 ①
Miss. 9
Ala. 11
Ga. 13
S.C. 9
N.C. 11
Fla. 4
W.Va. 6
Va. 12
Penn. 32
N.Y. 36
Vt. 4
Me. 6
N.H. 4
Mass. 15
R.I. 4
Conn. 6
N.J. 10
Del. 3
Md. 8

Nor was the pendulum about to swing back to the Democrats any time soon. The old ethnocultural balance of American politics had toppled. The election of 1894 had begun to solidify a critical realignment first noticeable in the state elections of 1893. The new alignment came less from mass changes in party loyalty, although there was party switching in the chaotic years between 1893 and 1897, and more from a combination of the ability of the Republicans to mobilize new voters and remobilize voters they had temporarily lost, and the decreasing ability of Democrats to muster their voters. In the mid-1890s the Republicans doubled the Democratic recruitment rate among new voters. Both parties kept their base, but the Democratic base grew smaller and less active. The Northeast and eastern sections of the Midwest led the movement into the Republican Party. Not until 1932 would the Democrats again take a majority of the congressional or presidential vote.[74]

Despite the mass turnout of 1896, fewer people would vote in the new electoral system taking shape in the 1890s. The Populists failed in the South, but they had terrified the Southern Bourbons, whose solution was to disenfranchise blacks through legal restrictions modeled after those in Mississippi and to partially extend them to poor whites through the poll tax. This did not end Southern antimonopolism, but it guaranteed that only virulently racist antimonopolism thrived among Southern Democrats. Tom Watson now advocated black disenfranchisement. He became a U.S. senator. Men who had collaborated in the murder of black people and embraced antimonopolism also sat in the U.S. Congress or in governors' chairs. The Bourbons could not eliminate their enemies, but they could curb them. In a strong antimonopolist state like Texas, voting rates fell precipitously.[75]

But more than Southern reaction was at work. The decrease in turnout was also due to electoral reforms such as those the Republicans pushed through in New York: registration laws, restrictions on naturalization, the Australian ballot, and literacy tests. These were intended to cut electoral participation, and they did. Another part of the decline arose from the declining competitiveness of the parties and demise of the old army campaigns. It became harder to mobilize voters. The country became an almost solidly Democratic South and, once the impact of the 1896 campaign faded, a Republican North, Midwest, and West. In 1896 Bryan had mobilized rural votes, but the Democrats' share of the votes in the cities had declined. By 1900 the Democratic rural gains had largely evaporated,

74. Kleppner, 71, 82, 89.
75. C. Vann Woodward, *Tom Watson: Agrarian Rebel* (New York: Oxford University Press, 1963), 370–71.

Turnout in National General Elections
Voting-Eligible Population Turnout Rates, 1789–2014

Sources: Stanley and Niemi, *Vital Statistics on American Politics*; Michael P. McDonald, United States Elections Project, University of Florida.

and Democratic advances in the Middle Border, Great Plains, and Mountain states proved transient. They faded with the silver issue. Republican urban gains, on the other hand, proved solid. By 1898 Republicans controlled nearly 70 percent of the non-Southern states. Republican dominance had been restored. About 34 percent of those who voted for Bryan in 1896 voted for McKinley in 1900.[76]

Republican dominance, however, was not synonymous with corporate dominance or the defeat of antimonopoly, which was bigger and more catholic than Populism or free silver. In California, Collis Huntington of the Southern Pacific rejoiced at Bryan's defeat. He thought Bryan "an unsafe man...on the worst platform probably ever made by any civilized nation." But the Southern Pacific's own political machine, "the Octopus," which had briefly dominated California, was in shambles. Despite heavy lobbying, bribery, and the mustering of political friends, the Southern Pacific had failed to win the legislation Huntington needed to secure Santa Monica harbor for the railroad. William Randolph Hearst had hired Ambrose Bierce, as fierce a satirist as the country possessed, to cover Huntington's attempts to win legislation in Congress, and Bierce had pilloried him. "Of our modern Forty Thieves," he wrote, "Mr. Huntington is

76. Kleppner, 26, 33, 63–78, 82, 224; Richard J. Jensen, *The Winning of the Midwest: Social and Political Conflict, 1888–1896* (Chicago: University of Chicago Press, 1971), 306–8.

the surviving 36." McKinley had won California, but the only congress-man supporting Huntington's bills lost. Huntington's operatives told him that of the six congressman elected in California in 1896, five were hostile to the Southern Pacific and the other one was "leery."[77]

The immediate fruits of antimonopolism's regional triumphs in 1896 proved limited. The Democratic-Populist sweep of much of the West failed to yield a harvest of reform legislation on the state level. In Kansas, the Populists controlled the Senate, but reform legislation on railroads, finance, and taxation went there to die. The large majority of Populist senators maintained their principles and devotion to the Populist Platform, although a minority of Populist senators, largely fusionists chosen to at-tract non-Populist voters, united with Democrats and Republicans to kill the legislation.[78]

In North Carolina, too, antimonopoly triumphed as the state-level fusion ticket of Republicans and Populists triumphed. It was the kind of victory that struck horror into the hearts of Southern Bourbons, and in 1898 a bloody horror was the result. The precipitating incident was an ed-itorial on interracial sex in the *Wilmington Daily Record*, edited by a black Republican. It made the same points that Ida Wells had been making for years: many interracial sexual relationships were consensual. This was read as a slander on white women. A white mob destroyed the offending press, murdered ten black men, and drove the remaining black Republican leaders out of town. Agrarian reform in North Carolina and elsewhere in the South would not vanish, but interracial reform alliances survived, largely among women.[79]

The new political system went beyond simple realignment. It was as regionally divided as the system that had emerged following 1876, but it showed less intense party loyalty outside the South. More voters split their tickets while voting than in the period following the Civil War, and such behavior was a sign that the passionate connection between identity and political affiliation was fraying.[80]

77. Richard White, *Railroaded: The Transcontinentals and the Making of Modern America* (New York: Norton, 2011), 450–52.
78. Peter H. Argersinger, "Populists in Power: Public Policy and Legislative Behavior," *Journal of Interdisciplinary History* 18, no. 1 (Summer 1987): 81–105; Argersinger, *Structure, Process, and Party: Essays in American Political History* (Armonk, NY: Sharpe, 1992), 206–8.
79. Glenda Elizabeth Gilmore, *Gender and Jim Crow: Women and the Politics of White Supremacy in North Carolina, 1896–1920* (Chapel Hill: University of North Carolina Press, 1996), 105–13; this is the argument of Elizabeth Sanders, 148ff.
80. Kleppner, 31–44, 46, 65–67, 81–82, 84, 86.

A third major change, one for which Bryan deserves much of the credit, reflected a shift in attitudes toward governance. The Populists had been a party of government activism and intervention, as well as democratization of governance. Bryan's charge that the Republicans were the party of corporate power and monopoly had an element of truth, but a deeper truth was that the Republicans had long been the party of government intervention and public welfare, which is one reason the Mugwumps had proved so restless within it. It was the party of corporate subsidies, of the tariff, and increasingly of an expanded military. It was also the party of the pension, of federal protection of civil rights against state attempts to limit them, and, less successfully, of federal monitoring of public morals. The Democrats had been the party of localism and of minimal federal power. Such Democrats remained, but after 1896 they did not dominate the Democratic Party, which under Bryan sponsored government intervention to improve the well-being of the mass of citizens.[81]

Few American elections had the drama of 1896; few since 1860 had taken on the air of a great crusade. The results were both anticlimactic and profound. The political structure had shifted under Americans' feet, but unlike 1860 no great struggle or immediately apparent change followed. Antimonopolism, which drove so many of the reforms of the Gilded Age, melted away as a separate party and as distinct factions within the old parties. Antimonopolists adjusted to new conditions and became a component of what would emerge as progressivism. The great symbolic issue of the election, the gold standard, lost its salience, in part because its practical significance lessened. The gold standard continued to be clumsy and unsustainable, but in the historical moment it survived because gold discoveries first in South Africa and then in the Klondike in 1896 dramatically increased supplies of that metal, easing deflationary pressures.[82]

It took time to recognize more-profound changes. The substructure of politics and the economy took on a new shape. Like the economic movement from producer goods to consumer goods and the Great Merger Movement, which signaled a new corporate dominance, the political system had realigned. The two parties remained, but in ideology, membership, and strength both differed from what they had been before. These realigned parties and the progressivism that came to dominate both of them were something new, but they were also children of the Gilded Age and could not be understood outside of it.

---

81. Sanders, 152; Kazin, 79.
82. For Klondike, see Kathryn Morse, *The Nature of Gold: An Environmental History of the Klondike Gold Rush* (Seattle: University of Washington Press, 2003).

Conclusion

At the end of the Gilded Age, as at its beginning, it was hard to escape Abraham Lincoln; he was everywhere in memorials, statues, and speeches. By the early twentieth century, he would be carried in every American purse and pocket, his image gracing the Lincoln penny. What he had achieved in 1865 remained intact. Under his leadership, the United States had ended slavery and maintained the Union.

Lincoln's Union had grown and expanded even beyond his dreams. Its symbolic center was no longer Springfield, but rather Chicago. Between the beginning of Lincoln's presidency and the end of the century, the country's population had gone from about 31 million to 76 million, and its gross domestic product had increased from $69 billion to $320 billion. In a generation, the United States had taken possession of the western part of the continent, which it had claimed but hardly controlled, and transformed it from Indian country into American states, territories, and a set of constantly shrinking Indian reservations.[1]

Yet the ubiquitous Lincoln of the *fin de siècle* United States was also a strangely diminished figure because his, and the Republicans', ambitions had been far greater than mere growth. They intended to create a free-labor republic of independent producers who shared a homogeneous national citizenship with rights guaranteed by the federal government, whose authority stretched from the Atlantic to the Pacific. Americans would continue to reference Lincoln to understand the end of slavery and their continental republic, but the republic he imagined at the end of the war had not been realized. The guarantee that freedpeople would enjoy rights equal to those of white citizens had proven largely empty. Despite the ex-slaves' successful resistance to the restoration of gang labor and

1. Table Ca9–19 — Gross domestic product: 1790–2002, table Aa1–5 — Population, population density, and land area: 1790–2000, in *Historical Statistics of the United States, Earliest Times to the Present: Millennial Edition*, ed. Scott Sigmund Gartner, Susan B. Carter, Michael R. Haines, Alan L. Olmstead, Richard Sutch, and Gavin Wright (New York: Cambridge University Press, 2006).

their impressive political mobilization, Reconstruction had not achieved its larger ambitions, having been undermined by stubborn racial prejudice and overwhelmed by terror and violence.

Jane Addams wrote that Lincoln had "cleared the title to our democracy," but Americans had grown less democratic than they had been at the passage of the Fifteenth Amendment. Most black men had been disenfranchised, and Addams, like all but a few Western women, was still denied the vote. Attempts to restrict suffrage, not expand it, were everywhere apparent in the 1890s.[2]

With slavery in its grave, Americans had imagined a largely egalitarian society emerging from the war. They feared and distrusted the dangerous classes—the very rich and the very poor—but both had grown. The original ambition of free labor was not great wealth but rather a competence attainable by all who were burdened by neither horrendous bad luck nor moral failure. The grail of their society's success remained for them, as it had been for Lincoln, the home, the cornerstone of the republic. All Americans would coexist in a largely Protestant world of independent work, a world of small farms and businesses with a flourishing countryside and idyllic small towns. But in the 1890s, the United States was less egalitarian and less a country of independent producers than it had been in the immediate aftermath of the Civil War. Workers everywhere in the nation feared a loss of independence.

Liberals had believed that laissez-faire, contract freedom, and competition would eliminate corruption, sustain independent production, and prevent the rise of the very rich and very poor. Contract freedom quickly revealed itself as a delusion when those negotiating contracts were so incommensurate in wealth and power.

Liberalism had been forged in opposition to a world of slavery, established religion, monarchy, and aristocracy, and the victory of liberals in that contest sealed their own doom. They assumed that once the necessary work of destruction was done, the new world would emerge under their guidance, as they supervised the working out of eternal laws of nature, the market, and society. They expected a self-regulating order and got near chaos. In opposition, liberalism had been active, creative, and progressive. With its old enemies largely vanquished, it had grown sclerotic and rigid.

Those Republicans descended from the Whigs partially filled the vacuum liberals created. Liberal ideas of the minimal state and free markets had played a negligible role in a Civil War that had created the Yankee Leviathan, the most powerful federal government that the country

2. Jane Addams, *Twenty Years at Hull-House* (New York: Macmillan, 1911), 42.

had ever seen, and fueled a policy of state-subsidized internal development. Following the war, the Republican mixture of Whiggish ideas advocating a key role for the government in stimulating the economy and producing prosperity with liberal ideas advocating laissez-faire and a minimal state had proved paradoxical.

The paradox produced a vibrant and expansive capitalism that proceeded with considerable public aid. The Homestead Act, the Mining Law of 1872, the railroad land grants, the tariff, and the Morrill Act all either facilitated the rapid distribution of public resources into private hands or protected favored industries. The federal government eliminated, by force when necessary, the obstacles Indian peoples threw in the way of development, which came at their expense. Government on all levels often determined the outcome of conflicts between labor and business, with the federal government increasingly coming down on the side of employers by the end of the century. Federal monetary and banking policy favored some areas of the country and some kinds of production over others. There were vigorous attempts at government regulation to correct inequities, but by the 1890s the courts were invalidating many of them.

Regular Republicans contributed to American growth, but they controlled it no more than the liberals did. The question of who did control the industrial Gilded Age world, which was most visible in the cities, where immiseration and environmental crisis contrasted with size, technology, and gaudy wealth, produced constant dispute. Antimonopolists at their most conspiratorial thought it was bankers and plutocrats, but anyone who has spent much time in their correspondence gets the sense of men riding an avalanche that they could neither control nor stop. Charles Francis Adams dismissed them as mere money-getters and traders, for good reason. It might seem that in this great age of invention and innovation, it was the inventors who pushed society forward. But Thomas Edison served more as a symbol of invention and less as the thing itself. Actual invention resulted from the hands and minds of tens of thousands of American tinkerers and mechanics. Invention proved to be cumulative and cooperative; it was one element of Howells's sufficiency of the common.

Once under way, American industrialization exerted a gravitational pull that drew in people from Europe, Asia, and North America; it unleashed forces that remade the continent. New technologies, new methods of production, and new ways of organizing work could not be traced to a single hand or mind; they were literally the work of millions. Those millions did not work as one; they split into identifiable classes whose struggles spawned social conflicts that wracked the society. As liberalism and Republican variants of a state-sponsored capitalism proved inadequate to these conflicts, Americans endeavored to find new ways of thinking about society and politics that might explain and contain them.

Intellectuals who in the twentieth century became pragmatists proved the most astute, and in many ways sympathetic, critics of the liberals. They acknowledged their debt to liberalism even as they broke with it. When he published *Pragmatism* in the early twentieth century, William James recognized that pragmatists inherited from liberals the reverence for facts that had produced the American Social Science Association. He also acknowledged Spencer's "fearful array of insufficiencies. His dry schoolmaster temperament, the hurdy-gurdy monotony of him, his preference for cheap makeshifts in argument, his lack of education even in mechanical principles, and in general the vagueness of all his fundamental ideas, his whole system wooden, as if knocked together out of cracked hemlock boards...."[3]

In 1891 John Dewey was more generous to Matthew Arnold, but then Arnold, far more than Spencer, had comprehended the utterly disorienting turn modernity took as Darwinism challenged divine creation and divine order. Evangelicals struggled to salvage that order, but religious dogma could no longer obtain a consensus on truth. The search for authority and meaning amid "the agnosticism, the doubt, the pessimism of the present day" preoccupied Dewey. He took as foundational text Arnold's couplet:

> Wandering between two worlds, one dead
> The other powerless to be born.

Yet for all Dewey's admiration of Arnold, he rejected what he called Arnold's "consciousness of a twofold isolation of man—his isolation from nature, his isolation from fellow-man." Arnold and other nineteenth-century liberals could not move beyond "the old isolated struggle of the individual."[4]

Dewey regarded "Mr. Arnold's interpretation of life" as "partial"; he thought "a deeper and more adventurous love of wisdom, should find community below all isolation." Dewey emphasized instead "a common idea, a common purpose, in nature and in man." John Patrick Diggins later saw in Dewey the emotional origins of pragmatism "as an effort to

3. William James, "A Defence of Pragmatism," *Popular Science Monthly* 70 (March 1907): 206.
4. John Dewey, "Poetry and Philosophy," *Andover Review* 16, no. 92 (August 1891): 108–10.

overcome the negations of modernism," which Diggins defined as the consciousness "of what was once presumed to be present and is now seen as missing."[5]

Antimonopoly in all its forms struggled to find common purpose, which seemed to have vanished. The antimonopolists substituted community for individualism and cooperation for competition, but the immediate political, economic, and social results of their efforts yielded increased conflict. If the Columbian Exposition reflected a dream of common meaning and common purpose, then the turmoil that followed in the streets of Chicago indicated a reality of division, disagreement, and struggle.

Trying to understand the meaning of the changes that she saw all around her in Chicago during the Pullman Strike of 1894 sent Jane Addams to the statue of Lincoln in Chicago's Lincoln Park. Cast in bronze by Augustus St. Gaudens in 1887, the statue caused critics to gush over both the bronze Lincoln and Lincoln the man. The *Century's* art critic, M. G. van Rensselaer, wrote that Lincoln possessed a mind that was "a very synonym for practical good sense; yet it was the mind of a poet, a prophet, too, and beneath it lay the heart of a child and the tender instincts of a woman." Father Abraham, without ceasing to be the symbol of masculine self-making, had also become the mother and child of the Republic. He had become both protean and reduced. To be everything to everyone, he had been largely emptied of historical content, and more than that, the failures of his vision, as well as the larger Republican vision, for the country had to be ignored.[6]

St. Gaudens's statue stood in a Chicago Lincoln would not have recognized. Lincoln's Republicans had courted immigrants, particularly Germans, but he had not envisioned most of the people who lived around Hull House as Americans. He had not foreseen the size of the factories in which they worked, nor the poverty that he had thought would be banished with the end of slavery. He had assumed that the material abundance pouring from American farms, factories, mines, and shops would translate into general prosperity. Lincoln believed that political freedom ensured a general prosperity and a general equality; all around Addams, as she walked to Lincoln Park, was evidence that it had not and did not. The differences extended to material things. Lincoln inhabited a world of wood, stone, and iron; they persisted, but Chicago was becoming a city of steel. Its grime and smoke bespoke the steam and coal that powered

5. John P. Diggins, *The Promise of Pragmatism: Modernism and the Crisis of Knowledge and Authority* (Chicago: University of Chicago Press, 1994), 7–8; Dewey, 112, 114.
6. M. G. van Rensselaer, "Saint Gaudens's Lincoln," *Century Illustrated Magazine* (November 1887): 37.

astonishing and productive machines whose effects were not always as intended.

Yet Addams was not willing to let Lincoln go. Her father had known the martyred president, and Hull House annually celebrated Lincoln's birthday. Addams knew she had to work to make Lincoln relevant in industrial and immigrant Chicago. She sought to perpetuate Lincoln's memory among people from Eastern and Southern Europe, largely Catholics and Jews, in what Lincoln had assumed would always be an overwhelmingly Protestant country. Lincoln mattered because Addams thought he had secured democracy and "democratic government, associated as it is with all mistakes and shortcomings of the common people, still remains the most valuable contribution America has made to the moral life of the world."[7]

"World" was a revealing word. Others placed Lincoln at the center of a national story, but Addams also placed him and the United States at the center of a global story. The very plot of the national story was at stake at the end of the nineteenth century. Grant's *Memoirs* and Hay and Nicolay's *Abraham Lincoln* made the Civil War the centerpiece of the American narrative, the axis on which it turned. Slavery had been the original sin of the American experiment, the cause of the rebellion, and the Civil War. Lincoln regarded that sin as national, but the more partisan Republican story placed the blame for the Civil War firmly on the South. Grant wrote that although he did not rejoice at the suffering of the South, whose soldiers had fought valiantly, their cause was "one of the worst for which a people ever fought, and one for which there was the least excuse." In 1888 the Blue-Gray reunion at Gettysburg had drawn few Southerners, and the editor of a Union veterans' journal cautioned against the "God-knows-who-was-right bosh...the men who won the victory there were eternally right, and the men who were defeated were eternally wrong." As the "Battle Hymn of the Republic" had it, Lincoln and the Union soldiers did God's work: "As he died to make men holy, Let us live to make men free."[8]

The meaning of the Civil War became contested. St. Gaudens, the sculptor of the softened Lincoln, complained to Richard Watson Gilder, the editor of the *Century*, that the installments of *Abraham Lincoln* appearing in his magazine had become too partisan. Gilder, in turn, urged Hay and

---

7. Addams, 42; Richard Wightman Fox, *Lincoln's Body: A Cultural History* (New York: Norton, 2015), 177–78.
8. Ulysses S. Grant, *Personal Memoirs of U.S. Grant* (New York: C. L. Webster, 1886), 2: 489; David W. Blight, *Race and Reunion: The Civil War in American Memory* (Cambridge, MA: Belknap Press of Harvard University Press, 2001), 203–8.

Nicolay to omit passages that might offend in coming installments and "to err on the side of calmness of tone and generosity."[9]

Gilder's strictures encouraged a literature that emphasized reconciliation and reunion. As Union veterans aged, their memories became nostalgic. As historian David Blight has put it, Union veterans held fast to the idea that they were "the saviors, the deliverers of the nation—that the republic had survived and been renewed by their blood." Confederates, for their part, threw out the actual history of the rebellion: "they had never fought for slavery, never really engaged in 'rebellion' at all." The Lost Cause had been a struggle for independence and was overwhelmed only by the greater numbers and resources of the North. Secession, slavery, and Reconstruction virtually vanished from this account. Whites commemorated the war as a white man's struggle. In memoirs, speeches at veterans' encampments, commemorations, and inscriptions on monuments, the myths of the war gradually eroded its history. This was the sanitized Lincoln and the sad but rosy past that gripped Jane Addams in Lincoln Park.[10]

The Lost Cause could never be a national story, and Clarence King, Frederick Jackson Turner, Buffalo Bill Cody, and others created an alternate narrative that resurrected free labor, restored its whiteness, relocated it to the West, and offered an account of homemaking and nation building. During the Gilded Age the Midwest had emerged literally and figuratively as the heartland of the country. Lincoln was a Midwesterner, as was Addams. Her contemporaries replaced the Lincoln of avenging Union armies with Lincoln the pioneer, and they made westering, interrupted but not diverted by the Civil War, the great story of the republic. Westering had created the Midwest, and now it continued in the trans-Missouri West. Those who went West often carried the Civil War with them, but in this telling the West became a refuge from the Civil War. Free labor would be judged not in the South or North, but in the West. In this story the threat to American homemaking continued to come, as it always had, from "savages," who would be vanquished. "Savage," a wonderfully capacious word, expanded to include immigrant workers. Southerners resumed their place among the ranks of the pioneers.[11]

9. John Taliaferro, *All the Great Prizes: The Life of John Hay from Lincoln to Roosevelt* (New York: Simon & Schuster, 2013), 250–51.

10. Blight, 164, 174–78, 189–90, 198–99.

11. Ibid., 164; William Deverell, "Redemption Falls Short: Soldier and Surgeon in the Post–Civil War Far West," in *Civil War Wests: Testing the Limits of the United States*, ed. Adam Arenson and Andrew R. Graybill (Oakland: University of California Press, 2015), 139–57; Clarence King, "The Biographers of Lincoln," *Century* 32 (Oct. 1886): 861–69.

Addams felt the pull of the new stress on forgiveness and reconciliation, but she stressed class rather than sectional conflict and American connections with the world from which the immigrants came. She visited the St. Gaudens statue, after all, to find solace and meaning in a period of class strife and violence; she sought an equivalency between the great sectional struggle of the Civil War and the industrial struggles of the 1890s, which Chicago knew so intimately. Halsted Street, where Hull House stood, had been the site of bloody fighting during the Great Strike of 1877. She walked near Haymarket on her way to the park, with troops and marshals brought in to break the Pullman Strike still filling the streets of Chicago. She wanted Lincoln, matured in a struggle to save the Union, to speak to her about the struggle over the shape of the Union that raged all around her. She wanted lessons on how to act and what to do. She quoted Lincoln's "immortal words...cut into the stone at his feet" at the base of the statue as a message to "a distracted town." She compared the "irrepressible conflict" raging between classes in Chicago with the "irrepressible conflict" of the Civil War. The lesson she derived from Lincoln was "with charity towards all," a noble lesson to be sure, but an oddly anodyne and timeless one from a man who was so very much of his time.[12]

Addams's view of the world sprang from a long American strain of providential thinking in which the United States was in, but not really of, the world. It gave, but rarely received. It was the country of the future, a place less enmeshed in the messy quarrels of other nations than a shining example of what the world would become. This was American exceptionalism, but in the Gilded Age exceptionalism seemed less naïve and innocent than dangerous. In it, as in Clarence King's version, ties to the larger world through immigration became threatening, and immigrants alien and destructive. Exceptionalism was the stuff of political campaigns; only a fool would rely on it to govern. The United States was enmeshed in the same messy industrial modernity as other countries. The hodgepodge of languages and customs on the streets of Chicago, the multiplicity of beliefs, the way the economy rose and fell with distant events, the ideas Americans absorbed from abroad and those they exported, all spoke to their connections with a world beyond American borders.

Henry Adams recognized that changes in Europe and the United States were linked. In his cynical way, he thought that American superiority consisted in lagging behind England and France in a march that would "change...our institutions at last to a pure monied regime." The United States was not a savior, only a laggard: "The essential problem is not changed. That belongs to the whole world, and we can do little to solve it.

12. Fox, 177–78; Addams, 32–34.

We are at most an outlying province of Europe, and in the long run we must follow where Europe goes. At present, I admit, she seems to me to be going to the devil, and dragging us after her; but such a race is apt to be a long one."[13]

Few besides Adams were ready to see America's fate in a Europe that the nation had always defined itself against. Jane Addams assumed there was a goal to American history, something Henry Adams could not discern, and she thought Lincoln's greatness consisted of his ability "to make clear beyond denial to the American people themselves, the goal towards which they were moving." That was an eloquent truth for 1865, when the goal for the victorious Union was the free-labor republic, but there was no similar common goal in the 1890s. Prosperity lacked a comparable resonance.[14]

William Dean Howells, like Addams, turned to Lincoln as a compass in order to chart American direction. This was what brought him to his conclusion that "If America means anything at all, it means the sufficiency of the common, the insufficiency of the uncommon."[15]

Relatively few others subscribed to the sufficiency of the common in the Gilded Age. Liberals would have no part of it, and neither would nativists nor many evangelical reformers. The people were diverse, rambunctious, and disorderly; they often hated each other. The well-to-do and middle classes feared the vibrant, dirty, tumultuous, and sometimes violent world around them. Judges tried to quell the poor, workers, angry farmers, and the reforms their advocates passed. American voters elected officials who disappointed them, and whom the country often ridiculed as hopelessly corrupt and venal.

Howells knew all that. He had been, through the 1870s, a leading liberal critic of the common, but two decades later he tentatively embraced a country where he believed that important things bubbled up rather than trickling down. This was the opposite of the world Matthew Arnold, Andrew Carnegie, and Charles Eliot Norton proposed. It was a working-class and middle-class world. It was a country of the shop, the common school, the church, the local community, the neighborhood, the labor union, the daily press, and the vast array of voluntary organizations that mobilized people and pushed reforms. It was a striving world that produced and nurtured American mechanics, evangelicals, Masons, and vernacular intellectuals.

13. H. Adams to Lucy Baxter, Oct. 27, 1896, in Henry Adams, *The Letters of Henry Adams*, ed. J. C. Levenson (Cambridge, MA: Belknap Press, 1982), 4: 435–36.
14. Addams, 27–38.
15. "Editor's Study," February 1891, in William Dean Howells, *Editor's Study*, ed. James W. Simpson (Troy, NY: Whitston, 1983), 298.

In different ways, Horatio Alger, Herbert Spencer, and to a lesser degree William Graham Sumner tried to disguise this America, reducing it to a seedbed for successful individuals. They took what was a social garden and noticed only the most flourishing plants. They treated Thomas Edison and Booker T. Washington as the victors in some inchoate struggle for existence, ignoring the soil that nurtured them. Edison ultimately was an extraordinarily able mechanic who organized a particularly successful shop before becoming a not particularly able businessman. Washington was the product of freedmen's thirst for education following the Civil War and a man whose goal was to provide an education, even if diminished to manual education, to others. In celebrating the shop, the home, and the church, all of them cooperative entities, most Americans embraced versions of cooperation and not unbridled individualism. Frances Willard, with her embrace of "Gospel Socialism," rather than Elizabeth Cady Stanton, who remained an unreconstructed liberal individualist, was the representative figure for women's rights and female reform.

The tension between individualism and cooperation and community was apparent in a talk that Frederick Douglass gave fifty times, and probably more, between 1859 and 1893. He entitled it "Self-Made Men," and it doubtless went through multiple iterations. It began as a paean to great men, with its moral the opposite of Howells's celebration of the sufficiency of the common. In other speeches and writings of the 1870s, Douglass understood his own life as an exercise in will, individualism, and self-making. Self-reliance became the keystone of his own self-presentation and his prescription for freedpeople. Work, self-discipline, and ambition produced great men, and "Self-Made Men," probably even more so in its earliest versions, echoed Ralph Waldo Emerson's "Self-Reliance."[16]

A copy of what must have been the final version of "Self-Made Men" is contained in Douglass's published papers. He delivered it to Indian students at Carlisle Indian School in 1893. The speech reflected his long intellectual journey. He was not willing to surrender free labor's concepts of individualism and manhood, but by the 1890s he had redefined them, and in doing so partially subverted them. He admitted that no men were purely self-made; individuals were as waves upon an ocean.[17]

16. I want to thank David Blight, who allowed me to read parts of his forthcoming biography of Frederick Douglass in manuscript. The material on Douglass after the Civil War owes much to his work. David W. Blight, *Frederick Douglass* (New York: Simon & Schuster, forthcoming).

17. "'Self-Made Men,' An Address Delivered in Carlisle Pennsylvania in March, 1893," in *The Frederick Douglass Papers: Series One, Speeches, Debates, and Interviews* (New Haven, CT: Yale University Press, 1979), 5: 545–75.

Douglass embraced the idea of free and equal competition. He praised labor and said all that black people deserved was fair play and a chance to improve themselves. But he also said, "It is not fair play to start the negro out in life, from nothing and with nothing, while others start with the advantage of a thousand years behind them." He implicitly embraced the old idea of a competence, rejecting Carnegie's Spencerian view of progress in which great wealth was the seed of civilization's progress and the results of the workings of natural law. He reached a very different conclusion about the relationship between personal success and larger social obligations, which, Gilded Age figure that he was, he would have defined as manhood. The goal of an individual's life should not be wealth or fame, but personal, family, and neighborhood well-being. The speech could only have arisen out of the free-labor vision whose individualism it subverted and found inadequate. In this, Douglass resembled Addams and Howells. The speech's final irony was that he delivered it to an audience of Indian students, to whom free labor was an ideology of conquest and forced transformation.

By *cooperation* Americans bent on reform initially meant voluntary social combinations, but they increasingly meant government. Evangelical reformers moved away from suasion and turned to the government to suppress drink, eliminate polygamy, and remove vice. Members of the Farmers' Alliance recognized that cooperative enterprises could succeed only with changes in laws and government aid giving cooperatives at least the same advantages corporations received. Antimonopolists, the largest and broadest of the era's reform groupings, turned to government to regulate railroads, reform the monetary system, and secure what they regarded as the legacy that could be salvaged from free labor.

The turn to government involved far more than just an increase in the role and power of government; the form of American governance was changing during the Gilded Age. The large powers granted the government beginning with the Civil War had always seemed less than they were because of lack of administrative capacity. They depended on fee-based governance, bounties, subsidies, and delegations of power for their execution. This gave appointed officials an interest in those administrative functions that yielded them a profit. Fee-based governance, subsidy, and delegation contributed to the very real corruption of the Gilded Age. Government converted public goods into private assets, with public officials often receiving private favors in exchange for those goods. It employed appointed officials whose search for fees and bounties led to widespread abuse and rent seeking.

There was a strong popular reaction against fee-based administration. Government was not a business. Citizens were not customers. A republican government could not serve only those citizens who yielded officials the greatest profit. Citizens were due equal treatment, and no group of Americans should be allowed to monopolize public services. The reaction encouraged the expansion of salaried administrators. Antimonopolists defined society as a clash of organized classes and interests, and the legitimacy of democratic government—and thus public compliance with the law—demanded that officials honor all legitimate interest group claims to public resources and not just the claims of those able to pay for them. Public officials had to be subject to democratic will, as expressed through Congress and legislatures, and not be available for purchase.[18]

Behind the sound and fury of the era's election campaigns, basic changes in governance took shape. The changing administrative capacity of the government, the gradual shift from fee-based governance to salaried administrators, the gradual development of increasingly detailed administrative law and procedures within government departments, and the growing role of the courts, for better or worse, were great hidden stories of the Gilded Age. The result was not the kind of expert bureaucracy free from democratic influence that liberals desired. The actual system proved far more complicated, and even distinctively American, suspended between popular influences in which the new bureaucracies had to cultivate constituencies and top-down administrative mandates that depended on internal rules and expertise.

The new administrative system both enabled and grew from a distinctive creation of space. Space was about movement, and how goods moved, people moved, commodities moved, and information moved depended not only on distance and technology but also on how people arranged schedules, prices, and access. It depended, too, on gender and race. As Ida Wells and Homer Plessy knew, the spaces of common carriers were not equally open to all, and as farmers complained, railroads manipulated rates to favor some and hurt others. Quarrels over the newly constructed American space were central to the age.[19]

Familiar boundaries remained, but their meanings had changed. The old states of the Union remained and new ones were added, but the powers of those states diminished because of both the enhanced, if contested, power of the federal government that came with Reconstruction amendments and the powerful corporations that operated within and

18. Nicholas R. Parrillo, *Against the Profit Motive: The Salary Revolution in American Government, 1780–1940* (New Haven, CT: Yale University Press, 2013), 360–62.
19. Mary P. Ryan, *Women in Public: Between Banners and Ballots, 1825–1880* (Baltimore, MD: Johns Hopkins University Press, 1990), 58–94; Sarah Deutsch, *Women and the City: Gender, Space, and Power in Boston, 1870–1940* (New York: Oxford University Press, 2000), 25–114.

outside their boundaries. Reconstruction expanded federal power at the expense of state power, at least in theory and often in practice. Corporations and the technologies they embodied slipped beyond the jurisdictional control of states. Railroads and steamships allowed the creation of national and international markets. In this and a thousand other ways, Americans were reconstructing the spatial parameters of the continent, determining what was near, what was far, and what was accessible and inaccessible, where authority applied and where it did not.

Where people could go and how quickly they could get there were far different in 1890 from what they had been in 1860, but movement was not equally accessible to all. Americans lived in a transnational world, though the common currents of that world—immigration, trade, the exchange of ideas, the movement of plants and animals—led to a reaction that increasingly strengthened borders and boundaries. American nationalism found expression in nativism, tariffs, and immigration restrictions.

The great pressures building in the 1890s erupted along the country's social fault lines, but what they left standing revealed an important ideological and practical agreement on the direction the country must go. The old United States of small government, localism, and independent production had vanished. Those who held most strongly to the legacy of free labor and the sanctity of independent labor and the home recognized that new means were needed to achieve them. Once the independent producer and the independent citizen had been two sides of a single coin; now wage labor and the absurdities of contract freedom had rendered the supposedly sovereign republican citizen a dependent laborer often unable to provide for and protect his home.

The practical turn to government arose most clearly in new cities like Chicago. The health and well-being of the urban home could never be fully protected by the unaided labor of husbands or the skilled housekeeping of wives. They could not guarantee pure water and clean air. They could not be sure of the removal of waste or sewage. They could not protect themselves or their children from disease. Gradually, incompletely, but relentlessly a municipal water and sewage system took shape. As judges limited the older powers of *Salus populi* employed by local governments, newer powers of municipal commissions and utilities arose. Without increased governmental powers, cities –the center of the new industrial economy—threatened to be unlivable.

The 1890s marked the tipping point in the turn toward government. In turning to government, particularly the federal government, reformers joined Whiggish Republicans and businessmen, who wanted aid and favors as well as assistance in reining in the era's destructive competition. Grover Cleveland and the Democratic Party remained the last bastion of localism and small government, but in the crisis of the 1890s even Cleveland turned to the courts and the army to crush labor, over the objections of state and local officials. When William Jennings Bryan captured the party and turned it toward reform, the ideological battle was effectively over. The older liberalism did not disappear. Liberals found their castle's keep in the judiciary, and unelected and interventionist judges battled reforms enacted by Congress and legislatures, though the fight was now between branches of the government, and not over the power of government itself. Antimonopolists and their opponents differed about what government should do and which branch should do it.

Where Henry Adams was pessimistic and cynical after the election of 1896, William Dean Howells was surprisingly hopeful. He summarized the mood of the country for *Harper's Monthly*. He compared American attitudes and hopes at the end of the Civil War to the country's current mood. He remembered the earlier outlook as rather arrogant and naïve. Americans had been sure that the free-labor republic would flourish. They were certain that with slavery erased they had perfected the republic. The ensuing years, however, had sobered them and turned them inward. They had become more inclined to self-scrutiny, fuller of experience, but not "morbid or despondent."[20]

When Howells defined "what we understand America to mean," his answer in 1897 remained Lincolnian. Whatever the answer to the American future, he thought it would be democratic and egalitarian: "We intend the good of all; that is what we understand America to mean." Current controversies and the tumultuous election of 1896 only reinforced that.

> We trust the republic with itself; that is we trust one another, and we trust one another the most implicitly when we affirm the most clamorously, one half of us, that the other half is plunging the whole of us in irreparable ruin. That is merely our way of calling all to the duty we owe to each. It is not a very dignified way, but the entire nation is in on the joke, and it is not so mischievous as it might seem.

He thought that over the course of the century American faith in the republic had only grown stronger. The founders could but believe it would work, yet it had weathered great crises and "we have found that it works."[21]

Another voice also addressed the changes of the Gilded Age and the possibilities of the future. In 1899 L. Frank Baum copyrighted what would

20. W. D. Howells, "The Modern American Mood," *Harper's New Monthly Magazine* (July 1897).
21. Ibid.

become a lasting work of American popular culture: *The Wonderful Wizard of Oz*. Baum announced in his introduction a "modernized fairy tale, in which the wonderment and joy are retained and the heart-aches and nightmares left out." In part, Baum was lying. The book began with heart-aches and nightmares and proceeded to tell the story of a quite violent journey.[22]

The book opened in "the midst of the great Kansas prairies." There lay no beneficent nature, no flourishing farms, and no return for hard work. The Middle Border had become a dystopia. The prairies were "gray," baked by the sun "into a gray mass, with little cracks running through it." Even the grass was gray. Dorothy, an orphan, lived with her Uncle Henry and Aunt Em in a small house, once painted, but the sun and rain had blistered and washed away the paint until it was as gray as its surroundings. It had a single barely furnished room with a "rusty looking cooking stove." This was the fruit of a lifetime of labor. Aunt Em had come there to live when "she was a young pretty wife," but the sun and wind had "taken the sparkle from her eyes and left them a sober gray; they had taken the red from her cheeks, and they were gray also. She was thin and gaunt, and never smiled now." Nor did Uncle Henry ever laugh: "He worked hard from morning till night and did not know what joy was." He was gray "from his long beard to his rough boots, and he looked stern and solemn, and rarely spoke."[23]

A cyclone carries Dorothy and her dog, Toto, to Oz, a "country of marvelous beauty" and a land in every way the opposite of Kansas. Dorothy, or rather her house, crushes the Wicked Witch of the East, freeing the Munchkins, whom the witch had held in bondage "making them slave for her night and day." She is welcomed as a savior, but all Dorothy wishes to do is return to Kansas, her home. Along the way she gathers figures reminiscent of the antimonopolist coalition: a farm worker (the Scarecrow), industrial workers (the Tin Man), and the Cowardly Lion (a caricature, perhaps, of Bryan and other insurgent political leaders).[24]

---

22. L. Frank Baum, *The Wonderful Wizard of Oz* (Chicago and New York: Geo. M. Hill, 1900). Introduction, no page number.

23. Ibid., 11–13.

24. Ibid., 20–23; David B. Parker, "The Rise and Fall of the Wonderful Wizard of Oz as a 'Parable on Populism,'" *Journal of the Georgia Association of Historians* 15 (1994): 49–63. This analysis is inspired by Henry Littlefield's article, but my interpretation differs from his, and I am not arguing that Baum intended the story as a parable on Populism. Parker has made clear the difficulties with any such interpretation. I do, however, think that it arose from the experience of the 1890s. Henry M. Littlefield, "The Wizard of Oz: Parable on Populism," *American Quarterly* 16, no. 1 (1964): 47–58.

The Scarecrow, who does not have a brain, explains the book's joke and its tension. He cannot "understand why you should wish to leave this beautiful country and go back to the dry, gray place you call Kansas."

"This is because you have no brains," answered the girl. "No matter how dreary and gray our homes are, we people of flesh and blood would rather live there than in any other country, be it ever so beautiful. There is no place like home."[25]

Baum gave a fairy-tale version of Howells's sufficiency of the common, but he had written a complicated fairy tale. It is a story to instill in children an appreciation for the formidable, if unrecognized, powers of the seemingly deficient, and the deficiencies of the powerful. The Scarecrow, who has no brains, turns out to be clever; the Tin Man, who has no heart, turns out to be compassionate; the Cowardly Lion turns out to be brave. Dorothy, "the Small and Meek," is far more impressive than Oz, "the Great and Terrible." And home? It is both longed for and insufficient.[26]

Dorothy does return from Oz, and the last lines of the book are "And oh, Aunt Em! I'm so glad to be at home again." But Kansas remained gray; Springfield was nowhere in sight. The Scarecrow, the Tin Man, and the Cowardly Lion, all ruling over a happy kingdom, existed only in Oz.[27]

The Wonderful Wizard of Oz turned the Gilded Age into a children's story and a parable. Baum preserved the values that Howells and antimonopolists thought would sustain the United States: cooperation, mutuality, the desire for improvement, inventiveness, and a democratic faith in the abilities of ordinary people. He tried to instill them in generations of children. But he also contrasted the hopes of what such values might yield with the Kansas of Auntie Em and Uncle Frank.

In the late twentieth century, scholars interpreted the Wizard of Oz as a parable on Populism, but Baum was probably more interested in proposing an alternative to Populism, not that different from Samuel Gompers's. Springfield might be nowhere in sight, but his Emerald City took inspiration from Chicago's White City, which he visited repeatedly. Baum himself was a traveling salesman who started a magazine entitled the *Show Window*, devoted to the art of window dressing: the artful display of goods in department stores and shop windows. The solution to the grayness of Kansas was ultimately to get out of Kansas, and, like Carrie Meeber, move to the city, strive, and shop. In the Oz books, Dorothy took Uncle Henry and Auntie Em back to Oz with her. It was, in Baum's telling, like living

25. Baum, 44–45.
26. Ibid., 127.
27. Ibid., 260.

in a department store. Consumption and desire, not production and thrift, would be the values looking forward.[28]

There were other ways forward. The hopes for improvement and reform continued to course strongly in both political parties after 1896, and they flowed toward the state. In that year, Woodrow Wilson, a reforming political scientist and president of Princeton University, delivered an address, "Princeton in the Nation's Service." He wrote it while partially paralyzed by a stroke. He began the talk by sounding like William Graham Sumner. "We cannot pretend to have formed the world," he said, "and we are not destined to reform it." But this was just a feint. He continued: "We cannot even mend it and set it forward by the reasonable measure of a single generation's work if we forget the old processes or lose our mastery over them. We should have scant capital to trade on, were we to throw away the wisdom we have inherited and seek our fortunes with the slender stock we have ourselves accumulated."[29]

As Wilson proceeded, he sounded increasingly like the Progressive he, and Theodore Roosevelt, would become. He stressed public duty, particularly a duty connected to the nation and the state. He declared that the university had an obligation to implant in citizens this sense of duty, particularly in a period of rapid social change, as well as "to illuminate duty by every lesson that can be drawn out of the past." The university could not stand apart from society.

> We must make the humanities human again; must recall what manner of men we are; must turn back once more to the region of practicable ideals. There is laid upon us the compulsion of the national life. We dare not keep aloof and closet ourselves while a nation comes to its maturity. The days of glad expansion are gone. Our life grows tense and difficult; our resource for the future lies in careful thought, providence, and a wise economy; and the school must be of the nation.[30]

Wilson was a Democrat and Roosevelt a Republican. Both were intellectuals turned to public life. They had grown to maturity in Reconstruction and the Gilded Age. Wilson had been deeply marked also by his Southern upbringing. He was racist to the core, but racism had hardly been separate from reform in the Gilded Age. Reformers had entrenched themselves in

---

28. Eli Wirtschafter, *The Wonderful Windows of Oz*, podcast audio, Counter Culture: A History of Shopping 2014, http://backstoryradio.org/shows/counter-culture.

29. Woodrow Wilson, "Princeton in the Nation's Service," in *The Papers of Woodrow Wilson*, ed. Arthur S. Link (Princeton, NJ: Princeton University Press, 1966), 10; T. J. Jackson Lears, *Rebirth of a Nation: The Making of Modern America, 1877–1920* (New York: Harper, 2009), 312–13.

30. Wilson, "Princeton in the Nation's Service."

the dominant factions of both political parties, and the fear of rising inequality, class conflict, declining well-being, and the loss of the power of ordinary citizens stirred them ever more deeply.

The Gilded Age currents still ran strong, but they had begun to shift direction. A country that imagined its natural endowment in terms of abundance had begun to think in terms of scarcity and conservation even as it paradoxically began to stress consumption over production in its economy. A country that had always thought of itself as thinly peopled began to worry about immigration. A country that had worked to keep foreign manufactures out while attracting capital began to think in terms of foreign investments and exports. Strands such as conservation and imperialism, which seemed unconnected, began to intertwine.[31]

It was time to begin again.

31. This is a leading theme of Ian R. Tyrrell, *Crisis of the Wasteful Nation: Empire and Conservation in Theodore Roosevelt's America* (Chicago: University of Chicago Press, 2015).

Bibliographical Essay

This essay describes the core scholarship that I consulted in writing this book, as well as some of the more influential earlier works on the late nineteenth century. It represents only a fraction of the sources that I used and excludes most of the primary sources consulted. It is designed for the general reader rather than the academic. I have not included much of the specialized journal literature, particularly in economics, political science, and demography. I have favored those articles that summarize the basic research. I have grouped the books and articles into a series of overlapping categories; many books span several categories, such as the city, the economy, and the environment. To save space, I have eliminated subtitles, and I have omitted most collections of essays. I have also tried to eliminate superlatives.

In framing the period and its themes, I relied heavily on Amy Dru Stanley, *From Bondage to Contract* (1998). I took the idea of the Greater Reconstruction—while altering the periodization—from Elliott West, "Reconstructing Race," *Western Historical Quarterly* 34, no. 1 (2003). I have been stealing from him for years. Political economy forms the foundation of this volume, and four books shaped my thinking about this period: Robin Einhorn, *Property Rules* (1991); Richard F. Bensel, *Yankee Leviathan* (1990); Bensel, *The Political Economy of American Industrialization, 1877–1900* (2000); and James Livingston, *Pragmatism and the Political Economy of Cultural Revolution, 1850–1940* (1994). The insistence of Mark Fiege, *The Republic of Nature* (2012), that all history involves environmental history shaped my emphasis on the great environmental crisis of the nineteenth century, and William Cronon's *Nature's Metropolis* (1991) altered my view of the world from the day it was published.

I have tried to ground this account on basic historical statistics for the period, knowing full well how tricky they can be. Scott Sigmund Gartner, Susan B. Carter, Michael R. Haines, Alan L. Olmstead, Richard Sutch, and Gavin Wright, eds., *Historical Statistics of the United States, Earliest Times to the Present: Millennial Edition* (2006) is the basic source. Also useful is Herbert S. Klein, *A Population History of the United States* (2004). Two recent articles that recalculate the impact of the Civil War are J. D. Hacker, "A

Census-Based Count of the Civil War Dead," *Civil War History* 57, no. 4 (2011); and Jim Downs, *Sick from Freedom* (2012) have dramatically revised upward the toll of the Civil War and Reconstruction.

In interpreting Reconstruction and the Gilded Age, I sought as guides people whose lives spanned the period and touched key events. The chief scout was William Dean Howells and his writings: *Selected Letters*, George Warren Arms, ed. (1979); the John Hay–Howells Letters (1979); *Years of My Youth, and Three Essays* (1975); and the collection of his columns from *Harper's, Editor's Study* (1983). Three of his novels particularly inform the text: *A Hazard of New Fortunes* (orig. ed. 1890, reprint 1965), *The Altrurian Romances* (orig. ed. 1892, reprint 1968), and *The Rise of Silas Lapham* (orig. ed., 1884, reprint 1968). A series of essays he published in the 1890s helped formulate the book's conclusion: "Who Are Our Brethren," in the *Century* magazine (April 1896); "Are We a Plutocracy?" in the *North American Review* 158 (1894); and "The Nature of Liberty," in the *Forum* 20 (December 1895). For secondary works on Howells, see William Alexander, *William Dean Howells* (1981) and Kenneth Schuyler Lynn, *William Dean Howells* (1971). I also revisited Alfred Kazin, *On Native Ground* (orig. ed. 1942, reprint 1956).

My second guide was Frances Willard, whose embrace of the home gave me one of my organizing ideas for the book. For her writings, *Writing out My Heart* (1995); *The Ideal of "the New Woman" According to the Woman's Christian Temperance Union* (1987), a compendium edited by Carolyn De Swarte Gifford; and *How to Win* (1987, orig. ed. 1886). Ruth Bordin, *Frances Willard* (1986) remains the standard biography of Willard.

Frederick Douglass figured in many of the events of the period. I relied on *The Frederick Douglass Papers* (1979–) and on William McFeely, *Frederick Douglass* (1991). David Blight generously allowed me to use portions of his draft of a major new biography of Douglass.

Henry Adams predictably emerged as a recurring presence in the book. The relevant works include *The Education of Henry Adams: An Autobiography* (1942, orig. ed. 1918); *Selected Letters of Henry Adams*, Ernest Samuels, ed. (1992); Adams, *Democracy* (1961, orig. ed. 1880); and Charles Francis Adams and Henry Adams, *Chapters of Erie and Other Essays* (1886, orig. ed. 1869). Edward Chalfant, *Better in Darkness* (1994) and *Improvement of the World* (2001) give an exhaustive account of Adams's life during these years. Patricia O'Toole, *The Five of Hearts* (1990) recreates Adams's world. Henry's life was largely inseparable from that of his wife, Clover; see Natalie Dykstra, *Clover Adams* (2012).

Francis Amasa Walker appeared at many of the critical junctures in the book as a statistician, economist, bureaucrat, and political thinker. Walker's *Discussions in Economics and Statistics* (1899); "The Indian Question," *North American Review* 116, no. 239; "The Colored Race in the United States," in the *Forum* (July 1891); and "Restriction of Immigration," *Atlantic Monthly* 77 (1896) all reveal aspects of the period. James P. Munroe, *A Life of Francis Amasa Walker* (1923) and Bernard Newton, *The Economics of Francis Amasa Walker* (1968) take on aspects of his life.

For a while the Gilded Age became the flyover country of American history, but at other times it has loomed large. There are older interpretations that I do not share but whose influence I respect. I used very little of Charles Beard and Mary Beard, *The Rise of American Civilization* (1930), but I relied on it for inspiration. I think Richard Hofstadter got very many important things wrong about the period, but there is no denying his craft as an historian and his influence, especially *The American Political Tradition* (1948, Vintage Books ed. 1954), *The Age of Reform* (1955), *Social Darwinism in American Thought* (1992), and *Anti-intellectualism in American Life* (1963). Finally, Robert Wiebe, *The Search for Order, 1877–1920* (1967) wrote an account that proved so influential that its interpretation of the period as one of nationalization, the decline of "island communities," and the rise of a professionalizing middle class reigned for years. I question large parts of his argument, but the book still stands as a daunting piece of historical writing.

This volume begins with Lincoln's funeral, and I had the good fortune to draw on Drew Gilpin Faust, *This Republic of Suffering* (2008); Martha Hodes, *Mourning Lincoln* (2015); and Richard W. Fox, *Lincoln's Body* (2015). I also used Robert Reed, *Lincoln's Funeral Train* (2002); Dorothy Kunhardt, *Twenty Days* (1965); Victor Searcher, *The Farewell to Lincoln* (1965); and Merrill D. Peterson, *Lincoln in American Memory* (1994).

Reconstruction has preoccupied my generation of American historians. W. E. B. Dubois, *Black Reconstruction* (1935) long ago laid out many of the elements of the new interpretation. Thomas Holt, *Black over White* (1977) did much to push black people to the front of Reconstruction. The scholarship of the 1970s and 1980s was extensive. Much of it focused on Reconstruction politics: Michael Les Benedict, *A Compromise of Principle* (1974) and *The Fruits of Victory* (1975); Martin E. Mantell, *Johnson, Grant, and the Politics of Reconstruction* (1973); Peter Kolchin, *First Freedom* (1972); and LaWanda Cox, *Politics, Principle, and Prejudice, 1865–1866* (1963).

The literature expanded to include economic and social history. See, for example, Leon F. Litwack, *Been in the Storm So Long* (1979); Mark W. Summers, *Railroads, Reconstruction, and the Gospel of Prosperity* (1984); and James L. Roark, *Masters without Slaves* (1977). Michael Perman's *Reunion without Compromise* (1973) and *The Road to Redemption* (1984) look at Southern reactions to Reconstruction. Roger Ransom and Richard Sutch, "Capitalists without Capital," *Agricultural History* 62, no. 3 (1988) looks at plantation owners. Mark Elliott, *Color-Blind Justice* (2006) examines Albion Tourgée, an important figure.

Eric Foner, *Reconstruction: America's Unfinished Revolution, 1863–1877* (1988) synthesized and interpreted the existing scholarship and formulated Reconstruction to achieve a second American Revolution. His book inspired much of the scholarship that followed. Subsequent local studies refined and gave variety to Reconstruction. For Louisiana, see Frank J. Wetta, *The Louisiana Scalawags* (2012); Rebecca Scott, "'Stubborn and Disposed to Stand Their Ground'," *Slavery and Abolition* 20, no. 1 (2003); and John C. Rodrigue, "Labor Militancy and Black Grassroots Political Mobilization in the Louisiana Sugar Region, 1865–1868," *Journal of Southern History* 67, no. 1 (2001). For South Carolina there is Julie Saville, *The Work of Reconstruction* (1994). For Georgia, see Lee W. Formwalt, "The Origins of African-American Politics in Southwest Georgia," *Journal of Negro History* 77, no. 4 (1992); Susan O'Donovan, *Becoming Free in the Cotton South* (2007); and Charles L. Flynn, *White Land, Black Labor* (1983). For Mississippi, see Nora Frankel, *Freedom's Women* (1999). For North Carolina, see Deborah Beckel, *Interracial Politics in Post-Emancipation North Carolina* (2011). This merely scratches the surface.

The literature has increasingly emphasized the violence of the era, which earlier scholars such as Allen W. Trelease, *White Terror* (1971) had begun to detail. See Stephen V. Ash, *A Massacre in Memphis* (2013); Giles Vandal, "Bloody Caddo," *Journal of Social History* 25, no. 2 (1991); George C. Rable, *But There Was No Peace* (1984); W. Fitzhugh Brundage, *Lynching in the New South* (1993); Hannah Rosen, *Terror in the Heart of Freedom* (2009); Carole Emberton, *Beyond Redemption* (2013); Steph Budiansky, *The Bloody Shirt* (2008); Leeanna Keith, *The Colfax Massacre* (2008); Charles Lane, *The Day Freedom Died* (2009); Michael Martinez, *Carpetbaggers, Cavalry, and the Ku Klux Klan* (2007); Scott Reynolds Nelson, *Iron Confederacies* (1999); and Lou Falkner Williams, *The Great South Carolina Ku Klux Klan Trials, 1871–1872* (1996).

Gender, largely absent from earlier literature, has become an essential analytical category. Laura F. Edwards, *Gendered Strife and Confusion* (1997); Thavolia Glymph, *Out of the House of Bondage* (2008); Carol Faulkner, *Women's Radical Reconstruction* (2006); and Faye E. Dudden, *Fighting Chance* (2011) are but a few of these studies. Others show up in different categories.

The Freedmen's Bureau had a brief life but lasting importance; see Paul A. Cimbala, *The Freedmen's Bureau* (2005); Cimbala, *Under the Guardianship of the Nation* (1997). There is also William S. McFeely, *Yankee Stepfather* (1968). For the Union League, see Michael W. Fitzgerald, *The Union League Movement in the Deep South* (1989).

Both the Freedmen's Bureau and the Union League touched deep traditions of Southern and national life, culture, and politics in quite complicated ways. See Gregory P. Downs, *Declarations of Dependence* (2011); William A. Blair, *With Malice Toward Some* (2014); Bruce Baker, Brian E. Kelly, and Eric Foner, eds., *New Perspectives on the History of the South* (2013); and Gregory Downs and Kate Masur, eds., *The World the Civil War Made* (2015). Although it reaches beyond Reconstruction, Dylan C. Penningroth, *The Claims of Kinfolk* (2003) is a particularly revealing account of African American social organization.

The explosion of literature in the years following Foner's *Reconstruction* has opened up opportunities for historians to attempt new syntheses, including Steven Hahn, *A Nation under Our Feet* (2003); Mark W. Summers, *The Ordeal of the Reunion* (2014); and the edited collection by James L. Roark, *After Slavery* (2013). Many scholars have connected Reconstruction to later twentieth-century civil rights struggles; Richard M. Valelly, *The Two Reconstructions* (2004) and J. Morgan Kousser, "The Voting Rights Act and the Two Reconstructions," in Bernard Grofman and Chandler Davidson, eds., *Controversies in Minority Voting* (1992), made the comparison explicit.

For me, the most influential of the recent books on Reconstruction has been Gregory Downs, *After Appomattox* (2015). It not only goes far beyond J. E. Sefton, *The United States Army and Reconstruction, 1865–1877* (1967) in its analysis of the military role in Reconstruction, but also offers a compelling explanation as to why and how Reconstruction retreated and failed. It should be read alongside analyses of the politics of Reconstruction, such as Andrew L. Slap, *The Doom of Reconstruction* (2006).

Two women, Mary Chesnut and Ella Thomas, provided diaries and letters that offer our most nuanced views of white life in the Reconstruction South. See Mary Boykin Miller Chesnut, *The Private Mary Chesnut* (1984); C. Vann Woodward, ed., *Mary Chesnut's Civil War* (1981); and on Ella Gertrude Clanton Thomas, see Virginia Ingraham Burr, *The Secret Eye* (1990) and Carolyn N. Curry, *Suffer and Grow Strong* (2014).

The North has long been present in Reconstruction literature but usually in a minor key. James Mohr, ed., *Radical Republicans in the North* (1976) was a significant early work. Heather Cox Richardson, *The Death of Reconstruction* (2001) and Kate Masur, *An Example for All the Land* (2010) have expanded Reconstruction's reach in the North.

The idea of a Greater Reconstruction has sparked new scholarship on Reconstruction in the West: Stacey Smith, *Freedom's Frontier* (2014); Joshua Paddison, *American Heathens* (2012); and Adam Arenson and Andrew R. Graybill, eds., *Civil War Wests* (2015).

That Andrew Johnson had one of the most disastrous presidencies in American history during Reconstruction has not stanched the flow of scholarship. Readers can consult Eric L. McKitrick, *Andrew Johnson and Reconstruction* (1960) and *Andrew Johnson* (1969); Hans L. Trefousse, *Andrew Johnson* (1989) and *Impeachment of a President* (1999); Annette Gordon-Reed, *Andrew Johnson* (2011); and Brooks D. Simpson, *The Reconstruction Presidents* (1998).

Ulysses S. Grant is a more complicated figure than he is often made out to be. William S. McFeely, *Grant* (1981), along with Brooks D. Simpson, *Let Us Have Peace* (1991) and Harold M. Hyman, "Stanton, and Grant: A Reconsideration of the Army's Role in the Events Leading to Impeachment," *American Historical Review* 66, no. 1 (1960), look at Grant after the war. *Personal Memoirs of U.S. Grant* (1886) does not cover Reconstruction, but it is essential to understanding the man. An odd document from the period proved quite illuminating: John Russell Young, *Around the World with General Grant . . .* (1879).

David W. Blight, *Race and Reunion* (2001) follows the legacy and reinterpretation of the war in which the South tried to turn military defeat into a cultural victory. It forms a kind of scholarly bookend to Eric Foner's *Reconstruction*.

Reconstruction conventionally ends with the Compromise of 1877, but it did not end so sharply. For the Compromise of 1877, see Alan Peskin, "Was There a Compromise of 1877?" *Journal of American History* 60, no. 1 (1973); and Michael Les Benedict, "Southern Democrats in the Crisis of 1876–1877," *Journal of Southern History* 46, no. 4 (1980). Both offer convincing alternatives to C. Vann Woodward, *Reunion and Reaction: The Compromise of 1877 and the End of Reconstruction* (1991, orig. ed. 1951). Gregory P. Downs, "The Mexicanization of American Politics," *American Historical Review* 117 (2012) emphasizes how dangerous the crisis was. Jane E. Dailey, *Before Jim Crow* (2000) and Charles W. Calhoun, *Conceiving a New Republic* (2006) stress continuing efforts to reform the South.

I am hardly the first to note that not only is African American history critical to American history, it *is* American history. Key figures in this book, from Frederick Douglass to Ida B. Wells, demonstrate this. Wells's writings are also central to key events in this narrative. First and foremost are her works on lynching, *Southern Horrors* (1892), but also, as Ida B. Wells-Barnett, her edited work, *The Reason Why the Colored American Is Not in the World's Columbian Exposition* (1999). For a biography of Wells, see Paula Giddings, *Ida* (2008). For secondary work on these issues, David Squires, "Ida B. Wells and Lynch Law," *American Quarterly* 67, no. 1 (2015). For an overview of African American history, see Thomas C. Holt, *Children of Fire* (2010).

The rise of Jim Crow dominated the Southern story as Reconstruction faded. Thomas A. Upchurch, *Legislating Racism* (2004); Marek D. Steedman, *Jim Crow Citizenship* (2012); Neil R. McMillen, *Dark Journey* (1989); and Stephen Kantrowitz, *More than Freedom* (2012) are studies of this period. Allyson Hobbs, *A Chosen Exile* (2014) is a penetrating look at racial passing during the Jim Crow era as well as other periods of American history. Also see Karl Jacoby, *The Strange Career of William Ellis* (2016), and for African Americans and Africa, James T. Campbell, *Middle Passages* (2006).

One of the many horrors of Jim Crow was convict leasing. See David M. Oshinsky, *Worse than Slavery* (1996); Matthew J. Mancini, *One Dies, Get Another* (1996); Alex Lichtenstein, *Twice the Work of Free Labor* (1995); and David A. Blackmon, *Slavery by Another Name* (2008). For a broader look at imprisonment, see Rebecca M. McLennan, *The Crisis of Imprisonment* (2008).

Black politics did not cease with Jim Crow. Glenda E. Gilmore, *Gender and Jim Crow* (1992) begins at the end of the Gilded Age but it is essential. Robert V. Riser II, *Defying Disenfranchisement* (2010) is also good. The attempts of black people to accommodate to Jim Crow still often focus on Booker T. Washington. There are several biographies, including Louis R. Harlan, *Booker T. Washington* (1972).

The Southern story involved more than Jim Crow. For the best overview, Edward L. Ayers, *The Promise of the New South* (1992). For two very different groups of white Southerners, see Lou Ferleger, *Cultivating Success in the South* (2014) and Nancy Isenberg, *White Trash* (2016). For attempts to replace black labor, Moon Ho-Jung, *Coolies and Cane*.

I think Reconstruction formed the first part of the Gilded Age, but many scholars have linked the period to the subsequent Progressive Era. Nell Painter, *Standing at Armageddon* (1987) adopted such a periodization, as did T. Jackson Lears, *Rebirth of a Nation* (2009). Alan Trachtenberg, *The Incorporation of America* (1982) and Rebecca Edwards, *New Spirits* (2006) gave the period a framing similar to the one I have adopted here. For a thoughtful account of periodization of the Gilded Age, Richard Schneirov, "Thoughts on Periodizing the Gilded Age" *Journal of the Gilded Age and Progressive Era* 5, no. 3 (2006). For a recent collection of essays reiterating the importance of the period, see Charles Calhoun, ed., *The Gilded Age* (2007).

T. Jackson Lears, Rebecca Edwards, and Alan Trachtenberg, in particular, have stressed major cultural and social changes during the Gilded Age, and Lears, *No Place of Grace* (1981) and Gail Bederman, *Manliness and Civilization* (1995) are both foundational works. Richard Slotkin's *The Fatal Environment* (1986) and *Regeneration through Violence* (1973) are two volumes in his influential trilogy on the American frontier that outline how one of the defining myths of American society both frames interpretations of events during this period and changes along with them.

Caroline Winterer, *The Culture of Classicism* (2002) looked at an enduring element of American culture. Jeffrey P. Sklansky, *The Soul's Economy* (2002); Daniel T. Rodgers, *The Work Ethic in Industrial America* (2014, orig. ed. 1978); and Ann Douglas, *The Feminization of American Culture* (1978) are other intellectual and cultural histories that influenced this book.

Intellectually, this also became the age of Darwinism and pragmatism. Ronald L. Numbers, *Darwinism Comes to America* (1998) is the best treatment of Darwin in American culture. For pragmatism in the Gilded Age, see John P. Diggins, *The Promise of Pragmatism* (1994) and Louis Menand, *The Metaphysical Club* (2001).

Gilded Age popular culture manifested itself in the various World Fairs of the period. Robert W. Rydell, *All the World's a Fair* (1984) remains the key study. There is also Christopher R. Reed, *All the World Is Here!* (2000). John Maass, *The Glorious Enterprise* (1973) looks at the Centennial Exhibition of 1876.

Lawrence W. Levine, *Highbrow/Lowbrow* (1988) gave a great boost to scholarly work on popular culture, but its study was already well under way. Neil Harris, *Humbug* (1973) covered a figure (P. T. Barnum) whose greatest fame came before the Civil War. John F. Kasson, *Amusing the Million* (1978) centered on the great urban popular resort of Coney Island. Louis Warren, *Buffalo Bill's America* (2005) is an incisive study of American popular culture during this period. The essays in James Grossman, ed., *The Frontier in American Culture* (1994) also touch on these themes. Scott Reynolds Nelson, *Steel Drivin' Man* (2006) sets a standard for the genre.

Gilded Age scandals that captivated the reading public are both fascinating and revealing. Joseph A. Conforti, *Lizzie Borden on Trial* (2015); Ann Schofield, "Lizzie Borden Took an Axe," *American Studies* 34, no. 1 (1993); and Cara W. Robertson, "Representing Miss Lizzie," *Yale Journal of Law and Humanities* 8 (2013) look at an ax murder and the trial that followed. Peg A. Lamphier, *Kate Chase and William Sprague* (2003) examines a Washington scandal. Richard W. Fox, *Trials of Intimacy* (1999) and Laura Hanft Korobkin, *Criminal Conversations* (1998) analyze why Henry Ward Beecher's trial for adultery captured national attention. Daniel Czitrom, *New York Exposed* (2016) shows the possibilities of the genre.

I have tried to make the home the cultural center of the era. Much of the literature on the home concerns marriage, women, and children. Hendrik Hartog, *Man and Wife in America* (2000) and Nancy F. Cott, *Public Vows* (2000) both provided critical overviews of marriage and its legal basis. See also Michael Grossberg, *Governing the Hearth* (1985) and Elizabeth H. Pleck, "Two Worlds in One: Work and Family," *Journal of Social History* 10, no. 2 (1976). Susan J. Matt, *Homesickness* (2011) looks at the cultural gravity of the home. For childhood, ideally centered on the home, see Steven Mintz, *Huck's Raft* (2004); Paula S. Fass, *The End of American Childhood* (2016); and Elliott West, *Growing Up with the Country* (1989).

Home and homelessness were closely linked, and homelessness centered on the tramp: Todd DePastino, *Citizen Hobo* (2003); Tim Cresswell, *The Tramp in America* (2001); Kenneth Kusmer, *Down and Out, On the Road* (2002); Frank Tobias Higbie, *Indispensable Outcasts* (2003); and Paul T. Ringenbach, *Tramps and Reformers, 1873–1916* (1973).

Scott A. Sandage, *Born Losers* (2005) looks beyond the tramp at the even larger category of failure among the middle classes. Failure loomed large in a country that emerged from the Civil War with the cultural belief that hard work and initiative guaranteed success. The popular apostle of this view was Horatio Alger, whose *Ragged Dick, or, Street Life in New York with Boot Blacks* (1910, orig. ed. 1868) contains the basic Alger plot. In *From Canal Boy to President, or the Boyhood and Manhood of James A. Garfield* (1881), he carried it over into political biography. Gary Scharnhorst's *Horatio Alger, Jr.* (1980) and *The Lost Life of Horatio Alger* (1985) together give a full account of Alger's life.

Alger espoused a popular individualism, but nineteenth-century Americans were great joiners and advocates of aid and cooperation. This was most apparent in fraternal societies. The best study of them is Mark Carnes, *Secret Ritual and Manhood in Victorian America* (1989), but also see David G. Hackett, *That Religion in which All Men Agree* (2014) and Mary Ann Clawson, *Constructing Brotherhood* (1989). There are as well Anthony D. Fels, "The Square and Compass" (Ph.D. dissertation, 1987) and Stephen Kantrowitz, "'Intended for the Better Government of Man'," *Journal of American History* 96, no. 4 (2010).

Organized sports rocketed into prominence as sporting shifted in meaning and became more respectable. Elliott Gorn, *The Manly Art* (2010); Alan M. Klein, *Baseball on the Borders* (1997); Steven A. Riess, *City Games* (1989); and Julie Des Jardins, *Walter Camp* (2015) are all important. I particularly relied on Peter Levine, *A. G. Spalding and the Rise of Baseball* (1985). See also Harold Seymour, *Baseball* (1960) and Thomas W. Zeiler, *Ambassadors in Pinstripes* (2006). Jeffrey P. Powers-Beck, *The American Indian Integration of Baseball* (2004) and Katherine Mooney, *Race Horse Men* (2014) couple sports and race.

The leading political figures of the age were smarter and shrewder than I thought when I began this book, but they remain a largely uninspiring lot. This has not deterred biographers. For Rutherford B. Hayes, there is Hans L. Trefousse, *Rutherford B. Hayes* (2002) and Kenneth E. Davison, *The Presidency of Rutherford B. Hayes* (1972). Also see Rutherford B. Hayes, *Diary and Letters of Rutherford Birchard Hayes, Nineteenth President of the United States* (1922). For Garfield, see Margaret Leech, *The Garfield Orbit* (1978); Ira M. Rutkow, *James A. Garfield* (2006); and Allan Peskin, *Garfield* (1978). Candice Millard, *Destiny of the Republic* (2011) focuses on Garfield's assassination. For Grover Cleveland, see Horace S. Merrill, *Bourbon Leadery* (1957); Richard E. Welch, *The Presidencies of Grover Cleveland* (1988); and Alyn Brodsky, *Grover Cleveland* (2000). William McKinley closes out the period; see Quentin R. Skrabec, *William McKinley, Apostle of Protectionism* (2008); Kevin Phillips, *William McKinley* (2003); H. Wayne Morgan, *William McKinley and His America* (2003); and Lewis L. Gould, *The Presidency of William McKinley* (1980). Homer F. Socolofsky, "Benjamin Harrison and the American West," *Great Plains Quarterly, Paper 1834* (1985) looks at Harrison, the only president of the period to lack numerous biographers.

Congressional leaders often loomed as large as presidents during the Gilded Age. See Carl Schurz, *The Reminiscences of Carl Schurz* (1907); Hans L. Trefousse, *Carl Schurz* (1982); David M. Jordan, *Roscoe Conkling of New York* (1971), John A. Garraty, *Henry Cabot Lodge* (1965), and William D. Mallam, "Butlerism in Massachusetts," *New England Quarterly* 33, no. 2 (1960). *John Sherman's Recollections of Forty Years in the House, Senate and Cabinet* (1895) is useful. James G. Blaine, Conkling's rival and a man who nearly became president, is the subject of some specialized studies but no full modern scholarly biography. For an important governor, Ray Ginger, *Altgeld's America, 1890–1905* (1958).

Clarence King was, along with John Wesley Powell, the country's first charismatic bureaucrat. Both are the subject of excellent studies. Donald Worster, *A River Running West* (2001) covers Powell. King led a double life, masterfully told in Marni A. Sandweiss, *Passing Strange* (2009). He was close friends with John Hay, later Theodore Roosevelt's secretary of state, who has two biographies: William Roscoe Thayer, *The Life and Letters of John Hay* (1915) and John Taliaferro, *All the Great Prizes* (2013). The literature on Theodore Roosevelt, even as a young man, is enormous. David G. McCullough, *Mornings on Horseback* (1981); Roger L. DiSilvestro, *Theodore Roosevelt in the Badlands* (2011); and Kathleen Dalton, *Theodore Roosevelt* (2002) are just a few for this period.

Herbert D. Croly, *Marcus Alonzo Hanna* (1912) is a study of a man far more complicated than the usual caricature. There is a more recent biography, William T. Horner, *Ohio's Kingmaker* (2010). Hanna deserves more attention. Also see Francis P. Weisenburger, "The Time of Mark Hanna's First Acquaintance with McKinley," *Mississippi Valley Historical Review* 21, no. 1 (1934).

The period began as a mixed democratic triumph, with the extension of suffrage to African American men and its denial to all women. For the rest of the period the franchise was in retreat; Alex Keyssar, *The Right to Vote* (2000) and Scott C. James and Brian L. Lawson, "The Political Economy of Voting Rights Enforcement in America's Gilded Age," *American Political Science Review* 93, no. 1 (1999) are both useful. Peter H. Argersinger, *Representation and Inequality in Late Nineteenth-century America* (2015) and J. Morgan Kousser, *The Shaping of Southern Politics* (1974) look at gerrymandering and suffrage restriction.

For women's politics, their role in public life, and women's suffrage, consult Nancy F. Cott, *No Small Courage* (2000); Aileen S. Kraditor, ed., *Up from the Pedestal* (1968); Anne Firor Scott, *Natural Allies* (1991); Ellen C. DuBois, *Feminism and Suffrage* (1978); Mary P. Ryan, *Women in Public* (1990); and Ruth Barnes Moynihan, *Rebel for Rights* (1983).

Overall the 1870s, 1880s, and 1890s were years of virtual deadlock between the two major parties. For a look at party systems and the workings of party politics, see Michael E. McGerr, *The Decline of Popular Politics* (1986); Mark W. Summers, *Party Games* (2004); Daniel Klinghard, *The Nationalization of American Political Parties, 1880–1896* (2010); James E. Campbell, "Party Systems and Realignments in the United States, 1868–2004," *Social Science History* 30, no. 3 (2006); and Scott C. James, *Presidents, Parties, and the State* (2000). Wesley Hiers, "Party Matters," *Social Science History* 37, no. 2 (2013) ties the legal forms of racial exclusion to the operation of the Gilded Age party system.

Peter Argersinger, *Structure, Process, and Party* (1992) has also written several key articles on electoral politics in the era, the most recent of which is "All Politics Are Local," *Journal of the Gilded Age and Progressive Era* 8, no. 1 (2009).

The main drivers of party affiliation were ethnocultural identities rather than policy issues. Paul Kleppner, *The Third Electoral System, 1853–1892* (1979); Kleppner, *Continuity and Change in Electoral Politics, 1893–1928* (1987); and Richard J. Jensen, *The Winning of the Midwest* (1971) created the cornerstone of the ethnocultural school. They certainly overreached, but their research yielded fundamental insights into American politics.

Although the two major parties stalemated after 1876, the Republican Party has dominated academic studies because its active and affirmative view of the role of government gave scholars something to study. The Democrats were simply the Party of No. See George H. Mayer, *The Republican Party, 1854–1964* (1964); Heather Cox Richardson, *To Make Men Free* (2014); Lewis L. Gould, *Grand Old Party* (2003); and Gould, *The Republicans* (2014). Jean H. Baker, *Affairs of Party* (1983) is an excellent study of the Democrats.

Issues were as likely to divide parties as to distinguish them. The tariff was the key Republican issue in the Northeast and parts of the Midwest, but it was a liability elsewhere. James L. Huston, "A Political Response to Industrialism," *Journal of American History* 70, no. 1 (1983); Joanne R. Reitano, *The Tariff Question in the Gilded Age* (1994); and Douglas A. Irwin, "Tariff Incidence in America's Gilded Age," *Journal of Economic History* 67, no. 3 (September 2007) all illuminate the tariff issue.

The monetary system provided another staple of political debate where positions did not split cleanly along party lines. James Livingston, *Origins of the Federal Reserve System* (1986) presents a view of what was at stake and the struggle's partial resolution.

For nonspecialists, monetary policy can be quite daunting. Two good guides to it are Gretchen Ritter, *Goldbugs and Greenbacks* (1997) and Walter T. K. Nugent, *Money and American Society, 1865–1880* (1968). Michael O'Malley, *Face Value* (2012) provides a cultural study of the money question. For the patient and curious, it is worthwhile to read William H. Harvey, *Coin's Financial School* (1894), the basic tract of the silver crusade. Samuel DeCanio, "Populism, Paranoia, and the Politics of Free Silver," *Studies in American Political Development* (2011) is a fascinating account of the so-called Crime of '73, which resulted in the abandonment of bimetallism.

The tariff and the currency question proved key issues in the ultimate realignment of American politics in favor of the Republicans by 1896, but that struggle swayed back and forth for nearly a decade. Charles W. Calhoun, *Minority Victory* (2008) and R. Hal Williams, *Realigning America* (2010) and *Years of Decision* (1978) provide accounts of this process.

Concentrating on only presidential and congressional politics in a federal system ignores state and local governments, which play key roles. Many of the key reform initiatives of the era played out in the cities and states. For important state and regional studies, see Richard L. McCormick, *From Realignment to Reform* (1981) and R. Hal Williams, *The Democratic Party and California Politics, 1880–1896* (1971). In addition there were the territories—in effect states with restricted powers and without real representation in Congress. John Lauck, *Prairie Republic* (2010) and Howard Lamar, *The Far Southwest, 1846–1912* (2000) are two among many studies of the territories.

Much of the importance of city and state politics arose from their regulatory powers under the common law doctrine of *Salus populi*, as William J. Novak, *The People's Welfare* (1996) emphasizes. Novak's work, along with that of Richard Bensel and now a group of younger scholars, many of them political scientists, has upset a consensus that the United States had only a weak state in the nineteenth century. The nature of the American state and American governance has produced one of the most fruitful historical debates of the last few years. Brian Balogh, *A Government out of Sight* (2009) looks at sources of federal power, and Nicholas Parrillo, *Against the Profit Motive* (2013) argues that federal power was always real, though it operated not through European-style bureaucracies and a large standing military of conscripted soldiers but through delegation of powers, subsidies, and above all fee-based governance. I have adopted this argument. William Novak, "The Myth of the 'Weak' American State," *American Historical Review* 113, no. 3 (2008) challenges Stephen Skowronek, *Building a New American State* (1982), which described the nineteenth-century United States as a country of courts and parties. Gary Gerstle does not deny all of Novak's arguments, but his *Liberty and Coercion* (2015) places the most important changes later. See also Peter Zavodnyik, *The Rise of the Federal Colossus* (2011).

Bureaucracy was growing even as fee-based governance held sway, and the leading scholar here has been Daniel P. Carpenter, *The Forging of Bureaucratic Autonomy* (2001). Recently Jerry L. Mashaw, *Creating the Administrative Constitution* (2012) has discovered another route to increasing bureaucratic power. For all the attention given to Civil Service reform, including recently by Francis Fukuyama, *Political Order and Political Decay* (2014), its effects in the Gilded Age were limited, as Scott C. James shows in "Patronage Regimes and American Party Development from 'The Age of Jackson' to the Progressive Era," *British Journal of Political Science* 36, no. 1 (2006). See also Ronald N. Johnson, *The Federal Civil Service System and the Problem of Bureaucracy* (1994).

This newer scholarship is part of a shift in focus from individual reforms and reformers to changes in the nature of governance itself. The age took its name from Mark Twain and Charles Dudley Warner's *The Gilded Age: A Tale of To-Day* (1915, orig. ed. 1873), a novel whose title is the best thing about it. The corruption of the period was quite real, but it was less the result of any breakdown in morality than a system of fee-based governance and subsidy that turned government into a source of profit. Susan Rose-Ackerman, *Corruption* (1978) examines corruption around the world. Mark W. Summers, *The Era of Good Stealings* (1993) details American corruption but ultimately does not regard it as very consequential. R. E. Mutch, *Buying the Vote* (2014) and Ari A. Hoogenboom, *Spoilsmen and Reformers* (1964) provide other examples. For a wonderful tale of financial corruption, see Geoffrey C. Ward, *A Disposition to Be Rich* (2012). Margaret Thompson, *The "Spider Web"* (1985) is an excellent guide to the emergence of the modern lobby, how it capitalized on the government's lack of administrative capacity, and how it contributed to corruption.

Industrialization and wage labor drew immigrants, shaped cities, and underlay class relations. Much of the historical literature on the economy has been written by economists. With a few exceptions, those historians who have paid attention to the economy have written business history or labor history. The so-called new history of capitalism is an attempt by historians to take back economic history by reinserting culture and social context to counter the powerful but reductionist models used by most economists. Relatively few economists cross easily between economic history and American business history, but one who does is Gavin Wright, whose work I have relied on heavily. Wright's *Old South, New South* (1986) is a critical text, as are his articles. I will list only two notable ones: "The Origins of American Industrial Success, 1879–1940," *American Economic Review* 80, no. 4 (1990); and with Paul A. David, "Increasing Returns and the Genesis of American Resource Abundance," *Industrial and Corporate Change* 6, no. 2 (1997).

Until quite recently, most economists assumed an ahistorical *homo economicus*, who remains essentially the same across time and space. Still, read critically, the literature remains essential. I give only a sampling here. In addition to his numerous articles on labor markets, there is Joshua L. Rosenbloom, *Looking for Work, Searching for Workers* (2002). Also see Suresh Naidu and Noam Yuchtman, "Labor Market Institutions in the Gilded Age of American Economic History," *Working Paper* 22117, National Bureau of Economic Research (NBER, 2016) for the changing labor market.

For financing and investment, Jeffrey G. Williamson, "Watersheds and Turning Points," *Journal of Economic History* 34, no. 3 (1974); Mira Wilkins, "Foreign Investment in the U.S. Economy before 1914," *Annals of the American Academy of Political and Social Science* 516, no. 1 (1991); William N. Goetzmann and Andrey D. Ukhov, "British Investment Overseas 1870–1913," *Review of Finance* 10, no. 2 (2006); Matthew S. Jaremski, "National Banking's Role in U.S. Industrialization, 1850–1900," NBER *Working Paper* 18789 (2013). For tax policy, see W. Elliot Brownlee, *Federal Taxation in America* (2004).

For general economic accounts of the era, *The Cambridge Economic History of the United States* (1996) is a standard reference. Also see Harold G. Vatter, *The Drive to Industrial Maturity* (1975); Jeffrey G. Williamson, *Late Nineteenth-century American Development* (1974); Jeremy Atack, *A New Economic View of American History* (1994); and Sidney Ratner, *The Evolution of the American Economy* (1980). Angus Maddison, *The*

World Economy (2006); Claudia Dale Goldin, *The Regulated Economy* (1994); Robert J. Gordon, *The Rise and Fall of American Growth* (2016); and Thomas Piketty, *Capital in the Twenty-first Century* (2014) are particularly important.

For economic histories by historians, see Heather C. Richardson, *The Greatest Nation of the Earth* (1997); Walter Licht, *Industrializing America* (1995); and Maury M. Klein, *The Genesis of Industrial America, 1870–1920* (2007). Jonathan Levy, *Freaks of Fortune* (2012) is a fine example of the new history of capitalism. For a collection of essays, see Michael Zakim and Gary J. Kornblith, eds., *Capitalism Takes Command* (2012).

Historians, sociologists, and economists have all looked at increasing inequality: Carole Shammas, "A New Look at Long-Term Trends in Wealth Inequality in the United States," *American Historical Review* 98, no. 2 (1993); Richard H. Steckel and Carolyn M. Moehling, "Rising Inequality," *Journal of Economic History* 61, no. 1 (2001); Jeffrey Williamson and Peter H. Lindert, "The Long-Term Trends in American Wealth Inequality," in J. D. Smith, ed., *Modeling the Distribution and Intergenerational Transmission of Wealth* (1980). Monica Prasad, *The Land of Too Much* (2012) is an interesting account by a sociologist.

Outside of railroads, corporations did not dominate the economy until the 1890s. See Naomi R. Lamoreaux, *The Great Merger Movement in American Business, 1895–1904* (1985); Olivier Zunz, *Making America Corporate, 1870–1920* (1990); William G. Roy, *Socializing Capital* (1997); David R. Meyer, "Midwestern Industrialization and the American Manufacturing Belt in the Nineteenth Century," *Journal of Economic History* 49, no. 4 (1989); R. Jeffrey Lustig, *Corporate Liberalism* (1982); and Gerald Berk, *Alternative Tracks* (1994).

Railroads formed the most dynamic sector of the American economy in the late nineteenth century, and the literature is abundant. My earlier book, *Railroaded* (2011), covers western railroads, but also see David H. Bain, *Empire Express* (1999); Albro Martin, *James J. Hill and the Opening of the Northwest* (1991); Richard C. Overton, *Burlington West* (1941); Richard J. Orsi, *Sunset Limited* (2005); Robert W. Fogel, *The Union Pacific Railroad* (1960); Maury Klein, *Union Pacific* (1987); and Arthur M. Johnson, *Boston Capitalists and Western Railroads* (1967). Albert J. Churella, *The Pennsylvania Railroad* (2013) is a recent study of the nation's most powerful and influential railroad. William G. Thomas, *The Iron Way* (2011) gauges the linked impact of railroads and the Civil War. See also James W. Ely, *Railroads and American Law* (2001).

The best description of how businesses worked comes from business historians, whose work has often been neglected by other historians, who too often only read Alfred D. Chandler, *The Visible Hand* (1977). As a devastating critique of the invisible hand, it has held up well, as an accurate description of American managerial practices in the nineteenth century less well. Far more useful than Chandler are the histories written by Philip Scranton: *Proprietary Capitalism* (1983), *Endless Novelty* (1997), and "Conceptualizing Pennsylvania's Industrializations, 1850–1950," *Pennsylvania History* 61, no. 1 (1994). I also found Pamela Walker Laird, *Pull* (2006) very helpful. A critical study is Richard R. John, *Network Nation* (2010), and John, ed., *Ruling Passions* (2006) is an interesting collection. Also see Joshua D. Wolff, *Western Union and the Creation of the American Corporate Order, 1845–1893* (2013); Daniel Nelson, *Managers and Workers* (1975); and Stanley Buder, *Capitalizing on Change* (2009).

For American finance, there is a mix of work by historians and economists. The work of Richard Sylla is fundamental to understanding American capital markets and banking, in particular "Federal Policy, Banking Market Structure, and Capital Mobilization in the United States, 1863–1913," *Journal of Economic History* 29, no. 4 (1969); *The American Capital Market, 1846–1914* (1975); and "American Banking and Growth in the Nineteenth Century," *Explorations in Economic History* 9 (Winter 1971–72).

For financial crises and business cycles, Yochanan Shachmurove, "Reoccurring Financial Crises in the United States," *Penn Institute of Economic Research Working Paper* 11-006 (2010); Joseph H. Davis, "An Improved Annual Chronology of U.S. Business Cycles since the 1790s," *Journal of Economic History* 66, no. 1 (2006); and Charles Amélie, Darné Olivier, and Claude Diebolt, "A Revision of the US Business Cycles Chronology, 1790–1928," in *NEP* (2011). For a narrative account, Elmus Wicker, *Banking Panics of the Gilded Age* (2000). Nicolas Barreyre, "The Politics of Economic Crises," *Journal of the Gilded Age and Progressive Era* 10, no. 4 (2011) is the best analysis of the political implications of the Panic of 1873. His dissertation contains a fuller analysis: "Sectionalisme et politique aux États-Unis: le Midwest et la Reconstruction, 1865–1877" (EHESS, 2008). See also Douglas Steeples, *Democracy in Desperation* (1998) and Scott Reynolds Nelson, *A Nation of Deadbeats* (2012).

This was an age of federal subsidies for business, but regulation remained largely a state and local function until late. For attempts to take back land grants, David Maldwyn Ellis, "The Forfeiture of Railroad Land Grants, 1867–1894," *Mississippi Valley Historical Review* 33, no. 1 (1946). Gabriel Kolko, *Railroads and Regulation, 1877–1916* (1965) gets part of the impetus for regulation right. For the Interstate Commerce Commission, Ari Hoogenboom, *A History of the ICC* (1976) and Keith T. Poole and Howard Rosenthal, "The Enduring Nineteenth-Century Battle for Economic Regulation," *Journal of Law and Economics* 36, no. 2 (1993).

There is considerable literature on bankers and entrepreneurs: Ellis P. Oberholtzer, *Jay Cooke* (1907); Henrietta M. Larson, *Jay Cooke* (1936); John Lewis Harnsberger, *Jay Cooke and Minnesota* (1981); Jean Strouse, *Morgan* (1999), and Susie Pak, *Gentlemen Bankers* (2013). Charles R. Geisst, *Wall Street* (1997) provides a popular account of Wall Street.

The literature on key entrepreneurs, businessmen, and managers is large. T. J. Stiles, *The First Tycoon* (2009) and Maury Klein, *The Life and Legend of Jay Gould* (1986) look at Cornelius Vanderbilt and Jay Gould, two men who became the face of vast wealth. David Nasaw, *Andrew Carnegie* (2006) is wonderfully written and full of detail; Harold C. Livesay, *Andrew Carnegie and the Rise of Big Business* (1975) is succinct and full of insight. Ron Chernow, *Titan* (1998) remains the standard life of John D. Rockefeller. Daniel Nelson, *Frederick W. Taylor and the Rise of Scientific Management* (1980) looks at an important figure, even if one who exaggerated his own accomplishments. For Collis P. Huntington, David S. Lavender, *The Great Persuader* (1998, 1st ed. 1970). For Henry Villard, D. G. Buss, *Henry Villard* (1978).

Business history often elides into the history of technology, whose specialized literature can sound pedestrian but is very revealing. Leo Rogin, *The Introduction of Farm Machinery in Its Relation to the Productivity of Labor in the Agriculture of the United States during the Nineteenth Century* (1931); Alan L. Olmstead, "The Mechanization of Reaping and Mowing in American Agriculture, 1833–1870," *Journal of Economic History* 35, no. 2

(1975); Lewis R. Jones, "The Mechanization of Reaping and Mowing in American Agriculture, 1833–1870: Comment," *Journal of Economic History* 37, no. 2 (1977); and Ross Thomson, *The Path to Mechanized Shoe Production in the United States* (1989) all detail how technology influenced the American economy. Although it ends at the beginning of this period, Thomson, *Structures of Change in the Mechanical Age* (2009) was also helpful.

Technology in the American imagination connects with invention, which was more often a collective process than an individual one, as Steven W. Usselman, *Regulating Railroad Innovation* (2002) and Thomas Park Hughes, *American Genesis* (1989) have shown. Thomas Edison as both an inventor and a businessman figures centrally in this book. I relied on A. J. Millard, *Edison and the Business of Innovation* (1990) and Neil Baldwin, *Edison* (1995). Also see William T. Hutchinson, *Cyrus Hall McCormick* (1930).

Edison was central to the development of electricity, which like the telephone, showed the considerable lag existing between invention and impact on the larger economy. Thomas Parke Hughes, *Networks of Power* (1983) is a classic work. See David E. Nye, *Electrifying America* (1990) and Steven W. Usselman, "From Novelty to Utility," *Business History Review* 66, no. 2 (1992) are also good. Electricity was only part of the revolution in lighting, which changed how people lived. See A. Roger Ekirch, *At Day's Close* (2005) and Peter Baldwin, *In the Watches of the Night* (2012).

Industrialization in the United States depended heavily on coal, steam, and iron. For coal, see Alfred D. Chandler, "Anthracite Coal and the Beginnings of the Industrial Revolution in the United States," *Business History Review* 46, no. 2 (1972); C. K. Yearley, *Enterprise and Anthracite* (1961); Richard G. Healey, *The Pennsylvania Anthracite Coal Industry, 1860–1902* (2007); Grace Palladino, *Another Civil War* (1990); and Christopher Jones, "A Landscape of Energy Abundance," *Environmental History* 15, no. 3 (2010). For the steel industry, Thomas J. Misa, *A Nation of Steel* (1995) and Michael Nuwer, "From Batch to Flow," *Technology and Culture* 29, no. 4 (1988).

Because so much of the growth of the period depended on producer goods, or the most basic requirements of consumers—food, clothing, and shelter—or goods aimed at the relatively small number of middle-class consumers, it is easy to lose track of the beginnings of a consumer economy. For the rise of new consumer products, Bartow J. Elmore, *Citizen Coke* (2014) is excellent. It is also a fine environmental history.

The Gilded Age was also the beginning of a mass popular press. See Paul Starr, *The Creation of the Media* (2004). Menahem Blondheim, *News over the Wires* (1994) is the best account of the rise of the Associated Press. Richard Junger, *Becoming the Second City* (2010) covers Chicago. On Joseph Pulitzer, the leading publisher of the age, see George Juergens, *Joseph Pulitzer and the New York World* (1966) and James McGrath Morris, *Pulitzer* (2010).

Agriculture remained the leading economic sector and source of American exports. For agriculture and changes in farming and rural life, see Clarence H. Danhof, *Change in Agriculture* (1969); Allan G. Bogue, *From Prairie to Corn Belt* (1963); John C. Hudson, *Making the Corn Belt* (1994); David Danbom, *Born in the Country* (2006); and Hal S. Barron, *Mixed Harvest* (1997). Cotton was at the center of the American agricultural economy after as well as before the war and critical to the development of capitalism. See Sven Beckert, *Empire of Cotton* (2014) and Brian Schoen, *The Fragile Fabric of Union* (2009).

Working for wages in the industrial economy quickly became the major driver of immigration, a central facet of the age. Immigration to the United States was part of a larger pattern of internal and external migration within Europe, as is shown by Annemarie Steidl, Engelbert Stockhammer, and Hermann Zeitlhofer, "Relations among Internal, Continental, and Transatlantic Migration in Late Imperial Austria," *Social Science History* 31 (Spring 2007). For push and pull factors, Charles Hirschman and Elizabeth Mogford, "Immigration and the American Industrial Revolution from 1880 to 1920," *Social Science Research* 38, no. 4 (2009); and Timothy J. Hatton and Jeffrey G. Williamson, "What Drove the Mass Migrations from Europe in the Late Nineteenth Century?" NBER Historical Paper 43 (1992). For studies of the large numbers of immigrants returned home, Gunter Moltmann, "American-German Return Migration in the Nineteenth and Early Twentieth Centuries," *Central European History* 13, no. 4 (1980).

John E. Bodnar, *The Transplanted* (1985) and Thomas J. Archdeacon, *Becoming American* (1983) remain standard accounts of immigration. Aristide R. Zolberg, *A Nation by Design* (2006) supplements older studies of immigration policy. For Ellis Island, see Vincent J. Cannato, *American Passage* (2009).

Immigration provoked a nativist reaction, which John Higham, *Strangers in the Land* (1988) surveyed. Restrictions on Chinese immigration are usually regarded as the first attempts at exclusion, but Hidetaka Hirota, *Exiling the Poor* (2017) points out the limits imposed earlier on Europeans. For Japanese immigration and attempts to restrict it, see Andrea Geiger, *Subverting Exclusion* (2011).

Over the course of the period, immigration shifted from Western Europe and China to Eastern and Southern Europe, and Japan. Tara Zahra, *The Great Departure* (2016) is a recent look at Eastern European migration to the United States and elsewhere. For the Irish, the literature is quite rich. The standard book is Kerby A. Miller, *Emigrants and Exiles* (1985). David M. Emmons, *Beyond the American Pale* (2010); David Thomas Brundage, *Irish Nationalists in America* (2016); and Hasia R. Diner, *Erin's Daughters in America* (1983) are also excellent. For Italian immigrants, see Donna R. Gabaccia, *Militants and Migrants* (1988) and *From Sicily to Elizabeth Street* (1984).

For Germans, the largest immigrant group, see Kathleen Conzen, *Germans in Minnesota* (2003) and "Making their Own America," in *German Historical Institute Annual Lecture Series* (1990). For Jewish immigrants, Moses Rischin, *The Promised City* (1962); Hasia Diner, *A New Promised Land* (2003); and Ellen Eisenberg, Ava Kahn, and William Toll, *Jews of the Pacific Coast* (2009). Irving Howe, *World of Our Fathers* (1990) is a popular account.

For relations between native-born workers and new immigrants, Gwendolyn Mink, *Old Labor and New Immigrants in American Political Development* (1986). Contract labor became a central political issue; Gunther Peck, *Reinventing Free Labor* (2000) provides the best examination of this issue. For a general consideration of labor conflict and ethnicity, Susan Olzak, "Labor Unrest, Immigration, and Ethnic Conflict in Urban America, 1880–1914," *American Journal of Sociology* 94, no. 6 (1989). On relations between black people and white immigrants, Stanley Lieberson, *A Piece of the Pie* (1980).

The history of immigration intersects with the history of American Catholicism and Judaism. John T. McGreevy, *Catholicism and American Freedom* (2003) formed my account of Catholicism, but see also Jon Gjerde, *Catholicism and the Shaping of Nineteenth-*

Century America (2012). The clash over Bible reading in the public schools and aid to parochial schools formed critical battlegrounds of the era. See Steven K. Green, *The Second Disestablishment* (2010) and *The Bible, the School, and the Constitution* (2012). For education during this period, see Allen J. Going, "The South and the Blair Education Bill," *Mississippi Valley Historical Review* 44, no. 2 (1957); James D. Anderson, *The Education of Blacks in the South, 1860–1935* (1988). For education in general, there is Lawrence Cremin, *American Education, the National Experience, 1783–1876* (1980).

For Judaism, see Jonathan D. Sarna, *American Judaism* (2004). For workers and religion, Bruce C. Nelson, "Revival and Upheaval," *Journal of Social History* 25, no. 2 (1991).

A disproportionate number of Gilded Age immigrants moved into the growing cities, thus contributing to another major change during the period. The literature on the cities is enormous and diverse, and some basic urban histories end up in other categories in this essay. Philip J. Ethington, *The Public City* (1994) and William Issel and Robert W. Cherny, *San Francisco, 1865–1932* (1986) are accounts of San Francisco. Edwin G. Burrows and Mike Wallace, *Gotham* (1999) is a magisterial achievement. For Philadelphia there is Sam Bass Warner, *The Private City* (1968). Cleveland, the home of John Hay, Mark Hanna, and John D. Rockefeller for part of the period, is a neglected site in Gilded Age history. Jan Cigliano, *Showplace of America* (1991) illuminates Euclid Avenue. For Pittsburgh there is Francis G. Couvares, *The Remaking of Pittsburgh* (1984). For Boston, see Michael Rawson, *Eden on the Charles* (2010). Sarah Deutsch, *Women and the City* (2000) also looks at Boston in important and innovative ways.

Chicago has developed the richest urban literature. Dominic A. Pacyga, *Chicago* (2009) gives an overview. John B. Jentz, *Chicago in the Age of Capital* (2012), Carl S. Smith, *Urban Disorder and the Shape of Belief* (1995), and Richard Schneirov, *Labor and Urban Politics* (1998) collectively give an idea of the depth of this literature. Karen Sawislak, *Smoldering City* (1995) and Joanne J. Meyerowitz, *Women Adrift* (1988) are both superb social histories. For the rise of modern urban architecture in Chicago, Hugh Morrison, *Louis Sullivan* (1998).

During the Gilded Age, urban began to also imply suburban. John R. Stilgoe, *Borderland* (1988) provides an overview. Sam Bass Warner, *Streetcar Suburbs* (1978) looks at Boston, and Elaine Lewinnek, *The Working Man's Reward* (2014) at Chicago.

Urban immigrants have gotten considerable attention in the rise of political machines. John M. Allswang, *Bosses, Machines, and Urban Voters* (1977) is a relatively early account. Tammany Hall has dominated studies of political machines: Alexander B. Callow, *The Tweed Ring* (1969); Seymour J. Mandelbaum, *Boss Tweed's New York* (1965); and Terry Golway, *Machine Made* (2014). James J. Connolly, *An Elusive Unity* (2010) and Steven P. Erie, *Rainbow's End* (1988) examine the central role of the Irish. William L. Riordon, *Plunkitt of Tammany Hall* (1905) captures Plunkitt's shrewdness and appeal. Chris McNickle, *To Be Mayor of New York* (1993) looks at the broad sweep of New York ethnic politics.

Ira Katznelson, *City Trenches* (1981) shows that immigration and urbanization were central to emerging class conflicts and deepening class divides. It was in this context that the labor movement took shape. For the history of labor, John R. Commons, *History of Labour in the United States* (1918) is dated but still important. Bruce Laurie, *Artisans into Workers* (1989) chronicles the rise of wage labor. With wage labor came unemployment: Alex Keyssar, *Out of Work* (1986).

David Montgomery's important book on work and working people spans topics from unionism to worker republicanism, and working-class life. *The Fall of the House of Labor* (1987) is a good place to start. Herbert Gutman, whose *Work, Culture, and Society in Industrializing America* (1977, orig. ed. 1966) contains many of his important essays. S. J. Kleinberg, *The Shadow of the Mills* (1989) is a social history in this tradition.

Montgomery's *Citizen Worker* (1993) and *Beyond Equality* (1981) are the best places to begin for labor politics. Richard Jules Oestreicher, "Urban Working-Class Political Behavior and Theories of American Electoral Politics, 1870–1940," *Journal of American History* 74, no. 4 (1988) looks at the working-class vote.

There are numerous local and regional studies of working-class politics. John P. Enyeart, *The Quest for "Just and Pure Law"* (2009); Melvin Dubofsky, "The Origins of Western Working Class Radicalism, 1890–1905," *Labor History* 7, no. 2 (1966); and David T. Brundage, *The Making of Western Labor Radicalism* (1994) are also good. Roseanne Currarino, *The Labor Question in America* (2011) is an essential book for understanding the centrality of labor and class in the Gilded Age. Richard Jules Oestreicher, *Solidarity and Fragmentation* (1986) looks at Detroit, while Eric Arnesen, *Waterfront Workers of New Orleans* (1991) looks at New Orleans.

Workers' concerns went well beyond wages, as Mark Wyman, *Hard Rock Epic* (1979) makes clear. Control over work and its conditions was a prime concern of workers at the time, in large part because of the dangers of the job: Mark Aldrich, *Death Rode the Rails* (2006) and "History of Workplace Safety in the United States, 1880–1970," *Encyclopedia of Economic History* (2003).

Most workers did not belong to unions, but unions were central to the conflicts at the time. James Livingston, "The Social Analysis of Economic History and Theory," *American Historical Review* 92, no. 1 (1987), shows that the unions could be quite formidable. David Brody, *Steelworkers in America* (1960) looks at steelworkers after their unions were broken. For unions and labor politics, Nick Salvatore, *Eugene V. Debs* (1982).

For strikes, see David Montgomery, "Strikes in Nineteenth-Century America," *Social Science History* 4, no. 1 (1980) and Shelton Stromquist, *A Generation of Boomers* (1987). For particular strikes, David O. Stowell, *Streets, Railroads, and the Great Strike of 1877* (1999); Philip S. Foner, *The Great Labor Uprising of 1877* (1977); Robert V. Bruce, *1877* (1959); Michael A. Bellesiles, *1877* (2010); Ruth Allen, *The Great Southwest Strike* (1942); Theresa Case, *The Great Southwest Railroad Strike and Free Labor* (2010); and Donald L. McMurry, *The Great Burlington Strike of 1888* (1956). For Homestead, see Leon Wolff, *Lockout, the Story of the Homestead Strike of 1892* (1965); Paul Krause, *The Battle for Homestead, 1880–1892* (1992); Paul Kahan, *The Homestead Strike* (2014); and Jonathan Rees, "Homestead in Context," *Pennsylvania History* 64, no. 4 (1997).

The Great Upheaval of 1886 and the eight-hour movement, which led to Haymarket, has received significant attention. See James R. Green, *Death in the Haymarket* (2006); Timothy Messer-Kruse, *The Trial of the Haymarket Anarchists* (2011); and William A. Mirola, *Redeeming Time* (2014). So too has the town of Pullman and the Pullman strike, in Stanley Buder, *Pullman* (1967). Almont Lindsey, *The Pullman Strike* (1942) has held up well.

Class conflict led to fears of the dangerous classes: the very rich and very poor. For a generation the Commune in Paris terrified middle-class Americans, who often linked radical politics with crime; E. E. Leach, "Chaining the Tiger: The Mob Stigma and the Working Class, 1863–1894," *Labor History* 35, no. 2 (1994). For the scholarship on crime and violence, Eric H. Monkkonen, *Crime, Justice, History* (2002) is a useful starting point. Also see Monkkonen, *Murder in New York City* (2000) and *Police in Urban America, 1860–1920* (1981).

Many Americans regarded class violence as European in origin and attributed labor violence to European organizations. The Molly Maguires were one of the first: F. P. Dewees, *Molly Maguires* (1877) is a contemporary account of that organization. Harold W. Aurand, *From the Molly Maguires to the United Mine Workers* (1971); Wayne Broehl, *The Molly Maguires* (1964), and Kevin Kenny, *Making Sense of the Molly Maguires* (1998) are useful. By the end of the century anarchists populated the nightmares of prosperous Americans. For anarchists, Bruce C. Nelson, *Beyond the Martyrs* (1988) and Timothy Messer-Kruse, *The Haymarket Conspiracy* (2012).

The working class has received the most study, and the very rich have also attracted attention, while the middle class has gotten less notice. A contemporary, and still hilarious, account of the rich is Frederick Townsend Martin, *The Passing of the Idle Rich* (1911). Sven Beckert, *The Monied Metropolis* (2001) usefully distinguishes the rich and those upper-middle-class professionals who served them as collectively forming a bourgeoisie in the European sense. The bourgeoisie were more elite than those included in Stuart M. Blumin's *The Emergence of the Middle Class* (1989). There were possible lines of cooperation between smaller businessmen and labor. The divisions were very real but depended on place and issues. See Jeffrey Haydu, *Citizen Employers* (2008).

One of the lasting and often fruitless arguments of the period is whether industrialization and urbanization helped or hurt most Americans. Usually, this has been fought out on the basis of real wages, which, given the economic statistics available, provides no clear answers, or over property accumulation over time, which is unreliable given the serious difficulties in tracking people. Stephan Thernstrom, *Poverty and Progress* (1964) was the most prominent of many early efforts to study mobility. See also John F. McClymer, "Late Nineteenth-Century American Working-Class Living Standards," *Journal of Interdisciplinary History* 17, no. 2 (1986).

I have followed the lead of many economists and demographers and turned to measures of American physical well-being as a better source of answers. As of now, it appears the changes apparent during the Gilded Age hurt more people than they helped. I have labeled the decline in height and lifespan and the fluctuations in the death rate an environmental crisis since it sprang from bad water, bad air, faulty infrastructure, and epidemic disease as well as dangerous working conditions. The origin of this work is Robert W. Fogel et al., "Secular Changes in American and British Stature and Nutrition," *Journal of Interdisciplinary History* 14, no. 2 (1983). The most recent summary is Dora L. Costa, "Health and the Economy in the United States from 1750 to the Present," *Journal of Economic Literature* 53, no. 3 (2015). The underlying literature is so voluminous that I will list only a few key sources: Michael R. Haines, "Growing Incomes, Shrinking People — Can Economic Development Be Hazardous to Your Health?" *Social Science History* 28, no. 2 (2004); Roderick Floud, Robert W. Fogel, Bernard Harris, and Sok Chul Hong, *The Changing Body* (2011); and Marco Sunder, "The Height Gap in 19th-Century America," *Economics & Human Biology* 11, no. 3 (2013).

Declining stature may link to poor nutrition, but this was different from a lack of food. For studies of the American diet, see Harvey Levenstein, *Revolution at the Table* (1988); Katherine L. Turner, *How the Other Half Ate* (2014); D. Logan Trevon, "Nutrition and Well-Being in the Late Nineteenth Century," *Journal of Economic History* 66, no. 2 (2006); Cindy R. Lobel, *Urban Appetites* (2014); and Hasia Diner, *Hungering for America* (2001). Although it concerns a slightly later period, Kendra Smith-Howard, *Pure and Modern Milk* (2013) is useful.

I have profited immensely from the history of medicine, particularly Sheila M. Rothman, *Living in the Shadow of Death* (1995); Charles E. Rosenberg, *The Cholera Years* (1987); George Rosen, *A History of Public Health* (1993); and Richard J. Evans, *Death in Hamburg* (1987). Samuel H. Preston and Michael R. Haines, *Fatal Years* (1991) and Irving Loudon, *Death in Childbirth* (1992) look at childbirth and children. See also Gretchen Long, *Doctoring Freedom* (2012) for medical care for freedpeople.

The solution to the environmental crisis may have come not only from improvement to urban infrastructure but also from something as simple as ice. For urban infrastructure of sewage and water, see Peter D. Groote, J. Paul Elhorst, and P. G. Tassenaar, "Standard of Living Effects Due to Infrastructure Improvements in the 19th Century," *Social Science Computer Review* 27, no. 3 (2009); Joel A. Tarr, *The Search for the Ultimate Sink* (1996); Martin V. Melosi, *The Sanitary City* (2000); May N. Stone, "The Plumbing Paradox," *Winterthur Portfolio* 14, no. 3 (1979); and David Soll, "City, Region, and in Between: New York City's Water Supply and the Insights of Regional History," *Journal of Urban History* 38, no. 2 (2012). For ice, Lee A. Craig, Barry Goodwin, and Thomas Grennes, "The Effect of Mechanical Refrigeration on Nutrition in the United States," *Social Science History* 28, no. 2 (2004). For a broad global overview, Angus Deaton, *The Great Escape* (2013).

The environmental change that put cities into crisis had a much wider sweep. For examinations of urban ecosystems and their connections to other regions, begin with Ted Steinberg, *Gotham Unbound* (2014) and Matthew W. Klingle, *Emerald City* (2007). For the role of urban fires, look at Christine Meisner Rosen, *The Limits of Power* (1986). Pollution of air and water became a widespread concern in late nineteenth-century: Frank Uekoetter, *The Age of Smoke* (2009); Carl S. Smith, *City Water, City Life* (2013); and Sarah S. Elkind, *Bay Cities and Water Politics* (1998).

The older literature on environmental history focused on conservation. Samuel P. Hays, *Conservation and the Gospel of Efficiency* (1975, orig. ed. 1959) is a classic study. Michael McCarthy, *Hour of Trial* (1977) remains important. John F. Reiger, *American Sportsmen and the Origins of Conservation* (2001) and Thomas R. Dunlap, *Saving America's Wildlife* (1988) offer contrasting views of hunting and conservation. Donald Worster, *A Passion for Nature* (2008) is a biography of John Muir and the best book on wilderness preservation. Roderick Nash, *Wilderness and the American Mind* (1967) is an earlier work. Joseph Taylor, *Making Salmon* (1999) provides a model for how to incorporate environmental science and political economy into a conservation study. Some of the newer literature brings out the class and racial biases of conservation, notably Karl Jacoby, *Crimes against Nature* (2001).

The concerns with health, water, and fire, so prominent in urban contexts, also played out in rural areas. For rural and wildland fires, Stephen J. Pyne, *Fire in America* (1982). For concern with health in Midwestern and Western settlement, Conevery Bolton Valenčius,

The Health of the Country (2002) has spawned much imitation. In the same vein, see Linda Lorraine Nash, *Inescapable Ecologies* (2006), a work of tremendous sophistication.

The dramatic reduction of wetlands during the late nineteenth century is the concern of Anne Vileisis, *Discovering the Unknown Landscape* (1997). See also Christopher Morris, *The Big Muddy* (2012) and Matthew M. Booker, *Down by the Bay* (2013).

Environmental history adds value and insight to topics that might not at first seem environmental. See for example, Kathryn Morse, *The Nature of Gold* (2003); Jennifer Price, *Flight Maps* (1999); and Thomas G. Andrews, *Killing for Coal* (2008).

One the newer and more fascinating trends in environmental history is to consider the influence of other species on the course of American history. Studies of the bison have a long pedigree, but they often (although not entirely) focus on the animals largely as a resource for Indians and whites or as a key species in grasslands ecosystems. See Dan Flores, "Bison Ecology and Bison Diplomacy," *Journal of American History* 78, no. 2 (1991); and Andrew C. Isenberg, *The Destruction of the Bison* (2000). Recently, attention has turned to the city: Andrew Robichaud, "The Animal City" (2015) and Clay McShane, *The Horse in the City* (2007). Catherine McNeur, *Taming Manhattan* (2014) sets the stage for later battles. Also see Janet M. Davis, *The Gospel of Kindness* (2016).

The great changes of the nineteenth century affected the country unevenly. The evolution of distinct regions beyond the Northeast and South is one theme of this book. It cannot be separated from how the movement of foreign immigrants into the United States merged with internal migration. Elliott R. Barkan, *From All Points, 1870s–1952* (2007); Walter T. K. Nugent, *Into the West* (1999); and Patricia Kelly Hall and Stephen Ruggles, "'Restless in the Midst of Their Prosperity'," *Journal of American History* 91, no. 3 (2004) all examine these movements.

The Midwest and Middle Border emerged as the heartland of the country during this period, but there is little self-conscious scholarship for the Midwest. I have cited many Midwestern studies in sections on labor, cities, and politics, but also see Jon Gjerde's *The Minds of the West* (1997) and *From Peasants to Farmers* (1985), and John Mack Faragher, *Sugar Creek* (1986). Mark Twain and William Dean Howells were Midwestern writers, but Hamlin Garland was the most self-consciously so: *Main-Travelled Roads* (1891), *A Son of the Middle Border* (1917), and *A Daughter of the Middle Border* (1921). On Garland, see Robert F. Gish, "Hamlin Garland's Dakota: History and Story," *South Dakota History* 9 (1979).

The West, larger in area but much smaller in population than the Midwest and Middle Border, has gotten far more attention. Many works on the West appear here under immigration, labor, etc. The modern reinterpretation of the American West began with Patricia N. Limerick, *The Legacy of Conquest* (1987). Robert V. Hine and John M. Faragher, *The American West* (2000) and Richard White, *"It's Your Misfortune and None of My Own"* (1991) provide overviews of the West.

William H. Goetzmann, *Exploration and Empire* (1966) details how civilian expeditions gradually replaced the army in the exploration of the West. The army, however, remained critical since it embodied an administrative capacity the government otherwise largely lacked. Edward M. Coffman, *The Old Army* (1986) and Kevin Adams, *Class and Race in the Frontier Army* (2009) analyze that army. For black soldiers, William A. Dobak and Thomas D. Phillips, *The Black Regulars, 1866–1898* (2001). For military views on

Indians, see Sherry L. Smith, *The View from Officers' Row* (1990). For generals who were sympathetic to the Indians, Richard N. Ellis, *General Pope and U.S. Indian Policy* (1970). For accounts of ordinary soldiers, Sherry L. Smith, *Sagebrush Soldier* (1989) and Don Rickey, *Forty Miles a Day on Beans and Hay* (1963). For Indian scouts, see Mark Van de Logt, *War Party in Blue* (2010).

The literature on Indians and Indian wars is extensive. Scholars have established that some Indian groups, the Comanches, Lakotas, and Apaches in particular, were capable of offering serious opposition to American expansion. For the break-up of Indian nations along the Middle Border and Great Plains, H. Craig Miner, *The End of Indian Kansas* (1978); Pekka Hämäläinen, *The Comanche Empire* (2008); and Richard White, "The Winning of the West," *Journal of American History* 65, no. 2 (1978) emphasize the power of key groups. For particular conflicts, William Y. Chalfant, *Hancock's War* (2010); Catharine Franklin, "Black Hills and Bloodshed," *Montana* 63, no. 2 (2013) and Ned Blackhawk, *Violence over the Land* (2006). Elliott West, *The Last Indian War* (2009) manages to be at once elegiac, analytical, and concise. Equally good is West's *The Contested Plains* (1998). It is both a superb environmental history and a classic study of the wars on the southern and central Great Plains. Jeffrey Ostler, *The Plains Sioux and U.S. Colonialism from Lewis and Clark to Wounded Knee* (2004) examines American relations with the Lakotas. T. J. Stiles, *Custer's Trials* (2015) is the most recent and best biography of George Armstrong Custer.

For particular battles, Shannon D. Smith, "'Give Me Eighty Men'," *Montana* 54, no. 3 (2004); Jerome A. Greene, *American Carnage* (2014) and *Washita* (2004); and Heather Cox Richardson, *Wounded Knee* (2010). Karl Jacoby, *Shadows at Dawn* (2008) reveals the complexities of racial violence in the West. For an important study over the contested memory of a nineteenth-century massacre, Ari Kelman, *A Misplaced Massacre* (2013). Also see David W. Grua, *Surviving Wounded Knee* (2016).

Benjamin Madley, *An American Genocide* (2016) makes a convincing argument that what happened in California can be classified as genocide, and Gary Clayton Anderson, *Ethnic Cleansing and the Indian* (2014) persuasively argues that the term *ethnic cleansing* fits a much wider swath of American policy.

There is a wealth of ethnohistorical studies of Indian peoples adopting to change during this period. See, for example, Richard White, *The Roots of Dependency* (1988). Alexandra Harmon, *Rich Indians* (2010) has looked at both native attitudes toward wealth and the paradoxes of rich Indians. Andrew R. Graybill, *The Red and the White* (2013) looks at the often tangled histories of Indians and whites. Among the best ethnohistories are Gregory Smoak, *Ghost Dances and Identity* (2006) and Raymond DeMallie, "The Lakota Ghost Dance: An Ethnohistorical Account," *Pacific Historical Review* 51 (November 1982). Also see DeMallie's edited work of teachings given to John G. Neihardt, *The Sixth Grandfather* (1984). There is also a set of new studies that look at Indian attempts to turn white arguments and beliefs to their own advantage. See Louis S. Warren, "Wage Work in the Sacred Circle: The Ghost Dance as Modern Religion," *Western Historical Quarterly* 46, no. 2 (2015). For urban Indians, see Coll-Peter Thrush, *Native Seattle*.

Francis Paul Prucha's work still dominates studies of Indian policy, particularly *American Indian Policy in Crisis* (1976) and *The Great Father* (1984). William T. Hagan, *Taking Indian Lands* (2003) was the last of his important books, which additionally include

American Indians (1961) and *The Indian Rights Association* (1985). Robert M. Utley, *The Indian Frontier of the American West, 1846–1890* (1984) has had wide influence, as has Brian W. Dippie, *The Vanishing American* (1991). Everett A. Gilcreast, *Richard Henry Pratt and American Indian Policy, 1877–1906* (1974) is a study of an important Indian reformer. Paul Stuart, *The Indian Office* (1979) was one of the first institutional studies of the Indian Office. Clyde A. Milner, *With Good Intentions* (1982) looks at the Quakers and the Peace Policy.

Frederick E. Hoxie is the leading contemporary student of Indian policy and Indian political thought. His A *Final Promise* (1984) looks at a racist turn in American Indian policy, and *This Indian Country* (2012) examines how Indian activists sought to use the legal and political system to their own advantage. One of those Indian activists was Sara Winnemucca, who wrote *Life Among the Piutes* (1883). C. Joseph Genetin-Pilawa, *Crooked Paths to Allotment* (2012) is an important recent study of a key part of American policy. Douglas W. Adams, *The Federal Indian Boarding School* (1975) looks at another policy tool during this period that caused considerable death and suffering. Recent studies have appraised American Indian policy through the lens of colonialism. Margaret D. Jacobs, *White Mother to a Dark Race* (2009) is a good example.

The army did more than fight Indians. Paul Andrew Hutton, *Phil Sheridan and His Army* (1985) looks at a critical figure in both Western and Southern Reconstruction and in repressing strikes. For the army and strikes, Jerry M. Cooper, "The Army as Strikebreaker," *Labor History* 18, no. 2 (1977). For the army and law enforcement, D. Laurie Clayton, "Filling the Breach," *Western Historical Quarterly* 25, no. 2 (1994). Jerry M. Cooper, *The Rise of the National Guard* (1997) looks at the creation of the modern National Guard.

Non-Indian settlement in the West took place on land the federal government wrested from the tribes and then surveyed and distributed. This was part of a larger process of border making. For establishing national borders and what they meant, a place to start is Rachel St. John, *Line in the Sand* (2011); Benjamin Hoy, "A Wall of Many Heights" (2015), and Beth LaDow, *The Medicine Line* (2002).

For land policy, the work of Paul Wallace Gates remains foundational, including "The Homestead Law in an Incongruous Land System," *American Historical Review* 41, no. 4 (1936); *History of Public Land Law Development* (1968); *Fifty Million Acres* (1966); and *The Jeffersonian Dream* (1996). Also important are Roy M. Robbins, *Our Landed Heritage* (1976, 2nd ed.); Benjamin Horace Hibbard, *A History of the Public Land Policies* (1965); and Vernon Carstensen, *Farms or Forests* (1958). For the Homestead Act, Fred A. Shannon, "The Homestead Act and the Labor Surplus," *American Historical Review* 41, no. 4 (1936), and for the survey system that would extend across the West, Hildegard B. Johnson, *Order upon the Land* (1976). For a conceptual mapping, Katherine G. Morrissey, *Mental Territories* (1997).

Next to Indians, Mexican Americans and Chinese were the big losers in the West. For the fate of Mexican Americans in California, see Leonard Pitt, *The Decline of the Californios* (1998). For New Mexico and Colorado, Maria E. Montoya, *Translating Property* (2002). For the Chinese, Alexander Saxton, *The Indispensable Enemy* (1995) and Erika Lee, *At America's Gates* (2003) are both important works, but I also relied heavily on Beth Lew-Williams, whose important forthcoming book, *The Chinese Must Go*, I read in manuscript. For a notorious violent incident, Craig Storti, *Incident at Bitter Creek* (1991). For a general history that goes well beyond the West, Ronald T. Takaki, *A Different Mirror* (1993).

For migration into the West and non-Indian agricultural settlement, Fred A. Shannon, *The Farmer's Last Frontier* (1968, orig. ed. 1945) remains useful, as is Gilbert Courtland Fite, *The Farmers' Frontier, 1865–1900* (1966). For the experience of settlers, see John Ise, *Sod and Stubble* (1996); Paula Nelson, "'All Well and Hard at Work': The Harris Family Letters," *North Dakota History* 57 (Spring 1990); Sherry L. Smith, "Single Women Homesteaders," *Western Historical Quarterly* 22, no. 2 (1991); and Donald J. Pisani, *From the Family Farm to Agribusiness* (1984) and *Water, Land, and Law in the West* (1996).

For the challenges that the Great Plains and the arid West presented to settlers, a good beginning for the environmental realities of the region is Cary J. Mock, "Rainfall in the Garden of the United States Great Plains, 1870–79," *Climatic Change* 44 (2000). David M. Emmons, *Garden in the Grasslands* (1971) is the classic account of "rain follows the plow," and H. Craig Miner, *West of Wichita* (1986) and John Hudson, "Two Dakota Homestead Frontiers," *Annals of the Association of American Geographers* 63, no. 4 (1973) look at the actual settlement. Geoff Cunfer, *On the Great Plains* (2005) is an original but controversial reevaluation of Great Plains agriculture.

For African American migration and settlement, Quintard Taylor, *In Search of the Racial Frontier* (1998) is outstanding. Nell Irvin Painter, *Exodusters* (1976) remains an important work of both Southern and Western history. See also Albert Broussard, Quintard Taylor, and Lawrence Brooks De Graaf, eds., *Seeking El Dorado* (2001).

The Mormons were a group whose importance in Western history far outweighed their numbers. For Brigham Young, see Leonard J. Arrington, *Brigham Young* (1985) and John G. Turner, *Brigham Young* (2012). By far the best discussion of the legal and political importance of the Mormons during this period is Sarah Barringer Gordon, *The Mormon Question* (2002).

Laura Ingalls Wilder's *Little House* series has created the most lasting cultural representation of western settlement, and scholars have contextualized her work: Penny T. Linsenmayer, "A Study of Laura Ingalls Wilder's Little House on the Prairie," *Kansas History* 24 (Autumn 2001); and Frances W. Kaye, "Little Squatter on the Osage Diminished Reserve," *Great Plains Quarterly* 23 (2000).

Mining and cattle raising joined agriculture as the cornerstones of the West's extractive economy. Ernest Staples Osgood, *The Day of the Cattleman* (1957); J. Orin Oliphant, "The Eastward Movement of Cattle from the Oregon Country," *Agricultural History* 20 (January 1946); and David Galenson, "The End of the Chisholm Trail," *Journal of Economic History* 34, no. 2 (1974) look at the movement of cattle. Robert R. Dykstra, *The Cattle Towns* (1968) examines the towns that served the industry. Margaret Walsh, *The Rise of the Midwestern Meat Packing Industry* (1982) and Louise Carroll Wade, *Chicago's Pride* (1987) look at how cattle became meat. Clyde Milner and Carol A. O'Connor, *As Big as the West* (2009) complicate the life of a man often presented as the iconic Western rancher. John Clay produced one of the great Western memoirs, *My Life on the Range* (1961).

Gordon Bakken, *The Mining Law of 1872* (2008) looks at the law that governed Western mining. Rodman W. Paul, *Mining Frontiers of the Far West, 1848–1880* (1963); Michael P. Malone, *The Battle for Butte* (1981); Elizabeth Jameson, *All That Glitters* (1998); and

James E. Fell, *Ores to Metal* (2009) look at the spread of mining and smelting and the social conflicts that followed.

Much of the literature emphasizes the environmental, financial, and human costs of the industry: Duane A. Smith, *Mining America* (1987); Timothy J. LeCain, *Mass Destruction* (2009); Joseph E. King, *A Mine to Make a Mine* (1977); Robert L. Kelley, *The Hydraulic Mining Controversy in California, 1856–1895* (1953); and Andrew Isenberg, *Mining California* (2005).

Many of these studies look at the social history of the West, and to them should be added Elliott West, *The Saloon on the Rocky Mountain Mining Frontier* (1979) and Anne A. Butler, *Daughters of Joy, Sisters of Misery* (1985), both of which illuminate far more than drinking and prostitution.

For Western violence, Robert R. Dykstra, "Quantifying the Wild West: The Problematic Statistics of Frontier Violence," *Western Historical Quarterly* 40, no. 3 (2009) argues for relatively minimal Western violence, at least in frontier towns. Richard Maxwell Brown, *Strain of Violence* (1975) casts a wider net. Richard White, "Outlaw Gangs of the Middle Border," *Western Historical Quarterly* 12, no. 4 (1981); Jonathan Obert, "The Six-Shooter Marketplace," *Studies in American Political Development* 28, no. 1 (2014); Roger D. McGrath, *Gunfighters, Highwaymen, and Vigilantes* (1984); Andrew Isenberg, *Wyatt Earp* (2013); Daniel Belgrad, "Power's Larger Meaning," *Western Historical Quarterly* 33, no. 2 (2002); and Lisa Arellano, *Vigilantes and Lynch Mobs* (2012) all look at aspects of Western violence. John Mack Faragher, *Eternity Street* (2016) is a chilling and important study essential to any study of Western violence even if it largely covers an earlier period.

Taken together, the rise of Jim Crow in the South, conquest of Indians in the West, pogroms against the Chinese in the West, dispossession of earlier Mexican American settlers, and reaction against Catholic and Jewish immigrants were all part of the larger phenomenon of the rise of a white nationalism. Restriction and exclusion were part of a resurgence of white nationalism: Edward J. Blum, *Reforging the White Republic, 1865–1898* (2005); Alexander Saxton, *The Rise and Fall of the White Republic* (1990); David R. Roediger, *The Wages of Whiteness* (1991); and Roediger and Elizabeth D. Esch, *The Production of Difference* (2012) all look at aspects of this. Matthew Frye Jacobson, *Whiteness of a Different Color* (1998) and *Barbarian Virtues* (2000) look at immigrants and American racial thinking. Also see Noel Ignatiev, *How the Irish Became White* (1995). For racial science, see Ann Fabian, *The Skull Collectors* (2010). Peggy Pascoe, *What Comes Naturally* (2009) is a brilliant study of miscegenation law and the construction of race. See also Louise Michelle Newman, *White Women's Rights* (1999). For a comparative study, George M. Fredrickson, *White Supremacy* (1981). For anti-Catholicism and immigration restriction, see Jo Ann Manfra, "Hometown Politics and the American Protective Association, 1887–1890," *Annals of Iowa* 55 (Spring 1996); and Donald Kinzer, *An Episode in Anti-Catholicism* (1964).

I have treated the period as an age of reform. Liberals were reformers — even revolutionaries — who morphed into conservatives as the world changed around them. For European socialists' appraisal of the United States during this period, see R. Laurence Moore, *European Socialists and the American Promised Land* (1970). John G. Sproat, *The Best Men* (1968) is an older analysis of the liberals. There is no discussing liberalism without Louis Hartz, *The Liberal Tradition in America* (1955). For all its overreach and blind spots, and though I often disagree with Hartz, it remains a shrewd and important book. James T. Kloppenberg, the leading American scholar on liberalism, is the author of *Uncertain Victory* (1986), *The Virtues of Liberalism* (1998), and *Toward Democracy* (2016). I found Nancy Cohen, *The Reconstruction of American Liberalism, 1865–1914* (2002) insightful even if I did not accept all her conclusions. Sidney Fine, *Laissez faire and the General-Welfare State* (1969, orig. ed. 1956) points out that the central liberal idea had only limited applicability in the actual operation of a heavily subsidized and protected American economy.

The influence of Herbert Spencer—the archetypical Gilded Age liberal—was apparent in the United States. See his *Collected Writings* (1996). Leslie Butler, *Critical Americans* (2007) and Barry Werth, *Banquet at Delmonico's* (2009) provide takes on the exchange between British and American liberal intellectuals.

James A. Henretta, "Isaac Sherman and the Trials of Gilded Age Liberalism," *American Nineteenth Century History* 4, no. 1 (2003) looks at a ubiquitous liberal. E. L. Godkin, for all his peculiarities, was a significant figure; *The Gilded Age Letters of E. L. Godkin* (1974) and William Armstrong, *E. L. Godkin* (1978) provide points of entry. William Graham, *What Social Classes Owe Each Other* (1883) was never as important as Richard Hofstadter made him. Far more important was Josiah Strong, a figure who incorporated strains of both evangelical and liberal reform and whose *Our Country* (1963, orig. ed. 1885) is a fundamental text for understanding the period. See Dorothea R. Muller, "Josiah Strong and American Nationalism: A Reevaluation," *Journal of American History* 53, no. 3 (1966). Adam-Max Tuchinsky, *Horace Greeley's New-York Tribune* (2009) looks at a man who loomed large at the beginning of the period.

As with Josiah Strong, liberal reform could shade into certain kinds of evangelical reform, but evangelicals were also changing. Clifford Edward Clark, *Henry Ward Beecher* (1978) and Debby Applegate, *The Most Famous Man in America* (2006) provide biographies of Henry Ward Beecher, the leading evangelical at the beginning of the age. Both he and his sister, Harriet Beecher Stowe, retreated from advocacy of black rights, as Joan D. Hedrick, *Harriet Beecher Stowe* (1994) shows. Bruce J. Evensen, *God's Man for the Gilded Age* (2003) provides a biography of Dwight Moody, the most famous evangelical at the end. The differences between them were significant.

The literature on evangelical Christianity and reform is extensive, including Gaines M. Foster, *Moral Reconstruction* (2002). Benjamin L. Hartley, *Evangelicals at a Crossroads* (2010) provides a particular study of Boston. It is necessary to look at Anthony Comstock as an important reformer whose influence, and that of the so-called purity movement, came from the centrality of the home. See Nicola Kay Beisel, *Imperiled Innocents* (1997); Paul S. Boyer, *Purity in Print* (2002); David J. Pivar, *Purity Crusade* (1973); and Alison M. Parker, *Purifying America* (1997).

The best study of American sexuality is Estelle Freedman and John D'Emilio, *Intimate Matters* (1988). George Chauncey, *Gay New York* (1994) illuminates how sexual categories come into being.

Women were particularly prominent in the drive for reform. Some were evangelicals, others embraced the Social Gospel with or without evangelicalism, and some were largely secular. Much of this reform was linked to temperance. Barbara Epstein, *The Politics of Domesticity* (1981) and Ruth Birgitta Anderson Bordin, *Woman and Temperance* (1981) were early studies. The Anti-Saloon League, quite distinct from the Woman's Christian Temperance Union, emerged at the end of this period, even if much of its influence came in the twentieth century; see K. Austin Kerr, "Organizing for Reform: The Anti-Saloon League and Innovation in Politics," *American Quarterly* 32, no. 1 (1980).

The Social Gospel was central to Gilded Age reform. Henry F. May, *Protestant Churches and Industrial America* (1967) is still useful, as are Charles H. Hopkins, *The Rise of the Social Gospel in American Protestantism, 1865–1915* (1940) and Donald Cedric White, *The Social Gospel* (1976). Although it mostly concerns a later period, I found Kevin M. Kruse, *One Nation under God* (2015) helpful. Jacob Henry Dorn, *Washington Gladden* (1967) looks at a leading reformer, as does Benjamin G. Rader, "Richard T. Ely: Lay Spokesman for the Social Gospel," *Journal of American History* 53, no. 1 (1966). It is also necessary to remember that the same age that saw the emergence of Social Gospel also witnessed a resurgence in faith healing. See Heather Curtis, *Faith in the Great Physician* (2007). The female army of reform was heavily Christian, but not all women reformers relied on evangelicalism. See Michael L. Goldberg, *An Army of Women* (1997).

Evangelical reformers, temperance reformers, and crusaders for women's suffrage overlapped with one another and with antimonopolists. To situate women reformers in the Civil War and its aftermath, see Stephen B. Oates, *A Woman of Valor* (1994); Peggy Pascoe, *Relations of Rescue* (1990); and Alison M. Parker, *Articulating Rights* (2010). For biographies of key figures, Lori D. Ginzberg, *Elizabeth Cady Stanton* (2009); J. Matthew Gallman, *America's Joan of Arc* (2006); and Sally G. McMillen, *Lucy Stone* (2015). A classic autobiography of the period is Charlotte P. Gilman, *The Living of Charlotte Perkins Gilman* (1975, orig. ed. 1935).

I regard antimonopoly broadly construed as the most significant political movement of the Gilded Age. They are among the radicals in Michael Kazin, *American Dreamers* (2011). Antimonopolism grew out of liberalism but also played on American ideas of wealth distribution, described in James L. Huston, *Securing the Fruits of Labor* (1998). Its central text was Henry George, *Progress and Poverty* (1942, orig. ed. 1879). George was the subject, in part, of John L. Thomas, *Alternative America* (1983) and of Edward J. Rose, *Henry George* (1968). Edward T. O'Donnell, *Henry George and the Crisis of Inequality* (2015) and Christopher W. England, "Land and Liberty" (2015) will, I hope, bring him back as a major historical figure. George himself was deeply marked by the squatter movement in California, as described in Tamara H. Venit Shelton, *A Squatter's Republic* (2008); Chester M. Destler, "Western Radicalism, 1865–1901," *Mississippi Valley Historical Review* 31, no. 3 (1944) remains an important interpretation of antimonopolism.

The Greenbackers and Grangers launched antimonopolism as a popular movement. For a contemporary account, Edwin Winslow Martin (pseud. for James Dabney McCabe), *History of the Grange Movement* (1874). George H. Miller, *Railroads and the Granger Laws* (1971) long ago recognized that railroad regulation involved merchants as much as farmers, as did Lee Benson, *Merchants, Farmers, and Railroads* (1955). Irwin Unger, *The Greenback Era* (1964) and Thomas A. Woods, *Knights of the Plow* (1991) provide introductions to the Greenbackers and the Grange, as does William D. Barns, "Oliver Hudson Kelley and the Genesis of the Grange," *Agricultural History* 41, no. 3 (1967).

The Knights of Labor were as much an antimonopolist reform organization as a labor union. They have spawned a considerable literature: Leon Fink, *Workingmen's Democracy*

(1977); Robert E. Weir, *The Knights Unhorsed* (2000) and *Beyond Labor's Veil* (1996); Michael J. Cassity, "Modernization and Social Crisis," *Journal of American History* 66, no. 1 (1979); Kim Voss, *The Making of American Exceptionalism* (1993); Melton Alonza McLaurin, *The Knights of Labor in the South* (1978); and Joseph Gerteis, "The Possession of Civic Virtue," *American Journal of Sociology* 108, no. 3 (2002). For Terence Powderly, see Craig Phelan, *Grand Master Workman* (2000); Edward T. James, "T. V. Powderly, a Political Profile," *Pennsylvania Magazine of History and Biography* 99, no. 4 (1975); and Vincent J. Falzone, *Terence V. Powderly* (1978). Terence Vincent Powderly, *Thirty Years of Labor, 1859–1889* (1967) gives his version.

Antimonopoly has tended to be collapsed into one of its manifestations: Populism. M. Elizabeth Sanders, *Roots of Reform* (1999) emphasizes its broader sweep, as does Matthew Hild, *Greenbackers, Knights of Labor, and Populists* (2007) and Joseph Gerteis, *Class and the Color Line* (2007). Melvin G. Holli, *Reform in Detroit* (1969) has looked at the complicated alliances in a major city, as have Alexander Saxton, "San Francisco Labor and the Populist and Progressive Insurgencies," *Pacific Historical Review* 34, no. 4 (1965) and Robert D. Johnston, *The Radical Middle Class* (2003).

Populism, nonetheless, has received the most historical attention. Jeffrey Ostler, *Prairie Populism* (1993) has interpreted it within the larger realm of antimonopoly, both in and outside the major parties. Steven Hahn, *The Roots of Southern Populism* (1983) looks at complicated origins in Georgia. I have relied heavily on Charles Postel, *The Populist Vision* (2007) over earlier interpretations. Lawrence Goodwyn, *Democratic Promise* (1976) and C. Vann Woodward, *Tom Watson* (1963) are foundational studies. Norman Pollack, *The Populist Mind* (1967) argues for the Populists as American socialists. Walter T. K. Nugent, *The Tolerant Populists* (1963) defends the Populists against charges of anti-Semitism and xenophobia. Michael Kazin, *A Godly Hero* (2007) makes a compelling case for how Bryan changed the Democrats and thus American politics. John Thompson, *Closing the Frontier* (1986) treats persistent radicalism in Oklahoma.

Economic historians and political scientists have tried to correlate agrarian unrest with price fluctuations and markets, with mixed results: Robert A. McGuire, "Economic Causes of Late-Nineteenth Century Agrarian Unrest," *Journal of Economic History* 41, no. 4 (1981); Anne Mayhew, "A Reappraisal of the Causes of Farm Protest in the United States, 1870–1900," *Journal of Economic History* 32, no. 2 (1972); and Robert Klepper, *The Economic Bases for Agrarian Movements in the United States, 1870–1900* (1978).

Carlos Schwantes, *Coxey's Army* (1985) and Benjamin F. Alexander, *Coxey's Army* (2015) look at Jacob Coxey. He was a peculiar man, but he cannot be easily dismissed. He, too, was a manifestation of antimonopolism.

Many of the figures in this book would later become prominent in Progressivism, part of whose roots lay in antimonopoly. Jane Addams, *Twenty Years at Hull-House* (1911) is a basic text of the age. The best biographies of her are by Louise W. Knight, *Jane Addams* (2010) and *Citizen* (2005). Jacob Riis also emerged as a prominent, rather conservative reformer, who never trusted antimonopolists. See his *How the Other Half Lives* (1957, orig. ed. 1890). Bonnie Yochelson and Daniel J. Czitrom, *Rediscovering Jacob Riis* (2007) is a superb study that places Riis in context and analyzes his appeal. Roy Lubove, *The Progressives and the Slums* (1974) has long been the standard account of urban reformers, but David Huyssen, *Progressive Inequality* (2014) looks at the conservative tendencies of

Progressive Reform. Philanthropy, although reformist in a certain sense, was ultimately a conservative response to social problems. See Olivier Zunz, *Philanthropy in America* (2012). See also Robert Hamlett Bremner, *From the Depths* (1956).

I consider Samuel Gompers to have been a labor leader as much as a reformer. He has been getting a more sympathetic reevaluation. His *Seventy Years of Life and Labor* (1984, orig. ed. 1925) remains well worth reading, and Harold C. Livesay, *Samuel Gompers and Organized Labor in America* (1978) provides the gold standard for a short biography.

Gompers changed the emphasis of the labor movement from production to consumption. Lawrence B. Glickman, *A Living Wage* (1997) is part of a reevaluation of Gompers, but it is also one of the basic books of the new labor history and among the works that turn attention from production to consumption. Kathleen G. Donohue, *Freedom from Want* (2003); Lawrence B. Glickman, *Buying Power* (2009); Roy Rosenzweig, *Eight Hours for What We Will* (1983); Susan Curtis, *A Consuming Faith* (1991); and Lendol G. Calder, *Financing the American Dream* (1999) all trace aspects of this transformation, as do the early chapters of Mark Hendrickson, *American Labor and Economic Citizenship* (2013).

By the end of the century, demands for state intervention to correct social and environmental problems had increased. Part of this rose from antimonopolism, but it also came from the growth of professional expertise. The rise of the professions was a central concern of Robert Wiebe in *The Search for Order* (1967), and the literature has continued to grow. Mary O. Furner, *Advocacy and Objectivity* (1975); Theodore M. Porter, *The Rise of Statistical Thinking, 1820–1900* (1986); James Leiby, *Carroll Wright and Labor Reform* (1960); Ian Hacking, *The Taming of Chance* (1990); and Margo J. Anderson, *The American Census* (1988) all cover aspects of expertise. Thomas L. Haskell, *The Emergence of Professional Social Science* (1977) is an example of how a seemingly narrow subject can illuminate an age. Engineers were a particularly important group; see Edwin T. Layton, *The Revolt of the Engineers* (1986). Peter Novick, *That Noble Dream* (1988) looks at the development of professional history.

For the growth of a regulatory state, see William R. Brock, *Investigation and Responsibility* (1984); Samuel DeCanio, *Democracy and the Origins of the American Regulatory State* (2015); John Fabian Witt, *The Accidental Republic* (2004); Jon C. Teaford, *The Unheralded Triumph* (1984); Terrence J. McDonald, *The Parameters of Urban Fiscal* (1986); and Michael Sandel, *Democracy's Discontent* (1996). The desire for reform had its antidemocratic as well as democratic aspects. See Michael H. Frisch, "Urban Theorists, Urban Reform, and American Political Culture in the Progressive Period," *Political Science Quarterly* 97, no. 2 (1982) and Kenneth Finegold, *Experts and Politicians* (1995).

For the origins of early versions of the welfare state in this period, see Michele Landis Dauber, *The Sympathetic State* (2013) and Theda Skocpol, *Protecting Soldiers and Mothers* (1995). The rise of the Grand Army of the Republic was fundamental to the pension system; Stuart McConnell, *Glorious Contentment* (1992).

The limits of antimonopolism came not so much from political failure as the growing conservatism of the courts. Research for this book led me profitably into legal history. A contemporary work, Christopher G. Tiedeman, *The Unwritten Constitution of the United States* (1890), helped me to understand constitutional thinking at the time and the great freedom judges and legal scholars gave the courts in interpreting the law. For a modern analysis of legal formalism and realism, Richard Posner, "Legal Formalism, Legal Realism, and the Interpretation of Statutes and the Constitution," *Case Western Reserve Law Review* 37, no. 2 (1986–87). Michael Les Benedict, "Laissez-Faire and Liberty," *Law and History Review* 3, no. 2 (1985).

The work of William E. Forbath was critical to my interpretations, including "The Ambiguities of Free Labor," *Wisconsin Law Review* (1985); *Courting the State* (2010); and *Law and the Shaping of the American Labor Movement* (1991). Herbert Hovenkamp, *Enterprise and American Law, 1836–1937* (1991) has also influenced my thinking. Morton J. Horwitz, *The Transformation of American Law, 1870–1960* (1992) is fundamental to shaping the scholarship on the period. William M. Wiecek, *The Lost World of Classical Legal Thought* (1998); Robert J. Steinfeld, *The Invention of Free Labor* (1991); Karen Orren, *Belated Feudalism* (1991); Kenneth M. Casebeer, *American Labor Struggles and Law Histories* (2011); and Joseph A. Ranney, *In the Wake of Slavery* (2006) all proved useful.

For the Slaughterhouse Cases, Michael A. Ross, "Justice Miller's Reconstruction," *Journal of Southern History* 64, no. 4 (1998) and Ronald M. Labbe and Jonathan Lurie, *The Slaughterhouse Cases* (2005). For the Fourteenth Amendment, William E. Nelson, *The Fourteenth Amendment* (1988). Ruth Bloch and Naomi R. Lamoreaux, "Corporations and the Fourteenth Amendment," unpublished paper (2015).

I pay considerable attention to American intellectual engagement with a wider world as well as to immigration and economic relations but give little attention to foreign relations. For the Dominican Republic, see Anne Eller, "Dominican Civil War, Slavery, and Spanish Annexation, 1844–1865," in D. Doyle, ed., *American Civil Wars* (2016).

Several transnational histories influenced my account. Ian Tyrrell's *Reforming the World* (2010), *Crisis of the Wasteful Nation* (2015), *True Gardens of the Gods* (1999), and *Woman's World/Woman's Empire* (2010) form a quartet of works that literally rearrange the usual perspective on evangelical reform and conservation and the environment. Daniel T. Rodgers, *Atlantic Crossings* (1998) has been one of the most influential historical works of the last twenty years. See also David G. McCullough, *The Greater Journey* (2011); Allison L. Sneider, *Suffragists in an Imperial Age* (2008) connects women's suffrage and imperialism. Howard L. Platt, *Shock Cities* (2005) compares two industrializing cities, Manchester and Chicago.

Index

Note: Page numbers in *italics* indicate photographs and illustrations in the primary text. References to *"insert"* indicate photographs and captions in the photographic insert.